Real Estate Finance

Real Estate Finance

Eighth edition

William B. Brueggeman, Ph.D.

Corrigan Professor of Real Estate
Edwin L. Cox School of Business
Southern Methodist University
and
Consulting Director of Real Estate Research
Goldman, Sachs & Co.

Jeffrey D. Fisher, Ph.D.

Associate Professor and Director
Center for Real Estate Studies
School of Business
Indiana University

Leo D. Stone, M.B.A., J.D.

Professor Emeritus of Business Finance
College of Administrative Science
The Ohio State University

1989

Homewood, IL 60430
Boston, MA 02116

Sponsoring editor: Michael W. Junior
Project editor: Waivah Clement
Production manager: Irene H. Sotiroff
Compositor: Carlisle Communications, Ltd.
Typeface: 10/12 Times Roman
Printer: R. R. Donnelley & Sons Company

Library of Congress Cataloging-in-Publication Data

Brueggeman, William B.
    Real estate finance / William B. Brueggeman, Jeffrey D. Fisher,
Leo D. Stone.—8th ed.
      p.   cm.
   Bibliography: p.
   Includes index.
   ISBN 0-256-03033-2
    1. Mortgage loans—United States.   2. Real property—United
States—Finance.   I. Fisher, Jeffrey D.   II. Stone, Leo D.
III. Title.
NG2040.5.U5B78 1989
332.7'2—dc19   88–31234
                                            CIP

Printed in the United States of America
2 3 4 5 6 7 8 9 0 DO 6 5 4 3 2 1 0 9

Preface

This edition represents a major revision of the seventh edition. We have increased coverage in many new areas, including an expanded treatment of mortgage instruments, real estate development, and investments in mortgage-backed securities. We have somewhat reduced legal and institutional coverage. Much of the institutional material contained in previous editions has been reduced because many colleges and universities now offer classes in both real estate law and financial institutions. We have retained only those facets of law and financial institutions that deal specifically with real estate finance.

Major changes in this edition include more extensive coverage of both fixed and adjustable rate mortgages (ARMs) in Part II. Part III includes a considerable expansion in the analysis of income-producing properties. Updated material has been included on valuation, financial analysis, investment analysis, federal income taxation, financial leverage, and a more complete treatment of real estate syndication. Material dealing with real estate development in Part IV has been increased to two chapters. We believe this material to be a significant addition that is lacking in most other texts. Part V contains a brief survey of sources of real estate financing from financial institutions. It also includes a brief chronological development of the secondary mortgage and what we believe to be the most thorough treatment of mortgage-backed securities available in a college textbook today. Part VI includes a completely new topic, measuring real estate investment performance and risk from a portfolio management perspective. Although it is only one chapter, it is a topic of current concern to institutional investors. Part I continues to provide the legal characteristics and financial implications of the use of the principal instruments involved in financing real estate, and Part II summarizes the principal methods of financing residential properties. The latter coverage has been expanded to include the more important FHA and VA programs, and it also provides the approaches used for FHA, VA, and conventional underwriting, which are not covered in earlier editions.

This edition is designed for academic and professional use. Its goal is to provide a basic orientation in commonly used instruments, institutional structures, and financing policies and to develop problem-solving capabilities in all areas of general discussion. The authors have worked together in the development of all chapters in this revision. Primary responsibility was divided as follows: Brueggeman, Chapters 1, 4, 5, 6, 7, 8, 17–23 and Fisher, Chapters 2, 3, 9–16. Much of Professor Stone's influence from earlier editions has been retained throughout. If readers have comments regarding coverage, they should contact the author with primary responsibility for the chapter in question.

The authors want to express their appreciation to the reviewers for many helpful comments and constructive suggestions. The reviewers included Steve Gardner of Steven Austin College; Jack Harris of Texas A & M University; E. Vincent Mahoney of Lumbleaux Real Estate School-California; Wade Ragas of the University of New Orleans; and Gary Wells of Idaho State University. We acknowledge the assistance of Scott D. Nafe, J. D. in the revision of the legal chapters. We also want to thank Walter C. Barnes III and Paige Mosbaugh, who aided greatly with their computational assistance. The authors also acknowledge the assistance of Ms. Mary Zotos, Ms. Susan Arvin, and Ms. Terri Blanton in the preparation of the revised manuscript. The authors also acknowledge a great debt of gratitude to the late Henry E. Hoagland, who wrote the first edition of this text and set the tone of the editions that have followed. He was a distinguished pioneer in real estate education. His absence is deeply felt.

William B. Brueggeman
Jeffrey D. Fisher
Leo D. Stone

Contents

Introduction.   The Nature of Real Estate Investment Data.   Sources of Data Used for Real Estate Performance Measurement.   Computing of Holding Period Returns.   Risk, Return, and Performance Measurement.   Elements of Portfolio Theory.   Real Estate Returns, Other Investments, and the Potential for Portfolio Diversification.

APPENDIXES

Chapter 1

Overview of Real Estate Finance

Real estate finance is a field of study that requires an understanding of many important subjects. It requires a basic understanding of property law, mortgage underwriting practices, mortgage insurance programs, financial analysis, valuation principles, federal income-tax laws, investment analysis, financial institutions, real estate development, and capital markets. This book is intended to provide the reader with a foundation in each of these areas. It is oriented toward the student who has some exposure to basic finance and, perhaps, real estate principles and who desires a more advanced treatment of the subject. The emphasis of the book is real estate financial analysis. However, descriptions of important institutional characteristics are given at various points in the text to complement analysis with some insights into business practice.

This chapter contains an overview of the contents of the book. Subjects addressed throughout the book form the basis for much of what is needed for professionals who are in, or about to enter, the field. Although the breadth of coverage may seem to include topics that are very diverse, these topics contain analytic approaches and methodologies that are transferable to many different problem areas. Many students find that they have a much better understanding of basic finance after they have learned to apply it to real estate.

LEGAL CONSIDERATIONS—PART I

In a free market economy when transactions involving a specific good or service occur repetitively, various institutional and legal arrangements evolve to standardize and facilitate such activity. Financing real estate is no exception to this rule. When the acquisition or development of residential or commercial properties is financed, the nature of the borrower's interest in the property, which is generally used as security for a loan, must be identified and acceptable to the lender who is being requested to advance funds. Real estate transactions are significant both in economic magnitude and societal importance. Because of the many interests in real estate that can either be conveyed or used as security for lending, our legal system has evolved so that in order for real estate transactions to be valid they must be documented, in writing, in the form of a contract. Commitments made to finance these transactions are also documented, usually in the form of a mortgage and a note. Mortgages identify the property being used to secure a loan and contain promises made by the borrower to fulfill certain other obligations to the lender. Notes identify the amount of indebtedness between lender and borrower and the terms of repayment.

Chapters 2 and 3 contain a summary of the rights and interests in real estate which may be conveyed or used as security for mortgage loans. The legal nature of mortgages and contents normally included in most mortgages are also covered in some detail. Because changes in property law are most important at the state and local levels, the nature of interests that are acquired by lenders and the remedies available to lenders, should borrowers default, will vary by state. While it is not possible to compare such differences between states in a text such as this one, the major differences in approach as to mortgage contracts, that is, lien theory versus title theory, are distinguished. Further, various covenants (promises) commonly included in mortgage agreements are described in some detail. In the case of residential financing, much of the necessary documentation has been standardized. This has been done to facilitate the eventual sale of many mortgages in the secondary mortgage market. In fact, the mortgage document and note used most frequently in today's market are illustrated in Chapter 2. In addition to this material, foreclosure and alternatives to foreclosure by the lender are explored and discussed in some detail.

FINANCING RESIDENTIAL PROPERTIES—PART II

While we now take home ownership and mortgage financing of residential properties for granted, it was not until after the Great Depression of the 1930s that Congress took upon itself the responsibility for improving the housing standards and providing the framework for the vast system of housing finance that we know today. With the evolution of mortgage insurance programs by the Federal Housing Administration (FHA), then the mortgage and guarantee programs by the Veterans Administration (VA), mechanisms for eliminating or vastly reducing possible losses on loans made to households seeking mortgage financing were put into place. This provided lenders with sufficient protection to encourage them to make mortgage loans in substantial volume.

Part II of the book deals with many important topics in residential financing. Exhibit 1–1 outlines the many considerations that borrowers must make when seeking residential mortgage financing. The process involves deciding on the type of mortgage with respect to repayment pattern (that is, fixed or adjustable interest rates) and whether a conventional mortgage loan or a mortgage with FHA insurance or a VA guarantee should be chosen. These decisions are sometimes complex, particularly when one must choose between fixed and variable interest rates and compare closing-cost requirements. Chapters 5 through 8 contain a detailed analysis of these topics for all the above-mentioned mortgages. One of the tools needed for calculating and evaluating various payment patterns discussed in these chapters, is a thorough understanding of the time value of money. This topic is covered in great detail in Chapter 4.

Deciding how a property should be financed at the time of acquisition is important, but other considerations at the time of acquisition and subsequently are also important to most borrowers. Chapter 9 deals with the following issues:

1. Computing the effective cost of financing, including loan fees and charges. Using this methodology allows a comparison to be made between loans with different terms, such as the interest rate, fees, and maturity.
2. Computing the marginal or incremental cost of acquiring additional loan amounts (i.e., 75 percent, 80 percent, 90 percent, 95 percent, etc. of value). This analysis will help one decide whether to make a large or small down payment when acquiring a property.
3. Calculating the benefits and costs of refinancing. This decision must be made if interest rates decline after a loan has been made. The borrower must usually decide whether benefits from savings due to lower payments will exceed the costs that must be paid to undertake refinancing.
4. Comparing financing options, which may be provided by the seller of a property or by the buyer, assuming a mortgage that was previously made by the seller. These alternatives, coupled with the possibility of acquiring second mortgage financing, are also a topic of concern to borrowers.
5. Identifying the many different tax treatments that apply to interest deductions for each type of mortgage. This is necessary because of the many mortgage payment alternatives that a borrower may choose from.

EXHIBIT 1–1 Residential Mortgage Financing (borrower and lender considerations)

Stage I *Loan*	*Stage II* *Loan* *Underwriting*	*Stage III* *Loan* *Closing*
A. Type of mortgage	A. Verification of income/assets	A. Documentation
1. Fixed interest rate	1. Determination of payment-to-income ratios	1. RESPA
2. Adjustable interest rate	2. Credit history	2. Federal Truth in Lending
	3. Other savings and assets	
B. Type of mortgage insurance/guaranty	B. Appraisal of property value	
1. None—conventional loan	1. Relationship to loan amount	
2. Private insurance	2. Determination of maximum loan-to-value amount	
3. FHA		
4 VA		

FINANCING INCOME PRODUCING PROPERTIES—PART III

Part III provides an in-depth look at some of the more important aspects of financing and investing in income-producing properties. Exhibit 1–2 provides an illustration of the topics and the techniques that are used to analyze income properties. Note that the outline shown in the exhibit is a logical progression of concepts and aspects of income properties that an investor would consider when (1) acquiring a property, (2) considering the tax conse-

---

EXHIBIT 1–2   Important Considerations in Analyzing Income-Producing Properties

---

A. Estimating Cash Flows from a Real Estate Investment
   1. Examining lease provisions; base rents, escalations, expense stops
   2. Developing pro forma operating statements
   3. Estimating operating cash flows
   4. Estimating cash flows when properties are sold
   5. Performing a "before-tax" profitability analysis
B. Considering Federal Income Taxes
   1. Classifying income according to the 1986 Tax Reform Act
   2. Methods of depreciation allowable for residential and commercial income-producing real estate
   3. Provisions applying to amortization of financing and other fees
   4. Rehabilitation and historic building tax credits
   5. Developing pro forma statements of after-tax income from operation and the sale of real estate
   6. Combining before-tax cash flows with after-tax income to arrive at after-tax cash flow
   7. Performing an "after-tax" profitability analysis
C. Evaluating the Role of Financing and Leverage in Real Estate Investment Analysis
   1. Identifying alternative types of debt financing
   2. Evaluating the impact of financial leverage on the return on equity — positive and negative leverage
   3. Computing the break-even or maximum interest rate that can be paid while retaining positive leverage
   4. Evaluating the impact of tax deductibility of mortgage interest in the analysis
D. Risk Analysis in Real Estate Investment
   1. Sensitivity analysis — an introduction
   2. Considering the relative importance of the components of investment returns
E. Valuation of Income Properties
   1. Three approaches to estimating value: cost, market, and income capitalization
   2. The relationship between appraisal and investment analysis
F. The Decision to Hold or Sell, Refinance, or Renovate
   1. Marginal rates of return for additional holding periods
   2. Refinancing in lieu of selling
   3. Comparing the costs versus the benefits of renovating
G. Real Estate Syndication
   1. The nature of limited partnership structuring
   2. The framework for distributing cash flow and taxable income and losses
   3. The importance of the equity interest in the partnership
   4. Tax rules, substantial economic effect, capital gains, and cash distributions upon dissolution of the partnership
   5. Tax treatment of fees and expenses of the partnership

---

quences of the transaction, (3) deciding what type and how much financing to use in making the acquisition, and (4) attempting to gauge the amount of risk being taken for a specific type of property and how that risk may change should financial leverage be applied. The four areas just detailed are usually undertaken when the investor is faced with the decision to purchase a property at a *specified price*. That is, the investor is usually asking the question, "If I pay a *specific price* for the property and I use a certain amount of debt, what will be my rate of return on equity (before and after taxes)?" Further, based on that price, what will be the risk associated with the investment? Part E of the outline shown in Exhibit

1–2 changes the point of view somewhat and asks the question, "How much *should be paid* for the investment if a specific *rate of return* on equity invested is desired?" In other words, rather than determining the rate of return on equity if a specific price *is paid* for the property in question, this chapter focuses on the the question, "How much should a typical investor be willing to pay?" These questions are important because an investor will not normally want to pay any more than other investors would pay for a given property. To accomplish this analysis, we explain in detail the three approaches (cost, market, and income capitalization) to estimating value. The lender, who must consider the value of the property being used as security for financing, must also be concerned with estimating value. Hence, this topic is of equal importance to the lender.

Finally, in most situations, each topic detailed in parts A–E of the outline has more relevance for individuals and institutional investors *at the time* they are considering the purchase of property. Topics shown in part F are considerations which are vital to decision making *after* the asset has been purchased and the investor is faced with taking action relative to (1) continuing to own the asset or selling it, (2) refinancing, or (3) renovating the project. The fundamental approach to the sell or hold decision is to first ascertain the market value of the investor's equity. A decision must then be made as to whether the cash that would be realized if the asset is sold can be reinvested in an alternative investment of equal risk. That new investment would have to earn a rate of return at least equivalent to the future cash flow that would be given up if the project was sold. This decision framework is the proper way to formulate the decision to continue to own or to sell. The decision to refinance is another topic of concern in real estate finance. This decision is usually based on whether the additional cost incurred when refinancing exceeds the capital gain tax that would be paid if the project were sold. In other words, refinancing may be viewed as a method of removing equity from a project free of taxes, as opposed to selling an asset in order to raise capital. The decision to refinance may also be a part of the renovation decision. The decision to renovate a property is only justified if the present value of additional cash inflow is adequate relative to the outlay needed for the renovation. These topics are explained in considerable detail in Part III.

The last item on the outline, real estate syndication, is a term used when a group of investors pool funds to acquire full or partial ownership of real estate assets. From the perspective of investors, such an investment should be evaluated on both a before- and after-tax basis in accordance with the techniques outlined in parts A, B, C, and D of Exhibit 1–2. However, from the perspective of a developer, or a property owner selling a full or partial interest in a property, syndication may be viewed as an alternative way of raising equity This technique is used by real estate developers when they desire to raise equity capital based on any appreciation in value that may have occurred after a project has been completed. By selling a full or partial interest to investors in a partnership, the developer may be able to meet the dual goals of raising needed capital and retaining some equity ownership in a project.

FINANCING REAL ESTATE DEVELOPMENT—PART IV

Real estate development and financing is a subject not well understood by many individuals working on the periphery of this activity. This is because the majority of business activities in real estate involve the resale, financing, and leasing of *existing* properties. Real estate development deals with either (1) the preparation of land with an intent to resell sites to project developers (as in a business park), (2) the development of a single, large-scale project on one specific site, or (3) the development of mixed-use projects (such as a shopping mall-office-hotel complex). These activities usually require interim financing during the development phase, and then, for project developments, permanent financing after improvements have been made and leased to tenants.

The goals of Chapters 17 and 18 are to provide (1) a brief introduction to the real estate development industry, (2) a basic understanding of the development process, (3) some insight into how such projects are underwritten by the lenders, and (4) a framework to ascertain whether projects are economically feasible. Very detailed analysis is provided on lending arrangements and requirements, as well as detailed schedules relating to the way in which funds are ''drawn down'' as needed to complete construction. A very useful approach to estimating construction period interest is presented in an appendix to Chapter 17. Construction interest, which may account for up to 15 to 20 percent of total development costs, must be estimated carefully. Because loans made during construction are based on interest rates tied to the prime rate, they can change significantly, particularly when interest rates are high and volatile. Methods of hedging used to control these costs, are discussed in the appendix to Chapter 18. Individuals aspiring to work in the field of development or to work for lenders who lend to development companies should have a general understanding of these concepts.

SOURCES OF REAL ESTATE FUNDING AND THE SECONDARY MORTGAGE MARKET—PART V

While a solid foundation in analytic techniques is the cornerstone of understanding finance and investments, knowledge of the various institutions that make real estate loans and invest in real estate is also important. Chapters 19 and 20 describe institutional lenders and investors who supply funds to real estate developers and finance and purchase existing real estate projects. These institutions include

- Savings and loan associations
- Commercial banks
- Life insurance companies
- Mutual savings banks
- Mortgage banking companies
- Real estate investment trusts
- Public and private pension funds and trusts
- Public and private syndications (limited partnerships)

Many of these institutions are intermediaries that operate by accepting deposits from savers then making loans on real estate purchases or developments, or, making loans to other businesses. Other firms, such as mortgage companies, act as correspondents who produce loans for consideration by intermediaries. Many trusts, pension funds, and partnerships also provide funds for investment in real estate. Each of these entities tends to specialize in various aspects of real estate finance (interim lending, permanent lending, direct investment, etc.), and each operates under certain federal and state regulations that enable the entity to compete in some real estate activities but not others. The goal of Part V is to introduce the operations of these institutions and to provide insights into which are likely sources of funding for various kinds of real estate transactions.

Chapters 21 and 22 deal exclusively with the subject of the secondary mortgage market, a market in which institutions originating mortgage loans either sell such loans or issue mortgage-backed securities against pools of loans, which are then sold to other intermediaries and institutions. This market has grown tremendously in recent years, and it is now estimated that approximately 35 percent of all residential mortgages in the United States have been pooled for the purpose of issuing securities for purchase by others. Two government-related agencies, the Federal National Mortgage Association (Fannie Mae) and the Federal Home Loan Mortgage Company (Freddie Mac) have been the dominant institutions providing capital to facilitate transactions in the secondary market. The Government National Mortgage Association (Ginnie Mae) has provided guarantees needed to facilitate much of the mortgage securitization that has occurred to date. These entities are largely involved with residential mortgage loans that are pooled and then securized. However, a parallel development in commercial mortgage-backed securities has been occurring more slowly and should eventually provide an opportunity for lenders and investors to make a significant new secondary market in those mortgages.

In addition to a description of the institutions operating in the secondary market, Chapters 21 and 22 analyze, in depth, the various types of securities used in that market. Securities currently being issued against mortgage pools are described in detail, and examples dealing with how mortgage pools are formed are given. Cash flow patterns in and out of such pools are described for each security type, and the methodology used to value such securities is carefully considered. The various securities considered include (1) mortgage-backed bonds, (2) mortgage pass-through securities, (3) mortgage pay-through securities, and (4) collateralized mortgage obligations.

REAL ESTATE INVESTMENT PERFORMANCE—PART VI

Although this topic only constitutes one chapter, it is becoming very important in the world of institutional real estate investment. Many institutions have amassed real estate investment portfolios in the billions of dollars and must know how to measure investment return and risk on such portfolios. They must also understand the trade-offs between risk and return that usually occur as portfolios are diversified to include many assets. In developing this chapter, we use statistical concepts to develop risk measures for individual investments as well as investment portfolios. Different portfolio weights are used to examine how risk and return vary in relation to the addition and deletion of various investments. Many very important sources or investment return data are explained and historic data on common stocks, corporate and government bonds, mortgage-backed securities, and so on, are also used to develop important concepts. For readers interested in institutional investment activity in real estate, this chapter is extremely important and timely.

PART I

Legal Instruments and Other Considerations in Real Estate Finance

Chapter 2

Property Rights: Estates and Mortgages

INTRODUCTION

This chapter introduces important legal considerations in real estate finance. The economic benefits expected to be received by lenders, investors, and other parties in a real estate transaction are affected by these legal factors. We first consider the legal rights associated with ownership of real estate and the various ways of defining and protecting these rights. We then consider the legal rights of lenders and how those rights are defined and protected by various clauses in the mortgage agreement. When reading this chapter try to see how these legal considerations ultimately affect the expected benefits and risk associated with investing in or financing a real estate investment.

PROPERTY RIGHTS AND ESTATES

The term *real estate* is often used to refer to the *physical* land and improvements constructed on the land. The *ownership rights* associated with the real estate are referred to as *real property*. Real property is contrasted with *personal property,* which refers to the ownership rights in property and is not land or property permanently attached to the land.[1]

It is important to distinguish between *physical* real estate assets and *ownership rights* in real property because many parties can have different ownership rights in a given parcel of real estate. When one is financing or investing in real estate, our legal system offers ways for the investor to be creative and apportion these various interests among

---

[1]Certain items known as fixtures are items that were personal property but have become real property because they have either been attached to the land or building in a somewhat permanent manner or are intended to be used with the land and building on a permanent basis. Examples include built-in dishwashers, furnaces, and garage door openers.

parties. For example, a person may have ownership rights to a property for his or her lifetime (a life estate), after which the ownership rights will be transferred to a different person (as a revision or remainder). A company may have the rights to the minerals under the land, and another person may have ownership rights to space above the land (e.g., ownership of a condominium unit on the upper floor of a building or even airspace above the building).

We generally refer to *property rights* as the right of a person to the possession, use, enjoyment, and disposal of his or her property. With respect to its application to real estate, *interest* is a broad legal term used to denote a property right. The holder of an interest in real estate enjoys some right, or degree of control or use, and, in turn, may receive payment for the sale of such an interest. Such an interest, to the extent that its value can be determined, may also be bought, sold, or used as collateral for a loan.

The value of a particular parcel of real estate can be viewed as the total price individuals are willing to pay for the flow of benefits associated with all of these rights. An individual does not have to be an owner per se to have rights to some of the benefits of the real estate. For example, a person who leases the land (a lessee) has the right to exclusive use of the property for a period of time. This right of use has value to the lessee, even though the term of the lease is fixed. In exchange for the right to use the property, the lessee is willing to pay a lease rental for the term of the lease. Another example of rights enjoyed by nonowners of real estate involves mortgage lending. A holder of a mortgage also has some rights in real estate pledged as security for a loan. These rights vary with state law and depend on the terms of the mortgage. But, in general, the lender (or mortgagee) has a right to repossess, or bring about the sale of, a property if the borrower defaults on the mortgage loan. The mortgage provides the lender with what is referred to as a *secured interest*. Obviously this right has value to the lender in the event of default and reduces the quantity of rights possessed by the owner.

It should be clear that some understanding of the legal characteristics of real estate is essential to analyzing the relative benefits which accrue to the various parties who have some rights in a particular property. In most real estate financing and investment transactions, we generally think in terms of investing, selling, or borrowing based on one owner possessing all property rights in the real estate. However, as we have discussed, all or a portion of these rights may be restricted or transferred to others. Remarkably, the various holders of these separate rights generally enjoy their respective rights in relative harmony. However, conflicts arise occasionally concerning the relative rights and priorities to be accorded to the holders of these interests. The potential for such conflicts may also affect the value or price individuals may be willing to pay for an interest in real estate and, ultimately, the value of property.

Definition of an Estate

The term *estate* is used to denote a *possessory or potentially possessory interest* in real estate, that is, an estate which is either presently possessory or may ripen into a possessory estate in the future (e.g., at the end of a lease). A possessory interest involves the general right to occupy and *use* the property during the periods of possession. The modern notion of an "estate" continues to retain the English common law connotation of any interest in real estate that carries the right of exclusive possession, which includes the right to sell, use, lease, or even exclude others from the property.

Not all interests in real property are estates. An *easement* is a *nonpossessory* interest in land. It is the right to use the land owned or leased by someone else for some special purpose, for example, as a right of way to and from one's property. An easement entails only a limited user privilege and not privileges associated with ownership. Another important example of an interest in real estate that is not deemed to be an estate is the interest of a lender (mortgagee) in the property of the borrower (mortgagor). Mortgages are generally regarded in contemporary American law to be mere liens on the estates of others.

Classification of Estates

Estates in Possession versus Estates Not in Possession. Two broad categories of estates can be distinguished on the basis of the nature of rights accompanying the ownership of such estates. An estate in possession (a present estate in land) entitles its owner to immediate enjoyment of the rights to that estate. An estate not in possession (a future estate in land), on the other hand, does not convey the rights of the estate until some time in the future, if at all. An estate not in possession, in other words, represents a *future* possessory interest in a property. Generally, it does not convert to an estate in possession until the occurrence of a particular event. Estates in possession are by far the more common. When most people think of estates, they ordinarily have in mind estates in possession. Obviously, lenders and investors are very interested in the nature of the estate possessed by the owner when considering the purchase or financing of a particular estate in property.

Freehold versus Leasehold Estates. Estates in possession are of two general types: freehold estates and leasehold estates. These types of estates are technically distinguished on the basis of the definiteness or certainty of their duration. A *freehold estate* lasts for an indefinite period of time; that is, there is no definitely ascertainable date on which the estate ends. A *leasehold estate,* on the other hand, expires on a definite date. Aside from this technical distinction, a freehold estate connotes *ownership* of the property by the estate holder, whereas a leasehold estate implies only the right to *possess* and *use* the property owned by another for a period of time.

Fee Simple Estate. A *fee simple estate,* also known as a fee simple absolute estate, is the freehold estate which represents the most complete form of ownership of real estate. A holder of a fee simple estate is free to divide up the fee into lesser estates and sell, lease, or borrow against them as he or she wishes, subject, of course, to the laws of the state in which the property is located. In addition to controls imposed by government, the use of property may also be controlled by *deed restrictions,* which are essentially private contractual agreements imposed by former owners (usually developers and sub-dividers of real estate) to use or not to use property in certain ways. Deed restrictions are usually used in an attempt to control use of the land so that a future owner would not act in a manner which would reduce the value of the surrounding property. Apart from controls which may be imposed by government or deed restrictions, no special conditions, limitations, or restrictions are placed on the right of a holder of a fee simple estate to enjoy the property, lease it to others, sell it, or even give it away. It is this estate in property which investors and lenders encounter in most investment and lending transactions.

Life Estates.   A *life estate* is a freehold estate which lasts only as long as the life of the owner of the estate or the life of some other person. Upon the death of that person, the property reverts back to the original grantor (transferor of property), his or her heirs, or any other designated person. Most life estates result from the terms of the conveyance of the property. For example, a grantor may wish to make a gift of his property prior to his death, yet he wishes to retain the use and enjoyment of the property until his death. This can be accomplished by making a conveyance of the property subject to a reserved life estate. A life estate can be leased, mortgaged, or sold. However, parties concerned with this estate should be aware that the estate will end with the death of the holder of the life estate (or that of the person whose life determines the duration of the estate). Because of the uncertainty surrounding the duration of the life estate, its marketability and value as collateral are severely limited.

Estates Not Yet in Possession (Future Estates)

The preceding discussion concerned estates in possession which entitled the owner to immediate enjoyment of the estate. Here we discuss estates not in possession, or future estates, which do not convey the right to enjoy the property until some time in the future. The two most important types of future estates are the reversion and the remainder.

Reversion.   A *reversion* exists when the holder of an estate in land (the grantor) conveys to another person (a grantee) a present estate in the property that has less ownership rights than his own estate and retains for himself or his heirs the right to take back, at some time in the future, the full estate which he enjoyed before the conveyance. In this case, the grantor is said to have a reversionary fee interest in the property held by the grantee. A reversionary interest can be sold or mortgaged because it is an actual interest in the property.

Remainder.   A *remainder* exists when the grantor of a present estate with less ownership rights than his own conveys to a third person the reversionary interest he or his heirs would otherwise have in the property upon termination of the grantee's estate. A remainder is a future estate for the third person. Like a reversion, a remainder is a mortgageable interest in property.

The Leasehold Estates

There are two major types of leasehold estates: estates for years, and estates from year to year. There are two other types, but they are not common.[2] Leasehold estates are classified on the basis of the manner in which they are created and terminated.

Estate for Years. An *estate for years* is the type of leasehold estate most likely to be encountered by investors and lenders. It is created by a lease that specifies an exact duration for the tenancy. The period of tenancy may be less than one year and still be an estate for years as long as the lease agreement specifies the termination date. The lease, as well as all contracts involving transactions in real estate, is usually written. Indeed, a lease is generally required by the statute of frauds to be in writing when it is for a term longer than one year. The rights and duties of the landlord and tenant as well as other provisions related to the tenancy are normally stated in the lease agreement.

An estate for years can be for as long as 99 years (by custom, leases seldom exceed 99 years in duration), giving the lessee the right to use and control the property for that time in exchange for the rental payment. To the extent that the specified rental payment falls below the market rental rate of the property during the life of the lease, the lease has value (leasehold value) to the lessee. The value of this interest in the property can be borrowed against or even sold. For example, if lessee has the right to occupy the property for $1,000 per year when its fair market value is $2,000 per year, the $1,000 excess represents value to the lessee which may be borrowed against or sold (assuming no lease covenants prevent it).

While a property is leased, the original fee owner is considered to have a *leased fee* estate. This means that he has given up some property rights to the lessee (the leasehold estate). The value of the leased fee estate will now depend on the amount of lease payments expected during the term of the lease plus the value of the property when the lease terminates and the original owner receives the reversionary interest. Hence, a lease fee estate may be used as security for a loan or may be sold.

Estate from Year to Year. An *estate from year to year* (also known as an estate from period to period, or simply as a periodic tenancy) continues for successive periods until either party gives proper notice of its intent to terminate at the end of one or more subsequent periods. A ''period'' usually corresponds to the rent-paying period. Thus, such a tenancy commonly runs from month to month, although it can run for any period up to one year. Such estates can be created by explicit agreement between the parties, although a definite termination date is not specified. Since these estates are generally short term (one year or less), the agreement can be (and frequently is) oral. But this type

---

[2]*Estate at Will*. An estate at will is created when a landlord consents to the possession of the property by another person but without any agreement as to the payment of rent or the term of the tenancy. Such estates are of indefinite duration. *Estate at Sufferance*. An estate at sufferance occurs when the tenant holds possession of the property without consent or knowledge of the landlord after the termination of one of the other three estates.

of an estate can also be created without the express consent of the landlord. A common example is when the tenant "holds over" or continues to occupy, beyond the expiration date of an estate for years, and landlord accepts payment of rent or gives some other evidence of his tacit consent.

If present tenants are to remain in possession after the transfer or sale of property, the grantee should agree to take title subject to existing leases. The agreement should provide for prorationing of rents and the transfer of deposits to the grantee. Buyers of property encumbered by leases should always reserve the right to examine and approve leases to ensure that they are in force, are not in default, and are free from undesirable provisions.

ASSURANCE OF TITLE

When considering the purchase of real estate, buyers must be in a position to assess the quantity and quality of ownership rights that they are acquiring. Title assurance refers to the means by which buyers of real estate "(1) learn in advance whether their sellers have and can convey the quality of title they claim to possess, and (2) receive compensation if the title, after transfer, turns out not to be as represented."[3] Lenders are also concerned about title assurance because the quality of title affects the collateral value of the property in which they may have a secured interest. But before we examine the mechanisms used for title assurance, we briefly review the concepts of title and deed.

The Meaning of Title

Title is an abstract term frequently used to refer to documents, records, and acts that prove ownership. Title establishes the quantity of rights in real estate being conveyed from seller to buyer. The previous section briefly examined some of the various types of ownership rights and possessory interests that can be involved in a parcel of real estate. We saw, for example, that one person may hold title in fee simple ownership, convey title to a life estate to someone else, and convey the right to reversion upon termination of the life estate to yet another person. Hence, there are many possible combinations of rights and interests.

An *abstract of title* is an historical summary of the publicly recorded documents that affect title. The quality of the title conveyed from seller to buyer depends upon the effect these documents have upon the seller's rightful possession of his property.

Essentially, title exists only for freehold estates. A leasehold estate, on the other hand, is typically created by a contract (called a lease) between a person who holds title (the lessor) and another person (the lessee), whereby possession of the property is granted by the owner to the other person for a period of time. The existence of leases on a property will, however, impact the nature of the rights that can be conveyed to a new buyer because lease terms are binding on the new owner unless waived by the lessee. Because investors and lenders are concerned about the nature and extent of the rights they are acquiring or

---

[3]Grant S. Nelson and Dale A. Whitman, *Real Estate Transfer, Finance and Development,* 2nd ed., West Publishing Co., St. Paul, Minn. 1981, p. 167.

financing, leases encumbering the property can have a profound impact on a property's value.

Deeds

Usually title is conveyed from one person (the grantor) to another (the grantee) by means of a written instrument called a *deed*.[4] (We use the term *grantor* rather than *seller* because title may also be transferred by the owner (grantor) to heir (grantee) by means of a will, hence the terms *grantor* and *grantee*.) All deeds must be in writing and meet certain other legal requirements of the state in which the property is located in order to be a valid conveyance of ownership interests in real property.

Generally, a purchaser wants the deed to convey a good *and* marketable title to the property. A good title is one that is valid in fact; that is, the grantor does in fact lawfully have the title he claims to have to the property. However, a good title, because of the lack of sufficient documentation (as in the case of title by adverse possession) or because of encumbrances on the property, may be unmarketable. A marketable title is one that is not merely valid in fact but is also "free from reasonable doubt," one that is "reasonably free from litigation," and "one which readily can be sold or mortgaged to a reasonably prudent purchaser or mortgagee (mortgage lender)."[5]

An encumbrance on a title does not automatically make it unmarketable. A purchaser may be willing to take title to the property subject to the encumbrance. But the deed should note all encumbrances on the title so that a potential purchaser can rationally decide whether to purchase the property and to arrive at the appropriate price given any risks, costs, or restrictions posed by the encumbrances.

METHODS OF TITLE ASSURANCE

There are three general ways in which a buyer has assurance that a title is good and marketable. First, the seller may provide a warranty as part of the deed. Second, there may be a search of relevant recorded documents to determine whether there is reason to question the quality of title. This is usually done by an attorney and is accompanied by a legal opinion. Third, title insurance may be purchased to cover unexpected problems with the title.

Title Covenants in Deeds

The major types of deeds can be distinguished on the basis of the types of guarantees that the grantor makes with respect to the quality of the title. Guarantees, or warranties

---

[4]A deed is not the only way by which ownership rights in real property are conveyed. Titles are also transferred by wills, by court decrees, and by grants of land from the government to private persons. In addition, lawful title to property can also be acquired by means of adverse possession.

[5]*Black's Law Dictionary*, 5th ed. West Publishing Co., 1979, St. Paul, Minn.

as they are more commonly called, pertaining to the quality of the title that are contained within the deed instrument take the form of deed covenants. Deed covenants are clauses in the deed in which the grantor makes a promise that something is either done, shall be done, or shall not be done, or stipulates the truth of certain facts. It is important to understand that any deed, no matter how complete the warranties contained therein, can only convey the quality of title that the grantor actually has to the property. This is why most buyers of real estate usually obtain independent assurance of the validity and marketability of the title from a third party. Nonetheless, deed covenants do represent a significant form of protection for the buyer because the law provides for recourse in the form of a suit for damages against the grantor should they be breached. Depending on the type of deed used in conveyance, the grantee may have extensive claims or no claim at all against the grantor for defects of title. There is, of course, the possibility that the grantor's ability to pay damages to the grantee may be insufficient to cover the grantee's losses and costs.

General Warranty Deed.   A general warranty deed is the most commonly used deed in real estate transactions and the most desirable type of deed from the buyer's perspective. It offers the most comprehensive warranties about the quality of the title. Essentially, the grantor warrants that the title he conveys to the property is free and clear of all encumbrances, other than those that are specifically listed in the deed. Probably the most significant covenants that are generally contained in such a deed are the following: (1) a covenant that the grantor has good (legally valid) title to the property; (2) a covenant that he has the right to convey the property; (3) a covenant to compensate the grantee for loss of property or eviction suffered by the grantee as a result of someone else having a superior claim to the property; and (4) a covenant against encumbrances on the property other than those specifically stated in the deed. In a general warranty deed, these covenants cover all conveyances of the property from the time of the original source of title to the present.

Special Warranty Deed.   A special warranty deed makes the same warranties as a general warranty deed except that it limits their application to defects and encumbrances which occurred only while the grantor held title to the property. They do not apply to title problems caused or created by predecessors in title as do the warranties in a general warranty deed.

Quitclaim Deed.   A quitclaim deed offers the grantee the least protection. Such a deed simply conveys to the grantee whatever rights, interests, and title that the grantor may have in the property. No warranties are made about the nature of these rights and interests or of the quality of the grantor's title to the property. The quitclaim deed simply says that the grantor "quits" whatever "claim" he has in the property (which may well be none) in favor of the grantee.[6]

---

[6]Quitclaim deeds are appropriate and frequently used to clear up technical defects or "clouds" on the title to a property. Where the record indicates a person may have any potential claim to the property, obtaining a quitclaim deed from him will eliminate the risk that such a claim will be made in the future.

Very few buyers of real estate rely solely on the guarantees of title provided in deeds of conveyance by the seller. The two methods that buyers employ most often to obtain assurance of title independent of the guarantees provided by the seller are an attorney's opinion of title and title insurance.[7]

Abstract and Opinion Method

Obtaining a lawyer's opinion of title used to be the most common method of title assurance before the widespread availability of title insurance. Although its use has been reduced by title insurance, this older method of title assurance is still widely used today, especially in the South and East.

Essentially, the abstract and opinion method is a two-step process. First, there is a search of the title record. A search of title involves locating and examining all of the instruments in the public records that have affected the title of the property in question.[8] Second, when the title search is completed, a lawyer studies the relevant public records and other facts and proceedings affecting title for the purpose of arriving at an expert opinion of the character of the title. Based upon his study of the abstract and/or the record, he will give his judgment whether the title is good and marketable. If the title is found to be "clouded," the opinion should state what defects and/or encumbrances were uncovered by an examination of the records, and it should also state what the lawyer thinks can and should be done to "cure" the defects uncovered.

Because a lawyer's responsibility is limited to what appears in the records, the lawyer cannot be held liable for any defect in title not disclosed therein. For example, a forged deed or one signed by a person judged to be incompetent would show good record title and a purchaser would have no recourse against the attorney or title company because abstracts and opinions are expressly limited to matters of public record. Any liability borne by the lawyer is based upon proof of his negligence or of his lack of professional skill in the examination of the records. Either would be difficult to prove. Rather than rely on the lawyer's opinion, most lenders and investors today prefer to purchase title insurance, which eliminates this risk.

---

[7]There are other types of deeds, such as the bargain and sale deed, and deeds that are given by third party fiduciaries, such as a sheriff's deed or a trustee's deed. For a thorough discussion of all the different types of deeds, see J. L. Sackman, *The Law of Titles* (Matthew Bender and Co., Inc., New York, 1959).

[8]Most of the instruments that affect title to real estate are recorded, in accordance with the recording acts of the various states, at what is typically called the county recorder's office. But some instruments that affect title may be recorded in other places. The nature of these other places where records are filed vary from state to state, but Nelson and Whitman cite the following as illustrative: "real property tax liens in the county treasurer or tax collector's office, assessment liens for streets, sewer, and other improvements in various city offices, wills in the office of the clerk of the probate or other relevant court, judgment liens in the office of the clerk of court, bankruptcies and federal condemnations in the office of the federal district court clerk, and zoning or other land use information (technically not an aspect of title, but equally important to real estate purchasers [especially those of commercial and industrial property]) in a city or county zoning administrator's offices" (Nelson and Whitman, p. 189). As should be apparent, the search process may not always be straightforward, and a thorough search of title can involve a great deal of time and effort.

The Title Insurance Method

Title insurance was developed to cure the inadequacies of title validation accomplished through an abstract and legal opinion. Title insurance does all that both a carefully drawn abstract and a well-considered opinion by a competent lawyer are expected to do. In addition, it adds the principle of insurance to the above services and undertakes to spread the risk of *unseen hazards* among all who benefit from it.

The elimination of risk arising from unseen hazards in the public record has caused many investors and lenders to prefer this method of title assurance. In fact, title insurance is required for any mortgage to be traded in the secondary mortgage market. The title insurance process starts with a careful analysis of the records. The information available to the commercial title insurance company may be even more complete than that found in the public records. Title insurance companies' skilled technicians examine all available evidence of the title to determine its character. If the conclusions warrant, the title company will insure the title to a property and assume risks that are not even disclosed in the public records or in its own files. In short, title insurance ensures that the title is good and marketable.

What title insurance is supposed to add to the abstract system and the opinion of skilled lawyers may be summarized as follows (1) definite contract liability to the premium payer; (2) reserves sufficient to meet insured losses; (3) supervision by an agency of the state in which the title insurance company operates; and (4) protection to the policyholder against financial losses that may show up at any future time because of title defects of any kind, disclosed or hidden. Despite these advantages, the abstract and opinion method may still be used because of its lower cost. In general, one method but not both, is used when purchasing property, to avoid the duplication of effort and cost.

Kinds of Title Insurance Policies.   There are two kinds of title insurance policies. The owner's policy insures the interest of a new property owner. The lender's (or mortgagee) policy insures the interests of the mortgage. The owner's policy is payable to the owner (or to the heirs of the owner); the lender's policy is payable to the mortgagee.

Both policies are paid for with a one-time premium. The one-time premium for the owner's policy may be paid for by either the seller or the buyer, depending on the terms of the purchase contract, which is influenced by local custom and market conditions. It is almost universal practice for the borrower to pay the cost of the mortgagee's policy.

RECORDING ACTS

All states have enacted statutes known as recording acts. Although the recording acts are not uniform among the states, these acts in general provide a publicly accessible system for assessing and establishing claims or interests in real estate as against all other parties. These statutes also provide a set of authoritative rules for resolving priority disputes among competing claimants to interests in real estate. As part of this system, procedures have been established for placing documents affecting claims to real estate interests on the public record and for maintaining these records to make available information concerning almost all interests in real estate. Once an instrument creating a claim on an interest in real estate has been duly recorded, the recording is deemed to give constructive notice of this interest "to the world." Constructive notice means that the recording acts deem a person to have whatever information is contained in the public records which could be obtained by a reasonably diligent investigation of the records, whether or not he or she actually has knowledge of the information so recorded. Instruments affecting virtually all interests in real estate, including deeds, mortgages, assignments of mortgages, liens on real estate, land contracts, long-term leases, easements, restrictive covenants, and options to buy, are covered by recording acts.

Most recording acts say that in order to establish and preserve a claim to an interest in real estate that will take precedence in law against future claimants, the instrument creating that claim must be recorded in accordance with state law. These acts were designed in part to protect an innocent person who purchased an interest in real estate in good faith unaware that the interest had already been acquired by another. For example, if A conveyed to B, who did not record the instrument establishing his claim, and later A conveyed the same interest to C, who did record, C's claim would be superior to B's if he was unaware of the prior conveyance and paid valuable consideration to A for the conveyance. B's only claim would be to file a suit against A for fraud.

One cloud on title which may not be disclosed by the public records is a *mechanics lien*. In general, mechanics liens give unpaid contractors, workmen, and material suppliers the right to attach a lien on the real estate to which they added their labor or materials. To obtain the payment owed them, they may foreclose such liens by forcing a judicial sale of the encumbered property and be paid from the proceeds of the sale. Use of mechanics liens exists in every state, although the nature of the mechanics lien statutes vary from state to state.

Mechanics liens are permitted to be recorded "after the fact." In other words, state laws generally give contractors, laborers, or suppliers of materials a certain period of time following the completion of work or delivery of materials during which to file their lien. When the lien is filed, it "relates back" and takes priority over all liens filed after the time when materials were first delivered or work first performed on the real estate. As a result, until the end of the time allowed for filing (generally 60 days), a purchaser of an interest in newly constructed or improved real estate cannot be sure that the interest will be unencumbered or that the interest will have the priority bargained for. As a precaution, lenders and purchasers of such real estate should require the seller to provide an affidavit stating that at closing, all monies due to contractors and subcontractors have been fully paid. In the event liens are filed after the closing, a breach of the vendor's covenants in the affidavit can easily be proven, and the vendor can be held liable for the discharge of those liens.

THE MORTGAGE INSTRUMENT

In the following discussion of mortgages we will concentrate on loans used for the purchase of owner-occupied residential property. Although much of the information covered here also applies to income other types of loans (e.g., construction and land development loans), additional material which relates specifically to these loans will be discussed in later chapters.

Utilization of mortgage financing has been the most common method of financing the purchase of real estate. Under this method, the buyer usually borrows funds from an institutional lender (e.g., a savings and loan association, a savings bank, a commercial bank, or life insurance company) and uses these and other funds to purchase a property. Real estate is generally regarded by lenders as excellent security for a loan, and lenders acquire a secured interest in the real estate with a mortgage.

Definition of a Mortgage

In its most general sense, a mortgage is created in a transaction whereby one party pledges real property to another party as security for an obligation owed to that other party. A promissory note is normally executed contemporaneously with the mortgage. This note creates the obligation to repay the loan in accordance with its terms and is secured by the mortgage. The elements essential to the existence of a mortgage are an *obligation* to pay or perform and a *pledge* of property as security for that obligation. The obligation secured by a mortgage need not be monetary. It may be, for example, an agreement to perform some service or to perform some other specified actions.[9]

Title Theory versus Lien Theory.   Historically there have been two general theories of the legal effect on title when a property is mortgaged. Under the *title theory,* title and the right to possession technically pass from the mortgagor to the mortgagee when the mortgage is executed. Even if the mortgagor retains physical possession, the mortgagee could dispossess him. Only upon payment of the debt was the mortgagee's title defeated. Where it still prevails,[10] this theory has been modified by most states to protect the mortgagor so that only when he is in default on his obligations is the mortgagee permitted to take possession.

The *lien theory* has become the dominant one throughout the United States today. Under this theory the mortgage is considered by the courts to be essentially in the nature of a lien. The mortgage merely conveys a security interest in a specifically designated property in return for a loan. It grants neither title nor the right of possession to the mortgagee. In the event the borrower fails to make the required payments on the underlying debt, the lender may have its security interest in the property (i.e., its lien) enforced.

The right of the mortgagee in title theory states to take possession of his property upon default by the mortgagor is likely to be restricted or circumscribed by terms and procedures established by state statutes. These restrictions are likely to take the form of required procedures and processes to ensure that all parties who have an interest in the property

---

[9]To be an obligation that can be secured by a mortgage, an obligation which is not itself an explicitly monetary one must be reducible to monetary terms. In other words, a dollar value must be placed on it.

[10]States espousing the title theory, at least in part, include Alabama, Arkansas, Connecticut, Illinois, Maine, Maryland, Massachusetts, Mississippi, New Hampshire, New Jersey, North Carolina, Ohio, Pennsylvania, Rhode Island, Tennessee, Vermont, and West Virginia.

receive notice of the enforcement of the lender's lien rights and that the property is sold in such a manner that its fair value is realized. This is not unlike the denial of the right of possession to the mortgagee, except with the consent of the owner, in lien theory states until the ownership of the property is determined as a result of the foreclosure sale. Under modern mortgage law, the differences between the rights of the parties to a mortgage in a lien theory state and in a title theory state are more technical than real.

Note versus Mortgage

Normally, the underlying obligation which is secured by a mortgage is evidenced by a separate promissory note. The note admits the debt and generally makes the borrower personally liable for the obligation. The mortgage is usually a separate document which pledges the designated property as security for the debt. If the lender is completely confident that the borrower has sufficient assets now, would continue to have those assets over the term of the loan, and would meet the underlying obligation, no mortgage would be necessary. In fact, in case of default the mortgagee may elect to disregard the mortgage and sue on the note. The judgment awarded him as a result of a suit on the note may be attached to other property of the mortgagor which, when sold to satisfy the judgment lien, may enable the mortgagee to recover the amount of his claim more readily than if he foreclosed his mortgage. In practice, the mortgagee will normally elect to sue on the note and foreclose his mortgage simultaneously.

Mortgages typically include clauses containing important covenants for both the mortgagor and mortgagee. These clauses are frequently repeated in the promissory note, or the note may incorporate these covenants by reference to the mortgage. Promissory notes typically contain clauses specifying the interest rate, repayment terms, maturity dates and other clauses dealing with notices of default, the rights of mortgagors and mortgagees upon default, late payment fees, prepayment fees, and other clauses. The note also generally empowers the mortgagee to require immediate and full payment of the entire amount of debt secured by the mortgage (referred to as acceleration) in case of the mortgagor's default. Without an acceleration clause the mortgagee could only sue for the amount of the payments currently in default. Another clause may be included in the note, which requires full payment of the entire debt upon the transfer of the mortgagor's interest in the property without the mortgagee's consent. This is referred to as a *due on sale clause*.

Interests Which Can Be Mortgaged

Most people are accustomed to thinking of a mortgage in relation to full, or fee simple, ownership. But any interest in real estate that is subject to sale, grant, or assignment—that is, any interest that can be transferred—can be mortgaged. Thus, such diverse interests as fee simple estates, life estates, estates for years, remainders, reversions, leasehold interests, and options to purchase real estate, among others, are all mortgageable interests as far as legal theory is concerned. Whether, as a matter of sound business judgment, mortgagees would be willing to lend money against some of the lesser interests in land is quite another question.

Minimum Mortgage Requirements

A mortgage involves a transfer of an interest in real estate. Accordingly, the statute of frauds requires that it must be in writing. The vast volume of mortgage lending today is institutional lending, and institutional mortgages are formal documents. There is, however, no specific form required for a valid mortgage. Indeed, although most mortgages are formal documents, a valid mortgage could be handwritten. The requirements of a valid mortgage document are (1) wording that appropriately expresses the intent of the parties to create a security interest in real property for the benefit of the mortgagee and (2) other items required by state law.

In this country, mortgage law has traditionally been within the jurisdiction of state law, and, by and large, mortgages continue to be governed primarily by state law. Thus, in order to be enforceable, a mortgage must meet requirements imposed by the law of the state in which the property offered as security is located.

Whether a printed form of mortgage instrument is used or an attorney draws up a special form, the following subjects should always be included:

1. Appropriate identification of mortgagor and mortgagee.
2. Proper description of the liened property.
3. Covenants of seizin and warranty.[11]
4. Provision for release of dower rights.[12]
5. Any other desired covenants and contractual agreements. All of the terms and contractual agreements recited in the note can be included in the mortgage as well by making reference to the note in the mortgage document.

Although the bulk of mortgage law remains within the jurisdiction of state law, there is a wide range of federal regulations that are operative in the area of mortgage law. Moreover, in recent years the federal government has acted to directly preempt state law in a number of areas (e.g., overturning state usury laws,[13] overturning state restrictions on the operation of due on sale clauses, and establishing conditions for allowing prepayment of the mortgage debt and for setting prepayment penalties).

In addition, the federal government has exerted a strong but indirect influence on mortgage transactions via its sponsorship of the agencies and quasi-private institutions that support and, for all practical purposes, constitute the secondary market for residential mortgages. The Federal National Mortgage Association (FNMA) and the Federal Home Loan Mortgage Corporation (FHLMC) have adopted joint standardized mortgage forms

---

[11]A *covenant* is a promise or binding assurance. *Seizin* is the state of owing the quantum of title being conveyed.

[12]*Dower* is the interest in a husband's real estate transferred by law to the widow after his death. The common law counterpart running in favor of the husband as a widower is called *curtesy.* Many states now have a statutory allowance from the decedent's estate in lieu of dower and curtesy.

[13]Usury laws prohibit charging unconscionable and exorbitant rates or amounts of interest for the use of money. A usurious loan is one whose interest rate exceeds that permitted by usury laws.

for the purpose of facilitating secondary market transactions on a nationwide basis. The joint FNMA-FHLMC uniform mortgage form has been so widely adopted by residential mortgage lenders that it has largely replaced the use of mortgage forms used by individual institutions. One reason for the popularity of this form with residential lenders is that it is readily acceptable by the major secondary market institutions, should the lender desire to sell the mortgage after it has been originated.

Typical Mortgage Clauses

The Federal National Mortgage Association single family dwelling form used in Indiana (see Exhibit 2–1 FNMA/FHLMC Uniform Instrument) contains the following provisions:

Paragraph 1. Payment of Principal and Interest: Prepayment and Late Charges.   This clause contains a covenant to pay the mortgage debt and any prepayment and late charges due according to the terms specified in the note.

Paragraph 2. Funds for Taxes and Insurance.   This clause requires the mortgagor to pay the amounts needed to cover the items required by clauses 4 and 5, plus mortgage insurance premiums, if required by the lender, in monthly installments in advance of when they are due, unless such payments are prohibited by state law. The purpose of this clause is to enable the mortgagee to pay these charges out of money provided by the mortgagor when they become due instead of relying on the mortgagor to make timely payments on his own. The mortgagee is thereby better able to protect its security interest against liens for taxes, which normally have priority over the first mortgage, and against lapses in insurance coverage. Such funds are generally held in an escrow or trust account for the mortgagor.

Paragraph 3. Application of Payments.   Under this paragraph payments under paragraphs 1 and 2 are applied first to the late charges due under the note; second, to prepayment charges due under the note; third, to amount due under paragraph 2; fourth, to interest due; and, last, to principal due.

Paragraph 4. Charges; Liens.   This clause requires the mortgagor to pay all taxes, assessments, charges, and claims assessed against the property that have priority over the mortgage and to pay all leasehold payments, if applicable. The reason for this clause is that the mortgagee's security interest can be wiped out if these claims are not paid or discharged, since they generally can attain priority over the interests of the mortgagee. For example, if taxes and assessments are not paid, a first mortgage on the property can be wiped out at a sale to satisfy the tax lien, unless the mortgagee is either the successful bidder at the tax sale or pays the tax due to keep the property from being sold at tax sale.

Paragraph 5. Hazard Insurance.   This clause requires the mortgagor to obtain and maintain insurance against loss or damage to the property caused by fire and other hazards,

EXHIBIT 2–1   FNMA/FHLMC Uniform Instrument

——————————————— [Space Above This Line For Recording Data] ———————————————

MORTGAGE

THIS MORTGAGE ("Security Instrument") is given on
19   The mortgagor is

("Borrower"). This Security Instrument is given to

which is organized and existing under the laws of   , and whose address is

("Lender").

Borrower owes Lender the principal sum of

Dollars (U.S. $). This debt is evidenced by Borrower's note
dated the same date as this Security Instrument ("Note"), which provides for monthly payments, with the full debt, if not
paid earlier, due and payable on   This Security Instrument
secures to Lender: (a) the repayment of the debt evidenced by the Note, with interest, and all renewals, extensions and
modifications; (b) the payment of all other sums, with interest, advanced under paragraph 7 to protect the security of this
Security Instrument; and (c) the performance of Borrower's covenants and agreements under this Security Instrument and
the Note. For this purpose, Borrower does hereby mortgage, grant and convey to Lender the following described property
located in   County, Indiana:

which has the address of

[Street]   [City]

Indiana

[Zip Code]   ("Property Address");

TOGETHER WITH all the improvements now or hereafter erected on the property, and all easements, rights
appurtenances, rents, royalties, mineral, oil and gas rights and profits, water rights and stock and all fixtures now or
hereafter a part of the property. All replacements and additions shall also be covered by this Security Instrument. All of the
foregoing is referred to in this Security Instrument as the "Property."

BORROWER COVENANTS that Borrower is lawfully seised of the estate hereby conveyed and has the right to
mortgage, grant and convey the Property and that the Property is unencumbered, except for encumbrances of record.
Borrower warrants and will defend generally the title to the Property against all claims and demands, subject to any
encumbrances of record.

THIS SECURITY INSTRUMENT combines uniform covenants for national use and non-uniform covenants with
limited variations by jurisdiction to constitute a uniform security instrument covering real property.

INDIANA—Single Family—FNMA/FHLMC UNIFORM INSTRUMENT   Form 3015 12/83

Form 81-5 Rev.

EXHIBIT 2–1 (*continued*)

UNIFORM COVENANTS. Borrower and Lender covenant and agree as follows:

1. Payment of Principal and Interest; Prepayment and Late Charges. Borrower shall promptly pay when due the principal of and interest on the debt evidenced by the Note and any prepayment and late charges due under the Note.

2. Funds for Taxes and Insurance. Subject to applicable law or to a written waiver by Lender, Borrower shall pay to Lender on the day monthly payments are due under the Note, until the Note is paid in full, a sum ("Funds") equal to one-twelfth of: (a) yearly taxes and assessments which may attain priority over this Security Instrument; (b) yearly leasehold payments or ground rents on the Property, if any; (c) yearly hazard insurance premiums; and (d) yearly mortgage insurance premiums, if any. These items are called "escrow items." Lender may estimate the Funds due on the basis of current data and reasonable estimates of future escrow items.

The Funds shall be held in an institution the deposits or accounts of which are insured or guaranteed by a federal or state agency (including Lender if Lender is such an institution). Lender shall apply the Funds to pay the escrow items. Lender may not charge for holding and applying the Funds, analyzing the account or verifying the escrow items, unless Lender pays Borrower interest on the Funds and applicable law permits Lender to make such a charge. Borrower and Lender may agree in writing that interest shall be paid on the Funds. Unless an agreement is made or applicable law requires interest to be paid, Lender shall not be required to pay Borrower any interest or earnings on the Funds. Lender shall give to Borrower, without charge, an annual accounting of the Funds showing credits and debits to the Funds and the purpose for which each debit to the Funds was made. The Funds are pledged as additional security for the sums secured by this Security Instrument.

If the amount of the Funds held by Lender, together with the future monthly payments of Funds payable prior to the due dates of the escrow items, shall exceed the amount required to pay the escrow items when due, the excess shall be, at Borrower's option, either promptly repaid to Borrower or credited to Borrower on monthly payments of Funds. If the amount of the Funds held by Lender is not sufficient to pay the escrow items when due, Borrower shall pay to Lender any amount necessary to make up the deficiency in one or more payments as required by Lender.

Upon payment in full of all sums secured by this Security Instrument, Lender shall promptly refund to Borrower any Funds held by Lender. If under paragraph 19 the Property is sold or acquired by Lender, Lender shall apply, no later than immediately prior to the sale of the Property or its acquisition by Lender, any Funds held by Lender at the time of application as a credit against the sums secured by this Security Instrument.

3. Application of Payments. Unless applicable law provides otherwise, all payments received by Lender under paragraphs 1 and 2 shall be applied: first, to late charges due under the Note; second, to prepayment charges due under the Note; third, to amounts payable under paragraph 2; fourth, to interest due; and last, to principal due.

4. Charges; Liens. Borrower shall pay all taxes, assessments, charges, fines and impositions attributable to the Property which may attain priority over this Security Instrument, and leasehold payments or ground rents, if any. Borrower shall pay these obligations in the manner provided in paragraph 2, or if not paid in that manner, Borrower shall pay them on time directly to the person owed payment. Borrower shall promptly furnish to Lender all notices of amounts to be paid under this paragraph. If Borrower makes these payments directly, Borrower shall promptly furnish to Lender receipts evidencing the payments.

Borrower shall promptly discharge any lien which has priority over this Security Instrument unless Borrower: (a) agrees in writing to the payment of the obligation secured by the lien in a manner acceptable to Lender; (b) contests in good faith the lien by, or defends against enforcement of the lien in, legal proceedings which in the Lender's opinion operate to prevent the enforcement of the lien or forfeiture of any part of the Property; or (c) secures from the holder of the lien an agreement satisfactory to Lender subordinating the lien to this Security Instrument. If Lender determines that any part of the Property is subject to a lien which may attain priority over this Security Instrument, Lender may give Borrower a notice identifying the lien. Borrower shall satisfy the lien or take one or more of the actions set forth above within 10 days of the giving of notice.

5. Hazard Insurance. Borrower shall keep the improvements now existing or hereafter erected on the Property insured against loss by fire, hazards included within the term "extended coverage" and any other hazards for which Lender requires insurance. This insurance shall be maintained in the amounts and for the periods that Lender requires. The insurance carrier providing the insurance shall be chosen by Borrower subject to Lender's approval which shall not be unreasonably withheld.

All insurance policies and renewals shall be acceptable to Lender and shall include a standard mortgage clause. Lender shall have the right to hold the policies and renewals. If Lender requires, Borrower shall promptly give to Lender all receipts of paid premiums and renewal notices. In the event of loss, Borrower shall give prompt notice to the insurance carrier and Lender. Lender may make proof of loss if not made promptly by Borrower.

Unless Lender and Borrower otherwise agree in writing, insurance proceeds shall be applied to restoration or repair of the Property damaged, if the restoration or repair is economically feasible and Lender's security is not lessened. If the restoration or repair is not economically feasible or Lender's security would be lessened, the insurance proceeds shall be applied to the sums secured by this Security Instrument, whether or not then due, with any excess paid to Borrower. If Borrower abandons the Property, or does not answer within 30 days a notice from Lender that the insurance carrier has offered to settle a claim, then Lender may collect the insurance proceeds. Lender may use the proceeds to repair or restore the Property or to pay sums secured by this Security Instrument, whether or not then due. The 30-day period will begin when the notice is given.

Unless Lender and Borrower otherwise agree in writing, any application of proceeds to principal shall not extend or postpone the due date of the monthly payments referred to in paragraphs 1 and 2 or change the amount of the payments. If under paragraph 19 the Property is acquired by Lender, Borrower's right to any insurance policies and proceeds resulting from damage to the Property prior to the acquisition shall pass to Lender to the extent of the sums secured by this Security Instrument immediately prior to the acquisition.

6. Preservation and Maintenance of Property; Leaseholds. Borrower shall not destroy, damage or substantially change the Property, allow the Property to deteriorate or commit waste. If this Security Instrument is on a leasehold, Borrower shall comply with the provisions of the lease, and if Borrower acquires fee title to the Property, the leasehold and fee title shall not merge unless Lender agrees to the merger in writing.

7. Protection of Lender's Rights in the Property; Mortgage Insurance. If Borrower fails to perform the covenants and agreements contained in this Security Instrument, or there is a legal proceeding that may significantly affect Lender's rights in the Property (such as a proceeding in bankruptcy, probate, for condemnation or to enforce laws or regulations), then Lender may do and pay for whatever is necessary to protect the value of the Property and Lender's rights in the Property. Lender's actions may include paying any sums secured by a lien which has priority over this Security Instrument, appearing in court, paying reasonable attorneys' fees and entering on the Property to make repairs. Although Lender may take action under this paragraph 7, Lender does not have to do so.

Any amounts disbursed by Lender under this paragraph 7 shall become additional debt of Borrower secured by this Security Instrument. Unless Borrower and Lender agree to other terms of payment, these amounts shall bear interest from the date of disbursement at the Note rate and shall be payable, with interest, upon notice from Lender to Borrower requesting payment.

EXHIBIT 2–1   *(continued)*

If Lender required mortgage insurance as a condition of making the loan secured by this Security Instrument, Borrower shall pay the premiums required to maintain the insurance in effect until such time as the requirement for the insurance terminates in accordance with Borrower's and Lender's written agreement or applicable law.

8. Inspection.   Lender or its agent may make reasonable entries upon and inspections of the Property. Lender shall give Borrower notice at the time of or prior to an inspection specifying reasonable cause for the inspection.

9. Condemnation.   The proceeds of any award or claim for damages, direct or consequential, in connection with any condemnation or other taking of any part of the Property, or for conveyance in lieu of condemnation, are hereby assigned and shall be paid to Lender.

In the event of a total taking of the Property, the proceeds shall be applied to the sums secured by this Security Instrument, whether or not then due, with any excess paid to Borrower. In the event of a partial taking of the Property, unless Borrower and Lender otherwise agree in writing, the sums secured by this Security Instrument shall be reduced by the amount of the proceeds multiplied by the following fraction: (a) the total amount of the sums secured immediately before the taking, divided by (b) the fair market value of the Property immediately before the taking. Any balance shall be paid to Borrower.

If the Property is abandoned by Borrower, or if, after notice by Lender to Borrower that the condemnor offers to make an award or settle a claim for damages, Borrower fails to respond to Lender within 30 days after the date the notice is given, Lender is authorized to collect and apply the proceeds, at its option, either to restoration or repair of the Property or to the sums secured by this Security Instrument, whether or not then due.

Unless Lender and Borrower otherwise agree in writing, any application of proceeds to principal shall not extend or postpone the due date of the monthly payments referred to in paragraphs 1 and 2 or change the amount of such payments.

10. Borrower Not Released; Forbearance By Lender Not a Waiver.   Extension of the time for payment or modification of amortization of the sums secured by this Security Instrument granted by Lender to any successor in interest of Borrower shall not operate to release the liability of the original Borrower or Borrower's successors in interest. Lender shall not be required to commence proceedings against any successor in interest or refuse to extend time for payment or otherwise modify amortization of the sums secured by this Security Instrument by reason of any demand made by the original Borrower or Borrower's successors in interest. Any forbearance by Lender in exercising any right or remedy shall not be a waiver of or preclude the exercise of any right or remedy.

11. Successors and Assigns Bound; Joint and Several Liability; Co-signers.   The covenants and agreements of this Security Instrument shall bind and benefit the successors and assigns of Lender and Borrower, subject to the provisions of paragraph 17. Borrower's covenants and agreements shall be joint and several. Any Borrower who co-signs this Security Instrument but does not execute the Note: (a) is co-signing this Security Instrument only to mortgage, grant and convey that Borrower's interest in the Property under the terms of this Security Instrument; (b) is not personally obligated to pay the sums secured by this Security Instrument; and (c) agrees that Lender and any other Borrower may agree to extend, modify, forbear or make any accommodations with regard to the terms of this Security Instrument or the Note without that Borrower's consent.

12. Loan Charges.   If the loan secured by this Security Instrument is subject to a law which sets maximum loan charges, and that law is finally interpreted so that the interest or other loan charges collected or to be collected in connection with the loan exceed the permitted limits, then: (a) any such loan charge shall be reduced by the amount necessary to reduce the charge to the permitted limit; and (b) any sums already collected from Borrower which exceeded permitted limits will be refunded to Borrower. Lender may choose to make this refund by reducing the principal owed under the Note or by making a direct payment to Borrower. If a refund reduces principal, the reduction will be treated as a partial prepayment without any prepayment charge under the Note.

13. Legislation Affecting Lender's Rights.   If enactment or expiration of applicable laws has the effect of rendering any provision of the Note or this Security Instrument unenforceable according to its terms, Lender, at its option, may require immediate payment in full of all sums secured by this Security Instrument and may invoke any remedies permitted by paragraph 19. If Lender exercises this option, Lender shall take the steps specified in the second paragraph of paragraph 17.

14. Notices.   Any notice to Borrower provided for in this Security Instrument shall be given by delivering it or by mailing it by first class mail unless applicable law requires use of another method. The notice shall be directed to the Property Address or any other address Borrower designates by notice to Lender. Any notice to Lender shall be given by first class mail to Lender's address stated herein or any other address Lender designates by notice to Borrower. Any notice provided for in this Security Instrument shall be deemed to have been given to Borrower or Lender when given as provided in this paragraph.

15. Governing Law; Severability.   This Security Instrument shall be governed by federal law and the law of the jurisdiction in which the Property is located. In the event that any provision or clause of this Security Instrument or the Note conflicts with applicable law, such conflict shall not affect other provisions of this Security Instrument or the Note which can be given effect without the conflicting provision. To this end the provisions of this Security Instrument and the Note are declared to be severable.

16. Borrower's Copy.   Borrower shall be given one conformed copy of the Note and of this Security Instrument.

17. Transfer of the Property or a Beneficial Interest in Borrower.   If all or any part of the Property or any interest in it is sold or transferred (or if a beneficial interest in Borrower is sold or transferred and Borrower is not a natural person) without Lender's prior written consent, Lender may, at its option, require immediate payment in full of all sums secured by this Security Instrument. However, this option shall not be exercised by Lender if exercise is prohibited by federal law as of the date of this Security Instrument.

If Lender exercises this option, Lender shall give Borrower notice of acceleration. The notice shall provide a period of not less than 30 days from the date the notice is delivered or mailed within which Borrower must pay all sums secured by this Security Instrument. If Borrower fails to pay these sums prior to the expiration of this period, Lender may invoke any remedies permitted by this Security Instrument without further notice or demand on Borrower.

18. Borrower's Right to Reinstate.   If Borrower meets certain conditions, Borrower shall have the right to have enforcement of this Security Instrument discontinued at any time prior to the earlier of: (a) 5 days (or such other period as applicable law may specify for reinstatement) before sale of the Property pursuant to any power of sale contained in this Security Instrument; or (b) entry of a judgment enforcing this Security Instrument. Those conditions are that Borrower: (a) pays Lender all sums which then would be due under this Security Instrument and the Note had no acceleration occurred; (b) cures any default of any other covenants or agreements; (c) pays all expenses incurred in enforcing this Security Instrument, including, but not limited to, reasonable attorneys' fees; and (d) takes such action as Lender may reasonably require to assure that the lien of this Security Instrument, Lender's rights in the Property and Borrower's obligation to pay the sums secured by this Security Instrument shall continue unchanged. Upon reinstatement by Borrower, this Security Instrument and the obligations secured hereby shall remain fully effective as if no acceleration had occurred. However, this right to reinstate shall not apply in the case of acceleration under paragraphs 13 or 17.

EXHIBIT 2–1 *(continued)*

NON-UNIFORM COVENANTS. Borrower and Lender further covenant and agree as follows:

19. Acceleration; Remedies. Lender shall give notice to Borrower prior to acceleration following Borrower's breach of any covenant or agreement in this Security Instrument (but not prior to acceleration under paragraphs 13 and 17 unless applicable law provides otherwise). The notice shall specify: (a) the default; (b) the action required to cure the default; (c) a date, not less than 30 days from the date the notice is given to Borrower, by which the default must be cured; and (d) that failure to cure the default on or before the date specified in the notice may result in acceleration of the sums secured by this Security Instrument, foreclosure by judicial proceeding and sale of the Property. The notice shall further inform Borrower of the right to reinstate after acceleration and the right to assert in the foreclosure proceeding the non-existence of a default or any other defense of Borrower to acceleration and foreclosure. If the default is not cured on or before the date specified in the notice, Lender at its option may require immediate payment in full of all sums secured by this Security Instrument without further demand and may foreclose this Security Instrument by judicial proceeding. Lender shall be entitled to collect all expenses incurred in pursuing the remedies provided in this paragraph 19, including, but not limited to, reasonable attorneys' fees and costs of title evidence.

20. Lender in Possession. Upon acceleration under paragraph 19 or abandonment of the Property, Lender (by judicially appointed receiver) shall be entitled to enter upon, take possession of and manage the Property and to collect the rents of the Property including those past due. Any rents collected by Lender or the receiver shall be applied first to payment of the costs of management of the Property and collection of rents, including, but not limited to, receiver's fees, premiums on receiver's bonds and reasonable attorneys' fees, and then to the sums secured by this Security Instrument.

21. Release. Upon payment of all sums secured by this Security Instrument, Lender shall release this Security Instrument without charge to Borrower.

22. Waiver of Valuation and Appraisement. Borrower waives all right of valuation and appraisement.

23. Riders to this Security Instrument. If one or more riders are executed by Borrower and recorded together with this Security Instrument, the covenants and agreements of each such rider shall be incorporated into and shall amend and supplement the covenants and agreements of this Security Instrument as if the rider(s) were a part of this Security Instrument. [Check applicable box(es)]

☐ Adjustable Rate Rider   ☐ Condominium Rider   ☐ 2–4 Family Rider

☐ Graduated Payment Rider   ☐ Planned Unit Development Rider

☐ Other(s) [specify]

BY SIGNING BELOW, Borrower accepts and agrees to the terms and covenants contained in this Security Instrument and in any rider(s) executed by Borrower and recorded with it.

_____   _____(Seal)
—Borrower

_____   _____(Seal)
—Borrower

———————————— [Space Below This Line For Acknowledgment] ————————————

STATE OF INDIANA,   County ss:

On this _____ day of _____, 19____, before me, the undersigned, a Notary Public in and for said County, personally appeared _____

_____, and acknowledged the execution of the foregoing instrument.

WITNESS my hand and official seal.

My Commission expires:

_____
Notary Public

This instrument was prepared by:

EXHIBIT 2–1   *(continued)*

NOTE

...., 19..........   ...., ...
[City]   [State]

....
[Property Address]

1. BORROWER'S PROMISE TO PAY

In return for a loan that I have received, I promise to pay U.S. $.. (this amount is called "principal"), plus interest, to the order of the Lender. The Lender is ....

.... I understand that the Lender may transfer this Note. The Lender or anyone who takes this Note by transfer and who is entitled to receive payments under this Note is called the "Note Holder."

2. INTEREST

Interest will be charged on unpaid principal until the full amount of principal has been paid. I will pay interest at a yearly rate of ....%.

The interest rate required by this Section 2 is the rate I will pay both before and after any default described in Section 6(B) of this Note.

3. PAYMENTS

(A) Time and Place of Payments

I will pay principal and interest by making payments every month.

I will make my monthly payments on the .... day of each month beginning on ...., 19......... I will make these payments every month until I have paid all of the principal and interest and any other charges described below that I may owe under this Note. My monthly payments will be applied to interest before principal. If, on ...., ..., I still owe amounts under this Note, I will pay those amounts in full on that date, which is called the "maturity date."

I will make my monthly payments at ....

.... or at a different place if required by the Note Holder.

(B) Amount of Monthly Payments

My monthly payment will be in the amount of U.S. $...

4. BORROWER'S RIGHT TO PREPAY

I have the right to make payments of principal at any time before they are due. A payment of principal only is known as a "prepayment." When I make a prepayment, I will tell the Note Holder in writing that I am doing so.

I may make a full prepayment or partial prepayments without paying any prepayment charge. The Note Holder will use all of my prepayments to reduce the amount of principal that I owe under this Note. If I make a partial prepayment, there will be no changes in the due date or in the amount of my monthly payment unless the Note Holder agrees in writing to those changes.

5. LOAN CHARGES

If a law, which applies to this loan and which sets maximum loan charges, is finally interpreted so that the interest or other loan charges collected or to be collected in connection with this loan exceed the permitted limits, then: (i) any such loan charge shall be reduced by the amount necessary to reduce the charge to the permitted limit; and (ii) any sums already collected from me which exceeded permitted limits will be refunded to me. The Note Holder may choose to make this refund by reducing the principal I owe under this Note or by making a direct payment to me. If a refund reduces principal, the reduction will be treated as a partial prepayment.

6. BORROWER'S FAILURE TO PAY AS REQUIRED

(A) Late Charge for Overdue Payments

If the Note Holder has not received the full amount of any monthly payment by the end of .... calendar days after the date it is due, I will pay a late charge to the Note Holder. The amount of the charge will be ....% of my overdue payment of principal and interest. I will pay this late charge promptly but only once on each late payment.

(B) Default

If I do not pay the full amount of each monthly payment on the date it is due, I will be in default.

(C) Notice of Default

If I am in default, the Note Holder may send me a written notice telling me that if I do not pay the overdue amount by a certain date, the Note Holder may require me to pay immediately the full amount of principal which has not been paid and all the interest that I owe on that amount. That date must be at least 30 days after the date on which the notice is delivered or mailed to me.

(D) No Waiver By Note Holder

Even if, at a time when I am in default, the Note Holder does not require me to pay immediately in full as described above, the Note Holder will still have the right to do so if I am in default at a later time.

(E) Payment of Note Holder's Costs and Expenses

If the Note Holder has required me to pay immediately in full as described above, the Note Holder will have the right to be paid back by me for all of its costs and expenses in enforcing this Note to the extent not prohibited by applicable law. Those expenses include, for example, reasonable attorneys' fees.

7. GIVING OF NOTICES

Unless applicable law requires a different method, any notice that must be given to me under this Note will be given by delivering it or by mailing it by first class mail to me at the Property Address above or at a different address if I give the Note Holder a notice of my different address.

Any notice that must be given to the Note Holder under this Note will be given by mailing it by first class mail to the Note Holder at the address stated in Section 3(A) above or at a different address if I am given a notice of that different address.

MULTISTATE FIXED RATE NOTE—Single Family—FNMA/FHLMC UNIFORM INSTRUMENT   Form 3200 12/83

44601 SAF SYSTEMS AND FORMS
CHICAGO, IL

EXHIBIT 2–1 (*concluded*)

8. OBLIGATIONS OF PERSONS UNDER THIS NOTE

If more than one person signs this Note, each person is fully and personally obligated to keep all of the promises made in this Note, including the promise to pay the full amount owed. Any person who is a guarantor, surety or endorser of this Note is also obligated to do these things. Any person who takes over these obligations, including the obligations of a guarantor, surety or endorser of this Note, is also obligated to keep all of the promises made in this Note. The Note Holder may enforce its rights under this Note against each person individually or against all of us together. This means that any one of us may be required to pay all of the amounts owed under this Note.

9. WAIVERS

I and any other person who has obligations under this Note waive the rights of presentment and notice of dishonor. "Presentment" means the right to require the Note Holder to demand payment of amounts due. "Notice of dishonor" means the right to require the Note Holder to give notice to other persons that amounts due have not been paid.

10. UNIFORM SECURED NOTE

This Note is a uniform instrument with limited variations in some jurisdictions. In addition to the protections given to the Note Holder under this Note, a Mortgage, Deed of Trust or Security Deed (the "Security Instrument"), dated the same date as this Note, protects the Note Holder from possible losses which might result if I do not keep the promises which I make in this Note. That Security Instrument describes how and under what conditions I may be required to make immediate payment in full of all amounts I owe under this Note. Some of those conditions are described as follows:

Transfer of the Property or a Beneficial Interest in Borrower. If all or any part of the Property or any interest in it is sold or transferred (or if a beneficial interest in Borrower is sold or transferred and Borrower is not a natural person) without Lender's prior written consent, Lender may, at its option, require immediate payment in full of all sums secured by this Security Instrument. However, this option shall not be exercised by Lender if exercise is prohibited by federal law as of the date of this Security Instrument.

If Lender exercises this option, Lender shall give Borrower notice of acceleration. The notice shall provide a period of not less than 30 days from the date the notice is delivered or mailed within which Borrower must pay all sums secured by this Security Instrument. If Borrower fails to pay these sums prior to the expiration of this period, Lender may invoke any remedies permitted by this Security Instrument without further notice or demand on Borrower.

WITNESS THE HAND(S) AND SEAL(S) OF THE UNDERSIGNED.

....(Seal)
-Borrower

....(Seal)
-Borrower

....(Seal)
-Borrower

[Sign Original Only]

such as windstorms, hail, explosion, and smoke. In effect, this clause acknowledges that the mortgagee as well as the mortgagor has an insurable interest in the mortgaged property. The mortgagee's insurable interest is the amount of the mortgage debt. The insurance clause in the uniform instrument limits the amount of coverage that may be required by the lender to the amount of the debt and gives the mortgagor some voice in selecting the insurer. In the case of a loss, the insurance proceeds must be applied to rebuilding the improvements if economically feasible. This is a departure from older forms that gave the mortgagee the right to apply the insurance money on the mortgage debt, leaving the mortgagor with a damaged home and no money to make needed repairs.

Paragraph 6. Preservation and Maintenance of the Property; Leaseholds; Condominiums.   This clause obligates the mortgagor to maintain the property in good condition and to not engage in or permit acts of waste.[14] This clause recognizes that the mortgagee has a valid interest in preventing the mortgaged property from deteriorating to the extent that the collateral value of the property is impaired.

If the mortgaged premises is a leasehold estate, this paragraph requires the mortgagor to comply with the conditions of the lease to ensure that the lease is not altered to the detriment of the mortgagee's security interest or even terminated, in which case the mortgagee could be completely without security. If the mortgaged property is a condominium, this clause will prohibit change of the owner's association bylaws, percentage ownership of common areas, termination of professional management, or other changes deemed to be detrimental to the interests of the mortgagee.

Paragraph 7. Protection of Lender's Security in Property; Mortgage Insurance.   This clause provides that if the mortgagor should fail to pay any taxes, assessments, insurance premiums, or other charges as required under this mortgage agreement, the mortgagee has the right to make such payments. Moreover, if the mortgagor should fail to act to protect the property against legal actions involving such things as eminent domain, code enforcement, and bankruptcy, the mortgagee has the right to take such actions, including employing legal counsel, to protect its interests in the property. This clause also gives the mortgagee the right to enter the property and make repairs if necessary to protect its security interest in the property. The mortgagor also covenants to pay the premiums required to maintain any private mortgage insurance in effect until such time as the requirement terminates if such interest is required as a condition of obtaining the loan. Any payments made by the mortgagee or other amounts of money disbursed by the mortgagee pursuant to this clause will be added to the amount of the outstanding debt, and interest normally will be charged on these sums at the interest rate of the mortgage.

Paragraph 8. Inspection.   This clause gives the mortgagor or its agents the right to enter and inspect the property. The lender must provide the mortgagor with prior notice of such inspection, and must provide the mortgagor with a reasonable cause for such inspection that is related to the mortgagee's interest in the property. The purpose of this

---

[14]*Waste* is the abuse or destructive use of property by one in rightful possession.

clause is obviously that of permitting the mortgagee to check on the condition of its security.

Paragraph 9. Condemnation.   This clause describes the rights of the mortgagee should there be a taking of the property by any governmental authority under the government's power of eminent domain. If there is a total taking of the property, any awards, including interest, made to the mortgagor are assigned to the mortgagee for payment of the mortgage debt. Amounts awarded in excess of the outstanding debt are given to the mortgagor. If there is only a partial taking, then, unless the mortgagor and mortgagee agree in writing to allocate the proceeds otherwise, the mortgagee is to receive a proportion of the proceeds equal to the ratio of the loan balance to the fair market value of the property immediately prior to the taking with the balance going to the mortgagor. Such payments are to be made to the mortgagee, notwithstanding the fact that the amount owing is not then otherwise due and payable.

Paragraph 10. Borrower Not Released; Forebearance by Lender Not a Waiver.   Under this clause, if there is an assumption of the existing loan, the borrower agrees to all extensions or modifications entered into by lender and any subsequent owner of the property. When a purchaser assumes the mortgage, he becomes personally liable for the payment of the debt. This often requires permission of the mortgagee. When a loan is assumed, the original mortgagor remains liable as a surety.[15] Absent an express consent to any extensions or modifications, if a mortgagee grants an extension of time for re-payment the original mortgagor will be released from any liability for the debt. This is so because under suretyship law the extension agreement is a material alteration of the contract with the original mortgagee. Therefore it is necessary to include a clause whereby the original mortgagee expressly consents to such extensions or modifications and agrees that no discharge of liability will result should the mortgage be assumed.

Paragraph 11. Successors and Assigns; Joint and Several Liability.   The successors and assigns clause states that the successors and assignees of both the mortgagee and mortgagor under the mortgage are bound by all of the obligations and are entitled to enjoy all of the rights specified by the covenants and agreements therein. However, since the bulk of the covenants and agreements represent *obligations* on the part of the mortgagor and *rights* on the part of the mortgagee, this clause really means that any person who takes over this mortgage from the mortgagor is obligated to keep all of the mortgagor's promises, and any person who takes over the mortgage from the mortgagee is entitled to all of the mortgagee's rights.

The joint and several liability clause also states that the covenants and agreements of the mortgagor(s) are joint and several. This means that if more than one person signs the mortgage as mortgagor, then each one is obligated to keep the obligations contained therein (not just their pro rata share thereof) and that the mortgagee can take action against any one, as well as all, of the mortgagors. Judgments rendered against co-

---

[15]A *surety* is one who is liable for payment or performance in the event that one who ought to have paid or performed fails to do so.

mortgagors can be enforced and collected entirely from one mortgagor (usually the most liquid and/or solvent of the co-debtors), who then may seek contribution from other co-mortgagors.

Paragraphs 12–16. These paragraphs contain clauses pertaining to usury, enactment, or repeal of legislation, the giving of notices, and governing law. They have more legalistic than economic significance, so they are not elaborated on here.

Paragraph 17. Transfer of Property or a Beneficial Interest in Borrower. This clause, known as the *due on sale clause*, allows the mortgagee to accelerate the debt (that is, to take action to make the outstanding loan balance plus accrued interest immediately due and payable) when the property, or some interest in the property, is transferred without the written consent of the mortgagee. The purpose of this clause is to enable the mortgagee to protect its security interest by approving any new owner. The clause also permits the mortgagee to increase the interest rate on the loan to current market rates. This, of course, reduces the possibility of the new owner assuming a loan with an attractive interest rate.

Paragraph 18. Borrower's Right to Reinstate. This clause deals with the mortgagor's right to reinstate the original repayment terms in the note after the mortgagee has caused an acceleration of the debt. It gives the mortgagor the right to have foreclosure proceedings discontinued at any time before a judgment is entered enforcing the mortgage (i.e., before a decree for the sale of the property is given) if the mortgagor

1. Pays to the mortgagee all sums which would then be due had no acceleration occurred
2. Cures any default of any other covenants or agreements
3. Pays all expenses incurred by the lender in enforcing its mortgage
4. Takes such action as the mortgagee may reasonably require to ensure that the mortgagee's rights in the property and the mortgagor's obligations to pay are unchanged

Important Nonstandard Mortgage Clauses

Many states have undertaken to enact statutes governing the rights and responsibilities of borrowers and lenders under certain circumstances. Since the following clauses have been the subject of such nonuniform legislation, these clauses have been placed among the nonstandard mortgage clauses.

Paragraph 19. Acceleration; Remedies. Since curing of defaults has been the subject of much nonuniform legislation, we have placed the covenant dealing with curing defaults and reinstating the mortgage after acceleration among the nonuniform covenants. This clause provides that notice must be given to the mortgagor, which specifies (1) the default; (2) the action required to cure the default; (3) the time by which the default must be cured; and (4) that failure to cure the default may result in acceleration of the debt secured by the mortgage. Absent this clause, a mortgagee can only sue a delinquent mortgagor for payments then in default.

Because of the harsh effects of acceleration on borrowers, there have been many judicial and legislative attempts to limit its application. Many recent court decisions have set aside an acceleration where the result would be unconscionable. In addition to these decisions, many states have enacted statutes permitting mortgagors to cure defaults and avoid acceleration by payment of the amounts in arrears.

Paragraph 20. Lender in Possession.   This clause provides that upon acceleration under paragraph 19 or abandonment of the property, the mortgagee (or a judicially appointed receiver) may enter the property and collect rents until the mortgage is foreclosed. Rents collected must be applied first to the costs of managing and operating the property, and then to the mortgage debt, real estate taxes, insurance, and other obligations of the mortgagor as specified in the mortgage.

Paragraph 21. Release.   The release clause obligates the mortgagee to discharge the mortgage and deliver written evidence to the mortgagor thereof when all amounts of indebtedness secured by the mortgage have been paid off. The certificate of release should be recorded in the proper official records to clear the title of the estate to which the mortgage had been attached. The mortgagor does not have to pay the mortgagee for the release, but he does have to pay the costs of recording the release.

Paragraph 22. Waiver of Valuation and Appraisement.   Under this clause the mortgagor waives all rights to have the property sold at foreclosure for a price judicially determined to be just and true. State law will dictate how this foreclosure sale must be conducted, but this clause eliminates any requirement that the property sell for its market value if the property is sold according to the procedure set forth in the state foreclosure statute.

Paragraph 23. Riders to This Security Instrument.   This clause incorporates into the mortgage all covenants and agreements in such other documents annexed to the mortgage and mentioned in this clause (e.g., adjustable rate or graduated payment riders).

Some Optional Clauses

There are a number of other clauses that may be included in a mortgage instrument. Some may be included in the uniform mortgage form for certain states. Others are not found in the single family uniform mortgage instrument but appear in other mortgage forms. We will not attempt to cover all of the various optional clauses, but will instead discuss some of the more common ones.

Waiver of Dower Clause.   In those states recognizing dower, the mortgagee should require the spouse to sign the mortgage, and the mortgage should contain a clause stating the the spouse waives any dower (and/or curtesy, if applicable) interests in the property as against the mortgagee.

Defeasance Clause.   This clause is included in mortgages in title theory states (states that have historically treated a mortgage as actually transferring title and the right of possession to the mortgagee rather than just a lien). It provides that the conveyance of title by the mortgagor to the mortgagee is defeated when all of the terms and conditions of the mortgage have been met. The defeasance clause provides, in short, that the title returns to the mortgagor when the mortgage debt has been discharged.

Lender's Right to Notice.   This type of clause is common in junior mortgages. It obligates the borrower to ensure that the junior mortgage lender is provided with notice of actions to foreclose on the part of the holder of any senior mortgage or other lien with priority over the lender's loan. The purpose of such a clause is to provide the junior mortgage lender with an opportunity to redeem the senior debt or to take other action to protect its security interest in the property.

Prepayment.   The lender is not required to accept advance payments unless there is a provision to this effect, known as a *prepayment clause*. The clause may permit prepayment in full or in part, and the lender, at his option, may choose to charge the penalty provided. Lenders will typically choose not to enforce the penalty provision when current interest rates exceed the rate on the mortgage note being prepaid. This clause can be viewed as giving the lender an option of accepting payment when it is advantageous.

Assignment of Mortgage with an Estoppel Certificate.   Since a mortgage is considered to be an asset owned by its holder, it follows that he may dispose of it as he would any other asset. The person who acquires it should make sure that he succeeds to the rights of the original mortgagee. This process is known as an *assignment*. In the absence of an agreement to the contrary, the right of assignment does not require the consent of the mortgagor. Presumably his rights and obligations are not affected. He merely owes the assignee instead of the assignor.

In order to make sure that an agreement reached in the assignment of a mortgage states exact facts, estoppel certificates are sometimes used to prevent subsequent representations about a different set of facts. For example, if A is about to purchase from B a mortgage on property owned by C, A would be better protected if he obtained a written statement from C, showing the unpaid balance of the mortgage. Otherwise, representations made by B might be intentionally or unintentionally erroneous. Or a verbal statement by C might later be denied, and C might produce evidence to show that the amount owed by him is less than A thought it was. The estoppel certificate protects the purchaser of the mortgage.

A covenant in the mortgage commonly requires the mortgagor to give the required estoppel certificate within a certain time upon proper request. This ensures availability of information necessary to support the assignment.

Future Advances.   While it is expected that a mortgage will always state the total amount of the debt it is expected to secure, this amount may be in the nature of a forecast of the total debt to be incurred in installments. In other words, a mortgage may cover future as well as current advances. For example, a mortgage may be so written that it will protect several successive loans under a general line of credit extended by the mortgagee to the mortgagor. In case the total amount cannot be forecasted with accuracy, at least the general nature of the advances or loans must be apparent from the wording of the mortgage.

From one of the mortgagor covenants of a mortgage form in common use, the following quotation indicates the intent of the mortgagor and the mortgagee on this subject:

> That the mortgagee or legal holder of this mortgage may make future advancements for the repair, restoration, and improvement of said buildings, and that the amount of funds so advanced may be added to the then unpaid balance on said loan and bear interest as provided by the terms of the original note, and shall be secured by and subject to all of the terms of this mortgage.

One excellent illustration of a mortgage for future advances (sometimes called an open-end mortgage) takes the form of construction loans. Here the borrower arranges in advance with a mortgagee for a total amount, usually definitely stated in the mortgage, that will be advanced under the mortgage to meet the part of the costs of construction which the owner of the property does not expect to meet from his own capital. As the structure progresses, the mortgagor has the right to call upon the mortgagee for successive advances on the loan.

Subordination Clause.   By means of this clause, a first mortgage holder agrees to make its mortgage junior in priority to the mortgage of another lender. A subordination clause might be used in situations where the seller provides financing by taking back a mortgage from the buyer, and the buyer also intends to obtain a mortgage from a bank (or other financial institution), usually to develop or construct an improvement. Financial institutions will generally require that their loans have first mortgage priority. Consequently, the seller must agree to include a subordination clause in the mortgage whereby the seller agrees to subordinate the priority of the mortgage to the bank loan. This ensures that even if the seller's mortgage is recorded before the bank loan, it will be subordinate to the bank loan.

For the protection of the seller, the subordination agreement should be specific about the conditions under which it agrees to subordinate its first mortgage to another mortgage. A further discussion of the use of subordination clauses in land development loans will be covered in a later chapter.

ASSUMPTION OF MORTGAGE

In the previous section we discussed several mortgage clauses which affect the ability of a mortgagor to sell his property and have the buyer continue to make payments on the mortgage loan. In particular, a due on sale clause may be contained in the mortgage instrument, which gives the lender the right to demand repayment of the balance due on the mortgage note if the property is sold or to require the mortgagee's approval of the buyer's credit if the buyer is allowed to assume the loan. There may also be a provision for changing the interest rate on the debt secured by the mortgage.

When the mortgagor transfers his rights to another, the question arises, ''Does the grantee agree to become liable for payment of the mortgage debt and relieve the mortgagor of his personal obligation?'' If this is the intention of both parties, the assumption of the obligation by the grantee may accomplish the purpose. The deed, after specifying the nature of the mortgage which encumbers the property, will contain a clause to the effect that the grantee assumes and agrees to pay the amount of the obligations owed to the mortgagee, as part consideration for the conveyance of title. Where an assumption is undertaken by the grantee, it should be couched in such language that there is no doubt about his intent.

An assumption agreement takes the form of a contract of indemnity. It shifts the responsibility for the payment of the debt from the grantor to the grantee. Thereafter, the grantor stands in the position of a surety for the payment of the debt. However, such an arrangement binds only the parties to it—the grantor and the grantee. Since the mortgagee is not ordinarily a party to such an agreement, he is not bound by it. As a consequence, he may still hold the original mortgagor liable. Thus, if a property is sold with a loan assumption, and the new owner defaults on the loan, the lender can hold the previous owner liable, unless he has released the previous owner from the debt.

Release of Grantor from Assumed Debt.   When a mortgagor owning property grants that property to another and the grantee assumes the grantor's mortgage, the lender may or may not release the grantor from personal liability for the mortgage debt. The decision of release will depend on the value of the property as security, the grantee's financial capabilities, and other factors affecting the lender's attitudes toward the transaction. A mortgagee cannot be expected to release an antecedent mortgagor if the result will be to increase the credit risk, unless the mortgagee is compensated in some way (e.g., a higher interest rate). In the absence of a release from the mortgagee when a mortgaged property is transferred, there is always one way for the grantor to obtain release from an assumed mortgage—that is, to sell the property free and clear of all encumbrances, letting the grantee do his own financing. Even this proposal is based upon two assumptions: (1) that the mortgage contains a prepayment clause, permitting the grantor to pay off at his discretion; and (2) that the grantee has access to funds that will permit him to refinance the mortgage. Sometimes, when there is a provision for prepayment penalties, the lender may choose not to enforce it if interest rates have increased since the mortgage was granted and the lender can invest the amounts prepaid in new mortgages at a higher interest rate.

ACQUIRING TITLE ''SUBJECT TO'' A MORTGAGE

In contrast to the assumption of the personal obligation to pay the debt, the grantee may not be willing to accept this responsibility. In this case he may ask the grantor to allow him to take title ''subject to'' the mortgage. So long as the grantee is financially able and thinks it will be to his advantage, he will keep up payments on the mortgage and observe its other covenants. Under normal conditions, if he purchased the property at a fair price, it will be to his advantage to avoid default on the mortgage to protect his own equity.

But should the grantee reach the conclusion that it will no longer be to his advantage to make further payments, or should he become financially unable to do so, he may default in his payments. By so doing, he runs the risk of losing whatever equity he has in the property. However, he cannot be held personally liable for the amount of the debt that he assumed. The grantor is still personally liable and may be held liable for any deficiency judgment resulting from the foreclosure sale.

It is obviously riskier for the grantor to sell property subject to the mortgage. Given a choice, he would generally prefer that a responsible grantee assume the mortgage unless he is compensated for the additional risk he undertakes as a surety (e.g., by receiving a higher price for the property).

Property Covered by a Mortgage

The property that is covered by the mortgage as security for the loan includes not only the land and any existing buildings on the land, but also easements and fixtures. In addition, the mortgage agreement may provide that property covered by the mortgage also includes rights to natural resources (such as mineral, timber, oil and gas, and water rights) and even rights to rents and profits from the real estate. An easement that runs with the property is generally regarded by the law as being covered by the mortgage, regardless of whether the easement is created before or after the mortgage is executed. Such an easement, if in existence at the time the property is mortgaged, is covered by the mortgage even if it is not mentioned in the mortgage. Foreclosure of the mortgage will not extinguish this easement. An easement created subsequent to the recording of a mortgage, however, will be extinguished by foreclosure.

Issues involving fixtures have generated a considerable amount of legal controversy. In general, a *fixture* is an item of tangible personal property (also referred to as a chattel) that has become affixed to and/or is intended to be used with the real estate so as to be considered part of the property. The law is in general agreement that fixtures are covered by the mortgage, with the exception of "trade fixtures"[16] installed by a tenant.

A mortgage will usually contain what is called an *after-acquired property clause* as part of its description of the type of property to be covered by the mortgage. This is a provision to the effect that property which is acquired subsequent to the execution of the mortgage that becomes part of the real estate is to be included in the security covered by the mortgage. Such after-acquired property includes additional improvements erected on the property or fixtures that become part of the property at any time in the future for as long as the debt remains outstanding. The courts have generally affirmed the validity of after-acquired property clauses, and the Uniform Land Transactions Act (the ULTA) expressly accepts the validity of after-acquired property clauses.[17]

---

[16]Trade fixtures are personal property used by tenants in business. Such fixtures retain the character of personal property (e.g., shelves used to display merchandise).

[17]For a discussion and case law materials related to after-acquired property clauses, see Nelson and Whitman *Real Estate Transfer, Finance and Development* pp. 633–639; see also Kratovil and Werner, *Modern Mortgage Law and Practice,* 2nd ed., pp. 114, 117.

Junior Mortgages

In simple real estate financing transactions, such as those involving single residences, the character of the mortgage structure is easily defined. The senior or prior mortgage is usually called a first mortgage. All others are given the class name of junior mortgages. In any particular situation, there may be one or more junior mortgages or none at all. One junior lien, usually called a second mortgage, is sometimes used to bridge the gap between the price of the property and the sum of the first mortgage and the amount of money available to the purchaser to use as a down payment. Traditionally, second mortgages are short term and carry a higher rate of interest than first mortgages because of the additional risk associated with their junior status.

Recording of Mortgages

Unless the statutes of the state require it, recording is not essential to the validity of a mortgage as between the mortgagor and the mortgagee. The act of recording creates no rights that did not exist before, but it does give others notice of the existence and effect of the mortgage. A recorded mortgage protects its holder by giving him priority over the subsequent acts of the mortgagor. For example, if a mortgagee failed to record his mortgage, the mortgagor could mortgage the property to a second lender. If this second lender had no notice of the prior unrecorded mortgage, the second lender would have a lien prior to that of the original mortgagee. In general, the priority of successive liens is determined by the time they are accepted for record.

As we have discussed, the recording acts provide opportunities for the protection of holders of interests in property, but at the same time they place responsibilities upon them to make use of these opportunities. Failure to inspect the records for prior liens or failure to record the mortgage may result in loss to the mortgagee. In most states *junior lienors* of record without notice of the existence of a senior mortgage will have priority over an unrecorded senior mortgage. Even subsequent recording of a senior mortgage lien will generally not elevate it to a higher priority.

OTHER FINANCING INSTRUMENTS

Purchase-Money Mortgage

A source of credit for a real property buyer is often the seller. If the seller is willing to take back a mortgage as part or in full payment of the purchase price, the seller has what is referred to as a purchase-money mortgage. Purchase-money mortgages are common where

1. Third-party mortgage financing is too expensive or unavailable.
2. The buyer does not qualify for long-term mortgage credit because of a low down payment or difficulty meeting monthly payments.

3. The seller desires to take advantage of the installment method of reporting the gain from the sale. (Installment sales are discussed in a later chapter.)
4. The seller desires to artificially raise the price of the property by offering a lower-than-market interest rate on the mortgage, thereby creating more capital gains and less interest or ordinary income.[18]

Any mortgage given by a buyer to secure payment of all or part of the purchase price of a property is called a purchase-money mortgage. It can be a first mortgage, which might be the case if the seller is providing all of the financing necessary to consummate the transaction. It is more likely to take the form of a second mortgage that is used to bridge the gap between an available first mortgage and the buyer's down payment. As such, it must be differentiated from mortgages given to secure a loan from a third party for the purchase of the property. The third-party lender (e.g., a financial institution), will normally want its mortgage to be a first mortgage. Thus the purchase-money mortgage must either be recorded after the third-party loan or contain a subordination clause as defined earlier.

Package Mortgage

Under the package mortgage concept, both the borrower and the lender sanction the financing of many items of personal property, such as ranges, refrigerators, cooling and ventilating systems, automatic washers and dryers, and garbage disposal units for homes, as a part of the realty. Similarly, personal property particularly adapted to the use of commercial and industrial buildings may be covered under the real estate mortgage.

The added items are annexed to the security for the real estate mortgage by enumerating, immediately following the land description in the mortgage, the things that are sought to be included, but about which there may be some doubt as to legal coverage. This enumeration is then followed by a declaration that such articles ''are and shall be deemed to be fixtures'' and are to be considered in all respects as a part of the real estate which serves as security for the mortgage.

In event there is some doubt that the recitals will adequately incorporate the personal property as security under a real estate mortgage, it may be possible to protect the lender by filing a copy of the mortgage at the appropriate office of public record for security instruments protected by personal property, as well as at the recorder's office for real estate mortgages.

LAND CONTRACTS

One form of financing real estate that has been commonly used over the years is commonly referred to as a land contract. The term *land contract* has a variety of aliases, including real estate contract, installment sales contract, agreement to convey, and contract for deed. As the latter term implies, the land contract seller promises to convey title at such

---

[18]The use of this technique has been limited by the ''unstated interest rule.''

time as the purchaser completes the performance of the obligation called for in the contract. Such performance usually means payment of the purchase price in stipulated installments, much the same way as under a note and mortgage.

It should be emphasized that a land contract is not a mortgage. Under the land contract, the seller retains the title in his name. So far as the deed record shows, he is still the owner of the property. But the land contract is supposed to tie the hands of the seller to make sure that he or his assigns must ultimately transfer title to the vendee or his heirs or assigns.

The land contract may be used as a substitute for either a vendor's lien (a lien implied by courts of equity arising from the fact that the purchaser has received property for which he has not yet fully paid) or a purchase-money mortgage. Like the former, it is often a fragile type of evidence of the vendee's equity and would normally not be preferred over the purchase-money mortgage if the latter is available. However, in cases where there is no down payment or a small down payment, or in states that have long redemption periods during which the vendee has the right to possession and to collection of rents even though in default, sellers of land may refuse to give a deed and take back a mortgage until a very substantial part of the purchase price has been paid.

Several points of comparison exist between purchase-money mortgages and land contracts. A land contract buyer does not have title to the property and therefore cannot control whether the property will be mortgaged subsequent to the execution of the land contract or be made subject to covenants, easements, or mechanics liens in the future by the contract seller. In fact, most land contracts contain a clause allowing the seller to mortgage property up to an amount equal to the buyer's indebtedness to the seller. The buyer would have this protection if mortgage financing were used because limits would be made explicit and the buyer would have title. Furthermore, the possibility of forfeiture of the land contract interest may exist without any of the procedural protections afforded mortgages. It is suggested that all such points of comparison should be considered in the decision whether to buy or sell on land contract or to obtain mortgage financing. In general, land contracts are used in many of the same situations as purchase-money mortgages (e.g., where the buyer has difficulty obtaining third-party financing).

Recording of Land Contracts.   State laws provide for the recording of conveyances of land and instruments affecting title. Land contracts generally are considered instruments affecting title and are consequently admissible to record. Recording land contracts is not essential to their validity; it merely gives notice of their existence to third parties.

In some cases the contract contains a stipulation that it shall not be recorded. This is normally included at the instance of the vendor, who receives only a small down payment or none at all. If such a contract is recorded and there is an early default, clearing the record may take time and involve expense to the vendor. Even so, such a contract is occasionally recorded, in violation of its terms. This does not invalidate the contract. It may subject the vendee to a suit for damages if the vendor suffers loss by being unable immediately to effect a sale to another buyer, who refuses to take title with the cloud of the recorded contract against it and who is unwilling to wait upon the purchase until the record can be cleared.

On the other hand, failure to record land contracts against vacant lots because of small down payments affords the vendor a particularly good opportunity to take advantage of the vendee, should he care to do so. The complete absence of possession by the vendee, or of any evidence of it, makes it easy for the dishonest vendor to sell the land and deliver good title to a third party, even though the vendee is not in default.

If, however, the vendee makes a substantial down payment or as he builds up an equity with subsequent payments, he may feel safer if his contract is recorded. Under either of these sets of circumstances, the recording of the contract should meet with little opposition from the vendor. However, immediate and continued possession of the property by the vendee will normally serve as a satisfactory substitute for a record of the contract. All parties who might wish to acquire a lien prior to the claims of the vendee are put on notice to determine by what right the vendee occupies the property. Physical possession is not necessary to protect the rights of the vendee if sufficient evidence of possession exists to warrant a further inquiry by other parties.

CONCLUSION

This chapter discussed legal considerations important in creating and defining various rights to real property. This is important in the study of real estate finance, since it is these rights which are purchased, sold, and mortgaged. Thus, an understanding of the various rights associated with real estate is necessary to properly evaluate a real estate financial decision. Legal considerations affect the risk of receiving the economic benefit associated with one's property rights. For example, we have discussed the importance of having a marketable title. Any defects in the title may result in a loss of benefits to the owner and jeopardize the collateral value of the real estate for the mortgage lender. To some extent this risk is controlled and minimized by the use of title assurance methods, including title insurance and the use of general warranty deeds.

Knowing the various ways of petitioning property rights may also result in maximizing the value of a particular property, since it allows parties with different needs (users, equity investors, lenders, etc.) to have a claim on the property rights which best meets those needs. Thus the total value of all the rights associated with a property may exceed that of a property where there could be no mortgage, no leases, or other ways to separate rights.

QUESTIONS

1. What is the difference between real estate and real property?
2. What is meant by an estate? Why are estates important in real estate finance?
3. How can a leased fee estate have a value which could be transferred to another party?
4. What is an abstract of title?
5. Name the three general methods of title assurance and briefly describe each. Which would you recommend to a friend purchasing a home? Why?
6. What purpose is served when a mortgage lender records its mortgage?
7. Would it be legal for you to give a quitclaim deed for the Statue of Liberty to your friend?
8. How is a note different from a mortgage?

9. What is the purpose and effect of each of the following clauses:
   a. Acceleration clause?
   b. Prepayment clause?
   c. Due on sale clause?
   d. Joint and several liability clause?
10. How can mortgages permit future advances?
11. How does a purchase money mortgage differ from a land contract?
12. How can mechanic's liens achieve priority over first mortgages which were recorded prior in time to the mechanic's lien?
13. Name several mortgageable interests in real estate and comment on their risk as collateral to lenders.

PROBLEMS

1. Five years ago Smith purchased a home from Jones. Smith's attorney, Able, examined the abstract of title and rendered his opinion that no defects or encumbrances existed against the home. Smith has now contracted to sell the home to Tims. Tims's attorney now determines that Able had overlooked a judgment lien against the home which was recorded before Smith purchased from Jones. What is Smith's recourse? What is Tims's recourse against Smith?

2. A owns the building at 123 City Avenue which has been vacant for many years. A leases the building to B on a long-term fixed-rate lease for $1,000 per month. B does not record his lease or any memorandum thereof. Before B moves in, General Motors announces it is building a large manufacturing plant next door. A then signs a lease with C, who is willing to pay $10,000 per month to lease the same building. C has no notice of A's prior lease with B. Who is entitled to occupancy? What can B do?

3. *a.* Sedgewick arranged for an open-end mortgage loan from the Second National Bank in amounts up to $50,000. The loan was closed, and Sedgewick drew down $30,000 initially. Three months later he drew the remaining $20,000. What is the position of the bank with regard to the possibility of intervening liens?

   b. Assume there was no definite agreement for future advances between Sedgewick and the bank at the time the initial $30,000 loan was closed. Would your answer be different?

4. Last year Jones obtained a mortgage loan for $100,000. He just inherited a large sum of money and is contemplating prepaying the entire loan balance to save interest. What are his rights to prepay the loan?

Chapter 3

Mortgage Default, Foreclosure, and Bankruptcy

MORTGAGE DEFAULT

The previous chapter discussed the various property rights associated with real estate. The remainder of this chapter considers some of the problems that result when one of the parties does not fulfill a contractual obligation associated with their property right. The legal ramifications of these problems affect the financial security of other parties' rights and is thus an important aspect of real estate finance.

One of the most important risks in making a mortgage loan is the possibility that the borrower will default on his or her obligation in some way so that the lender may not receive the expected mortgage payments. The risk associated with mortgage loans depends in part on the rights of the lender if and when such default occurs. Thus, it is important to understand the legal ramifications of mortgage default.

What Constitutes Default?

An ordinary dictionary definition of a *default* is "a failure to fulfill a contract, agreement, or duty, especially a financial obligation." From this it follows that a default in a mortgage contract can result from any breach of the contract. The most common is the failure to meet an installment of the interest and principal payments. But failure to pay taxes or insurance premiums when due may also result in a default, which may precipitate an acceleration of the debt and a foreclosure action. Indeed, some mortgages have clauses which make specific stipulations to this effect as discussed in the previous chapter. Even a failure to keep the security in repair may constitute a *technical default*. We speak of this as a technical default because it would seldom result in an actual foreclosure sale. It might be difficult for the mortgagee to prove that the repair clause in the mortgage had been broken unless the property showed definite evidence of the effects of waste.

From another point of view, default is defined first in the breach of the letter of the contract and then in the attitude of the mortgagee. By this it is meant that even though there is a breach of contract, the mortgagee may see fit to ignore it or to postpone doing something about it. In case of default accompanied by abandonment, the probabilities are that the mortgagee will act quickly to protect his interests against vandalism, neglect, and waste. If, on the other hand, the mortgagor is of good character, has generally met his obligations promptly in the past, wishes to retain his interest in the property, and is only temporarily unable to meet his obligations, a default is not likely to be immediately declared by the mortgagee.

ALTERNATIVES TO FORECLOSURE

Foreclosure involves the sale of property by the courts to satisfy the unpaid debt. The details of this process are discussed later. Because of the various costs associated with foreclosure, lenders often prefer to seek an alternative to actual foreclosure.

Although mortgage contracts normally indicate definite penalties to follow any breach therein, experience has shown that in spite of provisions for prompt action in case of a default in mortgage payments, many such commitments are not met in strict accordance with the letter of the contract. Instead, whenever mortgagors get into financial trouble and are unable to meet their obligations, adjustments of the payments or other terms are likely to follow if both the borrower and lender believe that the conditions are temporary and will be remedied. When market value is less than the amount of the debt, it may be best for the mortgagor to sell his property immediately and take the loss rather than prolonging the period of default and incurring potentially larger losses in the event of foreclosure. Some of these adjustments best meet the needs of the mortgagee, to be sure. Others are accepted at times when strict adherence to the letter of the contract would give the mortgagee a financial advantage.

Mortgage Adjustments

Various types of mortgage adjustments are discussed, including

1. Recasting of mortgages by mortgagee
2. Transfer of mortgage to a new owner
3. Voluntary conveyance to mortgagee

Recasting of Mortgages.   Once a mortgage is executed and placed on record, its form may change substantially before it is redeemed. It may be recast for any one of several reasons. A mortgage can be renegotiated at any time, but most frequently is recast by changing the terms of the mortgage (either temporarily or permanently) in order to avoid or cure a default.

Where mortgage terms, such as the interest rate, amortization period, or payment amounts are changed, mortgagees must exercise care to avoid losing their priority over intervening lienors. The mere extension of time of payment will not generally impair the priority of the extended mortgage. Courts, however, are watchful to protect intervening lienors against prejudice, and mortgages may lose priority to the extent that changes in the interest rate, payment amounts or the amount of indebtedness place additional burdens on the mortgagor.[1]

Extension Agreements.   Occasionally, a mortgagor in financial difficulty may seek permission from the mortgagee to extend the mortgage terms for a period of time. A mortgagor may request a longer amortization period for the remaining principal balance or temporary grace period for the payment of principal or interest payments or both. In responding to such a request, the mortgagee needs to consider the following issues:

1. What is the condition of the security? Has it been reasonably well maintained, or does it show the effects of waste and neglect?

2. Have there been any intervening liens? These are liens recorded or attaching after the recordation of the mortgage but before any modifications to it. If so, what is their effect upon an extension agreement? If such liens exist, it is possible that the extension of an existing mortgage may amount to a cancellation of the mortgage and the making of a new one. If so, this could advance the priority of intervening liens.

3. What is the surety status of any grantees who have assumed the mortgage? Will an extension of time for the payment of the debt secured by the mortgage terminate the liability of such sureties? The best way for the mortgagee to protect himself against the possibilities implied in these questions is to secure the consent of the extension agreement from all sureties to the extension. As parties to it, they can have no grounds for opposing it. But if they are not made parties to the extension, and particularly if changes in the terms of the mortgage through the extension agreement tend to increase the obligations for which the sureties are liable, then care should be exercised to ensure that those sureties who refuse to sign the agreement are not released by the extension agreement. The possibility of foreclosure and the possibility of a deficiency judgment against them may be a sufficient inducement to obtain their agreement to be parties to the extension.

The exact nature of an extension agreement depends upon the bargaining position of mortgagor and mortgagee. If the mortgagor can refinance the loan on more favorable terms, he will probably not apply for an extension agreement. Alternatively, he may have to make changes that favor the mortgagee, such as an increase in the interest rate.

Alternative to Extension Agreement.   As an alternative to an extension agreement, the mortgagee may agree informally to a temporary extension, without making any changes in the formal recorded agreement between the parties. If the mortgagor is unable to meet all of monthly mortgage payments, these too may be waived temporarily or forgiven in whole or in part. For example, the fact that the question of such an agreement is raised suggests that the mortgagor cannot pay the matured principal of the loan. Therefore, some informal arrangement may be made to permit him to retain possession of the property in return for meeting monthly payments which may or may not include principal installments. The use of such informal agreements can be troublesome, but, in general, if such an informal agreement is reached, the amounts demanded will be adjusted

---

[1] Recasting of mortgages to admit interests not present at the time the mortgages were executed is sometimes necessary. For example, the mortgage may make no provision for an easement of a public utility company which requires access to the rear of the site covered by the mortgage. Since the installation of the services of the utility will normally add to rather than subtract from the value of the security, the mortgagee will usually be glad to approve the change. Nevertheless, it will require a recasting of the mortgage to the extent indicated.

to the present payment capacities of the borrower, and should the borrower's financial condition improve the lender may again insist that the originally scheduled payments resume.

The use of such an alternative to a definite extension agreement may serve the temporary needs of both mortgagor and mortgagee. If the latter feels that the security amply protects his lien, he can afford to be lenient in helping the mortgagor to adjust his financial arrangements during a difficult period. If the mortgagor also feels that any real equity exists in the property, he will wish to protect it if at all possible.

Transfer of Mortgage to a New Owner.   A mortgagor who is unable or unwilling to meet his mortgage obligation may be able to find someone who is willing to purchase the property and either assume the mortgage liability or take the property "subject to" the existing mortgage. (Recall the discussion in the previous chapter of the legal distinction between these two alternatives.) The new purchaser may be willing to do this if he thinks the value of the property exceeds the balance due on the mortgage. In either case, the seller retains personal liability for the debt. However, if the seller is about to default and expects to lose the property anyway, he may be quite willing to take a chance on a new purchaser being able to fulfill the mortgage obligation. The risk is that the new buyer will default, and the seller will again have responsibility for the debt and have the property back.

Recall that if the purchaser acquires the property "subject to" the existing debt, he does not acquire any personal liability for the debt. Thus, he can only lose any equity personally invested to acquire the property. This equity investment may be quite small in a situation where the seller is financially distressed and faces foreclosure. Thus, the buyer may have little to lose by taking a chance on acquiring the property subject to the mortgage. If it turns out to be a good investment, he will continue to make payments on the debt. But if he finds that the value of the property is unlikely to exceed the mortgage debt within a reasonable time frame, he can simply stop making payments and let the seller reacquire the property. Thus, we see that in this situation the buyer of the property "subject to" a mortgage has in effect purchased an option. The equity he invests is payment for this option, which allows him to take a chance on the property value increasing after it is acquired. We can therefore see why a purchaser might even give the seller money to acquire a property subject to a mortgage even if the *current* value of the property is less than the mortgage balance.

For example, suppose a property has a mortgage balance of $100,000. Property values in the area are currently depressed, and the owner believes that only $99,000 could be obtained on an outright sale. However, a buyer is willing to acquire the property at a price of $101,000 "subject to" the existing mortgage. Thus, $2,000 is paid for the option of tying up the property in hopes that property values rise above there current level.[2] If the property does not rise in value to more than $100,000, the purchaser could simply walk away, and the original owner again becomes responsible for the mortgage. If the property rises in value to more than $101,000, the purchaser stands to make a profit and would continue to make payments on the mortgage.

---

[2] The seller would receive $1,000 in cash, but since the seller had −$1,000 in equity he receives the economic benefit of $2,000, which is also the difference between the price paid and the market value of the property.

It should be clear that knowledge of various legal alternatives (e.g., being able to purchase a property ''subject to'' versus assuming a mortgage) can allow a buyer and seller to arrive at an agreement which best meets their financial objectives. Thus, legal alternatives can often be evaluated in a financial context.

Voluntary Conveyance.   A borrower (mortgagor) who can no longer meet the mortgage obligation may attempt to ''sell'' his equity to the mortgagee. For example, suppose that the mortgagor is unable to meet his obligations and faces foreclosure of his equity. To save time, trouble, and expense associated with foreclosure, the mortgagee may make or accept a proposal to take title from the mortgagor. If they both agree that the property value exceeds the mortgage balance, a sum may be paid to the mortgagor for his equity. If the value is less than the mortgage balance, the lender may still be willing to accept title and release the mortgagor from the mortgage debt. This might be done because cost of foreclosure may exceed the expected benefit of pursuing that course of action.

When voluntary conveyances are used, title is usually transferred with a warranty or quitclaim deed from mortgagor to mortgagee. The mortgagor should insist upon a release to make sure that he is no longer bound under his note and mortgage, especially in situations where the mortgage balance is near or in excess of the property value. Otherwise, he may find that he still has a personal obligation to pay the mortgage note. The conveyance to the mortgagee in exchange for a release from the mortgage debt is frequently referred to as giving *deed in lieu of foreclosure* of the mortgage.

In addition to the legal questions involved in voluntary conveyances, the mortgagee frequently faces very practical financial issues as well. If there are junior liens outstanding, they are not eliminated by a voluntary conveyance. Indeed, their holders may be in a better position than before if the title to the property passes to a more financially sound owner. Unless in some manner these junior liens are released from the property in question—possibly by agreement with their holders to transfer them to other property owned by the mortgagor or even on occasion to cancel them—the mortgagee may find it necessary to foreclose instead of taking a voluntary conveyance because the title conveyed is subject to junior liens. Through foreclosure the mortgagee has a lawful method of becoming free from the liens of the junior claimants.

FORECLOSURE

In practice, most mortgagees are not anxious to take property from mortgagors, particularly where the mortgagor has candidly communicated with the mortgagee concerning the default and has made realistic proposals to cure the default over a reasonable period of time. Because the management and disposal of property requires skills that are usually outside of the range of expertise of most lenders, and therefore costly to acquire, mortgagees prefer to collect the amounts owed them and are likely to be lenient and patient when circumstances warrant it. Seldom does the mortgagee insist upon the exact letter of his contract. Nor does he rush into court to insist upon foreclosure at the first evidence of default. But after patience and leniency have been extended to delinquent mortgagors, eventually a settlement becomes necessary and foreclosure proceedings are started.

Judicial Foreclosure

In general, the mortgagee possesses two types of remedies to protect his interests in case of default by the mortgagor. First, the lender may sue on the debt, obtain judgment, and execute the judgment against property of the mortgagor. In this case property subject to attachment and execution[3] is not limited to the mortgaged property. This judgment may be levied against any of the mortgagor's property not otherwise legally exempt[4] from execution.

Second, the lender may bring a foreclosure suit and obtain a decree of foreclosure and sale. If the sale of the mortgaged property realizes a price high enough to meet the expenses of the sale and the claims of the mortgagee and still leave a balance, this balance goes to the mortgagor. While foreclosure and sale of the property may be undertaken in two separate actions, they are usually pursued simultaneously in practice.

Redemption

Redemption[5] can be accomplished by paying the full amount of the debt, interest, and costs due to the mortgagee. The *equity of redemption*[6] must be asserted prior to foreclosure. Once the foreclosure sale has been confirmed, the mortgagor can no longer redeem the property, except in states which provide for a statutory period for redemption after foreclosure. The right to redeem after foreclosure is called the right of *statutory redemption,* which exists in about half of the states. Generally, the period for statutory redemption runs about six months to one year after the foreclosure sale. In a number of states, instead of granting the mortgagor a right to redeem after the foreclosure sale, state laws postpone the sale to provide a longer period of time to pay a debt that is in default.

Sales of Property

The advertising of the sale, the place where it takes place, and the method of sale are all matters that are governed by state law. While details differ, the results are approximately the same in all localities.

---

[3] *Attachment* is the act or process of seizing property of a debtor by court order in order to secure the debt of a creditor in the event judgment is rendered. *Execution* is the process of authorizing the sheriff or other competent officer to seize and sell property of the debtor in satisfaction of a judgment previously rendered in favor of a creditor.

[4] Most states provide by statute that a certain amount of a borrower's property shall be free from all liability from levy and sale as a result of the enforcement (execution) of a money judgment. These statutes typically provide that some amount of personal property and equity in a borrower's home not secured by a purchase-money lien shall be set off and free from seizure and sale in order to provide the borrower with a minimum amount of property to maintain his family on their road to financial recovery.

[5] Redemption is the process of canceling or annulling a title conveyed by a foreclosure sale by paying the debt or fulfilling the other conditions in the mortgage.

[6] The *equity of redemption* is the right of a mortgagor to redeem his property from default, the period from the time of default until foreclosure proceedings are begun.

Fixing a Price. Mortgage foreclosure sale emanates from the assumption that a public auction is a satisfactory way to realize the best possible price in selling property. Hence, in some jurisdictions the highest bidder gets the property irrespective of its cost, the amount of liens against it, or any other consideration. Despite this requirement of a public sale, in most cases only the mortgagee or the mortgagee and a small number of bidders appear at the foreclosure sale, and, as a result, the mortgagee is usually the successful bidder. He can use his claims as a medium of exchange in the purchase, except for costs, which must be paid in cash. Others must pay cash for their purchases (which may be in the form of a loan obtained from another lender with an agreement granting to it the new mortgage), unless the successful bidder can arrange with the mortgagee to keep his lien alive by renegotiating or assuming the existing indebtedness. As a consequence, it is frequently the case that only the mortgagee makes any serious bid for the property. Because lenders generally prefer to avoid owning and liquidating foreclosed properties, they will normally bid the full amount of their claim only where it is less than or equal to the market value of the security less foreclosure, resale, and holding costs. Rarely will lenders bid in excess of their claim in an attempt to outbid other buyers at the sale.

In a few states an "upset" price is fixed in advance of the sale. By this it is meant that an appraisal by agents of the court fixes a minimum value for the property that must be reached in the bidding or the court will refuse to confirm the sale. This is not a common practice. It is quite difficult for the court to fix the price that the property must bring at the foreclosure sale. On one hand, the court is interested in doing justice to the mortgagor. Since a deficiency judgment may be decreed in case the mortgagee is not completely satisfied from the proceeds of the sale, the lower the price, the larger the deficiency judgment. On the other hand, the mortgagee's rights must be protected also. If the court should attempt to insist upon too high a price, no sale would be effected, and hence the mortgagee would receive no satisfaction of his claims.

Deed of Trust. By reason of the historical development of the law, in some jurisdictions real estate is commonly financed by a deed of trust instead of a regular mortgage. There are three parties to a loan secured by a deed of trust. The *borrower* (creator of the trust) conveys the title to the property to be used as security to a *trustee,* who holds it as security for the benefit of the *holder of the note* executed by the borrower when the loan was made. The conveyance to the trustee is by deed, but the transfer is accompanied by a trust agreement, either as a part of the deed or in addition to it, setting forth the terms of the security arrangement and giving the trustee a power of sale in event of default.

The deed of trust is commonly used in Alabama, Arkansas, California, Colorado, District of Columbia, Delaware, Illinois, Mississippi, Missouri, Nevada, New Mexico, Tennessee, Texas, Utah, Virginia, and West Virginia. Deeds of trust are not used extensively in other states because their courts have held that any conveyance of real estate given to secure a debt is a mortgage, irrespective of the form of the instrument used. Such an interpretation greatly restricts the trustee's power of sale, often requiring the expense and delay of a court process up to and including foreclosure. States imposing this restriction have sought to ensure that a reasonable sale price and all other appropriate benefits are obtained for both borrower and note holder before the property is sold.

Where the deed of trust is used according to its terms, in case of default the trustee is authorized to foreclose the borrower's equity by a sale of the property at public auction. After a proper time period for advertisement, the trustee must account to both parties for the proceeds of the sale. Each is entitled to his share as his interest may appear, after expenses of the sale, including compensation to the trustee, have been met. An advantage of the deed of trust is that this action is normally more expeditious than where a mortgage foreclosure action is used.

Deed of Trust and Mortgage Compared.   The deed of trust is such a mixture of trust and mortgage law in concept that anyone using it should act under the counsel of a local real estate lawyer. In general, however, the legal rules surrounding the creation and evidence of the debt in the form of a note, rights of the borrower left in possession, legal description of the property, creation of a valid lien on after-acquired property, and recording are the same for both mortgages and deeds of trust. Similarly, a property subject to a deed of trust may be sold subject to the deed of trust either with or without an assumption of the debt by the purchaser. The borrower may sell his interest or borrow money using the interest as security. Technically, the borrower has a reversionary interest in the property, and title to the property revests in him upon payment of the debt. In event of failure or refusal of a trustee to execute a reconveyance when the borrower repays his debt, the trustee may be forced to act by legal process whereby the borrower would obtain a court order forcing the trustee to act.

In California, where deeds of trust and mortgages are used side by side, several distinctions are made between the two instruments. Whereas a mortgage may be discharged by a simple acknowledgment of satisfaction on the record, a reconveyance of title is considered necessary to extinguish a deed of trust.[7] Recording requirements for mortgages and deeds of trust also differ. Under the recording laws of most states, mortgage assignments may be, and in some states must be, recorded. Assignments of a deed of trust, however, need not be recorded and in some states are not eligible for recordation. The recording of the original deed of trust gives notice of the lien against the property, and only the trustee has the power to clear the record through a reconveyance of the property.

Nature of Title at Foreclosure Sale.   The purchaser of property at a foreclosure sale is, in effect, the purchaser of the rights of the mortgagor whose interests are cut off by the sale. Even though the sale is conducted under court supervision, the court makes no representation concerning the nature of the title that a buyer will receive. Any title defects that existed prior to the foreclosure sale will continue with the title as it passes to the purchaser. If a junior lienor has been omitted in the suit for foreclosure, his claims will

---

[7] Some states do not require reconveyance to extinguish a deed of trust. Instead, the secured beneficiary of the trust (noteholder) signs a request for release of the deed of trust, which is presented by the borrower to the trustee together with the canceled note and the deed of trust. The trustee issues a release of trust, which is then recorded at the appropriate office of public records for the county.

not be cut off by such suit. As long as lienor claims are not cut off, the purchaser, instead of acquiring a fee simple unencumbered, acquires the property subject to those liens.

Parties to Foreclosure Suit. When the holder of a senior mortgage brings suit to foreclose his mortgage, he must join in the suit all who share the mortgagor's interest. These include not only junior mortgage holders but judgment creditors, a purchaser at an execution sale, and a trustee in bankruptcy, if any. Failure to include all of these might improve their position with the foreclosure of the senior lien. For example, should the senior mortgagee become the successful bidder at the foreclosure sale, and should a junior lienor of record be not joined in the suit, it is possible that when the senior mortgagee takes title to the land the junior mortgagee may acquire the position of a senior lienor. To avoid this possibility, every foreclosure action should be preceded by a careful search of the record to discover all junior lien claimants who should be joined in the foreclosure suit.

Should any junior lienor think that he has an equity to protect, he has the right to purchase the property at a foreclosure sale, paying off or otherwise providing for the interests of the claimants whose liens are superior to his. It might be, for example, that a senior mortgagee has a $50,000 lien on a property that a junior mortgagee with a $10,000 lien considers to be worth more than $50,000. If the junior lienor does not bid for the property, the senior mortgagee may bid it in for $50,000 (in the absence of other bidders) and cut off the junior lienor's equity, causing him loss. By taking over responsibility for the senior mortgage, the junior lienor could bid up to $60,000 for the property without providing additional funds. In this event, it is not uncommon for a senior claimant to agree in advance upon the method of settlement of his claims. This may include an agreement to renew the senior mortgagee's claim, either with or without a reduction in the amount.

The purchaser at the foreclosure sale takes over the property free of the lien of the mortgage being foreclosed, but also free of all holders of junior liens who have been joined in the foreclosure action. If the senior mortgage holder or a third party purchases the property at a foreclosure sale, all such junior liens are of no further force or effect.

If a junior lienholder brings suit for foreclosure, he should not join the senior lienholder in the suit. Instead, he should sue subject to the senior lien. By this means he is not obligated to pay off the senior lienholder. He may prefer to keep the senior mortgage alive. The holder of the senior lien may join the action voluntarily, and sometimes does so to make sure that his interests are fully protected. He may wish to have determined by the court the amount due him to be assumed by the purchaser. Or should there be any questions about the order of priority of his lien, he may join the foreclosure action to have this question answered. Again he may have a side agreement with the junior lienor to continue his mortgage unchanged in amount. In case the junior mortgage holder plans to buy the property at the foreclosure sale, he may prefer to pay off the senior lien as well. This must be done with the consent of the lienholder if he is not a party to the suit. This practice represents a redemption of the senior mortgage and follows the English maxim of "redeem up, but foreclose down." This concept is fairly obvious. It simply means that the junior mortgagee must honor the prior position of the senior mortgagee, but he may wipe out liens junior to his. For example, say a property now worth $100,000 is encumbered as follows:

First mortgage, A	$ 90,000
Second mortgage, B	20,000
Third mortgage, C	10,000
Total mortgage liens	$120,000

In a foreclosure action, mortgagee B has a buying power of $110,000 without raising additional funds if he is able to keep the first mortgage undisturbed, or if he refinances it. If he buys the property at the foreclosure sale for not over $110,000, the third mortgage lien will be completely cut off by foreclosure.

Holders of junior liens which are destroyed in a foreclosure action are entitled to have the surplus of sale price over senior mortgage claims applied to their claims. If there is no surplus, then they are entitled to a judgment for the full amount of their claims. From that time on, they are merely general, unsecured creditors of the mortgagor, unless the latter should own other real estate to which such judgments would attach.

Effect of Foreclosure on Junior Lienors

If a senior mortgage holder brings foreclosure suit and joins junior claimants in the suit, the question arises, "What happens to the claims of those cut off by the foreclosure sale?" Any surplus remaining after satisfying the costs of foreclosure and the claims of the senior lienor is distributed according to the priority rights of junior claims. Sometimes the distribution of this surplus is not as simple as it sounds. Frequent disputes concerning the order of priority require action by the court to establish the order of settlement.

Where a senior mortgage is properly foreclosed, it extinguishes the *lien* of the junior mortgage, but the *debt* secured by the mortgage is unaffected. Where there is no surplus from the foreclosure sale, or where it is insufficient to meet all claims, the holders of such claims still maintain their rights to pursue the mortgagor on whatever personal obligation he has incurred in establishing their interests (e.g., on the mortgage note). This legal right may or may not result in satisfaction of the claims of lien holders. Such obligations are not extinguished and may be enforced at some future time should the mortgagor ever recover his economic status sufficiently to make pursuit of claims against him worthwhile.

Default and Foreclosure of Land Contracts

Because of the frequency with which land contracts are not completely executed in accordance with their provisions, consideration of what happens in event of default and foreclosure is particularly important. Courts, in the application of principles of equity, will often interpret provisions of land contracts in a manner somewhat at variance from what the contract would seem on its face to provide.

Default by Vendee. Because of the informality frequently surrounding the execution of land contracts, the vendee may interpret the contract to be a kind of option. He may assume that if he decides to default on his contract, all he needs to do is forfeit his rights under it and walk away from it. He may find that conditions established by his signature on the contract are not quite this simple. In fact, most land contracts specifically provide the vendor with several options upon the vendee's default. Under one such option, upon the vendee's default, the vendor reserves the right to retain as rent and liquidated damages any amounts paid by the vendee, including any improvements to the property made by him. Unless the circumstances are such that the enforcement of this provision would amount to a penalty, it will be enforced and the vendee will not be entitled to credit for any of the purchase price paid or improvements made.

The vendor may not exercise this option to repossess the property. If he thinks the unpaid portion of the debt exceeds the value of the property, and if he thinks the vendee is financially responsible, he may have the option to bring suit to recover a judgment for past due installments and, if the contract so provides, declare the entire balance of the purchase price immediately due and payable and recover a judgment for this amount. The judgment can then be satisfied out of other assets of the vendee.

On the other hand, if substantial equity exists because of considerable paydown of the amounts due on the contract or because the project has appreciated in value, he may decide not to forfeit any equity he may have in the property. Even though he has technically violated the contract by defaulting in his payments, he may insist upon retention of possession of the property and may actively resist any effort on the part of the vendor to dispossess him. By bargaining, in lieu of legal action, he may agree to vacate and release the vendor only upon consideration that the vendor pay all or a part of this equity.

While negotiations are in progress, the vendee generally continues in possession of the property. Depending upon a combination of circumstances, including the condition of the real estate market, the likelihood of the property not being maintained, and the forecast of a favorable or unfavorable decision in court, the vendor may be willing to pay a persistent vendee in default something to purchase a release from the contract.

Loss of Payments under Land Contracts. Under a long-term land contract, regular payments over a considerable period of time may have reduced the original indebtedness substantially. Because it is customary to stipulate in the contract that in case of a default on the part of the vendee all payments made may be retained by the vendor in lieu of liquidated damages, it would appear that a default might lead to a forfeiture of all the equity the vendee has built up in the property. Courts, however, may construe a land contract as an equitable mortgage and determine that the vendee may possess certain rights in relation to payments already made.

Foreclosure Sale. Failing to dispossess a vendee in default, either by a request for observance of the forfeiture clause in the land contract or by an offer of compensation for release from the contract, the vendor may pursue his rights in court. Because the law on the subject is not well defined, a court may render any one of several decisions. It may grant the vendor the relief he or she asks for, decree that the forfeiture clause in the contract be made effective, and dispossess the vendee from the property. It may even render judgment against the vendee for any installments in default.

As an alternative, the court may decree that the land contract is, in effect, an equitable mortgage. As such, it must be foreclosed like other mortgages to determine what disposition shall be made of the proceeds of the sale. Where such an alternative is followed, the procedure from then on follows the path taken by mortgage foreclosure and sale of the security, which was discussed previously. In general, courts tend to protect the interest of the vendee in default wherever the vendee has built up a substantial equity in the property. The courts have not defined the words "substantial equity" and have given us only general outlines to follow. A reading of the cases conveys the impression that the court's ultimate inquiry is whether a forfeiture under the circumstances is found to be constant with notions of fairness and justice under the law.

Deficiency Judgment

While a sale of the mortgaged property may result in a surplus to which the mortgagor is entitled, it may, on the contrary, be sold at a price that fails to satisfy the claims of the mortgagee. Since courts have arrived at the conclusion that the mortgagor is entitled to the surplus, they have followed this with the correlative decision that any deficit should constitute a continuing claim by the mortgagee against the mortgagor. The mortgagor, after all, is personally obligated to pay the debt evidenced by the promissory note and gave the mortgage only as security for payment. Since mortgages may involve one or more specific properties, the mortgagee will normally look to such property to provide primary security for his claim, but any deficiency remains the obligation of the mortgagor. Any deficit remaining after a foreclosure and sale of the property is known as a *deficiency judgment*.

Deficiency judgments are unsecured claims—unless the mortgagor owns other real estate—and take their place alongside other debts of the mortgagor. Unlike the mortgage from which such judgment springs, the latter gives the holder no right of preference against any of the non-real estate assets of the debtor.[8] Hence the value of deficiency judgments is always open to serious question. This is true in part because of the ways by which they can be avoided or defeated.

A debtor seeking to avoid the deficiency judgment may plan accordingly. Since such judgments attach only to real estate or other property which the debtor holds or may acquire in the future, a debtor may see to it that he does not acquire any future property interests, or, if he does so, he will be careful to have titles recorded in names other than his own.

---

[8] Deficiency judgments become a lien on all real estate owned by the judgment debtor in the county or counties where the judgment is entered. To the extent that there is equity in the real estate that is not exempt from execution, the judgment can be considered secured and the creditor can enforce his lien through foreclosure and sale of the property to which the lien attaches.

In some quarters there is considerable sentiment in favor of legislation to abolish deficiency judgments altogether, leaving the mortgagee with only the property to protect his claims. Several states strictly limit the applicability of deficiency judgments. Of course, this increases the possibility that a borrower will walk away from a property if its market value falls below the loan balance.

Taxes in Default

Payment of property taxes is an obligation of the mortgagor. As such, taxes constitute a prior lien against the security. Transfers of title always take into account accrued but unpaid taxes. Mortgages commonly contain tax clauses giving the mortgagee the right to pay taxes not paid regularly by the mortgagor. The amounts so paid are then added to the claims of the mortgagee. While the lien of taxes gives tax-collecting authorities the right to foreclose in case of default, this right is seldom exercised on first or even second default. Instead, the taxing authority from time to time may pursue an alternative policy of selling tax liens with deeds to follow. Since they constitute superior liens prior to the claims of mortgagees if the taxing authorities have observed statutory procedure, and since they customarily carry high effective rates of interest, the mortgagee may prefer to maintain its priority claim by paying delinquent taxes and adding them to his claims.

If foreclosure becomes necessary, the mortgagee includes all taxes paid by him. Usually at the time of a foreclosure sale the purchaser is expected to pay all delinquent taxes, thus making the tax status of the property current.

Tax Sales.   Where the mortgagee does not act to protect his interests against tax liens, it is expected that sooner or later pressure will be brought by taxing authorities to collect delinquent taxes. In effect, if not in form, the procedure followed is intended to parallel that in the foreclosure of mortgages. At the time of the tax sale, the purchaser receives a tax certificate, which is then subject to redemption in nearly all states. The period of redemption is usually two or three years. If the property is not redeemed by the delinquent taxpayer within this period, the purchaser at the tax sale is then entitled to receive a deed to the property.

Tax titles are usually looked upon as weak evidence of ownership. The interest of the tax collector is to find someone willing and able to pay taxes for someone else in return for a claim against the property. The collector is not greatly concerned about passing good title. There is no suggestion of warranty. In addition to any defects in title irrespective of delinquent taxes, the unconcern of the tax collector may in turn result in added clouds on the title. Among the latter the following may occur:

1. Because of inaccurate description of the property or incorrect records of ownership, the notice of sale may be defective.
2. The property owner may have been denied due process, or his day in court.
3. The line of authority for the sale may not be clear.
4. Irregularities and carelessness, even in minor procedural matters, may give rise to an invalidation of the tax sale.

All of these depend in part upon the recuperative powers of the delinquent taxpayer. If he has lost interest in the property or if he lacks the financial resources to protect his interests, he may interpose no objections that will interfere with the plans of the purchaser at the tax sale. Nevertheless, the risk is great enough to suggest caution and due attention even to minor details before purchasing tax liens.

In the absence of bidders at a tax sale—which might occur in periods of depression or in the sale of inexpensive vacant land—the property usually reverts to the state, the county, or some other local governmental unit. State and local units can be careless and neglect to take steps to realize a fair price when they dispose of property so acquired. A sale by the governmental unit, given full compliance with statutory requirements, normally offers a very short period of redemption after which the mortgagor and the mortgagee lose all rights to the property to the purchaser at the sale from the governmental unit. Mortgagees should diligently monitor tax sale notices to ensure that their lien rights on property sold at tax sales are not affected.

BANKRUPTCY

The potential for bankruptcy under Chapters 7, 11, and 13 of the Bankruptcy Code affects the value of real estate as collateral. Lenders must be aware of the possibility that a borrower may file bankruptcy and must know how such a filing will change their positions. Both real estate investors and lenders must have a basic understanding of their rights in a bankruptcy proceeding in order to effectively negotiate with one another and resolve their differences short of a bankruptcy proceeding. Although a comprehensive examination of the Bankruptcy Code is beyond the scope of this text, several areas of bankruptcy law which are of particular importance to real estate investors and lenders are discussed below.

Chapter 7 Liquidation

The purpose of Chapter 7, or "straight bankruptcy," is to give the debtor a fresh start by discharging all of his debts and liquidating his nonexempt assets. Chapter 7 is available to any person regardless of the extent of their assets or liabilities. A Chapter 7 petition can be filed voluntarily by a debtor or involuntarily by petitioning creditors, except that a farmer may not be forced into an involuntary proceeding.

Upon the filing of a Chapter 7 petition, the court appoints an interim trustee who is charged with evaluating the financial condition of the debtor and reporting at the first meeting of creditors whether or not there will be assets available for liquidation and distribution to unsecured creditors. It is the trustee's job to oversee the liquidation of nonexempt assets and to evaluate claims filed by creditors. The ultimate objective of a Chapter 7 bankruptcy is the orderly liquidation of the debtor's assets and the distribution of the proceeds according to the legal rights and priorities of the various creditor claimants.

A lender whose loan to the debtor is secured by a mortgage on real estate will normally be paid in full if the value of the security exceeds the balance due under the mortgage. In order to foreclose its mortgage and sell the debtors properly, the lender must first petition the bankruptcy court to do so. If the debtor is not behind in his mortgage payments and desires to retain the property, he may do so by reaffirming the mortgage debt. This means that, although the debtor's obligation to repay the debt has been discharged in bankruptcy, the debtor makes a new agreement, after the discharge, to repay the debt.

Chapter 11

A Chapter 11 bankruptcy is an alternative to Chapter 7, which is available to owners of a business. Whereas a Chapter 7 bankruptcy normally results in the liquidation of the debtor's assets, a Chapter 11 proceeding looks to the preservation of the debtor's assets while a plan of reorganization to rehabilitate the debtor is formulated. Within 120 days after filing a Chapter 11 bankruptcy petition, this plan of reorganization must be filed by the debtor with the court. The plan must classify the various claims against the debtor's assets and specify the treatment of the debts of each class. In a typical reorganization plan, the rights and duties of the parties are redefined in one of two ways. The plan may restructure the debt to provide for reduced payments over an extended period, or the plan may scale down the debt, reducing the debtor's obligation to an amount less than the full claim.

Once a plan is filed, the proponent of the plan, usually the debtor, must solicit creditor acceptance of the plan. Once holders of two thirds of the total amount of the claims and a majority of the total number of claim holders assent to the plan, the court will analyze the plan and determine whether it meets the technical prerequisites for judicial confirmation. Even if one or more creditor classes dissent, the court can still confirm the plan if it meets certain statutory requirements. This alternative method of confirmation is known as *cramdown.*

The cramdown provisions under Chapter 11 provide borrowers with the ability to restructure their secured (e.g., mortgage) and unsecured indebtedness by executing a plan of reorganization which outlines the mechanics for getting the borrower back on its feet and states how different classes of claims and interests will be treated. The cramdown provisions are essential to keeping the borrower whole during a reorganization. Without a cramdown provision, secured lenders could always block the proposed reorganization by refusing to approve the plan and foreclose on the major assets of the borrower.

Under the Code, a plan of reorganization may seriously impact the secured lender by impairing his claim. Despite this impairment, the plan may be confirmed by the court over the objections of the secured lender. The law, however, does make some provision for secured lenders who do not approve the plan. One such provision allows the borrower to keep the secured property but requires that the lender must receive present or deferred payments having a present value equal to the value of the collateral. A second method provides for a sale of the collateral with the lender's lien attaching the proceeds of the sale. A final catch-all provision requires the secured lender's realization of the "indubitable equivalent" of his claims.

Chapter 11 bankruptcy proceedings are of great concern to lenders who may find that their security is tied up for years during the reorganization of the debtor's financial affairs.

Even lenders holding mortgages on a Chapter 11 debtor's personal residence may find that they are unable to foreclose on their liens where such a foreclosure would interfere with the debtor's plan of reorganization. The basic object of a Chapter 11 bankruptcy, then, is to provide for a court-supervised reorganization, rather than a liquidation, of a financially troubled business.

Chapter 13

A Chapter 13 petition in bankruptcy, also know as a *wage earner proceeding,* represents an attractive alternative to liquidation, as in Chapter 7. Like Chapter 11, a Chapter 13 proceeding envisions the formulation of a plan designed for the rehabilitation of the debtor. Such plans provide that funding of the plan will come from future wages and earnings of the debtor. Any debtor with regular income who has unsecured debts of less than $100,000 and secured debts of less than $350,000 qualifies for Chapter 13 relief. Thus a Chapter 13 bankruptcy is the one most likely to be used by an individual, as opposed to a business which would use Chapter 13.

The heart of Chapter 13 is the repayment plan, which is proposed by the debtor and, assuming it meets certain tests and conditions, is subject to confirmation by the court over objections of creditors. In a Chapter 13 plan the debtor proposes to pay off his obligations and reorganize his affairs. The plan may call for payments over a three- to five-year period. Unlike a Chapter 7 or Chapter 11 bankruptcy, which can be filed by a debtor only every six years, a Chapter 13 plan can be filed immediately after completion of a prior bankruptcy liquidation or payment plan as long as it is filed in good faith.

During the period covered by the plan, creditors must accept payment as provided in the plan and may not otherwise seek to collect their debts. Assuming successful completion of the plan, the debtor receives a discharge of all debts provided for in the plan other than long-term obligations for payments which continue beyond the period of the plan's duration. However, the plan may not modify the rights of a mortgagee whose lien is secured only by property used by the debtor as his personal residence. This "preferred treatment" for such mortgagees under Chapter 13 is justified because the success of a plan of reorganization could be jeopardized if foreclosure of this mortgage disrupts the affairs of the debtor by forcing him to seek other shelter. Although the plan may not "modify" such a secured lender's right, lenders desiring to accelerate the balance of any indebtedness upon default to raise the interest rate should be aware of the borrower's right to cure a default in bankruptcy (by making arrangements to pay amounts currently in default over the period of the plan) and reinstate the mortgage. Thus, although a plan may not "modify" the rights of lenders whose debt is secured by liens on the debtor's personal residence, the filing of a Chapter 13 will likely prevent an eminent foreclosure and allow for the repayment of arrearages existing on the date of the filing to be carried over a reasonable period of time. Where the plan calls for curing the arrearages and no modification of the schedule of current payments, courts will normally approve the plan because it does not materially affect the rights of such lenders.

Automatic Stay Provisions

Automatic stay provisions apply in all liquidations or reorganization proceedings in bankruptcy. These provisions prohibit the commencement or continuation of proceedings against the debtor, including the creation, perfection, or enforcement of any liens or judgments, any act to collect a claim, any act to obtain possession of property, or the foreclosure of mortgages.[9] A secured party may petition the court and receive a court order modifying or dissolving the stay under a variety of circumstances, such as (1) where the debtor does not have an equity in the property being foreclosed by the lender *and* the property is not necessary to an effective reorganization; or (2) where the interest of the lender in the property subject to the stay is not adequately protected. Where the court finds this ''adequate protection'' to be lacking, the Code provides three ways the stay can be modified to provide it. First, the bankruptcy trustee[10] may be required to make periodic payments to the party entitled to the protection in amounts sufficient to compensate for the decrease in the value of the party's interest in the collateral due to the stay. Second, the party may receive alternative or additional liens to compensate for the same decrease in value. Finally, the court may grant any other relief that will give the party entitled to protection the ''indubitable equivalent''[11] of its interest in the property. In summary then, the court balances the harm to the lender against the harm to the debtor when ruling on whether to lift or modify the stay. Absent a judicial vacation or modification, stays operate from the date of the bankruptcy filing until either (1) the case is closed or dismissed or (2) the property is abandoned or declared exempt by the court. Although most liquidation-type bankruptcy proceedings are consummated quickly, in the reorganization of business entities these provisions may tie up mortgaged property for years.

Lease Termination

In many cases, a bankrupt mortgagor may have executed a number of leases with tenants in a real estate project. Although still effective in nonbankruptcy insolvency proceedings, the Bankruptcy Code, for all practical purposes, nullifies the effect of nonassignability clauses and default clauses, which provide that bankruptcy, insolvency, or related events will be deemed a default by the lessor. The Code precludes termination of these lease agreements despite express language to the contrary. Once a bankruptcy has been filed, the trustee in bankruptcy is, with the court's approval, empowered to assume or reject executory contracts[12] or unexpired leases of the debtor. The leases are considered property of the bankruptcy estate.

---

[9] The trustee is appointed by the Bankruptcy court to take charge of a bankrupt's estate, collecting its assets, and bringing or defending claims against it.

[10] Other than mortgages held by HUD covering five or more living units.

[11] The phrase ''indubitable equivalent'' is a term of art used in the bankruptcy field. The term has evolved on a case-by-case basis, and even the authorities are split on its definition.

[12] Executory contracts are contracts that have not yet been fully completed or performed.

Where the bankrupt debtor is a tenant (lessee), the trustee of a bankrupt tenant may assume and assign the lease to obtain any benefits of favorable lease terms. The trustee, however, must first cure any defaults or give assurance that the defaults will be cured in order to approve assumption of the lease. Where the *debtor* is the *lessor* and the lease is rejected by the trustee, the tenant may treat the lease as terminated and quit the premises or remain in possession for the balance of the lease term, and deduct from the rent any damages caused by the lessor's nonperformance of his obligations under the lease.

The Code specifically deals with the treatment of shopping center leases. A *trustee* for a bankrupt lessee (tenant) cannot *assume* such a lease unless he can provide adequate assurance (1) as to the source of rent, (2) that the percentage rent will not substantially decline, (3) that lease assignment or assumption will not breach lease or other valid shopping center restrictions, and (4) that there will be no disruption, by assignment or assumption of the lease, of tenant mix at the center.

If an unfavorable lease is terminated by the tenant's trustee, the landlord's only recourse is to file a claim for damages against the whole estate. The amount of the claim is limited to the rent for the greater of one year or 15 percent of the remaining lease term, not to exceed three years. The value of such an unsecured claim is limited by the ability of the estate to satisfy the claim. Furthermore, where the lease provides that the landlord is to retain a security deposit as liquidated damages, the court may refuse to permit the landlord to file any claim for rent on the theory that the liquidated damages retained were complete compensation for the lease termination. Landlords should take precaution to avoid these risks by monitoring the financial condition of tenants, taking security interests in tenants personal property, or seeking lease guarantees by responsible third parties.

Preferential Transfers

One other area of the bankruptcy law important to lenders and investors is preferential transfers. The trustee has the power to set aside preferential transfers (and here "transfers" include liens of all sorts) which occur when the property of the debtor is given (1) while the debtor was insolvent; (2) to or for the benefit of a creditor; (3) for or on account of an antecedent debt; (4) such that the creditor is able to receive more than it would be allowed to receive under the Bankruptcy Code; (5) within 90 days of bankruptcy (or within one year if transferee was an "insider" or had reason to believe that the debtor was insolvent.)

A transfer for present consideration cannot be a preference because the transferee is not preferred over other creditors and there is no depletion of assets from the estate. But notice that mortgages, security interests, and other liens given to secure an antecedent debt are subject to avoidance by the trustee as preferences. A lender who obtains such a lien may lose his security if the borrower files bankruptcy within 90 days. Common examples of preferences include unsecured loans where the lender obtains a lien after a 10-day grace period and within 90 days of bankruptcy and loan payments in excess of normal amortization payments within this 90-day period. Even a deed given in lieu of foreclosure can be avoided as a preference if given within 90 days of the filing and when there was an equity in excess of the mortgage debt.

CONCLUSION

This chapter discussed many of the legal ramifications associated with default, foreclosure, and bankruptcy. The probability of one or more of these events occurring and the rights of the parties if it occurs ultimately affects the value of the various property rights. These legal considerations should be kept in mind as we discuss the risks associated with mortgage lending in later chapters. Clearly, the legal rights of borrowers and lenders affect the degree of risk assumed by each party and, thus, the value of entering into various transactions.

The availability of various legal alternatives can be viewed as a way of controlling and shifting risk between the various parties to a transaction. The probability of default or bankruptcy by a borrower and the legal alternatives available to each party affect the expected return to the lender from the loan. In later chapters we will discuss how the amount of loan relative to the value of the property is used by the lender to control risk. The reader should keep in mind the fact that loan covenants as discussed in this chapter also control the risk.

QUESTIONS

1. What is meant by mortgage foreclosure, and what alternatives are there to such action?
2. Explain the difference between a buyer assuming the mortgage and his taking title ''subject to'' the mortgage?
3. What dangers are encountered by mortgagees and unreleased mortgagors when property is sold ''subject to'' a mortgage?
4. In general, how may the surety status of a previous grantee who has assumed the mortgage be affected by an extension of the existing mortgage?
5. What is the difference between the equity of redemption and statutory redemption?
6. What special advantages does a mortgagee have in bidding at the foreclosure sale where the mortgagee is the foreclosing party? How much will he normally bid at the sale?
7. May a foreclosure sale sometimes be desirable or even necessary when the mortgagor is willing to give a voluntary deed?
8. What remedies does a seller under a land contract have in event of a default in payment of the purchase price by the buyer?
9. Under what circumstances may a court refuse to enforce a clause in a land contract calling for the foreclosure of all payments made in the event of default.
10. What is a deficiency judgment and how is its value to a lender affected by the Bankruptcy Code?
11. What are the differences between Chapter 7, Chapter 11, and Chapter 13 petitions in Bankruptcy?
12. What is an automatic stay, and how does it affect a lender whose borrower has filed bankruptcy?

PROBLEMS

1. First Bank Company holds a note from X and a first mortgage on real estate owned by X to secure it. X sold his property to Y, and Y assumed the mortgage. The bank did not give X a release from his debt. Subsequently Y defaulted in payment on the note. After some negotiating, the bank extended the term of the note and increased the interest rate. What is X's position at this stage of the transaction?

2. Mort owns a property. A holds a first mortgage against it, and B holds a second mortgage. Mort defaults on his mortgage payments. A forecloses without joining B in the foreclosure suit. The property is sold to C at the foreclosure sale. What are B's rights?

3. In problem 2 what would your answer be if B's mortgage were not recorded?

4. In Problem 2, what if B was joined in the foreclosure suit but forgot to attend the sale and bid? Does B have any other way of getting A to pay?

5. B entered into a land contract to purchase real estate from S. The purchase price was to be paid over a 10-year period by monthly amortization. At the end of five years, B defaulted, failing to make his required payments. The contract provided that in event of default for a period of 30 days the seller could declare a forfeiture under the contract and repossess the property. If the courts should consider the land contract an equitable mortgage, what might be the rights of B and S?

6. Debtor has filed a plan to reorganize his affairs under Chapter 13 of the Bankruptcy Code. The plan calls for payment of 10 cents on the dollar to all unsecured creditors over the next three years. The only secured creditor is Last Bank and Trust, whose lien is secured by debtor's personal residence. The plan calls for curing the present payment arrearages over one year and reducing the scheduled payments by 50 percent for three years. Will the court approve debtor's plan? Why or why not?

PART II

Financing Residential Properties

Chapter 4

The Interest Factor in Financing

Financing the purchase of real estate usually involves borrowing on a long- or short-term basis. Because large amounts are usually borrowed in relation to prices paid for real estate, financing costs are usually significant in amount and weigh heavily in the decision to buy property. Individuals involved in real estate finance must understand how these costs are computed and how various provisions in loan agreements affect financing costs and mortgage payments. Familiarity with the mathematics of finance is essential in understanding mortgage payment calculations, how loan provisions affect financing costs, and how borrowing decisions affect investment returns.

This chapter provides an introduction to the mathematics of finance. It forms a basis for concepts discussed in financing single family properties, income-producing properties, and in funding construction and development projects. Although the subject matter of mathematics sometimes appears burdensome and difficult, this chapter will provide a fundamental approach to problem solving. From the concrete applications and illustrations provided here, the necessity for understanding these subjects will become readily apparent to anyone seeking a professional level of competency in the field of real estate finance.

COMPOUND INTEREST

Understanding the process of compounding in finance requires the knowledge of only a few basic formulas. At the root of these formulas is the most elementary relationship, compound interest. For example, if an individual makes a bank deposit of $10,000 that is compounded at an annual interest rate of 6 percent, what will be the value of the deposit at the end of one year? In examining this problem, one should be aware that any compounding problem has four basic components:

1. An initial deposit, or present value of an investment of money
2. An interest rate
3. Time
4. Value at some specified future period

In our problem, the deposit is $10,000, interest is to be earned at an annual rate of 6 percent, time is one year, and value at the end of the year is what we would like to know. We have, then, four components, three of which are known and one that is unknown.

Compound or Future Value

In the preceding problem, we would like to determine what value will exist at the end of one year if a single deposit or payment of $10,000 is made at the beginning of the year and the deposit balance earns a 6 percent rate of interest. To find the solution, we must introduce some terminology:

PV = present value, or principal at the beginning of the year
  i = annual interest
  I = dollar amount of interest earned during the year
FV = principal at the end of n years, or future value
  n = number of years

In this problem, then, $PV = \$10,000$, $i = 6$ percent, $n =$ one year, and FV, or the value after one year, is what we would like to know.

The value after one year can be determined by examining the following relationship:

$$FV = PV + I_1$$

or the future value, FV, at the end of one year equals the deposit made at the beginning of the year, PV, plus interest I_1 earned in the first period. Because $PV = \$10,000$, we can find FV by determining I_1. Since we are compounding annually, FV is easily determined to be $10,600, which is shown in Exhibit 4–1.

Multiple Periods.   To find the value at the end of two years, we continue the compounding process by taking the value at the end of one year, $10,600, making it the deposit at the beginning of the second year, and compounding again. This is shown in Exhibit 4–2.

EXHIBIT 4–1   Compound Interest Calculation (one year)

$$I_1 = PV \cdot i$$
$$= \$10,000(.06)$$
$$= \$600$$

Future value at the end of one year ($n = 1$ year) is determined as

$$FV = PV + I_1$$
$$= \$10,000 + \$600$$
$$= \$10,600$$

or

$$FV = PV(1 + i)$$
$$= \$10,000(1 + .06)$$
$$= \$10,600$$

EXHIBIT 4–2   Compound Interest Calculation for Two Years

$$\$10,600 \, (.06) = I_2$$
$$\$636 = I_2$$

and value at the end of two years, or $n = 2$ years, is now

$$\$10,600 + I_2 = FV$$
$$\$10,600 + \$636 = \$11,236$$

From Exhibit 4–2 it can be seen that a total future value of $11,236 has been accumulated by the end of the second year. Note that in the second year, not only is interest earned on the original deposit of $10,000, but interest is also earned on interest ($600) earned in the first year. *The concept of earning interest on interest is the essential idea that must be understood in the compounding process and is the cornerstone of all financial tables and concepts in the mathematics of finance.*

From the computation in Exhibit 4–2, it should be pointed out that the value at the end of year 2 could have been determined directly from *PV* as follows:

$$FV = PV(1+i)(1+i)$$
$$PV(1+i)^2$$

In our problem, then, when $n = 2$ years:

$$FV = PV(1+i)^2$$
$$= \$10,000(1+.06)^2$$
$$= \$10,000(1.123600)$$
$$= \$11,236$$

From this computation, value at the end of two years, or $11,236, is identical to the result that we obtained in Exhibit 4–2. Being able to compute *FV* directly from *PV* is a very important relationship because it means that the future value, or value of any deposit or payment left to compound for any number of periods, can be determined from *PV* by simple multiplication. Therefore, if we want to determine the future value of a deposit made today, when left to compound for any number of years, we can find the solution with the general formula for compound interest, which is

$$FV = PV(1 + i)^n$$

By substituting the appropriate values for *PV*, *i*, and *n*, we can determine *FV* for any desired number of years.[1]

Other Compounding Intervals.   In the preceding section, the discussion of compounding applies to cases where funds were compounded only once per year. Many savings accounts, bonds, mortgages, and other investments provide for monthly, quarterly, or

---

[1] At this point, the reader may realize that these problems can be solved with a financial calculator. Students should acquire a financial calculator and consult the manual to solve compounding and discounting problems. (The instructor should consult the manual accompanying this textbook for supplemental problems and materials.)

semiannual compounding. Because we will be dealing with mortgage loans extensively in a later chapter, which almost exclusively involves monthly compounding, it is extremely important that we consider these other compounding intervals.

When compounding periods other than annual are considered, a simple modification can be made to the general formula for compound interest. To change the general formula

$$FV = PV(1 + i)^n$$

where

   n = years
   i = annual interest rate
   PV = deposit

to any compounding period, we divide the annual interest rate (i) by the desired number of compounding intervals *within* one year. We then increase the number of time periods (n) by multiplying by the desired number of compounding intervals *within* one year. For example, let m be the number of intervals within one year in which compounding is to occur, and let n be the number of years in the general formula. Then we get

$$FV = PV \left[1 + \frac{i}{m} \right]^{n \cdot m}$$

Hence, if interest was earned on the $10,000 deposit at an annual rate of 6 percent, compounded monthly, to determine the future value at the end of one year, where $m = 12$, we would have

$$FV = \$10,000 \left[1 + \frac{.06}{12} \right]^{1 \cdot 12}$$
$$= \$10,000(1.061678)$$
$$= \$10,616.78$$

If we compare the results of monthly compounding with those of annual compounding, we can see the benefits of monthly compounding immediately. If our initial deposit were compounded monthly, we would have $10,616.78 at the end of the year, as opposed to $10,600.00 when annual compounding was used.

Another way of looking at this result is to compute an effective annual yield on both investments. This is done by assuming that $10,000 is deposited at the beginning of the year and that all proceeds are withdrawn at the end of the year. For the deposit that is compounded monthly, we obtain

$$(EAY) \text{ Effective annual yield} = \frac{FV - PV}{PV}$$
$$= \frac{\$10,616.78 - \$10,000.00}{\$10,000}$$
$$= 6.1678\%$$

The result can be compared with the annual yield obtained when annual compounding is used, or

$$EAY = \frac{\$10,600 - \$10,000}{\$10,000}$$
$$= 6\%$$

From this comparison, clearly we can conclude that the effective annual yield is higher when monthly compounding is used. This comparison should point out immediately the difference between computing interest at a *nominal* annual rate of interest and computing interest at the same nominal annual rate of interest, *compounded monthly*. Both deposits are compounded at the same nominal annual rate of interest (6 percent); however, one is compounded 12 times at a monthly rate of $(.06 \div 12)$, or .005, on the ending monthly balance, while the other is compounded only once, at the end of the year at the rate of .06. It is customary in the United States to use a nominal rate of interest in contracts, savings accounts, mortgage notes, and other transactions then to specify how payments will be made or interest accumulated (that is, annually, monthly, daily, etc.). It is then up to the parties involved in the transaction to ascertain the effective annual yield or rate of interest.

From the above analysis, one result should be very clear. Whenever the nominal annual interest rates offered on two investments are equal, the investment with the more frequent compounding interval within the year will always result in a higher effective annual yield. In our example, we could say that a 6 percent annual rate of interest compounded monthly provides an effective annual yield of 6.168 percent.[2]

Some other investments offer semiannual, quarterly, and daily compounding. In these cases, the basic formula for compound interest is modified as follows:

Compounding Interval		*Modified Formula*
Semiannually,	$m = 2$	$FV = PV\left[1 + \dfrac{i}{2}\right]^{n \cdot 2}$
Quarterly,	$m = 4$	$FV = PV\left[1 + \dfrac{i}{4}\right]^{n \cdot 4}$
Daily,	$m = 365$	$FV = PV\left[1 + \dfrac{i}{365}\right]^{n \cdot 365}$

Hence if a deposit or $10,000 is made and an annual rate of 6 percent *compounded daily* is to be earned, we would have

$$FV = \$10,000\left[1 + \frac{.06}{365}\right]^{1 \cdot 365}$$
$$= \$10,000(1.061831)$$
$$= \$10,618.31$$

---

[2]Because of this fact, many savings institutions that compound savings monthly or daily quote a nominal annual rate of interest but immediately point out that if funds are left on deposit for one year, a higher effective annual yield will be earned.

and the effective annual yield would be 6.1831%. If the money were left on deposit for two years, the exponent would change to 2 · 365, and *FV* at the end of two years would be $11,274.86.

We will also follow the convention of using nominal rates of interest in all problems, examples, and so on. Hence, the term *interest rate* means a *nominal* rate of interest. Thus, when comparing two alternatives with *different* compounding intervals, do not use the nominal interest rate as the basis for comparison. Instead, use the effective annual yield concept in developing solutions.

Use of Compound Interest Tables

Finding a solution to a compounding problem involving many periods is very awkward because of the amount of multiplication involved. To provide a shortcut for finding solutions to compound interest problems, a series of interest factors have been developed in tables in Appendixes A and B. Appendix A contains interest factors for selected nominal interest rates and years based on the assumption of annual compounding intervals. Appendix B contains interest factors for selected nominal interest rates and years based on the assumption of monthly compounding intervals. These two compounding periods were chosen because they represent the compounding intervals that are most frequently used throughout this book.[3]

In both appendixes, the interest factors used for compounding single deposits are contained in column 1, amount of $1 at compound interest. Essentially, these interest factors have been computed from the general formula for compound interest for annual compounding and from the formula, as modified, for monthly compounding for various combinations of *i* and years.

To familiarize the student with the use of these tables, interest factors (now referred to as *IF*) for the future value (*FV*) of $1 for various interest rates are shown in Exhibit 4–3. These factors for annual compounding have been taken directly from column 1 in each table for respective interest rates contained in Appendix A.

In the problem discussed earlier, we wanted to determine the future value of $10,000 deposit compounded at an annual rate of 6 percent after one year. Looking to the 6 percent column in Exhibit 4–3 to the row corresponding to one year, we find the interest factor 1.060000. This interest factor when multiplied by $10,000 gives us the solution to our problem.

$$FV = \$10,000(FVIF,6\%,1 \text{ yr.})$$
$$= \$10,000(1.060000)$$

The interest factor for the future value of $1, at 6 percent for one year (abbreviated as *FVIF*, 6%, 1 yr.) is 1.060000, which is the same result that we would obtain if we

---

[3]More complete tables for these and other compounding intervals, such as quarterly, semiannual, daily, and so on, can be computed with a financial calculator or may be found in *Thorndike Encyclopedia of Banking and Financial Tables* (Boston: Warren, Gorham & Lamont, Inc., 1973), with supplements.

EXHIBIT 4–3   Amount of $1 at Compound Interest (column 1, Appendix A) Annual Compounding Factors

Year	6%	10%	15%	20%	25%
			Rate		
1	1.060000	1.100000	1.150000	1.200000	1.250000
2	1.123600	1.210000	1.322500	1.440000	1.562500
3	1.191016	1.331000	1.520875	1.728000	1.953125
4	1.262477	1.464100	1.749006	2.073600	2.441406
5	1.338226	1.610510	2.011357	2.488320	3.051758

computed $(1 + .06)^1$ or 1.06 from the general formula for compound interest. In other words,

$$(FVIF, 6\%, 1 \text{ yr.}) = (1 + .06)^1 = 1.06$$

The interest factors in the tables in Appendix A allow us to find a solution to any compounding problem as long as we know the deposit (PV), the interest rate (i), and the number of periods (n) over which annual compounding is to occur. Students may also find this solution by using a financial calculator.

Question: What would be the future value of $5,000 deposited for four years compounded at an annual rate of 10 percent?

Solution: $FV = \$5,000(FVIF, 10\%, 4 \text{ yrs.})$
                                          $= \$5,000(1.464100)$
                                          $= \$7,320.50$

As was the case with the interest factors for annual compounding, interest factors for *monthly compounding* for selected interest rates and years have been computed from the modified formula $PV(1 + i/12)^{n \cdot 12}$ and are compiled in tables contained in Appendix B. To familiarize the student with these tables, interest factors for selected interest rates and periods have been taken from column 1, *amount of $1 at compound interest,* from tables in Appendix B and are shown in Exhibit 4–4.

In our earlier problem, we wanted to determine the future value of $10,000 deposit that earned interest at an annual rate of 6 percent, compounded monthly. This can be easily determined by selecting the appropriate interest factor from the 6 percent column for 12 months, or 1 year, in Exhibit 4–4. That factor is 1.061678. Hence, to determine the value of the deposit at the end of 12 months, or 1 year, we have

$$FV = \$10,000(MFVIF, 6\%, 12 \text{ mos.})$$
$$= 10,000(1.061678)$$
$$= 10,616.78$$

EXHIBIT 4–4   Amount of $1 at Compound Interest (column 1, Appendix B, monthly compounding factors)

		Rate		
Month	*6%*	*7%*	*8%*	
1	1.005000	1.058330	1.006670	
2	1.010025	1.011701	1.013378	
3	1.015075	1.017602	1.020134	
4	1.020151	1.023538	1.026935	
5	1.025251	1.029509	1.033781	
6	1.030378	1.035514	1.040673	
7	1.035529	1.041555	1.047610	
8	1.040707	1.047631	1.054595	
9	1.045911	1.053742	1.061625	
10	1.051140	1.059889	1.068703	
11	1.056396	1.066071	1.075827	
12	<u>1.061678</u>	1.072290	1.083000	
Year				*Month*
1	<u>1.061678</u>	1.072290	1.083000	12
2	1.127160	1.149806	1.172888	24
3	1.196681	1.232926	1.270237	36
4	1.270489	1.322054	1.375666	48

In other words, the interest factor for a 6 percent rate of interest compounded monthly for one year (*MFVIF*, 6%, 12 mos.) is 1.061678, which is the same result that we would obtain if we expanded $(1 + .06/12)^{1 \cdot 12}$ by multiplying, or

$$(MFVIF, 6\%, 12 \text{ mos.}) = \left[1 + \frac{.06}{12} \right]^{1 \cdot 12} = 1.061678$$

Note the letter *M* in our abbreviation for the *monthly compound interest equation*. Instead of writing $(1 + .06/12)^{1 \cdot 12}$ and expanding the equation to obtain the monthly interest factor, we simply indicate that a monthly interest factor was either calculated or obtained from Appendix B when we use the abbreviation (*MFVIV*, 6%, 12 mos.). When *M* is not included in the abbreviation, *annual* compounding is assumed, and those annual interest factors should be calculated or obtained from Appendix A. Hence calculating or using the interest factors shown in column 1 in the tables contained in Appendix B allows us to find to solution to any monthly compounding problem as long as we know the deposit (*PV*), the interest rate (*i*), and the number (*n*) of months or years over which compounding is to occur.

Question: What would be the future value of a single $5,000 deposit earning 8 percent interest, compounded, monthly, at the end of two years?

Solution:

$$FV = \$5,000\left[1 + \frac{.08}{12}\right]^{2 \cdot 12}$$
$$= \$5,000(MFVIF, 8\%, 24 \text{ mos.})$$
$$= \$5,000(1.172888)$$
$$= \$5,864.44$$

PRESENT VALUE

In the preceding section dealing with compounding, we were concerned with determining value at some time in the future; that is, we considered the case where a deposit had been made and compounded into the future to yield some unknown future value.

In this section we are interested in the problem of knowing the future cash receipts for an investment and trying to determine how much should be paid for the investment at *present*. The concept of *present value* is based on the idea that money has time value. Time value simply means that if an investor is offered the choice between receiving $1 today or receiving $1 in the future, the proper choice will always be to receive the $1 today. This is true because the $1 received today can be invested in some opportunity that will earn interest, which is always preferable to receiving only $1 in the future. In this sense, money is said to have *time value*.

When determining how much should be paid *today* for an investment that is expected to produce income in the *future*, we must apply an adjustment called *discounting* to income received in the future to reflect the time value of money. The concept of present value lays the cornerstone for calculating mortgage payments, determining the true cost of mortgage loans, and finding the value of an income property, all of which are very important concepts in real estate finance.

A Graphic Illustration of Present Value

An example of how discounting becomes an important concept in financing can be seen from the following problem. Suppose an individual is considering an investment that promises a cash return of $10,600 at the end of one year. In the investor's evaluation, this investment should yield an annual rate of 6 percent. The question to be considered here is how much should be offered or paid *today* if $10,600 is to be received at the end of the year and investor requires a 6 percent return compounded annually on the amount invested?

The problem can be seen more clearly by comparing it with the problem of finding the compound value of $1 discussed in the first part of this chapter. In that discussion we were concerned with finding the future value of a $10,000 deposit compounded monthly at 6 percent for one year. This comparison is depicted in Exhibit 4–5.

EXHIBIT 4–5 Comparison of Future Value and Present Value

					Month							
	1	*2*	*3*	*4*	*5*	*6*	*7*	*8*	*9*	*10*	*11*	*12*

Compounding   Future
 at 6% . . . . $10,000 ————————————————————➤ value(?)
Discounting Present
 at 6% . . . . value (?) ◄———————————————————— $10,600

Note from Exhibit 4–5 that, when compounding, we are concerned with determining the *future value* of an investment. With discounting, we are concerned with just the opposite concept; that is, what *present value* or *price* should be paid *today* for a particular investment, assuming a desired rate of interest is to be earned?

Because we know from the preceding section that $10,000 compounded annually at a rate of 6 percent results in a future value of $10,600 at the end of one year, $10,000 would be the present value of such an investment. However, had we not done the compounding problem in the preceding section, how would we know that $10,000 equals the present value of the investment? Let us again examine the compounding problem we considered in the previous section. To determine future value, recall the general equation for compound interest:

$$FV = PV(1 + i)^n$$

In our present value problem *PV* becomes the *unknown* because *FV*, or the future value to be received at the end of one year, $n = 1$ year, is known to be $10,600. Because the interest rate (i) is also known to be 6 percent, *PV* is the only value which is not known. *PV*, the present value or amount we should pay for the investment today, can be easily determined by rearranging terms in the above compounding formula as follows:

$$FV = PV(1 + i)^n$$

$$PV = FV \frac{1}{(1 + i)^n}$$

In our problem, then, we can determine *PV* directly by substituting the known values into the above expression as follows:

$$PV = FV \frac{1}{(1 + i)^n}$$

$$= \$10,600 \frac{1}{(1 + .06)^1}$$

$$= \$10,600 \frac{1}{1.06}$$

$$= \$10,600 \times (.943396)$$

$$= \$10,000$$

Note that the procedure used in solving for the present value is simply to multiply the future value, *FV*, by 1 divided by $(1 + i)^n$. We know from the previous section on compounding that in our problem $(1 + i)^n$ is $(1 + .06)^1$ or (*FVIF*, 6%, 1 yr.), which equals 1.06. Dividing 1.06 into 1 gives .943396. This last result is important in present value analysis because it shows the relationship between future value and present value.

Because we have seen from Exhibit 4–5 that the discounting process is a process that is the opposite of compounding, to find the present value of any investment is simply to compound in a "reverse sense." This is done in our problem by taking the reciprocal of the interest factor for the compound value of $1 at 6 percent, $1 \div 1.06$ or .943396, which we abbreviate as (*PVIF*,6%, 1 yr.), multiplying it by the future value of our investment to find the present value of the investment. We can now say that $10,600 received at the end of one year, when discounted by 6 percent, has a present value of $10,000. Alternatively, if an investment is offered which promises $10,600 to us after one year and we want to earn a 6 percent annual return on our investment, we should not pay more than $10,000 for the investment (it is on the $10,000 present value that we earn the 6 percent interest).

Use of Present Value Tables.   Because the discounting process is the reverse of compounding, and the interest factor for discounting $1 \div (1 + i)^n$ is simply the reciprocal of the interest factor for compounding, a series of interest factors has been developed that enables us to solve directly for present value (*PV*) instead of having to multiply out the term $(1 + i)^n$ and to divide the result into 1 each time we want to discount. In fact, all of that work has been done for us and compiled in column 4 in tables in Appendix A, present value reversion of $1, for annual compounding (monthly factors are contained in Appendix B). Exhibit 4–6 contains a sample of these factors to be used for discounting, taken directly from column 4 in tables for selected interest rates in Appendix A.

In our problem we want to know how much should be paid for an investment with a future value of $10,600 to be received at the end of one year if the investor demands an annual return of 6 percent. The solution can be found by calculating or selecting the (*PVIF*, 6%, 1 yr.) or from the 6 percent column in Exhibit 4–6, or .943396. The $10,600

EXHIBIT 4–6 Present Value Reversion of $1 (column 4, Appendix A, annual discounting factors)

Year	5%	6%	10%	15%	20%
			Rate		
1	.952381	.943396	.909091	.869565	.833333
2	.907029	.889996	.826446	.756144	.694444
3	.863838	.839619	.751315	.657516	.578704
4	.822702	.792094	.683013	.571753	.482253
5	.783526	.747258	.620921	.497177	.401878
6	.746215	.704961	.564474	.432328	.334898

future value can now be multiplied by .943396, resulting in a present value (*PV*) of $10,000.

Question: How much should be paid today for a real estate investment that will return $20,000 at the end of three years, assuming the investor desires an annual return of 15 percent interest on the amount invested?

Solution:
$$PV = \$20,000 \times \frac{1}{(1 + .15)^3}$$
$$= \$20,000(PVIF,15\%,3 \text{ yrs.})$$
$$= \$20,000(.657516)$$
$$= \$13,150.32$$

The investor should pay no more than $13,150.32 today for the investment promising a return of $20,000 after three years if a 15 percent return on investment is desired.[4]

Because we can use the discounting process to find the present value of a future value when annual compounding is assumed, we can also apply the same methodology assuming monthly discounting is required. For example, in our illustration involving monthly compounding, the future value of $10,000 when interest was earned at an annual rate of 6 percent compounded monthly was $10,616.80. An important question to be considered by an investor would be, how much should be paid today for the future value of $10,616.80 received at the end of one year, assuming that a 6 percent return *compounded monthly* is required?

We could answer this question by finding the reciprocal of the formula used to compound monthly, $1 \div (1 + i/12)^{1 \cdot 12}$, and multiplying that result by the future value of $10,616.78 to find the present value (*PV*). This factor may be calculated, or, following the procedure used in annual discounting, we could use the series of factors that have been calculated and included in table form. These factors, assuming a monthly discounting process, are contained in column 4 in tables in Appendix B. A sample of factors for selected interest rates and years is shown in Exhibit 4–7.

In our problem, then, we want to determine the present value of $10,616.80 received at the end of one year, assuming a desired rate of return of 6 percent, *compounded monthly*. By going to the 6 percent column and the row corresponding to one year (12 months) and selecting the interest factor .941905, we can now multiply $10,616.80 (.941905) = $10,000 and see that $10,000 is the maximum one should be willing to pay today for the investment.

Question: How much should an investor pay to receive $12,000 three years (36 months) from now, assuming that an annual return of 9 percent *compounded monthly* is desired?

---

[4]There is an accepted convention in finance that when one refers to a percentage return on investment, a nominal annual interest rate is assumed. If solutions are computed based on different compounding intervals within a year, such as monthly, the solution should be designated as an *annual rate of interest compounded monthly*. The latter solution may then be converted, if desired, to an effective annual yield, as shown previously.

EXHIBIT 4–7　Present Value Reversion of $1 (column 4, Appendix B, monthly discounting factors)

Month	6%	7%	8%	9%	
			Rate		
1	.995025	.994200	.993377	.992556	
2	.990075	.988435	.986799	.985167	
3	.985149	.982702	.980264	.977833	
4	.980248	.977003	.973772	.970554	
5	.975371	.971337	.967323	.963329	
6	.970518	.965704	.960917	.956158	
7	.965690	.960103	.954553	.949040	
8	.960885	.954535	.948232	.941975	
9	.956105	.948999	.941952	.934963	
10	.951348	.943495	.935714	.928003	
11	.946615	.938024	.929517	.921095	
12	.941905	.932583	.923361	.914238	
Year					Month
1	.941905	.932583	.923361	.914238	12
2	.887186	.869712	.852596	.835831	24
3	.835645	.811079	.787255	.764149	36
4	.787098	.756399	.726921	.698614	48

Solution:

$$PV = \$12,000(MPVIF, 9\%, 36 \text{ mos.})$$
$$= \$12,000(.764149)$$
$$= \$9,169.79$$

The investor should pay no more than $9,169.79 for the investment, or the present value (*PV*) of the investment is $9,169.79. (Again note the use of *M* in our abbreviation which designates monthly discounting.)

COMPOUND OR FUTURE VALUE OF AN ANNUITY

The first section of this chapter dealt with finding the compound or future value of a *single deposit* or payment made only once, at the beginning of a period. An equally relevant consideration involves a series of equal deposits or payments made at equal intervals. For example, assume deposits of $1,000 are made at the *end* of each year for a period of five years and interest is compounded at an annual rate of 5 percent. What would be the future value at the *end* of the period for a series of deposits plus all compound interest? In this case the problem involves equal payments (*P*), or deposits, made at equal time intervals. This series of deposits or payments is defined as an *annuity*. Because we know how to find the answer to a problem in which only one deposit is made, it would be logical and correct to assume that the same basic compounding process applies when dealing with *annuities*. However, that process is only a partial solution to the problem because we are dealing with a series of deposits which occur annually.

To compute the sum of all deposits made in each succeeding year and include compound interest on deposits only when it is earned, the general formula for compounded interest must be expanded as follows:

$$FVA = P(1 + i)^{n-1} + P(1 + i)^{n-2} + \cdots + P$$

This may also be written as

$$FVA = P \cdot \sum_{t=1}^{n-1} (1 + i)^t + P$$

which simply means that we may take the constant payment or annuity P and multiply it by the "sum of" the series $1 + i$ expanded from time $t = 1$ to the period $n - 1$, plus P.[5] Hence, the symbol Σ represents the "sum of" that series and is simply a shortcut notation to be used in place of writing $1 + i$ repetitively.

In this expression, *FVA* is the future value of an annuity or the sum of all deposits P compounded at an annual rate i for n years. The important thing to note in the expression, however, is that each deposit is assumed to be at the *end* of each year and is compounded through year n. The final deposit does not earn interest because it occurs at the end of the final year. In our example, since we are dealing with a series of $1,000 deposits made over a five-year period, the first $1,000 deposit would be compounded for four periods $(n - 1)$, the $1,000 deposit made at the beginning of the second year would be compounded for three periods $(n - 2)$, and so on, until the last deposit P is reached. The last deposit is not compounded because it is deposited at the end of the fifth year.[6]

To compute the value of these deposits, we could construct a solution like that shown in Exhibit 4–8. Note that each $1,000 deposit is compounded from the end of the year in which the deposit was made to the end of the next year. In other words, as shown in our expanded formula above, the deposit at the end of year 1 is compounded for four years, the deposit made at the beginning of the second year is compounded for three years, and so on. By carrying this process out one year at a time, we determined the solution, or $5,525.63, when the compounded amounts in the extreme right-hand column are added.

Although the future value of $1,000 per period, *FVA*, can be determined in the manner shown in Exhibit 4–8, careful examination of the compounding process reveals another, easier way to find the solution. Note that the $1,000 deposit occurs annually and never

---

[5]The formula shown here is the formula for an *ordinary annuity* which assumes all deposits are made at the *end* of each year. The final P in the expression means that the last payment is not compounded. The letter *A* in *FVA* signifies that an annuity is being evaluated.

[6]As previously indicated, the reader should be aware that this formulation is used for *ordinary annuities* or when payments or receipts occur at the end of a period. This is different from the formula for an *annuity due*, which assumes deposits are made at the *beginning* of the year. For additional applications of an ordinary annuity and an annuity due, the instructor should consult the instructor's manual accompanying this textbook.

EXHIBIT 4–8   Future Value of an Annuity of $1,000 Per Year Compounded at 5 Percent Annually (column 1, Appendix A)

Year	Deposit	IF	Future Value
1	$1,000 × (FVIF, 5%, 4 yrs.)	= $1,000 × 1.215506	= $1,215.51*
2	1,000 × (FVIF, 5%, 3 yrs.)	= 1,000 × 1.157625	= 1,157.63*
3	1,000 × (FVIF, 5%, 2 yrs.)	= 1,000 × 1.102500	= 1,102.50
4	1,000 × (FVIF, 5%, 1 yr.)	= 1,000 × 1.050000	= 1,050.00
5	1,000 × 1.000000	= 1,000 × 1.000000	= 1,000.00
	Also	= 1,000 × 5.525631	= 5,525.63*

*Rounded.

changes; that is, it is constant. When the deposits are constant, it is possible to sum all of the individual *IF*s as 5.525631. By multiplying $1,000 by 5.525631, a solution of $5,525.63 is obtained, as shown in Exhibit 4–8 at the bottom of the right-hand column.

Use of Compound Interest Tables for Annuities

Because the *IF*s in Exhibit 4–8 can be added when annuities are being considered, a series of new interest factors has been calculated for various interest rates in column 2 of Appendix A, *accumulation of $1 per period*. A sample of these factors, now referred to as *FVIFA,i%*, yrs., has been taken directly from column 2 in Appendix A and compiled in Exhibit 4–9 (note the use of the letter *A* after *FVIF*, which designates that the series of deposits being considered is an *annuity* and not the deposit of a single amount).

EXHIBIT 4–9   Accumulation of $1 per Period (column 2, Appendix A, annual compounding factors)

Year	Rate 5%	6%	10%	15%
1	1.000000	1.000000	1.000000	1.000000
2	2.050000	2.060000	2.100000	2.150000
3	3.152500	3.183600	3.310000	3.472500
4	4.310125	4.374616	4.641000	4.993375
5	5.525631	5.637093	6.105100	6.742381
6	6.801913	6.975319	7.715610	8.753738
7	8.142008	8.393838	9.487171	11.066799
8	9.549109	9.897468	11.435888	13.726819

In the problem at hand, to determine the future value of $1,000 deposited annually at 5 percent for five years, note that if we go to the 5 percent column in Exhibit 4–9 and obtain the *IF* that corresponds to five years, we can find the solution to our problem as follows:

$$
\begin{aligned}
FVA &= P(FVIFA, 5\%, 5 \text{ yrs.}) \\
&= \$1,000(FVIFA, 5\%, 5 \text{ yrs.}) \\
&= \$1,000(5.525631) \\
&= \$5,525.63
\end{aligned}
$$

This amount corresponds to the solution obtained from the long series of multiplications carried out in Exhibit 4–8.

Question: What would be the future value of $800 deposited each year for six years, compounded annually at 10 percent interest after six years?

Solution:
$$
\begin{aligned}
FV &= \$800(FVIFA, 10\%, 6 \text{ yrs.}) \\
&= \$800(7.715610) \\
&= \$6,172.49
\end{aligned}
$$

The same procedure used for compounding annuities for amounts deposited or paid annually can also be applied to monthly annuities. A very simple modification can be made to the formulation used for annual annuities by substituting $i \div 12$ in place of i and adding the number of compounding periods per period (m) in the annual formulation, as follows:

$$
FVA = P\left[1 + \frac{i}{12}\right]^{n \cdot m - 1} + P\left[1 + \frac{i}{12}\right]^{n \cdot m - 2} + \cdots + P
$$

or

$$
FVA = P \cdot \sum_{t=1}^{n \cdot m - 1}\left[1 + \frac{i}{12}\right]^{t} + P
$$

However, in this formulation, $n \cdot m$ represents months. Deposits or payments P are made monthly and are constant in amount. Hence, the interest factors used to compound each monthly deposit may be added (as they were for annual deposits in Exhibit 4–8), and a new series for compounding monthly annuities can be computed. This has been done for selected interest rates and years. The factors for compounding monthly annuities are contained in column 2 in Appendix B.[7]

Question: An investor pays $200 per month into a real estate investment which promises to pay an annual rate of interest of 8 percent *compounded monthly.* If he makes consecutive monthly payments for five years, what will be the future value at the end of five years?

---

[7]As was the case with annual compounding, this formulation assumes that deposits are made at the *end* of each month, or that an ordinary annuity is being compounded.

Solution:
$$FVA = \$200(MFVIFA, 8\%, 60 \text{ mos.})$$
$$= \$200(73.476856)$$
$$= \$14,695.37$$

Hence, in this case the value of these payments earning interest at an annual rate of 8 percent compounded monthly can be found by multiplying the $200 monthly annuity by the interest factor for the accumulation of $1 per period in column 2 in Appendix B, or $200(73.476856) = $14,695.37.

PRESENT VALUE OF AN ANNUITY

In the preceding section, our primary concern was to determine the *future value* of an annuity, or constant payments received at equal time intervals. In this section we want to consider the *present value* of a series of annual receipts as the investment produces income over time. Because an investor may have to consider a series of income payments when trying to decide whether to invest, this is an important problem. Recalling that when dealing with the present value of a single receipt, or ending value, *PV*, we took the basic formula for compounding interest and rearranged it to determine the present value of an investment as follows:

$$FV = PV(1 + i)^n$$
$$PV = FV \div (1 + i)^n$$
$$PV = FV \cdot \frac{1}{(1 + i)^n}$$

To consider the present value of an annuity, defined as *PVA*, we need only consider the sum of individual present value for all receipts. This can be done by modifying the basic present value formula as follows:

$$PVA = R \frac{1}{(1 + i)^1} + R \frac{1}{(1 + i)^2} + R \frac{1}{(1 + i)^3} + \cdots + R \frac{1}{(1 + i)^n}$$

or this can be written as

$$PVA = R \cdot \sum_{t=1}^{n} \frac{1}{(1 + i)^t}$$

Note in this expression that each receipt R is discounted for the number of years corresponding to the time at which the funds are actually received. In other words, the first receipt would occur at the end of the first period and would be discounted only one period, or $R \cdot [1 \div (1 + i)^1]$. The second receipt would be discounted for two periods, or $R \cdot [1 \div (1 + i)^2]$, and so on.

Assuming an individual is considering an investment which will provide a series of annual cash receipts of $500 for a period of six years, and the investor desires a 6 percent return, how much should be paid for the investment today? We can begin by considering the present value of the $500 receipt in year 1, as shown in Exhibit 4–10. Note that the present value of the $500 receipt is discounted for one year at 6 percent. This is done

---

EXHIBIT 4–10   Present Value of $500 per Year (discounted at 6 percent annually)

Year	Receipt	IF*		Present Value
1	$500 × (*PVIF*, 6%, 1 yr.)	= $500 ×	.943396	= $ 471.70
2	500 × (*PVIF*, 6%, 2 yrs.)	= 500 ×	.889996	= 445.00
3	500 × (*PVIF*, 6%, 3 yrs.)	= 500 ×	.839619	= 419.81
4	500 × (*PVIF*, 6%, 4 yrs.)	= 500 ×	.792094	= 396.05
5	500 × (*PVIF*, 6%, 5 yrs.)	= 500 ×	.747258	= 373.63
6	500 × (*PVIF*, 6%, 6 yrs.)	= 500 ×	.704961	= 352.48
	Also	500 × 4.917324		= 2,458.66†

*Column 4, Appendix A.
†Rounded.

---

because the first year's income of $500 is not received until the end of the first period, and our investor only wants to pay an amount today (present value) which will assure a 6 percent return on the amount paid today. Therefore, by discounting this $500 receipt by the interest factor in column 5 for one year in the 6 percent tables in Appendix A, or .943396, the present value is $471.70. Note that the second $500 income payment is received at the end of the second year. Therefore, it should be discounted for *two* years at 6 percent. Its present value is found by multiplying $500 by the interest factor in column 5 in the 6 percent tables for two years, or .889996, giving a present value of $445. This process can be continued for each receipt for the remaining three years, as shown in Exhibit 4–10. The present value of the entire series of $500 income payments can be found by adding the series of receipts discounted each month in the far right-hand column, which totals $2,458.66.

However, as also shown in Exhibit 4–10, because the $500 series of payments is constant, we may simply sum all interest factors to obtain one interest factor that can be multiplied by $500 to obtain the same present value. The sum of all interest factors for 6 percent in Exhibit 4–10 is 4.917324. When 4.917324 is multiplied by $500, the present value, $2,458.66, found in the lengthy series of multiplications carried in Exhibit 4–10, is again determined.

Use of Present Value of an Annuity Table

Because the interest factors in Exhibit 4–10 may be summed, as long as the income payments are equal in amount and received at equal intervals, this combination obviously takes a lot of work out of problem solving. The sums of *IF*s for various interest rates, now referred to as (*PVIFA,i%,*yrs.), have been compiled in table form and are listed in column 5, present value ordinary annuity $1 per period, in the tables in Appendix A. To familiarize the student with discounting annuities, Exhibit 4–11 has been developed showing the *IF*s for the present value of $1 per period (annuity). These *IF*s were taken

EXHIBIT 4–11 Present Value of Ordinary Annuity $1 per Period (column 5, Appendix A, annual discounting factors)

Year	Rate			
	5%	*6%*	*10%*	*15%*
1	.952381	.943396	.909091	.869565
2	1.859410	1.833393	1.735537	1.625709
3	2.723248	2.673012	2.486852	2.283225
4	3.545951	3.465106	3.169865	2.854978
5	4.329477	4.212364	3.790787	3.352155
6	5.075692	4.917324	4.355261	3.784483
7	5.786373	5.582381	4.868419	4.160420
8	6.463213	6.209794	5.334926	4.487322

directly from column 5 in the tables contained in Appendix A for a sample of interest rates. In our problem, then, we want to determine the present value of $500 received annually for six years, assuming an annual rate of return of 6 percent is desired. How much should an investor pay for this total investment today and be assured of earning the desired return? We can solve this problem by computing the solution with a calculator or by looking at Exhibit 4–11, finding the 6 percent column, and looking down the column until the *IF* in the row corresponding to six years is located. The *IF* is 4.917324. Thus

$$PVA = \$500(PVIFA,6\%,6 \text{ yrs.})$$
$$= \$500(4.917324)$$
$$= \$2,458.66$$

This solution corresponds to that obtained in Exhibit 4–10.

Question: An investor has an opportunity to invest in a rental property which will provide net cash returns of $400 per year for three years. The investor believes that an annual return of 10 percent should be earned on this investment. How much should be paid for the rental property?

Solution: $$PVA = \$400(PVIFA,10\%,3 \text{ yrs.})$$
$$= \$400(2.486852)$$
$$= \$994.74$$

No more than $994.74 should be paid for the investment property. If the investor pays $994.74, a 10 percent return will be earned on the investment. (Again note the use of the letter *A* after *PVIF*, indicating an *annuity* is being evaluated.)

Based on the logic used above in discounting annuities paid or received annually, the same procedure can be applied to cash receipts paid or receiving *monthly*. In this case the formula used to discount annual annuities is simply modified to reflect monthly receipts or payments, and the discounting interval is changed to reflect monthly compounding:

$$PVA = P\left[\cfrac{1}{1+\cfrac{i}{12}}\right]^1 + P\left[\cfrac{1}{1+\cfrac{i}{12}}\right]^2 + \cdots + P\left[\cfrac{1}{1+\cfrac{i}{12}}\right]^{12 \cdot n}$$

where payments (P) occur monthly, the exponents represent months running from 1 through $n \cdot m$, and *PVA* represents the present value of an annuity received over $n \cdot m$ months.

As was the case with annual discounting, computation of the present value of an annuity can be very cumbersome if one had to expand the above formula for each problem he faced, particularly if the problem involved cash receipts or payments over many months. Hence, a series of interest factors have been computed by expanding the above formula for each monthly interval and adding the resulting interest factors as was done with discounting annual annuities in Exhibit 4–10. These factors are contained in column 5 in tables in Appendix B, and, like the annual tables, the column is labeled present value of ordinary annuity of $1 per period; however, the period in this case is one month. A sample of these factors for given interest rates and years has been taken directly from column 5, Appendix B and included in Exhibit 4–12. Hence, if an investor wanted to know how much should be paid today for an investment that would pay $500 at the end

---

EXHIBIT 4–12   Present Value Ordinary Annuity of $1 per Period (column 5, Appendix B, monthly discounting factors)

Month	Rate			
	6%	7%	8%	
1	.995025	.994200	.993377	
2	1.985099	1.982635	.980176	
3	2.970248	2.965337	2.960440	
4	3.950496	3.942340	3.934212	
5	4.925866	4.913677	4.901535	
6	5.896384	5.879381	5.862452	
7	6.862074	6.839484	6.817005	
8	7.882959	7.794019	7.765237	
9	8.779064	8.743018	8.707189	
10	9.730412	9.686513	9.642903	
11	10.677027	10.624537	10.572420	
12	11.618932	11.557120	11.495782	
Year				*Month*
1	11.618932	11.557120	11.495782	12
2	22.562866	22.335099	22.110544	24
3	32.871016	32.386464	31.911806	36
4	42.580318	41.760201	40.961913	48

of each month for the next 12 months and earn an annual rate of 6 percent compounded monthly on the investment, the solution can be easily computed with a calculator or determined by consulting Exhibit 4–12. Looking to the 6 percent column and dropping down to the row corresponding to 12 months, the factor 11.618932 is found. Multiplying $500 by 11.618932 results in $5,809.47 or the amount that the investor should pay today if a 6 percent rate of return compounded monthly is desired.

Question: A real estate partnership predicts that it will pay $300 at the end of each month to its partners over the next six months. Assuming the partners desire an 8 percent return compounded monthly on their investment, how much should they pay?

Solution: $PVA = \$300(MPVIFA, 8\%, 6 \text{ mos.})$
                                              $= \$300(5.862452)$
                                              $= \$1,758.74$

ACCUMULATION OF A FUTURE SUM

The previous two sections have dealt with compounding and discounting single payments on annuities. However, in some instances, it is necessary to determine a series of payments necessary to *accumulate a future sum*, taking into account the fact that such payments will be accumulating interest as they are deposited. For example, assume we have a debt of $20,000 that must be repaid in one lump sum at the end of five years. We would like to make a series of equal annual payments (an annuity) at the end of each of the five years such that when we accumulate all deposits, plus interest, we will have $20,000 at the end of the fifth year. Assuming that we can earn interest on those deposits at the rate of 10 percent per year, how much should each annual deposit be?

Basically, we are dealing with accumulating a future sum in this case, which from Exhibit 4–5 indicates that we will be compounding a series of deposits (P), or an annuity, to achieve that future value. Hence, we can work with the procedure for determining future values by compounding as follows:

$$P(FVIFA, 10\%, 5 \text{ yrs.}) = \$20,000$$
$$P(6.105100) = \$20,000$$
$$P = \$20,000 \div 6.105100$$
$$= \$3,275.95$$

This computation merely indicates that when compounded at an annual interest rate of 10 percent, the unknown series of equal deposits (P) will result in the accumulation of $20,000 at the end of five years. Given the interest factor for compounding an annual annuity (*FVIFA*) from column 2 in Appendix A, or 6.105100, we know that the unknown deposit P when multiplied by that factor will result in $20,000. Hence, by dividing $20,000 by the interest factor for compounding an annual annuity, we can obtain the necessary annual payment of $3,275.95. The result tells us that if we make deposits of $3,275.95 at the end of each year for five years, and each of those deposits earns interest at an annual rate of 10 percent, a total of $20,000 will be accumulated at the end of five years.

In examining the above computation, we can see that dividing $20,000 by 6.105100 is equivalent to multiplying $20,000 by (1 ÷ 6.105100), or .163797, and the same $3,275.95 solution results. The factor .163797 is referred to in real estate finance as a sinking-fund factor (*SFF*), which is used in problems such as the one we are dealing with as well as other applications in real estate. These sinking-fund factors (or reciprocals of interest factors for compounding annuities) have been computed and are contained in column 3 in Appendix A for annual deposits (the reader should either locate or compute the factor .163797) and Appendix B for monthly deposits. In the latter case, if we wanted to know what monthly payments would be necessary to pay off the $20,000 debt at the end of five years, taking into account that each deposit will earn an annual rate of 10 percent compounded monthly, we can easily solve for the solution by multiplying $20,000 times (.012914) (the sinking-fund factor, column 3, Appendix B), and we would obtain $258.28 per month as the required series of deposits.

DETERMINING YIELDS OR INTERNAL RATES OF RETURN ON INVESTMENTS

Up to now, this chapter has demonstrated how to determine future values in the case of compounding and present values in the case of discounting. Each topic is important in its own right, but they have also provided tools for determining an equally important component used extensively in real estate financing, that is, calculating rates of return or *investment yields*. In other words, the concepts illustrated in the compounding and discounting processes can also be used to determine rates of return, or yields, on investments, mortgage loans, and so on. These concepts must be mastered because procedures used here will form the basis for much of what follows in succeeding chapters.

In the prior sections of this chapter, we have concentrated on determining the future value of an investment made today when compounded at some given rate of interest, or the present investment value of a stream of cash returns received in the future when discounted at a given rate of interest. In this section we are concerned with problems where we know what an investment will cost today and what the future stream of cash returns will be, but we do not know what *yield* or *rate of return* will be earned if the investment is made.

Investments with Single Receipts

In many cases investors and lenders are concerned with the problem of what rate of compound interest, or investment yield, will be earned if an investment is undertaken. To illustrate the *investment yield* concept, assume an investor has an opportunity to buy an unimproved 1-acre lot for $5,639 today. The lot is expected to appreciate in value and to be worth $15,000 after seven years. What rate of interest (or investment yield) would be earned on the $5,639 investment in the property if it were made today, held for seven years, and sold for $15,000?

To solve for the unknown rate, we can formulate the problem as follows:

$$PV = R \cdot \frac{1}{(1 + i)^n}$$

$$\$15,000 = \$5,639 \cdot \frac{1}{(1 + i)^7}$$

In other words, we would like to know the annual rate of compound interest i that when substituted into the above expression will make the $15,000 receipt equal to the $5,639 investment outlay, or present value, today.

Unfortunately, there is no "easy way" of finding a solution to the unknown, or i, directly. What follows are a number of approaches to finding i. (For readers using electronic calculators or who have access to computers, the material that follows may be lightly reviewed.)

One approach to solving for i is trial and error. That is, a value for i is estimated; then the equation is solved to ascertain whether the future value, or $15,000, when discounted to present value, PV, will equal $5,639. When the correct value for i is found, the solution for present value should yield $5,639.

How do we begin the search for i? One way is to simply guess for a solution. Let's try 10 percent. Mathematically we ask, for

$$PV = \$15,000 \frac{1}{(1 + .10)^7}$$

is $PV = \$5,639$?

Solving for PV, we have

$$PV = (\$15,000)(.513158)$$
$$= \$7,697$$

We note that $7,697 or PV is much greater than the desired PV, or $5,639. This means that the yield, or rate of compound interest being earned on the investment, is *greater* than 10 percent. Hence, we must continue the discounting process by increasing i.

Our next "trial" will be 15 percent. Substituting, we have

$$PV = \$15,000 \frac{1}{(1 + .15)^7}$$
$$= \$15,000(.375937)$$
$$= \$5,639$$

This time PV equals $5,639. Hence, we know that this "guess" was correct. From this result, we have determined that the yield or internal rate of return i earned on the investment is equal to 15 percent. We have, in essence, "removed" interest compounded at the rate of 15 percent for seven years from the $15,000 receipt of cash, leaving the initial deposit, or present value, of $5,639.

When working with financial tables and when trying to find the yield when only one future value is involved, we can use an alternative approach, where the interest factor in the tables, *PVIF,* is first determined as follows:

$$\$5,639 = \$15,000(PVIF,?\%,7 \text{ yrs.})$$
$$\$5,639 \div \$15,000 = (PVIF,?\%,7 \text{ yrs.})$$
$$.375933 = (PVIF,?\%,7 \text{ yrs.})$$

From the above calculations the interest factor is .375933, but we still do not know the interest rate *i*. However, we do know that the time period over which the investment is to appreciate in value is seven years. Because *PVIF* is .375933 and the term of investment is seven years, by consulting the interest tables in Appendix A we can easily find the correct interest rate. Since the cash return of $15,000 is a single receipt, we need only locate an *IF* for the present value reversion of $1 equal to .375933 in column 4 in the row corresponding to seven years for some interest rate. We begin the search for the interest rate by choosing an arbitrary interest rate, say 5 percent. Looking to the 5 percent table in Appendix A, we see the *IF* in column 4 for seven years is .710681, which is larger than .375933. Moving to the 10 percent table, the *IF* for seven years is .513158, which is lower than the *IF* at 5 percent but comes closer to the *IF* we are looking for. Continuing this trial-and-error process, by looking to the 15 percent table we see that the *IF* in column 4 for seven years is .375937; therefore the interest rate we desire is 15 percent. We know this is the correct interest factor because $15,000 (.375937) = $5,639. This proves that 15 percent is the yield on this investment.

What does this interest rate, or yield, mean? It means that if the $5,639 investment is made today, then held for seven years and sold for $15,000, this would be equivalent to investing $5,639 today and letting it compound annually at an interest rate of 15 percent (note the correspondence between the terms *interest rate* and *yield*).[8] This fact can be determined with the following computation:

$$FV = \$5,639(FVIF,15\%,7 \text{ yrs.})$$
$$= \$5,639(2.660020)$$
$$= \$15,000$$

This calculation simply shows that $5,639 compounded annually at an interest rate of 15 percent for seven years is $15,000. Hence, making this investment is equivalent to earning a rate of return of 15 percent. This rate of return is usually referred to as the *investment yield* or the *internal rate of return.*

The internal rate of return integrates the concepts of compounding and present value. It represents a way of measuring a return on investment over the entire investment period, expressed as a compound rate of interest. For example, if an investor is faced with making an investment in an income-producing venture, regardless of how the cash returns are patterned, the internal rate of return provides a guide or comparison for the investor. It

---

[8]Note that we are now using the terms *yield* and *internal rate of return* for *i,* instead of the interest rate. It is generally accepted practice to use these terms when evaluating most *investments.* The term *interest rate* is generally used when a *loan* is being evaluated. While the two concepts are very similar, the reader should become accustomed to these differences in the usage.

tells the investor what compound interest rate the return on an investment being considered is equivalent to. In our example of the unimproved 1-acre lot, the 15 percent yield or internal rate of return is equivalent to making a deposit of $5,639 and allowing it to compound monthly at an annual interest rate of 15 percent for seven years. After seven years the investor would receive $15,000, which includes the original investment of $5,639 plus all compound interest. With the internal rate of return known, the investor can make an easier judgment as to what investment should be made. If the 15 percent return is adequate, it will be made; if not, the investor should reject it.[9]

The concepts of the internal rate of return or yield, present value, and compounding are indispensable tools that are continually used in real estate finance and investment. The reader should not venture beyond this section without firmly grasping the concepts that have been explained. These concepts form the basis for the remainder of this chapter and the chapters which follow.

Yields on Investment Annuities

The concepts just illustrated for a single receipt of cash (when the unimproved lot was sold) also apply to situations where a *series* of cash receipts is involved. Consequently, a yield or internal rate of return also can be computed on these types of investments.

To illustrate, suppose an investor has the opportunity to make an investment in real estate costing $3,170 that would provide him with cash income of $1,000 at the end of *each year* for four years. What would be the investment yield, or internal rate of return, that the investor would earn on the $3,170 invested? In this case we have a series of receipts that we wish to discount by an unknown rate which will make the present value of the $1,000 annuity equal the original investment of $3,170. We would like to find a solution for i in this problem, or the rate of interest which will make the present value of the $1,000 four-year annuity equal to $3,170. Using our shorthand notation, we have

$$\$3,170 = \$1,000(PVIFA, ?\%, 4 \text{ yrs.})$$

Recalling the notation for the present value of an annuity *PVA*, we have

$$PVA = R \cdot \sum_{t=1}^{n} \frac{1}{(1 + i)^t}$$

Substituting gives

$$\$3,170 = 1,000 \cdot \sum_{t=1}^{n} \frac{1}{(1 + i)^t}$$

We would like to find a solution to i in this problem, or the rate of interest that will make the present value of a $1,000 four-year annuity equal to $3,170. Using our shorthand notation, we can express our problem as follows:

---

[9]When different investments are being compared, any differences in risk must also be considered. This topic is discussed in later chapters.

$$PVA = R(PVIFA, ?\%, 4 \text{ yrs.})$$
$$\$3,170 = \$1,000(PVIFA, ?\%, 4 \text{ yrs.})$$
$$\$3,170 \div \$1,000 = (PVIFA, ?\%, 4 \text{ yrs.})$$
$$3.170000 = (PVIFA, ?\%, 4 \text{ yrs.})$$

This procedure is similar to solving for the yield or internal rate of return on single receipts discussed in the preceding section, except that we are now dealing with an annuity (note the use of the letter *A* after *PVIF* in our abbreviated formula). As before, using the same procedure we solve for the interest factor for a four-year period that will correspond to some interest rate. To determine what the interest rate is, one must search the tables in Appendix A (column 5) in the four-year row until a factor very close to 3.1700 is found. A careful search reveals that the factor will be found in the 10 percent tables (the reader should verify this). Hence, based on this procedure, we have determined that the investment yield or internal rate of return (*IRR*) on the $3,170 invested is 10 percent. A more in-depth analysis of what the internal rate of return or investment yield means is presented in Exhibit 4–13.

Note from Exhibit 4–13 that when the investment yield or internal rate of return is computed, two characteristics are present. One is the *recovery of capital* in each period, and the other is *interest earned* in each period. In other words, when the *IRR* is computed based on the $3,170 investment and the $1,000 received each year, *implicit* in the *IRR* computation is the *full recovery* of the $3,170 investment *plus* interest compounded annually at 10 percent. Hence, the 10 percent investment yield is really a rate of compound interest earned on an outstanding investment balance from year to year. Of the total $4,000 received during the four-year period, total interest earned is $830 and $3,170 is capital recovery.

Monthly Annuities—Investment Yields.   A similar application for investment yields can be made in cases where monthly cash annuities will be received as a return on

EXHIBIT 4–13   Illustration of the Internal Rate of Return *(IRR)* and Components of Cash Receipts

	Year			
	1	*2*	*3*	*4*
Investment (balance)	$3,170	$2,487	$1,736	$ 910
IRR or yield at 10%	317	249*	174*	91*
Cash received	$1,000	$1,000	$1,000	$1,000
Less: Cash yield at 10%	317	249	174	90*
Recovery of investment	$ 683	$ 751	$ 826	$ 910
Investment (beginning of year)	$3,170	$2,487	$1,736	$ 910
Less: Recovery of investment	683	751	826	910
Investment (end of year)	$2,487	$1,736	$ 910	0

*Rounded.

investment. For example, assume that an investor makes an investment of $51,593 to receive $400 at the end of each month for the next 20 years (240 months). What annual rate of return, compounded monthly, would be earned on the $51,593? The solution can be easily determined with the following procedure:

$$R(MPVIFA,?\%,20 \text{ yrs.}) = PVA$$
$$\$400(MPVIFA,?\%,20 \text{ yrs.}) = \$51,593$$
$$(MPVIFA,?\%,20 \text{ yrs.}) = \$51,593 \div \$400$$
$$= 128.9825$$

As was the case with finding the *IRR* for investments with annual receipts, we find the interest factor for the present value of an ordinary annuity of $1 per month for 20 years for an interest rate compounded monthly (note the *M* in our shorthand notation), which is 128.9825. Looking to column 5 in Appendix B in the 20-year row for various interest rates, we find that the interest rate that corresponds to that factor is 7 percent. Hence the *IRR* is 7 percent compounded monthly on the $51,593 investment. Both the recovery of $51,593 plus $44,407 in interest was embedded in the stream of $400 monthly cash receipts over the 20-year period.

Linear Interpolation.   In the previous two examples involving yields on single receipts and annuities, either Appendix A or B was used because they corresponded to an interest rate for which tables are provided. Because it is possible to include only a small number of tables for interest rates in a textbook, in many cases where interest factors are computed tables for the exact interest rate that corresponds to the computed interest factor may not be contained in the book. In that event, a procedure known as linear interpolation must be used to solve for the interest rate. For example, assume that an investor can purchase a vacant lot for $5,000 today and expects to sell it five years from now for $9,000. What would be the internal rate of return? Assuming the investor wants the investment yield or internal rate of return expressed in terms of an annual rate of compound interest, we set the problem up as follows:

$$\$9,000(PVIF,?\%,5 \text{ yrs.}) = \$5,000$$
$$(PVIF,?\%,5 \text{ yrs.}) = \$5,000 \div \$9,000$$
$$= .555555$$

From this calculation, we obtain the interest factor of .555555 that corresponds to some rate of interest for a five-year period. Since this involves a single receipt of cash ($9,000), we use column 4 in Appendix A to find the appropriate factor. However, the interest factor is not contained in any of the available tables, hence the need for interpolation. A careful examination of the available tables shows that the interest factor we are seeking falls between the factor found in the 12 percent table (.567427) for five years and the factor found in the 15 percent tables (.497177). Hence, we know that because the interest factor we are looking for (.555555) falls between the factors at 12 percent and 15 percent, our yield must also be between 12 percent and 15 percent. The question is, how do we find it? We proceed as follows:

(*PVIF*,12%,5 yrs.)	= .567427	*PVIF*,12%,5 yrs.)	= .567427
(*PVIF*,15%,5 yrs.)	= .497177	Desired *IF*	= .555555
A. Difference	= .070250	B. Difference	= .011872

1. Ratio of B ÷ A = .011872 ÷ .070250 = .17 (rounded).
2. Difference in interest rates 15% − 12% = 3%.
3. Multiply ratio of B ÷ A by the difference in interest rates and add to the base (lower) interest rate or

$$(.17 \times 3\%) + 12\% = \underline{12.51\%}$$

In using this procedure, we first express B, which is the difference between the desired interest factor and the base interest factor, as a proportion of A or the difference in interest factors for the entire range (12%–15%). We then assume that the internal rate of return falls between 12 percent and 15 percent in the same proportion. Hence, in this case the internal rate of return would be 12.51 percent.

Space limitations do not permit the inclusion of numerous tables in Appendixes A or B. The accuracy of desired solutions has influenced the tables we have chosen to include in this book. For example, as can be seen from Appendix A, the differences between interest rates generally range from 2 percent, while in Appendix B, the differences are generally 1 percent. This is because Appendix B will be used extensively in the chapters dealing with mortgage lending, where a high degree of accuracy is desired. Tables in Appendix A, however, will be used in investment analysis, where we make many estimates in such things as annual rent, expense, and appreciation in property values. Because of the many uncertainties involved when estimating such variables, the degree of accuracy in computation is not as important when determining internal rates of return on investment projects as is the case when dealing with mortgage loans. When doing investment analysis then, slightly larger interpolation errors are acceptable. For students using financial calculators with adequate storage capacity, the internal rate of return may be solved *directly;* hence the use of tables is unnecessary in most cases. In cases where calculators do not have adequate capacity or when problems being solved have inputs that exceed its capacity, interpolation may be required. In that case the student must understand interpolation and the problems associated with the accuracy of the solution. (Additional examples and calculator solutions are provided in the instructor's manual accompanying this book. The instructor may desire to reproduce examples from this manual for student use.)

Effective Annual Yields—Extensions

In Chapter 4, we dealt with the problem of determining equivalent annual yields in cases where there were more than one compounding interval within a year. In our example, we showed the effective annual yield for a $10,000 investment compounded annually, monthly, and daily to be 6, 6.1678, and 6.1831 percent, respectively. In many situations, we may already know the *effective annual yield* and would like to know what the *nominal annual rate* of interest compounded monthly (or for any period less than one year) must be to earn the desired effective annual yield. For example, in the chapter we considered a problem in which compounding occurred monthly based on a nominal annual rate of interest of 6 percent. Because compounding occurred in monthly intervals, an effective annual interest rate larger than the nominal rate resulted. Assuming that we wanted to know what the nominal annual rate of interest, compounded *monthly,* would have to be to provide a desired (*EAY*) of 6 percent, we can employ the following formula, where *ENAR* = equivalent nominal annual rate:

$$ENAR = [(1 + EAY)^{\frac{1}{m}} - 1] \cdot m$$

In our problem we would have

$$
\begin{aligned}
ENAR &= [(1 + .06)^{\frac{1}{m}} - 1] \cdot 12 \\
&= [(1 + .06)^{.083333} - 1] \cdot 12 \\
&= [1.004868 - 1] \cdot 12 \\
&= .0584106 \text{ or } 5.84106\% \text{ (rounded)}
\end{aligned}
$$

To illustrate this concept, if we have investment A, which will provide an effective annual yield of 6 percent, and we are considering investment B, which will provide interest *compounded monthly,* we would want to know what the equivalent nominal annual rate (*ENAR*) of interest, compounded monthly, would have to be on investment B in order to provide the *same* effective annual yield of 6 percent. That rate would be an annual rate of 5.84106 percent compounded monthly.

$$
\begin{aligned}
FV &= \$1(MFVIF, 5.84106\%, 12 \text{ mos.}) \\
&= \$1 \left[1 + \frac{.0584106}{12} \right]^{12} \\
&= \$1.06 \text{ (rounded)}
\end{aligned}
$$

From our example in the chapter, we know that the *EAY* would be ($1.06 − $1.00) ÷ $1.00, or 6 percent. Hence, we now know that if we are considering an investment of equal risk, with returns that will be *compounded monthly,* its annual nominal rate of interest must be at least 5.84106 percent to provide us with an equivalent, effective annual yield of 6 percent. Obviously, this application can be modified for any investment with different compounding periods by altering *m* in the above formula.

QUESTIONS

1. What is the essential concept in understanding compound interest?
2. How are the interest factors in column 1, Appendix B, developed?
3. What general rule can be developed concerning maximum values and compounding intervals within a year? What is an equivalent annual yield?
4. What does the time value of money mean? How is it related to present value? What process is used to find present value?
5. How does discounting, as used in determining present value, relate to compounding, as used in determining future value? How would present value ever be used?
6. What are the interest factors in column 4 in Appendix A? How are they developed?

7. What is an annuity? How is it defined? What is the difference between an ordinary annuity and an annuity due?
8. When evaluating the present value of an uneven series of receipts, why can we not use interest factors for annuities? What factors must be used to discount a series of uneven receipts?
9. What is the sinking-fund factor? How and why is it used?
10. What is linear interpolation? What is the basic assumption made when it is used? What error should the user be concerned about when using this technique?
11. What is an internal rate of return? How is it used? How does it relate to the concept of compound interest?

PROBLEMS

Note: The instructor may wish to consult the instructor's manual for supplemental material on financial calculators before assigning these problems.

1. Jack Samuels makes a deposit of $9,000 in a bank account. The deposit is to earn interest *annually* at the rate of 6 percent for five years.
   a. How much will Mr. Samuels have on deposit at the end of five years?
   b. Assuming the deposit earned a 6 percent annual rate of interest compounded *monthly,* how much would he have at the end of five years?
   c. In comparing (a) and (b), what are the respective effective annual yields? (Hint: consider the value of each deposit after one year only.) Which alternative is better?
2. Ms. Bette Schmidler has the option of making a $10,000 investment that will earn interest either at the rate of 6 percent compounded semiannually or 5.5 percent compounded quarterly. Which would you advise? (Again, consider one year only.)
3. Roger Starbuck is considering the purchase of a lot. He can buy the lot today and expects the price to rise to $25,000 at the end of six years. He believes that he should earn an investment yield of 12 percent annually on his investment. The asking price for the lot is $11,000. Should he buy it?
4. An investor can make an investment in a real estate development and receive an expected cash return of $30,000 after eight years. Based on a careful study of other investment alternatives, he believes that a 12 percent annual return compounded monthly is a reasonable return to earn on this investment. How much should he pay for it today?
5. An investor can deposit $3,000 at the end of each year for the next 15 years and earn interest at an annual rate of 7 percent. What will the value of the investment be after 15 years?
6. Jason Smith deposits $1,000 at the end of each month in an account which will earn interest at an annual rate of 10 percent compounded monthly. How much will he have at the end of five years?
7. An investor will deposit $1,000 at the end of year 1, $500 at the end of year 2, $5,000 at the end of year 3, and nothing in year 4. Assuming that these amounts will be compounded at an annual rate of 8 percent, how much will the investor have on deposit at the end of 4 years?

8. Arco Supreme is considering an investment which will pay $1,000 at the end of each year for each of the next 12 years. It expects to earn an annual return of 20 percent on its investment. How much should the company pay today for the investment?

9. Easy Mark has the opportunity to make an investment in a real estate venture with Swampland Enterprises. Swampland is expecting to pay investors $1,000 at the end of each month for the next six years. Mark believes that a reasonable return on his investment should be 15 percent compounded monthly.
   a. How much should he pay for the investment?
   b. What will be the total sum of cash he will receive over the next six years?
   c. Why is there such a large difference between (a) and (b)?

10. The Gee Bee Corporation is evaluating an investment that will provide the following returns at the end of each of the following years: year 1, $10,000; year 2, $6,000; year 3, $0; year 4, $9,000; and year 5, $3,500. Gee Bee believes that it should earn an annual rate of 15 percent on its investments. How much should Gee Bee pay for this investment?

11. Starstrek Enterprises has a loan of $60,000 coming due eight years from now. It wants to make annual payments into a sinking fund which will earn interest at an annual rate of 8 percent. What will the annual payments have to be? Suppose that Starstrek makes monthly payments earning interest at 8 percent compounded monthly. What would those payments have to be?

12. The Landco Development Company is considering the purchase of an apartment project for $30,000. Landco estimates that it will receive $7,500 at the end of each year for the next seven years. If it purchases the project, what will be its internal rate of return? If the company insists on a 15 percent return compounded annually on investment? Is this a good investment?

13. Arcane Corporation is considering the purchase of an interest in a real estate syndication at a price of $60,000. In return, the syndication promises to pay $540 at the end of each month for the next 20 years (240 months). If purchased, what would Arcane's internal rate of return, compounded monthly, be on its investment? How much total cash would be received on the investment? How much is profit, and how much is capital recovery?

14. The Henry Stabler Company is making an investment in a real estate venture that will provide returns at the end of the next three years as follows: year 1, $9,000; year 2, $9,000; and year 3, $12,000. The company wants to earn a 15 percent annual return on its investment. How much should it pay for the investment? How does Stabler know that he is earning an annual rate of 15 percent on his investment? Now assume Mr. Stabler wanted to earn an annual rate of 15 percent compounded monthly. How much should be paid?

15. Hoosier Investment Company is making an investment of $10,000 today and expects to receive $4,000 at the end of each year for the next three years. What is the internal rate of return on this investment?

16. An investor has the opportunity to make an investment that will provide an effective annual yield of 8 percent. He is considering two other investments of equal risk that will provide compound interest monthly and semiannually, respectively. What must the equivalent nominal annual interest rate (*ENAR*) be for each of these two investments to ensure that an equivalent annual yield of 8 percent is earned?

Chapter 5

Fixed Interest Rate Mortgage Loans: Pricing, Payment Patterns, and Effective Borrowing Costs

This chapter deals with various approaches to pricing and structuring fixed interest rate mortgage loans. By *pricing* a loan, we refer to the rate of interest, fees, and other terms that lenders offer and that borrowers are willing to accept when mortgage loans are made. As a part of the pricing process, we also stress the supply and demand for loanable funds, the role of inflation, and how both affect the rate of interest. As to loan structuring, we review the many innovations in mortgage payment patterns that have evolved from changes in the economic environment.

Another major objective of this chapter is to illustrate techniques for determining the yield to the lender and actual cost to the borrower when various provisions exist in loan agreements. When lending on real estate, lenders commonly include various charges and fees in addition to the interest rate as a condition of making a loan. These charges may include loan discounts, origination fees, prepayment penalties, and/or prepaid interest. In addition, various amortization or loan repayment schedules can be agreed on by the borrower and lender to facilitate financing a particular real estate transaction. Because these provisions often affect the cost of borrowing, the methodology used to compute the yield to the lender (cost to the borrower) is stressed in this chapter.

DETERMINANTS OF MORTGAGE INTEREST RATES— A BRIEF OVERVIEW

The real estate finance industry has gone through an important evolution brought about by changing economic conditions. These changing conditions require lenders and borrowers to have a better understanding of the sources of funds used for lending and the nature of how risk, economic growth, and inflation affect the availability and cost of mortgage funds.

When considering the determinants of interest rates on mortgage loans used to finance single family residences, we must also consider the demand and supply of mortgage funds. Most mortgage lenders are intermediaries or institutions that serve as conduits linking flows of savings from savers to borrowers of those savings in the form of mortgage credit. The market rate of interest on mortgage loans is established by what borrowers are willing to pay for the use of funds over a specified period of time and what lenders are willing to accept in the way of compensation for the use of such funds. On the demand side of the market, it can be safely said that the demand for mortgage loans is a *derived demand,* or determined by the demand for housing.

The demand for housing is generally determined by the number of households desiring housing, their income, size, age, tastes, preferences for other goods and the interest rate that must be paid to acquire mortgage credit. Hence the demand for housing establishes, in large part, the demand for mortgage credit at various rates of interest.

The supply side of the mortgage market is established by what interest rates lenders are willing to accept when providing funds to borrowers. The amount of credit that they are willing to supply is a function of their cost of attracting funds from savers, the cost of managing and originating loans, losses from loan defaults and foreclosures, and, in the case of fixed interest rate loans, potential losses due to unexpected changes in interest rates after a loan is made.

When supplying funds to the mortgage market, lenders also consider returns and the associated risk of loss on alternative investments in relation to returns available on mortgages. Hence, the mortgage market should also be thought of as part of a larger capital market, where lenders and investors evaluate returns available on mortgages and on all competing forms of investment and the relative risks associated with each. Should lenders believe that a greater return can be earned by making more mortgage loans (after taking account of costs and the risk of loss) than would be the case if they invested in other developments such as corporate bonds or business loans, more funds will be allocated to mortgage loans, and vice versa. Hence, lender decisions to allocate funds to mortgages are also made relative to returns and risk on alternative loans and investment opportunities.

The Real Rate of Interest—Underlying Considerations

When discussing market interest rates on mortgages, we should keep in mind that these interest rates are based on a number of considerations. In the above discussion, we have pointed out that the supply of funds allocated to mortgage lending in the economy is, in part, determined by the returns and risks on all possible forms of debt and investment opportunities.

One fundamental relationship that is common to investments requiring use of funds in the economy is that they earn at least the real rate of interest.[1] This is the minimum rate

---

[1]If the reader can visualize an investment portfolio containing investments in all productive activities in the economy based on the weight that any particular activity has to the total value of all productive activity in the economy, the rate of current earnings on such a portfolio would be equivalent to the real rate of interest. Such a rate would also be the rate required by economic units to save rather than consume from current income.

of interest that must be earned by savers to induce them to divert the use of resources (funds) from present consumption to future consumption. To convince individuals to make this diversion, income in future periods must be expected to increase sufficiently because of interest earnings to divert current income from consumption to savings. If expected returns earned on those savings are high enough to provide enough future consumption, adequate amounts of current savings will occur.

The production of investment income interest, rents, and profits occurs through a process by which individuals, business, and government, or users of savings, compete for those savings based on returns that they expect to earn on various investments and other uses. The real rate of interest can be thought of as being ''imbedded in'' all interest rates and investment returns, as the basic or minimal return that productive uses of funds must earn to attract savings for investment.

Interest Rates and Inflation Expectations

In addition to the real rate of interest, an additional concern that all investors have when making investment decisions is how *inflation* will affect investment returns. The rate of inflation is of particular importance to investors and lenders making or purchasing loans made at fixed rates of interest over long periods of time. Hence, when deciding whether to make such commitments, lenders and investors must be convinced that interest rate commitments are sufficiently high to compensate for any expected loss in purchasing power during the period that the investment or loan is outstanding, otherwise, an inadequate real return will be earned. Therefore, a consensus of what lenders and investors expect inflation to be during the time that loans and investments are expected to be outstanding is also incorporated into interest rates at the time such investments and loans are made.

To illustrate the relationship between the *nominal interest* rate, or the contract interest rate agreed on by borrowers and lenders, and *real rates of interest,* suppose a $10,000 loan is made at a nominal or contract rate of 10 percent with all principal and interest due at the end of one year. At the end of the year the lender would receive $11,000, or $10,000 plus $10,000 times (.10). If the rate of inflation during that year was 6 percent, then the $11,000 received at the end of the year would be worth about $10,377 ($11,000 ÷ 1.06). Thus, although the *nominal* rate of interest is 10 percent, the *real* rate on the mortgage is just under 4 percent ($377 ÷ $10,000 = 3.77%). We would therefore conclude that if the lender wanted a 4 percent real rate of interest, the lender would have to charge a nominal rate of approximately 10 percent to compensate for the expected change in price levels due to inflation.[2]

---

[2]Actually the nominal rate of interest should be $(1.06 \times 1.04) - 1$, or 10.24 percent, if a real rate of 4 percent is desired. Throughout this text we will *add* the real rate and premium for expected inflation as an approximation to the nominal interest rate for convenience. We should point out that the relationship of expected inflation and interest rates has long been a subject of much research. While we show a very simple, additive relationship in our discussion here, there may be interaction between real interest rates and inflation. The specific relationship between the two is not known exactly. Hence, the student should treat this discussion at a conceptual or general level of interpretation.

We can summarize by saying that the nominal interest rate on any investment is partially determined by the real interest rate *plus a premium* for the expected rate of inflation. In our example, the real rate of 4 percent plus an inflation premium of 6 percent equals 10 percent. Note that this premium is based on the rate of inflation *expected* at the time that the loan is made. The possibility of inflation being more or less than expected is one of many risks that must also be considered by lenders and investors.

Interest Rates and Risk

In addition to expected inflation, lenders and investors are also concerned about various *risks* undertaken when making loans and investments. Hence, in addition to expected rates of future inflation, an additional concern that lenders and investors have is whether interest rates and returns available on various loans and investments compensate adequately for risk. Alternatively, will a particular loan or investment provide an adequate risk adjusted return?

Many types of risk could be discussed for various investments, but they are beyond the scope of this book. Consequently, we will focus on risks affecting mortgage loans. Many of these risks are, however, present to greater and lesser degrees in other loans and investments.

Default Risk.   When making mortgage loans, one major concern of lenders is the risk that borrowers will default on obligations to repay interest and principal. This is referred to as *default risk,* and it varies with the nature of the loan and the creditworthiness of individual borrowers. The possibility that default may occur means that lenders must charge a premium, or higher rate of interest, to offset possible loan losses. Default risk relates to the likelihood that a borrower's income may fall after a loan is made, thereby jeopardizing the receipt of future mortgage payments. Similarly, a property's value could fall below the loan balance at some future time, which could also result in a borrower defaulting on payments and a loss to the lender.

Interest Rate Risk.   An additional complication in lending and investing arises due to the fact that we live in a world where the future supply of savings, demand for housing, and future levels of inflation are not known with certainty. Thus interest rates at a given point of time can only reflect the market consensus of what these factors are expected to be. An additional risk incurred by investors and lenders is the risk that the interest rate charged on a particular loan may be insufficient should economic conditions change drastically *after* a loan is made. The magnitude of these changes may have warranted a higher interest rate when the loan was made. For example, inflation may have been *expected* to be 6 percent at the time the $10,000 loan in our above example was made. But if *actual* inflation turns out to be 8 percent, this means the interest rate that should have been charged is 12 percent. In this case we would say that the *anticipated* rate of inflation at the time that the loan was made was 6 percent. However, because *unanticipated* inflation of 2 percent occurred, the lender will lose $200 in purchasing power (2 percent of $10,000) because the rate of interest was too low. This does *not* mean that the "correct" interest rate was not charged *at the time the loan was made*. At that time, the market expected inflation to be 6 percent. Therefore, to be competitive, a 10 percent interest rate had to be charged. However, in this case the additional 2 percent was unanticipated by all lenders in the market. It is unanticipated inflation that constitutes a major component of interest rate risk to all lenders.

The possibility that the interest rate charged at the time a loan is made may turn out to be too low after a loan is made is a major source of risk to the lender. Hence, a premium for this risk must also be charged or reflected in the market rate of interest. The uncertainty as to what interest rate should be charged when a loan is made can be referred to as *interest rate risk*. It affects all loans, particularly those that are made with fixed interest rates, that is, where the interest rate is set for a lengthy period of time at the time the loan is made. Being averse to risk, lenders must charge a premium to incur this risk.

Other Risks.   In addition to the default risk, there are additional risks that lenders and investors consider that may vary by type of loan or investment. For example, the *liquidity* or *marketability* of loans and investments will also affect the size of the premium that must be earned. Securities that can be easily sold and resold in well-established markets will require lower premiums than those that are more difficult to sell.

Legislative risks, such as changes in the regulatory environment in which markets operate is another risk associated with mortgage lending that also may result in a premium. For example, regulations affecting the tax status of mortgages, rent controls, state and federal laws affecting interest rates, and so on, are all possibilities that lenders face after making loans for specified periods of time. Lenders must assess the likelihood that such events may occur and be certain that they are compensated for undertaking these risks when loans are made.

A Summary of Factors Important in Mortgage Pricing

From the above discussion we can now see that the interest rate charged on a particular mortgage loan will depend on the real interest rate, expected inflation, interest rate risk, default risk, and other risks. These relationships can be summarized in general as follows:

$$i = r + p + f$$

In other words, when pricing or setting the rate of interest i on a mortgage loan, the lender must charge a premium p sufficiently high enough to compensate for default and other risks and a premium f which reflects expected inflation in order to earn a real rate of interest r that is competitive with real returns available on other investment opportunities in the economy. If lenders systematically *underestimate* any of the components in the above equation, they will suffer real economic losses.

The fact that the mortgage loans under discussion are made at fixed interest rates for long periods of time makes pricing decisions by lenders complex. For example, if we assume for the moment that a mortgage loan is to be made with a one-year maturity, the interest rate charged at origination should be based on what the lender expects each of the components discussed above to be during the coming year. More specifically,

$$i_t = r_1 + p_1 + f_1$$

or the mortgage interest rate i at origination (time t) would be based on the lender's expectations of what the real rate of interest, the rate of inflation, and risk premiums (for risks taken in conjunction with making the mortgage loan over and above the level of risk reflected in the real rate of interest) should be for the coming year (designated with the subscript 1). For loans with longer maturities, an assessment of what these components of interest rates would be each year that the loan is expected to be outstanding must be made. Alternatively, this process could be viewed as the lender forming expectations of what interest rates on a series of one-year loans would be over the maturity period, or

$$(1 + i_t)^n = (1 + i_1)(1 + i_2)(1 + i_3) \ldots (1 + i_n)$$

or the interest rate i charged upon origination (time t) on a mortgage loan expected to remain outstanding for n years will be based on an expected series of interest rates for each year that the loan is expected to be outstanding. To illustrate, let's assume that at the time of origination, a lender *expects* that a mortgage loan will be outstanding for four years and *expects* a series of one-year interest rates during those four years to be 9, 10, 12, and 11 percent, respectively. The composite rate that should be charged *today* in order for the lender to earn the same rate of interest that would be earned on a series of individual, one-year loans at the above interest rates can be determined as follows:

$$(1 + i_t)^4 = (1 + .09)(1 + .10)(1 + .12)(1 + .11)$$
$$= 1.4906$$

and

$$i_t = \sqrt[n]{1.4906} - 1$$
$$= 10.49 \text{ or } 10.5\% \text{ rounded}$$

This formulation is equivalent to finding an interest rate at which an amount invested today can be compounded, such that the future value (year 4) will be equivalent to the future value found by compounding the same beginning amount by each of the annual interest rates in the series.[3] Hence, in our example the interest rate i that would be charged on the day of origination t, based on the expected series of one-year interest rates over four years ($n = 4$), is 10.5 percent (rounded). More will be said about the relationship between interest rates, inflation and the loan period later in this and in the following chapter.

---

[3] This formulation assumes that an amount loaned today $1 earns interest for one year at the first rate of interest in the series (9 percent), resulting in a total of $1.09 at the end of the year. That amount is then *reinvested* at 10 percent in the next year, resulting in a total accumulation of $1.20 at the end of that year. This process, if continued, results in a total accumulation of $1.49 at the end of four years. This is equivalent to (1) loaning $1 today at 10.49 percent and reinvesting annual payments at 10.49 percent each year for the number of years remaining, or (2) finding the *FV* of $1, or $1(*FVIF*,10.49%,4 yrs.), or $1(1 + .1049)^4 = $1.49. The 10.49 percent in this example is also referred to as the *geometric mean* of the annual interest rate series shown in the example. It can also be thought of as a single rate of compound interest that will yield the same future value that would be obtained if an amount were compounded by each rate of interest in the series during each year in the series.

DEVELOPMENT OF MORTGAGE PAYMENT PATTERNS

Given the many types of financial instruments that have evolved in recent years, there is no longer a "common" or "standard" mortgage pattern available in residential financing. Generally speaking, prior to the 1970s, changes in mortgage instruments occurred gradually, and when changes did occur they were considered to be of major significance. This pattern of gradual change existed for many years because of a relatively stable economic environment characterized by *very low rates of inflation*. Because of volatility in interest rates and inflation during the 1970s, changes in the design of mortgage loan instruments have now become very common. To gain insight into the structural changes in mortgage loan payment patterns and why they have evolved into the various forms available today, we briefly review the history of this evolutionary process and the economic influences which have forced the many changes that we observe today.

Early Mortgage Lending Patterns

Prior to the 1930s and 1940s a very common practice in mortgage lending was for lenders to require a substantial down payment from borrowers trying to purchase housing. Lenders would limit maximum loan amounts to 50 percent of property value, and the term of the loan would vary, with five years commonly being the maximum term available. Payments were generally "interest only," with the full loan balance due after five years. At that time, it would be expected that another loan would be made, usually for a lesser amount as the borrower saved on his own account and applied those savings to reduce the amount of the loan.

Based on the above description, a few relationships should become obvious to the reader. First, mortgage loans were considered to be very risky, and only relatively wealthy individuals could qualify for a mortgage loan because of the large down payment required by the lender. Second, lenders considered the borrower's ability to repay the loan far more important than the collateral value represented by the real estate; consequently, the borrower's ability to earn income and retire the debt "on his own" was critical in the lending decision. Finally, the fact that the loan could be called, or not renewed, after five years presented the possibility that if economic conditions were not favorable the borrower could be required to repay the full loan balance at that time.

The Constant Amortization Mortgage Loan (*CAM*)

After the Depression, the U. S. economy experienced a relatively long period of economic prosperity characterized by relatively high real growth and low rates of inflation. As employment and real income increased, lenders began to recognize the possibility that longer-term loans could be made because households were earning increasing real incomes. This influence resulted in lower risks to lenders, since households were more likely to repay their debt and housing values were not likely to decline. Hence, lenders were willing to make a longer-run assessment of both the borrower and the collateral when making lending decisions.

EXHIBIT 5–1   Monthly Payments and Loan Balance (constant amortization loan)

(1)	(2)	(3)	(4)	(3) + (4)	(2) - (4)
	Opening	*Interest*		*Monthly*	*Ending*
Month	*Balance* ×	*(.12 ÷ 12)*	*Amortization*	*Payment**	*Balance*
1	$60,000.00	$600.00	$166.67	$766.67	$59,833.33
2	59,833.33	598.33	166.67	765.00	59,666.66
3	59,666.66	596.67	166.67	763.34	59,499.99
4	59,499.99	595.00	166.67	761.67	59,333.32
5	59,333.32	593.33	166.67	760.00	59,166.65
6	59,166.65	591.67	166.67	758.34	58,999.98
•	•	•	•	•	•
•	•	•	•	•	•
•	•	•	•	•	•
360	166.67	1.67	166.67	168.34	–0–

*Monthly payments decline by $1.67, or the amount of monthly amortization ($60,000 ÷ 360) times the monthly interest rate (.12 ÷ 12). In this case we have ($60,000 ÷ 360)(.12 ÷ 12), or $1.67.

Given the economic environment just described, lenders devised what was referred to as a *self-amortizing* loan, or one that would be made for a *longer term,* with monthly payments that would consist of partial repayment of principal (*amortization* means the process of loan repayment over time). Indeed, a first effort to accomplish this was referred to as the *constant amortization mortgage (CAM) loan.* Payments on Constant Amortization Mortgages were determined first by computing a constant amount of each monthly payment to be applied to principal. Interest was then computed on the monthly loan balance and added to the monthly amount of amortization. The total monthly payment was determined by adding the constant amount of monthly amortization to interest on the outstanding loan balance. An example of a *CAM* is as follows: a loan was made for $60,000 for a 30-year term at 12 percent (annual rate compounded monthly); payments were to be made monthly and were to consist of *both* interest and amortization (or reduction of principal), such that the loan would be repaid at the end of 30 years.[4]

Amortization was determined by dividing the number of months or term of the loan (360) into the loan amount ($60,000) resulting in a reduction of principal of $166.67 per month. Interest would be computed on the outstanding loan balance and then be added to amortization to determine the monthly payment. An illustration of the payment pattern and loan balance is shown in Exhibit 5–1.

From the computations shown in Exhibit 5–1, it can be seen that the initial monthly payment of $766.67 included amortization of $166.67, plus interest computed on the outstanding loan balance. The total monthly payment would decline each month by a constant amount or $1.67 (.01 × $166.67). The loan payment and balance patterns are shown in Exhibit 5–2.

---

[4]Actually, mortgage interest rates were much lower than 12 percent in the postdepression period, and the term of the loan would have been closer to 20 years. We are using 12 percent interest and a 30-year term so that our later examples will be comparable with this one.

EXHIBIT 5–2   Loan Payment and Balance Patterns (constant amortization loan)

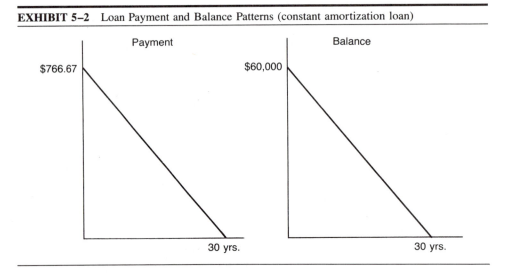

By instituting the constant amortization mortgage, lenders recognized that in a growing economy, borrowers could partially repay the loan over time, through the *amortization process,* as opposed to being left to their own devices to reduce the loan balance when the term of the loan ended, as was the case with the shorter-term, "interest only," loan pattern previously discussed.

While the constant amortization payment pattern was considered an improvement, it was still very conservative in that it placed primary emphasis on the amortization of the loan, as opposed to giving recognition to the fact that in an economy with long periods of sustained real growth, a borrower's income was more likely to increase, rather than decline. Therefore, the prospect that a borrower's ability to repay debt more slowly from an income stream that was expected to grow seemed to be reasonable enough to warrant further modification in mortgage lending instruments. Indeed, the constant amortization loan was a relatively short-lived phenomenon and quickly gave rise to the more familiar *fully amortizing, constant payment mortgage* loan, to which we now turn.

Fully Amortizing, Constant Payment Mortgage Loans

The most common loan payment pattern used in real estate finance from the postdepression era to the present, and one which is still very prevalent today, is the fully amortizing, *constant payment mortgage* (*CPM*). This loan payment pattern is used extensively in financing single family residences and is also used in long-term mortgage lending on income-producing properties such as multifamily apartment complexes and shopping centers. This payment pattern simply means that a level, or constant, monthly payment is calculated on an original loan amount at a fixed rate of interest for a given term. Like the CAM, payment includes interest and *some* (though not a constant) repayment of principal. At the end of the term of the mortgage loan, the original loan amount or principal is completely repaid, or fully amortized, and the lender has earned a fixed rate of interest on the monthly loan balance. However, with this loan the amount of amortization varies each month.

To illustrate how the monthly loan payment calculation is made, we turn to our previous example of a $60,000 loan made at 12 percent interest for 30 years. What will be the constant monthly mortgage payments on this loan, assuming it is to be fully amortized (paid off) at the end of 30 years? Based on our knowledge of discounting annuities from the preceding chapter, the problem is really no more than finding the present value of an annuity and can be formulated as follows:

$$PV = R \cdot \sum_{t=1}^{n} \left[\frac{1}{1 + \frac{i}{12}} \right]^t$$

where PV = present value

R = annuity
i = fixed interest rate on mortgage
n = number of months loan will remain outstanding

In this case, we are interested in solving for R, or the constant monthly payment (annuity) that will fully repay the loan amount (PV) and earn the lender 12 percent interest, compounded monthly. Using the shorthand notation developed in the previous chapter, we can also determine the monthly payment on the $60,000 loan as shown in Exhibit 5–3.

Looking again at the calculation of the monthly mortgage payment in Exhibit 5–3, we should give particular attention to the following step in the solution:

(MP) Monthly payment = $60,000 ÷ 97.218331

which is also equivalent to

= $60,000(1 ÷ 97.218331)
= $60,000(.010286126)
= $617.17

Note that dividing the *IF* 97.218331 into $60,000 is identical to multiplying $60,000 by (1 ÷ 97.218331), or .010286126. This simple fact enables us to simplify calculations of this kind considerably.

EXHIBIT 5–3   Determining Constant Monthly Payments—Fully Amortized Mortgage

Monthly payments × (MPVIFA, 12%, 360 mos.) = $60,000
Monthly payments × 97.218331 = 60,000
Monthly payments = 60,000 ÷ 97.218331
= $617.17

EXHIBIT 5–4   Monthly Mortgage Loan Constants (column 6, Appendix B)

Years	Months	Interest Rate 9%	10%	11%	12%
5	60	.020758	.021247	.021742	.022244
10	120	.012668	.013215	.013775	.014347
15	180	.010143	.010746	.011366	.012002
20	240	.008997	.009650	.010322	.011011
25	300	.008392	.009087	.009801	.010532
30	360	.008046	.008776	.009523	.010286

Mortgage Loan Constants.   Prior to the widespread use of financial calculators, manually performing multiplication was easier and more convenient than dividing, particularly when decimals were involved. Consequently, a series of new interest factors, called *loan constants,* were developed for various interest rates and loan maturities. These loan constants enable a simple multiplication to be made ($60,000 × .010286126) to determine monthly mortgage payments, rather than the more awkward division ($60,000 ÷ 97.218331). The factor used for multiplication in our example, .010286126 is the *loan constant* for 360 months at 12 percent interest. In Appendixes A and B, column 6 is titled installment to amortize $1. This means that a factor multiplied by the original principal gives the payments necessary to amortize, or pay off, principal and earn interest on the unamortized loan balance at a given interest rate over a prescribed number of years. It is customary to refer to this factor as the *loan constant* in mortgage lending. Factors are provided for loans requiring annual payments (Appendix A) and for monthly payments (Appendix B) in those tables. Given an interest rate and term of a loan, one can find the appropriate loan constant by looking down column 6 and finding the factor in the row corresponding to the number of years for which the loan is to be made. The loan constant can then be multiplied by any beginning loan amount to obtain the monthly mortgage payments necessary to amortize the loan fully by the maturity date.[5]

Exhibit 5–4 provides a sample of monthly loan constants for various interest rates and loan maturities. Returning to our problem of finding the monthly mortgage payment for a $60,000 loan made at 12 percent for 30 years, by locating the 12 percent column and looking down until we find the row corresponding to 30 years, we see that the loan constant in that position is .010286 (rounded).[6]

---

[5]With a financial calculator, the mortgage payment can be determined as follows: $360 = n$, $.12 ÷ 12 = i$, $60,000 = PV$, compute $PMT = \$617.17$. If needed, the loan constant can be calculated as $360 = n$, $.12 ÷ 12 = i$, $1 = PV$, compute $PMT = .010286126$.

[6]Because of rounding (to six decimal places), the loan constant is .010286. When we multiply $60,000 by the rounded constant, we get a monthly payment of $617.16. The more exact solution is $617.17. In many problems in future chapters we use mortgage constants in column 6 in tables in Appendixes A and B. Hence, readers should be aware that small discrepancies between their solutions and ours may occur when financial calculators are used, because calculator solutions may be rounded off to eight or more decimal places. We have attempted to carry out solutions to at least six decimal places.

Analysis of Principal and Interest.   It should be obvious that the sum of all mortgage payments made over the 30-year (360 months) period is $617.27 × 360, or $222,181.20. This amount is far greater than the original loan of $60,000. Why are the total payments so much higher than the amount of the loan? The reason for this is that interest must be paid monthly over the entire term of the loan on the outstanding loan balance. This relationship is shown in Exhibit 5–5.

The pattern developed in Exhibit 5–5 shows in month 1 a beginning mortgage balance, or loan principal, of $60,000. The monthly payment, which was calculated to be $617.17, includes interest of $600.00 in the first month. Interest is determined by multiplying the beginning loan amount of $60,000 by the annual rate of 12 percent divided by 12 months (.12 ÷ 12) to obtain monthly interest of $600. The difference between $617.17, (column 2) and $600.00 (column 3) gives the amount of loan amortization or principal reduction (column 4) of $17.17 during the first month. The beginning loan balance of $60,000 less the principal reduction in the first month of $17.17 gives the balance at the end of the first month of $59,982.83, which provides the beginning balance for the interest calculation in the second month. This process continues through the 360th month, or end of the 30th year, when the loan balance diminishes to zero.

The initial, relatively low, principal reduction shown in column 6 in Exhibit 5–5 results in a high portion of the early monthly payments being interest charges. Note that the ending loan balance after the first six months (column 6) is $59,894.36; thus only $105.64 has been amortized from the original balance of $60,000 after six months. Interest paid during the same six-month period totals $3,597.38. The reason for such a high interest component in each monthly payment is that the lender earns an annual 12 percent return (1 percent monthly) on the outstanding monthly loan balance. Because the loan is being

EXHIBIT 5–5   Loan Amortization Pattern, $60,000 Loan at 12 percent Interest for 30 Years

Month	Beginning Loan Balance	Monthly Payment	Interest (.12 ÷ 12)	Amortization*	Ending Loan Balance
1	$60,000.00	$617.17	$600.00	$ 17.17	$59,982.83
2	59,982.83	617.17	599.83	17.34	59,965.49
3	59,965.49	617.17	599.65	17.52	59,947.97
4	59,947.97	617.17	599.48	17.69	59,930.28
5	59,930.28	617.17	599.30	17.87	59,912.41
6	59,912.41	617.17	599.12	18.05	59,894.36
.	.	.	.	.	.
.	.	.	.	.	.
.	.	.	.	.	.
358	1,815.08	617.17	18.15	599.02	1,216.06
359	1,216.06	617.17	12.16	605.01	611.06
360	611.06	617.17	6.11	611.06	–0–

*Amortization increases each month by the factor $1 + i/12$; that is $17.17(1.01) = 17.34$, etc.

repaid over a 30-year period, obviously the loan balance is reduced only very slightly at first and monthly interest charges are correspondingly high. Exhibit 5–5 also shows that the pattern of high interest charges in the early years of the loan reverses as the loan begins to mature. Note that during the last months of the loan, interest charges fall off sharply and principal reduction increases.

Interest, Principal, and Loan Balance Illustrated.   To illustrate the loan payment pattern over time, Exhibit 5–6 Panel A shows the relative proportions of interest and principal in each monthly payment over the 30-year term of the loan. Exhibit 5–6 Panel B shows the rate of decline in the loan balance over the same 30-year period. It becomes clear from the exhibit that the relative share of interest as a percentage of the total monthly mortgage payment declines very slowly at first. Note in Panel A that halfway into the term of the mortgage, or after 15 years, interest still makes up $514.24 of the $617.17 monthly payment and principal would be the difference or $617.17 − $514.24 = $102.93. Further, the loan balance (Panel B) is approximately $51,424. Total mortgage

EXHIBIT 5–6   Monthly Interest and Principal Components of a Constant Payment Mortgage

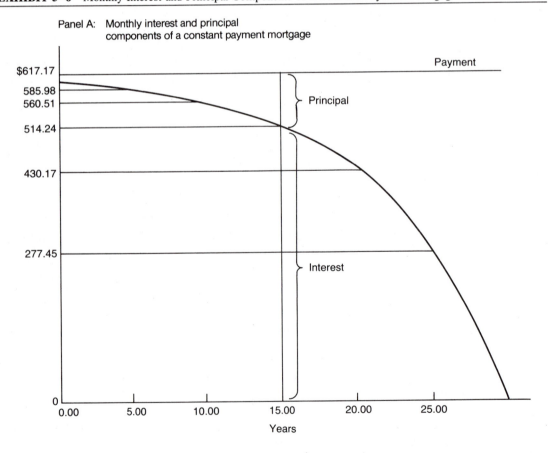

Panel A: Monthly interest and principal
           components of a constant payment mortgage

payments of $111,090.60 or ($617.17 × 180 months) have been made through the 15th year, with approximately $8,576 or ($60,000 − $51,424) of the loan having been repaid at that point. This pattern reverses with time. Note in Panel A that after 25 years, interest makes up only $277.45 of the monthly payment, and the loan balance (Panel B) has declined sharply to $27,745.

CONSTANT PAYMENT AND CONSTANT AMORTIZATION LOANS— A COMPARISON

At this point, it is useful to compare the payment and loan balance patterns of the constant payment and constant amortization loans. It is instructive to do this because, although

EXHIBIT 5–6   (*concluded*)

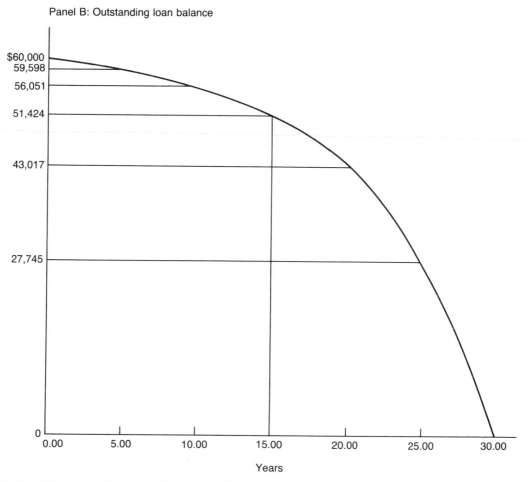

Panel B: Outstanding loan balance

the constant amortization mortgage was not used for an extensive period of time, the change to the constant payment mortgage was a dramatic modification in mortgage lending instruments and the forces that brought this change about, and its impact on borrowers and lenders should be understood.

Exhibit 5–7 contains a comparison of loan payment patterns (Panel A) and mortgage loan balance patterns (Panel B) for types of mortgages with the same loan terms. To make this comparison, we consider the same $60,000 loan made at 12 percent for 30 years. A very important pattern shown in Panel A is the significant reduction in the initial monthly payment for the constant payment mortgage (*CPM*) when compared with the constant amortization mortgage (*CAM*). Recall that if the *CAM* were made, the initial monthly payment would have been $766.67. If a *CPM* were made, however, the initial monthly payment would be $617.17. The reason for such a large difference in initial payments ($149.50) is that the $766.67 *CAM* payment *declines* through time, however the $617.27 *CPM* remains *level* throughout the life of the loan. It should be stressed however, that the present value of *both* payment streams is equal to $60,000. This equivalency results from the fact that although the *CPM* is below that of the *CAM* for approximately 10 years (dashed line, Panel A), beyond the 10th year the *CPM* payment exceeds the *CAM* payment. Hence, the present value of the difference between all monthly payments prior to the 10th year, or where *CAM* > *CPM*, is eventually offset by the present value of monthly payments beyond year 10, or where *CPM* > *CAM* for the next 20 years.

EXHIBIT 5–7   Comparison of Monthly Payments and Loan Balances (constant payment versus constant amortization loans)

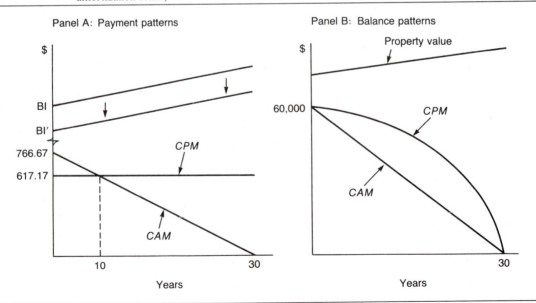

Another important pattern emerges in Panel B of Exhibit 5–7. The *CPM* loan balance always exceeds that of the *CAM* prior to the 360th month, because the rate of amortization for the *CPM* is far less than that of the *CAM*. In other words, with a *CAM*, more of each monthly payment is amortization of principal when compared with the *CPM*. Hence, the *CPM* loan balance is reduced more slowly. This can be seen easily, as the initial monthly interest charge for both loans would be 12 percent ÷ 12, or .01 × ($60,000) = $600. For the *CAM*, amortization would be $766.67 − $600 = $166.67, leaving a balance of $59,833.33. In the case of the *CPM* we would have $617.17 − $600.00 = $17.17, leaving a balance of $59,982.83. Hence the *CPM*, with its lower payment, reduces the loan balance more slowly. More total interest will be earned by the *CPM* lender over the 30-year loan period, although the lender's return will be 12 percent, compounded monthly, in each case.

While the mechanics of the payment and balance patterns are interesting, an *economic interpretation* of the difference in the two mortgage payments and its impact in the marketplace is equally important. Looking back to Panel A of Exhibit 5–7, we have already pointed out the fact that the initial monthly payment for a *CPM* was considerably less when compared with a *CAM*. This significant reduction in payment also meant that more households could *qualify* for a *CPM* loan than for a *CAM*. This point is illustrated in Panel A, which shows that if borrowers were required to have a minimum income of *BI* to qualify for a *CAM*, lenders could require a lower income (*BI'*) if a *CPM* were made and still have the same cushion or protection against default, or *BI* − *CAM* = *BI'* − *CPM*. In this case, borrower income could be lower by $149.50 or an amount equal to the difference in the initial *CAM* payment of $766.67 and the *CAM* payment of $617.17. This shift to the *CPM* pattern, however, was based on the fact that lenders were convinced that borrower incomes would increase and that property values (*PV*, Panel B) would either remain steady or increase over time. In an economy experiencing real economic growth with relatively stable prices, increases in income and property values would reduce borrower default risk associated with *CPM* loan. Hence, this fundamental change to the *CPM* pattern occurred after lenders realized the ability of households to meet mortgage payments from *future income*, as well as *current* income, was not as risky as first believed. Further, as real incomes increased, property values were likely to remain higher than the outstanding loan balance over the term of the loan; hence the collateral value of the real estate relative to the more slowly declining mortgage loan balance was considered by lenders to be adequate.

It should also be stressed that Federal Housing Administration (FHA) was instrumental in the willingness of lenders to make *CPM*s, as they created a borrower default insurance program immediately after the depression. This program provided an insurance pool based on premiums collected as a part of the monthly mortgage payments made by borrowers. This pool, or reserve, provided reimbursements to lenders for any losses from loan defaults. This concept was based on the idea that *small* premiums collected from *many* borrowers would create a pool from which lenders would be compensated for losses in the relatively few cases where house prices realized from foreclosures sales were less than mortgage loan balances. This insurance program is still functioning today and is considered to be one of many reasons for the large volume of home building that has occurred since World War II.[7]

Determining Loan Balances

Because most mortgage loans are repaid before they mature, mortgage lenders must be able to determine the balance on a fully amortized *CPM* loan at any time. As previously indicated, even though most loans are made for terms of 25 or 30 years, statistics gathered on a national basis indicate that households move because of job changes, purchases of different houses, etc. Hence mortgages are usually repaid from 8 to 12 years after they are made. Therefore, it is very important to know what the loan balance will be at any time when financing real estate with this type of mortgage.

To illustrate, let us return to the previous example of the $60,000 *CPM* loan made at 12 percent interest for a term of 30 years. After 10 years, the borrower decides to sell the property and to buy another one. In order to do so, the existing loan must be paid off. How much will have to be repaid to the lender after 10 years? We could construct a loan balance schedule as in Exhibit 5–5; however, this is quite time consuming and unnecessary. Finding loan balances for *CPM*s can be accomplished in two, easier ways. First, one can simply find the present value of the $617.17 payments at the 12 percent contract rate of interest *for the 20 years remaining until maturity.* For example:

$$\text{Mortgage balance } (MB) = \$617.17(MPVIFA, 12\%, 20 \text{ yrs.})$$
$$= \$617.17(90.819416)$$
$$= \$56,051.02$$

The unpaid balance after 10 years is $56,051.02. This exercise also points out another interesting fact. Because the payments include interest and a reduction of principal each month, by "removing" all interest from all remaining payments, it follows that only the principal can remain. Discounting the $617.17 monthly payments at an annual rate of 12 percent compounded monthly is a process that really amounts to "removing interest" from the payments.[8] Hence, after "removing interest" by discounting, we ascertain that the unamortized or unpaid balance must be $56,051.02.

An alternative method for finding mortgage balances at any time in the life of mortgage is to divide the interest factor for the accumulation of $1 per period (*FVA*), from column 2 in Appendix B for the year in which the balance is desired, by the accumulation of $1 per period factor for the original term of the mortgage, and then to subtract that result from 1. The result of this computation is the loan balance expressed as a percentage of the original amount. To illustrate:

$$1 - [(MFVIFA, 12\%, 10 \text{ yrs.}) \div (MFVIFA, 12\%, 30 \text{ yrs.})]$$
$$= \text{Percent mortgage balance}$$
$$1 - (230.03869 \div 3494.96451) = 93.42\%$$

---

[7]The mortgage insurance fund for single family housing is described in the Federal Housing Administration's Section 203 program. This is covered in more detail in Chapters 7 and 8.

[8]If a financial calculator is being used, the loan balance would be determined with the following sequence: $240 = n$, $12 \div 12 = i$, $\$617.17 = PMT$, compute $PV = \$56,051.02$.

This is a more general formula that can be used regardless of the original dollar amount of the loan or payments because it gives a solution in percentage form. In this case we determine that approximately 93.42 percent, or $56,052, of the original loan balance ($60,000) is still outstanding. This solution is nearly the same result that we obtained by discounting. The difference is due to rounding.

To assist the reader in finding loan balances more quickly, we have included a series of loan balance factors in Appendix C. These factors are useful for constant monthly payment loans with original terms of 25 years or 30 years only, which are very common maturity periods for mortgage loans. The factors in the columns should be converted to percentages and multiplied by the original loan balance to obtain the loan balance for the year desired. Hence, in our example we would go to the 12 percent column for a 30-year loan and obtain the factor for 10 years, .9342. This factor should be multiplied by the original loan amount to obtain the approximate outstanding balance.[9]

For loans with maturities different from 25 or 30 years, no loan balance factors in table form are provided. Hence, in those cases either of the two computational procedures described above should be used to find loan balances. Also, for loans requiring annual rather than monthly payments, outstanding balances may be found using the same computational procedure. Of course, *i* would not be divided by 12 and the number of years (not months) would be used for *n*.

Loan Closing Costs and Effective Borrowing Costs—Fully Amortized Loans

Closing costs are incurred in many types of real estate financing, including residential property, income property, construction, and land development loans. Closing costs can generally be placed in one of three categories: statutory costs, third-party charges, and additional finance charges. These categories are discussed more fully in a later chapter; however, they are briefly reviewed here to point out their relationship to effective borrowing costs.

Statutory Costs.   At the same time that a mortgage loan is closed between borrower and lender, certain charges for legal requirements pertaining to title transfer, recording of the deed, and other fees required by state and local law are usually charged to the buyer of the property, who is usually the borrower. These charges are usually collected at the title closing which may occur at the same time as the loan closing. In fact, in some states the lender may conduct both the loan and title closing. These charges are made for services performed by governmental agencies for the borrower, and consequently do not provide income to the lender. As such, they generally should not be included as additional finance charges because they do not affect the cost of borrowing. These charges would generally have had to be paid even if a property was bought for cash and no financing was involved.

---

[9]The loan balance factors are rounded to four decimal places because of space limitations. Hence, the factors will provide only a close approximation to the actual loan balance. The loan balance *factor* can be found with a calculator (if desired) by substituting $1 = PMT$ and repeating the sequence as outlined in footnote 8.

Third-Party Charges. Third-party charges generally include charges for such services as legal fees, appraisals, surveys, past inspection, and title insurance. Like statutory charges, these charges may occur even if the buyer paid cash to buy a property. If a loan is made, charges for these services may be collected by the lender or title company at a title closing, but are in turn paid out to third parties; hence, they usually do not constitute additional income to the lender. As such, they are usually not charges associated with financing the real estate being purchased.

Additional Finance Charges. Closing costs that *do* affect the cost of borrowing are additional finance charges levied by the lender. These charges constitute additional income to the lender and as a result must be included as a part of the cost of borrowing. Generally, lenders refer to these additional charges as loan fees. Such fees are intended to cover expenses incurred by the lender for processing loan applications, preparation of loan documentation and amortization schedules, obtaining credit reports, and any other expenses which the lender believes should be recovered from the borrower. Sometimes these charges are itemized separately in the loan closing statement, and sometimes they are grouped under the general category of loan origination fees. These fees are generally the "fixed cost" element of originating mortgage loans.

Lenders usually charge these costs to borrowers when the loan is made, or "closed," rather than charging higher interest rates. They do this because if the loan is repaid soon after closing, the additional interest earned by the lender as of the repayment date may not be enough to offset the fixed costs of loan origination. For example, assume that the prevailing interest rate on a $60,000 mortgage is 12 percent and that it will cost the lender $1,000 to close the loan. If the lender chose to increase the interest rate to 12.25 percent to recover these origination costs, an additional $150 (approximately) would be collected during the first year ($60,000 · .0025). If the loan was repaid after the first year, the lender would not recover the full $1,000 in origination costs. This is why lenders attempt to "price" these origination costs separately.

Another item, which may be itemized separately or included in the overall category of loan origination fees, is loan discount.[10] This charge also represents an additional finance charge, but its primary purpose is to *raise the yield* on a mortgage loan. In the context of real estate lending, loan discounting amounts to a borrower and lender negotiating the terms of a loan based on a certain loan amount. The lender then discounts the loan by charging a fee, which will be deducted from the contract loan to the borrower. Payments made by the borrower, however, are based on the contract amount of the loan. For example, assume a borrower and lender agree on a $60,000 loan at 12 percent interest for 30 years. The lender actually disburses $58,200 to the borrower by including a loan discount charge of 3 percent (points), or $1,800. The borrower is required to repay $60,000 at 12 percent interest for 30 years. However, because the borrower actually

---

[10]Lenders in some areas of the country refer to loan discount as "discount points" or simply "points." In conventional mortgage lending, the borrower usually pays this charge, which adds to financing costs. When FHA and VA mortgages are involved, however, the seller of the property pays the discount points. In this chapter we are concerned with conventional lending situations where the borrower pays the loan discount as a part of origination fees.

receives $58,200 but must repay $60,000 plus interest, it is clear that the actual borrowing cost to the buyer is greater than 12 percent.

Why do pricing practices such as discounting to increase yields, exist? Many reasons for these practices have been advanced. One reason given by lenders is that mortgage rates tend to be somewhat "sticky" in upward and downward moves. This means that if the prevailing rate is 12 percent and market pressures push upward on rates, rather than one lender making a move to perhaps 12.25 or 12.50 percent, 12 percent may still be quoted as the loan rate but loan discount points may be charged.

Many mortgage loans are originated by lenders then sold to investors. These loans may be sold to yield the investor the same rate of interest that the lender expects to charge borrowers. However, if interest rates rise before the date that the loan is originated but after the date on which the lender and investor agree on the yield on mortgages to be sold, the lender will add discount points to profit from the increase in interest rates. In this case the loan will be originated at an interest rate equal to the yield promised to the investor, and the lender will earn the discount points.

Another reason for loan discount fees is that lenders believe that, in this way, they can better price the loan to the *risk* they take. For example, in the beginning of this chapter we referred to the risk premium component (p) of the interest rate. However, the risk for some individual borrowers is slightly higher than others, further, these loans may require more time and expense to process and control. Hence, discount points may be charged by the lender (in addition to origination fees) to compensate for the slightly higher risk.

The practice of using loan origination and discount fees has historically prevailed throughout the lending industry. It is important to understand (1) that these charges increase borrowing costs, and (2) how to include them in computing effective borrowing costs on loan alternatives when financing any real estate transaction.

Loan Fees and Borrowing Costs.   To illustrate loan fees and their effects on borrowing costs in more detail, consider the following problem: A borrower would like to finance a property for 30 years at 12 percent interest. The lender indicates that an origination fee of a 3 percent of the loan amount will be charged to obtain the loan. What is the actual interest cost of the loan?

We structure the problem by determining the amount of the origination fee or .03 × ($60,000) = $1,800. Second, we know that the monthly mortgage payments based on $60,000 for 30 years at 12 percent will be $617.17. Now we can determine the effect of the origination fee on the interest rate being charged as follows:

Contractual loan amount	$60,000
Less: origination fee	1,800
Net cash disbursed	$58,200
Amount to be repaid:	
Based on $60,000 contractual loan amount, $617.17 for 30 years.	

In other words, the amount actually disbursed by the lender will be $58,200, but the repayment will be made on the basis of $60,000 plus interest at 12 percent compounded monthly, in the amount of $617.17 each month. Consequently, the lender will earn a yield on the $58,200 actually disbursed, which must be greater than 12 percent. To solve for the effective interest cost on the loan, we proceed as follows:

$$\text{Monthly payment} \times (MPVIFA, ?\%, 30 \text{ yrs.}) = \text{Amount disbursed}$$
$$\$617.17 \times (MPVIFA, ?\%, 30 \text{ yrs.}) = \$58,200$$
$$(MPVIFA, ?\%, 30 \text{ yrs.}) = \$58,200 \div \$617.17$$
$$= 94.301408$$

Using the procedure in the previous chapter when solving for yields on investment annuities, we see that this calculation results in an interest factor of 94.301408. We know that the loan will be outstanding for a period of 30 years. Therefore, to find the actual interest cost of this loan we want to locate an interest factor in column 5 for 30 years in Appendix B that equals 94.301408. A close inspection of Appendix B reveals that the interest factor that we are looking for falls between factors in the 12 percent and 13 percent tables.

To find a more exact interest rate, we must interpolate to find the solution.

$(MPVIFA, 12\%, 30 \text{ yrs.}) = 97.218$	$(MPVIFA, 12\%, 30 \text{ yrs.}) = 97.218$
$(MPVIFA, \underline{13\%}, 30 \text{ yrs.}) = \underline{90.400}$	Desired $MPVIFA = \underline{94.301}$
Difference $\underline{1\%} = 6.818$	Difference $= \underline{2.917}$
$(2.917 \div 6.818) \times 1\% = .43\%$	
$12\% + .43\% = 12.43\%$	

From the above calculation we can see that the effective cost of the loan, assuming it is outstanding until maturity, is approximately 12.43 percent compounded monthly. (A more accurate solution of 12.41 is obtained with a financial calculator.) This yield is obviously higher than the 12 percent contract, or nominal, rate of interest specified in the note or mortgage.

This computation forms the basis for a very widely used rule of thumb in real estate finance; that is, for every 2 percentage points in origination fee charged the borrower, the effective cost to the borrower, or investment yield earned by the lender, increases by approximately one fourth of a percent above the contract rate.[11] Note that in our solution, we obtained an effective rate of 12.43 percent, versus 12.5 using the approximation. While this estimate is close to the yield calculated in one example, we have assumed that the loan remains outstanding until maturity. However, most loans, on the average, are "prepaid," or paid off long before maturity. Hence, this rule of thumb, while helpful, generally provides an underestimate of the effective cost (yield) of most mortgage loans.[12]

---

[11]Using a financial calculator to solve for the actual interest rate, we follow sequence $360 = n$, $\$617.17 = PMT$, $\$58,200 = PV$, compute $i = 1.034329$ (solution) $\times 12 = 12.41\%$. Note that the solution is given as an effective monthly rate (1.034329). This must be multiplied by 12 to determine the annual rate of interest, compounded monthly. Also note the rounding difference between the slightly more accurate solution obtained with the calculator and the solution obtained using financial tables and linear interpolation. When possible, the calculator solution should be used for greater accuracy.

[12]This rule of thumb was developed when the level of interest rates was much lower than they are today. As the level of interest rates is lowered, this rule of thumb becomes more accurate.

Truth-In-Lending Requirements and the Annual Percentage Rate

Because of problems involving loan fees and the potential abuse by some lenders of charging high fees to unwary borrowers, Congress passed a federal Truth-in-Lending Act.[13] As a result of this legislation, the lender must disclose to the borrower the annual percentage rate being charged on the loan. Calculation of the annual percentage rate (*APR*) is generally made in the manner as shown in the preceding example. The annual percentage rate in this case would be disclosed at closing to the borrower by rounding the effective interest rate up or down to the nearest one-eighth percent. In this case, the 12.43 effective rate would be rounded and disclosed to be 12.5 percent. The *APR*, then, does reflect origination fees and discount points and treats them as additional income or yield to the lender regardless of what costs, if any, the fees are intended to cover.[14]

Loan Fees and Early Repayment—Fully Amortized Loans

An important effect of loan fees and early loan repayment must now be examined in terms of the effect on interest cost. In this section it will be shown that when loan fees are charged and the loan is paid off before maturity, the effective interest cost of the loan increases even further than when the loan is repaid at maturity.

To demonstrate this point, we again assume our borrower obtained the $60,000 loan at 12 percent for 30 years and was charged an $1,800 (3 percent) loan origination fee. At the end of *five years*, the borrower decides to sell the property. The mortgage contains a due on sale clause; hence, the loan balance must be repaid at the time the property is sold. What will be the effective interest cost on the loan as a result of both the origination fee and early loan repayment?

To determine the effective interest cost on the loan, we first find the outstanding loan balance after five years to be .9766 (12 percent column, balance, 30-year loan, Appendix C) × $60,000 = $58,596. To solve for the yield to the lender (cost to the borrower), we proceed by finding the rate at which to discount the monthly payments of $617.17 *and* the lump-sum payment of $58,596 after five years so that the present value of both sums equals $58,200, or the amount actually disbursed by the lender.

This presents a new type of discounting problem. Here, we are dealing with an annuity in the form of monthly payments for five years *and* a loan balance, or single lump-sum receipt of cash, at the end of five years. To find the yield on this loan, we proceed as follows:

$$\$58,200 = \$617.17(MPVIFA,?\%,5 \text{ yrs.}) + \$58,596(MPVIF,?\%,5 \text{ yrs.})$$

---

[13]See Regulation Z of the Federal Reserve Board, 12 C.F.R., sec. 226, as amended.

[14]Generally the *APR* disclosed to the borrower is the effective interest rate computed under the assumption that the loan will be outstanding until maturity, rounded to the nearest one-eighth percent. If the reader desires greater accuracy in these computations, consult *Computational Procedures Manual for Supplement 1 to Regulation Z of the Federal Reserve Board: Calculator Instructions* (Office of the Comptroller of the Currency, February 1978).

This formulation simply says that we want to find the interest rate (?%) that will make the present value of *both* the $617.17 monthly annuity and the $58,596 received at the end of five years equal to the amount disbursed. The student should take special note that the *two* interest factors used in the above formulation are different. One factor (*MPVIF*) is used to discount the single receipt or loan balance. While *MPVIFA* will be used to discount the payments, or monthly annuity. Hence, we cannot use the method of dividing the monthly annuity into the disbursement to find an interest factor, as we did above, because we also have the loan balance of $58,596 to take into account. How do we solve this problem? We find the answer by trial and error; that is, we must begin choosing interest rates and then select the interest factors for five years corresponding to (*MIFPVA*) in column 5 and (*MIFPV*) in column 4. We then multiply these factors by the cash payments and determine whether the calculated present value is equal to $58,200. When we have found the interest rate that gives us a present value of $58,200, we have the solution we want.

This trial-and-error process is not as ominous as it may seem. Some careful thought about the problem tells us that because loan fees are being charged, the yield we are seeking must be greater than the contract interest rate of 12 percent compounded monthly. Also, careful thought will lead us to conclude that the yield is going to be greater than 12.43 percent. This is because, as we have seen from the *APR* computed above, a 12.43 percent yield would be earned by the lender if the loan were repaid at the end of *30* years. Because the loan is being repaid over *5* years, the origination fee of $1,800 is being earned over 5 years as opposed to 30 years; hence, the effective interest cost to the borrower (yield to the lender) will be higher than 12.43 percent. How much higher? Probably not more than 13 percent because, based on the rule of thumb discussed earlier, it would take a fee of about 8 points to increase the yield from 12 percent to 13 percent over 30 years, and since we are dealing with a 3 percent origination fee, it is very unlikely that the yield would be in excess of 13 percent, even after only five years. Therefore, we will use the interest factors at 12 percent and 13 percent and interpolate for the solution as follows:

1. Discounting at <u>12%</u>: $617.17(44.955038) + $58,596(.55045) = *PV*
   $60,000 = *PV*
   Discounting at <u>13%</u>: $617.17(43.950107) + $58,596(.523874) = *PV*
   $57,822 = *PV*
   Difference = <u>1%</u> $ 2,178 = Difference
2. Desired present value = $58,200
3. Difference in *PV* at 12 percent and desired *PV*, or
   $60,000 − $58,200 = $1,800
4. Interpolating: ($1,800 ÷ $2,178) × 1% = .83, and 12% + .83% = 12.83%

We have employed a slightly different form of interpolation than was shown in previous examples. This approach must be used anytime *two or more* different cash flow patterns, such as an annuity and a single receipt, are encountered in a problem in which the yield must be determined. With a financial calculator, a more precise solution of 12.82 percent is obtained.[15] Also, note that when the cash flows are discounted at 12 percent, the original $60,000 balance is determined. The detail can be eliminated in future computations.

---

[15]If a financial calculator is used to solve for an internal rate of return or yield, it must have the capacity to input and store the monthly payment ($617.17), *PMT,* the loan balance of $58,596, *FV,* the initial outlay *PV*

From the above analysis, we can conclude that the actual yield (or actual interest cost) that we have computed to be approximately 12.82 percent, is higher than *both* the contract interest rate of 12 percent and the 12.43 percent yield computed assuming that the loan was outstanding until maturity. This is true because the $1,800 origination fee is earned over only 5 years instead of 30 years. Earning this $1,800 fee over 5 years as opposed to 30 years is equivalent to earning a higher rate of compound interest on the $58,200 disbursed. Hence, when this additional amount earned is coupled with the 12 percent interest being earned on the monthly loan balance, this increases yield to 12.82 percent.[16]

Another point is that the 12.82 percent yield is not reported to the borrower as being the "annual percentage rate" required under the Truth-in-Lending Act. The reason is that neither the borrower nor lender knows for certain that the loan will be repaid ahead of schedule. Therefore, 12.50 percent will still be reported as the annual percentage rate and 12 percent will be the contract rate, although the actual yield to the lender in this case will be 12.82 percent. It should be remembered that the annual percentage rate under truth-in-lending requirements never takes into account early repayment of loans. The *APR* calculation takes into account origination fees, but always assumes the loan is paid off at maturity.

Relationship between Yield and Time. Based on the preceding discussion, we can make some general observations about the relationship of mortgage yields and the time during which mortgages are outstanding. The first observation that we should make is that the effective interest cost on a mortgage will always be equal to the contract rate of interest when no finance charges are made at the time of loan origination or repayment. This follows because, as we saw in Exhibit 5–6, the level payment pattern ensures the lender of earning only a given annual rate of interest, compounded monthly, on the monthly outstanding loan balance. Hence the outstanding mortgage balance can be repaid at any time, and the lender's yield (borrower's cost) will not be affected. It will be equal to the contract rate of interest.

The second observation is that if origination or financing fees are charged to the borrower, the following occurs: (a) the effective yield will be higher than the contract rate of interest, and (b) the yield will increase as repayment occurs sooner in the life of the mortgage. These relationships can be explained by referring to Exhibit 5–8. The two curves, *A* and *B,* shown in the exhibit, represent the mortgage yield pattern under two assumptions. Curve *A* represents the effective yield, or cost, when no financing fees are charged to the borrower. In our previous example, then, the yield would remain at 12 percent, equal to the contract rate of interest, regardless of when the loan is repaid; hence, the horizontal line is over the range of 0 to 30 years. Curve *B* represents a series of loan

---

of $58,200, and to find the rate of discount *i* which will make the payments *and* loan balance equal to *PV* for *n* (60) months. The student should read parts of the manual accompanying the calculator dealing with internal rate of return, present value, computing the yield for an annuity with a balloon, and computing bond yields. If the calculator does not have the capability to compute internal rates of return in cases involving a series of payments and a lump sum or balance, the trial-and-error approach must be used. This is done by finding the present value of the payments and balance that is closest to the initial outlay, and interpolating.

[16]If the loan is repaid in less than one year, the yield becomes larger and approaches infinity should the loan be repaid immediately after closing.

EXHIBIT 5–8   Relationship between Mortgage Yield and Financing Fees at Various Repayment Dates

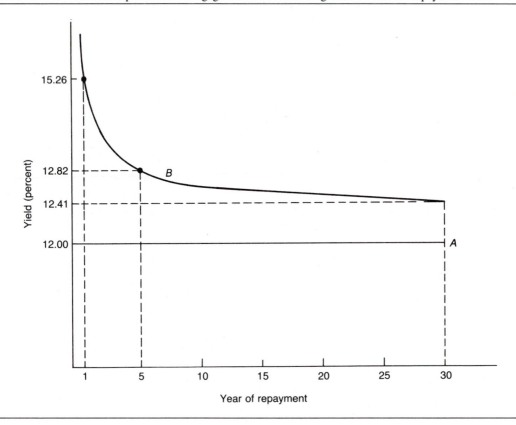

yields computed under the assumptions that a 3 percent origination fee is charged to the borrower and that the loan is prepaid each year prior to maturity. In our example, then, we note that the yield earned by the borrower is 15.26 percent if the loan is repaid one year after closing and that it diminishes and eventually equals 12.41 percent after 30 years, per our calculation in the preceding section. Hence, we can again conclude that if financing fees are charged to the buyer, the effective yield to the lender (cost to the borrower) can range from one that is extremely high if repaid, say, after one year (the yield in that case would be approximately 15.26 percent) to a yield that would be considerably lower if repaid at maturity, or 12.41 percent. If a borrower knows when he expects to repay a loan, this method of computing the effective borrowing cost should be used. This is particularly important if he is comparing alternative loans with different terms.

Prepayment Penalties.   Many borrowers mistakenly take for granted that a loan can be prepaid in part or in full anytime before the maturity date. This is not the case; and if the mortgage note is silent on this matter, the borrower may have to negotiate the privilege of early repayment with the lender. However, many mortgages do provide explicitly that a penalty can be paid by the borrower should the borrower desire to prepay the loan.

One rationale for a prepayment penalty is that the lender may be trying to recover a portion of loan origination costs not charged to the borrower at closing. This may have been done by the lender to compete for the loan by making initial closing costs lower for the borrower. Another reason for prepayment penalties is that the lender has agreed to extend funds for a specified time, 30 years in our present example. Early payment from the lender's view may represent an unanticipated inflow of funds that may or may not be readily reinvested in periods when mortgage rates are stable or are expected to decline. However, if interest rates undergo a sustained increase over long periods of time, lenders usually welcome early repayments since they may be able to loan out funds again at higher rates of interest.

Another reason for such penalties is that they are not included in the computation of the *APR;* hence they are not included in the APR disclosure to the borrower. Some argue that borrowers may not be able to determine the effect of these penalties on borrowing costs and the penalties merely represent a technique used by lenders to increase yield. Because of this, some states have begun prohibiting the enforceability of prepayment penalties to individuals financing residencies, if the loan has been outstanding more than some specified minimum number of years. Also in areas where penalties are allowed, lenders will waive them if the buyer of a property agrees to originate a new loan with the same lender.

Because of the use of prepayment penalties, we want to know the effective mortgage loan yield (interest cost) when both a loan discount fee and a prepayment penalty are charged on the loan. To illustrate, we consider both the effects of the 3 percent loan discount and a 3 percent prepayment penalty on the outstanding loan balance for the $60,000, 30-year loan with a contract interest rate of 12 percent used in the preceding section. We assume the loan is repaid early, at the end of five years, and would like to determine the effective interest cost to the borrower (yield to the lender). To solve for the yield, mortgage funds actually disbursed in this case will be $60,000 minus the origination fee of $1,800, or $58,200. Taking the loan discount fee into account, we want to find the discount rate which, when used to discount the series of monthly payments of $617.17 plus the outstanding loan balance of $58,596 and the prepayment penalty of $1,758 (3 percent of $58,596), or a total of $60,354, will result in a present value equal to the amount of funds actually disbursed, $58,200.

This is done as follows:

$$\$58,200 = \$617.17 \ (MPVIFA, ?\%, 5 \text{ yrs.}) + \$60,354(MPVIF, ?\%, 5 \text{ yrs.})$$

Following the same thinking used in the previous section, we note that a 3 percent origination fee and a 3 percent prepayment penalty are unlikely to increase the yield of this loan beyond 14 percent; therefore we discount using the monthly interest factors at 13 percent and 14 percent and interpolate as follows:

A. Discounting at 13 percent
$$PV = \$617.17(43.950107) + \$60,354(.523874)$$
$$PV = \$58,743$$

B. Discounting at 14 percent
$$PV = \$617.17(42.977016) + \$60,354(.498601)$$
$$PV = \$56,617$$

1. Difference in interest rates $= 1\%$
2. Difference in PVs $= \$2,126$
3. Difference in PV in (A)
    and desired PV $= \$58,743 - \$58,200 = \$543$
4. $(\$543 \div \$2,126) \times 1\%$ $= .26$,
    adding $13\% + .26\% = 13.26\%$

From the discounting procedure used above, we see that with a 3 percent origination fee, early payment in the fifth year, and a 3 percent prepayment penalty, the effective yield on the loan will increase to about 13.26 percent.

In this case the *APR* will still be disclosed at 12.5 percent, which reflects the loan discount only, not the prepayment penalty, and assumes the loan is repaid at the end of 30 years. The actual yield computed here of 13.26 percent is a marked difference from both the loan contract rate of 12 percent and the disclosed *APR* of 12.5 percent.

Charging Fees to Achieve Yield, or Pricing *CPMs*

In the preceding examples, we have developed the notion of the effective borrowing costs and yield from a given set of loan terms. However, we should consider how fees are determined by lenders when "pricing" a loan. As we discussed earlier in the chapter, lenders generally have other alternatives in which they can invest funds. Hence, they will determine available yields on those alternatives for given maturities and weigh those yields and risks associated with those alternatives against yields and risks on mortgage loans. Similarly, competitive lending terms established by other lenders establish yields that managers must consider when establishing loan terms. By continually monitoring alternatives and competitive conditions, management establishes loan offer terms for various categories of loans, given established underwriting and credit standards for borrowers (underwriting standards are discussed in the next chapter). Hence a set of terms designed to achieve a competitive yield on categories of loans representing various ratios of loan to property value (70 percent loans, 80 percent loans, etc.) are established for borrowers who are acceptable risks. These terms are then revised as competitive conditions change.

To illustrate, if, based on competitive yields available on alternative investments of equal risk, managers of a lending institution believe that a 13 percent yield is competitive on 80 percent mortgages with terms of 30 years and expected repayment periods of 10 years, how can they set terms on all loans made in the 80 percent category to ensure a 13 percent yield? Obviously, one way would be to price all loans being originated at a contract rate of 13 percent. However, management may also consider pricing loans at 12 percent interest and charging either loan fees or prepayment penalties or both to achieve the required yield. Why would lenders do this? Because (1) they have fixed origination costs to recover, and (2) competitors may still be originating loans at a contract rate of 12 percent.

To illustrate how fees for all loans in a specific category can be set, we consider the following formula:

$$ND = MLC(MPVIFA, 13\%, 10 \text{ yrs.}) + MLB (MPVIF, 13\%, 10 \text{ yrs.})$$

where

MLC = monthly loan constant factor at 12 percent contract rate for 30 years
MLB = loan balance factor for a 30-year loan, after 10 years, at 12 percent
ND = net disbursement (unknown) as percent of total loan

Substituting values for a 13 percent, 30-year loan in the above expression, we have

$$ND = .010286(66.974419) + .9342 (.27444)$$
$$= .9453$$

The result $ND = .9453$ means that the net disbursement at loan closing should be 94.53 percent, or 94.5 percent (rounded), of the loan amount. This means that if the loan is priced by offering terms of 12 percent interest and a 5.5 percent origination fee (100% − 94.5%) and the loan is repaid in 10 years, management will have its 13 percent yield.

The above formula can be used for any loan category for which a solution is desired. The application used here was for the 80 percent loan category. However, note that the numerical value of 80 percent does not appear in the formula. Hence, it can be used for all 13 percent, 30-year loans.

INFLATION AND MORTGAGE PRICING PROBLEMS

As stated previously, the fully amortizing, constant payment mortgage has been the most widely used mortgage instrument in the United States for some time. However, in more recent times, particularly during the 1970s and early 1980s, inflation and its effect on this "standard" mortgage instrument have caused problems for both lenders and borrowers. Because of these problems, a number of different mortgage instruments have been proposed as alternatives to the standard mortgage instrument. In this section we outline the problems that inflation has brought for both borrowers and lenders who have relied on the standard mortgage instrument. Also included is a detailed description of the graduated payment mortgage. This mortgage is also a fixed interest rate mortgage and has been used in place of the constant payment mortgage, particularly during periods of rising interest rates.

Effects on Lenders and Borrowers

How does inflation relate to mortgage lending and cause difficulty for lenders and borrowers desiring to make constant payment loan with fixed interest rates? The answer to this question can be easily illustrated. Let's initially assume that a $60,000 loan is being made at a time when no inflation exists. The loan is expected to be outstanding for a 30-

year period. Because there is no inflation, an inflation premium (*f*) is not required; hence the lender will earn a return equivalent to the riskless interest rate (*r*), plus a premium for risk (*p*) over the period of the loan.[17] We *assume* that the interest rate charged under such assumptions would be 4 percent, representing a 3 percent real rate of interest and a risk premium of 1 percent over the period of the loan. Assuming a constant payment, fixed interest rate loan made in an inflationless environment, the lender would collect constant payments of approximately $286 per month, based on the loan constant for 4 percent and 30 years. This amount is shown in Exhibit 5–9 as a straight line (*RP*) over the life of the loan and represents the series of *constant real payments* necessary to earn the lender a 4 percent fixed real return plus a risk premium each year that the loan is outstanding.

Now assume that the same loan is made in an inflationary environment where a 6 percent rate of inflation is expected to prevail during each year that the loan is outstanding. The interest rate on the mortgage loan would now have to increase to approximately 10 percent for the lender to earn the same real return. This includes the base rate of 4 percent earned when no inflation was expected, plus an inflation premium of 6 percent percent.[18] Given that the standard mortgage instrument is to be used, the lender must now collect approximately $527 a month (rounded). This new payment pattern is shown in Exhibit 5–9 as the horizontal line labeled *NP*, representing a constant series of nominal payments received over the term of the loan. Hence, included in the series of nominal payments are amounts that will provide the lender with a 4 percent basic rate of interest representing a real return and risk premium, plus a 6 percent inflation premium over the 30-year loan term.

In our example an expected inflation rate of 6 percent caused an 84 percent rise in the monthly mortgage payments from $286 to $527, or $241 per month. Why is there such a significant increase in these monthly payments. The reason can be easily seen by again examining curve *NPD* in Exhibit 5–9. This curve represents the real value of the monthly payments that the lender will receive over the 30-year loan period. It is determined by "deflating" the $527 nominal monthly payments by the rate of inflation.[19] The *NPD* curve is important because the lender, realizing that inflation is going to occur, expects that the constant stream of $527 payments to be received over time will be worth less and less because of lost purchasing power. Hence, in order to receive the full 10 percent interest necessary to leave enough for a 4 percent real return and risk premium over the life of the loan, more "real dollars" must be collected in the *early* years of the loan (payments collected toward the *end* of the life of the mortgage will be worth much less in purchasing power).

---

[17]Actually the interest rate charged will be related to the expected repayment period that may occur before maturity. However, this will not alter the concept being illustrated. The figures chosen here are arbitrary. Some studies indicate that the real rate of interest has historically been in the 1 to 3 percent range and risk premiums on mortgages in the 2 to 3 percent range.

[18]The nominal interest rate would actually be $(1 + .04)(1 + .06) - 1$ or 10.24 percent. However as indicated earlier, we use 10 percent to simplify calculations.

[19]Deflating an income stream is done by computing the monthly inflation factor $.06 \div 12$, or .005, and multiplying $527(1 \div 1.005)^1$ in the first month, $527(1 \div 1.005)^2$ in the second month, and so on, until the end of year 30.

EXHIBIT 5–9   Real and Nominal Values of Mortgage Payments

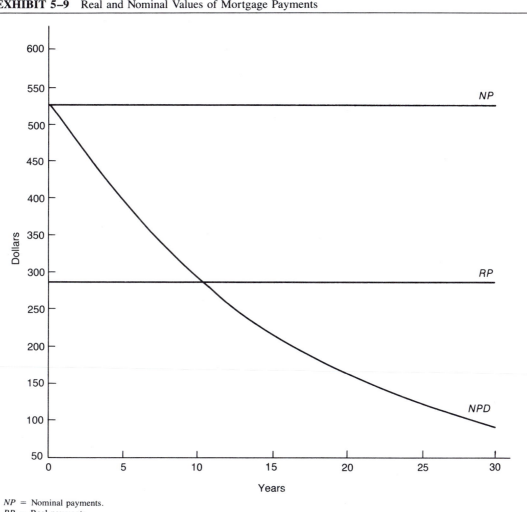

NP = Nominal payments.
RP = Real payments.
NPD − Nominal payments discounted.

To illustrate, let's examine the deflated or real value of the $527 payments collected each month, as represented by the curve *NPD*. Note that for about the first 10 years of the loan life, the real value of these payments is greater than those for the 4 percent loan. However, after 10 years, the real value of these payments falls below the payments required on the 4 percent loan. However, even though the two payment streams differ, the real value of the nominal payment stream is equal to the required real payments at 4 percent, or *NPD* = *RP*. This means that from the stream of nominal $527 monthly receipts, the lender will ultimately earn the same real value as a stream of $286 payments or 4 percent on investment after deflating the nominal payments by the inflation rate. However, in order to earn the same real interest rate, the real value of the payment stream (*NPD*) must be greater than *RP* in the early years, since it will fall below *RP* in the later years. This relationship is referred to as *tilting* the real payment stream in the early years to make up for the loss in purchasing power in later years.

This "tilt effect" also has a considerable impact on the borrower. Recall that, with no inflation, the borrower faced a $286 payment; however with inflation a $527 monthly payment is necessary. When the loan is first originated, the difference in the two payments is about $241 per month and represents an additional amount of real or current dollars that the borrower must allocate from current real *income* to meet mortgage payments.

Over time, this burden moderates. For example, by the end of the first year, the real value of the $527 payments deflated by the 6 percent rate of inflation would be about $497 per month, and the borrower's real income will have increased by 3 percent, or by the real rate of growth in the economy. At that time, the borrower will have more real income to pay declining real mortgage payments. The important point here is that even though the borrower's income is increasing both in real and nominal terms each year, it is not enough to offset the tilt effect in the early years of a loan. From this analysis, it becomes very apparent from Exhibit 5–9 why it is so difficult for first-time home buyers to qualify for constant payment, fixed interest rate loans during periods of rising inflation. With the general rate of inflation and growth in the economy, borrower incomes will grow gradually or on a year-by-year basis. However, as expected inflation increases, lenders must build estimates of the full increase into current interest rates "up front," or *when the loan is made*. This causes a dramatic increase in required real monthly payments relative to the borrower's current real income.

One final observation about the tilt effect is that, as the rate of inflation increases, the tilt effect increases. This can be easily seen from Exhibit 5–10. In this case, we show the effect of an increase in inflation from 6 percent in our previous example to 8 percent per year. Note that nominal monthly payments increase from $527 to $617 per month, the latter figure based on an increase in the mortgage interest rate to 12 percent. The impact of the tilt effect on a constant payment loan when inflation is expected to be 8 percent can be seen relative to the effect when inflation was expected to be 6 percent. Note that when the $617 monthly payments are deflated at 8 percent (*NPD* @ 8%) for inflation, the burden of the real payments to be made by the borrower increases relative to the real payments required when inflation was 6 percent in the early years of the loan. This can be seen in Exhibit 5–10, as the curve corresponding to monthly payments deflated at 8 percent indicates that the real value of monthly payments on the 12 percent mortgage exceeds the real value of payments on the 10 percent mortgage for about the first 10 years of the loan term. This is true even though the lender will earn a 4 percent real return on *both* mortgages after inflation. Further, if we again assume that the "average" borrower's real income will increase by 3 percent, regardless of the rate of inflation (recall real growth is assumed to be 3 percent in our example), as inflation increases from 6 percent to 8 percent it is clear that the borrower will have to allocate even more current real income to mortgage payments. This indicates that in the early years of the mortgage, the burden of the tilt effect on borrowers increases as the rate of inflation increases. This

EXHIBIT 5–10   Relationship between Real and Nominal Mortgage Payments at Various Rates of Inflation

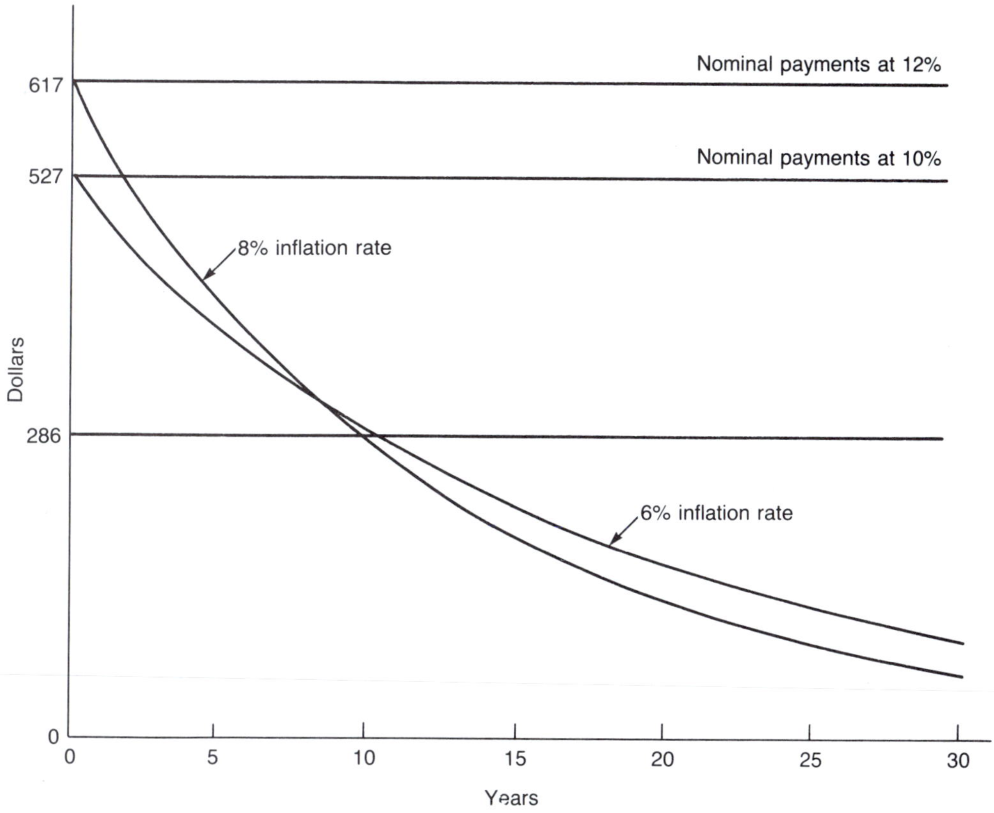

increased burden is due solely to (1) the nature of the mortgage instrument, that is, a constant payment, fixed interest rate mortgage, and (2) the rate of inflation. Further, the tilt problem makes it even more difficult for borrowers to qualify for loans based on their current income and make payments from current income.

The Graduated Payment Mortgage

In an attempt to deal with the problem of inflation and its impact on mortgage interest rates and monthly payments, lenders have instituted new mortgage instruments. One such instrument is the graduated payment mortgage (*GPM*). The objective of *GPM* is to provide for a series of mortgage payments that are *lower* in the initial years of the loan than they would be with a standard mortgage loan. *GPM* payments then gradually increase at a predetermined rate as borrower incomes are expected to rise over time. The payment pattern thus offsets the tilt effect to some extent, hence reducing the burden faced by

EXHIBIT 5–11 Comparison of *GPM* Payments and Standard Constant Payments ($60,000, 30-year maturity, various interest rates)

Interest Rate	10%	11%	12%	13%	14%
Constant Payments	$526.54	$571.39	$617.17	$663.72	$710.94
GPM payments graduated (7.5% annually)					
1	400.22*	436.96*	474.83*	513.71*	553.51*
2	430.24	469.73	510.44	552.24	595.03
3	462.51	504.96	548.72	593.66	639.65
4	497.19	542.83	589.87	638.18	687.63
5	534.48	583.55	634.11	686.04	739.20
6–30	574.57	627.31	681.67	737.50	794.64

*Computed based on formula in appendix to this chapter.

households when meeting mortgage payments from current income in an inflationary environment.[20]

An example of the payment pattern for the graduated payment mortgage is illustrated in Exhibit 5–11. That exhibit contains information on how payments should be structured for the 30-year, $60,000 loan used in our previous examples at various interest rates and different annual rates of graduation. *GPM*s can have a number of plans allowing for differences in initial payment levels, rates of graduation, and graduation periods.[21] Exhibit 5–11 contains information on *one* of the more popular payment plans in use today. This plan allows for a 7.5 percent rate of graduation in monthly payments over 5 years, after which time the payments level off for the remaining 25 years. The computation of initial payments on a mortgage of this kind is a complex undertaking. A procedure for determining initial payment levels is provided in the appendix to this chapter.

Looking at the information contained in Exhibit 5–11, we see that for a standard mortgage loan of $60,000 originated at 12 percent for 30 years, the required constant monthly payments would be $617.17. A *GPM* loan made for the same amount and interest rate where the monthly payments are increased (graduated) at the end of each year at a predetermined rate of 7.5 percent begins with an initial payment of approximately $474.83. This initial payment will then increase by 7.5 percent per year, as shown in the exhibit, to an amount equal to $681.67 at the beginning of the sixth year and will remain constant from that point until the end of year 30. When compared with the $617.17 standard, or constant mortgage payments, shown in the exhibit, *GPM* payments are initially lower by $142.34 in the first year. The difference becomes smaller over time. The graduated

---

[20]The Federal Housing Administration initiated the first widely accepted graduated payment plan under its Section 245 program. For more detail, the reader should obtain the *HUD Handbook 4240.2*, Rev., Graduated Payment Mortgage Program, Sect. 245. These handbooks are available from HUD regional insuring offices.

[21]For a current update on plans available, the reader should contact a regional insuring office of the FHA which is a division of the U.S. Department of Housing and Urban Development.

payment level reaches approximately the same payment under the standard mortgage between the fourth and fifth years after origination. *GPM* payments exceed constant payments by $64.50($681.67 − $617.17) beginning in year 6. *GPM* payments then remain at the $681.67 level for the remaining 25 years of the loan term.

The graph in Exhibit 5–12 provides a comparison of payment patterns for a GPM, a standard constant payment mortgage, and a constant amortization mortgage. *GPM* payments are based on the 7.5 percent graduation plan. All three loans are assumed to be originated for $60,000 at 12 percent interest for 30 years. Note that the *GPM* payment mortgage (*CPM*) is below that of the standard level payment mortgage (*CPM*) for approximately five years, at which point the *GPM* payments begin to exceed *CPM* payments. The reason for this pattern should be obvious. Under either payment plan, the yield to the lender must be an annual rate of 12 percent compounded monthly (assuming no origination fees, penalties, etc.) Therefore, because the *GPM* payments are below that

EXHIBIT 5–12　Comparison of Mortgage Payment Patterns (loan amount = $60,000, maturity = 30 years, interest 12% GPM add: 7.5% graduation rate, 5 years)

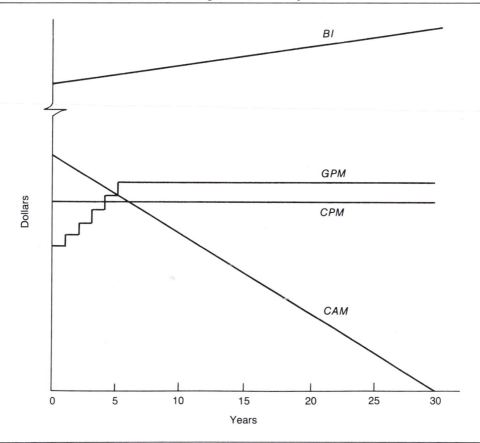

of the *CPM* in the early years, *GPM* payments must eventually exceed the level payment on the *CPM* loan to "make up" for the lower payments on the *GPM* in the early years. Hence, if the borrower chooses the GPM in our example, the payments will exceed those of a standard *CPM* mortgage from years 6 to 30.

The advantages of the *GPM* program are very obvious from the borrower's standpoint. The initial payment level under the GPM plan shown in Exhibit 5–12 is significantly lower than with the *CPM*. Further, in the early years, *GPM* payments correspond more closely to increases in borrower's income *BI* (as shown in the exhibit). Hence, the burden of the tilt effect requiring borrowers to allocate more current real dollars for mortgage payments from current real income in an inflationary environment is reduced somewhat with the *GPM*. Based on this analysis, it is easy to conclude that the *GPM* significantly reduces monthly payments for borrowers in the early years of the mortgage loan, corresponds more closely to increases in borrower income, and therefore may increase the demand for mortgage credit by borrowers.

When judged relative to the *CAM,* both the *CPM* and *GPM* clearly provide for initial payments that are far below payments required for the *CAM* with the same terms. It is important to stress that higher rates of inflation have caused a modification in mortgage instruments over time. Even though all *three* mortgage instruments provide the same yield (12 percent), changes in mortgage payments have clearly been structured to reduce initial payments. This has been done with the expectation that growth in real incomes and expected inflation will extend into the future, resulting in sufficiently high borrower incomes to repay the debt while reducing initial payments sufficiently to reduce the payment burden at the time of loan origination.

Outstanding Loan Balances—GPM.   Because the initial loan payments under *GPM* plans are usually lower than payments necessary to cover the monthly interest, the outstanding loan balance under the *GPM* will *increase* during the initial years of the loan. It will remain higher than that of the standard mortgage until full repayment occurs at maturity. A comparison of loan balances for a *GPM* and a standard mortgage, based on the 12 percent, $60,000, 30-year terms used in our previous example, are shown in Exhibit 5–13.

Based on Exhibit 5–13, we can see that the mortgage balance with the *GPM increases* until approximately year 4. It then begins to decline until it reaches zero in the 30th year. Hence, if a borrower sold this property during the first four years after making a *GPM* loan, more would be owed than originally borrowed. The reason why the loan balance increases during the first four years after origination is because the initial *GPM* payments are lower than the monthly interest requirements at 12 percent. Therefore, no amortization of principal occurs until payments increase in later periods. To illustrate, in our previous example, the interest requirements under a *GPM* after the first month of origination would be $60,000 × (.12 ÷ 12), or $600.00. The *GPM* payments during the first year of the loan are only $474.13, which are less than the monthly interest requirement of $600.00. The difference, or $125.17 must be added to the initial loan balance of $60,000, as if that difference represented an additional amount *borrowed* each month. This $125.17 monthly difference is referred to as *negative amortization*. Further, this shortfall in interest must also accumulate interest at the rate of 12 percent compounded monthly. Hence,

EXHIBIT 5–13 Determining Loan Balance on a *GPM* ($60,000 loan, 12% 30 yrs. 7.5% rate of graduation)

Year	Beginning Balance	Required Monthly Interest Payment	GPM Payment	Loan (amort.)	Change in Balance	Ending Balance
1	$60,000.00	$600.00	$474.83	$125.17	$1,587.47	$61,587.47
2	61,587.47	615.87	510.44	105.43	1,337.12	62,924.59
3	62,924.59	629.25	548.72	80.53	1,021.32	63,945.91
4	63,945.91	639.46	589.87	49.59	628.93	64,574.84
5	64,574.84	645.75	634.11	11.64	147.62	64,722.46*
6	64,722.46	647.22	681.67	(34.45)	(436.91)	64,285.55

*Maximum balance. During the sixth year, the payments ($681.67) will exceed required interest ($647.22), and loan amortization will begin.

during the first year, $125.17 per month plus monthly compound interest must be added to the $60,000 loan balance. This process amounts to compounding a monthly annuity of $125.17 at 12 percent per month and adding that result to the initial loan balance to determine the balance at year-end. The amount added to the loan balance at the end of the year will be $125.17 (*MFVIFA*,12%,12 mos.) or $125.17(12.682503) = $1,587.47.

The importance of the increasing *GPM* loan balance and negative amortization can be seen in relationship to the property value also shown in Exhibit 5–14. It is important to note the "margin of safety," or difference between property value and loan balance. This margin is much *lower* when a *GPM* loan balance is compared with that of a *CPM*. This makes a *GPM* loan riskier to the lender than a *CPM* is, because more consideration must be given to *future* market values of real estate and *future* borrower income. For example, let's assume that the *GPM* borrower decides to sell a property after five years. When compared with the *CPM*, the lender will have received relatively lower monthly payments up to that point. Further, the proceeds from sale of the property must be great enough to repay the loan balance that has increased relative to the original amount borrowed because of negative amortization. In short, with a *GPM*, the lender must now be more concerned about trends in real estate values because resale value will constitute a more important source of funds for loan repayment.

GPM Mortgages and Effective Borrowing Costs. A closing note in this chapter has to do with the question of the effective interest cost and *GPMs*. In the absence of origination fees and prepayment penalties, the yield on *GPMs*, like yields on *CAMs* and *CPMs*, is equal to the contract rate of interest as specified in the note. This is because like the *CPM*, the *GPM* is a fixed interest rate mortgage. As with *CAM* and *CPM* loans, this is true whether the *GPM* loan is repaid before maturity or not. However, to the extent points or origination fees are charged, the effective yield on a *GPM* will be *greater* than the contract rate of interest, and it will increase the earlier the loan is repaid. When computing yields on *GPMs* originated with points, the same procedure should be followed

EXHIBIT 5–14   Constant Payment, Graduated Payment and Constant Amortization Loan Balances Compared with House Value

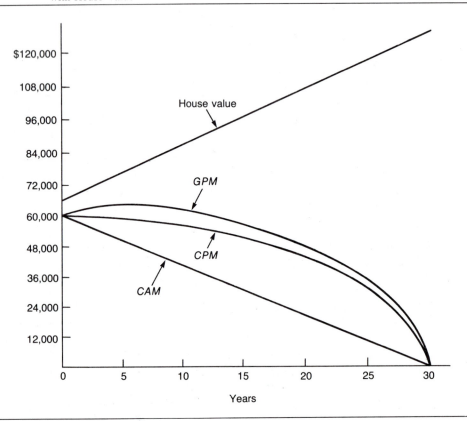

as described with the standard *CPM;* that is, the interest rate making the stream of *GPM* payments equal to the funds disbursed after deducting financing fees is the effective cost of the loan. Based on computations made by the authors (not shown) in cases where origination fees are charged on *GPMs,* results are very close to those computed for standard mortgage loans with the same terms and origination fees. This is true regardless of the loan amount or rate of graduation on the *GPM.* For example, for the *GPM* discussed above, if 3 points are charged and the loan is repaid after 5 years, the effective cost would be about 12.78 percent, as compared with 12.82 on a *CPM* with the same terms.[22]

---

[22]Computations for the effective interest cost on *GPMs* are much more difficult than for the *CPM* because the amount disbursed must be set equal to a series of seven annuities, representing different payments for 12 periods in each of the six years, with the final annuity payment covering years 6 to 30. Similarly, when finding loan balances, we may use for *GPMs* the same procedure demonstrated for *CPMs;* that is, the remaining payment streams would be discounted at the contract rate of interest, and the present value would be determined. However, determining loan balances on *GPMs* may involve discounting a series of one or more annuities spanning many different 12-month intervals if any remaining *GPM* payments differ.

Given the rather detailed discussion on *GPMs*, is a borrower better off or worse off with a *GPM* or a *CPM* loan? Generally speaking, if a standard loan and a *GPM* are originated at the same rate of interest, with the same fees, then there will be little, if any, difference in the effective cost of each. However, because the graduated payment pattern reduces tilt effect, the borrower is definitely better off with a *GPM* *if it can be obtained at the same interest rate* as the standard mortgage.

Would a *GPM* generally be available at the same interest rate as a standard mortgage? It would appear that because of the additional risk taken by the lender, in the form of an increasing loan balance due to negative amortization in the early years of the loan *and* lower initial monthly cash flows received from reduced payments, the *GPM* lender would require a *higher risk premium* than would the *CAM* lender. Hence, all else equal, a slightly higher interest rate may be required on a *GPM* relative to the *CPM*. This would tend to neutralize some of the positive features of the *GPM* when compared to the *CPM*. As to disclosure requirements to the borrower, because the effective interest cost on a *GPM* can be computed using the procedure discussed in the previous section, disclosure of the *APR* as part of the truth-in-lending documentation is essentially the same as described earlier in the chapter.

QUESTIONS

1. What are the major differences between the *CAM, CPM,* and *GPM* loans? What are the advantages to borrowers and risks to lenders for each? What elements do each of the loans have in common?
2. Define *amortization*.
3. Why do the monthly payments in the beginning months of a *CPM* loan contain a higher proportion of interest than principal repayment?
4. What are loan closing costs? How can they be categorized? Which of the categories influence borrowing costs, and why?
5. Does repaying a loan early ever affect the actual or true interest cost to the borrower?
6. Why do lenders charge origination fees, especially loan discount fees?
7. What are the Truth-in-Lending Act and the annual percentage rate (*APR*)?
8. Does the annual percentage rate always equal the effective borrowing cost?
9. What is meant by a real rate of return?
10. What is a risk premium in the context of mortgage lending?
11. When mortgage lenders establish interest rates through competition, an expected inflation premium is said to be part of the interest rate. What does this mean?
12. Why do monthly mortgage payments increase so sharply during periods of inflation? What does the tilt effect have to do with this?
13. As inflation increases, the impact of the tilt effect is said to become even more burdensome on borrowers? Why is this so?
14. A mortgage loan is made to Mr. Jones for $30,000 at 10 percent interest for 20 years. If Mr. Jones has a choice between a *CPM* and a *CAM,* which one would result in a greater amount of total interest being paid over the life of the mortgage? Would one of these mortgages be likely to have a higher interest rate than the other? Explain your answer.

15. A borrower makes a *GPM* mortgage loan. It is originated for $50,000 and carries a 10 percent rate of interest for 30 years. If the borrower decides to prepay the loan after 10 years, would he be paying a higher yield, lower yield, or the same yield as the contract rate originally agreed on? How would this yield compare with that on a *CPM* or *CAM* made on the same terms?

16. Would a lender be likely to originate a *GPM* at the same rate of interest as a standard *CPM* loan?

17. What is *negative amortization?* Why does it occur with a *GPM?* What happens to the mortgage balance of a *GPM* over time?

PROBLEMS

1. Alice Cooper makes a fully amortized *CPM* mortgage loan for $100,000 at 13 percent interest for 25 years. What will be the monthly payment on the loan? What would the initial six payments be with a *CAM?*

2. John Brown made a 30-year mortgage loan five years ago for $30,000 at 9 percent interest. He would like to paydown the mortgage balance by $5,000.
   a. Assuming he can reduce his monthly mortgage payments, what will the new mortgage payment be?
   b. Assuming the loan maturity is shortened, what will the new loan maturity be?

3. James Doe wants to buy a property for $90,000 and wants an 80 percent loan for $72,000. A lender indicates that the loan can be obtained for 25 years at 13 percent interest; however, a loan origination fee of $1,500 will also be necessary for Doe to obtain the loan.
   a. How much will the lender actually disburse?
   b. What is the effective interest cost to the borrower, assuming that the mortgage is paid off after 25 years (full term)?
   c. What is the annual percentage rate (*APR*) which the lender must disclose to the borrower?
   d. If Doe pays off the loan after five years, what is the effective interest charge? Why is it different from the *APR* in (c)?
   e. Assume the lender also imposes a prepayment penalty of 1.5 percent of the outstanding loan balance if the loan is repaid within eight years of closing. If Doe repays the loan after five years with the prepayment penalty, what is the effective interest cost? Why is it different from the *APR* in (c)?

4. A lender is considering what terms should be allowed on a loan to Charles Good. Current market terms are 11 percent interest for 30 years, and the loan amount Good has requested is $80,000. The lender believes that extra credit analysis and careful loan control will have to be exercised in this since Good has never borrowed such a large sum before. In addition, the lender expects that market rates will move upward very soon, perhaps even before the loan with Good is closed. To be on the safe side, the lender decides to extend a *CPM* loan commitment to Good for $80,000 at 11 percent interest for 30 years; however, he wants to charge a loan origination fee to make the mortgage loan yield 11.5 percent. What origination fee should be charged? What if the loan is expected to be repaid after 10 years?

5. Flirt Reynolds purchases a property for $80,000. He finances the purchase with a *GPM* carrying an 11 percent interest rate. A 7.5 percent rate of graduation will be applied to monthly payments beginning each year after the loan is originated for a period of five years. The initial payment will be $509.78 per month. The initial loan amount is $70,000 for a term of 30 years. Reynolds expects to sell the property after seven years.

   a. If he can sell the property for $90,000, what will the net proceeds be from the sale?

   b. What would the payment be if a *CPM* loan was available?

   c. Assume the loan is originated with two discount points, what would be the effective yield on the *GPM?*

6. A borrower is faced with choosing between two loans. Loan A is available for $100,000 at 12 percent interest for 30 years, with 2 points to be included in closing costs. Loan B would be made for the same amount, but for 11.5 percent interest for 30 years, with 6 points to be included in the closing costs.

   a. If the loan is repaid after 15 years, which loan would be the better choice?

   b. If the loan is repaid after five years, which loan is the better choice?

Appendix: Graduated Payment Mortgages—Extensions

As explained in the chapter, the mechanics of determining monthly payment streams and loan balance are relatively straightforward for *GPM*s. However, when designing a *GPM* program, the reader should be aware that the rate of graduation, number of years during which payments will graduate, term, and interest rate will vary, depending on the goals of the borrower and lender and the loan market that it is being designed to serve.

Perhaps the most complex problem associated with a *GPM* program is establishing the initial monthly payment. For example, in Exhibit 5–11, the monthly payments for various *GPM*s were illustrated. Each group of monthly payments was assumed to increase at the rate of 7.5 percent beginning in year 2. However, the reader may be wondering how the initial payment is determined in year 1. For example, in the case of our 12 percent *GPM* mortgage, we note that the initial payment would be $474.83. How was that payment determined?

To answer this question, we provide what appears to be a difficult solution. Upon closer examination, however, we will see that it is an application of the present value formulas that we have learned. It is important to recall that for the *GPM*, as was the case with the *CAM*, the present value of all payments discounted at the contract rate of interest will equal the initial loan amount. This concept is very important and must be kept in mind as we work through the problem at hand. What follows is a general formula for determining the initial monthly payment for a *GPM:*

$$PV = [MP_1 \cdot \sum_{t=1}^{12} \frac{1}{(1 + i/12)^t}]$$

$$+ [MP_1(1 + g)^1 \cdot \sum_{t=1}^{12} \frac{1}{(1 + i/12)^t} \cdot \frac{1}{(1 + i/12)^{12}}]$$

$$+ [MP_1(1 + g)^2 \cdot \sum_{t=1}^{12} \frac{1}{(1 + i/12)^t} \cdot \frac{1}{(1 + i/12)^{24}}]$$

$$+ [MP_1(1 + g)^3 \cdot \sum_{t=1}^{12} \frac{1}{(1 + i/12)^t} \cdot \frac{1}{(1 + i/12)^{36}}]$$

$$+ [MP_1(1 + g)^4 \cdot \sum_{t=1}^{12} \frac{1}{(1 + i/12)^t} \cdot \frac{1}{(1 + i/12)^{48}}]$$

$$+ [MP_1(1 + g)^5 \cdot \sum_{t=1}^{300} \frac{1}{(1 + i/12)^t} \cdot \frac{1}{(1 + i/12)^{60}}]$$

where

PV = loan amount
i = contract interest rate
MP_1 = monthly payments during year 1
g = rate of graduation in the monthly payment

While the computation appears to be complex, a relatively simple solution for MP_1 is obtainable for our $60,000, 12 percent, 30-year *GPM* with a graduation rate of 7.5 percent. Note that the expressions containing the Σ's are simply the interest factors for the present value of an annuity (*MPVIFA*) presented in Chapters 4 and 5. The terms $1 \div (1+i/12)^{12}$, $1 \div (1 + i/12)^{24}$ and so on, are simply the *MPVIF* factors also discussed in Chapters 4 and 5. These factors correspond to various 12-month intervals during which monthly payments will be greater than the previous 12-month period. However, in any given year, monthly payments (unknown) will remain constant during that year. Hence, what we have in our case example are six different groups of unknown monthly annuities, which, when discounted by the contract rate of interest on the mortgage (i), must equal the initial amount of the loan. This discounting process is usually referred to as discounting *grouped cash flows* and is a problem encountered frequently in real estate finance.

Essentially, our problem involves finding MP_1, which is the only unknown. We know the loan amount $60,000, the monthly interest rate $i \div 12 = .01$, and the term of the loan (360 months). Further, we know that *MP* in years 2, 3, 4, 5, and 6 will be equal to MP_1, increased by $(1 + g)^1$, $(1 + g)^2$, $(1 + g)^3$, $(1 + g)^4$ and $(1 + g)^5$, respectively where $g = .075$. Given this information, MP_1 can be found by assembling the information as shown in Exhibit 5A–1.

EXHIBIT 5A–1   Worksheet for Solving for Initial *GPM* Payments

(1) Payment Period	*(2)* Payment	*(3)* Graduated Payment Factor	*(4)* MPVIFA	*(5)* MPVIF	*(6)* $(3 \times 4 \times 5)$
MP_1	= $MP_1(1.0)$	1.0	11.255077	—	11.255077
MP_2	= $MP_1(1 + .075)$	1.075000	11.255077	.887449	10.737430
MP_3	= $MP_1(1 + .075)^2$	1.155625	11.255077	.787566	10.243594
MP_4	= $MP_1(1 + .075)^3$	1.242297	11.255077	.698925	9.772473
MP_5	= $MP_1(1 + .075)^4$	1.335469	11.255077	.620260	9.323008
MP_{6-30}	= $MP_1(1 + .075)^5$	1.435629	94.946551	.550450	75.030751
				Total	126.362333

Looking at Exhibit 5A–1, we see that column 1 corresponds to the payments for years 1 to 30. Column 2 merely indicates that payments during each year will be increased at the rate of 7.5 percent per year, which is equivalent to compounding MP_1 (unknown) by 1.075 for each year's set of payments *beginning* in year 2. In other words, we are solving for payments in year 1 which will remain the same for 12 months, then increase by 1.075 beginning in year 2. Hence, column 3 is simply the compound interest factor for the rate of graduation (7.5 percent) applied to MP_1.

In Exhibit 5A–1, column 4 contains the *MPVIFA* at 12 percent. This factor is, in effect, being used to discount the six different series of monthly payments *within* the interval during which they will occur. For example, in each of the first five years, 12 monthly payments will be received and must be discounted for that 12-month interval, hence the factor 11.255077. From years 6 to 30, 300 payments will be received and must be discounted for that interval, hence the factor 94.946551.

Column 5 contains the *MPVIF* factor which must be used to discount each series of monthly annuities back to time period zero or present value. In other words, column 4 discounts the 12 monthly payments *within* the 12-month interval. Column 5 is necessary because each series of grouped payments is not received all at once; instead the series received during the second year has a lower present value than the series received in the first year. Hence, each series must be discounted again by the *MPVIF* factor for one year, the third year must be discounted for two years, and so on.

Finally, column 6 is simply the product of columns 3, 4, and 5. Note that these factors are additive because we have been able to express each series of payments (MP_2, MP_3, MP_4, MP_5, and MP_{6-30}) in terms of MP_1 because we know that each succeeding period's payment will increase by same rate of graduation $(1 + g)$. Careful inspection of the equation shows that *MPVIFA, MPVIF,* and $1 + g$ may be factored, multiplied, and added. This is in essence what we have done in Exhibit 5A–1. Hence the equation reduces to

$$MP_1(126.362333) = \$60,000$$
$$MP = \$474.83$$

Because we know that MP_2 will be 1.075 times greater than MP, we have \$474.83(1.075) or \$510.44 and so on. The reader may now complete the calculations and verify the payments in the 12 percent column in Exhibit 5–11.

This formula and procedure have widespread application in real estate finance whenever one is faced with a series of payments which are scheduled to increase after given time intervals at any specified rate of increase.[1] The student is also encouraged to think about how the schedule and formula may change if different rates of graduation over different periods of time are desired.

Regarding loan balances for *GPMs*, once the mortgage payments are known, balances can be determined at any time by finding the present value of the remaining payments. This is done by discounting those payments by the contract rate of interest, taking into account any grouped cash flows in the remaining series, and discounting them appropriately. As for effective interest costs, any origination fees should be subtracted from the loan amount (PV). Then, given the *GPM* payments and balance, a new series for *MPVIFA* and *MPVIF* at a rate higher than 12 percent would be used to discount the payments and balances until the present value of all cash inflows equals the net amount of funds disbursed.

---

[1] This procedure can be programmed into many financial calculators. Many calculator manufacturers have already preprogrammed this procedure in memory. An explanation can usually be found in the accompanying manual under graduated payment mortgages and/or discounting grouped cash flows.

Problems

A-1. Mr. Qualify is applying for a $100,000 *GPM* loan for 25 years at an interest rate of 9 percent. Payments would be designed so as to graduate at the rate of 7.5 percent for three years beginning with payments in the second year.

    a. What would monthly payments be for Mr. Qualify in each of the first five years of the loan?

    b. What would the loan balance be on the *GPM* at the end of year 3?

    c. If the lender charged 4 points at origination, what would be the effective interest cost on this loan after five years?

Chapter 6

Adjustable Rate and Variable Payment Mortgages

In the preceding chapter, we discussed the evolution of fixed interest rate mortgage instruments, giving particular attention to payment patterns. We saw how payment structures have evolved in response to changes in the economic environment, particularly when the impact of inflation on interest rates and mortgage payments was considered. While many of those changes alleviated problems faced by *borrowers,* depending on the degree of uncertainty in expectations of inflation and interest rates, those remedies may be inadequate from the viewpoint of *lenders.* These inadequacies stem from the fact that although payment patterns can be altered to suit borrowers as expectations change, the *CAM, CPM,* and *GPM* are all originated in *fixed interest rates* and all have *predetermined payment patterns.* Consequently, neither the interest rate nor payment pattern will change, regardless of economic conditions. Loans made at fixed interest rates (*FRMs*) may cause serious problems for lenders who must pay market interest rates on savings. This is because market interest rates may change suddenly, and lenders who have made an overabundance of fixed interest rate mortgages may encounter serious difficulty as interest costs on savings rise relative to interest revenues from mortgage loans.

This chapter deals with a variety of mortgages that are made with either *adjustable* interest rates (called adjustable rate mortgages—*ARMs*) or with variable payment provisions that change with economic conditions. These instruments differ from fixed interest rate mortgages (*FRMs*) in that they are designed to adjust in one or more ways to changes in economic conditions. Rather than making mortgages with fixed rates of interest over long periods of time, these mortgages provide an alternative method of financing through which lenders and borrowers *share* the risk of interest rate changes, or interest rate risk. This enables lenders to match changes in interest costs with changes in interest revenue more effectively and thus provide borrowers with potentially lower financing costs.

In this chapter, we begin by discussing the price level adjusted mortgage (*PLAM*), which is one type of variable payment mortgage. Although not used widely, the *PLAM* illustrates many of the problems that must be considered by lenders and borrowers in financial decision making. We then consider *ARMs* and deal with issues relative to how they are "priced." As a part of the analysis of *ARM*s, we investigate the effects of limitations on (1) interest rate changes, (2) payment increases, and (3) negative amortization and the resultant effects on *ARM* loan yields. We also consider how these mortgages should be priced relative to *FRM*s and other *ARM*s made on different loan terms. At the conclusion of the chapter, we consider the shared appreciation mortgage (*SAM*), whose repayment terms are partially based on appreciation in property values. While this latter instrument is not as prevalent as *FRM*s and *ARM*s, it should also be understood by serious students of real estate finance.

*ARM*s AND LENDER CONSIDERATIONS

To this point, we have considered *borrower* concerns regarding mortgage loans. More specifically, we have concerned ourselves with how payment patterns have been modified to offset problems caused by the "tilt effect," thereby making more households eligible for loans. To complete the discussion of mortgage lending, we must briefly consider problems faced by *lenders* and their cost of funds.

Recall in the previous chapter that when we dealt with the tilt effect and *GPM*s with fixed interest rates, we approached it from the perspective of *borrowers*. We indicated that because of the tilt problem, borrowers had an increasingly difficult time qualifying for loans in inflationary times, even though their incomes may have been rising. When viewed by *lenders,* fixed interest rate mortgages are a potential problem regardless of what the payment pattern may be (that is, a *CAM, CPM,* or *GPM*). One major problem with *FRM*s lies in the fact that the interest rate on such loans is fixed on the date of origination and remains fixed until the loan is repaid. Hence, from the day of origination, lenders are underwriting the risk of any significant changes in the implicit components of mortgage interest rates, that is, the real rate of interest r, the risk premium p, and the premium for expected inflation f. To the extent that lenders underestimate any or all of these components at the time of mortgage origination, they will incur a financial loss. For example, assume that a mortgage loan for $60,000 is made for 30 years at 10 percent interest with an expected repayment period of 10 years. Such a mortgage would require monthly payments of about $527 per month (rounded). Should such a loan be made, it must follow that it is the consensus of lenders in the marketplace at the time the loan is made that a 10 percent rate of interest is sufficiently high to compensate them for all forms of risk bearing expected to occur over the time that the loan is expected to be outstanding. If over that time, one or more of the components of the mortgage interest rate i are significantly higher than was anticipated at the time of origination, lenders will suffer a loss.[1] If, for example, lenders make an inaccurate prediction of inflation and

---

[1]There are many reasons why lenders may inaccurately predict the components of i over the expected repayment period. Monetary growth may expand or contract, causing changes in the rate of inflation (f). General economic activity may expand (contract), resulting in a change in the general level of investment and employment, thereby affecting real interest rates and default risk (r and p).

EXHIBIT 6–1   Hypothetical Breakdown of Mortgages and Savings Accounts by Expected Maturity

	Mortgages			Deposits	
Percent of Total	*Expected Yield (percent)*	*Expected Maturity (years)*	*Percent of Total*	*Interest Rate (percent)*	*Maturity (years)*
33.3	11	2–3	33.3	9	0*
33.3	12	4–5	33.3	10	1
33.3	13	6–7	33.3	11	2
Weighted Average	12	4.5		10	1

*Withdrawable without notice.

unanticipated inflation occurs, warranting a 12 percent interest rate instead of 10 percent, the magnitude of the loss to the lender would be determined as follows:

$$PV = \$527(MPVIFA, 12\%, 120 \text{ mos.}) + MB(MPVIF, 12\%, 120 \text{ mos.})$$
$$= \$527(69.700522) + \$54,563(.302995)$$
$$= \$53,264$$

The loss would be equal to $60,000 − $53,264 = $6,736. Hence, in this case, a 2 percent rate of *unanticipated inflation* would result in a financial loss of $6,736 or 11.2 percent of the loan amount. Based on this example, it should be easy to see the relationship between *interest rate risk* and potential losses to lenders. The fact that there is always some additional risk because of the *uncertainty* about expected levels of each of the components of i is one of the reasons why a risk premium p is demanded by lenders. To the ex⁺ent that this *uncertainty* about future levels of r and f increases, p will also increase, and vice versa.[2]

It should be noted that losses incurred by lenders result in gains to borrowers. Of course, one could argue that if interest rates declined then lenders would gain. However, when this occurs, borrowers usually try to refinance their loans. This pattern implies that with fixed interest rate lending, risk bearing is not "symmetric," or evenly balanced; that is, lenders bear the risk of loss when interest rates increase which is not equally offset by gains if interest rates decline. This problem has also motivated lenders to turn to *ARMs* and other loan instruments.

Another serio⁻is problem faced by lenders during periods of rising interest rates is illustrated in Exhibit 6–1. In the exhibit, we present two components of a hypothetical, abbreviated balance sheet for a savings institution. On the asset side of the balance sheet,

---

[2]The reader should realize that there will always be some likelihood that expected levels of r and f will not always be accurate because of *unanticipated* changes. During some time periods, when economic conditions are stable, the uncertainty in these estimates is likely to be less, whereas in other periods, uncertainty may be greater. Hence, the *uncertainty* of these estimates is what causes interest rate risk and, in turn, larger or smaller risk premiums.

we assume that the institution has made only *FRM* loans. We also provide estimates of loan maturities and yields that will be earned on those loans. On the liability side, we detail the deposit accounts by maturity and also show the interest cost paid to savers for each maturity category. From this hypothetical, partial balance sheet, we compute a weighted average yield for *FRM* mortgages on the asset side which is 12 percent, with an average expected maturity of four to five years. On the deposit, or liability side, of the balance sheet, we compute a weighted average cost of funds, which is equal to 10 percent with an average maturity of one year. An estimate of the lender's net revenue before operating costs, or ''spread,'' would be approximately equal to 12 percent minus 10 percent, or 2 percent of assets. From this net revenue, the institution would have to meet its operating costs, cover loan default losses and earn a profit.

Difficulties that a savings institution may encounter during a period of unexpected changes in interest rates can be seen if we consider a 2 percent increase in interest cost associated with the deposit category with a zero maturity, or where savings deposits can be withdrawn at any time. Should that sudden, unanticipated increase in interest rates occur, we note in Exhibit 6–2 that the new weighted average cost of funds increases to 10.7 percent. On the asset side of the balance sheet, however, the weighted average yield on *FRM* loans does not change. Net revenue would decline from 2.0 to 1.3 percent of assets (12 percent minus 10.7 percent). This savings institution would now have a smaller amount of income, or spread, from which to pay operating costs and earn a profit. Clearly, this organization will find it more difficult to earn a profit after the sudden increase in interest rates than it did previously. Further, as time passes, if interest rates on deposits continued to rise, this would cause even more difficulty. Even if rates did not continue to rise, the spread will continue to narrow as deposits mature before mortgages are repaid. For example after one year the rate on new deposits, which was 10 percent, will also rise as deposits mature and are replaced with new one-year deposits. Of course, some new mortgages might be made during the year to partially offset this reduction.

It should be obvious to the reader that this lender's profitability problem was brought about by an *imbalance* in the maturity structure of assets and liabilities. The weighted average maturity of assets is much greater than the weighted average maturity of liabilities.

EXHIBIT 6–2   Hypothetical Breakdown of Mortgages and Savings Accounts by Expected Maturity (after interest rate charges)

Mortgages			Deposits		
Percent of Total	*Expected Yield (percent)*	*Expected Maturity (years)*	*Percent of Total*	*Interest Rate (percent)*	*Maturity (years)*
33.3	11	2–3	33.3	11	0*
33.3	12	4–5	33.3	10	1
33.3	13	6–7	33.3	11	2
Weighted Average	12	4.5		10.7	1

*Withdrawable without notice.

Over time this imbalance, or "gap," can become even more acute if interest costs rise and deposit maturities become shorter relative to asset maturities. This imbalance is sometimes referred to as the classic problem of a savings institution—"borrowing short and lending long." This means that the savings institution has accepted deposits, certificates of deposits, and so on, with relatively short maturities and has used most of the funds to finance fixed rate mortgage loans with longer maturities.[3] To the extent that this imbalance, sometimes referred to as the *maturity gap,* exists between assets and liabilities for savings institutions, they are exposed to a considerable risk that the cost of deposits may change relative to the yield on assets. Clearly, if deposit costs for lenders increase relative to yields on their assets, lenders are worse off.[4]

For many years, this maturity gap did not present serious difficulty for savings institutions. This is because they were protected by Regulation Q of the Federal Reserve Act, which set specific rates of interest that lenders were allowed to pay savers on deposits at all savings institutions. These regulations kept interest rates that lenders could pay depositors relatively low and allowed for changes in these rates very infrequently. Further, this period was characterized by relatively low rates of inflation, and the incentive for savers to withdraw deposits to invest in higher-yielding investments was not a serious concern. Hence. all deposits were thought to be "longer-term" liabilities.

In recent years, because of high rates of inflation, extremely high and volatile interest rate patterns occurred in the 1970s and early 1980s which caused even small savers to withdraw deposits and to seek higher-yielding investment opportunities. Congress eliminated protections under Regulation Q, and savings institutions had to increase interest rates paid on deposits during these periods to compete for savings.[5] As we have discussed, most savings institutions had been making constant payment mortgage loans with relatively long maturities, and the yields on those mortgages did not keep pace with the cost of deposits. These problems prompted savings institutions (lenders) to change the mortgage instruments to what they now use. In today's market environment, more mortgages are being made with adjustable interest rate features that will allow adjustments in *both* interest rates and payments so that the yields on mortgage assets will *change* in relation to the cost of deposits. This change amounts to lenders shifting at least part of the risk of unexpected interest rate changes to borrowers.

To accomplish the shifting of *interest rate risk,* mortgage lenders have devised adjustable interest rate mortgage (*ARM*) instruments with many different features. When developing these instruments, lenders have generally attempted to accomplish two goals: first, to

---

[3]Obviously lenders could protect themselves by investing in shorter-term assets, such as Treasury bills, to "match" zero maturity deposit accounts. Indeed, most lenders attempt to do this and still maintain a significant proportion of mortgages in their loan portfolio. Nonetheless, it is still very difficult to make an "exact" match. To reduce this risk, lenders have turned to designing lending instruments, including *ARM*s, with interest rates that change with market conditions and deposit costs.

[4]Of course, to the extent interest rates fall, they are better off. However, the risk is in not knowing what the outcome will be.

[5]Even if Regulation Q had not been changed, savings institutions would have had difficulty retaining deposits because savers would have withdrawn them and invested in higher-yielding securities, thereby reducing the flow of deposit funds.

make these more complex mortgage instruments acceptable to the borrowers and, second, to make mortgage instruments flexible enough, in terms of interest rate and payment features, so that problems that lenders face regarding deposit instability and cost of funds are alleviated. In the sections that follow, we will discuss many types of mortgage instruments, some which fully pass interest rate risk to the borrower and some which partially pass interest rate risk to the borrower. We will also discuss how these various mortgages are "priced," that is, how the initial interest rate and other fees vary in accordance with risks shared by the borrower and lender. Rather than attempting to detail or describe specific details on the many varieties of *ARM*s, we provide a generic framework which focuses on how changes in payments, interest rates, loan balances, and maturity occur in relation to market conditions. In this way, the student should be able to deal with mortgages containing many combinations of features that change in response to market conditions over time.

THE PRICE LEVEL ADJUSTED MORTGAGE

One concept that has been discussed as a remedy to the imbalance problem for savings institutions is the price level adjusted mortgage (*PLAM*). Recall in the previous chapter, when the determinants of mortgage interest rates, i, were discussed, that is an expected real rate of interest r, a risk premium p and expected inflation f, we displayed the following equation:

$$i = r + p + f$$

We also indicated that perhaps the most difficult variable in the equation to predict was a premium for expected inflation f. To help reduce interest rate risk, or the uncertainty of inflation and its effect on interest rates, it has been suggested that lenders should *originate* mortgages at interest rates that reflect lender expectations of the real interest rate plus a risk premium for the likelihood of loss due to default on a given mortgage loan, or $r + p$.

After specifying initial values for r and p, the *PLAM* loan balance would be adjusted up or down by a price index. Payments would then be based on a new loan balance, adjusted for inflation. This would shift the risk of changes in market interest rates brought about by inflation f to borrowers and relieve lenders of the difficult task of forecasting future interest movements when originating loans. The lender would still bear the risk of any unanticipated change in r or p.[6]

---

[6]Although we are treating each of these variables making up i as independent and additive, they may not be independent and may well interact with one another. For example, the risk premium p is partially dependent on the likelihood that a borrower's income and wealth will rise or fall, which may depend on changes in the economy and, hence, the underlying real riskless rate of return (r). Changes in income would affect the likelihood of default on a loan because of payments rising relative to income (which may rise or fall) and/or the loan balance exceeding the market value of the house. Similarly, we do not fully understand the relationship between inflation f and real growth r and possible interaction between them. Hence, the reader should be aware that we are dealing with these influences in a conceptual way to illustrate the importance of each component, but we do not mean to imply that the specification of i is this simplistic.

PLAM—Payment Mechanics

An example of a *PLAM* loan would have payments based on a rate of interest consisting only of expectations for *r* and *p* for an expected maturity period. Payments would be adjusted periodically, based on the indexed value of the *mortgage balance* for the remaining loan term. To illustrate, assume that a mortgage is made for $60,000 for 30 years at an interest rate of 4 percent, or a lender's estimate of *r* + *p*. The lender and borrower may agree that the *loan balance will be indexed* to the consumer price index (*CPI*) and adjusted annually. Initial monthly payments would be based on $60,000 at 4 percent for 30 years or, approximately $286. After one year, the loan balance, based on a 30-year amortization schedule for the 4 percent interest rate would be about $58,943. If it is assumed that the *CPI* increased by 6 percent during the first year of the loan, the *loan balance* at the end of year 1 would become $58,943(1.06), or $62,480. This balance would be repaid over 29 remaining years. Monthly payments, beginning in the second year, would be based on the higher-indexed loan balance of $62,480 at the same 4 percent interest rate for 29 years, or $304 per month. This process of (1) computing the loan balance using an amortization schedule based on a 4 percent interest rate for the remaining term, (2) increasing the balance by the change in the *CPI* during the next year, and (3) computing the new payment over the remaining loan term would continue each year thereafter.

Assuming inflation continued at an annual rate of 6 percent for the remaining loan term, Exhibit 6–3 shows the nominal payment and loan balance pattern every year for the *PLAM* loan. There are many patterns that should be pointed out in Exhibit 6–3. Note that the *PLAM* payments shown in Panel A increase at approximately the same rate as

---

EXHIBIT 6–3 Payments and Loan Balance Patterns $60,000, *PLAM*, 4%, Inflation = 6% per year, versus $60,000 *CPM*, 10% Interest, 30 years

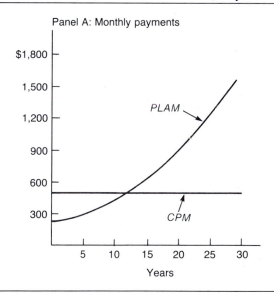

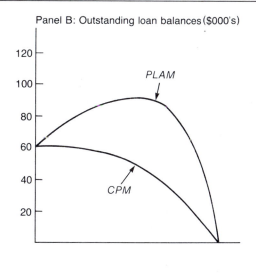

the change in the price level, or 6 percent over the life of the loan. This increase in payments continues over the life of the loan even though loan amortization begins to occur as the number of remaining years to maturity declines (see Panel B). This pattern of rising payments occurs because (1) of the effect of the increasing price index on the loan balance and (2) each succeeding year's payment is computed over a shorter remaining loan term.[7] It is also interesting to compare the payments on this *PLAM* to a $60,000, constant payment *FRM* made at 10 percent for 30 years. Payments on the *FRM* would be approximately $527, as compared to the initial *PLAM* payment of $286. Thus, it would appear that many more households could qualify to purchase housing with *PLAM*s when compared to *CPM*s. Further, *PLAM*s would appear to help remedy problems of savings imbalance and interest rate risk faced by savings institutions. This is because mortgage yields would correspond more closely with changes in interest rates on deposits.

The *PLAM* is not without problems, however. Panel B in Exhibit 6–3 shows that the loan balance on the *PLAM* increases to about 155 percent of the original loan amount, or from $60,000 to approximately $93,000, after 15 years. Although housing prices have appreciated considerably during the 1960s and 1970s, housing is only one of many components making up the *CPI*. Hence, should prices of other goods represented in the *CPI* increase faster than housing prices, indexing loan balances to the *CPI* could result in loan balances increasing faster than property values. If this occurred, borrowers would have an incentive to default. This possibility would place a considerable burden on lenders because now, instead of dealing with inflation and fixed interest rate loans, they would have to establish adequate down payment levels for all borrowers, forecast future housing prices, and be assured that the value of the property, which serves as collateral for the mortgage, would always be greater than the outstanding loan balance. Hence, it is questionable as to whether the *CPI* is the proper index to use when adjusting *PLAM* balances.

A second problem with *PLAM*s has to do with the relationship between mortgage payments and borrower incomes. It would appear that the tilt problem discussed earlier would be greatly reduced, because payments would be matched more closely with borrower income. However this assumes that both the *CPI*, used to index the *PLAM*, and borrower incomes change in the same way. A desired ratio between mortgage payments and borrower incomes may be easy to maintain as long as incomes keep pace with increases in the *CPI*. Over the long run this relationship may be possible, as increases in income and mortgage payments may "balance out." However, should inflation increase sharply, it is not likely that borrower incomes would increase at the same rate in the short run. During such periods, the payment burden may increase and households may find it more difficult to make mortgage payments. Because of this possibility, lenders would have to estimate future income for households in different occupational categories and relationship of that income with inflation in order to develop a desired relationship to mortgage payments. The problems of rising loan balances and payments just discussed make estimating the risk premium *p* that lenders must charge extremely difficult.

---

[7]The reader should realize that the process of adjustments occurring at the end of each year can be viewed as an annual series of new mortgage loan originations. As such, payments may be modified based on different rates of interest and/or maturities, with the outstanding loan balance always representing the new amount being borrowed. Hence, it is possible for changes in interest rates and/or maturities to be renegotiated or varied by the lender and borrower at any time to moderate or increase monthly payments.

A third problem with *PLAM*s is that the price level chosen for indexation is usually measured on an historical, or ex post (after the fact) basis, that is based on data collected in the *previous period* but published currently. Inasmuch as mortgage payments are to be made in the future, historic prices may not be an accurate indication of future prices. To illustrate, the change in the *CPI* may have been 10 percent during the past year (published currently). This would be used to index the outstanding mortgage balance, which will determine payments during the *next* year. If the rate of increase in the *CPI* subsequently slowed to 2 percent during the next year, it is easy to see that mortgage payments would be rising at a faster rate (10 percent) than current prices (2 percent) and, perhaps, faster than borrower incomes. Although borrower incomes may have increased by 10 percent in the previous year, there would still be a problem caused by the lag between realization of income in one period and higher payments in the next. This lag problem could become even more distorted in our example if the *CPI* were to decline and then increase. For this reason, many observers believe that if the *PLAM* programs were adopted extensively, the time intervals between payment adjustment periods would have to be shortened considerably.

A final problem with *PLAM*s as viewed by lenders would involve a modification in the types of deposits that are offered. If *PLAM*s were used to a large extent, lenders would probably have to develop new types of deposit accounts which would also be made available at some basic rate of interest and indexed to the price level. This would have to occur so that when prices and interest rates increase, yields on both *PLAM* loans and savings deposits would rise together. Otherwise, revenue from mortgages could fluctuate more than deposit costs, and a profit squeeze could develop.

While *PLAM*s offer the potential for a better match between the costs of deposit and returns on assets than is the case with fixed interest rate mortgages, *PLAM*s have not been tried to any significant extent because of the problems listed above. Further, savers can achieve their desired objectives through a variety of savings instruments presently available in the marketplace, which are not indexed to price levels. They can invest their savings in short-term securities and reinvest them very frequently, thereby reducing their interest rate risk exposure. Such investments could include Treasury bills, certificates of deposit, or unit shares in money market funds. By having a choice among short-term investment vehicles with yields that are very sensitive to changes in inflation, savers may believe that they can hedge adequately against the risk of unanticipated inflation without requiring price-indexed deposits. Lenders, on the other hand are probably willing to bear some of the interest rate risk associated with inflation; therefore they have not seen the need to shift this risk completely to borrowers by implementing *PLAM*s. Many *PLAM* features are, however, very attractive, and *these features form the framework* for understanding *ARM*s that are now being offered in the marketplace.

*ARM*s—A GENERAL OVERVIEW

Rather than using changes in the price level as a mechanism to adjust mortgage interest rates and payments, lenders have chosen a variety of mortgages with *interest rates* that are *indexed to other market interest rates*. By choosing indexes based on interest rates rather than on a price index, lenders partially avoid having to estimate real interest rates and risk premiums for the entire period that loans are expected to be outstanding. With *ARMs*, lenders are, in effect, making a loan, with terms which are updated to current interest rate levels at the end of each adjustment period. By using an interest rate index instead of an ex post measure of inflation based on the *CPI* or any other price index, lenders earn expected yields based on *expected future values* for *r, p,* and *f* over a future period of time. This is because interest rates are a reflection of lender and borrower expectations of *r, p,* and *f* over specific future periods of time. Hence, by tying the terms of a mortgage to an index of such rates which are continuously updated in market and used to revise the *ARM,* such revisions are always based on future expectations. Hence an *ARM* provides for adjustments that are more timely for lenders than a *PLAM* because values for *r, p,* and *f* are revised at *specific* time intervals to reflect market expectations of future values for *each* component of *i between adjustment dates.* For example, the value for *f,* or expected inflation, is based on an estimate of *future* prices rather than an ex post, or past, measure as exemplified in the *CPI* or other price indexes. Similarly, values for *r* and *p* are based on the market's current assessment of borrower incomes, housing values, and other risks in the prospective economic environment between adjustment dates.

ARMs Illustrated

We can begin to illustrate *ARM* mechanics with a simple example. An *ARM* for $60,000 with an *initial* interest rate of 10 percent is originated with a term of 30 years, but its payments are to be adjusted at the end of each year based on an interest rate determined by a specified index at that time. Based on these initial loan terms, monthly payments would be approximately $527 per month for the first year. If at the end of one year, the market index were to rise and change the interest rate on the *ARM* to 12 percent, payments would be determined based on the outstanding loan balance for 29 years as follows:

$$MP = \$59,666(MLC,12\%,348 \text{ mos.})$$
$$= \$59,666(.010324)$$
$$= \$616 \text{ (rounded)}$$

Hence, the new 12 percent interest rate on the *ARM* at the end of the first year is an updated estimate or consensus of all lenders and borrowers as to what the components of *i* will be for the *coming year.*

At least three observations should be made concerning our simple example. *First,* the use of *ARMs* does not completely eliminate the possibility of lenders realizing losses because of *interest rate risk.* To illustrate, in our example the yield to the lender on the *ARM* during the first year was 10 percent. If market rates move to 12 percent *the day after* the *ARM* is originated, the lender would sustain a 2 percent loss for the 12-month period. Obviously, this loss would be eliminated if the adjustment period was reduced to one day, or the loss could be reduced to the extent the adjustment period was less than one year. This leads us to the *second* point, that is, the longer the adjustment interval the greater the interest rate risk to the lender. Hence the expected yield on such a mortgage should be greater. This idea will be elaborated later in the chapter. One final point is that, depending on the nature of the index chosen and the frequency of payment adjustments, as the lender assumes *less* interest rate risk the borrower incurs *more* interest rate risk. This latter point can be appreciated if one thinks of an *FRM* where the lender assumes the full risk of future interest rate changes and compares it to an *ARM* with payments adjusting freely with market conditions. Clearly in the latter case the borrower would be assuming more interest rate risk, and the lender less. Because the borrower assumes more risk, the *initial interest rate* on an *ARM* should generally be *less* than that on an *FRM*. Further, because the lender is shifting interest rate risk to the borrower, the lender should also expect, at the time of loan amortization, to earn a lower yield on an *ARM* over the term of the loan.

Anytime the process of risk bearing is analyzed, it goes without saying that individual borrowers and lenders differ in the degree to which they are willing to assume risk. Consequently, the market for *ARMs* contains a large set of mortgage instruments which differ with respect to how risk is to be shared between borrowers and lenders.

ARM **Indexes.**   One differentiating feature among *ARMs* is the range of *indexes* used to establish future mortgage terms. Some commonly used indexes are:

- Interest rates on six-month Treasury bills.
- Interest rates on one-year Treasury securities.
- Interest rates on three-year Treasury securities.
- Interest rates on five-year Treasury securities.
- The weighted average national cost of funds (deposits) index, as compiled by the Federal Home Loan Bank Board (FHLBB).
- The national average of fixed interest rates on mortgage loans made on previously existing homes, as compiled by FHLBB.

There are many other components of *ARMs* in addition to indexation and interest rate adjustments which must be discussed if *ARMs* are to be adequately understood. These characteristics also determine how much interest rate risk is being passed from lenders to borrowers and, therefore, how much risk the borrower accepts.

Other *ARM* Characteristics.   The following list contains a description of some of the general characteristics frequently found in *ARMs*:

- *Initial interest rate.* The initial rate on an *ARM* will usually be determined based on market conditions at the time that the loan is made. However, it will almost always be *lower* than the prevailing rates on fixed interest rate mortgages. An *ARM* lender should also expect to earn a lower yield because with an *ARM* loan the lender is assuming less interest rate risk. Hence, at the time of origination, because an *ARM* lender should expect to earn a lower yield, the initial interest rate on the *ARM* will usually be lower than that on an *FRM*.[8]

---

[8]One exception to this rule would occur if the yield curve, discussed in the previous chapter, is inverted or "humped." This would mean that short-term interest rates are higher than long-term interest rates, and hence the initial interest rate on an *ARM* tied to an index with a shorter maturity would be greater than that on an *FRM* with a longer maturity.

- *Index.* This is the interest rate series (such as one from the above list) agreed on by both the borrower and the lender and over which the lender has no control. This index may be very short term or long term in nature.
- *Adjustment interval.* The period of time between mortgage payment adjustments. This time period is usually six months or one year. However, it could be as long as every three to five years, or it could be as short as one month or less.
- *Margin.* A constant spread, or premium in addition to the index chosen for an ARM.
- *Composite rate.* The sum of the index plus the margin which is used to establish the new rate of interest for *ARM*s after each adjustment interval. It can differ from the initial interest rate on the date of origination.
- *Limitations or caps.* Maximum *increases* allowed in payments, interest rates, maturity extensions, and negative amortization (or loan balances) between adjustment intervals and/or over the life of the loan, as provided for in an ARM agreement.
- *Negative amortization.* Depending on the type of ARM being used, to the extent the composite rate exceeds either (1) an interest rate cap or (2) would result in payments exceeding a payment cap, the difference in interest may be compounded at current rates and added to the outstanding loan balance. When additions to the outstanding loan balance are allowed, such amounts are referred to as negative amortization (see discussion of *GPM*s in the previous chapter).
- *Floors.* Maximum *reductions* in payments and/or interest rates between adjustment intervals and/or over the life of the loan.
- *Assumability.* The ability of borrower to allow a subsequent purchaser of a property to assume a loan under the existing terms.
- *Discount points.* As is the case with *FRM*s, these points, or fees, are also used with *ARM*s to change yield in relation to risk.
- *Prepayment privilege.* As is the case with *FRM*s, the borrower usually has the right to prepay the loan. This prepayment privilege is usually allowed *without penalty.*

To acquaint the reader with *ARM* terminology, a brief illustration of how these various provisions might be used in quoting *ARM* terms is as follows: A loan is made for $60,000 for a period of 30 years at an *initial interest rate* of 10 percent. Payments will be *adjusted annually* based on the *index* of yields on one year U.S. Treasury obligations on the payment adjustment date, plus a *margin* of 2 percent. Payment increases will be *capped,* based on a maximum increase of a 2 percent increase in the interest rate in any one year, or a total increase of 5 percent over the life of the mortgage (this is sometimes referred to as a 2/5 rate cap). Should the composite rate exceed the interest rate cap at the time of payment adjustment, *negative amortization* will be computed and added to the outstanding loan balance. There will be a 2 percent floor, or limit on the extent to which the interest rate may fall each year, regardless of the decline in the market index. The loan will *not be assumable;* that is, the outstanding loan balance must be repaid in the event the property is sold. Later in the chapter, we will show how future payments and loan balances are calculated on a loan like the one described above.

Clearly, many other combinations of the above provisions could be used to allocate interest rate risk between the lender and borrower, depending on borrower qualifications and willingness to assume risk. Space does not allow for an in-depth analysis of all of these combinations. What we will provide, however, is a framework which, after the reader thoroughly understands it, should provide the necessary tools that can be used to analyze any given set of *ARM* provisions.

Problems with *ARM*s Faced by Lenders and Borrowers

There are many problems regarding adjustable rate mortgages of concern to both lenders and borrowers. With respect to borrowers, these features are more complex and difficult to understand than provisions usually present in a constant payment mortgage. This complexity is compounded by the fact that many *ARM*s contain more than one feature (as listed above) that may change in response to changes in conditions in the mortgage market. It is more difficult for borrowers to determine the effect of each feature, both individually or combined, on borrowing costs. Some of these features will be more important than others, and the relative importance of each feature may change over an interest rate cycle.

Lenders also face significant uncertainty when making *ARM*s. They must find the proper combination of options to include in the mortgage instrument to satisfy borrower requirements, including how much risk borrowers are willing to bear. Lenders must also estimate the yields they expect to earn on these loans and how the pattern of yields corresponds to expected changes in their cost of funds. While lenders may pass much of the interest rate risk to borrowers with *ARM*s, to the extent that they improperly price or establish too low an initial interest rate on these loans, they still may earn an inadequate yield and have difficulty paying market interest rates to savers. In this sense, while they may be better off because of being able to add *ARM*s to their asset portfolios, lenders have, to a degree, replaced the problems that they faced with standard, fixed interest rate *CPM* loans with a different set of problems. In other words, *ARM*s may not completely relieve lenders from the possibility of making loans with *expected yields* that may be inadequate in relation to future deposit costs. To the extent that lenders select inappropriate indexes, margins, adjustment periods, and so on, they may still be underwriting a considerable amount of *interest rate risk* which may adversely affect profitability.

Borrowers also face the decision regarding *ARM*s lacking market experience. On the positive side, these loans will generally be priced at an *initial* interest rate *below* that of an *FRM*. Hence in periods of very high long-term interest rates, the tilt problem is reduced and more households should be able to qualify for loans with *ARM*s than would be the case with *FRM*s. As a result, a more continuous flow of funds should be available to borrowers than would be the case if only *FRM*s were available. On the other hand, households must also budget a more uncertain monthly payment flow from their incomes from year to year, a requirement that they have not had to deal with when *FRM*s were available.

Finally, because of the fact that *ARM*s may shift all or part of the interest rate risk to the borrower, the *risk of default* will generally increase to the lender, thereby reducing some of the benefits gained from shifting interest rate risk to borrowers. For example, if a lender were to shift all interest rate risk to a borrower by requiring payments in accordance with any changes in interest rates without limit, it is clear that the risk of default would increase considerably. Similarly, the way in which *ARM* payment patterns are structured may also affect default risk. As a result, in practice, lenders must assess the likelihood that a borrower will default under a number of different *ARM* plans that shift all or a part of the interest rate risk to borrowers. In the remainder of this chapter, we focus on interest rate risk and default risk change in relation to the types of ARMs negotiated by lenders and borrowers. We do not consider how such mortgage loans are underwritten in relation to borrower characteristics such as borrower income, type of employment, the value of the house being purchased, etc. This aspect of default risk is considered in detail in the two chapters that follow.

Risk Premiums, Interest Rate Risk, and Default Risk on *ARM*s

It is very difficult to determine how expected yields will vary among *ARM*s containing different repayment characteristics. However, for any given class of borrowers, the expected yield (cost) of borrowing with an *ARM* generally depends on the *ARM* provisions described above; these are (1) the initial interest rate, (2) the index to which the interest rate is tied, (3) the margin, or spread, over the index chosen for a given *ARM,* (4) discount points charged at origination, (5) the frequency of payment adjustments, and (6) whether caps or floors on the interest rate, payments, and/or loan balances are included. The loan amount and each of the six characteristics listed will determine the cash outflow or amount loaned, expected monthly payments, and the expected loan balance for an expected time period from which an expected yield (internal rate of return) can be computed. In addition to understanding how each of the above relationships are likely to affect the expected yield (or cost of borrowing), further complications include understanding how combinations of these terms may *interact* over time and possibly amplify or reduce *default risk* to the lender.

While much has been said about benefits to lenders from shifting *interest rate risk* to borrowers, there are added risks that lenders must assume with *ARM*s. The combination of the above six characteristics also affect *default risk* either (1) by affecting the borrower's ability to make mortgage payments or (2) if negative amortization is allowed, by increasing the loan balance too high in relation to the value of the house. While we discuss lender underwriting standards used to gauge default risk in more detail in the next chapter, we also want to stress the importance of default risk in our present discussion.

A useful way to approach the relationships between interest rate risk and default risk for an individual and lender is to examine Panel A of Exhibit 6–4. In the exhibit, we show the risk premium p demanded by the lender on the vertical axis and interest rate risk, assumed by the lender on the horizontal axis. Looking at the curve in the exhibit, we see that as more interest rate risk is assumed by the lender (less by the borrower), the lender will demand a higher risk premium. Hence, the interest rate risk curve is positively sloped. In the extreme, if the lender assumes all interest rate risk (point B) this would be equivalent to the amount of interest rate risk assumed with an *FRM*. Note that when the lender assumes no interest rate risk, the borrower is assuming all interest rate risk. This is represented by the intersection of the interest rate risk curve at the origin of the diagram (point A).

EXHIBIT 6–4   The Relationship between Interest Rate Risk, Default Risk, and Risk Premiums

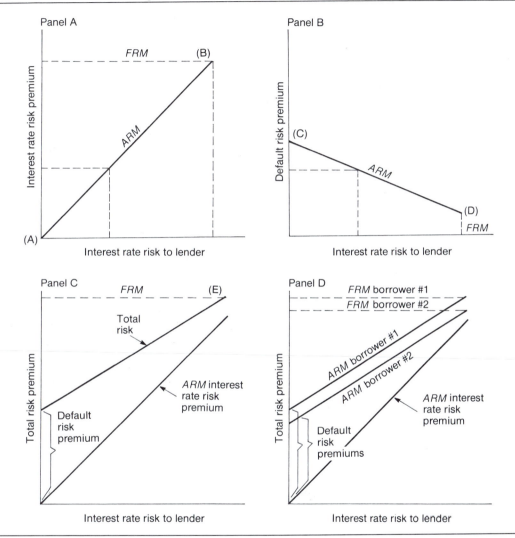

When interest rate risk assumed by the borrower increases (as would be the case with an *ARM* with *no cap* on payments or the interest rate), *default risk* assumed by the lender increases (see panel B). Default risk is greatest at point C when there are no restrictions on *ARM* interest rates or payments. This is because the borrower faces a greater likelihood that unanticipated changes in interest rates may cause significant increases in payments (''payment shock'') relative to income. Hence, the likelihood of default is greater when the borrower assumes all interest rate risk. However, as more interest rate risk is assumed by the lender, we should note in Panel B that risk of borrower default declines. This is because payment shock to the borrower is restricted when caps on payments and/or interest rates are used. In essence, by assuming more interest rate risk, the *lender* absorbs more shock, thereby reducing *borrower* default risk. This pattern is exhibited in Panel B with the default risk curve being shown as negatively related to the risk premium demanded by the lender as interest rate risk to the lender increases. However, the level of default risk never declines below the risk assumed by the lender on a fixed rate mortgage (point *D*), which is also coincident with the lender's assumption of all interest rate risk (point (B) Panel A).

The total risk curve, shown in Panel C of Exhibit 6–4, establishes the risk premium demanded by the lender for *both* risks (interest rate risk plus default risk) being assumed under various *ARM* terms. The total amount of risk assumed by the lender corresponds to various combinations of *ARM* terms ranging from the case where all interest rate risk is assumed by the borrower (Panel A, point A) to the case where all interest rate risk is assumed by the lender (Panel A, point B) coupled with the amount of default risk incurred by the lender *given* different levels of interest rate risk (Panel B). Hence, Panel C shows the total risk premium that should be earned by the lender, given levels of interest rate risk *and* default risk that correspond to various levels of interest rate risk. However, the total risk premium should not exceed the total premium that would be earned on an FRM (Panel C, point E).

Panel D in Exhibit 6–4 shows the relationship between total risk and the risk premium demanded by the lender for *different borrowers*. Note that the amount *interest rate risk* remains the same for each borrower; however, *default risk* differs for each borrower. Hence, the premium charged by the lender on *ARM*s will vary, depending on the amount of default risk being assumed for each ARM borrower, (1) or (2) and how that default risk varies, or interacts, with expected changes in interest rate risk. We should point out that many other noninterest rate factors can cause default such as loss of employment, divorce, etc. Our focus here has been only on how default risk changes with fluctuations in interest rates.

The example diagrammed in Exhibit 6–4 is only appropriate for specific borrowers, however. To date, the exact relationship between default risk and interest rate risk for many different classes of borrowers has not been studied extensively. Hence the reader may not generalize the example shown in the exhibit to all borrowers and lenders in the mortgage market. However, *it is safe to say that ARM loans will only be made to an individual borrower as long as the expected benefits to the lender from shifting interest rate risk exceed potential default losses associated with doing so. Similarly, as long as a given borrower is willing to undertake interest rate risk in exchange for paying a lower risk premium to a lender, the ARM will be acceptable to the borrower.*

While Exhibit 6–4 graphically portrays the risk/return trade-off faced by lenders and borrowers, it should be pointed out that *ARM* terms may be structured in many ways to provide a trade-off between interest rate and default risk that is satisfactory to both. These terms could include many possible combinations of initial interest rates, margin, points, the index chosen, frequency of payment adjustment, caps on payments, and so on. We will explore various combinations of *ARM* terms later in this chapter.

From the above discussion, then, mortgage lending (borrowing) can be viewed as a process of *pricing risk,* with the expected yield being the return received (paid) by lenders (borrowers) for making loans with terms under which lenders and borrowers bear various amounts of risk. The terms utilized in construction of an *ARM* (e.g., initial rate, index, adjustment period, caps) are simply the variables or "tools" at the disposal of borrowers and lenders to negotiate and allocate the amount of interest rate and default risk being shared.[9]

Expected Yield Relationships and Interest Rate Risk

While the contracting process used by lenders and borrowers to allocate risk is a complicated one, there are some general relationships regarding interest rate risk and yields that can be employed in this process. What follows are some general relationships regarding *interest rate risk* that may be useful when comparing *ARMs* with *FRMs* and comparing *ARMs* containing different loan provisions with one another. The relationships focus on the effects of interest rate risk on *ARM* yields, given the conclusion arrived at in the preceding section. The conclusion was that an *ARM* will never be made unless the expected benefit to a lender from shifting interest rate risk to a borrower exceeds expected losses from default risk. Proceeding with this assumption in mind, when evaluating *ARM* terms, interest rate risk, and expected yields to lenders, we should consider the following relationships:

1. At the time of origination, the *expected* yield on an *ARM* should be less than the *expected* yield on an *FRM;* to the extent that benefits to lenders from shifting interest rate risk exceed increases in default risk to borrowers. Otherwise, the borrower and lender will always prefer an *FRM*. Coincident with the lower expected *ARM* yield, the *initial interest rate* on an *ARM* will *usually* be less than that of an *FRM*.[10]

2. *ARMs* that are tied to *short-term* indexes are generally riskier to borrowers than *ARMs* that are tied to long-term indexes. This is because short-term interest rates are generally more variable than long-term interest rates. Therefore, *ARM* borrowers who are more risk averse will generally prefer *ARMs* tied to a longer-term index and should be willing to pay more (a higher risk premium and expected yield to the lender). Less risk-averse borrowers will prefer a shorter-term index and will expect to pay less for taking additional interest rate risk. Borrowers who prefer no interest rate risk will choose an *FRM* and will pay the highest total risk premium, or yield to the lender.

3. Coincidentally with (2), *ARMs* with shorter time intervals *between* adjustments in payments are generally riskier to borrowers than those with longer periods of time between

---

[9]If risk could be quantified, or reduced to some unit quantity such as dollars, an agreement could be devised that would specify exactly how much risk was being shared. However, because risk is an abstract concept, this is not possible. This is the reason why borrowers and lenders include various provisions in contracts to share risk under any set of unknown future economic conditions.

[10]Although the initial interest rate on an *ARM* should generally be less than that of an *FRM*, in cases where short-term interest rates are greater than long-term rates and an *ARM* is tied to a short-term rate, it is possible that the initial rate on an *ARM* may be greater than an initial interest rate on an *FRM*. However, the *expected yield* on an *ARM* should be lower because yields are computed to maturity, which includes expected future interest rate patterns.

adjustments. This is because, although an *ARM* may be tied to a short-term index, the adjustment period may not coincide with the index. For example, an *ARM* may be adjusted every *three* years based on the value of the *one*-year index at the time of adjustment. Hence, the more frequent the adjustment interval, the lower the interest rate risk to lenders because *ARM* payments will reflect current market conditions, irrespective of the index chosen. Borrowers preferring no adjustment in payments will choose *FRM*s.

4. Regarding caps, to the extent *ARM*s contain maximum limitations on interest rate or payment adjustments, the interest rate risk incurred by borrowers will be lower. Hence, the expected yield realized by lenders should be higher than if no restrictions were present. The expected yield will vary with the size of the limitations. When floors are used, the risk to the borrower is greater because of the limit placed on the decline in interest rate used to compute *ARM* payments in any given year. For borrowers preferring certainty in payments and interest rates, they will choose an *FRM,* which will always have the highest *expected* yield to the lender.

5. Coincident with (4), if an *ARM* has a provision for negative amortization, then the effect of interest rate or payments caps will not materially reduce interest rate risk to borrowers or the expected yield to lenders, relative to *ARM*s with no caps or floors. This is because with negative amortization any interest forgone because of limitations or caps will be deferred and become a part of the loan balance. Any amounts of negative amortization will also accrue compound interest and must be eventually paid by borrowers.

6. If caps on payments and/or interest rates exist on an *ARM* and no negative amortization is permitted, borrowers assume less interest rate risk than would be the case if no caps existed. Hence, the expected yield to the lender should be greater on *ARM*s that do not allow negative amortization than on *ARM*s that do allow negative amortization.

7. Similarly, if a cap is placed on the amount of negative amortization on an *ARM,* the borrower is assuming less interest rate risk. In this event, the expected yield to the lender should be greater, depending on the probability that the cap will be exceeded.

Initial *ARM* Terms.   In the preceding section, we described some general relationships regarding *ARM* loan terms, risk bearing, and what lenders (borrowers) should expect to yield (pay) *over the life of the ARM contract, or repayment period*. We must point out, however, that lenders and borrowers also negotiate certain *initial* loan provisions that (1) will be known at the point of origination and (2) will affect expected yields. Once the index frequency of payment adjustments, rates of payments, and negative amortization have been negotiated, the magnitude of the effect on lenders and borrowers will be determined solely by future market conditions. However, the *initial terms* on *ARM*s, or the loan amount, maturity, initial interest rate, margin, and discount points, are quantifiable and can be negotiated with complete certainty at the time the loan is made. These initial loan terms will reflect the net effect of (1) amount of interest rate risk assumed by the lender as determined by the index chosen, adjustment period, any caps and/or negative amortization, and (2) the amount of default risk assumed by the lender as determined by the amount of interest rate risk shifted to a specific borrower. To illustrate, Exhibit 6–5 contains a summary of hypothetical loan terms being quoted on different *ARM*s and one *FRM*.

A careful review of these loans reveals considerable differences in terms. Looking to the exhibit, we note that the *initial* interest rate for *ARM* I is 8 percent, for *ARM* II it is

EXHIBIT 6–5 Comparison of Hypothetical Loan Terms

Contents	ARM I	ARM II	ARM III	FRM
(a) Initial interest rate	8%	9%	11%	14%
(b) Loan maturity	30	30	30	30
(c) Maturity of instruments making up index	1 year	1 year	1 year	—
(d) Percent margin above index	2%	2%	2%	—
(e) Adjustment interval	1 year	1 year	1 year	—
(f) Points	2%	2%	2%	2%
(g) Payment cap	None	7.5%	—	—
(h) Interest rate cap	None	None	2%, 5%*	—
(i) Negative amortization	—	Yes	None	—
(j) Negative amortization cap	—	Yes†	—	—

*2 percent maximum annual increase, 5 percent total increase over the loan term.
†Up to a maximum of 125 percent of the initial loan balance.

9 percent, and for *ARM* III it is 11 percent. We see that fixed interest rate mortgages are quoted at 14 percent. Why is this the case?

A quick review of terms for *ARM* I shows that it has the same terms (b)–(f) as *ARMs* II and III, however, characteristics (g)–(j) reveal that future payments and interest rates are *unrestricted* since there are no caps on payments or interest rates. These terms may now be compared to *ARM* II, which has a cap, or maximum increase in payments of 7.5 percent between any adjustment period plus a provision for negative amortization. *ARM* III has payment caps determined by an interest rate cap of 2 percent between adjustment periods and 5 percent over the life of the loan and no negative amortization. When all three *ARMs* are compared it is clear that the borrower is assuming more interest rate risk with *ARM* I than would be case with any of the other *ARMs* in the exhibit. Hence, the expected yield on *ARM* I to the lender should be *less*, when compared to other *ARMs*, for an otherwise qualified borrower (that is, a borrower with an acceptable level of default risk under all three ARM choices).

Because the *expected yield* should be *less* for *ARM* I, the *initial interest rate* will also generally be *lower* than each of the initial rates shown for the other *ARM* alternatives in Exhibit 6–5. Given that all *ARMs* in the exhibit are tied to the same index and have the same margin and discount points, the only way to "price" *ARM* I to achieve a lower expected yield is to *reduce* the initial interest rate relative to the other *ARMs*. *ARM* I should also have the largest discount, or spread, relative to the interest rate on the *FRM*. This would be expected because the borrower is bearing all interest rate risk; hence, the lender should expect to earn a lower risk premium and therefore a lower *yield* on *ARM* I when compared to the *FRM* (again, default risk is assumed to be acceptable for this borrower if ARM I is made).

It should be obvious that using a lower initial rate as an inducement to borrowers to accept more interest rate risk and unrestricted payments in the future is only one of many combinations of terms that may be used to differentiate *ARM* I from *ARMs* II and III and from the *FRM*. For example, the lender could keep the initial rate on *ARM* I the same as that offered on *ARM* II, but reduce the margin on *ARM* I or charge fewer discount points, or both. Other terms, such as the choice of index, payment adjustment intervals, and so on, could also be varied with these three terms to accomplish the same objectives.[11]

Moving to *ARM*s II and III in Exhibit 6–5, we note that both have initial interest rates that are greater than the initial rate on *ARM* I. The interest rate on *ARM* II is greater when compared to *ARM* I because *ARM* II has a cap on payments. Further, even though *ARM* II has provision for negative amortization, it is capped at 125 percent of the initial loan balance. The latter provision means that if the index rises high enough and the cap is exceeded, interest forgone will be added to the loan balance, up to the 125 percent limit. This cap serves to reduce interest rate risk to the borrower to some degree, as the lender would lose any interest beyond that allowed by the amortization cap. Hence, even though default risk may be lower in this case, *ARM* II should have a higher initial rate of interest than *ARM* I.

When *ARM* III is compared to *ARM*s I and II, the interest rate risk being assumed by the lender is clearly greater because payments are limited by interest rate caps and *no negative amortization is allowed*. In this case, should market interest rates rise, the interest rate cap would restrict interest payments and not allow the lender to recover any lost interest with negative amortization. Hence, when compared to *ARM*s I and II, *ARM* III provides that more interest rate risk will be borne by the lender. Hence, it should be originated at a higher initial rate of interest.

Important note should be taken of other possibilities in Exhibit 6–5. While we have chosen to concentrate on differences in payment and on negative amortization rate caps in our discussion thus far, it is important to realize that if other terms, such as the index and adjustment interval, were to be changed, we would also expect changes in the initial loan terms. For example, if in the case of *ARM* I, an index based on securities with longer maturities were to be chosen and/or payment intervals were longer than those shown, we would expect either, or all of, the initial rate, index, or points to *increase* because of lower interest rate risk to the borrower. This is because indexes tied to securities based on longer maturities are not as volatile as those based on shorter maturities. Obviously the same would be true for the other *ARM*s, if a longer-term index and payment interval were used. Indeed, the reader should now see that if such changes were made to the other *ARM*s, they would become *more* like an *FRM*. If longer-term indexes and lower caps were used on *ARM*s II and III, interest rate risk bearing would become greater for the lender; hence the expected yield earned by the lender should approach that of an *FRM* as of the date of origination.

Expected Interest Rate Adjustments—*ARM*s. While the preceding analysis aids us a great deal in understanding how initial *ARM* terms should be priced relative to *FRM*s

---

[11]From about 1980 until the present, there have been approximately 70 different *ARM* programs that have combined many of the features discussed here. While that number has diminished as *ARM*s become more standardized, there are more examples than we could include in a basic text. Hence, we treat this subject in a more general way, focusing on only the major *ARM* features.

and other *ARMs*, selecting *actual values* for the initial interest rate, points, and margin, such as those shown in Exhibit 6–5 is not that simple. For example, at the time of origination, when we select a set of *ARM* loan terms, how do we know whether the *expected yield* on an *ARM* will be greater or less than that on an *FRM?* Even though the initial rate on an *ARM* may be lower than that on an *FRM,* there is no certainty that the expected yield on the *ARM* will be lower than that of an *FRM,* because future rates of interest are unknown. However, there is additional, valuable information that we do know at the time an *ARM* is originated. This information is the *expected* pattern of future interest rates *at the time* the *ARM* is originated. This information is important and represents a reference point that may help lenders and borrowers when pricing *ARMs* and calculating *expected* yields *at the time ARMs are made.*

How can we obtain information concerning future interest rates? One answer to this question involves examining future interest rate expectations that are *implicit* in the yield curve. These implicit rates are referred to as *forward rates* and reveal investor expectations of interest rates between any two maturity periods on the yield curve. To illustrate, Exhibit 6–6 contains a *hypothetical* yield curve for U.S. government securities with maturities ranging from one to five years. The vertical axis shows yields available today if we purchased securities with maturities shown on the horizontal axis. We can see that the yield for a security maturing one year from now is 8 percent, and the yield for a security

EXHIBIT 6–6   Hypothetical Yield Curve for Riskless Securities with Various Maturities

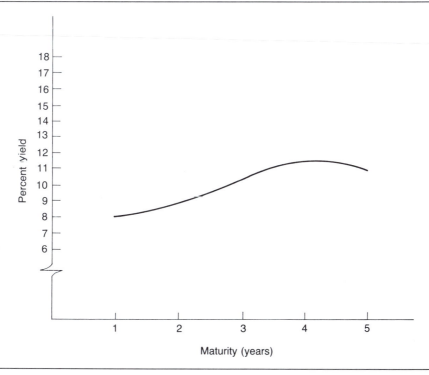

that matures two years from now is 9 percent. Based on these two yields, we can compute a forward rate, or rate that an investor who invests in a one-year security can expect to reinvest funds for one additional year. As we will see, this forward rate will be 10 percent because if investors have the opportunity to invest today in *either* the one- or the two-year security and are indifferent between the two choices, the investor buying a one-year security must be able to earn 10 percent on funds available for reinvestment at the end of year 1. If 10 percent could not be earned during the next years reinvestment, the investor would choose the two-year security today. This relationship can be easily shown for a $100 investment as follows: (1) For a two-year investment providing a yield (internal rate of return) of 9 percent, the future value at the end of two years would be

$$FV = \$100(FVIF,9\%,2 \text{ yrs.})$$
$$= \$100(1.09)^2$$
$$= \$118.81$$

(2) For a one-year investment providing a yield of 8 percent,

$$FV = \$100(FVIF,8\%,1 \text{ yr.})$$
$$= \$100(1.08)^1$$
$$= \$108$$

Therefore, for the investor in (2) to reinvest $108 at the end of year 1 and earn $118.81 at the end of year 2, a one-year investment yielding at least ($118.81 ÷ $108) − 1 = 10 percent must be available; otherwise the investor would be better off making the two-year investment today at 9 percent. In this case, the *expected* one-year *forward rate at the end of year 1* is 10 percent.

We should point out there are varying points of view on whether the procedure that we have followed here produces reasonable estimates of future interest rates. Assuming that the only determinant of this expected forward rate is the reinvestment rate required to equalize yields between maturity periods, we can use this as our best estimate of the interest rate on one-year obligations, one year from now. However, investors may not be indifferent between choosing two, one-year investments and one, two-year investment. If they demand a ''liquidity premium'' for the loss of the use of funds when purchasing a security with a two-year maturity, then the expected forward rate just referred to would be overstated by the amount of such a premium. Further, many financial economists assert that the market for securities with different maturities is a segmented one, based on the demand by investors who must match liabilities with specific maturities by investing in assets with the same maturities. If this is the case, the yield on securities would vary in relation to maturities preferred by investors at specific times. Hence, in a segmented market, using a security with a two-year maturity to predict interest rates one year from now may not be relevant. This is because the demand, and hence the yield, for securities with one-year maturities could change relative to securities with two-year maturities, and vice versa.[12]

---

[12]There are at least three schools of thought dealing with the determinants of the term structure of interest rates as exemplified in the yield curve. The expectations theory holds that expected forward rates can be estimated from the term structure as we have discussed it. The liquidity preference theory holds that investors

Continuing our analysis, assuming that the one-year forward rate *can* be estimated from the yield curve when an *ARM* is being originated, we ascertain the one-year forward rates at the end of years 1, 2, 3, and 4, by using the following procedure:

End of Year	Yields from Exhibit 6–6	Expected Forward Rate	Computed as:
1	8%	—	—
2	9	10	$(1.09)^2 \div (1.08)^1 - 1$
3	10.33	13	$(1.1033)^3 \div (1.09)^2 - 1$
4	11.48	15	$(1.1148)^4 \div (1.1033)^3 - 1$
5	11.18	10	$(1.11181)^5 \div (1.1148)^4 - 1$

This procedure is used to "extract" the series of one-year future rates at the end of each year that would be available for reinvestment and make an investor indifferent between making one-five year investment or rolling over a series of investments at the end of each year for five years. In both cases the total yield would be the same.

From the above computation of forward rates, if a given *ARM* has a *margin* of 2 percent, such as those indicated in Exhibit 6–5, our "best estimate" of what the forward *ARM* composite rate will be one year from now would be the estimated forward rate plus the 2 percent margin, or 12, 15, 17 and 12 percent as shown in Exhibit 6–7. Even though the structure of interest rates may change immediately after making an *ARM* loan, if the expectations theory is a reasonable one, it should generally be the case that *on the date of origination*, the expected yield on an *ARM* based on these forward rates, should be *less* than the rate available on an *FRM*. If the expected yield on an *ARM* is greater than that on an *FRM* on the date of origination, the borrower would have little incentive to make an *ARM*.

ARM Payment Mechanics

To illustrate how payment adjustments and loan balances are determined over the term for the *ARMs* in Exhibit 6–5, we consider the following example. The loan amount is

---

demand a premium for the loss of liquidity and that premium increases with the maturity period being purchased. Hence, all or part of the differences between yields by maturity period may be attributable to this premium. According to this school, premiums for loss of liquidity would be larger for securities with longer maturities. However, the size of the premium would vary from time to time, depending on the opportunity cost of liquidity loss. The last explanation of the term structure is the market segmentation theory, which asserts that each maturity class is subject to the demand by investors desiring a specified asset to match a liability with a specific maturity. In this sense, many investors need short-term securities because they have funds to invest temporarily, while others have funds available for long-term investment only. This is because capital investments and liabilities that firms must pay, require cash outlays at specific times. Because the demand for short-term and long-term securities can change, using the present distribution of interest rates from the yield curve to predict forward rates may be very inaccurate. This latter point of view has been highly criticized, however, because it tends to ignore the use of hedging, arbitrage, and other operations which tend to integrate, rather than segment, financial markets. For a good review of these ideas and criticisms of each, see William F. Sharpe, *Investments*, 3rd ed. (Englewood Cliffs, N.J.: Prentice-Hall, 1985).

EXHIBIT 6-7   Summary Data and Results: *ARM* I (unrestricted case)

(1)	(2)		(3)		(4)	(5)	(6)	(7)
					Interest		*Percent Change*	
Year	*Index*	+	*Margin*	=	*Rate*	*Payments*	*in Payments*	*Balance†*
1					8%*	$440.28		$59,502
2	10%		2%		12	614.30	+39.5	59,260
3	13		2		15	752.27	+22.5	59,106
4	15		2		17	846.21	+12.5	58,990
5	10		2		12	617.60	−27.0	58,639

*Initial rate.
†Rounded.

$60,000 and the term is 30 years. We assume that the *ARM* interest rate will be adjusted annually. Hence, the first adjustment will occur at the beginning of the second year. At that time, the composite rate on the loan will be determined by the index of one-year U.S. Treasury securities, *plus* a 2 percent margin. If we *assume* (1) that, based on forward rates in existence at the time each *ARM* is originated, the index of one-year Treasury securities takes on a pattern of 10, 13, 15, and 10 percent for the *next* four years and (2) that monthly payment and interest rate adjustments are made annually, what would payment adjustments, loan balances, and expected yields be for an *ARM* with these assumed characteristics?

No Caps or Limitations on Payments or Interest Rates.   The first case we want to consider is *ARM* I, where payments are unrestricted or allowed to move up or down with the index without limit. What would be the payment pattern on such an *ARM* given that the expected distribution of future interest rates actually occurred? This unrestricted case, where no limitations apply to payments or interest, is straightforward to deal with.

The first four columns of Exhibit 6-7 contain the data needed for our computations. Note that we *assume* that the initial interest rate is quoted to be 8 percent for the first year, but after the first year the index *plus* the 2 percent margin establish what the payment will be. Hence, as indicated in the preceding section, from the beginning of year 2 through the beginning of year 5 the interest rates that will be used to determine payments are 12, 15, 17, and 12, respectively, based on our assumptions. *As previously pointed out, ARMs tied to the same index may vary with respect to the initial rate of interest, the margin, and, perhaps, discount points offered by lenders.* As we have discussed, these latter components are usually set by competitive conditions in the lending area and are the primary variables (along with caps or other restrictions) with which lenders compete when pricing loans. This is because lenders have no control over the index and, therefore, *must rely on other components to compete with when pricing the loan.*

The payments column of Exhibit 6-7 is based on a series of relatively simple computations. They are carried out as though at the end of each year a new loan is originated based on a new rate of interest, as determined by the index plus the margin, applied to the outstanding loan balance. For example, the initial mortgage payment (*MP*) is determined as

$$MP = \$60,000(MLC, 8\%, 360 \text{ mos.})$$
$$= \$60,000(.007338)$$
$$= \$440.28$$

The mortgage balance (*MB*) at the end of the first year will be

$$MB_1 = \$440.28(MPVIFA, 8\%, 348 \text{ mos.})$$
$$= \$440.28 \ (135.145031) \text{ (rounded)}$$
$$= \$59,502$$

At the beginning of year 2, payments would be computed based on a new interest rate of 12 percent for the remaining loan term of 348 months. Hence, the new payment would be

$$MP_2 = \$59,502(MLC, 12\%, 348 \text{ mos.})$$
$$= \$614.30$$

The mortgage loan balance at the end of the second year would be

$$MB_2 = \$614.30 \ (MPVIFA, 12\%, 336 \text{ mos.})$$
$$= \$614.30(96.468019)$$
$$= \$59,260$$

This process of (1) computing the loan balance, based on the interest rate applicable during the year for which the balance is desired, and (2) computing the new payment, based on any change in the index at the end of the appropriate adjustment interval, would continue after each adjustment interval over the remaining life of the loan.

Looking again to Exhibit 6–7, we carry out the computations using the hypothetical interest rate pattern. Assuming no restrictions or caps on interest rates or payments, we see considerable variation in the payment pattern. Payments increase by as much as 39.5 percent and decline by as much as 27 percent during the first five years. For borrowers who have a strong aversion to interest rate risk and the coincident variability in payments, the unrestricted *ARM,* tied to a short-term instrument, may not be desirable. One final pattern should be noted in Exhibit 6–7; that is, regardless of the interest rate pattern chosen, the loan is amortizing. The rate of amortization will differ, however, depending on the rate of interest in effect at each adjustment interval.

The default risk associated with *ARM* I should also be clear from Exhibit 6–7. Note that although the initial payment level is low, the variation in payments over the five-year period is great. Clearly, for a borrower to take this risk, future income or present and future wealth must be viewed by the lender to be sufficient enough to cover significant changes in monthly payments.

Payment Caps and Negative Amortization.   We now consider *ARM* II where the lender and borrower have agreed that to moderate possible interest rate fluctuations in the future there will be a cap, or maximum rate, of 7.5 percent at which *payments* can increase between adjustment intervals. In this case, however, any difference between payments and interest that should be earned, based on unrestricted changes in interest rates, will be *added* to the loan balance. As previously discussed, this type of *ARM* contains a payment cap and *negative amortization*. Negative amortization will be allowed until subsequent loan balances reach 125 percent of the initial loan balance, at that point payments will be allowed to increase in excess of 7.5 percent.

Because this *ARM* allows for a payment cap and negative amortization, the receipt of more cash flow is pushed further into the future than in the unrestricted case. Therefore, interest rate risk to the lender is somewhat greater than with *ARM* I, so we assume that the initial rate on the mortgage is quoted to be 9 percent while the margin will remain at 2 percent. Exhibit 6–8 contains computations of the payment and loan balance patterns for the *ARM* just described. As indicated, we assume that 7.5 percent is the maximum rate at which payments can increase each year. As shown in the exhibit, based on an unrestricted change in our hypothetical pattern of interest rates, monthly payments in the second year would be $615.18, or 27.4 percent higher than the $482.77 payment required during the first year. A payment of $615.18 would obviously be greater than the 7.5 percent maximum allowable increase; hence the payment would be capped at $518.98, or 7.5 percent more than $482.77. However, because this *ARM* requires negative amortization, the difference between interest charged during year 2, or 12 percent, and the amount actually *paid* will be added to the outstanding loan balance plus *compound interest*.

EXHIBIT 6–8 Determination of Payment Limits (negative amortization: *ARM* II, with payment cap = 7.5 percent annually)

(1) Beginning of Year	*(2)* Balance (rounded)	*(3)* Uncapped Payment	Percent Change in Payments	*(4)* Payment Capped at 7.5 percent
1	$60,000	$482.77		$482.77
2	59,590	615.18	+27.4	518.98
3	60,566	768.91	+48.2	557.90
4	63,128	903.79	+62.0	599.74
5	66,952	700.96	+16.8	644.72

(5) Monthly Interest Rate	*(6)* Monthly Interest (5) × (2)	*(7)* Monthly Amortization (4)–(6)	*(8)* Annual Amortization (7) × MFVIFA in (5)
.09 ÷ 12	$450.00	$32.77	$ 409.87
.12 ÷ 12	595.90	(76.92)	(975.54)
.15 ÷ 12	757.08	(199.18)	(2,561.53)
.17 ÷ 12	894.31	(294.57)	(3,823.69)
.12 ÷ 12	669.52	(24.80)	(314.53)

Negative amortization is computed by using the method shown for the *GPM* in the previous chapter. Exhibit 6–8 contains a breakdown of interest and amortization for *ARM* II. Note in the exhibit that during the first year when loan payments are computed at 9 percent interest, monthly amortization occurs and the loan balance is reduced. After the first year, monthly payments must be computed *first* based on the unrestricted interest rate (col. 3) to determine whether payments will increase at a rate greater than 7.5 percent. If uncapped payments would exceed 7.5 percent, then the payment cap (col. 4) becomes operative and actual payments will be restricted to a 7.5 percent increase. The monthly *interest* that is accruing on the loan balance at the unrestricted rate is $(.12 \div 12)\$59,590 = \$595.90$ (col. 6). However, the payment that will actually be made is \$518.98. The difference, \$76.92 (col. 7), must be *added* to the loan balance *with compound interest*. Hence as shown in the exhibit, the difference in year 2, \$76.92 per month, is compounded at 12 percent per month (col. 8) resulting *in an increase* of \$975.54 in the loan balance.[13]

Payments in the third year of the *ARM* are determined by again establishing whether uncapped payments would increase by more than 7.5 percent. To determine this, we find that the loan balance, which includes the previous year's negative amortization, is \$59,590 + \$975.54 = \$60,566 (rounded). The *unrestricted* interest rate of 15 percent for the remaining 336 months is used to compute the uncapped payment. Uncapped payments based on the unrestricted rate of 15 percent would be \$768.91. This is a 48 percent increase from \$518.98; hence the payment will again be capped at a 7.5 percent increase, and negative amortization will be computed on the interest shortfall, compounded at 15 percent monthly, and added to the loan balance. This process is repeated for each adjustment interval over the life of the loan.[14] Actual loan balances with payments capped at 7.5 percent are shown in Exhibit 6–9.

Another observation regarding *ARM* II that can be seen in Exhibit 6–8 has to do with the fact that in year 5 an increase in both the payment *and* loan balance occur, even though there is a significant decline in the interest index from 17 to 12 percent. This occurs because the loan balance has increased, due to past negative amortization, to \$66,952 at the end of year 4. Even though the interest rate declines to 12 percent, monthly interest will be \$669.52, which is in excess of the maximum 7.5 percent increase from the \$599.74 payment in the preceding year. Hence, payments would increase by 7.5 percent, even though interest rates have declined.[15]

---

[13]It would be possible, however, to moderate fluctuations in monthly payments to some degree by extending the loan maturity. This could be done by simply substituting the desired maturity at any adjustment interval and computing payments based on the prevailing index and the new maturity desired. If the maturity was extended, it would reduce monthly payments somewhat, thereby moderating fluctuations in monthly payments.

[14]Many *ARMs* with negative amortization provisions limit increases in the loan balance to 25 percent over the initial loan balance during the life of the loan. Lenders and borrowers must agree that if that maximum is reached, the lender must either forgo further accumulation of interest in the loan balance or require that monthly payments be increased at that time. We should also point out that when *payment caps* are used on an *ARM*, negative amortization is usually always required by the lender. In cases where negative amortization is not required, the lender and borrower must agree how future amortization will occur during periods when payment caps are binding. Because this is very awkward to do, negative amortization is usually always required.

[15]Needless to say, this point may be difficult for an unsophisticated borrower to understand.

EXHIBIT 6–9 *ARM* II: Loan Balances When Payments Are Capped at 7.5 Percent Annually (negative amortization allowed)

Year	Index	Margin	Interest Rate	Payments	Percent Change in Payments	Loan Balances	Percent Change in Balance†
1			9%*	$482.77			
2	10%	2%	12	518.98	+7.5	$60,566	+ .6
3	13	2	15	557.90	+7.5	63,128	+4.2
4	15	2	17	599.74	+7.5	66,952	+6.1
5	10	2	12	644.72	+7.5	67,267	+ .5

*Origination rate.
†Rounded.

Interest Rate Caps. The final case that we consider with *ARM*s is a common pattern in which interest rates are capped or limited. We consider one case, *ARM* III, where the increase in interest rates is limited to 2 percent during any one adjustment interval (year in our example) and to a *total* of 5 percent over the life of the loan. If interest rates ever exceed these caps, payments are limited. Hence, the interest rate cap really acts as a payment cap because the maximum increase in interest rate determines the maximum increase in mortgage payments. If interest rate caps are exceeded we assume that *no* negative amortization will be allowed. Lenders will take this added risk of loss. This means that if the index plus the margin exceeds these caps, the lender will lose any amount of interest above the capped rates.[16] To illustrate the payment mechanics of *ARM* III, it can be seen from Exhibit 6–10 that the interest rate quoted at origination, 11 percent, is higher than was the case with *ARM*s I and II. This is because the latter two *ARM*s were unrestricted with respect to the interest rate while *ARM* III has interest rate caps. Therefore the lender is taking more *interest rate risk* with *ARM* III because of the possibility that the cap will be exceeded and interest will be lost. To compensate for this possibility, the lender will charge a higher initial interest rate and should expect to earn a higher expected yield.

The payment patterns shown in Exhibit 6–10 are determined from the loan balance established at the end of each adjustment interval. Payments are then computed based on the indicated rate of interest for the remaining term. Results of computations shown in Exhibit 6–10 show that, compared with *ARM* I (the unrestricted case), payments on *ARM* III are higher initially, then remain generally lower than payments on *ARM* I for the remaining term. Hence, borrowers would have to have more income to qualify for *ARM* III, and default risk to the lender should be lower. The loan balances for both *ARM*s are

---

[16]In many cases, *ARM*s may contain floors as well as a cap. In our example this would mean that a maximum reduction of 2 percent in the mortgage rate would be allowed, regardless of the decline in the index. These floors have limited effectiveness, however, because if a significant decline in the index occurred, borrowers may refinance with a new mortgage loan.

EXHIBIT 6–10   Summary Data and Results: *ARM* III Interest Rates Capped at 2 percent, 5 percent (no negative amortization allowed)

Year	Index + Margin	Capped Interest Rate	Payments	Percent Change in Payments	Balance
1		11%	$571.39		$59,730
2	12%	12	616.63	+7.9	59,485
3	15	14	708.37	+14.9	59,301
4	17	16	801.65	+13.2	59,159
5	12	12	619.37	−22.7	58,807

about the same in year 5. When *ARM* III payments are compared with those of *ARM* II, *ARM* III payments begin at a higher level (because of the higher initial rate of interest) and remain higher over the term of the loan. However, because of negative amortization, loan balances over time for *ARM* II are significantly higher than for *ARM* III.

Expected Yields on *ARMs*—A Comparison

In the preceding sections we examined three kinds of *ARMs* with provisions commonly used in real estate lending. Other considerations are also important to lenders and borrowers. One important issue is the *yield* to lenders, or *cost* to borrowers, for each category of loan. Given the changes in interest rates, payments, and loan balances, it is not obvious what these yields (costs) will be.

Computing Yields on *ARMs*.   To compare yields on *ARMs*, the yield (cost) to the lender (borrower) must be computed for each alternative. This is done by solving for the internal rate of return, or the rate of discount, that makes the present value of all expected mortgage payments and the loan balance in the year of repayment equal to the initial loan amount less discount points (or $58,800) for each alternative. To illustrate, consider the case of the *unrestricted ARM* I which is paid off in year 5. To compute the internal rate of return in that example, we use data from Exhibit 6–7 and compute the yield as shown in Exhibit 6–11.

From the computations shown in Exhibit 6–11, we see that the solution is approximately 13.0 percent.[17] This means that even though the *initial* rate of interest was 9 percent and the forward rates of interest are expected to range from 9 to 17 percent over the five-year period, the *expected* yield (cost) is 13.0 percent. Hence by computing the internal rate of return, which means the same thing as the yield, we have a result which can be compared among alternative *ARMs*.

[17]Using a financial calculator yields a solution of 13.0 percent. We will rely on this result in our discussion.

EXHIBIT 6–11   Computing the *IRR* Unrestricted *ARM*, Payoff at End of Year 5

(1)	*(2)*	*(3)*	*(4)*	*(5)*
	Monthly	*MPVIFA,*	*MPVIF,*	
Year	*Payments*	*13 Percent, 12 Months*	*13 Percent, Years 1–5*	*PV*
1	$ 440.28	× 11.196042	× —	= 4,929.39
2	614.30	× 11.196042	× .878710	= 6,043.53
3	752.27	× 11.196042	× .772130	= 6,503.22
4	846.21	× 11.196042	× .678478	= 6,428.04
5	617.60	× 11.196042	× .596185	= 4,122.43
5	$58,639.00	× —	× .523874	= 30,719.45
				$58,746.06*

*Desired *PV* = $58,800; *IRR* approximately 13 percent.

Before comparing results for each *ARM* considered, we examine the computational procedure used in Exhibit 6–11. Essentially, we are discounting a series of grouped cash flows. In the present case we are dealing with five groups of monthly cash flows *and* a single receipt (the loan balance). Note in the exhibit that we discount each group of monthly cash flows by using the present value of a monthly annuity factor of 13 percent (column 3). However, this procedure gives us a present value for a *one-year group* of 12 monthly payments and does not take into account the fact that the cash flows occurring from the second through fifth years are not received during the first year. Hence, each of the grouped cash flows must be discounted again by the present value of $1 factor to recognize that the present value of each group of cash flows is not received at the same time. This is carried out in column 4. The loan balance, or $58,639, is then discounted as a lump sum, as has been shown many times in previous chapters.

The process of finding the yield (cost) for each *ARM* has been carried out and is summarized in Exhibit 6–12. Yields were also computed and are detailed for each *ARM* as though repayment occurred at the end of *each* of years 1 through 5. This was done in the same way as illustrated in Exhibit 6–11 assuming repayment at the end of *each* year. This summary shows what we would expect given the nature or risk bearing shared between lender and borrower. For *ARM* I, which represents the case where the borrower takes most of the interest rate risk, the yield to the lender is lowest (13 percent).

The expected yield is higher for *ARM* II than for *ARM* I because interest rate risk taken by the lender is slightly higher with *ARM* I, due to the caps on payments and negative amortization. The expected yield to the lender then is 13.3 percent. Note that this is very close to the yield for *ARM* I even though *ARM* II required payment caps and had a higher initial rate of interest. The reason for this is that, with negative amortization, all interest not received currently is compounded at the current rate of interest and added to the loan balance. The outstanding loan balance then earns the market rate of interest in each successive period. Hence, even though the full amount of cash interest payments is not received when earned, as is the case with the unrestricted *ARM,* all payments not received currently earn interest and are eventually received over the remaining term of the loan,

EXHIBIT 6–12   Expected Yields (*IRR*) on *ARMs* on Origination Date, Given Forward Rates Implicit in Yield Curve and Mortgage Terms from Exhibit 6–2

Case	Loan Type	Interest Rate	Repayment in Year				
			1	2	3	4	5
ARM I	Unrestricted "no caps"	8.0	10.1	11.0	12.2	13.1	13.0
ARM II	Payment cap, with negative amortization	9.0	11.1	11.5	12.6	13.5	3.3
ARM III	Interest rate cap, no negative amortization	11.0	13.2	12.6	13.0	13.6	13.4
FRM	Fixed interest rate, constant payment	14.0	16.2	15.2	14.8	14.7	14.6

or in the loan balance, if the loan is prepaid. Finally, results in Exhibit 6–12 show that of the *ARMs* used in our example, *ARM* III provided the lender highest expected yield. This is because of the interest rate cap and no provision for negative amortization, which increases interest rate risk to the lender. The initial rate of 11 percent was higher than the other three *ARMs*, and, based on the forward rate projections, an expected yield of 13.4 percent resulted.

When all *ARM* yields are compared to the expected yield on the *FRM* (14.6 percent with discount points), the reader can get an idea of how *ARMs* are priced relative to *FRMs*. All *ARMs* indicate that a lower expected yield will be earned by the lender, which is constant, with ARM borrowers bearing more interest rate risk than FRM borrowers.

Concluding Observations: *ARMs*, Borrower, Lender, and Market Behavior.   From the results in Exhibit 6–12 we can see that there is a consistency between the expected yield (cost) to the lender (borrower) and the amount of risk that borrowers and lenders are sharing. We can attribute the differences in these yields to differences in the initial loan terms shown in Exhibit 6–5. Differences in those terms are the *primary reason* why the yields resulted as they did. Recall that in our discussion of those terms, we adjusted the *initial interest rates* in our examples based on the interest rate risk and default risk inherent in each *ARM*. In reality, *competition* between lenders in the marketplace will determine the spread in the initial interest rate, margin, and points for each *ARM* and relative to *FRMs*. Recalling the graphic analysis of the risk premium and the relationship between interest rate and default risk in Exhibit 6–4, we now show how risk premiums demanded for *ARMs* I–III would fall on the total risk curve in Exhibit 6–13. This diagram basically indicates that moving from *ARM* I–III, interest rate risk to the lender increases. However, based on Panel B in Exhibit 6–4 we should recall that as interest rate risk increases to the lender, default risk for a specific borrower due to interest rate changes declines. Following the market rule that benefits to the lender from shifting interest rate risk to the borrower *must exceed* expected default risk in order for the *ARM* to be originated, we see in Exhibit 6–13 that the total risk premium, and hence the expected yield to the

EXHIBIT 6–13   Ranking *ARMs* Based on Total Risk

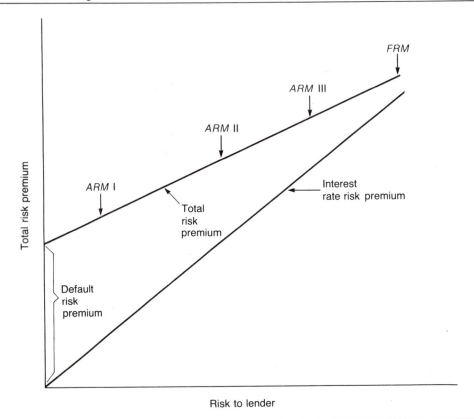

lender, increases as we move from *ARM* I to *ARM* III. All expected *ARM* yields remain below that of the *FRM,* as should also be the case.

We also know that, in general, the initial interest rate and expected yield for all *ARMs* should be lower than that of an *FRM* on the day of origination. The extent to which the initial rate and expected yield on an *ARM* will be lower than that on an *FRM*, or another *ARM*, is dependent on the terms relative to payments, caps, etc. Terms that are more unrestricted and shift more interest rate risk to the borrower will generally have initial interest rates that are discounted farthest from *FRMs*. They will also be discounted from *ARMs* containing caps on payment and interest rate increases. Hence, when a borrower is faced with selecting from a given set of *ARMs* with different terms and expectations of forward interest rates, an expected yield must be calculated before a comparison among *ARMs* and an *FRM* can be accomplished. While there is no guarantee that the *expected* yield calculated at origination will be the *actual* yield or cost of funds over the term of the *ARM,* the expected yield represents the *best estimate* of the cost of an *ARM based on information available at the time of origination.*

One of the major concerns of borrowers and lenders is the possibility of a shift in the level and distribution of forward interest rates implicit in the yield curve *after an ARM is originated*. The combination of *ARM* terms selected at the time of origination affects not only the *initial* terms and expected yields at the time of origination but also the degree of risk *after* the loan is made. While we have shown how *ARM* pricing may be carried out, given the information available at the origination date, as we have stated previously it is only our "best guess" at the time of origination and helps us to ascertain (1) whether the expected yield on an *ARM* is less than that on an *FRM,* and (2) whether expected yields on *ARM*s which require the borrower to take *more risk* (through the structure of loans to *ARM*s) have lower expected yields than *ARM*s that do not. In summary, there will always be some borrowers preferring *FRM*s and some preferring *ARM*s, based on their relative assessment of the future and their aversion to interest rate risk.

After making *ARM*s, borrowers should always monitor the current rate of interest that they are paying relative to rates available on *FRM*s and assess their expectations of future interest rates. Because current federal regulations presently require lenders to give borrowers the option to repay *ARM*s with no penalty, many borrowers may change from *ARM*s to *FRM*s or opt to change from one type of *ARM* to another over time. This option clearly increases choices that borrowers and lenders can make through time, which in turn makes for more options available in the mortgage market and more benefits to society at large.

SHARED APPRECIATION MORTGAGES

The final type of mortgage that we will consider in this chapter is one which is referred to as the shared appreciation mortgage (*SAM*). This mortgage design is also intended to deal with the problem of uncertain future inflation. It is similar in some ways to the *PLAM* considered earlier in this chapter in that it has a lower contract interest rate that is then adjusted for inflation. However, the nature of the adjustment is quite different. Recall that the *PLAM* had the loan balance adjusted periodically based on the change in a price level index. With the *SAM* the lender receives an agreed upon percentage of the appreciation in the value of the home used as collateral for the loan.

To illustrate this loan, we return to our example of $60,000 loan first introduced in the previous chapter. When we considered this loan as a *CPM,* we assumed it had a 12 percent interest rate with a 30-year loan term. Let us assume the same lender is willing to make a *SAM* at a 9 percent contract rate with the lender receiving one third of any appreciation in the value of the home. (The lender will not share in any depreciation, however.) The loan will be amortized over 30 years, but the payment to the lender for price appreciation is due either at the end of 10 years or whenever the home is sold, if it is sold before the 10 years are up. If the home is not sold by the end of the 10 years, an appraisal is made to determine what amount is due to the lender.

Payments on the loan based on the 9 percent contract rate will be $482.77 per month. Recall that the payment based on the 12 percent market rate was $617.17. We will assume that the home is currently worth $90,000 and that it is expected to increase at the inflation rate of 6 percent per year. After 10 years the home will be worth $90,000(1.06)^{10} = $161,176$. Thus the appreciation is $161,176 - $90,000 = $71,176$, and the lender will receive one third of this, or $23,725. In addition, the lender will receive the loan balance based on the initial 9 percent, 30-year terms of $53,657.

One of the first things we should consider when analyzing this loan is what the effective yield will be, based on the payments and price appreciation assumed above. This is a relatively simple calculation. The payment stream will consist of annual payments and the sum of the loan balance at the end of the 10 years plus the amount of appreciation paid to the lender at the end of the 10 years. We want to find the discount rate that equates these payments with the $60,000 loan amount. We have

$$\$60,000 = \$482.77(MPVIFA, ?\%, 10 \text{ yrs.}) + \$77,382(MPVIF, ?\%, 10 \text{ yrs.})$$

Using a financial calculator, we find the yield to be 11.24 percent, which is slightly higher than the fixed rate *CPM*. The actual yield will depend on what the actual appreciation in the home is over the 10-year period and, thus, could be greater or less than 11.24 percent.

Like the *PLAM*, the *SAM* begins with payments based on a lower interest rate. With the *PLAM*, the payments are adjusted after the first year, however, based on inflation for the previous year. With the *SAM* the payments remain the same. The adjustment for inflation is made all at once at a preagreed future time, 10 years in our example. The inflation premium is usually paid by the borrower from the sale of the home or from funds obtained by refinancing. Thus the borrower is not faced with continually increasing mortgage payments as in the case of the *PLAM*. The adjustment is also based on the inflation rate for the home rather than a more general inflation index which may not correlate with the increase in value of the home.

From the foregoing discussion it is clear that the *SAM* provides an alternative way for the lender to be compensated for increases in inflation and thus transfers much of the risk of price level increases to the borrower. The *SAM* has not been used extensively by borrowers and lenders, for several possible reasons. First, lenders may prefer not to wait years before receiving compensation for price level increases. Second, while borrowers may like the idea of the inflation adjustment depending only on the increase in the value of the home rather than on a more general price index, lenders may be concerned with how well a particular house will keep up with inflation. Clearly, there are many factors in addition to inflation that affect the future value of a house. Third, the amount of appreciation in the value of the home depends on actions by borrowers after the loan is closed, such as how well the property is maintained. Borrowers may have less incentive to maintain homes because the lender shares in any increase in house value as a result of the maintenance. Fourth, until recently, it was not clear whether the appreciation paid to a lender would be considered ''contingent'' interest or a reduction in the capital gain from the sale of the home. This is important for tax purposes. It has recently been ruled that appreciation is contingent interest and is therefore deductible against ordinary income. This is more attractive than if it only reduced capital gains, which are taxed at a lower effective rate.

QUESTIONS

1. In the previous chapter, significant problems regarding the ability of borrowers to meet mortgage payments and the evolution of fixed interest rate mortgages with

various payment patterns were discussed. Why didn't this evolution address problems faced by lenders? What have lenders done in recent years to overcome these problems?

2. What is meant by the "spread" and "maturity gap" problems faced by savings institutions who supply much of the funds made available for mortgage loans?

3. How do inflationary expectations influence interest rates on mortgage loans?

4. How does the *PLAM* address the problem of uncertainty in inflationary expectations? What are some of the practical limitations in implementing a *PLAM* program?

5. Why do *ARM*s seem to be a more suitable alternative for mortgage lending than *PLAM*s?

6. List each of the main terms likely to be negotiated in an *ARM*. What does pricing an *ARM* using these terms mean?

7. What is the difference between interest rate risk and default risk? How do combinations of terms in *ARM*s affect the allocation of risk between borrowers and lenders?

8. Which of the following two *ARM*s is likely to be priced higher (that is, offered with a higher initial interest rate)? *ARM* A has a margin of 3 percent, and is tied to a three-year index with payments adjustable every two years, payments cannot increase by more than 10 percent from the preceding period, no negative amortization is allowed, the term is 30 years, and no assumption or points will be allowed. *ARM* B has a margin of 3 percent, is tied to a one-year index with payments to be adjusted each year, payments cannot increase by more than 10 percent from the preceding period, negative amortization is allowed, the term is 30 years, no assumption or points are allowed.

9. What are forward rates of interest? How are they determined? What do they have to do with indexes used to adjust *ARM* payments?

10. How do *ARM*s help lenders with their gap management problem? What would be a strategy that lenders would like to use in structuring *ARM* terms with deposit liabilities?

11. Distinguish between the initial rate of interest and yield on an *ARM*? What is the general relationship between the two? How do they generally reflect *ARM* terms?

12. If an *ARM* is priced with an initial interest rate of 8 percent and a margin of 2 percent (when the *ARM* index is also 8 percent at origination) and an *FRM* (constant payment) is available at 11 percent, what does this imply about inflation and the forward rates in the yield curve at the time of origination? What is implied if an *FRM* were available at 10 percent? 12 percent?

13. What is a *SAM*? Contrast it with a *PLAM* and an *ARM*.

PROBLEMS

1. A price level adjusted mortgage (*PLAM*) is made with the following terms: amount = $80,000, initial interest rate-3 percent, term-30 years, points = 2 percent and payments are to be adjusted at the beginning of each year. Assuming inflation is expected to increase at the rate of 6 percent per year for the next five years:

   a. Compute the payments at the beginning of each year.

   b. What would the loan balance be at the end of the fifth year?

   c. What would be the yield to the lender on such a mortgage?

2. An adjustable rate mortgage (*ARM*) is made for $100,000 with the following terms:

Initial interest rate = 9 percent	Term = 25 years
Index = 1-year Treasury	Payment cap = none
securities	Interest rate cap = none
Payment adjusted each year	Negative amortz. = none
Margin = 2 percent	Discount points = 2 percent

Based on estimated forward rates computed from the yield curve on U.S. Treasury bills, the index to which the *ARM* is tied is forecasted to be as follows: end of year (*EOY*) 1 = 10 percent, *EOY* 2 = 9 percent, *EOY* 3 = 12 percent, *EOY* 4 = 13 percent.

a. Compute the payments, loan balances, and yield for an unrestricted *ARM* for the five-year period.

b. Assuming that payment increases are capped at 7.5 percent per year and negative amortization is allowed, recompute the requirements in (a).

c. Assume conditions in part (b), however the 7.5 percent payment adjustments will only be allowed beginning in year 2, then at the beginning of year 4. Recompute the requirements in (a). Are results different from (b)? Why or why not?

d. Assume that the *ARM* provides for a 2 percent annual cap and a cap of 5 percent over the life, and that negative amortization is allowed. What would the payments, balance, and expected yield be for the five-year period now?

e. Given assumptions in (d) assume that negative amortization is *not* allowed. What would the expected yield be now? Is it different from your answer in (d)? If so, why?

f. Based on the fact that each *ARM* in (a–e) was assumed to be "priced" at the same initial interest rate (for simplicity), yield results will not be consistent with risk bearing by lenders and borrowers. Why is this so? Prepare a ranking based on an initial interest rate for each *ARM* category (a–e) that would *better reflect* the allocation of risk between the borrower and lender (numerical estimates are not necessary, simply rank each category a–e with the lowest to highest initial interest rate).

3. An *ARM* for $120,000 with the following terms is made:

Initial interest rate = 6 percent	Payment cap = none
Index = 1-year treasuries	Interest rate cap = none
Margin = 2.75 percent	Negative amortz. = none
Term = 25 years	Discount points = 2 percent

The index is expected to change during each of the next *six-month* intervals as follows: 9, 11, 14, 15, 13 percent. Compute payments, balances, and yields for *each* of the following *ARMs*, assuming the loan is repaid after three years:

a. The payment adjustment interval is (a) six months, (b) one year, (c) two years. Is it likely that each of these *ARMs* would be priced at the same initial interest rate? If not, what would be a more realistic ranking for these *ARMs* (initial interest rate only)?

b. Assuming that an interest rate cap of 2 percent per year and 5 percent over the life of the *ARM* are the maximum increases allowed for *each* mortgage, what would payments, balances, and yields be now? What would be a more realistic pricing structure for each of the payment intervals (consider ranking initial interest rates only, do not rework problems)?

4. A lender is trying to "price" an *ARM* by substituting various loan terms. He has three variables to work with: (1) the initial interest rate, (2) the margin, and (3) points. The loan will be made for $100,000 for 30 years, and the interest rate will be tied to a one-year index. Payment adjustments will be made annually, with no limit on payment or interest rate increases. The interest rate index is expected to be 9, 10, 12 percent at the end of years 1, 2, and 3, and the loan will be originated at 10 percent with a margin of 2 percent and origination fees of 2 percent.

   a. What would be the expected yield on this *ARM* after four years?
   b. What if, in (a), the initial rate was 10 percent and the margin was reduced to 1 percent. What would the origination fee/points have to be in order to realize the same yield?
   c. Given your answer in (a) and given the expected index pattern, the lender would like you to "reprice" (select an initial interest rate to achieve same yield in (a) by increasing the origination fee to 3 percent and increasing the margin to 3 percent). (Optional problem available only to students with access to a computer.)

5. A *SAM* is made for $80,000 at an initial rate of 10 percent for 30 years. The lender will have a 20 percent share in any increase in the value of the property over the next five years. The property value is expected to increase a total of 30 percent over its initial value of $100,000.

   a. What would be the lender's yield, assuming that the property is sold after five years?
   b. Assuming that the lender desires a 12 percent yield over the next five years, at what rate would the property have to appreciate to provide this desired yield?

6. You are trying to estimate forward rates of interest that may be used in estimating an expected *ARM* yield. You consult the financial page of the newspaper and find that yields on U.S. Treasury obligations are as follows: one-year maturities = 7 percent, two-year maturities = 8 percent, three year = 9 percent, four year = 10 percent. What would one-year forward rates be, given this yield structure? Assume the structure is 7, 7.5, 8, and 8.5 percent. What would forward rates be now? Comparing the two structures, what does this imply for expected *ARM*s yields, assuming the same margin would be used on each *ARM*?

   Now assume that the Treasury yield pattern is 12, 11, 10, and 9 percent. How would *ARM* yields compare to each of the two patterns assumed above? How would *ARM* yields compare to *FRM* yields given this structure? How would initial rates of interest on *ARM*s compare with interest rates on *FRM*s under this pattern? (Discuss the last two questions; no further computations are needed.)

Chapter 7

Underwriting and Financing Residential Properties

This chapter deals with the process of seeking long-term mortgage financing for owner-occupied residential properties. Here we focus on two aspects of this process: loan *underwriting* and *closing*. When discussing the underwriting process, we consider borrower and property characteristics and how loan terms are established. Consideration is also given to: size of the loan relative to property value; loan payments relative to borrower income; and default risk undertaken by lenders. In cases where the total risk of lending to a specific borrower is too great for a given lender to undertake, we consider the use of *mortgage insurance* or *guarantees* that may be necessary to grant a given loan request. Insurance may be provided by private insurers, or, depending on the property and borrower characteristics, insurance or guarantees may be available from various government agencies.

The loan closing process is discussed in terms of the necessary accounting between the borrower, lender, seller, and other parties that must be done in a transaction in which transfer of title and a loan closing occur simultaneously. Consideration is given to federal regulations that require from the lender certain practices regarding uniform disclosure of interest charges, closing statements, and collection of credit and other information about the borrower.

UNDERWRITING DEFAULT RISK

The process of evaluating a borrower's loan request in terms of potential profitability and risk is referred to as *underwriting*. This function is usually performed by a loan officer at a financial institution, such as a savings and loan association, commercial bank, mutual savings bank, or mortgage banking company. The loan officer performs this analysis based on information contained in (1) the loan application submitted by the borrower and (2) an appraisal of the property. This analysis is made also in the context of a lending policy, or guidelines, which a particular institution specifies. In some cases, lenders will require that borrowers obtain *default insurance*. This insurance policy is purchased by the borrower to protect the lender from potential losses should the borrower default on the loan. In such cases, the lender is not willing to bear the total risk of borrower default, or the loan may be sold to a third party investor (recall the process of assignment of the note and mortgage discussed in Chapter 2). In the latter case, the lender must consider underwriting standards required by such investors; otherwise the lender may lose the option of selling mortgages later. In deciding whether a loan application should be accepted or rejected, the loan officer follows some fundamental concepts in loan risk analysis.

Before beginning a detailed discussion of specific underwriting standards and policies, we first consider some basic relationships and terms used in mortgage underwriting. Two fundamental relationships that must be assessed by any lender when considering the risk of making a mortgage loan are the expected *payment-to-income* ratio and the *loan-to-value ratio*. The payment-to-income ratio is simply the monthly payment on the loan amount being applied for plus other housing expenses divided by the borrower's income. The loan-to-value ratio is the loan amount requested divided by the estimated property value.

The first ratio is important because the borrower will generally be personally liable on the note, and must be able to make payments either as scheduled (in the case of an *FRM*) or as market conditions change interest rates (in the case of *ARM*s). Clearly, the greater the ratio of mortgage payment to income for a given borrower, the greater is default risk. Hence, a higher risk premium must be earned by the lender. Similarly, because the property being acquired by the borrower also serves as security for the note, as the loan-to-value ratio increases, the likelihood of loss increases. This is because the property may not bring a sufficient price at a foreclosure sale to cover the outstanding loan balance, any past due payments, and foreclosure costs. Therefore, the major problems facing a lender when reviewing a loan request made by a borrower are (1) assessment of the many variables that affect default risk, (2) determining whether a fixed interest rate or adjustable rate mortgage can be made, and (3) if the total risk on a particular loan request is too great, to decide whether the loan should be refused, or made with default insurance or guarantees from third parties.

CLASSIFICATION OF MORTGAGE LOANS

In previous chapters, we discussed and classified mortgage loans mainly in terms of interest rate risk, that is, whether a loan was a fixed rate mortgage (*FRM*) or an adjustable rate mortgage (*ARM*). While basic discussion of default risk was also included in those chapters, specific methods and procedures for assessing borrower default risk are primary topics in this chapter.

Recall from the previous chapter that default risk was defined as a potential loss that could occur if the borrower failed to make payment on a loan. This could be caused by a borrower having insufficient income or because the market value of the property falls below the outstanding mortgage balance, or both. There are several ways that default risk can be shared. Default risk may be fully assumed by the lender, shared by the lender and a third-party insurer, or fully assumed by a third-party insurer or guarantor. To facilitate discussion, we use the following classification:

1. Conventional mortgages.
2. Insured conventional mortgages.
3. FHA insured mortgages.
4. VA guaranteed mortgage loans.

Conventional Mortgage Loans

Conventional mortgage loans are negotiated between a borrower and lender. From these negotiations, the loan-to-value ratio, interest rate (or *ARM* terms), and the payment-to-income ratio are established. The loan-to-value ratio establishes the borrower's down payment, or equity. Should the borrower default on the loan, both the lender and borrower may incur losses. Losses usually include any past due interest, costs of selling the property, and the extent to which the sale price is less than the mortgage balance. In the event of loss, the borrower absorbs such losses first to the extent of any equity. If losses exceed the amount of borrower equity, the lender will then incur a loss which then becomes a claim against the borrower and (depending on state law) may be used to attach other assets owned by the borrower (recall the discussion of deficiency judgments in Chapter 3).

Typically, if a conventional loan is desired, the maximum loan amount that the borrower can obtain will be 80 percent of the value of the real estate being purchased. Because the lender must look to the sale of the property for repayment of the mortgage loan should the borrower default, regulations governing the operation of most savings institutions generally require that for conventional loans, equity of at least 20 percent of value must be provided by the borrower.[1] Therefore, such losses must exceed 20 percent of the original property value before the lender would suffer a loss.

Insured Conventional Mortgage Loans

In many instances, borrowers do not have the necessary wealth accumulation to make a down payment of 20 percent of value when purchasing a property. However, if the income-earning ability of the borrower and the location of the property being acquired are satisfactory, lenders may be willing to grant a loan request in excess of 80 percent of value with a condition that *insurance* against default risk be purchased by the borrower. There are many firms that provide this insurance for a premium which is paid by the borrower and is based on the amount of risk assumed by the mortgage insurer. A useful way of thinking about mortgage insurance is to view the borrower negotiating for a larger loan from the lender, then paying an insurer to assume the increase in default risk above that taken by the lender on a conventional loan. In other words, only the amount of the loan in *excess* of 80 percent of the property value at the time of loan origination is usually

---

[1] Federal regulations require that residential mortgages cannot be made in excess of 80 percent of value without mortgage insurance. For further information see the Code of Federal Regulations, 12 CFR Section 545. 32(d)(2).

covered under the mortgage insurance policy. Therefore, if a mortgage is made for 95 percent of value and private mortgage insurance is purchased, the borrower would make an equity down payment of 5 percent of the property value and the mortgage lender would make a 95 percent loan. However, the lender would have 80 percent of the loan amount at risk and the mortgage insurer would insure any losses to the lender in an amount equal to 15 percent of the property value. The interest rate charged on this type of loan is likely to be higher than the rate on an uninsured conventional loan because the amount of the loan is greater (95 percent versus 80 percent).

Mortgage insurers are private companies that operate by collecting premiums from borrowers based on the incremental risk being assumed as loan amounts rise in excess of 80 percent. These insurers maintain reserves that are used to pay claims to lenders should mortgage defaults occur. These companies can usually take this additional risk at a premium that would be lower than individual lenders would have to charge, because they insure mortgage loans nationally while individual lenders usually make loans in only one geographic region. Consequently, mortgage insurers are able to diversify the additional default risk more effectively than a single lender can. Lenders could be more adversely affected should an economic decline occur in a particular region.

When an insured conventional mortgage is made, the maximum loan that a borrower is likely to obtain will be 95 percent of value. Because a greater potential for loss exists, and much of the risk of loss is being assumed by the mortgage insurer, underwriting requirements that the lender uses to evaluate the borrower are also likely to be heavily influenced by the insurer. Lenders must rigidly adhere to these standards when this type of loan is considered. Premiums will be based on the extent to which the loan-to-value ratio exceeds 80 percent for any given borrower.

FHA Insured Mortgage Loans

It is also possible for a mortgage loan to be insured by the Federal Housing Administration (FHA). Unlike conventional insurance, which protects the lender against some portion of the potential loan loss, FHA mortgage insurance *completely* insures the lender against any default losses. It should be stressed that FHA does not make loans but provides insurance. Because FHA accepts the entire risk of borrower default, it maintains strict qualification procedures before the borrower and property will be acceptable under its insurance program.

The FHA was created in 1934 with the passage of the Federal Housing Act.[2] The original intent of the FHA was to stabilize the housing industry after the depression of the early 1930s. It also has had a long-standing policy objective to make housing affordable to lower- and middle-income families. This has been accomplished by allowing such families to purchase homes with lower down payments than would be required under conventional lending standards. The FHA operates as an insurance program, collecting premiums and maintaining reserves for payment of lender claims. Because FHA mortgage

---

[2]The National Housing Act of 1934, as amended.

loans are made with higher loan-to-value ratios than conventional uninsured loans are and because the FHA assumes the entire risk of default, mortgage insurance premiums charged by FHA are usually higher than conventional premiums reflecting the additional risk taken by FHA.

The reader may wonder why a need exists for both FHA and private mortgage insurance. Regulations place loan maximums on FHA insured mortgage loans which may not be sufficient for many borrowers desiring to purchase higher-priced properties.[3] Hence, for qualified borrowers, in cases where larger loans are necessary to purchase higher-priced properties with low down payments, a conventional, privately insured loan will normally be chosen. The net effect of these two insurance programs tends to result in borrowers with higher incomes, who desire to purchase higher-valued properties with low down payments, opting for private mortgage insurance. The loan amount will be greater than the maximum available under FHA at a lower insurance cost. FHA borrowers are likely to have lower incomes and are desirous of purchasing properties in lower price ranges, within the maximum loan limits set by FHA. Because of their lower incomes, lenders may insist that the entire mortgage loan be insured; consequently these borrowers will pay higher insurance premiums to FHA.

FHA offers a number of programs under which insurance can be extended to borrowers. The most commonly used of these programs is Section 203b, which insures loans on one to four family single family detached residences. This program requires fixed interest rate financing with a term of between 15 and 30 years. Other FHA loan programs include Section 251, an *ARM* program, Section 243c, a condominium insurance program, and Section 245, a graduated payment mortgage insurance program.[4]

VA Guaranteed Mortgage Loans

For qualified veterans who desire to purchase property with a down payment of less than 20 percent of value, there is an alternative to the three categories of mortgages discussed above. Veterans who meet certain length of service tests[5] may obtain a *guaranteed* mortgage from the Veterans Administration (VA). Loan guarantees for eligible veterans were first authorized under The Servicemen's Readjustment Act of 1944. Under this program, the VA *guarantees* a mortgage lender repayment of a specified maximum amount, should a VA mortgage result in a loss to the lender. It should be stressed that like FHA, VA generally does not make mortgage loans but guarantees the lender a maximum payment in the event of default. Also, VA *guarantees* default losses as opposed to *insuring* the lender against losses. This means that VA does not operate an insurance fund and does not collect insurance premiums. Other than a small qualifying fee charged

---

[3]For a discussion of FHA maximum insurable loan amounts see *Hud Handbook 4000.2* and revisions. FHA maximum insurable loan amounts depend on the geographic region in which the loan is made. These amounts also change from time to time.

[4]For a detailed listing of FHA mortgage insurance programs, see *Hud Handbook 4000.2*.

[5]For a discussion of VA loan guarantee eligibility requirements, see title 38, U.S. Code of Federal Regulations, Section 1801.

to eligible borrowers, any default losses paid by VA are subsidy benefits made available by the U.S. Government. The maximum dollar amount which lenders can claim in the event of a loan loss on a VA guaranteed mortgage varies based on statutory limits.[6]

Generally, the VA loan guarantee amount will be either 60 percent of the loan request or the maximum amount of guarantee that a veteran is eligible for, whichever is less. For example, if an eligible borrower desires a $60,000 mortgage, and has never used any VA loan guarantee benefits, $27,500 would be the maximum amount of the guarantee to the lender. This is because $27,500 is less than 60 percent of the $60,000 loan request. In this case, should a default occur, the first $27,500 of lender losses would be paid by VA.[7]

The primary advantage to a borrower in obtaining a VA loan is that under most circumstances, no down payment will be required by the lender. As of this writing, the VA requires that a minimum of 25 percent of the loan balance on all VA mortgages be composed of either VA mortgage guarantee or borrower equity. As a result, if the veteran has never used VA loan guarantee benefits, a loan of up to $110,000 or $27,500 ÷ .25 can be obtained with no down payment. However, the maximum mortgage amount possible under VA regulations with any size down payment is presently $130,000.[8]

THE UNDERWRITING PROCESS

Regardless of the type of mortgage (conventional, conventional insured, FHA, or VA), much of the underwriting process is common to each type of mortgage loan. The underwriter begins by collecting the data for deciding whether credit should be extended. The goal of this process is to determine whether the loan-to-value ratio, the payment-to-income ratio, assets of the borrower, and borrower credit history are acceptable to the lender, or the lender and insurer. What follows is a discussion of (1) how borrower income is estimated, and the relationship of that income to the proposed mortgage payments and other obligations of the borrower, and (2) how the value of the property is established through an appraisal.

Borrower Income

The underwriting process usually begins with the underwriter obtaining the data needed to make a decision about credit extension. An item of primary importance will be borrower

---

[6]Currently, guarantees range from a minimum of $4,000 to a maximum of $27,500. The amount of guarantee available to the lender will depend upon the period in which the loan was originated. In the event of default, the lender may never collect more than the maximum guarantee available at the time a VA mortgage was originated. These maximums also change from time to time. For more information see title 38 of the U.S. Code of Federal Regulations, as amended, Section 1801.

[7]If the mortgage amount in this example was $40,000, then the maximum guarantee would be (.60 times $40,000) or $24,000 because this amount is less than the maximum guarantee of $27,500 in the example.

[8]VA does not make the same distinction concerning high-cost areas as FHA does. As a result, the VA maximum mortgage amount usually applies to all areas of the country. Maximum loan amounts change from time to time based on changes in maximum VA loan guarantees.

income. To gather the necessary data regarding income, the borrower is requested to allow the lender to (1) verify place of employment, (2) verify wages, and (3) inquire as to whether employment is likely to continue into the future. Typically, where a borrower is employed on a full-time basis and obtains regular income from this employment, there is little problem in verifying income. In cases where a borrower's income is derived from more than a single source, the process of verifying the amount and the likelihood of that income to continue is more difficult.

A list of other possible income sources is listed below:

- Part-time employment.
- Working spouse.
- Rentals.
- Alimony or child support.
- Commissions.
- Self-employment.
- Bonuses.
- Dividends or interest.
- Retirement annuity.
- Social security.
- Public assistance.

Generally, two tests must be met before any of these sources will be included in establishing borrower income in the underwriting process. First, in the judgment of the underwriter, the income will have to be considered likely to continue. This usually means that a source of income must have already occurred continuously for a sufficient time for the underwriter to judge whether that income will continue. Second, the income must be verifiable. This is usually done by reviewing the borrower's federal income tax returns for at least two years. When the income is nontaxable, such as distributions from retirement annuities, canceled checks or verification of deposits may be used to verify the existence of the income.

In addition to deciding what sources of income should be included, difficulties also arise when determining how much of such income should be used in the underwriting process. The amount of income from a particular source may vary from period to period. When income is variable in nature, such as the earnings from commission sales positions, rentals, or self-employment, a borrower's income will generally be averaged over a period of at least two years from amounts shown on tax returns. Any expenses incurred in earning that income will be deducted from the amount of income earned.

When two individuals are employed, the question arises of what constitutes income. The general rule applied by the lender takes a long-run viewpoint, that is, whether both individuals will remain employed indefinitely, or at least until the income of one is sufficient to meet the monthly mortgage payments. This question often presents difficulty when the value of the property and the corresponding loan amount being requested are high in relation to the income of only one of the earners. Obviously, a judgment by the lender as to the future stability of the joint incomes will have to be exercised. Generally, if both parties have been employed for several consecutive years, there is a greater likelihood of future income stability. If the intent of one of the parties is to end employment after a given number of years, and this individual is presently employed in a professional activity that lends to employment stability, both incomes may be included for the time both expect to remain employed. An estimate may then be made as to what the primary worker's total income will be at the time the other party ceases employment.

While income forms much of the basis for risk analysis by the lender, recent federal regulations have limited the extent to which lenders may obtain information or make inferences concerning a loan applicant's background. Regulation B of the Board of Governors of the Federal Reserve System provides guidelines that lenders must comply with when gathering information about potential borrowers.[9]

Verification of Borrower Assets

Another step in the data collection process is the verification of borrower assets. Assets of the borrower must at least be sufficient to close the transaction. This means that borrower assets must be sufficient to pay closing costs and make a down payment. Moreover, gifts, or borrowed funds, are usually not allowed to be used as the borrower's down payment. Thus, how long a borrower's assets have been on deposit will be used as an important indicator of whether the borrower is planning to use borrowed funds or gifts to make a down payment. Any assets which are not required to close the lending transaction will reflect favorably upon the creditworthiness of the borrower.

Other assets of the applicant also play an important role in the rating loan quality by the lender. The rating is improved if the applicant has demonstrated a consistent ability to save as evidenced by savings accounts or investments in other property, ownership of life insurance (cash value), purchase of securities, and the like, as well as the ability to carry the obligations associated with the acquisition of these assets. For example, an older applicant whose remaining life expectancy is less than the term of the mortgage being sought may be granted a loan with the desired maturity, even though it exceeds the years

---

[9](a) The use of sex, marital status, race, religion, age, or national origin in a credit underwriting procedure is prohibited. (b) Creditors may not inquire into birth control practices or into childbearing capabilities or intentions, or assume, from her age, that an applicant or an applicant's spouse may drop out of the labor force due to childbearing and thus have an interruption of income. (c) A creditor may not discount part-time income but may examine the probable continuity of the applicant's job. (d) A creditor may ask and consider whether and to what extent an applicant's income is affected by obligations to make alimony or child support or maintenance payments. (e) A creditor may ask to what extent an applicant is relying on alimony or child support or maintenance payments to repay the debt being requested, but the applicant must first be informed that no such disclosure is necessary if the applicant does not rely on such income to obtain the credit. Where the applicant chooses to rely on alimony, a creditor shall consider such payments as income to the extent the payments are likely to be made consistently. (f) Applicants receiving public assistance payments cannot be denied access to credit. If these payments and security provided for the loan meet normal underwriting standards, credit must be extended. (g) An individual may apply for credit without obligating a spouse to repay the obligation, as long as underwriting standards of the lender are met. (h) A creditor shall not take into account the existence of a telephone listing in the name of an applicant when evaluating applications. A creditor may take into account the existence of a telephone in the applicant's home. (i) Upon the request of an applicant, creditor will be required to provide reasons for terminating or denying credit.

of life expectancy remaining, if adequate life insurance exists to pay off the mortgage loan in the event death occurs before the loan is repaid. In most cases, the lender will request that the applicant sign a request allowing other financial institutions, investment companies, and credit agencies to disclose to the lender the nature and amount of the applicant's assets. These could include stocks, bonds, savings accounts, and any recent activity in the accounts.

Assessment of Credit History

Typically a judgment will also be made by the underwriter as to the acceptability of the borrower's past payment history on other obligations. Credit reports from a central credit bureau, located in most cities, will give history on a borrower's payment habits for up to 10 years. Such things as slow payment of past borrower obligations may reflect unfavorably upon the loan applicant. Large amounts of adverse credit experience will surely cause the loan application to be rejected. However, a brief interruption in an otherwise acceptable credit history caused by explainable events such as divorce or interruption in income will sometimes be overlooked by the underwriter if an explanation is provided. This implies that the borrower has recovered financially from the adverse circumstances that caused this problem. Even bankruptcy may be allowed in some cases if there were extenuating circumstances and the borrower has had several years of acceptable history since the problem occurred.

Estimated Housing Expense

Determining the housing expense that is used in establishing the payment-to-income ratio that a borrower is proposing to undertake is relatively straightforward. The following is a list of items which are likely to be included in the estimate of monthly housing expense:

- Principal and interest on the mortgage being applied for.
- Mortgage insurance (if any).
- Property taxes.
- Hazard insurance.
- Condominium or cooperative homeowners association dues (if applicable).

Many of these items will have to be estimated by the underwriter because their exact amounts will not be known at the time of underwriting. Very often the lender may require that the borrower pay monthly, prorated installments toward mortgage insurance, hazard insurance, and property taxes, in addition to the mortgage payment. Judgment concerning the risk associated with making the mortgage loan will depend upon the total cost of home ownership relative to borrower income. If this total cost of home ownership is too high, then an applicant's loan application may be rejected. Specific examples of how these expenses are estimated and related to income will be discussed later in the chapter.

Other Obligations

In most cases borrowers will have other obligations in addition to the mortgage loan being applied for. Obvious examples would include auto loans, credit card accounts, insurance premiums, other mortgage debts, or alimony and child support payments. The underwriter will request that the borrower disclose all debts at the time of application, then verify these commitments by obtaining a credit report with the approval of the borrower. Courthouse records in the borrower's county of residence also may be checked to determine whether there are any judgments outstanding against the borrower for unpaid debts. Another item on the credit report of importance to the underwriter will be whether the borrower has ever filed for bankruptcy.

If the household is attempting to obtain mortgage credit for the first time, there may be additional items included when estimating total obligations. These could include the costs of furnishings, or landscaping and fencing if the property is newly constructed. Because these purchases may be likely to occur soon after the acquisition of a residence, then additional payments for these items may be included in the total obligations of the borrower.

Compensating Factors

It is possible that the underwriter will find other favorable factors about the borrower which can offset certain unfavorable factors during the underwriting process. Typically, it is considered favorable for a borrower to have in his possession liquid assets which could be used to make his monthly mortgage payment should the borrower's income be interrupted. If the borrower is employed in a field where his skills are in high demand and the likelihood is that his income will increase over time, this is considered favorable. These factors may prove sufficient to allow a borrower to devote more of his income to housing expenses, even if the borrower's proposed housing expense ratio is higher than is the case for other borrowers with similar incomes. Of course, if the borrower is also making a substantial equity down payment as part of the purchase price, this is considered favorable as well. When any or all of the above conditions exist, it is possible that the enforcement of underwriting policies may be relaxed to some degree.

After all of the factual data described above has been determined, then the loan underwriter will consider whether or not the loan in question should be granted. The process of making this evaluation will generally vary, depending upon the kind of loan the borrower is seeking. The following examples of underwriting process in conventional, conventional insured, FHA, and VA loan transactions should help to illustrate this point.

THE UNDERWRITING PROCESS ILLUSTRATED

This section of the chapter illustrates how each of the four types of mortgage loans described above are generally underwritten by lenders. As indicated earlier, one goal of underwriting is to establish whether the risk of borrower default is acceptable and whether the loan should be granted. Each type of mortgage (conventional, insured conventional, FHA, and VA) will be considered separately. In this section, we consider how the maximum mortgage amount is established, how it is related to property value, and how that relationship varies under each type of mortgage. An assessment also is made of (1) proposed housing expenses and other obligations relative to borrower income, (2) the criteria used to establish acceptable relationships between these outlays and income which will serve as the basis for the lending decision, and (3) the role of appraisals in establishing the loan-to-value ratio.

To facilitate the discussion, we use the sample borrower information contained in Exhibit 7–1 to illustrate the underwriting process for each category of mortgage loans. The underwriting criteria will be presented in sufficient detail to allow it to be generalized beyond the cases used in our discussion.

Underwriting Standards—Conventional and Insured Conventional Mortgages

Looking to the data shown in Exhibit 7–1 we see that in addition to the verification of income and outstanding debts, the lender has estimated both property taxes and hazard insurance (fire, storm, etc.), which are also used in estimating housing expenses. These expenses are used to establish the monthly payment-to-income ratio for the borrower-applicants. Looking to Exhibit 7–2, we see some of the *general* underwriting standards that will be applied by lenders in making the decision to grant or deny the loan request. In other words, after assembling the facts necessary to establish monthly housing expenses and other obligations, the lender will compute the necessary ratios and compare them to the general standards used by the lenders and mortgage insurers. This will help determine whether the default risk is acceptable, given the prevailing rate of interest. These underwriting standards, or maximum allowable ratios, are established by lenders and insurers based on loss experience from previously underwritten loans. These ratios should be

---

EXHIBIT 7–1   Sample Underwriting Illustration: Borrower and Property Characteristics

Name of borrower:	John and Jane J. Jones
Income:	$3,542 monthly from salaried employment of both spouses, $42,500 annually
Debts:	Installment obligation of $181 per month with 35 months remaining
	Credit card obligations, $50 per month with more than 12 months remaining
Sale price:	$76,700
Appraised value:	$77,000
Estimated property taxes:	$797 annually
Hazard insurance:	$552 annually
Desired mortgage:	*FRM* with a 30-year term, constant payment

EXHIBIT 7–2 General Industry Standards for Underwriting Conventional and Insured
Conventional Loans

	Conventional		Insured Conventional	
	FRMs	ARMs	FRMs	ARMs
	(percent)		*(percent)*	
Maximum ratios allowed:				
Loan to value	80	80	95	90*–95
Payment to income	28	25†–28	28	25†–28
Total obligations to income	36	33†–36	36	33†–36

*Conventional *ARMs* with loan-to-value ratios in excess of 90 percent and expected negative amortization are generally not available. Graduated payment mortgages (*GPMs*) are usually limited to 90 percent loan-to-value ratios because of scheduled negative amortization.

†Generally, the higher ratios are allowed; however, if the conventional *ARM* or *GPM* allows for the possibility of maximum increases in monthly payments beyond prescribed limits, the lower ratios must be met for the loan to be insured.

interpreted by the reader as a general guide, however, because there may be other assets or compensating factors to be considered as a part of the underwriting process.

It should also be noted in Exhibit 7–2 that, in the case of *ARMs*, there may be more stringent underwriting standards to be met in certain cases. As the notes to the exhibit indicate, in cases where an *ARM* is originated at an initial rate of interest which is *lower* than the composite rate, or the sum of the current *ARM* index plus the margin at the time of origination, the likelihood of a sharp increase in payments or negative amortization on the first scheduled payment adjustment date is very high (unless interest rates comprising the index fall before the first adjustment period). In cases where negative amortization is *expected,* lenders refer to this as "scheduled amortization" and will usually take it into account when underwriting the ARM by requiring a *lower* loan-to-value ratio. If payments are likely to be adjusted because the composite rate at the time of origination is higher than the initial interest rate, the underwriter is likely to take account of the scheduled payment increase when reviewing the payment-to-income ratio.[10] It should also be noted that conventional *GPMs* are usually underwritten on the basis of scheduled amortization, which is known at the time of origination, and the loan-to-value ratio is usually restricted to 90 percent. Also, in the case of *ARMs*, initial maximum payment-to-income ratios may be lowered if the mortgage agreement provides for the possibility

---

[10]When the composite rate is much higher than the initial rate at the time of origination, the latter rate is referred to as the *teaser rate,* because lenders may be using it as an incentive for borrowers to make *ARMs*. When first payment adjustment occurs payments will increase substantially, if the composite rate is still considerably higher than the initial rate. This increase in *ARM* payments is referred to as *payment shock* in the lending industry.

of monthly payments exceeding prescribed maximums. For example, if an *ARM* is made with a payment cap greater than 15.0 percent annually, or the interest rate cap exceeds 2 percent annually or 5 percent over the life of the mortgage, lower ratios will usually be required. This latter restriction also applies to *GPMs*.

When computing these ratios for the conventional and insured conventional cases, we take relevant information from Exhibit 7–1 and compute the necessary ratios shown in Exhibit 7–3. The reader should note that in the two cases being considered, the insured conventional loan is larger (95 percent versus 80 percent) and is made at a higher interest rate. Also, the insured loan requires a monthly mortgage insurance premium, and the conventional loan does not. The ratios calculated and shown at the bottom of the exhibit indicate that the borrower would probably qualify for either a conventional loan or an insured conventional loan, given that those ratios fall well below the maximum ratios allowed under the general underwriting standards shown in Exhibit 7–2. Whether the borrower will prefer the conventional or insured conventional loan depends on the amount available for a down payment (20 percent or 5 percent of appraised value) and whether the borrower wants to pay additional interest and insurance charges. The latter choice also depends on whether the borrower has sufficient funds to make either down payment requirement. If the borrower could afford to make either down payment, the borrower

EXHIBIT 7–3   Computation of Borrower Qualification (conventional and insured conventional loan examples)

	Conventional	*Conventional Insured*
Loan amount requested	$61,360	$72,865
Terms	*FRM* 30 yr., 9.25 percent	30 yr., *FRM*, 9.5 percent
Loan-to-value ratio	80%	95%
Borrower income (*A*)	$3,542	$3,542
Housing expenses		
Principal and interest	$ 505	$ 613
Property taxes	66	66
Hazard insurance	46	46
Mortgage insurance	—	21*
Housing expense (*B*)	617	746
Add:		
Installment debt[†]	181	181
Credit cards	50	50
Total obligations (*C*)	$ 848	$ 977
Housing expense ratio $B \div A$	17%	21%
Total obligation ratio $C \div A$	24%	28%

*Based on the second year's premium, or .35 percent of the loan balance outstanding at the end of the first year, divided by 12 months. The first year's premium is likely to be higher (.8 percent) and is usually collected in advance as a part of closing cost (to be discussed).

[†]Usually defined as an obligation with at least 11 remaining monthly payments. However, any obligation which in the judgment of the underwriter requires a large monthly outlay relative to income may be included, even if the number of remaining payments is less than 11.

must decide whether the difference (15 percent) can be reinvested at a rate of interest in excess of the added interest and insurance charges. (A procedure that may be used to choose between loans that differ in amount and interest rates will be presented in detail in Chapter 9.)

Underwriting Standards—FHA Insured Mortgages

If the borrower in our example is considering an FHA insured mortgage, a similar approach is used to underwriting, with some notable exceptions. To begin our general discussion of FHA underwriting, we point out that unlike the conventional underwriting process, which provides for loan amounts as a percentage of appraised value (80 percent, 95 percent, etc.), FHA has a specific procedure that is used to establish the *maximum insurable loan amount* for which they are willing to issue an insurance binder. This process is generally described in Exhibit 7–4.

Looking to Exhibit 7–4, it can be seen that FHA provides for a closing cost allowance (to be discussed) in its definition of total acquisition cost, which is used as a basis for establishing the maximum loan amount.[11] To the extent the borrower pays closing costs that are equal to or greater than the FHA allowance, the acquisition cost is allowed to increase. The reader should note that FHA also gives the borrower the option to finance the entire 3.8 percent mortgage insurance premium. This additional amount financed is added to the maximum mortgage amount to arrive at the total amount financed, $77,485. Monthly payments are calculated on this latter amount. It should also be noted that the maximum loan amount is computed on a graduated basis, that is, 97 percent of the first $25,000 which is equal to $24,250, then 95 percent of the remainder, subject to an absolute maximum loan amount that FHA is willing to insure. These graduated rates and maximums are subject to change by FHA at any time, based on prevailing economic conditions.

As to qualifying ratios, FHA uses an *after-tax* definition of income, whereas conventional underwriters generally do not. Note in Exhibit 7–4 that the underwriter estimates federal, state, and local income taxes in arriving at net effective income, the key figure around which FHA relates both housing expense and total obligations. The latter two categories also differ somewhat in that FHA's definition of housing expense includes an estimate of monthly housing maintenance and utilities, and total obligations include an estimate of social security taxes.

It should be stressed that FHA has established its own standards for both of these qualifying ratios (see bottom of the exhibit), which it uses uniformly for *FRM, GPM,* and *ARM* loans. This practice of computing ratios based on current income at the time of loan originations is followed even though, with a *GPM* or *ARM* monthly payments may change in future periods. However, in order for *ARMs* to be insurable by FHA, they must conform to very rigid specifications. For example, *ARMs* cannot have negative

---

[11]Examples of various closing costs to be discussed later in the chapter include loan origination fees, discount points, appraisal fees, credit report fees, and transfer taxes.

EXHIBIT 7–4   Determination of Maximum Loan Amount and Borrower
Qualification Ratios (FHA example)

Lower of price or appraised value		$76,700
Plus closing cost allowance*		1,350
Acquisition cost		78,050
97 percent of 1st $25,000	$24,250	
95 percent of remainder	$50,398	
Maximum loan amount†		74,648
Add mortgage insurance premium @ 3.8%‡		2,837
Amount financed		77,485

Computation of Qualifying Ratios

Gross income (monthly)	3,542
Less federal income taxes	602
state and local income taxes	106
Net effective income (A)	2,834

Housing expense

Principal and interest loan and insurance	
($77,485, 9.5%, 30 yrs.)	652
Property taxes	66
Hazard insurance	46
Maintenance and utilities	192
Total housing expense (B)	956

Other obligations

Social Security tax	266
Installment debt§	181
Credit cards	50
Total obligations (C)	1,453

Qualifying ratios *(percent)*	*Applicant ratios* *(percent)*	*FHA maximum ratios* *(percent)*
Housing expense ratio $B \div A$	34	36
Total obligations ratio $C \div A$	51	53

*The FHA provides for a closing cost allowance in determining the loan amount. Limits on this amount vary by region.
†The maximum loan amount may not exceed limits set by FHA regulations. These limits vary by city and change over time.
‡Limits are reduced to 3.661 percent if paid in cash at closing and not included in amount financed.
§Usually debt with 12 installments remaining. However, this can be increased or decreased by the underwriter depending on his assessment of the total number of obligations outstanding and the relationship to borrower income.

amortization, and are currently subject to interest rate caps of 1 percent annually and 5 percent over the term of the loan. *GPM*s are also subject to specific limits on allowable payment increases. The current allowable scheduled increases in payments are

Plan 1   2.5 percent payment increases annually for 5 years.
Plan 2   5 percent payment increases for 5 years.
Plan 3   7.5 percent payment increases for 7 years.
Plan 4   2 percent payment increases for 10 years.
Plan 5   3 percent payment increases for 10 years.

Further, the original mortgage balance for a *GPM* at the time of origination plus all interest which is scheduled to be accrued over the life of the loan may not exceed 97 percent of the original appraised value.

Because of the very limited variations in payments allowed by FHA in its *ARM* and *GPM* programs, a single set of underwriting ratios (bottom of Exhibit 7–4) is generally used on both types of mortgages, as well as *FRM*s. This stands in contrast to the range in ratios used by underwriters when reviewing conventional *ARM*s (see Exhibit 7–2).

As in the case of conventional lending, the underwriter is likely to take into account other assets, the credit history, and offsetting factors when deciding to accept or reject a loan application. Because FHA requires tax adjustments in its underwriting process, the reader should note that the qualifying ratios used as standards in determining the adequacy of borrower income are higher than those used in the conventional cases. These ratios are also based on FHA's loss experience in the operation of its insurance fund. Based on our hypothetical borrower-applicants, we see that they would likely qualify for an FHA insured loan. There is one additional underwriting test, however, that FHA utilizes that is also utilized in VA underwriting. This test is discussed in the next section.

Underwriting Standards—VA Guaranteed Mortgages

The underwriting process followed by the Veterans Administration differs considerably in its approach to establishing the adequacy of borrower income in relation to the loan request. The VA procedure stresses the notion of *residual income,* which is a process whereby gross income is reduced by all monthly outlays for housing, expenses, taxes, all debt obligations, and recurring job related expenses (see Exhibit 7–5). The difference, or residual income, is then examined to establish whether VA deems it adequate for supporting the borrower's family.

There are a few items of particular importance that should be elaborated. The mortgage loan amount is equal to the sale price, $76,700, plus a funding fee usually equal to 1 percent of the loan request to help the borrower fund closing costs (to be discussed).[12]

---

[12]VA typically allows the 1 percent funding fee which is paid to VA to be included in the veteran's loan amount. The funding fee of .01 times 76,700, or $767, is included in the loan amount of $76,700 + $767, or $77,467. Any closing costs in excess of $767 would be required of the borrower at closing. However, the VA also monitors what it considers to be excessive closing costs when considering whether to extend its guarantee.

EXHIBIT 7–5 Determination of Borrower Qualification
(VA guaranteed loan example)

Residual income technique

Gross income	$3,542
Less federal income taxes	602
State income taxes	106
Social Security taxes	266
All debts*	231
Maintenance	58
Utilities	134
Principal and interest payment[†]	651
Property taxes	66
Hazard insurance	46
Job-related, or child care expense	50
Residual income	$1,332

Residual income must equal for family of:		
	1	$ 400
	2	570
	3	670
	4	760
	5	850
	6	940
	7	$1,030

*Usually includes obligations with six monthly installments remaining; however, the underwriter may include any obligations considered material relative to the borrower's income.
[†]Based on a loan amount of $77,467 at 9.5 percent for 30 years (rounded).

Because the loan request is less than both the maximum loan VA will guarantee with no down payment and the maximum loan amount with down payment, it would qualify for a guarantee.[13] In addition, because the VA is providing a guarantee, there is no monthly

---

[13]The down payment plus VA guarantee must always equal 25 percent of the lesser of purchase price or appraised value. Because the current maximum guarantee is $27,500, a loan of up to $110,000 can be made with no down payment. Buyers of properties with prices in excess of $110,000 must make down payments equal to 25 percent on amounts in excess of $110,000. In no case may the mortgage loan exceed $130,000, however.

VA loans are also fully assumable. There are two types of assumptions: (1) nonqualifying assumptions, where the buyer may or may not be a veteran nor qualify with VA before assuming the loan; (2) qualifying assumptions, where the buyer assumes the loan with VA approval. In the former case, the veteran who originated the loan remains personally liable on the note. In the latter case, the veteran has no liability because the buyer qualified with VA prior to assuming the loan. FHA loan assumption policies are the same as those just described.

When a VA mortgage loan is assumed, the buyer is not required to be a veteran and is not charged for the mortgage guarantee. If, however, the buyer is a veteran and the seller can induce him to substitute his guarantee for the guarantee used by the seller, then the seller's VA guarantee is fully restored and can be used again. Also, in many instances, increases in VA guarantees provided for by Congress are retroactive. As a result, a

mortgage insurance premium required of the borrower. Based on the borrower-applicant information in Exhibit 7–1, with a family size of two and no minor dependents, they should qualify for a VA guaranteed loan. They would also meet the supplemental test as used as a secondary underwriting tool by the FHA.

Underwriting and Loan Amounts—A Summary

It is useful at this point to summarize some pertinent data before moving on to the next topic, closing costs. Exhibit 7–6 provides a summary breakdown of some of the more important characteristics considered thus far. The first item to be noted is that although we begin with the same appraised value in all cases, the loan amount will vary by mortgage category. This variation is based on the fact that we have assumed that a loan-to-value ratio of 80 percent is to be used in the case of the conventional loan, 95 percent loan is to be made and in the insured conventional loan with any additional closing costs to be paid by the borrower in both cases. In the FHA case the loan amount is higher because of the higher-to-value ratio allowed by FHA (97 percent and 95 percent of portions of the loan request) *and* because a closing cost allowance may be financed under this program. In the case of VA, the loan amount is 100 percent of the lower of price or appraised value, plus an allowance for closing costs. The reader will also note that an additional term, *amount financed,* is used in the exhibit. This is the amount upon which the monthly interest and principal will be calculated. In three of the cases it is equal to the loan amount. In the FHA case, the amount financed includes the total insurance premium or 3.8 percent of the loan balance (or an additional $2,874) which the lender is also financing and which must be repaid as a part of monthly principal and interest on the total loan amount.

Other items of importance in Exhibit 7–6 are the interest rates, and notes regarding insurance costs. In our example, we have *assumed* that the interest rate on the conventional loan will be 9.25 percent, or lower than the rate charged in all other cases. This is because the amount of funds being loaned is lower than in all other cases. Another important item in the exhibit relative to the interest rates is that, with the exception of the VA interest rate, which is *regulated* by the VA, all of these rates are competitively determined through negotiation between borrower and lender and will change over time. The reader should not infer from our example that there is fixed spread between interest rates on conventional and other loan types. These illustrations are used as *examples only.* Similarly, the terms of the mortgages are assumed to be 30 years. While FHA and VA loans are available in 15- to 30-year terms, 30-year loans are used most frequently under these programs. Conventional mortgages, however, are frequently made for 15, 20, and 25

---

veteran who used his maximum VA guarantee in one period may have an additional VA guarantee in a subsequent period.

In the case of an FHA assumption, if the seller paid the FHA one time insurance premium the buyer will pay the seller for a prorated share of the insurance in relation to the number of months remaining until maturity. However, FHA loans with annual insurance premiums must continue to be paid by the buyer as a part of the monthly payment.

EXHIBIT 7–6   Summary of Underwriting Results

	Conventional	Insured Conventional	FHA Insured	VA Guaranteed
(a) Lower of price/ appraised value	$76,700	$76,700	$76,700	$76,700
(b) Loan amount	61,360	72,865	74,648	76,700
(c) Amount financed	61,360	72,865	77,485	77,467
(d) Interest rate	9.25%	9.5%	9.5%	9.5%
(e) Term	30 years	30 years	30 years	30 years
(f) Insurance fee	N.A.	*	†	N.A.

*.8 percent of loan at closing, .35 percent per year, payable monthly.
†3.8 percent if included in financing, 3.661 percent if paid by borrower at closing.

years. Finally, the reader should keep in mind that in developing the estimates of housing expenses, total obligations, and other expenses used in underwriting, we have assumed the same estimates in many of our examples for similar expense categories (utilities, maintenance, debts, etc.). We caution the reader that in reality these estimates may differ, depending on the specific regulations, policies, cost manuals, and guidelines used by the various insurers and lenders involved in the underwriting process.[14] While there are many other peculiarities associated with underwriting each type of loan, we have attempted to limit the technical detail and to focus on the major differences between underwriting approaches and regulations in order to help the student understand the more important attributes of the process.

Property Appraisal

At some point in the application and underwriting process, the lender must estimate whether the market value of the property serving as security for repayment of the debt is sufficiently high to pay the loan balance in the event of default. This estimate of value is usually made by an appraiser on the staff of the lender or by an independent fee appraiser. The latter individual is someone who specializes in performing appraisals for lenders and investors for a fee. Such an individual must be unrelated to the parties to the transaction and must have no vested or financial interest in the property being appraised. Lenders use independent appraisers when the volume of appraisals required by loan applications is not sufficiently high to warrant employing one permanently on staff or

---

[14]FHA and VA closing cost estimates may vary regionally, or even locally, and are updated continuously. In some instances, an appraiser may even make specific estimates of utilities and maintenance items for a given property.

when staff appraisers face a temporary overload of appraisal requests. Such appraisals are then reviewed by the lending institution.

The objective of the appraisal is to establish a market value, usually meaning the most probable price that would be paid for a property under competitive market conditions. The reader should understand that this notion of *value* may be different from the *price* that an individual buyer (such as the loan applicant) may be willing to pay for the property. For example, the borrower-applicant's *individual preference* for attributes of the property being acquired may be such that he may be willing to pay a significantly higher price for a property than the *majority* of potential buyers in the market. Because the lender is more concerned about what the market price would be in the event of default, the appraiser must make an independent estimate of the most probable price that a property would bring if it were sold under competitive market conditions, where individuals other than the borrower would be bidding. In a sense, the appraiser's estimate of value will help the lender to determine whether the price being offered by the borrower-applicant is an "outlier," or a price that is significantly different from what would be paid by most buyers in the market for similar properties. Although there are some differences in appraisal requirements used in conventional, FHA, and VA mortgage underwriting, the general approaches to estimating value are similar.

To accomplish an estimate of value, the appraiser will generally begin with an assessment of national, regional, and local economic conditions, stressing income, population, employment, and interest rate trends, which form the determinants of demand for the property in question. Supply is examined by assessing the relative cost of land and the factors of production (wages, capital). Current market equilibrium conditions in the housing market are then considered by examining the current availability (inventory) of housing units, absorption rates, rental vacancies, and trends in rents to gauge the likelihood of any short-run price movements that may affect the estimate of value. Finally the submarket, usually encompassing the neighborhood, including nearby retail, educational, and religious facilities, is examined to establish any premiums that might be paid for the subject because of its proximity to those facilities.

In estimating the value for the specific property (usually referred to as the "subject" property), the appraiser will rely on three approaches: the market, cost, and income capitalization approaches, although in residential appraisals only two, cost and market, are usually reliable. The market approach involves selecting properties that have sold most recently and that are *most comparable* to the subject. Adjustments are made for dissimilarities (such as size of dwelling, lot, amenities) which the appraiser attempts to keep at a minimum, in accordance with the concept of comparability. This approach is based on the principle that buyers should be willing to pay the same price for otherwise identical properties. By adjusting the sale price of comparable properties for dissimilarities, the appraiser is trying to make properties that have recently sold as identical as possible to the subject. The adjusted price of the comparables can then be used to price the subject.

The second approach involves estimating the cost to reproduce the structure (less depreciation), then adding the value of the land (site) to it in arriving at a value. The rationale for this approach is that no knowledgeable buyer would pay more for a property than it can be reproduced for. Finally, the income approach is a process whereby comparable residences that are currently *renting* for income are used to estimate the value of the subject. This process usually involves establishing a ratio between the selling price and income of such recently sold comparables. The rent is then adjusted for dissimilarities with the subject. A comparable rent for the subject is then established, and the ratio of price to rent for comparables is then used to convert the adjusted rent into a value for the subject. This latter approach is not frequently used because it is generally the least reliable method, since the number of comparable residences that are rented are few and not sold as often as owner-occupied residences.

Based on these approaches, the final estimate of value is made and reported to the lender. The lender will review the report and, if he is in agreement with the approach used by the appraiser, use the *lower* of appraised value or the market price in establishing the maximum loan amount. The loan amount is also subject to the adequacy of the borrower's income to carry the monthly payments based on prevailing loan terms. For a more detailed examination of each of these approaches, we now consider a problem example. In the example, we use the uniform appraisal form (see Exhibit 7–7, Panels A and B) required by the Federal National Mortgage Association and Federal Home Loan Mortgage Corporation. Most residential mortgages made today utilize this form, since it is a part of the required documentation should any lender desire to sell a loan to either of these entities after origination.[15]

The Market Approach. As previously indicated, when using this method the appraiser estimates the value of a property by comparing the selling prices of properties similar to, and near, the property being appraised. Because no two properties are exactly alike, the values of similar properties (called *comparable* properties) are adjusted by the appraiser for dissimilarities. These differences are isolated, and adjustments are made by the appraiser, who, using his judgment and knowledge of current market conditions, establishes what the market value is for each major attribute of a comparable that is different from the subject property. Because the value of the subject property is unknown, the price of the *comparables* will be adjusted until all differences have been taken into account. If this process is carried out correctly, the adjusted value of the comparable properties should then be approximately equal to the price of the subject property. In selecting the comparables, the appraiser must be careful to establish that the sale of the comparable properties were arm's-length transactions between the buyer and seller. For instance, if the seller were under duress as in a foreclosure situation, or if a sale were between relatives, such sales would not be desirable for use as comparables because buyers may

---

[15]For more detailed information see *Underwriting Guidelines, Home Mortgages,* Federal Home Loan Mortgage Corporation, July 1985. The sale of mortgages to institutions in the secondary mortgage market will be covered in a later chapter. While all residential appraisals are made using the three approaches to value discussed above, additional specifications concerning condition and construction quality of the dwelling being appraised are sometimes included in FHA and VA appraisals. While such specifications are too numerous to be considered here, the following sources provide additional information: (1) for an overview of FHA appraisal policies, see *HUD Handbook 4150.1,* "Valuation Analysis for Home Mortgage Insurance," April 1983; (2) for VA appraisal standards, see *VA Bulletin CNU-2-86,* "Procedures for Making VA Appraisals," March 21, 1986 and Department of Veterans Benefits Circular 26–86–9, "Appraisal Review Guidelines," March 10, 1986.

EXHIBIT 7–7 (Panel A) Property Description

Property Description & Analysis **UNIFORM RESIDENTIAL APPRAISAL REPORT** File No.

SUBJECT

Property Address 482 Liberty Street	Census Tract 1005.00	LENDER DISCRETIONARY USE
City Anytown, USA. County State Zip Code		Sale Price $
Legal Description Lot 78,1st Section Happy Acres Farm		Date
Owner/Occupant John and Jane J. Jones	Map Reference 33-84	Mortgage Amount $
Sale Price $ 76,700 Date of Sale 3-01-86	PROPERTY RIGHTS APPRAISED	Mortgage Type
Loan charges/concessions to be paid by seller $ None	[x] Fee Simple	Discount Points and Other Concessions
R.E. Taxes $ 797.00 Tax Year HOA $/Mo. None	[ ] Leasehold	Paid by Seller $
Lender/Client XYZ Federal Savings and Loan Assoc.	[ ] Condominium (HUD/VA)	
	[ ] De Minimis PUD	Source

NEIGHBORHOOD

LOCATION					NEIGHBORHOOD ANALYSIS	Good	Avg.	Fair	Poor
BUILT UP	[ ] Urban	[x] Suburban	[ ] Rural		Employment Stability		[x]		
GROWTH RATE	[x] Over 75%	[ ] 25-75%	[ ] Under 25%		Convenience to Employment		[x]		
PROPERTY VALUES	[ ] Rapid	[x] Stable	[ ] Slow		Convenience to Shopping			[x]	
DEMAND/SUPPLY	[ ] Increasing	[x] Stable	[ ] Declining		Convenience to Schools	[x]			
MARKETING TIME	[ ] Shortage	[x] In Balance	[ ] Over Supply		Adequacy of Public Transportation		[x]		
	[ ] Under 3 Mos.	[x] 3-6 Mos.	[ ] Over 6 Mos.		Recreation Facilities			[x]	

PRESENT LAND USE	%	LAND USE CHANGE	PREDOMINANT	SINGLE FAMILY HOUSING					
			OCCUPANCY	PRICE $ (000)	AGE (yrs)	Adequacy of Utilities		[x]	
Single Family	80	Not Likely [x]				Property Compatibility		[x]	
2-4 Family	10	Likely	Owner [x]			Protection from Detrimental Cond.		[x]	
Multi-family	10	In process	Tenant	55 Low	10	Police & Fire Protection			[x]
Commercial		To:	Vacant (0-5%)	80 High	20	General Appearance of Properties		[x]	
Industrial			Vacant (over 5%)	65 Predominant	15	Appeal to Market		[x]	
Vacant									

Note: Race or the racial composition of the neighborhood are not considered reliable appraisal factors.

COMMENTS: shopping is approximately two miles away at I-75 and Colerain,City Park one mile north. Other recreational facilities of a private nature. Fire protection is voluntary unit. Other aspects average or better.

SITE

Dimensions 60x125x72x140

Site Area 8,745 Sq.Ft.		Topography Level
Zoning Classification R-2 (Min.Size 7500 Sq.Ft.) Zoning Compliance Yes	Corner Lot Yes	Size Typical in neighborhood
HIGHEST & BEST USE: Present Use Single family res. Other Use		Shape Typical in neighborhood
		Drainage Good
		View Average

UTILITIES	Public	Other	SITE IMPROVEMENTS	Type	Public	Private	
Electricity	[x]		Street	Macadem	[x]		Landscaping Typical in neighborhood
Gas	[x]		Curb/Gutter	Concrete		[x]	Driveway
Water	[x]		Sidewalk	Concrete		[x]	Apparent Easements
Sanitary Sewer	[x]		Street Lights				FEMA Flood Hazard Yes* No [x]
Storm Sewer			Alley				FEMA* Map/Zone

COMMENTS (Apparent adverse easements, encroachments, special assessments, slide areas, etc.): None

IMPROVEMENTS

GENERAL DESCRIPTION		EXTERIOR DESCRIPTION		FOUNDATION		BASEMENT		INSULATION	
Units	1	Foundation	Concrete	Slab	Concrete	Area Sq. Ft. 1316		Roof	[x]
Stories	1	Exterior Walls	Brick	Crawl Space	None	% Finished 0		Ceiling	[x]
Type (Det./Att.)	Det.	Roof Surface	Cedar Shingle	Basement	Yes	Ceiling		Walls	[x]
Design (Style)	Rambler	Gutters & Dwnspts	Galv. Iron	Sump Pump	No	Walls		Floor	[x]
Existing	Yes	Window Type Dbl.	Hung Wood	Dampness	None	Floor	Concrete	None	
Proposed		Storm Sash	Yes	Settlement	None	Outside Entry Yes		Adequacy	[x]
Under Construction		Screens	Yes	Infestation	None			Energy Efficient Items:	
Age (Yrs.)	10	Manufactured House	No					▸R-38 Ceiling	
Effective Age (Yrs.)	10-12							R-19 Walls	

ROOM LIST

ROOMS	Foyer	Living	Dining	Kitchen	Den	Family Rm.	Rec. Rm.	Bedrooms	# Baths	Laundry	Other	Area Sq. Ft.
Basement												
Level 1	x	x	x	x		x		3	2			
Level 2												

Finished area **above** grade contains: 7 Rooms; 3 Bedroom(s); 2 Bath(s); 1645 Square Feet of Gross Living Area

INTERIOR

SURFACES	Materials/Condition	HEATING		KITCHEN EQUIP.		ATTIC		IMPROVEMENT ANALYSIS	Good	Avg.	Fair	Poor
Floors	Hardwood/Good	Type	FWA	Refrigerator	[x]	None		Quality of Construction	[x]			
Walls	Plaster	Fuel	Gas	Range/Oven	[x]	Stairs		Condition of Improvements	[x]			
Trim/Finish	Wood	Condition	Good	Disposal	[x]	Drop Stair	[x]	Room Sizes/Layout		[x]		
Bath Floor	Ceramic Tile	Adequacy	x	Dishwasher	[x]	Scuttle		Closets and Storage		[x]		
Bath Wainscot	Ceramic	COOLING		Fan/Hood	[x]	Floor		Energy Efficiency	[x]			
Doors		Central	x	Compactor		Heated		Plumbing-Adequacy & Condition		[x]		
		Other		Washer/Dryer		Finished		Electrical-Adequacy & Condition		[x]		
		Condition		Microwave	[x]			Kitchen Cabinets-Adequacy & Cond.		[x]		
Fireplace(s)	#	Adequacy	x	Intercom				Compatibility to Neighborhood		[x]		
CAR STORAGE	Garage	Attached		Adequate	[x]	House Entry		Appeal & Marketability		[x]		
No. Cars 1	Carport	[x]	Detached	Inadequate		Outside Entry		Estimated Remaining Economic Life	45		Yrs.	
Condition	None	Built-In		Electric Door		Basement Entry		Estimated Remaining Physical Life	60		Yrs.	

Additional features: Fireplace in living room; rear concrete covered patio (22x12);4 ft. high chain link fence around rear yard.

COMMENTS

Depreciation (Physical, functional and external inadequacies, repairs needed, modernization, etc.): Additional insulation (floor and ceiling) and automatic thermostat were added in 1979

General market conditions and prevalence and impact in subject/market area regarding loan discounts, interest buydowns and concessions:

EXHIBIT 7–7 (Panel B) Property Valuation

UNIFORM RESIDENTIAL APPRAISAL REPORT   File No.

Valuation Section

Purpose of Appraisal is to estimate Market Value as defined in the Certification & Statement of Limiting Conditions.

COST APPROACH

BUILDING SKETCH (SHOW GROSS LIVING AREA ABOVE GRADE)
If for Freddie Mac or Fannie Mae, show only square foot calculations and cost approach comments in this space.

Measurements		No. Stories	=	Sq.Ft.
42x37	x	1		1,554
24x3.8	x	1		91

Total gross living area   1,645sq.ft

ESTIMATED REPRODUCTION COST - NEW - OF IMPROVEMENTS:	
Dwelling 1,645 Sq. Ft. @ $ 38.09	= $62,658
1,316 Sq. Ft. @ $ 7.89	= 10,383
Extras soft wtr.sys.;d/w, disp. =	
range/oven;f/h; fireplace =	3,240
Special Energy Efficient Items R-30 Insultn.	500
Porches, Patios, etc. and fence	1,800
Garage/Carport 200 Sq. Ft. @ $ 6.50	1,300
Total Estimated Cost New	= $ 79,881

	Physical	Functional	External	
Less Depreciation	13,500		7,500	= $21,000

Depreciated Value of Improvements .... = $58,881
Site Imp. "as is" (driveway, landscaping, etc.) = $ 3,050
ESTIMATED SITE VALUE .... = $15,500
(If leasehold, show only leasehold value.)
INDICATED VALUE BY COST APPROACH .... = $77,431

(Not Required by Freddie Mac and Fannie Mae)
Does property conform to applicable HUD/VA property standards? [X] Yes [ ] No
If No, explain: _____

Construction Warranty [ ] Yes [X] No
Name of Warranty Program _____
Warranty Coverage Expires _____

The undersigned has recited three recent sales of properties most similar and proximate to subject and has considered these in the market analysis. The description includes a dollar adjustment, reflecting market reaction to those items of significant variation between the subject and comparable properties. If a significant item in the comparable property is superior to, or more favorable than, the subject property, a minus (−) adjustment is made, thus reducing the indicated value of subject; if a significant item in the comparable is inferior to, or less favorable than, the subject property, a plus (+) adjustment is made, thus increasing the indicated value of the subject.

SALES COMPARISON ANALYSIS

ITEM	SUBJECT	COMPARABLE NO. 1	+ (−)$ Adjustment	COMPARABLE NO. 2	+ (−)$ Adjustment	COMPARABLE NO. 3	+ (−)$ Adjustment
Address	482 Liberty	478 Liberty St.		225 West 17th Street		110 East 16th Street	
Proximity to Subject		Adjacent		2 blocks West		3 blocks SE	
Sales Price	$ 76,700	$ 65,000		$ 73,500		$ 67,500	
Price/Gross Liv. Area	$ 46.63	$ 46.43		$ 44.54		$ 42.19	
Data Source	Sales contract	Present Owner		Appraiser's Files		Selling Broker	
VALUE ADJUSTMENTS	DESCRIPTION	DESCRIPTION	+ (−)$ Adjustment	DESCRIPTION	+ (−)$ Adjustment	DESCRIPTION	+ (−)$ Adjustment
Sales or Financing Concessions		None	−	None	−	None	−
Date of Sale/Time	3-1-86	1-29-86	−	2-14-86	−	12-17-85	−
Location	Avg.Suburb	Similar		Similar		Similar	−
Site/View	Corner Lot	Inside Lot	1,950	Inside Lot	1,950	Corner Lot	−
Design and Appeal	Rambler-Avg.	Similar		Similar		Similar	−
Quality of Construction	Good	Good		Good		Good	
Age	20 years	19 years		20 years		13 years	(3,250)
Condition	Good	Good		Good		Int.Paint Fair	950
Above Grade Room Count	Total 7 / Bdrms 3 / Baths 2	Total 6 / Bdrms 1 / Baths 1.5	7,500	Total 7 / Bdrms 3 / Baths 2	−	Total 7 / Bdrms 3 / Baths 1	2,800
Gross Living Area	1,645 Sq.Ft.	1,400 Sq.Ft.		1,650 Sq.Ft.		1,600 Sq.Ft.	
Basement & Finished Rooms Below Grade	80% BsmtArea Unfinished	Full Bsmt Rec. Room	(1,950)	Full Bsmt,Rec Rm,½ Bath	(2,800)	50% Bsmt Unfinished	3,200
Functional Utility	Good	Good	−	Good	−	Fair	2,800
Heating/Cooling	Central	Central	−	None	2,500	Central	−
Garage/Carport	1Car att.C/P	Similar	−	2 Car att.Gar.	(4,000)	2 Car att.Gar.	(4,000)
Porches, Patio, Pools, etc.	Fence, Rear Patio	Fence, Rear Screen Porch	(1,200)	Fence, Rear Patio	−	No Fence,Rear Screen Porch	(500)
Special Energy Efficient Items	R-38 Ceiling Ins. Solar HW Heater	No solar HW Heater	3,900	No solar HW Heater	3,900	Inf.Insulatn. No solar HW Heater	4,600
Fireplace(s)	Living Room	Similar	−	No Fireplace	1,800	No Fireplace	1,800
Other (e.g. kitchen equip., remodeling)	Range/Oven Disp.,Dish Washer	Similar	−	Similar	−	No Built-in Appliance	500
Net Adj. (total)		[X] + / − $ 10,200		[X] + / − $ 3,350		[X] + / − $ 8,900	
Indicated Value of Subject		$ 75,200		$ 76,850		$ 76,400	

Comments on Sales Comparison: Sale No. 1 is recent sale of smaller house next door to subject and indicated value reflects considerable net adjustments as does sale No. 3. Sale No.2 is most comparable to subject and required only a few moderate size adjustments consequently most weight is assigned to its indicated value.

INDICATED VALUE BY SALES COMPARISON APPROACH $ 76,850
INDICATED VALUE BY INCOME APPROACH (If Applicable) Estimated Market Rent $ 650 /Mo. x Gross Rent Multiplier = $ 75,400

This appraisal is made [X] "as is" [ ] subject to the repairs, alterations, inspections or conditions listed below [ ] completion per plans and specifications.
Comments and Conditions of Appraisal: Property is at the top of the neighborhood value, but at estimated value it is readily saleable.

RECONCILIATION

Final Reconciliation: Most weight is given to market approach as the comps are recent sales and are fairly similar and in close proximity to subject. Less weight is assigned to cost approach due to the difficulty in reliably establishing depreciation. Least weight given to income approach.

This appraisal is based upon the above requirements, the certification, contingent and limiting conditions, and Market Value definition that are stated in
[ ] FmHA, HUD &/or VA instructions.
[ ] Freddie Mac Form 439 (Rev. 7/86)/Fannie Mae Form 1004B (Rev. 7/86) filed with client December 1, 19 85 [ ] attached.
I (WE) ESTIMATE THE MARKET VALUE, AS DEFINED, OF THE SUBJECT PROPERTY AS OF March 7, 19 86 **to be $** 77,000

I (we) certify: that to the best of my (our) knowledge and belief the facts and data used herein are true and correct; that I (we) personally inspected the subject property, both inside and out, and have made an exterior inspection of all comparable sales cited in this report; and that I (we) have no undisclosed interest, present or prospective therein.

Appraiser(s) SIGNATURE _____   Review Appraiser SIGNATURE _____   [X] Did [ ] Did Not
NAME _____   (if applicable) NAME _____   Inspect Property

Freddie Mac Form 70 10/86 12Ch.   Forms and Worms Inc.® 315 Whitney Ave., New Haven, CT 06511 1(800) 243-4545   Fannie Mae Form 1004 10/86

not have paid a fair market price for the properties. Once the appraiser has determined that the comparable sales were arm's-length transactions, the process of adjusting the comparable sales by the appraiser can begin.

To illustrate how the appraiser will adjust the comparable sales for any differences between the subject property and the comparable properties, Exhibit 7–7 contains a property description in Panel A, and an example of the three approaches to value used in the appraisal process is shown in Panel B. Note that Part A contains the identification of the property and a general description of the property. Section II, Panel B provides an example of the market approach to value. Some of the items that the appraiser will have to adjust the comparable properties for are (1) time since the comparable has been sold, (2) location, (3) view, (4) design appeal, (5) quality of construction, (6) age of the property, (7) condition, (8) size of rooms, (9) quality of interior finish, (10) functional utility, (11) type and condition of major systems such as central heat and air, and (12) sale or financing concessions.

When making these adjustments, the appraiser adds or subtracts from the value of the *comparable properties* to reflect the difference in market value between comparable and subject property that are caused by different attributes. If the subject property is superior to the comparable property with regard to a particular attribute, then the appraiser will *add* to the value of the *comparable property*. If the subject property has attributes which are inferior to the comparable property, then the appraiser will *subtract* from the value of the *comparable property*. Recall that the value of the subject is unknown; hence *adjustments must be made to the comparable properties*. After all adjustments have been made to the comparables, the adjusted values of the comparables should be approximately equal to the value of the subject.

The amount that the appraiser adds to or subtracts from the price of a comparable property is an estimate of the *market value* of attributes that are different when comparing the subject with comparable property. For example, in dealing with differences in the *site*, in Panel B (middle) we see that comparables 1 and 2 are both ''inferior'' to the subject in the sense that the subject is a corner location while the comparables are not. The appraiser judges that such a difference is worth $1,950 in additional market value for the subject, hence the prices of the *comparables* are *increased* or adjusted up by $1,950. On the other hand, we note that comparable 2 has a two-car garage while the subject has only a one-car garage. In this case, the price of the *comparable* is adjusted *down* by the difference in the value of a two-car versus a one-car garage ($4,000). Again, the idea is to adjust the *comparables* until all positive and negative characteristics are priced and added to or subtracted from the comparables, leaving a residual value (after adjustments) that should be equal in price to the bundle of characteristics contained in the subject property. The residual values of all comparables, after adjustments, should approach the value of the subject which is unknown.

How does the appraiser estimate the value of these characteristics? It is done on the basis of experience, judgment, and knowledge of how individual buyers and sellers tend to *price* these attributes in various neighborhoods, given the site and other property characteristics. In other words, the appraiser must be able to *identify* and *defend* the estimated increase or decrease in the total price of a property, given the addition or removal of one or more characteristics (garage, bedroom, bath, etc.). This may seem to the reader to be a difficult task; however, in many housing markets hundreds of properties are sold each week and the appraiser generally has access to this data. A process of comparison and continuous updating of information makes the estimation possible. It should be stressed that under the market approach to value, adjustments are *not* based on the *cost* of constructing improvements. This is because the *market* may not value the addition the same way that an individual may. For example, the cost of adding a swimming pool to a property in an area of small, older, lower-priced homes may not be recovered in the market price when the property is sold. This may be the case, even though the current owner may believe that the value of this addition is at least equal to its cost. In this case, the addition to *market value may not be equal to the cost of constructing the pool* because the appraiser may judge that buyers comprising the market for the property are not willing to pay as much for such an improvement as the current owner. Hence the swimming pool may be referred to as an *overimprovement* to the property, and its full cost may not be reflected in the sale price.[16]

To obtain the final estimate of value under the market approach, the appraiser gives a *qualitative* weight to the residual price for each comparable. The weight assigned to each price depends on how many adjustments were made to each comparable. If many adjustments were made to a comparable, it would be given less weight, and vice versa. The appraiser then assesses the final estimates for each comparable in relation to the qualitative weights (see comments at the bottom of Panel B, Exhibit 7–7) given to each, and arrives at a final estimate of value.

A common concern of appraisers when using the market approach to value is the possibility that a comparable sale price may contain financing benefits paid for by the seller of a property. This situation occurs when the seller of a comparable is attempting to help the buyer qualify for a loan and has paid points or discount fees for the buyer, or has taken back a second mortgage at a below market rate of interest, which usually reduces the borrower's-buyer's monthly payments and cost of financing the property.[17] Sellers often recover such financing costs by charging a higher price for the property. If this property is used later by an appraiser as a comparable to estimate the value of another property, its price may be overstated. This is a difficult situation for appraisers because unless the conditions upon which a property is sold are known, it will not always be clear whether the seller of a property has paid some of the buyer's financing costs. During times when interest rates are rising and buyers find it difficult to qualify, seller-paid financing is common. During these times, appraisers usually verify that a comparable

---

[16]Overimprovements occur when individuals make improvements which they may prefer and/or believe will add value to the property. However, the market may not agree and hence will not pay for the cost of the improvement. Similarly, an underimprovement can also be made by an individual. This could happen if too small a house is built on a large site. In this case, individuals may not be willing to pay as much for the property than would be the case had the relationship between the site and the improvement been in conformity with other properties in the market area. If the reader wished to pursue the topic of appraising, in more detail, there are many available textbooks on the subject.

[17]This is sometimes referred to as "creative" financing in residential transactions. This problem is more prevalent in periods of high interest rates, when buyers have a difficult time qualifying for a loan. In these situations, sellers may finance all or part of the purchase at below market rates of interest or contribute in some way to the buyer's cost of financing.

transaction does not include seller financing by speaking directly with one of the parties to the transaction or the settlement agent before using the comparable in the appraisal process. If seller financing has been used in the transaction, the appraiser must reflect this in his estimate of value by estimating the cost of the seller financing and subtracting this amount from the comparable value.[18] In the example shown in our exhibit, we see that no seller financing was present in any of the comparable sales. Based on the various adjustments to comparables and the appraisers' weighting of these estimates, a value of $76,850 is assigned to the property being appraised under the market approach.

The market approach gives the most reliable indication of value when there are a number of current sales of highly comparable properties and information regarding the nature of circumstances surrounding the transaction are easy to obtain. When these conditions are prevalent, use of the market approach is preferred by the appraiser.

The Cost Approach.   When using the cost approach, the appraiser establishes a value for the site on which the improvement is located, then determines the cost of reproducing the improvement and adds the two. After the cost of the improvement and land value are added, the appraiser deducts an amount for any depreciation (if appropriate) that improvements have suffered since they were constructed. If the improvement has just been completed, the latter adjustment is usually unnecessary unless it was poorly designed or located. This procedure is illustrated at the top of Exhibit 7–7, Panel B.

In arriving at the estimate of land value, a procedure similar to that followed in the market approach just described is used. Comparable sites that have been recently sold are selected, and adjustments are made for differences in location, size, shape, and topography. In estimating the improvement cost, the appraiser will usually consult cost manuals for material, labor, and profit (overhead) as well as verifying with local construction companies the costs associated with constructing improvements with specific physical and qualitative dimensions. Based on these sources, estimates of construction costs per square foot are made for living space, basements, garages, and second floors. Individual estimates are then made for fixtures (kitchen, bath, etc.), landscaping, and additional improvements (pool, porches, etc.).

In the event the improvement is not newly constructed, there are three types of depreciation that the appraiser will deduct from the cost estimate just described. The first is depreciation in the property's value resulting from normal wear, and is referred to as physical depreciation. Examples of physical depreciation would include curable items, such as worn carpeting or walls needing paint, or incurable items, such as foundation settling, which may detract from a property's appearance but does not affect the usefulness of the structure. The second is depreciation resulting from internal property characteristics which make the property less livable or marketable than it was when first constructed. This is referred to as functional obsolescence. Examples of incurable functional obsolescence may include excessive amounts of hallway space. Curable obsolescence would include replacement of lighting fixtures. The third type of depreciation the appraiser will consider is called economic depreciation. Economic depreciation is caused by charac-

---

[18]This will be analyzed in detail in the next chapter.

teristics external to the property, such as changing land uses in a neighborhood which will cause a structure to become obsolete before the actual building would wear out. Examples of external factors which would cause economic depreciation to occur include pollution, shifting land uses, or changing legal restrictions on land use.

The older a property becomes the more difficult it is for the appraiser to estimate the amount of depreciation which should be used in the appraisal process. In the example shown in Exhibit 7–7, Panel B, we see that the appraiser has estimated that for the subject property (which is 10 years old), physical depreciation amounts to $13,500 and economic depreciation is $7,500 while no functional obsolescence was apparent. Based on the cost approach to value, we see that the appraiser assigns a value of $77,400 to the subject property.

The cost approach to value usually provides the most reliable estimate of value when comparable properties are newly constructed and require very few adjustments for depreciation. The cost approach will also be considered heavily by appraisers when determining value if only a few transactions involving comparable properties exist and the market approach to value is difficult to use.

The Income Approach.   A third appraisal method establishes market value of property by determining how much an investor is willing to pay for the income stream that a property produces. Using this method, the appraiser attempts to establish the relationship between a property's sale price and the monthly income stream it would produce, if rented. The appraiser typically uses sales of a rental property similar to the subject property and determines the ratio of sale price to monthly rental income. This ratio is referred to as the *gross rent multiplier*. The value of the subject property would then be estimated by judging what the subject property should rent for (again by looking at comparable rental units and adjusting for dissimilarities), then multiplying this estimate by the ratio established from comparable sales.

In our example we see in the lower portion of Panel B in Exhibit 7–7, that the appraiser has estimated that, if rented, the subject would bring $650 per month. Given that comparable properties have recently sold for 116 times their monthly rents, it is reasonable that the same relationship would hold for the subject also. Hence a value of $75,400, or $650 $\times$ 116, is arrived at by using the income approach.

Typically, income approach is difficult to use because sales of single family, rental properties are rare in an area. When this is the case, the *market* and *cost* approaches to value tend to be more heavily relied upon in establishing value. However, it should be stressed that for some properties, such as condominiums, where many units are frequently rented, the income approach may provide a reliable estimate of value.

Final Estimate of Value.   The appraiser must reconcile the different estimates of value provided by the market, income, and cost approaches to value when making a final estimate of value. This is accomplished by using a qualitative weighting method, much in the same way as used in the market approach. The appraiser assigns subjective weights to each of the three values based on the reliability of the data and the number of adjustments that had to be made in each technique. More weight would be given to the method requiring fewer adjustments where data is verifiable, current, and complete. In our example, we see that the final estimate of value is $77,000, which, as the appraiser points out, is closest to the market and cost approaches.

Property Appraisal and Actual Sale Price.   In our example the sale price of a property agreed on between a buyer and seller does not exactly correspond to the lender's appraised value. For example, a buyer and a seller agreed on a price of $76,700 for the property and the appraised value obtained by the lender was $77,000. The lender will generally use $76,700, or the lower of sale price or appraised value, as the value on which the loan will be based, unless there is convincing evidence to change it.

Property Values over Time.   A cardinal rule followed by lenders is that the value of a mortgaged property should never fall below the outstanding loan balance at any time during the life of the mortgage. In other words, the lender wants to be assured that the market value of the property will always be higher than the loan balance in the event of default by the borrower.

An additional consideration for the lender when considering the relationship of the mortgage balance and property value over time will be the potential effect of any *increases* in the mortgage balance relative to property value. This may present problems in the case of mortgage programs in which loan balance may, or will, increase after the time of loan origination. Recall the discussion in Chapter 5 of the effects of negative amortization in graduated payment mortgage programs and of adjustable rate mortgage programs in Chapter 6.

While the lender may consider the factors outlined above in the appraisal process, the lender may not make a lending decision based upon the racial or national origin of individuals living in an neighborhood. This discrimination in making mortgage loans in a neighborhood is known as *redlining* and is prohibited under the Equal Credit Opportunity Act (EEOC). Under this act, the lender may not discourage loan applications from borrowers or use discriminatory appraisal practices relative to the neighborhood where the borrower resides. Enforcement of EEOC appraisal guidelines may represent a problem for lenders when neighborhoods (1) have had declining value patterns over time and the risk that this pattern will continue is high, and (2) a large protected minority resides in the neighborhood. EEOC requirements do not prevent lenders from refusing to make loans in such areas, but they do prohibit racial or ethnic considerations from being determining factors in the lending decision.[19]

Loan Commitments

The initial loan application, completed by the borrower and submitted for evaluation by the lender, does not represent a binding contract. Normally it represents a mechanism to gather information concerning the loan, the borrower, and the property. After completion of the underwriting process and after negotiation between the borrower and lender, if the

---

[19]For an expanded discussion of the EEOC, see 12 CFR 202.1.

loan application is approved, the lender will issue a loan commitment. The loan commitment is binding and details the loan amount and the terms on which the lender is willing to lend. The commitment usually carries an expiration date, setting the time by which the borrower must accept the terms of the loan offer or lose the commitment.

QUESTIONS

1. What does underwriting mean in real estate lending?
2. Describe the residual income, net effective income, and gross income approaches to underwriting. What kinds of mortgage loans are usually associated with each?
3. Why would a lender be concerned about payment shock, negative amortization, and the existence of a teaser rate, when underwriting an adjustable rate mortgage?
4. Compare the differences between private and FHA mortgage insurance from the lender's perspective. What similarities exist?
5. How do private or public mortgage insurance, hazard insurance, and mortgage cancellation insurance each serve to reduce default risk from the lender's perspective?
6. Under Regulation B of the Board of Governors of the Federal Reserve Board, what guidelines must a lender follow when underwriting a loan?
7. Why is the income approach to value often difficult to use on a single family residential appraisal?
8. What are the differences between the cost and market comparison approaches to appraising property?

PROBLEMS

1. Ms. Sally Strutter is considering the purchase of a residence for $60,000. She desires a fixed rate, constant payment 30-year mortgage. Ms. Strutter requests some information from you concerning what types of loans are available on her proposed purchase. After questioning her you determine that she is single, a veteran, and is eligible for a VA guaranteed mortgage. The amount of guarantee available to her would be the current VA maximum because Ms. Strutter has never used any of her loan guarantee benefits. Her current occupation is stockbroker, and she has earned $36,000 annually over the last several years. Typically, Ms. Strutter has incurred expenses of $5,000 annually in earning that income. Her credit record is exceptional, and her only current obligation is an auto loan with payment of $100 monthly for the next 36 months. Ms. Strutter has $7,000 in savings at the current time.

   After some research you are able to compile the following information about the borrower and the property in the proposed transaction:

Borrower Data

Monthly federal income taxes	$439
Monthly state income taxes	$78
Monthly FICA withholding	$194

Property Characteristics

Current owner's hazard insurance premium	$36 monthly
Property taxes	$33 monthly
Maintenance expenses	$45 monthly average
Utilities monthly	$105 average

In addition, you decide that should the borrower desire an FHA 203b mortgage, the closing cost allowance authorized by FHA in this region for determining the mortgage balance would be about $1,000.

a. Calculate the *maximum* mortgage amount for conventional insured, FHA and VA mortgages for the borrower. Do not include any costs of mortgage insurance in these mortgage amounts.

b. You determine that the appropriate FHA one-time mortgage insurance premium on the loan requested is 3.8 percent of the mortgage amount. Furthermore, you determine that the renewal premium on conventional mortgage insurance will be .35 percent of the mortgage balance outstanding annually. You believe that the available interest rate on each of the three loan types being considered will be 9.5 percent. Also, Ms. Strutter indicates she would like to finance the FHA insurance premium or the VA funding fee in the loan amount rather than pay them in cash at closing. What effect does this have on the mortgage amounts? What would Ms. Strutter's monthly payment for principal, interest, and mortgage insurance or guarantee be on each of the loans being considered?

c. Would Ms. Strutter qualify for each of the loans being considered?

d. Which loan appears to be best for Ms. Strutter? Give specific reasons.

2. As a new appraiser with the firm of Smith, Turner, and Brown, you have been given your first appraisal assignment. The subject property is located at 322 Rock Creek Road in a new suburb of a large metropolitan area. The property is like many others in the area, with three bedrooms, two baths, a living room, a den, a large kitchen, and a two-car garage. The residence has about 1,800 square feet of air-conditioned space and is of traditional design. The property is located on an interior lot with no potential flooding problems. The quality of construction appears to be about average for the market area.

From the office file you have obtained the locations of and driven by comparable properties to use in the appraisal process which have the following characteristics:

	Comparable I	*Comparable II*	*Comparable III*
Address	123 Clay St.	301 Cherry Lane	119 Avenue X
Sale price	$85,000	$79,000	$75,000
Time of sale	6 months ago	7 months ago	13 months ago
Design	Modern	Traditional	Traditional
Parking	2-car garage	2-car carport	1-car garage
Location	Corner lot	Interior lot	Interior lot
Drainage	Good	Below average	Good
Bedrooms	Four	Three	Two
Baths	Two	Two	Two
Construction	Average	Average	Below average

After discussing the matter with your boss, you have come to some conclusions concerning what you believe the different attributes of the comparable properties are likely to be worth in the market area. Appreciation in house values in the area has been very low over the past eight months, and you think that any properties which have sold within that period would probably not require any adjustments for the time of sale. However, one of the comparable properties sold over a year ago, and you think it will require a $1,500 upward adjustment. Your boss has also indicated that properties in the area which are located near the creek sell for about $1,200 less than other properties in the area because of a slower rate of runoff after heavy rains. Properties on corner lots generally sell for a premium of about $1,000. Houses with the fashionable modern design usually bring about $1,000 more than those which have traditional design characteristics. Because three-bedroom homes are considered desirable by buyers in the area, an additional fourth bedroom will generally only add about $1,200 in value to a property. However, properties which only contain two bedrooms are rather difficult to sell, and often bring $2,000 less than their three-bedroom counterparts when they are sold. Most homes in the area have a two-car garage, but when properties have a one-car garage, they usually sell for about $800 less. A two-car open carport generally reduces the value of the property by a similar amount, or $800. The inferior construction quality exhibited by comparable III should reduce its value by about $1,500.

a. Complete the market comparison approach to value and assign an estimate of value to the subject property. Give specific reasons for your choice of value.

b. Assume that the value of the lot the subject property is constructed on is $13,000. Air-conditioned space in the dwelling would cost about $36.00 per square foot to reproduce, and the garage would cost approximately $3,700 to reproduce. Complete the *cost* approach to value, assuming that, because the property is new, no depreciation of the structure is required.

Chapter 8

Residential Real Estate Closings

In the previous chapter, we considered underwriting and financing residential properties. Another important aspect of residential financing is the loan closing process and the attendant regulatory requirements. In this chapter, we consider this process. More specifically, we describe (1) the many charges and fees that are incurred by the borrower when acquiring and financing a residence, (2) the proration of costs that are the obligation of the seller when title is transferred, and (3) the standardized reporting of closing costs and financing costs that are required by federal regulation.

To provide continuity with the previous chapter, we utilize the same examples for conventional, insured conventional, *FHA* insured, and *VA* guaranteed mortgages. We provide a comparative treatment of closing and financing costs for each case as well as extending the necessary disclosure of financing costs to include *GPM*s and *ARM*s.

THE CLOSING PROCESS

After the loan commitment has been accepted by the buyer, the usual next step is for all interested parties to gather, execute, and exchange the documents necessary to close the loan and to transfer title to the property. Generally, such closings are attended by (1) buyer and seller (perhaps each with legal counsel), (2) any real estate brokers involved, and (3) the settlement agent. The settlement agent is usually a representative of a title insurance company, if such insurance is being purchased, or a representative of the lender, if no title insurance is purchased.[1] The purpose of the closing, then, is to make final settlement between buyer and seller for costs, fees, and prorations associated with the real estate transaction prior to the transfer of title.

To summarize the many sources, disbursements, charges, and credits associated with the closing, a settlement of closing statement is prepared by the settlement agent. This statement summarized the expenses and fees to be paid by the buyer and seller, and it shows the amount of funds that the buyer must pay and the amount of funds that the

---

[1]Brokers and lawyers are usually also permitted to conduct real estate closings.

seller will receive at closing. Before illustrating the closing statement, we summarize some of the costs associated with real estate closings.

Fees and Expenses

Expenses associated with loan closings must be paid either by the buyer or the seller, depending somewhat on custom in a particular lending area. There is no generally established practice in the area of expense settlement, and in many cases payment of any, or all, expenses is negotiated between buyer and seller. What follows is an identification of various expenses associated with real estate closings, followed by an illustration of a settlement statement.

Financing Costs.   These charges are generally paid to the lender and are made in connection with services performed by the lender when underwriting and approving the loan. Sometimes many of these services are performed by the lender without charge, depending on how competitive the market is for mortgage loans at the time. During periods when ample funds are available for lending, lenders may not charge for some services; when funds are scarce, however, lenders may charge for all services performed in connection with making a loan. What follows is an extensive list of possible charges that may be made by the lender.

1. Loan application fee. Charge made for processing the borrower's loan application.
2. Credit report fee. Charge made for compilation of the borrower's credit statement.
3. Loan origination fee. Charge which compensates the originator of a mortgage loan for handling paperwork, preparing mortgage documents, and dispensing funds to the borrower.
4. Lender's attorney's fees. For preparing loan documents–mortgage/note; also for examining title documents presented to the lender.
5. Property inspection and property appraisal fee required by the lender. (This does not include fees for appraisals desired by the buyer or seller. Those fees are usually paid directly by the buyer and seller outside of the closing.)
6. Fees for property survey and photos when required by the lender.
7. Fees for preparation of loan amortization schedule by the lender from the borrower.
8. Loan discount points. Additional charge paid to the lender to increase the loan yield (per discussion in the preceding chapter).
9. Prepaid interest. Interest charged from the date of closing until the date that interest begins accruing under the terms of the note. The latter date usually coincides with the day of the month that the borrower and lender prefer to make payments, which may be different from the day of the month that the closing occurs.

Prorations, Escrow Costs, and Payments to Third Parties

Property Taxes, Prorations, and Escrow Accounts.   Because the dates on which property taxes are due to a particular governmental unit rarely coincide with the title closing date, a portion of the taxes that come due at the next collection date is payed by the seller at closing. In other words, the buyer usually pays taxes only from the date that title to the property is transferred. For example, if a county collects taxes on January 1 and July 1 of each year, and the loan closing date is April 1, the seller should pay half of the taxes (January through March), which will be due on July 1 because the seller owned the property for half of the tax period. A proration of taxes is usually made at closing by deducting the seller's share of taxes from the purchase price paid by the buyer. In this way the seller pays the buyer for taxes up until the closing date.

Depending on the loan-to-value ratio in the transaction, the lender may require that an escrow account be established. An escrow account is a noninterest-bearing account into which is deposited prorated taxes from the seller and into which the borrower prepays a monthly share of property tax along with the monthly mortgage payment. These funds are accumulated until taxes are due; then a disbursement is made by the lender to pay the tax bill when due. In addition to these monthly payments, the lender may also require that two additional monthly payments be prepaid and escrowed at closing. This is done to insure the lender of a "cushion," or reserve, in the event that the borrower falls behind in payments or is in default. This provision assures the lender that no tax liens will be attached to the property as a result of the borrower's failure to pay property tax, and is usually required in cases where the loan-to-value ratio exceeds 80 percent.[2]

Mortgage Insurance and Escrow Accounts. When mortgage insurance (for either conventional or FHA loans) is made as a requirement of obtaining a loan, it will be paid in one of two ways. Either the full policy premium will be paid by the borrower at closing, or, if the borrower plans to make premium payments over time, the premium for the first year will be prepaid by the borrower at closing then disbursed to the insurer. The premium for the second year is also determined at closing, and the borrower will be required to prepay an amount equal to two monthly premiums into escrow. Monthly premium payments are then prepaid into escrow each month after the closing. In this way, when the annual policy premium comes due each year after closing, the lender will always have a full year's premium for payment plus premiums for two additional months in escrow. The escrow or reserve may be needed should the borrower fall behind in mortgage payments and default becomes a possibility. The escrow insures that the default insurance policy will not lapse should the borrower be in danger of default. This is the objective of requiring a default insurance policy, and the lender wants to be certain that it does not lapse and coverage is lost while the loan is about to go into default.

Hazard Insurance and Escrow Accounts. Hazard insurance against property damage is required by the lender as a condition for making the loan, and the mortgage usually carries a provision to that effect. For loans made in excess of 80 percent of value, however, the lender usually requires that the premium for the first year be collected at closing, which is then disbursed to the insurer. An escrow account will also be established for

---

[2]A lender may require that escrow accounts be established on any mortgage regardless of the loan-to-value ratio, but loans with loan-to-value ratios above 80 percent will always require escrow accounts, see Title 12 CFR, Section 54532(b)(6).

pro rata payments made by the borrower toward the next annual premium due on the policy renewal date. In other words, like the collection of property taxes and mortgage insurance premiums, the lender collects monthly installments equal to $\frac{1}{12}$ of the annual premium, along with the mortgage payment, and credits the insurance payment to the borrower's escrow account. When the policy renewal date arrives, the lender then disburses the 12 monthly payments accumulated to the property insurance company. In this way the lender is certain that the property is always insured against damage. This in turn insures the loan collateral. In addition to these requirements, the lender will also require that two months premiums be prepaid at closing and escrowed. In this way the lender has a hazard insurance reserve with which to pay premiums should the borrower default.

Mortgage Cancellation Insurance and Escrow Accounts.   Mortgage cancellation insurance is usually optional, depending on whether the borrower desires it. Essentially, it amounts to a declining term life insurance policy which is taken out at closing and runs for the term of the mortgage. Because with a fully amortized mortgage the outstanding loan balance declines as monthly payments are made, the insurance coverage also declines with the loan balance. In the event of the borrower's death, the insurance coverage is equal to the outstanding loan balance. The mortgage loan is repaid with insurance proceeds. Premiums are usually paid monthly and are added to the monthly mortgage payment. The lender then disburses those payments to the life insurance company. Although mortgage cancellation insurance is usually bought at the borrower's option, if the borrower's age is a critical factor in the lender's loan analysis, purchase of such insurance may be necessary to obtain the loan.

Title Insurance, Lawyer's Title Opinion.   Premiums are charged by the title insurance company to search, abstract, and examine title to a property and to issue an insurance policy that indemnifies the buyer against loss arising from claims against the property. Attorneys may perform a similar service for a fee and render an opinion as to the validity of the title held by the seller and whether it is merchantable. Normally the full premium or fee for the insurance policy or abstract opinion is paid at closing. Depending on the policy of the lending institution and government regulations, either title insurance or an attorney's opinion is required as a condition for granting a loan.

Release Fees.   Release fees are associated with canceling outstanding liens, such as the seller's mortgage lien, mechanics' liens, and so on, and for services rendered by third parties in negotiating and obtaining such releases.

Attorney's Fee.   When incurred by the buyer or seller, legal fees may be paid directly by each party outside of the closing or may be included in the closing.

Pest Inspection Certificate.   A pest inspection may be made at the insistence of the lender or buyer. In some states, such as Florida, an inspection is required before title is transferred. The inspection fee may be paid directly or included in the closing settlement.

Real Estate Commission.   When a seller of a property engages the service of a real estate agent to sell a property, the seller usually pays the commission for such service at the closing.

Statutory Costs

Certain costs may be imposed by a local or state government agency and must be paid before deeds can be recorded, which include

1. Recording fees. Fees paid for recording of the mortgage and note in the public records.
2. Transfer tax. A tax usually imposed by the county on all real estate transfers.

THE REAL ESTATE SETTLEMENT AND PROCEDURES ACT (RESPA)

From the preceding discussion of settlement costs, it is apparent that with the many possible fees and disbursements involved in a residential real estate closing, the event can become a fairly complex undertaking. Because of the lack of buyer sophistication in real estate transactions and because of past abuses in the form of exorbitant closing and referral fees charged mainly to buyers, Congress passed Public Law 95-522, known as the Real Estate Settlement and Procedures Act of 1974 (which became effective June 20, 1975), and Public Law 94-205 (effective July 1976), which amended the 1974 Act. These laws established federal control over settlement and closing procedures in transactions involving the purchase of residential real estate. This control is clearly for consumer protection, and the purpose of the Act is to effect certain changes that attempt to accomplish the following objectives:

1. More effective advance disclosure of settlement costs.
2. Elimination of kickbacks or unearned fees.
3. A reduction in the amount of escrow placed in accounts by homeowners.

Coverage of the Act

There are two requirements that a mortgage transaction must meet before it will be covered by the provisions in RESPA. First, the lender making the mortgage loan will have to be a *covered lender* as defined in the Act. Generally a lender is covered by the provisions of RESPA if the lender originates federally related mortgage loans totaling $1 million or more annually. Generally a federally related loan is one that is originated by an institution with federally insured deposits or an institution supervised by the Federal Home Loan Bank Board. Most of the usual sources of mortgage credit would be deemed covered lenders under the Act. Second, the mortgage transaction must be considered a covered transaction under the provision of RESPA. Most 1-to-4-unit residential dwellings being financed by traditional sources of first lien financing would be covered under the

Act. Loans on unimproved land, assumptions, construction loans (when made to dealers), and home improvement loans are generally excluded from coverage under the Act.[3] The general intent of RESPA is to require that the disclosures under the Act be limited to a buyer's first mortgage transaction on a residental dwelling. It should be stressed, however, that RESPA does not require that the property being mortgaged be the residence of the borrower, and as a result the purchase of small-income properties which have less than four units may be covered under the Act if they meet all the criteria discussed above.

Requirements under the Act

Although RESPA includes many provisions, only those directly associated with the closing are covered here. The essential aspects of RESPA fall into six areas which are used here to facilitate discussion:

1. Consumer information.
2. Advance disclosure of settlement costs.
3. Title insurance placement.
4. Prohibition of kickbacks and referral fees.
5. Uniform settlement statement.
6. Advance inspection of uniform settlement.

Consumer Information.   Under provisions in RESPA, lenders are required to provide prospective borrowers with an information booklet containing information on estate closings and RESPA when a loan application is made. This booklet contains information provided by the U.S. Department of Housing and Urban Development. It provides a description of closing costs and contains various illustrations designed to inform a prospective buyer-borrower of the nature of the costs. It describes the function of the parties usually involved in a real estate transaction, as well as fees likely to be charged by lenders. It also provides information on the responsibility of all parties engaged in the closing under RESPA provisions.

Advance Disclosure of Settlement Costs.   At present, the lender is required to mail to the borrower within *three days after* the time of application, good faith estimates of certain closing costs for which information is available. The lender must provide information on the basis of actual costs known at that time,[4] or estimates based on past experience in the locality where the property is located.

---

[3]No hard and fast rules can be made here; for instance, even though a construction loan to a developer is not covered under RESPA, if the same loan is later converted to a permanent mortgage and assumed by an individual then RESPA disclosures would be required. However, all other types of assumptions are generally excluded from coverage; for example, assumptions which are generally permitted on FHA and VA mortgages are excluded. For more detailed discussion see *United States Leagues of Savings Institutions,* "Special Management Bulletin," June 24, 1976.

[4]Under RESPA, the lender is only required to disclose exact amounts of settlement costs when the lender requires a specific third party to provide a settlement service. If the borrower is free to choose providers of services, the lender need only disclose a range of what an acceptable fee for the service might be.

The estimates provided by the lender generally cover costs in the following categories: (a) title search, (b) title examination and opinion, (c) title insurance, (d) attorney's fee, (e) preparation of documents, (f) property survey, (g) credit report, (h) appraisal, (i) pest inspection, (j) notary fees, (k) loan closing service fee, (l) recording fees and any transfer tax, (m) loan origination fees, (n) discount points, (o) mortgage insurance application fees, (p) assumption fees, (q) mortgage insurance premiums, (r) escrow fees (fees charged for setting up escrow accounts), and (s) prepaid mortgage interest.

In addition, it is suggested, but not required, that the lender disclose (a) hazard insurance premiums and (b) escrow deposits for mortgage insurance, hazard insurance, and property taxes, if these amounts are known at the time of the advance disclosure. In practice, it would be difficult for the lender to know these latter two amounts three days after the borrower has applied for a loan. Although these two items are not likely to be estimated by the lender at the time of the advance disclosure, they will be charged to the borrower at the time of closing.

The form of the advance disclosure may vary from lender to lender and still remain within the requirements of the Act. Typically the disclosure will be made in dollar amounts which will be estimates of the cost of settlement services which are to be performed. However, it is also acceptable for the lender to disclose *ranges* for settlement costs. For instance, a loan origination fee could be stated as ranging from $1,500 to $2,000 in the lending area where the settlement is to occur. However, the lender may not disclose a range if a *specific party* is required by the lender to provide a settlement service. In this case, a specific dollar amount is required. Also, the lender is under no requirement to redisclose if the estimates of settlement services provided to the borrower change prior to the time of closing.

Title Insurance Placement. Under RESPA, a seller may not require that a buyer use a specific title insurance company as a condition of sale. This regulation is aimed primarily at developers who may have obtained a very favorable title insurance rate on undeveloped land, with the understanding that after development, buyers would be required to place the title insurance with the same company. This part of the Act prohibits such requirements and insures the freedom of the buyer to place title insurance with any title company.

Prohibition of Kickbacks and Unearned Fees. Under RESPA, no person can give or receive a kickback or fee as a result of a referral. If any person refers a buyer-borrower to any specific party involved in the closing (lender, title company, attorney, real estate broker, appraiser, etc.) and receives a fee for the referral, receipt of such a fee violates the Act. RESPA also prohibits fee splitting by parties associated with the closing unless fees are paid for services actually performed. This latter part of RESPA has probably caused more confusion than any other provision of the Act because of the vagueness of the term ''services actually performed.'' However, the intent was to prohibit any circumvention of payments that would have been normally called referral fees by simply splitting fees.

Uniform Settlement Statement. Under RESPA provisions, a uniform settlement statement must be used by the settlement agent at closing. The responsibility for preparation of this statement lies with the lender, and it must be delivered to the borrower and seller at closing. Other closing statements, such as a company form, can also be used for closing purposes, if desired, but the uniform statement must be completed.

This statement is uniform in the sense that the same form must be used in all loan closings covered under RESPA. This form coupled with the information booklet received by the borrower when the loan application is made, which defines and illustrates costs on a line-by-line basis, should enable the borrower to make a better judgment concerning the reasonableness of the closing costs to be paid.

Advance Inspection of Uniform Settlement Statement.   Not only must a uniform settlement statement which details all closing costs be used at the closing, but the borrower has the right to inspect this statement one day prior to closing. At that time, information on the additional closing costs not required to be disclosed when the loan application is made must be disclosed to the borrower. These costs include hazard insurance premiums and any required escrow deposits, whatever their intended use is to be.

All of these costs must be disclosed to the extent that they are known to the lender on the day prior to closing. Also, the good faith estimates of other closing costs made when the loan application was completed by the borrower must be revised, if necessary, to reflect actual costs at that time. Both groups of costs must be entered on the uniform disclosure statement for inspection by the borrower.

Although the borrower has the right to advance disclosure, under RESPA the borrower is deemed to have *waived* the right of advance inspection unless a request is made in writing to see the settlement statement on or before the business day prior to settlement. If no request has been received, the lender is under no obligation to prepare the advance disclosure statement.

Escrow Deposits.   RESPA limits the amount that a creditor may require the borrower to pay as an initial deposit into the escrow account. The maximum that a lender may require from the borrower as an escrow deposit is one sixth of the annual amount to be paid on the borrowers behalf. For example, if the lender forwards premiums on the borrower's hazard insurance annually, then the maximum escrow deposit that the borrower can be required to make is one sixth (two monthly premiums) of the annual hazard insurance premium. Lenders are not allowed to earn or pay the borrower interest on the initial deposit or monthly payments made into the escrow account.

SETTLEMENT COSTS ILLUSTRATED

To help the reader understand how settlement costs are allocated between buyer and seller, we present an example involving the acquisition of the property used in our base example. We demonstrate first how closing costs are determined for the *conventional loan case,* illustrated in the previous chapter. We then make a comparison of these costs for all other cases in the next section. The basic information for the closing transaction is shown in Exhibit 8–1. Essentially, these costs must be disclosed to the borrower on the uniform settlement statement shown in Exhibit 8–2.

EXHIBIT 8–1   Information for RESPA Closing Statement

Buyer: John and Jane J. Jones
482 Liberty Street
Anytown, USA

Seller: Ralph and Pearl Brown
200 Heavenly Drive
Anytown, USA

Lender: ABC Savings and Loan Association
Anytown, USA

Settlement agent: Land Title Company
Anytown, USA

Loan application date: March 1— conventional loan

Advance disclosure date: March 3

Borrower may request advance copy of actual settlement statement on March 24

Actual settlement date (closing date): March 25

I. Buyer and seller information
  a. Purchase price $76,700.00
  b. Deposit 1,000.00
  c. Real estate tax proration (taxes due January 1)
    $797 per year; taxes unpaid by seller 181.24
    (January 1–March 25 or 83 days/365 days times $797 = $181.24)

II. Buyer-borrower and lender information
  a. Amount of loan (9.25% interest,30 years,conventional loan) 61,360.00
  b. Prepaid interest March 25–31 (7 days) or
    (.0925 ÷ 365) times $61,360 times 7 = ... 108.85
  c. Property tax (escrow) (2 months @ $66.42 month) 132.84
  d. Loan origination fee (1%) 614.00
  e. Loan discount (1%) 614.00
  f. Application fee 50.00
  g. Appraisal 125.00
  g. Credit report 45.00
  i. Hazard insurance (escrow) 92.00

III. Transactions between buyer-borrower and others
  a. Recording fees 31.00
  b. Hazard insurance (1 yr.) 552.00

IV. Transactions between seller and others
  a. Land Title Company — closing fee 75.00
  b. Release statement — seller's mortgage 5.00
  c. Payoff-seller's mortgage (Anytown State Bank) 21,284.15
  d. Real estate brokerage fee (6%) (Bobbie Broker) 4,602.00
  e. Pest inspection (Anytown Pest Co.) 20.00
  f. Title insurance — Land Title Company 350.00

EXHIBIT 8–2   RESPA Closing Statement

OMB No. 2502-0265 (Exp. 12-31-86)

A.	U.S. DEPARTMENT OF HOUSING AND URBAN DEVELOPMENT **SETTLEMENT STATEMENT**	B.		TYPE OF LOAN

B. TYPE OF LOAN

1. ☐ FHA   2. ☐ FMHA   3. ☒ CONV. UNINS.
4. ☐ VA   5. ☐ CONV. INS.

6. FILE NUMBER: 7. LOAN NUMBER:

8. MORTGAGE INS. CASE NO.:

C. NOTE: *This form is furnished to give you a statement of actual settlement costs. Amounts paid to and by the settlement agent are shown. Items marked "(p.o.c.)" were paid outside the closing; they are shown here for informational purposes and are not included in the totals.*

D. NAME OF BORROWER: / ADDRESS OF BORROWER:
John and Jane J. Jones
482 Liberty Street
Anytown, USA

E. NAME OF SELLER: / ADDRESS OF SELLER:
Ralph and Pearl Brown
200 Heavenly Drive
Anytown, USA

F. NAME OF LENDER: / ADDRESS OF LENDER:
ABC Savings & Loan
Anytown, USA

G. PROPERTY LOCATION:
200 Heavenly Dr.
Anytown, USA

H. SETTLEMENT AGENT: / PLACE OF SETTLEMENT:
Land Title Co.
100 North Street
Anytown, USA

I. SETTLEMENT DATE: 3-25-86

J. SUMMARY OF BORROWER'S TRANSACTION		K. SUMMARY OF SELLER'S TRANSACTION	
100. GROSS AMOUNT DUE FROM BORROWER:		400. GROSS AMOUNT DUE TO SELLER:	
101. Contract sales price	76,700.00	401. Contract sales price	76,700.00
103. Settlement charges to borrower *(Line 1400)*	2,364.69	403. Reserves transferred	
104.		404.	
105.		405.	
Adjustments for items paid by seller in advance:		*Adjustments for items paid by seller in advance:*	
106. **School** / City, town tax to		406. **School** / City, town tax to	
107. **State** / County tax to		407. **State** / County tax to	
108. School tax to		408. School tax to	
109. Prorations (Rent, Tax, Ins.)		409. Prorations (Rent, Tax, Ins.)	
110. Assessments		410. Assessments	
111.		411.	
120. GROSS AMOUNT DUE FROM BORROWER:	79,064.69	420. GROSS AMOUNT DUE TO SELLER:	76,700.00
200. AMOUNTS PAID BY OR IN BEHALF OF BORROWER:		500. REDUCTIONS IN AMOUNT DUE TO SELLER:	
201. Deposit or earnest money	1,000.00	502. Settlement charges to seller *(Line 1400)*	5,052.00
202. Principal amount of new loan(s)	61,360.00	503. Existing loan(s) taken subject to	
203. Existing loan(s) taken subject to		504. Payoff to first mortgage loan	21,284.15
204. Settlement cost paid by Seller		505. Payoff of second mortgage loan	
205. Add.amts. financed by lender		506. Deposit or earnest money	
206.		507. Settlement cost paid for borrower	
207.		508.	
208.		509.	
Adjustments for items unpaid by seller		*Adjustments for items unpaid by seller*	
210. **School** / City, town tax to		510. **School** / City, town tax to	
211. **State** / County tax to		511. **State** / County tax Jan. 1 toMar.25	181.24
213. School tax to		513. School tax to	
214. All Taxes to		514. All Taxes to	
215.		515.	
216.		516.	
		520. TOTAL REDUCTION AMOUNT DUE SELLER	26,517.39
220. TOTAL PAID BY / FOR BORROWER	62,360.00		
300. CASH AT SETTLEMENT FROM / TO BORROWER		600. CASH AT SETTLEMENT TO / FROM SELLER	
301. Gross amount due from borrower *(Line 120)*	79,064.69	601. Gross amount due to seller *(Line 420)*	76,700.00
302. Less amounts paid by / for borrower *(Line 220)*	(62,360.00)	602. Less reductions in amount due seller *(Line 520)*	(26,517.39)
303. CASH (☒ FROM) (☐ TO) BORROWER	16,704.69	603. CASH (☒ TO) (☐ FROM) SELLER	50,182.61

Southwest Land Title Co., acting as Escrow Agent, has assembled on this Statement, information and figures representing your transaction as understood by it. It is the responsibility of the Escrow Agent to make such settlement as agreed to by all parties to this transaction. Tax prorations have been based on figures for the preceding year, or estimates for the current year, and in the event of change of taxes for the current year, all necessary adjustments must be made between Seller and Purchaser and / or Borrower and Lender, with the understanding that Southwest Land Title Co. will not be liable for any adjustments. In the event a Real Estate Agent negotiated this transaction, or in the event a loan is involved, such agent and lender may be furnished a copy of this statement. If the foregoing statement is satisfactory to you, please signify your approval, and authorization of payments and receipt of a copy hereof, by signing your name in the space provided.

EXHIBIT 8–2 (*Concluded*)

L. Settlement Charges			Paid From Borrower's Funds at Settlement	Paid From Seller's Funds at Settlement
700.	**Total Sales / Broker's Commission based on price $**	@ =		
	Division of Commission (line 700) as follows:			
701.	$	to		
702.	$ 4,602.00	to Bobbie Broker		
703.	Commission paid at Settlement			4,602.00
704.				
800.	**Items Payable In Connection With Loan**			
801.	Loan Origination Fee 1 %to ABC Savings		614.00	
802.	Loan Discount 1 %to ABC Savings		614.00	
803.	Appraisal Fee $125.00 to I.M.Sharp Co.		125.00	
804.	Credit Report $ 45.00 to Will Check Co.		45.00	
805.	Lender's Inspection Fee to			
808.	Amortization Schedule to			
810.	Photos to			
811.	Warehouse Fee to			
812.	Tax Research Fee to			
813.	Mortgage Application Fee $50 to ABC Savings		50.00	
814.				
815.				
816.				
817.				
900.	**Items Required By Lender To Be Paid In Advance**			
901.	Interest from 3-25-86 to 3-31-86 @ $ 15.55 per/day		108.85	
902.	Mortgage Insurance Premium for months to			
903.	Hazard Insurance Premium for 1 years to Safety First, Inc.		552.00	
905.				
1000.	**Reserves Deposited With Lender**			
1001.	Hazard Insurance 2 months@$ 46.00 per month		92.00	
1002.	Mortgage Insurance months@$ per month			
1003.	City/school property taxes months@$ per month			
1004.	County property taxes 2 months@$ 66.42 per month		132.84	
1005.	Annual assessments months@$ per month			
1007.	months@$ per month			
1008.				
1100.	**Title Charges**			
1101.	Settlement or closing fee to Land Title Co.			75.00
1102.	Abstract or title search to			
1103.	Title examination to			
1104.	Title insurance binder to			
1105.	Document preparation to			
1107.	Attorney's fees to			
	(includes above items numbers: 1105			
1108.	Title insurance to Land Title Co.			350.00
	(includes above items numbers: 1102, 1103			
1109.	Lender's coverage $ 350.00			
1110.	Owner's coverage $			
1111.	Restrictions			
1112.	Escrow Fee			
1113.	IRS Reporting Fee			
1114.				
1115.				
1116.				
1200.	**Government Recording and Transfer Charges**			
1201.	Recording fees: Deed $ 10.00 ; Mortgage $ 15.00 ; Releases $ 5.00		25.00	5.00
1204.				
1300.	**Additional Settlement Charges**			
1301.	Survey to			
1302.	Pest inspection to Pests-R-Us, Co.			20.00
1303.	Tax Certificates		6.00	
1304.	State of Texas Policy Guaranty Fee			
1305.	Courier / Messenger Fees			
1306.				
1307.				
1308.				
1309.				
1400.	**Total Settlement Charges (enter on lines 103, Section J and 502, Section K)**		2,364.69	5,052.00

I have carefully reviewed the HUD-1 Settlement Statement and to the best of my knowledge and belief, it is a true and accurate statement of all receipts and disbursements made on my account or by me in this transaction. I further certify that I have received a copy of the HUD-1 Settlement Statement.

_____   _____
Borrowers   Sellers

The HUD-1 Settlement Statement which I have prepared is a true and accurate account of this transaction. I have caused or will cause the funds to be disbursed in accordance with this statement.

_____   _____
Settlement Agent   Date

Warning: It is a crime to knowingly make false statements to the United States on this or any other similar form. Penalties upon conviction can include a fine and imprisonment. For details see: Title 18 U.S. Code Section 1001 and Section 1010.

As shown in Exhibit 8–1, closing costs are separated into four categories, the first three of which involve the buyer. These are: the amount to be paid to, or received from, the seller, lender, and third parties. The fourth category involves costs that must be paid by the seller to third parties. Most items have been previously explained; however, a few computational procedures deserve mention.

In Section I of Exhibit 8–1 note that a property tax proration is made for the 83 days that the property has been owned by the seller since the last property tax payment was made. This tax is paid by the seller at closing. This amount will be paid by the seller to the buyer and ultimately escrowed by the lender for payment on the next due date. Prepaid interest for seven days will be collected by the lender, as monthly payments are scheduled to commence on May 1 (Section II). Interest included in the first, regular payment on May 1 spans the period of April 1–30; hence interest for March 25–31 (inclusive) must be paid at closing. The reader should also note that two monthly installments for hazard insurance and property taxes are to be prepaid by the buyer and escrowed by the lender. Finally, the lender is also requiring evidence of a binder and one full year's hazard insurance be prepaid at closing to the insurance carrier. The amounts shown in Exhibit 8–1 are summarized on the uniform settlement statement in Exhibit 8–2. As previously indicated, this statement must be used by lenders to disclose closing costs in most residential transactions.

A Comparison of Settlement Costs

Exhibit 8–3 illustrates the primary distinction between closing costs for our four types of mortgages. We have used the descriptions and numbering from Exhibit 8–2 so that the reader can relate the summary shown in Exhibit 8–3 to the uniform statement. In the far left column, we repeat the description of the types of costs that are likely to be encountered by the buyer-borrower. Looking to the first cost category for all four loans, we see that a loan origination fee of 1 percent and loan discount (points) equal to 1 percent are to be charged in each case. Because the loan amounts vary for each mortgage type, the dollar amount will also vary. We should also point out that, depending on market conditions, lenders could vary the origination and discount points higher or lower than the 1 percent amount shown in our example. Also, it may be the case that the seller may be willing to pay all or some of these points for the buyer. In the case of VA, however, there is currently a restriction on what the borrower may pay at closing which is equal to a 1 percent funding (origination) fee plus a 1 percent discount fee. Any additional discount points must be paid by the *seller*. We should also point out that both FHA and VA are very concerned about the *reasonableness* of closing costs and may reject an insurance or guarantee request if these costs are too high. This is because FHA allows a portion of the closing costs (see the $1,350 in our example shown in Exhibit 7–4) to be included in the loan amount and therefore attempts to keep these costs to a minimum so that more of the funds paid in by the borrower are applied to equity. VA is also concerned about these costs because it is guaranteeing a loan with no down payment and it does not want the veteran to become overextended at the time of closing.

EXHIBIT 8–3 Comparison of Closing Costs and Funds Required (rounded) from the Borrower/Buyer under Four Mortgage Alternatives

	Conventional	Insured Conventional	FHA	VA
A. Purchase price	$76,700	$76,700	$76,700	$76,700
Financing fees (Section 800)				
(801) Loan origination (1 percent)	614	729	746¶	767
(802) Loan discount (1 percent)	614	729	775	767†
(803) Appraisal	125	125	125	125
(804) Credit report	45	45	45	45
(808) Application	50	50	50	50
Prepaids required by lender (900)				
(901) Prepaid interest — 7 days	109	133	141	141
(902) Mortgage insurance (total)			2,837*	
(902) Mortgage insurance (year 1)	—	583	—	—
(903) Hazard ins. (escrow) 1 year	552	552	552	552
Reserves deposited with lender (1000)				
(1002) Mortgage ins. (escrow)—2 months	—	42	—	—
(1003) Hazard ins. (escrow)—2 months	92	92	92	92
(1004) Property tax (escrow)—2 months	133	133	133	133
Statutory charges (1200)				
(1201) Recording fee	31	31	31	31
B. (1400) Total charges	$ 2,365	$ 3,244	$ 5,527	$ 2,703
C. (120) Total funds required (A + B)	$79,065	$79,944	$82,227	$79,403
less:				
Amounts paid by or on behalf of borrower (200)				
(201) Earnest money	1,000	1,000	1,000	1,000
(202) Mortgage loan	61,360	72,865	74,648	76,700
(205) Additional amounts financed by lender	–0–	–0–	2,837‡	767†
(303) Total borrower requirements at closing	$16,705	$6,079	$ 3,742	$ 936
D. Monthly payments:				
Loan amount [202 + 205]	$61,360	$72,865	$77,485	$77,467
Interest rate	9.25%	9.50%	9.50%	9.50%
Payment on loan (30 years)	$504.79	$612.69	$651.54	$651.38
add:				
Mortgage insurance	—	21.00‡	—§	—
Hazard insurance	46.00	46.00	46.00	46.00
Property taxes	66.42	66.42	66.42	66.42
Total collected by lender	$617.21	$746.11	$763.96	$763.80

*FHA mortgage insurance is also financed based on 3.8 percent of loan amount with interest computed at 9.5 percent and repayment over 30 years. Mortgage insurance payments are included with monthly principal and interest payment. If paid at closing, the amount would be 3.66 percent of the loan amount and would be included in closing costs.

†The 1 percent fee is funded in the loan amount.

‡Estimated based on loan balance at the end of year 1. ($72,415) times .0035 (premium rate second year) or $253.45 ÷ 12 = $21 (rounded). This amount is subject to change each year as the loan balance declines.

§Mortgage insurance payment included in monthly payment.

¶Based on amount financed (see: Exhibit 7–6).

Other categories show fees for processing the loan application ($50), the cost of an appraisal ($125), obtaining a credit report ($45), and seven days of prepaid interest, which will vary with the loan amount and the interest rate in each case. In the case where *private mortgage insurance* is required, the entire first year's premium will be collected at closing and disbursed to the insurer. Monthly premiums for the next year (second year's premium) are determined, and two additional monthly premiums are then prepaid and escrowed.[5] For FHA mortgage insurance, the full premium for the life of the mortgage is charged at closing; however, additional funds are loaned by the lender and are then paid to FHA. The borrower then repays the lender (with interest) for the prepaid insurance premium which is added to the loan balance. Subsequent monthly payments include repayment of this additional amount financed with interest, using the same interest rate and amortization pattern as the mortgage loan. In both the private insurance and FHA cases, the borrower may elect to pay the full premium in cash. We do not assume this in our example, since in practice most borrowers elect to use the installment option just described.[6]

As shown before, in all cases, the first year's premium for hazard insurance will be collected and disbursed to the insurance carrier. Also, an additional amount equal to two months' payment will be escrowed by the lender as a reserve in case of borrower default. As before, an escrow for property taxes will also be required in our example. The additional two months' escrows required for mortgage insurance, hazard insurance, and property taxes are repaid to the borrower when the property is eventually sold. Finally, we show the filing fee charged by the public entity for processing and recording the change in title and mortgage lien in the public record.

In reconciling the various flow of funds under the four loan categories shown at the bottom of Exhibit 8–3, we see that when closing costs (B) are added to the purchase price (A), total funds required from the buyer (C) results. When the earnest money deposit, loan amount, and additional amounts financed by the lender are subtracted, the result becomes the total amount due from the borrower *on the day that the transaction is closed.*

In Section D of Exhibit 8–3, we present the monthly payment to be received by the lender beginning one month and seven days after closing. The total monthly payment is composed of principal and interest (*P & I*) on the loan amount and any additional amounts financed, plus monthly prepayments of mortgage insurance, property taxes, and hazard insurance. The latter amounts are escrowed. Each year, these monthly prepayments to escrow accounts may be adjusted, depending on the lender's estimate of amounts likely to be due when annual disbursements must be made to the appropriate entities. With the FHA insured loans, the full insurance premium is added to the loan amount as additional financing and the monthly payment is simply computed at 9.5 percent for 30 years; hence the lender is also earning 9.5 percent on the total FHA insurance premium which has

---

[5] Private mortgage insurance may cease to be required when the mortgage balance declines below 80 percent of the initial purchase price, or the current appraised value of the property, depending upon the agreement of the lender and borrower. Unless the point at which mortgage insurance may be canceled is specified in the mortgage agreement, the lender may continue to purchase it on the borrower's behalf and charge the borrower for it.

[6] Under some circumstances, if a borrower prepays an FHA mortgage, a refund of the remaining mortgage insurance premium included in the amount financed may be made.

been loaned to the borrower. The VA example shows no insurance premium paid either at closing or in monthly payments because the guarantee is provided as a benefit by VA. Also, because VA funds up to 1 percent of the loan amount for added financing costs, the borrower will be required to pay only a 1 percent funding fee plus other closing costs. Hence, the VA borrower makes no equity down payment in this example, only closing costs of $936 are paid at closing.

As to the difference between funds required at closing and monthly payments as the four alternatives are compared, a general pattern is apparent for the first three alternatives. The reader can see that in those cases, as the amount of funds required of the borrower at closing decreases, the monthly payment increases. This pattern does not hold for the VA case because the borrower is required to make a smaller cash commitment at closing than would be the case with the FHA insured loan, but the monthly payment is essentially the same. This is because of the "free" loan guarantee provided by VA, which is absorbed by the U.S. Government and which is available only to qualified veterans. The reader should also keep in mind that we have dealt with a case example where the purchase price of the dwelling and required financing is sufficiently low enough to qualify under all four scenarios. In practice, both the FHA and VA place restrictions on either (1) the maximum purchase price or (2) the loan amount which may be lower than the borrower desires. Should the purchase price and/or required loan amount exceed these limits, an FHA or VA mortgage may not be a viable option for the borrower. In that event, conventional loans may be the only financing alternatives available. Finally, in cases where all four types of financing are options to a borrower, a choice which considers the trade-off between funds required at closing and monthly payments must also be made. In other words "how does one analyze whether a lower down payment and larger monthly payments are better than a higher down payment with lower monthly payments?" The procedure for examining this trade-off is presented in the next chapter.

Federal Truth-in-Lending (FTL) Requirements

In addition to disclosure requirements affecting settlement costs under RESPA, disclosure requirements under the federal Truth-in-Lending Act which deals with the cost of mortgage credit, has been a requirement affecting lenders since 1968.[7] The intent of FTL legislation is to require that lenders disclose to borrowers financial information contained in loan agreements in a uniform manner. This is required so that borrowers can compare the cost of different loan agreements. It should be stressed that FTL legislation does not attempt to regulate the cost of mortgage credit, but it mandates uniform disclosure of the cost of credit. This section begins with a description of mortgage transactions that are covered under the Act. Next, disclosure and timing requirements of FTL are discussed. The remainder of the section deals with how the annual percentage rate (*APR*) is determined. In addition, sample FTL disclosures for our four example loans—conventional, insured conventional, FHA, and VA—will be presented to illustrate differences in the FTL disclosure process.

---

[7]USC 1601; Stat. 146; Pub. L. 90-321 (May 29, 1968), as amended.

EXHIBIT 8–4   *FTL* Disclosure Requirements (numerical disclosures (*FRM*))

Disclosure Item	Description
Annual percentage rate	The effective cost of credit to the borrower on an annual basis as determined by an actuarial method prescribed in the Act.
Finance charges	The sum of (1) all interest paid over the term of the loan including discount points, (2) loan application fees*, (3) *required* mortgage insurance or guarantee, credit life, or disability, and hazard insurance†, (4) loan origination fees, (5) discount points, (6) escrow charges made for establishing an escrow account, (7) prepaid mortgage interest, (8) assumption fees, (9) fees for the preparation of an amortization schedule, when *paid for by the borrower.*
Amount financed	The mortgage amount less any of the finance charges described above which are paid at closing.
Total of payments	The borrower's total monthly payment over the loan term, including interest and principal reduction and fees for required mortgage insurance or credit life insurance, but typically excluding charges for property taxes and hazard insurance.
Amount of payments	The dollar amount of borrower monthly payments. When the monthly payment varies due to the cost of mortgage insurance, typically the highest and lowest payment amounts will be disclosed. When payment increases are known, as would be the case on a *GPM,* all payment amounts must be disclosed to the borrower.
Number of payments	For a constant payment, fixed rate mortgage the term of the mortgage times 12. For a *GPM,* the number of times a borrower must make a payment must be disclosed.

*When an application fee is charged to all applicants, rather than just to applicants who receive loan approval, this fee need not be included in the finance charge.

†Credit life or disability insurance need not be disclosed with the finance charge unless it is required by the lender. Hazard insurance is included in the finance charge only when the lender requires that a specific insurer must be used.

Coverage of the Truth-in-Lending Act

Truth-in-lending legislation generally requires that lenders disclose financial information contained in mortgage loan agreements to individuals. Mortgage transactions which require RESPA disclosure usually require FTL disclosure also. However, in certain circumstances it is possible for a mortgage transaction to be covered by either RESPA or FTL but not both. For instance, if the borrower in a mortgage transaction is a *business entity* such as a corporation or partnership or the mortgage transaction involves a one- to four-family residential *rental property,* RESPA disclosure, but not FTL disclosure, will generally be required. In these cases a business entity is the purchaser and not an individual borrower. In some cases, such as when an individual applies for a mortgage to refinance a residence or to assume another individual's mortgage, FTL disclosure, but

EXHIBIT 8–4   *concluded. FTL* Disclosure (contents in loan agreement)

Disclosure Item	Description
Security interest	The lender must describe the nature of any interest he will require in the borrower's property should the loan be granted. Typically the lender must describe any assets which he places a lien against.
Assumption policy	The lender must inform the borrower whether the mortgage is assumable by a subsequent purchaser of the property and whether the loan terms might change at the time of assumption.
Variable rate	If the interest rate on the mortgage is not fixed, the lender must disclose this fact.
Filing fees	The lender must disclose any statutory fees for filing liens against loan assets.
Late charge	The lender must disclose the existence and amount of any late payment fees.
Payment due date	The date after which the lender will charge late fees.
Prepayment policy	Whether or not a penalty will have to be paid should the borrower repay the loan before the term has expired. The amount of any penalty need not be disclosed.
Hazard insurance	The lender must disclose whether insurance is required.
Mortgage insurance	Premium amount of any such insurance if the lender either requires or offers it for sale to borrowers.

not RESPA disclosure, would generally be required. These transactions are excluded from coverage under RESPA. But, since the borrower is an individual, FTL disclosure would still be required.

Nature of Truth-in-Lending Disclosure

There are two types of disclosures made to consumers under FTL requirements: (1) numerical disclosures concerning the cost of mortgage credit provided for the benefit of the borrower, and (2) disclosures of certain terms of the mortgage agreement. Exhibit 8–4 describes both requirements for a fixed rate, constant payment mortgage. With other mortgage types, such as *ARMs* and *GPMs*, additional disclosure is required. Disclosure requirements on *GPMs* and *ARMs* will be discussed in detail in the next section.

Timing of Federal Truth-in-Lending Disclosure

The FTL disclosures described in Exhibit 8–4 must be made by lenders three days after application for a mortgage is made by the borrower. Recall that this time requirement is the same as the RESPA disclosure for closing costs. However, unlike the RESPA disclosure, which are estimates, the FTL disclosure, particularly the *APR,* must be accurate to one eighth of a percent. As a result, market interest rates and, hence, the *APR* may change from the time of application until the loan is closed. If this happens, the lender must make additional disclosures prior to the date of loan closing.

Truth-in-Lending Sample Disclosure

Exhibit 8–4 contains a description of disclosures that must be made under FTL regulations. Referring to Exhibit 8–5 will aid the reader in establishing what financing costs are included under each disclosure item.

EXHIBIT 8–5   Federal Truth-in-Lending Disclosure requirements (*FRM* transactions)

	Conventional	Conventional Insured	FHA	VA
(*a*) Prepaid finance charges				
Loan origination fee	$ 614	$ 729	$ 746	$ 767
Discount fee	614	729	775	–0–
Prepaid interest	109	133	141	141
Prepaid mortgage insurance	–0–	583	–0–	–0–
Prepaid finance charge	$ 1,337	$ 2,174	$ 1,662	$ 908
(*b*) Payment amount				
Constant	$ 504.79	N/A	$ 651.53	$ 651.38
Highest		$ 633.94		
Lowest		$ 612.69		
(*c*) Number of payments	360	360	360	360
(*d*) Total of payments				
(*c* times *b*)	$181,724	$223,919	$234,551	$234,497
(*e*) Total finance charge*	121,701	153,228	161,565	158,705
(*f*) Amount financed				
(1) *first method:*				
original loan balance	61,360	72,865	74,648	76,700
less :				
prepaid finance charge	(1,337)	(2,174)	(1,662)	(908)
amount financed	$ 60,023	$ 70,691	$ 72,986	$ 75,792
(2) *second method:*				
total payments	$181,724	$223,919	$234,551	$234,497
less:				
total finance charge	$121,701	153,228	161,564	158,705
amount financed	$ 60,023	$ 70,691	$ 72,986	$ 75,792
(*g*) APR	9.5%	10.19%	10.20%	9.75%

*This amount includes all interest and mortgage insurance premiums, as well as all prepaid finance charges.
†Based on amount financed.

Establishing the *APR* under Federal Truth-in-Lending Requirements

The *APR* is the most important required disclosure under FTL, because not only must it be disclosed to loan applicants, it also must be used when the lender advertises specific loan programs. Accuracy of calculation is also important because in the case of fixed rate, constant payment mortgages the stated *APR* may vary from the true *APR* by only one eighth of a percent. The calculation performed to determine the *APR* is essentially the same as the internal rate of return calculation developed in previous chapters.

By using the information provided in Exhibit 8–5, determining the *APR* on the sample conventional mortgage developed in Chapter 7 is fairly straightforward. The *APR* is found by taking the amount financed from the exhibit shown as item (f), then setting this amount equal to the borrower's monthly payment, shown as item (b), and solving for the interest rate that makes the present value of the monthly payments equal to the amount financed. This is done as follows:

$$PV = MP(MPVIFA, \ ? \ \%, \ 360 \ mos.)$$
$$\$60{,}023 = \$504.79(MPVIFA, \ ? \ \%, \ 360 \ mos.)$$
$$i = 9.5\%$$

Determining the *APR* on the conventional insured mortgage is more difficult. This is because of multiple, uneven payments that occur as annual premiums for mortgage insurance change at the end of each year. Exhibit 8–6 illustrates the payment pattern on a conventional insured mortgage, where the annual mortgage insurance premium is based as a percentage of the outstanding loan balance each year. To find the *APR*, 30 groups of 12 monthly payments listed in the exhibit must be discounted until the present value equals the amount financed. The procedure for discounting grouped cash flows has been presented in an earlier chapter, and the student should refer again to that material. The *APR* on the mortgage used in the example and the payment pattern shown in Exhibit 8–6 is 10.19 percent.

The calculation of the *APR* on the FHA or VA mortgages is done the same way as was shown for the conventional mortgage. The *APR* for the FHA insured mortgage is 10.2 percent; it is 9.75 percent for the VA mortgage example.

*ARM*s and Truth-in-Lending Disclosure

In addition to the required disclosure for an *FRM* outlined in Exhibit 8–4, slightly more disclosure is required when a borrower applies for an *ARM*. Additional items that must be disclosed are listed in Exhibit 8–7. The intent of the additional disclosure on *ARM*s is to illustrate to the borrower the effect of one increase in the composite rate (the index plus the margin) on monthly payments and the loan balance. However, determining the *APR* is more difficult on an *ARM*. The difficulty arises because, as discussed in the previous chapter, future interest rates on *ARM*s are *unknown*.

Because the future pattern of interest rates is unknown, the method required when determining the *APR* on an *ARM* requires that the margin plus index *at the time of origination* be used as the assumed interest rate over the entire term of the loan. An example should help clarify this point. We make the following assumptions:

EXHIBIT 8–6   Mortgage Insurance Premiums (conventional mortgage)

Year	Mortgage Balance Beginning of Year	Annual Mortgage Insurance Premium	Annual Mortgage Insurance Payment	Borrower Monthly Payment	Current Mortgage Balance as a Percentage of the Original Mortgage Balance
Closing	$72,865.19	$582.92			100.00%
1	72,865.19	255.03	$21.25	$633.94	100.00
2	72,415.87	253.46	21.12	633.81	99.38
3	71,921.96	251.73	20.98	633.67	98.71
4	71,379.03	249.83	20.82	633.51	97.96
5	70,782.22	247.74	20.64	633.33	97.14
6	70,126.17	245.44	20.45	633.14	96.24
7	69,405.01	242.92	20.24	632.93	95.25
8	68,612.28	240.14	20.01	632.70	94.16
9	67,740.87	237.09	19.76	632.45	92.97
10	66,782.98	233.74	19.48	632.17	91.65
11	65,730.02	230.06	19.17	631.86	90.21
12	64,572.55	226.00	18.83	631.52	88.62
13	63,300.21	221.55	18.46	631.15	86.87
14	61,901.59	216.66	18.05	630.74	84.95
15	60,364.17	211.27	17.61	630.30	82.84
16	58,674.15	205.36	17.11	629.80	80.52
17	56,816.41	0.00	0.00	612.69	77.97
18	54,774.29	0.00	0.00	612.69	75.17
19	52,529.50	0.00	0.00	612.69	72.09
20	50,061.91	0.00	0.00	612.69	68.70
21	47,349.43	0.00	0.00	612.69	64.98
22	44,367.73	0.00	0.00	612.69	60.89
23	41,090.11	0.00	0.00	612.69	56.39
24	37,487.19	0.00	0.00	612.69	51.45
25	33,526.70	0.00	0.00	612.69	46.01
26	29,173.13	0.00	0.00	612.69	40.04
27	24,387.48	0.00	0.00	612.69	33.47
28	19,126.87	0.00	0.00	612.69	26.25
29	13,344.15	0.00	0.00	612.69	18.31
30	6,987.52	0.00	0.00	612.69	9.59
31	0.00	0.00	0.00	-0-	0.00

Conventional *ARM*.

$60,000 loan amount.

2 percent annual interest rate cap.

5 percent over the life of the mortgage cap.

8 percent initial rate.

 7 percent index at origination.

 2 percent margin.

30-year term.

$1,200 prepaid finance charge.

$59,498.76 balance at the end of year 1.

Negative amortization is allowed.

The following illustrates the calculation of an *APR* on the loan described above:
 (A) Payment year 1:

$$PMT = \$60,000(MLC, 8\%, 360 \text{ mos.})$$
$$= \$440.28$$

 (B) Payment year 2 through year 30:

$$PMT = \$59,498.76(MLC, 9\%, 348 \text{ mos.})$$
$$= \$482.06$$

The payments in (B) are based on the index (7%) plus margin (2%) at origination. Using a financial calculator, we get

$$\$58,800 = \$440.28(MPVIFA, ?\%, 12 \text{ mos.})$$
$$+ \$482.06(MPVIFA, ?\%, 348 \text{ mos.})(MPVIF, ?\%, 12 \text{ mos.})$$
$$APR = 9.12\%$$

EXHIBIT 8–7   Federal Truth-in-Lending Additional Required Disclosures or *ARM*s

---

· Index
· Margin
· Composite rate at the time of origination
· Adjustment period
· Payment caps at each adjustment period (if any)
· Payment caps over the term of the loan (if any)
· Interest rate caps over the life of the loan (if any)
· Interest rate caps at each adjustment period (if any)
· Whether composite rate increases will affect payment amounts, the loan balance, or both
· An example of the effect that an increase in the composite rate would have on payment amounts or the loan balance or both (depending upon payment and rate caps, as well as any limits on negative amortization the loan may feature).

Recall that disclosure of the *APR* on a fixed rate mortgage must be accurate to one eighth of a percent; however, on an *ARM*, the *APR* may vary as much as one fourth of a percent from the actual *APR*.

It should be stressed that this method of computing the *APR* on an *ARM* will almost certainly *not* reflect the true cost of funds to the borrower. Clearly, a decrease or increase in the index over the loan term would cause the stated *APR* to be incorrect. Moreover, the lender is not required to redisclose the *APR* after closing. As a result, the borrower should be aware that using the *APR* for an *ARM* for comparison with *FRM*s or *ARM*s with substantially different terms is not advisable. Indeed, the usefulness of an *APR* for an *ARM* is quite limited since it assumes that the composite rate (9 percent) in existence at the time that the loan is originated will be the same at the end of the first adjustment interval and for every succeeding period for the term of the loan.

QUESTIONS

1. What is the legislative intent of federal truth-in-lending disclosures, and what specific disclosures are required under the Act?
2. When would the cost of credit life insurance be included in the finance charge and *APR* calculations for federal truth-in-lending disclosures?
3. What assumption about the future composite rate of interest on an adjustable rate mortgage is made when determining the *APR* for federal truth-in-lending disclosures?
4. List the closing cost items which require RESPA disclosure. What items may be excluded from disclosures under the Act? What form can these disclosures take?
5. What types of fees and conditions are prohibited under RESPA?
6. How can a borrower waive the right to advance inspection of the actual uniform settlement statement which will be used at closing under RESPA?
7. For what items may a lender require escrow accounts from a borrower?
8. Under the Real Estate Settlement and Procedures Act requirements, how large an escrow account deposit may a lender require?

PROBLEMS

1. A loan with the following terms is being made:

   Fixed rate, constant payment.

   10% interest rate.

   $80,000 desired mortgage amount.

   $2,000 prepaid finance charge.

   30-year term, monthly payments.

   a. Calculate the *APR* for federal truth-in-lending purposes.
   b. Do you think that the *APR* calculated in (a) reflects the likely return that the lender will receive over the term of the loan? List specific reasons that the lender's actual return might be different than the *APR*.

2. As a new loan officer with ABC Mortgage, the manager of the loan department has just presented a problem to you. He is unable to complete the *APR* calculation on an adjustable rate mortgage which a borrower applied for yesterday. The loan features initial payments based upon an 8 percent rate of interest, while the current composite rate on the loan is 11 percent. No discount points have been paid by any party to the transaction, and any difference between borrower payments and the interest payment required at the composite rate will be accrued in the mortgage balance in the form of negative amortization. The mortgage amount desired by the borrower is $50,000 for a 30-year term, but a one-time mortgage insurance premium of $2,700 is being funded as a part of the loan amount, making the total loan balance $52,700. The borrower is paying $1,400 in prepaid finance charges at closing.

   a. Determine the *APR,* assuming that the *ARM* is made with a 2 percent annual and 5 percent over-the-life interest rate cap.

   b. When do you have to finish your assignment to remain within federal truth-in-lending guidelines?

   c. In what way does the *APR* disclosure aid the borrower in understanding the terms of this specific loan agreement? What are some of the problems with the *APR* calculations on *ARM*s?

3. On August 20, Mr. and Mrs. Gould decided to buy a property from Mr. and Mrs. Booth for $115,000. On August 30, Mr. and Mrs. Gould obtained a loan commitment from ABC Savings and Loan for a $92,000 conventional loan at 10 percent for 30 years. The lender informs Mr. and Mrs. Gould that a $2,300 loan origination fee will be required to obtain the loan. The loan closing is to take place September 22. In addition, escrow accounts will be required for all prorated and prepaid property taxes and hazard insurance; however, no mortgage insurance is necessary. The buyer will also pay a full year's premium for hazard insurance to Rock of Mutual Insurance Company. A breakdown of expected settlement costs has been provided by ABC Savings and Loan when Mr. and Mrs. Newton request and inspect the uniform settlement statement as required under RESPA on September 21, as follows:

I.	Buyer and seller information	
	a. Purchase price	$115,000.00
	b. Deposit paid by Newton's to Oldton's (paid in escrow to ABC Savings and Loan)	1,000.00
	c. Real estate tax proration (taxes due to county January 1 and July 1. $800 per year, $400 per half) (July 1–September 22 unpaid by seller) 83 days or (83/365 · $800)	181.77
II.	Buyer-borrower and lender information	
	a. Amount of loan	92,000.00
	b. Prepaid interest (regular monthly) payments to begin on November 1 from closing through September = 9 days [(.10 · $92,000) ÷ 365] · 9	226.85
	c. Property tax escrow—2 months required	133.33
	d. Hazard insurance escrow—2 months @ $20 required	40.00
	e. Loan origination fee	2,300.00

III.   Transactions between buyer-borrower and third parties

    a. Title insurance fee (Landco Title Co.) $ 300.00

    b. Recording fees—mortgage and deed   25.00

    c. Real estate transfer tax   200.00

    d. Barry Barrister—attorney   100.00

    e. Hazard insurance—one year policy—Rock of Mutual
Ins. Co.   240.00

IV.   Transactions between seller and third parties:

    a. Landco Title Co.—closing fee   95.00

    b. Release statement—seller's mortgage   5.00

    c. Payoff—seller's mortgage (XYZ State Bank)   15,215.00

    d. Real estate brokerage fee (6% Plain Deal Realty)   6,900.00

    e. Linda Lawyer—attorney   150.00

    f. Pest inspection   20.00

a. What are the amounts due from the borrower and due to the seller at closing?

b. What would the disclosed annual percentage rate be required under the Truth-in-Lending Act?

Chapter 9

Analysis of Residential Finance

In previous chapters we have considered the analytics of various types of mortgages used in real estate finance. This chapter extends those concepts to various questions related to the financing of owner-occupied residential properties. Topics to be examined include questions such as how to compare two loans with different loan terms (amount of loan, interest rate, etc.), how to decide whether to refinance or prepay a loan, and whether or not a loan assumption is desirable. The effect of below market financing on the sale price of a house will also be evaluated. This is important because one must often pay a higher price for a home which appears to have favorable financing.

INCREMENTAL BORROWING COST

We begin by considering the question of how to evaluate two loan alternatives where one alternative involves borrowing additional funds relative to the other alternative. For example, assume a borrower is purchasing a property for $100,000 and faces two possible loan alternatives. A lender is willing to make an 80 percent first mortgage loan, or $80,000, for 25 years at 12 percent interest. The same lender is also willing to lend 90 percent, or $90,000, for 25 years at 13 percent. Both loans will have fixed interest rates and constant payment mortgages. How should the borrower compare these alternatives?

To analyze this problem, emphasis should be placed on a basic concept called the *incremental* or *marginal cost* of borrowing. Based on the material presented in earlier chapters, we know how to compute the effective cost of borrowing for one specific loan. However, it is equally important in real estate finance to be able to compare financing alternatives, or situations in which the borrower can finance the purchase of real estate in more than one way or under different lending terms.

In our problem at hand we are considering differences in the amount of the loan and the interest rate. A loan can be made for $80,000 for 25 years at 12 percent, or $90,000 can be borrowed for 25 years at 13 percent interest. Because there are no origination fees, we know from the preceding chapter that the effective interest cost for the two loans will be 12 percent and 13 percent, respectively. However, an important cost that the borrower should compute is the cost to acquire the incremental or additional $10,000, should he choose to take the $90,000 loan over the $80,000 loan. At first glance the reader may think that because the interest rate on the $90,000 loan is 13 percent, the cost of acquiring the additional $10,000 is also 13 percent. This is *not* so. Careful analysis of the two loans reveals that when compared to the $80,000 loan available at 12 percent interest, if the borrower wants to borrow the additional $10,000, he also must pay an *additional* 1 percent interest on the first $80,000 borrowed. This increases the cost of obtaining the additional $10,000 considerably. The $90,000 loan has a larger payment due to the fact that an additional $10,000 is being borrowed *and* the fact that a higher interest rate is being charged on the entire amount borrowed. To determine the cost of the additional $10,000, we must consider how much the additional payment will be on the $90,000 loan versus the $80,000 loan. This difference should then be compared with the additional $10,000 borrowed. This can be done as follows:

	Loan Amount		Loan Constant		Monthly Payments
Alt. II at 13%	$90,000	times	.011278	=	$1,015.05
Alt. I at 12%	80,000	times	.010532	=	842.57
Difference	$10,000		Difference		$ 172.48

We want to find the annual rate of interest, compounded monthly, that makes the present value of the difference in mortgage payments, or $172.48, equal to $10,000, or the incremental amount of loan proceeds received. As previously discussed, one approach is to solve directly for the interest factor. We have

$$\$172.48(MPVIFA, \ ?\%, \ 25 \ \text{yrs.}) = \$10,000$$
$$(MPVIFA, \ ?\%, \ 25 \ \text{yrs.}) = \$10,000/\$172.48 = 57.977737$$

As seen from above, we have computed the monthly *interest factor* for the $172.48 annuity to be 57.977737. Looking to column 5 in Appendix B, we see that this factor is close to the 25-year factors in the 20 percent interest rate table. Using a financial calculator indicates that the answer is 20.57 percent. Hence, if our borrower desires to borrow the additional $10,000 with the $90,000 loan, the cost of doing so will be over 20 percent, a rate considerably higher than 13 percent. This cost is referred to as the *marginal or incremental cost of borrowing.*

The borrower must consider this cost when evaluating the decision as to whether the additional $10,000 should be borrowed. If the borrower has sufficient funds so that the $10,000 would not have to be borrowed, it tells the borrower what rate of interest must be earned on funds *not* invested in a property because of the larger amount borrowed. In other words, by obtaining a larger loan ($90,000 versus $80,000), this means that $10,000 less will be required as a down payment from the borrower than would have been the case had the $80,000 loan been made. Hence, unless the borrower can earn 20.57 percent interest *or more* on a $10,000 investment of equal risk on funds not invested in the property, he would be better off with the smaller loan of $80,000.

If the borrower does not have sufficient down payment for an $80,000 loan and needs to borrow $90,000, the incremental borrowing cost indicates the cost of obtaining the extra $10,000 by obtaining a larger first mortgage. There may be alternative ways of obtaining the extra $10,000. For example, if the borrower could obtain a second mortgage for $10,000 at a rate *less* than 20.57 percent, this may be a better alternative than a 90 percent loan.[1] Therefore, the marginal cost concept is also an *opportunity cost* concept in that it tells the borrower the minimum rate of interest that must be earned, or the maximum amount that should be paid, on any additional amounts borrowed.

It should be noted that the 20.57 percent figure we calculated above also represents the *return* that the lender earns on the additional $10,000 loaned to the borrower. That is, the *cost* of a loan to the borrower will reflect the *return* on the loan to the lender. Of course it should be kept in mind that the figures we are calculating do not take federal income tax considerations into account, which are also important in determining returns and costs. For example, if the borrower is in a higher tax bracket than the lender, then the after-tax cost to the borrower will be less than the after-tax return to the lender.

Early Repayment

We should also note that in this example, the incremental cost of borrowing will depend on when the loan is repaid. For example, if the loan is repaid after one year, instead of being held for the entire loan term, the incremental borrowing cost increases from 20.57 to 20.97 percent. To see this, we modify the above analysis to consider the fact that if the loan is repaid after one year, the amount that would be repaid on the $80,000 loan will differ from the amount that would be repaid on the $90,000 loan. Thus in addition to considering the difference in payments between the two loans, we must also consider the difference in the loan balances at the time the loan is repaid. We can find the incremental borrowing cost as follows:

	Loan Amount		Loan Constant		Monthly Payments	Loan Balance after One Year
Alt. II at 13%	$90,000	times	.011278	=	$1,015.05	$89,489.68
Alt. I at 12%	80,000	times	.010532	=	842.57	79,459.99
Difference	$10,000		Difference		$ 172.48	$10,029.69

Computing the marginal cost, we have

$172.48 *(MPVIFA, ?%,* 1 yr.) + $10,029.69*(MPVIF, ?%,* 1 yr.) = $10,000

---

[1] A lower effective cost for a second mortgage means that the borrower pays less interest each month. However, if the second mortgage has a term less than 25 years, the total monthly payments will be higher with the $80,000 first mortgage and a $10,000 second mortgage than for a $90,000 first mortgage. Thus, some borrowers may prefer to choose a higher effective borrowing cost to have lower monthly payments.

In this case we cannot simply solve for an interest factor and use the tables to find the interest rate. This is because there are two present value factors in the above equation. To find the answer we must find the interest rate which makes the present value of the monthly annuity and lump sum equal to $10,000. This method for doing this has been presented in Chapter 5. The reader should be able to verify that the incremental borrowing cost is now 20.97 percent. Thus early repayment has increased the incremental cost of borrowing from 20.57 percent to 20.97 percent. As we will see in the next section, the impact of early payment may be greater when there are also points involved on one or both of the loans.

Origination Fees

It should be apparent that the incremental borrowing cost concept is extremely important when deciding how much should be borrowed to finance a given transaction. In the preceding section, the two alternatives considered were fairly straightforward with the only differences between them being the interest rate and the amount borrowed. As discussed in the preceding chapter, in most cases financing alternatives under consideration will have *different* interest rates as the amount borrowed increases and, possibly, *different* loan maturities. Also, loan origination fees will usually be charged on the loan alternatives. This section considers differences in loan fees on two loan alternatives. The next section considers differences in loan maturities.

The first case we wish to consider is the incremental cost of borrowing when loan origination fees are charged on the two 25-year loan alternatives. For example, if a $1,600 origination fee (two points) is charged on the $80,000 loan and a $2,700 fee (three points) is charged on the $90,000 loan, how does this affect the incremental cost of borrowing? These differences can be easily included in the cost computation as follows.

Differences in amounts borrowed and payments:

	Loan	−	Fees	=	Net Amount Disbursed	Loan		Loan Constant		Monthly Payments
Alt. II at 13%	$90,000	−	$2,700	=	$87,300	$90,000	times	.011278	=	$1,015.03
Alt. I at 12%	$80,000	−	$1,600	=	78,400	$80,000	times	.010532	=	842.57
			Difference	=	$ 8,900			Difference	=	$ 172.46

As we did previously, we want to find an annual rate of interest, compounded monthly, that makes the present value of the difference in mortgage payments, or $172.46, equal to $8,900, or the incremental amount of loan proceeds received. Using a financial calculator, we find that the exact answer is 23.18 percent. Hence, the marginal cost increases to about 23.2 percent when the effects of origination fees are included in the analysis. This results from the fact that $1,100 in additional fees are charged on the $90,000 loan. Thus, the borrower only benefits from an additional $8,900 instead of $10,000.

As before, the marginal or incremental cost of borrowing increases if the loan is repaid before maturity. For example, if in the above problem, the loan were repaid after 10 years, the incremental cost would increase to about 23.57 percent.

Differences in Maturities

In the above examples, the loan alternatives considered had the same maturities (25 years). How does one determine the incremental cost of alternatives that have different maturities as well as different interest rates? Do differences in maturities materially change results? We examine these questions by changing our previous example and assuming that the $90,000 alternative has a 30-year maturity as well as a higher interest rate. How would the analysis be changed? We first must compute the following information:

	Loan	Payments Years 1–25	Payments Years 26–30
Alt. III at 13%, 30 yrs.	$90,000	$995.58	$995.58
Alt. I at 12%, 25 yrs.	80,000	842.57	–0–
Difference	$10,000	$153.01	$995.58

In this case we compute the monthly payment for a $90,000, 30-year loan at 13 percent interest, which is $995.58. However, there are two differences in the series of monthly payments relevant to our example. For the first 25 years, should alternative III be chosen over alternative II, the borrower will pay an additional $153.01 per month. For the final five-year period, or years 26 through 30, the difference between payments will be the full $995.58 payment on alternative III because the $80,000 loan would be repaid after 25 years. Hence the incremental cost must be computed by considering the payment differences as two annuities or grouped cash flows as follows:

$153.01(*MPVIFA*, ?%, 25 yrs.)
+ $995.58(*MPVIFA*, ?%, 5 yrs.) (*MPVIF*, ?%, 25 yrs.) = $10,000

In the above formulation, the second annuity of $995.58 runs for 5 years, but it is not received until the end of year 25 and therefore must also be discounted for 25 years.[2] We cannot solve directly for the interest factor because there are two unknown factors. Thus, we must use the procedures outlined in Chapter 5 to calculate the yield (cost). Using an estimate of 19 percent and discounting, we get

---

[2]Alternatively we could compute the present value of the second annuity as follows: $995.58(*MPVIFA*, ?%, 30 yrs. − 25 yrs.).

$$PV = \$153.01(62.590755) + \$995.58(38.549682)(.008980)$$
$$= \$9,921.65$$

Because the desired present value is $10,000, the answer must be slightly *less* than 19 percent. Using a calculator which can solve for an *IRR* with uneven, or grouped cash flows, we find the solution is 18.86 percent. Hence the marginal or incremental cost of borrowing the additional $10,000 given the interest rate increases from 12 percent to 13 percent but the loan term increases from 25 years to 30 years will be about 18.86 percent. This compares to the incremental cost of 20.57 percent in the first example where there also were no fees charged but both maturities were 25 years. The reason the marginal cost is lower in this case is that although a higher rate must be paid on the $90,000 loan, it will be repaid over a longer maturity period, 30 years. Even though the borrower pays a higher rate for the $90,000 loan versus the $80,000 loan, there is a benefit of a longer amortization period (and thus lower monthly payments) on the $90,000 loan.

We should point out that if the loan is expected to be repaid before maturity, both the difference in monthly payments and loan balances in the year of repayment must be taken into account when computing the marginal borrowing cost. Also, should any origination fees be charged, the incremental funds disbursed by the lender should be reduced accordingly.

LOAN REFINANCING

On occasion, an opportunity may arise for an individual to refinance a mortgage loan at a reduced rate of interest. For example, during 1986 interest rates fell substantially relative to what they had been for many years. Many borrowers had existing home mortgage loans at rates of 14 percent or more, but could refinance with loans at rates less than 11 percent. Thus many borrowers took advantage of the opportunity to refinance. In fact, for a while the demand for loans to refinance existing mortgages exceeded the demand for loans to purchase a home.

The fundamental relationships that must be known in any refinancing decision include at least three ingredients: (1) terms on the present outstanding loan, (2) new loan terms being considered, and (3) any charges associated with paying off the existing loan or acquiring the new loan (such as prepayment penalties on the existing loan or origination and closing fees on the new loan). To illustrate, assume a borrower made a mortgage loan 5 years ago for $80,000 at 15 percent interest for 30 years (monthly payment). After 5 years, interest rates fall, and a new mortgage loan is available at 14 percent for 25 years. The loan balance on the existing loan is $78,976.50. Suppose that the prepayment penalty of 2 percent must be paid on the existing loan, and the lender who is making the new loan available also requires an origination fee of $2,500 plus $25 for incidental closing costs if the new loan is made. Should the borrower refinance?

In answering this question, we must analyze the costs associated with refinancing and the benefits or savings which all accrue due to the reduction in interest charges, should the borrower choose to refinance. The costs associated with refinancing are as follows:

Cost to refinance:
Prepayment penalty: 2% times $78,976.50 =	$1,580
Origination fee, new loan	2,500
Recording, etc., new loan	25
	$4,105

Benefits from refinancing are obviously the interest savings that result from a lower interest rate. Hence, if refinancing occurs, the monthly mortgage payment under the new loan terms will be lower than payments under the existing mortgage. Monthly benefits would be $60.88 as shown:

Monthly savings due to refinancing:
Monthly payments, existing loan, $80,000, 15%, 30 Years	$1,011.56
Monthly payments, new loan, $78,976.50, 14%, 25 years	950.68
Difference in monthly payments	$ 60.88

The issue faced by the borrower now becomes whether it is worth "investing," or paying out, $4,105 (charges for refinancing) to save $60.88 per month over the term of the loan. Perhaps the $4,105 could be invested in a more profitable alternative? To analyze this question, we should determine what rate of return is earned on the investment of $4,105 for 25 years, given that $60.88 per month represents a savings. Using a financial calculator, we find that the yield on our $4,105 investment, with savings of $60.88 per month over 25 years, would be equivalent to earning 17.57 percent per year. If another alternative equal in risk cannot be found which provides a 17.57 percent annual return, the refinancing should be undertaken.

Early Repayment—Loan Refinancing

One additional point must be made concerning refinancing if the property is not held for the full 25 years. In that event, monthly savings of $60.88 do not occur for the entire 25-year term, and therefore the refinancing is not as attractive. To demonstrate, if we assume the borrower plans to hold the property for only 10 more years after refinancing, is refinancing still worthwhile? To analyze this alternative, note that the $4,105 cost will not change should the refinancing be undertaken; however, the benefits (savings) will change. The $60.88 monthly benefits will be realized for only 10 years. In addition, since the refinanced loan is expected to be repaid after 10 years, there will be a difference between loan balances on the existing loan and the new loan, due to different amortization rates.

Loan balance, 15th year—existing loan*	$72,275
Loan balance, 10th year—new loan†	71,386
Difference	$ 889

*Based on $80,000, 15 percent, 30 years, prepaid after 15 years.
†Based on $78,796, 14 percent, 25 years, prepaid after 10 years.

The new calculation comparing loan balances under the existing loan and under the new loan terms shows that if refinancing occurs, the amount saved because of a lower loan balance is $889, should the new loan be made. Hence, total savings in the event of refinancing would be $60.88 per month for 10 years, plus $889 at the end of 10 years. Do these savings justify an outlay of $4,105 in refinancing costs? To answer this question, we compute the return on the $4,105 outlay as follows:

$$\$60.88 \ (MPVIFA, \ ?\%, \ 10 \ \text{yrs.}) + \$889 \ (MPVIF, \ ?\%, \ 10 \ \text{yrs.}) = \$4,105$$

Because the loan is repaid early and the monthly savings of $60.88 will not be received over the full 25-year period, the yield must be below the 17.57 percent yield computed in the previous example. The yield earned due to refinancing in this case will be 14.21 percent per year for the 10-year period.

Obviously, this return is lower than the 17.57 percent computed by assuming the loan was repaid after 25 years. This is true because the refinancing cost of $4,105 remained the same, while the savings stream of $60.88 was shortened from 25 years to 10 years. Although an additional $889 was saved because of differences in loan balances, it did not offset the reduction in monthly savings that will have occurred from the 10th through the 25th year. In analyzing refinancing decisions, then, not only must costs and benefits (savings) be compared, but the time period one expects to hold a property must also enter into the decision.[3]

Effective Cost of Refinancing

The refinancing problem can also be analyzed by using an extension of the effective cost concept discussed in the previous chapters. From this previous discussion, we know that points increase the effective cost of a loan. In our problem the borrower would be making a new loan for $78,976.50, but must pay $4,105 in "fees" to do so. Although these fees include the prepayment penalty on the old loan, this can be thought of as a cost of making a new loan by refinancing. Thus, the borrower in effect receives $78,976.50 less

---

[3]Obviously, the shorter the time period that the borrower expects to be in the home after refinancing, the lower the return on "investing" in refinancing. In fact if the period of time is relatively short, the return could be negative. Hence, if a borrower expects to sell a property within a short time after refinancing, it will be difficult to justify refinancing.

$4,105 or $74,871.50. Payments on the new loan would be $950.68. To find the effective cost for the case where the loan is held to maturity, or 25 years, we proceed as follows:

$$\$950.68(MPVIFA, \ ?\%, \ 25 \ yrs.) \ = \ \$74,871.50$$

Using the tables or a financial calculator, we obtain an interest rate of 14.86 percent. This can be interpreted as the effective cost of obtaining the new loan by refinancing. Since this cost is *less* than the rate on the old loan (15 percent), refinancing would seem . to be desirable.[4]

Borrowing the Refinancing Costs

In the above analysis we assumed that the borrower had to pay (as a cash outlay) the refinancing costs of $4,105. But it is likely that if the borrower were going to go to the trouble of refinancing, he may also be able to borrow the refinancing costs.[5] How does this effect our analysis?

The borrower now gets a loan for the loan balance of $78,976.50 *plus* the fees of $4,105.00 for a total of $83,081.50. Payments at the 14 percent rate (assuming the interest rate is still the same) would be $1,000.10.[6]. What do we compare this to now that the borrower has no cash outlay when refinancing? The answer is simple. These payments are still less than those on the old loan ($1,011.56). Given that the borrower has lower payments ($11.46) for 300 months without any cash outlay, it is desirable to refinance.[7]

We could, of course, also compute the effective cost of refinancing as we did in the previous section. In this case, the total amount of the loan is $83,081.50; however, the borrower, in effect, only benefits from $78,976.50 (the loan amount less the refinancing costs). Using the payment of $1,000.10 and assuming the new loan is held for the full loan term, we can calculate the effective cost as follows:

$$\$1,000.10 \ (MPVIFA, \ ?\%, \ 25 \ yrs.) \ = \ \$78,976.50$$

Solving for the effective interest rate, we obtain an answer of 14.81 percent, which is virtually the same as we obtained in the previous section. In fact, the only reason the answer is slightly lower is that the origination fee on the new loan was assumed to remain at $2,500 even though the amount of the loan was increased to cover the refinancing costs.

---

[4]Any points that *had* been paid on the *old* loan would *not* be relevant in this analysis since they are a "sunk cost." That is, they have already been paid and are not affected by refinancing. Thus, only the current interest rate on the old loan should be compared with the effective cost of the new loan.

[5]The borrower will probably have sufficient equity in the home to do so since if the old loan was held for several years he has reduced the balance on the old loan and the home may have increased in value.

[6]If this approach were used to analyze the case where the loan was to be repaid early, the additional loan balance on the refinanced loan would have to be considered. This would *reduce* the benefit of the lower payments.

[7]If the interest rate was higher, then we would also want to consider the incremental cost of the additional $4,105, as considered earlier in the chapter.

Note that assuming the refinancing fees are borrowed does not affect our conclusion, even though we analyzed the problem a little differently. Often there are many ways of considering a problem that leads to similar conclusions. It is informative to look at a problem several ways to gain skill in handling the wide variety financial alternatives one may encounter. Knowing alternative ways of analyzing a problem also reduces the chance of applying an incorrect solution technique.

EARLY LOAN REPAYMENT—LENDER INDUCEMENTS

After a period of rising interest rates, borrowers may have a loan that has an interest rate that is below the market rate. Earlier we considered the situation where interest rates had fallen and the borrower may find it beneficial to refinance at a lower interest rate even if additional fees and penalties have to be paid to the lender. In a situation where interest rates have risen considerably the situation may be opposite. Banks may be willing to ''pay'' the borrower to induce him or her to repay the loan early. That is, the lender may offer the borrower a discount to pay off the balance of a below market interest rate loan.[8] How much of a discount should be offered?

To illustrate, suppose a borrower has a loan which was made 10 years ago. The original loan amount was $75,000 to be amortized over 15 years at 8 percent interest. The balance of the loan is now $35,348, and the payments are $716.74 per month. If the current market interest is 12 percent, then the lender would like to have the loan paid off early so that funds could be loaned to someone else at the market rate. The borrower has no incentive to prepay the loan even if he has $35,348 available to do so. However, the bank may be willing to offer the borrower a discount to prepay the loan. Suppose the lender discounts the loan by $2,000 so that only $33,348 must be paid to the lender. Is this attractive to the borrower?

By accepting the discount, the borrower, in effect, earns a return on the funds used to repay the loan. That is, by making a payment of $33,348 to the lender the borrower saves $716.74 per month. To calculate the return earned by prepaying the loan, we have

$$\$716.74(MPVIFA, \text{ ?}\%, 5 \text{ yrs.}) = \$33,348$$

Scanning the tables for the MPVIFA, or using a financial calculator, we find the return to be about 10.5 percent. Thus the interest savings represent a 10.5 percent return on the ''investment'' made to repay the loan.[9] Whether this represents an attractive proposition for the borrower depends on what alternatives he or she has for investing the $33,348.

---

[8]This is particularly true if the loan is assumable.

[9]The above analysis does not consider the impact of federal income taxes. The IRS has ruled that when a lender discounts a loan such that the borrower does not have to repay the contract loan balance, the discount represents ''loan forgiveness'' and as such is considered taxable income. Thus the borrower would have to pay taxes on the $2,000 discount. For a 40 percent investor, the taxes would be $800. Thus, the net result is as if the borrower only received a discount of $2,000 − $800 = $1,200. This clearly reduces the benefit to the borrower to repay the loan.

In the above example, we assumed that the borrower had the funds ($33,348) to prepay the below market rate loan. Several other possibilities could be considered. One possibility is that the borrower would refinance some, or all, of the loan at the market rate. Another possibility is that the borrower wants to increase the loan balance by refinancing. In either case the lender may still be willing to provide an inducement for him to refinance since his existing loan is at a below market rate. However, the approach that would be taken to analyze the problem depends on whether, on balance, the borrower gives funds to the lender to reduce the loan balance in exchange for the lower payments or if the borrower receives additional funds in exchange for an additional loan payment.

MARKET VALUE OF A LOAN

We have considered several problems in which the balance of a loan was determined after payments had been made for a number of years. The balance of the loan represents the amount that the borrower must repay the lender in order to satisfy the loan contract. (Any prepayment penalties would of course have to be added to the loan balance.) The loan balance may be interpreted as the "contract" or "book value" of the loan. However, if interest rates have changed since the origination of the loan, the loan balance will probably not represent the "market" value of the loan.

The market value of a loan is the amount that a new lender or investor would pay to receive the remaining payments on the loan. It can be thought of as the amount that could be loaned so that the remaining payments on the loan would give the lender a return equal to the current market rate of interest.

Finding the market value of a loan simply involves calculating the present value of the remaining payments at the market rate of interest. For example, suppose a loan was made 5 years ago for $80,000 with an interest rate of 10 percent and monthly payments over a 20-year loan term. Payments on the loan are $772.02 per month. As we know, one way of finding the current balance of the loan is to compute the present value of the remaining loan payments at the *contract* interest rate of 10 percent. We have

$$\text{Loan balance} = \$772.02 \ (MPVIFA, 10\%, 15 \text{ yrs.})$$
$$= \$772.02 \ (93.057439)$$
$$= \$71,842$$

To find the market value of the loan, we compute the present value of the remaining payments at the market interest rate. Suppose that rate is currently 15 percent. We have

$$\text{Market value} = \$772.02 \ (MPVIFA, 15\%, 15 \text{ yrs.})$$
$$= \$772.02 \ (71.449643)$$
$$= \$55,161$$

Thus the market value of the loan is $55,161, as compared to the loan balance of $71,842. The market value or $55,161 is the amount that the lender would receive if the loan were sold to another lender, investor, or the secondary market.[10] We could say that the above loan is selling at a "discount." The amount of the difference in this case would be $71,842 − $55,161 = $16,601. We could also say that the mortgage is selling at a discount of 23 percent of its "face" value.

The market value of the loan is lower than the contract loan balance in this example because interest rates have risen relative to the interest rate (10 percent) at which the loan was originated at some 10 years ago. However, the borrower is required to make payments based on 10 percent even though market rates have risen to 15 percent. This is one reason why adjustable rate mortgages have become more attractive to lenders (see Chapter 6). With an adjustable rate mortgage, the market value of the outstanding loan will not differ as much when compared to a new loan originated at market rates of interest. In fact, if the interest rate on the outstanding loan could be adjusted at each payment interval and there were no limitations (caps) on the amount of the adjustment, then the contract rate on the loan would always equal the market rate. In this event, the loan balance and market value for such a loan would always be equal because future payments would be based on current rates of interest.

EFFECTIVE COST OF TWO OR MORE LOANS

There are many situations where the buyer of a home may be considering a combination of two or more loans (e.g., a first and a second mortgage to finance the home). One situation where this could arise is when a loan is being assumed because a favorable rate of interest exists on the first mortgage.[11] However, the amount of cash necessary for the buyer to assume a mortgage may be prohibitive. This can occur because the seller has already paid down the balance of the loan, and because the home has appreciated in value since it was originally financed by the seller. Thus the seller must use a second mortgage to bridge the gap between the amount available from the loan assumption and the desired total loan amount.

Suppose an individual bought a $100,000 property and made a mortgage loan 5 years ago for $80,000 at 10 percent interest for a term of 25 years. Due to price appreciation the market value of the property has risen in value over the past five years to $115,000. The amount of cash equity required by the buyer to assume the seller's loan would be $39,669, determined as follows:

---

[10]It is informative to look at an alternative approach which yields the same answer. Suppose we were to make a loan for $71,842 at the market rate of 15 percent for the remaining loan term of 15 years. The payment would be $1,005.49. This is $233.47 higher than the contract payment. If we discount this *difference* in payments for the 15-year period at the market rate, we get a present value of $16,681. Subtracting this difference from the loan balance results in the market value of the loan.

[11]In many areas of the United States, properties are sold on assumption. However, in many other areas, the right to sell on assumption is precluded explicitly in the mortgage or by the lender not approving the new buyer. Lending practices vary widely, depending on tradition and economic conditions in a given area.

Purchase price	$115,000
Seller's mortgage balance	
($80,000, 10%, 25 yrs., after 5 yrs.)	75,331
Cash equity required to assume	$ 39,669

If the buyer does not have $39,669 in cash, even though he desires an assumption, he may be unable to complete the transaction. One alternative open to the buyer who could not make the large cash outlay in the above example may be to obtain a second mortgage. However, using a second mortgage will be justified in this case only if the terms of the second mortgage, when combined with the terms on the assumed mortgage, will make the borrower as well or better off than if the entire purchase had been financed with a new mortgage. If the entire purchase can be financed with a new $92,000 loan (80 percent of value) at 12 percent for 20 years, we must know how to combine a second mortgage with the assumed mortgage to determine whether or not the assumption would be as attractive as the new mortgage loan. Suppose a second mortgage for $16,669 ($92,000 − $75,331) could be obtained at a 14 percent rate for a 20-year term. To analyze this problem, we compute the combined mortgage payments on the assumed loan and a second mortgage loan made for 20 years at 14 percent.

Monthly payment assumed loan*	$726.96
Monthly payment second mortgage loan[†]	207.28
	$934.24

*Based on original $80,000 loan, at 10 percent, for 25 years.
[†]Based on second mortgage loan of $16,669 at 14 percent, for 20 years.

The combined monthly payments equal $934.24. We now want to compute the effective cost of the combined payments which are made on the combined loan of $92,000. We have

$$\$934.24 \ (MPVIFA, \ ?\%, \ 20 \ \text{yrs.}) = \$92,000$$
$$MPVIFA = 98.475766$$

Using a financial calculator, we find an answer of 10.75 percent. This is the cost of obtaining $92,000 with the loan assumption and second mortgage. Since this is less than the cost of obtaining $92,000 with a new first mortgage at a rate of 12%, the borrower is still better off with the loan assumption and a second mortgage.[12] It is important to

---

[12]It should be apparent that such a high interest rate can be paid on the second mortgage because $75,331, the amount assumed, carries a 10 percent rate and represents about 82 percent of the $92,000 to be financed, while the second mortgage of $4,669 represents only 18 percent. When weighted together by the respective interest rates, the total rate paid on the combined amounts is influenced more by the amount assumed at 10 percent. As an approximation of the average of "blended" rate for the two loans, we have (.82 times 10%) + (.18 times 14%) = 10.72%, which is approximately the same as the answer we found using the present value factors above.

note, however, that the above analysis does not consider the fact that the *seller of the home may have raised the price of the home* to capture the benefit of his below market rate loan which could be assumed. Later in the chapter we will consider how this could be considered in our analysis.

Second Mortgages and Shorter Maturities

In most cases second mortgages may not be available for a 20-year period. If a five-year term were available on a second mortgage loan at 14 percent interest, would the borrower still be better off by assuming the existing mortgage and making a second mortgage? To answer this question, we must determine the combined interest cost on the assumed mortgage which carries a rate of 10 percent for 20 remaining years and the second mortgage which would carry a rate of 14 percent for 5 years. This combined rate can then be compared to the current 12 percent rate for 20 years presently available, should the property be financed with an entirely new mortgage loan.

To combine terms on the assumable mortgage and second mortgage, we add monthly payments together as follows:

	Monthly Payments
Assumed loan*	$ 726.96
Second mortgage[†]	387.86
Total	$1,114.82

*Based on original terms: $80,000, 10 percent, 25 years.
[†]Based on $16,669, 14 percent, 5 years.

The sum of the two monthly payments is equal to $1,114.82. However, the combined $1,114.82 monthly payments will be made for only five years. After five years, the second mortgage will be completely repaid, and only the $726.96 payments on the assumed loan will be made through the 20th year.

Whether or not the combined mortgages should be used by the borrower can now be determined by again solving for the combined cost of borrowing. This cost is based on the monthly payments under both the assumed loan and second mortgage, for the respective number of months payments must be made, in relation to the $92,000 amount being financed. This can be seen easily to be the monthly payments of $118.56 on the second mortgage for *5 years* and the $726.96 payments on the assumed mortgage for *20 years,* both discounted by an interest rate that results in the present value of $92,000.

$387.86(*MPVIFA,* ?%, 5 yrs.) + 726.96(*MPVIFA,* ?%, 20 yrs.) = $92,000

We must find the interest rate that makes the present value of the combined monthly mortgage payments (grouped cash flows) equal to $92,000. Using a financial calculator, we find that the combined interest cost on the existing mortgage if assumed for 20 years and the second mortgage made for 5 years is 10.29 percent. This combined package of financing must again be compared to the 12 percent interest rate currently available on an $80,000 mortgage for 20 years. Because the effective cost of the two combined loans is less than the market rate, this is the best alternative. It should be noted, however, that for the first 5 years the combined monthly payments of $1,114.82, should the assumption and second mortgage combination be made, would be higher than payments that would be made with a new mortgage for $92,000 at 12% for 20 years, which would be $1,013.00 per month. Although this is offset by the lower $726.96 payments after 5 years, the borrower must decide which pattern of monthly loan payments fits his income pattern, in addition to simply choosing the loan alternative with the lower effective borrowing cost. A borrower may be willing to pay a higher effective cost for a loan (or combination of loans) which has lower monthly payments.

EFFECT OF BELOW MARKET FINANCING ON HOUSE PRICES

There are many situations where a home buyer may have an opportunity to purchase a home and obtain financing at a below market interest rate. One case which we have already discussed occurs when the seller of the house has a below market rate loan which can be assumed by the buyer. Below market financing might also be provided by the seller of the home with a *purchase money mortgage*. In this case, the seller provides some or all of the financing to the buyer at an interest rate lower than currently available in the market. Indeed this type of financing is quite common during periods of tight credit and high interest rates.

It should be obvious to the reader that below market rate loans have value to the buyer. However, because the informed seller of the home also recognizes the value of such financing, we would expect the seller to increase the price of the house to reflect this value. That is, the ''price'' of the house would be higher when accompanied with below market financing than it would be with market rate financing.

We now consider how a buyer would analyze whether to purchase a house with below market financing if the house price is higher than that of an otherwise comparable home that does not have below market financing. To illustrate, suppose a home could be purchased for $105,000 subject to an assumable loan at a 9 percent interest rate with a 15-year remaining term, a balance of $70,000 and payments of $709.99 per month. A comparable home without any special financing costs $100,000, and a loan for $70,000 could be obtained at a market rate of 11 percent with a 15-year term. Which alternative is best for the buyer? Note that we are assuming that the two loans amounts are the same. In analyzing this problem, we must consider whether it is desirable for the buyer to pay an additional $5,000 in cash for the home (additional equity invested) in order to receive the benefit of lower payments on the below market loan. The calculations are as follows:

	Down Payment	Payment
Market rate loan	$30,000	$795.62
Loan assumption	35,000	709.99
Difference	$ 5,000	$ 85.63

$85.63 times (*MPVIFA*, ?%, 180 mos.) = $5,000

Using a financial calculator, we find that making the additional $5,000 down payment would result in earning the equivalent of 19.41 percent because of the lower monthly loan payments. Alternatively, should the buyer decide not to pay the additional $5,000, he would have to find a return of 19.41 percent on the $5,000 in an investment comparable in risk. Because the 19.41 percent rate is higher than the 11 percent market rate, it appears to be desirable.

Assuming a Lower Loan Balance

For simplicity, it was assumed in the above example that the balance of the assumable (below market) loan was the same as the amount available for a new loan at the market rate. As discussed previously, an assumable loan may have a lower balance than that which would be obtained with a new market rate loan because the seller has paid down the loan and the home may have increased in value. To continue our example, suppose the balance on the assumable loan is only $50,000. The buyer, however, needs financing of $70,000, the amount that can normally be borrowed at market rates. The borrower may also obtain a second mortgage of $20,000 for 15 years at a 14 percent rate, with payments of $266.35 per month. Is it still desirable to assume the loan, take a second mortgage, and pay $5,000 more for the house? We can make the following calculations:

	Down Payment	Payment
Market rate loan	$30,000	$795.62
Loan assumption + second	35,000	773.48*
	− $ 5,000	$ 22.14

*$507.13 on the $50,000 loan assumption plus $266.35 on the second mortgage.

The return is now − 2.90 percent. The buyer is clearly better off by *not* paying $5,000 more for the house to assume the loan. How much more would the buyer be willing to pay? This is the subject of the next section.

CASH EQUIVALENCY

In the previous section we considered how a buyer could analyze whether a premium should be paid for a home with a below market rate loan. We now extend that discussion to consider how much the buyer *could* pay to be indifferent between purchasing the home with a below market loan versus one which must be financed at the market rate.

We will reconsider the example first considered in the last section, where a $70,000 loan could be assumed at a 9 percent rate with a remaining term of 15 years and payments of $709.99 per month. Recall that a comparable home with no special financing available would sell for $100,000 and could be financed at a market rate of 11 percent. How much more than $100,000 could the buyer pay if he chose to assume the 9 percent loan and still be as well off if he purchased the property for $100,000 and financed it with an 11 percent loan? We first find the present value of the payments which can be assumed using the *market* rate.

$$PV = \$709.99 \ (MPVIFA, \ 11\%, \ 180 \ \text{mos.})$$
$$= \$709.99(87.981937)$$
$$= \$62,466.30$$

This is the market value or *cash equivalent* value of the assumable loan. It represents the price that the old loan could be sold for to a new lender/investor.

By assuming the existing loan balance, the buyer of the house would obtain financing equal to $70,000 instead of $62,466.30 for the same $709.99 payment. Thus, he receives a net benefit of $70,000 − $62,466.30 = $7,533.70. Therefore, the buyer could pay $7,533.70 more for the home, or $107,533.70.

In the previous section, we calculated that the return to the buyer would be 19.41 percent if he paid an additional $5,000 more for the home or $105,000. The student should verify that by paying $107,533.70 for the home the return to the buyer would be exactly 11 percent, the same as the market interest rate on the loan.

Based on the above analysis, the home with the assumable loan could probably sell for as high as $107,500 (rounded). The buyer would be paying $100,000 for the house plus an additional *financing premium* of about $7,500 to obtain the benefit of the below market loan. It is important to realize that the "price" that the house sells for includes the financing premium. The recognition of this premium is important, because if we knew that the property under consideration had actually sold for $107,500, but did *not* consider the fact that it had an assumable below market rate loan, we would have an inflated opinion as to what the *house* was really worth. Alternatively, the buyer would never want to agree to pay $107,500 for the property unless the 9 percent below market financing could be obtained. During the early 1980s when below market rate loans were common, appraisers were criticized for not taking financing premiums into consideration when using sales of homes with below market rate loans as comparables when determining the value of houses which did *not* have special financing.

CASH EQUIVALENCY: LOWER LOAN BALANCE

In the previous section we determined the indifference price for a property in a situation where a below market rate loan could be assumed. The loan balance was the same as would be obtained with a market rate loan. However, as discussed earlier in the chapter, when loan assumptions occur, it is likely that the loan balance is significantly less than would normally be desired. We would now like to modify the example in the last section by considering the case where balance of the assumable 9 percent loan is only $50,000 and the buyer would have to borrow an additional $20,000 through a second mortgage to obtain the $70,000 needed. We assume that the second mortgage could be obtained at a 14 percent rate for a 15-year term. We continue to assume that a $70,000 new first mortgage (70 percent of the house value) could be obtained at an 11 percent rate with a 15-year term.[13] Now how much could the buyer pay for the house and be indifferent to the two methods of financing?

We now find the present value of the *sum* of the payments on the assumable loan ($507.13) plus payments on the second mortgage ($266.35), using the 11 percent market rate.

$$PV = \$773.48(MPVIFA, 11\%, 180 \text{ mos.})$$
$$= \$773.48(87.981937)$$
$$= \$68,052.27$$

The difference between this present value ($68,052.27) and the $70,000 available at the market rate is $1,947.73. Thus, the buyer would now only pay an additional $1,947.73 for the home to get the below market rate loan. Thus, the home would probably sell for no more than $101,950 (rounded). This is considerably less than the $107,500 obtained in the case where the assumable loan had a balance of $70,000 instead of $50,000. There are two reasons that the premium is less: First, because the balance of the assumable loan is less, the saving (from lower payments) is less. Second, because this balance is less than the balance which could be obtained at the market rate, the benefit from lower payments on the assumable loan is reduced by the necessity of obtaining a second mortgage at a higher interest rate than the rate on a new first mortgage. It is important to realize that when carrying out this analysis, the need for a second mortgage must be considered; otherwise the benefit of the loan assumption would be overstated.

CASH EQUIVALENCY: CONCLUDING COMMENTS

In the previous two sections we showed how to analyze the impact of below market financing on the sale price of a property. It is important to recognize that there is a relationship between the price a property sells for and any special (e.g., below market)

---

[13]Even if the buyer didn't *need* a second mortgage, we can only evaluate the benefit of the loan assumption by comparing it with what is currently available in the market. Since market rates are usually based on a loan-to-value ratio of 70 percent or more, a second mortgage must be considered in the analysis.

financing that might be available. Although we have considered several examples of cash equivalency calculations, we have only introduced the possible situations that could arise in practice. At least two additional situations could arise that would affect the analysis. First, should below market financing ever not be transferable to a subsequent buyer, this would mean that a previous buyer may not benefit from the below market rate loan for its remaining term. This would obviously affect any financing premiums that would be paid for properties.

Second, even if below market loans were always assumable by subsequent buyers, the value of such financing over the remaining term of the loan to a subsequent buyer depends on the market rate of interest at the time of subsequent sales. These rates may be higher or lower than rates prevailing at the time that the existing owner purchased the property. Hence, the likelihood of subsequent sales and interest rates at such points in time adds an element of uncertainty to the benefit of assuming any loan, and should tend to reduce the amount buyers are willing to pay for such loans.

Both of the situations discussed above would tend to reduce the premium a buyer would pay for a below market interest rate loan. Thus, our analysis presented in the previous two sections is likely to indicate the *upper limit* on the premium associated with below market loans. The best way to verify the value of such premiums is by observing how much more buyers actually pay for below market financing versus houses without special financing.

WRAPAROUND LOANS

Wraparound loans have been used by borrowers as an alternative way of obtaining additional financing without obtaining a second mortgage and without disturbing an existing mortgage on the property. The way the wraparound loan works is best explained with an example. Suppose a homeowner named Smith has an existing loan with monthly payments of $322.38. The interest rate on the loan is 10 percent, and the remaining loan term is 15 years. The current balance of the loan is $30,000. From the time Smith originally obtained this loan, the home has risen in value such that it is now worth $65,000. Smith would like to borrow an additional $20,000, which would increase his debt to $50,000. He has found that the current rate on first mortgages is 13 percent and that on second mortgages is 15 percent.

A lender, different from the holder of the current $30,000 loan, indicates to Smith that he can obtain a wraparound loan for $50,000 at a 12 percent rate and a 15-year term. Payments on this loan would be $600.08 per month. If Smith makes this loan, the wraparound lender will take over the payments on Smith's current loan. That is, Smith will pay $600.08 to the wraparound lender, and the wraparound lender will make the $322.38 payment on the original loan. Thus, Smith's payment would increase by $277.70 ($600.08 − $322.38) as compared to what he would make before the wraparound loan. Because the wraparound lender is taking over the payments on the old loan, Smith will actually only receive $20,000 in cash (the $50,000 amount for the wraparound loan less the $30,000 balance of Smith's current loan).

The question now is whether the wraparound loan is an attractive alternative for Smith to obtain an additional $20,000. It is obvious that the wraparound rate (12 percent) is less than the market rate (13 percent) on a new first mortgage for $50,000. However, the real issue is the cost of the *additional* $20,000. That is, from Smith's point of view, he wants to obtain an additional $20,000 at the lowest effective cost. The cost can be determined by finding the interest rate that equates the present value of the additional payment with the additional funds received. We have

$$\$277.70(MPVIFA, ?\%, 18 \text{ mos.}) = \$20,000$$
$$MPVIFA = 72.0202$$

Using the tables and interpolating, or using a financial calculator, we find that the interest rate is 14.84 percent. This should be compared with alternative ways of receiving the additional $20,000. For example, compared to the second mortgage with a rate of 15 percent, the wraparound is a more attractive alternative.

The reader should realize that the 14.84 percent rate we calculated as the effective cost of the wraparound loan also represents the rate of return earned by the wraparound lender. Still, we should ask why the wraparound lender is willing to make the loan at a more attractive rate than a second mortgage? After all, the wraparound loan is, in effect, a second mortgage with the original loan still intact.

One reason could be because the wraparound lender makes the payments on the first mortgage loan. Hence, control is retained over default in its payment, whereas if a second was made the second mortgage lender would not necessarily be aware of a default on the first mortgage loan and may not be included in foreclosure action resulting from such a default. In a typical wraparound mortgage agreement, the wrap lender obligates itself to make payments on the original mortgage only to the extent that payments are received from the borrower, and the borrower agrees to comply with all of the covenants in the original mortgage except for payment. Any default by the borrower will be realized by the wraparound lender, who may not want to see the property go into foreclosure. The wrap lender may make advances on the first mortgage and add them to the balance on the wrap loan, foreclose on its mortgage, or negotiate for the title to the property in lieu of foreclosure, while still making payments on the first lien.

Thus, the wraparound loan may be an attractive alternative for both Smith and the wraparound lender. It should be noted, however, that the original mortgage may contain a prohibition against further encumbrances or a due on sale clause which may preclude use of a wraparound loan to access equity in, or finance the sale of property. In the absence of such restrictions the original lender may also be willing to work out a deal with Smith that would be attractive to both of them. For example, this lender might offer Smith a new first mortgage at a 12 percent rate if Smith borrows the additional $20,000. Since the 12 percent rate applies to the entire $60,000 (not just the additional $20,000), the lender is now earning a return which is closer to the 13 percent market rate. At the same time the borrower is paying a lower rate than if he refinanced the entire $60,000 at the market rate.

BUYDOWN LOANS

The final type of loan situation that we will consider in this chapter is what is referred to as a *buydown* loan. With a buydown loan, the seller of the home (frequently a builder) pays an amount to a lender to buy down or lower the interest rate on the loan for the borrower for a specified period of time. This may be done in periods of high interest rates in an attempt to help borrowers qualify for financing. For example, suppose interest rates are currently 15 percent and a purchaser of a builder's home only has enough income to qualify for financing based on payments that would result from a loan at a 13 percent fixed rate. Let's assume that the loan will be for $75,000 with monthly amortization based on a 30-year term. Payments based on the market rate of 15 percent would be $948.33 per month. Payments at a 13 percent rate would only be $829.65 per month. The buyer's income would qualify him at $829.65 but not at $948.33. Suppose the lender wanted to buy down the interest rate from 15 to 13 percent, thereby enabling the bank to make the loan such that payments are only $829.65 per month for the first five years of the loan term, increasing to $948.33 for the remaining loan term. To accomplish this the builder would have to make up the difference in payments ($118.68 per month for the five-year period). If this difference were paid by the builder to the lender at the time the loan closed, the amount paid would have to be the present value of the difference in payments, discounted at the market rate of 15 percent. Thus we have

$$
\begin{aligned}
\text{Buydown} &= \$118.68(MPVIFA, 15\%, 60 \text{ mos.}) \\
&= \$118.68(42.034592) \\
&= \$4,988.67
\end{aligned}
$$

The builder would therefore pay $4,988.67 to the lender to buy down the loan. When coupled with the payments received from the buyer, the lender would earn a market rate of 15 percent and be willing to qualify the buyer.

As indicated above, one advantage of the buydown is that it may allow borrowers to qualify for the loan whose current income might not otherwise allow them to meet the lender's payment-to-income criteria. However, the reader should also realize based on our discussion of cash equivalent value, that the builder will probably have added part or all of the buydown amount to the price of the home. Thus, the borrower might be better off bargaining for a lower price on the home and obtaining his or her own loan at the market rate. For example, suppose the same home or a similar one could be obtained for $6,000 less without a buydown. In this case, if the borrower can qualify, he would probably be better off obtaining a loan at the market rate, since we have determined that the value of the buydown is only about $4,988.67. Of course, the borrower may still choose the buydown if he would not qualify for a loan at the market rate due to the higher payments. Assuming the borrower bought the home for $6,000 less and thus only needed to borrow $69,000, his payments at the market rate of 15 percent would be $872.47 per month, which is higher than the initial payment on the buydown. Of course, after five years payments on the buydown jump to $948.33 per month, whereas they would remain at $872.47 on a market rate loan for $69,000.

It should also be noted that many buydowns are executed with graduated payments for three or five years. That is, they may be initiated with monthly payments of $829.65 and step up each year by a specified amount until $948.33 is reached in the fifth year.

Some buydown programs are also used in conjunction with *ARM*s, where the *initial* rate of interest will be bought down. Because initial rates on *ARM*s are typically lower than those on *FRM*s, this results in even lower initial payments, thereby allowing more buyers to qualify. However, this latter buydown practice has been discouraged because payments may increase considerably, particularly if there is an increase in the market rate of interest. In these cases payments would rise because of higher market rates and because future payments have not been bought down.

CONCLUSION

This chapter has illustrated a number of problems having to do with residential financing situations which borrowers and lenders might face. In today's era of "creative financing," there are many other examples that could be discussed. However, we have chosen examples which illustrate the main concepts and approaches to solving problems that are important and can be applied to other situations that the reader might want to analyze. Thus, this chapter should be viewed as introducing various tools that can be used to handle other types of residential financing problems.

To keep our analysis as straightforward as possible and focus on the key new concepts we wanted to introduce in this chapter, we have used fixed rate mortgages in all our examples. However, the student should realize that the analyses would apply to other types of mortgages as well.

As a final comment, although we have only analyzed residential financing problems in this chapter, all of the concepts apply equally as well to the analysis of income-producing or investment real estate. Thus in later chapters which deal with income property, we will again refer to many of the concepts introduced in this chapter.

QUESTIONS

1. Why do points increase the effective interest rate for a mortgage loan more if the loan is held for a shorter time period?
2. What factors must be considered when deciding whether to refinance a loan after interest rates have decreased?
3. Why might the market value of a loan differ from its outstanding balance?
4. Why might a borrower be willing to pay a higher price for a home that had an assumable loan?
5. What is a buydown loan? What parties are usually involved in such a loan?
6. Why might a wraparound lender provide a wraparound loan at a lower rate than a new first mortgage?
7. Under what conditions might a lender be willing to accept a lesser amount from a borrower than the outstanding balance of a loan and still consider the loan paid in full? (Assume the borrower is in no danger of default on the loan.)

8. Under what conditions might a home with an assumable loan sell for more than that of comparable homes with no assumable loans available?
9. What is meant by the incremental cost borrowing additional funds?
10. Is the incremental cost of borrowing additional funds affected significantly by early repayment of the loan?

PROBLEMS

1. A borrower can obtain an 80 percent loan at a 10 percent interest rate with monthly payments amortized over 15 years. Alternatively, he could obtain a 90 percent loan at a 10.5 percent rate with the same loan term. The borrower plans to stay in the home for the *entire loan term*.
    a. What is the incremental cost of borrowing the additional funds? (Hint: The dollar amount of the loan doesn't affect the answer.)
    b. How would the answer change if two points were charged on the 90 percent loan?
    c. Would the answer to part (*b*) change if the borrower only planned to be in the home five years?
2. A potential homeowner has $30,000 to invest in a $140,000 home. He can obtain either a $110,000 loan at 11 percent for 20 years or a $90,000 loan at 10 percent for 20 years and a second mortgage of $20,000 at 14 percent for 20 years.
    a. Which alternative should he choose, assuming he will be in the house for the full loan term?
    b. Would the answer change if he plans to be in the home only five years?
    c. Would the answers to (*a*) and (*b*) change if the second mortgage had a 10-year term?
3. A homeowner obtained a mortgage 5 years ago for $95,000 at a 12 percent rate amortized over 30 years. Mortgage rates have dropped so that a 25-year loan can be obtained at a 10 percent rate for 25-year loans. There is a 3 percent prepayment penalty on the mortgage balance of the original loan, and two points will be charged on the new loan.
    a. Should the borrower refinance if he plans to be in the home for the remaining loan term? Assume the homeowner only borrows an amount equal to the outstanding balance of the loan.
    b. Would the answer change if he only planned to be in the home 10 additional years?
4. Secondary Mortgage Purchasing Company wants to buy your mortgage from the local savings and loan. The original balance of your mortgage was $140,000 and was obtained 6 years ago at 12 percent interest for 30 years.
    a. What should they pay if market rates are currently 14 percent?
    b. How would the answer change if Secondary Mortgage expected the loan to be repaid after three years?
5. You have a choice between the following two identical homes: Home A is priced at $150,000 with 80 percent financing at an 11 percent interest rate for 20 years. Home B is priced at $160,000 with an assumable mortgage of $100,000 at a 9 percent interest rate with 20 years remaining. Monthly payments are $899.73. A second mortgage for $20,000 can be obtained at a 14 percent rate for 20 years.

    a. With no preference other than financing, which house would you choose?

    b. How would your answer change if the *seller* of home B provided a second mortgage for $20,000 at the same 9 percent rate as the assumable loan?

    c. How would your answer change if the seller of home B provided a second mortgage for $30,000 at the same 9 percent rate as the assumable loan so that no additional down payment would be required by the buyer if the loan were assumed?

6. A homeowner has lived in a home for 15 years, and the value of the home has risen from $50,000 to $90,000. The balance on the original mortgage is $40,000, and the monthly payments are $440 with 15 years remaining. The homeowner would like to obtain $35,000 in additional financing. A second mortgage for $35,000 can be obtained at a 14 percent rate with a term of 15 years. Alternatively, a wraparound loan for $75,000 can be obtained at a 12 percent rate and a 15-year term. Which should the homeowner choose?

7. A home builder is offering $100,000 loans for his homes at 11 percent for 25 years. Current market rates are at 15 percent for 25-year loans. The home would normally sell for $110,000 without any special financing.

    a. At what price should the builder sell the homes in order to, in effect, earn the market rate of interest on the loan? Assume that the buyer would have the loan for the entire term of 25 years.

    b. How would your answer to part (*a*) change if the home would be resold after 10 years and the loan repaid?

8. A home is available for sale that could normally be financed with an $80,000 loan at a 12 percent rate with monthly payments over a 25-year term. The builder is offering buyers a mortgage that reduces the payments by 50 percent for the first year and by 25 percent for the second year. After that the regular payments would be made.

    a. How much would you expect the builder to have to give the bank to buy down the payments as indicated?

    b. Would you recommend the home be purchased if it was selling for $5,000 more than similar homes that do not have the buydown available?

Appendix: After-Tax Effective Interest Rate

The preceding chapters have dealt with numerous situations where financing alternatives were evaluated. In all cases the analysis was done without considering the fact that mortgage interest is tax deductible. An obvious question is whether consideration of federal income taxes affects the conclusions from our analyses. To gain insight into this question we first consider the after-tax effective cost of a standard fixed rate mortgage loan.

EXAMPLE

Suppose a borrower makes a $100,000 loan with *annual* payments at a 10 percent rate and a 10-year term. We will assume that payments are made on an *annual* basis to simplify the initial illustration. The annual loan payment is calculated as follows:

$$\text{Annual payment} = \$100,000 \ / \ (PVIFA, \ 10\%, \ 10 \text{ yrs.})$$
$$= \$100,000 \ / \ 6.14439$$
$$= \$16,275$$

A loan schedule is calculated below (Exhibit 9A–1) for the 10-year loan term.

The before tax cost of this loan is simply 10 percent because there are no points or prepayment penalties. We now want to see the effect of interest being tax deductible. The tax benefit of the interest tax deduction is calculated by multiplying the loan interest each year by the borrower's tax rate. For example, the first year the interest is $10,000. At a 28 percent tax rate this means that the borrower can reduce taxes by $2,800 by being able to deduct the interest.

The after-tax cost of the loan is can now be found by subtracting the tax savings from the loan payment. The after-tax cost is calculated in Exhibit 9A–2.

To calculate the after tax effective cost of borrowing, we need to find the annual compound interest rate that equates the after-tax payments to the initial amount of the loan ($100,000).

EXHIBIT 9A–1   Loan Schedule

End of Year	Payment	Interest	Principal	Balance
1	$16,275	$10,000	$ 6,275	$93,725
2	16,275	9,373	6,902	86,823
3	16,275	8,682	7,592	79,231
4	16,275	7,923	8,351	70,880
5	16,275	7,088	9,187	61,693
6	16,275	6,169	10,105	51,588
7	16,275	5,159	11,116	40,472
8	16,275	4,047	12,227	28,245
9	16,275	2,825	13,450	14,795
10	16,275	1,480	14,795	0

EXHIBIT 9A–2   After-Tax Cost of Loan Payment

Year	Payment	After-Tax Value of Deduction*	After-Tax Payment
1	$16,275	$2,800	$13,475
2	16,275	2,624	13,650
3	16,275	2,431	13,843
4	16,275	2,218	14,056
5	16,275	1,985	14,290
6	16,275	1,727	14,547
7	16,275	1,444	14,830
8	16,275	1,133	15,141
9	16,275	791	15,484
10	16,275	414	15,860

*Interest times tax rate.

EXHIBIT 9A–3   Net Present Value of After-Tax Payments

Year	ATCF	PVIF	Present Value
0	$ – 100,000	$1.00000	$ – 100,000
1	13,475	0.93284	12,570
2	13,650	0.87018	11,878
3	13,843	0.81174	11,237
4	14,056	0.75722	10,644
5	14,290	0.70636	10,094
6	14,547	0.65892	9,585
7	14,830	0.61466	9,115
8	15,141	0.57338	8,682
9	15,484	0.53487	8,282
10	15,860	0.49894	7,913
Total present value			0

Calculating this rate indicates an after tax cost of borrowing of exactly 7.2 percent. This is verified in Exhibit 9A–3.

Adding the present value column in Exhibit 9A–3 results in a net present value of zero, which verifies that the after-tax cost is 7.2 percent.

Now that we have performed the calculations the "long way," the reader may wonder if the before- and after-tax costs are related in some way to the borrower's tax rate. There is in fact a very simple relationship in this situation. The relationship is

$$\text{After-tax effective cost} = (\text{Before-tax effective cost}) (1 - \text{tax rate})$$
$$7.2\% = 10\% (1 - .28)$$

We see that the after-tax borrowing cost is inversely proportional to the complement of the borrower's tax rate. That is, if the tax rate is 28 percent the complement of the tax rate is 72 percent and the after-tax cost is 72 percent of the before-tax cost. (In effect, we are saying that the entire interest cost is tax deductible.) This relationship will hold even if the loan is repaid early. Even in cases where it doesn't hold exactly,[1] it is usually a good approximation of the effective cost. It should also be clear that the higher the borrower's tax rate, the more the benefit of the interest tax deduction.

MONTHLY PAYMENTS

The above example assumed that the payments on the loan were made annually—for example, at the end of the year, which coincided with the time when the borrower received the tax deduction. If the loan payments were monthly, would the answer differ significantly? If we assumed that the

---

[1] For example, if points are charged on loans for income property, the relationship may not hold exactly. This is because the timing of the tax deduction for the points may not correspond with the actual payment of the points. Whereas the points are paid at the time the loan is closed, they must be amortized over the loan term for tax purposes.

buyer realized tax benefits from the interest deductions monthly, then the answer would not change at all. It could be argued that taxes are only paid once each year (or April 15 of the following year!) and thus the tax deduction is not received at the exact same time as the loan payment. However, knowing that the tax benefit from the interest deduction will affect tax forms at the end of the year may also mean *less* estimated taxes may be paid by the borrower during the year.[2] Furthermore, the taxpayer may have less taxes withheld from his monthly pay because he knows the interest will reduce his taxable income at the end of the year. Because of these possibilities, assuming that interest deductions occur at different points in time than the mortgage payment may be more realistic when calculating the after-tax cost of financing. However, even if the tax deduction was not assumed to occur until the end of the year, it would not affect the calculated effective interest rate significantly. Thus, for practical purposes, we can conclude that the after-tax effective monthly interest cost is equal to the before-tax effective monthly cost multiplied by the complement of the investor's tax rate $(1 - \text{tax rate})$.

EFFECT OF AFTER-TAX INTEREST COST ON LOAN DECISIONS

We have seen that the after-tax effective interest rate is directly proportional to the borrower's tax rate. This will be true as long as the interest is tax deductible in the year it is paid.[3] When this is true, tax considerations will *not* affect any of the conclusions regarding selection from alternative mortgages, because taxes affect each loan in a similar manner. Thus, we can still compare before-tax effective interest costs when choosing a loan and be confident that tax considerations will not affect financing decisions. Similarly, we can compute the incremental borrowing cost, the effective cost of refinancing, and other decision criteria discussed in the preceding chapter on a before-tax basis. We do *not* mean to imply that interest deductions for tax purposes are an unimportant consideration when deciding to borrow money. Clearly, a borrower should be aware of the cost of making borrowing decisions after consideration of the tax deductibility of the interest payments. In fact, the *higher* a borrower's tax rate, the *lower* the after-tax cost of borrowing. This affects one's willingness to borrow on investment real estate as we will see later in the book when we evaluate financial leverage.

NEGATIVE AMORTIZATION LOANS

We have seen that the after-tax effective cost of a loan is equal to the before-tax effective cost multiplied by the complement of the investor's tax rate. This is true as long as all interest "charged" on the loan is tax deductible in the year that the interest is paid. By interest charged we mean the portion of each monthly payment which is *not* principal.

In the case of loans with negative amortization, interest charged will exceed the payment during some or all of the loan term. One example we have discussed is the graduated payment mortgage (*GPM*). We will now see how the after-tax effective cost is calculated for a loan with negative amortization. To illustrate, consider a loan for $100,000 at a 10 percent interest rate with

---

[2]The IRS requires taxpayers to estimate their tax liability and in many cases quarterly payments must be made to the IRS.

[3]Some alternative mortgages such as the graduated payment mortgage have interest charged (due to negative amortization) which is not deductible in the year it is paid. This is discussed later in this appendix.

EXHIBIT 9A–4   Loan Schedule

Year	Beginning Balance	Payment	Interest	Amortization
1	$100,000	$ 8,000	$10,000	$(2,000)
2	102,000	8,000	10,200	(2,200)
3	104,200	8,000	10,420	(2,420)
4	106,620	8,000	10,662	(2,662)
5	109,282	8,000	10,928	(2,928)
6	112,210	12,000	11,221	779
7	111,431	12,000	11,143	857
8	110,574	12,000	11,057	943
9	109,631	12,000	10,963	1,037
10	108,594	12,000	10,859	1,141
11	107,453	12,000	10,745	1,255
12	106,198	12,000	10,620	1,380
13	104,818	12,000	10,482	1,518
14	103,300	12,000	10,330	1,670
15	101,630	12,000	10,161	1,837
16	99,793	12,000	9,979	2,021
.	.	.	.	.
.	.	.	.	.
.	.	.	.	.

annual payments of $8,000 per year for the first five years, followed by payments of $12,000 per year until the entire balance is repaid.

Because interest charged would be $10,000 (.10 times $100,000) the first year, and the payment is only $8,000, there will be negative amortization of $2,000. This increases the balance of the loan to $102,000 after one year. Interest the second year is, therefore, $10,200 (.10 times $102,000). Proceeding in this manner we can construct the loan schedule in Exhibit 9A–4.

From the exhibit we see that the balance increases due to the negative amortization for the first five years. In year six, when the payments increase to more than the interest charged, the loan balance begins to decline. However, it takes until year 15 before the balance decreases below the initial $100,000 balance.

The question now is how much interest can the borrower deduct for tax purposes each year? Most borrowers, at least for owner occupied homes, compute taxes according to a "cash basis." That is, their income and expenses for tax purposes is based on actual cash income and expenditures.[4] For these borrowers, *current tax regulations require that interest deductions may not exceed the amount of payments.* Thus, in our example, only $8,000 could be deducted each year during the first five years. Starting with the sixth year, we see that the payment exceeds the interest. The reader may be wondering what happens to the interest that could *not* be deducted during the first five years (due to the negative amortization). The answer is that the borrower can continue to deduct the entire loan payment *until the loan balance is reduced to its initial balance,* in this case $100,000. Thus, the borrower can deduct the $12,000 payment until year 14. In year 15 the

---

[4]The alternative is an "accrual basis," where an accrual-based accounting system is used to determine income and expenses.

EXHIBIT 9A–5   Tax Deductions Negative Amortization Loan

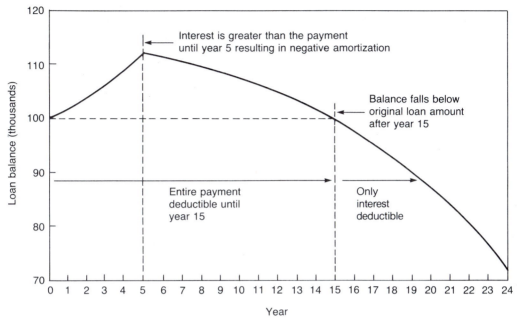

borrower can deduct the $10,161 interest, plus the remaining negative amortization that will reduce the balance to $100,000, or $1,630. After year 15, interest is deductible at the rate in the same manner that it is on any constant payment mortgage. Exhibit 9A–5 illustrates the relationship between the mortgage payment, interest charges, and loan balance in the example discussed above.

After-Tax Effective Cost

We now have the information we need to calculate the tax deductions and after-tax effective cost of the loan. We can create the schedule in Exhibit 9A–6.

We could compute the effective cost for the entire loan term or considering repayment of the loan at any time prior to the end of the loan term. For purpose of illustration, we will compute the after-tax effective cost for repayment of the loan at the *end* of year 15 when the balance is $99,793. We have the following cash flows:

Year	After-Tax Cash Flow
0	− $100,000
1–5	5,760
6–14	8,640
15	108,492

EXHIBIT 9A–6   After-Tax Payments

Year	Payment	Interest Deductions	Tax* Savings	After-Tax Payment
1	$ 8,000	$ 8,000	$2,700	$5,760
2	8,000	8,000	2,700	5,760
3	8,000	8,000	2,700	5,760
4	8,000	8,000	2,700	5,760
5	8,000	8,000	2,700	5,760
6	12,000	12,000	3,600	8,640
7	12,000	12,000	3,600	8,640
8	12,000	12,000	3,600	8,640
9	12,000	12,000	3,600	8,640
10	12,000	12,000	3,600	8,640
11	12,000	12,000	3,600	8,640
12	12,000	12,000	3,600	8,640
13	12,000	12,000	3,600	8,640
14	12,000	12,000	3,600	8,640
15	12,000	11,791	3,302	8,699

*28 percent tax rate.

The *IRR* for the above cash flows is 7.32 percent. Recall, that the before-tax effective cost in this case was 10 percent, thus, we see that the after-tax effective cost is slightly higher than it would be for a fully amortizing loan which would have an after-tax effective cost of exactly 7.2 percent. The higher after-tax effective cost for the negative amortization loan occurs because of the *deferral* of interest deductions. During the period of time that the loan balance was increased, less interest is deducted than is being charged. The portion of interest that is not deductible during those years becomes deductible from the time the loan balance begins to fall until it reached the original balance.

CONCLUSION

The tax deductibility of interest payments reduces the after-tax cost of debt. As long as the entire amount of interest charged in a given year is tax deductible that year, there is a very simple relationship between the before-tax cost of a loan and the after-tax cost. The after-tax cost is equal to the before tax cost multiplied by the complement of the borrower's tax rate. That is,

$$\text{After-tax cost} = (\text{Before-tax cost}) (1 - \text{Tax rate})$$

If the entire amount of interest charged is *not* deductible, as was illustrated for negative amortization loans, the effective after-tax cost will be higher than it would be for the fully amortized loan. This results from the delay in receiving the tax deduction. However, even in this situation, multiplying the before-tax cost times the complement of the borrower's tax rate provides a close approximation of the after-tax borrowing cost.

If all loans being evaluated are treated about the same for tax purposes, taxes do not have to be considered in the analysis since they affect all loans in the same manner and thus "wash out" in the final analysis. Thus the types of analyses discussed in previous chapters can still be done without explicitly considering taxes. However, the fact that interest is tax deductible is still important when deciding whether to borrow in the first place since the tax deductibility of interest reduces the cost of using debt to finance the purchase of real estate. As we will see in later chapters, this is particularly important when determining whether to borrow money for investment property since the after-tax cost of the funds borrowed must be compared with the after-tax return on the property (before considering borrowing money) to see if it is favorable to use debt to finance the purchase.

PROBLEMS

1. A $100,000 loan can be obtained at a 10 percent rate with monthly payments over a 15-year term.
    a. What is the after-tax effective interest rate on the loan assuming the borrower is in a 20 percent tax bracket and the loan is held only three years? Assume that the benefit of interest deductions for tax purposes occurs at the same time payments are made.
    b. Calculate the after-tax effective cost for the above loan assuming 5 points are charged and that the points are tax deductible at the time they are paid.
    c. How does the after-tax cost in part (*b*) compare with the before-tax effective cost of the loan?
2. A mortgage for $100,000 is made with *initial* payments of $700 per month for the first year. The interest rate is 9 percent. Payments will increase after the first year to an amount such that the loan can be fully amortized over the remaining 24 years with constant monthly payments.
    a. Calculate the interest deductions for the loan for the first year.
    b. How much, if any, interest must be deferred until the second year?
    c. How much interest will be deducted in the second year?

Financing and Investing in Income-Producing Properties

Chapter 10

Introduction to Analysis of Income Properties

The previous section of this book dealt with the analysis of various mortgage instruments and issues related to the financing of residential real estate. In this chapter we will begin to focus on the analysis of income properties. By *income properties* we mean properties that are purchased as an investment for the purpose of receiving income. In this chapter we will deal strictly with existing properties. Development projects are considered in Chapters 17 and 18.

Many variables must be considered by the investor when acquiring income properties. Market factors, occupancy rates, tax influences, the level of risk, the amount of debt financing, and the proper procedures to use when measuring return on investment all constitute major questions that must be considered by equity investors. Lenders are concerned with many of the same questions because these factors affect the value and marketability of the properties which are being used as collateral for loans. In addition, lenders will be concerned with the ability of properties they finance to generate enough cash flow to cover the loan payments. This chapter also provides the framework for analyzing additional issues addressed in many of the remaining chapters in this text.

PROPERTY TYPES

Exhibit 10–1 outlines major classifications used to identify and group different types of real estate. The two major categories used to classify property are residential and non-residential. As we will see in the following chapter, this distinction is also important when determining federal income taxes because the tax code also differentiates between residential and nonresidential properties for purposes of specifying allowable depreciation deductions.

Residential properties include *single family houses* and *multifamily properties* such as apartments. Condominiums and co-ops are also included as residential property. In gen-

EXHIBIT 10–1   Classification of Real Estate Uses

I. Residential
　　Single family
　　　Detached
　　　Cluster developments
　　　Zero lot line developments
　　Multifamily
　　　High rise (usually *CBD*)
　　　Low rise
　　　Garden apartments (usually suburban)

II. Nonresidential
　　Commercial
　　　Office building
　　　　Major multitenant — *CBD*
　　　　Single or Multitenant—Suburban
　　　　Single tenant — built to suit
　　　　Combination office/showroom
　　　Retail
　　　　Regional shopping centers/malls
　　　　Neighborhood centers
　　　　Strip centers
　　　　Specialty centers
　　　　Discount centers
　　Industrial
　　　Heavy industrial
　　　Light industrial warehouse
　　　Office/warehouse
　　　Warehouse
　　Hotel/Motel
　　　Business/Convention
　　　Tourist/Resort
　　Recreational
　　　Country clubs
　　　Marinas/resorts
　　　Sports complexes
　　Institutional (special purpose)
　　　Hospital/convalescent
　　　Universities
　　　Government
　　　Other

III. Mixed use developments
　　　Combinations of one or more of the above areas

eral, residential properties are properties that provide residences for individuals or families. Although hotels and motels can also be thought of as providing residences for people, they are considered to be transient or temporary residences and thus are not categorized as residential property. In our discussion to follow, we will follow the same categorization, which is logical from an economic perspective because factors that affect the supply and demand for hotels and motels are quite different from those that affect residential properties used as a residence.

Single family dwellings are usually thought of as individual, detached units developed in subdivision tracts. Other variants include cluster home developments where owners share ''green space'' in outdoor areas and ''zero lot line'' developments that contain single family and detached units.

The second major category of residential housing is referred to as multifamily housing. It is usually differentiated by location (urban or suburban) and size of structure (high rise, low rise, or garden apartments). High-rise apartments are usually found near or close to the central business district (*CBD*) of cities because land costs are greater than in suburban areas.

Nonresidential properties are typically broken down into five major subcategories: commercial, industrial, hotel/motel, recreational, and institutional. *Commercial* real estate includes both office buildings and retail space. As is the case for many of the categories, the same *building* can contain both commercial and retail space. In fact, the same building could contain residential as well as nonresidential uses of space. A combination of end uses in one property is usually referred to as a *mixed use development*. Thus, the categories being discussed should be viewed more as a convenient way of categorizing the use of space for the purpose of analyzing supply, demand, and thus investment potential for that space.

Office buildings range from major multitenant buildings found in the central business district of most large cities to single tenant buildings often built with specific tenant needs in mind. An example of the latter would be a medical office building near a hospital.

Retail space varies from large regional shopping centers containing over a million square feet of retail space to small stores with single tenants found in almost every town. As indicated earlier, it is also common to find retail space combined with office space, particularly on the first floor of office buildings in major cities.

Industrial real estate includes property used for light or heavy manufacturing as well as associated warehouse space. This category includes special-purpose buildings designed specifically for industrial use which would be difficult to convert to another use, buildings used by wholesale distributors, and combinations of warehouse/showroom and office facilities. Older buildings that were initially used as office space often ''filter down'' to become warehouse or light industrial space.

Hotels and motels vary considerably in size and facilities available. Motels and smaller hotels are used primarily as a place for business travelers and families to spend a night. These properties may have limited amenities, such as swimming pools or limited dining facilities or meeting space. The property will often be located very close to a major highway. Hotels designed for tourists who plan to stay longer will usually provide dining, a swimming pool, and other amenities. They will also typically be located near other attractions that are visited by tourists. Hotels at ''destination resorts'' provide the greatest amount of amenities. These are resorts that are away from major cities where the guests usually stay for several days or even several weeks. Facilities at these resort hotels can be quite luxurious, with several dining rooms, swimming pools, nearby golf courses, and so forth. Hotels that cater to convention business may be either a popular destination resort, or could be located near the center of a major city. People who go to conventions usually want a variety of choices for dining and want to be able to "combine business with pleasure."

Recreational real estate includes uses such as country clubs, marinas, sports complexes, and so on. These are very specialized uses, usually associated with retail space which complements the recreational activity (e.g., golf shops). Dining facilities and possibly hotel facilities may also be present.

Institutional real estate is a general category for property that is used by a special institution such as a government agency, a hospital, or a university. The physical structure could be similar to other properties; government office space, for example, would be similar to other offices, and in fact be in the same building. However, space used by institutions such as universities and hospitals is usually designed for a specific purpose and not easily adaptable for other uses.

MOTIVATIONS FOR INVESTING

We have seen that there are many different categories of income property. We now consider why investors and lenders make investments in one or more of these properties. We first consider the equity investor. The term *equity* refers to funds invested by an "owner" or the person acquiring the property. The particular form of ownership could be any of the freehold estates discussed in Chapter 2. That is, equity funds could be invested in a fee simple estate, a leased fee estate, a leasehold estate, and so forth. Equity funds are contrasted with debt, which is provided by a lender with the real estate used as collateral for the loan as discussed in Chapter 2.

What motivates the investor to make an equity investment in income properties? First, investors anticipate that market demand will be sufficient enough for space in the property being considered such that after collecting rents and paying operating expenses sufficient net income will be produced. This income constitutes part of an investor's return (before considering taxes and financing costs).

Second, the investor anticipates selling properties after holding them for some period of time. (The determination of how long a property will be held is discussed in Chapter 16.) Investors often expect prices to rise over the holding period, particularly in an inflationary environment. Thus any price increase also contributes to an investor's return.

A third reason for investing in real estate is to achieve diversification. By this we mean that most investors want to hold a variety of different types of investments such as stocks, bonds, money market funds, and real estate. Diversification tends to reduce the overall risk of a portfolio of investments, as we will discuss later in the text.

A final reason for investing in real estate that may be more important to some investors than others is any preferential tax benefits enjoyed by virtue of investing in real estate. Because of favorable tax treatment of real estate, investors paid little or no taxes on returns from real estate investments for many years. As we will see in Chapter 11, many of these favorable tax benefits were eliminated by the Tax Reform Act of 1986. Understanding real estate tax law is important. Investors must be able to understand changes in such laws and interpret their interaction on rents and real estate values. As tax laws change, investor decisions regarding purchase prices, how much financing should be used, and when to sell the property are also affected.

PROJECTING CASH FLOWS

We will now look more closely at how investors and lenders project expected cash flows when they consider investing in income-producing properties. This will be followed by a discussion of various performance measures that are used to determine the attractiveness of a particular property.

Projecting Operating Income

We have already indicated that income from operating a property before it is sold is one component of an investor's return. What this income will be for a particular property depends on several factors such as expected market rents, expenses associated with operating the property, and the nature of any leases on the property. The following discussion considers these factors in more detail.

Market Rents

The starting point for an analysis of income for a property is usually a study of market rents for competitive properties. What is the level and trend in rents for similar properties? Rents for the property being considered may be established by determining rents being paid for similar properties in the current market. However, the trend in future rents will be more difficult to assess because it depends on many unknown factors, including (1) the outlook for the national economy, (2) the economic base of the area in which the property is located, (3) the demand for the type of space provided by the property in the location being analyzed, and (4) the supply of similar competitive space.

Past trends in market rents are often used to predict future rents. However, this can be dangerous in that it assumes that what happened in the recent past is indicative of what will happen in the future. When forecasting future rents, a more complete analysis requires one to relate rents for the type of property being analyzed in a particular area with factors which affect those rents. For example, the rent on apartments may depend on the demographic makeup of the population and median income of families in the area in which the property is located, among other things. The analyst would therefore project trends in population and median incomes and use this information to project rents. Chapter 14 considers the estimation of market rents in further detail.

Vacancy

All space available in a building may not be leased at a particular time. This is because tenants leave after their lease has expired (or walk away from their lease before it expires!), or it could be that the space was never rented, especially if it is a newly constructed building. To project income for a property, it is therefore necessary to project how much of the space will be occupied by tenants during the anticipated holding period for the project. There should always be some allowance for vacant space, even in markets where leasing activity is strong, because as tenant turnover occurs it takes time to make space ready and to re-lease space to new tenants. Hence, there will always be some loss in rents, even in buildings occupied by a few larger tenants.

It is more difficult to project vacancy for newly constructed properties. While some leases may be signed before a project is completed, it is possible that less than full occupancy will be achieved immediately after construction is completed. In these cases, projections must be made as to how long it will take for remaining space to be "absorbed" by the market. That is, how long will it take for occupancy to reach a normal level? Obviously the longer it takes for space to be rented, the less income the investor will receive during the initial years of the project. Because this affects cash flows in the early years of the holding period, it will also have a significant impact on the investment value of a property.

Expenses

There are many different expenses associated with operating income properties. Categories commonly used to classify expenses are summarized in Exhibit 10–2.

Variable expenses are expenses which fluctuate with the level of occupancy. For example, management fees are typically based on a percentage of rental income. Utility expenses usually depend on how many tenants are in the building and hence are usually

---

EXHIBIT 10–2   Categories of Operating Expenses

Fixed expenses:

Property taxes	Taxes paid to state and local governments based on the assessed value of the real estate
Insurance	Payments to insurance companies for property and liability insurance
Repairs and maintenance	Expenses associated with normal repair and maintenance of the property such as painting, driveway repaving, etc.
Advertising and promotion	Expenses associated with keeping potential tenants aware of space which may be available in the building

Variable expenses:

Utilities	Payment for water, electricity, gas, etc.
Management	Fees paid to property managers for leasing the property, collecting the rents, overseeing maintenance, legal, etc.
Cleaning	Expenses for cleaning areas of the building used by the tenants

categorized as variable. However, there may be some minimum amount paid for utilities (heat and light) even if the building is vacant. Thus it should be pointed out that these categories are not intended to be exact, but general categories that are useful for making expense projections.

Fixed expenses do not fluctuate with the level of occupancy. For example, real estate taxes are determined by the assessed value of the property. Because this tax will not change with the level of occupancy, it is a fixed expense. Similarly, amounts that must be paid for insurance are usually based not on the level of occupancy but on the replacement cost of the project. Repairs and maintenance expenditures are usually classified as fixed expenses because they are not directly related to the level of occupancy (i.e., weather, age of the project, etc., result in a need for normal repairs). Also, maintenance and repairs are often done *after* a tenant leaves to ''make ready'' for the next tenant. So within the normal range of occupancy for a project, repairs and maintenance are relatively fixed.

The primary reason for categorizing expenses is to make it easier to project future expenses. That is, different categories of expenses may change differently over time, and, as we have discussed, some expenses are affected by changes in occupancy more than others.

LEASES

Income properties are usually purchased by investors subject to existing leases. Such investors also lease space as it becomes available in their building to businesses or individuals. The nature of lease agreements tends to vary considerably among different categories of income property. Terms in a lease can vary in a number of ways, including (1) the length or term of the lease, (2) the base rent, (3) additional charges on expenses that may be added to the base rent, (4) the manner in which the base rent may increase over the term of the lease, (5) provisions for additional rents based on some measure of a tenant's sales activity, (6) options that a tenant may have to renew the lease at the end of the initial lease term, and (7) expense stops, or a base level of operating expenses above which the tenant must pay. The ways in which these factors are combined may be viewed as ways of *pricing* a lease. For example, a tenant might expect to pay a higher rental if a lease contains a renewal option than if the lease did not contain a renewal option. In contrast, other things being equal, the initial rent may be lower if there are provisions in the lease which allow future rent to automatically increase over the term of the lease. The following discussion will outline some of the general ways in which leases differ among different types of properties.

Hotel and motel rooms are typically rented on a day-to-day basis for obvious reasons. Rental housing and apartments are usually leased on an annual basis, although shorter or longer leases may occur. Lease terms are usually renegotiated after the end of each lease term.

Office space tends to be leased for three- to five-year terms with the tenant often having the option to lease for one additional three- to five-year term. There may be a provision for rent increases each year by either a specified dollar amount or an amount based on inflation adjustment. Tenants are often responsible for paying their share of certain expenses such as property taxes, insurance, and maintenance.

Lease terms in retail space vary considerably. Smaller retail establishments may only lease space for one or two years, whereas larger establishments may be willing to commit to much longer lease terms. Retail leases may also have a *percentage lease* clause which provides that rents will also be based on a percentage of the tenants' sales. A "minimum" rent is usually specified in the lease, to which is added an additional amount of rent based on a percentage of the tenants sales. This additional rent is usually referred to as *overage rent*.

Leases for industrial property are often highly individualized due to the special-purpose nature of the building. Although three- to five-year leases are common, many tenants will prefer longer-term leases, especially when equipment is to be installed which is expensive and inconvenient to move over relatively short periods of time. This is particularly true for manufacturing firms. The leases are typically *net* leases, which means that the tenant is responsible for paying taxes, insurance, and maintenance. The tenant is also usually responsible for paying utilities costs because this can be a significant and uncertain amount for many users of industrial space.

OFFICE BUILDING EXAMPLE

To illustrate how a projection of income is made, we consider the possible purchase of a 100,000-square-foot office building by an investor for $8,500,000. Construction of the Monument office building was completed two years ago. The first tenants signed five-year leases at that time (two years ago). The remaining space was leased at various times during the past two years. Additional assumptions are as follows:

Current market rent (per square foot)	$15.00
Gross square feet	100,000
Projected increase in market rent per year	4.00%
Management costs (percent of effective gross income)	5.00%
Estimated annual increase in the consumer price index	4.00%

The importance of these assumptions should become clear as we discuss the example. A summary of the leases that would be honored by the investor if the building is purchased is shown in Exhibit 10−3.

Base Rent

From Exhibit 10−3 we see that there are six tenants, occupying a total of 96,000 square feet of rentable space. The remaining 4,000 square feet of space is used for heating, air conditioning, stairs, elevators, and so on, and is not rentable. The first three tenants to

EXHIBIT 10–3   Summary Lease Information: Monument Office Building

Tenant	Square Feet	Current Rent Square Feet	Current Rental	Remaining Lease Term (years)	CPI Adjustment (percent)
Tenant 1	30,000	$14.00	$ 420,000	3	50.00
Tenant 2	25,000	14.00	350,000	3	50.00
Tenant 3	15,000	14.00	210,000	3	50.00
Tenant 4	10,000	14.50	145,000	4	50.00
Tenant 5	10,000	15.00	150,000	5	50.00
Tenant 6	6,000	15.00	90,000	5	50.00
Total	96,000		$1,365,000		

Note: Additional assumptions about the tenant's responsibility for increases in operating expenses (expense stops) will be discussed later.

occupy the building leased most of the space. The market rate at the time they signed the lease (two years ago) was $14.00 per square foot. These leases were made for five years, and thus there are three years remaining on each lease. A fourth tenant signed a lease last year at $14.50 per square foot. The last two tenants just signed their leases at a rate of $15.00 per square foot, the current rental rate for comparable space.

CPI Adjustment

In an inflationary environment, the real value of the rental income will decline each year. Hence, office leases often provide for a rent adjustment based on increases in the consumer price index (*CPI*). That is, the rental rate is adjusted each year based on any increase in the *CPI* that occurred that year. One possibility is that rents are increased by the same percentage amount that the *CPI* increases. For example, if the *CPI* rises 4 percent as projected in our example, then the base rent would be increased 4 percent. However, lease payments are not always increased by the full amount of the increase in the *CPI*. Inclusion of inflationary adjustments in lease terms will depend on market conditions and the willingness of tenants to bear the risk of unanticipated inflation. Inflation adjustments may be limited by caps or by specific step-ups in base rents. Further, as we will discuss in detail later, many building operating expenses incurred by owners are passed through to tenants. Because tenants will be paying a portion of these expenses (which will increase with inflation), it is not always necessary for a building owner to charge rents that fully adjust to the rate of inflation. On the other hand, if the market is experiencing an oversupply of space, no adjustment in base rent for inflation may be possible. Another reason rents may not be adjusted by the full amount of the *CPI* is that there can be a separate provision in the lease to reimburse the tenant for any increase in expenses. This is discussed in the following section.

EXHIBIT 10–4 Projected Base Rental Income

Year	1	2	3	4	5	6
Tenant 1	$ 420,000	$ 428,400	$ 436,968	$ 506,189	$ 516,313	$ 526,639
Tenant 2	350,000	357,000	364,140	421,824	430,260	438,866
Tenant 3	210,000	214,200	218,484	253,094	258,156	263,319
Tenant 4	145,000	147,900	150,858	153,875	175,479	178,988
Tenant 5	150,000	153,000	156,060	159,181	162,365	182,498
Tenant 6	90,000	91,800	93,636	95,509	97,419	109,499
Total	$1,365,000	$1,392,300	$1,420,146	$1,589,672	$1,639,992	$1,699,809

In our example, we assume that rents will increase by 50 percent of any increase in the *CPI*. Because we assumed that the *CPI* will increase at a rate of 4 percent per year, this means that the base rental payment will increase by 2 percent per year (50 percent of 4 percent).

Based on our assumptions, the base rental income can be projected as shown in Exhibit 10–4. The reader should verify some of the numbers in the exhibit. As discussed above, base rents depend on (1) the initial base rent at the time the lease is signed, (2) *CPI* adjustments to the base rent, and (3) the market rent prevailing at the time of lease renewals.

Market rent for our example is $15 per square foot during the first year. This is also the base rent for leases signed that year. Base rent on the leases is projected to increase at 2 percent per year because of the *CPI* adjustment (half of 4 percent). However, a 4 percent annual rate of increase is used for projecting market rents that will be in effect when leases are renewed. This is because space will be re-leased at market rates at the expiration of each of the leases, and it is assumed that market rates will increase at the same rate as the *CPI*.

It appears that a tenant will face much higher rents when the lease is renewed because the new lease is based on a market rate which is projected to rise by the full amount of the *CPI*, whereas the tenant's rent was only increased by half the *CPI* over the term of the lease. However, we will see in the next section that there may also be a reduction in the amount of expenses for which the tenant must reimburse the owner when the lease is renewed.

In the case of the first tenant, the initial base rent is $420,000, which is projected to increase 2 percent per year due to the *CPI* adjustment until the lease expires in the third year. The base rent in year 4 is projected to be $506,189,[1] which assumes the market rent (which applies to new leases) of $15 per square foot will have increased 4 percent per year by that time.

---

[1] $15(1.04)^3$ times 30,000 s.f. = $506,189.

Expense Stops

We have discussed the use of a *CPI* adjustment to increase rents for unanticipated inflation. It is also common in office leases to include a provision which protects the owner from increases in operating expenses beyond what they were during the year the lease was signed. In our example, each lease for the office building has an *expense stop*. These stops place an upper limit on the amount of operating expenses that will have to be paid by the owner. Any operating expenses in excess of the stop must be paid by the tenant. The amount of the stop is usually based on (1) the tenant's pro rata share (percent of total leasable area), (2) categories of expenses that the lessor and lessee agree will be included in the stop, and (3) the actual amount of operating expenses at the time the lease is signed.

For a newer property the tenant and property owner usually negotiate the amount of the stop. For older properties the owner will generally provide the prospective tenant with operating expense statements, and the stop will be based on the tenants pro rata share of actual expenses on such statements plus an estimate of any expected increase during the first year of the lease.

In this case it has been agreed that the stop will include all operating expenses. However, the owner of the property will incur property management expenses which will not be chargeable to the tenants. All amounts in excess of the expense stop must be paid by the tenant in addition to the base rent specified in the lease. For example, if the expense stop in the lease is $4.00 per square foot and current expenses are $4.45 per square foot, then the tenant must pay the owner $.45 per square foot as an expense reimbursement. The reason for an expense stop is obviously to assure the owner that net income in subsequent years will be at least equal to the initial net income. Using expense stops is particularly important when leases containing fixed base rents (i.e., no *CPI* adjustments) are signed. If expense stops are not used, operating expenses may rise during the term of the lease and net income will decline. The particular expenses passed through to the tenants are negotiable and vary with market conditions. In our example, we have assumed that all expenses except property management expenses will be passed through. Tenants are usually reluctant to have increases in property management expenses passed through, because these expenses are the responsibility of the building owner and any attempt to pass these through to tenants could lead to excessive management fees.

Expense stops in the existing lease are assumed to be as follows:

Lease	Stop
Tenant 1	$4.00
Tenant 2	4.00
Tenant 3	4.00
Tenant 4	4.25
Tenant 5	4.45
Tenant 6	4.45

Panel A of Exhibit 10–5 shows the current expenses for the office building and the estimated annual increase in the expenses.

We can see from Panel A of Exhibit 10–5 that total operating expenses subject to expense stops are projected to be $427,200 or $4.45 per rentable square foot. Projections are also shown for the increase in each expense category in Panel B of the exhibit. Future rates of increase depend on estimates of how each cost is expected to change. In our example, utilities (heat and air conditioning) are expected to increase at a higher rate

EXHIBIT 10–5   Summary of Operating Expenses

Panel A: First-Year Expenses and Projected Increases

	Dollars	*Dollars per Square Foot*	*Projected Increases*		
Property tax	$148,800	$1.55	Level 2 yrs,	10%	Increase, then level
Insurance	14,400	0.15	Increase	4.00% per yr.	
Utilities	120,000	1.25	Increase	5.00% per yr.	
Janitorial	76,800	0.80	Increase	3.00% per yr.	
Maintenance	67,200	0.70	Increase	3.00% per yr.	
Total	$427,200	$4.45			

Panel B: Projection of Expenses

Operating Expenses	*Year*					
	1	*2*	*3*	*4*	*5*	*6*
Property tax	$148,800	$148,800	$163,680	$163,680	$163,680	$163,680
Insurance	14,400	14,976	15,575	16,198	16,846	17,520
Utilities	120,000	126,000	132,300	138,915	145,861	153,154
Janitorial	76,800	79,104	81,477	83,921	86,439	89,032
Maintenance	67,200	69,216	71,292	73,431	75,634	77,903
Total operating expense	$427,200	$438,096	$464,325	$476,146	$488,460	$501,289
Per square foot	$ 4.4500	$ 4.5635	$ 4.8367	$ 4.9599	$ 5.0881	$ 5.2218

Panel C: Projected Expense Reimbursement

	Year					
	1	*2*	*3*	*4*	*5*	*6*
Tenant 1	$13,500	$16,905	$25,101	$ 0	$ 3,848	$ 7,857
Tenant 2	11,250	14,088	20,918	0	3,207	6,548
Tenant 3	6,750	8,453	12,551	0	1,924	3,929
Tenant 4	2,000	3,135	5,867	7,099	0	1,336
Tenant 5	0	1,135	3,867	5,099	6,381	0
Tenant 6	0	681	2,320	3,059	3,829	0
Total	$33,500	$44,396	$70,625	$15,256	$19,189	$19,670

than the other items. We assume that property taxes will be level for two years, but then will increase with a reassessment of property values that is scheduled to take place at that time. They are expected to be level again for at least four years after the reassessment.

The information on expense projections and expense stops is used to project expense reimbursements as shown in Panel C of Exhibit 10–5. Note that in year 1 the first four tenants will be making expense reimbursements to the owner because actual expenses are $4.45 per square foot, which exceed the $4.00 expense stops in their leases. Also note that there is no expense reimbursement projected for the year that leases are renewed because the stops included in lease renewals will be based on actual expenses at that time.

Net Operating Income

Based on the information in Exhibits 10–4 and 10–5, we can now make a projection of net operating income (*NOI*) for the office building. Exhibit 10–6 contains a projection of net operating income for the next six years. Recall that management expenses are assumed to be 5 percent of effective gross income (*EGI*). *EGI* is the actual rent expected to be collected after allowing for any vacancy. In our example, vacancy is projected to be 5 percent of the base rent, beginning in the fourth year when the original leases are renewed. The management expense may be incurred by the owner or paid to a property management company. In either case it is not passed on to the tenant, so the owner has an incentive to control management expenses.

Note that net expenses (before management) are level ($393,700) after gross expenses are netted against the expense reimbursement (before management expenses) for the first three years. Expenses rise in years 4 and 5, since some of the leases are being renewed at new (higher) expense stops which reflect the estimated expenses per square foot at the time of the lease renewal.

EXHIBIT 10–6   Projected Net Operating Income

	Year					
	1	*2*	*3*	*4*	*5*	*6*
Base rent	$1,365,000	$1,392,300	$1,420,146	$1,589,672	$1,639,992	$1,699,809
Vacancy	0	0	0	79,484	82,000	84,990
EGI	1,365,000	1,392,300	1,420,146	1,510,189	1,557,992	1,614,819
Operating expenses	427,200	438,096	464,325	476,146	488,460	501,289
Less reimbursements	33,500	44,396	70,625	15,256	19,189	19,670
Subtotal	393,700	393,700	393,700	460,890	469,271	481,619
Add management expenses	68,250	69,615	71,007	75,509	77,900	80,741
Total expenses	461,950	463,315	464,707	536,399	547,170	562,360
NOI	$ 903,050	$ 928,985	$ 955,439	$ 973,790	$1,010,822	$1,052,459

Although expense stops protect owners against increases in expenses, it does not provide for any increase in *NOI* to offset inflation. An expense stop simply guarantees that *NOI* will not decline. Thus we see why it is also desirable to have a *CPI* adjustment as in our example. *This allows the NOI to increase each year even if no leases are renewed.* We can now also see why the *CPI* adjustment does not have to be for the *full* amount of the increase in *CPI*. This is because, as we have seen, the effect of any increase in expenses due to inflation or any other factors has already been adjusted for by the expense stop. In general, expense stops and inflationary adjustments should be considered along with the initial base rent as part of the "price" of using space.

INTRODUCTION TO DEBT FINANCING

Usually an investor will pay for a property by combining his own money (equity) with a loan (debt); purchase price = debt + equity. In Chapter 13 we will discuss reasons why both equity investors and lenders often find this desirable for real estate ownership. For now we will focus on how the use of debt affects the cash flows expected to be received by a real estate investor.

To illustrate, we again return to our previous example of the Monument office building example. Let us assume that a loan can be obtained at a 10 percent interest rate to be amortized over 20 years with monthly payments. The amount of the loan is 70 percent of the proposed purchase price (.70 · $8,500,000), or $5,950,000. Monthly payments would be $57,418.79, or $689,025 per year. It is traditional in investment analysis to compute loan payments based on monthly payments (assuming that is the way the payments will be made), but when financial projections are made all cash flows are summarized on an annual basis.

Exhibit 10–7 shows a summary loan schedule for the property for the first five years. From this point on projections will be made for five years under the assumption that the property will be sold after five years. The reason for projecting *NOI* for an *additional* year will become apparent when we discuss estimating the sale price of the property at the end of the five-year holding period.

Exhibit 10–8 shows the results of including the financing costs in the calculation of cash flows to the equity investor.

EXHIBIT 10–7   Summary Loan Information

| | *End of Year* | | | | |
	1	*2*	*3*	*4*	*5*
Payment	$ 689,025	$ 689,025	$ 689,025	$ 689,025	$ 689,025
Mortgage	5,851,543	5,742,776	5,622,620	5,489,883	5,343,245
balance	590,569	580,259	568,869	556,288	542,388
Interest	98,457	108,767	120,156	132,738	146,637
Principal					

EXHIBIT 10–8 Estimates of Cash Flow from Operations

	Year				
	1	*2*	*3*	*4*	*5*
Net operating income (*NOI*)	$903,050	$928,985	$955,439	$973,790	$1,010,822
Less debt service (*DS*)	689,025	689,025	689,025	689,025	689,025
Before-tax cash flow	$214,025	$239,960	$266,414	$284,765	$ 321,797

Subtracting debt service from *NOI* results in before-tax cash flow from operations (*BTCF_o*). This is also referred to as the *equity dividend* because it represents the cash flow that will actually be received by the investor each year, analogous to a dividend on common stocks.

INTRODUCTION TO INVESTMENT ANALYSIS

In general, when we refer to *investment analysis* in real estate we are referring to analysis of a particular property to evaluate its investment potential. This analysis should also help in answering other important questions, such as: Should the property be purchased? How long should it be held? How should it be financed? What are the tax implications of owning the investment? How risky is the investment?

We will provide the reader with the analytic tools to answer these questions in the next several chapters. However, we can now begin to answer the first question: Should the property be purchased at a price of $8,500,000? To illustrate how we might approach this question, we continue with the pro forma statements from the office building example introduced above.

Measures of Investment Performance Using Ratios

We first consider several common measures of investment performance that might be referred to as ratio measures. They are relatively simple measures, yet they provide a starting point for our analysis. They are also often used to screen an investment. That is, if one of the ratios indicates a poor investment, then the analyst may not take the time to do a more comprehensive analysis.

Price per Square Foot. A preliminary measure of the reasonableness of the proposed purchase price for the property is the price per square foot. For our property, we have an asking price of $8,500,000 and gross building area of 100,000 square feet. This results in a price per gross square foot of $85. Similarly, the *rentable* square footage is 96,000, resulting in a price per rentable square foot of $88.54. These prices may also be compared with comparable properties to determine if they are in line with what other investors have paid for similar space. Of course, this assumes that the similar space is in fact comparable and will command the same income and resale potential. We are looking for significant departures from the norm. Another way of determining whether the asking price is reasonable would be to consider what a new office building on a comparable would cost per square foot. If it could be built for $70.00 per square foot (including land), we would have to question whether the asking price of the building is reasonable. If the cost of a new building was $85.00 per square foot of rentable area, however, we might feel that a premium of $3.54 per square foot ($88.54 − $85.00) is justified, considering that our building is fully leased and may therefore be less risky than building and leasing a new one.

Capitalization Rate.   Another preliminary test of reasonableness of the purchase price for the property is the ratio of first-year *NOI* to the asking price. This is referred to as the *capitalization rate* or cap rate. In this case we have $903,050/$8,500,000, or 10.62 percent, which is just under 11 percent. What does this mean? It certainly is *not* a rate of return on investment (e.g., like an *IRR*) because it doesn't consider future income from operations and resale of the property at the end of the holding period. However, this ratio or cap rate can be compared with rates for comparable office buildings that have recently sold. For example, a nearby office building may have recently sold for $10,000,000. An analysis of its leases at the time it sold indicates that it would produce a *NOI* of about $1,100,000 for the upcoming year. Its ratio of *NOI* to sale price reflects a capitalization rate of 11 percent and provides a rough indication that the price for our property may be competitive. Of course, we have to be careful when using this approach for a number of reasons. First, the nature of the leases for the two properties may be quite different (i.e., different expiration dates, renewal options, escalations, etc.). Operating expenses over time may also be different for various reasons (the building may be older, less functionally efficient, and have a different type of mechanical system, etc.). Further, because the location of the two properties may be slightly different, and because future income and expenses may not be the same for the two properties, the potential for price increases may be quite different. Thus the capitalization rate is only a starting point in our analysis. It does, however, represent a benchmark or a norm from which we are looking for significant deviations. For example, if the capitalization rates were in the range of 15 percent for most similar properties as compared to 10 percent for our property, this would probably indicate that the asking price for the property we are considering may be too high relative to what other investors have recently paid for comparable properties.

Equity Dividend Rate.   The capitalization rate discussed above relates the entire *NOI* to the value of the property. An analogous measure from the equity investor's point of view is the equity dividend rate. It is calculated by dividing the *BTCF* (recall that this is also referred to as the equity dividend) in the first year by the initial equity investment. The investor's initial equity in the project is equal to the purchase price less the amount borrowed. Thus the equity is $8,500,000 − $5,950,000 = $2,550,000. The equity dividend rate is therefore $214,025/$2,550,000 = 8.39%. This is a rough measure of current return on equity. Note, however, that it is not an investment yield because it does not take into account future cash flows from operation or sale of the property. The difference between the equity dividend rate and an investment yield or *IRR* for the equity investor is an important one, which we will discuss later in the chapter.

Debt Coverage Ratios.   To obtain financing on the property, the lender must be satisfied that it is a good investment. One consideration obviously is the rate of return received by the lender over the term of the loan, which depends on factors such as the interest rate charged, points, and so forth, as discussed earlier in this text. But the lender's rate of return is only one consideration. The lender will also evaluate the riskiness of the loan. One widely used indication of the riskiness of the loan is the degree to which the *NOI* from the property is expected to exceed the mortgage payments. The lender would like a sufficient cushion so that if the *NOI* is less than anticipated (e.g., from unexpected vacancy) the borrower will still be able to make the mortgage payments without using his personal funds.

A common measure of this risk is the *debt coverage ratio (DCR)*. The *DCR* is the ratio of *NOI* to the mortgage payment. When *NOI* is projected to change over time, the first-year *NOI* is typically used. For the office building example, *NOI* in year 1 is projected to be $903,050. The mortgage payment (debt service) is $689,025. This results in a debt coverage ratio of 1.31. Lenders typically want the debt coverage ratio to be at least 1.2. Exhibit 10–9 shows the *DCR* for each of the five years.

EXHIBIT 10–9   Debt Coverage Ratios

	Year				
	1	*2*	*3*	*4*	*5*
DCR	1.31	1.35	1.39	1.41	1.47

From the exhibit we see that this project has a debt coverage of about 1.3 for the first year, and it is projected to increase each year thereafter. Thus it meets the minimum debt coverage ratio typically required by lenders.

Estimated Sale Price

To calculate measures of investment performance over an investment holding period, we must also estimate what our property might sell for. We first need to choose a holding period over which to analyze the investment. For now we will choose five years. (In Chapter 16 we will consider this question more closely.) When estimating a sale price, there are two general procedures that investors commonly use. The first procedure is to estimate a rate at which property values in general are expected to increase in the area. This is often closely related to expected inflation rates, although depending on future employment in office buildings some areas may do better or worse than the overall inflation rate for the economy. For our office building, it was assumed that the market rental rate would increase 4 percent per year. However, the rate at which *NOI* increases depends on the nature of the expense stops and the degree to which the lease payments are adjusted with the *CPI*. In our example the increase in *NOI* for the five-year-lease term is about 3 percent per year. It seems reasonable, therefore, that the price for our property would also increase about 3 percent per year. Using the asking price as a starting point, this would result in a sale price after five years of about $9,850,000.[2]

A second way of estimating a resale price is to use the capitalization rate concept discussed above. Recall that the capitalization rate (cap rate for short) for our property was 10.62 percent. This is sometimes referred to as the "going-in" cap rate, since it applies to the rate at the time of purchase. Similarly, a "terminal" cap rate, when the property is sold can also be estimated. It is defined as the ratio of *NOI one year after* the property is expected to be sold to the sale price. Note that the *NOI* one year after the property is sold is the *NOI* for the *first* year of a *new* investor. When using a terminal cap rate to determine a sale price, the investor is making an assumption that if no significant changes have occurred in the market for office space during the holding period, another investor should be willing to pay a price that reflects the same ratio of net operating income at the end of the fifth year that the initial investor paid when the property was acquired. This reflects the cap rate to the next buyer. However, in many cases terminal cap rates used by investors are slightly higher than going-in cap rates to reflect the uncertainty associated with estimating a resale price.[3]

In this case for example, we might use 11 percent (versus a going-in capitalization rate of 10.62 percent). Of course, *NOI* during the sixth year (the first year of ownership for the next buyer) would be higher than it was in year 1. Using *NOI* of $1,052,459 in year 6 and a terminal cap rate of 11 percent results in an estimated resale price of $9,567,809.

We now have two separate estimates of the resale price. Using a growth rate, we arrived at an estimate of $9,850,000. Using a terminal cap rate, we arrived at an estimate of about $9,550,000. Considering both prices that we estimated, we might conclude that for purposes of analysis an estimated resale price about midpoint between these two estimates or about $9,700,000 would be reasonable. Clearly, the analyst must use some judgment at this point regarding what is a reasonable estimate for the resale price. We are simply pointing out some of the considerations that might go into the investor's thought process. There is no single precise methodology that can be rigidly followed. It is also common to round off the numerical estimate to convey the subjective nature of the estimate.

Before-Tax Cash Flow from Sale

When the property is sold, the mortgage balance must be repaid from the sale proceeds. This results in before-tax cash flow from sale (*BTCF_s*). After the fifth year, the mortgage

---

[2]$8,500,000 times $(1.03)^5 = 9,853,830$.

[3]Use of a capitalization rate can be viewed as a shortcut to finding the present value of an income stream. That is, instead of *multiplying* the *NOI* by an appropriate present value factor (e.g., *PVIFA* if the *NOI* is level), the *NOI* is *divided* by a capitalization rate.

balance is $5,343,245. Subtracting this from the sale price of $9,700,000 results in before-tax cash flow ($BTCF_s$) of $4,356,755. This is summarized as follows:

Estimates of Cash Flows from Sale in Year 5	
Sales price	$9,700,000
Mortgage balance	5,343,245
Before-tax cash flow ($BTCF_s$)	4,356,755

Measures of Investment Performance Based on Cash Flow Projections

We now consider measures of investment performance that make use of the cash flow projections we have developed. These measures are more comprehensive than the ratio measures considered earlier because they explicitly consider cash flows over the entire investment holding period.

Net Present Value (NPV).   We now have the necessary information to calculate different measures of investment performance for the property which consider the entire holding period. To simplify calculations, it is common practice to assume that all cash flows will be received at the end of the year (the sum of all monthly cash flows received during the year). We begin with a calculation of the net present value (*NPV*). Because our analysis will not consider federal income taxes (this is considered in the next chapter), it is a before-tax analysis. We will refer to the net present value being calculated as the *BTNPV.*

A summary of the cash flows for our office building (assuming it is purchased at the asking price) is as follows:

Year	Cash Flow
0 (equity)	($2,550,000)
1	214,025
2	239,960
3	266,414
4	284,765
5	4,678,551

The cash flow in year 5 includes *both* the cash flow from operating the property in year 5 ($321,797) plus the estimated sales proceeds ($4,356,755).

The *NPV* is found by first calculating the present value (PV) of all the estimated future cash flows. The initial cash outlay (equity) invested to acquire the investment is then subtracted from (netted against) this present value to obtain the net present value. Thus, *NPV* measures the extent, if any, that the present value of cash flows to be received from the investment exceeds the equity invested in the office building. A positive *NPV* indicates that the value of the investment, in present value terms, exceeds the equity investment. The *NPV* obviously depends on the discount rate used to calculate the present value of the cash inflows. This discount rate should reflect the minimum rate of return required by the investor to make the investment, considering the riskiness of the investment. It is an opportunity cost concept in that the return required for the investment being analyzed should be at least as good as the return available on comparable investments. By investing in the property being analyzed, the investor must forgo the return that could have been earned on alternative investment opportunities.

Let's assume that the appropriate discount rate for the office building being analyzed is 18 percent. What is the *BTNPV?* Using the cash flows calculated above, the *BTNPV* is as follows:

Year	Cash Flow	Present Value (18%)
1	$ 214,025	$ 181,377
2	239,960	172,335
3	266,414	162,148
4	284,765	146,878
5	4,678,551	2,045,038
Total present value		2,707,776
Less initial equity investment		2,550,000
Net present value (*NPV*)		$ 157,776

We see that the *BTNPV* is $157,776. What does this mean? First, it indicates that the expected return for the investment is greater than the 18 percent discount rate. Second, we can say that the investor could invest $157,776 more equity capital and still earn the required 18 percent rate of return.

Profitability Index.   An investment measure closely related to the *NPV* is the profitability index (*PI*). The profitability index is the ratio of the present value (PV) of cash inflows to the initial equity invested. Like the *NPV,* it is based on a specified discount rate used to find the *PV.* The difference is that the initial equity is divided into the *PV* instead of subtracted from the *PV.* Using the above cash flows and present value, we find the profitability index as follows:

$$PI = \frac{2,707,776}{2,550,000} = 1.06$$

A profitability index greater than 1 has the same implication as an *NPV* which is greater than 0; that is the expected return exceeds the discount rate.

Internal Rate of Return.   Based on material covered in earlier chapters, we have already seen that an investment yield or *IRR* is found by finding the discount rate which equates the present value of the future cash inflows with the initial cash outflow. Recall that the initial equity investment is $2,550,000, found by subtracting the $5,950,000 loan amount from the $8,500,000 purchase price. The cash flows are repeated in Exhibit 10–10.

EXHIBIT 10–10   Cash-Flow Summary

	End of Year					
	0	*1*	*2*	*3*	*4*	*5*
Before-tax cash flow		$214,025	$239,960	$266,414	$284,765	$4,678,551
Equity	− $2,550,000					
Total	− $2,550,000	$214,025	$239,960	$266,414	$284,765	$4,678,551

The student should confirm that this results in an *IRR* of 19.64 percent, which we will refer to as the *BTIRR* since it is a before-tax *IRR*. This is the before-tax yield that the investor may expect to earn on equity over the investment period.

Is the return adequate? This depends on what the investor can earn on comparable investments, such as similar office buildings or even other real estate investments with similar risk characteristics. We have discussed comparing capitalization rates and price per square foot with comparable properties. Similarly, we could also ask what rate of return we would expect to earn had we bought another property at the price paid by another investor. This may give us some idea on what returns other investors are expecting. Of course, we would have to make our own projections of *NOI* and resale price unless the other investor told us exactly what he was thinking. We would also make similar projections and *IRR* calculations for other properties that are for sale, using their asking price. That is, we should earn a return that is at least as good as the return we could earn on other properties that are for sale that have similar risk characteristics.

Another test of the reasonableness of the *BTIRR* is to compare it with the effective interest cost of any mortgage financing that could be obtained to purchase the property. Normally, we would expect the return on the property to be greater than the effective cost of financing on the property, because the investor accepts more risk than the lender. The lender assumes less risk because a lender would have first claim on income and proceeds from sale of the property should there be a default. For example, we should expect that the *IRR* for the office building (*BTIRR* of 19.64 percent) would be more than the 10 percent mortgage interest rate. Otherwise, the investor would be better off lending on real estate rather than investing in it. In Chapter 12 we will discuss approaches to measuring and evaluating risk to investors. Then in Chapter 13 we will show how debt effects that risk and return for equity investors.

Adjusted (Modified) IRR.   A variation of the *IRR* calculated by many investors is a performance measure referred to either as the adjusted *IRR* or modified *IRR*. It differs from the *IRR* by making assumptions about how cash flows from the investment during the operating years (before it is sold) are *reinvested*. If the cash cannot be reinvested at the same rate as the *IRR*, the *IRR* to the investor will be different than calculated. To calculate the adjusted *IRR*, the investor must make an assumption as to the rate at which cash flows can be reinvested at each year. However, some investors prefer to assume cash flows will be reinvested at a rate which reflects the "typical" investment opportunity (e.g., the rate of return normally expected on real estate investments). Others believe that the annual cash flows are not enough to buy additional real estate investments, so they assume a reinvestment rate which represents putting the funds into short-term securities (referred to as a *safe rate*) until the property is sold and another purchased. The latter assumption might make sense for individual investors, whereas the former would be more appropriate for institutional investors like insurance companies or pension funds.

To illustrate the calculation of the adjusted *IRR*, assume that cash flows are reinvested at a 6 percent rate, representative of putting funds in short-term securities. Using the cash flows above, we have the following calculation:

Year		Future Value (6%)
1	$ 214,015	$ 270,201
2	239,960	285,796
3	266,414	299,342
4	284,765	301,850
5	4,678,551	4,678,551
Total future value		$5,835,741

The cash flow in year 1 is assumed to be reinvested for four additional years (end of year 1 to end of year 5), the cash flow in year 2 for three additional years, and so on. The cash flow in year 5 (operations and reversion) is not reinvested since it is already assumed to be received at the end of the fifth year. The total future value of $5,835,741 represents all of the funds from the investment, including interest earned from funds temporarily reinvested. How much does the investor earn considering that he has accumulated $5,835,741 after five years? We compare this future value with the $2,550,000 initial equity investment. That is, we find the discount rate which equates $5,835,741 received after five years with $2,550,000 invested in year 0. This is like an *IRR* for an investment with a *single* cash inflow. The student should confirm that the rate is 18.01 percent.

It should be no surprise that the adjusted *IRR* is less than the unadjusted *IRR* which was 19.64 percent. This is because the adjusted *IRR* is, in a sense, a weighted average of the *IRR* and the reinvestment rate. It is not much lower than the *IRR* in this case, because a substantial portion of the cash flow comes from sale of the property in year 5, and this does not have to be reinvested at the lower reinvestment rate.

Whenever the reinvestment rate is lower than the *IRR*, the adjusted *IRR* will be lower than the *IRR*. Conversely, if the reinvestment rate was higher than the *IRR* (not usually the case), then the adjusted *IRR* would be higher than the *IRR*. Finally, the adjusted *IRR* will be exactly the same as the *IRR* only if the reinvestment rate happens to be the same rate as the *IRR*. For this reason people often say that the *IRR* implicitly assumes that cash flows can be reinvested at a rate equal to the *IRR*. If the cash flows could not be reinvested at this rate, the adjusted *IRR* will not be equal to the *IRR*, implying that the investor's return is not what it was expected to be.

Summary of Performance Measures

A summary of the calculations for the office building is shown in Exhibit 10–11. The performance measures in Exhibit 10–11 should all be compared with other investment alternatives. This will give a good indication of whether acquisition of the office building is a good investment. However, these measures may still not be sufficient to allow us to decide whether we should purchase the investment. This is because we have not yet considered how *federal income taxes* might affect the results. Federal income tax considerations are included in the following chapter along with a discussion of what ownership forms might be considered (e.g., individual, partnership, or corporate). We may also want to know more about the *riskiness* of the investment so that we can be reasonably sure that we are comparing the performance measures in Exhibit 10–11 with alternatives of comparable risk. Risk is discussed in Chapter 12. We will also want to know whether we should borrow more or less money, and whether there are other, better ways of financing the property. This is covered in Chapter 13. Being able to obtain a loan on the property will also depend on the appraised value arrived at by an independent appraiser. This value may be more or less than the investor is willing to pay. If the appraised value is too low, it will be difficult to finance the property with the amount of debt that we have assumed in our projections. The appraisal of income properties is considered in Chapter 14.

EXHIBIT 10–11   Summary of Office Building Investment Analysis Measures

Price/gross square foot	$85.00
Price/net square foot	$88.54
Capitalization rate	10.62%
IRR (BTIRR)	19.64%
Adjusted *IRR* (6% reinvestment rate)	18.01%
NPV (18% discount rate)	$157,776.00
Profitability index (18% discount rate)	1.06

It should be obvious that we have only begun to do the in-depth analysis that must be done when analyzing the potential acquisition of our office building. Whether investors consider all of these issues in practice depends on the level of sophistication of the investor. Our objective will be to cover all the issues that *should* be considered to be certain of making an intelligent investment decision.

CONCLUSION

This chapter has introduced concepts and techniques important in the analysis of real estate income property. We discussed ways of projecting cash flows for an investor and ways of evaluating those cash flows with various measures of investment performance. The performance measures discussed in this chapter (*IRR, NPV, DCR,* etc.) will be used throughout the remainder of the text. Although the techniques in this chapter provide a good initial analysis of a project, as demonstrated by the office building example, there are many remaining questions to explore in more depth. For example: "How will taxes affect the performance of the property? Are there alternative ways of financing the property that would be better? How risky is the investment? These and other questions will be covered in the remaining chapters of this part of the text.

QUESTIONS

1. What are the primary benefits from investing in real estate income property?
2. What factors affect a property's projected *NOI?*
3. What factors would result in a property increasing in value over a holding period?
4. How do you think expense stops and *CPI* adjustments in leases affect the riskiness of the lease from the lessor's point of view?
5. Why should investors be concerned about market rents if they are purchasing a property subject to leases?
6. Discuss the pros and cons of using growth rates versus terminal cap rates to project a resale price.
7. What is the rationale for applying a terminal cap rate to the income one year after the end of the investment holding period?
8. Why is an overall rate not an *IRR?* In general, what factors could cause an *IRR* to be higher than an overall rate?
9. When might it be incorrect to apply a growth rate to the initial value to estimate the reversion?
10. What is meant by equity?
11. What are the similarities and differences between an overall rate and an equity dividend rate?
12. What is the significance of a debt coverage ratio?

PROBLEMS

1. An office building has three floors of rentable space with a single tenant on each floor. The first floor has 20,000 square feet of rentable space and is currently renting for $15.00 per square foot. There are three years remaining on the lease. The lease has an expense stop at $4.00 per square foot. The second floor has 15,000 square feet of rentable space and is leasing for $15.50 per square foot and has four years remaining on the lease. This lease has an expense stop at $4.50 per square foot. The third floor has 15,000 of leasable space and a lease just signed for the next five years at a rental rate of $16.00 per square foot, which is the current market rate. The expense stop is at $5.00 per square foot, which is what expenses per square foot are estimated to be during the next year (excluding management). Management expenses are expected to be 5 percent of effective gross income and are not included in the

expense stop. Each lease also has a *CPI* adjustment that provides for the base rent to increase at half the increase in the *CPI*. The *CPI* is projected to increase 4 percent per year.

Estimated operating expenses for the next year include the following:

Property taxes	$100,000
Insurance	10,000
Utilities	75,000
Janitorial	25,000
Maintenance	40,000
Total	$250,000

All expenses are projected to increase 4 percent per year. The market rental rate at which leases are expected to be renewed is also projected to increase 4 percent per year. When a lease is renewed, it would have an expense stop equal to operating expenses per square foot during the first year of the lease.

To account for any time that may be necessary to find new tenants after the first leases expire, 5 percent vacancy is estimated for the last two years (years 4 and 5).

a. Project the effective gross income (*EGI*) for the next five years.

b. Project the expense reimbursements for the next five years.

c. Project the net operating income (*NOI*) for next five years.

d. How much does the *NOI* increase (average compound rate) over the five years?

e. Assuming the property is purchased for $5,000,000, what is the overall capitalization rate (going-in rate)?

2. You are an employee of Multiplex Properties, Ltd., and have been given the following assignment. You are to present an investment analysis of a new small residential income-producing property for sale to a potential investor. The asking price for the property is $1,100,000; rents are estimated at $185,000 during the first year and are expected to grow at 4 percent per year. Vacancies and collection losses are expected to be 5 percent of rents. Operating expenses will be 35 percent of effective gross income. A 75 percent loan can be obtained at 11 percent interest for 30 years. The property is expected to appreciate in value at 3 percent per year and is expected to be owned for five years and then sold.

a. What is the investor's expected before-tax internal rate of return on equity invested (*BTIRR*)?

b. What is the first-year debt coverage ratio?

c. What is the terminal capitalization rate?

d. What is the *NPV* using a 12 percent discount rate? What does this mean?

e. What is the profitability index using a 12 percent discount rate? What does this mean?

Appendix: Multiple **IRR** *and Ranking Issues*

Chapter 10 introduced several performance measures used in investment analysis, including the *IRR, NPV,* and profitability index. This appendix discusses two important issues that the reader should be aware of when using these performance measures. These are referred to as the *multiple IRR* and *ranking* issues.

The multiple *IRR* issue has to do with the fact that, in certain situations, there can be more than one *IRR* for the same investment. The ranking issue has to do with using the performance measures to choose among investment alternatives. We will find that in some cases the conclusion can be ambiguous. In both of these situations, the student needs to know how to interpret the results.

Multiple *IRR*

We have discussed several measures of investment performance. One of the key measures we discussed was the *IRR*. Although this is a widely used measure of investment performance, we would be deficient in our discussion if we did not point out some of the issues surrounding use of the *IRR*. One of these issues is referred to as the "multiple rate of return" problem. This problem can occur when there is an "unconventional" cash flow pattern associated with an investment. A nonconventional cash flow pattern is one that involves a change in the sign of the cash flows (plus to minus) after the initial investment is made and positive cash flows were being received.

Exhibit 10A–1 shows an example of a project where cash flow may change signs.

Recall that by definition, the *IRR* is the discount rate which results in a net present value of zero. Exhibit 10A–2 calculates the *NPV* for various discount rates using the cash flows from Exhibit 10A–1. We see that the *NPV* is zero when two discount rates, about -8 percent and $+16$ percent, are used. Which is the correct *IRR?* Both are mathematically correct. The question is whether this is a good investment. One way of deciding is to look at the *NPV* at the discount rate that represents

---

EXHIBIT 10A–1   Multiple *IRR*

Year	Cash Flow
0	$-100,000
1	50,000
2	40,000
3	30,000
4	10,000
5	9,000
6	8,000
7	7,000
8	6,000
9	5,000
10	$-50,000

EXHIBIT 10A–2   Net Present Value Profile

Discount Rate (percent)	NPV	Discount Rate (percent)	NPV
− 12.00	$ − 30,082	5.00	$12,026
− 11.00	− 19,804	6.00	11,041
− 10.00	− 11,436	7.00	9,986
− 9.00	− 4,678	8.00	8,879
− 8.00	723	9.00	7,734
− 7.00	4,981	10.00	6,564
− 6.00	8,277	11.00	5,380
− 5.00	10,765	12.00	4,190
− 4.00	12,575	13.00	3,003
− 3.00	13,817	14.00	1,823
− 2.00	14,584	15.00	657
− 1.00	14,956	16.00	− 492
.00	15,000	17.00	− 1,621
1.00	14,773	18.00	− 2,727
2.00	14,325	19.00	− 3,807
3.00	13,695	20.00	− 4,861
4.00	12,919	21.00	− 5,887

the investor's target rate. For example, suppose a discount rate of about 12 percent reflects the investor's opportunity cost. Since the *NPV* is positive at this discount rate, we can conclude that this is a favorable investment. Because the *NPV* does not give us an ambiguous conclusion about the desirability of an investment when there is a sign change (and possibly a multiple *IRR*), many analysts believe the *NPV* is superior to the *IRR* in decision making. Exhibit 10A–3 shows a graph of the *NPV* for different discount rates. This is referred to as an *NPV profile*. We could also calculate an adjusted *IRR* for the above cash flows. This is shown in Exhibit 10A–4. Because the adjusted *IRR* reduces the cash flows after year 0 to a single cash inflow at the end of the holding period, there will be no multiple *IRR* problem. In this case we find that the adjusted *IRR* is 10.77 percent when calculated with a 10 percent reinvestment rate.

A multiple *IRR* does not occur often in practice, even if the cash flows are unconventional. However, it is a problem that investment analysts should be aware of since it can lead to a wrong interpretation of an investment if multiple rates are present but not accounted for. For example, we may have rejected the above investment if we thought the *IRR* was − 8 percent.

RANKING INVESTMENTS

Investors are often faced with many properties to choose from when making investment decisions. Hence they must rank, or prioritize, various alternatives before deciding which one to invest in. Given that the investor has selected several investments to choose from, the proper way of ranking them is very important. Any of the performance measures we have discussed could be used to do the ranking; that is, we could rank based on the *IRR*, the adjusted *IRR*, the *NPV*, the profitability

EXHIBIT 10A–3 Illustration of the Multiple *IRR*

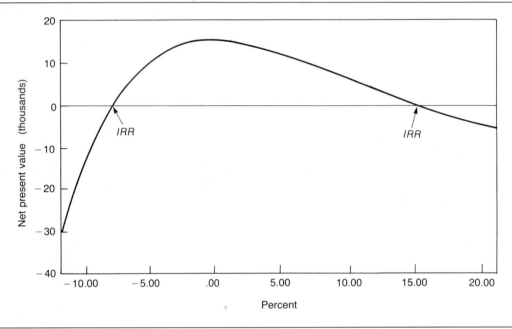

index, the overall capitalization rate, and so forth. A problem that sometimes occurs is that we can get different rankings depending on which criteria we use. This is illustrated for two investment alternatives shown in Figure 10A–5.

Investment A has relatively high cash flows in the beginning, but the cash flows decrease rapidly over time. Cash flows from investment B begin slower, but increase over time until the investment is sold in year 10. Exhibit 10A–6 shows the *NPV* profile for the two alternatives.

Note that the *IRR* is higher on Investment A, but the *NPV* is higher on investment B (using a 10 percent discount rate). Which one is better? Investment A has a higher return, but requires more cash flows to be reinvested during the early years than investment B. Thus one suggestion to resolve this dilemma is to explicitly consider the rate that cash flows can be reinvested. This could be done with an adjusted *IRR* calculation. In fact, if we believe that the reinvestment rate is the same as the rate that was used to calculate the *NPV* (10 percent in this example), then choosing the project with the highest *NPV* is identical to choosing the project with the highest adjusted *IRR*. This is illustrated in Exhibit 10A–7, where project B has the highest adjusted *IRR* with a 10 percent reinvestment rate.

Similarly, if the reinvestment rate is expected to be at least as much as the *IRR* for investment A, then choosing the investment with the highest *IRR* will also be identical to choosing the one with the highest adjusted *IRR*. This is related to the concept that the *IRR* implicitly assumes cash flows can be reinvested at a rate equal to the *IRR*. This is illustrated in Exhibit 10A–8, where the *IRR* for investment A is used as the reinvestment rate.

EXHIBIT 10A–4   Adjusted *IRR* for the Nonconventional Cash Flows (reinvestment rate 10.00 percent)

Year	Cash Flow	Future Value
1	$50,000	$117,897
2	40,000	85,744
3	30,000	58,462
4	10,000	17,716
5	9,000	14,495
6	8,000	11,713
7	7,000	9,317
8	6,000	7,260
9	5,000	5,500
10	− 50,000	− 50,000
Total future value		$278,102
Initial investment		$100,000
Adjusted *IRR*		10.77%

EXHIBIT 10A–5   Ranking Investments

	Investment A		Investment B	
Year	Cash Flow	Year		Cash Flow
0	$ − 100,000	0		$ − 100,000
1	25,000	1		5,000
2	25,000	2		8,000
3	20,000	3		12,000
4	15,000	4		14,000
5	10,000	5		14,000
6	5,000	6		14,000
7	2,500	7		16,000
8	1,500	8		16,000
9	1,000	9		16,000
10	100,000	10		135,000
Performance measures:				
IRR	13.96%			12.97%
NPV at 10%	$18,653			$20,839
Profitability index at 10%	1.19			1.21

EXHIBIT 10A–6 Analysis of Two Investments: A Conflict in Ranking

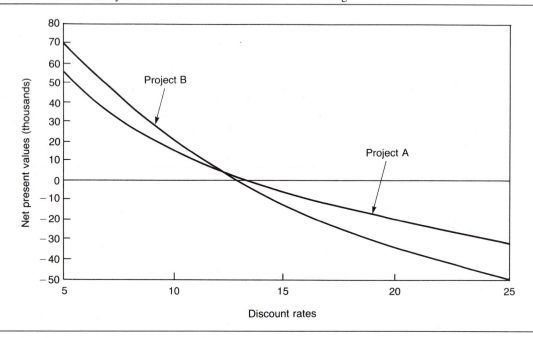

EXHIBIT 10A–7 Reinvestment Rate Calculations (reinvestment rate 10.00 percent)

	Investment A			Investment B	
Year	Cash Flow	Future Value	Year	Cash Flow	Future Value
1	$ 25,000	$ 58,949	1	$ 5,000	$ 11,790
2	25,000	53,590	2	8,000	17,149
3	20,000	38,974	3	12,000	23,385
4	15,000	26,573	4	14,000	24,802
5	10,000	16,105	5	14,000	22,547
6	5,000	7,321	6	14,000	20,497
7	2,500	3,328	7	16,000	21,296
8	1,500	1,815	8	16,000	19,360
9	1,000	1,100	9	16,000	17,600
10	100,000	100,000	10	135,000	135,000
Total future value		$307,754			$313,425
Initial investment		$100,000			$100,000
Adjusted *IRR*		11.90%			12.10%

EXHIBIT 10A–8   Reinvestment Rate Calculations (reinvestment rate 13.96 percent)

	Investment A			Investment B	
Year	*Cash Flow*	*Future Value*	*Year*	*Cash Flow*	*Future Value*
0	$ – 100,000		0	$ – 100,000	
1	25,000	$ 81,022	1	5,000	$ 16,204
2	25,000	71,099	2	8,000	22,752
3	20,000	49,913	3	12,000	29,948
4	15,000	32,850	4	14,000	30,660
5	10,000	19,218	5	14,000	26,905
6	5,000	8,432	6	14,000	23,610
7	2,500	3,700	7	16,000	23,678
8	1,500	1,948	8	16,000	20,778
9	1,000	1,140	9	16,000	18,233
10	100,000	100,000	10	135,000	135,000
Total future value		$369,320			$347,767
Initial investment		$100,000			$100,000
Adjusted *IRR*		13.96%			13.27%

In cases like this, the most logical assumption is probably that the reinvestment rate is the same as the discount rate that would be used to calculate the *NPV* to begin with. This is the basis for selecting a discount rate in the first place (e.g., it reflects what the investor can normally expect to earn). Thus, using the *NPV* to choose the alternative is the recommended method. Again, this is equivalent to using the adjusted *IRR if the reinvestment rate is the same as the discount rate used to calculate the NPV.*

QUESTIONS

A–1.   What is meant by the ranking problem? What causes a difference in ranking?

A–2.   What causes a multiple rate of return? When this occurs, what criteria should an investor use to make a decision?

A–3.   Why is it argued that the *IRR* assumes cash flows can be reinvested at a rate equal to the *IRR?* Do you agree with this argument?

A–4.   What is meant by an adjusted rate of return?

A–5.   Why is it argued that the *IRR* assumes cash flows can be reinvested at a rate equal to the *IRR?*

A–6.   What is the rational for assuming cash flows can be reinvested at a rate which is different from the *IRR?*

PROBLEMS

A–1. Cash flows for an investment are projected as follows:
  a. What is the *IRR?*
  b. What is the *NPV* at a 12 percent discount rate?
  c. Is this a desirable investment?

Year	Cash Flow
0	$ – 23,000
1	10,000
2	10,000
3	10,000
4	10,000
5	0
6	0
7	0
8	0
9	0
10	– 20,000

A–2. Two different investment alternatives have cash flow projections as follows:

Investment A		Investment B	
Year	Cash Flow	Year	Cash Flow
0	$ – 100,000	0	$ – 100,000
1	30,000	1	0
2	20,000	2	2,000
3	15,000	3	10,000
4	11,000	4	15,000
5	8,000	5	17,000
6	7,000	6	20,000
7	6,000	7	20,000
8	5,000	8	20,000
9	4,000	9	20,000
10	100,000	10	135,000

The investor only has enough funds to make one of the investments.
  a. Which one has the highest *IRR?*
  b. Which one has the highest *NPV* at a 10 percent discount rate?
  c. Which one has the highest profitability index at a 10 percent discount rate?
  d. What is the adjusted *IRR* for each using 10, 13, and 16 percent reinvestment rates? Does knowing the reinvestment rate help determine which investment is better?

Chapter 11

Taxation of Income-Producing Real Estate

Chapter 10 introduced investment analysis of income-producing property. Measures of investment performance such as the *IRR* and *NPV* were calculated. However, these calculations did not consider the effect of federal income taxes on the investment and financing decision; consequently, the analysis in Chapter 10 is referred to as a before-tax analysis. This chapter extends investment analysis introduced in Chapter 10 to include the effect of federal income taxes and is referred to as an after-tax analysis.

Our discussion of taxes will focus on the tax treatment of real estate based on the Tax Reform Act of 1986 (TRA). However, we will discuss some of the ways TRA differs from tax treatment that existed prior to 1986 for several reasons. First, the reader should have an appreciation as to why real estate has for many years been considered to be a "tax-sheltered" investment. Second, there are many investors who purchased real estate under previous tax laws, and who are, therefore, still affected by some of those provisions. Hence, their decision as to whether or not to sell the investment will be affected by both TRA and previous tax rules. Third, because tax laws are changed frequently, it is important to have a sense of how future changes may impact the desirability of real estate investment. As we will see, one element of risk of the desirability of real estate investment is the possibility of a tax law change which would reduce the after-tax rates of return.

CLASSIFICATION OF REAL PROPERTY

From the perspective of federal taxation, real estate can generally be classified as follows:

1. Owned as a personal residence by individuals.
2. Held for resale to others.
3. Held for the production of income or investment (capital asset).
4. Held for use in trade or business (Section 1231 asset).

This chapter does not deal with real estate held as a *personal residence* by individuals. However, the reader should realize that there are special rules that apply to the taxation of personal residences. For example, personal residences cannot be depreciated for tax purposes.

Property *held for resale to others* is viewed as inventory and profit from the sale of the inventory is treated as ordinary income. Individuals holding property for resale to others in the ordinary course of business are referred to as *dealers, not investors*. Examples of individuals or firms with *dealer* status would be developers who develop lots for resale, builders of houses for resale, or other activities in which real estate is not intended to be held as an investment; rather it is held for immediate resale. Real property held for resale by a dealer is *not depreciable* for tax purposes. (Depreciation rules are discussed later in this chapter.)

Under federal tax provisions, when real estate is held only for income or investment (item 3 above) and is not *operated* by its owner in a trade or business, it is classified as a *capital asset* for tax purposes. This could be a situation in which an investor will receive income from the investment but will *not* be actively engaged in *operating* the property. This is much like owning stocks or bonds. For example, an investor may own raw, unimproved land as an investment with an intent to sell it at a later time, or he may collect rents from a lease made to another individual or business, on a "net" lease basis. In the latter case, the investor owns the property for the production of income, but the property is not used in a trade or business. In this case, the owner does not have management responsibility, and the tenant would be responsible for all maintenance and operating costs. Hence the return to the investor would be "net" of operating expenses over some specified period. This is similar to an investor who receives a dividend payment on stock or interest on a bond, as the investor is purchasing the warehouse with the intention of *investing* and not for the purpose of operating it in trade or business to *produce income*.

In contrast to real estate categorized as a capital asset, we now consider property held for use in trade or business (classification 4 above). *Most income-producing real estate investments are included in this category*. In this case, an owner acquires real estate with the intent to operate, modify, or do whatever necessary to produce income in a trade or business. This may also be done by individuals in other occupations who also own and operate rental properties, although they must be actively engaged in the management of the property. This may also be done by investors in a partnership, corporation, or trust. Ownership forms are discussed later in this chapter. Real estate used for the production of income in a trade or business are categorized as Section 1231 assets. Section 1231 assets also applies to capital equipment (such as a machinery) purchased by businesses who use such assets in the production of income. Real estate used in trade or businesses include land and improvements such as income-producing rental properties and commercial properties which are subject to depreciation. This category of real estate is the primary focus of the chapter.

Owners of real estate used in the production of income in a trade or business report income from rents and may deduct expenses incurred with the operation of the property, such as maintenance, repair, and utilities. They may also deduct property taxes and interest on mortgage loans made to acquire property and loans made in the operation of the business. In addition, they are allowed deductions for depreciation, and when properties are sold, certain capital gain and loss provisions (discussed in a later section) also

---

EXHIBIT 11–1   Marginal Tax Rates for a Married Taxpayer Filing Jointly

---

Taxable Income	*Marginal Tax Rate*
$ 0–$29,750	15%
$ 29,751–$71,900	28%
$ 71,901–$149,250*	33%
$149,251–$182,850	33%
Over $182,851	28%

*The 5 percent surcharge on all taxable income from $71,901 to $149,250 is equivalent to increasing the tax rate on the first $29,750 of income from 15 percent to 28 percent; i.e., ($29,750)(.13) = $3,867 = (0.5)(149,250 − 71,900). Similarly, on incomes from $149,250 to $182,850 the benefit of $6,000 of personal exemptions is eliminated. Because these exemptions would have reduced taxes at a 28 percent rate—i.e., ($6,000)(.28) = $1,680— eliminating them amounts to raising the marginal rate by 5 percent; i.e., (0.5)(182,850 − 149,250) = $1,680. Hence for all income from $71,901 to $182,850 the effective rate of tax is 33 percent. Beyond $182,850, however, the marginal rate is 28 percent. We will refer to this (28 percent) as the maximum tax rate, since it is the rate which applies to the highest income categories.

---

apply. Later in the chapter we will see that the classifications above, especially whether the real estate is held as a capital asset versus an asset used in a trade or business, is important for determining the way gains from the sale of such assets are categorized for tax purposes.

INDIVIDUAL TAX RATES

To understand the impact of federal income taxes on investors who own real estate, we must first consider the tax rates faced by individuals. Later in the chapter we will consider alternative forms of holding real estate (such as corporate ownership). Effective with the 1988 tax year, there will be two statutory tax rates for individuals, 15 percent and 28 percent.[1] In addition, once individuals reach a certain income level, an additional 5 percent "surcharge" raises the individual's effective marginal tax rate to 33 percent. This surcharge is in effect until the individual's income has reached the point where, first, the benefit of having income taxed at the 15 percent rate is eliminated, and second, the benefit of personal exemptions ($2,000 per exemption after 1990) is eliminated. For example, for married taxpayers filing jointly with three exemptions, the marginal tax rates at various levels of taxable income can be summarized as in Exhibit 11–1.

The tax rate that corresponds to a particular tax bracket is referred to as a *marginal* tax rate since it is the rate that applies to an *additional* or *marginal* dollar of income that falls in a particular bracket. For investment decisions, we want to know how the additional income by adding the particular investment under consideration will affect the investor's

---

[1]During 1987, the maximum rate was 38.5 percent.

taxes. Thus, we are interested in knowing what marginal tax rate (or rates) applies to the investment. For example, suppose the individual for which the rates in Exhibit 11–1 applies already has taxable income of $72,000. Furthermore, suppose a real estate investment being considered would produce taxable income of $5,000 in 1990. According to the exhibit, the additional $5,000 of income would be taxed at a 33 percent rate, resulting in $1,650 of taxes. The investor's *average* tax rate will be 23.31 percent, which is lower than the marginal rate because income earned by the investor earned below $71,901 is subject to a lower tax rate.[2] Hence the average is the sum of all taxes calculated at different tax brackets divided by total taxable income.

If the income from the investment under consideration spans several brackets, then the calculations are slightly more complicated, but the concept is the same. In other words, we want to know what tax brackets are affected by income produced by the investment. For example, suppose the investor has $65,000 in other income and the investment would add $10,000 in taxable income. In this case, the investor would have total income of $75,000. From the exhibit we see that the first $6,900 of additional income (up to $71,900) would be taxed at a 28 percent rate, and the remaining $3,100 would be taxed at a 33 percent rate. Thus, the additional or marginal tax from the investment would be $2,955. The marginal rate would be $[(\$6,900)(.25) + (\$3,100)(.33)]/\$10,000$, or 29.6%.

We will see in a later section that if the investment produces tax losses instead of taxable income, calculating the marginal tax rate will be more involved. This is because the Tax Reform Act of 1986 introduced a distinction between different categories of income, and losses in one category may not be able to reduce income from a different category. It should also be pointed out that the 1986 tax law reduced both the number of tax brackets and the maximum tax rate paid by individuals. Prior to its passage, there were 14 tax brackets for married individuals filing joint returns, ranging from 11 percent to 50 percent.[3]

TAXABLE INCOME FROM OPERATION OF REAL ESTATE

Recall that in Chapter 10, we discussed at length how to calculate net operating income (*NOI*) for income producing property. Recall also that the calculation of *NOI* involved deducting expenses associated with *operating* a property, such as property taxes, insurance, maintenance, management, and utilities. Then, after subtracting the mortgage payment from the *NOI*, before-tax cash flow from operating the property ($BTCF_o$) results. We will now see that *taxable income* from operating real estate income property differs

---

[2]The total tax is calculated as follows:

$$.15(29,750) + .28(71,900 - 29,750) + .33(77,000 - 71,900) = 17,945.50.$$

Dividing this by $77,000 results in the average tax rate of 23.31 percent.

[3]See 1986 *Federal Tax Course*, Commerce Clearing House, Inc., for a discussion of the tax law in effect during 1986.

from $BTCF_o$ for two main reasons.[4] First, only the *interest* portion of a loan payment, not the total payment, is deductible from *NOI* for tax purposes. Second, the tax code allows owners to deduct an allowance for *depreciation* from *NOI*. Thus, taxable income from operating a real estate income property can be stated as follows:

$$\text{Taxable income} = NOI - \text{Interest} - \text{Depreciation allowance}$$

The amount of interest deductible in a given taxable year is equal to the total interest paid to the lender during that year. We have discussed the separation of loan payments into principal and interest in considerable detail in earlier chapters.[5] The calculation of depreciation allowances for tax purposes has not been covered as yet and will be discussed in the following section.

Depreciation Allowances

Physical assets like buildings suffer from physical depreciation over time which, ceteris paribus, reduces their economic value. Because buildings must ultimately be replaced, and because investment in improvements is allowed to be recovered before income produced from the improvement is taxed, a deduction for capital recovery (depreciation) from net operating income is allowed prior to the determination of taxable income. Otherwise, net operating income and taxable income would be overstated by an amount equal to the annual decrease in value due to economic depreciation. Thus, in theory, investors should only be taxed on the income net of this economic allowance for depreciation. This is the theoretical basis for tax depreciation. (The appendix to this chapter will elaborate on this concept.)

However, because of inflation, changes in supply and demand, and other economic factors which also affect the value of real estate, it is difficult to know what portion of any net change in value is caused by physical depreciation. Further, our tax system has historically provided for depreciation allowances that are greater than any actual decline in the economic value of the property. As we will see, to the extent that tax depreciation *allowances* exceed *actual* economic depreciation, tax benefits will be realized by investors. Exhibit 11–2 summarizes the methods that have been allowed to compute depreciation allowances under various tax laws in effect in recent years.

It should be obvious from the exhibit that tax policy has varied considerably with respect to depreciation allowances. As indicated, this is because, historically, Congress has provided for allowances in excess of economic depreciation to stimulate investment in real estate in the belief that this would increase construction and, hence, the supply of rentable space in the economy. Unfortunately, it may also have contributed to much of the overbuilding that occurred during the early 1980s. As shown in the exhibit, TRA, which passed in 1986, lengthened the depreciable life relative to what it was during the period from 1981 to 1986 and is one of several features in the 1986 law that reduced the

---

[4]Additional differences will be shown in later chapters.

[5]The reader may want to review the appendix to Chapter 9 at this time.

EXHIBIT 11–2   Depreciation Rules for Real Estate

Years	Depreciable Life	Methods Allowed
1969–1980	Useful life approximately 30–40 years	Accelerated or* straight line
1981–1983	15 yrs	ACRS based on 175% of straight-line depreciation†
1984–1985	18 yrs	ACRS based on 175% of straight-line depreciation†
1986	19 yrs	ACRS based on 175% of straight-line depreciation†
1987–	27.5 yrs for residential	Straight line
	31.5 yrs for nonresidential	Straight line

*Investors generally selected accelerated depreciation methods that ranged from 125 to 200 of straight-line depreciation, depending on whether the property was residential or nonresidential, new or existing.

†Because of severe "recapture" rules that affected investors who used accelerated depreciation on nonresidential real estate, straight-line depreciation was used by most investors in nonresidential real estate during this period.

favorable tax treatment that real estate had enjoyed previously. Later in this chapter we will see that depreciation is one source of tax benefits to investors in real estate.

Depreciable Basis.   The amount that can be depreciated for real estate improvements depends on the depreciable basis of the asset. The basis for a real estate investment is generally equal to the *cost* of the improvements (unless inherited or acquired by gift). Cost is generally defined to include the acquisition price of the improvements plus any installation costs associated with placing it into service. The cost of any capital improvements to the property made during the ownership period are also included in the basis when such outlays are made. Only improvements can be depreciated. The cost of land cannot be depreciated. In this chapter, we focus on the tax treatment for existing properties. (Differences for properties to be *developed and constructed* are discussed in Chapter 17.)

Depreciation of Personal Property

When investors acquire real estate for use in trade or business, they also often purchase furniture and fixtures in addition to the land and building. For example, when an apartment is acquired, it may include stoves and refrigerators. Hotel acquisitions usually include beds, tables, lobby furniture, kitchen equipment, and other items. This distinction is important for tax purposes, because furniture and fixtures are categorized as *personal property,* not real property. Under the Tax Reform Act of 1986, furniture and fixtures may be depreciated over seven years using the 200 percent declining balance method. Depreciation schedules for various categories of personal property are published by the IRS. These schedules assume that such property is purchased in the middle of the year, regardless of when the property is actually purchased. The schedules for furniture and fixtures also assume that the investor switches to straight-line depreciation in the fourth year.[6]

The following table shows the percent of the depreciable basis that would apply for personal property purchased after December 31, 1987:

Year	Depreciation (percent)
1	14.286
2	24.490
3	17.493
4	12.495
5	8.925
6	8.925
7	8.925
8	4.461
Total	100.00 %

The first year depreciation allowance is lower than the second year because of the midyear convention mentioned above. Because of this assumption (i.e., that the property is purchased in the middle of the year), the property is not fully depreciated until the eighth year.

Loan Points

Points paid in connection with obtaining a loan to purchase, refinance, or operate a real estate income property investment must be deducted ratably over the term of the loan. For example, suppose a loan for $800,000 is made to purchase an office building. The loan is to be amortized over a 25-year term. Suppose two points, or $16,000 is paid on the loan. For tax purposes, the $16,000 would have to be amortized over 25 years, or $640 per year. If the property is sold before the points are completely amortized, the balance can be expensed in the year of sale. Thus in the above example, if the property is sold and the loan is repaid after five years, $12,800 could be expensed.

It should be noted that the deductibility of points is based on the *term* of the loan, not on the amortization period. If the loan in our example had a balloon payment due in the 10th year, then the points could be deducted over 10 years, even though the loan payments are based on 25-year amortization.

---

[6]This provision is a carryover from previous tax laws when the investor could choose to switch to straight-line depreciation in the year that the depreciation calculated by the straight-line method resulted in more depreciation than would have resulted by maintaining the declining balance method.

The reader might note that points paid when obtaining financing for the purchase of a personal residence are generally fully deductible in the year they are paid. However, points paid to *refinance* a personal residence must be deducted ratably over the loan term, as discussed above for income property.

TAXABLE INCOME FROM DISPOSAL OF DEPRECIABLE REAL PROPERTY

In establishing whether a taxable gain or loss has occurred when a property is sold, we must determine the gross sales price. The gross sales price is equal to any cash or other property received in payment for the property sold, plus any liabilities against the property assumed by the buyer. Any selling expenses (e.g., legal fees, recording fees, and brokerage fees) may then be deducted to establish *net sales proceeds*. To determine gain or loss, subtract the *adjusted basis* of the property from net sales proceeds. The adjusted basis of a property is its *original basis* (cost of land and improvements, acquisition and installation fees), plus the cost of any capital improvement, alterations, or additions made during the period of ownership, less accumulated depreciation taken to date. Any excess of the net sales proceeds over the adjusted basis results in a taxable gain, and any deficit results in a taxable loss.

As previously indicated, how a property is classified—that is, personal residence, held for resale, capital asset or used in trade or business—is important when establishing capital gains and losses. Detailed discussion of these classifications is beyond the scope of this chapter.[7] In the case of depreciable real estate held for use in trade or business (Section 1231 assets), *net* gains on the sale of such property are treated as long-term capital gains. *Net* losses from the sale of such property are treated as *ordinary losses*.[8] This distinction has historically been important because Congress has either made the effective tax rate on gains and losses from the *sale* of property different from tax rates applied to income and losses produced from the *operation* of property, or this has been done by using various exclusions applied to long-term capital gains. For example, prior to the Tax Reform Act of 1986 (TRA) capital gains received very favorable tax treatment. Prior to TRA, if such property had been held more than six months, 60 percent of the gain on sale was totally excluded from taxation. Thus, only 40 percent of the gain was taxed, resulting in a maximum effective tax on capital gains of 20 percent (40 percent exclusion multiplied by a 50 percent maximum tax rate). The Tax Reform Act of 1986 eliminated the capital gain exclusion, and by 1988 capital gains are scheduled to be taxed at the same rate as ordinary income, (i.e., at rate of up to 28 percent).[9]

---

[7]The reader should consult a general reference on federal income taxes for more information. See *Federal Tax Course—1987* (Englewood Cliffs, N.J.: Prentice-Hall).

[8]The term net means after *all* gains and losses from sales (if more than one occurs) in a tax year are combined.

[9]However, even after TRA passed in 1986, while the capital gain *exclusion* was immediately eliminated, Congress chose to apply different tax rates to ordinary income and capital gains in 1986 and 1987. Barring any future changes in legislation by Congress, this difference is scheduled to disappear by 1988, when the maximum tax rates on ordinary income *and* capital gains will be 28 percent.

Even though tax rates are scheduled to become the same, the distribution between capital gains and losses and between ordinary income and losses remains important. This is because (1) TRA calls for special treatment of losses produced from the operation of real estate for certain "passive investors" and capital gains upon sale, and (2) for properties acquired prior to 1986, certain recapture of excess depreciation rules apply before the calculation of capital gains. The application to passive investors will be discussed in more detail later in the chapter. Calculation of taxable income from the operation and disposition of real estate are illustrated in the following section.

AFTER-TAX INVESTMENT ANALYSIS

We now consider the effect of federal income taxes on the office building investment analysis example from Chapter 10. Our example applies to a depreciable property held by an *individual* to produce income in a trade or business (Section 1231 asset). As a starting point for our discussion, Exhibit 11–3 summarizes the calculation of before-tax cash flow from Chapter 10.

After-Tax Cash Flow from Operation

We have estimated *before-tax* cash flows from the investment and now must determine the increase or decrease in the investor's taxable income as a result of undertaking this investment. Because taxes will either be increased or decreased as a result of undertaking the investment, that increase or decrease must be combined with before-tax cash flows to determine how much cash flow will result in an *after-tax* basis. To do this we must consider how much taxable income is produced each year from operations and then

EXHIBIT 11–3   Estimates of Before-Tax Cash Flow from Operations and Sale

	Year				
	1	*2*	*3*	*4*	*5*
Cash flow from operations:					
Net Operating Income (*NOI*)	$903,050	$928,985	$955,439	$973,790	$1,010,822
Less debt service (*DS*)	689,025	689,025	689,025	689,025	689,025
Before-tax cash flow	$214,025	$239,960	$266,414	$284,765	$ 321,797
Estimates of cash flows from sale in year 5:					
Sales price					$9,700,000
Less mortgage balance					5,343,245
Before-tax cash flow (*BTCFs*)					$4,356,755

EXHIBIT 11–4   Taxable Income and After-Tax Cash Flow from Operations

Taxable income:					
Net operating income (*NOI*)	$903,050	$928,985	$955,439	$973,790	$1,010,822
Less interest	590,569	580,259	568,869	556,288	542,388
depreciation	229,365	229,365	229,365	229,365	229,365
Taxable income (loss)	83,116	119,361	157,204	188,137	239,069
Tax (at 28%)	$ 23,273	$ 33,421	$ 44,017	$ 52,678	$ 66,939
After-tax cash flow:					
Before-tax cash flow (*BTCF*)	$214,025	$239,960	$266,414	$284,765	$ 321,797
Less tax	23,273	33,421	44,017	52,678	66,939
After-tax cash flow (*ATCF*)	$190,752	$206,538	$222,396	$232,086	$ 254,857

consider taxes in the year that the property is sold. Exhibit 11–4 shows the calculation of taxable income and after-tax cash flow from operating the property. In Exhibit 11–4 we see that taxable income is found by subtracting interest and depreciation from the *NOI*. Note that only the interest, not the total loan payment, is tax deductible. In our example, interest was based on having a $5,950,000 loan amortized over a 20-year term with monthly payments based on a 10 percent interest rate. Exhibit 11–5 reproduces the summary loan schedule from Chapter 10.

Depreciation.   Taxable income is also affected by an allowance for *depreciation*. As discussed earlier in the chapter, under the TRA of 1986, residential properties may be depreciated over 27.5 years, and nonresidential real property must be depreciated over 31.5 years. Both must be depreciated in a straight-line basis.[10] Also recall that only the improvements, not land, can be depreciated. Thus, we need to know what portion of the $8,500,000 purchase price of the office building represents building improvements as opposed to land. For our case example, we assume that land cost requirements are 15 percent of the purchase price or $1,275,000, leaving improvements of $7,225,000. Dividing improvement cost by 31.5 results in an annual depreciation deduction of $229,365.[11]

Recall that depreciation allowances represent recovery of capital and do not represent an actual cash outflow for the investor (that occurs when the property is acquired). The deduction only affects taxable income and not operating cash flows. In our example, taxable income is $83,116 in year 1. Assuming the investor is in a 28 percent tax bracket, the increase in tax liability as a result of owning the property will be $23,273 (.28 · $83,116).

---

[10]In the case of mixed use properties (i.e., those with both residential and nonresidential uses), if 80 percent of revenues are produced by *one* of the uses, the total improvement may be depreciated over the tax life corresponding to that use.

[11]The IRS publishes tables that taxpayers must use to calculate depreciation deductions. The tables assume that the investor purchases the property in the middle of the month, and they pro rate the first-year depreciation according to the actual month of the year the property is purchased. We are simply dividing by 31.5 years.

EXHIBIT 11–5 Summary Loan Information

	End of Year				
	1	*2*	*3*	*4*	*5*
Payment	$ 689,025	$ 689,025	$ 689,025	$ 689,025	$ 689,025
Mortgage balance	5,851,543	5,742,776	5,622,620	5,489,883	5,343,245
Interest	590,569	580,259	568,869	556,288	542,388
Principal	98,457	108,767	120,156	132,738	146,637

Subtracting this from before-tax cash flow results in after-tax cash flow of $190,752 in year 1.

Note that taxable income is *positive* during each year in this example. If the taxable income was negative (i.e., a tax loss), additional assumptions must be made regarding the investor's ability to use the losses to offset other taxable income. This is discussed later in this chapter.

After-Tax Cash Flow from Sale

Exhibit 11–6 illustrates how sale of the property affects the investor's taxable income. When determining the investor's capital gain from sale of the property, we should keep in mind that the investor will have depreciated the property for five years. Hence, the investor's *cost basis* in the property will be reduced. In our example, depreciation was $229,365 per year for five years, resulting in total depreciation (accumulated depreciation) of $1,146,825. Subtracting the accumulated depreciation from the original cost basis of the property (cost of the land and improvements) results in an adjusted basis of $7,353,175. (This is also sometimes referred to as the *book value* of the property.) The difference between the adjusted basis ($7,353,175) and the sale price ($9,700,000) is the capital

EXHIBIT 11–6 After-Tax Cash Flow from Sale

Sale price			$9,700,000
Less mortgage balance			5,343,245
Before-tax cash flow (*BTCF*s)			4,356,755
Taxes in year of sale			
Sale price		$9,700,000	
Original cost basis	$8,500,000		
Accumulated depreciation	1,146,825		
Adjusted basis		7,353,175	
Capital gain		2,346,825	
Tax on gain at 28%			657,111
After-tax cash flow from sale (*ATCF*s)			$3,699,644

EXHIBIT 11–7   Cash Flow Summary

	End of Year					
	0	*1*	*2*	*3*	*4*	*5*
Before-tax cash flow	$ − 2,550000	$214,025	$239,960	$266,314	$284,765	$4,678,551
After-tax cash flow	− 2,550000	190,752	206,538	222,396	232,086	3,954,501

Before-tax *IRR*
(*BTIRR*)   =   19.64%
After-tax *IRR*
(*ATIRR*)   =   15.17%

gain, $2,346,825. As discussed earlier, under current tax law the entire taxable gain is taxed at the same rate as ordinary income. Thus, assuming the investor is still in the 28 percent tax bracket upon sale of the property (and assuming tax laws haven't changed again), taxes resulting from sale of the property would be $657,111. Subtracting the tax from the before-tax cash flow results in after-tax cash flow of $3,699,644.[12]

After-Tax IRR

Using the information from Exhibits 11–4 and 11–6, we may now calculate the after-tax *IRR*. The cash flows are summarized in Exhibit 11–7 along with the before-tax cash flows for comparison. As we might expect, the after-tax *IRR* is *lower* than the before-tax *IRR*. However, although the investor's tax rate was 28 percent, the after-tax *IRR* is not 28 percent lower than the before-tax *IRR*. Rather, it is about 23 percent lower (1 − 15.17/19.64 = 22.76%).

Effective Tax Rate

In the previous section, we indicated that the after-tax *IRR* is 23 percent lower than the before-tax *IRR*, even though the investor had a 28 percent marginal tax rate. In this case we would say that if the investment being analyzed was undertaken, its income and gain would be taxed at an *effective tax rate* of 23 percent. Why is the effective tax rate on this investment lower than the marginal tax rate? There are two reasons. First, depreciation deductions lowered the investor's taxable income each year. Had the property actually

---

[12]The reader should be aware that for some properties acquired before 1986, if depreciation was taken based on ACRS or accelerated depreciation methods, certain recapture rules apply before capital gains are calculated. These rules require that the difference between depreciation allowances taken and straight-line depreciation be taxed at ordinary tax rates. In these situations, the reader must take into account the year the property was acquired, the method of depreciation used, and recapture rules in the year of sale. For more information see *Federal Tax Course*, Commerce Clearing House, Inc., various years, Section 1250 and Section 1245 property.

depreciated in value at the same rate; that is, had the property sold at a price equal to its adjusted basis, there would have been no tax benefits. (This is illustrated in the appendix to this chapter.) However, the nominal property value has actually increased. Thus, the investor is taking annual depreciation allowances each year the property is operated, which results in lower taxable income and hence lower taxes, although the property value is increasing. While these allowances also reduce the adjusted basis of the property each year and will eventually result in an increase in taxes paid on the capital gain in the year of sale, because of the "time value of money" lower taxes paid on income each year is a benefit to the investor. It is as if the investor received an interest-free "loan," or use of funds each year equal to the amount of depreciation deductions. The "loan" is repaid when the property is sold.

The second reason that the effective tax rate is lower than the marginal tax rate is not quite so obvious. It also stems from the fact that the property is increasing in value. We have already discussed the fact that depreciation deductions are a benefit as long as the property does not decline in value at a rate equal to or greater than depreciation allowances. If the property actually increases in value, there is a further benefit because such increases in value are not taxed each year. Rather, the increase in value is not taxed until the property is sold. Hence, for an investment to have an effective tax rate equal to the investor's marginal tax rate, the investor would have to be taxed each year on the increase in the value of the property from the previous year. Thus, there is an additional tax deferral benefit associated with holding real estate when it increases in value.

Before-Tax Equivalent Yield

From the discussion above it should be apparent that despite the Tax Reform Act of 1986, all investments are not treated alike when it comes to federal income taxes. Thus, taxes must be considered when comparing returns for investments which are not taxed in the same manner. One obvious way to do this is simply compare after-tax rates of return for each investment. Alternatively, we can compare investments on a before-tax basis by computing what is referred to as the *before-tax equivalent yield*. For a given investment that is expected to produce a given after-tax *IRR* (*ATIRR*), the before-tax equivalent yield is defined as the before-tax yield (*BTIRR*) that would have to be earned on the investment to produce the *same* after-tax *IRR if* the investment was fully taxable. By "fully taxable" we mean that the effective tax rate for the investment would be the same as the investor's marginal tax rate (t). With this definition, the before-tax equivalent yield (*BTEY*) would be

$$BTEY = \frac{ATIRR}{1 - t}$$

For example, the *ATIRR* for the office building was 15.17 percent, and the investor was assumed to have a marginal tax rate of 28 percent. The before-tax equivalent yield is therefore 21.07 percent. That is, a 21.07 percent before-tax *IRR* would have to be earned for the investor to earn 15.17 percent after tax if there were no tax benefits. Note that the before-tax equivalent yield is higher than the actual expected *BTIRR* of 19.64 percent. This is because the office building can earn a lower *BTIRR* and still produce a 15.17 percent *ATIRR* due to the tax benefits.

After-Tax NPV

In Chapter 10, we calculated a net present value for the office building example, using before-tax cash flows. Similarly, we can calculate the *NPV*, using after-tax cash flows. Exhibit 11–8 summarizes the calculations. Note that a lower, *after*-tax discount rate was applied to the *after*-tax cash flows to obtain the after-tax net present value. With the investor in a 28 percent tax bracket, his after-tax return on fully taxable investments would be reduced by 28 percent. Thus if the before-tax required return was 18 percent, the investor might want to earn about 13 percent after tax [.18(1 − .28) = 12.96%]. The after-tax discount rate depends on the after-tax return that can be earned on alternative investments of comparable risk.

CLASSIFICATION OF INCOME

The Tax Reform Act of 1986 requires that income and loss from all sources, including real estate, be divided into three categories as follows:

1. *Passive income (or loss)*: Income or loss from a trade or business where the investor does not materially participate in the management or operation of the property. Material participation is defined as "involvement in the operations of the activity on a regular, continuous and substantial basis." Real estate investment is considered to be a passive activity. Hence, unless an investor materially participates in the operation of the property, income and losses earned from such activity is categorized as passive income or loss. Income (or loss) received by a limited partner in a partnership is considered passive by definition.

2. *Active income (or loss)*: Salaries, wages, fees for services, and income from a trade or business in which the investor materially participates. However, even if a taxpayer materially participates, income or loss from "rental activity" is not considered active income. Thus, income from rental housing, office buildings, shopping centers, and other real estate activities in which a taxpayer is a landlord are not classified as active income (or loss). This income or loss is classified as *passive income*. However, the operation of

---

EXHIBIT 11–8   After-Tax Net Present Value (13% discount rate)

Present value of *ATCF* from operations (Exhibit 11–5)	$ 765,358
Present value of *ATCF* from reversion (Exhibit 11–6)	2,008,018
Original equity investment	− 2,550,000
After-tax net present value	223,376

a hotel, other transient lodging, or a nursing home is *not* a rental activity, and therefore its owners will have active income if they materially participate.

3. *Portfolio income (or loss)*: Interest and dividend income from stocks, bonds and some categories of real estate which are classified as *capital assets*. Recall that most real estate investments are usually Section 1231 assets and are not capital assets, as discussed earlier. Examples of portfolio income from real estate activity that would be (1) dividends received on shares in a real estate investment trust (REIT) or (2) income received on long-term land leases or net leases on real estate where the owner does not materially participate in its operation.

The above classifications of income are very important because, in general, passive losses cannot be used to offset income from another category. This is referred to as the *passive activity loss limitation* (PALL). Prior to the 1986 Tax Reform Act, many investors purchased real estate that was held as a trade or business by a limited partnership where the individual investor (limited partner) did not materially participate. These investments often produced (and may still be producing) tax losses which were used by the investor to offset other taxable income. This can no longer be done with the passive activity loss limitation.[13] Passive losses produced from real estate investments and other passive activities must now be used to offset passive income earned during the tax year. Any remaining or unused passive losses must be "suspended" and carried forward to offset any passive income earned in future years.

When an investment producing passive income is *sold* and a capital gain occurs, any unused or suspended losses from that activity (1) must first be used to offset any capital gain from the sale of that activity, (2) must then be used to offset any other passive income produced from other passive activities during that year, and (3) can then be used to offset *any income,* including active and portfolio income earned during that year. To the extent that unused losses remain, they may be carried forward into succeeding years as capital losses, not subject to passive loss rules. For Section 1231 property, any remaining losses would be deductible as ordinary losses.

In cases where the sale of a passive activity, such as real estate, produces a capital loss, *and* unused suspended losses from previous years also remain, the unused passive losses may be used to offset any other sources of income (active, passive, or portfolio). Of the capital loss portion, $3,000 of the loss may be used to offset any other source of income that year. Any excess must be carried forward to the next taxable year as a capital loss. It would no longer be subject to passive loss rules, and the excess as well as any unused passive losses may be deducted from ordinary income as a Section 1231 loss.[14]

---

[13]For investors that purchased real estate or because limited partners in entities that acquired real estate prior to 1986, this change in characterization is important. Such investors have probably used ACRS or accelerated depreciation in methods which may have produced large top losses. These losses are passive losses and may not be used any longer to reduce ordinary income for tax purposes. They are subject to PALL.

For property purchased prior to October 22, 1986, there is a phase-in of the passive loss limitations. Prior to 1991, only a proportion of the investor's passive losses are subject to the passive loss limitation rules as follows: 35 percent in 1987, 60 percent in 1988, 80 percent in 1989, and 90 percent in 1990. After that all of the investor's passive losses are subject to the limitations.

[14]For further explanation see P. Fass, R. Haft, L. Loffman, and S. Presant, *Tax Reform Act of 1986* (New York: Clark Boardman Co., Ltd., 1986).

Excess Passive Activity Losses

As noted in the previous section, the 1986 tax law requires that any excess passive activity losses be classified as suspended losses. These losses can be carried forward and used in subsequent years against passive activity income. If an investor has passive income from an activity in a given year, that income is first reduced by any passive losses which occurred that year. Any remaining passive income can be reduced by any accumulated suspended losses from previous years. If the individual has more than one activity (e.g., multiple real estate investments) producing passive losses and passive income, then the passive income must be allocated to each activity with losses on a pro rata basis. For example, suppose the investor has $5,000 in suspended losses from building A and $10,000 in suspended losses from building B. If the investor also has $6,000 in passive income from building C for the current year, then the accumulated suspended losses on buildings A and B will be reduced as follows:

Building A:
$$\frac{5,000}{15,000} \times \$6,000 = \$2,000$$

Building B:
$$\frac{10,000}{15,000} \times \$6,000 = \$4,000$$

The investor will report zero taxable income from these three investments and after allocation of the passive income, the suspended losses on building A will be $3,000 and the suspended losses on building B will be $6,000. This pro rata allocation is important because it affects the amount of suspended passive losses remaining for each property. This, in turn, becomes important if one of the properties is sold and unused losses are used to offset capital gains from the sale of that property.

When a property is sold, any suspended losses are allowable as a deduction against income in the following order: (1) any income or gain from that passive activity for the taxable year, including any gain recognized on the sale; (2) any net income or gain (including Section 1231 gains from other investments) for the taxable year from other passive activities; and (3) *any other* income or gain (i.e., from active of portfolio income). Thus when the asset is sold suspended losses are effectively treated like an ordinary loss in the sense that it can offset other taxable income.

Special Exceptions: Loss Allowances for Rental Real Estate

One special exception that was included in the 1986 Tax Reform Act applies to individual rental property owners (other than limited partners). These investors are allowed to offset active income with up to $25,000 of passive activity losses (to the extent they exceed income from passive activities) from rental real estate activities in which the individual *actively* participates. Active participation is less restrictive than the material participation standard referred to earlier and requires less personal involvement. In general, the individual must own a 10 percent or greater interest in the activity and be involved in management decisions, selection of tenants and determination of rents or arrange for others to provide services (e.g., a property manager to manage the property on a day-to-day basis).

This special rule is phased out for individuals with adjusted gross incomes between $100,000 and $150,000. The $25,000 loss allowance is reduced by 50 percent of the amount the individual's adjusted gross income when such income for the taxable year exceeds $100,000. Thus individuals with an adjusted gross income of $120,000 would only be allowed to use up to $10,000 of any passive losses to reduce active income. An individual with adjusted gross income in excess of $150,000 would receive no loss allowance.

EFFECT OF PASSIVE LOSS LIMITATION ON THE *ATIRR*

In the previous section we discussed the passive loss rules that were introduced in the Tax Reform Act of 1986. Recall that the passive loss rules limit the amount of losses that an investor can use to offset other income. In general, passive losses can only be used to offset passive income. This means that the investor may not be able to realize full benefits from any tax losses generated by the investment. To illustrate, we return to the office building example with all assumptions the same except for the financing. We now assume that an 85 percent loan can be obtained (versus the 70 percent loan in the original example) from a lender that is willing to make a larger loan. To compensate for the additional risk, the lender now requires a 10.75 percent interest rate instead of 10 percent. As shown in Exhibit 11–9, the larger interest deductions resulting from the use of a larger loan and the higher interest rate results in *tax losses* for the first three years. In this illustration, assume that the investor is not affected by passive loss limitations; that is, the investor has other passive income available from other passive activities, such as other real estate investments currently producing taxable income. Thus Exhibit 11–9 assumes that losses produced by this investment can be used to offset other passive income, thereby reducing taxes each year. Note that for the first three years, a taxable loss is produced which will serve to reduce the investor's *total tax liability*. This reduction in tax liability means that the investor will have a larger cash outflow for taxes in these years, if the investment is made. Hence, this reduction in net cash outflow must be actual cash flow after taxes that will occur as a result of taking on this additional investment.

Note that the effective tax rate drops from 23 percent in the case where 70 percent financing was used to 19 percent in the current example. This results from larger interest deductions and the additional tax benefits created by the ability to use the losses to offset other income. The use of high amounts of debt to create tax losses was common prior to the Tax Reform Act of 1986, or before the passive loss limitation rules were introduced. As we have discussed, because of the passive loss limitation rules many investors may no longer be able to use such passive losses in the year they occur. To illustrate, in Exhibit 11–10 we assume that the investor has (1) no other passive income and (2) is not in a position to benefit from the special rule for rental real estate discussed above.

As can be seen in the cash flow from operation, the before-tax cash flows are obviously the same as in the previous example (see Exhibit 11–9). Annual tax losses are also the same, but because the investor has no other passive income those losses cannot be used to offset other taxable income. These losses must now be suspended. Thus the tax is zero for each year that there is negative taxable income. The unused losses will be accumulated

EXHIBIT 11-9 After-Tax Cash Flows Assuming No Passive Loss Limitation

	Year				
	1	*2*	*3*	*4*	*5*

Estimates of Cash Flow from Operations

A. Before-tax cash flow					
Net operating income (*NOI*)	$ 903,050	$ 928,985	$ 955,439	$973,790	$1,010,822
Less debt service (*DS*)	880,204	880,204	880,204	880,204	880,204
Before-tax cash flow	$ 22,846	$ 48,781	$ 75,235	$ 93,586	$ 130,618
B. Taxable income or loss					
Net operating income (*NOI*)	$ 903,050	$ 928,985	$ 955,439	$973,790	$1,010,822
Less interest	771,432	759,145	745,471	730,251	713,313
depreciation	229,365	229,365	229,365	229,365	229,365
Taxable income (loss)	− 97,747	− 59,525	− 19,397	14,173	68,144
Tax	$ − 27,369	$ − 16,667	$ − 5,431	$ 3,969	$ 19,080
C. After-tax cash flow					
Before-tax cash flow (*BTCF*)	$ 22,846	$ 48,781	$ 75,235	$ 93,586	$ 130,618
Less tax	− 27,369	− 16,667	− 5,431	3,969	19,080
After-tax cash flow (*ATCF*)	$ 50,216	$ 65,449	$ 80,667	$ 89,618	$ 111,538

Estimates of Cash Flows from Sale in Year 5

Sale price		$9,700,000	
Less mortgage balance		6,543,595	
Before-tax cash flow (*BTCFs*)		3,156,405	
Sale price		$9,700,000	
Original cost basis	$8,500,000		
Less accum. depreciation	1,146,825		
Adjusted basis		7,353,175	
Capital gain		2,346,825	
Tax from sale (at 28%)			657,111
After-tax cash flow from sale (*ATCFs*)		$2,499,294	

	End of Year					
	0	*1*	*2*	*3*	*4*	*5*

Cash Flow Summary

Before-tax cash flow	$ − 1,275,000	$22,846	$48,781	$75,235	$93,586	$3,287,024
After-tax cash flow	− 1,275,000	50,216	65,449	80,667	89,618	2,610,833
Before-tax *IRR* = 23.50%						
After-tax *IRR* = p$19.00%						
Effective tax rate = 19.13%						

as shown in the exhibit, and by the end of the third year there will be $176,669 in suspended losses. During the fourth year, the investment generates *positive* taxable income (passive income). Thus some of the suspended loss can be used at this time, so the taxes are still zero. There are enough suspended losses from the first three years so that no taxes will be paid on taxable income from operation during the fifth year. After considering the taxable income from operation during the fifth year, there still remains $94,352 of suspended losses as shown in Section B of the exhibit. This balance can be used to reduce the capital gain from the sale of the property in the fifth year, as shown in the calculation of tax from sale in Exhibit 11–10.

Although the before-tax *IRR* (*BTIRR*) is the same whether or not the passive losses can be used when they occur, the after-tax *IRR* (*ATIRR*) is *lower* when the passive loss limitations affect the investor (see Exhibits 11–9 and 11–10). This is obviously due to the fact that the present value of the tax deduction is less when passive losses cannot be used immediately. Clearly the investor must take the passive loss rules into consideration when evaluating an investment and the amount of financing. Additional financing considerations are discussed in Chapter 13.

AT RISK RULES

At risk rules may also act to limit total losses which can be deducted by taxpayers, irrespective of the existence of passive income from other activities. The term *at risk* refers to investment amounts which taxpayer-investors are deemed to have placed at risk of economic loss when undertaking a specific investment. The amount that is considered at risk includes (1) cash contributions to the activity, (2) adjusted basis of any property contributed to the activity, and (3) amounts borrowed for use in the activity with respect to which the taxpayer has personal liability (recourse debt) or has pledged property not used in the activity. In addition, third party nonrecourse debt (debt for which the taxpayer is not personally liable) can be included in the amount the investor is considered to have at risk if it is from a third party, commercial lender and is made on current market terms. The reader should note that seller financing would *not* be included in the amount the investor is considered to be at risk. After the property is purchased, the amount at risk is increased by any additional cash contributions, income earned, or gain recognized. The amount at risk is reduced by any cash withdrawals or losses incurred. If the amount at risk is reduced to zero, additional losses cannot be deducted. These losses must be accumulated and carried forward until the activity generates income, is sold for a gain, or additional cash contributions are made.

The amount at risk is determined separately for *each* activity. The at risk rules are designed to prevent investors from using *tax* losses (which exceed any actual *cash* losses) to reduce other taxable income beyond amounts invested in the project, or amounts deemed to be at risk in the investment. Losses from real estate will not usually be so great that the at risk rules will affect most individual taxpayers. However, if a large amount of seller financing is used, amounts at risk will be substantially lower than would be the case if conventional financing is used, and the at risk rules may limit the amount of losses the investor can deduct.

EXHIBIT 11–10 *ATIRR and Effective Tax Rate Assuming No Passive Income*

	Year				
	1	*2*	*3*	*4*	*5*

Estimates of Cash Flow from Operations

A. Before-tax cash flow					
Net operating income (*NOI*)	$ 903,050	$ 928,985	$ 955,439	$ 973,790	$1,010,822
Less debt service (*DS*)	880,204	880,204	880,204	880,204	880,204
Before-tax cash flow	$ 22,846	$ 48,781	$ 75,235	$ 93,586	$ 130,618
B. Taxable income or loss					
Net operating income (*NOI*)	$ 903,050	$ 928,985	$ 955,439	$ 973,790	$1,010,822
Less interest	771,432	759,145	745,471	730,251	713,313
Depreciation	229,365	229,365	229,365	229,365	229,365
Taxable income (loss)	− 97,747	− 59,525	− 19,397	14,173	68,144
Tax	0	0	0	0	0
Accumulated loss	$− 97,747	$− 157,272	$− 176,669	$− 162,495	$ − 94,352
C. After-tax cash flow					
Before-tax cash flow (*BTCF*)	$ 22,846	$ 48,781	$ 75,235	$ 93,586	$ 130,618
Less tax	0	0	0	0	0
After-tax cash flow (*ATCF*)	$ 22,846	$ 48,781	$ 75,235	$ 93,586	$ 130,618

Estimates of Cash Flows from Sale in Year 5

Sale price		$9,700,000
Less mortgage balance		6,543,595
Before-tax cash flow (*BTCF*s)		3,156,405
Sale price		$9,700,000
Orig. cost bases	$8,500,000	
Accum. depreciation	1,146,825	
Adjusted basis		7,353,175
Capital gain		2,346,825
Less suspended losses		− 94,352
Taxable portion of gain		2,252,474
Tax from sale (at 28%)		630,693
After-tax cash flow from sale (*ATCF*s)		$2,525,713

Cash Flow Summary

	End of Year					
	0	*1*	*2*	*3*	*4*	*5*
Before-tax cash flow	$− 1,275,000	$22,846	$48,781	$75,235	$93,586	$3,287,024
After-tax cash flow	− 1,275,000	22,846	48,781	75,235	93,586	2,656,331

Before-tax *IRR* = 23.50%
After-tax *IRR* = 18.67%
Effective tax rate = 20.55%

REHABILITATION INVESTMENT TAX CREDITS

Investment tax credits are available for certain rehabilitation expenditures in the year (or when expenditures occur). Investment tax credits reduce the investor's *tax liability* (e.g., a dollar of tax credit generally reduces a dollar of taxes otherwise payable). Thus a dollar of tax credit is usually more valuable to an investor than a dollar of additional deductions (e.g., depreciation). This is because an additional deduction reduces taxable income which would be taxed at the investor's marginal tax rate. For an investor in the 28 percent tax bracket a dollar of deduction reduces taxes by 28 cents. However, a $1 tax credit reduces taxes by $1.

In general, the credits available for rehabilitation are as follows:

Category	Credit
Placed in service before 1936	10%
Certified historic structures	25%

The credit is available to the investor in the year the property is placed in service—when the property is open for tenants to occupy. The depreciable basis for the property is reduced by the *full* amount of the credit in the year it is deducted. For example, suppose $50,000 is spent to rehabilitate a property that is a certified historic structure and meets the necessary requirements for a rehabilitation tax credit. The amount of tax credit will be $12,500 (i.e., 25 percent of $50,000). The depreciable basis for the rehabilitation expenditures must be reduced by the amount of credit or by $12,500. The depreciable basis will therefore be $37,500 ($50,000 − $12,500).

There is no age requirement for the certified historic structures. However, the building must be located in a registered historic district and approval must be obtained from the secretary of the interior. The rehabilitation must also be "substantial," which means that the amount of rehabilitation exceeds the *greater* of (1) the adjusted basis of the property prior to rehabilitation, or (2) $5,000. (Note that this favors investors who have owned the property for a long time and have a low adjusted basis.) Furthermore, at least 75 percent of the existing external walls of the building must have been retained (at least 50 percent remaining external walls) after the rehabilitation. Also, at least 75% of the building's internal structural framework must be retained.

If a rehabilitation investment tax credit was taken, and the property is disposed of during the first five years after the rehabilitated building was placed in service, some of the credit will be recaptured. The amount of recapture as a percent of the original tax credit is as follows:

Year of Disposition	Recapture Percent
One full year after placed in service	100%
Second year	80
Third year	60
Fourth year	40
Fifth year	20

Low-Income Housing

A new tax credit that was introduced with the Tax Reform Act of 1986 allows a tax credit to be claimed by owners of residential rental property providing low-income housing. The credits are claimed annually for a period of 10 years. The *annual* credit has a maximum rate of 9 percent for new construction and rehabilitation, and a maximum rate of 4 percent for the acquisition cost of existing housing. To qualify, the expenditure for construction or rehabilitation must exceed $2,000 per low-income unit. For the property to qualify for the credit, either (1) at least 20 percent of the housing units in the project are occupied by individuals with incomes 50 percent or less of the area median income, or (2) at least 40 percent of the housing units in the project are occupied by individuals with incomes of 60 percent or less of area median income. The basis for project depreciation is *not* reduced by the amount of low-income credits claimed.

OVERVIEW OF OTHER ORGANIZATIONAL FORMS FOR OWNERSHIP OF REAL ESTATE

Thus far, we have focused our discussion on the taxation of real estate held by individual taxpayers. However, real estate may be owned in many different organizational forms. There are both financial and legal advantages and disadvantages associated with each form. We now briefly consider two additional organizational forms that are often used for investment real estate: the partnership and corporation.

Corporations

Incorporation of a business generally provides such advantages as continuity of life, marketability of ownership shares, and ease of estate planning, since security values are generally more ascertainable. It also limits the liability of the shareholders to the amount of the cost of their shares. A major disadvantage of this form, however, is the exposure of the investor to double taxation. Corporations pay income tax on all income produced by the firm, and investor-shareholders pay income tax on any dividends at the individual marginal tax rate as they are paid. For this reason, the corporate form of ownership is less attractive than others in allowing investors to receive the tax benefits associated with real estate.

Individuals, or individuals owning partnership interests (discussed below) in entities operating Section 1231 assets (assets used in a trade or business), used to have a distinct advantage over corporations. Formerly operating losses could be combined with other personal income in the year of occurrence, thereby reducing personal income taxes. This stands in contrast to the possibility of having to carry such losses back or forward as corporations must do. Unlike partnerships, corporations cannot pass through losses to shareholders like partnerships can pass through losses to partners. With the passive activity loss limitation rules introduced in 1986 (discussed earlier), this may no longer be as advantageous for individual investors in partnerships. Furthermore, corporations may consolidate losses from real estate investments to offset other corporate income. Thus, from a tax perspective, the corporate form of organization may not be as disadvantageous relative to individual or partnership ownership as it was previously.

Individual taxpayers and individuals owning partnership interests in such entities will retain an advantage over corporations in that such income is taxed only *once,* that is, at the individual level. Should such assets be owned and operated by a corporation, operating income is taxed at the corporate level and then at the individual level if dividends are paid to stockholders. Hence, the advantages of corporate ownership and operation of real estate relative to a partnership are not as great if any portion of corporate income produced from the operation of real estate is paid as a dividend to shareholders.

General Partnerships

A partnership is not a taxable entity, but serves as a conduit through which income, gains, losses, deductions, and credits are passed through to the individual partner. Partners then pay tax on their respective incomes after taking account of their shares in each of these items. As will be discussed later, a partner's share of these tax items is determined by the partnership agreement and may vary from item to item. A partnership also has the advantage over joint ownership in that the partnership agreement will usually ensure that the death or bankruptcy of a partner will not force a termination of the business or cloud title to partnership property. One disadvantage of a general partnership is that none of the partners have *limited liability*. In addition, actions taken by any one of the partners may be binding on the others. Any one can act in behalf of the partnership, and external parties have enforceable contracts against the partnership. Other partners have recourse against partners who overstep authority delegated to them in the partnership agreement that binds them. For these reasons and others, a general partnership is not usually an appropriate investment vehicle for a large group of investors.

Limited Partnerships

Limited partnerships are widely used as vehicles for raising equity capital for real estate ventures from the public. They combine the limited liability feature of an investment in a corporation with the advantages of a general partnership discussed above. Unlike general partnerships, a limited partnership provides limited partners with limited liability. That is, liability is limited to the initial contribution of capital plus any unpaid contributions that must be made in the future. Furthermore, the responsibility for the management of the partnership and unlimited liability rests with the general partners who are frequently knowledgeable in real estate matters, thus providing the partnership with professional management.

The limited partnership is the most widely used legal form of organization for public and private syndications. Such syndications can frequently be used to raise equity capital for real estate investments. As indicated earlier, the limited partnership also has a major advantage enjoyed by a corporation; that is, liability for business obligations is limited to a specific capital contribution. However, unlike corporations, which are not allowed to pass business operating losses through to stockholders, partnership losses are distributable directly to the partners. Further, corporations must carry such losses forward, thereby offsetting them against corporate income of other periods. In the case of a limited partner such losses may be used to offset other passive income, or suspended and used to offset future passive income.

At Risk Rules. As was the case for individual taxpayers, at risk rules also act to limit losses which can be deducted by either general or limited partners to amounts for which they are economically at risk of loss. However, in the case of a partnership, each partner has an amount which is at risk in the partnership. The amount the partner has at risk normally includes all equity contributions plus the partner's share of partnership debt.

In the case of a limited partnership where limited partners are not personally liable for the debt, the at risk amount includes the partner's share of partnership debt for which *no one* is liable (nonrecourse debt). As in the case of individual taxpayers, nonrecourse debt provided by the seller of a property may not be included in the amount at risk.

Safe Harbor Rules. A general partner of a limited partnership may be a corporation. The advantage of this arrangement lies in limiting personal liability of the general partner who may be incorporated (recall that corporations have limited liability) while acting as a general partner in a limited partnership. In many cases, limited partners have created corporations in which such partners are stockholders, thereby creating a general partner while retaining limited liability. Further, if such a corporation was created having very few assets (sometimes referred to as a *shell corporation*), the substance of such an action may be interpreted as effectively having no general partner in the limited partnership. The absence of a general partner would make the creation of a limited partnership invalid.

To avoid this possibility while keeping the opportunity available for corporations to be general partners, the Internal Revenue Service follows internal guidelines (called *safe harbor rules*) imposing certain ownership and minimum capital requirements. In regard to ownership, limited partners may not own, individually or in the aggregate, more than 20 percent of the corporate stock. The net worth requirement of the corporate general partner depends upon the total contributed capital of the partnership. If the contributed capital is less than $2.5 million, the corporate general partner must have a net worth at least equal to 15 percent of the total partnership capital but not greater than $250,000. Where the contributed partnership capital is $2.5 million or more, the corporate general partner must maintain at all times a net worth of at least 10 percent of the partnership capital.

S Corporations

Some corporate forms of ownership can retain many of the tax advantages of partnerships and some of the limited liability benefits of corporations. The Internal Revenue Code permits certain corporations to elect S Corporation treatment if they qualify as a small business corporation under the provisions of the Code. As an S Corporation, the tax consequences of the corporate operations pass through to its shareholders much in the same way as with partnerships. The corporation pays no tax, but there are some limitations that apply to an S Corporation which do not apply to partnerships.

A critical difference between an S Corporation and a partnership is that the corporation's income or loss is ratably allocated to stockholders in an S Corporation in proportion to their ownership of the corporation. In contrast, partnerships have much more flexibility in specially allocating items of income or deduction according to each partner's tax situation. Consequently, the use of the S Corporation is generally not feasible when disproportionate allocations are necessary to reflect the different contributions by stockholders.

Ownership Comparison Summary

Exhibit 11–11 summarizes, in very general terms, the advantages and disadvantages of the various ownership forms we have discussed. These advantages and disadvantages must be evaluated in view of the investor's particular objectives with respect to the ownership of a particular property or properties.

Tax Treatment as a Partnership versus a Corporation

The Internal Revenue Service does not want individuals to form an association that appears to be a partnership for tax purposes (to pass through losses to partners and avoid double

EXHIBIT 11–11   Ownership Form Comparison Summary

Investor Objective	*Corporation*	*S Corporation*	*Partnerships*	
			General	*Limited*
Avoid double taxation	No	Yes	Yes	Yes
Avoidance of management responsibility	Yes	Yes	No	Yes
Flexibility in allocating gains/losses	No	No	Yes	Yes
Limited liability	Yes	Yes	No	Yes
Ability to pass through losses	No	Yes	Yes	Yes
Easy transfer of interests	Yes	Yes	No	No

taxation) when, in fact, the association acts like a corporation. An association that has *more* corporate than noncorporate characteristics will be classified as a corporation for tax purposes. Four nontax criteria are used to determine whether there are more corporate than noncorporate characteristics.

1. Centralization of management.
2. Continuity of life.
3. Limited liability.
4. Free transferability of interest.

Most limited partnerships have a centralization of management in the general partner which is similar to the management of corporations, so differentiation normally will take place in the remaining three criteria. To avoid being classified as a corporation for tax purposes, at least two of these three criteria must be missing.

Under the Uniform Partnership Act, after which most states statutes are patterned, the general partner has the power to dissolve the partnership at any time, thus denying it continuity of life. Otherwise, a terminal date may be provided for in the partnership articles. The criterion of limited liability is negated by the very fact that one partner is a general partner with unlimited liability. Finally, free transferability of interests can be limited by requiring permission of the general or other limited partners to effect a change of ownership. This latter restriction has been deemed by treasury regulations to constitute an adequate curtailment of transferability of interests. A proper combination of these provisions will usually result in the partnership being treated as a partnership for tax purposes.

CONCLUSION

This chapter has identified the key tax considerations that affect real estate investment decisions. These considerations include determining the appropriate marginal tax rate, rules for depreciating real and personal property, treatment of gains and losses from the disposition of real estate, and tax credits available to real estate investors. These tax considerations will enter into different types of analyses that will be addressed in many of the remaining chapters of the text. In several cases we will be applying the tax rules introduced in this chapter to see how they affect investment issues such as: What is the optimal time to dispose of a property? Is it profitable to renovate a building? Additional tax considerations, such as the taxation of limited partnerships and development projects will also be introduced as needed in future chapters.

QUESTIONS

1. What is meant by tax shelter?
2. What are the limitations on the use of losses from real estate to reduce other sources of taxable income?
3. What is meant by passive income? Why is this important to real estate investors?

4. How is the gain from the sale of real estate taxed?
5. What is meant by an effective tax rate? What does it measure?
6. Do you think taxes affect the value of real estate versus other investments?
7. What were the major changes in the 1986 Tax Reform Act that affected income-producing real estate?
8. What is the significance of real estate being held as a trade or business versus being held for the production of income?
9. What are the tax ramifications of being classified as holding real estate "for resale to others?"
10. What tax benefits are available for renovation of older real estate properties?
11. What tax benefits are available for investment in low-income housing?
12. What happens to passive losses that become suspended? What are the possible ways that they can eventually be used?

PROBLEMS

1. (Extension of problem 2 in Chapter 10). You are still an employee of Multiplex Properties, Ltd., and are doing an investment analysis of a new small residential income-producing property for sale to a potential investor. As before, the asking price for the property is $1,100,000; rents are estimated at $185,000 during the first year and are expected to grow at 4 percent per year. Vacancies and collection losses are expected to be 5 percent of rents. Operating expenses will be 35 percent of effective gross income. A loan for 75 percent of the purchase price can be obtained at 11 percent interest with constant monthly payments over a 30-year term. The property is expected to appreciate in value at 3 percent per year and is expected to be owned for five years and then sold.

   The investor tells you he would also like to know how tax considerations affect your investment analysis. You determine that the building represents 90 percent of value and would be depreciated over 27.5 years (use 1/27.5 per year). The potential investor indicates that he is in the 28 percent tax bracket, and has enough passive income from other activities so that any passive losses from this activity would not be subject to any passive activity loss limitations.

   a. What is the investor's expected before tax internal rate of return on equity invested (*BTIRR*)? (Note: This is the same answer as for problem 2 in Chapter 10.)
   b. What is the investor's expected after-tax internal rate of return on equity invested (*ATIRR*)?
   c. Using the results from parts (*a*) and (*b*), what is the effective tax rate and before-tax equivalent yield?
   d. How would you evaluate the tax benefits of this investment?
   e. Recalculate the *ATIRR* in part (*b*) under the assumption that the investor can*not* deduct any of the passive losses (they all become suspended) until the property is sold after five years.
   f. What could be done to restructure the financing so that there would be no passive losses?

2. An investor has two projects with suspended passive losses that have accumulated from prior years. Investment A has $10,000 of suspended losses and investment B has $20,000 of suspended losses. The investor makes a third investment that produces $15,000 of passive income during the year. How is the passive income allocated between investments A and B?

3. An investor is considering renovating an old warehouse that was originally placed in service in early 1920s. The investor could purchase it for $500,000 (land and building). He would then spend about $800,000 renovating the property to convert it into apartments.

   a. What tax credits would be available if the property was not a certified historic structure?

   b. How much of the renovation cost could be depreciated?

   c. How would the answers to parts (a) and (b) change if the property was a certified historic structure?

Appendix: Depreciation and Effective Tax Rates

In Chapter 11 we indicated that, in theory, depreciation allowances should be allowed for tax purposes to the extent of the expected decrease in the economic value of the improvement each year, and to the extent such allowances exceed economic depreciation, benefits are realized by investors. The purpose of this appendix is to illustrate this concept with a simple example.

To focus on the tax effect of depreciation allowances, we will make assumptions in the example as simple as possible. Because land is not depreciable, we assume that only a building is purchased (the land is leased). We also assume that there will be no debt financing because the use of financing does not affect the point we want to make. We assume that a building will be purchased for $100,000. We assume that there will be no inflation and, therefore, all the values and depreciation charges are in "real" terms. The impact of inflation on our analysis will be discussed later.

We assume that the building is an older special-purpose structure and that it is expected to actually decrease in value by 5 percent each year over the next 10 years. Net operating income (*NOI*) during the first year is expected to be $20,000, but thereafter it is expected to decrease at the same 5 percent rate as the building. We also initially assume that depreciation allowances will be equal to economic depreciation each year, that is, by an amount which is equal to the 5 percent expected loss in value. Exhibit 11A–1 illustrates the resulting after-tax cash flow for an investor who is in the 28 percent tax bracket.

Exhibit 11A–2 illustrates the calculation of after-tax cash flow from sale of the property after 10 years. Note that there is no capital gain or loss on the sale because the adjusted basis of the property is *exactly* equal the estimated sale price. Exhibit 11A–3 shows the before- and after-tax *IRR* for the property as well as the effective tax rate. Note that the effective tax rate is exactly the same as the marginal tax rate we assumed for the investor. This is because depreciation allowances were exactly the amount necessary to reduce annual taxable income to reflect the loss in value of the building.

EXHIBIT 11A–1 Depreciation Allowance Equals Economic Depreciation

	Year									
	1	2	3	4	5	6	7	8	9	10
	Estimates of Cash Flow from Operations									
A. Before-tax cash flow										
Net operating income (NOI)	$20,000	$19,000	$18,050	$17,148	$16,290	$15,476	$14,702	$13,967	$13,268	$12,605
B. Taxable income or loss										
Net operating income (NOI)	$20,000	$19,000	$18,050	$17,148	$16,290	$15,476	$14,702	$13,967	$13,268	$12,605
Less depreciation	5,000	4,750	4,513	4,287	4,073	3,869	3,675	3,492	3,317	3,151
Taxable income (loss)	15,000	14,250	13,538	12,861	12,218	11,607	11,026	10,475	9,951	9,454
Tax	$ 4,200	$ 3,990	$ 3,791	$ 3,601	$ 3,421	$ 3,250	$ 3,087	$ 2,933	$ 2,786	$ 2,647
C. After-tax cash flow										
Before-tax cash flow (BTCF)	$20,000	$19,000	$18,050	$17,148	$16,290	$15,476	$14,702	$13,967	$13,268	$12,605
Less tax	4,200	3,990	3,791	3,601	3,421	3,250	3,087	2,933	2,786	2,647
After-tax cash flow (ATCF)	$15,800	$15,010	$14,260	$13,547	$12,869	$12,226	$11,614	$11,034	$10,482	$ 9,958
D. Projected property value										
Property value	$95,000	$90,250	$85,738	$81,451	$77,378	$73,509	$69,834	$66,342	$63,025	$59,874
Decrease in value	−5,000	−4,750	−4,513	−4,287	−4,073	−3,869	−3,675	−3,492	−3,317	−3,151

EXHIBIT 11A–2   Estimates of Cash Flow from Sale in Year 10

Sale price			$59,874
Taxes in year of sale			
Sale price		$59,874	
Original cost basis	$100,000		
Less accumulated depreciation	40,126		
Adjusted basis		59,874	
Capital gain		0	
Tax from sale			0
After-tax cash flow from sale (*ATCF*$_s$)			59,874

To emphasize that this amount of depreciation is necessary to reduce annual taxable income to reflect the loss in value of the building, we now make an extreme assumption to prove the point. We now assume that *no depreciation allowances* will be allowed for tax purposes. Exhibit 11A–4 illustrates the impact that this has on the after-tax cash flows from operations and reversion, shown in the previous example, and how the after-tax *IRR* and effective tax rate are affected. The before-tax *IRR* remains 10 percent because eliminating depreciation deductions only affects after-tax cash flow. Note that the after-tax *IRR* is now 10.23 percent, which is lower than the 10.80 percent rate in the previous example. The effective tax rate is also higher, 31.77 percent versus 28 percent. The higher effective tax rate will occur because the investor is not allowed any annual capital recovery and is, therefore, overpaying taxes each year. Although the investor will benefit from a capital loss when the property is sold (assuming the loss can be used to offset other taxable income), this does not make up for the overpayment of taxes in the previous years because the loss is not recognized until the end of the 10th year.

Effect of Accelerated Depreciation

In the example illustrated in Exhibit 11A–1, we showed that the effective tax rate will be equal to the statutory tax rate when depreciation allowances are *exactly equal* to the annual change in value. In the second example, we saw that if the decrease in value was greater than the depreciation allowed, then the effective tax rate was greater than the statutory tax rate. It follows that if depreciation allowances are *greater* than the annual change in value, the effective tax rate will be *lower* than the statutory tax rate. This is illustrated in Exhibit 11A–5. In the exhibit, we use the *same* 5 percent annual depreciation allowances used in the first example, however, the *NOI* and property value are assumed to remain *constant* instead of actually declining. That is, we assume that there is no economic depreciation during the first 10 years. In this case, the effective tax rate decreases to 22.85 percent versus the statutory tax rate of 28 percent.

The reader should now see that accelerated depreciation is clearly a benefit to investors. As noted in the chapter, Congress has frequently used accelerated depreciation on real estate income property to encourage investment. With accelerated depreciation the investor's effective tax rate is lowered and the before-tax return necessary to justify making the investment is reduced. However, this also can lead to investors making investments that would not be feasible on a before-tax basis and may lead to overinvestment in real estate.

EXHIBIT 11A–3 Cash Flow Summary

						End of Year					
	0	1	2	3	4	5	6	7	8	9	10
Before-tax cash flow	$ – 1,0C0,000	$20,000	$19,000	$18,050	$17,148	$16,290	$15,476	$14,702	$13,967	$13,268	$72,479
After-tax cash flow	–1,0C0,000	15,800	15,010	14,260	13,547	12,869	12,226	11,614	11,034	10,482	69,832

Before-tax *IRR* = 15.00%
After-tax *IRR* = 10.80%
Effective tax rate = 28.00%

EXHIBIT 11A–4 No Depreciation Allowances

	Year									
	1	2	3	4	5	6	7	8	9	10
	Estimates of Cash Flow from Operations									
A. Before-tax cash flow										
Net operating income (*NOI*)	$20,000	$19,000	$18,050	$17,148	$16,290	$15,476	$14,702	$13,967	$13,268	$12,605
B. Taxable income or loss										
Net operating income (*NOI*)	$20,000	$19,000	$18,050	$17,148	$16,290	$15,476	$14,702	$13,967	$13,268	$12,605
Depreciation	0	0	0	0	0	0	0	0	0	0
Taxable income (loss)	20,000	19,000	18,050	17,148	16,290	15,476	14,702	13,967	13,268	12,605
Tax	$ 5,600	$ 5,320	$ 5,054	$ 4,801	$ 4,561	$ 4,333	$ 4,117	$ 3,911	$ 3,715	$ 3,529
C. After-tax cash flow										
Before-tax cash flow (*BTCF*)	$20,000	$19,000	$18,050	$17,148	$16,290	$15,476	$14,702	$13,967	$13,268	$12,605
Less tax	5,600	5,320	5,054	4,801	4,561	4,333	4,117	3,911	3,715	3,529
After-tax cash flow (*ATCF*)	$14,400	$13,680	$12,996	$12,346	$11,729	$11,142	$10,585	$10,056	$ 9,553	$ 9,076
D. Projected property value										
Property value	$95,000	$90,250	$85,738	$81,451	$77,378	$73,509	$69,834	$66,342	$63,025	$59,874
Decrease in value	−5,000	−4,750	−4,513	−4,287	−4,073	−3,869	−3,675	−3,492	−3,317	−3,151

Estimate of Cash Flow from Sale in Year 10

Sale price		$ 59,874
Taxes in year of sale		
Sale price	$59,874	
Original cost basis	$100,000	
Less accumulated depreciation	0	
Adjusted basis	100,000	
Capital gain	−40,126	
Tax from sale (at 28%)		−11,235
After-tax cash flow from sale ($ATCF_s$)		$ 71,109

Cash Flow Summary

	0	1	2	3	4	5	6	7	8	9	10
							End of Year				
Before-tax cash flow	$ − 100,000	$20,000	$19,000	$18,050	$17,148	$16,290	$15,476	$14,702	$13,967	$13,268	$72,479
After-tax cash flow	− 100,000	14,400	13,680	12,996	12,346	11,729	11,142	10,585	10,056	9,553	80,185
Before-tax IRR	= 15.00%										
After-tax IRR	= 10.23%										
Effective tax rate	= 31.77%										

EXHIBIT 11A–5 Tax Depreciation Greater Than Economic Depreciation

	Year									
	1	2	3	4	5	6	7	8	9	10
	Estimates of Cash Flow from Operations									
A. Before-tax cash flow										
Net operating income (NOI)	$20,000	$20,000	$20,000	$20,000	$20,000	$20,000	$20,000	$20,000	$20,000	$20,000
B. Taxable income or loss										
Net operating income (NOI)	$20,000	$20,000	$20,000	$20,000	$20,000	$20,000	$20,000	$20,000	$20,000	$20,000
Depreciation	5,000	4,750	4,513	4,287	4,073	3,869	3,675	3,492	3,317	3,151
Taxable income (loss)	15,000	15,250	15,488	15,713	15,927	16,131	16,325	16,508	16,683	16,849
Tax	$ 4,200	$ 4,270	$ 4,337	$ 4,400	$ 4,460	$ 4,517	$ 4,571	$ 4,622	$ 4,671	$ 4,718
C. After-tax cash flow										
Before-tax cash flow (BTCF)	$20,000	$20,000	$20,000	$20,000	$20,000	$20,000	$20,000	$20,000	$20,000	$20,000
Less tax	4,200	4,270	4,337	4,400	4,460	4,517	4,571	4,622	4,671	4,718
After-tax cash flow (ATCF)	$15,800	$15,730	$15,664	$15,600	$15,540	$15,483	$15,429	$15,378	$15,329	$15,282
D. Projected property value										
Property value	$95,000	$90,250	$85,738	$81,451	$77,378	$73,509	$69,834	$66,342	$63,025	$59,874
Decrease in value	−5,000	−4,750	−4,513	−4,287	−4,073	−3,869	−3,675	−3,492	−3,317	−3,151

Estimates of Cash Flow from Sale in Year 10

Sale price $120,000

Taxes in year of sale

Sale price		$100,000
Original cost basis	$100,000	
Less accum. depreciation	40,126	
Adjusted basis	59,874	
Capital gain		40,126
Tax from sale		11,235

After-tax cash flow from sale ($ATCF_s$) $108,765

Cash Flow Summary

					End of Year						
	0	1	2	3	4	5	6	7	8	9	10
Before-tax C.F.	$-100,000	$20,000	$20,000	$20,000	$20,000	$20,000	$20,000	$20,000	$20,000	$20,000	$140,000
After-tax C.F.	-100,000	15,800	15,730	15,664	15,600	15,540	15,483	15,429	15,378	15,329	124,047

Before-tax *IRR* = 20.74%
After-tax *IRR* = 16.00%
Effective tax rate = 22.85%

THE EFFECT OF INFLATION ON EFFECTIVE TAX RATES

For simplicity, our example thus far has focused on *real* depreciatior.. We found that tax depreciation must be equal to real economic depreciation to have the effective tax rate equal to the statutory tax rate, a criteria for tax neutrality. We now consider how inflation affects this conclusion. Suppose that it is assumed that real depreciation will be 5 percent, as in our first example, but inflation will be 10 percent per year. This means that the net increase in *NOI* and value will be 10 percent each year relative to what they would have been in real terms (i.e., in the absence of inflation). In other words, the real *NOI* and property value will decline by 5 percent each year, but nominal *NOI* and the nominal property value will increase because the rate of inflation (10 percent) is greater than the economic depreciation (5 percent). For example, to obtain the *NOI* in year 2, the *NOI* in year 1 is still reduced by 5 percent for economic depreciation (i.e., multiplied by 0.95). But the resulting real *NOI* for year 2 is increased by 10 percent for inflation to obtain the nominal *NOI*. Similar calculations are used to obtain the value each year. Exhibit 11A–6 shows the nominal *NOI* and value each year.

As can be seen, the nominal *BTIRR* and nominal *ATIRR* are 24.5 percent and 19.01 percent, respectively. Using these returns to calculate the effective tax rate, we obtain 22.43 percent versus 28 percent in Exhibit 11A–1. Thus it appears that the effective tax rate decreases as a result of inflation. However, we have calculated the effective tax rate using *nominal* rates of return. We now calculate the effective tax rate using *real* rates of return. The real *BTIRR* and *ATIRR* are obtained by subtracting the inflation rate from both of these nominal returns. The result is shown in the exhibit. Using these returns, we now obtain a *real* effective tax rate of 37.89 percent $(1 - 9.01/14.50)$, which is significantly higher than the investor's marginal tax rate of 28 percent. Why does the effective tax rate *increase* in real terms? The answer is that the nominal increase in property value is being taxed, inflationary gains are taxed rather than just the real gain. This raises serious issues regarding the taxation of investments. Should nominal gains due to inflation be taxed? Further, this has serious implications for depreciable assets such as real estate, because although depreciation allowances are provided each year, if the rate of inflation is equal to or exceeds the rate of depreciation allowed for tax purposes, there will be no *real* capital recovery. That is, the investor will be taxed on a nominal value that is equal to or greater than the initial investment.

It could be argued that when inflation is present, the real value of depreciation deductions is reduced each year. This is because depreciation is based on the historical cost of the investment. One way of compensating for this tax on inflation would therefore be to *index* the depreciation deductions each year by the inflation rate (i.e., increase the deductions for inflation). Indeed, this has been proposed by many economists. It has also been argued that the use of accelerated depreciation is a roundabout way of adjusting depreciation ·for the effects of inflation (i.e., by allowing for a depreciation charge that is greater than real depreciation). Congress has historically tended to permit accelerated depreciation for real estate (e.g., ACRS with the Economic Recovery Act of 1981) during periods of high inflation. The problem, of course, is that this results in a tax law based on what inflation was in the past, which is not necessarily what it will be in the future.

CONCLUSION

It should be clear that the relationship between depreciation allowances permitted as a tax deduction relative to the rate of economic depreciation in property values has an effect on the effective tax rate faced by the investor. Favorable tax benefits result when the depreciation allowance is greater than any decrease in the real value of the property. However, when inflation is present, nominal increases in property values may lead to a tax on capital gain which tend to offset the tax savings

EXHIBIT 11A–6 Effect of Inflation on the Effective Tax Rate

	Year									
	1	2	3	4	5	6	7	8	9	10

Estimates of Cash Flow from Operations

	1	2	3	4	5	6	7	8	9	10
A. Before-tax cash flow										
Net operating income										
(*NOI*)	$ 20,000	$ 20,900	$ 21,841	$ 22,823	$ 23,850	$ 24,924	$ 26,045	$ 27,217	$ 28,442	$ 29,722
B. Taxable income or loss										
Net operating income										
(*NOI*)	$ 20,000	$ 20,900	$ 21,841	$ 22,823	$ 23,850	$ 24,924	$ 26,045	$ 27,217	$ 28,442	$ 29,722
Depreciation	5,000	4,750	4,513	4,287	4,073	3,869	3,675	3,492	3,317	3,151
Taxable income (loss)	15,000	16,150	17,328	18,536	19,778	21,055	22,370	23,736	25,125	26,571
Tax	$ 4,200	$ 4,522	$ 4,852	$ 5,190	$ 5,538	$ 5,895	$ 6,264	$ 6,643	$ 7,035	$ 7,440
C. After-tax cash flow										
Before-tax cash flow										
(*BTCF*)	$ 20,000	$ 20,900	$ 21,841	$ 22,823	$ 23,850	$ 24,924	$ 26,045	$ 27,217	$ 28,442	$ 29,722
Less tax	4,200	4,522	4,852	5,190	5,538	5,895	6,264	6,643	7,035	7,440
After-tax cash flow										
(*ATCF*)	$ 15,800	$ 16,378	$ 16,989	$ 17,633	$ 18,313	$ 19,028	$ 19,782	$ 20,574	$ 21,407	$ 22,282
D. Projected property value										
Real property value	$ 95,000	$ 90,250	$ 85,738	$ 81,451	$ 77,378	$ 73,509	$ 69,834	$ 66,342	$ 63,025	$ 59,874
Nominal property value	104,500	109,203	114,117	119,252	124,618	130,226	136,086	142,210	148,610	155,297
Real decrease in value	−5,000	−4,750	−4,513	−4,287	−4,073	−3,869	−3,675	−3,492	−3,317	−3,151

EXHIBIT 11A–6 (Concluded)

	Year									
	1	2	3	4	5	6	7	8	9	10

Estimates of Cash Flows from Sale in Year 10

Sale price $155,297

Taxes in year of sale
Sale price		$155,297
Original cost basis	$100,000	
Less accum. depreciation	40,126	
Adjusted basis	59,874	
Capital gain	95,423	
Tax from sale	26,719	

After-tax cash flow from sale (ATCFs) $128,578

Cash Flow Summary

					End of Year						
	0	1	2	3	4	5	6	7	8	9	10
Before-tax cash flow	$–100,000	$20,000	$20,900	$21,841	$22,823	$23,850	$24,924	$26,045	$27,217	$28,442	$185,019
After-tax cash flow	–100,000	15,800	16,378	16,989	17,633	18,313	19,028	19,782	20,574	21,407	150,861

Nominal Rates of Return

Before-tax IRR (BTIRR) = 24.50%
After-tax IRR (ATIRR) = 19.01%
Effective tax rate = 22.43%

Real Rates of Return

Before-tax IRR (BTIRR) = 14.50%
After-tax IRR (ATIRR) = 9.01%
Effective tax rate = 37.89%

realized from accelerated depreciation deductions based on original costs. Historically, Congress has provided depreciation allowances for real estate income property that have been greater than rates of economic depreciation. Real estate income properties probably decrease in value at a relatively slow rate and last at least 50 years in most cases. Yet, even under the current tax law, properties can be depreciated over 28.5 years for residential property and 31.5 years for nonresidential property. This may be an attempt by Congress to compensate for taxing any inflation which may occur. In any event, effective nominal tax rates for real estate income property are usually lower than the statutory tax rate.

QUESTIONS

A–1. How would depreciation allowances have to be determined for the effective tax rate for real estate to be equal to the investor's marginal tax rate?

A–2. Why do you think depreciation allowances have historically been at an "accelerated" rate?

A–3. What effect does inflation have on the tax benefits associated with depreciation?

Chapter 12

Risk Analysis

In the previous two chapters we have dealt with the before- and after-tax analysis of real estate income property. We have discussed how to calculate the *IRR*, *NPV*, *PI*, and other measures of investment performance. We have also discussed some of the issues associated with ranking different investment alternatives (i.e., choosing the investment with the best performance based on criteria such as the *IRR* or *NPV*). In this chapter we will see that choosing between investment alternatives also requires knowing something about the *risk* associated with the investment relative to other investment alternatives. We will provide a brief discussion of sources of risk and how they may differ among investment alternatives. Because of risk differences, simply comparing *IRR*s or *NPV*s when making choices among alternative investments is usually not possible. Indeed such a comparison may only be made if we assume that the risk associated with the different investments being analyzed is the same. Because risk usually is not the same, we provide some techniques for evaluating risk so as to enable a more complete basis for making comparisons among alternatives.

COMPARING INVESTMENT RETURNS

To begin our discussion, we will briefly explore considerations that investors should take into account when comparing measures of return on investment on a specific real estate investment with *other* real estate investments, and *other* investments generally.

After the investor has gone through a reasonably detailed illustration of an investment analysis of an income-producing property, and after having developed measures of return on investment, a decision must be made as to whether an investment in such a project will provide an "adequate" or "competitive" return. The answer to this question will depend on (1) the nature of alternative real estate investments, (2) other investments available to the investor, (3) the respective returns that those alternatives are expected to yield, and (4) differences in *risk* between the investment being considered relative to those alternative investments available to the investor.

In Exhibit 12–1, we have constructed a hypothetical relationship between rates of return and risk for various classes of alternative investments. The vertical axis represents

EXHIBIT 12–1 Risk and Return (alternative investments)

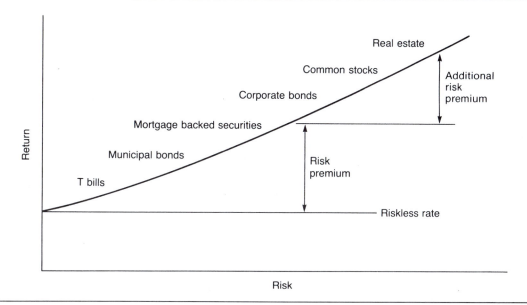

the expected return,[1] and the horizontal axis represents the degree of risk inherent in each category of investment. It should be noted that we are dealing with the average risk for entire classes of assets. There are obviously significant differences in risk within each class. For example, some bonds will be riskier than other bonds within the general bond category. Also, there is less variance within some asset classes than others (e.g., Treasury bills are considered to be riskless). There may also be assets within one category that have more risk than some of the assets in a higher risk category. For example, some bonds are riskier than some stocks, even though as a *class* stocks are riskier than bonds.

Risk, as presented in Exhibit 12–1, is considered only by class of investments in relative terms; that is, as one moves to the right on the axis, an investment is considered riskier, to the left less risky. Hence, investments with higher risks should yield investors higher expected returns and vice versa.

Based on the risk-return ranking indicated in Exhibit 12–1, the reader should note that the security with the lowest return, U.S. Treasury bills, also has the lowest risk.[2] As we move out on the risk-return line in the exhibit, we see that expected before-tax returns

---

[1]As emphasized in Chapter 11, to be comparable, returns should either all be calculated on an after-tax basis or before-tax equivalent yields used. The returns should also be based on similar assumptions as to how the investment is financed. This is because, as will be emphasized in this chapter, financing affects both the risk and return, and thus the position of the investment on the diagram.

[2]Treasury bills are usually considered riskless, although they are subject to some interest rate risk and inflation risk.

on investments in real estate offer a considerably higher expected return but are also much riskier than investing in U.S. Treasury bills. What are the investment characteristics peculiar to real estate that make it riskier than investing in government securities? Similarly, what risk characteristics differentiate real estate investment from the other alternatives such as common stock, corporate bonds, and municipal bonds also shown in Exhibit 12–1? To answer this question we must consider some of the characteristics that are the source of risk differences among various categories of investments. What follows is a brief summary of major investment risk characteristics that must be considered by investors when deciding among alternative investments.

Business risk—risk of loss due to fluctuations in economic activity and its effect on the variability of income produced by the investment. In the case of real estate, business risk would be factors that effect the *NOI* and resale price of the property. Changes in economic conditions such as a recession may affect some properties more than others. Those affected to a greater degree than others would be riskier.

Financial risk—risk of loss due to the use of debt financing (referred to as financial leverage). Financial risk increases as the amount of debt on a real estate investment is increased. The risk depends on the extent of prior claims of lenders on income and proceeds upon liquidation of the investment.

Liquidity risk—occurs to the extent of the lack of a continuous market with many buyers and sellers and frequent transactions. The more difficult an investment is to liquidate, the greater the risk that a price concession may have to be given to a buyer should the seller have to dispose of the investment quickly.

Purchasing power risk—occurs to the extent income from a security does not adjust to inflation, thereby reducing the *real* value of the underlying security. Certain types of business activity are more favorably or adversely affected by inflation than others. Hence, this is a source of risk that must be considered in an investment analysis.

Management risk—based on the capability of management and its ability to innovate, respond to competitive conditions, and operate the business activity efficiently.

Interest rate risk—changes in interest rates will affect the price of all securities and investments. However, depending on the relative maturity (short-term versus long-term investments), some investment prices will repond more than others, thereby increasing the potential for loss or gain.

Legislative risk—comes about in the form of tax law changes, rent control, zoning, and other restrictions imposed by government that could adversely affect the profitability of investments.

Essentially, these risk characteristics are, in large part, the reasons for differences in returns between the alternative investments shown in Exhibit 12–1. For example, U.S. Treasury bills are a very short-term investment (90 or 180 days). They are free from business risk, management risk, and financial risk because they are guaranteed by the U.S. government. Because the government has the potentially unlimited ability to tax, it is not likely to default on its obligations. Further, because of the vast, continuous market in government securities, the risk of loss due to the inability to sell a government security when a sale is desired or necessary is very low. Regarding inflation and interest rate risk, because of the extremely short-term nature of these investments, these risks are thought to be minimal. Consequently, Treasury bills, with extremely short maturities, are thought to be the closest thing to a riskless investment available in the economy. Hence, as shown in the exhibit, this investment is shown to have essentially zero risk and a very low return relative to other securities. In theory, then, a Treasury bill with a given maturity should carry an interest rate that provides the investor with a real rate of interest, plus a premium for expected inflation at the time of purchase, with *no* risk premium for any of the categories of risk discussed above.

Considering each of the investment categories in Exhibit 12–1 in conjunction with the list of risk characteristics just discussed makes it slightly easier to place real estate investment into an overall, risk-return context with alternative investments. For example, when considering a real estate investment, it is clear that many of the risks included in the above list are very important for an investor to consider. Business risk is a very important influence to consider because a sudden downward turn in the economy could cause unemployment, a slowdown in business expansion, and perhaps reduced demand for rental space. Financial risk is present in real estate when there is debt financing (referred to as financial leverage). Should excessive leverage be used and should default occur, mortgage lenders have prior claim in proceeds from a foreclosure sale, thereby increasing the risk of loss to equity investors. There is considerable liquidity risk present should an equity investor desire to suddenly sell an interest in a real estate project. It could take a considerable period of time to sell, or the investor may have to sell at a below-market price should funds be needed quickly. As to purchasing power risk, because leases on income property often have provisions to adjust for inflation (recall the *CPI* adjustment discussed in Chapter 10), this risk may be somewhat lower when compared to other investments paying a fixed income to investors. Also, management risks in real estate are present and would have to be carefully considered when making an investment choice.

Looking to Exhibit 12–1, then, we can now understand why the return on mortgage-backed securities, corporate bonds, and equity investments should be considerably higher than the return on U.S. Treasury bills. In general, mortgage-backed securities are considered riskier than Treasury bills and thus should command a risk premium in their yield. Furthermore, since equity investments such as common stock and real estate are riskier than debt investments, there should be an additional risk premium for equity investments.

The risk premium concept shown for real estate relative to Treasury bills also applies to all other investments shown in Exhibit 12–1. The risk premium concept also applies *among* individual investment categories shown in the exhibit (see the risk premium as represented by the difference in return on real estate relative to common stock in the exhibit). Each investment type differs in the extent to which the sources of risk described above influence each investment's expected return.

Contrasting the above investment types and assessing the risk of each, we should note that municipal bonds are issued by municipalities that have limited powers to tax (such power is limited by voter approval or limited to specific projects or districts). Although some of the business risk is eliminated by this power of taxation, financial risk is present to the extent that a municipality overissues debt and defaults (New York City bonds, for example). Further, there is generally not as continuous a market for these securities when compared to U.S. obligations; hence, there must be a risk premium for the lack of liquidity.

Common stock, mortgages, and corporate bonds usually have good marketability. However, they are also significantly affected by business risk, management risk, financial risk, and all of the remaining categories of risk previously discussed. Hence, they should also command a premium over both Treasury obligations and municipal bonds, but not as high a premium as an equity investor would earn on real estate, which is riskier in many ways.

We again stress that we are discussing investment alternatives in very broad *categories*. It may be very possible to find *individual* investments *within* a category where expected returns are below those expected in another category (a specific real estate investment may provide a lower return on investment than a specific common stock, for example). These categories were chosen in order to facilitate a discussion of major risk characteristics affecting each investment type. In the final analysis, a prospective investor in a specific real estate project must estimate and compute an expected return on that project and compare that return with expected returns on other *specific* real estate investments as well as all other investments. Any risk differentials must then be carefully considered relative to any risk premium, or difference in expected returns, in all such comparisons. Investors must then make the final judgement as to whether an investment is justified.

There are also many characteristics in real estate *markets*, however, that differentiate it from markets for the other investments shown in Exhibit 12–1. Many of these market characteristics make investment decisions in real estate more difficult and therefore more risky relative to other investments. Some of these market characteristics are:

1. *Highly technical product.* Many categories of real estate include improvements that are of a technical nature in design, construction, or use. Generally, the more complex a real estate investment is the more difficult it is to value. Hence, in these cases, there will be greater differences in prices investors are willing to pay. On the other hand, for more homogeneous properties (houses, apartment buildings, etc.) with fewer complexities, there will be greater agreement on property value.

2. *Continuous information—volume of buying and selling.* Contrary to many other markets such as the market for wheat, other commodities, and common stock, the real estate market does not present a continuous flow of investment opportunities. Real estate investments of all types are not always available at all times. Purchases and sales in a local market occur less frequently than in many other markets. Hence, prices and market conditions may change between sales of property. The investor does not have access to a more continuous flow of information as to how changes in those market conditions are changing prices.

3. *Changes in local and regional growth patterns.* Many regions of the country and locations within cities experience differences in the rate of growth due to changes in demand, population changes, and so on. Because of the lack of continuous price and other market data, such changes are not easily determined.

SENSITIVITY ANALYSIS

We have discussed various types of risk that must be considered when evaluating different investment alternatives. Unfortunately, it is not easy to *measure* the riskiness of an investment. We will learn that there are different ways of measuring risk, depending on the degree and manner in which the analyst attempts to quantify the risk.

One of the most straightforward ways of analyzing risk is to do what is referred to as *sensitivity analysis* or a "what if" analysis of the property. This involves changing one or more of the key assumptions for which there is uncertainty to see how sensitive the investment performance of the property is to changes in that assumption. For example, how would a higher vacancy rate in future years affect the *IRR*?

Assumptions that are typically examined in a sensitivity analysis are:

Future market rent levels—affects the future rents at which leases will be renewed. It may also affect the estimated resale price for the property (e.g., when a terminal capitalization rate is used to estimate the sale price).

Inflation—may affect lease payments, depending on whether there is a *CPI* adjustment in the lease. Inflation will affect the resale price if it is assumed that the resale price depends on inflation in the value of the property over time. It may also affect future interest rates on mortgage loans, particularly when such loans are not made at fixed interest rates.

Vacancy rates—assumptions about the rate of vacancy for the property obviously affect the property's *NOI*. Vacancy rates may be higher when leases expire due to tenant turnover.

Operating expenses—assumptions about any change in the level of the operating expenses (or a component of the operating expenses) affect the *NOI*.

Resale price—the estimated resale price may be varied directly, or as indicated above, may change when one of the above assumptions are changed due to the way the resale price is estimated.

When doing a sensitivity analysis, one first starts with a "base case," a set of assumptions for which the analysis is made that will provide a frame of reference for the sensitivity analysis. This set of assumptions will usually represent the analysts best estimate of the "most likely" situation. For example, the analyst may feel that a 5 percent vacancy rate is the most likely or best estimate of what the vacancy rate will be in future years.[3]

Once the base case set of assumptions is identified, the analyst will first compute the *IRR, NPV,* and other measures of investment performance using this base set of assumptions. Then one or more of the inputs will be varied at a time to see how this change affects the results. Usually one of the following approaches is taken when changing assumptions:

1. *Change a* single *assumption at a time.* The advantage of this approach is that it allows the analyst to isolate the impact of a specific input assumption. For example, the base case vacancy might be 5 percent. The analyst might then want to know how much the *IRR* would fall if the vacancy increases to 10 percent per year.

---

[3]In a statistical sense the most likely case would be the one with the highest probability of occurrence. We will consider probabilities in more detail in a later section.

2. *Analyze a pessimistic and an optimistic scenario.* We have indicated that the base case should be a most likely scenario. Similarly, one could conceive of a pessimistic scenario where the assumptions reflect a situation where things don't go as well as the most likely case. For example, vacancy might be higher, which in turn might also mean future market rents are lower, and the resale price is lower. This allows the analyst to see how much investment performance is effected by a combination of negative or worst-case assumptions. Likewise, a set of optimistic assumptions would be identified which indicates how good the investment would perform if everything goes well.

To illustrate the use of sensitivity analysis, consider an investment in a small rental house which is rented to students at the local university. Based on an analysis of the market, the following base case assumptions are made:

Purchase price	
Building value	$50,000
Land value	10,000
Total value	$60,000
Financing	
Loan amount	75% of value
Interest rate	10%
Loan term	20 years (monthly payments)
Current rent (first year)	$600 per month
Vacancy	5% of potential gross income
Initial expenses	
Management	7% of effective gross income
Maintenance	$600 per year
Insurance	$300 per year
Property taxes	$500 per year
Annual increase in	
Rent	3% per year
Taxes, insurance, and maintenance	4% per year
Property value	3% per year
Tax assumptions	
Marginal tax rate	28%
Depreciation	27.5 years (st. line)

Exhibit 12–2 shows the projected cash flows under the above assumptions. The before-tax return on equity (*BTIRR*) is 14.16 percent, and the after-tax return on equity (*ATIRR*) is 11.22 percent for a five-year holding period.

To illustrate the use of sensitivity analysis, we first consider a change in the vacancy rate. Exhibit 12–3 shows what the *IRR* would be for a range of vacancy rates from *no* vacancy to 16 percent. We see that the *BTIRR* ranges from 15.97 percent to 10.20 percent, and the *ATIRR* ranges from 12.63 percent to 8.11 percent. Thus, even with vacancy as high as 16 percent, the *ATIRR* only falls to about 8 percent.

EXHIBIT 12–2   Cash Flow Projections for Rental House

	Year				
	1	2	3	4	5

Estimates of Cash Flow from Operations

	1	2	3	4	5
Potential gross income	$ 7,200	$ 7,416	$7,638	$7,868	$8,104
Less vacancy	360	371	382	393	405
Effective gross income	6,840	7,045	7,257	7,474	7,698
Management	479	493	508	523	539
Maintenance	600	624	649	675	702
Insurance	300	312	324	337	351
Property taxes	500	520	541	562	585
Net operating income (*NOI*)	4,961	5,096	5,234	5,376	5,522
Less debt service (*DS*)	5,211	5,211	5,211	5,211	5,211
Before-tax cash flow (*BTCF*)	$ − 250	$ − 115	$ 23	$ 165	$ 311
Net operating income (*NOI*)	4,961	5,096	5,234	5,376	5,522
Less interest	4,466	4,389	4,302	4,207	4,102
Depreciation	1,818	1,818	1,818	1,818	1,818
Taxable income (loss)	− 1,323	− 1,111	− 886	− 649	− 398
Tax	$ − 371	$ − 311	$ − 248	$ − 182	$ − 112
Before-tax cash flow (*BTCF*)	− 250	− 115	23	165	311
Less taxes	− 371	− 311	− 248	− 182	− 112
After-tax cash flow (*ATCF*)	$ 121	$ 196	$ 271	$ 347	$ 422

Estimates of Cash Flows from Sale in Year 5

Sale price		$69,556
Mortgage balance		40,411
Before-tax cash flow (*BTCF_s*)		$29,145
Taxes in year of sale		
Sale price		69,556
Original cost basis	$60,000	
Less accum. depreciation	9,091	
Adjusted basis		50,909
Capital gain		18,647
Tax from sale		5,221
After-tax cash flow from sale (*ATCF_s*)		$23,924

	End of Year				
	0	1	2	3	4	5

Cash Flow Summary

	0	1	2	3	4	5
Before-tax cash flow	$ − 15,000	$ − 250	$ − 115	$ 23	$165	$29,456
After-tax cash flow	− 15,000	121	196	271	347	24,346

Before-tax *IRR* (*BTIRR*) = 14.16%
After-tax *IRR* (*ATIRR*) = 11.22%

EXHIBIT 12–3   Sensitivity Analysis (*IRR* versus vacancy)

Vacancy Rate percent	BTIRR percent	ATIRR percent
0.00	15.97	12.63
2.00	15.25	12.07
4.00	14.52	11.50
6.00	13.79	10.93
8.00	13.07	10.37
10.00	12.35	9.80
12.00	11.63	9.24
14.00	10.91	8.68
16.00	10.20	8.11

Exhibit 12–4 shows a graph of the information in Exhibit 12–3. Note that the *ATIRR* is not quite as sensitive to changes in the vacancy rate as *BTIRR*.

Exhibit 12–5 shows the sensitivity of the *BTIRR* and *ATIRR* to a range of annual rates of *price appreciation* from −4 to 40 percent per year. In this case the *BTIRR* ranges from −10.4 to 16.71 percent, and *ATIRR* ranges from −7.26 to 13.34 percent. Clearly the *IRR* is much more sensitive to a change in estimated value than to a change in the vacancy rate. Exhibit 12–6 graphs the relationship in Exhibit 12–5. Again we see that the *BTIRR* is more sensitive to changes in the growth than the *ATIRR*.

EXHIBIT 12–4   *IRR* versus Vacancy Rate

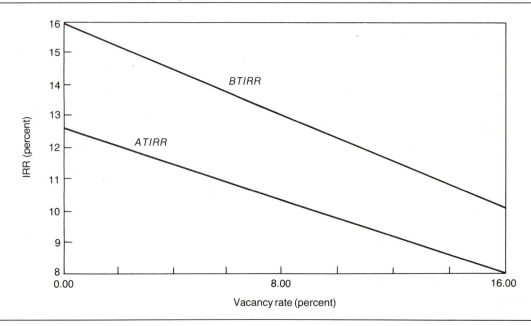

EXHIBIT 12–5   *IRR versus Property Growth Rate*

Growth Rate	*BTIRR*	*ATIRR*
percent	*percent*	*percent*
−4.00	−10.23	−7.26
−3.00	−5.50	−4.01
−2.00	−1.41	−1.05
−1.00	2.24	1.70
.00	5.55	4.27
1.00	8.61	6.70
2.00	11.47	9.01
3.00	14.16	11.22
4.00	16.71	13.34

THE EFFECT OF FIXED VERSUS VARIABLE COSTS ON RISK

In Chapter 10 we discussed how operating expenses for a real estate income property can be allocated into two main categories: fixed expenses and variable expenses. Recall that variable expenses vary with the level of occupancy, whereas fixed expenses do not vary with the level of occupancy. Fixed expenses could, of course, still increase each year due to other factors besides the occupancy of the property (e.g., inflation).

EXHIBIT 12–6   *IRR versus Price Appreciation*

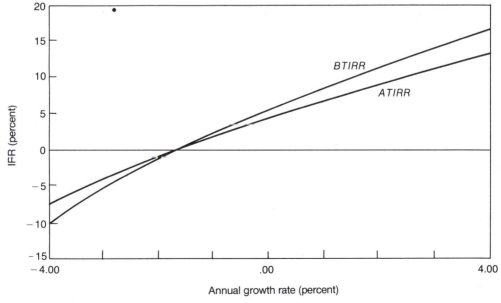

Differences in the amount of variable expenses verses fixed expenses can affect the riskiness of the property. This is because the greater the proportion of fixed expenses, the more the *NOI* is affected by a change in the level of occupancy. Alternatively, the lower the proportion of fixed expenses, the less *NOI* is affected by a change in the level of occupancy. This is because with lower levels of occupancy, expenses will also be lower, resulting in less of a decrease in *NOI* than if there were less variable expenses and more fixed expenses. Similarly at higher levels of occupancy, *NOI* does not increase as much because variable expenses also increase.

Purchase price	
Building value	$ 900,000
Land value	100,000
Total value	$1,000,000
Financing	
Loan amount	$750,000
Interest rate	10.00%
Term	20 years (monthly payments)
Potential gross income (year 1)	$200,000
Expected increase in potential gross income	3% per year
Tax assumptions	
Ordinary income rate	28.00%
Depreciation	27.5 years
Expected increase in property value	2.00% per year
Expenses	
Option 1	
Variable expenses	25% of effective gross income
Fixed expenses	$42,500 increasing 3% per year
Option 2	
Variable expenses	None
Fixed expenses	$85,000 increasing 3% per year
Vacancy	Could range from 0 to 50%

Note that two options for variable expenses are shown. Option 1 would result in $42,500 of fixed expenses which are projected to increase at a rate of 3 percent per year due to inflation. Variable expenses would be 25 percent of effective gross income each year. Option 2 has $85,000 of fixed expenses, still increasing 3 percent per year, but no variable expenses. There are various reasons why the owner might have options regarding the proportion of fixed and variable expenses, for example, payment of a fixed salary for a manager rather than a salary based on a percent of effective gross income, or the use of maintenance contracts for expenses. The point is that the effect of different vacancy rates on rates of return will be quite different depending on the makeup of the expenses. This is true whether we are evaluating different expense options for the same property or two different properties with a different makeup of expenses.

We now show what the *ATIRR* would be for each expense option for a range of vacancy rates from 0 to 50 percent. Exhibit 12–7 summarizes the results. These results are graphed in Exhibit 12–8. At a 15 percent vacancy rate, the *ATIRR* is the same for both options. Below a 15 percent rate *ATIRR* is higher with option 2, which has all fixed costs. Above a 15 percent vacancy rate, however, *ATIRR* is higher with option 1, which has fewer fixed costs and more variable costs. Of course, if we knew what the level of vacancy was going to be, we would know which option is best. But if the level of vacancy is uncertain, then the analyst should know how sensitive the return will be in each case. Note in the diagram that the *ATIRR* is more sensitive to the vacancy rate for option 2, when there is a greater proportion of fixed expenses.

Partitioning Internal Rates of Return

In Chapter 11, a considerable amount of attention was given to the development of the after-tax internal rate of return on equity invested in real estate projects. While this measure of return is useful in helping the investor to decide whether to invest in a project, it is helpful to break down or *partition* that rate of return into some meaningful components. This partitioning allows the investor to obtain some idea as to the relative weights of components of the return.

To illustrate what is meant by partitioning the return, recall that the after-tax internal rate of return on equity investment in real estate comprises two sources of cash flow: (1) after-tax cash flow from operations and (2) after-tax proceeds from the sale of the investment. In Exhibit 12–7, we present the after-tax cash flow from operating the property ($ATCF_o$) and the after-tax cash flow from sale of the property ($ATCF_s$) for a real estate project requiring an equity investment of $72,170. The internal rate of return on equity

EXHIBIT 12–7   Effect of Vacancy on *ATIRR* for Two Expense Options

Vacancy Rate (percent)	Option 1 (percent)	Option 2 (percent)
0.00	14.73	17.76
5.00	13.06	15.09
10.00	11.40	12.42
15.00	9.77	9.77
20.00	8.16	7.13
25.00	6.57	4.50
30.00	5.00	1.88
35.00	3.44	−0.72
40.00	1.91	−3.32
45.00	0.40	−5.90
50.00	−1.10	−8.47

EXHIBIT 12–8   *ATIRR* versus Vacancy Rate

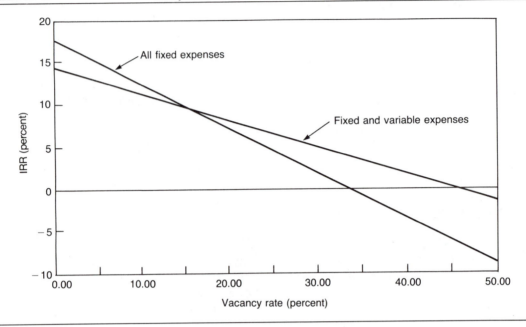

for the next five years is computed to be 11 percent. However, because both of the above-mentioned components make up the 11 percent internal rate of return, we have no way of knowing what proportion *each component bears to the total return*. A breakdown of each component would be useful to an investor concerned with how much of the return is made up of after-tax cash flow from *operations* realized from the project and how much is due to after-tax cash flow proceeds from *sale* of the property.

To consider these questions, it is a simple matter to reconsider the present value of the $ATCF_o$ and $ATCF_s$ in a slightly different manner as shown in Exhibit 12–9. We should note that all cash flow components expected to be received from the project are discounted to find the after-tax internal rate of return of 11 percent. Then the *PVs* of $ATCF_o$ and $ATCF_s$ are summed to get the total *PV* of $72,171. The ratios of the *PV* of $ATCF_o$ and the *PV* of $ATCF_s$ can now be taken to the total present value. These ratios now represent the respective proportion of the internal rate of return made up by after-tax cash flow (28 percent) and after-tax cash flow from appreciation and sale after five years (72 percent).

Why is partitioning an internal rate of return important? Because it helps the investor to determine how much of the return is dependent on annual operating cash flow and how much is dependent on expected appreciation in the value of the property.[4] It would

---

[4]It should also be pointed out that other components of *ATIRR* could be partitioned in addition to *ATCF* and $ATCF_s$. For example, tax shelter effects could be partitioned separately, and so on.

EXHIBIT 12–9 Partitioning the Internal Rate of Return (project 1)

Year	$ATCF_o$	IFPV at 11 Percent	PV
1	$ 4,852	.900901	$ 4,371
2	5,205	.811622	4,224
3	5,563	.731191	4,068
4	5,926	.658731	3,904
5	6,294	.593451	3,735
Total			$20,302
	$ATCF_s$		
5	$87,403	.593451	$51,869

PV of $ATCF_o$	$20,302
PV of $ATCF_s$	51,869
Total *PV*	$72,171

Ratio of
   PV, $ATCF_o$ / Total *PV* = 28%
   PV, $ATCT_s$ / Total *PV* = 72%

seem that the greater a proportion of the internal rate of return is made up of *expected appreciation in the future*, the greater the risk facing the investor. For example, the investment returns for this project, with its 11 percent *ATIRR*, is made up of 28 percent annual $ATCF_o$ and 72 percent $ATCF_s$. A second project is shown in Exhibit 12–10 that also requires an investment of $72,170 and has also provided the investor with the same *ATIRR* of 11 percent. However, when the *ATIRR* is partitioned, we can see that the proportions of the return are 3 percent for annual $ATCF_o$ and 97 percent for the estimated appreciation in value of the project in five years on an after-tax basis. Hence, it can be seen that even though *both* investments have an 11 percent *ATIRR*, a much higher proportion of the return in the second case is dependent on future appreciation in property value.[5] Given this outcome, the investor may want to compare any differences in risk between projects more carefully, because even though the two projects are estimated to yield the same *ATIRR* there is a strong likelihood that there are significant risk differences between the two.

DURATION

In the previous section we discussed partitioning as a way of measuring the relative contribution of $(ATCF_o)$ and $(ATCF_s)$ to the after-tax *IRR (ATIRR)* of the property. Because

---

[5]The reader should be aware that it is possible to have some negative *ATCF* and still have a *positive ATIRR*. Hence the operating cash flows are an important consideration that must be taken into account in addition to the *ATIRR*.

EXHIBIT 12–10   Partitioning the Internal Rate of Return (project 2)

Year	$ATCF_o$	PV at 11 percent
1	$ 500	$ 450
2	600	487
3	700	512
4	800	527
5	900	534
Total		$ 2,510

	$ATCF_s$	
5	$117,381	$69,660

PV of $ATCF_o$	$ 2,510
PV of $ATCF_s$	69,660
Total PV	$72,170

Ratio of
    PV, $ATCF_o$ / Total PV =   3%
    PV, $ATCF_s$ / Total PV = 97%

$ATCF_s$ may be less certain than $ATCF_o$, partitioning the *ATIRR* is one way of analyzing the riskiness of an investment. Another way of analyzing the timing of cash flows received by an investment is to calculate the *duration* of the cash flows. An introduction to the concept of duration and its calculation for project 1 is illustrated in Exhibit 12–11. To calculate the duration of an investment, we first determine the *PV* of the cash flow received each year as was done in Exhibit 12–9 for project 1. The second step is to multiply the *PV* for each year by the year. Thus, as shown in the exhibit, the *PV* in year 1 ($4,371) is multiplied by 1. The *PV* in year 2 ($4,224) is multiplied by 2, and so on. For the fifth year, both the *PV* from $ATCF_o$ and the *PV* from $ATCF_s$ are multiplied by 5. In effect

---

EXHIBIT 12–11   Duration of the Cash Flows for Project 1

Year	ATCF	IFPV at 11 percent	PV	PV · Year
1	$ 4,852	.900901	$ 4,371	$ 4,371
2	5,205	.811622	4,224	8,448
3	5,563	.731191	4,068	12,204
4	5,926	.658731	3,904	15,616
5	6,294	.593451	3,735	18,675
5	$87,403	.593451	51,869	259,345
Total			$72,171	$318,659
	$ATCF_s$			

$$\text{Duration} = \frac{\$318,659}{\$72,171} = 4.42 \text{ years}$$

EXHIBIT 12–12   Duration of the Cash Flows for Project 2

Year	ATCF	PV at 11 percent	PV · Year
1	$ 500	$ 450	$ 450
2	600	487	974
3	700	512	1,536
4	800	527	2,108
5	900	534	2,670
5	$117,381	69,660	348,300
Total		$72,170	$356,038

$$\text{Duration} = \frac{\$356,038}{\$72,171} = 4.93 \text{ years}$$

---

what we are doing is weighting each year by the contribution of that year's cash flow to the total present value of all of the cash flows received from the project.

The final step in our calculation of duration is to add the *PV* weighted years and divide the result by the total present value. As shown in the exhibit, the result is 4.42 years. Thus, we would say that the duration of the cash flows is 4.42 years. This is a measure of the average time it takes to receive the cash flows from the investment. To the extent that more of the cash flows are received during the early years of the investment, the duration will be shorter. Vice versa, to the extent that cash flows are received during the later years of the investment (including sale), the duration will be longer. Thus, we would expect the duration for project 2 to be longer than that for project 1. This is illustrated in Exhibit 12–12. The duration for project 2 is 4.93 years. It is close to five years, the length of the holding period, because most of the cash flows for project 2 are received in the final year when the project is sold. The longer duration for project 2 versus project 1 indicates that, on average, we have to wait longer to receive the cash flows from project 2, and that the return for project 2 depends more on the sale of the property.

The duration of an investment is also a measure of how much the value of the investment would be affected by changes market interest rates and thus the rate of return required by investors. For example, suppose there is a rise in the level of interest rates such that investors would require a 15 percent rate of return to invest in projects 1 and 2 rather than 11 percent. How does this change the present value for each of the investments? Exhibits 12–13 and 12–14 show the results for projects 1 and 2, respectively.[6] Note that the value of project 1, which has the shorter duration, does not decrease as much as project 2, which has the longer duration. The value of project 2 must decrease more than project 1 for an investor to achieve the same 15 percent return because it takes longer

---

[6]To isolate the effect of the change in the required discount rate on the value, we have assumed that the expected cash flows will stay the same. However, the reader should realize that if there is a change in interest rates, there could also be a change in the expected cash flows.

EXHIBIT 12–13   Present Value of Cash Flows for Project 1 at 15 Percent

Year	ATCF	PV at 15 Percent
1	$ 4,852	$ 4,219
2	5,205	3,936
3	5,563	3,658
4	5,926	3,388
5	6,294	3,129
5	$87,403	43,455
Total		$61,785

on average to receive the cash flows from project 2. Thus, in general, projects with a longer duration are more subject to interest rate risk.

VARIATION IN RETURNS AND RISK

Many of the sources of risk discussed in this chapter, such as business risk, financial risk, and so on, affect returns on real estate investment by making such returns more *variable*. Generally speaking, the higher the variability in returns, the greater the risk in a project. For example, assume that we have two properties being considered for investment. The first is an office building located in a part of town that is rapidly growing, rents are steadily increasing, and vacancies are low. If the office building is purchased, it is expected that good-quality leases will be executed with triple A corporate tenants, who are looking for branch office space, and vacancies will be minimal. The second property is a special-purpose convention hotel which is used for conventions, exhibitions, and related activities. The latter facility is located near a growing middle-income residential development. In the event of an unsuccessful venture in the latter case, the hotel property can be converted to some other commercial use, but not without significant expense for redeveloping the land.

EXHIBIT 12–14   Present Value of Cash Flows for Project 2 at 15 Percent

Year	ATCF	PV at 15 Percent
1	$ 500	$ 435
2	600	454
3	700	460
4	800	457
5	900	447
5	$117,381	58,359
Total		$60,612

A close examination of these alternatives would indicate that the office building would probably be less risky than the hotel. The office building would be less influenced by business risk than the hotel property because consumer spending on hotel activity is more sensitive to economic trends and personal income. The income produced by the hotel property will be highly dependent on the state of the national and local economy. Proper management and marketing may also be important to its success. On the other hand, the office building is located in a growing area and will be secured by leases with strong tenants. While there may be some losses in the latter case, the likelihood of such losses, when compared to the hotel property, would be lower. Given this characterization, we could say that the income stream expected from the hotel property could be more *variable* over time than the office building, given changes in the economic environment.

To illustrate, Exhibit 12–15 contains an estimate of the after-tax internal rate of return over a 10-year investment period for the office building and the hotel property under three different economic senarios. Essentially, what Exhibit 12–15 contains is estimates of the *ATIRR* made for both investments under three general economic scenarios that could occur over the investment period. That is, estimate of rents and expenses would be made for both investment alternatives under three assumptions regarding economic conditions. Then, given the debt-service and tax effects appropriate for each investment, the *ATCF* would be compiled as well as an estimate of the property value at the end of the investment period.

After compiling the *ATIRR* under each case, the investor could then make an estimate of the probability that each of the economic scenarios that affect the income-producing potential for both alternatives will occur. The estimated *ATIRR*, when multiplied by the probability that a given economic scenario will occur, produces expected or most likely return for each investment.

EXHIBIT 12–15 Payoff Matrix—Two Investment Alternatives

(1) *State of* *Economy*	*(2)* *Probability of* *Economic State (1)* *Occurring*	*(3)* *Estimated ATIRR* *Given State in* *(1) Occurs*	*(4)* *Expected Rate of* *Return (2) × (3)*
A. Commercial Office Building			
Rapid growth	.20	.17	.034
Slow growth	.60	.12	.072
Decline	.20	.07	.014
	1.00	Expected return	.120
B. Hotel Property			
Rapid growth	.20	.35	.070
Slow growth	.60	.15	.090
Decline	.20	− .05	− .010
	1.00	Expected return	.150

Based on the results in Exhibit 12–15, we see that the hotel property produces the highest return, 15 percent, compared to the 12 percent expected return for the office building. Does this mean that the hotel property should be selected over the office building? Not necessarily. At this point the reader should recall our discussion of risk characteristics in the chapter and how each investment may be affected by those considerations. A property that provides a high expected return may also be riskier relative to investments with somewhat lower returns.

In dealing with the problem of comparing risk and return among investments, there are some techniques that can be used to complement the qualitative considerations discussed at the end of the chapter. We now turn to a more quantitative discussion of the treatment of project risk.

In trying to deal with all risk characteristics particular to an investment, some researchers and market analysts argue that in combination these risks (e.g., business risk, financial risk, etc., discussed in the chapter) serve to induce *variability in a project's rate of return*. In our above example, the hotel project is clearly riskier than the commercial property, and in fact if one closely examines the estimates of *ATIRR* under each economic scenario, a much *wider range* in possible *ATIRR*s is encountered with the hotel property when compared to the office building. In fact, if we diagrammed the relationship between the probability of the possible economic states of nature and the expected *ATIRR* for that state of economic nature, we would have a pattern such as that shown in Exhibit 12–16. In that exhibit, we have plotted the probability of the state of the economy and expected *ATIRR* on each investment, given the state of the economy. We have "smoothed" the curves in the diagram between each probability point to show what the *ATIRR* would

EXHIBIT 12–16   Probability Distribution of *ATIRR* (Office Building and Hotel Property)

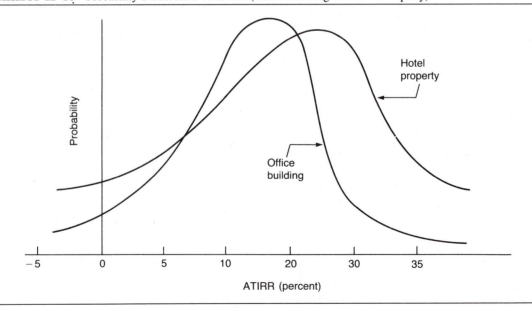

EXHIBIT 12–17   Meaures of Risk

(1) Estimated Returns	(2) Expected Return	(3) Deviation (1)–(2)	(4) Squared Deviation	(5) Probability	(6) Product (4) × (5)
		Office Building			
17.00	12.00	5.00	25.00	0.20	5.00
12.00	12.00	0.00	0.00	0.60	0.00
7.00	12.00	−5.00	25.00	0.20	5.00
				Variance	10.00
				Standard deviation	3.16
		Hotel Property			
35.00	15.00	20.00	400.00	0.20	80.00
15.00	15.00	0.00	0.00	0.60	0.00
−5.00	15.00	−20.00	400.00	0.20	80.00
				Variance	160.00
				Standard deviation	12.65

most likely be at points in between those specifically estimated. The key concept one should grasp from the exhibit is that even though the expected return for the hotel property is higher than that computed for the office building, the range of expected returns for the hotel property is far greater than that for the office building. The "narrowness" in the range of outcomes for the office building relative to the outcomes for the hotel property indicates that there is *lower variability* in expected returns for the office building than is the case with the recreation property. *Lower variability* in returns is considered by many analysts to be associated with *lower risk*, and vice versa. Therefore, by using a statistical measure of *variance*, one has an indication of the extent risk is present in an investment.

Measures of variance and risk.   Computing the statistical variance in returns is a very simple procedure and is done for the hotel property and for the office building as shown in Exhibit 12–17. Taking the square root of the variance, 160.0, we have the standard deviation (s) of 12.65 for the hotel property and 3.16 for the office project. What does the variance mean? What does the standard deviation, or s mean? Looking first to the measure of variance, we find that the *variation about the mean return* for the hotel property of 160.0 is *far greater* than that for the office building, which is only 10.0. This measure of *dispersion* tells us that the actual return for the office building is *more likely* to be *closer* to its expected return of 12.0 percent when compared to the hotel property. Since the measures for the hotel property were $s^2 = 160.0$ and $s = 12.65$, this tells us that the actual return for the hotel property is *less likely* to be closer to its expected return of 15 percent, when compared to the office building. Hence, if variation in returns is a good indicator of risk, then the recreational property is clearly the more risky of the two investments.

If the probability distribution of *ATIRR*s for the two investments being considered is normal, the standard deviation of returns for each investment also gives us valuable information. The standard deviation gives us a specific range over which we can expect the actual return for each investment to fall in relation to its expected return. For example, for the hotel property, we can expect its *actual* return to fall within ±1*s* of its expected return of 15 percent, 68 percent of the time. This means that we can expect the return on the hotel property to fall between 27.65 and 2.35 percent, 68 percent of the time. We can expect its actual return to fall within ±2*s* from its expected return approximately 95.5 percent of the time and ±3*s* from its expected return approximately 99.7 percent of the time.[7] In contrast, the actual return on the office building will fall in a much more narrow range of ±1*s* from its expected return, or 12% + 3.16% = 15.16% and 12% − 3.16% = 8.84%, 68 percent of the time, and so on.

Risk and return.   The relevance of these statistical measures, in addition to giving the investor a more quantitative perspective on dispersion and variance as proxies for risk, can also be related to the *ATIRR* in developing a measure of *risk per unit of expected return*. This is done for both investments by dividing the standard deviation of the *ATIRR*s by the expected mean *ATIRR*. For the office building this computation would be 3.16/12.0 = .263; for the hotel property it would be 12.65/15.0 = 0.843. This statistic, called the *coefficient of variation*, is a measure of relative variation; that is, it measures *risk per unit of expected return*. In the case of the hotel property, the coefficient of variation is much higher than that of the office building. This simply means that although the expected return for the hotel property is higher than that of the office building, when the *variation* in returns, or risk, is taken into account, the *reward* per unit of risk is not as high as it is for the office building.

Risk, reward, and project selection.   Based on the preceding analysis, we have concluded that the hotel property, when compared to the office building, does not provide the same return *per unit of risk taken*. Does this mean that the office building should be chosen over the hotel property? For many investors, the answer would be yes. Unless the coefficient of variation for the hotel property were at least *equal* to the coefficient computed for the office building, there would be a tendency for many investors to select the investment with the *lower* coefficient of variation.

However, we should stress that not all investors view risk the same way. For some investors, the incremental risk of hotel property may not appear to be that significant relative to the higher expected return. These investors would be those who could be characterized as more aggressive or less risk averse. On the other hand, investors who greatly fear the probability of failure or loss would not choose the hotel property over the office building. These investors are sometimes characterized as being more conservative, or more risk averse. Hence, even though we have developed a way to quantify risk, we are still unable to state with complete confidence that one investment should always be chosen over another, based on its risk-return relationship. Nonetheless, this

---

[7]The percentages associated with the standard deviations which set out the intervals in which the actual returns are likely to fall assume the distribution of returns is normal.

treatment of risk is useful when thinking about the relative risk among investments and does aid in decision making.

Other extensions and considerations.   While the above discussion of risk has been limited to investment analysis, there are other applications that would be useful to lenders, such as those interested in assessing the extent to which the degree of financial leverage may affect the variability in returns and related issues.

We should also point out that certain problems are encountered in the above analysis when, unlike the assumption made in our illustration, possible returns on investment in a project are not normally distributed. When this condition occurs, problems in interpreting the coefficient of variation arise and information provided by the risk-return analysis is not as helpful in decision making.

Finally, we have not considered here the possibility of reducing risk by combining investments into a *portfolio*. By developing a portfolio of *different* investment properties, and also including stocks and bonds, a significant reduction in risk can come about due to *diversification*. By diversifying among investment types, some of the risk discussed in the chapter can be eliminated by combining returns from many investments in a portfolio. Diversification usually serves to lower the variance of total returns from all investments in a portfolio because high and low expected returns tend to offset one another when combined. This results in less variation about an expected mean return for the entire investment portfolio. This type of analysis is an interesting aspect of real estate finance and will be explored in Chapter 23.

CONCLUSION

This chapter pointed out the importance of considering risk when analyzing investments. Rates of return for alternative investments cannot be compared if the investments have different degrees of risk. This chapter introduced several ways the investor can attempt to evaluate the riskiness of a real estate investment. These include sensitivity analysis, partitioning the return, and the use of probability distributions to compute the expected return and standard deviation of the return.

QUESTIONS

1. What is meant by partitioning the internal rate of return? Why is this procedure meaningful?
2. What is a risk premium? Why does such a premium exist between interest rates on mortgages and rates of return earned on equity invested in real estate?
3. What is meant by duration? How can it be used as a risk measure?
4. If a greater portion of the *ATIRR* on an investment is received later in its economic life, would that investment generally be riskier or less risky than an investment paying a greater portion of the return earlier in its economic life? Why?
5. Why could the measure of variance in expected returns for an investment be a proxy measure for risk?

6. What is the coefficient of variation? How is it measured? Why is it useful for comparative purposes?
7. What are some of the types of risk that should be considered when analyzing real estate and other categories of investment? Why is real estate investment generally riskier than other investments discussed in the chapter?
8. What are some of the market characteristics that make real estate investment riskier than other investments?
9. Do you think the *IRR* is usually more sensitive to a change in the growth rate for income or the growth rate for the reversion?
10. How can sensitivity analysis be used to evaluate the riskiness of an investment?
11. What is the difference between business risk and financial risk?
12. Identify some of the main sources of business risk.
13. Why is the variance (or standard deviation) used as a measure of risk? What are the advantages and disadvantages of this risk measure?

PROBLEMS

1. Two investments have the following pattern of expected cash flows from operations for years 1 to 4 respectively:

   Investment A: $5,000 $10,000 $12,000 $15,000

   Investment B: $2,000 $4,000 -0- $5,000

   Investment A requires an outlay of $110,000, and investment B requires an outlay of $120,000. At the end of the fourth year Investment A is expected to sell for $120,000 and Investment B is expected to sell for $182,700.
   a. What is the *ATIRR* on each investment?
   b. If the *ATIRR* were partitioned based on *ATCF* and *ATCF$_s$*, what proportions of the *ATIRR* would be represented by each?
   c. What do these proportions mean?
   d. Calculate the duration of each investment. What does this mean?
2. Mike Riskless is considering one of two projects. He has estimated the *ATIRR* under the three possible economic scenarios and assigned probabilities of occurrence to each scenario.

State of Economy	Probability	Estimated ATIRR Investment I	Estimated ATIRR Investment II
Growth	.10	.15	.25
Stability	.80	.10	.15
Decline	.10	.05	.05
	1.00		

Riskless is aware that the pattern of returns for investment II looks very attractive relative to investment I; however, he believes that investment II could be riskier than investment I. He would like to know how he can compare the two investments considering both the risk and return on each. What do you suggest?

3. An investor has projected three possible scenarios for a project as follows:

Pessimistic—NOI will be $200,000 the first year then decrease 2 percent per year over a five-year holding period. The property will sell for $1,800,000 after five years.

Most likely—NOI will be level at $200,000 per year for the next five years (level *NOI*), and the property will sell for $2,000,000.

Optimistic—NOI will be $200,000 the first year and increase 3 percent per year over a five-year holding period. The property will then sell for $2,200,000.

The asking price is $2,000,000. The investor thinks there is about a 30 percent probability for the pessimistic scenario, a 40 percent probability for the most likely scenario, and a 30 percent probability for the optimistic scenario.

a. Compute the *IRR* for each scenario.
b. Compute the expected *IRR*.
c. Compute the variance and standard deviation of the *IRR*s.
d. Would this project be better than one with a 12 percent expected return and a standard deviation of 4 percent?

Chapter 13

Financial Leverage and Debt Structure

In Chapter 9 a number of issues related to analyzing financing alternatives were introduced. Important concepts from that chapter included the effective cost of borrowing (before and after tax), and the incremental cost of borrowing additional funds. We also discussed how to evaluate whether a loan should be refinanced when interest rates decline. Although this discussion focused on *residential* property, all of the above concepts also apply to the analysis of income property. The reader may want to review the material in Chapter 9 before proceeding with this chapter.

The three preceding chapters have dealt with analyzing investment returns and risk on income property. In that analysis, we introduced financing and alluded to its affect on the before- and after-tax cash flow to the equity investor.

The purpose of this chapter will be to extend the discussion of debt from the earlier chapters in two main ways. First, we consider how the level of financing affects the investor's before- and after-tax *IRR*. Second, we consider several different financing alternatives that are used with real estate income property. Since it is impossible to discuss all the varieties of loans that are used in practice, we will concentrate on the primary alternatives and focus our discussion on concepts and techniques that the reader can apply to any type of financing alternative that might be considered.

INTRODUCTION TO FINANCIAL LEVERAGE

Why should an investor use debt? One obvious reason is simply that the investor may not have enough equity capital to buy the property, or the investor may have enough equity capital, but may choose to borrow anyway. In the latter case, the excess equity could then be used to buy other properties. Because equity funds could be spread over several properties, the overall risk of an investor's portfolio may be reduced. A second reason to borrow is to take advantage of the tax deductibility of mortgage interest. This amplifies tax benefits to the equity investor. The third reason that is usually given for using debt is to realize the potential benefit associated with what is referred to as *financial leverage*. Financial leverage is defined as benefits that may result to an investor by borrowing money at a rate of interest that is lower than the expected rate of return on total funds invested in a property. If the return on the total investment invested in a property is greater than the rate of interest on the debt, the return on equity is magnified.

To examine the way financial leverage affects the investor's rate of return, we consider investment in a small commercial property with the following assumptions:

Purchase price	
Building value	$ 85,000
Land value	15,000
Total value	$100,000
Loan assumptions	
Loan amount	$ 80,000
Interest rate	10.00%
Term	Interest only
Income assumptions	
NOI	$12,000 per year (level)
Income tax rate[1]	28.00%
Depreciation	31.5 years (straight line)
Resale price	$100,000
Holding period	5 years

Using the above assumptions, we obtain the cash flow estimates as shown in Exhibit 13–1.

Exhibit 13–2 shows the cash flow summary and *IRR* calculations for the cash flows in Exhibit 13–1. From Exhibit 13–2 we see that the before-tax *IRR* (*BTIRR*) is 20.00 percent and the after-tax *IRR* (*ATIRR*) is 15.40 percent. This result was obtained with an 80 percent loan. We now consider how these returns would be affected by a change in the amount of debt. Exhibits 13–3 and 13–4 show the cash flow and return calculations for the example assuming *no loan* is used.

From Exhibit 13–4 we see that both the *BTIRR* and *ATIRR* have fallen. That is, both returns are higher with debt than without debt. When this occurs, we say that the investment has positive or favorable financial leverage. We now examine the conditions that result in positive financial leverage more carefully. To do so, we first look at the conditions for positive leverage on a *before-tax* basis (i.e., the effect of leverage on *BTIRR*). Later, we examine the relationship on an *after-tax* basis (i.e., on *ATIRR*).

---

[1]It is assumed that the investor will not be subject to any passive loss limitations.

EXHIBIT 13–1 Cash Flow for Commercial Building

	Year				
	1	*2*	*3*	*4*	*5*

Estimates of Cash Flow from Operations

A. Before-tax cash flow					
Net operating income (*NOI*)	$12,000	$12,000	$12,000	$12,000	$12,000
Less debt service (*DS*)	8,000	8,000	8,000	8,000	8,000
Before-tax cash flow	$ 4,000	$ 4,000	$ 4,000	$ 4,000	$ 4,000
B. Taxable income or loss					
Net operating income (*NOI*)	$12,000	$12,000	$12,000	$12,000	$12,000
Less interest	8,000	8,000	8,000	8,000	8,000
Depreciation	2,698	2,698	2,698	2,698	2,698
Taxable income (loss)	1,302	1,302	1,302	1,302	1,302
Tax	$ 364	$ 364	$ 364	$ 364	$ 364
C. After-tax cash flow					
Before-tax cash flow (*BTCF*)	$ 4,000	$ 4,000	$ 4,000	$ 4,000	$ 4,000
Less tax	364	364	364	364	364
After-tax cash flow (*ATCF*)	$ 3,636	$ 3,636	$ 3,636	$ 3,636	$ 3,636

Estimates of Cash Flows from Sale in Year 5

Sale price			$100,000
Less mortgage balance			80,000
Before-tax cash flow (*BTCF*$_s$)			$ 20,000
Taxes in year of sale			
Sale price		$100,000	
Original cost basis	$100,000		
Less accumulated depreciation	13,492		
Adjusted basis		86,508	
Capital gain		$ 13,492	
Tax from sale			3,778
After-tax cash flow from sale (*ATCF*$_s$)			$ 16,222

EXHIBIT 13–2 Cash Flow Summary and *IRR*

	End of Year					
	0	*1*	*2*	*3*	*4*	*5*
BTCF	$ – 20,000	$4,000	$4,000	$4,000	$4,000	$24,000
ATCF	– 20,000	3,636	3,636	3,636	3,636	19,858

Before-tax *IRR* (*BTIRR*) = 20.00%
After-tax *IRR* (*ATIRR*)   = 15.40%

EXHIBIT 13–3   Cash Flow Estimates (no loan)

	Year				
	1	2	3	4	5

Estimates of Cash Flow from Operations

	1	2	3	4	5
A. Before-tax cash flow					
Net operating income (*NOI*)	$12,000	$12,000	$12,000	$12,000	$12,000
Less debt service (*DS*)	0	0	0	0	0
Before-tax cash flow	$12,000	$12,000	$12,000	$12,000	$12,000
B. Taxable income or loss					
Net operating income (*NOI*)	$12,000	$12,000	$12,000	$12,000	$12,000
Less interest	0	0	0	0	0
Depreciation	2,698	2,698	2,698	2,698	2,698
Taxable income (loss)	9,302	9,302	9,302	9,302	9,302
Tax	$ 2,604	$ 2,604	$ 2,604	$ 2,604	$ 2,604
C. After-tax cash flow					
Before-tax cash flow (*BTCF*)	$12,000	$12,000	$12,000	$12,000	$12,000
Less tax	2,604	2,604	2,604	2,604	2,604
After-tax cash flow (*ATCF*)	$ 9,396	$ 9,396	$ 9,396	$ 9,396	$ 9,396

Estimates of Cash Flows from Sale in Year 5

Sale price			$100,000
Less mortgage balance			0
Before-tax cash flow (*BTCF$_s$*)			$100,000
Taxes in year of sale			
Sale price		$100,000	
Original cost basis	$100,000		
Less accumulated depreciation	13,492		
Adjusted basis		86,508	
Capital gain		$ 13,492	
Tax from sale			3,778
After-tax cash flow from sale (*ATCF$_s$*)			$ 96,222

EXHIBIT 13–4   Cash Flow Summary and Rates of Return (no loan)

	End of Year					
	0	1	2	3	4	5

Cash Flow Summary

	0	1	2	3	4	5
Before-tax cash flow	$ −100,000	$12,000	$12,000	$12,000	$12,000	$112,000
After-tax cash flow	−100,000	9,396	9,396	9,396	9,396	105,618
Before-tax *IRR* (*BTIRR*) = 12.00%						
After-tax *IRR* (*ATIRR*) = 8.76%						

Conditions for Positive Leverage—Before Tax

In the example when no debt was used, the *BTIRR* was 12 percent. We will refer to this as the *unlevered BTIRR*, since it equals the return when no debt is used. In the case where 80 percent debt was used, the *BTIRR* increased to 20.00 percent. Why does this occur? It occurs because *the unlevered BTIRR is greater than the interest rate paid on the debt.*[2] The interest rate on the debt was 10 percent, which is less then the 12 percent unlevered *BTIRR*. We could say that the return on investment (before debt) is greater than the rate that has to be paid on the debt. This differential (12 percent versus 10 percent) means that positive leverage exists that will magnify the *BTIRR* on equity.

We now show a formula which formalizes this relationship, a formula for estimating the return on equity, given the return on the property and the mortgage interest rate:[3]

$$BTIRR_E = BTIRR_P + (BTIRR_P - BTIRR_D)\left(\frac{D}{E}\right)$$

where

$BTIRR_E$ = before-tax *IRR* on equity invested
$BTIRR_P$ = before-tax *IRR* on total investment in the property (debt and equity)
$BTIRR_D$ = before-tax *IRR* on debt (effective cost of the loan considering points)
D/E = ratio of debt to equity

Using the numbers for our example we have

$$BTIRR_E = 12.00\% + (12.00\% - 10.00\%) \cdot \left(\frac{80\%}{20\%}\right)$$
$$= 20.00\%$$

This formula indicates that as long as $BTIRR_P$ is greater than $BTIRR_D$, then $BTIRR_E$ will be greater than $BTIRR_P$. This is referred to as favorable or positive leverage. Whenever leverage is positive, the greater the amount of debt, the higher the return to the equity investor. From this result many investors conclude that they should borrow as much as possible. (We will see later that this conclusion is not necessarily valid when risk is considered.) The graph in Exhibit 13–5 illustrates the effect of different loan-to-value ratios on the *IRR* for our example.

While the relationships in Exhibit 13–5 are relatively straightforward, there are limits to the amount of debt that may be used. What are the limits? First, for various amounts of debt the debt coverage ratio may exceed the lender's limits, as discussed in Chapter 10. Because the *NOI* does not change when more debt is used, increasing the amount of debt increases the debt service relative to the *NOI*. Second, at higher loan-to-value ratios and declining debt coverage ratios, risk to the lender increases. As a result, the interest

---

[2]More precisely, the unlevered *IRR* is greater than the *effective cost* of the loan. Recall that the effective cost of a loan reflects points, prepayments, and other factors which affect the borrower.

[3]This is an approximation when the ratio of debt to equity changes over time.

EXHIBIT 13–5   Before- and After-Tax Leverage

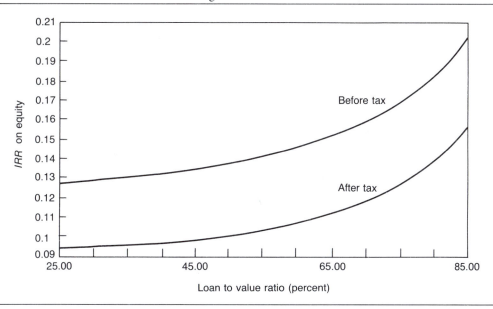

rate on additional debt will also increase. Indeed, at some point $BTIRR_P$ may no longer exceed $BTIRR_D$ (i.e., leverage will no longer be favorable). Third, there is additional risk to the equity investor associated with additional borrowing. The effect of leverage on risk will be dealt with more formally later in this chapter. However, we will now point out that leverage works both ways in the sense that it can magnify either returns or losses. That is, if leverage is unfavorable, or $ATIRR_D > BTIRR_P$, the use of more debt will magnify losses on equity invested in the property. We saw earlier that $BTIRR_P$ must exceed $BTIRR_D$ for the leverage to be favorable. Suppose that the interest rate is 14 percent instead of 10 percent. This will result in negative leverage because the unlevered $BTIRR_E$ (12 percent) is now less than the 14 percent cost of debt. Exhibit 13–6 illustrates the effect that different loan-to-value ratios will have on the before- and after-tax *IRR*s. Note that when $BTIRR_P$ is less than $BTIRR_D$, then $BTIRR_E$ is also less than $BTIRR_D$ and declines even further as the amount borrowed (debt-to-equity ratio) increases. The next section develops this relationship more formally.

Conditions for Positive Leverage—After Tax

Looking at the after-tax *IRR* (*ATIRR*) in Exhibits 13–2 and 13–4, we see that $ATIRR_p$ (on total investment) is 8.76 percent and *ATIRR* on equity invested is 15.4 percent. Thus, there is also *favorable* or *positive* leverage on an *after-tax* basis. That is, the expected after-tax *IRR* is higher if we can borrow money at a 10 percent rate as assumed in the example. How can leverage be favorable if the unlevered *ATIRR* (8.76 percent) is less

EXHIBIT 13–6   Before- and After-Tax Leverage

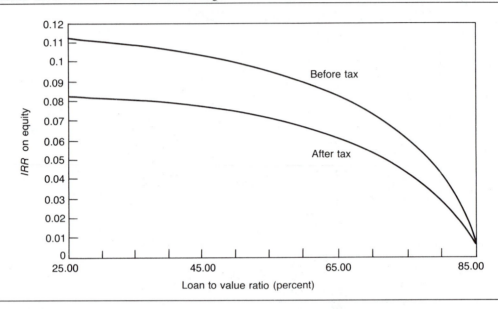

than the cost of debt (10 percent)? The reason is because interest is tax deductible; hence we must consider the *after-tax* cost of debt. Because there are no points involved in this example, the after-tax cost of debt is equal to the before-tax cost times $(1 - t)$, where t is the tax rate. Thus the after-tax cost of debt is

$$.10(1 - .28) = 7.2\%$$

In the previous section we showed a formula to estimate the return on equity, given the return on the property and the mortgage interest rate. That formula can be modified to consider taxes as follows:

$$ATIRR_E = ATIRR_P + (ATIRR_P - ATIRR_D)\left(\frac{D}{E}\right)$$

where

$ATIRR_E$ = after-tax *IRR* on equity invested

$ATIRR_P$ = after-tax *IRR* on total funds invested in the property

$ATIRR_D$ = after-tax *IRR* on debt (effective after-tax cost of the loan)

D/E = ratio of debt to equity

Using the above equation we have

$$ATIRR_E = 8.76\% + (8.76\% - 7.2\%)\left(\frac{80\%}{20\%}\right)$$

$$= 15.00\%$$

Hence the approximation is 15.00 percent versus the actual *ATIRR* of 15.40 percent, as shown in Exhibit 13–2. The formula is an approximation because the debt-to-equity ratio increases over the holding period. That is, although the initial debt-to-equity ratio is 4.0 ($80,000/$20,000), when the property is sold, the debt is still $80,000, but the equity is $16,222 (sale price of $96,222 less the loan of $80,000), resulting in a debt-to-equity ratio of 4.93. Thus, the average *D/E* for the holding period is greater than the initial *D/E* of 4 that we used in the formula. However, using the initial *D/E* is still a good approximation. And the pivotal point for leverage is still the after-tax cost of debt. That is, for leverage to be favorable on an *after-tax* basis, the after-tax return on total funds invested must exceed the after-tax cost of the debt. For example, in our illustration, if the $ATIRR_P$ was less than 7.2 percent, leverage would be unfavorable.

It is useful to summarize the various *IRR* calculations we have made for the office example. Exhibit 13–7 shows the before- and after-tax *IRR* with and without a loan. It is important to understand the difference between each of these returns. When using the term *return* (or *IRR*), it is obviously very important to specify whether that return is before tax or after tax, and whether it is based on having a loan (e.g., a *levered* return) or not having a loan (e.g., an *unlevered* return).

BREAK-EVEN INTEREST RATE

In the previous discussion we saw that the relationship between the after-tax *IRR* on the property (before debt) and the after-tax cost of debt determines whether leverage is favorable or unfavorable. It is sometimes useful to determine the maximum interest rate that could be paid on the debt before the leverage becomes unfavorable. This is referred to as the *break-even interest rate* and represents the interest rate where the leverage is neutral (neither favorable or unfavorable). By examining the after-tax leverage equation in the previous section, we see that the point of neutral leverage can be expressed as follows:

$$ATIRR_D = ATIRR_P$$

Based on this relationship, we want to know the interest rate that will result in an after-tax cost of debt that is equal to the after-tax *IRR* on total funds invested in the property. In general, recall from Chapter 9 that the after-tax cost of debt, $ATIRR_D$ can be estimated as follows:

$$ATIRR_D = BTIRR_D(1 - t)$$

EXHIBIT 13–7   Summary *IRR* Measures

	$BTIRR_E$	$ATIRR_E$
No loan*	12.00%	8.76%
70% loan	20.00%	15.40%

*Note that $IRR_E = IRR_P$ when there is no loan.

Solving this for the before-tax cost of debt, we have

$$BTIRR_D = \frac{ATIRR_D}{1 - t}$$

Because the break-even point for leverage occurs when $ATIRR_D = ATIRR_P$, we can substitute $ATIRR_P$ for $ATIRR_D$ in the above equation and obtain a break-even interest rate

$$BTIRR_D = \frac{ATIRR_P}{1 - t}$$

For our example, the break-even interest would be

$$\frac{8.76\%}{1 - .28} = 12.17\%$$

This means that regardless of the amount borrowed, or degree of leverage desired, the maximum rate of interest that may be paid on debt and not reduce the return on equity is 12.17 percent. To demonstrate this concept further, Exhibit 13–8 shows the after-tax *IRR* for interest rates ranging from 10 to 16 percent for three different loan-to-value ratios. Note that for interest rates above the break-even interest rate of 12.17 percent, the after-tax IRR for equity investor ($ATIRR_E$) is less than the after-tax *IRR* on total investment ($ATIRR_P$), which is 8.76 percent. Conversely, for interest rates below the break-even interest rate the after-tax *IRR* for the equity investor is greater than the after-tax *IRR* on the property.

Exhibit 13–9 graphs the information in Exhibit 13–10 and shows the break-even interest rate. Again note that the break-even interest rate remains 12.17 percent regardless of the amount borrowed (that is, 60, 70, or 80 percent of the property value).

EXHIBIT 13–8   Effect of Interest Rates on the After-Tax *IRR* on Equity

Interest Rate (%)	$ATIRR_E$ (%) Loan to Value		
	60.00%	*70.00%*	*80.00%*
10.00	10.83	11.86	13.73
10.50	10.36	11.16	12.61
11.00	9.89	10.45	11.48
11.50	9.41	9.73	10.32
12.00	8.92	9.01	9.16
12.50	8.44	8.27	7.98
13.00	7.95	7.53	6.78
13.50	7.45	6.79	5.57
14.00	6.95	6.03	4.34
14.50	6.45	5.27	3.10
15.00	5.95	4.50	1.85
15.50	5.44	3.73	0.58
16.00	4.92	2.94	−0.70

EXHIBIT 13–9   After-Tax *IRR* versus Interest Rates

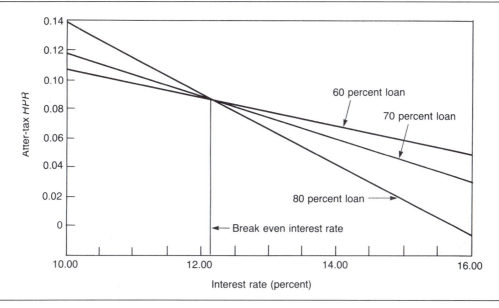

If an investor borrowed funds at an effective interest rate that was just equal to the break-even interest rate, leverage would be neutral; that is, it would not be unfavorable or favorable. However, it should be noted that at the break-even interest rate $ATIRR_P$ is exactly equal to $ATIRR_D$ (by definition), which means that $ATIRR_E$ will exactly equal $ATIRR_D$. That is, the investor just earns the same after-tax rate of return as a lender in the same project. But borrowing at the break-even interest rate will not provide a risk premium for the equity investor. A risk premium will normally be required by equity investors because they bear the risk of variations in the performance of the property. This will be shown more formally in the section following the next one.

LEVERAGE AND THE INCREMENTAL COST OF DEBT

As mentioned earlier in this chapter, at high amounts of debt a higher interest rate may have to be paid to obtain additional financing. We know that favorable leverage occurs as long as the effective cost of debt is less than the break-even interest rate. Thus we might conclude that it is advantageous to borrow additional funds as long as the cost of those funds is less than the break-even interest rate. We now show that this is not necessarily true. Recall that in Chapter 9 we discussed the concept of the *incremental cost of debt* as it related to loans on residential property. We showed that the decision to borrow additional funds should be made by considering the incremental or marginal cost of the additional funds obtained. Knowing the incremental cost of funds is equally important in analyzing the amount to borrow on income property.

EXHIBIT 13–10   Conventional Loan

	Year				
	1	2	3	4	5

Estimates of Cash Flow from Operations

	1	2	3	4	5
A. Before-tax cash flow					
Net operating income (*NOI*)	$100,000	$103,000	$106,090	$109,273	$112,551
Less debt service (*DS*)	90,267	90,267	90,267	90,267	90,267
Cash flow before partic	9,733	12,733	15,823	19,006	22,284
Participation	0	0	0	0	0
Before-tax cash flow	$ 9,733	$ 12,733	$ 15,823	$ 19,006	$ 22,284
B. Taxable income or loss					
Net operating income (*NOI*)	$100,000	$103,000	$106,090	$109,273	$112,551
Less Interest	69,045	66,823	64,368	61,656	58,660
Participation	0	0	0	0	0
Depreciation	32,727	32,727	32,727	32,727	32,727
Taxable income (loss)	−1,772	3,450	8,995	14,890	21,164
Tax	$ −496	$ 966	$ 2,519	$ 4,169	$ 5,926
C. After-tax cash flow					
Before-tax cash flow (*BTCF*)	$ 9,733	$ 12,733	$ 15,823	$ 19,006	$ 22,284
Less tax*	−496	966	2,519	4,169	5,926
After-tax cash flow (*ATCF*)	$ 10,229	$ 11,767	$ 13,305	$ 14,837	$ 16,358

Estimates of Cash Flows from Sale in Year 5

Sale price			$1,159,274
Less mortgage balance			569,216
Before-tax cash flow (*BTCF*s)			$ 590,058
Taxes in year of sale			
Sale price		$1,159,274	
Original cost basis	$1,000,000		
Accumulated depreciation	163,636		
Adjusted basis		836,364	
Capital gain		$ 322,910	
Tax from sale			90,415
After-tax cash flow from sale (*ATCF*s)			$ 499,643

Cash Flow Summary

	End of Year					
	0	1	2	3	4	5
BTCF	$−3,00,000	$ 9,733	$12,733	$15,823	$19,006	$612,342
ATCF	−3,00,000	10,229	11,767	13,305	14,837	516,001

Before-tax *IRR* = 18.37%
After-tax *IRR* = 14.30%

*It is assumed that the investor is not subject to passive activity loss limitations.

In the example we have been using, an 80 percent loan was available at a 10 percent interest rate. This was less than the break-even interest rate of 12.17 percent; thus we concluded that there was favorable leverage. Now suppose that an 85 percent loan can be obtained, but the interest rate would be 10.25 percent instead of 10 percent. We assume it would also be an interest only loan for simplicity. We might conclude that it is desirable to borrow the additional funds because the rate on the 85 percent loan (10.25 percent) is less than the break-even interest rate of 12.17 percent. However, the *incremental* cost of the additional $5,000 received on the 85 percent loan is 14.25 percent.[4] This cost is greater than the break-even interest rate of 12.17 percent. Thus, it is not desirable to obtain the additional loan. Looking only at the 10.25 percent rate on the entire loan would not lead to the correct decision because it does not focus on the cost of the additional funds received. Recall from Chapter 9 that whenever the investor has a choice of obtaining a higher loan amount at a higher interest rate, there is an incremental cost associated with obtaining the additional funds. Thus it is this increment cost that we should compare with the break-even interest rate when deciding to borrow additional funds.

RISK AND LEVERAGE

We have seen how favorable financial leverage can increase $BTIRR_E$ and $ATIRR_E$. We also saw that increasing the amount of debt magnifies the effect of leverage. It is no wonder that many people conclude that they should borrow as much as possible (as evidenced by the number of "no money down" seminars and advocates of using "OPM," or other people's money). The point of the following discussion is to emphasize that *there is an implicit cost associated with the use of financial leverage.* This cost comes in the form of *higher risk.* To illustrate, consider the following investment opportunity:

Total project costs (land, improvements, etc.) will be $1,000,000. In our initial example, no debt is used to finance the project. The investor has projected three possible scenarios for a project as follows:

Pessimistic—NOI will be $100,000 the first year and decrease 2 percent per year over a five-year holding period. The property will sell for $900,000 after five years.

Most likely—NOI will be level at $110,000 per year for the next five years, and the property will sell for $1,100,000.

Optimistic—NOI will be $120,000 the first year and increase 5 percent per year for five years. The property will then sell for $1,300,000.

---

[4]Interest on the 85 percent loan is $(.1025)(\$85,000) = \$8,712$. Subtracting the $8,000 interest on the 80 percent loan $(.10)(\$80,000)$, we obtain a difference of $712.50 per year. Dividing this by the additional funds received of $5,000 results in an incremental cost of 14.25 percent. Note that because it is an interest only loan, the total payments are the same as the interest payments. And because the balance of the loan does not change, the *IRR* can be found by simply dividing the payment by the loan amount, rather than using present value factors.

The investor thinks there is about a 20 percent probability for the pessimistic scenario, a 50 percent probability for the most likely scenario, and a 30 percent probability for the optimistic scenario.

Using the above information, we have computed (calculations not shown) $BTIRR_P$ for each scenario, the expected $BTIRR_P$, the variance of the $BTIRR_P$'s, and the standard deviation of the $BTIRR_P$'s. The results are as follows:

	Unlevered					
	(1) *Estimated* *BTIRR$_P$*	*(2)* *Expected* *BTIRR$_P$*$*$	*(3)* *Deviation* *(1)–(2)*	*(4)* *Squared* *Deviation*	*(5)* *Probability*	*(6)* *Product* *(4)(5)*
Pessimistic	7.93	13.06	−5.13	26.31	0.20	5.26
Most likely	12.56	13.06	−0.50	0.25	0.50	0.12
Optimistic	17.31	13.06	4.25	18.07	0.30	5.42
					Variance	10.81
					Standard deviation	3.29

$*$7.93(.2) + 12.56(.5) + 17.31(.3) = 13.06%.

We now assume the same investment is financed with a loan for $900,000 which is obtained at a 10 percent interest rate for a 15-year term. What will be the expected $BTIRR_E$ and the standard deviation of the $BTIRR_E$? The results are as follows:

	Levered					
	(1) *Estimated* *BTIRR$_E$*	*(2)* *Expected* *BTIRR$_E$*$*$	*(3)* *Deviation* *(1)–(2)*	*(4)* *Squared* *Deviation*	*(5)* *Probability*	*(6)* *Product* *(4)(5)*
Pessimistic	−5.09	26.49	−31.58	997.36	0.20	199.47
Most likely	25.99	26.49	−0.50	0.25	0.50	0.13
Optimistic	48.38	26.49	21.89	479.13	0.30	143.74
					Variance	343.34
					Standard deviation	18.53

Note that under the most likely and optimistic scenarios, estimated *IRR*s are higher with the loan (levered) than with no loan (unlevered), indicating that there is favorable leverage in these cases. In the pessimistic case, however, the estimated return is lower, indicating that if that scenario occurs, leverage will be very unfavorable. Looking at the range in expected $BTIRR_E$, however, which is higher with the loan, one might think that it is still a good idea to borrow. Note, however, that the standard deviation is considerably higher in the levered case, 18.53 percent versus 3.29 percent. Thus, the investment is clearly riskier when leverage is used. (This would also be true regardless of whether the leverage is favorable or unfavorable.) The point is that the decision to use leverage cannot be made by only looking at $BTIRR_P$ and $BTIRR_E$. The investor must ask whether the higher expected return with leverage is commensurate with the higher risk. Alternatively, the investor should ask if there is a way to realize the higher return with less risk, such as another investment in a different property or in the same property but with a different way of financing the property, a topic we consider next.

PARTICIPATION LOANS

We begin our discussion of financing alternatives by introducing what are referred to as *equity participation loans,* also referred to as *participations* or *equity kickers.* Actually the term *equity participation* is somewhat of a misnomer because the lender does not actually acquire an ownership interest in the property. Rather, in return for a lower stated interest rate on the loan, the lender *participates* in some way in the income or cash flow from the property. Thus the lender's rate of return depends, in part, on the performance of the property.

There are many ways of determining the amount of participation. For example, the lender might receive a percentage of one or more of the following: (1) potential gross income, (2) net operating income (*NOI*), and (3) cash flow after regular debt service (but before the participation). In addition, there might be a participation at the time the property is sold based on (1) total sale proceeds, or (2) the appreciation in property value since it was purchased.

It is often the case for newly developed properties for participation in cash flows to begin after some preagreed amount of leasing and rental achievement is reached. For example, the participation might be based on a percentage of all *NOI in excess* of $100,000. In the case of existing properties, the break-even point is typically set so that the participation begins after the first operating year. For example, *NOI* might be expected to be $100,000 during the first year. Thus the lender would receive a participation only when *NOI* increases to more than $100,000, which might occur in the second year.

In return for receiving a participation, the lender charges a lower stated interest rate on the loan. How much lower depends on the amount of participation. Participations are highly negotiable, and there is no standard way of structuring them.

Lender Motivations

Why would a lender be willing to make a participation loan? As we will discuss, the lender will want to structure the participation in such a way that the lender's rate of return (including the expected participation) is at least comparable to what the return would have been with a fixed interest rate loan (no participation). Whether the lender will accept a lower expected return with the participation or demand a premium depends on how risky the participation loan is perceived relative to a fixed interest rate loan. There is clearly some uncertainty associated with the receipt of a participation since it depends on the performance of the property. At the same time, however, the lender does not participate in any losses. The lender still receives some minimum interest rate (unless the borrower defaults). Furthermore, the participation provides the lender with somewhat of a hedge against unanticipated inflation because increasing *NOI*, resale prices, and so on, for an income property is often a result of inflation. Thus to some extent a participation protects the lender's ''real'' rate of return.

Investor Motivations

Why would an investor-borrower want a participation loan? As indicated above, participation loans are often structured so that the participation is based on income or cash flow above some specified break-even point. This means that the participation may be very little or zero for one or more years. During this time period the borrower will be paying less than would have been paid with a straight loan. This may be quite desirable for the investor since *NOI* may be lower during the first couple of years of ownership, especially on a new project that is not fully rented. Thus the investor may have more cash flow during the early years of a participation loan than with a straight loan. This also increases the debt coverage ratio. That is, the investor may be better able to meet debt service during the initial years of the loan with a participation.

The reader may wonder why the investor wouldn't accept a participation loan with a lower rate and a participation that doesn't kick in for a couple of years, and sell the property before the participation kicks in! This problem is handled by having a ''lock-in'' period during which the property cannot be sold or refinanced without a prepayment penalty to compensate the lender.

Participation Example

To illustrate a participation loan, we assume that an apartment project being considered for purchase by an investor is projected to have *NOI* of $100,000 during the first year. After that the *NOI* is projected to increase 3 percent per year. The property can be purchased for $1,000,000. This price includes a building value of $900,000, which will be depreciated over 27.5 years. The property value is projected to increase 3 percent per year over a five-year holding period.

The lender has offered the following alternatives:

1. A conventional, fixed rate, constant payment loan for $700,000 at 10 percent interest rate (monthly payments) over a 15-year term.
2. A loan for $700,000 at 8 percent interest with monthly payments over 15 years and a participation in 50 percent of any *NOI* in excess of $100,000 plus a participation in 45 percent of any gain (sale price − original cost) when the property is sold.

It should be noted that the *amount* of the loan for the two alternatives is the same. This is important because otherwise there would be differences in risk due to financial leverage. At this point we want to focus on analyzing different ways of *structuring* the debt independent of the decision about the *amount* of debt, which we have already discussed.

Exhibit 13–10 shows the cash flows for the conventional loan. It should be noted that the debt coverage ratio (*DCR*) during the first year of the conventional loan is only 1.11. This is lower than many lenders would find acceptable. Recall that lenders typically require a minimum *DCR* of 1.2. Thus the borrower may have difficulty borrowing $700,000 with a conventional loan. Of course, the amount of the loan could be reduced to increase the debt coverage ratio. As we will see, however, a participation loan may be structured to alleviate the *DCR* problem.

Exhibit 13–11 shows the cash flows for the participation loan. The cash flow patterns differ significantly due to the different nature of the participation. Note that with the participation loan, there are lower payments (debt service plus participation payments) during the early years. This is because of the lower interest rate on the participation loan plus the fact that the participation does not start until the second year. Also, part of the payments to the lender from the participation loan do not come until the property is sold.

Despite the difference in payment patterns, the before-tax *IRR* (*BTIRR$_E$*) is virtually the same for both the conventional loan and the participation loan. This is a result of the amount of terms for this particular participation loan.

EXHIBIT 13–11 Participation Example

	Year				
	1	*2*	*3*	*4*	*5*
Estimates of Cash Flow from Operations					
A. Before-tax cash flow					
Net operating income (*NOI*)	$100,000	$103,000	$106,090	$109,273	$112,551
Less debt service (*DS*)	80,275	80,275	80,275	80,275	80,275
Cash flow before participation	19,725	22,725	25,815	28,998	32,276
Participation	0	1,500	3,045	4,636	6,275
Before-tax cash flow	$ 19,725	$ 21,225	$ 22,770	$ 24,362	$ 26,001
B. Taxable income or loss					
Net operating income (*NOI*)	$100,000	$103,000	$106,090	$109,273	$112,551
Less Interest	55,090	53,000	50,736	48,284	45,629
Participation	0	1,500	3,045	4,636	6,275
Depreciation	32,727	32,727	32,727	32,727	32,727
Taxable income (loss)	12,183	15,773	19,582	23,625	27,919
Tax	$ 3,411	$ 4,417	$ 5,483	$ 6,615	$ 7,817
C. After-tax cash flow					
Before-tax cash flow (*BTCF*)	$ 19,725	$ 21,225	$ 22,770	$ 24,362	$ 26,001
Less-tax	3,411	4,417	5,483	6,615	7,817
After-tax cash flow (*ATCF*)	$ 16,314	$ 16,809	$ 17,287	$ 17,747	$ 18,183

EXHIBIT 13–11   *(Concluded)*

Estimates of Cash Flows from Sale in Year 5

Sale price		$1,159,274
Less mortgage balance		551,364
Cash flow before participation		607,910
Less participation in gain from sale		71,673
Before tax cash flow ($BTCF_s$)		536,237
Taxes in year of sale		
Sale price	$1,159,274	
Participation	71,673	
Original cost basis	$1,000,000	
Accumulated depreciation	163,636	
Adjusted basis	836,364	
Capital gain	$ 251,237	
Tax from sale		70,346
After-tax cash flow from sale ($ATCF_s$)		$465,891

Cash Flow Summary: Investor

	End of Year					
	0	*1*	*2*	*3*	*4*	*5*
Before-tax cash flow	$ −300,000	$19,725	$21,225	$22,770	$24,362	$562,238
After-tax cash flow	−300,000	16,314	16,809	17,287	17,747	484,074

Before-tax *IRR* = 18.36%
After-tax *IRR* = 14.07%

Cash Flow Summary: Lender

Month	*0*	*1–12*	*13–24*	*25–36*	*37–48*	*49–60*	*60*
Loan amount	$ −700,000						
Debt service		$6,690	$6,690	$6,690	$6,690	$6,690	
Participation		0	125	254	386	523	$ 71,673
Loan balance							551,364
Total	$ −700,000	$6,690	$6,815	$6,944	$7,076	$7,213	$623,037

Lender's *IRR* 10%.

EXHIBIT 13–12   Summary of Returns to the Lender and Investor

	Before-Tax IRR	*After-Tax IRR*	*DCR*	*Lender's IRR*
Conventional loan	18.37%	14.30%	1.11	10.00%
Participation loan	18.36%	14.07%	1.25	10.17%

For a participation loan to be attractive to the lender, the expected rate of return to the lender, which is also the effective cost of the loan, must be attractive relative to the interest rate available on conventional loans. In this case, the lender's *IRR*, considering both debt service and participation payments, is about 10 percent.[5] This is the same as the conventional loan, which would also provide the lender with a 10 percent *IRR* (the same as the interest rate on the loan because there are no points.)

Although the lender's *IRR* is also about the same for each alternative, the reader should note that the *DCR* for the first year is 1.25 for the participation loan, whereas it is only 1.11 for the conventional loan. Recall that lenders typically require a *DCR* of at least 1.2. Thus the participation loan might be much more acceptable to the lender. This payment pattern may also be preferred by the investor because the pattern on debt service (regular mortgage payment plus the participation) is a better match with the pattern of *NOI*. In an inflationary environment, the nominal increase in *NOI* will be greater than the real increase in *NOI*. The reader should recall our discussion in Chapter 5 of problems associated with a constant payment mortgage in an inflationary environment. A participating mortgage helps alleviate the tilt effect by allowing the nominal debt service to start at a lower amount than necessary for a conventional loan, and then increase in nominal terms as a function of the nominal increase in the *NOI*.

Note that because part of the lender's return is dependent on the likelihood of income being produced by the property, the participation payments are referred to as *contingent* interest. Because the contingent interest is contingent on the performance of the property and its ability to produce income, this interest is also tax deductible, as shown in Exhibit 13–11. Thus, one feature of a participation loan is that the entire participation payment is tax deductible, whereas only the interest portion of a conventional loan is deductible. However, because the amount of participation is lower during the early years in this case, the present value of the interest deductions on the conventional loan is greater than the present value of the deductions for interest and participation payments on the participation loan. This results in an after-tax *IRR* ($ATIRR_E$) that is lower for the participation loan even though the before-tax *IRR* ($BTIRR_E$) is virtually the same for each loan alternative. Exhibit 13–12 summarizes the *IRR*s for each financing alternative. The *DCR* for each case (based on first-year cash flows) is also shown.

---

[5]This is found by calculating the interest rate which equates the amount of loan ($700,000) with the present value of *both* the debt service paid each year ($80,275) *plus* the participation paid each year *plus* the loan balance and participation paid at the end of the holding period. The cash flows differ each year due to the participation. The answer we calculated (10.17%) was based on the assumption that the debt service and participation were paid monthly.

From the foregoing analysis, it appears that the participation loan is a viable alternative to the conventional loan. The lender receives virtually the same *IRR,* and the *DCR* is higher. The expected *BTIRR* for the investor is also virtually the same for each, and the expected *ATIRR* is only slightly less. Furthermore, the borrower might have difficulty obtaining the conventional loan due to the low *DCR*.

SALE-AND-LEASEBACK OF THE LAND

Up to this point in this chapter we have considered alternative ways of financing acquisition of a property (land and building). We have assumed that both the land and building are financed with the same loan. It is possible, however, to obtain financing on the building only (e.g., with the building as collateral for the loan). A separate loan may be obtained on the land, or the land may be financed with a land lease. That is, the investor would own the building but lease the land from a different investor. If the land is already owned, the land can be sold with a simultaneous agreement to lease the land from the party it is sold to. This is referred to as a *sale-and-leaseback of the land.* Either way, the investor is, in effect, financing the land.

To illustrate the use of a sale-and-leaseback of the land, we will use the same example used in the previous section. We now assume that the land could be sold for $100,000 and leased back at an annual payment of $7,800 per year for 25 years. The building would be financed for $630,000 (70 percent of the *building* value) at a 10 percent rate and a 15-year term. The amount of equity invested is therefore equal to the purchase price ($1,000,000) less the price the land was sold for ($100,000) less the amount of loan on the building ($630,000), resulting in equity of $270,000. The cash flows for this alternative are shown in Exhibit 13–13. Note that the resale price is now lower because only the building is being sold.[6]

There are several reasons an investor may find a sale-and-leaseback an attractive financing alternative. First, it is, in effect, a way of obtaining 100 percent financing on the land. For example, if a loan is made on the entire property (land and building) for 70 percent of the value, then this also amounts to a 70 percent loan on the land. With the sale-and-leaseback, funds would be received in an amount equal to 100 percent of the value of the land. Instead of a mortgage payment on the land, the investor would make lease payments on the land.

A second benefit of a sale-and-leaseback is that lease payments are tax deductible. Recall that with a mortgage only the interest is tax deductible (not the principal portion of the payment).

Third, whereas the building can be depreciated for tax purposes, the land cannot be depreciated. Thus the investor may deduct the same depreciation charges whether or not

---

[6]It was assumed that the building will still increase in value 3 percent per year, the same rate that the property value (land and building) was assumed to grow. Obviously the building value may grow at a slower rate than the land, with the 3 percent growth rate for the property being a weighted average of the land and building growth rates. Using a rate of 3 percent for the building, the sale price is $(\$900,000)(1.03)^5 = \$1,043,347$.

EXHIBIT 13–13   Sale-and-Leaseback of the Land

	Year				
	1	*2*	*3*	*4*	*5*

Estimates of Cash Flow from Operations

A. Before-tax cash flow

Net operating income	$100,000	$103,000	$106,090	$109,273	$112,551
Less debt service	81,240	81,240	81,240	81,240	81,240
Less land lease payment	7,800	7,800	7,800	7,800	7,800
Before-tax cash flow	$ 10,960	$ 13,960	$ 17,050	$ 20,233	$ 23,511

B. Taxable income or loss

Net operating income (*NOI*)	$100,000	$103,000	$106,090	$109,273	$112,551
Less interest	62,140	60,140	57,931	55,490	52,794
Land lease payment	7,800	7,800	7,800	7,800	7,800
Depreciation	32,727	32,727	32,727	32,727	32,727
Taxable income (loss)	(2,668)	2,332	7,632	13,255	19,230
Tax	$ (747)	$ 653	$ 2,137	$ 3,711	$ 5,384

C. After-tax cash flow

Before-tax cash flow (*BTCF*)	$ 10,960	$ 13,960	$ 17,050	$ 20,233	$ 23,511
Less tax	(747)	653	2,137	3,711	5,384
After-tax cash flow (*ATCF*)	$ 11,707	$ 13,307	$ 14,913	$ 16,521	$ 18,126

Estimates of Cash Flow from Sale in Year 5

Sale price			$1,043,347
Less mortgage balance			512,295
Before-tax cash flow			$ 531,052
Taxes in year of sale			
Sale price		$1,043,347	
Original cost basis	$900,000		
Accumulated depreciation	163,636		
Adjusted basis		736,364	
Capital gain		$ 306,983	
Tax from sale			85,955
After-tax cash flow from sale (*ATCF$_s$*)			$ 445,097

Cash Flow Summary

	End of Year					
	0	*1*	*2*	*3*	*4*	*5*
Before-tax cash flow	$ − 270.000	$10,960	$13,960	$17,050	$20,233	$554,563
After-tax cash flow	− 270,000	11,707	13,307	14,913	16,521	463,223

Before-tax *IRR* = 19.16%
After-tax *IRR*   = 14.98%

the land is owned. Because, as discussed above, less equity is required with a sale-and-leaseback of the land, the sale-and-leaseback results in the same depreciation for a smaller equity investment.

Finally, the investor may have the option to purchase the land back at the end of the lease. This provides the investor the opportunity to regain ownership of the land if it is desirable to do so.

Whether or not the sale-and-leaseback is a desirable financing alternative depends on the "cost" of obtaining funds this way. One of the obvious costs is the lease payments that must be made. Another aspect of the cost is the "opportunity cost" associated with any appreciation in the value of the land over the holding period. That is, by doing a sale-and-leaseback the investor gives up the opportunity to sell the land at the end of the holding period along with the building.

Effective Cost of the Sale-and-Leaseback

Calculating the effective cost of the sale-and-leaseback (before-tax return to the investor who purchases the land) is similar to the calculation for other financing alternatives. However, we must consider the opportunity cost of the proceeds from sale of the land.

When the land is sold at the time of the sale leaseback, $100,000 is received by the building investor. During the five years of the holding period, lease payments of $7,800 are made. At the end of the five-year holding period, the investor receives $115,927 *less* than if he had not done the sale-and-leaseback (Exhibit 13–13). That is, the entire property could be sold for $1,159,274 without the sale-and-leaseback (see Exhibit 13–11). In other words, if the sale-and-leaseback is used, the building alone will sell for $1,043,347 at the end of the holding period. The difference is $115,927. We can now solve for the effective cost as follows:

$$100,000 = 7,800 \ (MPVIFA, \ ?\%, \ 5 \ \text{yrs.}) + 115,927 \ (MPVIF, \ ?\%, \ 5 \ \text{yrs.})$$

The resulting yield rate is 10.25 percent. Thus the cost of the sale-and-leaseback of the land (return to the purchaser-lessor of the land) is 10.25 percent, which is about 25 percentage points more than the conventional loan. At the same time, the building investor's return on equity invested is greater than that for a straight loan. Furthermore, the lender on the building is still receiving the 10 percent return that would have been available on a straight loan on the land and building, and the building lender's risk is slightly less if the land lease is subordinated to the building loan.

SUMMARY SALE-AND-LEASEBACK VERSUS OTHER ALTERNATIVES

One way to compare the sale-and-leaseback with other financing alternatives, such as the conventional loan and participation loan considered earlier, is to compare the *IRR*s for each alternative. Exhibit 13–14 contains results for the *IRR*s for the alternatives considered earlier along with that for the sale-and-leaseback of the land. In this case we see that the

EXHIBIT 13–14 Summary of Performance Measures

	$BTIRR_E$	$ATIRR_E$	DCR	IRR_D*
Straight loan	18.37%	14.30%	1.11	10.00%
Participation loan	18.36%	14.07%	1.25	10.17%
Sale leaseback of land	19.16%	14.98%	1.12†	10.25%‡

*Based on monthly cash flows for debt service and participation payments.

†Includes land lease payment with debt service. The *DCR* is 1.23 when land lease payments are not included.

‡This is the yield to the purchaser of the land who provides the sale leaseback financing. The yield (IRR_D) on the building loan is 10 percent.

before- and after-tax returns for the sale-and-leaseback are higher than the conventional loan and higher than participations. Why is the investor's *IRR* higher? This occurs for several reasons. First of all, the effective cost of receiving funds by using the sale-and-leaseback is 10.25 percent, which is only slightly higher than the conventional loan. Second, less equity ($30,000) is required when there is a sale-and-leaseback of the land. This is because equity is only needed for the building. Finally, the payments on the land lease are less than debt service on a loan on the land. This is because there is no amortization involved with the sale-and-leaseback. Furthermore, a significant portion of the cost of the sale-and-leaseback is reflected in the opportunity cost associated with the increase in land value. But this opportunity cost is not a factor until the property is sold.

The debt coverage ratio for the sale-and-leaseback is 1.2, which is about the same as a conventional loan. This is calculated with the land lease payments added to the mortgage payments in the calculation of the *DCR*. The sale-and-leaseback of the land is usually done with an investor that is different from the lender that provides a loan on the building. Furthermore, the land lease payments might be subordinated to the loan on the building loan. This means that the lender on the building has first priority to be paid from the *NOI*. Thus, from the building lender's point of view, the debt coverage ratio is even higher, 1.23 in this case.

CONCLUSION

This chapter illustrated the concept of financial leverage and discussed the conditions for favorable leverage on both before-tax and after-tax bases. It was also shown that the use of financial leverage in the hopes of increasing the rate of return on equity is *not riskless*. That is, increasing the level of debt increases the riskiness of the investment. This was illustrated by showing that debt increases the variance of the rate of returns. Thus when investors use leverage they must consider whether the additional risk is commensurate with the higher expected return (assuming positive leverage).

Financial leverage deals with the *amount* of financing. The chapter also discussed several financing alternatives, including different types of participation loans as well as a sale-and-leaseback of the land. We also considered the effect of each of these alternatives on the investor's cash flows, rates of return, and the debt coverage ratio. The effective cost of each alternative was also calculated. These calculations are used to make decisions regarding the type of financing alternative to choose (i.e., the *structure* of the debt).

It is impossible to discuss all the possible types of financing alternative. However, the concepts discussed in this chapter should help the reader analyze any alternative encountered in practice.

QUESTIONS

1. What is financial leverage? Why is a one-year measure of return on investment inadequate in determining whether positive or negative financial leverage exists?
2. What is the break-even mortgage interest rate (*BEIR*) when viewed in the context of financial leverage? Would you ever expect an investor to pay a break-even interest rate when financing a property? Why or why not?
3. What is meant by *positive* and *negative* financial leverage? How are returns or losses magnified as the degree of leverage is increased? How does leverage on a before-tax basis differ from leverage on an after-tax basis?
4. In what way does leverage increase the riskiness of a loan?
5. What is meant by a participation loan? What does the lender participate in? Why would a lender want to make a participation loan? Why would an investor want to obtain a participation loan?
6. What is meant by a sale-and-leaseback? Why would a building investor want to do a sale-and-leaseback of the land? What is the benefit to the party that purchases the land under a sale-and-leaseback?
7. Why might an investor prefer a loan with a lower interest rate and a participation?
8. Why might a lender prefer a loan with a lower interest rate and a participation?
9. How do you think participations affect the riskiness of a loan?
10. What is the motivation for a sale-and-leaseback of the land?
11. What criteria should be used to choose between two financing alternatives?
12. What is the traditional cash equivalency approach to determine how below market rate loans affect value?
13. How can the effect of below market rate loans on value be determined using investor criteria?

PROBLEMS

1. K. C. Sunshine is concerned over a financing problem he is currently facing. He would like to purchase a new warehouse-office property for $2,000,000. However, he is faced with the decision over whether he should use 65 percent or 75 percent financing. The 65 percent loan can be obtained at 10 percent interest for 25 years. The 75 percent loan can be obtained at 11 percent interest for 25 years.

   NOI is expected to be $190,000 per year and increase at 3 percent annually, the same rate at which the building is expected to increase in value. The building and improvements represent 80 percent of value and will be depreciated over 31.5 years

(1/31.5 per year). The project is expected to be sold after five years. Sunshine's tax bracket is 28 percent.

a. What would the *BTIRR* and *ATIRR* be at each level of financing (assume annual mortgage amortization)?

b. What is the break-even interest rate (*BEIR*) for this project?

c. What is the marginal cost of the 75 percent loan? What does this mean?

d. Is there favorable financial leverage for each loan? Which would you recommend?

2. Bette Fidler is considering the purchase of a shopping center complex. However, interest rates have just risen very sharply in a matter of months, and she is concerned as to whether the project is financially feasible.

Mutual of Bigrock Insurance Company has made a 75 percent loan proposal to Fidler. The proposal calls for a base interest rate of 10 percent for 25 years and an equity participation of 40 percent in cash flow over break-even (or the excess of cash flow remaining after the base debt service is subtracted from *NOI*) for a period of 10 years. In the event the loan is repaid before that time, a prepayment penalty of 10 percent of the outstanding loan balance (based on 10 percent amortization) will be required.

The property is expected to cost $5,500,000. *NOI* is estimated to be $475,000, including overages during the first year, and to increase at the rate of 5 percent per year for the next five years. Fidler estimates she will be able to realize $6,000,000 at that time. The improvement represents 80 percent of cost, and depreciation will be based on the current tax law. Bette is in the 28 percent tax bracket. She has approached you for advice on this project. She plans to hold the project for five years and sell.

a. Compute the *BTIRR* and *ATIRR* after five years, taking into account the equity participation.

b. What would the *BEIR* be on such a project? What is the projected cost of the equity participation financing, including the prepayment penalty?

c. Is there favorable leverage with the proposed loan?

3. Use the same information as problem 3 in Chapter 12. Now assume a loan for $1,500,000 is obtained at a 10 percent interest rate and a 15-year term.

a. Calculate the expected *IRR* on equity and the standard deviation of the return on equity.

b. Contrast the results from part *a* with those from problem 3 in Chapter 12. Has the loan increased the risk? Explain.

Appendix: Alternative Loan Structures—Income Producing Properties

The reader should recall the discussion of expected inflation and its effect on interest rates from Chapters 5 and 6. In those chapters we also discussed the evolution of Graduated Payment and Adjustable Rate Mortgages (*GPMs* and *ARMs*) in response to the tilt effect. We indicated that one of the reasons why these mortgage instruments developed was because of a need for repayment terms that would enable households to qualify for loans during periods of rising interest rates. Investors desiring to purchase income producing properties also face problems when interest rates suddenly increase. What follows is a discussion of how loan terms on mortgages being negotiated by such borrowers may be modified during periods of rising interest rates. The reader will recognize many of the concepts developed in Chapters 5 and 6 in application involving income producing properties.

To introduce some of the more generic approaches to structuring loan terms for income properties during periods of rising interest rates, we begin with the basic example shown in Exhibit 13A–1. This exhibit is based on a conventional, fully amortizing, fixed interest rate loan made for 75 percent of the purchase price ($1,000,000). The interest rate is 10 percent, and the amortization period is 25 years, however, the loan will mature at the end of 10 years.[1] Projections indicate that during the first year, the debt coverage ratio (*DCR*) will be 1.20. Further, the coverage ratio is expected to improve with time, as net operating income is projected to increase at 3 percent per year. Note that by year 5, the *DCR* is 1.35. Based on the projections shown in Exhibit 13A–1, and assuming that all other assumptions are acceptable, a lender would have little problem underwriting the $750,000 loan request because of the very favorable debt coverage ratio.

Exhibit 13A–2 shows what happens to the projections when inflation is assumed to be two percent higher each year, resulting in an increase in the nominal interest rate to 12 percent from 10 percent. Note that when the interest rate in this example increases to 12 percent, debt service increases from $6,815.26 per month ($81,783 per year) shown in Exhibit 13A–1 to $7,899.18 per month ($94,790 per year). The *DCR* shown in Exhibit 13A–2 falls to 1.03 during the first year, or to a level that would be unacceptable to most lenders. Even when the two percent increase in inflation is reflected in both the net operating income and the property value (note the increase from 3 percent to 5 percent for each beginning in year 2 in Exhibit 13A–2), debt coverage does not materially improve until year 4. Hence, the short term effect on the *DCR* makes it difficult for lenders to make loans. This is true even though vacancy rates may be very low and tenant demand for space may be excellent. The reader should also note that if the expected increase in inflation actually occurred as projected in the exhibit, the *spread* between the before-tax yield to the lender and yield to the investor shown in Exhibit 13A–2 would remain approximately the same as it was in Exhibit 13A–1. (In Exhibit 13A–1 the lender's yield is 10 percent and the investor's yield is 19.5 percent. In Exhibit 13A–2 these yields increase to 12 percent and 20.92 percent, respectively.) In other words, over the five year period of analysis, the nominal return to the lender and investor increase, however, the pattern of cash flows is considerably different. Thus, it is entirely possible for a project to remain economically feasible and profitable because of strong demand for rental space, but because of sudden changes in interest rates they appear not to be financially feasible when being underwritten for a loan (due to the low *DCR* during the initial years).

---

[1] Prior to the 1980s, it was possible to obtain loans with maturities ranging from 15 to 25 years. Since then however, most fixed-interest rate loans on income properties have been made with maturities ranging from 5 to 15 years. This is because lenders have generally been unwilling to accept the interest-rate risk on long-term loans made at fixed rates of interest. By requiring shorter loan maturities on fixed interest rate loans, lenders preserve the option of being able to either refinance loans with existing borrowers or to reinvest funds from loan repayments at prevailing interest rates more frequently. These shorter-term loans have come to be called "bullet loans". They generally include a monthly amortization schedule of 25 to 30 years, even though the loan balance will be "called", or mature, 5 to 15 years after origination. Some loans, when made for very short terms, say five years, will be made on an "interest only" basis, with the full loan amount coming due at that time.

EXHIBIT 13A–1 Conventional Loan, 10 Percent Interest Rate

Purchase price	$1,000,000
Loan to value	75%
Interest rate	10%
Amortization period	25 years
Maturity	10 years
Annual increase in *NOI*	3.00%
Annual increase in value	3.00%
Monthly payment	$6,815.26

		End of Year			
	1	2	3	4	5
NOI	$ 98,000	$ 100,940	$ 103,968	$ 107,087	$ 110,300
Debt service	81,783	81,783	81,783	81,783	81,783
BTCF	$ 16,217	$ 19,157	$ 22,185	$ 25,304	$ 28,517
DCR	1.20	1.23	1.27	1.31	1.35
Sale price	$1,030,000	$1,060,900	$1,092,727	$1,125,509	$1,159,274
Mortgage balance	742,898	735,051	726,383	716,807	706,229

		Investor Before-Tax Cash Flow Summary			
	0	1	2	3	4	5
Equity	($250,000)					
BTCF		$ 16,217	$ 19,157	$ 22,185	$ 25,304	$ 28,517
BTCFs						453,045
Total	($250,000)	$ 16,217	$ 19,157	$ 22,185	$ 25,304	$ 481,562

Investor *BTIRR* = 19.50%
Lender *BTIRR* = 10.00%

MODIFYING LOAN TERMS—INTEREST ONLY LOANS

In an attempt to structure loan repayments that are acceptable to lenders and borrowers in such circumstances, one approach that is commonly used is to make a loan with "interest only" payments. By making a monthly payment that includes only interest and no amortization of principal, the debt service will obviously be lower. Further, because no amortization is required, the ratio of *NOI* to debt service (or *DCR*) will improve.[2] Note in Exhibit 13A–3 that if monthly payments of (.12 ÷ 12) × $750,000, or $7,500 per month are made, the debt service coverage would improve from 1.03 to 1.09. Of course, there would be no reduction in the loan balance while the interest only payments are being made. If a lender believed the 1.09 coverage would provide a sufficient amount of protection against borrower default and that the property value should increase, such a loan might be made. However if the loan was made, payments would not remain interest only

---

[2]Obviously, another approach to improving the *DCR*, would be for the borrower to make a smaller loan. However, the borrower would have to make a larger down payment which may not be possible. Further, a lower loan amount would reduce the expected benefits of financial leverage.

EXHIBIT 13A–2   Conventional Loan, 12 Percent Interest Rate

Purchase price	$1,000,000
Loan to value	75%
Interest rate	12%
Amortization period	25 years
Maturity	10 years
Annual increase in *NOI*	5.00%
Annual increase in value	5.00%
Monthly payment	$7,899.18

	Year				
	1	*2*	*3*	*4*	*5*
NOI	$ 98,000	$ 102,900	$ 108,045	$ 113,447	$ 119,119
Debt service	94,790	94,790	94,790	94,790	94,790
BTCF	$ 3,210	$ 8,110	$ 13,255	$ 18,657	$ 24,329
DCR	1.03	1.09	1.14	1.20	1.26
Sale price	$1,050,000	$1,102,500	$1,157,625	$1,215,506	$1,276,282
Mortgage balance	744,937	739,233	732,804	725,561	717,399

Investor Before-Tax Cash Flow Summary

	0	*1*	*2*	*3*	*4*	*5*
Equity	($250,000)					
BTCF		$ 3,210	$ 8,110	$ 13,255	$ 18,657	$ 24,329
BTCFs						558,883
Total	($250,000)	$ 3,210	$ 8,110	$ 13,255	$ 18,657	$ 583,212

Investor *BTIRR* = 20.92%
Lender *BTIRR* = 12.00%

---

indefinitely. A common condition for making such a loan would be for amortization to begin as cash flows improve, such as they do in years 3 through 5 (note that the *DCR* ranges from 1.20 to 1.32 during that period). Amortization would usually be based on a schedule of from 20 to 25 years. The loan would generally mature at the end of 5 to 10 additional years.

USING DEFERRED INTEREST TO MEET DEBT COVERAGE RATIO TARGETS

Lowering the Pay Rate Relative to the Accrual Rate.   In the event that the interest only loan illustrated in Exhibit 13A–3 would not provide adequate debt service coverage for the lender, loan payments may be structured to meet a target debt coverage ratio. Any interest deficiency would then be deferred and added to the loan balance to assure that the lender would earn a specified rate of interest. One approach that is used to achieve this goal is to select a rate to compute payments (referred to as a "payment rate" or "pay rate") which is less than the rate used to calculate interest on a loan (referred to as the "accrual rate"). The pay rate will be lowered until payments are reduced to a sufficiently low level in order to meet debt coverage requirements. Any interest

EXHIBIT 13A–3   Interest Only Loan, 12 Percent Interest Rate

Purchase price	$1,000,000		
Loan to value	75%		
Interest rate	12%		
Maturity	10 years		
Annual increase in *NOI*	5.00%		
Annual increase in value	5.00%		
Monthly payment	$7,500.00		

	Year				
	1	*2*	*3*	*4*	*5*
NOI	$ 98,000	$ 102,900	$ 108,045	$ 113,447	$ 119,119
Debt service	90,000	90,000	90,000	90,000	90,000
BTCF	$ 8,000	$ 12,900	$ 18,045	$ 23,447	$ 29,119
DCR	1.09	1.14	1.20	1.26	1.32
Sale price	$1,050,000	$1,102,500	$1,157,625	$1,215,506	$1,276,281
Mortgage balance	750,000	750,000	750,000	750,000	750,000

	Investor Before-Tax Cash Flow Summary				
	0	*1*	*2*	*3*	*4*	*5*
Equity	($250,000)					
BTCF		$ 8,000	$ 12,900	$ 18,045	$ 23,447	$ 29,119
BTCFs						526,281
Total	($250,000)	$ 8,000	$ 12,900	$ 18,045	$ 23,447	$ 555,400

Investor *BTIRR* = 21.07%
Lender *BTIRR* = 12.00%

deficiency (negative amortization) will then be added to the loan balance, plus interest on all deficiencies.

To illustrate, Exhibit 13A–4 contains a modification to the examples used in Exhibit 13A–2 and 13A–3. In this case, the initial pay rate on the loan is 10.5 percent, while the accrual rate is 12 percent. That is, payments are calculated by multiplying the outstanding loan balance by 10.5 percent. However, interest is calculated by multiplying the outstanding balance by 12 percent. The 10.5 percent pay rate is chosen because monthly payments based on that rate will result in a *DCR* of 1.24 in year 1, which is in the range desired by the lender. Note also in Exhibit 13A–4 that the pay rate of 10.5 percent will provide payments for the first year in an amount of $6,562.50 per month ($78,750 per year). However, based on the contract or accrual rate, interest owed will be (.12 ÷ 12) × $750,000 or $7,500 per month. Hence, payments made based on the pay rate of $6,562.50 per month will be less than 12 percent interest on the loan balance. In order for the lender to earn a required yield of 12 percent, interest will be deferred and added to the loan balance. Further, all interest amounts that are deferred must also earn interest at the required 12 percent interest rate. (Recall from Chapter 5 that when dealing with single family mortgages, this was referred to as "negative amortization"). Hence, at the end of the first month, the interest deficiency will be $7,500 − $6,562.50 or $937.50. This monthly amount, when compounded for 12 months at an annual rate of 12 percent yields total deferred interest of $11,889.85. When this amount is

EXHIBIT 13A–4 Deferred Interest Loan—Payment Rate Less Than Accrual Rate

Purchase price	$1,000,000	
Loan to value	75%	
Accrual rate	12.00%	
Amortization period	25 years (beginning in year 5)	
Maturity	10 years	
Annual increase in *NOI*	5.00%	
Annual increase in value	5.00%	

	Year				
	1	*2*	*3*	*4*	*5*
NOI	$ 98,000	$ 102,900	$ 108,045	$ 113,447	$ 119,119
Debt service	78,750	83,808	88,543	92,881	97,825
BTCF	$ 19,250	$ 19,092	$ 19,502	$ 20,566	$ 21,294
DCR	1.24	1.23	1.22	1.22	1.22
Accrual rate	12.00%	12.00%	12.00%	12.00%	12.00%
Pay rate	10.50%	11.00%	11.50%	12.00%	12.00%
Sale price	$1,050,000	$1,102,500	$1,157,625	$1,215,506	$1,276,281
Mortgage balance	761,890	769,942	774,011	774,011	768,786

	Investor Before-Tax Cash Flow Summary					
	0	*1*	*2*	*3*	*4*	*5*
Equity	($250,000)					
BTCF		$ 19,250	$ 19,092	$ 19,502 $	20,566 $	21,294
BTCFs						507,495
Total	($250,000) $	19,250	$ 19,092	$ 19,502 $	20,566 $	528,789

Investor *BTIRR*	=	21.37%
Lender *BTIRR*	=	12.00%
Year amortization starts	=	5

added to the initial loan balance of $750,000, the balance at the end of year 1, or $761,890 (rounded) is determined.

In this case, the borrower and lender may also agree that pay rates will graduate at a rate of .5 percent annually, thereby keeping the *DCR* in a range of 1.20. It should be noted that at the beginning of the fourth year, the pay rate is scheduled to equal to the accrual rate. Also, monthly interest only payments on the outstanding loan balance of $774,011 at the accrual rate (12 percent) will be $7,740.11 (annual payments = $92,881). *NOI* will be $113,447 or sufficient enough to pay interest and to *begin some amortization* of principal, while retaining a desired *DCR* in a range of 1.20. In this example, the amount of *NOI* that is allocated to debt service in year 5 while retaining the desired *DCR* is $119,119 ÷ 1.20 or $99,266 (rounded), which is equal to $8,272 per month. At that point, regularly scheduled fully amortizing payments for a term of *25 years* would be $8,158.30 per month. Thus, monthly payments can be made and regular amortization of principal would begin.

Based on the above exercise, it should be clear that by properly structuring loan terms and selecting a pay rate low enough to provide a satisfactory *DCR,* then graduating that rate, an acceptable *DCR* can be achieved in the initial years of ownership. However, it should be stressed that this structuring would generally be used during periods of high interest rates. The lender would still have to be convinced that market demand for leasable space is strong. If projections of *NOI* do not materialize and scheduled loan payments do not occur, the borrower will be in default. If *NOI* and property values increase as projected, however, the *spread* between the projected yield to the lender and the yield to the borrower remain very close to the initial projections made in Exhibit 13A–1.

Finally, it should be stressed that because interest is being deferred and made a part of the loan balance, the lender is likely to demand a higher rate of interest than would be the case on a straight, or conventional loan.[3] Further, even though the loan is scheduled to start amortizing for a 25-year period during the fifth year, the loan maturity date will still likely be in a range of 10 years. This is because even though the property may be performing well and loan repayments are occurring as scheduled, the lender will prefer to call the loan and refinance it at rates of interest prevailing at that time.

Structuring Payments to Meet Debt Coverage Targets—Deferred Interest Loans.

Another way of deferring interest on a loan when trying to achieve a desired debt coverage ratio is to *structure the payments,* rather than selecting a pay rate to achieve the target *DCR*. In other words, a specified dollar amount is negotiated as the required mortgage payment as opposed to selecting a pay rate to establish the payment when using this approach.

To illustrate this approach to loan structuring, Exhibit 13A–5 contains an example which shows how payments can be constructed to achieve a constant *DCR* of 1.20. This is accomplished by taking *NOI* during year 1, or $98,000 and dividing by 1.20 to find the maximum dollar amount of debt service that can be paid, while still retaining the *DCR* at 1.20. That amount is $6,805.58 per month ($81,667 annually). Hence, by setting initial monthly payments at that amount, then increasing them at the end of each year by the same rate that *NOI* is expected to grow, a constant *DCR* is achieved. However, like the previous case which utilized the pay rate approach, deferred interest must also be considered as a part of the structuring.

Recall that monthly interest at 12 percent is equal to $7,500, which when compared to the actual payments of $6,805.58 results in $694.42 in deferred interest during year 1. Of course, interest must also be earned on this amount at a rate of 12 percent and added to the loan balance. At the end of the first year then, $694.42 compounded at a rate of 12% ÷ 12 per month for 12 months yields $8,807 (rounded) in deferred interest. This amount, when added to the original loan amount of $750,000, yields the ending balance for the first year of $758,807.

Looking to year 2 in Exhibit 13A–5, payments are scheduled to increase at 5 percent, or to $7,145.86 per month. This means that (12% ÷ 12) × $758,807 less $7,145.86, or $442.21 must be accrued each month. When compounded in the same way as explained above, the addition to the previous year's loan balance will be $5,608.34 yielding an outstanding balance of $764,416 (rounded) at the end of year 2. This process continues until the 5 percent increases in payments are sufficiently high enough to cover interest requirements. This occurs during year 4, when scheduled monthly payments are $7,878.33 and interest requirements are $766,204 × (12% ÷ 12) or $7,662.04. At that point, loan amortization begins in the amount of $216.29 per month. Hence the loan balance declines at the end of year 4 to $763,461. During the fifth year, regular amortization over a 25-year schedule is possible while the *DCR* remains in a desirable range. At

---

[3]We assume a 12% interest rate here to facilitate comparison with other loan structures illustrated in this Appendix.

EXHIBIT 13A–5   Deferred Interest Loan—Payments Structured to Meet Desired Debt Coverage Ratios

Purchase price	$1,000,000
Loan to value	75%
Accrual rate	12%
Amortization period	25 years (3 years interest only)
Maturity	10 years
Desired *DCR*	1.2
Annual increase in *NOI*	5.00%
Annual increase in value	5.00%
Initial monthly payment	$6,805.58

	Year				
	1	*2*	*3*	*4*	*5*
NOI	$ 98,000	$ 102,900	$ 108,045	$ 113,447	$ 119,119
Debt service	81,667	85,750	90,038	94,540	96,491
BTCF	$ 16,333	$ 17,150	$ 18,007	$ 18,907	$ 22,628
DCR	1.20	1.20	1.20	1.20	1.23
Accrual rate	12.00%	12.00%	12.00%	12.00%	12.00%
Sale price	$1,050,000	$1,102,500	$1,157,625	$1,215,506	$1,276,281
Mortgage balance	758,807	764,416	766,204	763,461	758,304

	Investor Before-Tax Cash Flow Summary					
	0	*1*	*2*	*3*	*4*	*5*
Equity	($250,000)					
BTCF		$16,333	$17,150	$18,007	$18,907	$ 22,628
BTCFs						517,977
Total	($250,000)	$16,333	$17,150	$18,007	$18,907	$540,605

Investor *BTIRR*	=	21.28%
Lender *BTIRR*	=	12.00%
Year amortization starts	=	4

the beginning of the fifth year, the loan balance is $763,461 and based on a 12 percent interest rate for 25 remaining years, regular payments of $8,040.96 per month ($96,491 annually) may commence while the *DCR* increases slightly to 1.23. Hence, by structuring payments in this way, both the lender and the borrower may be able to negotiate a satisfactory repayment schedule.

LOAN STRUCTURING SUMMARIZED

Thus far, we have presented a series of alternatives that can be used in loan structuring should the economic and interest rate environment require it. Exhibit 13A–6 provides a comparison of monthly loan payments (panel A) and loan balances (panel B) for all cases considered. It should be clear that when compared to the conventional loan repayment pattern, the trade-off that is made in each case is to lower initial monthly payments. This is done by either making interest only payments and keeping the outstanding loan balance constant, or by deferring interest and allowing the loan

EXHIBIT 13A–6

Panel A: Monthly payments under alternative loan structures

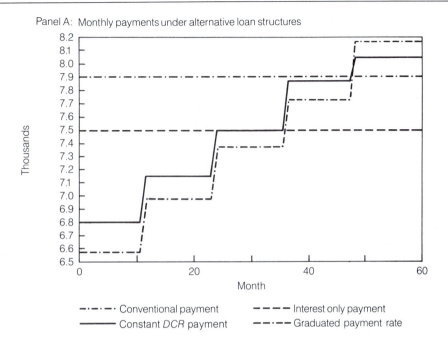

Thousands

Month

 $-\cdot-\cdot-$ Conventional payment $-\,-\,-$ Interest only payment

 $\longrightarrow$ Constant *DCR* payment $-\,-\cdot-$ Graduated payment rate

Panel B: Outstanding balances under alternative loan structures

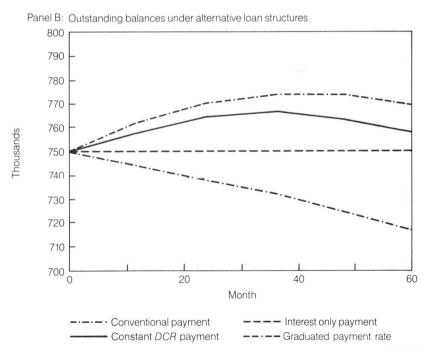

Thousands

Month

 $-\cdot-\cdot-$ Conventional payment $-\,-\,-$ Interest only payment

 $\longrightarrow$ Constant *DCR* payment $-\,-\cdot-$ Graduated payment rate

balance to increase. In all cases the lender will have to judge whether the *DCR* is in a desirable range, whether too much interest is being deferred and whether projected *NOI* will be sufficiently high enough to meet debt service. The reader should also understand that we have presented only a limited number of possibilities regarding structuring of loan terms. Many other terms such as loan to value ratios, loan maturity, rates of amortization, and so forth, may also be varied when considering alternative structures.

It should also be emphasized that many of these same techniques can be used in *loan workouts*, or in situations where the borrower has defaulted on a loan. Rather than foreclosing, taking possession of a property or having it auctioned, the lender may prefer to restructure the loan terms by reducing payments or the interest rate, lengthening the amortization period, deferring interest, or some combination of all of these variables. These changes can be made for a specified period of time, then, as market rents and trends in property values improve, regular payments and amortization would begin again.

BALLOON PAYMENTS—A FINAL NOTE

In the two cases that utilized deferred interest as part of an approach to payment structuring (Exhibit 13A–4 and 13A–5), increasing loan balances were an integral part of those patterns. Generally, when outstanding loan balances increase relative to the initial loan amount and the loan matures, the borrower must make what is referred to as a "balloon payment." This term is frequently used in income property lending when the amount due at maturity from a borrower exceeds the initial amount borrowed.

In cases when fixed interest rate loans are made, balloon payments due on the maturity date can be easily determined by simply manipulating the familiar present value equation that we have used in conjunction with mortgage payment patterns. For example, if we assume that a loan is made for $1,200,000 with a contract rate of 12 percent and payments are scheduled to be $10,000 per month for the first year, $10,500 for the second year and the loan is prepaid after two years, what will the balloon payment be? This can be easily solved. Recall from Chapter 5 that for fixed interest rate loans that the present value of all payments and the outstanding balance for any time interval must equal the initial loan balance. Hence, given the initial loan amount (*MLA*), monthly payments (*MP*) and the discount rate (12 percent), the balloon payment (or mortgage balance, *MB*) may be determined as follows:

$$MLA = MP_1 (MPVIFA, 12\%, 12\,\text{mos.}) + MP_1(1 + .05)^1 (MPVIFA, 12\%, 12\,\text{mos.}) \times$$
$$(MPVIF, 12\%, 12\,\text{mos.}) + MB\,(MPVIF, 12\%, 24\,\text{mos.})$$
$$\$1,200,000 = \$10,000(11.255077) + \$10,500(11.255077)(.887449) + MB(.787566)$$
$$= \$112,550.77 + \$104,877.22 + MB(.787566)$$
$$\$982,572.01 = MB(.787566)$$
$$MB = \$1,247,606 \ (\text{rounded})$$

Based on this calculation,[4] the balloon payment (*MB*) at the end of two years will be $1,247,606 as compared with the initial loan balance of $1,200,000. In practice, the increase in this balance (about 2 percent per year) would be compared to the projected increase in property value to ascertain whether the ending loan to value ratio is acceptable to the lender. This aspect of the analysis when structuring loan repayments is just as important as looking at the debt service coverage ratio. This

---

[4]This solution may also be found by using a financial calculator.

is because if the debt service is materially reduced, debt coverage ratios will obviously improve. However, the deferred interest may cause the balloon payment to rise too high and result in an unacceptable loan to value ratio. This is an additional trade-off that lenders must consider when structuring repayment terms.

In some cases the borrower and lender may, for some reason, agree to set the amount of the *balloon payment first,* then schedule payments needed to provide the lender with the required yield. In our example then, if the borrower and lender set the balloon payment after two years to be a maximum of $1,247,606, we would have the following:

$$\$1,200,000 = MP_1 (11.255077) + MP_1 (1 + .05)^1 \times (11.255077)(.887449)$$
$$+ \$1,247,606(.787566)$$
$$\$217,427.93 = MP_1 (21.742799)$$
$$\$10,000 = MP_1$$

Based on the 5 percent rate of graduation, the mortgage payment in the second year would be $10,000(1.05) or $10,500.

PROBLEMS

A–1 A developer wants to finance a project costing $750,000 with a 70 percent, 25-year loan at an interest rate of 8 percent. The project's *NOI* is expected to be $60,000 during year 1 and the *NOI*, as well as its value, is expected to increase at an annual rate of 3 percent thereafter. The lender will require an initial debt coverage ratio of at least 1.20.

    a. Would the lender be likely to make the developer the loan? Support your answer with a cash flow statement for a five-year period. What would be the developer's before-tax yield on equity (*BTIRR*)?

    b. Suppose that mortgage interest rates suddenly increase from 8 percent to 10 percent. *NOI* and value will now increase at a rate of 5 percent. If the desired *DCR* is 1.20, will the lender be as willing to make a conventional loan now? Support your answer with a cash flow statement.

    c. Assume that the lender is willing to consider an interest only loan. However, a debt coverage ratio of 1.20 will still be required. Would the lender be likely to make the loan now?

    d. Assume that the lender is agreeable to a deferred interest loan, with an initial pay rate of 9 percent which will increase in increments of .25 percent each year until it equals the accrual rate of 10 percent. Payments will be "interest only" until amortization begins. Assume that the lender would like the loan to begin to amortize over a 25-year period after the pay rate reaches 10 percent. However, no amortization will occur unless the *DCR* after payments for the year in which the amortization is to occur is equal to 1.20 or greater. What will the mortgage payments be during the first five years? When will *full* amortization begin? What will be the before-tax yield to the lender and developer? What will be the loan balance at the end of year 5?

    e. Now assume that the mortgage payments in year 1 will be fixed at the level needed to provide the lender with a 1.20 *DCR*. All amounts of deferred interest also earn interest at 10 percent. The payments are scheduled to increase at 5 percent per year until they are large enough to fully amortize the remaining loan balance over a 25-year period and still retain a *DCR* of at least 1.20. What will the monthly payments be? What year will amortization start? How does this structure differ from that described in part (*d*)?

A–2 Ace Development Company is trying to structure a loan with the First National Bank. Ace would like to purchase a property for $2,500,000. The property is projected to produce a first year *NOI* of $200,000. The lender will only allow up to a 75 percent loan on the property, and requires a *DCR* in the first year of at least 1.25. All loan payments are to be made monthly, but will increase by 7.5 percent at the beginning of each year for 5 years. The contract rate of interest on the loan is 12 percent. The lender is willing to allow the loan to negatively amortize, however the loan will mature at the end of the 5-year period.

    a. What will the balloon payment be at the end of the fifth year?

    b. If the balloon payment in part (*a*), is retained, and the first year's *NOI* fell by 10 percent, how much debt could the property support and still maintain the lender's requirement of a 1.25 *DCR*?

A–3 Certainty Asset Management Corp. wants to purchase multifamily property for $1,000,000 and operate it for 4 years. The Last National Bank of Texas has agreed to be the lender on the project if the loan can be structured as follows. Certainty agrees to: (1) make 48 monthly payments which will increase annually the rate of 5 percent and (2) make a balloon payment at the end of the 48th month equal to 115 percent of the initial loan balance (the lender is willing to allow the loan to negatively amortize up to this limit). If Certainty agrees to the terms of the loan, the bank will underwrite a loan on the property for up to 70 percent of the initial purchase price with a contract interest rate of 13 percent.

    a. Given the terms of the loan agreement, what will be the initial monthly payment? What will be the monthly payment at the beginning of the fourth year?

Chapter 14

Valuation of Income Properties

A key consideration when financing or investing in income-producing properties is the market value of the property. A property's market value is the basis for the lending decision because the property will be either the full or partial security for the loan. When making investment decisions, the investor will not normally want to pay more than the market value of the property. Similarly, the lender will not want to loan more than a proportion of the market value of the property because if the property must eventually be sold due to foreclosure of the loan, it would probably not sell for more than its market value. In the context of real estate finance, appraisal reports on properties are a part of the documentation required by lenders when considering whether to make mortgage loans. Because lenders and borrowers-investors use appraisals in decision making, they should be familiar with the generally accepted approaches to appraisal or valuation. The purpose of this chapter is to explain the appraisal process and the three approaches ordinarily used in valuation.

APPRAISAL PROCESS

An appraisal is an *estimate* of value. In making this estimate, appraisers use a systematic approach. First, they ascertain the physical and legal identification of the property involved. Second, they identify the property rights to be appraised or valued. For example, the property rights being valued may involve fee simple ownership of the property or something less than fee simple such as a leased fee estate. Third, appraisers specify the purpose of the appraisal. Besides an estimate of market value, appraisals are also made in such situations as those involving condemnation of property, insurance losses, and property tax assessments. Fourth, appraisers specify the effective date of the estimate of value. Since market conditions change from time to time, the estimate must be related to a specific date. Fifth, appraisers must gather and analyze market data, then apply appropriate techniques to derive the estimate of value. This process is the main concern of this chapter.

In the appraisal process, a considerable amount of market data must be collected and analyzed. Market data on rents, costs, vacancies, supply and demand factors, expenses, and any other data considered to be an important influence on property values must be collected, summarized, and interpreted by the analyst when making an estimate of value. It is not the intent of this book to cover how to conduct market studies and to collect data for making appraisals. In real estate finance, it is more commonly the case that lenders, borrowers, and investors will use the appraisal report to make lending and investment decisions. However, the user must understand the approach used by the appraiser in estimating value. By understanding these approaches, the user will be in a better position to decide whether the appropriate market data has been used and whether appropriate techniques have been used to estimate the value.

APPROACHES TO VALUATION

The role of appraisals cannot be overemphasized because appraised values are used as a basis for lending and investing. Methods and procedures used in establishing values are thoroughly reviewed and evaluated by lenders to prevent overborrowing on properties and by investors to avoid overpaying for properties. Lenders want to be assured that both the initial property value and the pattern of property value over time exceed the outstanding loan balance for any given property over the term of the loan.

In income property appraisals at least two of three approaches are normally used: the *cost approach,* the *market approach,* and the *income capitalization approach.* The essentials of each approach are reviewed here to provide insight into the process followed by appraisers in establishing the values considered as a basis for financing by lenders.

Cost approach

The rationale for using the cost approach to valuing (appraising) properties is that any informed buyer of real estate would not pay more for a property than what it would cost to buy the land and build the structure. For a new property the cost approach ordinarily involves determining the construction cost of building a given improvement, then adding the market value of the land. In the case of existing buildings, the cost of replacing the building is first estimated. This estimate is reduced by estimating any physical, functional, or economic depreciation (discussed below) in arriving at the estimated value of the building. This approach is procedurally identical to the cost approach detailed in the chapter on residential financing. In the case of income-producing property, however, structural design and equipment variations and locational influences make the cost estimation process much more complex. Consequently, the cost approach may at times be difficult to apply, particularly if the property is not new.

Many techniques can be used in conjunction with the cost approach to value. The technique chosen to estimate value will generally depend on (1) the age of the structure being valued, (2) whether the structure is highly specialized in design or function, and (3) the availability of data to be used for cost estimating. Generally if a project is in the proposal stage, cost data will be developed from plans and drawings by an appraiser or

EXHIBIT 14-1 Cost Breakdown—Hypothetical Office-Warehouse Complex (73,500 square feet): (8,000 office, 65,500 warehouse; 3 land acres; projected economic life 50 years)

Component	Cost	PSF
Hard Costs		
Excavation—back fill	$ 31,500	
Foundation	47,250	
Framing (steel)	160,500	
Corrugated steel exterior walls	267,750	
Brick facade (front)—glass	51,000	
Floor finishing, concrete	61,000	
Floor covering offices	17,500	
Roof trusses, covering	115,040	
Interior finish offices	57,400	
Lighting Fixtures, electrical work	83,400	
Plumbing	114,500	
Heating–A/C	157,500	
Interior cranes, scales	139,060	
Loading docks, rail extension	96,000	
Onsite parking, streets, gutters	176,000	
Subtotal	$1,575,000	$21.43
Soft Costs		
Architect, attorney, accounting	$ 200,000	
Construction interest	125,000	
Builder profit	250,000	
Subtotal	$ 575,000	
Land cost (by comparison)	$ 350,000	
Value per cost approach	$2,500,000	$34.00

estimator.[1] If a project is in the proposal stage, specifications for material and equipment will have been set out in detail, usually making it possible to arrive at a relatively accurate cost estimate. Exhibit 14–1 contains a breakdown of direct and indirect costs for a hypothetical office-warehouse complex which is in the proposal state of development. The cost breakdown shown in Exhibit 14–1 is based on categories that generally correspond to how various subcontractors would make bid estimates on improvements. This procedure is quite common for new, nontechnical construction.

---

[1]Cost estimation services are available for use by appraisers. Companies providing such services are the Marshall and Swift Company and the Boeckh Division of the American Appraisal Company.

In addition to the hard-cost categories shown in Exhibit 14–1 for our hypothetical office-warehouse complex, we see two additional categories. One represents a soft-cost category, which includes estimated outlays for services and intangible costs necessary when designing and developing a project. The other category represents land cost. Estimates of land value are made from comparisons with other, recent, land sales. These sales should be based on transactions where the land is *comparable* to the land underlying the improvement which is being valued.

In cases where the project to be appraised includes an *existing* improvement, the detailed cost breakdown shown in Exhibit 14–1 is more difficult to use. The reason is that the problem of physical and economic depreciation on the component parts must be estimated by the appraiser. Generally, when the cost approach to value is used for an existing improvement, the cost to replace the improvement is made and adjusted downward for depreciation caused by (1) physical deterioration, (2) functional or structural obsolescence due to the availability of more efficient layout designs and technological changes that reduce operating costs, and (3) economic depreciation which may result from style changes and external influences such as excessive traffic, noise, or pollution. These three categories of depreciation are very difficult to determine and, in many cases, require the judgment of appraisers who specialize in such problems. This particularly applies to industrial properties, special-use facilities such as public buildings, and properties that are bought and sold infrequently.

To illustrate how adjustments must be made to reflect physical, functional, and economic depreciation, we consider a different property, a 15-year-old office-warehouse complex. The improvement, if constructed today and ''costed out'' at *current prices* using a procedure similar to that shown in Exhibit 14–1, would be $1,750,000. However, because the structure is 15 years old, certain adjustments must be made for necessary repairs, changes in design technology, and depreciation, as shown in Exhibit 14–2.

The essence of the cost approach for existing properties is first to price the improvement at its current replacement cost. Then that amount is reduced by any costs (a) that can be expended to upgrade the improvement or to cure obvious deterioration due mainly to needed maintenance or (b) that correspond to the economic loss associated with nonrepairable (or incurable) factors due to changes in design or layout efficiency that may make newer buildings less expensive to operate.

Hence, in our example, the appraiser estimates that a purchaser of the property would have to incur a cost of $47,700 simply to replace worn-out items, the result of deferred maintenance and replacement. However, because the structure is 15 years old and the economic life was 50 years when the building was constructed, the appraiser estimates that structural nonrepairable or incurable depreciation due to wear and tear would represent about 30 percent of current reproduction cost. This percentage was developed in the example by the ratio of age to economic life, or 15 divided by 50. This estimate assumes that the building will wear out *evenly* (a rate of 2 percent per year—100 percent divided by 50 years) over its 50-year life. Because 15 years have passed, based on these assumptions, the building would be 30 percent depreciated. Estimates of physical depreciation are not always based on these simple assumptions. Many structures may wear out faster or slower over time. In such cases the appraiser should consider the ''effective'' age of the property rather than its actual age.

EXHIBIT 14–2   Estimates of Depreciation and Obsolescence on Improved Property

Replacement cost estimate	$1,750,000
1. Physical deterioration	
a. Repairable (curable)	
Interior finish	25,500
Floor covering	5,200
Lighting fixtures	17,000
Total	$ 47,700
b. Nonrepairable (incurable)	
15 years divided by 50 years (age to economic life)	30%
2. Functional obsolescence	
Layout design (inefficiency)	
Increasing operating cost (annually)	$ 15,600
3. Location—economic obsolescence	
Loss in rent per year*	$ 4,000
Site value by comparison	$ 200,000

*Portion attributable to the building.

As for functional obsolescence in our example, it is estimated that operating costs will be $15,600 higher on the existing structure when compared with a completely new building. The higher costs could be caused, for example, by the lack of suspended ceilings in an older structure, by posts and columns that might affect traffic and storage patterns, or by an older conveyor system designed into the initial structure. This $15,600 additional annual expense could represent added costs in manpower, machinery costs, and so on, due to functional inadequacies. This additional expense is treated as a discounted annuity because the increase in operating costs is expected to be $15,600 per year for the next 35 years. Assuming the buyer could earn 10 percent annually on other investments, the adjustment for functional obsolescence would reduce the total operating costs to a present value of $150,449.[2]

Finally, an estimate of $4,000 per year has been made for locational (economic) obsolescence. This cost comes about because of environmental changes, such as pollution, noise, neighborhood changes, and other *external* influences which result in lower rents (or higher expenses) when present. Estimates for these characteristics must be obtained from comparable sites where none of these external influences are present. Because the land value is being estimated separately from the building value, the effect of economic obsolescence on the land value will already be accounted for in the estimated land value. Thus, during the adjustment for the effect of locational obsolescence on the *building* value, the estimated rent loss should represent only that portion of the total rent loss

---

[2]It is assumed that the owner could invest in a similar real estate venture or an investment of equal risk and earn 10 percent on total investment. This is discussed in more detail in the income capitalization approach later in the chapter.

EXHIBIT 14–3 Adjustment of Reproduction Cost Estimate

Reproduced improvement costs at current prices	$1,750,000
Less Repairable physical depreciation	47,700
Subtotal	$1,702,300
Nonrepairable (incurable) physical depreciation, 30%	510,690
Functional obsolescence (incurable):	
$15,600 (*PVIFA,* 10%, 35 yrs.)	
$15,600 (9.644159)	150,449
Economic-locational obsolescence:	
$4,000 (*PVIFA,* 10%, 35 yrs.)	
$4,000 (9.644159)	38,577
Add: Site value (by comparison)	200,000
Value per cost approach	$1,202,584
Or (rounded)	$1,200,000

(land and building) that applies to the building. For example, the appraiser might estimate that the rent for the entire property will be $5,000 per year less due to the locational obsolescence. However, if there were separate leases on the building and the land, the appraiser might expect that the building would rent for $4,000 less, whereas the land would rent for $1,000 less. This loss in building rent is capitalized and used to reduce the building value. In our example, we assume this rent loss to be $4,000 per year. As was the case with functional obsolescence, this loss in income will also be discounted at 10 percent. The discounted value of this loss is $38,577.[3]

Adjustments to the reproduction cost estimate for the existing improvement in our example is shown in Exhibit 14–3. Note that any repairable or curable depreciation or obsolescence should be subtracted from the reproduction cost estimate *before* any reduction is made for nonrepairable or incurable costs (30 percent in our example). In other words, even with the curable items adjusted for, productivity loss due to functional obsolescence and structural depreciation would still exist. The estimate for those incurable items must be made based on the assumption that all curable items are repaired.

In summary, the cost approach is most reliable where the structure is relatively new and depreciation does not present serious complications. However, when adjustments have to be made for depreciation and obsolescence, and when it is difficult to find comparable land sales, the cost approach is less desirable. This usually occurs where older, improved properties are being valued. However, where there are very few sales and market data are scarce, the cost approach to valuing older, existing properties may be the only method available.

---

[3]In practice, this estimate is extremely difficult to make. The appraiser must often use considerable judgment as to what the total rent loss would be and how much would be allocated to the building.

Market Approach

The market approach to value is based on data provided from recent sales of properties *highly comparable* to the property being appraised. This approach is often referred to as the "sales comparison approach" because it relies on the sales of comparable properties. These sales must be "arm's-length" transactions, or sales between unrelated individuals. They should represent normal market transactions with no unusual circumstances, such as foreclosure, or sales involving public entities, and so on.

To the extent that there are differences in size, scale, location, age, and quality of construction between the project being valued and recent sales of comparable properties, adjustments must be made to compensate for such differences. Obviously when this approach is used, the more differences that must be adjusted for, the more dissimilar are the properties being compared, and the less reliable the market approach. The rationale for the market comparison approach lies in the principle that an informed investor would never pay more for a property than what other investors have recently paid for comparable properties. Selection of data on properties that are truly comparable along all important dimensions, and that require relatively minor adjustments because of differences in building characteristics or locational characteristics, is critical to the successful use of this approach.

In developing the market approach to valuation, data on comparable properties from the market area analysis is summarized and used in the development of expected rents and value estimates for the property being appraised. An example of some of the data that could be used in the development of a market comparison approach is illustrated in Exhibit 14–4 for a hypothetical small office building and three comparable properties. Value is determined as of December 1986.

Based on the data developed from the market area analysis shown in Exhibit 14–4, we see that the subject property being appraised is very comparable to three small office buildings that have recently sold. A careful analysis of the data reveals relatively minor deviations in gross square footage, location, front footage on major streets, construction type and quality, parking space, and age of structures. The goal of the appraiser is now to adjust for the deviations between the property being appraised and the comparables. This adjustment can usually be accomplished in one of two ways. The price per square foot paid for each comparable can be adjusted to determine the market value for the subject, or the relationship between gross rental income and sale prices on the comparable can be applied to the subject with appropriate adjustment. Exhibit 14–5 shows how the price per square foot adjustment could be carried out.

In such adjustments on a square footage basis, adjustments for any major physical or locational deviations between the property being valued and the comparables recently sold must be made. Adjustments on the square footage cost should be made *relative* to the property being valued; that is, the comparable data must be adjusted as though one wants to make the comparables identical to the subject property. Positive features that comparables possess relative to the subject property require negative adjustments, and negative features require positive adjustments. All percentage adjustments are made by the appraiser based on knowledge of current market values and how various favorable

EXHIBIT 14–4   Market Area Analysis and Sales Data (market approach, hypothetical office building)

Item	Subject Property	Comparable Properties		
		1	2	3
Sale date	—	9/86	1/86	12/86
Price	—	$355,000	$375,000	$413,300
Gross annual rent	—	58,000	61,000	69,000
Gross square feet	13,300	14,500	13,750	15,390
Percent leasable square feet	90%	91%	93%	86%
Price per square foot*	—	$ 24.48	$ 22.27	$ 26.86
Rent per square foot*	—	$ 4.00	$ 4.44	$ 4.48
Proximity to subject†	—	2 mi.	2.5 mi.	.5 mi.
Frontage square feet	300	240	310	350
Parking spaces	130	140	130	155
Number floors	2	2	2	2
Number elevators	1	1	1	1
Age	New	3 yrs.	4 yrs.	2 yrs.
Exterior	Brick	Brick	Stucco	Brick
Construction‡	Average	Average	Average	Average
Landscaping‡	Average	Average	Average	Average

*Gross square footage (rounded).

†In this example the subject property is considered to be at the best location, and locations further away are less desirable.

‡Quality.

EXHIBIT 14–5   Adjustments from Comparables to Subject Property

	Comparable		
	1	2	3
Sale price	$355,000	$375,000	$413,300
Square footage	14,500	13,750	15,390
Sale price per square foot	$ 24.48	$ 27.27	$ 26.86
Adjustments			
Sale date	—	+4%	—
Leasable square footage	−5%	−10%	+9%
Location	+7%	+12%	+5%
Frontage	+10%	−8%	−10%
Age of structure	+8%	+10%	+6%
Net difference	+20%	+8%	+10%
Adjusted price	$426,000	$405,000	$454,630
Adjusted price per square foot	$ 29.38	$ 29.45	$ 29.54

Estimated price per square foot for subject   = $29.50

Indicated market value $29.50 · 13,300 square feet = $392,350

and unfavorable attributes of comparable properties would affect the value of the subject. When adjusting for age differentials, front footage, or differences in the percentage of leasable square footage, the appraiser must be able to estimate the value of such attributes and how the addition or deletion of those attributes affect the value of properties. It should be stressed that the *cost* of these attributes cannot be determined and added or subtracted to ascertain value. This is because buyers of properties establish what the value of each attribute of a property is and how each attribute interacts with others. Hence the appraiser should be concerned with the effect that the addition or deletion of an attribute will have on total property value, holding all other attributes constant. Alternatively, the appraiser is concerned with the marginal change in value. This marginal change in value may not correspond to the cost of adding or deleting an attribute. This is a subjective process and such adjustments should be justified with evidence based on recent experience with highly comparable properties; otherwise, serious errors can result.

In the above example the price of each of the comparable properties was divided by the number of square feet of the building to adjust for differences in the size of the property. This was done under the assumption that the price for an office building is directly related to its size in square feet. In this case the "price per square foot" is considered a "unit of comparison." Many other units of comparison may be more appropriate for a property. For example, price per cubic foot may be more appropriate for warehouse space, price per bed is often used for hospitals, and price per room is used for hotels.

Gross Income Multipliers.   A second technique used in conjunction with the market approach to valuation is to develop what are referred to as *gross income multipliers*. These are relationships between gross income and sale prices for all comparable properties that are applied to the subject property. This technique also requires that an estimate of the gross income be made for the subject property. The gross income multiplier (*GIM*) is defined as

$$GIM = \frac{\text{Sale price}}{\text{Gross income}}$$

or simply the ratio of sale price to gross income. Development of such multipliers is carried out for the properties comparable to the office building being valued. In this case "gross income" can be considered a unit of comparison. From the data developed in Exhibit 14–6, we can see that the *GIM*s range from 5.99 to 6.15, or it can be said that the comparable properties sold for 5.99 to 6.15 *times* current gross income. If the subject property is comparable, it too should sell for roughly a price that bears the same relationship to its gross income.

In arriving at a value for the subject property, then, the appraiser must develop an estimate of gross income based on the market data on comparables shown in Exhibit 14–4. For the comparable properties the gross income should be annual income at the time the property is sold (i.e., what it will be during the first year for the purchaser). Similarly, gross income for the subject will be for the first year of operation after the date for which the property is being appraised.

EXHIBIT 14–6   Development of *GIM* (comparable properties)

	Comparable		
	1	*2*	*3*
Date of sale	9/86	1/86	12/86
Sale price	$355,000	$375,000	$413,300
Current gross income	58,000	61,000	69,000
GIM	6.12×	6.15×	5.99×

Some appraisers use *potential* gross income (which assumes all the space is occupied) when developing *GIM*s. Others use *effective* gross income, which is based on occupied space (potential gross income less vacancies). The results should be similar if the appraiser is consistent for the comparable and subject properties. If there are significant differences in the vacancy rates among the comparable properties, then using effective gross income may be more appropriate. Of course, this may indicate that the properties are not really very comparable and may be in different market segments.

The *GIM* is based on prices *before adjustments* for the date of sale, location, and so on. This is because these factors would affect *both* the gross income *and* the price of the property. For example, if a comparable property is at a better location than the subject, then, all else being equal, the owner should be able to charge a higher rent and the gross income will be higher. At the same time, investors would be expected to pay a higher price for a property that is at a better location and produces a higher gross income. Consequently, the better location of the comparable property increases both the price and the rent relative to the subject property. Because the *GIM* is the ratio of the actual sale price of the comparable property to the gross income at the time of sale, it should therefore not be necessary to adjust the price of the comparable property.

In Exhibit 14–4 we see that annual rent per square foot ranged from $4.00 to $4.48 on the comparable properties. If, based on current competitive conditions, the appraiser estimates that the subject office building can be rented for $4.45 per square foot, then its gross rent should be $4.45 times 13,300 square feet, or $59,185.[4] From the range of *GIM*s shown in Exhibit 14–6, the appraiser also must select an appropriate *GIM* for the subject property. This is done by observing the range in *GIM*s for the comparable properties as shown in Exhibit 14–6. Rather than simply average the *GIM*s in the table, the appraiser would normally give more or less weight to a particular comparable when choosing a rate to apply to the subject property. For example, the appraiser may believe that of the three comparable properties, the third one should be given the most weight because it was the most recent sale. Thus the appraiser might believe the *GIM* should be closer to that for the third comparable property. The experience and judgment of the appraiser is an important part of this process. Assuming that the appraiser chooses a *GIM*

---

[4]Care should be taken here to ensure that significant changes in lease agreements are not expected to occur. For example, if a major increase in rent is expected on a comparable due to a lease expiration in the near future, this must be taken into account and adjusted for.

of 6.00 times as "appropriate" for the subject property, its indicated value would be $59,185 times 6.00 or $355,110.

Income Capitalization Approach

The third approach used in income property appraising is the income capitalization approach. The rationale for the income capitalization approach to value is based on the premise that because improved real estate is capable of producing a flow of income over its economic life, investors will pay a price that reflects the income potential of the property. That is, there is a relationship between income and value. In appraisal, the term *capitalization* refers to the conversion of income into an estimate of value. We will see that there are many *techniques* that are used in implementing the income capitalization approach to valuation. This chapter is limited to the more common techniques, but the reader should be aware of other methods.[5]

Because the income capitalization approach does involve estimates of income, utilizing this approach relies heavily on the operating statement that must be developed for any property being appraised.

Development of the Operating Statement.   In developing the operating statement, the economic studies of supply and demand are heavily drawn upon by the appraiser. Data from the market area analysis and surveys on comparable projects, similar to the data utilized in establishing comparisons under the market approach (see Exhibit 14–5), must be used to establish what expected rents will be. Estimates must also be made for normal vacancy and collection losses based on economic conditions expected to exist at the time of the appraisal.

Operating expenses are broken down into specific categories when possible, and a percentage relationship is established relative to effective income. Generally, data of this type are available through local property management firms, apartment owner associations, or from information collected from firms operating on a national basis. In cases where an existing property is being valued, past operating statements serve as a point of departure for the appraiser. These statements can be used to project future operating statements based on expected economic conditions in the local economy and market area. The development of operating expense relationships will depend on the type of property being appraised. Exhibit 14–7 details some sources of data available on a regional and national basis for many categories of property use that can be consulted in the development of such operating statements.

To develop and explain techniques used in the income capitalization approach, we show an operating statement for a hypothetical apartment project in Exhibit 14–8. The operating statement is made with the assumption that the property will be efficiently managed. The use of data and averages for properties in the market area are reasonable.

---

[5]For example, *The Appraisal of Real Estate,* 9th ed. (Chicago: The American Institute of Real Estate Appraisers, 1988).

EXHIBIT 14–7 Data Sources Useful for Income Property Research

Type of Property	Source
Apartment, condominium, cooperative	Income and Expense Analysis: Apartments, Condominiums and Cooperatives (Chicago, IL: Institute of Real Estate Management, annually).
Office buildings	Office Building Experience Exchange Report (Washington, D.C.: Building Owners and Managers Association International, annually)
Shopping centers	The Dollars and Cents of Shopping Centers (Washington, D.C.: Urban Land Institute).
Industrial parks	Site Selection Handbook (Atlanta, Georgia, Conway Publications, Inc.).
Hotels/leisure and recreation property	U.S. Lodging Industry, (Philadelphia, PA, Laventhol & Horwath); Trends in the Hotel Industry (Houston, TX, Pannell, Kerr & Forster)

As will be seen in the analysis that follows, the estimate of net operating income is critical in the income capitalization approach. In general, holding all else equal, the higher the estimate of net operating income, the higher will be the estimated property value. Hence, regardless of how much more "efficiently" optimistic investors believe that they will be able to manage properties in comparison to the competition, appraisers should recognize that competitive forces in the local market for wages, materials, and so on, should result in operating costs tending toward the same percentage of effective gross income for most comparable properties.

In the development of the operating statement, some appraisers include a "reserve for replacements" as an additional deduction from *NOI* to account for replacement of long-lived items such as a new furnace or replacement of a roof. For example, if a furnace is expected to last 10 years, the appraiser would include one tenth the cost of replacing the furnace as an annual expense. Other appraisers prefer that only items of income and expense expected to occur in annual operation of the property should be included. If the appraiser is consistent in the treatment of such items when calculating *NOI* for the property being appraised and the comparable properties, the resulting value estimate should be the same. Since a reserve for replacements is not normally included in expenses by investors when doing investment analysis calculations, the authors prefer to exclude it for appraisal purposes. If the appraiser expects that an item such as a roof or furnace will have to be replaced during the normal investment holding period, the estimated value of the property can be reduced by the present value of the cost of replacing the item in arriving at a final estimate of value.

Other items are also excluded in developing net operating income. Federal or state income taxes, interest expense, and mortgage payments are not considered to be operating expenses. As we saw in Chapter 10, these items are extremely important in investment analysis where investors are concerned with the after-tax return on equity invested.

EXHIBIT 14–8   Hypothetical Apartment Building, Operating Statement

Gross potential income	$600,000	
Vacancy and collection loss	30,000	5.0%
Effective gross income	$570,000	100.0%
Operating expenses:		
Personnel-wages	$ 39,900	
Utilities, common areas	22,800	
Management expense	28,500	
Paint and decorating	17,100	
Maintenance-repairs	45,000	
Miscellaneous	5,700	
Insurance	7,000	
Real estate taxes	65,200	
Total operating expenses	$231,200	40.6%
Net operating income	$338,800	59.4%

However, in valuation, appraisers often do not explicitly consider the effects of financing and depreciation on income. We will discuss the rationale for this later in the chapter.

Direct Capitalization with an Overall Rate.   This technique is a very simple approach to the valuation of income-producing property. It is based on the idea that at any given point in time the current *NOI* produced by a property is related to its current market value. Symbolically,

$$R = \frac{NOI_1}{V}$$

where NOI_1 is net operating income in the first year of the holding period, as developed from the operating statement, V is property value, and R is the overall rate which was introduced in Chapter 10. As discussed in Chapter 10, an overall rate expresses the relationship between income at a particular time and the value of the property at that time. It is not a rate of return on investment (*IRR*) because it does not explicitly consider projected future income or changes in the value of the property over time. The overall rate (*R*) may be a useful measure of value, however, if it is derived from the information about what investors have been paying for comparable properties. That is, if properties which are similar to the property we are appraising are producing a given *NOI* and selling at a price which results in a particular overall rate, then this approach assumes that the property being appraised would also sell with the same overall rate.

How should the analyst go about using *R* in determining *V* in the relationship *V* = *NOI*/*R*? Using our hypothetical apartment project example to develop *NOI*, we have already seen from Exhibit 14–8 that projected *NOI* is $339,500. How does the estimate of *R* come about? Based on Exhibit 14–9, we assume that the analyst has information

---

EXHIBIT 14–9   Comparable Sales Data Used in the Direct Capitalization Approach

| | *Comparable* | | |
	1	*2*	*3*
Date of sale	10/86	8/86	12/86
Price	$3,500,000	$2,750,000	$3,625,000
NOI	343,000	239,250	333,500
NOI/Price = *R*	9.8%	8.7%	9.2%

---

on three comparable sales prices and on the estimated rents for each of these complexes. If the appraiser can also estimate operating expenses for each, an *NOI* figure can be developed. Or, if the appraiser has access to the operating statement for each project, the *NOI* can be estimated directly from these statements. If the complete statements are not available, estimated vacancy rates and operating expense ratios based on the same sources cited in the development of the operating statement for the subject property may be relied on. The *R* for each comparable project is developed as shown in Exhibit 14–9. The value of *R* is based on the *unadjusted NOI* and sale price for the comparable properties for the same reason that we discussed with respect to the *GIM*. That is, differences in size, location, and so forth, should already be reflected in both the *NOI* and the sale price of the comparable property.

Based on data shown in Exhibit 14–9, the overall rate ranged from 8.7 percent to 9.8 percent. The appraiser will examine these rates and make a judgment as to which is most appropriate for the subject. That is, as pointed out in our discussion of *GIM*s, the appraiser must use judgment as to which of the comparables are most indicative of the value for the subject property. These comparables will then be given more weight in the selection of a final overall rate. Assuming that 9.5 percent is chosen as the "appropriate" overall capitalization rate for the subject, then the estimated value using this approach would be $338,800 divided by .095, or $3,566,316.

Sensitivity of Value Estimate to Overall Rate.   It should be stressed that estimates of value are highly sensitive to the overall rate chosen for capitalization. For example, in the above case, a capitalization rate that is 0.5 percent too low, or 9.0 percent, will result in an estimated value of $3,764,404, or a difference of $198,128 from the estimate made at 9.5 percent. This represents a difference of over 5 percent in the estimate of value. Clearly, choice of an appropriate overall capitalization rate is extremely important in the determination of value and should be carefully analyzed and supported in an appraisal.

The Band of Investment Approach to Developing an Overall Rate.   In the preceding discussion we illustrated the use of an overall rate to estimate the value of a property being appraised (subject property). The overall rate was obtained by observing what the overall rate was for comparable properties that had recently sold. A key assumption was that the overall rate should be the same for the comparable properties and the property being appraised (subject property). Our analysis did not take into consideration whether all of the comparable properties as well as the subject property were financed in a similar manner. That is, was the same amount of debt financing available for each of the properties, and was the cost of that debt the same? If the amount and cost of debt were not the same for all the properties, would this result in a difference in the overall rates? If financing does affect the overall rate, then any differences in financing must be taken into consideration in the valuation process.

What follows is an approach that is sometimes used by appraisers to explicitly take into account any differences in the financing for comparable properties relative to that for the subject property. It is referred to by appraisers as the "band of investment approach" and, as we will see, is based on taking into consideration investment criteria of both the lender and the equity investor involved in a project.

To understand the rationale for the band of investment approach, the reader should recall that the development of R is based on estimated *NOI,* and that *NOI* represents income *before* any account is taken of mortgage payments or cash return to equity investors. For example, if we wanted to estimate the current cash return to an equity investor who purchased a property, we would determine the before-tax flow to the equity investor as follows:

$$
\begin{array}{ll}
& \text{Effective gross income} \ (EGI) \\
- & \underline{\text{Operating expenses}} \qquad (OE) \\
& \text{Net operating income} \ (NOI) \\
- & \underline{\text{Debt service}} \qquad\qquad (DS) \\
& \text{Before-tax cash flow} \quad (BTCF)
\end{array}
$$

Using this format, an investor who financed the property with mortgage debt (M) and made an equity investment (E) would earn a current before-tax cash flow equal to *BTCF,* or *NOI* less the required debt service (DS).

The equity dividend rate or current return on equity for the equity investor would be as follows:

$$\frac{BTCF}{E} = \text{Percent cash return on invested equity}$$

$$(ROE \text{ or equity dividend rate})$$

The equity dividend is a measure of the current annual cash return to the equity investor as a percentage of the amount of equity invested. Similarly, a measure of the current annual cash return to the lender is

$$\frac{DS}{M} = \text{Annual percent mortgage payments}$$

This is simply the mortgage constant, expressed on an annual basis.

The values of M and E must add up to the purchase price of the property. If the property is being used as a comparable sale in an appraisal, this price is assumed to reflect the value (V) of that property. For example, if an investor obtained a 70 percent loan, then $M/V = 70\%$ and the equity invested must be 30 percent, $E/V = 30\%$, because $M/V + E/V$ must equal 100 percent.

By weighting the measures of current cash return to the equity investor and lender by the proportion of equity and debt used to acquire the property, we can obtain an overall rate R. This can be seen as follows:

	Component		Weight		Weighted Average
Mortgage	$\dfrac{DS}{M}$	$\times$	$\dfrac{M}{V}$	$=$	Debt component of R
					$+$
Equity	$\dfrac{BTCF}{E}$	$\times$	$\dfrac{E}{V}$	$=$	Equity component of R
				$=$	Overall rate (R)

Thus, we see that an overall rate can be developed by taking a weighted average of the equity dividend rate expected by the investor and the mortgage loan constant (expressed on an annual basis) required by the lender.

To illustrate the development of R for the apartment building considered earlier, we reconsider the comparable sales that were shown in Exhibit 14–9. This information is reproduced in Exhibit 14–10 along with information about how each of the comparable properties was financed *at the time it was purchased.*

From the exhibit we see the equity dividend rates range from 6.20 to 6.37 percent. The range of equity dividend rates is not as great as the range of overall rates or the range of interest rates on the loans. This implies that investors may be buying more on the basis of equity dividend rates than on overall rates. That is, they are willing to pay a price that provides an expected current return on equity of about 6.25 percent, regardless of the terms of the loan.

EXHIBIT 14–10   Comparable Sales Data Used in the Band of Investment Approach

	Comparable		
	1	*2*	*3*
Date of sale	10/86	8/86	12/86
Price	$3,500,000	$2,750,000	$3,625,000
Mortgage	$2,450,000	$1,950,000	$2,537,500
Interest rate/term	10.5%, 25 yrs	9%, 30 yrs	9.5%, 25 yrs
Equity	$1,050,000	$ 800,000	$1,087,500
NOI	$ 343,000	$ 239,250	$ 333,500
DS (annual)	$ 277,589	$ 188,282	$ 266,041
BTCF	$ 65,411	$ 50,968	$ 67,459
NOI/Price = R	9.80%	8.70%	9.20%
Equity dividend rate (R_E)	6.23%	6.37%	6.20%

Now assume that, based on current mortgage market conditions, it is believed that the apartment building we are appraising can be financed with a 70 percent mortgage with a 10 percent interest rate and a 25-year term (monthly payments). The mortgage constant for the loan would be 10.9044 percent. This is found by taking the monthly mortgage constant for a 10 percent, 25-year loan, or 0.009087 from Appendix B, and multiplying by 12 months to get the appropriate *factor,* .109044, that corresponds to annual mortgage payments. Even though we do not know the dollar amount of the mortgage, we expect it will be 70 percent of value. Hence, by weighting the mortgage constant 0.109044 times 70 percent, the debt component of *R,* or .07633, can be estimated.

The next step in the estimation of *R* is to estimate a value for the current cash return on *invested equity,* or *ROE.* Based on the analysis above, the appraiser may feel that an equity dividend rate of 6.25 percent would be appropriate. If the properties which sold are not comparable, adjustments to the current yield would have to be made (either up or down) (1) by perceived differences in *risk,* and (2) by differences due to current market conditions that could make for differences in current equity yields.

Assuming it is determined that a 6.25 percent current cash return on *equity (BTCF* divided by *E)* invested is "appropriate" for the shopping center being valued, the estimate of *R* can be completed as follows:

	Component		*Weight*		*Weighted Average*
Mortgage	.109044	×	.70	=	.07633
Equity	.0625	×	.30	=	.01875
					.09508 = *R*

Based on expected *NOI* of $338,800, the shopping center value could be estimated at $338,800 divided by .09508, or $3,563,315. Based on this value, we would expect that the mortgage amount would be $2,494,321, or 70 percent of value. Total debt service of $271,991, leaving *BTCF* of $66,809 *(NOI − DS)* as the current return to the investor. This would represent a 6.25 percent current cash yield on equity ($66,809 divided by $1,068,995).

Note that the value estimated by the weighted average approach is virtually the same as that estimated by using overall rates from the comparable sales. There may be differences in the value estimates in practice due to limitations in the accuracy of the data that the appraiser has to deal with in obtaining overall rates and equity dividend rates from comparable sales. Furthermore, the weighted-average approach assumes that the investor's motivation for purchasing the property can be captured by the equity dividend rate, and that this rate will be the same for the comparable properties and the subject property. It is only reasonable to make this assumption if the properties have similar expectations for changes in income and value over time and similar risk.

As pointed out earlier, the current equity yield (6.25 percent in the above case) does not represent the return that an investor would expect to earn on equity invested in such a project over the entire investment period. This is because no account is taken of potential appreciation or depreciation in property value, nor is any trend in *NOI* considered beyond the current year. The estimate of value under this approach is based on *current cash yields* prevailing in the marketplace, and as such are not intended to provide investors with estimates of long-term rates of return on equity investment Rather, these current yields are intended to serve as market benchmarks that can be used in establishing property values. Since the purpose of this technique is to determine value, it should *not* be relied upon as an indication of what the potential yield could be from investing in a particular property for the entire investment period. The remainder of this chapter considers how yield rates over the entire investment holding period can be used to estimate value.

The Present Value Method and Income Capitalization. As indicated previously, the rationale for the income capitalization approach is that there is a relationship between the value of an income property and its expected future income potential. The income approach uses various techniques to estimate the value of the property based on its projected income. In Chapter 10 we discussed that when purchasing an income-producing property, an investor will pay an amount which provides a competitive return on investment for a particular holding period. A competitive return on investment means a return equivalent to what investors in comparable properties and other investments comparable in risk are receiving on their investment. The resale price at the end of a particular holding period reflects the income potential of the property for the *next* investor, as we also discussed in Chapter 10. Thus, one obvious way of estimating the value of an income property is to determine the price that would result in a specified rate of return. This return should be the return that the appraiser feels is necessary to attract the "typical" or "most likely" investor to purchase the property being appraised. Viewed in this way, the income approach to appraisal essentially involves replication of the investment analysis process. The essential difference is that instead of starting with a purchase price and estimating a rate of return for a particular investor as we did in investment analysis, we specify the rate of return for a typical investor, then determine what price would be necessary to produce this rate of return (given the estimated income and resale price for the property).

The techniques illustrated above for the income approach used the concept of an overall rate as the basis for estimating the value of the property. It was stressed that the overall rate is *not* an investment yield because it does not explicitly account for changes in the *NOI* or value of the property over an investor's holding period. However, the overall rate *implicitly* reflects investor yield requirements. That is, an investor may accept an overall rate of about 9.5 percent today, as in the apartment example considered earlier, because the investor *expects* the *NOI* and property value to increase, and eventually expects to earn an investment yield rate greater than 10 percent. Hence there is correspondence between the overall rate and an investor's expected investment yield (i.e., the *BTIRR* discussed in Chapter 10). However, these two values may not be, and rarely are, the same. The same logic would apply to the interpretation of an equity dividend rate of only 6.25 percent as it was when the band of investment method was illustrated. Low-equity dividend rates may be observed in markets where expectations of rising income and property values has caused investors to pay a high price for properties relative to their *current* income potential, resulting in low-equity dividend rates.

As we have discussed, the use of overall rates and equity dividend rates relies on availability of comparable sales. When such sales are available, this can provide a reliable indication of value. Unfortunately, recent sales of comparable properties are not always available. This situation frequently occurs with *special-purpose* properties, such as recreational property, large hotels, or properties involving agricultural or mineral production. In such cases, a present value method to capitalization may have to be used in establishing value. The present value method (also referred to as discounted cash flow method) involves projecting the *NOI* for the property over a typical investment holding period. The resale price at the end of the holding period must also be estimated. The *NOI* and proceeds from resale are then discounted at an appropriate yield rate to arrive at a present value estimate. The discount rate should reflect a competitive investment yield for the type of property being valued. That is, it should be a rate that the typical investor would normally require as a minimum return over the life of the investment to be willing to purchase the property.

To illustrate, consider appraisal of an office building that, based on current market rents and typical operating expenses, would produce *NOI* of $500,000 during the first year. Due to the use of expense pass-throughs and *CPI* adjustments (as discussed in Chapter 10), *NOI* is expected to increase 3 percent per year over a five-year holding period. Since we do not know the current value of the property (this is the purpose of the appraisal), we would also not know the resale price at the end of the holding period. Appraisers who are knowledgeable about a particular market should be able to estimate the rate at which property values would be expected to increase over the holding period. In this case we will assume that the property value will increase 3 percent per year, the same rate as the *NOI* is increasing. Finally, we assume that a 13 percent investment yield would be necessary to attract investment capital to the office building. It is important to realize that in this case the yield is a before-tax yield (*BTIRR*), assuming that the investor is paying all cash for the entire property. Thus it does not explicitly reflect the effects of either federal income taxes or financial leverage. (These factors will be further discussed later in the chapter.)

Based on the above assumptions, we can estimate the income and resale proceeds from the property as follows:

Year	NOI	Resale Price
1	500,000	
2	515,000	
3	530,450	
4	546,364	
5	562,754	$(1.03)^5 \times V$

Note that in year 5, we have expressed the resale price as a function of the unknown present value (*V*). This is because we do not know the resale price until we know the present value. As we will see next, this means that we will have to use algebra to solve for the present value. Our valuation premise is that the value of the property (*V*) is equal to the present value of the above cash flows. Thus we can write the following algebraic expression:

$$V = \frac{\$500{,}000}{1.13} + \frac{\$515{,}000}{(1.13)^2} + \frac{\$530{,}450}{(1.13)^3} + \frac{\$546{,}364}{(1.13)^4} + \frac{\$562{,}754}{(1.13)^5} + \frac{(1.03)^5 \times V}{(1.13)^5}$$

Solving the above expression for V, we have

$$V = \$442{,}478 + \$403{,}321 + \$367{,}628 + \$335{,}095 + \$305{,}441$$
$$+ \ (0.629207 \times V)$$
$$V = \$1{,}853{,}962 + (0.629207 \times V)$$
$$.370792 \ V = \$1{,}853{,}962$$
$$V = \$5{,}000{,}000$$

Now that we know V, we can calculate the resale price as follows:

$$\text{Resale price} = \$500{,}000 \times (1.03)^5 = \$5{,}796{,}370$$

Shortcut Approach 1. To solve for value in the above example, we needed to calculate the present value of the *NOI* and the present value of the sale proceeds. If the *NOI* had been level, we could have used the present value of an annuity factor (*PVIFA*) to find the present value of the income portion. However, because the *NOI* was not level, we had to discount each year separately. Recalling the formula for discounting increasing cash flows from the appendix to Chapter 4, we can find the present value of the stream of *NOI* in our example as follows:

$$PVNOI = NOI_1 \ \frac{1 - \dfrac{(1 + g)^n}{(1 + r)^n}}{r - g}$$

where

$PVNOI$ = Present value of the changing income stream
NOI_1 = the first-year *NOI*
g = annual change in income
r = discount rate for present value
n = number of years being discounted

For the above example, we have

$$PVNOI = \$500{,}000 \ \frac{1 - \dfrac{(1.03)^5}{(1.13)^5}}{.13 - .03} = \$1{,}853{,}962$$

To find the value for the property, we now go directly to the algebraic expression which equates V with both the present value of the *NOI* (*PVNOI*) and the present value of the sale proceeds (*PVSALE*). We have

$$V = PVNOI + PVSALE$$
$$V = \$1{,}853{,}962 + (0.629207 \times V)$$

$$.370792 \ V = \$1,853,962$$
$$V = \$5,000,000$$

This is the same answer as before. This shortcut may be used only when the *NOI* is changing at the same rate each year.

Shortcut Approach 2. For the above example it was assumed that *both* the *NOI* and the property value were increasing at the *same* annual rate (e.g., 3 percent per year). This may be a very reasonable assumption for properties that are being valued on a fee simple basis or in situations where leases do not prevent *NOI* from changing with the market. It may also be reasonable to assume that when the leases are such that rents can be adjusted (with *CPI* adjustments and expense pass-throughs) that *NOI* will closely reflect market conditions. When this simplifying assumption can be made (e.g., *NOI* and property values are changing at the same annual rate), a very simple formula can be used to estimate the value. The formula is

$$V = \frac{NOI_1}{r - g}$$

or

$$
V = \frac{\$50,000}{.13 - .03}
$$
$$
= \frac{\$50,000}{.10}
$$
$$
= \$5,000,000
$$

Recall that the overall capitalization rate (R) expresses the relationship between the first-year *NOI* and value. Thus we have, in effect, used a formula to arrive at the capitalization rate of 10 percent. That is, $R = r - g$, or $10\% = 13\% - 3\%$. In this case the capitalization rate is based on a yield rate rather than being derived from comparable sales. This relationship should help emphasize the difference between yield rates and capitalization rates. As has been stressed several times, the difference has to do with expected changes in income and property value. In the above example, the difference is 3 percent, the rate we assumed that income and property values would increase over the holding period.

Capitalization rates will always differ from yield rates when income and/or property value is expected to change over the holding period. The relationship between these two rates will not be as simple as indicated above, however, when income and property values are not both expected to change at the same rate.

Although we may not know what rate of return (*IRR*) investors expect over a holding period, this return expectation is reflected in the overall rate. That is, although investors may purchase properties on the basis of an internal rate of return (before or after tax), the ratio of the property's current *NOI* to that price will be a function of that return and should be the same for properties that have the same future income potential and risk characteristics. This latter point is very important. If properties do not have similar future income potential, then although investors may be willing to purchase the properties for the same rate of return over a holding period, the resulting present value will not necessarily result in the same overall rate. This should be obvious if one thinks about two properties that have the same initial income when they are purchased, but the income for one of the properties is expected to increase over time whereas the income for the other property is expected to remain stable. If the properties have similar risk, then surely an investor will pay more for one that will have increasing income.[6] Thus when the overall rate is calculated, it will be lower for the property that is expected to have increasing income. Similarly, it should be clear that if properties do not have the same level of risk, the return required by investors would be different, and their values and overall rates would be different even if they had the same initial income.

Valuation of a Leased Fee Estate

In the office building example above it was assumed that the leases were such that *NOI* would increase each year to reflect current market conditions. Thus the value would be representative of that for fee simple ownership. Properties are often purchased with leases that are producing rents that are below current market rates. This can happen when the lease is such that market rents cannot fully adjust with increases in market rents, or expenses have risen more than the lease permits to be passed through to tenants. Because properties are always purchased subject to leases, and it is this leased fee estate that is being purchased, appraisers must estimate the value of the property subject to leasehold interests.

To illustrate, assume that for our office building example valued above, there is a lease on the entire property (e.g., a single tenant) that results in *level NOI* of $400,000 per year. The lease expires in five years. How does this affect our approach to finding the value? It may appear that we merely need to repeat the above analysis with the new *NOI* projection. We will see, however, that this would probably be incorrect. First, consider the resale price. Recall that the resale price depended on the unknown value, which we assumed was increasing 3 percent per year. Should we still assume it is increasing 3 percent per year? Or should we assume it does not change, since the income for the leased fee estate is level? Neither answer is correct, because the lease expires after the five-year holding period and the value at that time will reflect the *NOI* to the new investor. That investor will renegotiate the lease and earn market rents prevailing at that time, much the same as it was for a fee simple estate. Thus the value at the end of the five years should be *the same as for a fee simple estate,* which we estimated to be $5,796,370. The value of the leased fee estate will equal the present value of the $400,000 per year *NOI* plus the present value of the estimated sale price of $5,796,370. Before we calculate this present value, one additional question must be considered. Should the discount rate still be 13 percent? The answer depends on whether the leased fee estate is considered more or less risky than a fee simple estate. This depends in part on the creditworthiness of the tenants. Having a single tenant may also be considered riskier than having multiple tenants. One must also consider the fact that the below market nature of the leases makes it highly unlikely that the tenant will default on the lease, especially if the property can

---

[6]It is assumed that its resale price will also be higher because of the rising income.

be subleased. Furthermore, if the tenant does default in this case, the owner will probably be able to increase the rent considerably. Thus it might be argued that for this particular situation a discount rate slightly lower than 13 percent would be justified. The appraiser obviously must use judgment on this issue. We will assume that a 12.5 percent discount rate is appropriate. The value of the leased fee estate would therefore be as follows:

$$V = \$400,000 \times (PVIFA, 12.5\%, 5 \text{ yrs.}) + \$5,796,370 \times (PVIF, 12.5\%, 5 \text{ yrs.})$$
$$= [\$400,000 \times 3.604776] + [\$5,796,370 \times .567427]$$
$$= \$4,640\ 801$$

In this case, the difference between the value of the fee simple estate ($5,000,000) and the value of the leased fee estate ($4,640,801) should reflect the value of the leasehold estate, which is $359,199. That is, the below market lease results in the value of the fee simple estate being divided among the leasehold and leased fee interests.

A Note on Terminal Capitalization Rates

Recall that in Chapter 10 we discussed the use of terminal capitalization rates as a way of estimating the resale price of a property as an alternative to using a growth rate. As discussed in Chapter 10, the terminal capitalization rate can be used to estimate the resale price by dividing the *NOI* for the year *after* the property is sold (the first year of *NOI* to the new investor) by the terminal capitalization rate. In our previous example, the *NOI* in year 6 would be $500,000 times $(1.03)^5$ or $579,637. Suppose the terminal capitalization rate was estimated to be 10 percent. The estimated resale price would therefore be $579,637/.10 = $5,796,370. Note that this value is the same resale price as was estimated by using a growth rate.[7] Whether the answers would be the same in practice depends on the terminal capitalization rate selected. The point is that appraisers may prefer to estimate the resale price by applying a terminal capitalization rate to the *NOI* as seen by the next investor. As discussed in Chapter 10, this is based on the premise that the reversion value should depend on what the new investor receives in income. In fact, this is the reason that we argued in the previous section that the resale price for the leased fee estate should be the same as that for the fee simple estate. This is because when leases expire after five years, the *NOI* for the sixth year and beyond would be the same for both estates; thus the terminal capitalization rates should be the same.

Mortgage-Equity Capitalization

In the above discussion, value was found by discounting the *NOI* and resale proceeds for the property. We did not consider how the property was financed (e.g., how much debt

---

[7]Note that in this case the terminal cap rate chosen, 10 percent, is the same as the going-in capitalization rate that resulted for the value of the fee simple estate. As discussed in Chapter 10, terminal cap rates are usually assumed to be the same as or slightly higher than going-in capitalization rates. The assumptions used in the example (i.e., that income and value would grow at the same annual rate) imply the going-in and terminal cap rates will be exactly the same.

versus equity was used). In effect, we discounted the entire income available from the property before considering how that income would be split among holders of debt (mortgage lenders) and equity investors. The discount rate used must be consistent with this assumption; for example, it should not be a rate of return expected on equity invested, which as shown in Chapter 13 must reflect the risk associated with financial leverage. We now discuss how the value of a property can be estimated by explicitly taking into consideration the requirements of the mortgage lender and equity investor, hence the term *mortgage-equity capitalization.*

This method for estimating value is based on the concept that total value (V) must be equal to the present value of expected mortgage financing (M) and the present value of equity investment (E) made by investors. This technique relies on expressing all mortgage-related components affecting M and E as a percentage of value, then solving for value algebraically. Although this technique has many steps in the process and appears somewhat complex, a close examination of the approach reveals its simplicity. In using the mortgage-equity approach to value, we begin with the relationship

$$V = M + E$$

This merely indicates that value must equal the sum of a mortgage (M) obtainable on a property plus the equity (E) required of an investor. However, because the amount of the mortgage depends on the value of a property (assuming the loan will be based on a loan-to-value ratio), the exact dollar amount for (M) is unknown. The *percentage* of mortgage financing that would typically be loaned on the property being appraised as well as the other terms (interest rate and amortization period) can be based on current mortgage interest rates and terms for comparable properties, discussions with lending institutions, and data published by lenders on properties recently financed. Given that we can estimate an expected loan-to-value ratio, or M/V, we can modify our basic mortgage-equity equation to incorporate that estimate as follows:

$$V = M + E$$
$$V = \frac{M}{V}(V) + E$$

Hence, if we expect that a 75 percent loan will be obtainable on a particular property, $M/V = 75\%$, then our equation would be

$$V = .75V + E$$

Given this relationship, if we can now obtain an estimate for E, we can easily solve for V.

How do we estimate E, that is, the present value of the cash flow to the equity investor? Recalling the earlier analysis in this chapter and previous chapters, we know that one of the components of return to an investor making an equity investment on a property is before-tax cash flow, which is as follows:

Net operating income	(*NOI*)
− *Debt service*	(*DS*)
Before-tax cash flow	(*BTCF*)

We know that to estimate E we must include *BTCF,* or *NOI − DS,* for each year that the property is owned. Finally, we know that when the property is sold, the investor will receive any excess of cash remaining after the outstanding mortgage balance is paid, or *BTCF_s*. In the year that the property is sold, *REV* or the price expected in the year of sale, must be reduced by any mortgage balance (*MB*) to get the net cash reversion to the investor at that time. Based on these modifications, we can rewrite our basic valuation relationship $V = M + E$ as

$$V = \frac{M}{V}(V) + \frac{NOI_1 - DS}{(1 + k)^1} + \frac{NOI_2 - DS}{(1 + k)^2} + \ldots + \frac{REV - MB}{(1 + k)^n}$$

This new relationship merely says that value is equal to the mortgage amount (*M*) stated as (*M/V*) *V*, or the loan-to-value ratio times value, plus the present value of all proceeds to be realized by the equity investor. The latter amounts to all *BTCF,* which is equal to *NOI − DS* in each year, plus any residual cash remaining from the sale of the property in year *N,* after repayment of any mortgage balance (*REV − MB*).

It is again emphasized that in the above formulation, proceeds to be realized by the equity investor are discounted at an investment yield rate $k,$ which is not the same rate as used for discounting *NOI* (r). This is because the equity that an investor is willing to invest in a project is equal to the discounted value of all cash returns to be realized on *equity* investment and not *total* investment. When we attempt to estimate $E,$ we must obtain an estimate for $k,$ or the before-tax internal rate of return (*BTIRR*) investors expect to realize on their equity over the entire period of investment. In the previous cases, no leverage was assumed. Hence the discount rate, $r,$ reflects the required return on a total investment, or ''all cash'' basis because the investor did not use debt financing. For this reason we would also expect $k > r$ because of the increased risk to the equity investor when financing is used.

As indicated previously, determining the mortgage interest rate and other mortgage terms and what percentage of value lenders would be willing to loan on a particular property is relatively straightforward. However, estimating the internal rate of return on equity (k) that investors expect to earn over an expected period of ownership is more complex. We do not normally know what cash flows were being estimated by an investor when a comparable property was purchased. Further, k based on *historical* data may not be indicative of *future* trends. However, there are a few general guidelines that can be followed when estimating $k.$

1. We know that the risk premium should be *greater* for an equity investor than it would be for the mortgage lender. This equity position is riskier because the equity investor takes more risk than the mortgage lender. This is because all debt-service (*DS*) requirements must be paid from *NOI* before the equity investor realizes any *BTCF.* Also, because the property serves as security for the loan, the lender has first claim against proceeds from the sale of a property; that is, the mortgage balance must be paid from the proceeds from sales before any cash is received by the equity investor. Hence, the equity investor is in a residual position, or one in which the claims of the lender must be met before the equity investor receives any return.

2. We know that the rate of return required by an equity investor (k) should be higher than that for the entire property (r) because of the risk associated with financial leverage.

Recall from Chapter 13 that risk, as measured by the variance of the rate of return, increases with the use of debt.

3. When estimating the required investment yield on equity for a particular project, yields on similar properties, or yields on other investments such as corporate bonds and stock can serve as a point of reference for estimation. Adjustments must be made for differences in risk between the property being valued and any benchmark or average yields developed from other markets. This topic will be discussed further in Chapter 23.

4. Many companies publish investor surveys in which investment criteria currently being used to acquire different types of investments are reported.[8] Information in these surveys often includes investment yield requirements, going-in capitalization rates, terminal capitalization rates, and other investment criteria.

Example. Now that the general framework for the mortgage-equity technique has been established, we can illustrate the technique by estimating the value for the same office building considered earlier. Recall that the property had *NOI* of $500,000 per year, which was expected to increase 3 percent per year, and property value was also expected to increase 3 percent per year. Under the assumption that the investor would pay cash for the property (i.e., no debt financing), we used a discount rate of 13 percent to find the present value of the *NOI* and sale proceeds from reversion (*REV*). We now make the additional assumption that a 75 percent mortgage can be obtained at 10 percent interest for 25 years. We will use the same five-year holding period. The appraiser believes that given the risk and other factors related to this investment, the investor should earn a before-tax rate of return on equity (*k*) of 20 percent. How do we incorporate this data into an estimate of value?

Repeating the formulation of the problem, we have

$$V = M + E$$

$$V = \frac{M}{V}(V) + \frac{NOI_1 - DS}{(1 + k)^1} + \frac{NOI_2 - DS}{(1 + k)^2} + \ldots + \frac{REV - MB}{(1 + k)^n}$$

Using the prefix *PV* to represent the present value of each of the cash flows above, we can write the following summary expression:

$$V = \frac{M}{V}(V) + PVNOI - PVDS + PVREV - PVMB$$

Because the initial loan amount *M*, represented by the term (*M/V*)*V* in the above expression, is a cash flow that occurs when the property is purchased, it represents the present value of the mortgage. Thus it does not need to be discounted. We have separated the present value of the *NOI* from the present value of the *DS* because it is easier to find the present values of each separately, due to the fact that *NOI* changes each year whereas *DS* is usually a level annuity.

---

[8]For example, Real Estate Research Corporation and Cushman & Wakefield both survey institutional investors throughout the nation on a quarterly basis to find out what *IRR* they require for investing in different types of real estate.

We now incorporate known values into the above formula. First, we expect that a 75 percent loan will be obtained. This means that $M/V = 75\%$, and $(M/V)V = .75V$. Although we know that $NOI - DS = BTCF$, a *dollar* value for DS cannot be obtained because the *dollar* amount of the mortgage is not known. Hence, we must express DS as a *percentage* of V. This can be done because we do know what the mortgage will be as a *percent* of value and we also know the expected interest rate and term of the loan. Because we expect the mortgage amount to be 75 percent of value, the annual debt service expressed as a percentage of value is

$$
\begin{aligned}
DS &= .75V(MLC, 10\%, 25 \text{ yrs.}) \times 12 \\
&= .75V(.009087) \times 12 \\
&= .081783V
\end{aligned}
$$

That is, expressed in a relationship to value, DS would be based on a mortgage amount equal to 75 percent of value multiplied by the monthly loan constant (MLC) for a 10 percent, 25-year loan (Appendix B). This loan constant, which is equal to 0.009087, is multiplied by 12 to obtain annual debt-service requirements as a percentage of V. As seen above, we ascertain that DS will be 8.1783 percent of value. This is true even though we do not know the dollar amount of the mortgage or the property value. Because DS is the same each year, its present value ($PVDS$) can be found by simply multiplying DS by the factor for the present value of an annuity. Thus we have

$$
\begin{aligned}
PVDS &= DS \times (PVIFA, 20\%, 5 \text{ yrs.}) \\
&= (.081783)(2.990612) \\
&= .244581
\end{aligned}
$$

Because the NOI is increasing at a constant rate, we can use the formula for discounting increasing cash flows to find the present value of the NOI. We have

$$
PVNOI = (\$500,000) \, \frac{1 - \dfrac{(1.03)^5}{(1.20)^5}}{.20 - .03} = \$1,570,923
$$

As for the dollar amount of mortgage balance in the year of sale, it too is unknown because it is based on the original mortgage amount, which in turn is based on the unknown. However, like DS, the mortgage balance can also be expressed as a percentage of V. If it is expected that a 75 percent loan will be obtained when the property is purchased, the mortgage balance factor (MBF) for a 10 percent, 25-year loan at the end of 10 years (Appendix C), which is equal to .8456, when multiplied by the original percentage of value borrowed, or 75 percent, represents the mortgage balance at the end of 10 years, expressed as a percentage of value. This is computed as follows:

$$
\begin{aligned}
MB &= .75V(MBF, 10\%, 10 \text{ yrs.}) \\
&= .75V(.941638) \\
&= .706228V
\end{aligned}
$$

Hence the mortgage balance after 10 years should be 94.16387 percent of the original mortgage amount and 70.6228 percent of the *initial* property value. The present value of the mortgage balance or *PVMB* is found by multiplying by the factor for the present value of $1. Thus,

$$PVMB = .706228V \times (PVIF, 20\%, 5 \text{ yrs.})$$
$$= .706228V(.401878)$$
$$= .283817V$$

Finally, an estimate of *REV* is required. Although we do not know *V*, it is estimated that whatever the present value of the property is today, it will appreciate in value by 3 percent per year or a total of $(1.03)^5 - 1 = 15.9274$ percent (the same as we assumed earlier), for the five-year holding period. Hence, *REV* will be 1.159274 times the current value (*V*), and the present value of the reversion will be

$$PVREV = 1.159274V \times (PVIF, 20\%, 5 \text{ yrs.})$$
$$= 1.159274V(.401878)$$
$$= .465887V$$

Now that we have values for *DS, MB, NOI, REV*, and *k*, we can estimate *V* as follows:

$$V = \frac{M}{V}V + PVNOI - PVDS + PVREV - PVMB$$
$$V = .75V + \$1,570,923 - .244581V + .465887V - .283817V$$
$$.312518V = \$1,570,923$$
$$V = \$5,026,664$$

Based on the estimates made for variables used in the present value approach, value is estimated to be $5,026,664 for the subject property. The answer is very similar to what we obtained earlier. This value is slightly different because an adjustment was made to the discount rate (20 percent versus 13 percent) to account for the difference in the methodology (i.e., discounting equity cash flows rather than the entire cash flow stream). In practice, a similar value should be obtained if the appropriate discount rate is used in each case.[9]

From the preceding analysis, it should be clear that this approach to income capitalization can be modified for any combination of *NOI*, mortgage terms, mortgage amounts (as percent of value), expected investment period, required investment yield on equity, and reversion value. It is a valuable tool for estimating value for income-producing property.

Now that we have seen how the algebra can be used to calculate our value estimate, it is useful to see what cash flows to the equity investor are implied by the analysis. Now that we know the value, the mortgage amount, debt service, and resale price can be determined. Using the assumptions for the problem, we obtain the cash flow projections shown in Exhibit 14–11.

---

[9]The discount rate used to discount the *NOI* (13 percent) is approximately a weighted average of the discount rate applied to the equity cash flows (20 percent) and the interest rate on the loan (10 percent). That is, if these rates are weighted by the amount of equity and debt, respectively, we have $(.75)(10\%) + (.25)(20\%) = 12.50\%$. This is approximately the same as the 13 percent discount rate that would result in approximately the same value estimate. As discussed in Chapter 13, this relationship is not exact because the loan-to-value ratio changes over time as the property value changes and the loan is amortized.

EXHIBIT 14–11   Cash Flow Projections for Office Building

	Year				
	1	*2*	*3*	*4*	*5*

Estimates of Cash Flow from Operations
Before-Tax Cash Flow

	1	2	3	4	5
Net operating income (*NOI*)	$500,000	$515,000	$530,450	$546,364	$562,754
Less debt service (*DS*)	411,096	411,096	411,096	411,096	411,096
Before-tax cash flow	$ 88,904	$103,904	$119,354	$135,268	$151,658

Estimates of Cash Flows from Sale in Year 5

Sale price	$5,827,281
Less mortgage balance	3,549,972
Before-tax cash flow (*BTCF_s*)	$2,277,309

Cash Flow Summary
End of year

	0	*1*	*2*	*3*	*4*	*5*
Before-tax cash flow	$ – 1,256,666	$88,904	$103,904	$119,354	$135,268	$2,428,967
Before-tax *IRR* = 20.00%						

Note that the *IRR* is 20 percent, which proves that we obtained the correct value estimate in our algebraic approach above.

Sensitivity to Assumptions.   The reader should be aware that solutions obtained using the present value method of income capitalization are highly sensitive to the values assumed in the computation of value. For example, if in the above example the value selected for k were 19 percent instead of 20 percent, the estimated property value would be $5,179,867. This is $153,203, or 3 percent greater than the $5,026,664 estimated when k is 20 percent. Note, however, that the error is not as great as when the overall rate was changed from 9.5 percent to 9 percent, which resulted in a 5 percent change in value. That is, the value is more sensitive to a variation in the overall rate than the same variation in the discount rate.

The value estimate will also be sensitive to changes in other critical values such as the expected *NOI* and reversion value. For example, in our previous example we estimated the value of $5,026,664 based on the assumption that income and property value would increase 3 percent per year. Exhibit 14–12 shows how the value estimate would change under different assumptions about these growth rates. (In each case both income and property value are assumed to change at the same rate.)

Looking at Exhibit 14–11, we observe a wide variation in value estimates. For example, if the growth rate for income and property value is expected to be 2 percent per year instead of 3 percent, the estimated value would decrease to $4,616,951 from $5,026,664. This is an 8 percent decrease in value. If no increase in income or property value was

EXHIBIT 14–12   Sensitivity of the Value to Income and Property Value Growth Rates

Growth (percent) Rate	Value Estimate	Overall (percent) Rate
0	$3,971,373	12.59
1	4,269,574	11.71
2	4,616,951	10.83
3	5,026,664	9.95
4	5,517,456	9.06
5	6,115,628	8.18
6	6,860,898	7.29

expected, the estimated value would decrease to $3,971,373, which is a 21 percent decrease in value. Clearly the value of the property is very sensitive to assumptions about these growth rates. To accurately estimate the market value of a property, the appraiser must consider the expectations of investors as to trends in income and property values in the market. These expectations can change very quickly when there is an unexpected change in the economic outlook that affects the demand for a particular type of property. Although these projections are difficult to make, they clearly affect what investors are willing to pay for a property.

Although the values estimated in Exhibit 14–12 are based on using discounted cash flow analysis (the mortgage-equity model), there is an *implied* overall rate for each value estimate. Exhibit 14–12 also shows these overall rates, which are calculated by dividing the first-year *NOI* ($500,000) by the estimated value. Note that the first-year *NOI* is the same in all cases because the projected change in *NOI* only affects the *NOI* after the first year. From the exhibit we see that the overall capitalization is very sensitive to our assumptions about growth rates. The point is that the overall rate that investors are willing to accept on properties are also affected by investors' expectations for future income and trends in the value of properties. When appraisers derive overall capitalization rates from the sale of "comparable" properties, as discussed earlier, rather than through discounted cash flow analysis, they should take into consideration whether *expectations* about future market conditions were similar when that property sold to what they are at the time of the appraisal.

After-Tax Analysis.   In the mortgage-equity example discussed in the previous section, the value was estimated under the premise that the typical investor required a 20 percent *before-tax IRR* (*BTIRR*) on equity over the investment holding period. We know, however, that many investors are concerned about the *after-tax IRR* (*ATIRR*) on the investment. Hence the investment must sell for a price that will also provide a competitive aftertax *IRR* for investors. If the typical investor for the property being appraised is such an investor, then a further test of the reasonableness of the value estimate is provided by considering the after-tax *IRR* that would result from an investor purchasing the investment at the value that was estimated. Exhibit 14–13 shows the after-tax cash flows and after-tax *IRR* that results from purchasing the office building at a price of $5,026,664. To calculate the after-tax *IRR*, we made a few additional assumptions. First, it was assumed that the land value was $1,000,000. Thus the depreciable portion of the total value was

EXHIBIT 14–13   After-Tax *IRR* Office Building

	Year				
	1	*2*	*3*	*4*	*5*

Estimates of Cash Flow from Operations

A. Before-tax cash flow					
Net operating income (*NOI*)	$500,000	$515,000	$530,450	$546,364	$562,754
Less debt service (*DS*)	411,096	411,096	411,096	411,096	411,096
Before-tax cash flow	$ 88,904	$103,904	$119,354	$135,268	$151,658
B. Taxable income or loss					
Net operating income (*NOI*)	$500,000	$515,000	$530,450	$546,364	$562,754
Less interest	375,393	371,654	367,524	362,962	357,921
Depreciation	127,831	127,831	127,831	127,831	127,831
Taxable income (loss)	− 3,223	15,515	35,095	55,571	77,002
Tax	$ − 903	$ 4,344	$ 9,827	$ 15,560	$ 21,561
C. After-tax cash flow					
Before-tax cash flow (*BTCF*)	$ 88,904	$103,904	$119,354	$135,268	$151,658
Less tax	− 903	4,344	9,827	15,560	21,561
After-tax cash flow (*ATCF*)	$ 89,800	$ 99,560	$109,527	$119,708	$130,098

Estimates of Cash Flow from Sale in Year 5

Sale price			$5,827,281
Less mortgage balance			3,549,972
Before-tax cash flow (*BTCF_s*)			2,277,309
Taxes in year of sale			
Sale price		$5,827,281	
Original cost basis	$5,026,664		
Less accum. depreciation	639,153		
Adjusted basis		4,387,511	
Capital gain		1,439,770	
Tax from sale			403,136
After-tax cash flow from sale (*ATCF_s*)			1,874,173

Cash Flow Summary
End of Year

	0	*1*	*2*	*3*	*4*	*5*
Before-tax cash flow	$ − 1,256,666	$88,904	$103,904	$119,354	$135,268	$2,428,967
After-tax cash flow	− 1,256,666	89,807	99,560	109,527	119,708	2,004,271

Before-tax *IRR* = 20.00%
After-tax *IRR* = 15.69%

$4,026,664, which according to the TRA of 1986 can be depreciated over 31.5 years using straight-line depreciation. Second, it was assumed that the investor has a marginal ordinary income tax rate of 27.5 percent and has sufficient passive income to offset any passive losses that occur from the acquisition of this investment.

From Exhibit 14–13 we see that *ATIRR* is 15.69 percent. For this property to sell for $5,026,664, this rate of return should be sufficient to attract a typical investor to purchase the property. If investors are unwilling to pay that price, this implies that a 20 percent before-tax *IRR* is not sufficient. On the other hand, if a 15.69 percent after-tax *IRR* is greater than would be necessary to attract the typical investor, this implies that the before-tax *IRR* would not have to be as high as 20 percent to attract investors.

It should be obvious that rather than doing a before-tax analysis in the first place, we could have solved for the value that would result in a 15.69 percent *ATIRR* on equity. This would have made the algebra even more complex. However, by using a computer approach to find the value as described below, the algebra can be avoided.

A NOTE ON COMPUTER APPROACHES TO ESTIMATING VALUE

Our approach to finding value using discounted cash flow analysis has been to use algebraic formulas to calculate the value. Once the value was calculated, the value simply represented a price that would produce a specified *IRR* for a given set of assumptions about the property and the typical investor. In effect, we have solved an investment analysis problem backwards. That is, instead of starting with a price and calculating the *IRR*, we started with the *IRR* and found the price that would produce that *IRR*. With this in mind, the reader should realize that we could have also solved for the value by a trial-and-error process of searching for the price that produced the desired rate of return. That is, we could calculate the *IRR* (either before- or after-tax) for a range of prices. The cash flows would be different for each price because the mortgage payments and resale price depend on the assumed price (which is why we cannot simply discount the cash flows to arrive at the value estimate in the first place). By a series of sensitivity analyses, however, we can find the price that produces the required rate of return for a given set of assumptions about the property and the typical investor. The problem with this approach is that it obviously would be very time consuming if done manually. With the use of a computer program designed for investment analysis, however, the task becomes very simple. Computer programs are available which automatically do the search process to solve for the value. Alternatively, a spreadsheet problem such as Lotus 1–2–3® can be used to do the analysis. All the exhibits in this chapter (and most of the other chapters) were actually produced with templates written by the authors using Lotus 1–2–3.®

A FINAL NOTE ON APPRAISAL METHODOLOGY

Three approaches to valuation have been demonstrated here along with many of the techniques used in conjunction with each. Even though there are many combinations of approaches and techniques to valuation, such approaches and techniques are chosen when they best complement the data available for estimation. Stated another way, *the availability and quality of data should always dictate the methods and approaches chosen for valuation.* If perfect information were available, then theoretically the same value would result regardless of the methods chosen, be it cost, market, or income capitalization. Even with imperfect information, there should be some correspondence between the three approaches to value, which is the reason appraisal reports will typically contain estimates of value based on at least *two* approaches to determining value. While this procedure helps to corroborate the opinion of value, in the final analysis, it is up to the *user* of the report to be able to interpret, understand, and critically analyze the assumptions, techniques, and methods used to estimate value. Appraisals are only estimates of market value based on market conditions and information available at the time of the appraisal. Economic conditions are subject to much uncertainty, and appraisals should be interpreted and used in light of that uncertainty. Lenders and investors should be familiar with the techniques used by appraisers and with the assumptions made in the development of the estimate of value. However, the appraisal should be viewed as a complement to, not a substitute for, sound underwriting or investment analysis by the lender or investor.

QUESTIONS

1. What is the economic rationale for the cost approach? Under what conditions would the cost approach tend to give the best value estimate?
2. What is the economic rationale for the market approach? What information is necessary to use this approach? What does it mean for a property to be comparable?
3. What is an overall rate? What are the different ways of arriving at an overall rate to use for an appraisal?
4. If investors buy properties based on expected future benefits, what is the rationale for appraising a property without making any income or resale price projections?
5. Why do you think appraisers have traditionally not considered federal income taxes in appraisal methodology?
6. What is the relationship between a discount rate and a capitalization rate?
7. What is meant by a unit of comparison? Why is this important?
8. Why do you think appraisers usually use three different approaches when estimating value?
9. Under what conditions should financing be explicitly considered when estimating the value of a property?
10. What is meant by depreciation for the cost approach?
11. Why is it important for the appraiser to be aware of any below market financing that was used when a comparable property was purchased?
12. Why might an appraiser be forced to rely on the cost approach to value an old special-purpose industrial plant even though a lot of adjustments have to be made for economic depreciation and functional obsolescence?

PROBLEMS

1. An investor is considering the purchase of an existing office complex approximately five years old. The building, when constructed, was estimated to have an economic life of 50 years, and the building-to-value ratio was 80 percent. Based on current cost estimates, the structure would cost $1,000,000 to reproduce today. The building is expected to continue to wear out evenly over the 50-year period of its economic life. Estimates of other economic costs associated with the improvement are as follows:

Repairable physical depreciation	$60,000 to repair
Functional obsolescence (repairable)	20,000 to repair
Functional obsolescence (nonrepairable)	7,500 per year rent loss
Locational obsolescence	5,000 per year rent loss
	to the building

The land value has been established at $300,000 by comparable sales in the area. The investor believes that an appropriate opportunity cost for any deferred outlays or costs should be 15 percent per year. What would be the estimated value for this property?

2. Barry Gladstone is considering the purchase of a 120-unit apartment complex in Steel City, Pennsylvania. A market study of the market area reveals that an average rental of $300 per month per unit could be realized in the appropriate market area. During the last six months, two very comparable apartment complexes have sold in the same market area.

   Complex I, a 140-unit project, sold for $4,704,000. Its rental schedule indicates that $280 per month per unit constitutes its average rent per unit. Briarwood, a 90-unit complex, is presently renting units at $310 per month, and its selling price was $3,214,080. The apartment mix for both complexes is very similar to that of the subject property and both appear to have normal vacancy rates of about 5 percent annually.

   a. Based on the data provided here, how would an appraiser establish an estimate of value for Gladstone?

   b. What other information would be desirable in reaching a conclusion about the probable sale price that he could receive for his property?

3. LTD Corporation wants to buy a 320,000-square-foot distribution facility on the northern edge of a large midwestern city. The subject facility is presently renting for $1.87 per square foot. Based on recent market activity, two properties have sold within a 2-mile distance from the subject facility and are very comparable in size, design, and age. One facility is 350,000 square feet and is presently being leased for $1.85 per square foot annually. The second facility contains 300,000 square feet and is being leased for $1.90 per square foot. Market data indicate that current vacancies and operating expenses should run approximately 50 percent of gross income for these facilities. The first facility sold for $3,600,000, and the second sold for $3,000,000.

    a. With an overall capitalization rate approach to value, how would an estimate of value be made for the subject distribution facility?

    b. What additional information would be desirable before the final overall rate (*R*) is selected?

4. Melissa Lancaster is considering the purchase of a commercial property containing five (5) units comprising retail-commercial establishments. One of these units she plans to lease out as the Studio Minus 54 Disco. The commercial strip in question is presently 18,500 square feet. Current leases indicate the gross rents should be in the range of $2.25 per square foot annually, vacancy at 5 percent, and operating expenses approximately 35 percent of effective gross income. Lenders have indicated that an 11 percent mortgage would be obtainable with a 20-year term for approximately 70 percent of value. An analysis of comparable sales and a survey of owners of small commercial strip centers reveal equity dividend rates in the range of 7 percent.

    a. How could an estimate of value be made for this property?

    b. How sensitive is this value to a 1 percent difference (up or down) from the 7 percent equity dividend rate?

5. A building is being appraised which has been leased to a single tenant for the past 10 years. The lease has five years remaining. *NOI* is level at $175,000 per year. The appraiser estimates that the building could be leased today at a higher rate such that *NOI* would be $200,000 during the next year, and the *NOI* would probably increase about 3 percent per year over the next five to six years. The appraiser estimates that after the lease expires five years from now, it could be sold on the basis of a 10 percent terminal capitalization rate applied to the sixth-year *NOI*. Finally, the appraiser believes that an investor who purchased the property today would require a 12 percent before-tax rate of return (*BTIRR$_p$*) whether or not it was being leased at the time of purchase.

    a. What is the fee simple value of the property?

    b. What is the value of the leased fee estate?

    c. What do the answers to parts (a) and (b) imply about the value of the leasehold estate?

6. Sportspectics Limited, a partnership, has recently been established with the intention of acquiring a multipurpose sports and entertainment facility. This facility will accommodate racketball, tennis, and squash, and swimming and clubhouse activities.

    The building is located in the heart of a suburban area of a large eastern city and has been operating for approximately five years. Based on financial records, effective gross income is $650,000 per year. The effective gross income is projected to increase 3 percent per year. Operating expenses are expected to be about 30 percent of effective gross income per year. The present lender, who holds the mortgage on the property, is agreeable to refinancing the complex at 12 percent interest for a period of 25 years at 70 percent of value. Other lenders have indicated an interest in financing the project on essentially the same terms.

    The appraiser believes in this case that an ownership period of about 10 years is typical for this type of facility and has found that similar complexes in other cities, as well as large hotel/motel and recreation properties, have appreciated in value at about 3 percent per year over the 10-year holding period and will continue to do so.

A major risk in property of this type is that rental revenues are tied to the discretionary income of consumers, which tends to be highly sensitive to changes in business conditions. However, inclement weather throughout much of the winter provides a strong demand for such activities. These two factors have a positive and a negative effect on value from the perspective of risk. Based on a survey of past common stock performance in the recreational industries and on historical returns estimated from similar operations in similar sized cities growing at the same rate as the local economy, the appraiser estimates that a 3 percent risk premium over and above the mortgage rate provides a reasonable before-tax investment yield on equity for an investor in a property of this type over the term of the investment.

a. Estimate the value of Sportspectics.

b. What does the answer to part (a) imply about the dollar amount of financing that would be used by the investor?

c. What is the first-year debt coverage ratio, assuming the property is financed at the amount determined in part (b)?

Appendix: Additional Financing Considerations in Valuation

MORTGAGE-EQUITY ANALYSIS: DEBT COVERAGE RATIO CONSIDERATIONS

Chapter 14 discussed a technique that can be used to estimate the value of a property based on satisfying both mortgage and equity criteria. That is, financing information was specified for the mortgage loan, and an equity yield rate (*IRR*) and investment holding period were specified for a typical investor. The following general formula was given in Chapter 14 for the value (*V*) of a property based on mortgage-equity criteria:

$$V = M + E$$

where

$$M = \text{the present value of the cash flows to the mortgage lender}$$
$$E = \text{the present value of the cash flows to the equity investor}$$

During the operating years of the property, the equity investor receives cash flow equal to the net operating income (*NOI*) less the debt service (*DS*) (assuming there are no participations). At the time of reversion (i.e., when the property is sold), the equity investor receives the sale proceeds (*REV*) less the outstanding mortgage balance (*MB*). Thus, the value of the property can be expressed in the following present value terms:

$$V = M + PVNOI - PVDS + PVREV - PVMB$$

Because the mortgage loan (*M*) is assumed to be made at the time the property is being valued, it is already equal to the present value of the cash flows to the mortgage lender.

In the example in Chapter 14, specific assumptions were made about how the mortgage (M) would be determined. It was assumed that the loan would be based on a percent of the unknown value (V) expressed by a loan-to-value ratio (M/V). Thus M could be written as (M/V)V, resulting in the expression

$$V = \frac{M}{V}(V) + PVNOI - PVDS + PVREV - PVMB$$

It must be emphasized that in the above expression, it is assumed that whatever the value (V) is for the property, the lender will loan a specified percentage of that value based on a given loan-to-value ratio. In most appraisal situations, this may be an appropriate assumption for the loan amount (M). This approach, however, does not explicitly consider that many lenders are reluctant to make a loan that would result in a debt coverage ratio (DCR) that is too high. The amount the bank may be willing to lend might be based on a specified DCR rather than on a loan-to-value ratio. For example, the bank might only be willing to make a loan such that the DCR based on the NOI for the first operating year is 1.25. In these cases the lender is using the DCR to determine the loan amount rather than using a loan-to-value ratio. If financing for the type of property being appraised is being based by lenders on a DCR at the time of appraisal, then the appraiser should base the value estimate on this criteria when applying mortgage-equity analysis. How does this change our expression for M? Recall from Chapter 10 that the debt coverage ratio is defined as

$$DCR = \frac{NOI}{DS}$$

We can therefore find the maximum debt service (DS) for a given first-year net operating income (NOI_1) and DCR as follows:

$$DS = \frac{NOI_1}{DCR}$$

We also know that DS is equal to M multiplied by the mortgage loan constant (MLC) for that loan. Thus we also know that the loan amount must be equal to the debt service divided by the mortgage constant:

$$M = \frac{DS}{MLC}$$

Combining the above expressions, we obtain

$$M - \frac{NOI_1}{(DCR)\,(MLC)}$$

The expression for the value of the property now becomes

$$V = \frac{NOI_1}{(DCR)(MLC)} + PVNOI - PVDS + PVREV - PVMB$$

The point to be emphasized is that the appraiser must know how financing is determined in the market for the type of property being appraised so that a proper approach is used to value the property. To illustrate, we will use the same information as the previous example, which used mortgage-equity capitalization, except that we do not use a debt coverage ratio to determine the loan amount. Recall that the property had NOI of $500,000 per year, which was expected to increase 3 percent per year, and property value was also expected to increase 3 percent per year. The loan had a 10 percent interest rate and was amortized over 25 years. It was assumed that the investor could borrow 75 percent of the value of the property. Using a 20 percent discount rate, we estimated a value of $5,026,664 for the subject property. This implies that a loan can be obtained for $3,769,998 (.75 × $5,026,664) with annual debt service of $411,096. Using the first-year *NOI* of $500,000, we can calculate a debt coverage ratio of 1.22 ($500,000/$411,096).

We now assume that the lender requires a first-year debt coverage ratio of at least 1.25. How does this change the value? Using the procedure outlined above, we can calculate the *DS* as follows:

$$DS = \frac{NOI_1}{DCR} = \frac{\$500,000}{1.25} = \$400,000$$

To find *PVDS*, we multiply the *DS* by *PVIFA*(20%, 5 yrs.). Thus

$$PVDS = (\$400,000)(2.990612) = \$1,196,245$$

The initial balance of the loan would be

$$M = \frac{DS}{MLC} = \frac{\$400,000}{(.0098087)12} = \$3,668,241$$

The mortgage balance (*MB*) would be found by multiplying the loan amount by the same loan balance factor (*MBF*) as before. We have

$$MB = (\$3,668,241)(.941638) = \$3,454,155$$

Multiplying this by *PVIF*(20%, 5 yrs.) results in the present value of the mortgage balance. Thus,

$$PVMB = (\$3,454,155)(.401878) = \$1,388,149$$

The *NOI* is not affected by the loan amount. Thus, the present value of the *NOI* (*PVNOI*) will be the same as calculated in the original example, $1,570,923. Similarly, *PVREV* will be the same percent of the unknown value as before (.465887*V*).

Combining all of this information, we have

$$V = \frac{NOI_1}{(DCR)\,(MLC)} + PVNOI - PVDS + PVREV - PVMB$$

$$V = \frac{\$500,000}{(1.25)(.009087)(12)} + \$1,570,923 - \$1,196,245$$
$$+ .465887V - \$1,388,149$$
$$V = \$3,668,241 + \$1,570,923 - \$1,196,245 + .465887V - \$1,388,149$$
$$.534113 = \$2,654,770$$
$$V = \$4,970,428$$

Note that the answer is slightly less than we obtained when a 75 percent loan was assumed to be available. That value was $5,026,664 versus a value of $4,970,428 when the loan is constrained by the 1.25 debt coverage requirement. This is because the investor is not able to use as much financial leverage as before, whereas we assumed that the investor required the same 20 percent rate of return (*BTIRR_e*). Of course, it might be argued that the discount rate should be lower than before because there is less risk with the lower loan amount. Depending on how much the discount rate is reduced, this will offset some or all of the reduction in value due to the debt coverage constraint. The point is that the appraiser should consider the possible effect of the availability of financing on the value of a property, especially in cases where less than typical financing is available.

ANALYSIS OF BELOW MARKET LOANS

In Chapter 9 we discussed the fact that below market rate loans can affect the price that a purchaser is willing to pay for a property. We also discussed a procedure for estimating the premium that would be paid for a property with a below market loan. At that time our analysis was based solely on considering the terms of the loan. That is, the value of the below market loan was a function of the difference between the interest rate on the below market loan as opposed to the market rate of interest. It could be said that this approach was based on *lender criteria.*

We now consider an alternative way of estimating the effect of below market financing on the price an investor would pay for a property. The approach will be based on what might be referred to as *investor criteria.* We will assume that the investor is willing to purchase a property based on some specified measure, such as an equity dividend rate or equity investment yield, regardless of whether a below market loan can be obtained. To illustrate, assume a property is being appraised which is estimated to have a first-year *NOI* of $100,000. The appraiser determines that the typical investor for this type of property requires an 8 percent equity dividend rate ($BTCF/E$). Lenders are willing to make a 75 percent loan (M/V) at a 10 percent interest rate with monthly payments over 25 years. This results in a mortgage constant of .109044. Using the band of investment approach to determine the overall R, as discussed in Chapter 14, we can obtain the following overall rate:

	Component		*Weight*		*Weighted Average*
Mortgage	.109044	×	.75	=	.08178
Equity	.0800	×	.25	=	.02000
					.10178 = R

Based on expected *NOI* of $100,000, the property value would be estimated at $100,000 divided by .10178, or $982,482. Based on this value, we would expect that the mortgage amount would be $736,861, or 75 percent of value.

Now suppose that the seller has a $700,000 assumable loan at an 8 percent interest rate with 20 years remaining on the loan. Payments are $70,261 per year. What price would the investor be willing to pay for the property? It is reasonable to assume that the investor would still require an 8 percent equity dividend rate on the equity invested in the property. With the below market rate loan, the cash flow available to the investor (*BTCF*) would be $100,000 less $70,261, or $29,739. Dividing this by the equity dividend rate of 8 percent results in an *equity* value of 371,737. This is how much the investor would be willing to invest in the property (E). The total value is the value of the equity (E) plus the amount of loan (M). With the assumable loan, the mortgage (M) is $700,000. Thus the total value is $371,737 + $700,000 = $1,071,737. This is $89,255 more than the value estimated with the market rate loan. This difference represents the *premium* that the investor would be willing to pay for the assumable loan.

Several comments must be made about the above analysis. First, the value of the *real estate* would still be $982,482. The higher *price* that the investor would pay for the property with the assumable loan includes the value of the property plus a ''financing premium'' representing the value of being able to assume the below market rate loan. Appraisers should be careful to make this distinction in an appraisal report. Had this sale been a comparable sale being used in an appraisal, and the appraiser observed the property actually sell for $1,071,737 with the below market rate loan, the appraiser would have to recognize that the price was affected by the below market loan. The appraiser would adjust the sale price downward to $982,482, which would be the cash equivalent value of the real estate. (Recall our discussion of cash equivalency in Chapter 9.)

Second, the analysis assumed that the equity dividend rate remained constant. This is only reasonable if the risk is the same for both the assumable loan and the market loan. Because the amount of loan is about the same in this case, this is probably reasonable. The reader is cautioned that if the amount of the assumable loan is much greater than the amount generally available from a conventional lender, the risk would be greater (as discussed in Chapter 12), and thus a higher equity dividend rate would be appropriate. Similarly, if the assumable loan were significantly lower than available in the market, the appraiser would have to either use a lower equity dividend rate or include a second mortgage in the analysis to equalize the loan amounts so that the same equity dividend rate could be used.

A final point is that the above example used the band of investment approach to estimate the effect of the below market loan. This approach assumes that the equity dividend rate can be used to reflect investment criteria (i.e., that the required investment yield rate would be implicit in the equity dividend rate). If the appraiser believes that a discounted cash flow approach using equity yield rates is more appropriate, then the mortgage-equity analysis approach discussed in Chapter 14 could be used. The logic would be similar to the above example; that is, the value would be estimated with market financing (as done in the chapter), then estimated with the below market loan. At this point, the reader may be somewhat bewildered with all the different ways that have been discussed to estimate the value of a property! Unfortunately, there is not simply *one way* of estimating value. Different types of properties in different locations under different economic conditions may have quite different economic forces which affect the value. It is the appraiser's job to determine which approaches are reasonable for a given appraisal. It is often said that this involves art as well as science. Certainly the ability of the appraiser to understand the market and use good judgment in the choice of appraisal methods is important. We have attempted to point out the key issues that an appraiser should consider in an appraisal report. As emphasized earlier, it is up to the owner of the report to determine if these issues have been properly addressed.

PROBLEMS

1. A property is being appraised which currently has *NOI* of $100,000 per year. Market rents are expected to increase such that the *NOI* and the value of the property are expected to increase five percent per year over the next five years. The property can be financed with a loan at a 10 percent interest rate and a 20-year term (monthly payments). The lender requires a minimum debt coverage ratio of 1.25. The appraiser believes that a 15 percent discount rate would be appropriate.
   a. What is the estimated value of the property?
   b. What loan-to-value ratio is implied by the answer to part (a)?

2. A property recently sold for $120,000. The purchaser assumed the seller's loan which had a balance of $90,000. The interest rate on the loan was 8 percent, and it had 15 years remaining. Payments are $860.09 per month, or $10,321 per year. The market interest rate for a $90,000 loan on the property would be 11 percent for a loan with a 15-year term. The current *NOI* on the property is $14,000 per year.
   a. What is the equity dividend rate for the purchaser?
   b. Assuming the equity dividend rate in part (a) is typical for this type of property. Also assume that a $90,000 loan at an 11 percent interest rate and a 15-year term would be typical for this type of property. What is the value of the *real estate*?

Chapter 15

Disposition and Renovation of Income Properties

In the preceding chapters dealing with income properties, much attention has been given to measuring returns on investment in real estate and the extent to which financial leverage, federal income taxes, and other factors affect that return. Returns were always calculated based on a projected holding period for the property. In this chapter we take a closer look at the factors which would affect an investor's decision to choose a particular holding period. We also consider alternatives to disposition, such as renovating and refinancing the property.

DISPOSITION DECISIONS

An investor purchases a real estate investment based on the benefits expected to be received over an *anticipated* holding period. That is, the investor computes the various measures of investment performance based on expectations at the time the property is purchased. After the property is purchased, however, many things can change which affect the actual performance of the property. These same factors may affect the investor's decision as to whether the property continues to meet his investment objectives. For example, market rents may not be increasing as fast as expected, thus reducing the investor's cash flow. Tax laws may have changed, as they did in 1986 (and in many years prior to that, as we saw in Chapter 11), thus changing the benefit for some investors more than others. The point is that a periodic evaluation should be made to determine whether properties should be sold.

Even if the investor's projections for a property are accurate, there may be factors that will influence the investor to sell after a specified number of years. One factor in particular relates to the potential benefits associated with leverage that we have discussed in several previous chapters. Assuming that the mortgage on the property has positive amortization, the outstanding mortgage balance decreases each year and the investor's equity position increases. Although this "equity buildup" may appear desirable in the sense that the investor will get more cash from the property when it is sold, it also means that each year the investor has more funds "tied up" in the property. Any increase in the value of the property over time, whether anticipated or not, will also contribute to an increase in the investor's equity buildup.

Equity buildup represents funds that the investor could place in another investment if the current property were sold. This is the *opportunity cost* of *not* selling the property. The proceeds that the investor could have received if the property were sold can be thought of as the amount of equity investment made to *keep* the property for an additional period of time. But unless the property is refinanced, a greater portion of equity capital remains invested in relation to the cash flow being received from continuing to operate the property. Further, while the total mortgage payment (debt service) remains the same, the interest portion of the payment decreases each year, resulting in lower tax deductions. Hence, the investor is also losing the benefits of financial leverage each year.

A Decision Rule for Property Disposition

What follows is a discussion of the factors that should be considered by investors to determine whether a property should be sold or whether ownership should be retained. It is based on an incremental, or marginal, return criteria that should be utilized by investors when faced with such decision making.

To illustrate the criteria that should be applied when making a decision to keep a property or to sell it, we assume that an investor acquired a very small retail property five years ago at a cost of $200,000. The Apex Center was 15 years old at the time of purchase and was financed with a 75 percent mortgage made at 11 percent interest for 25 years. Depreciation is being taken on a straight-line basis with 80 percent of the original cost ($160,000) allocated to the building and 20 percent allocated to land. We assume that the property was purchased *prior* to the Tax Reform Act of 1986.[1] Thus, straight-line depreciation was used over a depreciable life of 19 years. The reader should also note that that marginal tax of 50 percent is being used. This was the maximum rate in effect from 1981 to 1986. Results during the *past five* years of operation are shown in Exhibit 15–1.

If Apex were sold *today,* it is estimated that the property could be sold for $250,000. Selling costs equal to 6 percent of the sale price would have to be paid. The cash flows from sale of the property (if sold today) are shown in Exhibit 15–2. Note that it is assumed that the capital gain from sale of the property is taxed as ordinary income in accordance with the Tax Reform Act of 1986. This is because the property is assumed to have been sold *after* the Tax Reform Act was passed. These assumptions are made in this illustration for two reasons. First, it represents the typical situation facing investors at the time this book is being revised. Second, the reader should understand the implication

---

[1]Although accelerated depreciation was available at that time, straight-line was typically used by investors for nonresidential real estate because of depreciation recapture rules that were in effect at that time which offset the benefits of using accelerated depreciation. For a discussion of the optimal depreciation method prior to 1986, see Brueggeman, William B.; Fisher, Jeffrey D.; and Stern, Jerrold S. "Choosing an Optimal Depreciation Method under 1981 Tax Legislation," *Real Estate Review,* Winter 1982.

EXHIBIT 15–1 Past Operating Results, Apex Center

	Year				
	1	*2*	*3*	*4*	*5*
A. Before-tax cash flow					
Rents	$ 39,000	$ 40,560	$ 42,182	$ 43,870	$45,624
Less operating expenses	19,500	20,280	21,091	21,935	22,812
Net operating income (*NOI*)	19,500	20,280	21,091	21,935	22,812
Less debt service (*DS*)	17,642	17,642	17,642	17,642	17,642
Before-tax cash flow	$ 1,858	$ 2,638	$ 3,449	$ 4,293	$ 5,170
B. Taxable income or loss					
Net operating income (*NOI*)	$ 19,500	$ 20,280	$ 21,091	$ 21,935	$22,812
Less interest	16,441	16,302	16,146	15,973	15,780
Depreciation	8,421	8,421	8,421	8,421	8,421
Taxable income (loss)	− 5,362	− 4,443	− 3,476	− 2,460	− 1,389
Tax	$ − 2,681	$ − 2,221	$ − 1,738	$ − 1,230	$ − 695
C. After-tax cash flow					
Before-tax cash flow (*BTCF*)	$ 1,858	$ 2,638	$ 3,449	$ 4,293	$ 5,170
Less tax	− 2,681	− 2,221	− 1,738	− 1,230	− 695
After-tax cash flow (*ATCF*)	$ 4,539	$ 4,859	$ 5,187	$ 5,523	$ 5,865

EXHIBIT 15–2 Estimates of Cash Flows from Sale Today

Sale price		$250,000
Less sale costs (at 6.00 percent)		15,000
Less mortgage balance		142,432
Before-tax cash flow (*BTCF*)		92,568
Taxes in year of sale		
Sale price	$250,000	
Sale costs	15,000	
Original cost basis	$200,000	
Less accumulated depreciation	42,105	
Adjusted basis		157,895
Capital gains tax at 28 percent		77,105
Tax from sale		21,589
After-tax cash flow from sale (*ATCF_s*)		$ 70,978

of purchasing a property under one tax law, then facing a decision to sell it under a different tax law.

Using the information in Exhibit 15–2, we can calculate the rate of return that the investor will have realized for the *past* 5 years if the property is sold. The cash flow summary is shown in Exhibit 15–3.

EXHIBIT 15–3   Cash Flow Summary Assuming Sale Today

| | End of Year | | | | | |
	0	*1*	*2*	*3*	*4*	*5*
Before-tax cash flow	$ – 50,000	$1,858	$2,638	$3,449	$4,293	$97,738
After-tax cash flow	– 50,000	4,539	4,859	5,187	5,523	76,843

Before-tax *IRR* = 18.26%
After-tax *IRR* = 14.83%

We see that if the property were sold today, the investor would earn an expost (historical) before-tax return (*BTIRR*) of 18.26 percent and an after-tax return (*ATIRR*) of 14.83 percent. But does this really help us decide whether to sell the property? For example, suppose that the investor had expected an after-tax return of 16 percent and now finds that if the property is sold a return of only 14.83 percent would be earned. Does that mean the property should be sold? We really cannot say. All we can say is that the property did not perform as well as originally expected. It may be a good investment in the future.

If the historic return calculated above is also an indication of *future* performance, then it will likely be reflected in the price that the property can be sold for today. This is because the current sale price of the property depends on expected *future* performance for a typical buyer. However, future performance does not necessarily have any relationship to historic returns.

IRR FOR HOLDING VERSUS SALE OF THE PROPERTY

If we are to determine whether the investor should keep the property, we must evaluate the *expected future performance* of the property. The essential question facing the investor at this time is whether Apex should be sold and funds from the sale invested in another property. Assuming that the investor believes that a reliable forecast for Apex can be made for the *next* five years, estimates of *ATCF* are made for years 6 to 10 and are presented in Exhibit 15–4. The investor believes that rents and expenses will *not* continue to grow at the same 4 percent per year rate as for the past five years. They are now projected to increase at a 3 percent rate for the next five years. Note in the exhibit that depreciation charges remain at $8,421 per year based on *original cost* and the *original depreciation method*. This is because the property was purchased prior to the Tax Reform Act of 1986, and the law did not require existing property owners to switch to the new (longer) depreciable life of 31.5 years for nonresidential property. However, the investor's tax rate is now assumed to be 28 percent because this is the maximum rate under the current tax law. Also note that mortgage payments and interest charges are still based on original financing.

If the forecast period is considered to be five years (ten years from the date of purchase), *ATCF*$_s$ must also be computed. Using a 3% per rate of price appreciation, the owner

EXHIBIT 15–4   Estimated Future Operating Results: Apex Center (if not sold)

	Year (since purchase)				
	6	*7*	*8*	*9*	*10*
A. Before-tax cash flow					
Rent	$47,449	$48,873	$50,339	$51,849	$53,405
Less expenses	23,725	24,436	25,170	25,925	26,702
Net operating income (*NOI*)	23,725	24,436	25,170	25,925	26,702
Less debt service	17,642	17,642	17,642	17,642	17,642
Before-tax cash flow (*BTCF*)	$ 6,083	$ 6,794	$ 7,528	$ 8,283	$ 9,060
B. Taxable income or loss					
Net operating income (*NOI*)	$23,725	$24,436	$25,170	$25,925	$26,702
Less interest	15,565	15,325	15,056	14,757	14,423
Depreciation	8,421	8,421	8,421	8,421	8,421
Taxable income (loss)	− 261	691	1,692	2,746	3,858
Tax	$ − 73	$ 193	$ 474	$ 769	$ 1,080
C. After-tax cash flow					
Before-tax cash flow (*BTCF*)	6,083	6,794	7,528	8,283	9,060
Less tax	− 73	193	474	769	1,080
After-tax cash flow (*ATCF*)	$ 6,156	$ 6,601	$ 7,054	$ 7,514	$ 7,980

estimates that Apex should increase in value to $289,819 by then. An estimate of what $ATCF_s$ will be is computed in Exhibit 15–5. Note that the mortgage balance and adjusted basis are based on a total period of 10 years, or from the date of acquisition.

To fully analyze whether a property should be sold also requires investigation into (1) the alternative investments available in which cash realized from a sale may be reinvested and (2) the tax consequences of selling one property and acquiring another. Clearly, if Apex is sold and an alternative investment is made, that investment will have to provide the investor with a high enough return to make up for the return given up if Apex is sold. The question is how much of an *ATIRR* must the alternative investment provide if Apex is sold?

If Apex is sold to acquire another property, capital gains taxes and selling expenses (if any) must be paid before funds are available for reinvestment. Hence, when considering the sale of one property and the acquisition of another, the first task facing the investor is to ascertain how much cash would be available for reinvestment should the Apex Center be sold. The estimated sale price for the Apex Center at this time is $250,000. However, the relevant data for the investor to consider is how much cash will be available for reinvestment after payment of the mortgage balance, taxes, and selling expenses. This is found by computing $ATCF_s$ as if the property were sold *immediately,* as we did before. We saw in Exhibit 15–2 that if the property were sold today the investor would net $70,978 after repayment of the mortgage and payment of capital gains taxes. Thus $70,978 would be available for reinvestment should the investor decide to *sell* Apex at this time. Note that capital gains tax rates are expected to remain at 28 percent for the next five

EXHIBIT 15–5   Calculation of After-Tax Cash Flow from Sale after Five
Additional Years

Sales price		$289,819
Mortgage balance		129,348
Selling expenses at 6.00 percent		17,389
Before-tax cash flow		143,081
Taxes in year of sale		
Sales price	$289,819	
Selling expenses	17,389	
Original cost basis	$200,000	
Accumulated depreciation	84,211	
Adjusted basis	115,789	
Total taxable gain	$156,640	
Capital gains tax at 28.00 percent		43,859
After-tax cash flow from sale ($ATCF_s$)		$ 99,222

years. Sale calculations should always be based on the tax laws that are expected to be
in effect when the property is sold. In our case, for example, even though the property
was *purchased* at a time when a 60 percent capital gains exclusion was available, because
the property is being sold under the new tax law, the capital gains exclusion is no longer
available. However, the maximum marginal tax has declined from 50 percent to 28 percent.

The owner must now consider whether or not the $70,978 can be reinvested at a greater
rate of return ($ATIRR$) than the return that would be earned *if Apex was not sold*. In other
words, we want to know what the *minimum ATIRR* would have to be on an alternative
investment (equivalent in risk to Apex) to make the investor indifferent between continuing
to own Apex and purchasing the alternative property.

The answer is relatively straightforward. We know that the cash available to reinvest
is $70,978 if Apex is sold. Also, we know that if Apex is sold, the investor gives up
$ATCF$ for the next five years (Exhibit 15–2) and the $ATCF_s$ of $99,222 at the end of the
five years. Hence the $70,978 must generate a high enough $ATIRR$ to offset the cash
flows that would be lost by selling Apex. The cash flow summary and return calculation
is as follows:

Cash Flow Summary

			Year			
	5	6	7	8	9	10
After-tax cash flow	– $70,978	$6,156	$6,601	$7,054	$7,514	$107,202
Internal rate of return = 15.60%						

Therefore, the investor would have to earn an *ATIRR* greater than 15.60 percent on the funds obtained from the sale of the Apex Center. These funds must be used to purchase some alternative investment, *equal in risk,* to justify selling Apex. In this case, if an alternative investment is equal in risk to Apex and the investor estimates that the $ATIRR_e$ from that alternative would *exceed* 15.60 percent, then the sale of Apex and the acquisition of the alternative would be justified. If the $ATIRR_e$ on the alternative is expected to be less than 15.6 percent, then Apex should be retained.

RETURN TO A NEW INVESTOR

To examine how incentives for the current investor to hold the property can differ from that of a new investor in the same property, even if both have the same expectations for future rents and expenses, we will assume a new investor purchases the property at the current value. Recall that Apex is currently worth $250,000 and was financed 5 years ago with a $150,000 loan which is being amortized over 25 years with monthly payments at 11 percent interest rate. To eliminate the effect of financing (leverage) on our comparison with the present owner, we assume that the new investor assumes the existing loan and does not obtain any additional financing. Thus, the only difference for a new investor will be the difference in the way the tax law affects the new investor versus the existing investor. First, the new investor will have a new adjusted basis in the property. Assuming that the building is still 80 percent of the total value in year 5, the new investor will be able to depreciate 80 percent of $250,000 or $200,000. This compares depreciation for the present owner, which is based on his original basis of $160,000. Second, a new investor must depreciate the property based on the tax law in effect at the time of purchase. Thus, if the new investor purchases under the Tax Reform Act of 1986, then a 31.5-year depreciable life must be used. This is a much longer period than the 19-year schedule that would still apply to the present owner. In summary, the new investor gets an increased depreciable basis but must use a longer depreciable life. How will these differences affect the *IRR* for a new investor? Exhibit 15–6 shows the projected cash flows and $ATIRR_e$.

Exhibit 15–6 shows that a new investor would earn an $ATIRR_e$ of 9.1 percent. Although this may be a competitive return for a new investor, given his opportunity cost, it is less than the current investor can earn (15.6 percent) by keeping the property, primarily because the existing investor can continue to use a depreciation schedule based on the old tax law. Thus we see that tax law changes affect the relative benefits of existing versus new investors in the same property. If the tax law becomes *less* favorable as it did in 1986, this tends to favor existing investors. If the tax law becomes *more* favorable, as it did in 1981 when *ACRS* was passed and depreciable lives were shortened considerably, then new investors tend to be favored. Thus tax law changes tend to affect the turnover, or sale of real estate. It is important for students to understand these concepts since tax laws are always subject to change, and these changes affect the relative risk and return opportunities for new and existing investors.

EXHIBIT 15–6   Projections for a New Investor

	Year				
	6	7	8	9	10

Calculation of After-Tax Cash Flow from Operations

	6	7	8	9	10
Rent	$47,449	$48,873	$50,339	$51,849	$53,405
Less expenses	23,725	24,436	25,170	25,925	26,702
Net operating income	23,725	24,436	25,170	25,925	26,702
Less debt service	17,642	17,642	17,642	17,642	17,642
Before-tax cash flow	6,083	6,794	7,528	8,283	9,060
Net operating income	23,725	24,436	25,170	25,925	26,702
Less interest	15,565	15,325	15,056	14,757	14,423
Depreciation	6,349	6,349	6,349	6,349	6,349
Taxable income	1,811	2,763	3,764	4,818	5,930
Tax	507	774	1,054	1,349	1,660
Before-tax cash flow	6,083	6,794	7,528	8,283	9,060
Tax	507	774	1,054	1,349	1,660
After-tax cash flow	$ 5,576	$ 6,021	$ 6,474	$ 6,934	$ 7,400

Calculation of After-Tax Cash Flow from Sale after 5 Years

Sale price		$289,819
Less mortgage balance		129,348
Less selling expenses at 6.00%		17,389
Before-tax cash flow ($BTCF_s$)		143,081
Taxes in year of sale		
Sale price	$289,819	
Less selling expenses	17,389	
Original cost basis	$250,000	
Less accumulated depreciation	31,746	
Adjusted basis	218,254	
Total taxable gain	54,175	
Capital gains tax at 28.00%		15,169
After-tax cash flow from sale		127,912

Cash Flow Year Summary

	5	6	7	8	9	10
ATCF	$− 107,568	$5,576	$6,021	$6,474	$6,934	$135,312

Internal rate of return ($ATIRR_e$) = 9.10%

Marginal Rate of Return

The return for selling versus holding the property calculated earlier (15.6 percent, using cash flows from Exhibits 15–4 and 15–5) is an $ATIRR_e$ based on holding the property for *five additional years*. This period of time was based on the assumption that if the property was sold the funds would be placed in an investment similar to the one being sold which would also be evaluated on the basis of a holding period of five additional years. A slightly different approach is to consider the return that would result from holding the property only *one* additional year. This return would be calculated the same way as above, but only one additional year of operating cash flow would be projected, and the $ATCF_s$ from a sale could be projected after one year. We refer to this one-year $ATIRR_e$ as the *marginal return*. For example, in the year that we are considering the sale of the property, we can ask, "what will the marginal return be if the property is held one more year"? Then (assuming the property has not been sold) at the end of that additional year we ask, "what is the marginal return for holding one more year"? This process can be continued until the property is actually sold (or renovated).

To illustrate calculation of the marginal return, we assume that *NOI* will actually increase 3 percent per year (the same rate used for our projections) over the next 10 years. We assume that the resale price will also actually increase 3 percent per year. Exhibit 15–7 shows the projected after-tax cash flows from operating the property over the next 10 years $(ATCF_o)$. For each of the 10 years (years 6 through 15), the exhibit also shows the projected after-tax cash flow $(ATCF_s)$ that would result *if* the property was sold at the end of that year.

The information in Exhibit 15–7 can be used to calculate the marginal rate of return for each of the next 10 years. Each year the marginal rate of return is based on the benefit of receiving $ATCF_o$ for one additional year and $ATCF_s$ at the end of the additional year. The cost of receiving this cash flow is $ATCF_s$ for the current year. Since only one year is involved, the return calculation is simply as follows:

$$MRR = \frac{ATCF_s(\text{year } t+1) + ATCF_o(\text{year } t+1) - ATCF_s(\text{year } t)}{ATCF_s(\text{year } t)}$$

Exhibit 15–8 shows what the *MRR* is for years 6 through 15. The *MRR*s shown in Exhibit 15–8 are plotted in Exhibit 15–9. We see that the marginal rate of return *(MRR)* rises until year 10 and then begins to fall. Increasing rents and increases in the value of the property tend to increase the *MRR*. Equity buildup from the price appreciation and loan repayment, however, tends to lower the *MRR*. After year 10 the effect of equity buildup dominates. How long should the property be held? The answer is that *the property should be sold when the marginal rate of return falls below the rate at which funds can be reinvested.* For example, suppose the investor believes that funds can be reinvested in a different property (with the same risk) at a rate of 15.5 percent. This means that the property should be sold in the 14th year, because the *MRR* falls below 15.5 percent after year 14.

The above analysis assumes that the reinvestment rate would be constant throughout the next 10 years. It is not necessary to make this assumption. For example, the rein-

EXHIBIT 15–7 Projections of ATCF_o and ATCF_s for 10 Additional Years

					Year (after purchase)					
	6	7	8	9	10	11	12	13	14	15
				Calculation of After-Tax Cash Flow from Operations						
Rent	$ 47,449	$ 48,873	$ 50,339	$ 51,849	$ 53,405	$ 55,007	$ 56,657	$ 58,357	$ 60,108	$ 61,911
Less expenses	23,725	24,436	25,170	25,925	26,702	27,503	28,329	29,178	30,054	30,955
NOI	23,725	24,436	25,170	25,925	26,702	27,503	28,329	29,178	30,054	30,955
Debt service	17,642	17,642	17,642	17,642	17,642	17,642	17,642	17,642	17,642	17,642
BTCF	6,083	6,794	7,528	8,283	9,060	9,861	10,687	11,536	12,412	13,313
NOI	23,725	24,436	25,170	25,925	26,702	27,503	28,329	29,178	30,054	30,955
Less interest	15,565	15,325	15,056	14,757	14,423	14,051	13,635	13,172	12,654	12,077
Depreciation	8,421	8,421	8,421	8,421	8,421	8,421	8,421	8,421	8,421	8,421
Taxable income	−261	691	1,692	2,746	3,858	5,032	6,272	7,586	8,978	10,457
Tax	−73	193	474	769	1,080	1,409	1,756	2,124	2,514	2,928
BTCF	6,083	6,794	7,528	8,283	9,060	9,861	10,687	11,536	12,412	13,313
Tax	−73	193	474	769	1,080	1,409	1,756	2,124	2,514	2,928
ATCF	$ 6,156	$ 6,601	$ 7,054	$ 7,514	$ 7,980	$ 8,453	$ 8,930	$ 9,412	$ 9,898	$ 10,385
				Calculation of After-Tax Cash Flow from Sale						
Sale price	$257,500	$265,225	$273,182	$281,377	$289,819	$298,513	$307,468	$316,693	$326,193	$335,979
Mortgage balance	140,355	138,037	135,452	132,567	129,348	125,757	121,750	117,280	112,292	106,727
Selling expenses	15,450	15,914	16,391	16,883	17,389	17,911	18,448	19,002	19,572	20,159
BTCF	101,695	111,274	121,339	131,928	143,081	154,845	167,270	180,411	194,330	209,093
Original cost basis	200,000	200,000	200,000	200,000	200,000	200,000	200,000	200,000	200,000	200,000
Accumulation depreciation	50,526	58,947	67,368	75,789	84,211	92,632	101,053	109,474	117,895	126,316
Adjusted basis	149,474	141,053	132,632	124,211	115,789	107,368	98,947	90,526	82,105	73,684
Sale price	257,500	265,225	273,182	281,377	289,819	298,513	307,468	316,693	326,193	335,979
Selling expenses	15,450	15,914	16,391	16,883	17,389	17,911	18,448	19,002	19,572	20,159
Adjusted basis	149,474	141,053	132,632	124,211	115,789	107,368	98,947	90,526	82,105	73,684
Total taxable gain	92,576	108,259	124,159	140,284	156,640	173,234	190,073	207,165	224,516	242,136
BTCF	101,695	111,274	121,339	131,928	143,081	154,845	167,270	180,411	194,330	209,093
Capital gains tax	25,921	30,312	34,765	39,280	43,859	48,505	53,220	58,006	62,865	67,798
ATCF_s	$ 75,774	$ 80,962	$ 86,575	$ 92,648	$ 99,222	$106,340	$114,050	$122,405	$131,465	$141,295

EXHIBIT 15–8   Marginal Rate of Return for the Next 10 Years

Year	Marginal Rate of Return (percent)
6	15.43
7	15.56
8	15.65
9	15.69
10	15.71
11	15.69
12	15.65
13	15.58
14	15.49
15	15.38

EXHIBIT 15–9   Holding Period Analysis

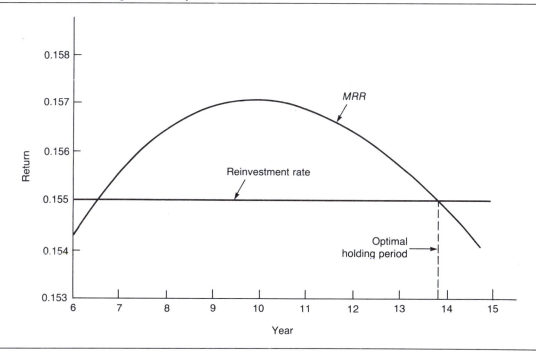

vestment rate may have been expected to rise through time due to an increase in the general level of interest rates and yields on alternative investments. This could obviously change the optimal holding period, as illustrated in Exhibit 15–10. Because of the rising reinvestment rate, the optimal holding period is now about 11 years.

REFINANCING AS AN ALTERNATIVE TO DISPOSITION

As we have discussed, after an investor has owned a property for a number of years, equity may build up as a result of increase in the property value and amortization of the loan. Thus, the loan balance relative to the *current* value of the property will be lower than when the property was originally purchased. This means that the investor has less financial leverage than when the property was originally financed. In this situation, the investor may consider *refinancing* the property. This would allow the investor to increase financial leverage. Because refinancing at a higher loan-to-current-value ratio may provide the investor with additional funds to invest, this is, to some extent, an alternative to sale of the property.

If the investor's equity has increased due to increase in the value of the property and amortization of the existing loan, then the investor should be able to obtain a new loan based on some percentage of the *current* property value. This would normally be based

EXHIBIT 15–10   Holding Period Analysis

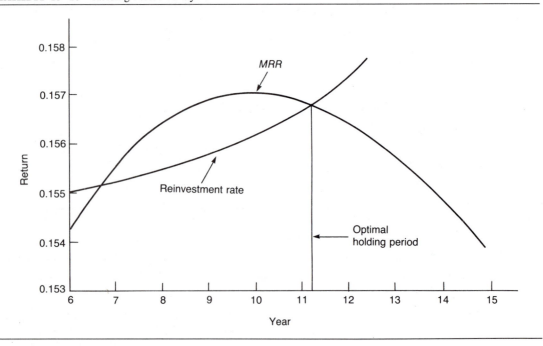

on an appraisal of the property. Of course, points, appraisal fees, and other expenses may be incurred to obtain the new loan. However, no taxes have to be paid on funds received by additional borrowing, whereas taxes would have to be paid if the property is sold.

How should an investor decide whether it is profitable to refinance? To answer this question we must first determine the cost of the additional funds obtained from refinancing. This is the topic of the next section.

Incremental Cost of Refinancing.

In Chapter 9 we discussed the importance of considering the incremental borrowing cost when the borrower is faced with a choice between two different amounts of debt. Recall that when the interest rate is higher on the larger loan amount, the incremental cost of the additional funds borrowed is even higher than the rate on the larger loan. This was due to the fact that the higher rate had to be paid on *all* of the funds borrowed, not just the additional funds.

The same concept applies to the analysis of refinancing. By refinancing we obtain *additional* funds. If the interest rate on the new loan is higher than that on the existing loan, the incremental cost of the additional funds will be even higher than the rate on the new loan. To illustrate, we return to the Apex Center example introduced at the beginning of this chapter. Now assume that Apex Center could be refinanced with a loan that is 75 percent of the current value of the property. Thus the loan would be for 75 percent of $250,000 or $187,500. Suppose the rate on this loan would be 12 percent with a 25-year term. We can calculate the incremental cost of refinancing as follows:

	Current Balance	Monthly Payment	Balance after Five Years
New loan	$187,500	$1,975	$179,350
Existing loan	142,432	1,470	129,348
Difference	45,068	505	50,002

$45,068 = \$505 \cdot (MPVIFA, \ ?\%, \ 5 \text{ years}) + \$50,002 \cdot (MPVIF, \ ?\%, \ 5 \text{ years})$

The difference between the new loan amount of $187,500 and the existing loan balance of $142,432 represents the additional funds obtained by refinancing, which is $45,068. The incremental cost of these funds depends on the additional payment made after refinancing ($505) and the additional loan balance after five years ($50,002). Solving for the interest rate we obtain 14.93 percent. We refer to this as the *incremental cost of refinancing*. To justify refinancing the investor must be able to reinvest the proceeds from refinancing Apex Center in another project earning more than 14.93 percent. Otherwise favorable financing leverage would not result from use of the funds obtained by refinancing Apex Center.

Refinancing at a Lower Interest Rate

The previous example assumed that the investor had to pay a higher interest rate when refinancing. The methodology would be the same if a lower rate could be obtained on the new loan. In this case the savings associated with the lower interest rate will be reflected in a lower incremental cost of the additional funds obtained from refinancing. To illustrate, suppose the rate on the loan used for refinancing Apex Center was at a 10½ percent rate for 25 years. The incremental cost of refinancing will now be as follows:

	Current Balance	Monthly Payment	Balance after Five Years
New loan	$187,500	$1,770	$177,321
Existing loan	142,432	1,470	129,348
Difference	45,068	300	47,973

$45,068 = \$300 \cdot (MPVIFA,\ ?\%,\ 5\ \text{years}) + \$47,973 \cdot (MPVIF,\ ?\%,\ 5\ \text{years})$

The incremental cost of refinancing is now 9.01 percent. Thus the investor would achieve favorable financial leverage by investing the funds obtained from refinancing Apex Center in a project earning more than 9.02 percent.

Diversification Benefits.   As we have pointed out, additional funds can often be obtained by refinancing a property because the property has increased in value since it was initially purchased and the loan balance has been reduced through amortization. The additional funds that are obtained from refinancing the property represents equity capital that can be reinvested in a second property. This enables the investor to increase the amount of property that is owned. Furthermore, the investor may be able to diversify investments further by owning more than two properties. This is especially true if different property types could be acquired in different locations. For example, suppose an investor currently owns a property that has a value of $1,000,000 and has an existing loan balance of $500,000. Equity in the project is therefore $500,000. By refinancing with a 75 percent loan the investor has $250,000 to reinvest in a second project. Assuming a 75 percent loan could also be obtained on the second project, the investor could purchase a second project that has a property value of $1,000,000. Note that the investor has the same total amount of equity capital invested ($500,000), but it is now being used to acquire *two* projects with a total value of $2,000,000. The investor has also incurred additional total debt of $1,000,000. Again, as stressed above, for refinancing to be a profitable strategy, the effective cost of this debt must be less than the unlevered return on the projects being financed. Diversification is discussed much more extensively in Chapter 23.

RENOVATION AS AN ALTERNATIVE TO DISPOSITION

Rather than selling one property to acquire another, an additional option that may be available to the investor would be to consider improving a property or altering it by changing its economic use. For example, depending on economic trends in the local market and in the location where the property is located, one may consider improving a property by enlarging it or by making major capital improvements to upgrade quality and reduce operating costs. Alternatively, one may consider converting the improvement to accommodate a different economic use, such as converting a small multifamily residence to a small professional office building in an urban neighborhood (assuming zoning allows such a conversion).

The issue that we want to address here is how to properly analyze such an option. To illustrate, we reconsider renovating the same property we analyzed in the first part of the chapter. Apex Center, which you recall is presently 20 years old and has been owned by an investor who purchased it five years ago at a cost of $200,000. It was financed 5 years ago with a $150,000 loan at 11 percent interest for 25 years. We know that the property could be sold today for $250,000 if it is *not* renovated (Exhibit 15–2). We also know what the return would be if the property was held for five *additional* years and not renovated (Exhibits 15–4 and 15–5). We will now see how to evaluate the return associated with making an additional investment to renovate the property.

The owner is considering renovation that would cost $200,000. We initially assume that, because of the risk involved in the project, the bank will only agree to refinancing the present loan balance ($142,432) plus 75 percent of the $200,000 renovation cost, for a total loan of $292,432.[2] The new mortgage would carry an interest rate of 11 percent for 15 years.[3]

If the owner, who is in a 28 percent tax bracket, undertakes the modernization project and wants to conduct an after-tax analysis of the investment proposal, the *additional* equity that the owner will have to invest in the property must be determined. This will equal the renovation cost less the additional financing (including both the financing for the renovation plus any existing financing on the remainder of the property. In this case, the lender would only provide additional financing to cover 75 percent of the renovation cost. However, it is also common on renovation projects to get an appraisal of what the entire property will be worth after the renovation and to borrow a percent of that value. This may allow the investor to get some equity out of the property.

In this case, the renovation cost is $200,000 and the additional financing amounts to 75 percent of the renovation cost or $150,000. Thus the *additional* equity investment is $200,000 − $150,000 = $50,000. What does the investor get in return for investing an additional $50,000 in the property? In general, renovation can have many benefits, including increasing rents, lowering vacancy, lowering operating expenses, and increasing the future property value.

Given the estimated cost of modernization and refinancing to be accurate, the critical elements now facing the investor are the estimates of rents, expenses, property values, and expected period of ownership. Obviously the results of this plan are dependent on such estimates, which require a careful market analysis and planning, as we have

---

[2]The lender will often make a loan based on the *present* market value rather than on the existing loan balance which was based on the market value at the time the loan was originally made, plus the cost of improvement. This is considered in the following section.

[3]Another alternative could be a second mortgage for $50,000. The procedure provided here would still be applicable to the problem.

previously discussed. Assuming such a plan is carried out, a five-year projection made by the owner-investor for the modernized Apex Center is shown in Exhibit 15–11.

Looking to Exhibit 15–11, we should note that, based on the modernization plan, *NOI* in year 1 is estimated to increase from $23,725 without renovation (see Exhibit 15–4) to $45,000 with modernization. Because of the renovation, *NOI* is now expected to increase at 4 percent per year instead of at 3 percent. Debt service is based on the new $292,432 mortgage loan made at 11 percent for 15 years. The depreciation charge of $14,770 is computed by first calculating depreciation for the renovation expenditure which increases the depreciable basis by $200,000. This is depreciated over 31.5 years,

EXHIBIT 15–11   Projections for Apex Center After Renovation

	Year					
	6	7	8	9	10	11
	Calculation of After-Tax Cash Flow from Operations					
Net operating income (*NOI*)	$45,000	$46,800	$48,672	$50,619	$52,644	$54,749*
Less debt service	39,885	39,885	39,885	39,885	39,885	
Before-tax cash flow	5,115	6,915	8,787	10,734	12,758	
Net operating income	45,000	46,800	48,672	50,619	52,644	
Less interest	31,766	30,827	29,779	28,609	27,304	
Depreciation	14,770	14,770	14,770	14,770	14,770	
Taxable income	−1,537	1,203	4,123	7,240	10,569	
Tax	−430	337	1,155	2,027	2,959	
Before-tax cash flow	5,115	6,915	8,787	10,734	12,758	
Tax	−430	337	1,155	2,027	2,959	
After-tax cash flow	$ 5,545	$ 6,578	$ 7,632	$ 8,707	$ 9,749	
	Calculation of After-Tax Cash Flow from Reversion					
Sale price						$547,494
Less selling costs at 6.00%						32,850
Less mortgage balance						241,290
Before-tax cash flow						273,354
Taxes in year of sale						
Sale price				$47,494		
Less selling expenses				32,850		
Original cost basis		$400,000				
Accumulated depreciation		115,957				
Adjusted basis				284,043		
Capital gain				230,601		
Capital gains tax at 28.00%						64,568
After-tax cash flow from sale						$208,786

*Projected *NOI* for year 11 is used to estimate the sale price at the end of year 10.

because the renovation is done with the Tax Reform Act of 1986 in effect. Thus the renovation results in depreciation of $200,000/31.5 = $6,349 per year. The depreciation for the existing building (e.g., the original depreciable basis) is not affected by the renovation. This depreciation is still $8,421 per year. Adding this to the $6,349 depreciation resulting from the renovation results in the total depreciation of $14,770.

A five-year expected investment period has been selected for analysis. To estimate the resale price, the investor uses a 10 percent terminal capitalization rate applied to an estimate of *NOI* six years from now. This is based on the assumption that the benefit of the renovation will be reflected in the future *NOI,* and a new investor purchasing the property after five years will purchase on the basis of *NOI* starting in year 11.

What we are now interested in is determining how much the after-tax cash flow increases as a result of the renovation. That is, how much greater, if any, is the after-tax cash flow *after* renovation, as compared with the after-tax cash flow *before* renovation. The after-tax cash flow assuming no renovation is the same as determined in Exhibits 15–4 and 15–5 when we analyzed Apex Center assuming no sale. Exhibit 15–12 summarizes the after-tax cash flows for each alternative (renovation versus no renovation).

From Exhibit 15–12 we see that after-tax cash flows are actually slightly less for the first two years if the property is renovated. After that, however, the after-tax cash flows are increasingly higher. And the after-tax cash flow from sale is higher if the property is renovated. Using the incremental cash flows, we can compute an *IRR* on the additional equity investment. The *IRR* is 17.58 percent. This means that the investor would earn 17.58 percent on the additional $50,000 spent to renovate the property. Whether this is a good investment depends on what rate the $50,000 could earn in a different investment of comparable risk.

It is important to realize that the 17.58 percent return we have calculated is not a return for the entire investment in Apex. It does not tell us anything about whether Apex is a good investment before renovation. That was the purpose of the analysis in the first part of the chapter. We are now assuming the investor already owns Apex and wants to know whether an additional investment to renovate the property is a viable investment.

RENOVATION AND REFINANCING

The previous example assumed that if the property was renovated, the additional financing would be for an amount equal to the existing loan balance of the property (before

---

EXHIBIT 15–12   Incremental Analysis—Renovation versus No Renovation

	Year					
	5	6	7	8	9	10
ATCF assuming renovation		$5,545	$6,578	$7,632	$8,707	$218,585
ATCF assuming no renovation		6,156	6,601	7,054	7,514	107,202
Incremental cash flow	− $50,000	− 611	− 23	578	1,193	111,382
IRR on incremental cash flows = 17.58%						

renovation) plus 75 percent of the renovation costs. When properties are renovated, the investor often uses that opportunity to refinance the entire property. For example, the existing loan balance on the Apex building is only 57 percent of the current value of the property ($142,432/$250,000). Thus the investor may be able to borrow funds in addition to what is needed for the renovation, especially if the investor plans to obtain a new loan on the entire property rather than a second mortgage to cover the renovation costs.

The total amount of funds that the investor will be able to borrow is usually based on a percentage of estimated value of the property after renovation is completed. This value would be based on an appraisal. If we assume that the *value* added by the renovation is equal to the *cost* of the renovation, then this value will be equal to the existing value of $250,000 plus the renovation cost of $200,000, or $450,000. If the investor can borrow 75 percent of this value, a loan for $337,500 could be obtained. Because the existing loan balance is $142,432, the net additional loan proceeds would be $195,068. Thus the investor will only have to invest $4,932 of his own equity capital to renovate the property. Obviously this is a highly leveraged situation, and the incremental rate of return should be significantly higher. Exhibit 15–13 shows the cash flows for Apex under the assumption that a loan is obtained for $337,500 at an 11 percent interest rate and a 15-year loan term.

Exhibit 15–14 shows the results of the incremental analysis. As indicated above, only $4,932 must be invested to complete the renovation. However, because the new loan is much higher than the existing loan, the additional payments result in negative incremental cash flows for each of the years until the property is sold. Because of the higher value resulting from the renovation, there is a significant amount of additional cash flow when the property is sold, resulting in an incremental *ATIRR* for the investor of 37.47 percent. Thus the additional financing (leverage) significantly increases the incremental return from renovating the property. As we know, however, there is also more risk now due to the additional debt. The investor must decide whether the additional return is commensurate with the additional risk. Some of the additional debt resulted from, in effect, bringing the original loan balance up to a 75 percent loan-to-value ratio. Thus although the renovation cost is highly levered, total leverage on the property is at a typical level. All of these factors must be considered by the investor so that an informed investment decision can be made.

CONCLUSION

The primary purpose of this chapter was to answer the following questions: (1) When should a property be sold? (2) Should a property be renovated? We saw that once a property has been purchased, the return associated with keeping the property might be quite different than the return originally estimated. The concept of a marginal rate of return was introduced to help evaluate whether a property should be sold or held for an additional period. The marginal rate of return considers what the investor could get in the future by keeping the property versus what he could get today by selling the property.

To determine whether a property should be renovated, we considered the incremental benefit associated with renovating the property versus not renovating the property. This

EXHIBIT 15–13   After-Tax Cash Flow from Renovation with Refinancing

			Year			
	6	7	8	9	10	11

Calculation of After-Tax Cash Flow from Operations

Net operating income	$45,000	$46,800	$48,672	$50,619	$52,644	$54,749*
Less debt service	46,032	46,032	46,032	46,032	46,032	
Before-tax cash flow	−1,032	768	2,640	4,587	6,611	
Net operating income	45,000	46,800	48,672	50,619	52,644	
Interest	36,662	35,578	34,368	33,018	31,512	
Depreciation	14,770	14,770	14,770	14,770	14,770	
Taxable income	−6,432	3,548	−466	2,831	6,361	
Tax	−1,801	−993	−131	793	1,781	
Before-tax cash flow	−1,032	768	2,640	4,587	6,611	
Tax	−1,801	−993	−131	793	1,781	
After-tax cash flow	$ 769	$ 1,761	$ 2,770	$ 3,794	$ 4,830	

Calculation of After-Tax Cash Flow from Reversion

Sale price						$547,494
Less selling costs (at 6.00%)						32,850
Less mortgage balance						278,477
Before-tax cash flow						236,168
Taxes in year of sale						
Sale price					$547,494	
Selling costs					32,850	
Original cost basis				$400,000		
Accumulated depreciation				115,957		
Adjusted basis					284,043	
Capital gain					230,601	
Capital gains tax at 28.00%						64,568
After-tax cash flow from sale						$171,599

*Projected *NOI* for year 11 is used to estimate the sale price at the end of year 10.

EXHIBIT 15–14   Incremental Analysis Assuming Refinancing

			Year			
	5	6	7	8	9	10
ATCF After renovation		$769	$1,761	$2,770	$3,794	$176,430
ATCF Before renovation		6,156	6,601	7,054	7,514	107,202
Incremental cash flow	$−4,932	−5,387	−4,840	−4,283	−3,720	69,227
IRR on incremental cash flow = 37.47%						

approach is appropriate when the investor already owns the property and the question is whether an *additional* investment made to renovate the property is justified. If the investor did *not* already own the property, a different approach would be taken. In this case the investor would want to know the total rate of return associated with both purchasing and renovating the property. The investor would also want to know the return for purchasing the property but not renovating it, since it still might make sense to purchase the property but not renovate it.

From the above discussion, it should be obvious that the approach we take when analyzing an investment depends on the particular question that we are trying to answer. Poor investment decisions are often made because the analyst did not do an analysis that answered the right question.

QUESTIONS

1. What factors should an investor consider when trying to decide whether to dispose of a property that has been owned for several years?
2. Why might the actual holding period for a property be different from the holding period that was anticipated when the property was purchased?
3. What is the marginal rate of return? How is it calculated?
4. What causes the marginal rate of return to change over time? How can the marginal rate of return be used to decide when to sell a property?
5. Why might the after-tax internal rate of return on equity ($ATIRR_e$) differ for a new investor versus an existing investor who keeps the property?
6. What factors should be considered when deciding whether to renovate a property?
7. Why is refinancing often done in conjunction with renovation?
8. Why would refinancing be an alternative to sale of the property?
9. How can tax law changes create incentives for investors to sell their properties to other investors?
10. How important are taxes in the decision to sell a property?
11. Are tax considerations important in renovation decisions?
12. What are the benefits and costs of renovation?
13. Do you think renovation is more or less risky than a new investment?
14. What is meant by the ''incremental cost of refinancing''?

PROBLEMS

1. Royal Oaks Apartments was purchased by Lonnie Carson two years ago. An opportunity has arisen for Carson to purchase a larger apartment project called Royal Palms, but Carson believes that he would have to sell Royal Oaks to have sufficient equity capital to purchase Royal Palms. Carson paid $2,000,000 for Royal Oaks two years ago, with the land representing approximately $200,000 of that value. A recent appraisal indicated that the property is worth about $2,200,000 today. When purchased two years ago, Carson financed the property with a 75 percent mortgage at 10 percent

interest for 25 years (monthly payments). The property is being depreciated over 27.5 years (1/27.5 per year for simplicity). Effective gross income during the next year is expected to be $350,000, and operating expenses are projected to be 40 percent of effective gross income. Carson expects the effective gross income to increase 3 percent per year. The property value is expected to increase at the same 3 percent annual rate. Carson is currently in the 28 percent tax bracket and expects to remain in the top bracket in the future. Because Carson has other real estate investments that are now generating taxable income, he does not expect any tax losses from Royal Oaks to be subject to the passive activity loss limitations. If he sells Royal Oaks, selling expenses would be 6 percent of the sale price.

a. How much after-tax cash flow ($ATCF_s$) would Carson receive if Royal Oaks was sold today (exactly two years after he purchased it)?

b. What is the projected after-tax cash flow ($ATCF_o$) for the *next* five years if Carson does *not* sell Royal Oaks?

c. How much after-tax cash flow ($ATCF_s$) would Carson receive if he sold Royal Oaks five years from now?

d. Using the results from parts (a) through (c), find the after-tax rate of return ($ATIRR_e$) that is expected to be earned by Carson if he holds Royal Oaks for five additional years versus selling it today?

e. What is the marginal rate of return (MRR) if Carson holds the property for *one additional year* (i.e., sells *next* year versus this year)?

f. Why do you think the MRR in part (e) is higher than the return calculated in part (d)?

g. Can you think of any other ways that Carson could use to purchase Royal Palms and still retain ownership of Royal Oaks?

h. What is your recommendation to Carson?

i. *Optional for computer users.* What is the MRR for each of the next 10 years? How can this calculation be used to determine when Royal Oaks should be sold?

2. Richard Rambo presently owns the Marine Tower Office building that is 20 years old and which he is considering renovating. He purchased the property two years ago for $800,000 and financed it with a 20-year, 70 percent loan at 10 percent interest (monthly payments). Of the $800,000, the appraiser indicated that the land was worth $200,000 and the building $600,000. He has been using straight-line depreciation over 31.5 years (1/31.5 per year for simplicity). At the present time Marine Towers is producing $90,000 in *NOI,* and the *NOI* and property value are expected to increase 3 percent per year. The current market value of the property is $820,000. Rambo estimates that if the Marine Tower Office building is renovated at a cost of $200,000, *NOI* would be about 20 percent higher next year (i.e., $120,000 versus $90,000) due to higher rents and lower expenses. He also expects that with the renovation the *NOI* would increase 4 percent per year instead of 3 percent. Furthermore, Rambo believes that after five years, a new investor would purchase the Marine Tower Office building at a price based on capitalizing the projected *NOI six* years from now at a 10 percent capitalization rate. Selling costs would be 6 percent of the sale price. Rambo is in the 28 percent tax bracket and expects to continue to be in that bracket. He also would not be subject to any passive activity loss limitations. If Rambo does the renovation,

he believes he could obtain a new loan at a 12 percent interest rate and a 20-year loan term (monthly payments). However, the amount of the loan is uncertain.

a. Assume that if Rambo does the renovation, he will be able to obtain a new loan that is equal to the balance of the existing loan plus 70 percent of the renovation costs. What is the *incremental* return ($ATIRR_e$) for doing the renovation versus not doing the renovation? Assume a five-year holding period.

b. Repeat part (a) but assume that Rambo is able to obtain a new loan that is equal to 70 percent of the *sum* of the existing value of the property ($820,000) plus the renovation costs ($200,000). (This assumes that after renovation the value of the property will at least increase by the cost of the renovation.)

c. Explain the difference between the returns calculated in parts (b) and (c). Is there a difference in the risk associated with each financing alternative?

d. What advice would you give Rambo?

Appendix: Convertible Mortgages—A Hybrid Method of Refinancing and Disposition

INTRODUCTION

Much of the material in Chapter 15 dealt at length with analytical approaches to decisions involving refinancing and the sale of properties. This appendix expands these ideas and introduces a "hybrid" approach to raising funds. This latter approach involves refinancing that includes the sale of an option to the lender to purchase the entire, or a partial interest in the property, at the end of some specified period of time. This purchase option allows the lender to convert its mortgage to equity ownership, hence the term "convertible mortgage". This approach also may be viewed by the lender as a refinancing combined with a call option, or right to acquire a full or partial equity interest for a predetermined price on the option's expiration date.

To illustrate, we assume that a property was purchased 10 years ago for $5,000,000. Its current market value is $6,500,000. It was originally financed with a conventional 75 percent mortgage loan made at 10 percent interest for 25 years. Depreciation on the improvements has been taken in the amount of $300,000 per year and will continue in that amount for 10 more years. Given that the property has appreciated in value during the past 5 years, the owner would like to raise equity capital from the appreciation in property value. As pointed out in the chapter, the owner could accomplish this with an outright sale. However, if a goal of the owner is to defer paying capital gain taxes, raising capital can be also be accomplished with either a conventional refinancing as also outlined in the chapter, or with a convertible mortgage. Further, if a large institutional lender would like to make a loan on the property *and* also obtain an eventual ownership interest in the property, a convertible mortgage may present a viable option to both parties.

Obviously, the convertible mortgage loan would have to be structured in such a way so as to meet the objectives of both parties. In order for the current owner to enter the transaction, lending terms (some combination of interest rate, payment, maturity, loan to value ratio, etc.) on the loan would generally have to be more favorable than what the owner could obtain with a conventional refinancing. These more favorable terms would be acquired in exchange for giving the lender a call option, that is, the option to purchase a full or partial interest in the property at a specified price at a future date.

To provide insight into how a decision may be made regarding the alternatives facing the owner and lender, we can consider the following alternatives:

Alternative	Terms
Conventional refinancing:	Loan to equal 70 percent of current market value, payments to be made at 10 percent interest for 25 years (fully amortizing), loan matures in 10 years.
Convertible mortgage:	Loan to equal 75 percent of current market value, interest only payments to be made at 8 percent over 5 years (call option expiration date). Lender also receives contingent interest equal to 50 percent of cash flow after payment of interest. If call option is exercised, lender will forgive the mortgage loan balance in exchange for a 65 percent ownership interest in the property.[1]

Based on these terms, the current owner can analyze whether a conventional refinancing or a convertible mortgage would be the preferential choice.

Looking to Exhibit 15A–1, cash flow from the three alternatives as of the time of either sale or refinancing is presented. As the exhibit shows, in order to establish what the owner's equity is at the time of refinancing, we see that if the property were to be sold, the owner would net $2,128,859 in equity after taxes. If the owner refinanced with either a conventional or convertible mortgage, lesser amounts of equity would be available after repayment of the existing mortgage. Of course, under the refinancing alternatives the property is still owned. Under both refinancing alternatives, capital gains taxes would be deferred until the project is sold five years into the future. To determine which choice may be best for the owner, we undertake an analysis of profitability and consider the cost of refinancing with either the convertible or conventional loan.

Exhibit 15A–2 provides a summary of the cash flows from operation and sale of the property after 5 additional years, assuming that conventional refinancing is undertaken. Debt service and interest expense are based on the new conventional mortgage terms, however, the owner continues to depreciate the property in the amount of $300,000 per year. It is also assumed that the owner is an active participant in a passive activity, hence ordinary losses during the operation of the property are offset against other ordinary income. A summary of after-tax cash flows (ATCF) for the conventional alternative is shown at the bottom of the exhibit. Essentially the summary indicates that if, instead of selling and removing all equity, the investor leaves $1,110,000 invested in the property, the property would earn an ATIRR of 18.9 percent on that equity. This should be compared with the return that would be earned on a new project that would be purchased if this property was sold.

---

[1]Generally, the Internal Revenue Service requires that the loan to value ratio on the date of refinancing must be greater than the conversion ratio. This is because if the conversion ratio is greater, the IRS considers the option to be "in the money." Although the lender may have to wait to exercise the conversion option, the lender may have the right to sell or assign the convertible mortgage after the refinancing date and before the exercise date.

EXHIBIT 15A–1   Net Cash Proceeds from Sale or Refinancing with a Conventional or Convertible Mortgage

Purchase price (5 years ago)	$5,000,000	Original mortgage amount =	$3,750,000
Current market value =	6,500,000	Original mortgage term =	25
Annual depreciation =	300,000	Original mortgage rate =	10.00%
Marginal tax rate =	28.00%	Original mortgage payment =	$34,076.28
			per month
		Current mortgage balance =	$3,531,141

	Immediate Sale	Conventional Mortgage (70 percent L/V)	Convertible Mortgage (75 percent L/V)
Gross proceeds from:	$6,500,000	$4,550,000	$4,875,000
Mortgage balance	3,531,141	3,531,141	3,531,141
BTCF	$2,968,859	$1,018,859	$1,343,859
Taxes:			
Sale price	$6,500,000	—	—
Adjusted basis	3,500,000	—	—
Gain on sale	3,000,000	—	—
Tax on gain at 28 percent	840,000	—	—
BTCF	$2,968,859	$1,018,859	$1,343,859
Taxes	840,000	—	—
ATCF	$2,128,859	$1,018,859	$1,343,859

Exhibit 15A–3 provides a detailed set of cash flows for the case where convertible financing is undertaken. Recall from Exhibit 15A–1 that if this approach is used, the owner would realize $1,343,859 in cash from the refinancing and would leave $785,000 invested in the project. It is the return on the $785,000 that we are interested in at this point. Based on the terms of the convertible mortgage the owner pays 8 percent interest only, plus 50 percent of cash flows remaining after the payment of interest to the lender. Depreciation expense of $300,000 per year is still deductible because no change in ownership has occurred. At the end of year 5, the lender will convert the $4,875,000 mortgage balance for a 65 percent equity interest in the project. As shown in the exhibit, 65 percent of the market value of the property, or $4,897,933, is greater than the $4,875,000 loan balance. This means that the lender's call option is ''in the money'' and the lender will most likely convert the outstanding debt to equity on the expiration date.[2] Note also that the lender realizes a capital gain of $22,933 on the conversion date.[3]

As for the owner, note that a total of $2,637,349 in cash flow (35 percent of the sale price) will be received on the conversion date. However, the owner must also recognize the forgiveness

---

[2]Although 65 percent of the property value exceeds the loan balance, the lender receives less cash flow until the property is sold. This is because at the time of conversion the debt service ($390,000) plus the participation ($114,515) exceeds 65 percent of the *NOI* (.65 × 619,030 = $402,369).

[3]In order to make the comparison with the conventional option, we assume that the property is sold at the end of the fifth year, even though the lender has just converted the debt to equity.

EXHIBIT 15A–2   Cash Flow from Conventional Refinancing

	Percent						
Annual increase in *NOI* =	3.00		New mortgage amount =			$4,550,000	
Annual increase in value =	3.00		New mortgage term =			25 years	
Loan to value =	70		New mortgage rate =			10.00%	
			New mortgage payment =			$41,345.88 per month	
			Mortgage balance (*EOY* 5) =			$4,284,451	

	Year						
	1	*2*	*3*	*4*	*5*	*Sale* (5)	
NOI	$550,000	$566,500	$583,495	$601,000	$619,030	Sale price	$7,535,281
Debt service	496,151	496,151	496,151	496,151	496,151	Mortgage balance	4,284,451
BTCF	$ 53,849	$ 70,349	$ 87,344	$104,849	$122,879	*BTCF*s	$3,250,830
						Taxes:	
NOI	$550,000	$566,500	$583,495	$601,000	$619,030	Sale price	$7,535,281
Interest	453,061	448,549	443,564	438,055	431,975	Adjusted basis	2,000,000
Depreciation	300,000	300,000	300,000	300,000	300,000	Capital gain	5,535,281
Taxable Income	(203,061)	(182,048)	(160,069)	(137,058)	(112,945)	Tax at 28 percent	1,549,879
Tax at 28%	(56,857)	(50,974)	(44,819)	(38,376)	(31,625)		
BTCF	53,849	70,349	87,344	104,849	122,879	*BTCF*s	3,250,830
Taxes	(56,857)	(50,974)	(44,819)	(38,376)	(31,624)	Taxes	1,549,879
ATCF	$110,706	$121,323	$132,163	$143,225	$154,504	*ATCF*s	$1,700,951

Incremental ATCFs from Refinancing with a Conventional Mortgage

	Year					
	0	*1*	*2*	*3*	*4*	*5*
Current sale	($2,128,859)					
Refinance	$1,018,859					
Operations		$110,706	$121,323	$132,163	$143,225	$1,154,504
Sale						1,700,951
	($1,110,000)	$110,706	$121,323	$132,163	$143,225	$1,855,455
ATIRR = 18.9%						

of $4,875,000 in indebtedness by the lender as a part of the consideration received on the conversion date. That is, the owner has in effect sold 65 percent of the property to the lender at a price equal to the outstanding mortgage balance. This means that the owner recognizes $7,512,349 in total consideration, against which the remaining $2,000,000 in adjusted basis is deducted in arriving at a capital gain of $5,512,349 in year 5. After paying capital gains tax, the investor realizes $1,093,891.

A summary of the investor's *ATIRR* for the case of convertible refinancing is shown in Exhibit 15A–4. Note that the owner would earn an *ATIRR* of 24.6 percent on equity. When compared to the 18.9 percent return earned if the conventional refinancing was used, the convertible alternative appears to be preferable. However, it should also be pointed out that the amount of leverage utilized

EXHIBIT 15A–3   Cash Flow from Convertible Refinancing

	Percent		
Annual increase in *NOI* =	3.00	New mortgage amount =	$4,875,000
Annual increase in value =	3.00	New mortgage rate =	8.00%
Loan to value =	75	New mortgage payment =	$32,500.00 per month
Conversion ratio =	65	Mortgage balance (*EOY 5*) =	$4,875,000
Lender participation of BTCF	50		

	Year				
	1	*2*	*3*	*4*	*5*
NOI	$550,000	$566,500	$583,495	$601,000	$619,030
Debt service	390,000	390,000	390,000	390,000	390,000
BTCF—owner (50%)	80,000	88,250	96,748	105,500	114,515
Lender participation (50%)	$80,000	$88,250	$96,748	$105,500	$114,515
NOI	500,000	566,500	583,495	601,000	619,030
Interest*	470,000	478,250	486,748	495,500	504,515
Depreciation	300,000	300,000	300,000	300,000	300,000
Taxable income	(270,000)	(211,750)	(203,253)	(194,500)	(185,485)
Tax at 28 percent	$(75,600)	$(59,290)	$(56,911)	$(54,460)	$(51,936)
BTCF	80,000	88,250	96,748	105,500	114,515
Taxes	(75,600)	(59,290)	(56,911)	(54,460)	(51,936)
ATCF	$155,600	$147,540	$153,659	$159,960	$166,451

	Owner	Lender
Sale Year (5)	*(35 percent interest)*	*(65 percent interest)*
Sale price	$2,637,349	$4,897,933
BTCFs	$2,637,349	$4,897,933
Taxes:		
Taxable interest	$7,512,349†	$4,897,933‡
Adjusted basis	2,000,000	4,875,000
Capital gain	5,512,349	22,933
Tax at 28 percent	1,543,458	6,421
BTCFs	$2,637,349	$4,897,933
Taxes	1,543,458	6,421
ATCFs	$1,093,891	$4,891,512

*Interest only = $390,000 + Lender participation in cash flow.
†Sum of mortgage balance $4,875,000 plus 35% of sale price.
‡ 65% of sale price.

with the convertible alternative is also higher, as is the risk (this will be discussed in more depth below). Looking to the lenders return, based on this alternative, a *BTIRR* of 10 percent, or the equivalent of a mortgage made at 10 percent interest would be earned by the lender. This return is comprised of payments based on the 8 percent interest rate, 50 percent participation in net cash flows from operation and the 65 percent ownership interest obtained in year 5.

Exhibit 15A–5 provides a comparison of the *ATIRR*s to the owner (a) under various combinations of loan-to-value ratios and conversion ratios for the convertible loan and (b) various loan-

EXHIBIT 15A–4 Summary of Cash Flows to Investor and Lender—Convertible Mortgage Refinancing

Summary of owner ATCF with Convertible Mortgage

	Year					
	0	*1*	*2*	*3*	*4*	*5*
Current sale	($2,128,859)					
Refinance	$1,343,859					
Operations		$155,600	$147,540	$153,659	$159,960	$ 166,451
Sale (year 5)						1,093,891
	($785,000)	$155,600	$147,540	$153,659	$159,960	$1,260,342

ATIRR = 24.6%

Summary of Lender's BTCF from Convertible Mortgage

	Year					
	0	*1*	*2*	*3*	*4*	*5*
Refinance	($4,875,000)					
Operations		$470,000	$478,250	$486,748	$495,500	$ 504,515
Sale (year 5)						4,897,933
	($4,875,000)	$470,000	$478,250	$486,748	$495,500	$5,402,448

Yield = 10.0%

EXHIBIT 15A–5 Summary of Yields to Owner and Lender Using Different Leverage and Conversion Options

I. Owner's ATIRR on Equity from Refinancing with a Convertible versus Conventional

	Percent			
Convertible Conversion Ratio	65	70	75	*Conventional*
Loan to value				
70	15.9	12.1	7.7	18.90
75	24.6	20.4	15.5	22.80
80	42.0	37.3	31.7	30.87

II. Lender BTIRR on Convertible Mortgage

	Percent		
Convertible Conversion Ratio	65	70	75
Loan to value			
70	11.6	12.8	14.0
75	10.0	11.3	12.4
80	8.6	9.8	11.0

to-value ratios for the conventional refinancing alternative. For example, in the case of the convertible loan just considered, which was based on a 75 percent loan to value and 65 percent conversion ratio, the exhibit shows that the investor would earn an *ATIRR* of 24.6 percent. This can be compared to the conventional loan example at a 70 percent loan to value ratio where the *ATIRR* is 18.9 percent. The purpose of this exhibit is to indicate what the trade-offs would be between the two approaches to refinancing. For example, at an 80 percent loan-to-value ratio, the investor would clearly earn a higher return with the convertible than with the conventional mortgage. However, if the loan-to-value ratio was reduced from 80 percent, to 70 percent, the conventional mortgage would be preferred by the owner, unless the conversion ratio was lowered. Similarly, the lender's *BTIRR* is shown in part II of the exhibit. Recall that in the conventional case, the yield was 10 percent. However, in the convertible cases, the yield will depend on the conversion ratio that the lender can negotiate. Depending on the ratio, the yield could range from as high as 14.0 percent to as low as 8.6 percent for the case being considered.

These trade-offs are illustrated further in Exhibit 15A–6. ATIRRs are provided for various combinations of loan-to-value and conversion ratios for the convertible loan and are compared to *ATIRR*s for the 70 percent loan-to-value ratio conventional case. Clearly the reader can see that, all else being equal, the owner would prefer to negotiate for the lowest possible conversion ratio and highest loan-to-value ratio in order to maximize return. The lender, on the other hand, will prefer the opposite. We should also point out that these results are dependent on the appreciation rate chosen for both *NOI* and property values. In Exhibit 15A–6, a 3 percent increase is assumed. However, if the expected appreciation rate increased, the conversion ratio becomes more important to both the owner and

EXHIBIT 15A–6 ATIRR on Equity at Various Conversion and Loan-to-Value Ratios

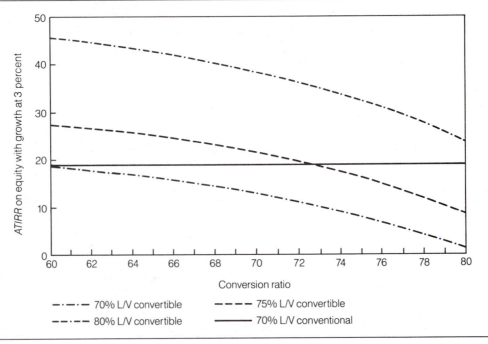

lender. Holding all else constant, as the appreciation rate increases, the lender will earn a higher rate of return relative to the owner for any given conversion and loan to value ratio.

Finally, in cases where the amount borrowed by the owner differs under the conventional and convertible loans, the comparison of *ATIRR*s must be interpreted more carefully. For example, in Exhibits 15A–2 and 15A–3, the owner's rate of return was greater for the convertible mortgage case. However, more leverage would be used in the convertible case. Recall that $325,000 less equity was required if the convertible alternative was chosen instead of the conventional loan. Hence, the risk is higher with the convertible and the return should be higher if that alternative is chosen. Another consideration that should be made when the amounts of financing are different is to consider the incremental borrowing cost (introduced in Chapter 9) on the incremental amount of funds borrowed in the convertible case. When comparing cash flows between the two cases, we have:

ATCFs to investor:

| | Year | | | | | |
	(0)	(1)	(2)	(3)	(4)	(5)
Convertible	$1,343,859	$155,600	$147,540	$153,658	$159,960	$1,260,342
− Conventional	1,018,859	110,706	121,323	132,164	143,225	1,855,455
difference	$ 325,000	$ 44,894	$ 26,217	$ 21,495	$ 16,735	($595,113)
ATIRR = 7.2%						

Based on this comparison, the owner receives more cash flow with the convertible (a) upon refinancing in the amount of $325,000 and (b) more cash flow from operations during years 1–4. However, during year 5, the owner will realize a $595,113 net cash outflow if the convertible is used because the conversion value is greater than the loan balance.

We can interpret the 7.2 percent *ATIRR* as the after-tax cost of borrowing additional funds if the convertible mortgage is used instead of the conventional mortgage. That is, the investor receives an additional $325,000 at the time of refinancing, an additional $44,494 in year 1, etc. The 7.2 percent after-tax cost is equivalent to a 10 percent before-tax cost [7.2% ÷ (1 − .28)].[4] This can be compared with alternative ways of borrowing the additional funds.

Based on the information contained in this appendix and the appendix to Chapter 13, the reader should be aware that there are many alternative ways that financing can be structured to accomplish the objectives of both borrowers and lenders. Indeed, many of the ideas introduced in the appendix to Chapter 13 can be used in conjunction with the alternatives considered here when structuring refinancing agreements.

PROBLEMS

A–1 Problematic Development Co. purchased an office building five years ago for $2,000,000. To finance the purchase, it made a 75 percent conventional mortgage for 25 years at an annual

---

[4]The incremental cost is exactly 10 percent because the cost of both the conventional and convertible loan is 10 percent.

interest rate of 12 percent. The current market value of the property is $3,000,000 and the current taxable basis is $1,000,000. It has been depreciating the property at $100,000 per year and expects to continue to do so for the next 10 years. Its marginal tax rate is 28 percent.

The developer would like to either sell the property or refinance with a convertible mortgage and continue to own the property for an additional five years. The terms on such a mortgage would be as follows:

Loan to value	= 70%
Conversion ratio	= 65%
Interest rate	= 10% (interest only)
Lender participation	= 50% of *NOI* less interest deduction

The first year *NOI* is expected to be $250,000. Both the *NOI* and the property value are expected to increase by 4 percent each year.

a. What would Problematic receive (after tax) from the sale today? What would it receive if the property was refinanced? If refinanced, what would be the 5 year *ATIRR* on equity?

b. What would be the lender's before-tax yield (*BTIRR*) on the convertible mortgage?

c. Assume that the developer could also refinance the property using a 60 percent L/V conventional mortgage with a 25-year amortization period and a 13 percent interest rate. Which refinancing alternative has the higher *ATIRR* on equity? What would be the marginal cost of refinancing with the convertible versus the conventional? Is this rate different from the *ATIRR* on equity for each alternative (conventional versus convertible)? If so, why?

Chapter 16

Raising Equity Capital: Syndications and Limited Partnership Investments

INTRODUCTION: WHAT IS A SYNDICATE?

The concept of real estate syndication extends generally to any group of investors who have combined their financial resources with the expertise of a real estate professional for the common purpose of carrying out a real estate project. A syndication is not an organization form per se. It may take any of the business forms discussed in Chapter 11 (e.g., corporation, limited partnership, or general partnership).

A syndicate can be formed to acquire, develop, manage, operate, or market real estate. Syndication can be viewed as a type of financing that offers smaller investors the opportunity to invest in ventures that would otherwise be beyond their financial and management capabilities. Syndicators benefit from the fees they receive for their services and the interest they may retain in the syndicated property. Many syndication firms are in the business of acquiring, managing, and then selling real estate projects. In order to acquire property, they bring in other investors with capital which forms the equity base with which the property is acquired. Syndicators do not usually invest much of their own capital. Rather, they act more as agent-managers earning fees for acquiring, managing, and selling properties owned by the investors who have contributed capital to the syndication.

Developers who need additional equity capital to undertake a project often raise funds through syndications, either directly or by using a firm that specializes in raising capital by selling interests in the syndication. The syndication may become involved during the development and construction of the project or after the building is completed and leased. In the latter case, the syndication provides a means for the developer to remove equity from the project, especially if the value of the project upon completion and lease-up is greater than the construction cost. The developer also typically receives a development fee. This strategy allows the developer to focus on developing projects, earning a development fee, retaining some ownership in the project, and going on to the next development project.

In cases where one or a small number of projects are to be syndicated, a limited partnership (introduced in Chapter 11) is often used. For a smaller project where a limited number of investors are needed, the capital for the partnership will usually be raised by what is referred to as a *private offering*. There are regulations that must be adhered to when offering ownership interests in partnerships to investors. These regulations are detailed in Chapter 20.

There are also cases where a syndicator may desire to raise a large amount of funds to acquire many properties. The particular properties to be acquired may or may not be identified when the funds are raised. In the latter case it is referred to as a *blind pool* offering, and it allows the syndicator to have discretion over what properties are purchased, subject to broad guidelines contained in an offering prospectus to investors. In cases where ownership interests will be sold to investors in many states, the syndication is usually undertaken through a *public offering*. This type of syndication is subject to numerous state and federal regulations and is also discussed further in Chapter 20.

The purpose of this chapter is to familiarize the student with basic approaches to understanding and evaluating investment in an ownership interest in a real estate syndication. This is important to both potential investors and developers. The investor must evaluate how the rate of return and risk for investment in a share of a syndicate compares with other investment opportunities. The developer must evaluate how the "cost" of obtaining equity funds through syndication (in terms of what the developer must give up) compares with other financing alternatives.

The focus of our discussion in this chapter will be on the analysis of a *private* offering in which a *single* property is to be acquired by a limited partnership. The emphasis is on understanding how ownership of shares in a partnership that owns the property differs from direct ownership of the property, as we have assumed in previous chapters.

USE OF THE LIMITED PARTNERSHIP IN PRIVATE AND PUBLIC SYNDICATES

Limited partnerships are widely used as vehicles for raising equity capital for real estate ventures. They combine the limited liability feature of an investment in a corporation with the advantages of a general partnership, such as the ability to make special allocations of income and cash flow to the partners. An investor's liability (limited partner) is limited to his initial contribution plus any unpaid contributions he has agreed to make in the future. Furthermore, the responsibility for the management of the partnership rests with the general partners who are frequently knowledgeable in real estate matters, thus providing the partnership with professional management.

PRIVATE SYNDICATION PROBLEM ILLUSTRATED

When embarking on a syndication with other investors, it is essential for all parties, be they investors or lenders, to understand the framework in which the venture will operate. What follows is a rather detailed analysis of a *private* real estate syndication that is being

EXHIBIT 16–1 Plaza Office Building Acquisition Cost and Financing Summary

Cost breakdown	
Land	$ 625,000
Improvements	3,375,000 (capitalized)
Points	60,000 (amortized over loan term)
Subtotal	$4,060,000
Organization fee	20,000 (amortized over 5 years)
Syndication expenses	100,000 (capitalized)
Total funding required	$4,180,000
Loan amount	$3,000,000 (71.77% of total funding)
Interest rate	12%
Term	25 years (monthly payments)
Points	$60,000
Annual debt service	$379,161

formed to acquire and operate the Plaza Office Building. In this syndication, 35 individuals have been approached by Dallac Investment Corporation, which has agreed to act as the sole general partner in a *limited partnership*.[1] Dallac is trying to raise sufficient equity capital to undertake the purchase and has decided to use the *limited partnership* form of organization, which will limit the liability of all partners to their agreed-upon capital contribution to the venture.

The venture to be undertaken and relevant cost and financial data are summarized in Exhibit 16–1. Dallac has obtained an option to purchase the property and has a commitment for a nonrecourse loan from Prudent Life Insurance Company. The loan requires prior approval of any change in the general partner at any time in the future.

Financial Considerations—Partnership Agreement

The financial aspects of the partnership agreement and the equity requirements of the general and limited partners for this example are summarized in Exhibit 16–2. The partnership agreement governs the business relationship among the general and limited partners and is often long and rather involved. At a minimum, partnership agreements should specify how and in what proportions the equity will be initially contributed, whether assessments will be made should the project experience a cash shortfall during operation, or should the improvement need substantial repair in the future. In this example, Dallac has agreed as general partner to contribute 5 percent of the required equity, with the 35

---

[1]For clarity of presentation we will consider all 35 limited partners as a single entity. As will be discussed in Chapter 20, when more than 35 investors become partners, this is generally considered a public offering.

EXHIBIT 16–2   Partnership Facts and Equity Requirements for Plaza Office Building Syndication

---

a. Organization: December 1987
b. Number of partners: 1 general partner and 35 limited partners.
c. Equity capital contribution: general partner, 5%; limited partners, 95%.
d. Cash assessments: none.
e. Cash distributions from operations: general partner, 5%; limited partners, 95%.
f. Taxable income and losses from operations: general partner, 5%; limited partners, 95%.
g. Allocation of gain or loss from sale: general partner, 10%; limited partner 90%.
h. Cash distributions at sale: Based on capital account balances. (Capital accounts will be explained in the following discussion.)

Initial equity requirements	
Land & improvements	$4,725,000
Points on mortgage loan	60,000
Organization fee	20,000
Syndication fees	100,000
Total cash requirements	4,180,000
Less mortgage financing	3,000,000
Equals equity requirements	1,180,000
General partner (5%)	59,000
Limited partners (95%)*	1,121,000

*As indicated earlier, it is common to allow limited partners to pay in their equity contribution over time. The general partner would then arrange for additional financing during this pay-in period, using the limited partner's notes as collateral. To keep this example manageable, we have not assumed such a pay-in.

---

limited partners investing 95 percent.[2] There is no provision for future assessments of the limited partners. Since limited partners are not liable for future capital contributions, Dallac will have to address the issue of what happens in the event the property generates negative before-tax cash flow. Dallac could guarantee to cover negative before-tax cash flow (and will likely charge a fee for doing so), raise sufficient equity capital initially to cover future negative cash flows, arrange for additional borrowings, or reserve the right to raise new capital by admitting additional partners.

The partnership agreement should also specify how income or loss from operating the property and capital gain or loss from sale of the property should be distributed. In our example, profits, losses, and cash flow from operations will be distributed 5 percent to the general partner (Dallac) and 95 percent to the limited partners. However, gain (or loss) from sale of the property is to be allocated 10 percent to the general partner and 90 percent to the limited partners. As mentioned earlier, an important characteristic of a partnership is that all items of income and loss (including gain or loss from resale) and cash do not have to be distributed in the same proportion. This is referred to as *special allocation* and allows flexibility in the ability to allocate the benefits of the real estate

---

[2]In this case, we assume each limited partner invests an equal percentage of the cash required from each partner. In practice, however, different proportional interests could be purchased by each partner. Also, in many syndications, the general partner may invest as little as 1 percent of the equity or no equity at all.

EXHIBIT 16–3   Plaza Operating and Tax Projections

Potential gross income (year 1)	$750,000
Vacancy and collection loss	5% of potential gross income
Operating expenses (year 1)	35% of effective gross income
Depreciation method	Straight line, 31.5 years
Amortization of loan points	$60,000 over 25 years or $2,400 annually
Amortization of organization fees	$20,000 over 5 years or $4,000 annually
Projected growth in income	3% per year
Projected resale price after 5 years	$5,000,000
Limited partners' tax rate	28%
General partners' tax rate	28%

---

investment between the general and limited partners. We will see that these allocations affect the rate of return to each of the partners and are therefore important considerations in the analysis of partnerships.

When special allocations are used to allocate items of income and cash flow in different proportions to different partners, it becomes important to know how to determine the amount of cash that should be distributed to each partner upon sale of the property. This is because this final cash distribution must take into consideration the initial equity contribution, allocations of cash flow during the operating years of the property, and allocations of income (or loss) from operation and sale of the property. These items are accounted for with what is referred to as the partner's *capital account*. The nature and importance of the capital account will be discussed in more detail later in the chapter. For now we point out that the partnership agreement specifies that the cash flow from sale of the property will be allocated according to the capital account balances at that time.

Operating Projections

Projections made by Dallac regarding operations are summarized in Exhibit 16–3. It should be stressed that all projections made in connection with a syndication offering must be carefully and prudently made, since any misrepresentation or failure to disclose all material risks of the investment may result in a lawsuit for recission of the partnership, for damages by investors, or an action by regulatory authorities.[3] Because of this scrutiny

---

[3] In the case of *public* offerings most states require that a prospectus be filed with the state securities and exchange commission, and such projections are carefully scrutinized before approval to offer the securities is granted. Interstate offerings must be filed with the U.S. Securities and Exchange Commission and undergo a similar examination. Review and examination of securities offerings by state or federal agencies in no way indicates their approval or disapproval of the economic merits of the investment, but only indicates that the offering substantially complies with the disclosure and other requirements for registration or exemption.

by public agencies and the potential for legal action by limited partners, many general partner-syndicators make very general projections regarding future results or provide only a description of the projects that will be invested in and give some information on the business background of the general partner or partners.

In addition to projections for rental income, operating expenses, management fees, etc., Dallac has also disclosed the method of depreciation to be used and has detailed the period over which loan fees and organization fees will be amortized and when syndication fees will be deducted for federal income tax purposes. These latter expenses cannot be deducted in the year in which payment occurs. These items must be capitalized and amortized over a prescribed time period established by tax regulations. These expenses are important from the investor's perspective because the cash flow requirement occurs when the expenses are paid; however, the tax influence of these items occurs over the period of years during which amortization occurs or when the item is appropriately deductable.

Statement of Before-Tax Cash Flow (BTCF)

An important projection to be considered when analyzing a partnership is the statement of cash flow. In addition to the $1,121,000 investment made by limited partners in 1987, the statement shown in Exhibit 16–4 summarizes the before-tax cash inflow (*BTCF*) or cash shortfalls expected from the operation of the Plaza Office Building.

Another aspect of the statement of cash flow that is important deals with the distribution of cash to partners. In 1988 the project is expected to generate $83,964 in cash for

---

EXHIBIT 16–4   Pro Forma Statement of Before-Tax Cash Flow for Plaza Office Building

	Year				
	1988	*1989*	*1990*	*1991*	*1992*
Potential gross income	$750,000	$772,500	$795,675	$819,545	$844,132
Less vacancy and collection	37,500	38,625	39,784	40,977	42,207
Effective gross income	712,500	733,875	755,891	778,568	801,925
Less operating expenses	249,375	256,856	264,562	272,499	280,674
Net operating income	463,125	477,019	491,329	506,069	521,251
Less debt service	379,161	379,161	379,161	379,161	379,161
Before-tax cash flow (*BTCF*)	$ 83,964	$ 97,858	$112,169	$126,909	$142,091
Allocation					
General partner	5%				
Limited partner	95%				
Distribution of *BTCF*					
General partner	$ 4,198	$ 4,893	$ 5,608	$ 6,345	$ 7,105
Limited partner	79,766	92,965	106,560	120,563	134,986

distribution. Of this amount $79,766 will be distributed to limited partners. This represents an equity dividend rate of about 7 percent.

Calculation of Net Income or Loss

To illustrate the tax effect of the projections made in Exhibit 16–3, we have constructed a statement of taxable income or loss in Exhibit 16–5 for the syndication-partnership investment in the Plaza Office Building. Hence limited partners making a $1,121,000 (total for all partners) investment at the end of December 1987 would have a $12,503 taxable *loss* to report during 1988. As discussed in Chapter 11, this will be a *passive loss* and subject to the passive activity loss limitation rules discussed in that chapter. In this example we assume that the partners each have sufficient passive activity income from other investments (e.g., other real estate partnership investments that now have taxable income) that their share of the loss (12,503/35) can be used in 1988. Beginning in 1989, investors would have to report taxable income, which would be subject to ordinary rates of taxation at that time.

Calculation of Capital Gain from Sale

The calculation of capital gains and the resulting tax due from sale of the property is the same for a syndicated investment property sale as it is for the sale of property held by an individual. Exhibit 16–6 shows the calculation of the capital gain and its allocation to the general and limited partners pursuant to the partnership agreement, which provides

EXHIBIT 16–5 Pro Forma Statement of Income (loss), Plaza Office Building Syndication

	Year				
	1988	*1989*	*1990*	*1991*	*1992*
Net operating income	$ 463,125	$477,019	$491,329	$506,069	$521,251
Less					
Interest	358,910	356,342	353,448	350,187	346,512
Depreciation	110,317	110,317	110,317	110,317	110,317
Amortization					
Organization fee	4,000	4,000	4,000	4,000	4,000
Loan fee	2,400	2,400	2,400	2,400	50,400
Taxable income	−$ 12,503	$ 3,959	$ 21,164	$ 39,165	$ 10,021
Distribution					
General partner	5%				
Limited partner	95%				
Distribution					
General partner	$ −625	$ 198	$ 1058	$ 1958	$ 501
Limited partner	−11,878	3,761	20,106	37,207	9,520

EXHIBIT 16–6 Calculation of Capital Gain and Allocation to Partners

Calculation of Capital Gain from Reversion in 1992

Sale price		$5,000,000
Selling costs		250,000
Original cost basis	$4,100,000	
Less accumulated depreciation	551,587	
Adjusted basis		3,548,413
Total taxable gain		1,201,587

Allocation of Gain

General partner (10% of gain)	120,159
Limited partner (90% of gain)	1,081,429

---

that 10 percent of the gain be allocated to the general partner and 90 percent of the gain be allocated to the limited partner.

CAPITAL ACCOUNTS

Capital accounts represent the partners' ownership equity in partnership assets. Capital accounts are maintained by *crediting* the account for all *cash contributed* to the partnership and all *income* and *gain* allocated to each partner. The account is then *debited* for *cash distributed* to the partner plus any loss allocated to the partner. Exhibit 16–7 shows the capital account balances for the partners after accounting for the initial equity contribution, all income allocated from operating the property, all cash distributed while operating the property, and the allocation of gain from sale of the property. Thus, capital account balances include everything but cash proceeds from sale of the property. This is because, according to the partnership agreement, the distribution of cash proceeds from sale of the property is to be based on this balance.

The capital account balance at the end of 1987 is $1,121,000 for the limited partner and $59,000 for the general partner. This represents the initial equity contributions. In 1988 those balances are reduced by both the losses allocated and the cash distributed. Of course, the reason that cash is available for distribution at the same time there are losses to allocate is because losses are due to noncash deductions (depreciations and amortization), as discussed in Chapter 11. Note that beginning in 1989, capital accounts are increased by income allocations, but are reduced by cash distributed. Finally, in 1992 capital accounts are increased by the gain from sale which is allocated to each partner. In an accounting sense, the balances in 1992 show what each partner has in the way of equity capital invested in the partnership at that time. This is important to know because cash proceeds from sale of the property will be distributed in accordance with these capital account balances. The importance of these capital accounts is further discussed later.

EXHIBIT 16–7 Capital Accounts Prior to Distribution of Cash Flow Sale

	Year					
	1987	1988	1989	1990	1991	1992
			Limited Partners			
Equity	$1,121,000					
Plus income	0	0	$ 3,761	$ 20,106	$ 37,207	$ 9,520
Less loss	0	$ −11,878	0	0	0	0
Plus gain from sale	0					1,081,429
Less cash distributed	0	−79,766	−92,965	−106,560	−120,563	−134,986
Total for year	1,121,000	−91,644	−89,204	−86,455	−83,357	955,963
Balance	$1,121,000	$1,029,356	$ 940,153	$ 853,698	$ 770,341	$1,726,304
			General Partner			
Equity	$59,000					
Plus income	0	0	$ 198	$ 1,058	$ 1,958	$ 501
Less loss	0	$ −625	0	0	0	0
Plus gain from sale						120,159
Less cash distributed	0	−4,198	−4,893	−5,608	−6,345	−7,105
Total for year	59,000	−4,823	−4,695	−4,550	−4,387	113,555
Balance	$59,000	$54,177	$49,482	$44,931	$40,544	$154,100

Distribution of Cash from Sale of Asset

Exhibit 16–8 shows a breakdown of the cash distribution from the sale of the property. As indicated in the agreement, after paying selling expenses and the outstanding mortgage, both the limited partners and the general partner will receive cash distributions from sale that are equal to their capital account balances. Capital account balances for all of the partners will be exactly zero after this distribution of cash because all prior allocations of income, cash flows, and losses have been accounted for in the partners' capital accounts (see Exhibit 16–7).

EXHIBIT 16–8 Cash Distribution from Sale

Sale price	$5,000,000
Less selling costs	250,000
Less mortgage balance	2,869,596
Before-tax cash flow	1,880,404
Distribution (based on capital account balances):	
General partner	154,100
Limited partners	1,726,304
Balance (should be zero)	0

Calculation of After-Tax Cash Flow and ATIRR on Equity

Based on all of the preceding exhibits and an assumed marginal tax bracket of 28 percent, after-tax cash flows from operations and reversion can be calculated and the ATIRR on the investment can be determined. This is done in Exhibit 16–9, where the initial equity investment is a cash outflow in 1985 and before-tax cash flows plus tax savings (or less taxes due) are cash inflows. After-tax cash flows from operations and reversion result in an ATIRR of 13.15 percent for limited partners and 22.24 percent for the general partner. The higher return to the general partner is due to the additional allocation of gain and, consequently, additional cash flow when the property is sold. That is, the general partner was allocated 10 percent of the gain from sale, whereas the general partner contributed 5 percent of the equity and received 5 percent of the income and cash flow during the operating years. If the allocation of gain was also 5 percent for the general partner, then the *ATIRR* would have been exactly the same for both general and limited partners. (This return would be 13.68 percent. Of course, the general and limited partners must also be in the same tax bracket for their after-tax returns to be the same.)

Based on our analysis of Dallac, the reader should have a general framework in mind, with which potential investments involving limited partnerships may be considered. We should stress that the Dallac case example is meant to be illustrative of one possible way in which an investment can be structured. Indeed, many consider the field of real estate syndication financing and partnerships one of the most complex areas of federal tax law, subject to great variation in structuring of terms among partners. Hence, much study in the law and federal taxation beyond what is presented here is required to gain expertise in the area.

However, there are a few underlying generalizations to keep in mind when evaluating such investments. One generalization is that syndication arrangements are subject to the same economic influences that all investments are subject to, that is, risk and return. Any real estate investment is capable of producing only so much income, regardless of whether or not it is syndicated. When syndicated under a limited partnership, cash flows and tax items from operating and the eventual sale of assets are simply split among different parties. The promoter of the syndicate, who in many cases becomes the general partner, will offer limited partners only what is necessary under current competitive conditions to induce them to invest in the project. Such a return must be commensurate with the risk and return available to investors from comparable syndication offerings or other investment opportunities. Hence the *ratios* used to establish contribution of equity assessments, splitting of cash flows, and so on, should be structured in such a way that given reasonable projections of income and property value, investors will earn a competitive return, as measured by the procedure described in this section of the chapter.

Investors should be in a position to compare terms offered by competing syndicators, given the risk and required equity investment, and to judge whether expected returns are adequate. However, it should be kept in mind that the general partner must also earn a competitive return in order to profitably perform the economic function of syndicating. Essentially, syndicators view their role in the investment process as more of an agent who seeks and finds properties for acquisition or development, finds equity investors, operates and manages properties during ownership by the syndication, and eventually

EXHIBIT 16–9   Calculation of After-Tax Cash Flow and *ATIRR*

	1987	*1988*	*1989*	*1990*	*1991*	*1992*
			Year			
			General Partner			
Operation						
BTCF*	− $ 59,000	$ 4,198	$ 4,893	$ 5,608	$ 6,345	$ 7,105
Taxable income†	0	− 625	198	1,058	1,958	501
Taxes (28%)	0	− 175	55	296	548	140
ATCF	− $ 59,000	$ 4,373	$ 4,837	$ 5,312	$ 5,797	$ 6,964
Reversion						
BTCF‡						$ 154,100
Capital gain§						120,159
Taxes (28%)						33,644
ATCF						120,455
Total *ATCF*	− $ 59,000	$ 4,373	$ 4,837	$ 5,312	$ 5,797	$ 127,419
ATIRR = 22.24%						
			Limited Partners			
Operation						
BTCF*	− $1,121,000	$ 79,766	$92,965	$106,560	$120,563	$ 134,986
Taxable income†		− 11,878	3,761	20,106	37,207	9,520
Taxes (28%)		− 3,326	1,053	5,630	10,418	2,666
ATCF	− $1,121,000	83,092	$91,912	$100,931	$110,145	132,320
Reversion						
BTCF‡						$1,726,304
Capital gain§						1,081,429
Taxes (28%)						302,800
ATCF						1,423,504
Total *ATCF*	− $1,121,000	$ 83,092	$91,912	$100,931	110,145	$1,555,825
ATIRR = 13.15%						

*From Exhibits 16–2 and 16–4.
†From Exhibit 16–5.
‡From Exhibit 16–7.
§From Exhibit 16–6.

disposes of them. Because syndicators perform these services, they must also be reasonably assured of being compensated. Hence, they attempt to charge *fees* for all services such as finding properties for purchase, renting up facilities, promoting the sale of partnership interests, managing and accounting for the partnership investment, in addition to legal and accounting costs of organizing the partnership.

Limited partners must consider the reasonableness of these fees, plus the general partner's share in cash flows and appreciation in property value, when comparing among syndication alternatives. The primary concern of the limited partner is whether the general partner is "carving out" too much in fees and participation in future cash flows which would make the return on investment unattractive to limited partners. On the other hand, the general partner must be assured of earning a reasonable return for the risk and time involved in promoting the investment. Further, if the syndicator is attempting to earn all compensation from fees and is not taking some equity risk in the project, it may appear to a limited partner that the syndicator-general partner really has no "stake" in the project and is acting more as a broker earning only a fee with little concern over the long-run performance of the investment. If *expertise* in the operation and management of the investment is part of the syndication that is appealing to the limited partner, then a "stake" in the profits in lieu of fees paid to the general partner may be more satisfactory to the limited partner. Clearly, there are many facets to be considered here, and some balance must be reached between partners to make for a satisfactory agreement. Although fees to the general partner may ultimately reduce the limited partner's rate of return, these fees represent the cost of transfering certain risks and responsibilities to the general partner. Thus, the limited partner should not expect as high a return as a situation where he or she must incur these risks and costs.

A PARTNER'S BASIS IN THE PARTNERSHIP

When a person invests in a partnership, he acquires an "interest in the partnership." A partnership interest can be acquired in many ways, for example, contributing directly to the partnership when it is formed, or acquiring an interest from another partner. The concept of a partnership interest is quite important in investment analysis and valuation because the owner of a partnership interest can have a gain or loss on the sale or disposition of his partnership interest that is separate from gain or loss allocated to him from the operation of the partnership itself. We did not have to consider the individual partner's basis in our analysis of the Plaza Office Building because we assumed that the partnership was set up for the sole purpose of acquiring a single property, and all of the partners remained in the partnership until the property was sold and the partnership was dissolved. However, had one of the partners (e.g., one of the 35 limited partners) sold his or her interest to another partner, prior to dissolution of the partnership, then the selling partner would have had to determine the gain on the sale of his or her partnership interest. The gain would be equal to the difference between the amount received for the partnership interest and the partner's basis in the partnership interest.

A partner's basis in his partnership interest is often referred to as *outside basis*. The original outside basis is defined as being equal to the amount of cash paid for the partnership interest, plus the partner's proportionate interest in the partnership's liabilities.

(It is also increased by the adjusted basis of any property that is transferred to the partnership, and reduced by any debt of the partner that is assumed by the partnership.)

The partner's basis in a partnership interest is increased each year by the partner's share of partnership income and by any additional cash contributed to the partnership. The basis is reduced by the partner's share of losses and by cash distributions received from the partnership. Increases in the partner's share of liabilities of a partnership are treated as contributions of cash to the partnership, and decreases in a partner's share of liabilities are treated as distributions of cash from the partnership.

In many cases the adjusted basis of a partner's interest in a partnership will equal the sum of his capital account and his share of the partnership's liabilities.[4] The main difference between the two is that a partner's capital account is unaffected by partnership liabilities whereas his basis in the partnership is increased by his share of partnership liabilities.

We will now return to our Dallac example in order to illustrate the calculation of a partner's basis in the partnership and the use of that basis for determining the gain on the sale of a partnership interest. We assume that one of the existing partners wants to sell his or her partnership interest at the end of the third year of operation of the partnership. Another investor is found who is willing to pay $40,000 for one of the limited partnership interests (1/35 of the total limited partnership interest). The new investor will also assume the selling partner's share of partnership liabilities.

Gain on the Sale of a Partnership Interest

To calculate the selling partner's gain on the sale of the partnership interest, we must first determine the selling partner's basis in the partnership interest. This is determined as follows:

Initial cash invested ($1,121,000/35)	$ 32,028.57
Share of liabilities (.95 · $3,000,000/35)*	81,428.57
Original basis	113,457.14
Less loss allocated from year 1 ($11,878/35)	339.37
Plus income allocated from yrs. 2 & 3 ($23,867/35)	681.91
Less cash distributed from yrs. 1–3 ($279,291/35)	−7,979.74
Less reduction in debt from loan amort. ($65,345[†]/35)	−1,866.94
Partner's basis at the end of the third year	$103,953.00

*The limited partners' share of the partnership debt is 95 percent (see footnote 5).

[†]95 percent of the reduction of the loan balance during the first three years; e.g., .95 · (3,000,000 − 2,931,218) = $65,343.

---

[4]In a limited partnership all nonrecourse debt is allocated among the general and limited partners in the same proportion as they share profits. Recourse liabilities are allocated in accordance with the partner's ratio for sharing losses. Nonrecourse debt is debt for which the lender agrees to look solely to the secured property, not the borrower personally, for payment in the event of default.

The partner's gain on the sale of a partnership interest can now be calculated as follows:

Cash received	$40,000.00
Plus liabilities transferred to new partner ($2,784,657*/35)	79,561.63
Amount realized	119,561.63
Amount realized	119,561.63
Less partner's basis	103,952.94
Gain on sale on partnership interest	$15,608.69

*95 percent of the loan balance at the end of the third year.

The selling partner would pay tax on this gain. Under the Tax Reform Act of 1986, it is taxed at the same rate as ordinary income. Assuming that the partner is still in the 28 percent tax bracket, tax on the gain is ($15,608.69)(.28) = $4,370.43.

What is the after-tax *IRR* to the selling partner? The calculations are as follows:

	1987	1988	1989	1990
ATCF from ownership of the partnership*	−$32,029	$2,374	$2,626	$ 2,884
Sale of the partnership interest				40,000
Tax on sale of the partnership interest				−4,370
Total *ATCF*	−$32,029	$2,374	$2,626	$38,514

*This is 1/35 of the *ATCF* shown in Exhibit 16–9 for the limited partners.

Calculating the after-tax *IRR*, we obtain 11.50 percent. This is less than the 13.15 percent return that was expected if the partner stayed in the partnership for the full five years. This is, of course, a function of how much the partnership interest can be sold for to a new partner. There is a very limited market for partnership interests, and they often have to be sold at a discount.

Tax Basis of New Partner

The previous section showed the calculation of a selling partner's basis in the partnership investment. We now consider the new partner's basis in the partnership interest that has been acquired. This is determined as follows:

Cash paid for partnership interest	$ 40,000.00
Share of liabilities incurred from selling partner	79,561.63
Basis in partnership interest	$119,561.63

The new partner's basis will change during years 4 and 5 as income is allocated and cash is distributed. The new partner's basis will also be increased by gain allocated from sale of the property in 1990. At the end of 1990, after gain is allocated to the partners, the partner's basis will be as follows:

Basis in partnership interest at time of purchase	$119,561.63
Plus income allocated from years 4 and 5 ($46,727/35)	1,335.06
Less cash distributed from years 4 and 5 ($255,549/35)	−7,301.40
Less reduction in debt from loan amort. ($58,541/35)	−1,672.60
Plus allocation of gain at sale ($1,081,429/35)	30,897.97
Partner's basis at the end of the fifth year	$142,820.66

The partner's gain on the sale of a partnership interest can now be calculated as follows:

Cash received from disposition of partnership ($1,726,304/35)	$ 49,322.97
Plus relief of liabilities after loan repayment ($2,726,116/35)	77,889.03
Amount realized	127,212.00
Amount realized	127,212.00
Less partner's basis	142,820.66
Gain (loss) on sale on partnership interest	($15,608.66)

Note that the new partner incurs a *loss* on the partnership interest. Furthermore, the amount of the loss is equal to the amount of the *gain* that the selling partner had on the sale of his or her partnership interest (slight difference due to rounding). This occurs because the purchasing partner paid the selling partner a price for the partnership interest that was greater than the selling partner's proportionate share of the adjusted basis of the property owned by the partnership. By recognizing the $15,609 (rounded) gain on the sale of the partnership interest in year 3, the selling partner has, in effect, recognized his or her share of the gain that occurred at that time by the amount that the value of partnership property (the Plaza Office Building) exceeded the adjusted basis of the property. The difference in value by the end of year 3 was reflected in the price that the purchasing partner was willing to pay for the partnership interest at that time. When the Plaza Office Building is sold after the fifth year, the new partner is allocated the same proportion of the gain from sale of the property that would have been allocated the old partner ($1,081,429/35), even though some of this gain is a result of the allocation of depreciation and increases in the property value *during the first three years*. Thus the loss on the partnership interest ($15,609), in effect, reduces the total gain allocated to the new partner by that portion that reflects the first three years of the partnership's operation.

Assuming the cash flow from operation of the Plaza Office Building is the same for years 4 and 5 as originally projected, the *ATCF* to the new partner will be as follows:

	Year		
	1990	*1991*	*1992*
Operation			
BTCF*	−$40,000	$3,445	$3,857
Taxable income†		1,063	272
Taxes (28%)		298	76
ATCF	−$40,000	3,147	3,781

*The partner's share (1/35) of the cash flow distributed.

†The partner's share (1/35) of the income allocated.

After sale of the Plaza Office building and dissolution of the partnership, the *ATCF* for the new partner is estimated as follows:

BTCF‡		$ 49,323
Capital gain		
Capital gain allocated§	$ 30,898	
Loss of partnership interest	− 15,609	
Net capital gain	15,289	
Tax (28%)		−4,281
ATCF		$ 45,042

‡The partner's share (1/35) of the before-tax cash flow from sale.

§The partner's share (1/35) of the capital gain allocated.

Combining the *ATCF* during operation of the partnership (years 4 and 5) with the *ATCF* received at dissolution of the partnership, we have the following summary cash flows and *ATIRR* for the new partner:

	Year		
	1990	*1991*	*1992*
Total *ATCF*	−$40,000	$3,147	$48,823
ATIRR = 14.48%			

The after-tax *IRR* (*ATIRR*) for the new partner is 14.48 percent. Note that this *ATIRR* is greater than the 11.50 percent that we calculated for the selling partner. It is also higher than the 13.14 percent *ATIRR* that we calculated as the return for a partner that held a partnership interest for the full five years. In effect, the 13.14 percent rate for the full five years is a weighted average of the rates for the old and new partners.

From the above analysis, the reader should have an appreciation of the complications involved with investment analysis of a real estate partnership interest. We have seen that the rate of return (*ATIRR*) on a partnership interest depends not only on the performance of the underlying real estate, but also on the structure of the partnership (e.g., special allocations), and whether the partnership interest is exchanged prior to dissolution of the partnership.

The Importance of the Partner's Basis for Tax Deductions

An extremely important consideration regarding a partner's basis in his partnership interest is the fact that *the partner's basis can never go below zero*. This differs from a partner's capital account, which can be negative if the partner's capital contributions plus allocations of profits are less than the partner's share of losses and cash distributions. Negative capital accounts are common in real estate partnerships where deductions in early years exceed a partner's capital contributions.

The fact that a partner's basis cannot be negative is important because it can limit the amount of tax losses that a partner can benefit from in a particular year. If the partner receives an allocation of loss which would result in a negative basis, that portion which would make the partner's basis negative cannot be deducted for tax purposes until such time as the partner's basis is increased (e.g., by future allocations of income or by additional cash contributions by the partner to the partnership). Thus the unused losses are "in suspension" and may not benefit the investor for many years.

Also note that if a partner receives cash distributions which would result in a negative basis, that portion of the cash distribution which would make the basis negative results in immediate recognition of income or gain. This income or gain must be recognized in the same year that the cash is distributed.

Special Basis Adjustments

As we have illustrated for the Dallac example, when a new investor purchases a share in a partnership interest, the partner's basis in the partnership interest is equal to the amount of cash paid plus the partner's proportionate interest in the partnership's liabilities. This outside basis may not equal the partner's share of the basis of partnership property. This can occur because (1) the partnership property has been depreciated for tax purposes prior to sale of the interest, and/or (2) the property has appreciated in value from the time the property was acquired by the partnership. The selling partner will recognize gain on the sale of his interest in this situation. However, the acquiring partner will only receive tax depreciation benefits based on the partnership's basis in its assets, which will not be affected by the sale. That is, the acquiring partner receives the same allocation of depreciation that the selling partner would have received. The acquiring partner also receives the same allocation of capital gain upon sale of partnership property that the selling partner would have received. As we have discussed, some of this gain is a result of depreciation allowances and price appreciation that occurred during the time the selling partner owned the partnership interest.

In the Dallac example, we saw that the acquiring partner's loss on his or her partnership interest at dissolution of the partnership offsets some of this gain. However, if partnership property is sold before dissolution of the partnership, the acquiring partner will have to recognize the gain that is allocated to him or her from the partnership before the loss on the partnership interest is recognized. If an offsetting loss on the disposition of the partnership interest does not occur in the same taxable year (e.g., where only part of a partnership's assets are sold and/or the partnership is not liquidated until a later date), an acquiring partner will incur a financial loss. This financial loss will be equal to the difference between the present value of the tax liability resulting from the sale of the partnership assets and the present value of the tax savings due to the eventual loss upon liquidation of his or her partnership interest.

Because the acquiring partner may be at a disadvantage when purchasing a partnership interest for the reasons discussed above, the tax code provides for an election to be made (IRC Section 754) which allows for an adjustment to the basis of partnership property on the transfer of a partnership interest. This election is commonly referred to as a *Section 754 election*. The election must be made in a written statement filed with the partnership return for the taxable year during which the transfer occurs. The election affects only the basis in the partnership property as to the purchaser of the interest. Once elected, this election applies to all subsequent taxable years unless revoked with consent of the IRS.

When a Section 754 election is *not* taken, as was assumed for the Dallac example, the partner's basis in partnership property is equal to the partner's proportionate interest in the adjusted basis of the partnership assets. If a Section 754 election would have been made by the partnership for the acquiring partner in the Dallac example, the acquiring partner's basis equal to the partner's proportionate interest in the adjusted basis of the partnership assets *plus* a "special basis" adjustment. This "special basis" adjustment is equal to the difference between the partner's basis in his partnership interest and his proportionate interest in the adjusted basis of the partnership property. This special basis adjustment affects only the purchaser of the partnership interest and has no effect on continuing partners. If the Section 754 election is made, the special basis is considered in determining gain or loss on the sale of partnership property and for determining depreciation. Thus the acquiring partner may receive additional depreciation benefits. Furthermore, instead of incurring an eventual loss on his or her partnership interest, the partner will have less gain allocated from the sale of partnership property. Any decision to make an election to adjust basis under Section 754 must be made after careful consideration of a number of factors. Once made, the election is irrevocable absent consent to the revocation by the IRS. Another drawback is the increased record-keeping requirements imposed upon the partnership. This burden in itself has caused many larger partnerships to specify in the partnership agreement that *no Section 754 will be made*. The impact of such a provision on a prospective purchaser of an interest in a partnership holding appreciated assets should be obvious from the above discussion.

SUBSTANTIAL ECONOMIC EFFECT

One of the advantages of a partnership is the ability to allocate profit and loss to different partners in different proportions than their equity contribution. However, certain guidelines must be followed to ensure the benefits of these allocations won't be disallowed. Syndicates typically attempt to allocate the greatest amount of tax loss from the venture as quickly as possible to the individuals (usually limited partners) who have contributed capital to the partnership. In effect, it is these tax losses that the investors have purchased. Various means, such as disproportionate allocations of specific items (such as depreciation deductions), have been used to accelerate the allocation of losses to limited partners.[5] A partner's distributive share of each item of income, gain, loss, deduction, or credit is generally determined by the partnership agreement. However, for the IRS to accept the allocations as valid, the allocations must result in what is referred to as a *substantial economic effect.* Where the allocation in the partnership agreement lacks substantial economic effect, the item that is subject to the allocation will be reallocated by the IRS according to the partner's "interest in the partnership."[6]

In determining whether an allocation had a substantial economic effect on the partners, the courts have long inquired whether the allocation was reflected by an appropriate adjustment in the partners' capital accounts. The new proposed regulations governing special allocations adopt this view and provide rules for the proper maintenance of the partners' capital accounts.[7] As we have seen, capital accounts are used for accounting purposes and reflect the economic contribution of partners to the partnership. In general, the proposed regulations provide that if an allocation to a partner is reflected in his capital account and the liquidation proceeds (cash flows from sale of the property) are distributed in accordance with the capital accounts, and following the distribution of such proceeds the partners are liable to the partnership (either pursuant to the partnership agreement or under state law) to restore any deficit in their capital accounts (by contributing cash to partners with positive capital account balances), the allocation has substantial economic effect and will be recognized by the IRS.

CAPITAL ACCOUNTS AND GAIN CHARGE-BACKS

Assume A and B form a partnership where A, the limited partner, contributes $100,000 and B, the general partner, contributes no cash. The partnership secures a $400,000 (10 percent interest only) nonrecourse loan and acquires AB Apartments for $500,000. Assume that the results from the first year of operations of AB Apartments are as follows:

---

[5]For a more complete discussion see Richard B. Peiser, "Partnership Allocations in Real Estate Joint Ventures," *Real Estate Review,* vol. 13, no. 3.

[6]A partner's "interest in the partnership" is determined by taking into account all of the facts and circumstances, including the partner's initial investment, interest in profits, losses, cash flow, and distributions of capital upon liquidation.

[7]Treasury Regulation Section 1.704–1.

Gross income	$70,000
Less vacancy and collection loss	−4,000
Effective gross income	66,000
Less operating expenses	−21,000
Net operating income	45,000
Less debt service (interest only)	−40,000
Before-tax cash flow	5,000

Assume that tax depreciation the first year is $50,000. This results in taxable income as follows:

Net operating income	$45,000
Less depreciation	50,000
Less interest cost	40,000
Taxable income	−$45,000

Now assume that the partnership agreement provides that 90 percent of all taxable income, loss, and cash flow from operations is to be allocated to A and 10 percent to B. At the end of year 1 the capital accounts of A and B would appear as follows:

Capital Accounts after First Year of Operations

	A's Capital Account	B's Capital Account
Initial equity contribution	$100,000	0
Less loss allocation	($40,500)	($4,500)
Less cash flow distribution	(4,500)	(500)
Ending balance	$ 55,000	($5,000)

Assume that AB Apartments are sold after year 1 for $550,000 with no expenses of sale. This results in a taxable gain as follows:

Sales price		$550,000
Purchase price	$500,000	
Depreciation taken	50,000	
Adjusted basis		450,000
Gain		$100,000

Cash proceeds from the sale would be as follows:

Sales price	$550,000
Less mortgage balance	400,000
Cash flow	$150,000

Now suppose that upon resale, taxable gains or losses are split 50–50 between A and B, and cash proceeds are distributed first to A in an amount equal to his original investment less any cash distributions previously received, and any remaining cash proceeds are split 50–50 between A and B. This would impact the capital accounts of A and B as shown in Exhibit 16–10. Notice that the *net* balance of the two capital accounts is zero (this will always be true if all items of income, cash, and so on, are properly accounted for), but A's capital account is negative and B's is positive. As mentioned above, for an allocation to have a substantial economic effect, liquidation proceeds to be distributed must reflect the disparities in the partners' capital accounts. Where A's capital account is negative and B's is positive, A has in effect recovered his investment at the expense of B. If A is not obligated to restore the deficit in his capital account (by a $17,500 cash payment to B), he may not have borne the entire economic burden equivalent to his share of the depreciation deductions and the allocations lack substantial economic effect. Therefore, in order for the allocations to be recognized the capital accounts of the partners must be equalized before the partners in this example can split the remaining cash 50–50. Two acceptable methods of equalizing the capital accounts are discussed below.

The first method of equalizing capital accounts is to adjust the cash distribution to the partners. This would be done by having A receive $17,750 less cash from sale and B receive $17,750 more cash. The accounts would now be equal. The second method would be to have A's capital account credited for an additional $17,750 in *gain from sale,* thereby

EXHIBIT 16–10   Capital Accounts after Sale of Building

	A's Capital Account	*B's Capital Account*
Balance prior to sale	$55,000	($5,000)
Return of original equity Less previous cash Distribution	– $95,500	NA
50 percent of gain	50,000	50,000
50 percent remaining cash proceeds	– 27,250	– 27,250
Ending balance	– $17,750	$17,750

reducing B's share of the gain proportionally. By allocating more gain to A, capital account balances will be zero after cash is distributed.

Exhibit 16–11 below illustrates a valid partnership allocation using the second approach or gain charge-back method, and shows its impact on the capital accounts of A and B.

Careful examination of the above example should make it clear that the requirements that capital account balances for both partners be zero is one way for the IRS to ensure that a partner who is allocated proportionately more losses for tax purposes is also either allocated more taxable gain at sale of the property or receives less cash. Otherwise, partnerships could be structured in such a way that the partners in higher tax brackets would receive most of the losses, whereas the partners in lower tax brackets would receive most of the gains! Furthermore, the partners in higher tax brackets would be willing to give up some of the cash flow in exchange for receiving the losses and not receiving the gains. The ending capital account balances would then most likely be negative for the higher tax bracket partners with a corresponding positive balance for the lower tax bracket partners. While the partners may be perfectly happy with this arrangement, the government loses tax revenue. Thus, as we have emphasized, partnership agreements must provide for ending capital account balances to be zero to avoid challenge from the IRS.

Recall that in the case of the Plaza Office Building, the gain was first allocated to the capital accounts, and then the final cash flow was based on the capital account balances. This ensured that the capital account balances would be zero for both partners after all allocations and distributions to partners. There are other ways that the partnership agreement could have been structured for Plaza Office Building and still result in zero capital account balances. For example, each partner could first be distributed a specified percentage of the *cash* available from sale; for example, the general partners in the Plaza Office Building could have received 10 percent and the limited partners 90 percent. Then to ensure zero capital account balances, the allocation of gain could be based on the capital account balances. (In this case the capital account balances would be negative after the distribution of cash. Allocation of gain to the partners would then eliminate the

---

EXHIBIT 16–11   Capital Accounts after Sale of Building Using Gain Charge-Back

	A's Capital Account	*B's Capital Account*
Balance prior to sale	$55,000	($5,000)
Return of original equity Less previous cash Distribution	− $95,500	
Gain charge-back	35,500	
50% of remaining gain*	32,250	32,250
50% remaining cash proceeds	− 27,250	27,250
Ending balance	0	0

*Total gain from sale is $100,000. After the gain charge-back, $65,000 remains to be distributed.

negative balance.) The point is that allocations of all items of income and cash flow cannot be made without some provision for ensuring that the capital account balances are zero after all allocations and distributions are made.

THE USE OF UP-FRONT DEDUCTIONS IN REAL ESTATE SYNDICATIONS

One major goal of most syndicates is to offer investors the greatest amount of deductions available from the investment in the early years of operations. Many types of fees have been developed and claimed as up-front deductions in syndicated transactions. As a result, the IRS has challenged many such deductions, and Congress has acted to limit their deductibility or require that they be added to the basis of property and be depreciated or amortized over an appropriate period of time.

Interest Expenses

Interest and real estate taxes incurred during construction of real property improvements must be included in the depreciable basis of the property. Interest *prepayments* (including ''points'')[8] must be amortized over the life of the loan with respect to which they were paid. Where a commitment fee or standby charge is paid to make funds available for a specific term, the IRS and the courts are in discord[9] and the tax treatment of the expense is unclear.

Retrocative Allocations

Prior to the Tax Reform Act of 1986 (TRA) syndicators typically attempted to increase investors' first-year write-offs by allocating deductions to incoming partners that related to periods prior to their entry into the partnership. Under the TRA incoming partners receive only deductions for their pro rata share of expenses, calculated on a daily basis, accruing after their entry.

Improper Accruals

One technique frequently employed by syndicators to increase up-front deductions was to have money loaned to an accrual basis partnership by a cash basis entity which was

---

[8]This differs from the tax treatment of points paid in connection with the purchase of the taxpayer's single family home which are currently deductible, where the charges for points are customary and reasonable and when the taxpayer actually pays the points at closing. Also, points charged on a loan calling for the payment of the entire remaining principal balance at the end of a certain term (commonly referred to as a *balloon payment*) are deductible over that term.

[9]See Rev. Rul. 81–60, 1981–1 C.B 312 and *Duffy* v. *Com.* 690 F2nd 889 (Ct. Cl. 1982).

owned or controlled by the syndicator. The accrual basis partnership would accrue (but not pay) interest on the loan and claim a deduction for it. The related cash basis entity would not have to report the income until it actually received payment. The 1984 Act greatly expanded the definition of related parties under Code Section 267, which precludes related party payors from deducting interest payments until actually paid.

Prepaid Expenses

Another change by the 1984 Act limiting up-front deductions requires "economic performance" as a precondition for the deductibility of prepaid expenses by certain "tax shelter" taxpayers. This economic performance test requires that when property or services are to be provided, the property must be used or the services rendered before sums paid in advance for the property or services can be deducted. In general there is an exception to this rule if economic performance occurs within 90 days after the end of the taxable year.

Covenants Not to Compete

Deductions for payments to a developer or syndicator for their covenants not to compete with a specific project are frequently included in real estate syndications. The IRS always carefully examines deductions of this type to ensure they are not "shams" where there was no real intention to compete or where the payment for the covenant was clearly excessive. Accordingly, where such a deduction is to be claimed by a syndicate, investors should ensure that the covenant is realistic and enforceable and that the deduction claimed clearly reflects its value.

Organizational and Syndication Fees

Under prior law many aggressive syndicators claimed an immediate write-off for both organizational and syndication expenses. Code Section 709 now requires that expenses incurred to organize a partnership or other investment vehicle must be amortized ratably over a period of not less than 60 months. Organizational expenses include legal fees for preparation of the partnership agreement, filing fees, and accounting fees for setting up the partnership accounting system.

Syndication fees are not currently deductible or amortizable, but must be capitalized and deducted only upon termination or liquidation of the partnership. Syndication fees include brokerage fees for the sale of partnership interests, registration fees, legal fees in connection with the issuance of the interests or for securities or tax advice pertaining to the adequacy of tax disclosures in the prospectus or offering memorandum, accounting fees for preparation of representations included in the offering materials, and the actual cost of printing the offering materials.

Maximizing Up-Front Deductions

Given the various restrictions on up-front deductions and the specific attempts by both the IRS and Congress to limit their availability in the recent past, what techniques remain for syndications to increase investor's early-year write-offs?

Although the 1984 Act placed numerous restrictions on the accrual of deductions, the adoption of the accrual method of accounting may still permit the acceleration of deductions in certain circumstances (e.g., where there is a cash flow shortage or due to a conscious business decision). There may also be limited circumstances where expenses can still be prepaid to accelerate their deductibility. Also, in the case of improved realty the underlying land can be leased to the partnership to provide deductible lease expenses rather than utilize investor's equity to support the cost of nondepreciable land.

Staged Pay-in

One final method frequently used by many private syndicators is to permit investors to make their capital contributions to the partnership in installments. By spreading contributions over a number of years, the write-off ratios (the ratio of tax deductions to equity investment each year) in each year of contribution can be increased and matched with items of deduction that must be amortized over a period of time, such as organizational expenses. To accomplish this, a syndicator usually (1) accepted a note from the investor and then sold the note to a financial institution or (2) arranged for an equivalent installment loan secured by a security interest in the investment units.

THE FUTURE OF REAL ESTATE SYNDICATION

Today is a period of change and transition for the real estate syndication industry. Many industry leaders have predicted that the Tax Reform Act of 1986 may seriously impair syndicators' abilities to raise the substantial amounts of capital that they have in the recent past. By removing many of the favorable tax benefits currently available, this legislation could affect the entire industry and may lead to a reduction in the number of syndicators.

However, several excellent new sources of investment capital have come into the marketplace in recent years. Potential investment dollars from Individual Retirement Accounts (IRAs) and Keogh plans have grown tremendously. Public syndication offerings have been designed to capture a share of these dollars. Several syndicators have started new funds specifically oriented toward IRA and Keogh investors by reducing their minimum investment from $5,000 or higher to $1,000 or $2,000. The ability to invest in real estate for as little as $1,000 should greatly broaden the market and serve the industry well in later years by exposing these smaller investors to the potential of real estate investment.

In addition to the increasingly large amounts of IRA and Keogh plan funds flowing into real estate, pension funds are also investing substantially in order to diversify their holdings and as a hedge against inflation. As the pension funds of both public and private retirement systems invest more broadly into real estate, they will become a major factor in real estate markets. (See Chapters 20 for further discussion of public syndications.)

New Sponsors of Syndicates

As the opportunity to make significant fees in sponsoring and selling syndicates has become readily apparent in the past several years, many new players have entered the rank of sponsors of real estate limited partnerships. Wall Street brokerage firms, who rarely acted as general partners prior to 1980, are now becoming more involved in sponsoring public offerings. Insurance companies are also now active sponsors of syndicates. The newest market force, and one that could become a major player in the syndications market, is the savings and loan industry. Now free from regulatory constraints that have long kept it from flexing its muscle in an area of real estate finance and equity ownership that is riskier, but potentially more profitable, than home mortgage lending, many savings and loans have jumped into the syndication business. Some have had separate ''service corporations'' that have been involved in such activity for years. Others are currently developing in-house development and syndication programs, and others have entered the business with experienced partners. Whatever the case, the current trend among aggressive and innovative savings and loans is toward doing more and more real estate syndications.

QUESTIONS

1. What is the advantage of the limited partnership ownership form for real estate syndications?
2. How can the general partner-syndicator structure the partnership to offer incentives to limited partners?
3. Why is the Internal Revenue Service concerned with how partnership agreements in real estate are structured?
4. What is the main difference between the way a partnership is taxed versus the way a corporation is taxed?
5. What are special allocations?
6. What causes the after-tax *IRR* ($ATIRR_e$) for the general partner to differ from that of the limited partner?
7. What is the significance of capital accounts? What causes the balance in a capital account to change each year?
8. How does the risk associated with investment in a partnership differ for the general partner versus a limited partner?
9. What are the different ways that the general partner is compensated?
10. Why do you think the Tax Reform Act of 1986 affected the desirability of investing in real estate syndications?
11. What is the significance of the partner's basis in a partnership interest?
12. Why is a Section 754 election important to investors who acquire an existing partnership interest?
13. Why might a partner who sells his or her partnership interest prior to dissolution of the partnership receive an after-tax rate of return that is different from that which would be expected if the investment is held until dissolution of the partnership?

PROBLEM

1. Venture Capital Limited has formed a *private* real estate syndication to acquire and operate the Tower Office Building, with Venture acting as the general partner. There would be 35 individual limited partners. The venture to be undertaken and relevant cost and financial data are summarized as follows:

Cost breakdown		
Land	$ 1,000,000	
Improvements	9,000,000	(capitalized)
Points	100,000	(amortized over loan term)
Subtotal	$10,100,000	
Organization fee	100,000	(amortized over 5 years)
Syndication expenses	100,000	(capitalized)
Total funding required	$10,300,000	

Financing		
Loan amount	$ 8,000,000	
Interest rate	12%	
Term	25 years	(monthly payments)
Points	$100,000	

Partnership facts and equity requirements

Organization: December, 1988.

Number of partners: 1 general partner and 35 limited partners.

Equity capital contribution: general partner, 10%; limited partners, 90%.

Cash assessments: none.

Cash distributions from operations: general partner, 10%; limited partners, 90%.

Taxable income and losses from operations: general partner, 10%; limited partners, 90%.

Allocation of gain or loss from sale: general partner, 15%; limited partner 85%.

Cash distribution at sale: based on capital account balances.

Operating and tax projections

Potential gross income (year 1)	$1,750,000
Vacancy and collection loss	5% of potential gross income
Operating expenses (year 1)	$35% of effective gross income
Depreciation method	Straight line, 31.5 years
Projected growth in income	3% per year
Projected resale price after 5 years	$13,500,000
Limited partners' tax rate	28%
General partners' tax rate	28%
Selling expenses	5%

a. Determine an estimated return ($ATIRR_e$) for a limited partner. (Hint: Consider all 35 limited partners as a single investor.)

b. Determine an estimated return ($ATIRR_e$) for the general partner.

c. Why do the returns differ for the general and limited partners?

Financing Real Estate Development

Chapter 17

Financing the Development of Income-Producing Properties

INTRODUCTION

This chapter deals with financing the development of income-producing real estate such as apartment complexes, office buildings, warehouses, and shopping centers. Project developers face changing conditions in the national and local economies, competitive pressures from other developments, and changes in locational preferences of tenants, all of which influence the long-run profitability of developing and operating an income-producing property. The ability of the developer to acquire land, build improvements, lease space to tenants and earn sufficient revenues to cover operating expenses and repay both a construction and a permanent mortgage loan is affected by all of these forces in combination.

THE DEVELOPMENT OF INCOME-PRODUCING PROPERTY— AN OVERVIEW

As pointed out in the introduction, there are many types of income property that may be developed (recall the exhibit depicting various categories of land use in Chapter 10), and each has its own special set of characteristics. This is particularly true of the differences in market demand that affect the economic feasibility of each. However, a few general concepts are common to all project developments.

Exhibit 17–1 contains a simplified diagram showing the nature of the typical development process. With the possible exception of the management phase, this process is generally applicable to most categories of project development. Essentially, a developer (1) acquires a site, (2) develops the site and constructs building improvements, (3) provides the finish-out and readies the space for occupancy by tenants, (4) manages the property after completion, and (5) may then eventually sell the project. How long after development the project will be sold depends on the business strategy employed by the developer when the development is undertaken. Generally, business strategies used by developers can be

EXHIBIT 17–1 Phases of Real Estate Project Development and Risk

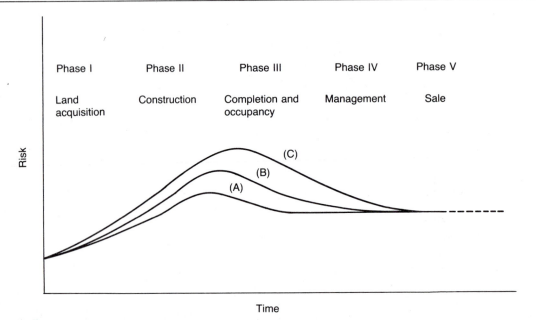

(A) Greater than normal pre-development leasing, completion ahead of schedule.
(B) Normal pre-development leasing, completion on schedule.
(C) Lower than normal pre-development leasing, completion behind schedule.

categorized in three ways; first, there are many development firms who undertake projects with the intention of owning and managing them for many years after completion. These developers view leasing and management as integral parts of their business in addition to the development function. Second, some developers expect to sell their developments after the lease-up phase, or when normal occupancy has been achieved. These projects are usually sold to institutional investors, such as insurance companies or other investment entities, or they may be fully or partially sold to syndication firms who form limited partnerships. In these cases, even though projects are sold, a development company may continue to manage the project. Third, some developers, particularly those involved in a combination of land development and developing commercial property such as business parks and industrial parks, normally develop land and buildings for lease in a master planned development. However, they may also "build to suit" for single tenants.

The point is that many developers intentionally *specialize* their business activities in one or more phases of the generalized diagram shown in Exhibit 17–1. Those developers intending to sell soon after lease-up rely heavily on external contractors, architects, real estate brokers, leasing agents and property managers to accomplish much of phases II, through V. Alternatively, very large, integrated development firms with activities in many regional markets find it profitable to provide most of the functions shown in the exhibit themselves, using external firms only wnen it is cost-effective to do so. For firms on both ends of the spectrum, however, it is possible that an unanticipated sale of a project may occur in any phase of development. Most developers are never adverse to considering a serious offer to purchase a project at anytime.

Market Risks

As to the risk profile of project development, Exhibit 17–1 depicts a typical risk scenario in a "normal" market, as represented by case B, or one in which market rents are believed to be sufficient enough to justify development (a subject that will be elaborated later in the chapter). Risk begins with land acquisition and increases steadily as construction commences and until expected cash flows from the leasing phase materialize. After lease-up is completed, occupancy takes place and the property management phase begins. At that point, project risk declines as tenants are committed to leases with terms of varying lengths. Assuming that the property is performing well, it is during phase IV that it may be described a "seasoned" property. An example of a market scenario with less risk is shown as case (A), where market demand for space is increasing and predevelopment leasing, or leasing *prior* to project completion, is occurring at an "above normal" rate, thereby increasing expected cash inflows. The expected increase in cash inflows usually reflects a greater than anticipated demand for the type of space being developed and, therefore, a reduction in project risk. Obviously, if market demand and expected revenues were to decline or if the time required for the leasing phase lengthened considerably, as in case (C), project risk would increase dramatically. Factors such as construction delays, price increases in materials, and interest rate increases may also cause increases and decreases in project risk.

Although the subject of regional and urban economics and the determinants of employment are not the focus of this book, it should be clear that factors determining the demand for the type of space (e.g., office, retail, warehouse) being developed is critical to project risk. These factors may manifest themselves in current market indicators, such as vacancy rate levels, rent levels, or the extent of predevelopment leasing commitments from tenants. A very good understanding of the underlying economic base of an urban or region is critical when assessing the viability of real estate development because not only is the demand for rental space important during development, but it is important long *after* development is completed. Demand may decline and rents may fall in markets at any time, and tenants may find more attractive space at lower rents. Simply because a project has been developed and leased up does *not* mean that it is no longer vulnerable to competition. As space in new developments is supplied to the market, owners of existing projects become subject to the possibility of a loss in tenants. Indeed, many developers are not willing to undertake this longer-term market risk and the intensive amount of property management necessary to retain tenants. As mentioned earlier, they may prefer to sell to institutional or other investors who are willing to specialize in that aspect of the real estate business and bear that risk.

Contrasted with developers who generally sell projects shortly after lease-up, larger, more geographically diversified developers may be willing to undertake management of projects in various regions. They view this risk in the context of a portfolio in which risks emanating from longer-term economic growth and declines in individual regions can be diversified sufficiently enough to provide an adequate risk-adjusted return on their total property holdings. There are other benefits that these firms may derive from continuing to perform the leasing and property management functions after development is completed. These include leads for future development opportunities that may be obtained from the existing tenant base under management. These leads can take the form of (1) expansion of existing tenant facilities, (2) expansion opportunities in other cities as the businesses in which existing tenants are engaged need facilities to pursue growth opportunities elsewhere, and (3) development of different product types (e.g., the development of an office building for a satisfied tenant who currently leases warehouse space elsewhere).

Project Risks

An understanding of the general market demand and leasing activity are not the only source of risk that developers must consider in project development. Obviously, the location of the site to be acquired for the project development is an important consideration, because its spatial proximity to other sites in an urban area will affect the cost of doing business for tenants and/or affect the demand for the product or service that tenants are selling. It follows that the better the spatial proximity, or location, as perceived by the tenant, the greater the value of site. When developers acquire sites in a given market, the cost of acquisition is an important determinant of the quality and cost of building improvements. Generally, as the cost of a given site increases, the building improvements will be of higher quality and will cost more to develop. Further, as the price of the land increases, the site is likely to be more densely developed. These basic economic relationships partially explain why certain areas of cities, such as downtowns, are more densely developed with high-rise office buildings while suburban areas are less densely developed (e.g., warehouses on relatively low-cost suburban or agricultural land).

Physical design, functionality in interior layout, quality of interior finish, density on the site and its adequacy of access and egress from transportation, amenities (dining, athletic, retail, etc.), landscaping, parking and circulation on the site, common areas, elevators, quality of HVAC (heat, ventilation, and air-conditioning), exterior finish (granite, aggregate, wood, etc.) are but a few of the major components that can be differentiated in cost and quality in anticipation of market demand for the type of space (office, retail, hotel, industrial, residential, etc.) being developed. Because there is uncertainty associated with how the quantity and quality of services provided as a part of the development should be combined or "packaged" to meet demand, each of these elements presents a potential source of project risk.

Not all new projects are initially constructed as luxury "class A" space, which is usually complemented with higher-quality interior, exterior, and mechanical components. Indeed, many large national corporations seeking to expand facilities will have set policies regarding the quality of space necessary for various categories of employees. Some employees involved with primary customer contacts (such as marketing) may be provided relatively high-quality space; on the other hand, the quality of space necessary for support services (accounting, computer, etc.) may not be as costly. Indeed, if the majority of the expansion space will be required for support service, not only will the corporate tenant be looking for a facility with average finish and construction quality in which support activities can be adequately provided, but the tenant may also prefer a suburban location. This is because proximity to residential location for its employees may be extremely important, since a support facility does not usually involve customer contact. On the other hand, a building to be occupied by tenants who have frequent face-to-face contact with customers (law firms, high-fashion retail shops) will generally require facilities with significantly higher finish costs.

The point is that the demand for space should be examined in terms of the characteristics of the demand by *end users* (tenants) in a given market. This demand will, in turn, depend on the type of employment in the local market and the nature of the functions that will be performed by tenants. Only by understanding the local economy and the nature of employment can the developer anticipate demand accurately and produce or supply the quantity and quality of space in the proper combination to satisfy market demand.

PROJECT DEVELOPMENT FINANCING—AN OVERVIEW

As far as financing development is concerned, in Phase I of Exhibit 17–1, the developer may use equity or combine equity with debt financing to acquire the land, perhaps after an option to purchase the land has been acquired (to be discussed in Chapter 18). Equity capital may be provided by the developer, or it may be provided from a partnership between the developer and the land owner or other investors. Should the developer expect to move forward on the project immediately after land acquisition, a loan providing funds for the cost of constructing improvements may be negotiated, with equity requirements met by one or a combination of entities just described. Generally, the loan used to construct the building and other site improvements is usually referred to as a construction, or interim, loan. This loan is usually provided by a commercial bank or a mortgage banking company and in some cases, a savings and loan association (these entities and other lenders are discussed in more depth in Chapters 19 and 20). It will generally be used to fund all "hard" construction costs, but may also cover some "soft costs," such as architect, planning, legal fees, and some of the costs of finishing the interior space for tenants through the lease-up stage.[1] After the lease-up stage is completed and when normal occupancy levels are achieved, the interim loan will usually be repaid from proceeds provided by a permanent mortgage loan. Permanent loans are usually provided by life insurance companies, pension funds, or in some cases by large commercial banks.

---

[1]It may be possible to obtain enough debt financing to pay for a portion of the land cost. As pointed out in the previous chapter, lenders may prefer to loan only on the cost of improvements; however, in a rapidly expanding market, competition among lenders may result in more flexible lending policies. Also, in most cases when interim financing is sought, the developer will be personally liable on the note. If the borrower is a good credit risk, the lender may be willing to advance some funds to acquire land.

These loans are usually closed after the property is developed, a preagreed percentage of the property space is leased, and other conditions that have been negotiated between the developer and lender have been met.

The Importance of a Permanent Funding Source to the Interim Lender

In many cases, a commitment for permanent debt financing, or financing that will come into effect *after* development and leasing is completed, is acquired *before* a commitment for the construction loan is obtained. This is because most construction lenders are *short-term lenders* and want assurance that a longer-term lender will be standing ready to retire the construction loan and to provide longer-term ("permanent") financing after the building has been completed and is leased. In some cases, however, if the demand for the space being developed in the local market is very strong, as evidenced by falling vacancy rates and significant amounts of space being leased prior to development, a construction lender may be willing to advance funds on an "open-ended" or "uncovered" basis. This means that the construction lender is willing to loan funds even though the developer does not have a permanent loan commitment. The interim lender either expects the developer to obtain a permanent loan commitment during the construction and lease-up phases or to sell the project before the maturity date of the interim loan. In cases where demand for space is strong and a lender makes such a construction loan, it is usually referred to as a *speculative* or "spec" loan. The only justification for such a loan would be if the demand for space in a local market is extremely strong and the likelihood of sale of a project upon lease-up is high, or, should the developer decide to retain ownership, a permanent loan will be easily obtained. Too much speculative and open-ended construction lending in a local market may result in significant overbuilding or an excess supply of space. This, in turn, may result in an increase in vacancies and a reduction in rents. Property values may then decline resulting in foreclosures.[2]

LENDER REQUIREMENTS IN FINANCING PROJECT DEVELOPMENT

When income properties are developed, the process of obtaining financing may be more complicated because in many cases *two* lenders are involved (construction and permanent). This means that the developer must satisfy *two* sets of lending criteria. While many components of these two criteria may be the same, some will be specific to each of the lenders. There is a further complication in that the nature of the agreement reached with the permanent lender may affect the nature of the agreement that must be reached with

---

[2]Many observers believe that the availability of funds is the primary determinant of development activity. Indeed, these observers believe if funds are available, developers will build regardless of general market indications because they are so optimistic that they believe that their individual project will always succeed in spite of the nature of competition and local market conditions.

the construction lender. This is because when a permanent lender is considering making a take-out commitment, that lender is literally "taking out" the construction lender and releasing that lender from any further lending responsibility to the developer. The take-out agreement may create a problem for a developer in that if the requirements of the commitment (lease-up requirements, lease approvals, etc.) are too stringent, it may be difficult to find a construction lender who is willing to comply with those conditions. This obviously narrows the developer's financing options and may result in considerable delay. To aid the reader in understanding the process of obtaining project financing and the nature of the documentation that is generally required by both lenders when developers seek financing, Exhibit 17–2 is provided.[3]

Loan Submission Information to Be Provided with Permanent and Interim Loan Requests— An Overview

While many of the items in Section (A) of Exhibit 17–2 are self-explanatory, the initial submission to the *permanent lender* will be more focused on what can be developed on the site, that is, a fairly detailed description of the size, design, and cost of the project. The submission will also provide a detailed market and competitive analysis, identify the team that will develop the project, and document all public approvals obtained or needed relative to zoning and permitting. Detailed pro forma operating statements and a set of financial statements from the borrower or borrowing entity will also be included. As just indicated, if the permanent lender gives the developer an indication of interest in financing the project, more detailed information will be requested and the developer will be required to support the assumptions used in the pro forma operating statements from the market analysis and provide other data requested by the lender. Assuming that this is done to the satisfaction of the lender, an *intent* to provide financing is usually provided by the lender, and the developer may proceed to work on much more detailed cost breakdowns, drawings, plans, and so on. This intent to finance is usually necessary before the developer invests additional funds needed to carry out more detailed planning. However, this detailed planning must be completed before a *commitment* is issued by the permanent lender and will certainly be required by the interim lender, who will be monitoring construction progress and compliance with plans and specifications. The methods used to underwrite and analyze market and financial data will be covered in a case example later in the chapter.

The information in Part A of the exhibit will generally not be complete when the developer first approaches a permanent lender for funding, because in most cases the development concept and strategy will not be finalized. The reader should keep in mind that the submission should contain as much information as possible; however, both lenders will have specific questions and requests for supporting data that the developer must

---

[3]The information contained in Exhibit 17–2 is not meant to be an exhaustive list of required documentation and requirements for obtaining loans. For a good treatment of legal considerations in construction lending, see Richard Harris, *Construction and Development Financing* (New York: Warren, Gorham and Lamont, 1982).

EXHIBIT 17–2   General Submission and Closing Requirements for Permanent and Interim Loans—
Project Development

A. General requirements for a loan submission package
  1. Project information
     a. Project description—legal description of site, survey, photographs of site, renderings of building and any parking facilities, development strategy and timing.
     b. Site and circulation plan, identification of any easements, availability of utilities, description of adjacent land uses, soil tests.
     c. Plans for building improvements, detailed list of amenities.
     d. Identification of architect, general contractor, principal subcontractors. Supporting financial data and past performance of parties. Copies of any agreements executed among parties. Description of construction and development procedures.
  2. Market and financial data
     a. Full set of financial statements on the borrower and any other principal project sponsors, past development experience; list of previous project lenders.
     b. A pro forma operating statement. Detail on proposed leasing terms to tenants, including base rent, escalations, expense stops, renewal options, common area expense allocation, overage (retail leases), finish-out allowances, other commitments.
     c. Detailed cost breakdowns, including
        · Any land acquisition costs.
        · Any necessary land development costs.
        · Any required demolition costs.
        · Direct or hard costs, breakdowns for excavation, grading, foundation, masonry, steel or other financing, drywall or plastering, HVAC, plumbing, electrical, elevator, and other mechanical, any special finish-out or fixtures.
        · Indirect or soft costs, including architects, engineering fees, legal fees, property taxes, interest-construction period, development fees, insurance and bonding fees, estimated contingency reserve, anticipated permanent loan fees.
     d. Any executed lease commitments or letters of intent from tenants detailing all terms of leases.
     e. Market study and appraisal including all comparables and detached schedule of rents charged by competitors.
     f. Loan request, terms, anticipated interest rate, amortization period, anticipated participation options.
     g. Equity to be provided by developer and/or other sponsors (cash and/or land); anticipated financing of draws/repayment.
  3. Government and regulatory information
     a. Statement as to zoning status.
     b. Ad valorem taxes, method or payment, reappraisal dates.
     c. All necessary permits, evidence of approved zoning variances, etc. (see list in Exhibit 18–2).
  4. Legal documentation
     a. Legal entity applying for loan (evidence of incorporation, partnership agreement).
     b. Statement of land cost, or contract evidencing purchase.
     c. Detail regarding deed restrictions, etc. (see Exhibit 18–2).
     d. Subordination agreements (see Exhibit 18–2).
     e. Force majeure provisions (events beyond the control of the developer such as an ''act of God''.)

EXHIBIT 17–2   (*Continued*)

B. Additional information needed for interim loan package
   1. A copy of the permanent or standby commitment from the permanent lender. Details on the amount, rate, term, fees, options relative to prepayment, calls, and participation. Details on contingencies that must be met by the developer before the commitment is binding (these are amplified in the chapter).
   2. *Detailed* architectural plans and specifications.
   3. *Detailed* cost breakdown.
   4. All data relative to requirements listed in Part A and *updated* as appropriate.

   Assuming that (1) upon review of all relevant materials in A and B, the interim lender makes a commitment and (2) that the developer goes forward with the project, the next step will be to close the interim loan.

C. Interim lender closing requirements
   1. Project information: *Final* drawings, cost estimates, site plan, etc.
   2. Market and financial information: Statement as to no adverse change in borrower's financial position since application date.
   3. Government and regulatory information: All necessary permits, notification of any approved zoning variances, etc. (also see list in Exhibit 18–2).
   4. Legal documentation
      a. Documentation indicating that the permanent lender has reviewed and approved all information in Part A and all updates in Part B.
      b. All documentation relative to contracts for general contractors, architects, planners, subcontractors. Evidence of bonding, conditional assignment of all contracts to interim lender, agreements of all contractors to perform for interim lender, verification of property tax insurance contracts, etc. (see list B in Exhibit 18–2 dealing with closing requirements in land development financing).
      c. Inventory of all personal property to also serve as security for the interim loan (particularly important for shopping centers and hotels).
      d. Any executed leases and approvals by permanent lender.
      e. Copies of ground leases and verification of current payment status by the lessor/owner.
      f. The interim lender will also insist on an assignment of all leases, rents, and other income in the event of default *and* a guarantee of loan payments by the borrower (personal liability). After review of all items indicated above, the interim lender will provide the borrower with a loan commitment detailing the terms of the loan, including amount, rate, term, fees, prepayment and call options, and any participations.

      However, with respect to the relationship with the *permanent* lender, certain agreements with the interim lender may be required; these include a buy-sell agreement or triparty agreement (discussed in chapter).

D. Permanent lender closing requirements
   This will occur *if* the developer (1) completes construction and (2) satisfies all contingencies (including lease-up requirements) contained in the permanent loan commitment before the expiration date of the permanent commitment.
   1. Market and financial data
      a. Statement of no material changes in financial status of borrower, or
      b. A certified list of tenants, executed leases and estoppel certificates indicating verification of rents currently being collected, any amounts owed, and any dispute relative to payments on finish-out costs agreement with the developer.

EXHIBIT 17–2   *(Concluded)*

---

2. Project information
   a. Final appraisal of project value.
   b. Final survey of building on site.
3. Government and regulatory information
   a. Updates on currency of property taxes.
   b. Certificate of occupancy issued by building inspector.
   c. Other permit requirements (fire, safety, health, etc.).
4. Legal documentation
   a. Delivery of the construction loan mortgage (if assigned to the permanent lender).
   b. Architect's certificate of completion with detailed survey and final plans, etc.
   c. Endorsements of all casualty and hazard insurance policies indicating permanent lender as new loss payee.
   d. Updated title insurance policy.
   e. Updated verification on status of ground rents (if relevant).
   f. An exculpation agreement, relieving the borrower of personal liability (if applicable).
   g. Lien releases from general and subcontractors—verification of any payments outstanding and proposed disposition.

---

provide. Hence, obtaining both permanent and construction financing should be viewed as a continuing process between all of the parties that may take several rounds of review by all concerned before any written commitments are made.

The Permanent or Take-Out Commitment.   Assuming that the loan submission proposal has been finalized and approved by the permanent lender, this commitment is made in writing by the permanent lender and will contain contingencies (to be discussed in more detail below) that must be met by the developer-borrower before the lender's commitment becomes legally binding. When these contingencies are met, the permanent lender will provide funds for the developer to repay the construction loan. If any of the contingencies in the take-out commitment are not met, the permanent lender is not obligated to fund the permanent loan. In this event, the developer must seek another permanent loan, or the construction lender may have to continue to carry financing on the completed project, or the developer may face a foreclosure proceeding initiated by the interim lender when the interim loan expires. The intent of the take-out commitment, then, is to create a legally binding agreement between the developer and permanent lender, whereby the permanent lender fully intends to make a long-term loan on the property after the building is completed, satisfactory levels of leasing have been accomplished and other contingencies have been satisfied.

Standby Commitments.   Standby commitments may be occasionally obtained by a developer from a lender when the developer cannot, or does not want to pay fees to, obtain a permanent loan commitment. Like the permanent loan, standby commitment funds are used to repay the construction loan. While standby commitments are similar to a permanent take-out loan in terms of the contingencies and other contents of the agreement, they differ from permanent take-outs in that neither the borrower nor the standby lender really expect the standby commitment to be used. This is because (1) the borrower expects to find a permanent loan commitment elsewhere, after construction is underway and preleasing occurs, on better borrowing terms, or (2) the developer is planning to sell the project upon completion and lease-up and does not believe a permanent loan will be needed. However, because the developer-borrower wants to begin development, and the interim lender wants assurance of a take-out, the developer may have to find a standby commitment at the insistence of the interim lender. If the developer does not sell the project, or a permanent take-out cannot be found upon completion of the project, then the standby commitment will be used and the permanent loan will be closed with the lender who made the standby commitment.

Even though permanent lenders who offer standby commitments charge a commitment fee and are legally bound to deliver mortgage funds on the completion date, many banks are unwilling to make construction loans when a borrower has only a standby commitment. This is because the commitment is made with a low expectation of being used. In many of these cases, should the borrower decide to use the commitment, the standby lender may be very inflexible concerning contingencies in the commitment. In situations such as these, lenders who have issued standbys may look for "technical violations" of contingencies in the commitment (for example, minor changes in construction plans and substitution of building materials that were not approved by the standby lender, and so on.) One problem faced by interim lenders is determining when a commitment is *intended* to be permanent and when it is *intended* as a standby, as between the developer and provider of permanent funding. Careful analysis of the permanent funding agreement provided by the developer is important, because if market conditions change, the developer and interim lender may consider the standby lender legally bound to provide funds, while the standby lender may balk because the intent of the agreement with the developer was not to have to deliver.

Contingencies in Permanent Funding Commitments

When a permanent loan commitment is obtained prior to actual development and prior to obtaining a construction loan, the permanent lender will usually include contingencies in the commitment. As pointed out, if the developer does not fulfill the requirements under these contingencies, the permanent lender does not have to fund the loan. Common contingencies found in take-out commitments obtained from permanent lenders are listed below:

a. The maximum period of time allowed for the developer to acquire a construction loan commitment.
b. Completion date for the construction phase of project.
c. Minimum rent-up (leasing) requirements and approval of all major leases in order for permanent financing to become effective.

d. Provisions for gap financing, should the rent-up requirement not be met.

e. Expiration date of the permanent loan commitment and any provisions for extensions.

f. Approval of design changes and substitution of any building materials by the permanent lender.

Essentially these items represent common contingencies that must be negotiated before a permanent loan commitment is issued. When financing is being sought on proposed projects, these contingencies are especially important because they establish that the permanent loan will be made after the developer has performed as promised.

These contingencies are indispensable to permanent lenders because they require that developers carry out certain responsibilities during development or prior to the expiration date of the permanent commitment. For example, provisions (a) and (b) require that the borrower have a specified time to find an interim lender willing to make a loan to cover construction and development costs, and that the project be completed by a specific date. Because large permanent lenders are usually life insurance companies, pension funds, and so on, they are not likely to be located in the city where the project is to be developed. Furthermore, the permanent lender must rely on a local lender to provide construction, or interim, funds and to monitor construction quality. The completion date contingency provides an incentive to developers to work as efficiently as possible toward completion of construction and leasing the building space or face the possibility of losing the loan commitment.

As for leasing requirements, this contingency is used to help assure permanent lenders that local economic conditions, which are being used to justify the appraised value and feasibility of the project, are favorable. The permanent lender requires a provision such as this in order to shift some project risk to the interim lender who should be very familiar with the local market and who specializes in construction lending in that market. The interim lender must carefully consider conditions in the local market because should the project not rent up to a specified percentage of occupancy by the expiration date, the rent-up contingency will not be met. This means that the permanent commitment will not have to be funded. Expiration would force the construction lender to extend its interim loan beyond the term originally intended and, perhaps, become a permanent lender. This is unless the permanent lender is willing to modify the terms of the permanent commitment.

In many cases, the permanent lender may agree that if the occupancy requirement is not met, funds will be advanced on a pro rata basis in proportion to occupancy achieved by the expiration date, with allowances made for full funding as occupancy increases. When the construction lender is unwilling to accept a pro rata funding take-out, however, the developer may have to find a third-party lender to stand by and provide a *gap financing* commitment. This gap financing commitment is usually obtained from a third lender. This commitment provides that the ''gap'' between any partial funding advanced by the permanent lender (because a rental achievement has not been met by the developer as of the date the permanent loan is scheduled to close) and the funds needed to repay the construction lender will be provided by a gap lender. The gap lender usually takes a second lien position and earns interest at a higher rate than both the interim and permanent lenders plus a nonrefundable gap commitment fee. Funds provided by the gap lender and permanent lender are used to repay the interim lender. As the project leases up and the permanent lender releases more funds, those funds are used by the developer to repay the gap lender.[4] Gap lending may also be used in cases where the developer faces cost overruns in excess of both the construction and permanent commitments, or if a permanent loan commitment is made for less than the construction loan. In either instance, the gap lender will analyze the project and, if convinced that it is acceptable risk, may take a second lien position.

The last item in the above list of contingencies, that is, approval of construction and design changes, is designed to assure permanent lenders that projects are developed substantially as agreed, that developers will not substitute substandard materials and use shortcuts to save costs that may jeopardize project quality. Poor project quality would obviously affect the collateral security of the permanent loan. For this reason, interim lenders usually insist that they retain the right to approve all substitutions of material and design changes.

The Construction or Interim Loan

As indicated previously, before construction loans on income-producing properties are negotiated between developers and lenders, the developer may have already obtained a commitment for a take-out, or permanent, loan, on a proposed project. Much of the same information on the proposed project that is used to obtain the permanent loan (shown in Part A of Exhibit 17–2) is also presented to the interim lender as support for obtaining financing. The permanent lender is generally not interested in making the interim loan because construction lenders are knowledgeable about local market conditions and are able to monitor construction progress and disburse funds as phases of the project are completed. This is an activity in development lending that requires knowledge of construction methods and materials and can be usually performed more cost-effectively by the construction lender. However, because of the contingencies required of the developer by the permanent lender, the construction lender must also evaluate the information used in permanent loan submission very carefully. In the event that the construction lender makes a commitment to fund the project's development and the take-out contingencies are not met by the developer, the permanent loan will not be funded and the construction lender will be forced to provide permanent funding for the project or call the construction loan due on the completion date, which could force the developer into bankruptcy.

In some cases, rather than negotiating a construction loan and a permanent loan, a *single* loan may be obtained from an interim lender and used to finance construction and operations for a year or two beyond the lease-up stage. These loans, which we have referred to as *miniperms* or *bullet loans* (see the appendix to Chapter 13) usually provide for a specific maximum construction loan amount and for interest only debt service. The

---

[4]In some cases, as the expiration date for closing the permanent loan nears, the construction lender may agree to become a ''gap lender'' if the rental achievement is not met. This is because the construction lender may prefer to keep the permanent commitment alive, particularly if the borrower cannot find a third-party gap lender.

full loan balance is usually due from five to seven years after the initial loan closing. This latter feature may take the form of a contractual maturity date or a call option. These loans are frequently used when a developer intends to sell the project soon after normal occupancy levels have been achieved, thereby reducing the cost and necessity of acquiring a permanent loan commitment prior to development.[5]

Methods of Disbursement—Construction Lending

Generally, the construction loan is secured by a mortgage for future advances or by an open-end mortgage. The construction lender will usually require a first lien on the land and all improvements as they are constructed on the site. A cardinal rule followed by construction lenders is never to advance loan funds in excess of the economic value of the property that serves as security for the loan. In other words, the construction lender never wants the developer "to get ahead" on a draw schedule, by drawing down funds in excess of the cost of construction improvements made to date.

The most commonly used method to disburse funds for commercial development is the *monthly draw method*. This method is used extensively in the construction of larger-scale projects requiring sizable loans. The developer requests a draw each month based on the work completed during the preceding month. If an architect or engineer verifies to the lender that such work is in place, the lender disburses the funds. Again, the collateral value for the loan increases simultaneously with the disbursement of funds.

In some cases, invoices may be submitted to a title insurance company, depending on whether the lender is using the services of a title company, who updates the title abstract between each draw and then approves payment on the invoices. As payments are made, contractors and subcontractors sign an agreement that they have been paid for work done to date.[6] This usually precludes them from filing mechanics' liens.[7]

Interest Rates and Fees

As is the case with many business loans, interest rates on construction loans are generally based on short-term interest rates that may vary considerably from period to period in response to current lending conditions. Most lenders, particularly commercial banks, usually rely on a system of floating interest rates on construction loans. Floating rates

---

[5]In cases where only one loan is negotiated, most of the material presented in the chapter is relevant, although some redundancy in documentation and other requirements is eliminated when one loan is used to finance a project.

[6]On a very large scale, projects that will take an extensive period of time to finish and involve many vendors and contractors, disbursements are frequently made by title companies who verify that no liens have been filed since the previous draw.

[7]Liens created during construction can cause problems for a developer when trying to close the permanent loan or sell the property when it is completed.

may be based on the bank's prime lending rate or the short-term interest rate charged on commercial loans to the bank's most creditworthy customers. However, some short-term loans are also based on Treasury bill rates, or the LIBOR (London Interbank Offering Rate). A construction loan normally is evaluated as to risk during the underwriting process, and the interest rate quoted on the loan reflects the short-term rate to which the loan will be tied *plus* a premium which is added to the prime rate. For example, an interest rate on a construction loan may be quoted as "two points over prime." This means that if the prime lending rate is 10 percent at closing, the interest rate charged on the construction loan will be 12 percent. Because the interest rate on construction loans is a "floating rate," the actual interest expense that the developer must pay can differ substantially from the amount budgeted or included in the loan request. In other words, the developer may bear the interest rate risk during the development period. (How developers manage this interest rate risk is the subject of the appendix to Chapter 18). The construction lender may also charge loan commitment fees.

Additional Information for Interim Loan Submission

Section B of Exhibit 17–2 contains a summary of some additional requirements for an interim loan submission which generally supplements and updates the material provided to the permanent lender. This additional information is provided by the developer, *assuming* that the preliminary data supplied to the permanent lender are satisfactory and the developer has obtained a permanent take-out commitment. Much of the documentation required by the *construction lender* depends on the terms and conditions contained in the permanent loan commitment. Hence, the interim lender must be in a position to review the permanent, or take-out, commitment as well as the final set of development plans and updated information for each component of the loan submission listed in Part A. Further, the interim lender will usually want assurance that the permanent lender reviews all of these updates prior to closing the construction loan.

Requirements to Close the Interim Loan

Although this chapter's focus is intended to be on financing, Part C in Exhibit 17–2 lists general requirements supplied by the developer to *close* the interim loan. Generally speaking, if the interim lender has expressed an interest to fund construction, a commitment letter will be issued containing all necessary requirements and documentation to close the loan.

Assignment of Commitment Letter. When commitments for two loans are obtained by a developer to finance a project, there is a legal obligation between the developer and the two lenders but no legal obligation between the two lenders. To create such an obligation, the construction lender may require that the borrower obtain the right to assign the take-out commitment from the permanent lender. Then the developer will be required to assign this commitment to the interim lender. In this way, if the project is finished by the completion date and all contingencies are met, the mortgage funds can be collected directly from the permanent lender by the construction lender, bypassing the developer. Also, should any disagreement occur between the developer and permanent lender, the construction lender, by obtaining assignment of the commitment, may pursue enforcement of the commitment directly with the permanent lender. This also limits the developer's ability to terminate the permanent loan commitment and seek another during construction.

Triparty Buy-Sell Agreement.   In lieu of assignment of the take-out commitment, the developer, construction lender, and long-term lender may enter into a more formal agreement in which (1) the permanent lender agrees to buy the construction mortgage loan directly from the construction lender on the completion date, assuming all contingencies are met, and (2) duties and responsibilities between the two lenders are created. This agreement goes beyond the assignment of the take-out commitment and provides that the permanent lender will notify the interim lender that the take-out commitment is in full effect, that the permanent lender will indicate whether all necessary plans and documents have been reviewed and approved prior to closing the construction loan, and, that the permanent lender will provide the construction lender with notice of any violations in the terms of the loan commitment by the developer and the time available to cure such a violation.

The goal of this agreement is to create legal responsibilities between the borrower, the permanent lender, and the construction lender. In this way, both lenders are more likely to be better informed as to the progress that the developer is making and whether any problems are likely to occur when it is time to close the permanent loan. Under this approach, the permanent lender also has more assurance that the permanent loan will be made at the agreed-on rate of interest and other terms. Inasmuch as the take-out commitment is made by the permanent lender, there may be some question as to whether the developer has a mandatory commitment to close the permanent loan. Indeed, if the developer finds another commitment on more favorable terms, he may choose to forfeit any commitment fees and close with the new lender. Inasmuch as funding will be available to repay the construction loan, that lender may not object. By using a triparty agreement, the construction lender agrees not to accept funding from any source other than the initial permanent lender.

The Permanent Loan Closing

After completion of the construction and lease-up period, and assuming that all contingencies enumerated in the take-out commitment are met, the permanent loan will be closed and the construction lender is "taken out," or repaid, with funds advanced from the permanent lender. From this point, the borrower will begin to make monthly mortgage payments from rental revenues. A list of some other general requirements for the permanent loan closing are listed in Part D of Exhibit 17–2. The reader must keep in mind that even though the permanent lender may have made a take-out or permanent commitment, that commitment will not be funded until the loan is ready to be closed, or after the project has been completed. Hence, the permanent lender will be in a position to evaluate whether all building and material specifications, leasing, and so on, have been carried out in conformance with what the developer promised when the permanent funding commitment was issued. Further, the permanent lender will also be in a position to ascertain whether all contingencies have been met before the permanent loan is closed.

A recent trend in the field of real estate finance has been to limit the liability of borrowers after all contingencies have been met, the permanent loan has been closed, and the project is operating normally. This is done by including an exculpation, or nonrecourse, clause in the permanent mortgage. Essentially, this clause limits the liability of borrowers by restricting the claim of lenders to proceeds from the sale of the real estate in the event of default. Because this relieves the developer of part, or all, personal liability, it potentially reduces the lender's ability to recover losses in the event of default and foreclosure. This is a point that is seriously negotiated by lenders and borrowers. This provision also places more underwriting emphasis on the quality of the property from the lender's perspective, since income produced from the property must repay the loan, and the property value must always be sufficiently high to repay the loan balance should a property become financially troubled.

If an exculpation clause is not a part of the permanent loan, the permanent lender will want to be very careful to ascertain that no material change in the financial status of the borrower has occurred since the commitment date. No lender wants to be in a position of funding a developer heading toward bankruptcy. This can present a problem, because the criteria used to ascertain what constitutes a ''material change'' may differ between the interim and permanent lenders and the permanent lender may refuse to close the loan. In some cases, enhancements, such as letters of credit or third-party guarantees, may be required of the developer by either the interim lender or the permanent lender at the outset, in anticipation of potential problems.

PROJECT DEVELOPMENT ILLUSTRATED

Project Description, Cost, and Permanent Loan Request

What follows is a case example of Rolling Meadows Center, a high-quality shopping center development located in an upper-income neighborhood proposed by Southfork Development Co. The Citadel Life Insurance Company has been approached by Southfork to provide permanent financing. Exhibit 17–3 contains a breakdown of land cost, site size, floor-to-area ratio, parking, and development costs. Percentage breakdowns are also provided for building coverage, parking, and open space and will be reviewed by the lender to ascertain whether the density of the project development on the site is too high and whether parking is adequate. Comparative data for this project will usually be available to Citadel from previous project financing files and from industry statistics.[8] Note that

---

[8]One important source of data is the Urban Land Institute's *Dollars and Cents of Shopping Centers.*

EXHIBIT 17–3   Project Description and Cost Breakdown for Rolling Meadows Center

I. General Description

A. Site and proposed improvements:

Site area: (in acres)	9.5
Gross building area *(GBA)*	120,000 sq. feet
Gross leasable area *(GLA)*	110,000 sq. feet
Percent leasable area	91.67%
Floor area ratio (Site Area)	29%
Parking spaces	550
Parking index	5 spaces/1,000 sq. ft. (GLA)

B. Development period: 24 months

C. Site plan:

Building coverage	29%
Streets parking	45%
Open space/landscaping	26%
Total	100%

II. Cost Information

			Percent of Total Cost	Cost per Sq. Ft. GBA
D. Land and site improvements:				
Site acquisition and closing cost		$ 2,500,000	19.6%	$ 20.83
Off-Site improvements	$ 250,000			
On-Site improvements				
Excavation and grading	$ 50,000			
Sewer/water	150,000			
Paving	200,000			
Curbs/sidewalks	100,000			
Landscaping	100,000			
On/Off site improvements		$ 850,000	6.7%	$ 7.08

development costs are broken down into land acquisition costs, off-site costs, "hard" costs, and "soft" costs. These costs are also broken down as a percentage of total cost and cost per square foot of gross building area *(GBA)*. Particular attention will also be paid to the site plan and ease of traffic circulation on the site.

Depending on the type of shopping center (e.g., strip, neighborhood, specialty, regional mall), lenders will want to know whether the relative breakdown of costs conforms to average breakdowns for recently developed neighborhood centers in comparable locations. Land costs that are too high or hard costs that are too low relative to land costs may mean that the total cost of developing an adequate mix of retail space of adequate quality may not be achievable at prevailing market rents. Similarly, common areas (difference

EXHIBIT 17–3 *(Concluded)*

E. Construction costs:

Hard costs:

Shell structure	$3,925,000		
HVAC	528,500		
Electrical	613,000		
Plumbing	221,580		
Fees	300,250		
Finish-out	1,400,600		
Graphics/signage	66,570		
Total hard costs	$ 7,055,500	55.4%	$ 58.80

Soft costs:

Architect engineering	$ 147,000		
Fees and permits	24,300		
Legal fees	26,900		
Construction interest	1,405,318		
Construction loan fees	194,286		
Permanent loan fees	291,430		
Leasing commissions	45,300		
Overhead direct	160,000		
Overhead indirect	30,800		
Total soft costs	$ 2,325,334	18.3%	$ 19.38
Total project costs	$12,730,834	100.00%	$106.09

between gross building area and gross leasable area) that are too large or too small may affect the ability to lease space and can be detrimental to profitability. The "correct" mix of location improvements, density, parking, circulation, and design is crucial to success.

In many cases, lenders will not fund any land acquisition costs or base loans as a percentage of appraised value only. In other words, lenders prefer to make loans to cover improvement costs only, and the developer may be expected to contribute the land as equity. Further, lenders will usually require a first lien on the land and all improvements made with the proceeds of the construction loan. This is because loans based on appraised value only may result in the lender advancing funds in excess of the market value of the property if the appraisal is in error. For example, if the lender agrees to loan 80 percent of the total project value and the appraisal (which the reader must realize is being done for a project that is still in the planning and design stages) results in an overestimate of value in the range of 130 percent of actual value upon completion, then the loan advances would equal 104 percent of actual value (80 percent of 130 percent). Further, if overestimate of project value was caused by an overoptimistic assessment of future rental achievement which does not materialize, the developer may have difficulty in servicing the mortgage debt. This obviously creates problems for the developer and for the interim lender who may be looking to a permanent lender to take out the construction loan. Recall

EXHIBIT 17–4 Summary of Loan Request for Rolling Meadows Center

A. Loan Summary

Total site improvements	$ 850,000
Total hard construction costs	7,055,500
Soft construction costs financed	
Architect/engineering	147,000
Fees and permits	24,300
Legal fees	26,900
Leasing commissions	45,300
Overhead direct	160,000
Total direct costs	$8,309,000
Estimated interest carry (from B. below)	1,405,318
Total loan amount	$9,714,318

B. Estimate of Interest Carry (interest rate 12%)

(a) Months	(b) Direct Cost Draws	(c) Draw Rate per Month	(d) Percent Repayment	(e) MPVIFA at 12 percent	(f) MPVIF at 12 Percent	(g) PV Draw Rates $(c)\times(e)\times(f)$	(h) PV PMT Rates $(d)\times(e)\times(f)$
Close	0	0.000000	0.000000	1.000000	1.000000	0.000000	
1–6	581,250	0.069954	0.000000	5.795476	1.000000	0.405417	
7–16	456,250	0.054910	0.000000	9.471305	0.942045	0.489929	
17–24	32,375	0.003896	0.000000	7.651678	0.852821	0.025423	
24			1.000000		0.787566	0.000000	0.787566
Totals	$8,309,000					0.920769	0.787566

TLF	=	.920769 ÷ .787566	= 1.169132
Total loan	=	$8,309,000 × 1.169132	= $9,714,318
TIC	=	1.169132 − 1.000	= 0.169132
Int carry	=	$8,309,000 × .169132	= $1,405,318
TPF	=	1.169132 + .169132	= 1.338264
Total PMT	=	$8,309,000 × 1.338264	= $11,119,636

that the take-out commitment may contain contingencies relative to leasing and rental achievement and may also contain a requirement that the final project appraised value exceed the permanent loan commitment by a specified percentage. If these provisions are not achieved, the interim lender and developer may have difficulty enforcing the take-out commitment.

We do not mean to say that lenders never consider appraised values in loan requests. Most lenders realize that the loan being represented must also represent a reasonable percentage of appraised value. This generally means that if the loan-to-value ratio for the proposed project is 80 percent, the lender anticipates that the improvement costs plus any other development costs that the lender is willing to fund should also be in the range of 80 percent. This, in turn, implies that land values and other costs that will not be funded in the loan should be in the range of 20 percent. In other words, the lender is looking for an equity contribution of 20 percent by the developer. This means that if improvement costs were estimated to be 90 percent of value, the lender may still be willing to fund only 80 percent of value. In this case, all improvement costs would not be funded. An alternative way of looking at the loan-to-appraised-value relationship is that a lender may, in our example, prefer to provide funds equal to the *lower* of either improvement costs or 80 percent of project value.

Many lenders will not fund off-site improvements that are part of a loan request because other parties may have title to the land on which improvements will be made. But even if the developer has title to the off-site land, the construction lender may have difficulty acquiring satisfactory lien security on the land where the improvements will be made. The ability to acquire funding for off-site costs depends on the lender's judgment regarding the value of the project, when completed, relative to the total loan amount. Most lenders will fund all hard costs if they can be documented and are commensurate with the overall quality of the development. Lenders, however, vary in their willingness to fund many soft-cost items. They may not be willing to fund closing fees associated with the land acquisition, financing fees, and, particularly, any overhead charges requested as a part of project cost by the developer. In most cases, however, an estimate of construction interest carry may be *included* in the loan request.

Exhibit 17–4 contains a breakdown of the *loan request* (Panel A) and an estimate of interest carry (Panel B). Note that no land cost has been included as a part of this particular loan request. Also, no request for indirect overhead or financing fees has been made; however, Southfork is requesting funding for off-site improvements. The total loan request is \$9,714,318, which represents about 76 percent of the \$12,730,834 estimate of total project cost (land plus all other outlays). The reader should note in Panel B that an estimate of construction period interest is made by computing the *monthly draw rate* for construction costs to be funded by the lender over the 24-month period (column c). The draw rates shown in column (c) are calculated by dividing each monthly direct cost draw column (b) by the total direct cost (\$8,309,000). The present value of those draw rates column (g) is calculated by multiplying the monthly draw rate by the *MPVIFA* for the appropriate number of months that draws are estimated to be the same amount (e.g., 6 months at \$581,250, or 6.9954%, then \$456,250, or 5.4910%, for 10 months, etc.). To find the present value of the draw rates as of the *loan closing date,* the factors in column (e) must be discounted by present value of one factor in column (f). This is because each set of grouped cash flows, when discounted by factors in column (*e*), are only being discounted for the time period during which the draws actually occur. To find the present value as of the loan closing date, these draws must be discounted again, by the present value of one. The factors in column (*f*) correspond to the end of the month preceeding the month when draw amounts change (e.g., 7, 17, and 24). The product obtained when figures in columns (*c*), (*e*), and (*f*) are multiplied is shown in column (*g*). The same procedure is used to obtain the present value of the payment rates shown in column (*h*). In this case, because there is only one repayment at the end of 24 months when the construction loan is to be repaid in full, only one factor is needed (.787566).

The procedure just explained must be followed because loan draw and loan repayment amounts are not equal and are received in different time periods. From the lenders point of view, repayment of the loan will not occur until the end of the 24th month. From the borrowers point of view, funds are received in various amounts throughout the 24-month period. Therefore, the present value of funds received by both the borrower and lender is found by discounting all amounts received back to the day of the loan closing. After finding the present value of payments and draws, we can now estimate the total loan amount that will be needed for Rolling Meadows.

The total loan amount that will be required to finance the development of Rolling Meadows can be determined by dividing the present value of the sum of the draw rates (*g*) by the present value of the repayment rate (*h*) to obtain the total loan factor *(TLF)*. This factor may be multiplied by total direct costs to obtain the total loan amount. The result, or (1.169132) × ($8,309,000) = $9,714,318, determines the total amount of the loan request, *including interest*. An estimate of total interest carry *(TIC)* can now be made by subtracting 1 from *TLF,* or 1.169132 − 1.000 = .169132, which is multiplied by the direct cost draws of $8,309,000, resulting in estimated interest of $1,405,318. (For a more detailed explanation on the computation of interest carry and lender yields, see the appendix to this chapter.) Hence, $9,714,318 will be the amount of the take-out loan commitment requested in our example. Finally, the reader should note that total cash interest payments that will be made by the borrower must equal monthly interest payments plus the loan balance at the end of the construction period, or $11,119,636, as shown in column (*f*) of Exhibit 17−4. Total payments may also be derived by adding *TLF* + *TIC,* which sums to 1.338264, then multiplying this total payment factor (TPF) by total construction costs to be borrowed, or $8,309,000. This results in the total repayment amount including interim interest payments, and loan principal, (which includes interest carry) of $11,119,636.

The reader should note in Exhibit 17−4 that the estimated interest is $1,405,318, or the difference between total draws used for direct development costs and the amount of the loan request. To elaborate on the interim financing at this point, we present Exhibit 17−5. While this exhibit contains information that would *not* accompany a loan request, it does lend some valuable insights to the reader. The exhibit contains a repayment schedule for the interim loan, *assuming* that all cost estimates are accurate as to the *amount and timing* of draws. Interest draws are computed on the outstanding monthly loan balance and are assumed to be taken down as a part of the construction cost draws at the end of each month. Cash interest payments are made by the developer to the bank each month. However, because the interest carry is borrowed and payments to be made by the developer

EXHIBIT 17–5 Construction Loan Draw and Repayment Schedule

	(a)	(b)	(c)	(d)	(e)	(f)	(g)
	Draws		Total Draw	Payments		Total Payment	Ending Balance: Prev Mo.Bal.
Month	Direct Cost	Interest	(a)+(b)	Principal	Interest (g)×(12%/12)	(d)+(e)	(g)+(c)−(d)
0	0	0	0		0	0	0
1	$ 581,250	0	$ 581,250		0	0	$ 581,250
2	581,250	$ 5,813	587,063		$ 5,813	$ 5,813	1,168,313
3	581,250	11,683	592,933		11,683	11,683	1,761,246
4	581,250	17,612	598,862		17,612	17,612	2,360,108
5	581,250	23,601	604,851		23,601	23,601	2,964,959
6	581,250	29,650	610,900		29,650	29,650	3,575,859
7	456,250	35,759	492,009		35,759	35,759	4,067,868
8	456,250	40,679	496,929		40,679	40,679	4,564,797
9	456,250	45,648	501,898		45,648	45,648	5,066,695
10	456,250	50,667	506,917		50,667	50,667	5,573,612
11	456,250	55,736	511,986		55,736	55,736	6,085,598
12	456,250	60,856	517,106		60,856	60,856	6,602,704
13	456,250	66,027	522,277		66,027	66,027	7,124,981
14	456,250	71,250	527,500		71,250	71,250	7,652,481
15	456,250	76,525	532,775		76,525	76,525	8,185,256
16	456,250	81,853	538,103		81,853	81,853	8,723,359
17	32,375	87,234	119,609		87,234	87,234	8,842,968
18	32,375	88,430	120,805		88,430	88,430	8,963,773
19	32,375	89,638	122,013		89,638	89,638	9,085,786
20	32,375	90,858	123,233		90,858	90,858	9,209,019
21	32,375	92,090	124,465		92,090	92,090	9,333,484
22	32,375	93,335	125,710		93,335	93,335	9,459,194
23	32,375	94,592	126,967		94,592	94,592	9,586,161
24	32,375	95,862	$ 128,237	$9,714,318	95,862	9,810,180	80
Total	$8,309,000	$1,405,398	$9,714,398	$9,714,318	$1,405,398	$11,119,716	80

Panel A. Interest Rate = 12.00%

Construction loan fees at 2 percent $194,286

Yield to lender on construction loan   14.00%

EXHIBIT 17–5 *(Concluded)*

Panel B. Summary of Loan Terms (permanent loan request)

Total loan	$9,714,318
Debt amortization period	25 years
Debt service/month	$102,314
Debt service/year	$1,227,768
Term of loan	10 years
Permanent loan fee at 3 percent	291,430
Construction loan fee at 2 percent	194,286
Interest rate	12.00%
Yield to lender	12.81%

will amount to interest only payments, no amortization of principal occurs. Hence, the loan balance will increase each month. The total ending loan balance $9,714,318 will be equal to the total construction loan amount at the end of the 24-month period. This amount will be funded by the permanent lender, thereby taking out the construction lender at that time. In most cases, the permanent loan and the interim loan commitments are usually made for the same amount. (The small remaining loan balance in Exhibit 17–5 results from rounding when calculating draw rates and repayment rates in part B of Exhibit 17–4. If carried out to enough decimal places, the estimated amounts for interest carry, total loan amount, etc. in Exhibit 17–4 and amounts shown in Exhibit 17–5 would be equal.)

Even though developers may estimate costs very carefully, the *actual* costs of development and interest carry will differ from such estimates because of uncertainties in the rate at which work will progress and because interest rates may change. Hence, it is likely that the *actual* interest draw pattern will deviate from the *estimated* pattern. Once the $9,714,318 commitment amount is reached however, the construction lender *is not required to fund any more draws, and the permanent lender is not required to fund any more than the committed amount*. If the developer does not want to bear the risk of unanticipated interest rate changes and, hence, the possibility or interest cost overruns, that risk can be eliminated, or at least reduced at a cost. This can be accomplished by either hedging or purchasing an interest rate swap (see the appendix to Chapter 18 for a discussion).

If the developer does not want to bear the cost of eliminating interest rate risk, additional funds will have to be provided (perhaps by attracting more partners to the venture), or a gap lender or equity partners will have to be found. If actual costs exceed estimated costs because of material and labor cost overruns, unanticipated changes in interest rates,[9] a longer than anticipated lease-up period because of a declining market, and so on, and the developer cannot find other sources of equity (through a partnership, etc.) or a gap loan, and the interim lender refuses to extend additional funds, the developer may face foreclosure.

A draw, interest, and repayment schedule similar to that shown in Exhibit 17–5 is generally used by lenders and developers as a tool for financial control. This schedule may be used in conjunction with field surveys completed by staff engineers to verify that the total percentage of *work in place* at the end of each month corresponds to the outstanding loan balance at the end of each month. If, in the view of the lender, total funds drawn down are in excess of construction in place, further draws will not be allowed until offsetting improvements are made. The reader should also note that because the construction lender charges a 2 percent loan origination fee the loan yield will be 14 percent, as compared with the 12 percent rate of interest used to compute interest on the loan. This yield is calculated by finding the rate of discount that makes the present value of monthly outflows in months 1–23 (column g) plus the lump sum inflow in month 24 equal to the loan fees charged at closing by the interim lender, or $194,286 (see the appendix for details).

---

[9] The methods used to hedge against interest rate risk when using floating interest rate loans is discussed in the appendix to Chapter 18.

A final note regarding the draw schedule has to do with the use of *hold backs* by lenders. Generally when project developers contract with various building contractors to perform work, developers generally hold back a percentage (10 percent) of each progress payment made to such contractors until all work is satisfactorily completed. This is done to assure the developer that all work has been completed in accordance with plans and specifications. When work is completed to the developer's satisfaction, the final payment is made to the contractors. Most lenders are aware of hold back practices and will in turn hold back a percentage (10 percent) of all loan draw requests from developers. This is done to prevent developers from drawing down funds at a faster rate than they must pay them to contractors. Holdbacks are not taken into account in Exhibits 17–4 and 17–5. However, the reader should be aware of this practice and take them into account in the draw schedule if applicable.

Market Data and Tenant Mix

Exhibit 17–6 contains a breakdown of the expected tenant mix for Rolling Meadows and the space that they are expected to occupy. For a neighborhood center, most lenders would expect at least one predevelopment lease commitment from a food chain and/or general merchandiser. Obviously, if favorable predevelopment lease commitments accompany the loan request, it is more likely that a commitment will be made. As for the other data in the exhibit, they are based on experience from U.S. data averages and with averages obtained from local market surveys. It should be stressed that exact comparability in tenant mix is not expected in each and every project submitted for review. However, past experience usually indicates that certain types of tenants are not compatible (e.g., auto parts and jewelry stores) in the same center, while others are (e.g., jewelry stores and furriers). A submission that indicates a lack of understanding regarding tenant mix may reveal inexperience on the part of the developer. Further, the tenant breakdown should be realistic in that if the developer projects too many "high-end" retail stores (which usually pay high rents), this may indicate overoptimism.

In addition to the data shown in Exhibit 17–6, the developer will have to provide more detail regarding the trade area expected to be served by the center, a competitive analysis of other centers, and proof that the addition of another center will not oversupply that market with retail space. Additional information relative to population growth, age, households, income, retail spending patterns, and so forth (not shown), in the trade area must also support the loan request. The importance of this data cannot be stressed enough.

Pro Forma Construction Costs and Cash Flow Projections

Another necessary ingredient in the submission of data to the permanent lender is a pro forma (estimate) of construction costs and net operating income. Exhibit 17–7 contains annual estimates for expenditures during the construction period for land acquisition, site improvements, hard costs, and soft costs. Total loan draws are based on the $9,714,318 loan request (including interest), for which financing is being sought, over the two-year

EXHIBIT 17–6 Market Survey Data—Shopping Centers (tenant information)

Classification	Number of Stores	Percent of Total Tenants*	Square Feet of GLA	Percent of GLA	U.S. Average Percent of GLA in Centers	Local Average Percent of GLA in Centers
General merchandise	1	3.57%	4,950	4.50%	5.60%	5.20%
Food	2	7.14%	37,400	34.00%	30.80%	36.00%
Food service	1	3.57%	8,800	8.00%	8.80%	7.00%
Clothing	3	10.71%	7,700	7.00%	5.00%	6.00%
Shoes	1	3.57%	1,155	1.05%	1.30%	0.70%
Home furnishings	1	3.57%	1,100	1.00%	2.60%	2.30%
Home appliances	1	3.57%	990	0.90%	2.40%	1.00%
Building materials	1	3.57%	1,320	1.20%	3.40%	2.00%
Automotive supplies		0.00%	0	0.00%	1.70%	1.50%
Hobby	1	3.57%	2,035	1.85%	2.70%	2.50%
Gifts & specialty	2	7.14%	2,860	2.60%	2.50%	2.30%
Jewelry & cosmetics	1	3.57%	1,650	1.50%	0.70%	2.00%
Liquor	1	3.57%	1,430	1.30%	1.50%	1.50%
Drugs	1	3.57%	9,900	9.00%	8.50%	8.00%
Other retail	6	21.46%	12,100	11.00%	4.40%	6.00%
Personal services	2	7.14%	8,910	8.10%	6.50%	7.00%
Recreational	1	3.57%	2,200	2.00%	3.50%	3.00%
Financial	1	3.57%	3,300	3.00%	4.10%	3.00%
Offices	1	3.57%	2,200	2.00%	4.00%	3.00%
Total	28	100.00%	110,000	100.00%	100.00%	100.00%

*Rounded.

EXHIBIT 17–7   Pro Forma Statement of Cash Flows (construction period Rolling Meadows Center)

	Draws per Year			
	(0)	*(1)*	*(2)*	*Total*
Cost breakdown				
Site acquisition and closing costs	$2,500,000			$ 2,500,000
Site improvements (on/off)		$ 636,806	$ 213,194	850,000
Hard costs		5,285,868	1,769,632	7,055,500
Soft costs				
Architect/engineering		110,130	36,870	147,000
Fees and permits		18,205	6,095	24,300
Legal and title fees		20,153	6,747	26,900
Leasing commissions		33,938	11,362	45,300
Direct overhead		119,869	40,131	160,000
Permanent loan fee	291,430			291,430
Construction loan fee	194,286			194,286
Construction interest*		377,704	1,027,614	1,405,318
Indirect overhead		15,400	15,400	30,800
Total	$2,985,716	$6,618,073	$3,127,045	$12,730,834
Total construction cash outflow	$2,985,716	$6,618,073	$3,127,045	$12,730,834
Less total draws	0	6,602,673	3,111,645	9,714,318
Total equity needed	$2,985,716	$ 15,400	$ 15,400	$ 3,016,516

*In year (1) interest is equal to the sum of the first 12 months shown in column (*e*) Exhibit 17–5. For the second year interest is equal to the total interest carry estimate $1,405,318–$377,704 or $1,027,614.

development period. Note that the developer will require $2,985,716 from internal sources at closing to cover land acquisition and loan fees, plus an additional $15,400 each year to cover indirect overhead, or total equity of $3,016,516. Citadel Life Insurance Co. will review Southfork's financial statements (not shown) to determine whether it has the ability to provide such funding from internal sources.

Exhibit 17–8 details the pro forma operating statement for Rolling Meadows. The lease-up or marketing effort should result in 70 percent occupancy during the third year and 95 percent thereafter. Southfork is estimating a base rent of $15.00 per square foot of gross leasable area, with average increases based on leases which are indexed to the *CPI* of 6 percent per year after the first year of operation (leases are expected to have terms ranging from one to five years). An overage provision requires tenants to also pay 5 percent of gross sales in excess of a base sales level each month.[10] In a retail operation,

---

[10]Overages are common in retail leasing. The breakpoint is commonly determined by dividing the tenant's base rental amount (rate per square foot times rentable area) by the percentage rent negotiated between the owner and tenant. For further discussion see *Shopping Center Development Handbook Series*. (Washington, D.C.) published by the Urban Land Institute.

EXHIBIT 17–8   Pro Forma Operating Statement for Rolling Meadows Center

Cash Flows (EOP)	*(3)*	*(4)*	*(5)*	*(6)*	*(7)*
INCOME					
Minimum rent*	$1,650,000	$1,749,000	$1,853,940	$1,965,176	$2,083,087
Overage (6% of gross sales)	30,000	124,800	129,792	134,984	140,383
TENANT REIMBURSEMENTS:					
Real estate taxes	137,500	143,000	148,720	154,669	160,856
Common area maintenance	385,000	400,400	416,416	433,073	450,396
Utilities	367,500	382,200	397,488	413,388	429,924
Insurance	33,000	34,320	35,693	37,121	38,606
GROSS POTENTIAL INCOME	$2,603,000	$2,833,720	$2,982,049	$3,138,411	$3,303,252
Vacancy allowance†	780,900	141,686	149,102	156,921	165,163
EXPECTED GROSS INCOME	$1,822,100	$2,692,034	$2,832,947	$2,981,490	$3,138,089
EXPENSES:					
Management + leasing fees	$104,500	$93,690	$99,187	$105,008	$111,174
General and administrative	77,000	80,080	83,283	86,614	90,079
Real estate taxes	137,500	143,000	148,720	154,669	160,856
Common area maintenance	385,000	400,400	416,416	433,073	450,396
Utilities	300,300	312,312	324,804	337,796	351,308
Insurance	33,000	34,320	35,693	37,121	38,606
Other	27,500	28,600	29,744	30,934	32,171
Total expenses	$1,064,800	$1,092,402	$1,137,847	$1,185,215	$1,234,590
NET OPERATING INCOME	$757,300	$1,599,632	$1,695,100	$1,796,275	$1,903,499
Less debt service	1,227,768	1,227,768	1,227,768	1,227,768	1,227,768
BTCF	($470,468)	$371,864	$467,332	$568,507	$675,731
RATIOS:					
Operating expense ratio		40.58%	40.16%	39.75%	39.34%
Debt-service coverage		1.30	1.38	1.46	1.55
Return on total investment		12.57%	13.31%	14.11%	14.95%
Return on equity		10.66%	13.40%	16.30%	19.38%
Vacancy-collection loss		5.00%	5.00%	5.00%	5.00%
Break-even occupancy rate		81.88%	79.33%	76.89%	74.54%
Base rent per square foot of *GLA*	$15.00				
Total rent per square foot of *GLA*‡	$23.66				

*Base rent $15.00 per square foot of *GLA*.
†70% occupancy during year 3.
‡Gross potential income divided by *GLA*.

rent is usually divided into two components. The first is a minimum rent per square foot. The other component is called percentage rent (sometimes also called overage). Percentage rent, or overage, is frequently charged by developers and is calculated as a percentage of the sales of a tenant in excess of a pre-determined breakpoint or sales volume. As long as the tenant's sales are below the breakpoint, the owner receives only the minimum rent. When a tenant's sales increase above the breakpoint, the percentage rent rate is applied to the sales volume in excess of the breakpoint and is added to the minimum rent, thus increasing the total rent. In this way, should the shopping center become very successful, the owner shares in the increased revenue produced by the tenants. The percentage rent shown in Exhibit 17–8 is estimated for all tenants in Rolling Meadows.

Tenant reimbursements are also shown in Exhibit 17–8. These amounts are based on negotiations between the owner and tenants and represent the amount of operating expenses over expense stops for which the tenant is responsible (recall the discussion of such stops in Chapter 10 for office buildings). Hence base rents, percentage rents and expenses for which tenants are responsible over some pre-agreed amount (stop) all represent gross income to the owner of Rolling Meadows.

Operating expenses are also detailed in Exhibit 17–8. These amounts represent the actual expenses that must be paid to operate Rolling Meadows. These amounts are deducted from rents, overage, and tenant reimbursements. All leases are to be *net to the tenant,* with a direct pass-through for insurance and property taxes. Tenants will also be billed for their share of common area maintenance (parking lot, circulation space in center, etc.) and utilities. An additional premium will be added to the utility charge to provide for a replacement reserve on HVAC equipment.[11] Tenants will pay these expenses to Southfork as reimbursement. Southfork management will, in turn, pay any expenses to third parties as they become due. Southfork will also incur expenses of its own for property management, leasing commissions, and general and administrative expenses that will not be recoverable from tenants. These amounts are deducted from rents, overage, and tenant reimbursements. It has been assumed in the projections that a sufficient number of leases will be signed at the end of the second year to warrant closing of the permanent loan.

The reader should also pay attention to the ratios that appear at the bottom of Exhibit 17–8. These ratios are calculated beginning with data for year 4, when "normal" operation is anticipated. These ratios, which have been defined in earlier chapters, indicate that after the third year, cash flow will be positive and debt service coverage will be in excess of 1.25. Occupancy is projected at 95 percent, which is in excess of the break-even point each year. Cash returns earned on total investment will be positive and exceed the mortgage interest rate.[12] These cash returns do not include any appreciation in project value. These and other ratios will be reviewed by the permanent lender to ascertain whether they fall into acceptable underwriting ranges. It should be stressed again that market data supporting rents and overages, proof of estimates of operating costs from the management of comparable centers, realistic estimates of the lease-up rate, and lease terms that tenants are willing to accept in the retail market are all critical to the underwriting process.

Assuming that the permanent lender makes the take-out commitment, the developer will incorporate the actual amount of the loan commitment into the pro forma statements

---

[11]Note the difference in utility income to be collected from tenants and actual costs to be paid by Southfork management. This difference is a depreciation charge for utility equipment. Depending on competition for space in the retail market, such a charge may or may not be possible for the developer to negotiate.

[12]Total project cost is estimated at $12,730,834. When divided into *NOI,* a 12.57 percent return on total investment results.

and seek out a construction lender.[13] During this time, the developer will refine and update cost and market estimates and provide more detailed construction plans in order to acquire interim financing. After the permanent financing commitment is acquired however, all changes in design, cost, predevelopment lease agreements, and so on, must be submitted to both the permanent and interim lenders for review.

FEASIBILITY, PROFITABILITY, AND RISK—ADDITIONAL ISSUES

Most of the analysis conducted by the interim and permanent lenders will focus on the pro forma statements and market data supplied with the loan requests. This is because lenders are concerned about market conditions, rents, and the ability of the project to cover expenses and debt service. Southfork is equally concerned with these issues; however, it is also interested in knowing how well this project will perform as an investment, both before and after taxes. Also, from the standpoint of assessing risk, it needs to know how sensitive the estimates provided in the pro forma statements are to various assumptions made in the analysis. Much of what follows are analytic tools that may be used to assess project performance. These tools may be used at any time during development as market data, building costs, interest rates, and so on, change. They may also be used to ascertain the maximum price that should be paid for the land *prior to its acquisition*. To illustrate these ideas, we will use the pro forma estimates presented thus far and change them by introducing sensitivity analysis.

Profitability Before and After Taxes

For Southfork to assess the profitability of the Rolling Meadows Center before and after taxes, additional assumptions regarding the number of operating periods and the appreciation rate on the property value must be made. We have assumed a holding period of five years after construction and a sale at that time.

Estimates of before-tax cash flow *(BTCF)* during the development and operating periods are summarized in Panel A of Exhibit 17–9, based on information contained in Exhibits 17–7 and 17–8. The before-tax estimate for *NPV* comprises all negative cash flows consisting of equity requirements at closing (land acquisition and loan fees), cash equity needed during development for costs not financed (indirect overhead), and cash requirements needed during year 3, or the lease-up phase. Positive cash flows are based on operations from years 4 through 7 plus cash flow from the sale of the project in year 7 (all figures are rounded).

---

[13]The actual take-out commitment will contain contingencies that may affect the pro forma statements presented here. Recall that all of the statements produced thus far are part of a *proposal* to the permanent lender. Should the lender decide to fund less than the total amount requested or insist on a higher lease-up requirement, among other things, those changes would have to be incorporated in the data submitted to potential interim lenders.

EXHIBIT 17–9   Profitability Analysis for Rolling Meadows Center in 000's

				Year				
	(0)	*(1)*	*(2)*	*(3)*	*(4)*	*(5)*	*(6)*	*(7)*
				Panel A				
NPV and BTIRR								
Equity needed	($2,986)	($15)	($15)					
BTCF				($470)	$372	$467	$569	$ 676
BTCF$_s$								7,574
Total *BTCF*	($2,986)	($15)	($15)	($470)	$372	$467	$569	8,250

BTNPV at 17% = $79

BTIRR = 17.4%

	(0)	*(1)*	*(2)*	*(3)*	*(4)*	*(5)*	*(6)*	*(7)*
				Panel B				
IRR after tax:								
Taxable income								
NOI				$ 757	$1,600	$1,695	$1,796	$1,903
Less:								
Interest				1,162	1,154	1,145	1,134	1,122
Depreciation								
Capital improvements				277	277	277	277	277
Tenant improvements				277	198	141	101	84
Amortization:								
Construction loan fees		97	97					
Permanent loan fees				29	29	29	29	29
Leasing commissions				9	9	9	9	9
Taxable income	$0	($97)	($97)	($997)	($67)	$94	$ 246	$ 382
Tax at 28%	0	(27)	(27)	(279)	(19)	26	69	107
ATCF:								
Total *BTCF*	($2,986)	($15)	($15)	($470)	$372	$467	$569	$8,250
Less taxes*		(27)	(27)	(279)	(19)	26	69	1,985*
ATCF	($2,986)	$12	$12	($191)	$391	$441	$500	$6,265

ATIRR = 14.5%

*Includes $1,878,287 in taxes from sale of Rolling Meadows in year 7.

EXHIBIT 17–10   Sale of Rolling Meadows Center

$BTCF_s$:

Sale price	$17,036,728
Selling expenses	170,367
Mortgage balance	9,292,098
$BTCF_s$	$ 7,574,263

Gain in year of sale:	
Sale price	$17,036,728
Selling expenses	170,367
Adjusted basis	10,158,192
Total gain	$ 6,708,169
Tax at 28 percent	1,878,287
$BTCF_s$	$ 7,574,263
Tax	1,878,287
$ATCF_s$	$ 5,695,976

Adjusted Basis

Item	Total Cost	Less: Accumulated Depreciation/ Amortization	Adjusted Basis
Land	$ 2,500,000	—	$ 2,500,000
Capital improvements	8,729,836	$1,385,688	7,344,148
Tenant improvements	969,982	801,652	168,329
Permanent loan fees	291,430	145,715	145,715
Leasing commissions	45,300	45,300	0
Construction loan fees	194,286	194,286	0
Total	$12,730,834		$10,158,192

Exhibit 17–10 contains estimates of before-tax cash flows when Rolling Meadows Center is sold to Mony Mutual Realty Advisors, who acquires projects and manages them on behalf of pension fund sponsors. Looking to the exhibit, we see that after paying selling expenses and repaying the mortgage loan balance to Citadel, Southfork will have $7,574,263 in cash before taxes *(BTCFs)*. The sale price for the project, $17,036,728, is based on the initial total project cost, $12,730,834 (Exhibit 17–7), compounded at an appreciation rate of 6 percent per year for five years.

From Panel A of Exhibit 17–9, an estimate for *NPV* before taxes is calculated based on all before-tax cash flows expected to occur from years one to seven, discounted at a required before tax rate of 17 percent. This results in a positive *NPV* of $79,000 (rounded). This 17 percent required rate of return represents a 5 percent risk premium over the mortgage interest rate which Southfork management believes to be a satisfactory return on its equity after recovery of all project costs and given the risk of the Rolling Meadows project.

The *after-tax internal rate* of return for Southfork is presented in Panel B of Exhibit 17–9. To arrive at net cash flow after tax during development and in each operating year, we need additional information to take income taxes into account.

Exhibit 17–11 provides information regarding depreciation and amortization of various project costs which are needed to estimate taxable income as shown in Panel B in Exhibit 17–9. Panel A in Exhibit 17–11 contains a list of costs that must be capitalized as part of the improvement and depreciated. Of total depreciable costs, we see in Panel B that 90 percent are capital improvements and, therefore, subject to depreciation on a straight-line basis over 31.5 years.[14] Southfork estimates 10 percent of these costs to be tenant improvements which are categorized as personal rather than real property. This category of improvement may be depreciated on a double declining basis over seven years.[15] Panel C contains a description of project soft costs that may be amortized. Because two loans are assumed to be used to fund the project, loan fees are amortized over the respective terms of each loan.[16] Finally, leasing commissions are capitalized and written off over the average of lease terms for the project.

After-tax cash flow in the year of *sale (ATCFs)* is also needed to complete the computation of the after-tax *IRR*. From Exhibit 17–10, tax in the year of sale ($1,878,287) is determined as the difference between the estimated net selling price less the adjusted basis times the 28 percent tax rate. The adjusted basis is computed as the cost of land plus all improvements, or $12,730,834, less the sum of all depreciation and amortization taken over the seven-year period.[17] The adjusted basis, or cost to be recovered from the sale of the asset prior to computing the tax on the gain, is $10,158,192. After-tax cash flow is then estimated to be $5,695,976.

Solving for the *ATIRR* shown in Exhibit 17–9 is accomplished by setting the equity requirements at closing equal to *ATCF* in each year and in the year of sale and solving for the rate of interest that makes the after-tax *NPV* = 0. The reader should note that although *BTCF* is negative in years 2 and 3, after-tax cash flow is positive during those years because of the tax deductibility of loan fees. Those deductions result in a net loss, or an offset against any other active income earned by Southfork during those years. Hence, they *reduce* taxes and *save* cash and are used to offset negative *BTCF* in those

---

[14]See Chapter 11 for an explanation of depreciation methods.

[15]An explanation of double declining balance depreciation may be found in the two previous editions of this book. Switching to straight-line is also allowed and carried out in the analysis here.

[16]The permanent loan fees are assumed to be paid when the commitment is obtained. However, amortization is assumed not to begin until the loan is closed at the beginning of the third year.

[17]In years prior to the 1986 Tax Reform Act, tax rates on capital gains and on ordinary income were different. Further, the tax treatment of construction period and interest and property taxes and certain other fees also differed. Because of these differences, interest, taxes, and fees were capitalized from the improvement, and the unamortized balance in the year of sale was either deducted as an ordinary expense or added to the undepreciated basis. The reader must stay informed regarding the taxation of real estate, particularly when *project development* is being analyzed, because the tax treatment of various cost categories change frequently.

EXHIBIT 17–11   Depreciation and Amortization Schedule for Rolling Meadows Center

A. Depreciable costs

Item			
Site improvements (on/off)	$ 850,000		
Hard costs	7,055,500		
Soft costs			
Architect/engineering	147,000		
Fees and permits	24,300		
Legal fees	26,900		
Construction interest	1,405,318		
Direct overhead	160,000		
Indirect overhead	30,800		
Total	$ 9,699,818		
		Depreciation Period	Method
B. Depreciation schedule			
Capital improvements (90 percent of total)	8,729,836	31.5	S/L
Tenant improvements (10 percent of total)	969,982	7	DDB
		Amortization period	
C. Amortization schedule		(years)	
Construction loan fees	194,286	2	
Permanent loan fees	291,430	10	
Leasing commissions	45,300	5	
Total depreciable/amortized costs	10,230,834		
Add land	2,500,000		
Total project cost	$12,730,834		

years. Taxes are calculated by assuming a tax rate of 28 percent,[18] and after-tax cash flows are determined and used to determine the *ATIRR,* which is 14.5 percent for Rolling Meadows. Note that this return is *not* equal to the *BTIRR* (shown in Panel A) times 1 - tax rate, or 17.4% (1 - .28) = 12.5%. This is because of the higher rates allowable for amortization of tenant improvements and fees (Exhibit 17–11) relative to the 31.5 year straight-line depreciation allowed for real property.

Sensitivity Analysis, Risk, Feasibility Analysis

Based on the preceding analysis, we have concluded that if Southfork is satisfied that a 17 percent before-tax rate return on equity is adequate to undertake the Rolling Meadows Center development, a positive *NPV* will be earned. This implies that the $2,500,000

---

[18]It is assumed that Southfork is a sole proprietorship or a partnership whose owners are taxed at ordinary rates. It is also assumed that Southfork's owners have other passive income which may be used to offset the passive losses produced by this project (see Chapter 11 for a discussion of passive income).

land acquisition price would be warranted, given estimates of construction costs, market rents, expenses, and the appreciation rate in property value. An interesting question that could be raised at this point is, "Suppose market rents were estimated to be $12 per square foot instead of $15 and all other assumptions remained constant (quantity of space, construction costs, interest rates, appreciation rates and operating expenses). Would the project still be feasible (i.e., cover all costs and provide the developer with a competitive return on equity)?

To consider this question, the reader should refer to Exhibit 17–12. This diagram represents the relationship between *BTNPV* (vertical axis) and market rents per square foot of leasable area (horizontal axis). Note that at the average rent of $15 per square foot assumed in our analysis, the *BTNPV* is slightly above zero (the discount rate is held constant at 17 percent). If, however, the market rent averaged $12 per square foot and all other assumptions remained the same, it is clear that the *NPV* would be negative (in the range of $650,000). In that case, Southfork would not be interested in pursuing the development. An even more critical aspect of this analysis becomes clear, if after both loan commitments were made, construction went forward on the project and market rents

EXHIBIT 17–12   *BTNPV* of Rolling Meadows Center and Rents

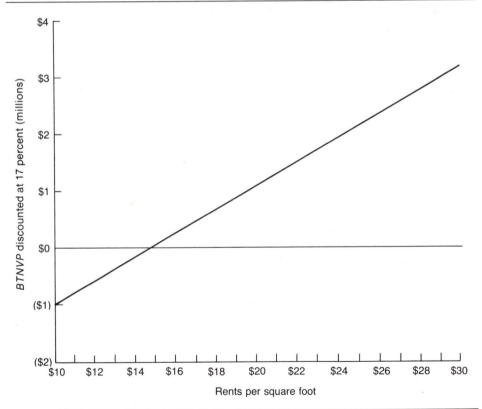

then fell from $15 to $12 per square foot as the lease-up phase was underway. In this event, Southfork would be facing a negative *NPV* and would be committed to the development. If it was not able to produce more equity or to find additional investors to provide equity at that point, it would not be able to meet project expenses and debt service. At that point, the interim lender would be faced with the prospect that the permanent lender may not be compelled to honor its take-out commitment because rental achievement would not be met by the developer. The interim lender must enter into a negotiation of the interim loan terms with the developer (sometimes referred to as a *workout*), or possibly foreclosing. The reader should now begin to see how changing market conditions can affect project risk.

Another consideration of importance can be seen by referring to Exhibit 17–13, where *BTNPV* is related to land cost (horizontal axis). As we know, a slightly positive *NPV* was estimated assuming that the land was acquired at $2.5 million. If Southfork was too optimistic and paid $3.0 million for the land, we can see from the diagram that the *NPV* would be negative (again discounting at 17 percent and holding all other variables constant). On the other hand, if the land could be acquired for less than $2.5 million, the

EXHIBIT 17–13   *BTNPV* of Rolling Meadows Center and Land Cost

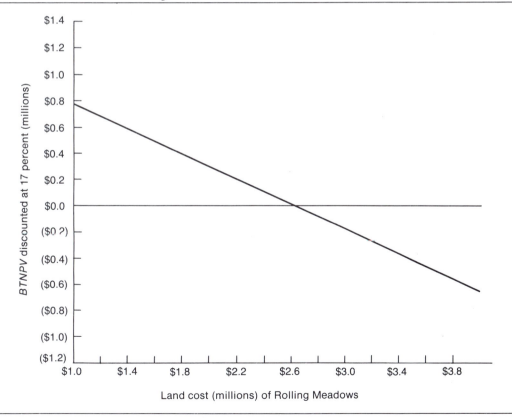

NPV would become more favorable. The value of the *sensitivity analysis* that we are undertaking should be obvious to the reader at this point.[19] This analysis is also referred to as feasibility analysis, or a determination of whether a project is commercially feasible at prevailing market rents, land prices, and construction and financing costs.

QUESTIONS

1. What are the sources of risk associated with project development?
2. What are some development strategies followed by many developers? Why do they follow such strategies?
3. How can development projects be differentiated from one another in the marketplace?
4. Describe the process of financing the construction and operation of a typical real estate development. Indicate the order in which lenders who fund project development financing are sought and why this pattern is followed.
5. What is a spec or open-ended construction loan? When is such a loan likely to be used?
6. What contingencies are commonly found in permanent or take-out loan commitments? Why are they used? What happens if they are not met by the developer.
7. What is a standby commitment? When and why is it used?
8. What is a miniperm or bullet loan? When and why is this loan used?
9. Gap financing is sometimes provided by third-party lenders in project developments. Why is this lending used? How does it work?
10. A presale agreement is said to be equivalent to a take-out commitment. What will the construction lender be concerned about if the developer plans to use such an agreement in lieu of a take-out?
11. Why don't permanent lenders usually provide construction loans to developers? Do construction lenders ever provide permanent loans to developers?
12. What is the difference between the assignment of a take-out commitment to the construction lender and a triparty agreement? If neither device is used in project financing, what is the relationship between lenders in such a case?
13. What is the major concern expressed by construction lenders regarding the income approach to estimating value? Why do they prefer that the cost approach be used when possible? In the latter case, if the developer has owned the land for five years prior to development is the cost approach more effective then? Why or why not?
14. What is meant by overage in a retail lease agreement? How might it be calculated?
15. What is sensitivity analysis? How might it be used in real estate development?
16. It is sometimes said that land represents "residual" value. This is said because improvement costs do not vary materially from one location to another, however rents vary considerably. Hence, land values reflect changes in rents (both up and down) from location to location. Do you agree or disagree?
17. Why is the practice of "holdbacks" used? Who is involved in this practice? How does it affect construction lending?

---

[19]The same analysis may be carried out by changing other variables, such as construction costs, interest rates, or operating expenses one at a time to assess the impact on before-tax *NPV*.

PROBLEMS

1. The CEO of Long Development Co. has just come from a meeting with his marketing staff where he was given the latest market study of their proposed new shopping center, Canyon Creek. The study calls for a construction phase of one year, and an operation phase of six years. The property is to be sold at the end of the sixth year of operation.

   Part I. *Construction Phase*

   The marketing staff has chosen a 15-acre site for the project and they believe they can acquire the land for $2 million. The initial studies indicate that this shopping center will support a floor to area ratio of 28.4 percent and a 88 percent leaseable area ratio. (This means that the gross building area (*GBA*) will be 185,265 square feet, and the gross leaseable area (*GLA*) will be 163,350 square feet.)

   The head of Long's construction division assures the CEO that they can keep hard costs to $50 per square foot (GBA) and soft costs (excluding interest carry and all loan fees) to $4 per square foot (*GBA*). They have decided to subcontract all of the site improvements at a total cost of $750,000.

   The Mercantile Bank has agreed to provide interim financing for the project. The bank will finance all of the construction costs and site improvements at an annual rate of 12 percent plus a loan commitment fee of two points. The construction division estimates that 75 percent of the total direct cost will be taken down evenly during the first six months of the construction phase. Long expects to obtain permanent financing from the Equitable Insurance Co. at an interest rate of 12 percent for 25 years with a 3 percent prepaid loan fee and a 10-year call. Long is expected to make monthly loan payments.

   a. What will the total project cost be for Canyon Creek (excluding loan commitment fees and interest carry)? What will the total direct costs be?

   b. What will the interest carry be for the Canyon Creek project? What will be the total loan amount that Long must borrow (including interest carry)? What will be the yield to the lender on this construction loan?

   c. What is the total project cost and how much equity must be put into the project each year during the construction phase? (Long will fund both loan commitment fees from project equity.)

   Part II. *Operations and Final Sale Phase*:

   Long estimates that they can lease Canyon Creek for $17 per square foot (*GLA*) base rent with a 2 percent overage on gross sales in excess of $200 per square foot (*GLA*). Rents are expected to increase by 4 percent per year during the lease period. Tenant reimbursements are expected to run $8 per square foot. (*GLA*) and will increase at the same rate as rents. They expect to have the shopping center 70 percent leased during the first year of operation. After that, vacancies should average about 5 percent per year. The vacancy losses should be calculated on the entire gross potential income, which includes minimum rents, percentage rents, and tenant reimbursements. Sales, which are expected to average $210 per square foot (*GLA*) for the first year of operation, should grow at 5 percent per year. The operating expenses are expected to average $13 per square foot of *GLA* for the first year and will increase at the same rate as the rents. Long will collect an additional 5 percent of *EGI* as an annual management fee.

The final sales price is expected to be $17,900,000 and Long will incur sales expenses of 2 percent. Included are two schedules: (1) the Gross Potential Income of Canyon Creek for the 6-year operation period; (2) the schedule of amortization and depreciation expenses for the project.

(1)	Pro Forma Operating Statement—Canyon Creek					
Cash Flows *(EOP)*	*(2)*	*(3)*	*(4)*	*(5)*	*(6)*	*(7)*
Income:						
Minimum rent	$2,776,950	$2,888,028	$3,003,549	$3,123,691	$3,248,639	$3,378,585
Percentage rent	32,670	66,974	102,992	140,812	180,522	222,218
Tenant reimbursements	$1,306,800	1,359,072	1,413,435	1,469,972	1,528,771	1,589,922
Gross potential income:	$4,116,420	$4,314,074	$4,519,976	$4,734,475	$4,957,932	$5,190,725

(2)	Item	Amortization period
	Construction loan fees	1 year
	Permanent loan fees	10 years
		Depreciation period
	Capital improvements − (90% of total)	31.5 years S/L
	Tenant improvements − (10% of total)	7 years DDB

    d. What cash flows would Long Development Co. earn before and after taxes for Canyon Creek if it were operated for six years (the marginal tax rate is assumed to be 28 percent)? What cash flows will Long realize before and after taxes from the sale of the project after six years?

    e. Assuming that Long's before tax required rate of return is 16 percent, should they develop Canyon Creek? Justify your answer based on BTNPV and *BTIRR*?

    f. Does this project provide any tax shelter? Explain.

2. As a financial advisor for the Emerald Development Co., you have been given the construction and marketing studies for the proposed Willow Run office project.
Several potential sites have been selected but the final selection has not been chosen. Your manager needs to know how much she can afford to pay for the land and still manage to return 16 percent on the entire project over its lifetime

The strategic plan calls for a construction phase of one year, and an operation phase of three years after which time the property will be sold. The marketing staff says that a 1.3-acre site will be adequate as the initial studies indicate that this site will support an office building with a gross leaseable area (*GLA*) of 25,000 square feet. The gross building area (*GBA*) will be 29,070 square feet, giving a leaseable ratio of 86 percent. The marketing staff further assures you that the space can be rented for

$20 per square foot. The head of the construction division maintains that all direct costs (excluding interest carry and all loan fees) will be $2,000,000.

The Second National Bank will provide the construction loan for the project. They will finance all of the construction costs, site improvements, and interest carry at an annual rate of 10 percent plus a loan origination fee of one point. The construction division estimates that the direct cost draws will be taken down in five equal amounts commencing with the first month after close. The permanent financing for the project will come at the end of the first year from the Reliable Co. at an interest rate of 12 percent with a 3 percent prepaid loan fee. The loan has an eight-year term and is to be paid back monthly over a 20-year amortization schedule. No financing fees will be included in either loan amount. Emerald is also expected to fund acquisition of the land with its own equity.

Tenant reimbursements for the project are expected to be $4 per square foot. The office building is expected to be 80 percent leased during the first year of operation. After that, vacancies should average about 5 percent per year. Rents, tenant reimbursement, and operating expenses are expected to increase by 5 percent per year during the lease period. The operating expenses are expected to be $10 per square foot. The final sales price is based on the NOI in the sixth year of the project (the fifth year of operation) capitalized at 14.5 percent The project will incur sales expenses of 4 percent. Emerald is concerned that it may not been able to afford to pay for the land and still earn 16 percent (before taxes) on its equity (remember that the land acquisition cost must be paid from Emerald's equity).

Requirements to consider project feasibility:

a. Estimate construction draw schedule, interest carry, and total loan amount for improvements.
b. Determine total project cost (including fees) less financing, or the equity needed to fund improvements.
c. Estimate cash flows from operations and eventual sale.
d. Establish whether a positive or negative *NPV* exists by discounting equity cash inflows and outflows in (c).
e. What does the *NPV* mean in this case? If the asking price of the land was $200,000 would this project be feasible?

Appendix: Estimating Interest Carry and Yields— Construction and Development Loans

INTRODUCTION

As discussed in Chapter 17, one of the components that lenders will generally fund as a part of "soft costs" is the estimated interest, or "interest carry" on funds advanced for development costs. This is generally made a part of loan advances because the project will not produce income while it is under development. If the lender is convinced that the "value added" by the developer exceeds the portion of all land, labor, and materials financed by the lender *by at least* the interest cost on the loan, then the lender will usually fund these interest costs.

To reiterate the importance of the interest carry estimate in financing, it should be kept in mind that (1) an interest carry reserve is *estimated* prior to loan closing and is included in the maximum loan amount and (2) to the extent that *actual* interest costs exceed the reserve, the developer must fund the excess. Hence it is possible that the amount of interest drawn may actually be less than amounts due.[1] Actual costs may be greater than estimated costs because of an increase in interest rates, or because the rate at which funds are drawn down exceed the estimated rate.

The goal of this appendix is to elaborate our discussion of interest carry in Chapter 17 by beginning with more basic examples and building up to more complex applications. The material in this appendix will also be useful in the next chapter which deals with land development loans. Finally, we quickly review the computation of lender yields on these more complex loan structures.

One problem that we are faced with when estimating interest carry is establishing what the total loan amount will be. This is complicated because interest carry will also be included in the total loan amount. Hence, both of the amounts are unknown. Therefore, we need a method whereby we can estimate interest and determine the total loan amount *simultaneously*. A second set of concerns has to do with the fact that rates at which loan funds are drawn down and repaid may vary from month to month. These patterns simply mean that cash inflows and outflows will not be level, and will depend on estimates.

Generally speaking, when estimating interest on a development loan, we must have information on the following variables: (1) the total of all other development costs that will be funded in the loan amount (exclusive of interest), (2) the monthly *rate* at which funds used for construction costs will be drawn down, (3) the interest rate, and (4) the monthly *rate* at which the loan principal will be repaid. As will be seen, the rates at which loan draws and the rates at which repayments of principal are made are the key to understanding the approach to estimating both interest and the total amount of the loan simultaneously.

To illustrate, in Panel A of Exhibit 17A–1, we have a loan request to finance $100,000 in project costs. To simplify, we assume that these costs will be drawn down annually over a 5-year period in *dollar amounts* shown in column (*b*) and at a *draw rate* shown in (*c*). However, the developer has requested that the loan also *include* an estimated amount of interest carry. In other words, the developer wants to borrow project costs plus interest. Hence, the total loan amount is to include all draws needed to cover development costs, plus interest on those draws which will be charged *as they are drawn*. Further, the loan will be repaid in *total* at the *end* of the 5-year construction period (we assume that funds for repayment will be supplied by a take out lender). The loan will be made at 9 percent interest (compounded annually).

One approach to the problem of *estimating* the total loan amount (*TLA*) which includes an unknown amount of interest, is to compound each draw from the period that it occurs to the end of the loan period as follows:

$$TLA = \$10,000 \ (1+.09)^5 + \$5,000 \ (1+.09)^4 + \$30,000 \ (1+.09)^3$$
$$+ \ \$5,000 \ (1+.09)^2 + \$45,000 \ (1+.09)^1 + \$5,000$$
$$= \$121,286$$

---

[1] This can also be seen by taking the 1st draw in our example of $10,000 and computing interest for the next year at 9 percent which is equal to $900. This $900 amount will also be borrowed and drawn down at that time. However, because the interest is borrowed, the loan balance at the end of the first year will still be $10,900. However, at that point, the borrower makes a cash payment of $900 in interest. The loan balance will remain at $10,900 because $900 in interest is borrowed and the $900 *cash payment is applied to interest and does not reduce the loan balance.*

EXHIBIT 17A–1 Estimating Interest Carry and Loan Yields Multiple Draw—Single Payment Loan

Panel A: Estimate of interest carry

(a)	(b)	(c)	(d)	(e)	(f)	(g)
		Draw Rate per Year	*Percent Repayment per Year*	*PVIF at 9*	*PV Draw Rate (c) × (e)*	*Percent PMT Rate (d) × (e)*
Year	*Direct Cost Draws*	*CDR*	*PAYR*	*Percent*	*PVDR*	*PVPAYR*
0	$ 10,000	0.10	0	1	0.100000	0.000000
1	5,000	0.05		0.917431	0.045872	0.000000
2	30,000	0.30		0.841680	0.252504	0.000000
3	5,000	0.05		0.772183	0.038609	0.000000
4	45,000	0.45		0.708425	0.318791	0.000000
5	5,000	0.05	1.000	0.649931	0.032497	0.649931
Total	$100,000	1.00	1.000		0.788273	0.649931

$$
\begin{aligned}
TLF &= PVDR \div PVPAYR \\
TLF &= 0.788273 \div 0.649931 = 1.212856 \\
\text{Total Loan} &= \$100,000 \times 1.212855 = \$121,286 \\
TIC &= TLF - 1.000 \\
TIC &= 1.212856 - 1.000 = 0.212856 \\
\text{Total Interest Carry} &= \$100,000 \times 0.212856 = \$21,286 \\
TPF &= TLF + TIC \\
TPF &= 1.212856 + 0.212856 = 1.425712 \\
\text{Total } PMT &= \$100,000 \times 1.425712 = \$142,571
\end{aligned}
$$

Panel B: Cash flow patterns

	(a)	(b)	(c)	(d)	(e)	(f)	(g)
							Total Ending Balance
	Draws		*Total*	*Payments*			*Previous Monthly*
			Draws		*Interest*	*Payments*	*Balance*
Year	*Direct Costs*	*Interest*	*(a)+(b)*	*Principal*	*(g)×(9%)*	*(d)+(e)*	*+(c)−(d)*
0	$ 10,000	$ 0	$ 10,000	$ 0	$ 0	$ 0	$ 10,000
1	5,000	900	5,900	0	900	900	15,900
2	30,000	1,431	31,431	0	1,431	1,431	47,331
3	5,000	4,260	9,260	0	4,260	4,260	56,591
4	45,000	5,093	50,093	0	5,093	5,093	106,684
5	5,000	9,602	14,602	121,286	9,602	130,887	0
Total	$100,000	$21,286	$121,286	$121,286	$21,286	$142,572	$ 0

Panel C: Yield to lender

Year	Loan Fees	Total Draws	Total Payments	Net Cash Flow to Lender (Out) In
0	$2,426	$(10,000)	0	$ (7,574)
1		(5,900)	$ 900	(5,000)
2		(31,431)	1,431	(30,000)
3		(9,260)	4,260	(5,000)
4		(50,093)	5,093	(45,000)
5		(14,602)	130,886	116,286
		Yield to lender =		10.52%

Hence, the total loan amount would be $121,286. Because $100,000 represents draw amount for costs, $21,286 represents the interest portion which is also borrowed. However, total cash flow payments by the borrower will be $121,286 plus $21,286 or $142,572. This is because interim cash payments totaling $21,286 in interest will also be made by the borrower. This may seem confusing at first. However because interest is also being borrowed and is included in the loan amount, then drawn down as a part of that amount, the borrower is making an interest draw to make a cash, "interest only" payment. Because this cash payment is "interest only," no reduction of loan principal occurs and the entire $121,286 will be the outstanding loan balance at the end of 5 years.[1]

As an alternative to the compounding approach shown above, Exhibit 17A–1 Panel A presents a method that provides an equivalent *estimate* of interest, the total loan amount, and total loan payments. The advantage of this approach is that it is a more generalized method and can be used where the borrower is required to make interim loan payments (principal) in addition to interest only. (This is particularly useful for land development loans, which are covered in the next chapter).

To amplify on this approach, the goal is to discount all draws *and* loan repayments back to present value (the loan closing date) by the rate of interest on the loan. After this is done, the ratio of the present value of draws (*PVDR*) to the present value of payments (*PVPAYR*) will yield a total loan factor (*TLF*). This factor can then be multiplied by the total direct costs to be funded ($100,000) to obtain the total loan amount. The loan amount includes construction period interest. To illustrate, let the cash draw rate per year (*CDR*) equal the *rate* at which *cost* draws are made. (If cost draws are made in, say, 5 equal payments, *CDR* would equal 20% per year.) PAYR equals the *rate* at which loan principal will be repaid and *i* equals the interest rate on the loan and *n* equals the term of the loan. Finding the present value of the draw rate (*PVDR*) and the payment rate (*PVPAYR*) we have:

$$PVDR = \sum_{t=i}^{n} \frac{CDR_t}{(1+i)^t}$$

$$PVPAYR = \sum_{t=i}^{n} \frac{PAYR_t}{(1+i)^n}$$

Note that the draw *rate,* which is the *percentage* of the total cost represented by each draw, and the payment *rate,* or the *percentage* of the total loan to be represented by each payment, are used in the calculation. Also note in this case that only one repayment of principal will be made at the end of the loan term, hence the repayment rate (*PAYR*) will be 100 percent in year 5. For our example in Exhibit 17A–1, we have:

$$PVDR = .788273 \text{ and}$$
$$PVPAYR = .649931$$

The ratio of the two present values gives us the total loan factor (*TLF*) or .788273 ÷ .649931 = 1.212856. We can now find the total loan amount that the developer will request by multiplying *TLF* by the costs to be loaned ($100,000) which equals $121,286. This amount *includes* the estimated interest amount that the developer wants to borrow. Total estimated interest carry will be $121,286 − $100,000, or $21,286. (Note that these results are equivalent to the results obtained when draws were compounded above). This is the amount that the developer will budget into the loan request as estimated interest. However, because the borrower will also be making interim annual cash *interest* payments (not principal payments)[2], the total cash payments that the developer will make *TPF* will be *TIF + TIC,* or 1.212856 + .212856, or 1.425712. This factor multiplied

---

[2] With regard to cash interest payments, we should note that in actual practice, after the loan is closed, interest would be computed on the daily loan balance at a rate of .09 ÷ 365. The interest draw, along with

by \$100,000, when rounded, results in \$142,571. The reader should review the proof for this calculation by reviewing the actual cash flow patterns in Panel B of Exhibit 17A–1.

To extend this analysis, we now consider the case shown in Exhibit 17A–2 Panel A where the draws will be taken down in stages and repayment of loan principal will *also* be made in stages. This pattern is frequently encountered in land development which is discussed in the next chapter. The question now becomes how do we estimate the total loan request, including interest, when we have simultaneous loan principal repayments occurring along with the draws? To answer this question, we provide an example in Exhibit 17A–2. This example assumes costs to be borrowed are \$100,000 over 5 years at 9 percent. Note that in this case that in addition to draw rates, we now have loan repayment rates (*PAYR*) shown in (column *d*). Using our present value approach, and discounting both the draw rate and repayment rate, we now have:

$$PVDR = .920783 \text{ (column } f\text{)}$$
$$PVPAYR = .765418 \text{ (column } g\text{)}$$
$$TLF = 1.202981$$

The total loan request, including interest which is computed on the outstanding loan balance which now reflects draws as they occur *and* loan repayments as they occur, will be \$100,000 × 1.202981 or \$120,298. As before the interest portion of the loan request (the unknown) will be \$120,298 − \$100,000 or \$20,298 and total cash payments to be made by the borrower (received by the lender) will be \$140,596. The reader should review the ''proof'' for this calculation by tracing the actual cash flow patterns shown in Panel B of this exhibit.

LENDER YIELDS ON CONSTRUCTION AND DEVELOPMENT LOANS

Panel C in Exhibits 17A–1 and 17A–2 provides a framework for finding the yield to the lender (cost to the developer) for our loan examples when points (loan fees) are charged by the lender. In both cases, we have assumed that the lender will charge 2 percent of the total loan amounts \$121,286 and \$120,298 respectively as a fee to the borrower. (In the event that no points or fees were charged, the yield on each of the loans would be 9 percent). Hence, when finding the yields on the two loans, we set all *net* cash flows received or disbursed by the lender equal to the net cash outflow at the time of closing and solve for the rate of interest that makes the *NPV* = 0. For example, in 17A–1 we would have:

$$0 = (\$7,574) + (\$5,000) \ (PVIF,?\%, \ 1 \text{ yr.}) + (\$30,000) \ (PVIF,?\%, \ 2 \text{ yrs.})$$
$$+ (\$5,000) \ (PVIF,?\%, \ 3 \text{ yrs.}) + (\$45,000) \ (PVIF,?\%, \ 4 \text{ yrs.})$$
$$+ \$116,286 \ (PVIF,?\%, \ 5 \text{ yrs.})$$

---

other cost draws, would occur at the end of each month. We have also assumed in our examples that the cash interest payment made by the borrower would be made to the bank *at the same time that the draw* is made. In practice, draws and interest payment may not occur exactly on the same date. For example, the interest and cost draw may occur on one date and the borrower may then be billed for interest which will be due on a later date. Therefore, the actual receipt of the cash interest payments by the lender may occur some days later than the draw. When this occurs, interest would continue to be charged on the loan balance at a daily rate until the lender actually receives the cash interest payment from the borrower. As a result, total interest charges will be slightly greater than what our methodology shows as the estimate. However, because we are making an *estimate* of interest carry, long before the project is developed, a detailed analysis of the daily receipt and disbursement of cash is unnecessary. This is particularly true in light other estimates of construction costs, completion dates, etc. all of which will affect the interest estimate more than the exact timing of payments and receipts.

EXHIBIT 17A–2 Estimating Interest Carry and Loan Yields Multiple Draw—Multiple Payment Loan

Panel A: Estimate of interest carry

(a)	(b)	(c)	(d)	(e)	(f)	(g)
		Draw Rate per Year	Percent Repayment per Year	PVIF at 9	PV Draw Rate (c) × (e)	Percent PMT Rate (d) × (e)
Year	Direct Cost Draws	CDR	PAYR	Percent	PVDR	PVPAYR
0	$ 40,000	0.40	0	1.000000	0.400000	0.000000
1	30,000	0.30	0	0.917431	0.275229	0.000000
2	20,000	0.20	0.350	0.841680	0.168336	0.294588
3	10,000	0.10	0.300	0.772183	0.077218	0.231655
4	0	0.00	0.200	0.708425	0.000000	0.141685
5	0	0.00	0.150	0.649931	0.000000	0.097490
Total	$100,000	1.00	1.000		0,920783	0.765418

$$TLF = PVDR \div PVPAYR$$
$$TLF = 0.920783 \div 0.765418 = 1.202981$$
$$\text{Total loan} = \$100,000 \times 1.202981 = \$120,298$$
$$TIC = TLF - 1.000$$
$$TIC = 1.202981 - 1.000 = 0.202981$$
$$\text{Total interest carry} = \$100,000 \times 0.202981 = \$20,298$$
$$TPF = TLF + TIC$$
$$TPF = 1.202981 + 0.202981 = 1.405962$$
$$\text{Total } PMT = \$100,000 \times 1.405962 = \$140,596$$

Panel B: Cash flow patterns

	(a)	(b)	(c)	(d)	(e)	(f)	(g)
							Ending Balance
							Previous Monthly
		Draws	Total Draws		Interest	Total Payments	Balance
Year	Direct Costs	Interest	(a) + (b)	Principal	(g) × (9%)	(d) + (e)	+ (c) − (d)
0	$ 40,000	0	$ 40,000				$40,000
1	30,000	$ 3,600	33,600	0	$ 3,600	$ 3,600	73,600
2	20,000	6,624	26,624	$ 42,104	6,624	48,728	58,120
3	10,000	5,231	15,231	36,089	5,231	41,320	37,262
4	0	3,353	3,353	24,060	3,354	27,413	16,556
5	0	1,490	1,490	18,045	1,490	19,535	(0)
Total	$100,000	$20,299*	$120,298	$120,298	$20,299*	$140,596	(0)*

*Rounded.

Panel C: Yield to lender

Year	Loan Fees	Total Draws	Total Payments	Net Cash Flow to Lender (Out) In
0	$2,406	$(40,000)	0	($37,594)
1		(33,600)	$ 3,600	(30,000)
2		(26,624)	48,728	22,104
3		(15,231)	41,320	26,089
4		(3,354)	27,414	24,060
5		(1,490)	19,535	18,045

Yield to lender = 10.37%

The rate of interest that makes all cash flows equal to zero is 10.52 percent in example 17A–1. The reader should note that the negative cash outflows (negative sign) and cash inflows (positive sign) are discounted in the same way. The points are netted against the first draw at closing ($10,000 − $2,426 = $7,574). This netting procedure should be used even if the borrower pays all points in cash. Finally, the last cash inflow and outflow in the pattern are also netted as they are both assumed to occur at the end of the 5th year. In example 17A–2, the reader should note that the patterns of positive and negative cash flows differ somewhat, however the procedure is the same and results in a yield (cost) of 10.37 percent.

PROBLEMS

A–1. The financial analyst for Sedco Development Company has determined that their latest project will require a direct cost outlay of five million dollars which will be taken down in one lump sum at the beginning of the loan. The project will last 2 years and will require monthly loan repayments, starting at the end of the first month. The first six payments are to be 2 percent of the total loan amount. Payments will increase every 6 months by a total of 1 percent until the loan is paid off at the end of two years. Note that the final month's payment will include a balloon payment of 16 percent of the total loan amount.

a. Assuming that Sedco can borrow funds at an annual rate of 11 percent, what will be the payment schedule on the loan. What is the interest carry?

b. What will the total payments be? Prove it with a repayment schedule of actual draws, repayments, and interest.

c. If the lender requires a 1.5 percent loan origination fee on the total loan, what will be the yield to the lender?

A–2. Canyon Development has decided to develop a large shopping mall on land that they already own. Total hard and soft costs excluding interest carry and loan origination fee will be $17 million. They estimate that the project will be completed in three phases of five months each. The first phase will require 50 percent of the total loan with draws spread evenly over the first five-month period. These draws will begin at the end of the first month after the loan is closed. The second phase will require 40 percent of the total draws evenly over the second five months. The remaining 10 percent will be spread evenly over the final five month period. The entire loan is to be repaid at the end of the construction period, but Canyon Development must also make monthly interest payments.

a. The Barnes Commercial Bank has agreed to finance Canyon's project at an annual interest rate of 13 percent. They will lend them the entire amount of both the hard and soft costs plus interest carry. What amount does Canyon need to borrow?

b. Will the total loan amount found in part *a.* be the total amount of Canyon's payments on the loan? If not, what will be the total? Why is there a difference (if any)?

c. If the Barnes Bank requires an effective yield on the construction loan of 15 percent, what will be the dollar amount of the loan origination fee? How much equity must Canyon put up for this project?

A–3. A local land development firm has contracted with you as an independent financial real estate consultant for financial analysis on their latest project. They estimate that the development will last for 10 years with a total direct cost of $35,000,000. They believe that the majority of these costs (60 percent) will be incurred over the first two years with the remaining costs spread evenly over the next seven years. The direct cost draws will follow this pattern with the first draw starting at the end of the first year. The Lifeco Life Insurance Company has agreed to provide construction financing for the project at an annual interest rate of 11.5 percent. The life insurance company requires annual interim interest payments based on a percentage of the loan outstanding. However, they will also require annual loan repayments. These are to be based on a percentage of the total loan and will start in the 6th year of the development with a repayment of 15 percent. Repayments will increase by a total of 5 percent each year thereafter until the 10th year when only a 10 percent payment is needed.

a. The development firm wants to know how much money they must borrow (including interest carry) in order to fund this project. How much of the total loan amount will be interest carry?
b. The development firm also needs to estimate their total payment loan, plus all interest payments. The CEO of the firm asks for proof of this total amount. Can you give it to him? (Hint: develop the repayment schedule).
c. The life insurance company requires a 3 percent loan origination fee. What will be the yield to the life insurance company?

Chapter 18

Land Development

As the last chapter indicated, real estate development is a very complex process to analyze, from the standpoint of both lenders and investors. This chapter deals with *land development,* which involves the acquisition of land with the intention of constructing utilities and surface improvements, then reselling some or all of the developed sites to project developers or, in the case of housing, homebuilders. As described in the previous chapter, *project development* deals with the acquisition of a specific site, then construction of an office building, shopping center, or other property type. This chapter contains a basic description of land development and financing. However, many attributes of real estate development are common to both types of development, so to avoid redundancy they are not repeated here. After completing both chapters the reader should have a general understanding of investment financing in the development process.

In this chapter, we provide insight into the land development process and how to determine on the feasibility of land development projects. We discuss how development loans are structured, how terms for disbursement and repayment are determined, and how profitability projections are made. Structuring loan agreements, repayment schedules, and estimating interest carry for land development projects is somewhat detailed and complex. The reader may want to refer to the appendix in the previous chapter for a more in-depth treatment of these subjects if difficulty is encountered when trying to master the material in the chapter.

CHARACTERIZATION OF THE LAND DEVELOPMENT BUSINESS

When generalizing about the land development process, it is useful to think of the land developer as an individual with a general development concept. Before proceeding with the development, however, there must be evidence that the project is feasible or that market acceptance of the end product (single family houses, offices, warehouses, etc.) is highly likely. This is important even though the land developer may, or may not, be the developer of the final product. In other words, in the land development phase, the developer must anticipate and understand the demand for the final product (or products in the case of a mixed use land development which may contain sites for sale to single family builders, apartment developers and/or shopping center developers, for example). This is necessary because demand will obviously affect the demand for individual sites, lots, or pads being developed within the land development. Every land acquisition decision must also be based on whether the tract of unimproved land on which the plan is to be executed is of sufficient size and contains adequate amounts of usable area to accommodate the development plan. While development plans will differ based on the general development concept, all plans include the subdivision, or platting, of sites within a tract of land to be acquired. Decisions as to how to subdivide the larger development into lot sizes and how to price individual sites are based on expected end uses that are envisioned as a part of the general development concept.

In residential land development, it is common to find firms specializing in the acquisition of raw land in suburban fringe areas and developing sites for single family detached units or for multiple uses, such as combinations of single family units, multifamily apartments, and cluster housing. Based on the market segment that the end use will likely sell in, the land developer acquires land, develops a land use and traffic circulation plan, then constructs streets, lighting, and subsurface improvements (utilities, drainage, sewer). Individual sites are then subdivided, and smaller sites are sold to builders and project developers. Some retail sites may be retained for later sale if the site has suitable highway frontage.

One point to be stressed here is that land developers and builders or project developers may, or may not, be the same entities. Land developers may or may not have the expertise to undertake building construction and/or project development. These functions differ in their respective production technologies and market risks. However, a few large firms may engage in both activities. For example, where residential sites are being developed for housing in lower price ranges, the land developer may also engage in some home-building. On the other hand, when land is more expensive, the land developer usually sells lots to custom home builders and engages in little, if any, homebuilding.

In business parks and industrial development, land developers (discussed in the previous chapter) may prepare sites for sale to project developers, but they usually retain some sites for project development of their own. For example, a major single tenant may want to have a building constructed in a business park. In this case, the park developer may design and ''build to suit'' a structure for the tenant and enter a long-term lease arrangement. Alternatively, the building may be constructed on a site and sold to the tenant on a ''turnkey'' basis. In business and industrial park development, the land developer may also construct some building improvements on a speculative basis to attract other tenants to the park. However, these developers usually stand ready to sell sites in the park to other project developers as long as those project developers abide by the development controls required by the park developer. These controls usually include construction of adequate building quality, maintenance, landscaping, and so on. These controls are usually carried out with deed restrictions and/or provisions in an agreement governing the operation of a business park owners association.

Another observation with respect to land development is that the industry is highly fragmented, localized, and competitive in nature. Many land development firms usually exist in a given urban market. They enter the market for raw land by contacting landowners or land brokers and obtain information on tracts of land available for sale. These developers then engage consultants to conduct market studies to assess the demand for end uses that should ultimately be developed and price ranges for each use. The developer then completes a preliminary land plan, estimates the land development cost, and conducts an analysis of whether the tract can be purchased and developed profitably. This process is referred to as a *feasibility study*. It should be stressed that in many cases the developer is more of a ''facilitator'' of the development process rather than a firm that undertakes all necessary functions in the land development process. This means that many functions required to complete a land development project may be done by consulting firms (land planners, civil engineers, landscape architects) and contractors (roads and utility construction). In these instances, the developer owns the land, obtains the necessary financing, and implements the overall development plan, but may not employ a staff that is directly involved in construction or design. The developer must also interact with public sector officials in obtaining various project approvals, changes in zoning when necessary, and then market sites to project developers and/or builders.

THE LAND DEVELOPMENT PROCESS—AN OVERVIEW

Exhibit 18–1 contains a general description of activities performed at various stages in the process. Generally, the process begins with the developer being contacted by a land broker who represents the owner of a tract of land available for sale. At this point (Stage I), a very preliminary investigation is made with respect to the site, the condition of the

EXHIBIT 18–1 Land Development Process

Stage I *Initial Contact* *by Land Broker*	*Stage II* *Option Period*	*Stage III* *Development Period*	*Stage IV* *Sales Period*
Site inspection	Soil studies, engineering	Purchase land	Implement marketing program
Preliminary market study	Feasibility, appraisal, and design strategy	Close on land development loan Begin construction of improvements	Additional coordination with builders
Preliminary cost estimates	Bidding and/or negotiation with contractors subject to closing	Implement financial controls	Implement design controls with builders
	Submit plan for public approvals, submit package for financing	Coordinate with contractors, consultants, public sector	Implement facility management and/or begin homeowner association

market, how a tract might be developed, and at what cost. Should sufficient interest exist to pursue negotiation, the developer will usually negotiate an *option* agreement with the landowner. An option usually provides that the developer will have the right, but no obligation, to purchase the land for a specific price at a future date. An option price is paid to the landowner which is usually applied to the purchase price of the land if the developer purchases it (exercises the option). In the event that the developer decides not to purchase the land on the expiration date, the landowner may keep the money paid for the option.

Acquisition of Land—Use of the Option Contract

The developer usually negotiates an option contract because it takes time to accomplish various tasks and activities prior to the decision to actually purchase the land. Some of these activities are shown in Stage II in the exhibit. Inasmuch as the developer's final decision to purchase will depend on the information provided from the activities indicated, the decision to purchase land obviously cannot be made quickly. Consequently, the developer would prefer to negotiate an option at the lowest price possible for the longest period of time possible, while accomplishing these tasks. Further, the developer will be incurring costs while the research is carried out to provide the needed information as to whether land should be purchased. The developer wants assurance that the land will not be sold while these costs are being incurred. On the other hand, if the landowner wants to sell as quickly as possible, an option with a short exercise period would be preferred at the highest possible price. While the option agreement provides the developer time to conduct research, it also ties up the land or precludes the landowner from selling it until the expiration date.[1] Consequently, the landowner may give up opportunities to sell the land during the option period, and has no assurance that the developer may actually close the transaction. Option periods can be very short (e.g., one month for small residential land developments) or as long as three years or more (e.g., regional shopping centers).[2]

---

[1]Because all terms of sale should be included in the option contract, in many cases a contract to purchase the land may be used instead of negotiating an option agreement. The contract would be executed with a closing date that would make it equivalent to the option period. All terms, conditions, contingencies, and so on, would be negotiated and included in the sale contract at the time that the contract is executed. This approach usually eliminates contractual ambiguities between the buyer and seller that could arise if an option is used.

[2]Options with assignment clauses have also been used in land speculation. In these cases, the prospective land buyer obtains an option from the landowner with little or no expectation of purchasing the land (although he may not indicate this). The owner of the option hopes to find another buyer to purchase the land at a price higher than the exercise price prior to the expiration of the option. If he can do so, he realizes a gain. If a buyer cannot be found, the speculator loses the option price. This practice has been referred to as *flipping* a contract. In some cases, developers with options with lengthy expiration dates inadvertently realize gains. This occurs when, after undertaking feasibility studies, they realize that land values have risen. In this case, they may engage a land broker or try to find a buyer prior to the option expiration date, or negotiate an extension period on the option with the landowner.

In some instances, landowners face situations in which a subsequent offer of a higher price is received after an option has been given to a developer. In this case, if the new bidder wants to close the transaction prior to the expiration date of the option, the landowner may try to repurchase the option from the developer and hope that the new buyer and the developer do not meet and negotiate directly.

Assuming that an option is obtained by the developer for an acceptable period of time and cost, some important activities must be undertaken before the expiration date, when the decision to acquire the land must be made. The site is studied to establish how much of the surface area needs excavating and grading, and at what cost. This is a function of the topography, drainage characteristics, soil condition, and subsurface characteristics. The market must be studied to estimate what the demand will be for a mix of lot sizes. The supply of sites coming into the market in competing areas must also be considered. An estimate of the project's value upon completion of development must be made to determine whether it will be profitable, or whether the market value will exceed the cost of the land plus all improvements, interest carry, and marketing costs. Improvement costs must be estimated by obtaining bids from contractors, consulting engineers, and land planners. These estimates are based on an anticipated land development plan, which usually has to undergo several iterations before it (1) complies with the overall development concept that is intended to meet market demand and (2) meets the approval of various public agencies (city departments, planning commissions, city council, etc.). Results from all of these activities must then be interpreted and used to develop a loan submission request. Without approval from a lender, who may be asked to provide a large portion of the funds necessary to acquire the land and construct improvements, the project is not likely to go forward.

One aspect of the process depicted in Stage II of Exhibit 18–1 should become clear at this point. The response time of the developer to accomplish these functions is critical and usually requires the commitment of other firms to the developer's time table. If the necessary approvals from public officials are not obtained or if a lender cannot be found, the developer may lose the cost of the option plus all fees and costs incurred while trying to accomplish the activities in Stage II. If approvals and the loan commitment are not secured by the expiration date, the developer may try to negotiate an extension of the option period with the landowner. Failing that, the developer may have to raise equity from partners to acquire the land with the expectation that approvals and/or a loan will be obtained shortly after the option period expires and the land acquisition is made. Clearly, this can be risky because if the land is acquired, long delays may occur before financing and necessary approvals are obtained. Market conditions and costs can also change during this time, thereby increasing the risk of development.

Financing and Development

Assuming that all activities in Stage II are successfully accomplished by the land developer, the purchase and financing of the land, the construction of utilities, and surface improvements must occur next as shown in Stage III. As discussed earlier, the developer is generally acting as a facilitator in coordinating, controlling, and paying for the construction of land improvements as funds are acquired from a lender. When financing the land acquisition and development process, a number of structures may be available to the developer; however, three of the more common alternatives are discussed here.

1. The land may be purchased by developer for cash. A loan may then be obtained for the cost of improvements and interest carry.

2. The land is purchased by the developer, who makes a down payment only. The seller finances all or a portion of the land sale by taking back a purchase-money mortgage from the developer. The developer then acquires a loan for improvements only. The seller of land (mortgagee) agrees to subordinate the lien represented by the purchase-money mortgage to the development loan, and the seller's mortgage is repaid from funds as parcels are sold and after payments on the development loan are made.
3. The land is purchased by the developer, who makes a down payment and obtains one loan based on a percentage of the appraised value of land plus improvements. Funds are used to pay off the seller and to construct improvements.

The extent to which each of these techniques is used partially depends on conditions in the market for land and the price paid for the land. If the demand for developable land is strong, sellers may demand cash and may not be willing to sell "on terms" or take back purchase-money mortgages. However, during such times, lenders are generally more willing to provide funds for improvements and a part of the land acquisition price. During periods when demand is not as strong, sellers of land are more willing to finance a portion of the sale price, however lenders are usually more cautious as uncertainty becomes more prevalent in the marketplace.[3]

Regardless of the financing technique used to acquire the land, loans for land improvements are usually made available by lenders who allow developers to "draw down" funds in stages, usually monthly, based on the percentage of development work completed and verified by the lender. An open-end mortgage is used as security for the loan. Such loans are usually made on a floating rate basis. That is, the lender will usually make the loan at 2 or 3 percent above the prime lending rate. Hence, the developer usually bears the risk of an interest rate change during the development period. As previously indicated, the lender providing the funds for improvements will insist on obtaining first lien on the land being developed and first lien on all improvements as they are completed and as funds are disbursed.

Repayment of land development loans ultimately depends on the sale of the subdivided sites to builders or other developers. Because repayments depend on lot sales and lenders view such loans as very risky, they must accurately assess the risk of projects and the rate at which parcels will be sold in order to determine whether such loans can be repaid. Financial statements, appraisal reports, and market studies are analyzed closely by lenders. In addition, as a development progresses, monthly inspections must be made to verify all work done before a draw can be made against a loan commitment.

As previously indicated, as funds eventually are obtained from the sale of individual parcels by the developer, a portion of the proceeds from each parcel sale must be used to repay loans used to make improvements and/or acquire the land. Amounts to be paid by developers to lenders for each type of developed site in a project are usually negotiated and are referred to as a *release schedule*. When a parcel is sold and a developer repays

---

[3]It is difficult to generalize how much a lender is willing to provide to a land developer. If the developer does not own the land and is in the process of acquiring it for development and if the lender is satisfied that the value of the land will not decline, the lender may be willing to make a land acquisition and development loan. Further, if the developer has considerable personal net worth and is personally liable on the loan, the lender may be more willing to advance a portion of the funds to acquire the land in view of the additional security behind the loan.

a lender or lenders, a release statement is obtained by the developer in which lenders waive all liens on the parcel to be sold. Clear title may then pass from the developer to the buyer of the parcel. Lenders use these release provisions as a control on development loans to ensure that repayment will occur as parcels are sold. Developers must also deal with risks of cost overruns, changes in market demand, and supply conditions causing delays and increases in carrying costs (interest on loans, taxes, etc.) during this phase.

In Stage IV, the final stage, promotion, marketing, and sales to builders or project developers will occur. Generally, the developer will have designed a marketing program utilizing various media (newspaper, trade publications, etc.) to advertise the development to the builders/developers that are constructing improvements based on nature of the land being developed (homesites, office parks, etc.).

LENDER REQUIREMENTS IN FINANCING LAND DEVELOPMENT

While the focus of this chapter is on financial analysis and the feasibility of land development projects, some understanding of the financing process and interaction between lender and borrower is essential. A general understanding of the documentation requirements associated with the development process also helps the reader understand the nature of the liability and performance requirements created when projects are financed and developed. Exhibit 18–2 contains a general list consisting of (A) typical requirements for a land development loan submission to the lender, (B) requirements for closing the loan, if the submission is approved, and (C) the final commitment and attendant terms of financing after closing. The reader should be aware that this is a very general list of requirements and that each land development will have unique requirements of its own. Also, during the process of trying to finance a project and close a loan, questions will be raised by the lender requiring additional documentation, verification, and so on, that the developer will have to supply during the application period. (Some of the material in Exhibit 18–2 is relevant to the land component of project development covered in Chapter 17. It was not included in Exhibit 17–2 to avoid redundancy.)

Much of the information required in Exhibit 18–2 deals with (1) the capacity of third parties to perform (contractors, architects), (2) verification by public sector officials that the use and density of the proposed development conforms with both appropriate zoning ordinances and the capacity of utilities on the site (the lender cannot rely on the developer to provide such information; the municipality or county must give an unambiguous statement on these issues since they will have to provide permits to allow development to commence), and (3) verification that third parties are committed to bear unforseen risks such as indicated by the items listed in part b in category 4. If the developer was unable to obtain any of these verifications, this would obviously be a signal to the lender that more factual information is necessary to support the loan application.

Detailed Cost Breakdowns

The developer usually must submit detailed cost estimates and plans for constructing the improvements. The cost breakdown will generally be verified by the lender, for accuracy in accordance with construction plans and specifications. The lender will usually require

---

EXHIBIT 18–2   General Loan Submission and Closing Requirements—Land Development and Closing

---

A. General requirements for *loan submission* package—land development

1. Project information
   a. Project description: all details for land use plan, aerials, soil reports, platting, circulation, amenities, renderings
   b. Survey and legal description of site showing property lines, easements, utility lines
   c. Preliminary plan for improvements and specifications
   d. Project cost breakdown
   e. Identification of architect, land planner, and general contractor with bank references and/or supporting data indicating their ability to complete the project if approved

2. Market financial data
   a. Requested loan terms: amount, rate, maturity period, proposed release schedule (to be dealt with later in chapter)
   b. Financial statements of borrowers (including bank references) and development background
   c. Feasibility study, including market comparables, appraisals, pro forma operating statement (latter will be dealt with later in chapter), schedule of estimated selling prices
   d. Projected loan closing date

3. Government and regulatory information
   a. Statement of zoning status: current zoning status and disclosure of any zoning changes required before undertaking development
   b. Ad valorem taxes: any impending change in the method of levy, any pending reappraisal and the current status of payment

4. Legal documentation
   a. Legal documents including corporate charters, partnership agreements (there should be no ambiguity as to the entity requesting the loan and where liability will rest)
   b. Statement of land cost and proof of ownership (deed), or impending ownership, as evidenced by an option or purchase agreement
   c. Detailed description of any deed restrictions or restrictive covenants regarding land use
   d. Subordination agreements: in the event of seller financing or debt financing used or to be used to acquire the land, evidence that such parties are willing to subordinate their liens to that of the development lender; if the land mortgages are to be repaid from advances from the development loan being requested, the exact amounts should be stipulated, and the nature of any releases being obtained should be disclosed

B. General requirements for *loan closing*—land development

1. Project information: land site plan containing platting, renderings, circulation, utility lines, landscaping, etc.

2. Market and financial data: statement that borrowers have had no adverse impact in financial condition since the initial loan submission

3. Government and regulatory information
   a. Copies of all permits from all relevant agencies and jurisdictions; includes building permits, approved zoning variances needed, health, water, sewer, environmental impact statements, etc.
   b. Availability of utilities: letters from appropriate municipal/county departments indicating extent of utilities available to the site. Any off-site utility extensions must be detailed and the extension cost disclosed

4. Legal documentation
   a. Detail on contracts to be let with general contractor and all subcontractors, including size of contracts
   b. Evidence of contractor performance and payment bond
   c. Agreement from general contractor, architect, and land planner to perform for the lender in the event of developer default

---

EXHIBIT 18–2   *(Concluded)*

---

   d. Evidence of all casualty, hazard, and other insurance policies naming the lender as loss payee
   e. Evidence of all liability and workman's compensation coverage needed by the developer
   f. Title insurance binder
C. Final commitment and agreements
   a. Loan commitment and terms: requirements for lender approval of draws, methods of calculating holdback requirements, prepayment options and any extension agreement
   b. Note and mortgage or deed of trust evidencing debt and lien status of lender
   c. Borrower's personal guarantee for repayment of loan
   d. Conditional assignment agreement covering all contracts made with architects, planners, and general contractor to be assigned the interim lender in the event of borrower default.

---

verification of all costs on a monthly basis as development work progresses and as the lender disburses funds.

General Contracts and Subcontracts

Normally, lenders prefer that developers obtain fixed-price contracts from subcontractors. The lender may require these contracts as a means of protecting against cost overruns that may occur if material or labor prices rise during development.

Labor and Material Payment Bonds and Completion Bonds.   Many lenders require that contractors purchase labor and material payment bonds and completion bonds. The first type of bond assures the lender that any unpaid bills for labor and material will be paid by the bonding company should a contractor default. The completion bond assures the lender that funds needed to complete the construction will be provided by the bonding company in the event that a contractor defaults during construction.

Title Insurance.   As a condition for obtaining a land development loan, title insurance generally must be purchased by the developer. This is to assure the lender that no liens superior to its lien exist on the property when construction commences.

Holdbacks.   As discussed in the previous chapter dealing with project development, land development loans may also provide for a holdback of a proportion of each disbursement payable to a developer. This occurs when the developer and/or a general contractor engage a number of subcontractors and hold back a portion of the funds due under subcontracts. The developer holds back to be sure that subcontractors perform all work completely before receiving final payment. Consequently, the lender holds back from the developer so that no excess funds are made available to the developer during the period the developer is holding back from subcontractors.

Extension Agreements.   Because it is possible that the loan will not be paid on time due to development problems or the slow sale of parcels, the lender will usually require an extension clause in the initial loan contract. This clause specifies that an additional charge will be made for any extra time needed to repay the loan. This amounts to gap financing or additional interim financing, and the lender will usually charge an extension fee in addition to interest on the outstanding loan balance if an extension is needed. In fact, these amounts may never be collectible. Indeed, if the project encounters extreme difficulty, the lender may have to foreclose and assume ownership of the development.

RESIDENTIAL LAND DEVELOPMENT—ILLUSTRATED

To illustrate one of the many land development scenarios that are possible, we have chosen a medium-size residential land development project. However, many of the same *general* concepts and the framework for analysis apply to business/office parks, and industrial/warehouse/distribution centers. Our illustration is based on the 50-acre Grayson tract, the availability of which has been brought to the attention of Landco Development Company by a land broker. Based on the combination of the description of the tract provided by the broker, Landco's knowledge of the area, and information obtained from the owner of the tract, a summary of important facts is provided in Exhibit 18–3.

Information in Exhibit 18–3 indicates that the tract is farmland at the fringe of suburban development 15 miles north of the central business district (CBD) with good proximity to highways. The present owner has recently had the property rezoned to allow for the development of single family detached units. Most of the surface area may be developed; however, 5 acres consists of creek and floodplain. Current zoning provides for an *average* maximum development density of one single family detached unit per 7,500 square feet of developable surface space (gross land area, less floodplain area, less circulation: roads,

---

EXHIBIT 18–3   Data on Grayson Tract

Size of tract	50 acres
Asking price	$40,000 per acre, for a total of $2,000,000
Option	30-day "free look", $20,000 for next 5 months
Current zoning	Single family detached, with a maximum average development density of 1 unit per 7,500 sq. ft. of developable area.
Legal status	No deed restrictions or easements are currently indicated; no encumbrances exist.
Site characteristics	Creek and floodplain comprise 5 acres of surface area. Terrain is gently rolling and moderately treed. A creek flows through the northeast quadrant, and the floodplain is contained within a channel to the edge of a steep embankment. The soil is stable with normal percolation.
Utilities	Water, sewer, electricity, and gas, all with adequate capacity, are extended to the site.
Proximity	1500 feet of highway frontage (state highway 66), 1 mile west of U.S. Interstate 166, 15 miles north of CBD.
Current use	Farmland in suburban fringe area.

alleys, etc). The terrain appears to present little, if any, problem to construct land improvements. The broker has indicated that the owner is willing to entertain an offer to sell the property for $2 million, and will give the developer an option to purchase it for 30 days at no cost. At the end of such time, another option may be acquired for an additional five months at 1 percent of the price of the land, or $20,000. Should the purchaser exercise the option to purchase the land, credit for the option price would be applied toward the purchase of the land.[4]

Inasmuch as the owner is allowing a 30-day "free look" at the property, Landco has decided to expend effort to determine if the project is feasible and whether the $2 million asking price is justified. To accomplish this, Landco must complete a preliminary development plan and conduct a market study to assess the demand for residential sites and the competitive supply conditions, both currently and in the near future. If results from the land plan and market study appear positive, information will be compiled to apply for a loan commitment and public approvals.

Market Conditions and Site Plan

As previously indicated, this illustration is intended to focus on approaches that can be used to evaluate the economic feasibility of residential land development. Estimates used to make projections for such developments are heavily based on market and cost information. While we do not provide the reader with an in-depth discussion of how to conduct market studies and how to make cost estimates, we do not mean to imply that these are minor considerations when one is deciding whether to enter into a land development project. Indeed, these studies are extremely important, and the reader should consult other sources of information if additional insights into this process are desirable.[5]

Exhibit 18–4 provides us with a brief summary of important facts that should be the objective of market and engineering studies. These studies should be carried out during the option period, before acquiring the land and applying for financing. In addition to gauging how strong builder demand for lots is before committing himself to purchase the land, the developer must have a clear vision of the proposed development and how it will be viewed by buyers, who have the choice of acquiring homes in competing developments.

Essentially, Landco's plan is to develop cluster-type housing sites, standard and oversized creek lots. The project will also include community facilities (pool, tennis courts). Inasmuch as 5 acres of the tract are not developable because they lie in a floodplain, to the extent competing land development projects do not have this loss in developable land, Landco may be at a competitive disadvantage unless (1) the loss of acreage is reflected in a lower acquisition price for the tract (holding all else equal), or (2) unless Landco can develop the creek area into a positive, complementary feature. If lots can be developed contiguous to the creek they may command a premium price. This may fully or partially

---

[4]In many cases, the buyer may be able to use a letter of credit in lieu of a cash option payment to the seller. This approach, if acceptable to the seller, is usually a lower-cost alternative to the buyer, who may have a more profitable use for the funds during the option period.

[5]For an illustration see John M. Clapp, *Handbook for Real Estate Market Analysis* (Englewood Cliffs, N.J.: Prentice-Hall, 1987).

EXHIBIT 18–4   Summary of Market Data and Development Strategy

---

A. Market conditions	Based on a survey of three land developments underway in the area, absorption of building sites appear to be excellent. Builder surveys indicate a strong desire to purchase sites for future development. Average lot sizes in competing developments are approximately 8,700 sq. ft.
B. Lot mix and development plan	Landco plans to utilize the creek area to enhance the development by configuring the circulation pattern to accommodate larger lot sizes on both sides of the creek. The lots for cluster-type housing units would be placed adjacent to the highway frontage as a buffer. These would be complemented with heavy landscaping. Cul-de-sacs would be utilized where possible in the interior of the development. Lot sizes would be ranging from 5,000 to 20,000 sq. ft. within the development with the average lot size being 8,712 sq. ft.
C. Deed restrictions	Private deed restrictions would be used to insure that detached housing units with a minimum of 2,000 sq. ft. would be constructed on each lot. Restriction regarding setbacks, external finish materials (% of brick and wood, roof composition), landscaping, fencing and future additions to structures would continue to apply after completion of the development to ensure neighborhood quality.
D. Developable area	50 acres less 5 acres of creek and floodplain, less an additional 20% for circulation (alleys, streets, amenities etc.) or 36 net acres. Lot yield should be 3.6 units per gross surface acre. Setbacks, lot lines, street and alley widths, and utility easements easily meet all city regulatory requirements.
E. Amenities	Clubhouse, two swimming pools, eight lighted tennis courts. A homeowners association will assume management upon completion and sell out of development.
F. Construction of land improvements	Paving, streets, curbing, water mains, hydrants, sewer, and all connections to be constructed in accordance with current city and county standards.
G. Development restrictions	Zoning allows an average of 1 unit per 7,500 sq. ft. of net developable area as the maximum density of development.

---

offset the loss of developable space in the floodplain. In any event, the developer must carefully consider how much of the land is developable relative to comparable sites and their respective prices, when deciding whether the development is economically feasible. In Landco's case, this means whether the asking price for the Grayson land ($2,000,000) plus development costs will be too high relative to the market value of competing homesites.

One aspect of the site plan that is considered when investing and financing land development is the percent of land available for lot development. For example, gross acreage in our case is 50 acres. However, the amount of land actually available for development is equal to gross land area, less floodplain area, less circulation requirements.

In our example, this would be $[(50 - 5) \times (1 - .20)] \div 50 = 72\%$, or 36 net acres of the total 50-acre tract. The lot yield in this case could be 180 lots $\div$ 50 or 3.6 lots to the acre. This also means that an average of 8,712 square feet of developable land would be available per developed lot (36 acres $\times$ 43,560 square feet per acre $\div$ 180 lots).

The value in knowing these relationships lies in conducting comparative analysis with competing developments. Large differences in developable land and lot yields may indicate that a development is to contain a relatively low density housing pattern or that the site has soil, terrain, or other characteristics that make a significant part of it unusable. These ratios also give us a basis to compare the *density* of housing that will be built with competing projects. For example, if Landco's estimated gross and net lot yield are greater or less than lot yields in competing developments, this may imply that Landco is over- or underdeveloping the tract relative to competing developments. A more careful analysis of market data and a competitive analysis should reveal why this is the case.

For example, if a developer overpays for a site relative to the competition, an attempt may be made to recapture the higher land cost with more density (higher net lot yield). However, this strategy may not be successful because it depends on the price that builders (and eventually homebuyers) are willing to pay for higher-density housing or smaller sites. One should not assume that developers always try to maximize net lot yield per acre. While this may appear to be a more "efficient" utilization of land and provide the developer with more lots to sell, market demand by homebuyers may be such that larger lot sizes and wider streets and alleys (circulation) and a lower development density are preferred. While this lower density may only be provided at higher prices, if household incomes and preferences will support the pattern, it would be a mistake to proceed with higher densities. On the other hand, if this tract were closer to the central business district, higher density may be acceptable to households who may have preferences for smaller lot sizes, higher density, but closer proximity to the center city. Hence, lot yield calculations should only be used as a tool to investigate why *deviations* from yields in comparable developments exist. In this way a better understanding of the market segment that developers are appealing to should result. There are no absolute maximum or minimum rules that apply.

The lot yield per acre is also generally used by public agencies to determine if zoning restrictions are being adhered to. As shown in Exhibit 18–4, we see that zoning provides that an *average* of 1 lot per 7,500 square feet of developable area is the maximum density allowed in this project. Landco projects an *average* of 8,712 square feet per unit is the maximum *average* density which easily meets zoning restrictions. This points out the fact that developers do not always design to the maximum density allowed by zoning regulations. In all cases, *market demand* and household preferences will dictate what densities should be developed. As previously indicated, homebuyers may prefer to pay higher prices for lower densities and corresponding increases in privacy (larger lots) and reductions in traffic and congestion. In this event, developers may be taking excessive risks if they attempt to increase densities, even if current zoning allows them to do so and lower average lot prices to buyers could result.

To consider some of the market conditions faced by Landco, the reader should refer to the competitive market analysis summary provided in Exhibit 18–5. For example, note that relative to Grayson, project A has about the same net development density, but

EXHIBIT 18–5   Competitive Market Analysis Survey: Project Name

	Grayson	*A*	*B*	*C*
Gross acres	50	40	70	100
number of lots	180	160	210	420
Density				
Percent developable	72%	80%	75%	80%
Lot yield	3.6	4.0	3.0	4.2
Range in sq. ft./lot	5–20,000	5–10,000	5–25,000	5–22,000
Average sq. ft./lot	8,712	8,712	10,890	8,300
Circulation				
requirements	20%	20%	25%	20%
Amenities				
Pools/cabanas	2	N/A	2	2
Tennis courts	8	N/A	10	12
Exercise rooms	N/A	N/A	1	2
Clubhouse	N/A	N/A	N/A	1
Other features	Creek sites	—	Bluff sites	—
Prices				
Cluster	$19,000	N/A	$36,000	$19,000
Standard	45,600	$40,000	$48,000	40,000
Creek/bluff	47,500	N/A	60,000	N/A

Gross project value/Grayson tract

	Number of parcels	*Price*	*Total*
Cluster	54	$19,000	$1,026,000
Standard	90	45,600	4,104,000
Creek	36	47,500	1,710,000
			$6,840,000

Construction period	6 months
Approval period	6 months
Likely financing terms:	50 percent of land acquisition cost, 100 percent of improvements costs (subject to appraisal and feasibility analysis). Loan draws are to be made as improvements are completed, interest is to be paid monthly. Interest rate: 12.00 percent or prime of 10 percent plus 2 percent with 3 points to be paid at loan closing.

it has no amenities or creek sites and it has a slightly lower average asking price per standard lot. Project B is larger in scale than Grayson, has much lower net density, larger average lot sizes, slightly greater circulation requirement (because of hilly terrain), a slightly better amenity package, and bluff sites as a special feature. Its sites are priced higher in each category. Development C is largest in scale and has no special topographic features. It has a higher development density and more amenities than the Grayson project. Landco believes that, based on this competitive analysis, its price structure is justified (all other important characteristics, such as access to schools, shopping, churches, etc., are thought to be equal).

From the above considerations, it should be apparent that estimating market demand and pricing the end product are very important. In cases where competing projects are very similar, pricing must be similar as the quantity or package of attributes being provided by each is the same. On the other hand, the more dissimilar projects are, the more variation in pricing is likely to be encountered. In these cases, pricing must be based on the desirability of the relative attributes of each development. In these instances pricing risk will be greater. Based on the estimated market prices for these lots, a preliminary estimate of the market value for the Grayson tract, *assuming all lots were completely developed and sold immediately,* would be $6,840,000.

Estimating Development Cost and Interest Carry

Landco has retained Robert Whole and Associates, an engineering firm to estimate direct development costs based on the anticipated land plan Landco has presented to them. Cost estimates are provided in Exhibit 18–6. These costs are broken down into (1) land cost,

---

EXHIBIT 18–6   Grayson Project Cost Estimates

Land: 50 acres at $40,000 per acre		$2,000,000
Other direct costs		
1. Grading/clearing	$ 390,000	
2. Paving	540,000	
3. Storm sewers	70,000	
4. Sanitary sewers	125,000	
5. Water	125,000	
6. Electricity	120,000	
7. Landscaping	90,000	
8. Other (signage, etc.)	90,000	
9. Amenities (pool, cabana, tennis)	390,000	
Other costs		
Engineering, land planning, studies	110,000	
Direct overhead—Landco	80,000	
Public approvals, tap fees, etc.	90,000	
Miscellaneous direct costs	80,000	
Legal and acounting fees	100,000	
Subtotal (direct costs)	$2,400,000	
Contingencies		
(10 percent of direct costs)	240,000	
Total direct development costs		$2,640,000
Total land and direct development costs		$4,640,000

(2) costs for constructing improvements (hard costs), and (3) other costs necessary to complete the project but not expended for improvements to the land (soft costs). To the extent that Landco borrows to finance these costs, interest carry will become a significant cost of the Grayson project, because it will take several years to complete.

Landco Development Company has approached Mid City Savings Association regarding its 50-acre Grayson tract. Mid City has reviewed the project and believes it to be viable. It has agreed to finance 50 percent of the land acquisition cost and up to 100 percent of all direct development costs, plus the interest carry on the project. The interest rate will be tied to the prime rate plus 2 percent. For the Grayson project, the interest rate will be 12 percent on the outstanding monthly loan balance. Landco also believes that the interest rate should remain the same during the development period.[6] As was the case in project development discussed in the preceding chapter, financing interest carry as a part of a land development loan is very common, even though no income will be earned by the developer until much of the development is complete and lots are sold to builders. As long as the lender is convinced that the value added to the site from development exceeds the cost of site plus the cost of improvements by more than the interest cost that will be incurred on the development loan, then making a loan that includes interest carry is feasible.

Draws and Revenue Estimates.   Estimating the amount of interest carry is somewhat complicated because (1) the loan will be taken down in "draws" or stages, and interest will be calculated only as funds are drawn down, (2) the revenue from the sale of each type of site varies, (3) the rate of repayment of the loan depends on when parcels are actually sold, and (4) as indicated earlier, the interest rate is usually tied to a floating rate and hence is subject to change. The procedure used to estimate interest carry is shown in Exhibit 18–7 (the reader may want to review the appendix to Chapter 17 at this point). Part I of the exhibit contains a schedule of dollar draws and draw rates for direct development costs as envisioned by Landco. Part II contains a sales revenue schedule for the three categories of lots. Note that although the cluster lots represent 30 percent of the sites to be developed, they will produce only 15 percent of total revenue. This is because the individual sites are smaller; hence the average cost of improving those sites is lower (not shown). Standard-size sites, which make up the majority of total sites, represent 60 percent of sites and will produce 50 percent of total revenue, while the creek sites represent only 20 percent of the sites but will produce 25 percent of total revenue. The latter sites are larger and require more than the average cost to develop.

It might be inferred from this allocation that the project may be more profitable if more standard and creek sites were developed. This would also lower the total density of the development. However, there may not be sufficient market demand to sell more of these sites. The point is that the *relative demand* for each type of homesite is important in determining the configuration of sites and prices that will maximize project value. For example, creek sites will also be most expensive to develop and consequently are priced

---

[6]The interest rate risk may be reduced by hedging interest rate futures or with interest rate swaps. These topics are discussed in the appendix to this chapter.

EXHIBIT 18–7 Loan Allocation and Parcel Release Schedule

I. Schedule of Estimated Monthly Cash Draws for Development Costs

Month	Amount	Rate (percent)
Closing	$1,019,200*	28.00
1	655,200	18.00
2	655,200	18.00
3	655,200	18.00
4	218,400	6.00
5	218,400	6.00
6	218,400	6.00
Total	$3,640,000	100.00

II. Allocation of Loan Draws to Development Costs

	(a) Percent of Total Revenue by Parcel Type	(b) Percent of Parcel Type
Cluster	15%	30%
Standard	60	50
Creek	25	20
	100	100

III. Estimated Monthly Absorption Rate after Loan Closing

Month	Cluster†	Standard‡	Creek§	Total Unit Sales	Cumulative Sales Volume	Monthly Sales Revenue	Monthly Revenue Rate (percent of total)
Close	0	0	0	0	$0		
1–3	0	0	0	0	$0		
4–6	2	0	0	6	$ 114,000	$ 38,000	0.555556%
7–12	3	2	1	42	$1,288,200	$195,700	2.861111
13–24	1	3	2	114	$4,297,800	$250,800	3.666667
25–36	1	2	0	150	$5,620,200¶	$110,200	1.611111
37–42	1	3	1	180	$6,840,000	$203,300	2.972222
Total	54	90	36				

*50% of land costs ($2,000,000), plus an additional draw of $19,200 for direct costs incurred by Landco to be funded at closing. 28% of $3,640,000 = $1,019,200.

†Price = $19,000.

‡Price = $45,600.

§Price = $47,500.

¶Loan repayment is scheduled to be complete in month 35 when sales reach 80% of projected total revenue (100% of loan amount ÷ 125% repayment rate = 80%). Repayment occurs when total revenue reaches $5,472,000 ($6,840,000 × .80).

highest. Cluster sites may be the only type of site amenable to the terrain on which the development of improvements must be constructed. In other words, the mix of all sites may be necessary to maintain an acceptable level of total development density, to utilize the sites along the creek, and to maximize total project value.

Sales and Repayment Rates.   Part III of Exhibit 18−7 provides a schedule of how sales of the three categories of lots are estimated to occur and how funds will be drawn down for direct development costs for the Grayson project. Sales estimates are made based on information obtained from market studies of competing projects and based on Landco's recent experience on its own similar projects. This sales estimate is necessary because the lender is to be repaid from revenue as lot sales occur.

Part III of the exhibit is very important. It shows that *monthly loan payments* will be based on the revenue produced from the sale of each type of lot and the number of lots sold per month. These monthly revenue rates are needed to estimate the interest carry, since they take into account the fact that as a parcel is sold the lender will receive a partial repayment of the loan that corresponds to the revenue produced from each sale. These monthly revenue rates are obtained by dividing the relative share of revenue produced by the sale of sites each month by the total revenue expected from sales of all sites in the project. For example, the two cluster sites sold each month during months 4−6 (Part III) will produce $38,000 each month. The lender would like to base principal and interest payments on the relative share of the revenue obtained from the sale of those sites, or .56 percent (rounded) of total revenues of $6,840,000. Monthly sales revenue rates for remaining parcel types for each sale period are listed in Part III of the exhibit. In essence, what lenders will generally do is *match* the loan repayment with the revenue produced from each parcel sale. Then, as parcels are sold, the lender will *release* the lien held on that parcel as a part of the loan security, thus clearing the way for the developer to sell to a builder. The amount that the borrower pays the lender to obtain this release is referred to as the *release price*.

Release Schedule.   Regarding the expected period that the loan will be outstanding, most lenders will insist that the loan be repaid *prior* to the time expected for the borrower to sell all parcels in the development. This is because the lender usually does not want to take the risk associated with a possible slowdown in sales in the later stages of the project. In many land developments, choice parcels are sold early and less desirable ones may remain unsold as time passes. Because some parcels may be more difficult to sell, the lender wants assurance that the developer takes this added risk. Consequently, the lender will bargain for a faster rate of loan payments thereby making sure that the loan will be repaid before all 180 parcels are sold.

Another reason for negotiating faster repayment rates is that because Mid City will put most of the ''front-end'' money into the development during the first six months it wants assurance that the loan repayment is given preference as sales proceeds are realized. Further, because the developer will realize some markup on each sale, there is some room for the lender to negotiate a satisfactory release schedule and still leave the developer with a reasonable amount of cash inflow.

In many land development loans, the repayment rate is set so that the loan would be repaid at the point where about 80 to 90 percent of total project revenue is realized. The exact schedule is negotiated based on how fast the lender wants the loan repaid, how much cash the developer must retain from each parcel sale to cover expenses not funded in the loan, and conditions in the loan market. In our example, the lender wants to be repaid when approximately 80 percent of project revenues, or $5,472,000, is realized. This means that the lender wants to be repaid at a rate equal to 125% of the rate at which monthly revenue is received (100% ÷ 80% = 125%). If the borrower and lender had agreed that the loan would be repaid over the entire life of the project (42 months), then 100 percent of the loan would be repaid when 100 percent of project revenues are received. Accelerating the repayment rate by 25% means that for every $1 of sales revenue realized, the loan will be repaid by an amount 125 percent greater than would be the case if the loan were repaid over the entire life of the project. In our illustration, based on the cumulative sales revenue shown in Part III of Exhibit 18–7, a total of about 80 percent of project revenues will be received during the 35th month. Hence the lender would like the loan to be repaid at that time.

Estimation of Loan Amount and Interest Carry.   Exhibit 18–8 provides a methodology for *simultaneously* determining the interest carry, total loan amount, and principal payments for each type of parcel, assuming that the release schedule will reflect loan repayments that are 125 percent of project revenue rates, or that the loan will be fully repaid when 80 percent of project revenues are received. Column *a* shows the months during which loan outflows and loan repayments are expected to occur as described in Exhibit 18–7. Column *b* shows the draw rate schedule for the land and direct development *costs*, and column *c* represents the repayment rate, per month, based on the *revenue* schedule shown in Part III of Exhibit 18–7 multiplied by 1.25. We do not yet know the exact dollar amount of principal repayment that must be paid to the lender from parcel sales because we do not know the total loan amount, which also includes the interest carry that we are estimating. However, we do know that repayment rates will reflect the amount of revenue produced by each parcel type and the monthly rate at which revenue is produced. Recall that these revenue rates will be .56 (rounded) percent for months 4–6 and a rate of 2.861 percent during months 7–12, and so on (see Part III, Exhibit 18–7). Hence the loan repayment rates will be .555556 percent × 1.25, or .694445 percent of revenues for months 4–6 and 2.861111 percent × 1.25 or .3576389 percent during months 7–12 as shown in column *c* of Exhibit 18–8. It should be noted that during months 3–5 when total revenues of $5,472,000 are reached, the .013194 repayment rate shown in column c is determined by finding the percentage of revenue needed during the 35th month to reach $5,472,000 and increasing it by 1.25. The amount needed in month 35 is equal to total revenue received through the 34th month, $5,399,800, plus the amount needed during month 35 to total $5,472,000. Hence when $72,200 is received in month 35, total revenues on which the final loan repayment will be based is achieved. Dividing $72,200 by $6,840,000 (total revenue) equals a revenue rate of .0105556, and when it is increased by 1.25, the required repayment rate (.01319433) needed to repay the loan during month 35 is determined.

Because the draw rates in column *b* and repayment rates in column *c* indicate that the cash draw and payment patterns will be annuities in various groups of months, column *d* in Exhibit 18–8 contains interest factors for the *PV* of $1 *per month* (*MPVIFA*) at 12

EXHIBIT 18–8   Estimate of Interest Carry Landco Development Co. Grayson Tract

---

I. Summary of Draw and Repayment Dates

(a)	*(b)*	*(c)*	*(d)*	*(e)*	*(f)*	*(g)*
		Monthly	*MPVIFA*	*MPVIF*		
	Direct Cost	*Repayment*	*at 12*	*at 12*	*PV Draw Rate*	*PV Repayment Rate*
Months	*Draws*	*Rate**	*Percent*	*Percent*	*(b)×(d)×(e)*	*(c)×(d)×(e)*
Close	0.28	0.00000000	1	1	0.280000	0.000000
1–3	0.18	0.00000000	2.940985	1	0.529377	0.000000
4–6	0.06	0.00694445	2.940985	0.970590	0.171269	0.019823
7–12		0.03576389	5.795476	0.942045		0.195257
13–24		0.04583334	11.255077	0.887449		0.457797
25–34		0.02013889	9.471305	0.787566		0.150222
35		0.01319433		0.705914		0.009314
Totals	1.00	1.00000000			0.980646	0.832413

II. Estimates of Interest Carry

TLF = PV of Draw Rate ÷ PV of Repayment Rate
TLF = .980646 ÷ .832413
TLF = 1.178076
Total loan = ($3,640,000)(1.178076)
Total loan = $4,288,197

$TIC = TLF - 1.000$
$TIC = 1.178076 - 1.000$
$TIC = .178076$
Interest carry = TIC × Total cost borrowed
Interest carry = ($3,640,000)(.178076)
Interest carry = $648,197

$TLP = TLF + TIC$
$TLP = 1.178076 + .178076$
$TLP = 1.356152$
Total loan payments = (TLP)($3,640,000)
Total loan payments = $4,936,393

*Monthly revenue rate (Exhibit 18–7, Part III) × 125% (rounded).

---

percent. Column *e* contains the factors for the *PV* of $1 which are used to discount the grouped annuities back to present value (the reader should recall our discussion of grouped cash flows in an earlier chapter). Both of these factors are multiplied by the rates shown in columns *b* and *c*. This ensures that when the principal repayment schedule is determined, amounts paid to the lender from each sale will be enough to earn the lender 12 percent on the monthly loan balance outstanding over the 34-month period. Although we do not yet know what the required repayment *amounts* will be for each parcel type, we do know that the *rate* of repayment will be based on the sales schedule and we know that the lender will insist on the loan being repaid at a rate 25 percent greater than the rate at which revenue is expected to occur. As noted previously, to match the rate of loan repayment, the factors in column *c* have been adjusted upward by multiplying 1.25 by the monthly revenue rates shown in Section III of Exhibit 18–7. The rates of inflow are discounted by 12 percent to account for the fact that loan repayments occur over time. Column *d* contains annuity factors for 3, 3, 6, 12, and 10 months, respectively. Columns *f* and *g* contain the present value of all inflows and outflows occurring over the 35-month expected loan period. It should now be clear that the unknown loan repayment schedule must be large enough to repay the initial $3,640,000 in loan draws and provide the lender 12 percent interest.

Loan Request Including Interest Carry

To arrive at the total loan request that Landco must make to acquire the land, pay for direct development costs, *and* pay interest carry, we can see the procedure for estimating the total loan amount at the bottom of Exhibit 18–8. The total loan factor *TLF* (recall from Chapter 17 and appendix) is 1.178076, which when multiplied by the total costs to be borrowed, or $3,640,000, yields $4,288,197 as the total loan amount *including* interest carry. Of this amount, $648,197 is interest. This total loan amount represents 63 percent of the gross project value ($6,840,000), and the interest carry represents about 15 percent of the total loan request. The reader may be wondering why so much attention is paid to estimating interest carry. This is because once this estimate is made, an interest reserve will be established by the lender as a part of the total loan commitment. Should actual sales be slower than anticipated, the outstanding loan balance will increase as repayments slow down. Actual interest draws on the loan balance will increase relative to the estimate and this reserve will be depleted sooner than scheduled. Any interest costs in excess of the reserve estimate of $648,197 must be paid by the developer from internal funds. Hence, an accurate estimate of interest carry is just as important as estimates of other hard and soft costs when making a loan request.

Estimating Release Prices per Parcel Sold

We have already indicated that the lender will generally insist on a loan repayment rate in excess of the rate at which revenue is estimated to be earned. Indeed, in our example we have indicated that the loan will be repaid at 125 percent of the rate at which revenue will be received. However, when lenders and developers negotiate land development loans, they also usually assign a *release price to each parcel* in the development. When each parcel is sold, that release amount is paid to the lender, who then releases the lien, thereby assuring the buyer of an unencumbered title. For the three categories of lots in our example, we can now calculate the release price as follows:

Cluster parcels:
(A) Repayment rate per parcel × (B) Loan amount = Release price
Step (1) (A) = [$19,000 ÷ $6,840,000] × 1.25 = .0034722
Step (2) (B) = $4,288,197
Step (3) Release price = .0034722 × 4,288,197 = $14,889 (rounded)

This computation is simply indicating that the release price for any parcel is based on its estimated selling price (as a percentage of total project revenue) multiplied by the rate in excess of the revenue rate that the lender demands. This is the desired repayment rate per parcel. Multiplying this rate by the total loan amount, we obtain the release price per parcel. For the cluster lots this amount is $14,889.

Following the same procedure for standard and creek sites, we obtain release prices for those categories of $35,735 and $37,224, respectively. Therefore, each time one of these parcel types sells, the lender expects to receive the appropriate release price for each parcel. Assuming that construction progresses and sales occur as planned, the full amount of the loan (including interest carry) will be repaid during the 35th month.[7]

Loan Repayment Schedule

To get some idea of what the monthly cash draw and loan repayment schedule would look like, assuming that all estimates of costs, interest rates, and lot sales are as estimated, see Exhibit 18–9. (This schedule would not have to be completed as a part of the loan request, but is included here to help the reader understand the pattern of cash flows associated with financing the project and repayment of the loan.) Note that during months 1–3 the interest draw pattern in column *b* is based on the interest rate (12 percent) divided by 12 months, or 1 percent of the previous month's ending loan balance. Also, note that because the interest carry is *borrowed,* it is accumulated in the loan balance. This is true even though the developer will be making cash "interest only" payments at the end of each month (see column *e*).[8] The ending monthly loan balance continues to increase until enough parcels are sold each month to provide a paydown of principal in excess of interest draws (month 7). However, monthly interest payments continue to be based on the preceding month's loan balance.[9] If sales were to slow down, the loan balance would

---

[7]Based on discussions that the authors have had with developers and lenders, we suspect that this approach to estimating interest carry, the total loan amount, and repayment schedules may be more sophisticated than what is actually done in practice. However, the availability of appropriate computer software now makes the approach just described more practical. Further, this approach can be used to make estimates, and the schedules may be updated as the project is being developed to ascertain any significant variances from budget estimates.

[8]The reader should recall that because the payment is interest only, no reduction in principal occurs. Because interest carry becomes a part of *principal* as it is drawn down, even though an exact payments equal to the amount drawn is made, the principal continues to increase. Only when payments exceeding the interest calculated on the outstanding loan balance are made will principal decline.

[9]We show in Exhibit 18–9 that interest draws are actually received in cash by the developer (column *b*). Then a cash interest payment is made by the developer simultaneously in an exact amount (column *c*). Notice that the same loan balance would result if the lender provided a draw for the direct cost only (column *a*), *computed* interest on those draws as in column *b*, added it to the loan balance (instead of actually paying out

increase rapidly because *actual* interest draws would increase at a faster rate than *estimated* draws. If this slowdown occurred, the interest reserve of $648,197 might be depleted. Further, if the loan balance ever reached $4,288,197, the lender would not allow further draws. The developer would have to make interest payments from other sources. This is one reason why the loan request is a low percentage of gross project value ($4,288,197 ÷ $6,840,000) = 63 percent. Indeed, most lenders prefer to keep the loan to value ratio for land development projects in the range of 70 percent, so that the loan balance has a better chance of being recovered should the project go into default.

PROJECT FEASIBILITY AND PROFITABILITY

From the developer's viewpoint, the economic feasibility of the project is based on whether the market value of the sites after development will exceed the acquisition cost of the land, plus direct improvement costs, plus the interest carry and any other costs not included in the loan provided by Mid City. Exhibit 18–10 summarizes total costs, including closing costs and other costs that Landco must pay for but that will not be funded in the loan for the Grayson project. The interest carry *is included* in the loan amount, and the estimated total cost for the Grayson project should be in the range of $6,156,343, leaving a total equity requirement from Landco of $1,868,146. Given that the market study for the project indicates that the sales prices for the project will yield a gross value of $6,840,000, the project appears feasible and will provide a gross margin over cost of about 11 percent. (This is calculated as total value, $6,840,000, less total cost, $6,156,343 or $683,657 divided by total cost). Relative to equity, this represents a gross return of about 37 percent (calculated as the total dollar margin, or $683,657, divided by equity of $1,868,146). These estimated margins do not take into account the time value of money, however. We now turn to a more appropriate technique for estimating the feasibility and profitability.

Schedule of Cash Flow

Based on the loan repayment schedule detailed above, the developer will retain all cash flow from sale proceeds beginning in month 35 through month 42. Although some cash flow will be retained from earlier sales, clearly the greatest profit will be earned by the developer during those months. However, from the beginning of the development period

---

cash), reduced the loan balance as principal repayments occur (column *d*), and did not require cash interest payments from the developer (column *e*). If this pattern were followed, the ending balance would be the same and no cash disbursement for interest would have to be made by the lender or repaid by the developer. In the pattern just described, interest carry is simply being accrued in the loan balance.

We believe the practice of actual cash disbursements is followed by most lenders instead of the accrued method just described. This may be due to a slight difference between the *actual days* on which draws are made and interest is due. This would make our example slightly inaccurate. Another reason could be that draws are made by one department in a bank, while interest is received by another. In any event, the *net* result is generally the same under either method.

EXHIBIT 18–9 Loan Repayment Schedule Landco Development Company

	(a)	(b)	(c)	(d)	(e)	(f)	(g)
	Draws		Total	Payments			Ending Balance
Month	Direct Cost	Interest	Draws (a)+(b)	Principal	Interest (g)×(.12/12)	Payments Total	(g)Previous Month Balance +(c)−(d)
Close	$1,019,200	0	$1,019,200				$1,019,200
1	$655,200	10,192	665,392		$ 10,192	$ 10,192	1,684,592
2	$655,200	16,846	672,046		16,846	16,846	2,356,638
3	$655,200	23,566	678,766		23,566	23,566	3,035,404
4	$218,400	30,354	248,754	$ 29,779	30,354	60,133	3,254,379
5	$218,400	32,544	250,944	29,779	32,544	62,323	3,475,544
6	$218,400	34,755	253,155	29,779	34,755	64,534	3,698,920
7		36,989	36,989	153,363	36,989	190,352	3,582,546
8		35,825	35,825	153,363	35,825	189,188	3,465,008
9		34,650	34,650	153,363	34,650	188,013	3,346,295
10		33,463	33,463	153,363	33,463	186,826	3,226,395
11		32,264	32,264	153,363	32,264	185,627	3,105,296
12		31,053	31,053	153,363	31,053	184,416	2,982,986
13		29,830	29,830	196,542	29,830	226,372	2,816,274
14		28,163	28,163	196,542	28,163	224,705	2,647,895
15		26,479	26,479	196,542	26,479	223,021	2,477,832

16	24,778	24,778	196,542	24,778	221,320	2,306,068
17	23,061	23,061	196,542	23,061	219,603	2,132,587
18	21,326	21,326	196,542	21,326	217,868	1,957,371
19	19,574	19,574	196,542	19,574	216,116	1,780,403
20	17,804	17,804	196,542	17,804	214,346	1,601,665
21	16,017	16,017	196,542	16,017	212,559	1,421,140
22	14,211	14,211	196,542	14,211	210,753	1,238,809
23	12,388	12,388	196,542	12,388	208,930	1,054,655
24	10,547	10,547	196,542	10,547	207,089	868,660
25	8,687	8,687	86,360	8,687	95,047	790,987
26	7,910	7,910	86,360	7,910	94,270	712,537
27	7,125	7,125	86,360	7,125	93,485	633,302
28	6,333	6,333	86,360	6,333	92,693	553,275
29	5,533	5,533	86,360	5,533	91,893	472,448
30	4,724	4,724	86,360	4,724	91,084	390,812
31	3,908	3,908	86,360	3,908	90,268	308,360
32	3,084	3,084	86,360	3,084	89,444	225,084
33	2,251	2,251	86,360	2,251	88,611	140,975
34	1,410	1,410	86,360	1,410	87,770	56,025
35	560	560	56,580	560	57,140	5
Totals	$648,204	$4,288,204	$4,288,199	$648,204	$4,936,403	$5
	$3,640,000					

*All entries subject to rounding.

EXHIBIT 18–10   Summary of Total Costs

Loan Summary	
Land at 50% of 2,000,000	$1,000,000
Total improvement costs	2,640,000
Interest carry	648,197
Maximum loan amount	$4,288,197
Total direct costs (see Exhibit 18–5)	$4,640,000
Add other project costs:	
Estimated interest carry	648,197
Loan fees (3 percent)	128,646
Closing costs	100,000
General and administrative overhead	210,000
Property taxes	87,500
Selling expenses (5% of gross sales)	342,000
Total project cost	$6,156,343
Less loan amount (Exhibit 18–6)	4,288,197
Total equity requirements	$1,868,146

until the 35th month, a question arises concerning the developer's ability to meet operating expenses and other cash outflow requirements not funded in the loan request from Mid City. The amount loaned to the developer is to cover only part of the land cost, direct costs, and interest carry. Other obligations, such as overhead and loan fees, must be paid during development. Sales commissions, property taxes, and general and administrative expenses were not funded as a part of the development loan and must also be covered from the cash retained by the developer from each parcel sale.

To investigate the developer's ability to carry this project until the loan is repaid and to establish whether the project is feasible for the developer to pursue and meet the expected return on investment, the lender must analyze a schedule of cash flows prepared by the developer. This statement should contain not only the direct cost elements but also additional day-to-day operating expenses that the Grayson project may require. In this way, the developer's cash position can be projected, and the risk of loan default can be better analyzed and the profitability of the project can be established. Exhibit 18–11 contains a quarterly summary of all cash inflows and outflows for Landco over the entire life of the project. The inflows are estimated based on the sales prices for each type of parcel, plus loan draws and equity required from the developer for the land purchase price and closing costs. The outflows include expenditures for direct development costs taken from the schedule of monthly draws (Exhibit 18–9). Loan repayments are taken from the schedule of loan repayments (Exhibit 18–9). Other operating expenses, including general and administrative expenses, sales commissions, and property taxes, have been estimated on a quarterly basis and included in the exhibit.

An analysis of Exhibit 18–11 provides insight into Landco's ability to carry the cash needs of the entire project. At closing and in the first quarter, Landco will have negative

EXHIBIT 18–11 Schedule of Cash Flow, Landco Development Co.

Quarter	Close	(1)	(2)	(3)	(4)	(5)	(6)	(7)
Inflow								
Sales	$0	$0	$114,000	$587,100	$587,100	$752,400	$752,400	$752,400
Loan draw	$1,019,200	2,016,203	752,852	107,463	96,779	84,471	69,164	53,394
Total inflow	$1,019,200	$2,016,203	$866,852	$694,563	$683,879	$836,871	$821,564	$805,794
Less: Outflow								
Land purchases	$2,000,000							
Closing costs	100,000							
Loan fees	128,646							
Repayment of principal		0	$ 89,336	$460,089	$460,089	$589,626	$589,626	$589,626
Direct costs		$1,965,600	655,200					
Interest costs		50,603	97,652	107,463	96,779	84,471	69,164	53,394
General and Administrative		15,000	15,000	15,000	15,000	15,000	15,000	15,000
Property tax					25,000			
Sales expense			5,700	29,355	29,355	37,620	37,620	37,620
Total outflow	2,247,846	2,031,203	862,888	611,907	626,223	726,717	711,410	695,640
Net cash in (out)	($1,228,646)	($15,000)	$3,964	$82,656	$57,656	$110,154	$110,154	$110,154
Net present value at 15%	$59,608							
Internal rate of return	16.89%							

Quarter	(8)	(9)	(10)	(11)	(12)	(13)	(14)
Inflow							
Sales	$752,400	$330,600	$330,600	$330,600	$330,600	$609,900	$609,900
Loan draw	37,146	23,722	16,590	9,243	1,970	0	0
Total inflow	$789,546	$354,322	$347,190	$339,843	$332,570	$609,900	$609,900
Outflow							
Repayment of principal	$589,626	$259,080	$259,080	$259,080	$142,939	0	0
Interest costs	37,146	23,722	16,590	9,243	1,970	0	0
General and administrative	15,000	15,000	15,000	15,000	15,000	15,000	15,000
Property tax	25,000				25,000		12,500
Sales Expense	37,620	16,530	16,530	16,530	16,530	30,495	30,495
Total outflow	$704,392	$314,332	$307,200	$299,853	$201,439	$ 45,495	$ 57,995
Net cash in (out)	$85,154	$39,990	$39,990	$39,990	$131,131	$564,405	$551,905

cash flow. However, from the 2nd through 14th quarters, cash flow is positive. It is during such periods that estimates concerning costs, sales, rates, and repayment conditions become crucial to both Landco and Mid City. If the time needed for development exceeds initial estimates, if actual development costs exceed estimates, or if sales do not materialize as projected, Landco's cash flow position during these months will change dramatically. Similarly, if Mid City demands a release schedule calling for loan repayments that are too high, cash flow to Landco from sales revenue would be reduced, which may jeopardize Landco's ability to carry out the project and to repay the loan. For this reason, Landco's own financial resources must be considered by Mid City in the event that any of these adverse factors materialize. Clearly, if Landco's cash position in this project becomes questionable, Landco will be expected to share in some of the risk by contributing working capital from its own resources to complete sale of the project successfully. To analyze Landco's ability to provide working capital, should it be necessary, Mid City will thoroughly review the company's income statement and balance sheet as well as possibly requiring additional loan security or guarantees from Landco beyond the land which serves as security for the loan.

Finally, based on Exhibit 18–11, Landco's profitability does not materialize significantly until the last three quarters of the project. This is in keeping with the way in which risk is taken during the project. Because the lender puts in front-end capital, it wants assurance of a high priority in the sales proceeds as the development matures. Consequently, Landco must wait until the lender's prior claim is satisfied before it realizes a return. However, from Landco's viewpoint, its equity in the project increases as value is added to the project as actual development occurs. Hence, most of its returns are appropriately deferred to the later stages of the project.

Project Net Present Value

Up to this point in the analysis, we have made some rough estimates as to the economic viability of the project. Recall that we estimated that the market value of the project if it were developed and all parcels were sold today was $6,840,000, and costs were estimated to be $6,156,343 indicating that a margin between total revenues and total costs existed. Although such a margin exists, the cash inflows and outflows related to the development and subsequent sales *do not occur immediately.* Consequently, the *time value of money* must be taken into account. To do this for this project, we *estimate* that a risk premium of at least 3 percent over the borrowing rate of 12 percent, or 15 percent, would be the *minimum* before-tax return that Landco is willing to accept on its equity investment at this time.[10] Applying this rate to the quarterly net cash flows shown in Exhibit 18–11 results in a net present value of $59,608. This indicates that the project

---

[10]The rate of return used for discounting is an annual rate of 15 percent, compounded quarterly. This discount rate represents the required return that Landco must earn as a development company or a going concern, *net of all direct and indirect costs* associated with this project. It represents a rate of return to the owners or shareholders of the Landco Company.

is economically feasible and meets Landco's required return.[11] Stated another way, based on the assumptions used in our analysis, Landco can pay $2,000,000 for the land and still earn a positive net present value.[12]

Entrepreneurial Profits

In the preceding section, we noted that revenues produced by the Grayson project, as projected by Landco, would cover all costs, and the resultant cash flows, when discounted by the required rate of return (assumed to be 15 percent before taxes in the example), would provide a positive *NPV* of about $60,000. When such estimates are made, *all costs* associated with development, *particularly general overhead costs* relating to time spent by all Landco staff, executives, and other personnel should be included (see Exhibit 18–10). The goal of the analysis is to produce an estimate of net cash flow that can be used to evaluate whether a required before-tax return of 15 percent (net of *all* relevant costs) will be earned on the $1,868,146 of equity invested by Landco in the Grayson project. This required return should be viewed as a minimum rate of return that Landco must earn to justify allocating the equity to the project.

Some professionals in the real estate field may also include in their projections an estimate for developer profit, say 10 or 15 percent, as an additional cost of development when projecting net cash flow. Net cash flow is then discounted by a required return on equity. This really amounts to a ''double counting'' of profit in the form of including a developer profit and discounting by a required return. We have included all costs relative to land, labor, and capital explicitly in our projections and have not included an estimate of markup or developer profit as an *additional* cost of development.

Sensitivity Analysis

Based on the analysis just concluded, because a positive *NPV* was estimated by Landco, this implies that the $2,000,000 land price is justified. Indeed, the analysis shows that based on the assumptions used to make projections for the project, Landco could actually

---

[11]Because the project shows a positive net present value, Landco could pay slightly more than $2,000,000 and still earn its required return. If the seller of the land, however, is satisfied with $2,000,000, Landco may be in a position to earn a higher return (assuming all projections materialize). Such a difference between what buyers and sellers are willing to pay and receive occurs because of differences in expectations concerning future development revenues, or because of differences in information (e.g., market knowledge) possessed by each party. The student should now see that the exhibits presented in this chapter can be linked in a spreadsheet format, and with a computer, various ''what if'' scenarios or simulation analyses can be carried out.

[12]To get some idea of the sensitivity of profitability to unexpected change in market conditions, suppose revenue from lot prices were to suddenly increase by 5 percent and all costs remained the same, the *NPV* for Landco's Grayson project would be over $300,000! On the other hand, if direct project costs (Exhibit 18–6) suddenly increased by 5 percent and lot prices could not be changed, *NPV* would decline and become a negative $66,500!

pay slightly more and still earn its desired return of 15 percent. However, sensitivity analysis should also be undertaken to determine how sensitive this return is to lower market prices, larger development periods, cost over-runs, higher interest rates, etc. before Landco proceeds to acquire the land. This analysis was discussed at the conclusion of the previous chapter. It applies to land development as well as project development.

QUESTIONS

1. How might land development activities be specialized? Why is this activity different from project development discussed in the preceding chapter?
2. What is an option contract? How is it used in land acquisition? What should developers be concerned with when using such options? What contingencies may be included in a land option?
3. What are some of the physical considerations that a developer should be concerned with when purchasing land? How should such considerations be taken into account when determining the price that should be paid?
4. In land development projects, why are lenders insistent on loan repayment rates in excess of sales revenue? What is a release price?

PROBLEMS

1. Community Development Corp. (CDC) is seeking financing for acquisition and development of 150 homesites. The land will cost $1,500,000, and direct development costs are estimated to be an additional $2,400,000. City Federal Bank is interested in making the loan covering 30 percent of the land acquisition cost, 100 percent of direct improvement cost, and interest carry. The loan would be made at 10 percent interest with a 3 percent loan origination fee.

   CDC has decided to split the development into *two* parcel types, standard and deluxe, with the standard parcel comprising 60 percent of the total parcels. Also, CDC thinks that the deluxe sites will be priced at an $8,000 premium over the standard parcel price of $32,000. Total project revenue will be $5,230,000. After making a 70 percent down payment for the land and incurring closing costs of $50,000, CDC believes that the remaining development costs will be drawn down at $600,000 a month for the first three months and $200,000 a month for the next three months. Parcel sales are expected to begin during the seventh month after closing. CDC estimates that they will sell three standard parcels and two deluxe parcels a month for the remainder of the first year, four standards and three deluxes per month for the second year, with the sales of the remaining parcel types equally distributed throughout the third and final year of the project.

   The company and the bank have agreed to a repayment schedule calling for the loan to be repaid at a rate 15 percent faster than the receipt of sales revenues; that is, the loan plus interest carry per parcel will be repaid when approximately 87 percent of all revenues are realized. Other costs to consider: sales expense (paid quarterly at a rate of 5 percent on parcels sold during the quarter); administrative costs of $7,500 per quarter; and property taxes of 1 percent at the end of each year (paid on the initial raw land value only).

a. Estimate the total loan amount including interest carry for CDC.

b. Based on your answer in (a), what will be the release price for each type of lot?

c. Based on (b) and the pattern of loan draws, prepare a schedule showing when CDC will have the loan fully repaid? What will be the total cash payments on the project loan?

d. What will total project costs be? What percentage of total project costs are being financed?

e. What will be the *NPV* and *IRR* of this project if CDC's before-tax required rate of return is 15 percent? (Hint: Prepare a cash flow analysis on a quarterly basis over the life of the project.)

2. Holsum Development Co. has found a site that they believe will support 81 homesites. They also believe that the land can be purchased for $100,000 while direct development costs will run an additional $1,000,000. The Last National Bank of Texas will underwrite 100 percent of the improvements plus the interest carry. The loan would be made at 12 percent interest with a 3 percent loan origination fee. Holsum believes that the development will sell faster with two types of parcels, standard and deluxe, with the standard parcel comprising 36 of the total parcels.

Holsum's marketing staff believes that the deluxe sites can be sold for $20,000 while the standard sites should bring $16,000. Holsum estimates that the direct cost draws will be taken down in four equal amounts, with the first draw commencing with the close of the loan. Other up front fees include closing costs of $10,000 and a 3 percent loan fee (not covered by the loan). Holsum's sales staff assures him that they can generate sales activity starting in the fourth month that will result in the sale of three standard parcels per month and two deluxe parcels per month for three months. Activity should then increase to six standard parcels per month and five deluxe parcels per month for the next six months. The Last National Bank wants its money out of the project early and wants Holsum to agree to a release price per parcel that will result in the loan being repaid at a rate 25 percent faster than sales revenue is expected to be earned. Other costs to consider: sales expense (paid quarterly on five percent of the sales price of parcels sold during the quarter); administrative costs of $7,500 per quarter; property taxes of 1 percent at the end of the year (paid on the initial raw land value only). None of these latter items are to be funded in the loan.

a. Develop a total monthly sales schedule for Holsum. What will be Holsum's total revenue? Compute the loan repayment schedule. How many months will it take Holsum to fully repay the loan?

b. What will be the total interest carry funded in the loan amount? What will be the release price for each type of lot? What will be the total cash payments made by Holsum to the Last National Bank?

c. Should Holsum undertake this project if its required return on equity is 16 percent? (Hint: Do a cash flow analysis on a quarterly basis for the life of the project.) What will be the *IRR* on the project?

Appendix: Managing Interest Rate Risk

A. Financial Futures
B. Interest Rate Swaps
C. Interest Rate Caps

Most large real estate development and construction loans are floating rate loans. They are usually tied to a short-term interest rate, such as the prime interest rate. A margin or premium for additional risk is usually added to this rate in establishing the interest rate on the loan. Because the loans are made at a floating rate, the cost of funds to the developer is uncertain and interest rate risk is created. This appendix presents three approaches that developers may use when hedging with interest rate risk: using financial futures, interest rate swaps and interest rate caps.

Many developers prefer having some assurance that the actual interest carry during the development period will be close to the amount projected when the loan is made. In other words, they would like to immunize themselves against adverse movements in interest rates during development.[1] Because their primary business is development and not the management of financial assets and liabilities, many prefer to hedge away interest rate risk. However, like any other type of insurance, a price must be paid to compensate someone else for bearing this risk.

A. HEDGING WITH THE FINANCIAL FUTURES MARKET

Hedging in the financial futures market is accomplished in the very same way as hedging with any other commodity. However, rather than dealing in a fungible good such as corn or wheat, the good being used to hedge with is usually a security such as a Treasury bill or Treasury bond.

Futures contracts are standardized contracts that are traded on commodities exchanges much like common stocks are traded on the stock exchanges. All contracts traded have standard dollar size and standard expiration date. This standardization facilitates trading and brings together a market of buyers and sellers. The commodity exchange regulatory boards set the initial terms of contracts and periodically update them as necessary.[2] Because the futures contract involves future delivery or sale of a commodity, when a futures contract is purchased or sold each buyer and seller of a contract is required to make a margin deposit with the appropriate commodity clearing house. This is done to guarantee performance on their future contract in much the same way parties to a real estate transaction require earnest money as a measure of good faith.[3] In many cases, this

---

[1]To illustrate the importance of adverse movements in interest rates, recall that in the land development example shown in Chapter 18, we showed that Landco would earn an *NPV* of about $60,000. If the floating rate on the development loan increased by just 1 percent, the *NPV* would fall by approximately 80 percent.

[2]There are many exchanges where trading occurs in financial futures. The exchange with the greatest transaction volume is the Chicago Board of Trade.

[3]In the futures market, the size of the margin requirement will be determined by the policy of the brokerage through which the contracts are traded. This is unlike buying stock, where the margin is regulated by the Board of Governors of the Federal Reserve System.

deposit can be met by pledging securities or other interest-bearing assets in lieu of cash. This enables the developer to earn interest on the deposit, thereby reducing the cost of undertaking the hedge.

Developers trying to hedge against interest rate risk use what is known as a *short hedge* because they want to protect themselves against additional interest expense in the event of unanticipated increases in interest rates. When entering into a ''perfect'' short hedge,[4] the particular commodity, in this case money, is bought on the spot or cash market and a corresponding amount of the same commodity is simultaneously sold or ''shorted'' on the futures market (the actual details of this transaction will be discussed later). When the hedger no longer needs protection against risk and wants to close out the hedge, the particular commodity that is sold does not actually have to be delivered. Instead, because the futures contracts are standardized, a reversing trade is made and the obligation is met by ''covering'' the *short position* in the futures markets. Thus, the legal, or contractual, commitment to deliver the commodity may be met by purchasing an identical contract to close out the *futures position.*[5]

As mentioned previously, interest rate risk is usually hedged with financial futures. *Financial futures contracts* are currently traded on a variety of instruments such as securities issued by the U.S. Treasury, commercial paper, and GNMAs (Government National Mortgage Association). The choice of a futures instrument is very important to the developer and will ultimately determine the success of the hedge. For a hedge to be successful, the developer must choose a financial instrument that most closely tracks or correlates with the index that the floating rate on the loan is tied to.

Most interest rates on development and construction loans are tied to the prime rate. Unfortunately, there is no futures contract traded on the prime rate. However, several financial instruments that are traded have a high degree of correlation with the prime rate index. For example, T bills tend to track the prime rate fairly well and will be used in our example of how to hedge a development loan. In such cases, where the futures contract used to hedge and the price or interest rate that is being hedged are different but highly correlated, the hedge is known as a *cross-hedge*. This lack of perfect correlation creates a new type of risk: *basis* risk. Basis risk is created when a futures instrument such as a T bill is used to hedge a cash or spot instrument such as the prime rate where the two instruments are not perfectly correlated. The existence of basis risk creates another problem dealing with the quantity of contracts needed to conduct the hedge. That is, because (1) T bill contracts are being used to hedge against the prime rate and (2) interest rates on T bills are more volatile than the prime rate, more than an equivalent amount of T bills will have to be shorted to hedge against movement in the prime rate. The dollar quantity of contracts necessary to cross-hedge relative to the loan amount is called the *hedge ratio*. As will be seen in our first example, a cross-hedge will be necessary. A hedge ratio greater than 1 will also be required because interest rate movements in T bills are not matched exactly by the movement in the prime rate. We will *assume* that the hedge ratio of prime rate to T bills is 1 to 1.3; that is, in order to hedge $1 of a loan against prime rate movement, the developer must use $1.30 of T bill futures.

As an alternative to the prime rate, many developers have negotiated loan agreements with banks to base the interest rate on the loan on an index such as the T bill rate, which has a future

---

[4]A perfect hedge is one in which the underlying commodity at risk is the same as the commodity future used to complete the hedge. For example, if a banker decides to invest $1,000,000 in a Treasury bill three months from now, the risk of the T bill rates decreasing during that time can be hedged by selling a T bill futures contract short. Because both the future and the commodity are the same, that is T bills, the banker has hedged away interest rate risk perfectly.

[5]According to the commodity exchanges, about 98 percent of all futures transactions do not result in actual delivery but are closed prior to expiration.

traded on it, or the LIBOR rate, which is quoted daily and varies more closely with the T bill rate. In this way, a more perfect hedge can be executed.[6]

HEDGING INTEREST RATE RISK—A SIMPLIFIED EXAMPLE

Before we look at an actual hedging transaction, some of the mechanics of T bills and T bill futures trading merit discussion, since there are some significant differences between financial futures and commodity futures. The 90-day T bills are the shortest U.S. Treasury security issued and are considered to be risk-free. Individual T bills are sold in denominations of $10,000; however, futures are traded in lots of 100 T bills or $1,000,000. Individual T bills are traded with the interest discounted from the initial price, since there are no interim interest payments on these short-term financial instruments. Thus, a single 90-day T bill with an annual interest rate of 6 percent would sell "net" of interest or at a price of $9,850. This is determined as (.06 ÷ 4) or an annual rate of 6 percent compounded quarterly, which is equal to 1.5 percent. The quarterly rate of 1.5 percent times $10,000, results in a discount of $150. However, because all interest on the T bill will be paid at the time of maturity, the total amount received by the investor at maturity will be $10,000. Price quotations on futures are quoted net of the yield demanded by the investors at the time of purchase. However, when prices are quoted, all such yields are annualized. This means that a 90-day T bill futures contract for 100 T bills will have a dollar value of ($9,850) times (100), or $985,000 (remember that T bill futures trade in lots of 100 T bills); however, the contract price will be quoted as 94.00. This corresponds to the annualized yield of 6 percent subtracted from 100 percent. This method of quoting futures prices is done to facilitate comparisons with yields on other securities which are also converted to annual yields. In other words, rather than quoting a yield of 1.5 percent quarterly and a contract price of $985,000, the instrument is quoted at 94.00 which implies an annualized interest rate of 6 percent. Should the annualized expected yields on 90-day T bills suddenly change to 7.5 percent, the futures contract price would be quoted at 92.50, but the actual price would be $981,250.

When a developer "shorts" a T bill future, a promise is made to deliver one hundred 90-day T bills on the maturity date of the futures contract. The T bills that are delivered on that date must have an identical maturity to those shorted. Hence, those delivered will have 90 days until maturity as of the date that the transaction is covered. Thus, the "commodity" in this transaction is a T bill with a maturity of 90 days from the time of delivery from the futures contract.

For contracts with short maturities, the annualized interest rates implied by the futures price will be close to the "spot," or current, market price of T bills currently trading in the market. The two prices, however, will usually differ. Future contracts with the longest term to maturity will typically have prices significantly different from the spot price. This difference will depend on market expectations with respect to forward interest rates. In other words, if the market expects

---

[6]These rates are preferable to the prime rate if the developer wants to hedge because the prime rate is a rate charged by banks to their best corporate clients. The prime rate does not change daily because there is no trading; rather, banks change the rate up or down by one-quarter or one-half a percent as conditions warrant. Because the T bill has a futures contract available for trading, it would be the better choice to base the interest rate on. The LIBOR rate is the London InterBank Offered Rate. It is a rate quoted daily by five London money center banks for loans with terms of three months, six months, or one year. Because it is quoted daily, it also varies more than the prime rate. Both of these rates would be preferred to the prime rate for basing the interest rate. Using the LIBOR rate allows a better cross-hedge, thereby reducing basis risk. Using the interest rate on U.S. Treasury securities would be most preferable because T bill futures contracts can be used to create a perfect hedge and thus eliminate basis risk.

interest rates to rise substantially in the future, future T bill interest rates will be higher than yields implied by current cash or spot prices.

A numerical example will demonstrate the use of a financial hedge using the T bill futures to hedge a variable rate loan based on the prime. We will assume that the developer has an adequate amount of interest bearing securities to deposit as margin.

Date	Transaction
Jan. 1	A developer borrows $20,000,000 at 8 percent prime + 2 percent, or a total of 10 percent, from a bank for 90 days. To hedge interest rate risk, he sells 26 T bill futures contracts (the 26 comes from 20 times $1,000,000 T bill future contract size times the assumed T bill prime rate hedge ratio of 1:3 to 1). The annualized yield on the futures contract due in 90 days is 6.5 percent, and the spot rate is 6 percent (this implies that the market expects interest rates to increase during the next 90 days).
Jan. 2	The prime rate suddenly increases 1.5 percent to 9.5 percent, and T bill interest rates increase 1.00 percent to 7.5 percent. Both rates remain the same through March 31.
March 31	The developer repays the loan plus all interest and covers the futures position by purchasing 100 T bills to cover the short sale.

An increase of $75,000 in interest costs would have occurred because of the change in the prime rate. This increase in interest cost would occur if the developer does not hedge interest rate risk. Let us see how an offsetting futures transactions will reduce this cost.

Financial Analysis of Transactions

No hedging:
Budgeted loan interest
($20,000,000 times 10% times 3 months $\div$ 12) $500,000

Actual loan interest
($20,000,000 times 11.5% times 3 months) $575,000
Increase in interest costs if unhedged: $ 75,000

Interest rate hedged:
Proceeds from the short sale of T bill futures contracts on Jan. 1
$26,000,000[100% $-$ (6.5% $\times$ 90 $\div$ 360)] $25,577,500

Price paid to cover short sale, or to buy back, T bill futures contracts on March 31

$26,000,000[100% $-$ (7.5% $\times$ 90 $\div$ 360)] $-25,512,500
Gain on hedge transaction $ 65,000

As the transaction shows, the developer has offset a higher interest carry of $75,000 with a $65,000 gain in the T bill futures. All but $10,000 of the interest rate risk has been eliminated with the hedge. However, had interest rates declined, the developer will have *sacrificed* the opportunity of reduced interest costs in the project financing, for more predictable borrowing costs. However, as previously pointed out, the developer is not in the business of taking interest rate risk and may prefer to hedge this risk and concentrate on development.

In our example, the prime rate and T bill interest rate did not move together exactly, so the developer did not realize the full benefits of the reduction in interest costs because a cross-hedge had to be used. While a hedge ratio of 1.3 to 1 was used to compensate, some risk remained because of the lack of perfect correlation between the prime rate and T bill rate. Therefore, if developers could persuade banks to tie variable rate contribution loans to a T bill or T bond which is traded in the futures markets, basis risk could be completely eliminated.

Another type of risk that arises in construction and development situations comes about because the loan is not taken down all at once, but cash draws are made to finance the project. Therefore, the developer will not hedge an entire amount of the construction loan because full exposure to risk on the entire loan does not occur at any time. Consequently, hedging in real estate development usually consists of making a number of smaller hedges (referred to as sequential hedging) as draws are taken down. This results in additional complications.

The first problem arises because T bill futures may usually be purchased with delivery dates of up to a maximum period of only 24 months into the future. Therefore, if T bills are used, the developer may hedge for only 24 months at any given time. Other instruments such as Treasury notes and bonds could be considered because their maturity periods are longer than T bill contracts. While such securities might be used to construct a hedge for longer periods, their yield patterns are more indicative of longer maturity instruments. Because construction and development loans are tied to prime which is a short term rate, a more serious *basis* risk problem would arise, even though the period over which the hedge is desired may be better. Hence, for projects with lengthy development periods, a material amount of interest rate risk *may still remain* because of (1) the cross-hedge and (2) the differences in maturities on security type available to construct the hedge. Further, each minihedge has its own transaction and rollover costs. The transactions costs and paperwork involved might negate the benefits incurred in a hedge of this type. However, many developers use these types of hedges successfully, even with the above-mentioned risks.

Sequential Short Hedging

This section of the appendix illustrates the use of a *sequential short hedging* of draws made on a construction loan utilizing the financial futures market. (We should point out that this discussion also applies to any variable interest rate loan. If a floating rate loan is made to acquire an existing project only one short sale of T bills would be required corresponding to the period during which interest rate protection is needed. When making development and construction loans, many contracts must be shorted because the loan amount increases as draws are made.) The floating rate loan will be based on the prime rate, but T bills will be used as the financial futures instrument for the cross-hedge. The developer's loan will consist of $20 million of principal as in the last example, however, funds will be taken down in a series of monthly draws. The entire loan will mature one year from the time of initial takedown. The entire construction loan balance (including interest) will be due at the end of the year. Because the total loan amount outstanding consists of principal plus interest carry, the developer must hedge the draw amount plus the preceding month's loan balance on the first of each month.

Date	Transaction
Jan. 1	The developer arranges to borrow $20 million through his bank at prime + 2 percent for one year. At this time, the prime rate is 8 percent and the 90-day T bill rate is 6 percent. The developer's cash draw schedule calls for $2 million per month for the first eight months and $1 million per month for the next four months. The amount budgeted for interest is $1,256,534 based on the 10 percent rate prevailing at the time the loan is negotiated (see Exhibit 18A–1). The developer decides to hedge interest rate risk with T bill futures.
Feb. 1	The prime rate rises to 8.5 percent, and the T bill rate rises to 6.25 percent.
July 1	The prime rate rises again to 9.0 percent, and the T bill rate rises to 6.5 percent.
	During each month, T bill futures are assumed to trade at 10 basis points higher than the spot rate.

As shown in Exhibit 18A–1, if the developer did not hedge against interest rate risk and interest rates moved adversely, actual interest carry would be $1,366,709, or an overrun of $110,175. To demonstrate how this risk might be averted, the next section will detail a sequential short hedge. As in our previous example, equity margin requirements will not be considered because it is assumed that the developer has enough interest bearing collateral (T bills and the like) on deposit with the commodity broker.

Futures Transactions Needed for Sequential Short Hedging

Exhibit 18A–2 illustrates the way in which a sequential short hedge would be done. Column (*b*) contains the monthly amount to be hedged. It is derived from the previous month's balance plus the current month's direct cost draw. For example, the amount to be hedged on February 1 consists of the January loan balance of $2,016,667 plus the $2,000,000 direct cost draw made on February 1. Column (*c*) shows the number of futures contracts corresponding to the expected ending loan balance each month. The number of contracts shown for each month is determined by first, multiplying the monthly outstanding loan balance by the hedge ratio, which we assume to be 2.0 in this case. This result is then divided by the standard futures contract amount for T bills, or $1,000,000, times number of months corresponding to the maturity of the instrument being used to execute the hedge. In this case, 90-day T bills are being used.[7] Therefore the number of months

---

[7]Note that the difference in the T bill spot rate of 6.0 percent and futures rate of 6.10 percent indicates that the market expects a rate increase in interest rates over the 90-day T bill maturity period. This is because the spot rate, or annualized yield, on a T bill purchased today is 6.0 percent, while the rate on the same security with a 90-day maturity due for delivery 90 days from now is 6.10 percent. Similarly, over the hedge period, a security with a 90-day maturity to be delivered one year from now has a current expected yield of 6.75 percent.

EXHIBIT 18A–1   Budgeted and Actual Construction Loan Draws ahd Interest

---

I. Pro Forma Estimate of Construction Loan Draws and Interest Carry

Date	Direct Cost	Budgeted Floating Interest Rate	Budgeted Monthly Interest	Monthly Change in Loan Balance	Total Loan Balance
Jan.	$ 2,000,000	10.00%	$ 16,667	$2,000,000	$ 2,016,667
Feb.	2,000,000	10.00	33,472	2,016,667	4,050,139
Mar.	2,000,000	10.00	50,418	2,033,472	6,100,557
Apr.	2,000,000	10.00	67,505	2,050,418	8,168,062
May	2,000,000	10.00	84,734	2,067,505	10,252,796
June	2,000,000	10.00	102,107	2,084,734	12,354,903
July	2,000,000	10.00	119,624	2,102,107	14,474,527
Aug.	2,000,000	10.00	137,288	2,119,624	16,611,815
Sept.	1,000,000	10.00	146,765	1,137,288	17,758,580
Oct.	1,000,000	10.00	156,322	1,146,765	18,914,902
Nov.	1,000,000	10.00	165,958	1,156,322	20,080,860
Dec.	1,000,000	10.00	175,674	1,165,958	21,256,534
Total	$20,000,000		$1,256,534		

II. Actual Loan Account and Interest Carry

Date	Direct Cost	Actual Floating Interest Rate	Actual Monthly Interest	Monthly Change in Loan Balance	Toal Loan Balance
Jan.	$ 2,000,000	10.00%	$ 16,667	$2,000,000	$ 2,016,667
Feb.	2,000,000	10.50	35,146	2,016,667	4,051,813
Mar.	2,000,000	10.50	52,953	2,035,146	6,104,766
Apr.	2,000,000	10.50	70,917	2,052,953	8,175,683
May	2,000,000	10.50	89,037	2,070,917	10,264,720
June	2,000,000	10.50	107,316	2,089,037	12,372,036
July	2,000,000	11.00	131,744	2,107,316	14,503,780
Aug.	2,000,000	11.00	151,285	2,131,744	16,655,065
Sept.	1,000,000	11.00	161,838	2,151,285	17,816,903
Oct.	1,000,000	11.00	172,488	1,161,838	18,989,391
Nov.	1,000,000	11.00	183,236	1,172,488	20,172,627
Dec.	1,000,000	11.00	194,082	1,183,236	21,366,709
Total	$20,000,000		$1,366,709		

Variance between actual and budgeted interest carry: $ 110,175

---

until the bill matures is *three,* which becomes the divisor. To illustrate, in May we would have $10,168,062 times 2, or $20,336,324, divided by $1,000,000 times 3, or $3,000,000, yielding a result of 6.78. This result is rounded to 7 contracts.

Another question that must be answered deals with when and how many contracts must be shorted. Column (*d*) shows that 101 contracts will be shorted in January. The reason for this is

EXHIBIT 18A-2 Analysis of a Sequential Short Hedge

(a)	(b)	(c)	(d)	(e) T Bill Rates		(f) Futures Prices		(g) Futures $ Value		(h)
Date	Monthly Amount to Be Hedged	Number of Contracts	Contracts Shorted per Month	Spot	Futures	Monthly Open	Monthly Close	Monthly Open*	Monthly Close†	Net Gain from Futures
Jan. 1	$ 2,000,000	1	101	6.00%	6.10%	93.90	93.65	$99,459,750	$99,396,625	$ 63,125
Feb. 1	4,016,667	3	100	6.25	6.35	93.65	93.65	98,412,500	98,412,500	0
Mar. 1	6,050,139	4	97	6.25	6.35	93.65	93.65	95,460,125	95,460,125	0
Apr. 1	8,100,557	5	93	6.25	6.35	93.65	93.65	91,523,625	91,523,625	0
May 1	10,168,062	7	88	6.25	6.35	93.65	93.65	86,603,000	86,603,000	0
June 1	12,252,796	8	81	6.25	6.35	93.65	93.40	79,714,125	79,663,500	50,625
July 1	14,354,903	10	73	6.50	6.60	93.40	93.40	71,795,500	71,795,500	0
Aug. 1	16,474,527	11	63	6.50	6.60	93.40	93.40	61,960,500	61,960,500	0
Sept. 1	17,611,815	12	52	6.50	6.60	93.40	93.40	51,142,000	51,142,000	0
Oct. 1	18,758,580	13	40	6.50	6.60	93.40	93.40	39,340,000	39,340,000	0
Nov. 1	19,914,902	13	27	6.50	6.60	93.40	93.40	26,554,500	26,554,500	0
Dec. 1	21,080,860	14	14	6.50	6.60	93.40	93.40	13,769,000	13,769,000	0
Total		101						Total gain from futures		$113,750

Gains from futures transactions $113,750

Less losses from interest rate increases on loan (Exhibit 18A–1)   110,175

Total gain (loss) from hedge $ 3,575

*[101 × ($1,000,000)][100% − (6.10%) (90/360)] = $99,459,750

†[101 × ($1,000,000)][100% − (6.35%) (90/360)] = $99,396,625

because each hedge position is opened at the beginning of the month (see monthly open of $99,459,750 in column *g*) and is closed at the end of each month (see monthly close of $99,396,625 in column *g*). The short position must be closed at the end of each month even though the construction loan will mature at the end of 12 months. This is because it would be possible for the interest rate to change on the construction loan immediately after the first draw, then remain level until the end of December. If this happened, interest would be calculated at the higher rate on each subsequent monthly loan draw until the loan matures. This would cause actual interest expense on the construction loan draws to exceed expected interest expense by a substantial amount. In order to hedge against this possibility, the borrower must be sure that enough profit will be earned on the hedge as soon as interest rates change, to offset the possibility of higher interest costs on all draws made during the next 11 months. Profits from the short sale are then held in reserve to offset possible higher interest costs on all future draws. Therefore, by shorting 101 contracts at the beginning of January when the first loan draw is made, then covering by purchasing 101 contracts at the end of January, the borrower would be sure to earn enough profit on the hedge to cover higher interest charges on all future loans draws. Hence, in Exhibit 18A–2, we see that at the beginning of January, 101 contracts would be shorted. Assuming that (1) the *actual* interest rate on the construction loan increased to 10.5 (see Panel B of Exhibit 18A–1), and that the T bill futures rate increased to 6.35 percent, or 25 basis points (column (*e*) in Exhibit 18A–2), the borrower would cover the hedge by purchasing 101 contracts at the end of January for 93.65. The difference between the purchase price of 93.65 and the proceeds from the short sale price, or 93.90, would result in a profit of $63,125. This amount would be kept in reserve in the event that interest on all future draws would be charged at 10.5 percent instead of 10.0 percent.

The reader should also note that the number of contracts that must be shorted declines at the end of each month. The decline is equal to the number of contracts corresponding to the previous month's amount to be hedged shown in column (*c*). This decline occurs because even if interest rates continued to increase, profits on subsequent monthly short sales would only have to be equal to incremental changes in the construction loan interest rate times the outstanding loan balance at the end of any particular month until the loan reaches maturity.

Based on the pattern of actual interest rate changes on the construction loan (Panel B of Exhibit 18A–1), it can be seen that because of higher interest charges, the construction loan will be over-budget by $110,175. Profits from hedging based on changes in T bill futures prices as shown in Exhibit 18A–2 would be $113,750. Hence, profits from hedging exceed higher interest costs by $3,575 and the developer will have "locked in" a rate of interest in the range of 10 percent, as budgeted for.

Based on the assumptions made in the example, hedging will be successful regardless of what future interest rates actually turn out to be. As interest rates rise, profits from hedging will offset higher construction loan interest costs and as interest rates fall, losses from hedging will be offset by lower interest costs on the loan. However, it must be kept in mind that the success of this hedge is based on the fundamental assumption that the assumed hedge ratio of 2.0 adequately captures the relationship between interest rates on T bills and the prime rate (basis risk). If it does not, the developer stands to gain or lose accordingly.

In addition to basis risk, maturity risk also exists because the trading pattern of the T bills futures themselves. T-bills are usually only traded for a maximum maturity of 24 months. Because of this limitation, the developer cannot use these instruments to hedge loans longer than 24 months. Any loan amount outstanding after the 24 months would be at risk to an adverse interest rate move and as such would partially defeat the developer's purpose of the original hedge. For these reasons, developers undertaking large developments with long development periods with loans tied to the prime interest rate may prefer another method of hedging interest rate risk that is not subject to the same constraints as hedging with financial futures markets. The ideal hedge should have the same cash flow timing sequence and maturity that the loan does and should be based on the same floating rate index that the loan is indexed to. This problem leads us into the next section on *interest rate swaps,* a more recent innovation in financial markets.

B. INTEREST RATE SWAPS

The concept of an interest rate swap is relatively new; however, the market is rapidly growing. During 1988, total swap volume was in the range of $1 trillion. Swaps used in real estate lending represent a sizable portion of total swap volume. Basically, an interest rate swap is a transaction in which two firms trade individual financing advantages (sometimes through financial intermediaries) to produce more favorable borrowing terms for each. In the classic swap, the holder of floating rate debt seeks to reduce interest rate exposure by swapping variable payments on the debt for fixed payments. The firm holding fixed rate debt seeks to match a liability that carries a variable repayment pattern with an asset that produces a variable stream of income by swapping a series of fixed payments for floating payments based on variable rate debt. In order for both parties to benefit from the swap, one party must have a comparative advantage in either the short- or long-term credit market. The mechanics of an interest rate swap may be illustrated with an example.

In this example, there are two parties. The first party, a large insurance company, would like to borrow funds at floating interest rates to make interest payments on liabilities to policy beneficiaries who have retirement contracts based on variable investment rates. The second party, such as a developer, would like to borrow fixed rate money to eliminate interest rate risk associated with construction loan borrowing at a rate tied to the prime. As stated above, each party hopes to benefit from the interest rate swap because of a comparative advantage that each one has in the financial market. This comparative advantage may exist because of differences in lender assessment of risk between the larger insurance company and relatively smaller developer in short-term and long-term credit markets.

To illustrate, an insurance company may be able to borrow floating rate funds from a bank at a prime rate of 8 percent + 0.5 percent, whereas the land developer would have to pay a higher rate, say prime 8 percent + 2 percent or 10 percent, for the same loan amount. Similarly, the insurance company may be able to issue fixed rate long-term bonds for 9 percent, but for a long-term fixed rate loan the land developer must pay 12.5 percent. Based on these borrowing relationships, the longer-term bond market which provides fixed rate financing requires a larger percentage differential from the land developer than does the short-term, floating rate credit market. This differential arises because investors providing funds to the long-term credit markets have a different perception of risk relative to long-term lending to the developer compared to that of the insurance company. Therefore, the 1.5 percent short-term floating rate differential widens to 3.5 percent in the longer-term fixed rate market. It is the net differential of 2.0 percent in this case (see Exhibit 18A–3) that could make a swap economically advantageous for both and will ultimately lower the cost of obtaining funds for *both* parties.

To begin the analysis of the swap process, we assume that the following sequence of events occurs:

Transaction 1	The land developer borrows $20 million from the bank for three years at a floating rate equal to a prime rate of 8 percent + 2 percent. (The developer could borrow at a fixed rate of 12.5 percent if desired.)
Transaction 2	The insurance company issues $20 million of three-year bonds at a fixed rate of 9 percent. (The insurance company

Transaction 3

could borrow at a floating prime rate of 8 percent + 0.5 percent.)

The two companies swap *interest payments*. Assuming that each party swapped payments based on their respective cost of borrowing, the net result would be as follows:

	Interest Payment after Swap	Interest Payment w/no Swap	Savings (Loss)
Developer	9.0%	12.5%	3.5%
Insurance Co.	10.0	8.5	(1.5)

It is clear that the developer would gain from a swap as longer-term funds at a fixed rate of interest would be acquired at a savings of 3.5 percent less than if the developer borrowed directly. However, this case shows that the insurance company would not benefit from the swap because it would be paying 1.5 percent more for variable interest payments than it could obtain by borrowing directly at 8.5 percent. Clearly, this swap would not work for the insurance company. However, if an arrangement could be made such that the insurance company could charge the developer a *premium* for the privilege of swapping for a fixed interest payment, while still making both the insurance company and developer better off (by lowering their respective interest costs below 8.5 percent and 12.5 percent), respectively, then a swap could be consummated.

To examine the potential for charging premiums and conducting a swap, we again refer to Exhibit 18A–3. In the exhibit we note that the developer cannot afford to pay more than a premium of 3.5 percent in addition to the rate obtained on the 9 percent fixed payment swap because the total cost would be 12.5 percent, or equal to the cost of raising funds directly. Alternatively, the insurance company must receive a premium greater than 1.5 percent, since the 10 percent cost of swapping for a variable payment stream exceeds the 8.5 percent cost of raising funds directly. Hence, the premium that the insurance company may charge must be greater than 1.5 percent but less than 3.5 percent. If the premium was 2.5 percent, for example, the cost of funds to the developer after the swap would be 9 percent + 2.5 percent, or 11.5 percent, which is less than 12.5 percent. The cost to the insurance company after the swap would be $10\% - 2.5\% = 7.5\%$. Hence, both parties would be able to reduce borrowing costs by 1 percent and obtain the floating rate and fixed rate funds that each desires. More formally we define

$DIWS$ = developer fixed interest rate with swap
$DINS$ = developer fixed interest rate if no swap occurs
$IIWS$ = insurance company variable interest rate with swap
$IINS$ = insurance variable interest rate if no swap occurs
P = premium charged by insurance company

EXHIBIT 18A–3   Interest Rate Swaps (interest rate differentials: fixed rate versus floating rate credit markets)

	Short-Term Floating Rate	Longer-Term Fixed Rate
Developer	10.0%	12.5%
Insurance Company	8.5	9.0
Difference	1.5	3.5

The swap can occur if

$$\text{DIWS} + P < \text{DINS} \text{ and } \text{IIWS} - P < \text{IINS}$$

If *IINS* < *IIWS* and *DIWS* > *DINS*, then *P* will be in the range of

$$\text{DINS} - \text{DIWS} > P > \text{IIWS} - \text{IINS}$$

One obvious issue that should come to mind is whether a premium of the type just discussed can persist over the long run as more firms realize that such an arbitrage opportunity exists between short-run variable rate markets and long-term fixed rate markets. Indeed, as more firms enter the market for swaps, it could follow that a smaller premium may be charged, thereby reducing the interest cost savings of the insurance company in our example.

Forward Swaps—Construction & Development Loans

With the basic foundation for the swap concept having been detailed in the previous section, an example of how such an agreement would be applied to a construction and development loan is detailed in this section. Referring back to Exhibit 18A–1, recall that the budgeted interest carry for the construction loan with a 10 percent interest rate on 12 monthly draws was $1,256,534. However, as explained earlier this is a floating interest rate loan subject to change at any time, hence the interest carry could change dramatically. Instead of using the futures market to hedge, we will assume that the borrower enters the *swap market* and agrees to exchange the variable interest payments on the construction loan for fixed payments with a counterparty who desires to make the exchange. In order to facilitate the draw pattern on the construction loan, however, a swap agreement will be made with *delays in the payment swaps* so that interest payments due from the developer will correspond to monthly draws on the construction loan which includes the budgeted interest carry. Hence, based on the pattern of draws and borrowed interest shown in Exhibit 18A–1 (part I), the developer will agree on January 1, to swap twelve monthly interest payments based on $2,000,000 of swap principal beginning in January. The amount of the twelve swap payments will be $17,000 or $2,000,000 × (.102 ÷ 12) as shown in Exhibit 18A–4. The next amount on which swap payments will be based is the increase in the monthly loan balance at the beginning of February or $2,016,667 (the sum of February's draw of $2,000,000 plus $16,667 in borrowed interest from January). Eleven swap payments will be made in the amount of $17,310 or $2,016,667 × (.103 ÷ 12). Total swap payments during February will be $34,310, or the sum of $17,000 committed to in January plus $17,310 in February. Total swap payments will amount to $1,324,202 over the entire loan period. This amount will be known with certainty because the series of fixed interest rates that will be charged on each of the swaps by the counterparty are established *as of the date of the swap agreement*. Hence, the pricing schedule shown in Exhibit 18A–4, beginning with 10.20 percent for the series of 12 swap payments and ending with 11.3 percent for 1 swap payment delayed until December, is agreed upon on the date that the swap agreement is made. The reason why the interest rate series charged for the swap increases is because of the delays built into the swap agreement.[8]

---

[8]In practice, swaps are usually constructed whereby actual interest payments are made quarterly, or semi-annually. We use monthly flows here to compare this method with the hedging examples used in the previous section. Actually, prices in the swap market are usually based on spreads over Treasury securities corresponding to the maturity period over which interest rate risk protection is desired. When delays in swap payments are built into the agreement, the counterparty usually demands a premium because a forward commitments on interest rates are being made today on payments that will be made in the future.

EXHIBIT 18A–4   Pro Forma Monthly Budget—Forward Swap Transaction (calculation of principal)

Date	(a) Monthly Change in Loan Balance (swap principal)	(b) Interest Rate on Swap	(c) Monthly Swap Payments	(d) Budgeted Monthly Interest	(e) Difference (c) − (d)	(f) Net Cash to Borrower— Direct Cost Draws Minus (e)
Jan.	$2,000,000	10.20%	$ 17,000	$ 16,667	$ 333	$1,999,667
Feb.	2,016,667	10.30	34,310	33,472	838	1,999,162
Mar.	2,033,472	10.40	51,933	50,418	1,515	1,998,485
Apr.	2,050,418	10.50	69,874	67,505	2,369	1,997,631
May	2,067,505	10.60	88,137	84,734	3,403	1,996,597
June	2,084,734	10.70	106,726	102,107	4,619	1,995,381
July	2,102,107	10.80	125,645	119,624	6,021	1,993,979
Aug.	2,119,624	10.90	144,898	137,288	7,610	1,992,390
Sept.	1,137,288	11.00	155,323	146,765	8,558	991,442
Oct.	1,146,765	11.10	165,931	156,322	9,609	990,391
Nov.	1,156,322	11.20	176,723	165,958	10,765	989,235
Dec.	1,165,958	11.30	187,702	175,674	12,028	987,972
Total			$1,324,202	$1,256,534	$67,668	
Effective cost of swap		10.54%				

How well would the borrower do with the swap hedge against interest rate risk? Note that in Exhibit 18A–4 total swap payments made to the counterparty under the swap agreement should be $1,324,202. The counterparty would have assumed variable payments on the construction loan. As shown in Exhibit 18A–1, if no change in interest rates would have actually occurred and the interest rate remained at 10 percent, then total interest paid by the counterparty would have been $1,256,534 (part I). Hence, the swap would have cost the developer $67,668 and would have been unnecessary. On the other hand, if interest rates would have changed as shown in part II of Exhibit 18A–1 the developer would have paid $1,366,709 in interest, hence, $42,507 would have been *saved* with the swap. Clearly in the latter situation, the developer would have been better off with the swap. The reader should also note that the effective interest rate on the construction loan hedged with the swap agreement is 10.54 percent. This is calculated by finding the internal rate of return on the monthly net cash flows received by the developer (cost draws less the excess of swap payments over interest draws) shown in column *f* of Exhibit 18A–4, less the repayment of loan principal from the permanent loan as budgeted ($21,256,534).[9]

Because the concept of one company exchanging interest payments with another may be foreign to many, several of the more interesting special aspects of interest rate swaps are mentioned.

1. Because the two parties exchange only the interest payments, and no swapping of principal is involved, the only amount at risk is the amount of interest payable. In the case of a default by one of the parties, the swap agreement would be nullified and each party would once again be responsible for its interest payment to its lender. This is a desirable feature because the idea of

[9]The reader should refer to Chapter 17 and the appendix to Chapter 17 for an explanation of how to calculate the effective interest cost in a construction loan.

interest swapping is to reduce interest rate risk and not change default risk. The swap partners would probably not enter a transaction whereby all are effectively trading interest rate risk for default risk.

2. Because there is no exchange of principal, the maximum default risk incurred by either party is the difference between the floating rate and fixed rate. At the present time, many of these swaps are done through intermediaries and not directly (as assumed in our simplified example). Many third party intermediaries offer protection against *interest payment default,* further limiting risk. This service is provided for a fee in the form of a flat rate, up front fee.

3. Because the swap is not considered to be a contingent liability, and the risk is unquantifiable, the transaction is done entirely on an off-balance sheet and as such does not negatively impact any financial ratios.[10] This provides confidentiality to the parties involved, but it does tend to make regulation and control by federal agencies difficult, if not impossible.

C. INTEREST RATE CAPS

In both of the preceding sections we have introduced basic approaches to hedging interest rate risk. We have shown that protection against upward movements in interest rates can be achieved (for a price) by using interest rate futures contracts or swapping interest rate payments based on one, or many, loan principal amounts. While both of these approaches are effective (with interest rate swaps being the preferred approach at the present time), the developer does not benefit from declines in interest rates under either. In other words when hedging with interest futures, as interest rates rise, profits from the futures hedge offset increases in interest costs on the variable rate loan. When rates decline, *losses* will occur on the futures transactions and offset savings in interest on the variable rate construction loan. Similarly, when using a swap agreement the interest rate or series of rates are "locked in" as of the date of the swap agreement. Hence, the developer is protected from upward movements in rates but loses the benefits should rates fall.

To allow the developer to profit from declines in interest rates and still buy some "up side" interest rate protection, a financial arrangement can be entered into between a developer and another party who agrees to sell an *interest rate cap.* In other words, the developer makes a variable rate construction loan and enters into an interest rate cap agreement, whereby the developer makes all payments as long as interest rates remain below the capped rate (say 11 percent). Should the rate ever exceed 11 percent, the counterparty agrees to pay the difference between payments required at prevailing rates and 11 percent. Hence with the cap, the developer purchases *upside protection only.* Benefits from downside movement in interest rates would be realized by the developer should interest rates decline on the construction loan.

When purchasing a cap, the fee is usually charged "up front". Hence, the borrower may easily calculate what the *maximum* interest cost will be on floating rate loans when an interest rate cap has been purchased. For example, if a cap is purchased for a one-year loan at a cost of 76 basis points and the rate is capped at 11 percent, then the maximum interest rate that can ever be paid by the developer for any loan amount would be:

$$1.00 - .0076 = (.11 \div 12) \ (MPVIFA, \ ?\%, \ 12 \ \text{months.})$$
$$+ \ 1.00 \ (MPVIF, \ ?\%, \ 12 \ \text{months.})$$
$$.992400 = .009167 \ (MPVIFA, \ ?\%, \ 12 \ \text{months.})$$
$$+ \ 1.00 \ (MPVIF, \ ?\%, \ 12 \ \text{months.})$$

---

[10]As of early 1987, the accounting profession does not even require that the swaps be footnoted in financial statements. However, this may be subject to further review.

This formulation is very similar to solving for the effective costs of borrowing discussed many times before except that payments in this case are interest only. Solving for ?%, yields .984158, which when multiplied by 12 = 11.81 percent.[11] Hence, if the borrower purchased an 11 percent interest rate cap for 76 basis points, the *maximum* effective interest rate that would be paid would be 11.81 percent. Obviously if interest rates increased above, or averaged over 11.81 percent during the 12-month period, the borrower made a wise choice in purchasing the cap. Further, the borrower would profit from any downside movements in interest rates by saving on the construction loan.

Swaps, Caps, and Floating Interest Rates Compared

Based on the preceding two examples, we have established that borrowers facing variable interest rates when obtaining loans can hedge all or a part of their interest rate risk. To compare the latter two approaches (swaps and caps) the reader should refer to Exhibit 18A–5.

To illustrate the trade-offs between using swaps, caps and floating rates when financing, Exhibit 18A–5 shows the effective cost of each under different interest rate scenarios. If, for example, a borrower wanted a one-year financing commitment and considered making a floating rate loan, the effective cost of floating rate financing could vary over a wide range (a range of 3 percent to 15 percent is used for purposes of illustration only). Alternatively, as our previous example indicated, the borrower could have entered into an interest rate swap agreement thereby locking in a 10.54 percent effective cost over the term of the loan. With a swap then, insurance against interest rate risk for the year could be purchased at a cost of 54 basis points over the prevailing prime rate of 10 percent. Exhibit 18A–5 shows, if over the one year term, the average of floating rates turns out to be greater than 10.54 percent, the borrower would be worse off without the swap, and vice versa.

As an alternative to the swap, a borrower could have purchased an interest rate cap of 11 percent for approximately 76 basis points upfront. Under this arrangement, the borrower would pay the floating rate up to a maximum of 11 percent interest, the point at which the rate would be capped. The maximum effective interest cost that the borrower would pay in this case would not exceed 11.81 percent (11 percent, plus a fee of 76 basis points). This means that if the average of floating rates over the term exceeded 11.81 percent, the borrower would be better off with the cap as opposed to the floating rate.[12] If the average interest rate exceeded 10.54 percent, the borrower would be better off with the swap when compared to the cap. This also means, however, that if the borrower wanted to purchase protection against interest rate risk and the floating rate averaged below 9.74, the cap would have been the better choice (see the point of intersection of the swap

---

[11] A calculator solution can be easily found by entering the following .992400 = *PV*, .009167 = *PMT*, 1.00 = *FV*, 12 = *n*, then calculate *i* and multiply by 12 to get the annual rate. If the term of the cap is greater than one year, *n* should be increased by the number of periods and *PV* will be lower to reflect a higher fee.

[12] In order to reduce the cost of *buying* an interest rate cap, many developers may also choose to *sell* a floor. This works as follows: The developer would agree to a minimum interest rate that would be paid on the loan principal regardless of what actual interest rates are. Hence, if the borrower agreed to sell a 9 percent floor to a counterparty, should interest rates fall below 9 percent, the borrower would continue to pay 9 percent to the counterparty. The counterparty would make payments should rates fall below 9 percent and realize a profit from any declines in rates below the floor rate. The proceeds that a borrower earns by selling a floor can be used to offset the cost of the cap and interest rate risk would be confined to a maximum and minimum range. These maximum and minimum rates are said to comprise an interest rate "collar", which has been created by purchasing the cap and selling the floor. However, in practice, the use of floors in real estate lending has not been used to a significant extent.

EXHIBIT 18A–5   Relative Cost of Hedging Alternatives

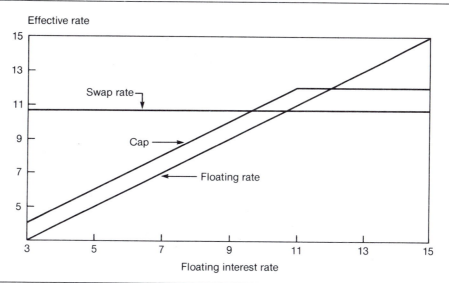

and cap rate curves relative to the horizontal axis).[13] Hence, the trade-off between a swap and an interest rate cap becomes clear. If a cap is purchased, the borrower still benefits from downward movements in interest rates. If a swap is purchased, the developer locks in a fixed rate but does not benefit if rates decline. Under either approach, however, the borrower obtains protection from potentially harmful interest rate risk.

After considering this analysis, one might ask "why not make a fixed interest rate loan?" This would eliminate the problem of interest rate risk from the borrowers perspective and no hedging would be necessary. There are a few additional considerations concerning why hedging may be desirable that should be made here. First, depending on market conditions and interest rate volatility, lenders may be generally unwilling to make fixed interest rate loans. Second, in the case of relatively straightforward permanent financing such as in the financing of an existing building which requires the disbursement of a single cash outflow at closing, fixed rate financing is certainly an option.

However, when *construction* and *development* loans are made and funds are taken down in draws over time, construction lenders have usually been unwilling to commit to fixed rate financing on each draw. This is because lenders view cash draws as the equivalent of a series of separate loans being made at future dates. The cost of funds that they will use to fund future loan draws can change if general interest rates change. Hence, they want to be able to change current rates on these draws, just as though they were making new loans. For this reason they are very reluctant to make a fixed interest rate commitment unless they can match such loan draws against a source of funds (deposit) that are equal in amount, have a known interest rate and have a maturity equal to the construction loan period. Finally, even if such a fixed rate loan is made, lenders will generally require that if such a loan is prepaid, that the borrower pay a penalty for doing so. This is because

---

[13] For the interested reader, 9.74 can be determined with a financial calculator as follows:
   $(1.00 - .0076) = PV$, $n = 12$, $FV = 1.00$, $(10.54 \div 12) = i$, compute $PMT \times 12$.

if the lender has been able to match the loan with a source of funds having a fixed cost and maturity and interest rates suddenly decline, the borrower will prepay the loan. The lender will be faced with the problem of having to reinvest funds at an interest rate below that of the fixed cost as funds that were initially used to match the loan. Because of this, lenders will include a provision in the loan agreement allowing them to charge a penalty. This penalty is usually based on a "yield maintenance" formula. This amounts to a penalty, such that when added to the income available at reinvestment rates available to the lender at the time of prepayment (usually specified as rates on Treasury Bonds with maturities equal to the remaining years to maturity on the fixed rate loan being prepaid, plus some premium) will make the remaining yield on reinvested amounts equal to the initial rate on the fixed rate loan. In this way, the lender does not lose any yield if the loan is prepaid and funds must be reinvested at interest rates that have declined.

In contrast to the fixed interest rate loan, when prepaying a swap the counterparty in the swap is likely to have the same problem as a fixed rate lender if such an agreement is terminated early. The counterparty has most likely used a source of funds to match the variable payments that have been assumed by the counterparty and early termination may present a reinvestment problem. In essence, if the borrower, who is making the fixed interest rate payments under a swap, wants to terminate the swap, another borrower must be found who is willing to enter into a swap for the remaining term of the agreement. Further, the party who is making the floating rate payments will benefit when interest rates decline and that party certainly does not want to assume the fixed payments based on a higher fixed interest rate. In order to induce someone to assume the fixed payments based on interest rates that are higher than prevailing rates, the borrower must pay a fee to the party assuming the higher fixed rate payments. This fee would be equal to the present value of the difference between remaining fixed payments based on prevailing interest rates and those made under the swap agreement, discounted at the prevailing swap rate for the remaining term of the swap agreement.

PROBLEMS

A–1. A developer must borrow $5 million on April 1 from the bank to finance a project for three months. The bank offers the loan at a floating rate of prime + 3 percent. The prime rate is at 10 percent, and the bank expects full repayment of *both* principal and the interest at the end of the loan period. One day after the developer receives the money, the prime rate increases to 10.5 percent.

  a. Calculate the developer's interest cost for the full term of the loan, given the increase in the prime rate.

  b. Assume that the developer wanted to hedge interest rate risk and that the T bill–prime rate hedge ratio is 1.20:1. How many T bill futures must the developer purchase? (Assume that there are no transaction costs on the purchase of T bill futures.)

  c. The developer is considering a hedge to reduce interest rate risk. What would be the total possible gain (loss) due to the change in the prime rate from 10 percent to 10.5 percent? If T bills are used, would this be a perfect hedge? Why or why not?

  d. Present an analysis of the hedging transaction. Assume that the initial rate on the spot T bill was 8 percent, and it increased to 8.5 percent on the day that the prime went up. Also, assume that the futures T bill interest rate demands a premium of five basis points (.05 percent) over the spot rate (there are 100 basis points in a percentage point). Remember that on the expiration of the futures, the spot rate and the futures rate will be the same.

A–2. Mead development company borrows $7.2 million on July 1 to finance a nine-month construction project. The bank will lend Mead the entire amount at prime + 1.75 percent compounded monthly, and Mead will take down the $7.2 million in nine equal monthly draws commencing July 1. The entire loan plus interest is to be paid at the loan's maturity. Initially, the prime rate was 10 percent, but it increased to 10.25 percent on July 2, where it remained until September 30. It rose again to 10.5 percent, where it remained for the remainder of the loan period.

    a. Calculate Mead's budgeted interest cost and actual interest cost. What is the difference between the two costs? What does this difference represent?

    b. Suppose that Mead decides to hedge away its interest rate risk by using T bills. How many T bill futures contracts will it have to sell for each monthly draw if it takes $1.25 of T bill futures to hedge $1.00 of prime rate price movement? Assume that the size of the T bill futures contracts is $1,000,000 and that Mead does not incur any transaction costs with the futures transaction.

    c. If Mead decided to use T bill futures to hedge its interest rate risk, what would be the gain from the futures portion of the hedge? Would this gain offset the loss from the increases in interest rates? Why or why not? (Assume that the spot T bill interest rate always remained 200 basis points below the prime and that the T bill futures rate was always at a 10-basis–point premium to the spot except at expiration when the spot rate equals the futures rate.)

A–3. Barnes Development Company can borrow $10,000,000 for a three-year project development from its bank at either a floating rate of LIBOR + 2 percent (LIBOR stands for *London InterBank Offered Rate*) or a fixed rate of 11.375 percent. A large pension fund would like to borrow $10,000,000 for three years also. It can either issue three-year bonds at 9.25 percent or borrow floating rate funds at LIBOR + 0.325 percent.

    a. What are the fixed rate differentials for the developer and the pension fund? What are the floating rate differentials?

    b. If the pension fund and Barnes development decided to swap interest payment and the pension fund required a fixed payment from Barnes, what is the maximum fee that Barnes could make to the pension fund and still be better off after the swap? What is the minimum fee that the pension fund must charge in order to benefit from the transaction? Demonstrate a case where the swap can occur and both parties benefit.

A–4 Placid Development Company would like to develop a property. It plans to borrow $6,000,000 in draws of $1,000,000 each for the next six months. It can make a standard construction loan at 10 percent interest (floating rate tied to prime) or can execute a series of delayed swaps with an initial rate of 10.2 percent and a schedule of rates increasing at .1 percent per month thereafter.

    a. What would be the effective cost of the swap?

    b. If the prime rate increased .5 percent at the end of the third month after the loan agreement was made, how would the cost of the floating rate loan compare to the cost of the swap?

A–5 Walton Investment Company must decide how to hedge interest rate risk on a $10,000,000 loan that it is using to purchase a property. It expects to need this financing for three years. It can (1) make a floating rate loan beginning at 10 percent interest, (2) it can make the floating rate loan and enter a swap agreement at a cost of 65 additional basis points, or (3) it can purchase an interest rate cap which would limit the monthly interest payments on the loan to 12 percent interest. The cap would cost 150 basis points.

    a. What would be the maximum effective interest cost payable if the cap is purchased?

    b. Under what conditions would the borrower be better off with the floating interest rate as opposed to the swap?

    c. What would the average floating interest rate have to be to make the cap preferable to the swap?

PART V

Institutional Sources of Funds and the Secondary Mortgage Market

Chapter 19

Sources of Mortgage and Equity Financing for Real Estate—Part I

This chapter serves as an introduction to the sources of funds that are available to finance the acquisition of existing properties (both residential and income producing) and the development of new properties. It includes a discussion of the sources of funds available for mortgage lending and the major institutional participants in the market for mortgage loans. The description of institutions is based on the types of loans in which they specialize their lending activity. In addition, the major causes of instability in the availability of mortgage credit from period to period are investigated.

FLOW OF FUNDS AND THE FINANCIAL SYSTEM

To understand the nature of the mortgage market, it is helpful to place it in context with other financial markets in our economy. Generally, when referring to financial markets, a distinction is made between *money* markets and *capital* markets. Money markets are usually defined as markets for financial claims with maturities of less than one year. Examples of claims with maturities of less than one year include U.S. Treasury bills, some securities of U.S. government agencies, and commercial paper issued by corporations. Capital markets generally refer to markets in which obligations with maturities greater than one year are bought and sold. Examples of these obligations include corporate bonds and stocks, mortgages, long-term bonds issued by the federal government, and long-term bonds issued by state and local governments. The stock market, bond market, and mortgage market can be thought of as component parts of capital markets.

While it is sometimes useful to analyze money and capital markets separately, a basic understanding of our financial system can be obtained through flow of funds analysis. Flow of funds analysis integrates money and capital markets into a framework that enables one to trace the primary flows between economic sectors in the economy. Exhibit 19–1 contains a simplified flow of funds diagram that enables one to trace money and capital flows from sources that supply funds to economic units that use or demand funds.

EXHIBIT 19–1   Simplified Flow of Funds Diagram

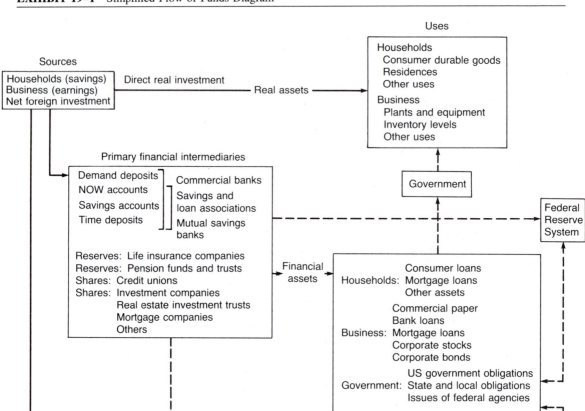

Sources and Uses of Funds

Over any given period of time, the primary sources of funds available for investment include savings of households and earnings from business.[1] Determinants of savings include the amount of income earned during the period and the amount of current consumption of that income. The amount consumed partially depends on interest that can be earned on income not consumed, or savings, and expected price levels. Determinants of business earnings are generally governed by competitive forces governing sales, cost of output, and expected capital investment less necessary dividend payments to investors. What remains after dividend payments is the amount of saving that business has for future investment.

---

[1] More specifically, this includes retained earnings plus capital consumption allowances.

Primary uses of funds are shown in the upper right-hand corner of Exhibit 19–1. Part of the demand for funds comes from households desiring to acquire consumer durable goods, (such as automobiles and appliances) and to construct, remodel, and renovate residences. In addition, businesses requiring expansion in production facilities, (new plants and machinery) and increases in inventory levels, result in an additional demand for funds. Therefore, a considerable amount of funds generated by businesses and households as sources is invested directly in real assets,[2] as shown at the top of the figure.

Channels of Funds Flows

One of the main purposes of the diagram in Exhibit 19–1 is to show how funds provided by individual households and businesses are channeled to other individual households and businesses, and perhaps government, which demand funds in excess of their current levels of savings and earnings. Many households and businesses that provide funds may not invest exactly the amount of funds at their disposal in real assets. Those households and businesses will have an excess or surplus of funds during any period. However, other households and businesses will have a need for funds in excess of amounts which they can derive from their own sources. Consequently, during any given time, some individual households and businesses will be seeking funds to use for investment in real assets while others will have excess funds the use of which they are willing to sell. Government at the federal, state, and local levels may also enter the market for funds, depending on their respective budgetary-expenditure patterns over a given time.[3]

To raise the necessary funds, households, business, and government create financial claims and obligations. For households these claims usually take the form of consumer and mortgage loans. Businesses generally make business and mortgage loans and issue stock, commercial paper, and bonds while government agencies usually issue bonds, bills, and notes.[4] These financial claims become *financial assets* for lenders who will supply funds for some specified period and earn either interest or dividends in return for the use of funds.[5] A summary listing of financial assets used by households, business, and government to raise funds in money and capital markets is shown in the lower right-hand corner of Exhibit 19–1.

Financial assets can be sold to suppliers of funds directly through the various bond or stock markets (see direct financial investment arrow at the bottom of Exhibit 19–1).[6]

---

[2]Real assets are meant here to include stocks of physical goods which are expected to produce a flow of services over time.

[3]Whether government enters the market for funds depends in large part on tax revenues and expenditures. If a governmental unit runs a budgetary deficit over a given period, it must raise funds. On the other hand, if a unit runs a budgetary surplus, it will enter the market to retire outstanding obligations from preceding periods.

[4]Depending on the maturity of these financial claims, they may be classified as money market instruments or capital market instruments.

[5]We refer here to new issues or additional amounts of financial assets only. Existing issues of stocks, bonds, and so on, that are traded among individuals provide no net increase in funds to households and businesses seeking to expand or invest in real assets.

[6]A direct purchase will generally require the services of a broker or investment banking firm. Nonetheless, in our discussion, it still constitutes a direct purchase.

However, most funds, available for investment in financial assets are channeled through financial intermediaries.

Financial Intermediaries and Funds Flow

Because direct financial investment of savings by households (shown at the bottom of Exhibit 19–1) requires (1) knowledge of financial assets (how to buy securities and other financial assets), (2) a willingness to take certain risks (price fluctuation on securities or default by the issuer), (3) some minimum amount of funds to buy certain financial assets (mortgages, for example), and (4) the necessary underwriting knowledge to make large business loans, mortgage loans, and so on, it is usually not practical for most households to invest in financial assets directly.[7] Most individuals do not meet one or more of these four criteria because of the specialization required to underwrite or purchase assets, or because they have small savings balances which they do not want to risk losing. Consequently, financial intermediaries have developed that specialize in (1) consolidating many small amounts of savings from individuals and making large loans (mortgages, business loans, etc.), (2) diversifying funds over many different types of financial assets so as not to risk all funds in one investment, and (3) underwriting and studying characteristics associated with investments which require managerial expertise. Clearly all of these functions could not be performed by individual households.

In the middle of Exhibit 19–1 an abbreviated list of major financial intermediaries and their primary methods of attracting savings from households is provided. Basically each institution, either by design or by government regulation, offers a certain inducement such as interest, dividends, or a service in return for savings flows. These flows are then aggregated and invested in a diversified portfolio of financial assets (loans, mortgages, bonds, etc.) on which a return is earned by the intermediary.[8] The intermediary, in turn, pays individual households in the form of interest, service, and so forth, for the use of savings flows and earns a profit for performing this intermediation function. As we will see later, the degree to which households choose to use financial intermediaries or purchase financial assets directly can drastically affect funds available for mortgage lending.

Government Debt and Financial Markets

Government influence is felt in financial markets when that sector (particularly the federal government) increases a budgetary deficit or surplus. Deficits occur when tax receipts

---

[7]Businesses with surplus funds also face some of these problems. However, these surpluses tend to be very short term in nature. Because of the dynamic nature of the economy, individual firms with surpluses in one period may be large borrowers in the next. Hence, most firms keep surplus funds in short-term investments. Since our focus here is on the mortgage market, which is a long-term capital market, we are more interested in long-term sources of savings. Hence, our discussion centers more on households.

[8]Most intermediaries are highly regulated by either state or federal government as to the types of financial assets they may invest in. This discussion must be interpreted by the reader in general terms at this point.

fall short of expenditures (see the government section in Exhibit 19–1). To finance a deficit, government, like households and business, must borrow by creating financial claims, since it is a net user of funds. When such deficits occur at the federal level, debt obligations are issued consisting of short-term U.S. Treasury bills, notes, and bonds which are bought by individuals and intermediaries. When budgetary receipts exceed expenditures, a surplus occurs. In this event, government usually repurchases obligations issued in previous periods or adds to the flow of funds.[9]

The impact of government deficits on financial markets partially depends on the magnitude of the deficit and its timing. If a large governmental deficit occurs simultaneously with rapid business expansion, for example, there is a tendency for interest rates on financial assets to increase in the short run, as households and businesses compete with the government for funds. On the other hand, in periods of declining economic activity, such deficits are used to stimulate investment in the business sector through increased government spending. In the latter case, the impact on interest rates tends to be slight because the reduction in the demand for funds by business is offset by the increased demand by government.

The Federal Reserve System and Financial Markets

Another significant way in which government can influence financial markets is through actions taken by the Federal Reserve System (see Federal Reserve System at the extreme right of Exhibit 19–1). This public agency is charged with management of the nation's monetary system while promoting the attainment of maximum economic income, minimum unemployment, and stable prices. The supply of money is generally defined as currency in circulation and demand deposits at commercial banks. Only about one-half of the commercial banks belong to the Federal Reserve System; however, they account for about 80 percent of deposits in all banks in the United States. All banks are required to keep a specific percentage of demand and time deposits on reserve in district Federal Reserve banks. This is referred to as the reserve requirement for member banks.[10] The Federal Reserve System, in turn, provides them with check-clearing services, transfer of funds services, and currency. It will also lend money to member banks and supervises and audits their performance. It also engages in the sale and purchase of treasury securities which, along with other tools it has at its disposal, influences the money supply.[11]

---

[9]Since World War II, government, particularly at the federal level, has been in the position of financing deficits.

[10]By reducing reserve requirements, more funds become available for investment at lower interest rates. With lower interest costs, the Federal Reserve hopes to stimulate investment.

[11]Purchases of treasury securities by the Federal Reserve have the following effect: Sellers of securities receive checks from the Federal Reserve which are deposited at banks. This increases demand deposits and hence loanable funds. When the Federal Reserve Board decides to contract the supply of money, it sells securities, thus receiving funds from purchasers, which it removes from the commercial banking system.

Flow of Funds Illustrated

To familiarize the reader with the flow of funds concept, Exhibit 19–2 is a summarized segment of a flow of funds statement for the period 1977–1986. This exhibit concentrates on the types of financial claims created by households, business, and government to raise funds. These claims, also listed in Exhibit 19–1, include (1) mortgages used by households and business for real estate improvements (2) bonds and stocks issued by corporations for plant expansions and equipment outlays, and (3) securities and obligations used by government at all levels to raise capital. Note the increases and decreases in funds invested in mortgages during each of the years from 1977 to 1986. This fluctuation is very important because it shows that the flow of funds into the mortgage market was greater in some periods when compared to others. The availability of mortgage funds has a direct bearing on residential construction and commercial real estate development, a point to be explored later. Funds flowing into each of the sectors detailed in the top half of the exhibit are also a reflection of the competition for funds. Each claim created by business, households, and government has either an interest or dividend rate, which reflects the price each borrower is willing to pay to raise funds and the rate that lenders demand to supply funds. Hence the relative share of total funds available for borrowing in each sector will be determined by competition.

GROWTH AND INSTABILITY IN THE SUPPLY OF MORTGAGE FUNDS

Growth in Mortgage Lending

As we have seen from Exhibit 19–2, mortgage loans constitute the largest type of private credit used in the United States. Further, residential mortgage loans constitute the largest category of loans among the various types of mortgages made in the United States.

From Exhibit 19–2, it can be seen that during 1986 total funds raised in the mortgage market totaled approximately $298.6 billion. Compared to the other major categories of credit use, mortgage credit is by far the single largest use of credit in the private sector of our economy. During 1986, mortgage credit accounted for about 25 percent of the long-term uses of credit in our economy. This far exceeds credit usage by corporations, state and local governments, and consumers.[12]

Changes in Interest Rates and the Flow of Mortgage Funds

While the growth in mortgage credit during 1977–1986 might be characterized as phenomenal by some, it must be stressed that during this same time period the availability

---

[12]Note that prior to 1981, the amount of mortgage funds raised in credit markets exceeded that of the federal government. Since that time, however, the trend has been reversed.

EXHIBIT 19–2 Funds Borrowed and Raised in Credit and Equity Markets, 1977–1986

	1977	1978	1979	1980	1981	1982	1983	1984	1985	1986
Funds borrowed by instrument ($ billions)										
Mortgages	$128.0	$151.2	$164.8	$131.1	$109.2	$ 85.4	$183.0	$217.8	$ 235.4	$ 298.6
Corporate and foreign bonds	39.9	33.1	26.6	30.1	32.6	37.8	31.2	70.7	114.4	143.5
U.S. government securities	79.9	90.5	84.8	122.9	133.0	225.9	254.4	273.8	324.2	388.4
State and local obligations	20.3	28.4	30.3	30.3	23.4	44.2	53.7	50.4	152.4	49.5
Consumer credit	38.1	46.7	42.7	4.5	22.6	17.7	56.8	95.0	96.6	65.8
Bank loans	29.3	60.6	54.1	48.5	61.2	49.3	29.3	74.2	41.0	74.0
Commercial paper	15.0	17.7	37.5	19.3	51.3	5.7	26.9	52.0	52.8	26.4
Other loans	30.7	41.2	50.0	47.5	68.0	27.6	24.8	67.6	41.0	45.8
Total borrowed	381.2	459.4	490.8	434.2	501.3	493.6	660.1	901.5	1,057.8	1,092.0
Funds raised by corporate equity	6.6	1.7	–3.9	21.2	–3.3	33.6	67.0	–31.1	37.5	119.5
Total funds borrowed/raised	$387.8	$471.1	$486.9	$455.4	$498.0	$527.2	$727.1	$870.4	$1,095.3	$1,211.5

EXHIBIT 19-2 (Concluded)

Funds borrowed by instrument

Mortgages	33.01%	32.10%	33.85%	28.79%	21.93%	16.20%	25.17%	25.02%	21.49%	24.65%
Corporate and foreign bonds	10.29	7.03	5.46	6.61	6.55	7.17	4.29	8.12	10.44	11.84
U.S. government securities	20.60	19.21	17.42	26.99	26.71	42.85	34.99	31.46	29.60	32.06
State and local obligations	5.23	6.03	6.22	6.65	4.70	8.38	7.39	5.79	13.91	4.09
Consumer credit	9.82	9.91	8.77	0.99	4.54	3.36	7.81	10.91	8.82	5.43
Bank loans	7.56	12.86	11.11	10.65	12.29	9.35	4.03	8.52	3.74	6.11
Commercial paper	3.87	3.76	7.70	4.24	10.30	1.08	3.70	5.97	4.82	2.18
Other loans	7.92	8.75	10.27	10.43	13.65	5.24	3.41	7.77	3.74	3.78
Total borrowed	98.30	99.64	100.80	95.34	100.66	93.63	90.79	103.57	96.58	90.14
Funds raised by corporate equity	1.70%	0.36%	−0.80%	4.66%	−0.66%	6.37%	9.21%	−3.57%	3.42%	9.86
Total funds borrowed/raised	100.00%	100.00%	100.00%	100.00%	100.00%	100.00%	100.00%	100.00%	100.00%	100.00%

Adapted from *Flow of Funds Accounts*, Federal Reserve System, (Washington, D.C.) various issues.

of mortgage credit in individual years fluctuated dramatically. Exhibit 19–3 provides some basic information concerning mortgage interest rates and the flow of mortgage funds. In general, the amount of funds raised in mortgage markets tends to be negatively correlated with interest rates. Although the interest rate shown in the exhibit is based on conventional single family residential commitments and mortgage amounts raised in credit markets are for all types of properties (residential, commercial, industrial, hotels, etc.), interest rates for the latter uses would also tend move very closely to residential rates.[13] Data in the exhibit indicate that as mortgage interest rates peaked during 1981–1982 the availability of mortgage funds sharply contracted. During 1986, however, interest rates approached the level that existed previously in 1978–1979 and the amount of funds raised in the form of mortgage loans tripled from the 1982 level. This significant increase in lending activity was brought about by an increase in demand for mortgage funds for new construction and by a tremendous volume of refinancing and additional funds loaned to borrowers who originated loans from 1980 to 1985.

The point is that the availability of mortgage funds is highly cyclical and depends on interest rates. This cyclical pattern has caused numerous problems in residential markets for households seeking financing for house purchases as well as for developers seeking financing for project development. Lenders have also faced serious problems because of an imbalance between their cost of funds and return on assets in these periods. Two influences not shown in Exhibit 19–3 that have contributed to this pattern have been a general decrease in the amount of savings by households. This decrease in savings has occurred because interest rates offered by financial intermediaries have not been high enough to induce savings from income earned by households. Further, in some years, most notably 1978–1982, potential losses in real purchasing power (based on the difference between the rate paid on savings and the change in the consumer price index) on amounts saved increased to a level that caused a significant reduction in the flow of funds into credit markets (see Exhibit 19–2) and a reduction in the proportion of funds saved at intermediaries. In those years, increasing amounts of savings were invested *directly* in other investments, such as stocks, bonds, and in real assets, which offered yields that were expected to keep pace with rising price levels. Even small savers began investing directly in financial assets or investing in money market mutual funds, whose growth during this period was tremendous. When substantial shifts in the flow of funds away from financial intermediaries directly into the market for securities and other assets occurs, this process is called *financial disintermediation.*[14]

INTERMEDIARIES IN THE MORTGAGE MARKET

From the discussion to this point, we have seen that the flow of funds from sectors of the economy with a surplus of funds to sectors with a net demand for funds depends, in

---

[13]Depending on the property type, there will be a *spread* between residential interest rates and interest rates for each category of property; however, the *direction* of movement should be the same.

[14]Many remedies have been used to circumvent financial disintermediation in recent years, including *ARMs* and allowing institutions more flexibility in asset investments. For a review, see the *Depositary Institutions Deregulation and Monetary Control Act of 1980,* and the *Garn-St. Germain Depository Institutions Act of 1982.*

EXHIBIT 19–3   Funds Raised in Mortgage Market and Interest Rates for 1977–1986

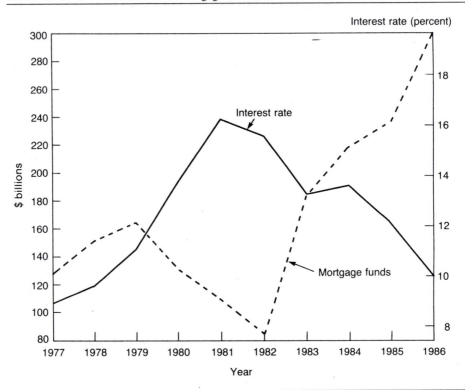

part, on a system of direct investment or through financial intermediaries. In addition, the flow of funds can be altered by actions taken by government financing debt and policies of the Federal Reserve System. Because the mortgage market is only one component of the financial system just described, it is definitely affected by changes that occur in the overall flow of funds. Although we focus the discussion on the mortgage market here, it must be kept in mind that it is a part of the overall financial system and is responsive to changes affecting that system.

In this section, we discuss the mortgage market separately from the remainder of the financial system and provide more detail on mortgage market participants. A simplified diagram of the mortgage market is presented in Exhibit 19–4. The intent of the diagram is to identify the major participants in the mortgage markets and to depict how the interaction of the supply and demand for mortgage funds sets the terms for mortgage lending and borrowing.

The Demand for Mortgage Funds

The demand for mortgage funds emanates from business and households desiring to make investments in real assets, such as single family residential housing, multifamily housing,

EXHIBIT 19–4 The Mortgage Market

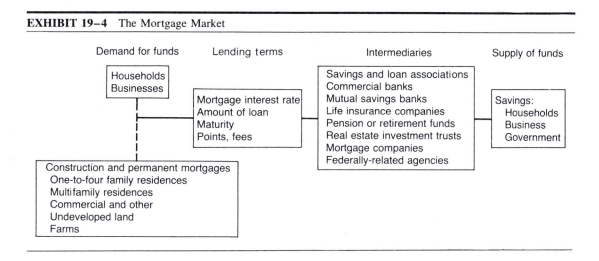

apartment complexes, and commercial developments (shopping centers, hotels, and office buildings) which require financing. This group is depicted in the left portion of Exhibit 19–4. There are many determinants of demands for housing and other real assets requiring mortgage financing. Many of these factors have been discussed throughout the text.

Exhibit 19–4 also shows lending terms offered by financial intermediaries. Although we refer to the mortgage interest rate in the exhibit, there are risk differentials among individual loan transactions, based on the relative financial strength of borrowers, geographic differences in project location, and other factors. These differences result in a *distribution* of mortgage interest rates and terms. Hence, when reference is made to the interest rate on mortgages, these risk differentials must be kept in mind. In addition, although the mortgage market diagram in Exhibit 19–4 excludes other sectors of the financial system, remember that the mortgage market is a part of the larger system. Further, the demand for mortgage funds is a part of the demand for all funds in the economy, and competition among all sectors influence mortgage interest rates.

The Supply of Mortgage Funds

Suppliers of mortgage funds are listed on the right-hand side of Exhibit 19–4. The institutions listed in the exhibit through which the supply of funds is channeled are the most important lenders in the mortgage market. While other institutions listed in Exhibit 19–1 may make some mortgage loans, they are not significant in dollar amount. Hence, our discussion will focus on only the most important intermediaries in the mortgage market.

The institutions listed in Exhibit 19–4 may be classified into one of three categories. Depository-type institutions, which include savings and loan associations, commercial banks, and mutual savings banks, offer a variety of deposit accounts to savers. Contractual-type institutions, which include life insurance companies and pension and retirement funds, usually provide retirement and death benefits to individuals that require a contractual commitment of savings over a long time. The third category, including mortgage companies, real estate investment trusts, and federally related agencies, might be called specialized mortgage market intermediaries. These intermediaries restrict their investment activity primarily to the mortgage market, and most of the funds that they use for making investments in mortgages do not come directly from savers.

Commercial Banks

Commercial banks can be characterized as a highly regulated business enterprise whose goal is to attract deposits and use those funds to make investments and loans. Its goal, like that of all financial intermediaries, is to earn a high enough return on investments and loans so that when interest is paid on their sources of funds, a profit results.

The primary sources of funds available to commercial banks for lending comprise demand deposits, NOW accounts, and money market accounts, which constitute 30 to 40 percent of the bank's total available funds. Because these funds tend to be very short term in nature, their availability expands and contracts with the business cycle and changes in interest rates. As a result, banks tend to hold these funds in cash, which usually constitutes 10 to 15 percent of the bank's assets, and primary reserves such as investments in short-term Treasury bills and tax-free municipal bonds. Those investments usually constitute an additional 15 to 20 percent of the bank's assets. Time deposits make up an additional 30 to 40 percent of funds available to commercial banks. These funds are provided in the form of savings certificates and money market certificates which have a fixed maturity and, therefore, represent funds which can be committed in longer-term loans and investments. With these funds, banks make commercial and industrial loans and provide lines of credit. These loans usually constitute 20 to 25 percent of total bank assets. However, real estate loans are also made from these sources and can constitute anywhere from 10 to 15 percent of bank assets and, as such, represent an important investment for commercial banks. Recall that much of the material in Chapter 18 on financing real estate development applies to commercial bank lending practices, so it will not be repeated here.

Current provisions of the law governing real estate loans by national banks include the following:

1. National banks may not make real estate loans in excess of the greater of unimpaired capital plus surplus, or time plus savings deposits. They are authorized to make real estate loans in excess of 70 percent of time and savings deposits if total unpaid loan amounts do not exceed 10 percent of the maximum amount that may be invested in real estate loans.

2. Under present law, national banks are authorized to make various loan-to-value ratio loans secured by first liens. They also may make loans secured by other than first liens, where the lien, when added to prior liens, does not exceed the applicable loan-to-value ratio for the particular type of loan.

3. National banks are not required to classify as real estate loans various loans insured, guaranteed, or backed by the full faith and credit of the federal government or a state.

4. Loans with maturities of less than 60 months are classified as commercial loans when made for construction of buildings and secured by a permanent, or takeout, commitment to advance the full amount of the loan upon completion.

5. Loans made for the construction of residential or farm buildings with maturities of not more than nine months are eligible for discount as commercial paper if accompanied by an agreement for firm take-out upon completion of the building.

6. National banks are permitted to make loans on leaseholds that have at least 10 years to run beyond the terminal date of the loan.

7. Loans made to manufacturing or industrial businesses are exempt from real estate loan limitations even though the bank takes a mortgage on real estate as security, where the bank relies primarily on the general credit standing and earning power of the business as the source of repayment.

As will be seen in the next section, commercial banks are the largest provider of funds to the real estate industry. However, because of deregulation of thrift institutions (to be discussed), banks found themselves facing additional competition in the construction and permanent loan markets. This was partially true for loans made on multifamily and commercial projects. Many observers maintain that this added competition resulted in more aggressive underwriting by banks, and these practices, combined with a short-term loan in the energy industry, resulted in massive overbuilding in Sunbelt markets during the early to mid-1980s.

After a decline in the energy industry, rental markets in these areas experienced severe difficulty, and many real estate loans went into default. These problems, in addition to others,[15] caused a rapid rise in the number of bank failures and a depletion in reserves of the FDIC and FSLIC which had to pay depositors up to insurance limits. This prompted a congressional review of the deposit insurance corporations (FDIC, FSLIC) and an infusion of reserves to the FSLIC, which insures thrift institutions, who as competitors of commercial banks, were more seriously affected. The outcome for the FDIC and commercial banking has yet to be determined. This issue is discussed further in the section on thrift institutions.

Loan Origination Activity.   Even though the real estate investment category only represents 10 to 15 percent of bank assets, commercial banks are by far the largest originator of total construction loans made in the United States and are the second largest originator of long-term, or permanent, real estate loans. Looking to Exhibit 19–5, we can see that in 1979 commercial banks originated over 50 percent of all construction loans made in the United States. By 1986, originations increased to almost 70 percent. Looking to Exhibit 19–6, we can see that commercial banks provided by far the largest amount of construction funding for commercial real estate projects. They were also the most important construction lenders on multifamily developments and were an important originator of one- to four-family loans.

---

[15]During this period banks also made loans to Third World countries, energy firms, and some agriculturally based companies. Many of these loans also went into default, thereby contributing to the demise of many commercial banks.

EXHIBIT 19–5 Origination of Construction Loans

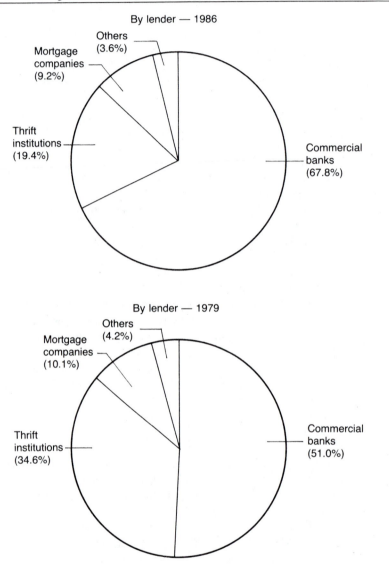

As far as origination of long-term or permanent loans, commercial banks are also a very important source of funding. As can be seen in Exhibit 19–7, commercial banks were the second largest provider of total long-term funds in the two periods shown in the exhibit. Exhibit 19–8 shows that, as with construction lending, commercial banks were the largest originators of long-term loans for commercial real estate projects. They did not provide long-term financing for multifamily projects and single family dwellings

EXHIBIT 19–6   Origination of Construction Loans

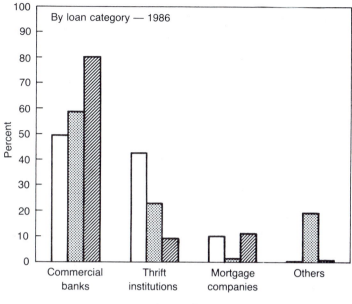

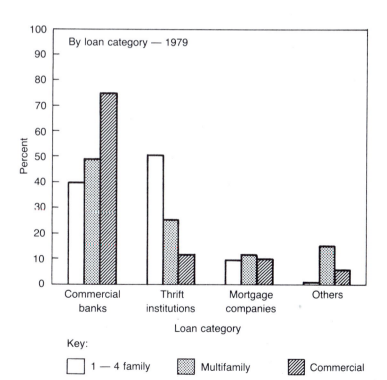

EXHIBIT 19–7 Origination of Long-Term Loans

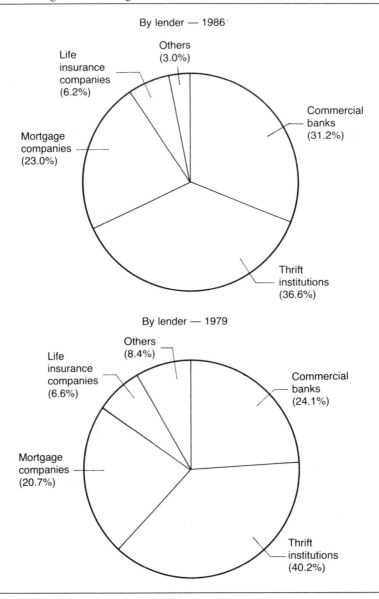

By lender — 1986

Others (3.0%)

Life insurance companies (6.2%)

Mortgage companies (23.0%)

Commercial banks (31.2%)

Thrift institutions (36.6%)

By lender — 1979

Others (8.4%)

Life insurance companies (6.6%)

Mortgage companies (20.7%)

Commercial banks (24.1%)

Thrift institutions (40.2%)

in the same proportion as construction funding was provided, however. In summary, because commercial banks have the largest deposit base of any category of intermediary in the United States, even though they allocate a relatively small percentage of those funds to real estate, they are, nonetheless, the largest provider of funds to the real estate industry.

EXHIBIT 19–8 Origination of Long-Term Loans

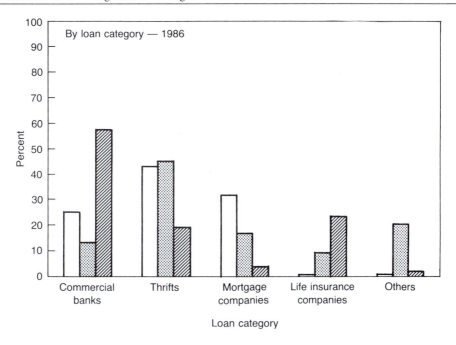

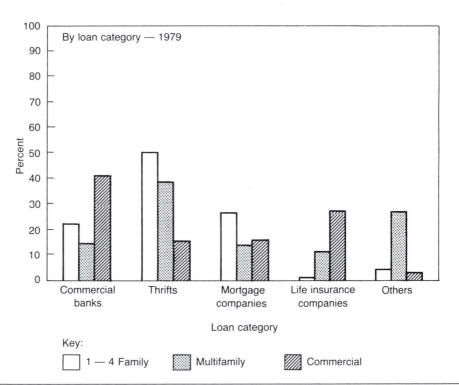

Thrift Institutions

When discussing thrift institutions, we are generally referring to three types of inter-mediaries: mutual savings banks, savings and loan associations, and credit unions. We differentiate these institutions from commercial banks in that the orientation of the latter has historically been toward servicing the financial needs of commercial enterprises while thrift institutions have had more of a tradition of servicing the savings and mortgage needs of households. However, as we will see, the distribution between thrift institutions and commercial banks has blurred considerably in recent years.

Mutual savings banks (MSBs) began in the early 1800s in the form of an institution with a primary function of providing a safe depository for small savings accounts of individuals. Indeed, names of early MSBs (e.g., Dime Savings Bank) reflect their ori-entation toward small savers whose first priority was for safe keeping of funds, plus an opportunity to earn some interest. They have historically remained concentrated in the northeastern part of the United States.[16] Savings and loan associations (S & L's), on the other hand, had their beginning during the 1830s but have always focused on providing funds for homeowners. Essentially, early associations were begun by members who pooled funds with the express purpose of homebuilding. Funds provided from savings from new members and repayments of loans previously made to members were the source of financing for the purchase of homes.

Credit unions were established in the early 1900s and focused on meeting consumer needs for loans that were not being met by commercial banks. Regulations governing the operations of such institutions have traditionally required them to be affiliated with groups that have similar occupations, are employed by the same firm, or that have other similar characteristics (members of unions, religious groups, teachers, etc.). Loans were generally made for installment purchases of consumer durables (autos, appliances, etc.). However, in recent times, loans have been expanded to include renovation and expansion of homes with second mortgage loans and some lending for members to acquire residences. Although the credit union is a possible source of credit, they provide a relatively small amount of funds to the real estate market, so we will not consider them any further.

Real Estate Lending by Thrifts. Thrifts have historically been *conventional* mortgage lenders. However, in some geographic lending areas, thrifts have originated significant numbers of FHA insured or VA guaranteed loans. In total, however, these intermediaries account for only about 15 percent of FHA and VA mortgage originations. In some cases, MSBs, because of their geographic concentration, may also purchase packages of FHA and VA loans or securities backed by such loans when residential development activity declines relative to the flow of savings in their regions.

With the advent of episodes of disintermediation started in the 1960s and the wave of deregulation begun during that period (including a more liberal attitude toward chartering

---

[16]Even today, mutual savings banks operate in only 17 states, and most are still concentrated in Massachusetts, New York, and Connecticut. All are chartered and regulated by the state, although most choose to be insured by the FDIC or FSLIC. As a result, they must also meet federal regulatory requirements regarding real estate loans.

new thrifts and banks), the nature of real estate and other lending by thrifts changed considerably, particularly in the post-1980 era. In addition to making commercial loans to business (an unprecedented change), thrifts were also allowed to make real estate loans on office buildings, shopping centers, industrial-warehouses, hotels and other non-residential uses. In short, they were allowed to loan on virtually any type of income-producing property. Further, they could structure construction and long-term loans to include equity participation (contingent interest) provisions. They were also allowed to engage in limited joint venture activities as an equity partner and to partially engage in brokerage, title insurance, and other activities through subsidiary service corporations. It is safe to say that the amount of deregulation that occurred during 1966–1986 was significant and changed (perhaps forever) how thrift institutions operate. Because of deregulation, many thrifts with limited underwriting experience proceeded too aggressively with these new lending vehicles in order to establish themselves and to acquire a share in these new markets. Indeed, during this period many thrifts virtually abandoned their role as originators and investors in single family loans. Instead they became originators of such loans, then sold them to other investors in the secondary mortgage market while retaining only loan servicing in some cases. Hence, many thrifts chose to earn fees and discount points on single family loans, sell them to other entities, and use available funds for commercial mortgage lending.

Many observers have also noted that a "moral hazard" was created by the new regulatory environment in which thrifts operated. Essentially, because of poor profitability brought about by traditional residential lending policies and the lack of regulatory change, during the 1960s and 1970s, managers aggressively diversified into what they believed were new and more profitable lending opportunities. They also reasoned that if they failed in this endeavor, depositors would be protected with insurance provided by the FSLIC or FDIC. This change also occurred coincidentally with the energy crisis brought on in the late 1970s and early 1980s, and a dramatic growth in economic activity in the Sunbelt area in the United States. Real estate development activity increased dramatically in these areas, and many thrifts made loans to developers and entered into joint ventures in their respective lending markets. In many cases, thrifts in other geographic areas bought participations in loans originated by Sunbelt thrifts. These thrifts encountered severe difficulty as the domestic energy market softened in 1985. Many were forced into bankruptcy. The FSLIC paid depositors in those failed institutions to such an extent that by 1987 its reserves were depleted. Congress passed emergency legislation in August of 1987 that provided the FSLIC with the ability to acquire $10 billion in additional reserves as the number of insolvent thrifts increased. We should hasten to add that numerous commercial banks who found themselves competing in this deregulated environment were also affected by the real estate development and energy boom. Indeed, as of mid-1987, reserves of the FDIC were at an all-time low due to an extensive amount of bank failures, and discussions regarding recapitalization and/or merging the FSLIC and FDIC were underway.

In the face of these difficulties, Congress reversed, to a degree, actions taken in 1985 regarding liberalization of deposit and lending regulations of thrifts. It did so by restricting the dollar volume of direct investment in real estate development activities of thrifts to twice the amount of their net worth. What follows is a list of other important lending regulations that characterize the real estate activities of thrifts as of 1987.

1. Mortgages on existing single family housing remain as the most important loan made by thrifts. Conventional loans for up to 90 percent of value and privately insured mortgages for up to 95 percent of value may be made.
2. Construction loans for up to 75 percent of value can be made with a conversion to a conventional permanent loan for up to 90 percent or 95 percent of value.
3. Second mortgage loans may be made provided total indebted does not exceed the 90 percent conventional lending limit.
4. Loans on commercial and industrial properties may not exceed 40 percent of thrift assets.
5. Direct commercial loans cannot exceed 10 percent of assets.
6. Limited lending on ground leases and unimproved land may still be undertaken.

Real Estate Originations by Thrifts.   From Exhibit 19–5, it should be apparent that thrifts were the second most active originator of construction loans during the periods being compared. From 1979 to 1986, however, their market share of originations in construction loans declined. These reductions came about in one-to-four family originations (Exhibit 19–6), which were absorbed by commercial banks. An even more important relationship can be seen in Exhibit 19–7. This exhibit shows that their market share of permanent loans also declined. This decline occurred primarily in single family loans (Exhibit 19–8) while they increased their share of multifamily originations and commercial loans considerably. This pattern is indicative of the previously discussed changes brought about in the marketplace from the mid-1960s through the mid-1980s. The increased market share in multifamily and commercial lending by thrifts appears to have come at the expense of mortgage companies and life insurance companies.[17]

Mortgage Banking Companies

As indicated earlier, these institutions have been classified as a specialized intermediary to match institutions willing to lend on real estate in various regions with developers and investors who are seeking funds to develop or acquire property. As such, mortgage bankers are *not* depository-type intermediaries. They accept no savings deposits, nor do they perform the transactional functions (checking, NOW accounts, etc.) that thrifts and commercial banks perform. They are more specialized in that their activities generally involve intermediation between parties engaging in real estate transactions only. Hence, the principal activity of the mortgage banker is originating and servicing loans on residential and income properties that are sold to institutional investors.

---

[17]Many loans are combined construction and permanent loans both for one-to-four family and income properties. (Recall the discussion of bullet and miniperm loans in Chapter 17.) These loans are believed to be reported as long-term loans; hence the data and trends shown in Exhibits 19–5 through 19–8 may be somewhat misleading if one category of lender increased its share of such combined loans. In such cases, the number of construction loans reported would fall while permanent loans reported would increase.

Operations and Sources of Funds.   As noted previously, mortgage banks (MBs) do not have access to savings as other intermediaries. These organizations are usually corporations or partnerships, who, like other businesses, raise equity capital through the sale of common stock or by capital contribution by its partners. This equity base then grows through retention of earnings (retained earnings). Further, they can issue debt securities, assuming that they have sufficient assets to do so.

Many services are provided by the mortgage banker. The mortgage banker acts as a regional correspondent for large institutional investors (particularly life insurance companies) who are seeking lending and investment activity in diverse areas of the country (and world). Mortgage bankers regularly contact developers and investors in their respective areas of business (some MBs have national coverage, but the vast majority are local in orientation) to determine what new projects are being proposed or what projects are available for sale. After many years of close contacts with institutions, MBs get to know the portfolio needs, underwriting practices, and types of real estate preferred for lending and investing (for example, some life insurance companies do not lend on apartment projects or hotels, yet others do). Hence, they can perform what amounts to the acquisition function for loans and real estate in their respective markets for specific institutional clients.[18] For acting in this capacity, MBs charge interest and earn fees and/or points on the loans that are placed with institutional lenders. From these funds, MBs must pay interest on any interim funds borrowed, cover operating expenses, and earn a profit.

When it makes construction loans, the MB acts in the same capacity as a commercial bank. It disperses funds, monitors progress, adherence to plans, and material specifications, and so on (see Chapters 17–18). However, unlike the commercial bank, upon completion of the project when the institutional lender honors its take-out commitment, the mortgage banker may continue to "service" the permanent loan. By this is meant that the MB will collect payments from the property owner, make dispersements to the institutional lender, and verify that all property taxes, insurance premiums, and any other contractual commitments that are a part of the transaction are honored. For this activity, the MB earns a fee based as a percentage of the outstanding mortgage balance being serviced.[19]

---

[18]Many MBs may have a close working relationship with only one large life insurance company, for example. However, if a life company has an investment policy that prohibits certain types of loans (e.g., hotel loans), the MB may represent another company for that property type only. In other cases, some MBs may have relationships with many smaller life companies who make investments in the region infrequently.

[19]We should clarify the difference between mortgage bankers and mortgage brokers. The latter are individuals or firms who specialize in placing loans on behalf of developers and investors who are seeking financing as a part of the purchase price. The broker develops a loan proposal or package based on data relative to the project and the client/borrower/investor and seeks out institutional lenders on behalf of the client. In many cases, the mortgage broker also acts as a real estate broker, who attempts to find financing for the purchaser of a project that was sold by the real estate broker. The impetus for the services of the broker usually emanates from the developer or investor, whereas the services of a mortgage banker are utilized by the institution providing the permanent funding.

In recent years, when dealing with income properties, the mortgage banker has also acted as an investment advisor to pension funds who also seek loans and investments on real estate. In these cases, the income-producing real estate will generally be an existing project, but occasionally it may be a "to be developed" project. The MB then acts as an advisor to the fund by recommending purchases and sales of specific properties for a specific pension fund or funds. At times the MB may have discretion over funds provided by a plan for investment, and at other times the role is more limited, in that the pension fund makes investments with the advice of the MB. In either case, the MB earns fees for this function, usually based on the amount of funds invested or under management. More will be said about the relationship with pension funds in the next chapter.

For one- to four-family residential lending, the mainstay of most mortgage bankers, the financing pattern is generally more institutionalized. Mortgage bankers utilize mortgage warehousing arrangements with commercial banks, whereby a commitment for a specified loan maximum is agreed on and the commercial bank releases funds as mortgage loans are originated by the MB. These mortgages, in essence, provide additional security for the warehouse loan. Simultaneously, the MB has received, or is attempting to secure, a purchase commitment for a package of such loans from a large institutional purchaser (such as a life company or, more likely, from the Federal National Mortgage Association (FNMA) or the Federal Home Loan Mortgage Corporation (FHLMC), to be discussed in the next chapter). Alternatively, the MB may assemble a package of loans and place them into a pool against which securities are issued and sold to the public or other purchasers (mortgage-backed securities are also discussed in the next chapter). In any event, the warehousing loan acts as an interim funding mechanism which allows MBs to originate loans, assemble them for sale, or securitize them. In most instances, the MB will retain the loan servicing function for the ultimate purchaser. Fees are earned on the servicing, and a profit may also be earned in packaging and securitization activities.[20]

From small beginnings before World War II, the growth in mortgage banking activities has been spectacular. The substantial postwar growth of mortgage bankers, as well as their present structure and operational methods, can be attributed largely to the federal mortgage assistance program. The Federal Housing Administration insurance and the Veterans Administration guarantee programs have offered what was needed to create a national mortgage market. These agencies provided minimum property requirements, subdivision standards, and credit review which gave insured or guaranteed mortgages a quality upon which distant lending institutions could rely with little individual review or investigation. The federal underwriting itself permitted institutional investors to make loans of higher risk than would otherwise be prudent or legally possible from the standpoint

---

[20]One risk that the MB takes during the warehousing period is that the interim loan from the commercial bank is usually made at a floating rate of interest. If the individual loans being originated are made at fixed interest rates, adverse movements in short-term rates on the interim loan may result in a loss. Hence, the MB may choose to hedge this risk by utilizing interest rate futures or swaps. Further, the MB may have a commitment to deliver the package of mortgages to a specified yield to the purchaser. Should long-term rates decline while the package is being assembled, loans in the packages may be originated at an interest rate below the yield promised to the buyer. Hence, the MB may suffer a loss. In this event, the MB may choose to hedge using GNMA futures.

of loan-to-value ratio or of distance from lender to liened property. Further, with this insurance or guarantee, a purchaser of a mortgage or an interest in a pool can be assured of safety of principal in the event the borrower defaults. This attribute, and the uniform underwriting procedures have made FHA and VA mortgages available for trading in the national marketplace. It has an additional unique feature. It is eligible, under certain limitations, for purchase by federally oriented secondary market facilities. Of particular significance to mortgage bankers in this respect is the Federal National Mortgage Association. The availability of this resource as a buyer in the market at times of temporary credit stringency has provided a stability in the supply of mortgage funds that did not previously exist.

Although the Federal Home Loan Mortgage Corporation (discussed in Chapter 22) has been developed in recent years as an additional secondary market facility, it was not until 1978 that it was permitted to buy directly from mortgage bankers. The addition of this resource in support of the secondary mortgage markets should greatly benefit the mortgage banking industry.

Servicing Mortgages. Mortgage bankers perform two functions for institutional investors: (1) They invest money safely, and (2) they recover the investment outlay according to the loan contract. Lending money is fairly simple. Getting it back may be more difficult. Servicing involves acting more as a clearinghouse for checks transmitted by the borrower. Adequate servicing involves at least four major operations:

1. Current payments made by the borrower must be processed, and the net proceeds, after retaining tax, mortgage, and hazard insurance premiums and service fees, must be transmitted to the investor who owns the mortgage. In rare cases the investor insists that all escrow deposits for taxes, mortgage insurance, and hazard insurance be transmitted to it to be held in trust for the borrower.

2. The security must be inspected to ascertain whether it is being subjected to waste or extraordinary depreciation.

3. When the property changes hands and the new owner assumes the mortgage debt, records in the office of the mortgage banker must be changed. If the mortgage is insured by the FHA or guaranteed by the VA, the proper governmental agency must be notified. Even where the present mortgage is completely paid off rather than assumed by the new owner, the mortgage banker must protect the interests of the holder of the mortgage until the lien is legally extinguished.

4. Finally, in serious cases of delinquency, steps must be taken to protect the holder of the mortgage, by foreclosure if necessary.

Fees. Mortgage bankers generally earn fees for loan origination and for servicing the loan during its existence. They also receive compensation for servicing the loan from the time it is made until it is paid off is collected by the mortgage banker out of the borrower's periodic payments. If the servicing fee is .375 percent, for example, and the contract interest rate on the mortgage note is 11.5 percent, when the borrower's payment is received by the mortgage banker, only 11.125 percent is forwarded to the lender as interest; the other .375 percent is retained as compensation for the collection service. All amortization of principal amount is forwarded to the lender. The servicing fee is based on the unpaid loan balance and decreases as the loan is amortized. Clearly, the incentive for mortgage bankers to continue to originate, package, sell, and securitize mortgages is obvious; this is because fee income from servicing is based on the size of the portfolio being serviced. However, this does not mean that the size of the portfolio should be increased by sacrificing loan quality. Defaults reduce the size of the portfolio and, hence, fees. Costs incurred by MBs pursuing delinquent borrowers, foreclosure proceedings, and so on, may substantially reduce profits from servicing income and origination fees.

Origination Activity. As mentioned earlier, mortgage bankers are the largest originators of FHA insured and VA guaranteed single family mortgage loans. This activity is clearly their most significant activity (see Exhibits 19–7 and 19–8). Recall that the data shown in these Exhibits 19–7 and 19–8 reflect *origination activity,* not the ultimate ownership of the mortgages. That data is presented in the next chapter, and it will be seen that most mortgages originated by MBs are *sold* to institutional investors. However, it is equally important to understand who originates mortgages, because that is the initial funding source that must be approached when seeking financing for the development or purchase of a project or residence.

In construction lending, MBs hold a significant market share in residential and commercial areas (Exhibit 19–6). Much of the multifamily construction lending done by MBs was taken over by state and county home finance agencies in 1986. These agencies usually engaged the services of mortgage bankers, however, since they lacked the underwriting and construction experience needed in this type of lending. Federal tax legislation passed in 1986 has limited the amount of tax-exempt mortgage financing that these agencies may now undertake. It is very likely that multifamily originations by MBs will again increase in response to this legislation.

Single family originations for total permanent financing by MBs were second only to those of thrifts, who are the dominant lenders in conventional single and multifamily markets. Also, the conventional mortgage market is far larger than the FHA-VA market. Hence, even though MBs dominate in originations in the latter market, the former is much larger in total dollar volume.

Life Insurance Companies

These contractual-type intermediaries enjoy a relatively high degree of stability in the availability of funds for investment when compared with both commercial banks and savings and loan associations. This stability follows from the contractual nature of premiums on insurance policies and the amount of benefit payouts required at any given time. Essentially, the business of life insurance companies is to offer individuals and businesses life insurance programs which involve the payment of premiums to life companies who, in turn, establish reserves for future payouts based on the projected mortality rates of policyholders. Insurance programs are too numerous to discuss here; however, the price of all insurance plans by life companies takes into account the fact that premiums will be collected on many individual plans, while payouts in any particular period (based on mortality rates) will be far less than premium income. The difference is usually invested by life companies in their ''general account'' in order to earn investment income. The ability to earn investment income is taken into account when establishing premiums for a particular insurance plan. The general account will contain diverse investments, including U.S. government bonds, corporate bonds, preferred and common stock, real estate mortgages (residential, commercial, and agricultural), and equity ownership of real estate (through outright acquisition or partial equity interests such as joint ventures, etc.).

Real Estate Lending and Property Acquisitions.   Life insurance companies, like commercial banks, make substantial investments in permanent commercial mortgage loans and loans on multifamily properties. Their commercial lending activity lies more in large shopping center developments, hotel and motels, larger-scale office buildings, warehouses, and industrial properties throughout the entire United States. This may be contrasted with more local, smaller-scale, permanent loans made by commercial banks. Life insurance companies tend not to be interested in underwriting smaller-scale projects, but they specialize in larger-scale projects that involve large outlays of funds. They rely on mortgage bankers and commercial banks to make construction loans and to monitor construction at the local level. Local lenders, because of their geographic proximity to the construction and development, are more efficient in performing that function. As a result, life insurance companies are more interested in only the permanent financing on large projects.

Because of an overriding concern over inflation, life insurance companies have increasingly insisted on equity participation features as a condition for making commercial mortgage loans. In recent years they have become more aggressive in seeking direct equity positions in real estate and have developed a growing stake in direct ownership of properties. A major reason for this trend toward equity investment, with its potential for price appreciation, was because yields on long-term fixed rate bonds and mortgages did not keep up with inflation. Furthermore, as effective marginal tax rates for life insurance companies have increased, the favorable tax treatment of real estate has been an added motivation for its inclusion as a general account investment.

Like other financial institutions, the investment objectives of life insurance companies are determined by the type of liabilities they incur while carrying on their business. As previously indicated, the traditional actuarial liabilities of life insurance companies have been long-term and *highly predictable,* with the result that they have had little need for liquid assets. These characteristics of life insurance companies made them well-suited for real estate investing.

But events associated with the relatively high inflation and high market interest rates of the late 1970s and early 1980s have resulted in increasing pressure to provide a more competitive rate of return to policyholders. This has led them to take on more equity investments in an effort to achieve higher returns. The apparent willingness of life insurance companies to undertake higher risks and sacrifice some safety of principal in pursuit of higher overall returns can be seen in a slight shift in their investment policies. Life insurance companies have changed their policy from being involved in the real estate field primarily as lenders and concentrating on relatively safe long-term mortgage lending, to undertaking riskier lending activities, such as shared equity lending and construction lending, and to investing in equity real estate directly. The latter includes taking an increasingly active role in real estate development, often in joint ventures with proven real estate developers. In their activity as equity investors, many life companies have initiated regional offices to initiate contracts with developers and acquire properties for investment. They have also initiated property management activities and have acquired considerable knowledge of local markets. This activity has also enabled them to provide leads for their commercial mortgage lending function for projects yet to be developed or on the resale of existing properties.

While there has been a willingness to sacrifice some safety of principal by more aggressively seeking higher returns, there is still great reluctance to significantly increase risk because of the high fiduciary standards[21] placed on life insurance companies by public opinion and public policy. Thus, these companies have placed a great deal of emphasis on diversification in order to minimize the risks associated with their strategy of more aggressively pursuing higher returns. Moreover, to decrease risk and to increase potential return, life insurance companies have concentrated their interest in properties considered to be high-quality investment-grade properties in prime locations.

Life insurance companies also invest in real estate *separate* accounts which they *administer* for individual pension funds (to be discussed in more detail in the next chapter). Another vehicle used by life insurance companies to invest in real estate on behalf of pension funds is through the so-called commingled real estate funds (CREF), whereby small investments received from pension plans are pooled, or commingled, enabling large real estate acquisitions, the returns from which are distributed in proportion to funds invested. These vehicles will be discussed in the next chapter.

Loan Origination Activity. Real estate lending by life insurance companies has changed dramatically in the post–World War II era. At one time they were the primary purchasers of FHA-VA mortgages originated by mortgage bankers. Indeed at one time such mortgages made up about 50 percent of all mortgages owned by insurance companies. Today, the percentage is about 15 percent or less.

From Exhibit 19–5, note that we have not broken data out separately for life companies because they are not significant construction lenders. Remember that commercial banks and mortgage bankers are the institutions that provide most of the interim financing for development, with life companies really being the source of permanent funding. As just indicated, permanent funding is negotiated through mortgage banking relationships, or in some cases life companies make commitments directly through a branch office operation.

---

[21]Most states have passed laws governing the operations of insurance companies. These fall into two classes: laws governing the operations of companies domiciled within the state, and those controlling activities of companies domiciled elsewhere but doing business within a state. The major purpose of both types of laws is the protection of the policyholders. With respect to real estate lending and investment, however, most states generally impose maximum individual loan limits that may be made on any real estate project to a specific percentage of life company assets. Also, real estate loans, in total, will also be restricted to a specific percentage of assets. As to its management of pension funds, life companies are regulated under the provision of ERISA (Employee Retirement Income Security Act). This act governs the activities of all fiduciaries investing funds on behalf of qualified pension plans (this is discussed in more detail in the next chapter).

As for permanent loans, Exhibit 19–7 indicates that life companies rank third in long-term originations; however as shown in Exhibit 19–8 life companies are second in importance in commercial real estate lending. The role and importance of life companies are not completely indicated by mortgage lending activity. These institutions have become extremely important in the commercial real estate industry through ownership for their own account and because of their longstanding expertise in real estate lending. The property management and leasing expertise that they have acquired from owning and operating income-producing real estate has enabled them to become the dominant investment advisor for pension funds. Pension funds are becoming the most important new source of funds to the real estate industry. This funding source is discussed in the next chapter.

Chapter 20

Sources of Mortgage and Equity Financing for Real Estate—Part II

PENSION FUNDS

One of the most important developments in the flow of funds into real estate has been the entry of pension funds as lenders and investors. Insurance companies, trust departments of commercial banks, and investment companies are becoming increasingly cognizant of the magnitude of the pension funds market, and they are more aware of their own excellent position to compete for fund investments.

In essence, pension funds are simply funds accumulated over the working life of individuals that provide income during retirement. Before World War II, these funds were largely established by corporations or by governmental units on a voluntary basis and on a relatively small scale. In the postwar labor climate, desirable pension plans became an important method of attracting employees to a particular firm. Pension plans pay no federal income taxes if they operate in accordance with regulations of the Treasury and Department of Labor.

As of 1986, assets held for investment by pension funds were estimated at $1.3 trillion. Because of the current demographic makeup of the population in the United States, these funds are growing at a multibillion dollar annual rate.

In recent years, because of their large and rapidly expanding pool of assets, pension funds have become recognized by the real estate industry as a potentially major force in real estate finance. But a pension fund represents a very special type of investor when it comes to real estate. Indeed, until the early 1980s the world of real estate seemed very different and even alien to pension fund sponsors, managers, and consultants. However, given the potentially large returns from real estate investments during periods of high price inflation and the potentially beneficial portfolio diversification benefits, pension funds have increased their real estate investment activity. Innovative investment arrangements, vehicles, and instruments are being developed as the real estate industry attempts to fashion investments suitable to the needs and characteristics of pension funds.

The Evaluation of Real Estate Acquisition by Pension Funds

In the past, pension funds have shied away from investing in mortgages because of the costs and administrative burdens involved with originating and servicing them. Mortgages were seen as being too complicated relative to bonds and had the added problem of illiquidity. As we will see, however, recent innovations in the mortgage market have made mortgage investments more attractive to pension funds.

In addition, there are a number of reasons why pension funds have been reluctant to become involved in real estate as equity investors. First, and perhaps most important, federal tax laws have historically provided incentives for real estate investors to make maximum use of leverage and make use of sizable tax shelter benefits. Because pension funds are tax-exempt and cannot take advantage of tax shelter benefits, real estate in the 1970s appeared overpriced to them because prices usually reflected the capitalized tax benefits that would accrue to taxable entities. That is, pension funds expected to be outbid by taxable investors who could use real estate tax benefits to increase their after-tax return. Moreover, pension funds have generally bought properties on an all-cash basis; thus, they have not been able to enjoy the effects of positive leverage (for reasons that will be explained later). The Tax Reform Act of 1986 drastically reduced these benefits, hence, tax considerations should now play a reduced role in the determination of real estate investment by pension funds.

Second, real estate was perceived as a high-risk investment area, ill-suited to the trustee-fiduciary character of pension funds. In other words, real estate was seen as an arena for entrepreneurs, where little regulation existed and where the principal approaches to investment seemed very different from those found in the traditional trustee-fiduciary setting in which pension fund managers were accustomed to operating.

Third, the labor-intensive demands involved in managing real properties have discouraged real estate investments by pension fund managers, who tend to be passive investors.

Fourth, and related to all of the above, the managers of and advisors to pension funds were trained in security (equities and fixed income) analysis and had little expertise in the intricacies of real estate investment, which appeared to be not only riskier but more complex than the world of securities investing.

Finally, the real estate market has been characterized by a *lack* of information of the type needed to *perform a comprehensive investment analysis*. Unlike information available in common stocks and bonds, a lack of information needed to analyze and measure the expected return and risk real estate assets in various market areas has inhibited the growth of real estate investment by pension funds. Without such data, quantitative tools developed to make prudent capital allocation decisions could not be used effectively, nor could performance be adequately measured.[1]

---

[1]The prudent man rules and guidelines established by ERISA, Labor Department regulations, and the conventions of the pension fund investment management community do not require the use of currently accepted investment analysis and measurement technology. Nonetheless, pension fund managers and advisors who can justify their investment decisions by such technology are in a better position to guard against charges of being imprudent.

There are several reasons why pension funds have tended to avoid leveraged investments: First, they had plenty of cash; second, being very conservative and risk-averse investors, they feared the impact of negative leverage on portfolio performance; and third, until late 1980 they were subject to an unrelated business *income tax* on the income generated by leveraged investments (properties purchased using debt) under Section 514 of the Internal Revenue Code. With the 1980 tax law change, however, the disincentive for pension fund investors to use leverage in real estate purchases has been removed.

Sources and Stability of Pension Fund Liabilities

In the opinion of many observers, pension funds may well be the best *matched* pool of assets that has ever existed for the real estate industry. This statement may be stronger than is warranted, but a few generalizations can be made about the characteristics that make pension funds well-matched to make real estate investments.

Many pension funds are recipients of funds provided from payroll deductions from beneficiaries, which tend to be relatively long-term and stable. This puts them in a favored position to purchase real estate and to provide capital to developers of real estate projects during periods of high interest rates. This characteristic offsets, at least to some extent, the disadvantages they may face in competing against taxable entities. In addition, except for more mature funds, pension funds normally do not need a great deal of liquidity; their liabilities are generally long-term and actuarially predictable. In this respect, pension funds resemble life insurance companies. Of all the institutional investors discussed, they are also probably least subject to disintermediation. During periods of high interest rates, pension funds contributions have continued to grow even while people tended to withdraw savings from thrifts and banks and to increase borrowing against their life insurance policies.

To illustrate the flow of funds between pension funds and investment, Exhibit 20–1 is a flowchart which generally represents the process. Essentially a pension plan will be either privately sponsored or publicly sponsored. The size of the plan can range from individual plans, which utilize IRA and Keogh accounts, to professional associations (doctors, dentists, etc.) to large corporate plans (General Motors, AT&T, etc.) or public plans (police, firemen, teachers) that can include thousands of beneficiaries. Contributions are made to the fund from employee wages, business income, or from the public sector through tax collections. Funds are invested in a myriad of investments, including real estate ownership and mortgage loans. Depending on the size and management experience of the pension plan, investments may be made directly, or portfolio plan funds may be turned over to investment advisors (whose selection may depend on the advice of consultants based on past performance and portfolio strategy). These advisors have varying degrees of discretion over how funds may be invested. Income from the investment portfolio is combined with contributions to provide benefits to beneficiaries when they retire.

Pension fund investment in real estate is usually one of three types: mortgages, hybrid debt, or equity investments. In September 1986, "fund managers reported total tax-exempt assets invested in real estate at $73.3 billion, an increase of 40.7% from $52.1

EXHIBIT 20–1   Flow of Funds and Asset Management—Pension Funds

Retirement Payments	Investments	Sources of Plan Funds	Plan Sponsor

Plan beneficiaries	Bonds
	Stocks
	Mortgages
	Real estate
	
	Methods of Investment Management
		Employee contributions
		Employer contributions
		IRAs
		Keogh
			Private
			  Corporations
			  Individuals
			  Unions
			  Self-employment

	Plan sponsor (Consultants)
	  and/or
	Investment advisors
	  Life insurance companies
	  Trust depts.—Commercial banks
	  Mortgage bankers
	  Investment companies
	Investment vehicles
	  Direct acquisition
	  Use of separate accounts
	  Use of commingled accounts
	    closed-end
	    open-end
			Public
			  State
			    Employees
			    Teachers
			  Local
			    Employees
			    Police/fire
			    Transit
			    Others

billion in the previous year. Of the total, approximately $45.2 billion or 61.7% was real estate equity; $12.2 billion or 16.6% was in hybrid debt; and $15.9 billion or 21.7% was in mortgages."[2] Standard mortgage investments include fixed interest rate loans on all types of commercial properties. Pension funds also invest in some VA guaranteed and FHA insured single family and multifamily mortgages and GNMA mortgage-backed securities. Most pension fund investment in hybrid debt takes the form of participating mortgages, variable rate mortgages, and convertible mortgages.

Equity investment in real estate by pension funds is by far the most popular form currently used to achieve high returns and optimal diversification effects. Equity investment is usually accomplished (1) by direct investment, (2) by using the services of an investment advisor who may aid with direct investment, or establish a separate investment account on behalf of the pension plan, or (3) by investing in a commingled real estate fund.

---

[2] See "Investors Place $5.6 Billion of New Business in Direct Accounts," *Pension and Investment Age,* Sept. 15, 1986.

Direct Investment

When a pension fund decides to make direct investments, it must then decide (1) whether to set up its own in-house staff to make such real estate investment decisions and to oversee the management of the real estate assets it acquires, or (2) to employ the services of an independent real estate advisor to handle its investments.

Only large pension funds have the resources to engage in direct real estate investments, and such investments may be restricted to mortgage loans. Only the largest funds have the resources to develop an internal staff with the real estate expertise necessary to make investment decisions and to oversee the management of real estate assets. Selecting and managing real estate assets requires knowledge of and competency in a wide range of real estate matters, including determining the quality of properties to make loans on or to purchase. Skills are also required in real estate investment analysis, property performance measurement, assessing risk diversification, property management, reporting techniques, appraisal procedures, and property disposition.

Large pension funds desiring real estate mortgages as an investment will often engage an independent advisor, who is often appointed a trustee of the fund. The independent advisor makes recommendations for investment decisions and may aid in the management of the fund's portfolio. Even if a pension fund employs the services of an independent advisor, the advisor is still considered to be included in ERISA's definition of a fiduciary. In these cases, the investment advisor also assumes liability for reasonable care of the pension fund's assets. But even when it chooses the independent advisor alternative, the fund will still require someone in-house who has real estate expertise to oversee the work of the advisor and to make the required final investment decisions.

Separate Accounts

In many cases the pension fund may engage the services of an investment advisor and will allocate a given amount of funds to the advisor, who establishes a separate account. Separate accounts are generally set up for only one specific pension fund client. The degree of discretion that a manager has with pension fund dollars also varies with the agreement made with the pension plan sponsor. If a single, separate account is established by a large pension plan, the advisor will receive a large allocation of funds to invest and manage.

Commingled Real Estate Funds

A commingled real estate fund (CREF) represents a pool of capital provided by a number of pension funds assembled to acquire real estate. A type of separate account, CREFs have been established primarily for pension fund clients by life insurance companies, commercial banks, and independent investment companies. Such accounts may be open-end or closed-end funds.

Commingled funds provide several advantages over direct investments for pension fund investors. They provide professional management and, if they are large enough, geographic and property-type diversification. In addition, open-end commingled funds usually provide a greater degree of liquidity than separate accounts provide, although, as will be discussed below, even the open-end CREF, the most liquid type, may appear more liquid than it really is.

The commingled real estate fund is a relatively new investment vehicle. The first, the Wachovia Bank Fund, was established in 1968. Prudential Insurance Company of America followed with its open-end CREF, known as PRISA, in 1970. Over half the funds in existence today were established after 1974. The growth in CREF assets has been dramatic, although figures available on the industry differ. Combining figures from several sources, we can roughly estimate that total assets of the largest CREFs were approximately $50 billion in mid-1986.

Open-End Commingled Real Estate Funds.   As with bond and common stock mutual fund vehicles, a major attraction of open-end CREFs is that they offer a potentially greater degree of liquidity than either direct real estate equity investments or closed-end CREFs (to be discussed). By retaining a small amount of assets in the form of cash and marketable securities, funds are available to buy out (or redeem) the units of participants who wish to leave the CREF. Funds used for redemption of units come from current income earned on investments, sale of properties, or money provided by new participants (investors).

Typically, however, this liquidity is far from being completely adequate for all situations that might arise, and redemption is usually subject to certain restrictions and conditions. These depend on the particular CREF's policy on redemptions as specified in the operating agreement established for its participants. Most importantly, virtually all open-end CREFs have provisions against permitting redemptions that would require forced liquidation of assets.[3] Therefore the degree of liquidity offered by open-end CREFs may diminish when market forces are such as to cause many participants to want to redeem at the same time. Under such conditions, CREFs can obtain the funds to meet redemption requests only from selling properties. Thus they become no more liquid than their underlying assets. In effect, the redemption capability of an open-end fund exists only as long as requests for liquidation do not exceed the liquid component of the real estate portfolio.[4]

Open-end funds have an additional problem with establishing the current value of their assets. Unlike mutual funds, which invest in stocks and bonds and are able to obtain daily market quotations to establish unit values, open-end real estate funds contain properties that are not sold frequently enough to provide them with timely, market price

---

[3]Advance notice to the CREF by the participant of its intention to withdraw is universally required (30 days is normally the minimum notice required). CREF units are normally redeemable at the end of calendar quarters. However, a waiting period that can be longer than 12 months may be required.

[4]Prior to 1982, essentially all major open-end CREFs freely honored requests for withdrawals. In mid-1982, however, one of the largest of the CREFs did not have enough funds on hand to promptly honor all requests for redemption, as it had done in the past. It notified clients requesting redemption that they may have to wait at least an additional quarter before redemption.

information. Consequently, they must rely largely on appraisals to establish a price for their participation units. Although substantial progress has been made toward developing a standardized body of procedures and techniques for estimating real estate values and for measuring the performance of real estate assets, the real estate appraisal process is a less than perfect way to solve the need for accurate market value data.

CREF real estate assets are appraised on a regular basis. External appraisals for each property are usually conducted by third-party independent-fee appraisers each year. Internal appraisals by the advisor are made quarterly, but may be made more frequently to establish the CREF's unit value. This appraisal unit value serves as the current price for both entry and withdrawal.[5]

Closed-End Commingled Real Estate Funds.   The other type of commingled real estate fund is the closed-end fund. The closed-end fund also provides a flexible vehicle for pension fund investors. For example, a closed-end fund can take a variety of organizational forms, such as group trusts, limited partnerships, and even real estate investment trusts (REITs). The choice of form is governed in part by the investment objectives of the fund. What these funds have in common is that they are organized with a fixed capitalization to serve the investment needs of pension funds.

Closed-end CREFs differ from open-end CREFs in several ways. First, unlike the open-end CREF, after a specified amount of capital is raised the closed-end CREF typically does not accept any new participants. Closed-end funds seek to initially raise a predetermined amount of money from investors, which they then commit to a predetermined real estate acquisition program. For example, the types and locations of properties expected to be acquired are disclosed by the investment manager of the fund when commitments from pension plans are solicited. Once the fund has sold the number of units needed to raise the amount of money it seeks, usually no additional participants are accepted. Thus, the asset size of the fund remains more or less static, subject to underlying asset value changes.

Second, unlike buying into a fund at a value set by an appraisal (as is the case with open-end funds), participants in closed-end funds acquire a share in a pool of properties that were purchased at market prices. The number of units they own is proportionate to the size of their investment in the fund. Thus, the value of each participant's investment in the fund, at least for the original investors, is established by the cost to enter the fund. Further, because closed-end funds do not admit investors after the initial amount of capital to undertake the investment program is raised, there is no need for frequent appraisals. Generally, closed-end funds use annual appraisals to update the value of their asset holdings. Such valuations are made to keep plan investors informed as to how well the portfolio is performing.

Third, closed-end funds are generally established for a specific period of time (which varies from 7 to 15 years), at the end of which they are liquidated. The only way a participant can redeem a share in a closed-end fund in the interim is to find some would-

---

[5]The annual appraisals for properties in the portfolio are staggered throughout the year (usually quarterly) so that at the end of each quarter at least one-fourth of the portfolio has been subjected to an outside appraisal.

be participant who is willing to buy its units. The price for such units may be more or less than the selling participant's cost basis in the fund. In this respect, participants in closed-end funds are analogous to investors in closed-end investment companies. Unlike the latter, however, there is no well-organized secondary market in which units of closed-end CREFs can be bought and sold.

Conflicts of Interest

Because of the simultaneous operation of general accounts and separate accounts by some investment advisors, there is a potential for conflicts of interest. Indeed, the decision as to which account should benefit from the acquisition of choice properties can develop into a moral hazard for investment advisors. To overcome this problem, advisors must adhere to regulations set forth in ERISA and pronouncements by the Department of Labor governing self-dealing, incentive fees, and so on. Further, many investment advisors have created real estate investment advisory subsidiaries to try and keep real estate activities for general accounts distinct from separate and commingled accounts. Advisors have also created commingled funds with very focused investment objectives to minimize competition with other commingled funds that they operate.

REAL ESTATE INVESTMENT TRUSTS

Background

The concept of the real estate investment trust goes back to the 1880s. In the early years, trusts were not taxed if trust income was distributed to beneficiaries. A Supreme Court decision in the 1930s, however, required that all passive investment vehicles that were centrally organized and managed like corporations be taxed as corporations. This included real estate investment trusts.

Stock and bond investment companies, also affected by the Supreme Court decision, promptly secured legislation (in 1936) which exempted regulated investment companies, including mutual funds, from federal taxation. At this time the real estate trusts were not organized to press for equal consideration, and the trust did not develop into importance as a legal form for investing in real estate.

After World War II, however, the need for large sums of real estate equity and mortgage funds renewed interest in more extensive use of the real estate investment trust (which also became known as the REIT, pronounced ''reet''), and a campaign was begun to achieve for the REIT special tax considerations comparable to those accorded mutual funds. In 1960 such legislation cleared Congress.

Legal Requirements

Effective January 1, 1961, special income tax benefits were accorded a new type of investment institution by an amendment to the Internal Revenue Code (Sections 856–

858). Under this amendment, a real estate investment trust meeting prescribed require ments during the taxable year may be treated simply as a conduit with respect to the income distributed to beneficiaries of the trust. Thus the unincorporated trust or association ordinarily taxed as a corporation is not taxed on distributed taxable income when it qualifies for the special tax benefits. Only the beneficiaries pay the tax on such distributed income. To qualify as a real estate investment trust for tax purposes, the trust must satisfy the following requirements:

1. Ownership must be in an unincorporated trust or association managed by at least one trustee, with transferable certificates of beneficial interest or shares, and ordinarily taxable as a domestic corporation.
2. There must be at least 100 beneficial owners; no more than 50 percent of outstanding shares may be owned by fewer than five individuals.
3. The trust must not be a personal holding company even though all of its gross income constitutes personal holding company income.
4. The trust may not hold any property primarily for sale to customers in the ordinary course of business, that is, dealer property.
5. It must elect to be treated as a real estate investment trust.

REIT regulations are intended to ensure that they will be *passive* investment vehicles. For example, REIT assets must satisfy certain diversification requirements. At least 75 percent of all assets must consist of real estate, loans secured by real estate, mortgages on real property, shares of other REITs, cash, or government securities. Therefore, no more than 25 percent of total REIT assets may be invested in other securities.

At least 75 percent of a REIT's annual gross income must be from qualifying real estate sources. This includes rents, mortgage interest, and gains from the sale of property, exclusive of gains from property held in the ordinary course of business. Further, 95 percent of a REIT's gross income must be derived from these qualifying sources and/or from dividends, interest, and capital gains from the sale of stock and other securities. The penalty for violation of these rules could jeopardize the REIT's tax status for current and past years. If violated, taxes may be recalculated as though the trust was operated as a regular corporation.

As insurance that REITs do not engage in speculative and short-term trading, there is a requirement that gains from the sale of property held for less than four years (excluding gains generated from foreclosures) must represent less than 30 percent of gross income. (There are exceptions to this rule in the case of sales pursuant to liquidation of the trust.) If a REIT is found to be involved in short-term trading, any gains from sales are subject to regular taxation (not allowed to be a part of distributed taxable income.)

To retain their tax-exempt status, REITs must distribute at least 95 percent of net annual taxable income to shareholders. This mechanism makes REITs pass-through investment vehicles. If a REIT is found to be in violation of its dividend requirement, it could be forced to pay catch-up dividends along with severe penalties.

A business activity restriction also exists which prohibits REITs from engaging in the *active* operation of a business such as land development, building homes for sale, or condominium conversion. As a general rule, REITs will lose their nontaxable status with respect to income received from the sale of properties developed, built, and/or held primarily for resale. However, the tax law has been modified to permit a REIT to sell its investment property (primarily for purposes of portfolio restructuring) free of income taxation to the REIT if certain conditions are met.

A management activity restriction also exists to ensure the passive nature of REITs. Trustees, directors, or employees of a REIT must not actively engage in managing or operating REIT property, rendering services to tenants of REIT property, collecting rents from tenants. These functions are to be performed by an independent contractor. With regard to this latter set of restrictions, the trustees or directors of a REIT, in keeping with their fiduciary and management responsibilities for the affairs of the REIT, are permitted to make decisions with respect to the property of the REIT if such decisions are involved with the conduct of the affairs of the REIT itself. For example, they may establish rental terms, choose tenants, enter into and renew leases, make decisions regarding taxes, interest, insurance, capital expenditures, and even repairs relating to REIT property.

Many REITs are organized and/or sponsored by a financial institution, such as an insurance company, a commercial bank, or a mortgage banker. The sponsoring institution also serves as an advisor to the REIT, either directly or through an affiliate. Responsibility is delegated to the advisor for managing the operations of the REIT, including management of the REIT's assets and liabilities. By the early 1980s, the use of advisors by REITs had become less common as REITs tended to become independent organizations.

Types of Trusts

The two principal types of real estate investment trusts are equity trusts and mortgage trusts. In the early years the equity trust was generally used, but later the mortgage trust became the more important, and more recently the equity trust has again grown in importance.

The difference between the assets held by the equity trust and those held by the mortgage trust is fairly obvious. The equity trust acquires property interests, while the mortgage trust purchases mortgage obligations and thus becomes a creditor with mortgage liens given priority to equity holders. As time has progressed, more heterogeneous investment policies have been developed, combining the advantages of both types of trusts to suit specific investment objectives. Such combinations are called hybrid trusts.

For purposes of description, equity trusts have generally been categorized into the following groups.[6] (Some REITs have more than one of the following attributes and could be classified under more than one category.)

1. Blank or ''blind pool'' check trusts. A blank trust is one that is organized to buy properties judged by the trustees to meet the investment goals of the trust. These goals and the nature of properties expected to be acquired are usually spelled out very generally in the offering prospectus. Participating interests in the trust are sold to investors based more on the strength of the reputations of the promoters, trustees, and independent

---

[6]John C. Williamson, ''The Real Estate Investment Trust Act—The Catalyst Which Is Making Real Estate 'Go Public','' *Journal of Property Management,* vol. 27, no. 2 (Winter, 1961), pp. 68–79.

contractors with management responsibility. The advantage of this type of trust is its flexibility, but a major disadvantage results from the lapse of time between the date the investor's shares are offered to the public and the time when the funds can be profitably invested.

2. Purchasing, or fully specified trusts. A purchasing trust is one that has been organized to purchase a specific property or properties described in a prospectus. The advantage of this form is that the potential investor is fully informed about the property to be acquired.

3. Mixed trusts. Mixed trusts are organized to invest part of the funds raised in specific properties and the balance on a "blank check" basis. Being mixed, this trust has the advantage of providing almost immediate income, but since a part of the funds will be invested over time, the overall return will be relatively low, at least until the total investment has been made.

4. Leveraged REIT's versus unleveraged REITs. When an equity REIT acquires properties, it may also seek mortgage financing to partially fund the acquisition. Financing may provide for up to 90 percent of the value of purchased assets. Unleveraged equity REITs do not use debt financing in their acquisitions. The offering prospectus should indicate whether a given REIT plans to use leverage as a part of its investment policy.

5. Finite-life versus non-finite-life REITs. A finite-life (or self-liquidating) REIT is undertaken with the goal of disposing of its assets and distributing all proceeds to shareholders by a specified date. These REITs were instituted in response to the criticism of many investors that the prices of REIT shares tended to behave more like shares of common stock; that is, they were based on current and expected future earnings rather than the underlying real estate asset value of the REIT. Hence, by the establishment of a terminal distribution date, it is argued that REIT share prices should more closely match asset values because investors can make better estimates of the terminal value of the underlying properties. This, it is argued, is not the case with non-finite-life REITs, which reinvest any sale and financing proceeds in new or existing properties and tend to operate more like a going concern, as opposed to an investment conduit.

6. Closed-end versus open-end REITs. Closed-end REITs specify a total dollar maximum that the trust will raise for investment; therefore, it limits the number of shares issued to the public at the initial offering. This limitation protects shareholders from possible future dilution of their equity interest, which could happen if more shares were later authorized for issue (as would be the case with an open-ended trust) and new funds could not be invested as profitably as funds invested from the initial offering.

Open-end REITs, on the other hand, create and sell new shares as they find new investment opportunities. Management and shareholders of these REITs assume that the total value of each share will ultimately increase with new investments undertaken and that dilution of earnings will not be a serious concern over the long term. Obviously, how much money can be raised with an initial offering is hard to determine in advance of the offering. Hence, many REITs reserve the right to sell additional shares to take advantage of operating economies that it may realize by operating a larger trust.

Further, it will also save underwriting and public registration fees that it would have to pay if it undertook a new issue each time capital is raised. The offering prospectus should clearly indicate whether an option exists to issue more shares, and the investor should assess the potential for distribution in earnings.

7. Exchange trusts. Exchange trusts involve the exchange of property for shares in the trust immediately after its organization. Such a transfer qualifies as a tax-free exchange for income tax purposes, and the trust acquires the shareholder's cost basis with respect to the property for depreciation purposes. The disadvantage of failing to acquire a stepped-up basis for higher depreciation deductions is offset by the tax-free diversification that the investor achieves. The trust also benefits in that it obtains a seasoned property with a known income potential.

8. Developmental-joint venture equity REITs. REITs may also participate in joint venture real estate development, which may provide shareholders higher returns than other types of REITs because of the ability to participate in development profits. However, these higher returns usually come at the expense of higher risk because of construction and lease-up time periods. In such cases one of the sponsors of such a REIT is a developer seeking funds for construction. The REIT raises funds in a public offering and advances them to a joint venture partnership comprising a developer and the REIT. Although the REIT commits itself to fund a specific portion of development costs, it usually funds the project in stages as work progresses. It must also invest the net proceeds from the offering in other projects on an interim basis until needed. As a joint venture partner, the REIT may receive preferential cash flow distributions, with the remaining cash flow shared between the REIT and the developer on the basis of a predetermined formula. Once a project is completed, the joint venture investment will usually be refinanced, and the REIT will recoup a substantial portion of its initial investment while retaining some ownership until the project is sold.

From the developer's point of view, a developmental joint venture with a REIT may provide a relatively inexpensive source of capital for construction and development. The initial dividend yield requirement of the REIT's shareholders may be lower than the cost of traditional construction financing. Further, the developer may be able to obtain more financing than would otherwise be available with a conventional loan.

A REIT may also participate in a development project through a land purchase-leaseback transaction. Under this arrangement, the REIT purchases the land that is to be developed and simultaneously leases it to the developer. The REIT earns income from the lease on the land and usually participates in income earned on the project through an income participation agreement based on a percentage of income from the improved property and a participation in any sale or refinancing of the project. The REIT may also obtain an option to purchase the improvement when the land lease expires.

The Appeal of Equity Trusts as an Investment

The equity-oriented real estate investment trust has provided investors with an opportunity to invest funds in a diversified portfolio of real estate under professional management while providing better liquidity than would be the case if a property was acquired outright. Because the individual investor has the opportunity to pool his or her resources with those of persons of like interests, funds are assembled to permit purchase of buildings, shopping centers, and land in whatever proportion that seems to offer the most attractive returns. Investment must be approved by a board of trustees who are ordinarily well qualified to make such decisions. The trust certificate holder buys an interest in diversified holdings, with shares that are usually readily salable in the over-the-counter market or on major stock exchanges. The tax exemption places the small shareholder in a position for tax payments similar to what might have occurred had the same investment been made as an individual real estate operator.

Caveats.   As described above, when an equity REIT is created, existing properties or projects to be developed will be acquired as investments. In addition, during the life of the REIT, management fees, advisory fees, and commissions will be paid to affiliates and other parties doing business with the trust. Typically a real estate owner working with an investment banker can form a REIT that is capitalized through a public securities offering. The REIT may then use the funds it has raised to acquire the owner's properties. Outside business entities that may be affiliated with the sponsors of the REIT can contract to provide property management and advisory services.

Obviously, the close association of REITs and real estate organizations or individuals who sponsor it can create potential conflicts of interest. The following safeguards attempt to protect investors against the problems of such conflicts. The articles of incorporation of most REITs provide that a *majority* of the trustees or directors may not be affiliated with the sponsors of a REIT. The articles also require that the REIT engage independent appraisers to determine whether the purchase prices of properties acquired from the sponsors are at fair market value, and whether "fees paid to the REIT's management and advisory companies are reasonable."

Tax Shelters and Real Estate Investment Trusts

In previous chapters, we have pointed out the tax advantages that may be derived from depreciation allowances deductible from taxable income. The fact that the functional or economic life of a property often extends far beyond the depreciable life used for income tax purposes may result in a tax shelter to investors. In many instances, the decline in value as a result of depreciation or obsolescence may be offset by rising replacement costs of similar properties when demand for such properties is high in relation to supply. Thus, older properties may sell today at prices above original cost of construction, and yet they may have been substantially depreciated for income tax purposes.

However, to the extent a depreciation charge is taken, the investor has recognized a return of capital and not income on investment. A statement of income and expenses may demonstrate why this is true:

Total revenues received	$100,000
Total cash expenses	60,000
Net cash earnings	$ 40,000
Depreciation charge allowable (write-off to reduce property carrying value)	30,000
Net taxable income	$ 10,000

If this property is managed by a tax-exempt real estate investment trust and the $40,000 of net cash earnings is distributed to trust certificate holders, only one-fourth of the earnings (in the ratio of $10,000 to $40,000) will be taxable to the individual recipients. The other three-fourths will constitute a nontaxable return of capital. For accounting purposes, the individual investor cannot measure a precise return on investment based on cash receipts. Distributions paid to the extent of depreciation (as the $30,000 above) instead of net income ($10,000 above) are considered a return of capital until the investor recovers the full acquisition cost of REIT shares or sells them. After full recovery of costs, taxable gains may be realized. If, in our example, investors initially paid $200,000 for all REIT shares one year ago, the tax basis of these shares after one operating period would become $200,000 − $30,000 = $170,000. If all shares were then sold for $220,000 a capital gain of $50,000 would be realized ($220,000 − $170,000). When REITs report operating losses, such losses may not be passed through to investors, but must be carried forward to offset income in future periods.

With respect to capital gains from the sale of property by a REIT, the law gives REITs the authority to either (1) retain the gain for future investment, in which case the gain is taxed at the appropriate corporate capital gains rate, or (2) to distribute the gain as a dividend to shareholders. In the latter case the REIT is not taxed on the distributed gain; however, such dividends are required to be designated as a capital gain distribution to shareholders, who must recognize it as a capital gain in their individual treatment. Capital losses may not be passed through to individual investors, but must be carried forward.

The Tax Reform Act of 1986 contains several features that will impact REITs as an investment vehicle. The reader may recall from Chapter 11 that one of the most important aspects in the Act is the passive loss limitation. This provision will not affect REITs because losses have never been allowed as a pass-through to investors. Note that REIT dividends are considered to be portfolio income under the Act and thus will *not qualify* as passive income to offset passive losses.

The Appeal of Mortgage REIT as an Investment

The mortgage trust is unlike the equity trust in that it does not own the real property. Rather, it owns mortgage paper secured by the underlying real property. Income generated by the mortgage paper is affected by the interest rate on the mortgage note, the discount (or premium) at which the obligation is acquired, and the amount of funds outstanding on loan. Trust expenses applicable against this income are, generally, interest paid for the funds derived to put out on loan, management company costs, and other lesser expenses incident to the operations of this kind of investment company.

During the late 1960s and early 1970s, this trust was used as a source of loans, particularly for construction and development, that were beyond the legal or policy limits of the highly regulated banks, savings and loans, insurance companies, or other real estate–oriented financing institutions. Because their lending policies were relatively un-regulated and because they had access to public securities markets, mortgage trusts were in a position to fill a void in the real estate financing market. Even though their cost of the short-term borrowed funds was relatively high, there was always the reasonable expectation that the trust could make construction or development loans at a 3.5 to 4 percent higher rate than rates available from other lending sources. The spread between borrowing costs and loan income thus held the promise of increasing earnings on the shareholders' equity as the loan portfolio grew. Such growth in earnings would support further sales of shares in the trust at higher prices, and so on. Following this pattern, the expansion of mortgage trusts during the early 1970s was spectacular.

However, during 1974 a general economic recession set in, and the prime bank lending rate rose to unprecedented heights. Because of the unanticipated rise in their cost of funds, many mortgage trusts were forced into an operating loss position because they were not able to pass on a sufficient amount of these higher costs to borrowers. Further, many advance mortgage commitments had already been made at lower rates with inadequate flexibility for upward rate adjustments. During this period of rising interest rates, many developers were unable to sell their completed units or could not complete their projects because of rapidly inflating construction costs and, consequently, were thrown into default on their construction loans. The share values of mortgage trusts fell dramatically, thus reducing the possibilities for further stock offerings as a source of funds.

Because of loan default expectations, the commercial paper market also dried up for the trusts and forced them to rely almost exclusively on bank credit lines. As the defaults continued to increase during 1975, many large commercial banks were placed in the position of having to extend the maturities on notes taken pursuant to these credit lines which had usually been extended by banks as a group under a revolving credit agreement. The extensions were granted to avoid the cumulative impact on the total financial system if the trusts were forced to undertake mass foreclosures in a time of serious business recession. A number of bank sponsors took large blocks of mortgages out of the trust portfolios and into their own loan and liquidation accounts to reduce trust debts where stringencies became so severe that commercial bank lines could not otherwise be reasonably renewed. Such actions had an impact on overall commercial bank liquidity and removed the mortgage trusts generally from the construction and development loan markets as a supplier of funds for the foreseeable future.

Caveats

As was the case with equity REITs there exists the potential for a conflict of interest when sponsors and affiliates of mortgage REITs are also originators of mortgage loans (mortgage companies, thrifts, commercial banks, etc.). In these instances, there may be incentives to sell REITs submarginal loans while charging fees for servicing them. As indicated earlier, the rules governing the appointment of nonaffiliated trustees and the use of outside appraisers must also be followed in the creation and operation of mortgage REITs.

SYNDICATION

The concept of real estate syndication extends generally to any group of investors who have combined their financial resources with the expertise of a real estate professional for the common purpose of carrying out a real estate project. A syndicate is not an organization form per se. It may take any of the business forms discussed in Chapter 11 (e.g., corporation, joint ownership, joint venture, or partnership).

A syndicate can be formed to acquire, develop, manage, operate or market real estate. Syndication can be viewed as a type of financing that offers smaller investors the opportunity to invest in ventures that would otherwise be beyond their financial and management capabilities. Syndicators benefit from the fees they receive for their services and the interest they may retain in the syndicated property.

Use of the Limited Partnership in Private and Public Syndicates

Limited partnerships are widely used as vehicles for raising equity capital for real estate ventures. They combine the limited liability feature of an investment in a corporation with the advantages of a general partnership, such as the ability to make special allocations of income and cash flow to the partners. An investor's liability (limited partner) is limited to the initial contribution plus any unpaid contributions agreed to in the future. Furthermore, the responsibility for the management of the partnership rests with the general partners who are frequently knowledgeable in real estate matters, thus providing the partnership with professional management.

In establishing the limited partnership, great care must be taken that the contractual terms identify it in effect as a partnership and not as an "association" as understood by the Internal Revenue Service. An association is taxed like a corporation. The six criteria for treatment like a corporation are

1. Business association.
2. An objective to carry on the business and divide the gains therefrom.
3. Continuity of life.
4. Centralization of management.
5. Limited liability.
6. Free transferability of interest.

A corporation must have more corporate than noncorporate characteristics to be classified as a corporation for tax purposes. Criteria 1 and 2 are common to corporations and partnerships. It is therefore commonly understood that a business firm will receive treatment as a partnership if two of the criteria 3 through 6 are absent.

Most limited partnerships have a centralization of management similar to corporations, so differentiation normally will take place in 3, 5, and 6. Under the Uniform Partnership Act, after which most state statutes are patterned, the general partner has the power to dissolve the partnership at any time, thus denying it continuity of life. Otherwise, a terminal date may be provided for in the partnership articles. The criterion of limited liability is negated by the very fact that one partner is a general partner with unlimited liability. Finally, free transferability of interests can be limited by requiring permission of the general or other limited partners to effect a change of ownership. This restriction has been deemed by the Treasury regulations as a legal curtailment of transferability of interests. By proper combination of these provisions, tax treatment as a partnership can be achieved.

Use of Corporate General Partners

The sole general partner of a limited partnership is often a corporation. The advantage of this arrangement lies in the limited personal liability the builder-sponsor of a project can achieve by holding his interest in the limited partnership in his corporation. An incorporated general partner can also provide better continuity of management. To avoid "dummy" characteristics in the sole corporate general partner, the Internal Revenue Service follows internal guidelines (called *safe harbor rules*) imposing certain ownership and minimum capital requirements. In regard to ownership, limited partners may not own, individually or in the aggregate, more than 20 percent of the corporate stock. The net worth requirement of the corporate general partner depends on the total contributed capital of the partnership. If the contributed capital is less than $2.5 million, the corporate general partner must have a net worth at least equal to 15 percent of the total partnership capital, but not to exceed $250,000. Where the contributed partnership capital is $2.5 million or more, the corporate general partner must maintain at all times a net worth of at least 10 percent of the partnership capital.

Private versus Public Syndicates

An important way to classify syndicates is as *private* and *public*. Most private offerings are issued under Regulation D of the Securities Act of 1933 so as to be exempt from the registration requirements of that Act. Regulation D was promulgated by the Securities and Exchange Commission in 1982 to simplify and expand the availability of exemptions from federal securities registration. Every private syndicator seeks to avoid the cost and regulatory burdens of federal securities registration. The significant costs of registration essentially eliminate all but the largest syndicated offerings, and the intent of Regulation D is to facilitate small and medium-sized offerings by exempting them from registration if they meet certain guidelines. Although Regulation D represents a codification and expansion of prior exemption statutes, it defines important concepts, including that of the "accredited investor," which is discussed below. Compliance with the regulation, however, does not by itself furnish exemption under state securities laws, but many states do have similar exemption statutes. The exemption provided by Regulation D is only the exemption from the registration requirement of the Securities Act and does not furnish an exemption from the full disclosure and antifraud provisions of the securities laws. Anyone involved in making an offering pursuant to the regulation should read and understand it thoroughly to ensure careful compliance with its provisions.

Accredited Investors—Regulation D

If the securities are sold only to accredited investors, it is not necessary to provide investors with the information otherwise required to obtain an exemption under Regulation D. Accredited investors purchasing securities are also not counted in determining the maximum number of potential purchasers that may be solicited to retain exemption from

Regulation D. Also, accredited investors do not need to meet the "sophistication and experience" requirements in financial and business matters that are applicable to other investors under the private placement exemption rule in Regulation D. General examples of criteria used to describe accredited investors include the following:

1. Any director, executive officer, or general partner of the issuer of the securities being offered or sold, or a director, executive officer, or general partner of a general partner of that issuer.
2. Any person who purchases at least $150,000 of the securities being offered, where the purchaser's total purchase price does not exceed 20 percent of the purchaser's net worth at the time of sale.
3. Any natural person whose individual net worth, or joint net worth with that person's spouse, at the time of purchase exceeds $1,000,000.
4. Any natural person who had an individual income in excess of $200,000 in each of the two most recent years and who reasonably expects an income in excess of $200,000 in the current year.

Private offerings are usually limited to 35 or fewer investors. A public offering, on the other hand, is characterized by rigorous compliance requirements of the federal and state securities divisions governing the sale of securities to the public. Numerous reports, brochures, prospectuses, and the like are required to qualify an issue for sale to the public. The minimum cost for a registration with the Securities and Exchange Commission is about $50,000 and can run as high as $300,000 to $500,000 for large syndications that register and sell shares in many states. Given the high cost of registering a public syndication under federal and state laws, it only makes sense to have a public syndication for large transactions where a large amount of capital is raised with one syndication.

Certificates of participation in public syndicates have been sold in units as low as $500, $1,000, or $5,000. Minimum investments in private syndicates are usually 10 times this amount. Recently, public syndicates have reduced their minimum investment amounts in an attempt to attract their share of Individual Retirement Account and Keogh (self-employed retirement plan) money. The result has been that instead of a few participants of substantial means and risk-taking ability, the syndicate membership may be composed of thousands of small investors. Individuals now have a chance to invest in prime real estate that would normally be beyond reach of all but the wealthy or institutional investors.

Caveats

In an operation of this kind, the syndication general partners usually share very few of the risks. They may have originally bought property through another business entity and sold it to the syndicate at a profit. Through other companies that they may also own, they may receive substantial remuneration for the sale of securities to the public, management services, and so on. As the general partners, all earnings and capital gains not contracted to the limited partners accrue to their benefit. These activities may or may not be fully disclosed to potential investors. This has been a matter of increasingly grave concern to state and federal securities sales regulators.

REGULATION OF SYNDICATES

The great flexibility of the limited partnership has led to abuses. In 1980 a statement of policy or guidelines that established standards for limited partnership offerings of real estate was adopted by the North American Securities Administrators Association (NASAA). State registration agencies, in those states where the guidelines are applicable, generally look with disfavor upon applications that do not conform to the standards contained in the guidelines. All states except California (which has even more stringent guidelines in some aspects) belong to NASAA, but not all states have adopted the NASAA guidelines. However, a substantial number of states follow the guidelines, and although the guidelines are intended to *apply only to public syndicates,* many securities administrators look to them for guidance when considering requests for exemptions from registration. The guidelines address syndicates' investment policies, promoters' and managers' compensation, and investor suitability standards. It is in these areas that federal and state regulatory authorities have expressed their greatest concern.

Investment Objectives and Policies

Syndicates differ widely in the investment objectives they seek to accomplish and policies they follow to achieve them. If targeted syndicate investors are in a low tax bracket and seek current income (e.g., IRA and pension fund investors), the syndicate will acquire properties which produce the greatest cash flow. Some of these properties may be purchased for all cash. Other investors may not need current income and seek properties (such as raw land in the path of urban growth) which offer the greatest potential for future capital gain. Still other investors may emphasize investments that generate tax shelters through high depreciation and mortgage interest deductions. The targeted investors for the syndicate will dictate the investment objectives and policies of the syndicator.

In the early experience with limited partnerships and until the late 1960s, capital was normally raised to finance identifiable parcels which are described in the prospectus or offering circular in detail and could be evaluated by the investor before he invested his money. Such syndicates are referred to as "specified property" syndicates. Other syndicates raise capital before any (or less than all of the) properties it will eventually own are identified. They are known as *blind pool* syndicates and should be recognized as pure venture capital funds, since there can be no property descriptions or relevant economic or financial data available for the investor's guidance. Specific investment criteria (e.g., type of property and geographic location) should be disclosed in the prospectus for such a blind pool syndicate, as well as the sponsor's background, experience, and previous results, because an investment in a blind pool is essentially an investment in the syndicator's track record and reputation. Investors in such offerings should carefully scrutinize the statement of investment objectives contained in the prospectus, as well as the background and track record of the syndicator.

Promoters' and Managers' Compensation

A major area of concern for syndicate investors arises in connection with promotional and management fees. Keeping these fees to reasonable levels becomes especially difficult because of the many ways in which compensation can be paid. Syndicators often charge fees for providing services such as acquiring properties for the portfolio, managing them, guaranteeing investors a minimum cash flow, selling properties, or arranging refinancing. Obviously the up front fees reduce the amount of funds available for investment in the actual real estate. Additional fees may also be charged on the "back end" out of proceeds from sale of the property.

Management fees have been based on gross assets, net assets, gross rentals, net income, and cash flow. Each method will yield its own unique results dependent upon the fortunes of the syndicate operation. Unfortunately, projections of results are often based on hypotheticals without valid underlying assumptions. Bad projections will distort judgments regarding what is appropriate compensation or, for that matter, what is a proper method for determining it. In all instances, full disclosure of conflicts of interest of principals, as well as all direct and indirect compensation payable by the partners to promoters, general partners, underwriters, and affiliates, should be made. This disclosure should describe the compensation as to time of payment and amount, and it should detail the service rendered to earn it.

As the preceding paragraphs point out, fees charged by syndicators and others promoting the syndicate vary widely. Because up front fees reduce amounts available for investment, investors should look closely at deals where more than 20 percent of the equity raised is paid out in such fees. Typical up front fees include 7 to 10 percent for sales commissions to brokers selling syndicate interests, 1 to 3 percent for legal and accounting expenses, and 5 to 15 percent for organizational and financing fees.

Investor Suitability Standards

An outstanding weakness of a limited partnership interest as an investment is its lack of liquidity or marketability. By virtue of the restrictions on the assignability of the capital interest, a new partner must have the consent of the existing partners to acquire and enjoy the full interest of a selling partner. Furthermore, state-imposed requirements of financial responsibility of potential investors have complicated the problem of developing a secondary market for such interests. Even an issue of certificates of beneficial interest[7] in a limited partnership is complicated by the fact that the limited partner selling an interest becomes a securities issuer and is subject to separate registration requirements. This lack of liquidity and marketability increases the riskiness of a limited partnership investment.

---

[7]A certificate of beneficial interest is a legal document which evidences a fractional or percentage interest in a partnership.

Another weakness of the syndicate lies in the fact that many syndications have limited appeal to any but the investor in the high tax brackets. Yields on other than a tax shelter basis may be negligible. The low-income investor may acquire such a syndicate interest with too little appreciation of the weak economic viability of the venture. Minimum suitability standards for investors as recommended by the NASSA guidelines include either (a) annual gross income of $30,000 and net worth (exclusive of home, furnishings, and automobiles) of at least $30,000 or (b) net worth of at least $75,000. In tax-oriented offerings, higher standards, such as being in the highest federal income tax bracket may be required, and higher income and net worth standards may be imposed on high-risk offerings. In any case, the nature of the investor's expected return in the traditional sense, as well as the potential tax savings, should be clearly presented in the prospectus.

FEDERAL AND STATE SECURITIES AUTHORITIES

The federal and state securities laws and regulations are relevant to any real estate syndication. Disclosure requirements under the Securities Act of 1933 and the Securities Exchange Act of 1934 set the federal basis for civil liability and criminal fraud liability for principals and their professional counsels for failure to disclose full information about a public issue. Most state laws[8] require securities salespersons to be registered in the local jurisdiction. These laws often go beyond the federal requirements in permitting the state commissioner to disqualify a securities offering on its merits, in addition to determining the required degree of disclosure of specific facts about the issue. Neglect by the issuer to qualify the issue may permit investors to rescind the whole transaction and demand their money back. Beyond these laws are the antifraud statutes which deal with fraudulent practices in connection with securities registration. Although the degree of applicability of federal or state laws and regulations differs with the characteristics of each issue, full and active compliance will yield the best results for both the syndicator and investors.

QUESTIONS

1. How have pension funds traditionally viewed real estate investment? How has that point of view changed in recent years? Why?
2. The match between pension fund assets and liabilities has been said to be ideally suited to real estate investment. What is meant by this statement?
3. What are the approaches to real estate investment that have been used by pension plan sponsors? How do these vehicles differ and why do they appeal to pension plan sponsors?
4. What is a REIT? How is it generally classified for tax purposes?

---

[8]State securities laws are commonly referred to as ''blue sky'' laws since their purpose is to prevent ''speculative schemes which may have no more basis than so many feet of blue sky.''

5. Describe the investment restrictions placed on REITs. If these restrictions are violated, what are the consequences to the trust?
6. What are the various descriptions used to categorize equity trusts?
7. From a federal income tax perspective, what are favorable features of REITs?
8. What does the term *syndication* mean in real estate investment? Does it have any legal significance?
9. What form of business organization is most frequently used by real estate syndications?
10. What concerns should an investor in a real estate syndication have regarding general partners?
11. Differentiate between public and private syndications. What is an accredited investor? Why is this distinction used?
12. How are general partners usually compensated in a syndication? What major concerns should investors consider when making an investment with a syndication?

Chapter 21

The Secondary Mortgage Market and Mortgage-Related Securities— Part I

INTRODUCTION

The very large volume of mortgage loan originations and the importance of such originations relative to other types of debt has been pointed out in the flow of funds data in Chapter 19. Along with the growth in originations, a secondary or ''after'' market in which mortgages are sold and resold has also developed. There are many reasons why this market has evolved and grown enormously in recent years. These reasons, as well as the structure, participants, operation, and investors are the focus of this chapter and the next.

We begin with a brief description of the evolution of the secondary market. Particular attention is paid to the need for such a market and identifying the major organizations that participate in it. We then describe the various types of mortgage-backed securities that have evolved in recent years and provide a framework for analyzing their investment characteristics. Although mortgage-related securities may be offered on many types of mortgage pools, we generally restrict our discussion to residential mortgage-backed pools. The chapter concludes with a section on ''pricing'' two types of mortgage-related securities, and provides an evaluation of characteristics that differentiate these more important security types. The next chapter is a continuation of this one. In addition to a detailed analysis of mortgage-backed securities, it also contains sections dealing with commercial mortgage-backed pools and important provisions in the 1986 Tax Reform Act which affected the secondary mortgage market.

EVOLUTION OF THE SECONDARY MORTGAGE MARKET

It is probably safe to say that the secondary mortgage market, as we know it today, evolved as a result of a combination of the following influences: (1) There existed a need for a market in which specialized mortgage originators, such as mortgage banking companies (a nonthrift intermediary discussed in Chapter 19), could sell mortgages and thereby replenish funds with which new loans could be originated. (2) A need also existed for a market mechanism to facilitate a geographic flow of funds. Such a market would allow lenders located in regions of the country where the demand for housing and mortgage financing far exceeded the availability of deposits to sell mortgages to other intermediaries in regions with a surplus of savings. (3) Beginning in the late 1960s, many innovations in securitization occurred in response to the trend toward deregulation of depository-type financial institutions. Because of this trend, savers were no longer limited to traditional methods of saving, such as savings accounts and certificates of deposits. Further, with the passage of legislation giving individual retirement accounts (IRAs) favorable tax treatment and the aging of the U.S. population, which increased the flow of funds to pension accounts, the market for investible funds became much broader. Hence, mortgage lenders, with the aid of organizations specializing in underwriting and selling securities to the public and institutional investors, were faced with the challenge of attracting savings from the public in different ways so as to replenish funds for new mortgage loans. (4) There has been a longstanding commitment on the part of the federal government to encourage homeownership and to provide support for a strong system of housing finance.

EARLY BUYERS OF MORTGAGE LOANS

There has always been a secondary mortgage market of some type. Prior to the mid-1950s, primary mortgage originators involved in the secondary market included mortgage companies and, to a lesser extent, thrift institutions. Investors who purchased these mortgages included large life insurance companies and eastern thrifts. The former generally purchased mortgages from mortgage companies, and the latter generally purchased from thrifts in other regions. By purchasing mortgages, these institutional investors helped to provide funds necessary for housing booms during the postwar era.

One major factor that enhanced the early development of the secondary market was the fact that the federal government, through programs initiated with FHA and later the VA, protected mortgage investors from losses by providing either default insurance (FHA) or loan guarantees (VA). (see Chapter 7 for discussion of these programs.) One outcome of these programs was a system of minimum underwriting standards regarding borrower qualifications, appraisals, and building specifications. Uniform administrative procedures required by the FHA and VA were followed by mortgage companies and helped to accommodate significant volumes of FHA and VA originations and facilitated servicing activities. Given (1) the availability of default insurance and loan guarantees, (2) the development of standardized loan underwriting, processing, and servicing, and (3) the availability of hazard and title insurance, investors in mortgages could acquire a large quantity of loans and expect to receive interest and principal payments with little or no risk. Administrative problems regarding defaults, late payments, and so forth, were usually handled for a fee by the servicer, making mortgage investments resemble those of a bond or fixed income security. With funds acquired from sales of mortgages to institutional investors, originators (primarily mortgage companies) replenished funds with which they could originate new loans.

GOVERNMENT'S ROLE IN MARKET DEVELOPMENT

Government involvement in the secondary mortgage market was formally established in 1916 when the first farmer's credit program was created at the Federal Land Bank as a result of federal concerns with rural housing finance. However, the two most important factors in the early development of the secondary mortgage market were the creation of the Federal Housing Administration (FHA) in 1934 and the chartering of the Federal National Mortgage Association (FNMA) in 1938. As previously indicated, FHA programs helped found a national mortgage market with the creation of mortgage underwriting standards and mortgage default insurance. This program, along with the creation of the Veterans Administration loan guarantee program in 1944, were very important events in the evolution of the secondary market.

In 1935, Congress authorized the Reconstruction Finance Corporation (RFC)[1] to form a subsidiary to be known as the RFC Mortgage Company, to initiate a secondary mortgage market. This venture was not successful, and in 1938 a subsidiary was formed to focus only on a secondary market for government insured residential mortgages. This institution, the Federal National Mortgage Association is now commonly known as "Fannie Mae," and is often designated by its initials FNMA.

FNMA was a subsidiary of the RFC until 1950, when it was transferred to the Housing and Home Finance Agency,[2] which had been created in 1942. By becoming a part of the federal agency primarily concerned with housing and home finance, FNMA's activities in the secondary market for home mortgages could be more closely coordinated with activities of the Federal Home Loan Bank Board and its affiliated agencies as well as with those of the FHA. It should be stressed that FNMA's role at this time was limited to very specialized activities, such as direct lending on FHA insured housing located in remote areas not reached by the existing mortgage market and selling these mortgages to private investors. During this time, it had no real comparative advantage in borrowing or purchasing relative to private entities and hence was not a major force in the secondary market.

THE SECONDARY MARKET AFTER 1954

In 1954, Congress rechartered FNMA. The new Charter Act assigned to FNMA three separate and distinct activities: (1) enhancement of secondary market operations in federally insured and guaranteed mortgages, (2) management of direct loans previously made

---

[1]This agency was charged with the responsibility of raising capital to provide loans for construction of new physical facilities after the Depression.

[2]This agency, along with FHA, would ultimately be combined as a part of the U.S. Department of Housing and Urban Development (HUD).

and, where necessary, liquidation of properties and mortgages acquired by default, and (3) management of special assistance programs, including support for subsidized mortgage loan programs. Each function was carried out as though it was operated as a separate corporation.

Throughout this and earlier periods, interest rates on FHA and VA mortgages were *regulated* by those agencies. Rather than deregulating interest rates on FHA and VA mortgages, Congress, in its attempt to keep mortgage interest rates as low as possible to would-be homebuyers, preferred to maintain a system under which FHA-VA interest rates would remain regulated. FNMAs role would be to raise capital by issuing debt when necessary to purchase mortgages, thereby replenishing capital to originators during periods of rising interest rates. It was thought that those mortgages would be sold at a gain when interest rates declined, thereby providing FNMA with funds to retire debt that was previously issued to acquire mortgages. FNMA was thus viewed as a vehicle which would provide liquidity to the home finance system when needed, and would assume the interest rate risk associated with its role as an intermediary between mortgage originators (primary originators of FHA and VA loans) and investors in its bonds. Ostensibly, over many periodic cycles of interest rate movements, it was hoped that FNMA would, on the average, earn a "spread" between interest earned on mortgages and interest paid on its bonds, while providing liquidity to the home finance system.[3]

FNMA's Changing Role

As market interest rates gradually increased and FHA-VA mortgage interest rates lagged, life insurance companies began to adopt a policy of shifting funds from mortgages to other investments. At the same time, life companies developed considerable interest in the acquisition of common stock, which was previously thought to be too risky. Hence, investment by life companies in common stocks and corporate bonds grew at the expense of mortgages. The traditional channel between mortgage companies and life insurance companies was seriously disrupted. Mortgage companies and other originators became concerned, since their traditional source of funds from secondary mortgage sales diminished. Recognizing these changes in investment policy, organizations such as the National Association of Home Builders, the Mortgage Bankers Association of America, the National Association of Real Estate Boards, and the United States Savings and Loan League advocated that FNMA's secondary market operations be expanded.

These influences prompted Congress to review the operations of FNMA and culminated in the 1954 rechartering. Among the provisions in the Act, however, was an additional provision that governmental participation in the operation of the principal secondary market facility should be gradually replaced by a private enterprise. The Act included a procedure whereby FNMA would, over a period of time, be transformed into a privately

---

[3]Obviously, the risk of such a strategy is that the *net* cost of bonds and notes used to raise funds over periods of rising and falling interest rates would exceed the *net* interest income from mortgages held in a portfolio. This could occur if, over several cycles, net purchases of mortgages exceeded net sales.

owned and managed organization. By converting FNMA to a private operation rather than setting up a new one, FNMA's years of experience in the secondary market could be utilized during the transition period and eventually would concentrate the whole operation in private hands.

To provide a financial base to operate FNMA, the Charter Act also authorized issuance of nonvoting preferred and common stock for the financing of secondary market operations. The preferred stock was issued to the Secretary of the Treasury. Sellers of mortgages to FNMA were required to purchase FNMA stock as a condition of sale which provided additional capital for operations and resulted in widespread ownership of FNMA. Additional funding for FNMA came from its issuance of notes and debt instruments. The Act provided that, if necessary, the U.S. Treasury would be permitted to acquire up to $2.25 billion of these notes. This "backstop" was intended to provide assurance of liquidity to FNMA bond and note purchasers and a price support for such securities, should FNMA's profitability or inability to issue more of these obligations ever come into question. It also provided FNMA with a distinct advantage when borrowing in capital markets to finance its activities. FNMA could now borrow at lower rates of interest than it otherwise could have in the absence of the Treasury backstop.

THE HOUSING AND URBAN DEVELOPMENT ACT OF 1968

Under the Housing and Urban Development Act of 1968, the assets, liabilities, and management of the secondary market operations were transferred to a completely private corporation.[4] This corporation became the Federal National Mortgage Association as we know it today. As previously indicated, prior to this time, FNMA had been jointly financed by the U.S. government and private investors. The 1968 law made it a government-sponsored corporation owned solely by private investors. All Treasury-held preferred shares provided for in the 1954 Act were retired, thereby eliminating government ownership in FNMA.

The special assistance and management and liquidating functions, largely dealing with subsidized mortgage purchases for special federal housing programs, remained in the Department of Housing and Urban Development. To perform these functions, the 1968 Act created another corporation titled the Government National Mortgage Association (GNMA), now familiarly known as "Ginnie Mae."

THE GOVERNMENT NATIONAL MORTGAGE ASSOCIATION

The Government National Mortgage Association was organized to perform three principal functions: (1) management and liquidation of mortgages previously acquired by FNMA,

---

[4]The board of directors of FNMA consists of 15 members, one-third of whom are appointed by the president of the United States and the remainder of whom are elected by the stockholders. All terms are for one year. The presidential appointments are required to include one person each from the homebuilding, real estate, and mortgage lending industries. All directors are removable by the president but only for good cause. Because of the nature of its charter and the support provided by the U.S. Treasury, FNMA must also be sensitive to national housing needs. Its work is conducted from agency offices strategically located across the country.

(2) special assistance lending in support of federal programs, and (3) provision of a guarantee for FHA-VA mortgage pools which would provide a guarantee for mortgage backed securities. Its operations are financed through funds from the U.S. Treasury and from public borrowing.

The management and liquidating functions of Ginnie Mae involve the holding, managing, and liquidating of a portfolio of mortgages and properties acquired from FNMA at the time of its partition. The liquidation of this portfolio comes through regular principal repayments and sales.

Ginnie Mae is also charged with the obligation to provide special assistance in connection with certain subsidized housing programs deemed desirable by the federal government. GNMA is authorized to purchase mortgages, which are originated under various housing programs designed by FHA, to provide housing in areas where it cannot be provided by conventional market lending.

Mortgage-Backed Securities and the GNMA Payment Guarantee

It is safe to say that the guarantee program provided for in 1968 was the most significant provision in development of the secondary mortgage market as we know it today. Essentially, GNMA was empowered to guarantee the timely payment of principal and interest on securities backed or secured by pools of mortgages insured by the FHA and the Farmers Home Administration, or guaranteed by the VA. One of the problem areas in the secondary mortgage market prior to this time was that even though FHA insured mortgages could be purchased by investors who received monthly payments of principal and interest (less servicing fees), investors often experienced delays in payments when borrower defaults occurred. In these cases, servicers would have to make a claim for any payments in arrears plus remittance of the loan balance from FHA or the guarantee from VA. Settlement of these claims could be time-consuming and required additional administrative effort on the part of investors.

Many investors in mortgage packages disliked this waiting period, which resulted in unanticipated cash flows and also resulted in a reduction in investment yields. By providing the buyer with a guarantee of timely payment of interest and principal, GNMA was, in essence, guaranteeing monthly payments of interest and principal from amortization, plus repayment of outstanding loan balances should a mortgage be prepaid before maturity, or should a borrower default. GNMA would make timely payments to the security purchaser, then take responsibility for settling any accounts with the servicer. This would relieve investors from administrative problems and delays in receiving mortgage payments. For this guarantee, the buyer was charged a guarantee fee, which provided GNMA with operating funds to perform this function.

As a result of this GNMA guarantee program, a virtual explosion in the secondary market occurred. This guarantee enabled originators of FHA and VA mortgages to pool or package mortgages and to *issue securities,* called *pass-through securities,* which were collateralized by the mortgages, and were based on the notion of investors buying an undivided security interest in a pool of mortgages with interest and principal being passed through to investors as received from borrowers. These securities would be underwritten by investment banking firms and sold to investors in markets that were not being reached prior to this innovation. Funds received by originators from the sales of pass through securities would be used to originate new mortgages.

Investors were attracted to these securities because default risk on such securities was minimized as a result of either FHA insurance or a VA guarantee. Securities issued against such pools were viewed by investors as being virtually riskless or very similar to an investment in a government security. With the added guarantee of timely payment of interest and principal by GNMA, these securities also took on the repayment characteristics of a bond, although repayment of the outstanding principal could occur at anytime. Repayment could occur when a borrower defaulted, refinanced, or repaid the outstanding loan balance.[5]

The Federal Home Loan Mortgage Corporation

By the early 1970s, the mortgage-backed securities market based on pools of FHA insured and VA home mortgages was well established under the operation of FNMA and GNMA. However, no such secondary market existed for the resale of *conventional* loans originated by thrifts. These mortgages have historically accounted for the vast majority of residential loan originations. For example, in 1986 (according to data obtained from FHLMC), conventional mortgage originations accounted for approximately 79 percent of total residential loans, while FHA and VA mortgages accounted for only 21 percent of the total. Thrifts originated the majority of conventional loans (58 percent), and mortgage companies originated the majority of FHA-VA mortgages (80 percent). Hence, finding a way to securitize conventional loans was very important if funds were to continue to flow to originators.

As described in Chapter 19, periods of intermittent interest rate volatility, particularly during the mid- and late 1960s, was also causing liquidity problems which plagued thrifts.[6] This resulted in a reduction in the flow of funds to the conventional mortgage market and prompted Congress, under Title III of the Emergency Home Finance Act of 1970, to charter the Federal Home Loan Mortgage Corporation (FHLMC), more commonly known as "Freddie Mac." Its primary purpose was to provide a secondary market and, hence, liquidity for *conventional* mortgage originators just as Fannie Mae and Ginnie Mae did for originators of FHA-VA mortgages. The corporation's initial capital came from the sale of $100 million in nonvoting common stock to the 12 district Federal Home Loan Banks. The FHLMC's board of directors was composed of the three members of

---

[5]Repayment could also occur if a property was sold and the loan was not assumed by the buyer, or, in the event of a hazard (fire, etc.), if proceeds from hazard insurance were used to repay the mortgage rather than to reconstruct the improvement.

[6]Ironically, it is likely that prior to the era of interest rate deregulation (on savings deposits) the small investor would have deposited funds in a thrift or bank, who would in turn originate and retain the mortgagor as an investment. During this period of regulated interest rates, savers withdrew deposits and began investing directly in financial securities. This change, as well as legislation allowing individuals to open individual retirement accounts (outside of savings institutions), forced thrifts to find a way to compete for funds that they once had been able to acquire by offering savings accounts.

the Federal Home Loan Bank Board, who are appointed by the president. The board of directors was given the authority to require that the district Federal Home Loan Banks guarantee Freddie Mac's obligations. However, this power has never been used.

Initially Freddie Mac was authorized to purchase and make commitments to purchase first lien, fixed rate conventional residential mortgage loans and participations. This bill also allowed Fannie Mae to purchase *conventional* mortgages, and Freddie Mac was given the authority to purchase FHA-VA loans as well. This provision would, in essence, allow both organizations to *compete* for all mortgage loans. However, the vast majority of Freddie Mac's business was, and continues to be, conventional mortgages, and FNMA continues to be the dominant purchaser of FHA-VA mortgages, although its acquisitions of conventional loans now exceeds its FHA-VA acquisition volume.

OPERATION OF THE SECONDARY MORTGAGE MARKET

To understand how the secondary mortgage market functions, remember that the primary function of this market is to provide a mechanism for replenishing funds used by mortgage originators. This, in turn, enables them to maintain a flow of new mortgage originations during periods of rising and falling interest rates. They may accomplish this by selling mortgages directly to Fannie Mae, Freddie Mac, or other private entities. Or they may form mortgage pools and issue various securities (to be described), thereby attracting funds from investors who may not otherwise make investments directly in mortgage loans. Hence, much like any corporation raising funds for doing business, the primary goal of mortgage originators in today's market is to replenish funds by reaching broader investor markets.

Direct Sale Programs

Exhibit 21–1 illustrates the direct sale approach used by mortgage originators to replenish funds. As previously indicated, prior to the mid-1950s, the secondary market was utilized by mortgage companies and some thrifts who originated FHA and VA mortgages, which were in turn sold to life insurance companies and some large eastern thrifts. These institutions utilized funds obtained from policyholder reserves and savings deposits, respectively, to acquire mortgage packages. This market changed during the mid-1950s as FNMA became the predominant purchaser of FHA-VA mortgages from mortgage bankers. The FHLMC entered the market by 1970, offering savings and loan associations the opportunity to sell conventional and FHA-VA mortgages.

At the present time, originators may now sell to both Fannie Mae and Freddie Mac, who now purchase a myriad of mortgages through their direct "standard purchase" programs. These standard programs include the purchase of 30-year fixed rate loans, various adjustable rate loans, participations in individual or packages of loans, and second mortgage loans. In addition to the standard purchase programs, both agencies offer their version of a negotiated purchase program in which they will purchase a loan that does not fit into any of the standard categories.

EXHIBIT 21–1   Funds Flow Analysis (direct purchase programs)

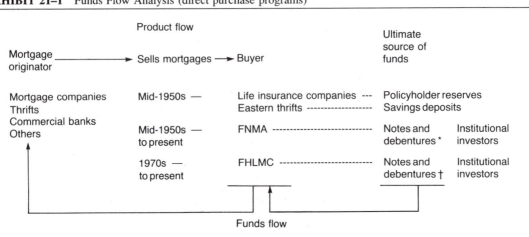

*US Treasury empowered to purchase up to $2.25 billion.

†Federal Home Loan Bank System empowered to guarantee securities if necessary.

A by-product of the standard purchase programs instituted by FNMA and FHLMC was the development of standardized procedures in such areas as qualifying borrowers, property appraisals, and obtaining insurance when originating loans. This came about because neither FNMA or FHLMC would purchase loans unless underwriting and documentation procedures conformed to their requirements. These requirements had to be followed by originators; otherwise the mortgage could not be sold. With the institution of standardized procedures came the recognition that a more standardized product was beginning to emerge that could be sold and resold in substantial market volumes.[7]

FNMA's current commitment program is divided into two parts: mandatory and optional. Under the mandatory commitment option, Fannie Mae is obligated to purchase a certain amount of mortgages at a certain price at a certain time, and mortgage originators are *obligated* to deliver the mortgages. Originators pay a commitment fee to Fannie Mae for the privilege of selling mortgages under the commitment program. Under the optional delivery program, originators paid Fannie Mae a fee (the amount would be higher than the corresponding commitment fee under the mandatory commitment program) for the *option* to deliver their mortgages to Fannie Mae. Under the mandatory commitment program, mortgage originators would benefit if market interest rates rose, but they could lose if market interest rates fell because they could have received a higher price elsewhere. On the other hand, the optional delivery commitment program gave the mortgage orig-

---

[7]Recall the use of the standardized appraisal forms in Chapter 7 and the mortgage form in Chapter 2. FNMA and FHLMC jointly agreed that lenders desiring to sell loans to either entity had to document loans by using these forms (and others not shown). Because most lenders wanted to retain the option to sell loans or to securitize them at a later time, these forms have become standardized throughout the industry.

inator the "right but not the obligation" of selling the mortgages to Fannie Mae. Hence, if interest rates increased, originators could sell mortgages to Fannie Mae, but if rates fell, they retained the option to sell mortgages to another party for a better price (or even to renegotiate a price with Fannie Mae). With the advent of these commitment programs, mortgage originators, were able to continue to shift most interest rate risk to Fannie Mae; however, this could now only be done for a fee. The program became so successful for Fannie Mae that Freddie Mac instituted a similar program in 1970.

The Development of Mortgage-Related Security Pools

As discussed previously, in addition to direct sales of mortgages from originators to investors, many large mortgage originators found that they could place mortgages in pools and sell securities of various types using the mortgages in these pools as collateral. With the aid of investment bankers, large originators could issue securities in small denominations which would be purchased by many more investors. Firms with smaller mortgage origination volumes could continue to sell mortgages directly to FNMA and FHLMC, who in turn would create large pools of their own and issue securities. To give some idea of the growth in the use of such pools, Exhibit 21–2 contains data on origination of 1–4 family mortgage loans by major category of lender for 1979 and 1986. In addition to originations, the exhibit contains data on net acquisitions (originations plus purchases, less sales and prepayments) that occurred during this period.

From the data presented in Exhibit 21–2, it is clear that the formation of mortgage pools has increased greatly. By 1986 all major originators of mortgages were either issuing mortgage-backed securities directly or selling mortgages to FNMA and FHLMC,

---

EXHIBIT 21–2 Mortgage Investment Activity of Selected Institutions for 1–4 Family Mortgages

	Thrift Institutions	*Commercial Banks*	*Mortgage Companies*	*Mortgage Pools*	*Other**
1986					
Originations†	$180,619	$102,962	$131,628	$ 0	$ 7,632
	42.72%	24.35%	31.13%	0.00%	1 80%
Net acquisitions	$ 94,635	$ 80,690	$ 33,502	$252,519	$28,799
	19.31%	16.46%	6.84%	51.52%	5.87%
1979					
Originations	$ 91,788	$ 41,415	$ 45,257	$ 0	$ 8,643
	49.06%	22.13%	24.19%	0.00%	4.62%
Net acquisitions	$ 87,400	$ 37,002	$ 6,468	$ 27,215	$22,168
	48.49%	20.53%	3.59%	15.10%	12.29%

*Other institutions include life insurance companies, private pension funds, REITs, state and local retirement funds, federal credit agencies, and state and local investment agencies.

†The first figure is the amount in millions of dollars. The second figure is the percentage.

who were creating pools and issuing mortgage-backed securities of their own. Creation of mortgage pools for securitization has clearly changed the previous pattern of thrifts *originating and holding* mortgages in their own portfolios and mortgage companies originating and selling mortgages directly to either life insurance companies or large thrifts in regions where a surplus of savings existed. As we will see, many originators are no longer willing to take the interest rate risk associated with originating loans with funds obtained from deposits and have found a way, through securitization, to raise funds and shift interest rate risk to various classes of investors who are willing to take that risk.

Differences between percentage originations and net acquisitions by each financial institution shown in Exhibit 21–3 indicate that in 1986 net acquisition by mortgage pools represented approximately 50 percent of all mortgages originated in that year. This stands in sharp contrast to the pattern shown for 1979 when mortgage pools accounted for only 15 percent of originations, and most of those net acquisitions could be accounted for by mortgage companies through creation of pools of FHA-VA mortgages or sales of such loans to FNMA, who in turn created such pools.

Mortgage Securitization

There are many types of mortgage-related securities that have been developed in recent years. The number and types of securities is continuing to increase as mortgage originators, investment bankers, and the three federally related institutions discussed thus far (FNMA, FHLMC, and GNMA) continue to innovate and reach investor markets that provide the ultimate source for much of the funds used in new mortgage originations. Exhibit 21–4 provides a breakdown of total mortgage-related securities outstanding by type of issuer. (In the case of GNMA, however, mortgage-related securities are actually issued by private entities, and a timely payment guarantee is provided by GNMA.)

In this chapter and the next we will deal in depth with the major types of mortgage-backed securities currently in use. These are

1. Mortgage-backed bonds (MBBs).
2. Mortgage pass-through securities (MPTs).
3. Mortgage pay-through bonds (MPTBs).
4. Collateralized mortgage obligations (CMOs).

MORTGAGE-BACKED BONDS

One approach to mortgage securitization that has been used by private mortgage originators such as mortgage companies, commercial banks, and savings and loans to replenish funds for new originators has been to issue mortgage-backed bonds (MBBs). When issuing MBBs, the issuer establishes a pool of mortgages (this pool usually includes residential mortgages, but commercial mortgages and other mortgage-related securities may also be used) and issues bonds to investors. The issuer retains ownership of the mortgages, but they are pledged as security and are usually placed in trust with a third-party trustee.

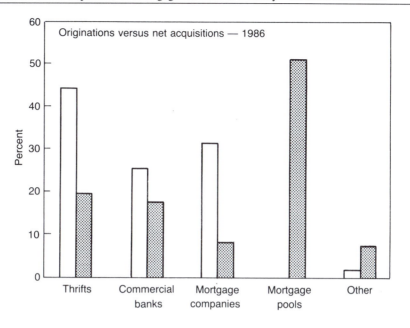

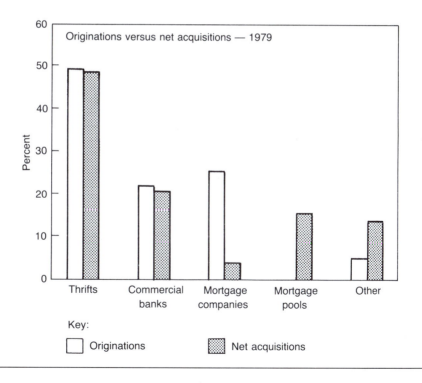

EXHIBIT 21–4   Mortgage-Related Securities in 1986 (total outstanding $784 billion)

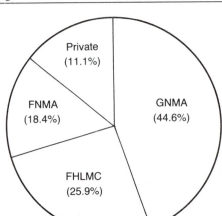

This trustee makes certain that the provisions of the bond issue are adhered to on behalf of the security owners. Like corporate bonds, MBBs are usually issued with fixed coupon rates and specific maturities.

To assure investors that the income from mortgages will be sufficient to pay interest on the bonds as well as repay principal on the maturity date, the issuer usually "over-collateralizes" the bond issue. This is done by placing mortgages in the pool with outstanding loan balances in excess of the dollar amount of securities being issued. Historically, issuers have pledged from between 125 percent to 240 percent in mortgage collateral in excess of the par value of securities issued. This practice is followed because some borrowers may default or fall behind in payments on mortgage loans in the pool. In this case the overcollateralization ensures that interest payments promised to security holders will continue, even though some mortgages may be in default. Further, some loans may be prepaid either before the maturity date of the mortgage or before the bond maturity date. Because mortgage-backed bonds are issued for a specified number of years, overcollateralization ensures that, as mortgages are prepaid, others will still be in the pool to replace them. Another reason for overcollateralization is because such bond issues usually provide that the trustee will "mark all mortgage collateral to the market." This is done periodically to make sure that the market values of mortgages used for overcollateralization are maintained at the level agreed on at time of issue (e.g., 125 percent or 240 percent) or at other levels agreed on throughout the life of the bond issue. Should the market value of the mortgages in trust fall below the agreed-on level of overcollateralization or be reduced because of an excessive number of defaults or prepayment on mortgages in the pool, the issuer must *replenish* the pool with additional mortgages of the same quality. If the issuer doesn't replenish or doesn't abide by the provisions of the security issue, the trustee may sell all collateral in the trust to protect the security owners.

Mortgage-backed bonds, like all mortgage-related securities, are usually underwritten by investment banking companies, given an investment rating by independent bond rating agency,[8] and sold through an underwriting syndicate.[9] The investment rating depends on (1) the quality of the mortgages in the underlying pool, which is a reflection of the types of mortgages (residential, commercial, second mortgages and their loan-to-value ratios,) and whether they are insured or guaranteed against default, either fully or partially; (2) the extent of geographic diversification in the mortgage security; (3) the interest rates on mortgages in the pool; (4) the likelihood that mortgages will be prepaid before maturity; (5) the extent of overcollateralization; and (6) in the case of commercial mortgages, the appraised value and debt coverage ratio (and the various financial guidelines discussed in Chapter 10).

Obviously for mortgage pools containing FHA-VA mortgages or conventional mortgages with private mortgage insurance, the risk of default losses would be lower than if such mortgages were not insured or guaranteed. However, in some cases, the issuer may include some additional types of credit enhancement from a third party as additional security against default losses to bondholders. This enhancement could be a letter of credit from a bank, based on the issuer's credit standing and deposit requirements maintained at the bank issuing the letter, or some types of surety in the form of an insurance or other agreement negotiated with a creditworthy third party for a fee. When credit enhancements are used, the investor must also evaluate the ability of the third party to perform on the guarantee or to evaluate the terms and conditions of letters of credit when provided by the issuer or third parties. The quality of the enhancement will generally affect the amount of overcollateralization required and/or the coupon rate offered on the bonds.

In summary then, the quality and types of mortgages in the pool are the primary determinants of whether the cash flows used to pay interest on the bonds and to eventually retire them will be adequate. These characteristics just described (which will be expanded in the next section) will affect the ability of the issuer to meet the requirements of the bond issue and hence affect the risk to investors. This risk will determine the yields required by investors on such bonds and, hence, the price that the issuer will receive for them. This pricing issue is the next topic in this section.

Pricing Mortgage-Backed Bonds

To illustrate how mortgage-backed bonds are priced by issuers when negotiating with underwriters, we assume that $200 million of MBBs will be issued against a $300 million pool of mortgages, in denominations of $10,000 for a period of 10 years. The bonds will carry a coupon, or interest rate, of 8 percent, payable annually,[10] based on the quality of the mortgage security in trust, the overcollateralization, and the creditworthiness of the issuer (and/or credit enhancement provided by the issuer). We assume that the securities

---

[8]Such agencies might be Moody's or Standard & Poor's Corporation.

[9]Prominent underwriters of mortgage-related securities have included First Boston Company, Salomon Brothers, and Goldman Sachs & Co.

[10]Most bonds pay interest semiannually. We are simplifying the analysis here.

receive a rating of Aaa or AAA.[11] To determine the *price* that the security should be offered for on the *date of issue,* we must discount the present value of the future interest payments and return of principal at the market rate of return demanded by investors (who will purchase them from underwriters) at the time of issue. This rate is obviously a reflection of the riskiness of the bond relative to other securities and the yields on other comparable securities in the marketplace.

More specifically, in our example the price of the security is determined by finding the present value of a stream of $800 interest payments (made annually for 10 years, plus the return of $10,000 in principal at the end of the 10th year). Assuming that the issuer, in concert with the underwriters, agrees that the rate of return that will be required to sell the bonds is 9 percent, then the price will be established as follows:

$$PV = \$800(PVIFA, 9\%, 10 \text{ yrs.}) + \$10,000(PVIF, 9\%, 10 \text{ yrs.})$$
$$= \$9,358$$

Hence, the bond would be priced at a discount of $642, or at 93.58 percent of par value ($10,000), resulting in a yield to maturity of 9 percent. The issuer would receive $187,160,000 from the underwriter,[12] less an underwriting fee, in exchange for the securities. On the other hand, if the required rate, or yield to maturity,[13] was deemed to be 7 percent, then the present value of the bonds would be $10,702 or they would sell at a premium of $702 and the issuer would receive $214,400,000. Hence, the price of the issue will depend on the relationship between the coupon rate on the bond and prevailing required rates of return. When market rates exceed the coupon rate, the price of the bond will be lower, and vice-versa. Exhibit 21–5 shows the relationship between price and the market yield or rate of return at the time that the 8 percent MBB is issued. Note the inverse relationship between prices and demanded rates of return.

Subsequent Prices

The bonds referred to will be traded after they are issued and although the prices at which they trade will no longer affect funds received by the issuer, these prices are important to investors as well as issuers who plan to make additional security offerings. For example, if we assume that two years after issue the required rate of return is again 9 percent, then the bond price would be

$$PV = \$800(PVIFA, 9\%, 8 \text{ yrs.}) + \$10,000(PVIF, 9\%, 8 \text{ yrs.})$$
$$= \$9,447$$

---

[11]This is the highest rating obtainable. An explanation of the meaning and determination of ratings can be obtained from Moody's or Standard & Poor's.

[12]We assume that the underwriter makes a firm commitment to purchase the entire offering from the originator for an agreed price. The underwriter then forms a syndicate with other underwriters, who then take the risk of reselling securities to the public and institutional investors through a network of securities dealers.

[13]The yield to maturity is a term used by bond investors which is identical to the internal rate of return. It is calculated based on whether the coupon (interest) payments are made semiannually, quarterly, and so on.

EXHIBIT 21–5   Prices for an 8 percent Coupon versus a Zero Coupon MBB at Varying Interest Rates

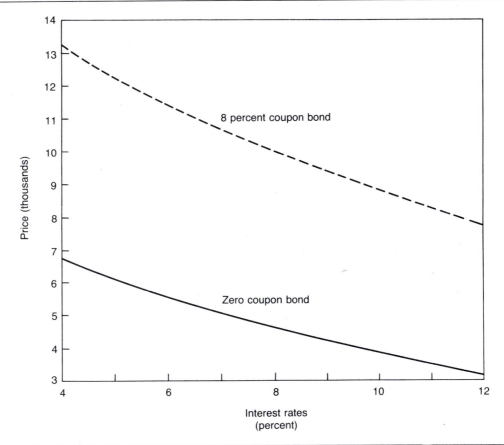

Hence, we can see that the price of security would now be 94.47 percent of par value. The discount is now lower than it was at time of issue. This is because the remaining number of years to maturity is now 8 as opposed to 10. Alternatively, if the demanded return was 7 percent after two years, then the premium would be $10,597, or the price (105.97 percent) of par. Hence, the extent of premium and discount when the maturity period is 10 years is different from the pattern illustrated when the remaining maturity is eight years. However, regardless of the remaining maturity period, when the market rate of return is 8 percent or equal to the coupon rate, the security will always sell at par value. (The student should verify this.)

Zero Coupon Mortgage-Backed Bonds.   In some cases, bonds issued against mortgages will carry zero coupons or will not pay any interest. These MBBs accrue interest until the principal amount is returned at maturity. To illustrate, we assume the bond in our previous example is to be issued with a zero coupon, but interest is to be accrued at 8 percent until maturity. At maturity, the *par value* of the security will be redeemed for $10,000. If, however, at the time of issue, the rate of return demanded by investors in these securities is 8 percent, then the security will be *priced* as follows:

$$PV = \$10,000(PVIF,\ 8\%,\ 10\ \text{yrs.})$$
$$= \$4,632$$

Based on this result, the security would be priced to sell for $4,632, or 46.32 percent of par value at maturity ($10,000). Should market rates of interest be 7.5 percent at the time of issue, the security would be priced at $4,852, or at 48.52 percent of par. Exhibit 21–5 also shows the relationship between prices and various market rates of return for a zero coupon MBB with a 10-year maturity period at the time of issue. When compared with the 8 percent coupon bond, the price sensitivity of a zero coupon bond, as a percentage of par value, is far greater than for the more standard bonds that pay interest currently. For example, when the required return is 4 percent, the 8 percent interest-bearing coupon bond would sell for 130 percent of par, while the zero coupon would sell for about 68 percent of par. The greater price sensitivity for zero coupon bonds relative to bonds carrying interest coupons occurs because for the zero coupon bond all income is deferred until maturity. Therefore, its present value will always be more sensitive to changes in interest rates than for investments returning some cash flows during the investment period.

Marking the Mortgage Portfolio to Market.   As mentioned previously, the trustee selected to oversee that the provisions of the bond issue are carried out must ascertain periodically whether the market value of the mortgages placed in trust is equal to the agreed-on level of overcollateralization. The pricing techniques used by the trustee to establish the market value of the pledged mortgages are very complex. This is because (1) there are generally many different interest rates on mortgages placed in trust, (2) those mortgages will be amortizing principal, (3) many of the mortgages in the pool may be prepaid because many of the mortgages may allow for the borrower to repay the outstanding loan balance at any time, and (4) some borrowers may default on loans. These latter two factors would obviously reduce the amount and number of mortgages in the pool.

To make an estimate of the value of mortgages in the pool (referred to as *marking the mortgages to market*), the trustee must value each of the mortgages in the pool by first establishing the number and outstanding balance of each mortgage in trust. The current market yield being demanded by investors for each type of mortgage must then be estimated based on assumptions about the period that each mortgage is expected to be outstanding (not the contract maturity period, because, as pointed out, most mortgages are prepaid as properties are sold, loans refinanced, borrowers default, etc.).[14] Hence, the valuation of the underlying security is a more complex undertaking, particularly when

---

[14]Other methods of principal repayment may also be used, such as sinking fund retirement and call provision. For a discussion see any basic text dealing with investments.

the prepayment patterns are considered. Many of the techniques that must be considered in evaluating such securities are also important when valuing mortgage pass-through securities.

MORTGAGE PASS-THROUGH SECURITIES

In 1968, the mortgage-backed security guarantee program was initiated by Ginnie Mae. This program represented an attempt to create a mortgage-backed investment capable of competing with corporate and government securities for investment funds. As previously pointed out in our discussion of GNMA, one of the most serious objections that had to be overcome with such a security was the issue of safety. Because mortgage-related securities would represent loans made by many individual borrowers with different income and household characteristics, an investment vehicle had to be created whereby the collateral underlying the mortgage security could be easily understood and yet be comparable to other securities.

As discussed earlier, mortgages are subject to two important types of risk: default risk and interest rate risk. Although fixed interest rate mortgage securities, like corporate and government bonds, would also be subject to interest rate risk, default risk could be eliminated by FHA insurance or dramatically reduced with a VA guarantee. Another characteristic of concern to potential investors in mortgage-related securities was the predictability of the income stream. Substitute investments, such as noncallable bonds, have very predictable interest payment schedules. As pointed out previously, mortgage payments can be delayed because of a household's inability to keep payments current or because of default. To overcome this lack of timeliness in payments, Ginnie Mae guaranteed the full and timely payment of principal and interest. GNMA's position as guarantor was that of a surety, with securities carrying the GNMA guarantee having full faith and credit of the United States government behind it. This full faith and credit guarantee meant that GNMA could borrow without limit from the Treasury should it ever be necessary. This unique guarantee has made the GNMA security the most liquid of all secondary mortgage market securities.

Before the advent of the first mortgage-backed security, the pass-through, the only way for an originator to sell a package of mortgage investments was to sell whole loans, which involved the transfer of ownership in addition to all of the investor concerns mentioned above. The mortgage pass-through overcame many of these problems. Mortgage pass-throughs are securities issued by a mortgage originator (mortgage company, thrift, etc.) and represent an undivided ownership interest in a pool of mortgages. The pool may consist of one or many mortgages. However, the usual minimum size of such a pool is $100 million, which could represent 1,000 or more residential mortgages. Each mortgage placed in the pool continues to be serviced by its originator or an approved servicer. A trustee is designated as the owner of the mortgages in the pool and ensures that all payments are made to individual security owners. Cash flows from the pool, which consists of principal and interest, less servicing and guarantee fees, are distributed to security holders. That is why the securities are called "pass-throughs" because cash flows are "passed-through" to the investors by the mortgage servicer.

EXHIBIT 21–6   Mortgage Pass-Through Securities: Issuance and Funds Flow

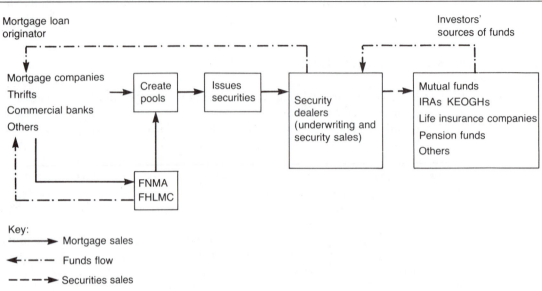

Exhibit 21–6 is a flowchart of how mortgage pass-through securities are originated and sold. Essentially, mortgages are originated by lenders and are pooled by them or sold to FNMA or FHLMC. If pooled by the originator, the originator will work with a securities underwriter to issue securities. These securities are then sold through security dealers to mutual funds, individuals with individual retirement accounts (IRAs) and Keogh retirement plans, trust and pension fund administrators, life insurance companies, or even thrifts and commercial banks in geographic areas with a surplus of savings. This pattern of securitization enabled originators of mortgages to ultimately reach the relatively small investor, who could now purchase an interest in a Ginnie Mae pass-through or another pass-through security by investing in a mutual fund or buying directly.

The pattern shown in the upper portion of Exhibit 21–6 represents the approach generally used for issuing mortgage-backed securities until 1970. After that time, both FHLMC and FNMA instituted their own mortgage pass-through programs (their securities were referred to as participation certificates (PCs) and mortgage-backed securities (MBS), respectively). These securities were backed by mortgage pools from direct purchases made under both the optional and mandatory commitment direct purchase programs. Guarantees for timely payment of interest and principal were also provided by FNMA and FHLMC. Rather than securitizing themselves, originators of small mortgage volumes would sell directly to FNMA and FHLMC, who would in turn create mortgage pools and issue securities. These securities could then be placed directly with large institutional buyers or sold through security dealers to generally the same investors that would purchase GNMA pass-throughs.

The process of mortgage securitization changed again in 1981 when Freddie Mac instituted its "swap program." A similar program was later implemented by Fannie Mae. The major information brought about with swaps is shown in Exhibit 21–7. Essentially, a swap program amounts to one originator pooling mortgages, then swapping them for pass-through mortgage securities issued simultaneously by Fannie Mae or Freddie Mac. Contrary to the direct sale programs discussed earlier in which mortgage packages are sold to either Fannie Mae or Freddie Mac for cash, the swap program allows for mortgages with the same interest rate to be swapped for securities guaranteed by Fannie Mae or Freddie Mac (for a fee), bearing the same coupon rate. Depending on market interest rates, the originator may then choose to sell part or all of the mortgage securities at a premium or discount. These securities could be sold directly by the originator to institutional investors, to security dealers or through the trading department operated by FHLMC. By swapping securities for mortgages, the originator has more flexibility when deciding whether to own securities or how and when such securities will be sold to raise cash. Further, in an attempt to provide a market outlet for such securities, Freddie Mac maintains a trading department which makes a market in mortgage-backed securities. During 1986, approximately $3 trillion of all types of mortgage-backed securities, including those guaranteed by Ginnie Mae and issued by Fannie Mae and Freddie Mac, were traded.

EXHIBIT 21–7   Mortgage Pass-Through Security Swaps

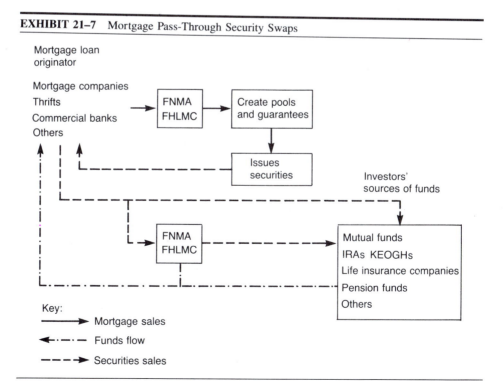

Important Characteristics of Mortgage Pools

Exhibit 21–8 provides important information on the four most important types of pass-through securities in use today. Although all pass-through securities have the same basic underlying structure, there are some major differences between the various securities that should be pointed out. These factors are extremely important to issuers when creating mortgage pools and are equally important to investors when they evaluate the possibility of investing in a mortgage pass-through security versus a government bond, corporate bond, or on other interest-bearing security.

Not all mortgage-backed securities are alike. When reviewing the characteristics listed in Exhibit 21–8, pay particular attention to how the market value of a pass-through security, which is backed by an underlying pool of mortgage loans made to borrowers, will respond to general changes in market interest rates. The change in market value of a particular security depends on the characteristics of the mortgages in the underlying pool, the response of borrowers to changes in interest rates, and the changes in borrower behavior in response to changes affecting their demand for housing, employment opportunities, and other influences. Borrowers may choose to refinance or repay their loans in response to changes in interest rates. Or as economic conditions change, they may sell their present house in order to buy another or to take a job transfer to another region. In these cases, they would very likely prepay their outstanding mortgages. These factors are extremely important to investors who must evaluate the timing of the receipt of cash flows when estimating value.

Security Issuers and Guarantors.   The first two security types listed in Exhibit 21–8 are referred to as GNMA I and II pass-throughs. These securities are usually issued by mortgage companies, thrifts, commercial banks, and other organizations who originate FHA and VA mortgages. The remaining two security types, participation certificates and mortgages-backed securities, are securities issued by FHLMC and FNMA, respectively. As previously mentioned, the latter two securities are backed by pools of mortgages that are purchased from originators by FHLMC and FNMA from who in turn, provide a timely payment guarantee. In these cases, FNMA and FHLMC act as intermediaries, purchasing smaller quantities of mortgages from many originators, then accumulating larger pools against which they issue securities.

Default Insurance.   The first pass-through securities, GNMA I's, are backed with FHA-VA mortgages which carry either insurance or a guarantee against any default losses. This program, when begun, was limited to FHA-VA pools because at that time private mortgage default insurance on conventional mortgages was not generally available. Even today, with the availability of private mortgage insurance, major issuers of pass-through securities generally do not mix *both* FHA-VA and conventional mortgages in the same pool. This is because of the greater depth of default insurance coverage provided by FHA and the depth of VA guarantee when compared to conventional default coverage.[15] As

---

[15]Recall from the earlier chapters on residential mortgages that FHA insures the entire loan amount in the event of default, VA provides a fixed dollar maximum (e.g., $27,500) guarantee, while private mortgage

shown in Exhibit 21–8, GNMAs still contain mortgages with FHA-VA backing whereas FNMA's and FHLMC's pass-throughs may be based on separate pools of either FHA-VA or conventional mortgages. In their conventional mortgage-backed programs, both FNMA and FHLMC require conventional mortgages with loan-to-value ratios greater than 80 percent to carry private mortgage insurance.

Payment Patterns and Security for Mortgages in Pools. As Exhibit 21–8 indicates, most mortgage varieties may be individually pooled for a pass-through security issue. This is true for mortgages with adjustable payment patterns such as adjustable rate mortgages (*ARMs*), graduated payment mortgages (*GPMs*), mortgages secured by single family, multifamily and mobile homes, and even second lien mortgages. However, the vast majority of mortgages used in the pass-through security market are fixed interest rate loans secured by mortgages on single family houses.

As previously pointed out, FHA-VA and conventional mortgages are generally not mixed in the same pool. This rule also generally applies to payment patterns and the nature of loan security and loan maturity. In other words, mortgage pools are also usually grouped based on (1) payment patterns (such as *ARMs*), (2) maturity (such as second mortgages with 10-year terms), or (3) security (single family homes, mobile homes, etc.). The reason is that investors must be able to predict, with some confidence, the cash flow pattern that they can expect to receive should they purchase a pass-through security. If pools contained mortgages with many different payment patterns, investors would have a more difficult time assessing the likely cash flow pattern that they could expect to receive. This is because the payment pattern of individuals making fixed interest rate loans may vary considerably from those making *ARMs*, second liens, and so on. As we will see in the material on pricing securities, expected prepayment patterns dramatically affect expected yields on mortgage securities. Hence, a general rule followed thus far in most security issues has been to keep mortgage pools as homogeneous as possible so that their prepayment patterns are somewhat easier for investors to assess.

Coupon Rates, Interest Rates, and Number of Seasoned Mortgages in Pools. Pass-through securities, like bonds and other fixed interest rate investments, promise a coupon interest rate to investors purchasing securities. In the case of mortgage pools containing only mortgages with the *same interest rate,* the coupon rate is based on the interest rate less any servicing and guarantee fees. Hence, in the case of GNMA I pools which allow no variance in interest rates on mortgages in the underlying pool (see Exhibit 21–8), the coupon is easily determined. If, for example, mortgages made at a 10 percent interest rate are included in the pool, the coupon rate will be 9.5 percent (after deducting the 50-basis-point, or .5 percent, servicing and guarantee fee shown at the bottom of the exhibit).

However, pass-through securities issues guaranteed by Fannie Mae and Freddie Mac have allowed for a mixture of *interest rates* on mortgages included in a pool. This has

---

insurers usually insure an amount equal to the loan amount in excess of 80 percent of property value at closing. Unless the issuer provides some additional enhancement, investors in privately insured and VA guaranteed pools are not completely free from losses in the event of default because of these limits. This is not true with FHA insured loans.

EXHIBIT 21–8 Selected Characteristics of Mortgage Pass-Through Securities

Security	GNMA I pass-through	GNMA II pass-through	Participation certificate	Mortgage-backed security
Issuer	Mortgage companies Thrifts, others	Mortgage companies Thrifts, others	FHLMC	FNMA
Date of first issue	1970	1983	1971	1981
Guarantor against default on mortgages	FHA, VA, FmHA	FHA, VA, FmHA	Private mortgage insurance, FHA/VA	FHA/VA Private mortgage insurance
Types of mortgages in pool*	FRM, GPM, GEM, MH, CL, PL	FRM, GPM, GEM, MH, ARM	FRM, GPM, ARM, MF seconds	FRM, GPM, ARM, MF seconds
Interest rate on mortgages in underlying pools allowed to vary?	No	Yes	Yes	Yes
Seasoned mortgages allowed in pools?	No	Yes	Yes	Yes
Nature of payment guarantee	Timely payment of P & I and prepayments	Timely payment of P & I and prepayments	Timely payment of P & I and eventual prepayments	Timely payment of P & I and prepayments

Guarantor	GNMA and credit of U.S. government	GNMA and credit of U.S. government	FHLMC only	FNMA only
Minimum certificate size	$25,000	$25,000	$25,000	$25,000
Servicing fee (basis points)	44	Dependent on range of interest rates in pooled mortgages; minimum is 44	Dependent on range of interest rates in pooled mortgages; minimum is 37.5	Dependent on range of interest rates in pooled mortgages minimum is 25
Guarantee fee (basis points)	6	6	25	25 min.

*Legend

FRM = 1–4 single family, 30-year fixed rate mortgages.

GPM = Graduated payment mortgage.

GEM = Growing equity mortgage.

ARM = Adjustable rate mortgages.

CL = Construction loan mortgages.

MH = Manufactured housing mortgages.

PL = Federally financed housing project loans.

MF = Multifamily housing mortgages.

Seconds = Mortgage pools secured by second mortgages.

been done to enable a faster accumulation of larger pools for securitization. This pattern has been followed by security issuers, who believe that the variation in cash flows caused by mixing such mortgages is not sufficiently large enough to offset the lower issuance costs on very large mortgage pools (i.e., economies of scale).

When Freddie Mac began its PC pass-through program, it allowed a variation of 200 basis points (from highest to lowest) in interest rates on mortgages packaged in the same pool. Fannie Mae allowed a 200-basis-point range with its first mortgage-backed security offering in 1981. The GNMA II pass-through program, which began in 1983, has also relaxed the stringent no-interest-rate variation rules of the GNMA I program and now allows a variation of 100 basis points on mortgages in the underlying pool. These ranges are subject to revision by the guarantors from time to time.

The variation in interest rates on a mortgage pool may be very important for investors to consider, because in each case the *coupon rate* promised to investors purchasing securities is generally based on the *lowest* interest rate on *any* mortgage in the pool, less servicing and guarantee fees. This means that for two security issues bearing the same coupon rate—the issue backed by a pool with different interest rates and one backed by a pool containing mortgages with the same interest rates—expected cash flows to investors in the pool containing mortgages with different rates will be less variable than for investors in the other pool. This is because each mortgage included in a pool with different interest rates will have a lower likelihood of prepayment than pooled mortgages with the same interest rate. This likelihood exists because mortgages with one interest rate are *all* more likely to be prepaid, should interest rates decline. This would obviously make the pattern of expected cash flows more variable.

Another important factor relating to the amount and timing of cash flows received by investors is the maturity distribution of mortgages and the extent to which "seasoned" mortgages are included in a pool. *Seasoning* is a term used to describe the age or number of years that a loan has been outstanding before it is placed in a pool. The scheduled maturity date for a pass-through security issue is generally stated to be the date on which the mortgage with the longest remaining maturity in the pool is scheduled to be repaid, that is, assuming no prepayment. Each guarantor listed in Exhibit 21–8 places limitations on the number of seasoned mortgages allowed in a pool. Most GNMA insured mortgage pools generally contain mortgages made within one year of pool formation. Fannie Mae and Freddie Mac generally allow for more variation in seasoning in pools that they guarantee. The concern over seasoning is important because, *ceteris paribus*, the more seasoned a mortgage is the greater the likelihood of prepayment. This is because the likelihood that borrowers will sell houses, change job locations, and so on, increases with the length of time the mortgage has been outstanding.

On the other hand, the risk of default is usually greatest in the early years of the life of a mortgage. Hence seasoned mortgages tend to reduce the possibility of prepayment because of default. However, to the extent seasoning reduces or increases the likelihood of prepayment, more variation in cash flows result, which makes evaluation of the security more difficult for investors. This will, in turn, affect the price investors are willing to pay for the security.

Number of Mortgages and Geographic Distribution. Other factors relating to mortgages in the underlying pool that may affect the predictability and, hence, the variability of the monthly cash flows on pass-through securities are the *number* and *geographic* distribution of mortgages in the pool.

Both of these factors may be critical when estimating the yield on a pass-through security because they influence the expected repayment of principal. Generally, the larger the dollar amount of the pool issue, the more individual mortgages will be contained in the pool; and the larger the number of mortgages in the pool, all else being equal, the more predictable the monthly cash flow. This means that the likelihood of a major change in cash flows because of default or prepayment of one or a few individual mortgages will not significantly impact future cash flows paid to investors. Most mortgage pools underlying pass-throughs are in minimum denominations of $100 million. If the average mortgage size is about $100,000, most pools of residential mortgages will contain at least 1,000 mortgages. This may be enough individual mortgages to assure investors that changes in cash flows caused by a small number of mortgages are minimal.

Geographic factors are also important because they also may affect the likelihood of prepayment and default. Certain regions of the country may be affected more by economic downturns than others and hence may have higher default rates because of unemployment. Prepayment rates, because of mobility by borrowers due to their age and family status, may be higher in some areas than others. A mortgage pool with more geographic diversity tends to insulate investors from such cash flow irregularities.

Borrower Characteristics and Loan Prepayment.   Perhaps as important as any of the other explicit pool characteristics discussed in conjunction with Exhibit 21–8 are borrower characteristics, or the socioeconomic makeup of individuals who have made the mortgage loans and are the ultimate source of cash flows for the mortgage pool. These characteristics are important because (1) households prepay existing mortgage loans as they adjust their consumption of housing over time in response to changes in income, family size, and tastes; (2) like other economic entities, households respond to changes in interest rates by refinancing their loans when interest rates fall and postponing adjustments in housing consumption when interest rates rise; and (3) households may default on loan obligations because of loss of employment, divorce, and so on, and, although most pools have default insurance, the mortgage balance is prepaid upon default. Therefore, changes in borrower behavior with respect to these characteristics will affect the expected cash flows on loans and expected maturities. Indeed, depending on borrower behavior, the expected maturity of a loan may vary significantly, therefore affecting the expected yield on the mortgage. Unfortunately, not much information relative to borrower characteristics for individual loans in an underlying mortgage pool is made available to investors in pass-through securities. Hence, even though it is an important variable affecting cash flows on mortgage securities, no reliable source of information is generally available to investors.[16]

Nuisance Calls.   Where the prepayment rate is such that a diminishing number and amount of mortgages remain in the pool, say about 10 percent of the initial pool amount, the servicer may call the remainder of the securities. This call is referred to as a *nuisance*

---

[16]Many researchers are interested in this question and are engaged in statistically based research projects at this time.

or *cleanup call* and is used when the cost of servicing begins to become large relative to servicing income received by the servicer.

Mortgage Pass-Through Securities: A General Approach to Pricing

As discussed in the previous section, many things influence the investment of a mortgage pass-through security (or any mortgage-backed security, in general). We can summarize these influences as follows:

1. Interest rate risk—Reductions in market value due to an unanticipated rise in interest rates. This risk is generally greatest for pools containing fixed interest rate loans.
2. Default risk—Losses due to borrower default. For single family loans, the likelihood of default losses is lowest for FHA insured mortgages, slightly greater for VA guaranteed mortgages, and generally greater for privately insured mortgages. As discussed earlier, this source of risk is also generally higher for *ARM*s and variable payment mortgages.
3. Risk of default—Timely payment of principal and interest. This source of risk can be evaluated in relation to the financial strength of the guarantor. This is because the guarantee of *timely payment* is only as good as the ability of the guarantor to perform on the guarantee. GNMA is backed by full faith and credit on the U.S. government. FNMA has a $2.25 billion commitment from the U.S. Treasury to purchase its notes and bonds, which provides some assurance that a market will be available for its ability to raise funds, maintain liquidity, and make good on its timely payment guarantee. FHLMC has the backing of the Federal Home Loan Bank System, which is owned by member savings and loan association, who have pledged to purchase securities if necessary. However, neither FNMA or FHLMC have the direct backing of the U.S. government.
4. Prepayment risk—Loss in yield because of greater than anticipated loan repayments. In general, most mortgage loans are prepaid before the stated maturity date. Hence, when investing in a pass-through, an investor must estimate expected cash flows, by including an assessment of the prepayment rate on loans in the underlying pools. In the case of fixed interest rate mortgage pools, the impact of prepayment on cash flows passed through to investors will vary according to the:
   a. Number of mortgages in the pool.
   b. Distribution of interest rates on such mortgages.
   c. Number of seasoned mortgages included in the pool.
   d. Geographic location of borrowers.
   e. Household (borrower) characteristics.
   f. Unanticipated events (flood, earthquake).

As previously indicated, although the above sources of risk are important to issuers and investors, information available on mortgage pool at this time is usually limited to very general borrower and mortgage characteristics. Information usually available on mortgage pools is discussed in the following sections.

Pass-Through Rates, Yields, and Servicing Fee.   The pass-through rate is the coupon or rate of interest promised by the issuer of a pass-through security to the investor. The yield to maturity, or internal rate of return, on such a security is equal to this rate only when it is issued at par value.

The coupon rate on pass-throughs is lower than the lowest rate of interest on any mortgage in the pool. The difference between the two rates is known as the *servicing fee*. For GNMA I's, which allow no variance in interest rates in the underlying pool, the total servicing fee is .5 percent, or 50 basis points below the interest rates on all mortgages in the pool. The servicing fee is divided between the guarantor fee and the loan services fee and is calculated as a percentage of the outstanding principal balance of the pool. As an example, GNMA takes .06 percent or 6 basis points of the outstanding principal balance of the pool as its fee for guarantee of timely payment of principal and interest, while the remaining 44 basis points of the servicing fee are retained by the servicer. For mortgage pass-through securities that allow a range of interest rates on mortgages in the pool such as GNMA II's, the coupon rate will be set lower than the lowest mortgage rate in the pool.

Weighted Average Coupon.   The weighted average coupon (WAC) is a measure of the homogeneity of the coupon rates on mortgages in a pool. It is calculated as the average of the underlying mortgage interest rates weighted by the dollar balance of each mortgage as of the security issue date. WACs are meaningful only for pools that allow a variance in interest rates on mortgages in the pool. In most instances, the servicing and guarantee fee can be approximated as the difference between the WAC and the pass-through coupon rate.

Stated Maturity Date of Pool.   The stated maturity date of the pass-through pool is the longest maturity date for any mortgage in the pool, assuming that no prepayments occur. For example, if 75 percent of the pool contained 15-year mortgages and the remaining 25 percent contained 20-year mortgages, the stated pool maturity would be 20 years. GNMA generally imposes more restrictions on the variance in mortgage maturities allowed in pools. FNMA and FHLMC pools may contain more seasoned loans with a wider range in stated maturity dates.

Weighted Average Maturity.   Because the remaining term to stated maturity of mortgages in a pool may affect the prepayment rate of mortgages and, consequently, the yield of securities issued against the pool, the concept of a weighted average maturity maturity (WAM) was developed. The weighted average maturity is calculated as the average remaining term of the underlying mortgages as of the pass-through issue date, with the principal balance of the mortgage as the weighting factor.

Payment Delays by Servicer.   Payment delay is the time lag between the time that the homeowners make their mortgage payment and the date that the servicing agent actually pays the investors holding the pass-through securities. This delay may range from 14 to 55 days. As with other securities, the timing of cash flows is important. Delays in payments received by investors obviously reduce yields.

Pool Factor.   The pool factor is defined as the outstanding principal balance divided by the original pool balance. This balance changes every month as mortgages are amortized and as balances are prepaid. The pool factor starts out as 1 and usually declines. (However, it may increase above 1 if the pool includes mortgages that allow negative amortization.) The pool factor is used to determine the current principal balance of the pool based on the outstanding balance of all mortgages remaining in the pool at any point in time. For example, if the pool factor is .9050 and the pool initially contained mortgages with $50,000 in balances outstanding, the current principal balance of the pool would be ($50,000)(.9050) = $45,250. This factor is particularly important when securities are traded *after* the issue date, when subsequent buyers are considering how much to pay for a security. For example, as the pool factor becomes smaller, the remaining balances on mortgages in the pool are also becoming smaller; hence the likelihood of prepayment becomes greater (holding all else constant).

Mortgage Pass-Through Payment Mechanics Illustrated

Exhibit 21–9 helps to illustrate cash flow patterns that are important when evaluating mortgage pass-through securities. In this exhibit it is assumed that $1,000,000 of 10 percent fixed interest rate mortgages have been pooled as security for an issue of pass-through securities. The pass-through will carry a coupon, or pass-through, rate of 9.5 percent. The difference between the pooled mortgage rates and coupon rate, or .5 percent, is the servicing fee, which is assessed on the outstanding loan balances. To simplify the discussion, we have assumed that mortgage payments, or cash flows and outflows in and out of the pool, occur annually.[17]

The cash flows passed through to individual security holders (column *g*) are based on annual mortgage payments for a 10 percent, 30-year mortgage on the initial pool balance of $1,000,000, resulting in total principal and interest payments generated by the pool (column *c*).[18] The servicing fee of .5 percent (column *e*) is then assessed on the outstanding loan balance at the end of each previous period and subtracted from total principal and interest payments. This results in actual payments to be made to all investors (column *f*). The interest component of total cash flows paid to investors (column *f*) is calculated by multiplying the coupon rate of 9.5 percent by the outstanding principal balance and subtracting the result from the total payment received by investors (column *d*) less servicing fees (column *e*). The residual remaining after deducting interest represents amortization of principal on the pass-through securities (also contained in column *f*). Note that because of the way servicing fees are calculated, payments passed through to investors (column *f*) are not the same from year to year, even though payments into the pool (column *c*) are level.[19] The exhibit also shows that if no mortgages in the pool are

---

[17]For most pass-through issues, payments are made to investors monthly.

[18]Because all mortgages in the pool are 10 percent, 30-year loans, the constant payment in column *c* can be computed as one annual payment on a $1,000,000 loan.

[19]Ordinarily, for fixed interest rate mortgages, principal and interest payments would be a level annuity. In this example, interest payments are computed at 9.5 percent interest on the pool balance. However, amortization

prepaid (column *b*), that is, all mortgages remain outstanding for their stated maturities, the principal balance in the pool will not reach zero until the end of the 30th year.

The amount of cash that will be received by an issuer when such a pool is formed and securitized depends on the prevailing market rate of return that investors demand on such an investment. If it is assumed that, based on the pool characteristics discussed above, the market or desired rate of return is *equal* to the coupon rate (9.5 percent), then the amount to be received (paid) by the issuers (investors) will be $1,000,000 (or 40 securities with a face value of $25,000 will be sold). This is based on the stream of annual cash flow payments in the exhibit, discounted at 9.5 percent. In this instance, the securities would be sold at par value or $25,000 each.

It is rarely ever true that the rate of return demanded by investors is *exactly* equal to the coupon rate on a security, however. As we know, market interest rates change continuously; hence it would only be coincidental that interest rates on mortgages originated at some previous time and placed in a pool would bear interest rates exactly equal to the market rate being demanded by investors at the time that the securities are issued. Inasmuch as the annual cash flows into the pool based on payments received by borrowers are known at the time of issue and passed through to investors, the price received by the issuer will depend on the present value of all payments received by investors, discounted at the prevailing market rate of return. As discussed earlier, this latter rate is determined by the real rate of interest, inflationary expectations, and a premium for the various sources of risk which we have discussed. It is also based on yields available on alternative investments. We shall also see that the period that mortgages are expected to remain outstanding is also very important in the determination of the prices that investors are willing to pay for pass-through securities.

To illustrate the effect that market interest rates have on the price of pass-through securities, note that if the stream of cash flows paid to investors (column *g*) in Exhibit 21–9 is discounted at a market rate of 8.5 percent, the securities will sell for a premium or $27,334 (Part B). This is a result of discounting payments in column *g* by 8.5 percent. If market rates were to rise to 10.5 percent at the time of issue, the security prices would reflect a *discount* of $22,987 (see Part C). Both of these calculations assume, however, that the expected maturity of the pass-through security is equal to the stated maturity of mortgages in the pool (30 years). Hence, the amortization of principal is assumed to occur over the full 30-year period; that is, no prepayment is assumed.

To give the reader some idea of the effect of the sensitivity of security prices to changes in market interest rates, Exhibit 21–10 shows the effect of rising and falling interest rates

---

of the pool balance is occurring based on the contract interest rate on the underlying mortgages (10 percent). Hence, investors receive amortization payments based on 10 percent loans and interest based on 9.5 percent of the remaining loan balances. This means that the pool is amortizing at a slower *rate* than would be the case if it were amortizing based on a 9.5 percent mortgage. The result is that relative to a level annuity, investors receive lower payments in the early years and greater payments in later years because of a slower amortizing pool balance. If market interest rates are 9.5 percent, however, the securities will be priced at par value even though payments to investors are not a level annuity because interest is always calculated at 9.5 percent on the loan balance and the pool is amortized to zero at the end of the 30th year.

EXHIBIT 21–9 Cash Flows Mortgage Pass-Through Security (constant payment, fixed rate, 30-year mortgage pool, interest rate = 10 percent, prepayment assumed to be 0 percent PSA, coupon rate = 9.5 percent rounded)

Period Years	(a) Pool Balance	(b) Principal due to Prepayment	(c) P & I Payments	(d) Total P & I Payments* (b)+(c)	(e) Guarantee and Service fees (a)×(0.5%)	(f) Total PMTs to Investors (d)−(e)	(g) Payment to Individual Investor (f)/40
0	$1,000,000						($25,000)
1	993,921	$0	$106,079	$106,079	$5,000	$101,079	2,527
2	987,234	0	106,079	106,079	4,970	101,110	2,528
3	979,878	0	106,079	106,079	4,936	101,143	2,529
4	971,786	0	106,079	106,079	4,899	101,180	2,529
5	962,886	0	106,079	106,079	4,859	101,220	2,531
6	953,095	0	106,079	106,079	4,814	101,265	2,532
7	942,325	0	106,079	106,079	4,765	101,314	2,533
8	930,478	0	106,079	106,079	4,712	101,368	2,534
9	917,447	0	106,079	106,079	4,652	101,427	2,536
10	903,112	0	106,079	106,079	4,587	101,492	2,537
11	887,344	0	106,079	106,079	4,516	101,564	2,539
12	870,000	0	106,079	106,079	4,437	101,643	2,541
13	850,920	0	106,079	106,079	4,350	101,729	2,543
14	829,933	0	106,079	106,079	4,255	101,825	2,546
15	806,847	0	106,079	106,079	4,150	101,930	2,548
16	781,453	0	106,079	106,079	4,034	102,045	2,551
17	753,519	0	106,079	106,079	3,907	102,172	2,554
18	722,791	0	106,079	106,079	3,768	102,312	2,558
19	688,991	0	106,079	106,079	3,614	102,465	2,562
20	651,811	0	106,079	106,079	3,445	102,634	2,566
21	610,913	0	106,079	106,079	3,259	102,820	2,571
22	565,925	0	106,079	106,079	3,055	103,025	2,576
23	516,438	0	106,079	106,079	2,830	103,250	2,581
24	462,003	0	106,079	106,079	2,582	103,497	2,587
25	402,124	0	106,079	106,079	2,310	103,769	2,594
26	336,257	0	106,079	106,079	2,011	104,069	2,602
27	263,803	0	106,079	106,079	1,681	104,398	2,610
28	184,104	0	106,079	106,079	1,319	104,760	2,619
29	96,436	0	106,079	106,079	921	105,159	2,629
30	0	0	106,079	106,079	482	105,597	2,640

A.
Value of cash flows to issuer if the required rate is 9.50 percent = $1,000,000
Value of cash flows to individual investors at 9.50 percent = $25,000
B.
Value of cash flows to issuer if the required rate is 8.50 percent = $1,093,345
Value of cash flows to individual investors at 8.50 percent = $27,334
C.
Value of cash flows to issuer if the required rate is 10.50 percent = $919,492
Value of cash flows to individual investors at 10.50 percent = $22,987

*Payments calculated on an annual basis.

on the issue *price* of the mortgage pass-through securities in our example. (The reader should keep in mind that the assumption regarding repayment of principal over the 30-year period remains the same.) Results show that for all rates of return desired by investors in excess of 9.5 percent, the pass-through will be issued at a discount, and when required rates decrease, the security would be sold at a premium. Note that only when the required rate of return is *equal* to the promised coupon rate (9.5 percent) does the security sell at par value (an amount equal to the initial pool balance of $1,000,000, or $25,000 per security).

Prepayment Patterns and Security Prices

As previously discussed, one problem area that affects how securities are priced by investors, and that is rather unique to the mortgage-backed securities market, is the option that most borrowers have to prepay or repay the outstanding mortgage balance at any

EXHIBIT 21–10 Relationship between Security Prices and Market Rates of Return

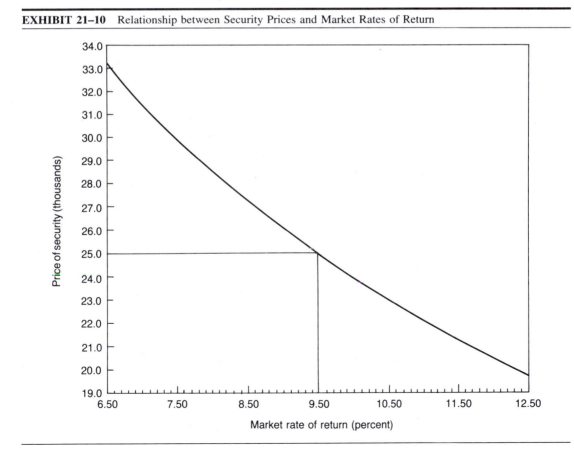

time.[20] This topic is important because when investors make comparisons between pass-throughs, corporate bonds, U.S. government bonds, and various state and local bond issues, the *expected* maturity period for pass-throughs is usually more difficult to estimate relative to these other investments. For example, when corporate bonds are issued, an option to call the outstanding principal is usually made explicit in the indenture agreement by specifying the price at which the bond may be called by the corporation each year that the bond issue is outstanding. Such options to call are usually included in the event that interest rates decline and the company wants to refinance the debt at a lower interest rate.[21]

As an alternative to call provisions, bond indentures issued by both corporations and state and local issuers may specify that a *scheduled* number of bonds will be called and retired in specific years after issue, regardless of what the current level of interest rates are at that time. Note that this is not an option but a requirement of the indenture agreement.[22] For U.S. Government securities, the vast majority are issued for a stated maturity and are generally not callable. In other words, they are generally issued to run until maturity.[23]

The point is that other fixed interest securities are generally more predictable with respect to when repayment of principal can be expected. This is not true for mortgage pass-through securities. Hence, when comparing yields on pass-throughs with other securities, there is definitely some additional uncertainty regarding the rate of repayment of principal that must be taken into account by investors.

Prepayment Assumptions—Mortgage Pass-Through Securities

Because some prepayments by borrowers are likely to occur over time, as outstanding balances on mortgages contained in pools are repaid, proceeds are passed through to

---

[20]There are some exceptions and additional facts that should be mentioned that affect mortgage prepayment. FHA and VA mortgages are assumable by buyers of properties. Hence, they are not always repaid when a property is sold. Conventional mortgages may contain a due on sale clause which prohibits assumptions; hence, they would be more likely to be repaid if a property is sold. Some older conventional fixed interest rate mortgages may also contain prepayment penalties which tend to discourage early repayment. Conventional mortgages made more recently and *ARM*s generally do not include such penalties.

[21]In order to include this option in the agreement with investors, however, the issuer usually includes a schedule of premiums in excess of par value that will be paid to bondholders if the option to call is exercised by the corporation. This premium is paid because (1) the market value of the bonds will have increased if market rates have fallen and calling in the bond would deprive bondholders of an increase in market value, and (2) if investors expect to own the bonds for the entire maturity period, refinancing by the company may represent an unanticipated interruption in cash flows and bondholders would have to reinvest at lower interest rates.

[22]Such retirements amount to an implicit method of amortization (such as that of a mortgage) and are usually accomplished with a sinking fund which is used to (1) call bonds as scheduled, by serial number at either a premium or at par value, or (2) call a percentage of the original issue at random by serial number at either par value or at a premium, or (3) use sinking funds to enter the market and repurchase bonds at market value.

[23]A limited number of U.S. government bond issues are callable for a specified number of years prior to maturity.

investors in pass-through securities. Such pass-throughs of mortgage balances can be zero in months when interest rates increase then accelerate rapidly when market interest rates decline. During the latter periods, many households choose to refinance. Mortgages are then paid off and removed from the pool as principal is passed through to investors.[24]

When issuing pass-through securities, the issuer generally specifies both a coupon rate of interest (9.5 percent in our preceding example) *and* an offering price on the securities being issued. This offering price may be above or below par value. This is done because although the security will pay interest at 9.5 percent on the outstanding pool balance, as we have discussed, investors may demand a rate of return that is different from the coupon rate as market conditions vary at the time of issue. As shown in Exhibit 21–10, even when no prepayments are assumed, the range in security prices may vary considerably, depending on the market rate of return demanded by investors. However, because investors realize that there is also a strong likelihood that some prepayments will occur while they own these securities, issuers usually price these securities, taking into account some *assumed prepayment pattern*. This is necessary in order to provide a more accurate estimate of cash flows (hence, yield to investors) rather than assuming that all borrowers will repay loans in accordance with a stated amortization schedule.

Methods that issuers use to include prepayment assumptions when pricing securities fall into four broad classes:

1. *Average maturity.* This method assumes, for example, that a pool of 30-year mortgages is scheduled to amortize principal based on a 30-year maturity but the pool is totally paid off after some average period of time, such as the 12th year. Hence, when calculating yields, or pricing securities, it is assumed that regular mortgage payments would be made for 12 years, and the principal due at that time would amount to a balloon payment. This method has the advantage of simplicity because an average prepayment rate is being chosen to represent all mortgages in the pool. Further, choosing an average maturity has the effect of facilitating comparison with traditional bonds.

The disadvantages of this technique far outweigh its advantages. There is considerable evidence, both empirical and theoretical, that the so-called 12-year average life convention is not an adequate method of handling the prepayment problem and will usually result in under- or overestimation of yield. As previously explained, prepayments are the product of numerous factors, including interest rate changes and household characteristics. Hence, using an average maturity may not reflect changes underlying these characteristics.

2. *Constant rates of prepayment.* This method of handling prepayment assumes that a constant percentage of the total mortgages in the pool will be paid off every year. The advantages of this model of prepayment assumption are that it is simple to understand and prepayments are easy to compute. However, empirical evidence suggests that prepayments due to defaults occur more frequently early in the life of most mortgages. Hence, most constant prepayment rates would tend to understate prepayment in earlier

---

[24]As interest rates declined during 1986 and 1987, it was estimated that 60 percent of all mortgages made during 1981–1985 were refinanced by borrowers. This unanticipated decline probably meant that investors in pass-through pools received principal payments much sooner than anticipated.

years and overstate it in later years. While this method may be preferable to an average maturity, it is also likely to not reflect underlying pool characteristics.

3. *FHA prepayment experience.* Prepayment assumptions based on empirical data based on actual prepayment experience collected by the FHA over several decades have been suggested as a guide for making more accurate prepayment assumptions. The FHA has developed an extensive data base on mortgage terminations as a part of its insurance program. This data base contains the total number of mortgage terminations during a single policy year, including information on the number resulting from defaults and repayments. Many argue that prepayment assumptions could be based on this FHA "experience." For example, if slower or faster prepayment on pools of mortgages is expected because of differences in investor expectations, those rates could be adjusted to be less than 100 percent or greater than 100 percent of FHA experience, and yields could be disclosed to investors. As shown in Exhibit 21–11, FHA data indicates that a rising prepayment rate exists in the early years of most mortgages, levels off to a fairly constant rate, then accelerates again as mortgages approach maturity.

However, the FHA data on prepayment experience is not without its shortcomings. Major problems are encountered when applying historic FHA experience to current mort-

EXHIBIT 21–11 PSA versus FHA Prepayment Assumptions

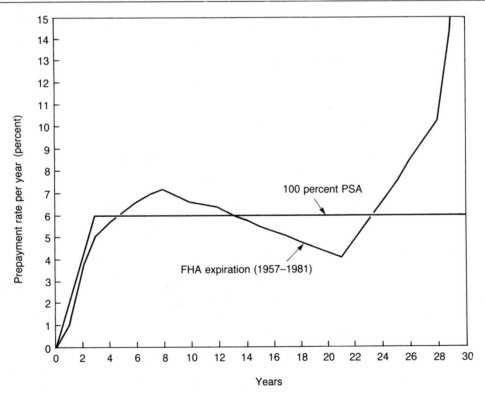

gage pools. This is because the precise causes of prepayment (e.g., changes in interest rates, borrowers employment, etc.) over time are difficult to determine. Further, there is no assurance that this pattern will repeat in the future. Further, the FHA does not keep enough detailed data for each mortgage and borrower to enable a systematic investigation of the causes of prepayment behavior.

4. *The PSA model.* The PSA model was developed by the Public Securities Association as an attempt to simplify the FHA experience prepayment model. Even though it suffers from the same shortcomings as the FHA prepayment experience does, it has become an industry standard for prepayment assumptions used by most issuers of mortgage-backed securities. Simply put, the model is based on monthly prepayment rates, which vary during the life of a mortgage pool underlying the security. At present, the standard PSA prepayment rate curve (referred to as "100 percent PSA") begins at 0.2 percent per month for the first year, then increases by 0.2 percent each month until month 30. It then remains at 0.5 percent per month, or 6 percent per year for the remaining stated maturity period of the pool. The model combines both the FHA experience and the constant rate of repayment approach. As Exhibit 21–11 shows, the initial rising prepayment rate for the PSA model closely tracks FHA experience in the early years of the life of the pool. In the latter years, the PSA rate levels off to a constant rate. Although it levels off at this point, the pool factor is rapidly approaching zero. Hence, the distortion in cash flows caused by this simplification is not material in relation to the repayment implied by the FHA experience.

As previously mentioned, because investors and issuers are aware that yields are likely to be affected by the rate of loan repayment, the PSA assumption shown in Exhibit 21–11 regarding repayment rate is widely used in the security industry as a standard approach to convey both price and yield information to investors at the time of issue. The PSA repayment pattern shown in Exhibit 21–11 is referred to in the industry as "100 percent PSA." To provide additional information to prospective security buyers at the time of issue, a series of yield quotes are generally provided in the prospectus based on various PSA repayment rates (e.g., 75 percent PSA, 150 percent PSA). This is done to provide the buyer with some idea of the sensitivity of yields to different prepayment rates. To illustrate the cash flows and the repayment pattern at 100 percent PSA, Exhibit 21–12 illustrates cash flows to the investor. Note that column *b* of the exhibit contains prepayment cash flows in accordance with approximately 100 percent PSA.[25] When column *g* in Exhibit 21–12 is compared with column *g* of Exhibit 21–9, it is clear that more principal is being "passed through" to investors at the end of each payment period. This pass-through of cash occurs at an increasing rate for the first three years in Exhibit 21–12, then levels off at a constant rate from that point until maturity.

Even though the 100 percent PSA assumption is being used in the analysis, if the securities were issued in a market in which investors expected a 9.5 percent return, the price would be equal to par value ($25,000). This is true even though cash flows in column g of Exhibit 21–12 (with the PSA assumption) are very different from cash flows

---

[25]To simplify calculations, we assume prepayments of 2 percent and 4 percent in years 1 and 2, then 6 percent each year thereafter.

EXHIBIT 21–12 Cash Flows Mortgage Pass-Through Security (constant payment, fixed rate, 30-year mortgage pool, interest rate = 10 percent prepayment assumed to be approximately 100 percent PSA, coupon rate = 9.5 percent)

Period Years	(a) Pool Balance	(b) Principal due to Prepayment	(c) P & I Payments	(d) Total P & I Payments* (b) + (c)	(e) Guarantee & Service Fees (a) × (0.5%)	(f) Total PMTs to Investors (d) − (e)	(g) Payment to Individual Investor (f)/40
0	$1,000,000						($25,000)
1	973,921	$20,000	$106,079	$126,079	$5,000	$121,079	3,027
2	928,411	38,957	103,945	142,902	4,870	138,032	3,451
3	865,789	55,705	99,759	155,463	4,642	150,821	3,771
4	806,692	51,947	93,728	145,676	4,329	141,347	3,534
5	750,902	48,402	88,058	136,459	4,033	132,426	3,311
6	698,213	45,054	82,725	127,780	3,755	124,025	3,101
7	648,430	41,893	77,711	119,604	3,491	116,113	2,903
8	601,373	38,906	72,995	111,901	3,242	108,659	2,716
9	556,868	36,082	68,560	104,642	3,007	101,635	2,541
10	514,755	33,412	64,388	97,800	2,784	95,015	2,375
11	474,883	30,885	60,463	91,348	2,574	88,774	2,219
12	437,107	28,493	56,771	85,264	2,374	82,889	2,072
13	401,295	26,226	53,297	79,523	2,186	77,337	1,933
14	367,320	24,078	50,027	74,105	2,006	72,098	1,802
15	335,063	22,039	46,950	68,989	1,837	67,152	1,679
16	304,413	20,104	44,052	64,156	1,675	62,480	1,562
17	275,267	18,265	41,323	59,588	1,522	58,066	1,452
18	247,526	16,516	38,752	55,268	1,376	53,891	1,347
19	221,099	14,852	36,328	51,179	1,238	49,942	1,249
20	195,902	13,266	34,041	47,307	1,105	46,202	1,155
21	171,856	11,754	31,882	43,636	980	42,657	1,066
22	148,889	10,311	29,841	40,153	859	39,293	982
23	126,936	8,933	27,908	36,842	744	36,097	902
24	105,940	7,616	26,073	33,690	635	33,055	826
25	85,853	6,356	24,325	30,681	530	30,151	754
26	66,639	5,151	22,648	27,799	429	27,370	684
27	48,282	3,998	21,023	25,021	333	24,688	617
28	30,799	2,897	19,415	22,312	241	22,071	552
29	14,285	1,848	17,746	19,594	154	19,440	486
30	0	0	15,713	15,713	71	15,642	391

A.
Value of cash flows to issuer if the required rate is 9.50 percent = $1,000,000
Value of cash flows to individual investors at 9.50 percent = $25,000
B.
Value of cash flows to issuer if the required rate is 8.50 percent = $1,066,111
Value of cash flows to individual investors at 8.50 percent = $26,653
C.
Value of cash flows to issuer if the required rate is 10.50 percent = $940,909
Value of cash flows to individual investors at 10.50 percent = $23,523

*Payments calculated on an annual basis.

in column *g* of Exhibit 21–9 (no prepayment assumption). This result occurs because even though the PSA assumption results in more cash flows early in the life of the pool, interest is still calculated at 9.5 percent on the outstanding balance at all times. Hence, the investor is receiving *principal* on the pass-through faster, but continues to earn interest on the outstanding balance at 9.5 percent. Hence, the present value of both columns *g* in Exhibits 21–12 and 21–9, when discounted at 9.5 percent, equals $25,000.

Exhibit 21–13 depicts cash flows from a pool assuming 50 percent, 100 percent, 150 percent PSA, and no prepayment, or 0 percent PSA. For 150 percent PSA, this would mean that repayment would be 3 percent in year 1, 6 percent in year 2, and 9 percent in year 3 and thereafter, all multiplied by the outstanding loan balances in the pool at the end of the preceding period. Obviously, the cash flow to investors will vary dramatically, depending on the repayment rate. Also, as previously discussed, in the unlikely event that the market rate of return demanded by investors is equal to the coupon rate on the pass-through security, the security will always sell at par value, or $25,000, regardless of the prepayment rate (the student should think about why this result is true).

EXHIBIT 21–13   MPT Cash Flows at Different Prepayment Rates

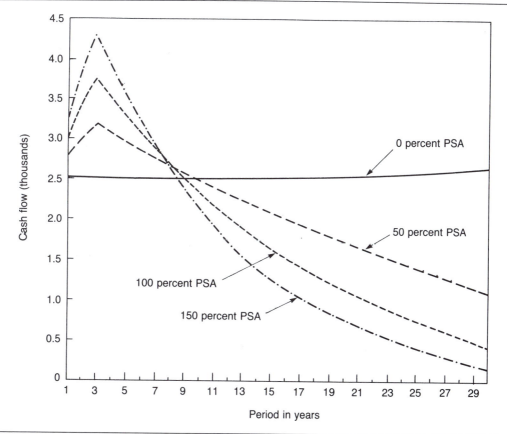

Security Prices and Expected Yields

As previously pointed out, when mortgage pass-through securities are priced by the issuer (with the advice of security underwriters), some assessment of yields expected by investors *at the time of issue* must be made. Further, this yield is likely to be different from the coupon rate on securities at the time of issue. This assessment is usually made by (1) establishing the extent of the premium that investors expect in excess of current yields on government securities with maturities in the same expected maturity range, or (2) considering the current yields on other pass-throughs currently trading in the market. In the former case, establishing the premium may be difficult because of the uncertainty in repayment rates on pass-throughs, and in the latter, pricing of other pass-throughs assumes that the characteristics underlying both pools are the same. Nonetheless, the securities must be priced to sell to investors at the time of issue.

Turning back to our example, if we *assume* that after considering all current market conditions and future expectations regarding repayment that the issuer decides that an expected yield of 8.5 percent will be required to successfully sell all securities to investors and that the prepayment rate will be 100 percent PSA, then the security price will be equal to the present value of cash flows in column g of Exhibit 21–12 discounted at 8.5 percent. This yields a price of $26,653, or a premium of $1,653 over the $25,000 par value (see Part B of Exhibit 21–12). The security is now said to be "priced at 106.61 percent of par ($26,653 ÷ $25,000) to yield 8.5 percent at 100 percent PSA." However, the issuer will usually provide yield information to the investor by assuming *faster* and *slower prepayment rates*. This is done by taking the offering price for the security ($26,653) and setting it equal to the expected cash flows that would occur above and below 100 percent PSA, then solving for the internal rate of return. Hence, in our example, in addition to the 8.5 percent yield (internal rate of return) at 100 percent PSA, the issuer may disclose a yield of 8.36 percent at 150 percent PSA and 8.64 percent at 50 percent PSA (calculations not shown).[26] The reader should think about why faster (or slower) rates of repayment will cause the yield to be lower (or higher) in this example. The investor is willing to pay a premium of $1,653 in this example because the coupon rate is higher than the investor's required yield. But because the mortgages in the pool are likely to be prepaid sooner than expected, the investor will not benefit from the higher coupon rate for very long because of the increase in prepayments. Hence, the premium must reflect not only the relationship between the coupon rate on the security and the market yield on similar investments demanded by investors, but also the expected rate of repayment by homeowners. On the other hand, if market yields indicated that at the time of issue the security should be priced to yield 10.5 percent at 100 percent PSA, it would be issued at a discount, or at a price of $23,523 (see Part C of Exhibit 21–12). In this case, mortgages are not likely to be prepaid by homeowners as fast, hence the expected rate of repayment decreases. Hence, the discount paid on the security must

---

[26]To reiterate, the price being asked for the security does not change in these calculations. Only cash flows from prepayments in the pool that are passed on to the investor are changed in accordance with the accelerated or reduced percentage of PSA in each case. The internal rate of return (yield) is then solved for by setting the price equal to the modified cash flows in each case.

reflect this factor as well as coupon rates and market yields. Exhibit 21–14 provides a range in expected yields at various PSA rates if the security is initially offered at a price of \$23,523 (discount) and \$26,653 (premium).

Market Interest Rates and Price Behavior on Mortgage Pass-Throughs

Note the following patterns in conjunction with Exhibit 21–14. It should be obvious that if a pass-through is priced at a premium and the rate of repayment accelerates (i.e., PSA > 100 percent), then the expected yield on the pass-through will be lower as the expected repayment rate becomes higher. The opposite result occurs when the prepayment rate is expected to be lower (i.e., PSA < 100 percent). On the other hand, when a mortgage pass-through is priced at a discount (original issue price is less than par value), the expected yield increases as the prepayment rate increases.

EXHIBIT 21–14 Range in Expected Yields for MPTs Issued at a Premium and at a Discount at Different Prepayment Rates

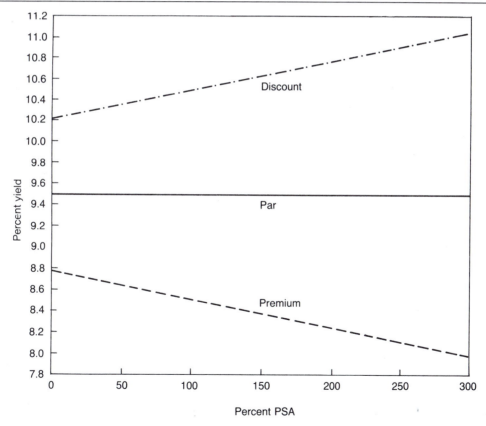

This very important relationship shown in Exhibit 21–14 should be elaborated further. While the exhibit shows that yields increase and decrease with the assumed repayment rate *at the time of issue,* it is generally the case that *after* securities are issued the price will vary with market interest rates. In other words, the price of a pass-through after issue will also respond to both changes in market interest rates and prepayment rates.[27]

To illustrate, Exhibit 21–15 shows that if the market rate of interest were to fall to 7.5 percent, for a 9.5 percent coupon rate pass-through security, investors would expect an increase in the *price* of the pass-through because of the decline in interest rates. Further, if there were no prepayment assumed (i.e., 0 percent PSA), the price of the pass-through would increase from $25,000 to approximately $30,000. However, if interest rates decline and the prepayment rate accelerates because more borrowers chose to refinance or pay off loans, the price will not rise to the extent that it would have if no increase in prepayments occurred. This can be seen by comparing prices at extreme rates of repayment, such as prices at 0 percent PSA (no prepayment), with prices at 1000 percent PSA for interest rates less than 9.5 percent. Note that even though interest rates may decline, if the prepayment rate accelerates to 1000 percent PSA,[28] the price at a 7.5 percent demanded yield would now be only slightly in excess of $26,000, as compared with $30,000 assuming no prepayment. On the other hand, when market interest rates are greater than the coupon rate, MPT prices will fall, and by a greater amount as repayments slow. This can also be seen by comparing prices for interest rates greater than 9.5 percent at 0 percent PSA and 1000 percent PSA. Hence, prices of MPTs are inversely related to interest rates; however, they are *less sensitive to declines in interest rates and more sensitive to increases in interest rates.* This is because rates of repayment are likely to accelerate as interest rates fall, and slow as interest rates rise. This asymmetry in the response of prices to interest rates, that is, a wider range of price responses to rising interest rates when compared to the range of prices likely to occur in required to falling interest rates, is likely to result in a maximum on premiums that can be earned on MPTs but no limit on discounts. This limit on premiums is referred to as *price compression.* Further, as interest rates decline and prepayments accelerate, all cash flows received by investors must be reinvested at lower interest rates. This prospect is perhaps the most serious problem that investors perceive when investing in mortgage pass-through securities. It is this problem, coupled with other factors, that has given rise to collateralized mortgage obligations (CMOs), one of the mortgage-related securities that we will cover in the next chapter.

---

[27]After a security is issued, subsequent buyers can determine whether it is selling at a discount or premium by comparing the current selling price against the pool factor multiplied by the original issue price of $25,000. Hence, if a security issued five years ago is currently selling for $19,500 and its pool factor is .8516, then the outstanding pool balance per security is $21,290. The security would be selling at a discount of $1,790.

[28]Our approximation to 1000 percent PSA would have repayment rates on pool balances of 20 percent at the end of year 1, 40 percent at the end of year 2, and 60 percent at the end of year 3 and thereafter. One thousand percent PSA is used to illustrate the wide range in discounts and premiums in MPTs that could result in the case of an extremely high repayment rate in contrast to another extreme—that is, a zero prepayment rate.

EXHIBIT 21–15   MPT Price versus Market Interest Rates for Different Prepayment Assumptions

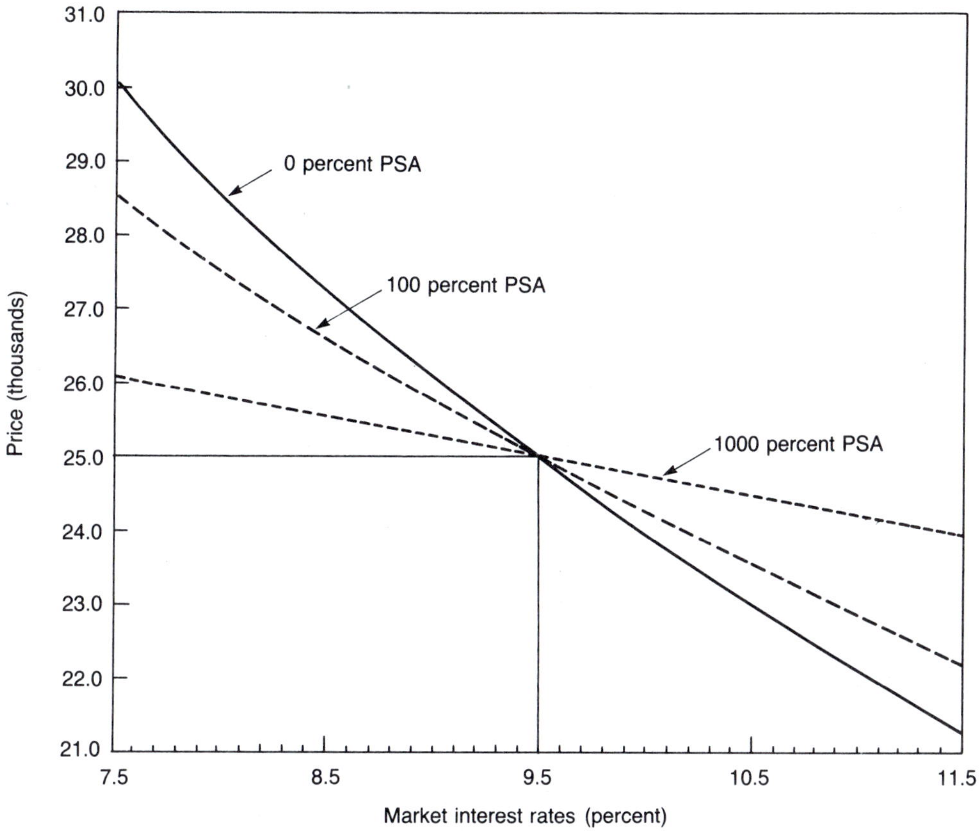

A Note on MBBs and MPTs

As indicated in the previous section dealing with mortgage-backed bonds, we indicated that the trustee was required to periodically "mark the mortgage collateral to the market" to determine whether the overcollateralization requirements of bond issues were being maintained. The methodology just outlined for pricing MPTs is the methodology that would generally be followed by such a trustee to establish the market value of the mortgage pool for an MBB issue. Further, for MBBs, *issuers bear prepayment risk* by virtue of the overcollateralization requirement. In other words, as prepayments accelerate and mortgages are prepaid, more mortgages must be replaced in the pool. For MPTs, *security holders bear prepayment risk* because all prepayments are passed through to investors. This means that (1) MBBs should be priced to provide lower yields than MPTs because the MBB issuer bears prepayment risk, and (2) as market interest rates change the price of MBBs will not reflect accelerated prepayment rates. As shown in Exhibit 21–15, this is not the case for MPTs. In fact, if all other terms of the MPT offering described in our example were exactly the same for an MBB offering, the price behavior for the MBB would be represented by the 0 percent PSA curve in Exhibit 21–15.

QUESTIONS

1. What is the secondary mortgage market? List three reasons why it is important?
2. What were the three principal activities of FNMA under its 1954 charter? What is its principal function now?
3. Name two ways that FNMA currently finances its secondary mortgage operations?
4. When did GNMA come into existence? What was its original function? What is its main function now?
5. Why was the formation of FHLMC so important?
6. What is a mortgage-related security? What are the similarities and differences between mortgage securities and corporate bonds?
7. Name the principal types of mortgage-related securities? What are the differences between them?
8. There are several ways that mortgages can be sold into the secondary market. Pick two of them, compare and contrast them as to length of distribution channel, relative ease of transaction, and efficiency as it relates to maximizing funds flow from sale.
9. What is the function of the optional delivery commitment?
10. What is a mortgage swap? Does it increase market efficiency?
11. Name five important characteristics of mortgage pools. Tell why each is important.
12. In general, would a falling rate of market interest cause the price of an MPT security to increase or decrease? Would the increase or decrease be greater if the security was issued at a discount? Would an increase in prepayment be likely or unlikely? Describe with an example.

PROBLEMS

1. Two 25-year maturity mortgage-backed bonds are issued. The first bond has a par value of $10,000 and promises to pay a 9.5 percent annual coupon, while the second is a zero coupon bond that promises to pay $10,000 (par) after 25 years including accrued interest at 9.5 percent. At issue, bond market investors require an 11 percent interest rate on both bonds.
   a. What will be the initial price on each bond?
   b. Assume both bonds promise interest at 9.5 percent, compounded semiannually. What will be the initial price for each bond?
   c. If market interest rates fall to 8.5 percent at the end of five years, what will be the value of each bond (state both as a percentage of par value and actual dollar value)?

  d. The issuer of the 9.5 percent coupon MBBs has decided to include a call provision that would give the issuer the right to call the issue after 10 years. Assuming that the call premium is 5 percent over par value, what would be the yield to investors if the issue was called? (Hint: Assume that the initial price of the bond is the same as in (a).)

  e. What would the equivalent decline in interest rates have to be in (d) in order for the market value of the bond to be equal to the call price?

2. The Green S & L originated a pool containing 75 ten-year fixed interest rate mortgages with an average balance of $100,000 each. Each mortgage in the pool carried a coupon of 11 percent, because that was the prevailing interest rate at the time they were originated. (For simplicity, assume all mortgage payments are made *annually* at 11 percent interest.) Green would now like to sell the pool to FNMA.

  a. Assuming a constant annual prepayment rate of 10 percent, (for simplicity assume that prepayments begin at the end of year 1) what would be the price that Green could obtain if market interest rates were 11 percent, 12 percent, 9 percent?

  b. Assume that five years have expired since the date in (a). What will the pool factor be? If market interest rates were 12 percent, what price could Green obtain now?

  c. Instead of selling the pool of mortgages in (a), Green decides to securitize the mortgages by issuing 100 pass-through securities. The coupon rate will be 10.5 percent and the servicing and guarantee fee will be .5 percent. However, the current market rate of return is 9.5 percent for such securities. How much will Green obtain for this offering of MPTs? What will each purchaser pay for an MPT security? (Assume the same prepayment rate as in (a).)

  d. Assume now that immediately after purchase in (c), interest rates fall to 8.0 percent, and that the prepayment rates are expected to accelerate to 20 percent per year, beginning at the end of the first year. What will the MPT security be worth now?

Chapter 22

Secondary Mortgage Markets and Mortgage-Related Securities— Part II

INTRODUCTION

Two additional securities have been recently introduced to securitize mortgage pools. The first is referred to as a mortgage pay-through bond (MPTB). It contains elements of both mortgage-backed bonds and mortgage pass-through securities. The second security, referred to as a collateralized mortgage obligation (CMO), was developed in conjunction with investment underwriters by Freddie Mac in 1983 and adopted by Fannie Mae in 1987. These securities should be viewed as a natural evolution or outgrowth of the initial success of the mortgage-backed bond and pass-through security programs. Recall that many risks and investor concerns with purchasing whole mortgages discussed in the previous chapter were alleviated to some extent by mortgage pass-throughs. However, several key concerns with prepayment risk and reinvestment risk remained for some investors. Innovators of mortgage-backed securities believed that new product types had to be developed to address these concerns.

MORTGAGE PAY-THROUGH BONDS (MPTBs)

These bonds can be best described as a hybrid security or one containing elements of both mortgage pass-throughs and mortgage-backed bonds. These bonds are issued against mortgage pools and, like MPTs, cash flows from the pool (that is, principal and interest) are passed through to security holders. However, unlike an MPT, this security is a *bond* and *not* an undivided *equity* ownership interest in a mortgage pool. That is, like the MBB, it is a debt obligation of the issuer, who retains ownership of the mortgage pool. However, like the MPT, cash flows paid to bondholders are based on a coupon rate of interest, while principal is passed through as it is received from normal amortization and prepayment of loans in the pool. Hence, an MPTB can be viewed as a MBB with the pass-through of principal and prepayment features of a MPT.

Most pay-through issues are based on residential pools and, like MBBs, will generally be overcollateralized by including (1) more mortgages in the pool than the sum of the securities issued against it or (2) additional collateral in the form of U.S. government bonds or other agency obligations. The income from this additional collateral is used as added assurance that sufficient cash flows will be available to service the bonds. As was the case with MBBs, MPTBs may be issued with either a coupon rate or on a zero coupon basis.

An MPTB credit rating depends on (1) the riskiness of mortgages in the pool, (2) the extent of overcollateralization, and (3) the nature of any government-related securities constituting the excess collateral. Emphasis is placed on the extent of cash flow that will be produced by the pool, the reinvestment period that the issuer faces between receipt of principal and interest from the mortgage pool and periodic (usually semiannual) payments to bondholders, the securities making up the overcollateralization, and its relationship to promised coupon payments. All of these features are evaluated relative to prepayment risk. Because of the pass-through of amortization and prepayments, the market value of the collateral is not as important as with MBBs. Hence, there is usually no need to mark the collateral to the market or to provide for replenishment of collateral as long as the amount of overcollateralization is adequate. Because of the pass-through of principal, overcollateral requirements are not as great as for MBBs. Credit enhancements in the form of letters of credit and third-party guarantees or insurance are used by MPTB issuers to acquire higher credit ratings. In the absence of such enhancements, the creditworthiness of the issuer is very important, because should the mortgage pool experience a high rate of default losses and prepayments, the issuer must be looked to for satisfaction by the debt security holders.[1]

Although we do not provide a detailed analysis of MPTBs, the cash flow patterns are similar to those shown in the illustrations used for MBBs and MPTs in Chapter 21. However, with respect to MPTBs, it should be clear that, contrary to the MBB, the issuer does not bear prepayment risk. It is born by the investor. Hence, when pricing MPTBs, the risks discussed regarding prepayment patterns and reinvestment rates that are so important when evaluating MPTs are equally important to MPTBs. This uncertainty regarding cash flows from prepayments has resulted in yet another security type, one that provides more protection against prepayment risk than MPTs and MPTBs, but less than that of an MBB. This security, referred to as the collateralized mortgage obligation (CMO), is the subject of the next section.

COLLATERALIZED MORTGAGE OBLIGATIONS

To understand how CMOs help to alleviate some of the reinvestment and prepayment risk for investors, we must understand the concept of a CMO and how it differs from MPTs and MPTBs. CMOs are debt instruments (like MBBs) that are issued using a pool

---

[1]Like other mortgage-related securities, default risk can be reduced by using FHA-VA mortgages or conventional loans with private mortgage insurance.

of mortgages for collateral. Contrary to the pass-through in which investors own an individual interest in the entire pool, in a CMO offering the *issuer retains the ownership* of the mortgage pool and issues the bonds as debt against the mortgage pool. However, like the MPT and MPTB, the CMO is a pay-through security in that all amortization and prepayments flow through to investors. This means that the security holder assumes prepayment risk, although the CMO modifies how this risk is allocated. Like both the MBB and MPTB, the difference between assets pledged as security and the amount of the debt issued against the pool constitutes the equity position of the issuer.

The major difference between CMOs and the previous securities discussed is that CMOs are securities issued in multiple maturity classes against the same pool of mortgages. These securities may have a number of maturity classes, such as 3, 5, or 7 years. Such maturities are chosen by the issuer to meet the investment needs of various classes of investors. By issuing multiple classes of securities, each with a different maturity, the issuer is effectively creating different securities with maturity and payment streams that are vastly different from the underlying mortgage pool. At the present time, CMOs are the fastest-growing type of mortgage related security, second only to MPTs in dollar volume. Of the $785 billion of mortgage-related securities outstanding at the end of 1986, CMOs constituted $75 billion.

There are several fundamental differences between CMOs and MPTs. In order to reduce prepayment risk (and the coincident reinvestment risk), a mechanism had to be developed for an entity other than the investor to assume this risk, while retaining the basic procedure of issuing securities against a mortgage pool. This was accomplished by the *issuer* retaining the ownership of the mortgage pool and prioritizing the payment of interest and principal among the various categories (classes) of debt securities issued against the pool. This prioritization is accomplished by issuing CMOs in classes referred to as *tranches* with different stated maturity dates. To achieve the desired number and maturity of these tranches a prioritization of interest, principal, and prepayment proceeds from the mortgage pool to bondholders is made. Based on this prioritization, some classes of CMO investors receive cash flows like investors in conventional debt securities, while other investors agree to defer cash flows to later periods. This allocation was designed to appeal to more investor groups than would be willing to invest in MPTs, but who also were willing to bear some prepayment risk at yields that would be higher than that earned on MBBs. Another way of characterizing a CMO would be to refer to it as a *multiple security class, mortgage pay-through security.*

CMOs Illustrated

Exhibit 22–1 shows provisions that a typical offering of a CMO security might contain. On the ''asset'' side of the exhibit, the pool used for the bond collateral is assumed to be either FHA, VA, or conventional mortgages with interest rates fixed at 10 percent interest over a 30-year maturity. As with pass-throughs, mortgages placed in CMO pools are generally secured by very similar kinds of real estate and have very similar payment patterns. It is also possible to pool GNMAs or other pass-through securities for a CMO

EXHIBIT 22–1 Contents of a CMO Security Offering (ABC Mortgage Corporation)

			Stated Maturity	Coupon Rate (percent)	Amount Issued
Assets:		Liabilities:			
Mortgages	$104,000,000	Class A Bonds	5–9	9.00	$ 30,000,000
		Class B Bonds	9–14	9.25	30,000,000
		Class C Bonds	12–17	9.75	25,000,000
		Class Z Bonds	28–30	10.50	15,000,000
		Total bonds			100,000,000
		Equity:			4,000,000
Total assets	$104,000,000	Total debt and net worth			$104,000,000

Major investors:
Class A—Thrifts, commercial banks, money market funds, corporations
Class B—Insurance companies, pension funds, trusts, international investors
Class C—Insurance companies, pension funds, trusts, international investors
Class Z—Insurance companies, pension funds, trusts, international investors and aggressive, long-term bond mutual funds

offering.[2] The latter securities can be used because they ultimately represent securities based on a pool of mortgages.

On the "liability" side of the exhibit, four classes of bonds are created with different maturities and different coupon rates. The amount of CMOs issued against the $104 million pool is $100 million. The difference ($4 million) is overcollateral, which is the equity contribution made by the issuer. The need for the overcollateralization will be apparent as the structure of the CMO issue is explained. Another observation that can be made in our example is that the 10 percent rate to be earned on the asset pool exceeds the coupon rates promised to each class of bondholders, except for the Z class. However, because the latter represents only 15 percent of the issue, a spread exists between the rate to be earned on the pool and the weighted average rate of interest promised to security holders. As we will see, this spread represents the source of profit to be earned by the issuer. This residual cash flow will represent a return on the $4 million in overcollateral, or equity, invested in the venture. The issuer earns a profit on the equity which is used for creating the security issue. Fees may be also earned for providing any credit enhancements, managing, and administering the mortgage pool.

To achieve the desired maturity pattern for the CMOs shown in Exhibit 22–1, the conditions of the issue are such that the coupon rate of interest is not paid currently on

[2]CMOs can be created based on many different mortgage pools (e.g., *ARM*s, *GPM*s), such as those listed in Exhibit 21–8 in the previous chapter.

all tranches. For example, interest is paid currently on tranches A, B, and C, but it is not paid on tranche Z until principal on the other tranches is repaid. For securities in tranche Z, interest will be accrued and accumulated into the investment balance. To ensure that the maturity of tranche A securities is kept relatively short, all interest accrued on the portion of the security offering contributed by the Z tranche ($15 million) is also allocated first to the A tranche security holders. Further, all current amortization of principal and prepayments from the *entire* mortgage pool will also be allocated *first* to tranche A. Hence, tranche A investors, representing $30 million of the CMO issue, will receive principal on all mortgages in the pool (including prepayments), plus interest that would have been paid to the Z tranche until the $30 million tranche is repaid, plus a coupon rate of 9 percent on their outstanding investment balance. Their investment balance is reduced by all principal payments from the pool plus the interest not currently paid but accrued on the Z class investment balance. As to the spread in stated maturities for tranche A securities (five to nine years), it represents (a) the maximum number of years (9) that it would take for class A investors to recover their principal, *assuming that no prepayments* occurred on the underlying mortgage pool, and (b) an *estimate* of the minimum number of years (5) that it would take them to recover their investment, assuming that the repayment rate was 100 percent PSA (as explained in the preceding chapter).[3] Of course, this latter estimate could be longer or shorter, depending on the *actual* rate of prepayment.

Until the A tranche is repaid, the B and C tranches receive "interest only" payments on their investment. After class A is repaid, all principal allocations are made to B, and so on. As pointed out, the Z class of security holders receive no interest payments *or* principal payments while the A, B, and C tranches are being repaid. Instead, interest is accrued on the $15 million invested by this class of investors and is compounded at the 10.5 percent coupon rate. The accrued interest is then added to the amount owed. After classes A, B, and C are repaid, cash interest payments are made to the Z class, and all principal payments from the pool are then directed toward this class.

The $4,000,000 in extra mortgages placed in the pool, which represents overcollateralization or equity invested in the issue, is required for several reasons. First, in addition to the cash flow patterns described, most CMO issues promise payments to investors either quarterly or semiannually; however, as we know, payments into the mortgage pool occur monthly. Because monthly mortgage payments may be reinvested by the issuer until semiannual payments are due to investors, the issuer usually promises a minimum rate of interest on these investable funds *in addition to* promised coupon payments and priority repayment of principal. Hence, in addition to the risk of prepayment, a reinvestment risk exists in the event that market interest rates fall dramatically. In this event prepayments into the pool would accelerate thereby repaying all tranches *much faster* than 100 percent PSA.[4] Further, the issuer may not be able to earn the promised rate of return on interim cash flows as interest rates fall (reinvestment risk). In this event, any

---

[3]Many CMO offerings indicate an average maturity for each tranche of securities. In our example for class A, it would be (5 years + 9 years) ÷ 2 = 7 years.

[4]Recall our earlier observations and analysis of repayment patterns in Chapter 21.

cash shortfall to CMO investors will be paid from the $4 million of additional mortgage collateral. Hence, as with MBBs and MPTBs, the extent of overcollateralization is an important consideration that must be made by investors when evaluating a CMO investment. Obviously, the greater the amount of overcollateralization, the more likely that promised coupon rates and rates on interim cash flows will be paid. However, this lower risk also implies that the coupon rate and rate on reinvested funds promised to the shorter-term tranches may also be lower.

Another important attribute of these securities is whether the CMO issuer is liable beyond the $4 million of equity. CMOs are debt instruments usually issued by a corporation and these debt instruments can be made with or without recourse to the issuer. Hence, like an issue of corporate bonds, CMO security owners may have recourse against the assets of the issuing corporation should the issuer become bankrupt and not perform as promised and liability exceeds $4 million.[5]

CMO Mechanics

Some idea of how cash flows from a CMO offering are patterned is given in Exhibit 22–2. The data from our example in Exhibit 22–1 are used to produce cash flows in Exhibit 22–2. To simplify this analysis, we have assumed that payments into the pool from mortgage borrowers occur annually. Consequently, we do not consider any reinvestment of interim cash flows between receipt of mortgage payments into the pool and payment to the various tranches of securities.[6] We begin by assuming a rate of prepayment equal to 0 percent PSA. Essentially, the exhibit details the source and composition of cash flows into the mortgage pool backing the CMO offering. Exhibit 22–3 provides a breakdown of cash flows for two tranches of securities, Class A and Z. Based on the assumption that no prepayments occur (0 percent PSA), tranche A security holders would be paid (a) interest at 9 percent of $30 million or $2,700,000, (b) all principal repayments of $632,242 flowing into the pool (see column *4* in Exhibit 22–2), plus (c) the $1,575,000 in interest that would have been paid to the Z class of securities, or a total of $4,907,242 at end of the first year. The amount owed to the A class of securities is now $30 million less $632,242 and $1,575,000, or $27,792,758. The cash flow pattern just described continues each year until the class A securities are repaid, which occurs at the end of the ninth year (this corresponds to the stated maximum maturity shown in Exhibit 22–1 for class A bonds). Note again that Z class investors receive no current cash payments because interest is being accrued in that class.

Exhibit 22–4 provides a similar breakdown for class B and C security holders. Note that class B securities receive current interest payments from years 1 to 9, but they do not receive any repayment of principal until class A is repaid. They then receive current

---

[5]Hence, in addition to overcollateralization, the investor will want to investigate the creditworthiness of the issuer if the issue is made with recourse to the issuer. If it is made without recourse, other enhancements, such as letters of credit and insurance policies purchased from third parties, should be carefully investigated.

[6]To do this requires more complex programming; however, it can be incorporated if desired. Our purpose is to provide the reader with a general understanding of CMOs.

EXHIBIT 22–2   Annual Cash Flows into CMO Mortgage Pool (prepayment = 0% PSA)

Period	(1) Mortgage Pool: 30-Year Term 10% Fixed Rate	(2) Principal and Interest Payments into Pool	(3) Assumed Prepayments End of Period (0% PSA)	(4) Total Amortization Excluding Prepayments	(5) Interest	(6) Amount Owed to Security Holders
0	$104,000,000					$100,000,000
1	103,367,758	$11,032,242	0	$ 632,242	$10,400,000	99,367,758
2	102,672,292	11,032,242	0	695,466	10,336,776	98,672,292
3	101,907,280	11,032,242	0	765,013	10,267,229	97,907,280
4	101,065,766	11,032,242	0	841,514	10,190,728	97,065,766
5	100,140,100	11,032,242	0	925,665	10,106,577	96,140,100
6	99,121,869	11,032,242	0	1,018,232	10,014,010	95,121,869
7	98,001,814	11,032,242	0	1,120,055	9,912,187	94,001,814
8	96,769,753	11,032,242	0	1,232,060	9,800,181	92,769,753
9	95,414,487	11,032,242	0	1,355,266	9,676,975	91,414,487
10	93,923,694	11,032,242	0	1,490,793	9,541,449	89,923,694
11	92,283,821	11,032,242	0	1,639,872	9,392,369	88,283,821
12	90,479,962	11,032,242	0	1,803,860	9,228,382	86,479,962
13	88,495,716	11,032,242	0	1,984,246	9,047,996	84,495,716
14	86,313,046	11,032,242	0	2,182,670	8,849,572	82,313,046
15	83,912,108	11,032,242	0	2,400,937	8,631,305	79,912,108
16	81,271,077	11,032,242	0	2,641,031	8,391,211	77,271,077
17	78,365,943	11,032,242	0	2,905,134	8,127,108	74,365,943
18	75,170,296	11,032,242	0	3,195,647	7,836,594	71,170,296
19	71,655,084	11,032,242	0	3,515,212	7,517,030	67,655,084
20	67,788,350	11,032,242	0	3,866,733	7,165,508	63,788,350
21	63,534,943	11,032,242	0	4,253,407	6,778,835	59,534,943
22	58,856,196	11,032,242	0	4,678,747	6,353,494	54,856,196
23	53,709,574	11,032,242	0	5,146,622	5,885,620	49,709,574
24	48,048,289	11,032,242	0	5,661,284	5,370,957	44,048,289
25	41,820,876	11,032,242	0	6,227,413	4,804,829	37,820,876
26	34,970,722	11,032,242	0	6,850,154	4,182,088	30,970,722
27	27,435,553	11,032,242	0	7,535,170	3,497,072	23,435,553
28	19,146,866	11,032,242	0	8,288,687	2,743,555	15,146,866
29	10,029,311	11,032,242	0	9,117,555	1,914,687	6,029,311
30	0	11,032,242	0	10,029,311	1,002,931	0

interest plus all amortization flowing into the pool and interest from the Z tranche accrual. Note that when no prepayment is assumed, the B class would have a maximum maturity period of 14 years based on normal amortization of the underlying mortgage pool. This pattern is followed for tranche C upon repayment of tranche B securities. Based on 0 percent PSA, the maximum maturity would be 17 years for that class of bonds.

EXHIBIT 22–3 Cash Flows to Class A and Z Investors (prepayment = 0 percent PSA)

Tranche A (coupon rate = 9.00%; amount invested = $30,000,000)

Period	Amount Owed at End of Period	Principal Allocation from Pool and Z Class	Coupon Interest at 9%	Total Payments
0	$30,000,000			
1	27,792,758	$2,207,242	$2,700,000	$4,907,242
2	25,356,917	2,435,841	2,501,348	4,937,189
3	22,668,790	2,688,127	2,282,123	4,970,250
4	19,702,235	2,966,555	2,040,191	5,006,746
5	16,428,399	3,273,836	1,773,201	5,047,037
6	12,815,439	3,612,960	1,478,556	5,091,516
7	8,828,208	3,987,230	1,153,389	5,140,620
8	4,427,919	4,400,289	794,539	5,194,828
9	0	4,427,919	398,513	4,826,432

Tranche Z (coupon rate = 10.50%; amount invested = $15,000,000)

Period	Amount Owed at End of Period	Accrued Interest	Accumulated Accrued Interest	Prepayments	Interest Payments	Total Payments
0	$15,000,000					
1	16,575,000	$ 1,575,000	$ 1,575,000			$ 0
2	18,315,375	1,740,375	3,315,375			0
3	20,238,489	1,923,114	5,238,489			0
4	22,363,531	2,125,041	7,363,531			0
5	24,711,701	2,348,171	9,711,701			0
6	27,306,430	2,594,729	12,306,430			0
7	30,173,605	2,867,175	15,173,605			0
8	33,341,834	3,168,229	18,341,834			0
9	36,842,726	3,500,893	21,842,726			0
10	40,711,213	3,868,486	25,711,213			0
11	44,985,890	4,274,677	29,985,890			0
12	49,709,408	4,723,518	34,709,408			0
13	54,928,896	5,219,488	39,928,896			0
14	60,696,430	5,767,534	45,696,430			0
15	67,069,556	6,373,125	52,069,556			0
16	74,111,859	7,042,303	59,111,859			0
17	74,365,943	254,084	59,365,943	($254,084)	$7,781,748	7,527,661
18	71,170,296	(3,195,647)	56,170,296	3,195,647	7,808,424	11,004,072
19	67,655,084	(3,515,212)	52,655,084	3,515,212	7,472,881	10,988,093
20	63,788,350	(3,866,733)	48,788,350	3,866,733	7,103,784	10,970,517
21	59,534,943	(4,253,407)	44,534,943	4,253,407	6,697,777	10,951,184
22	54,856,196	(4,678,747)	39,856,196	4,678,747	6,251,169	10,929,917
23	49,709,574	(5,146,622)	34,709,574	5,146,622	5,759,901	10,906,523
24	44,048,289	(5,661,284)	29,048,289	5,661,284	5,219,505	10,880,790
25	37,820,876	(6,227,413)	22,820,876	6,227,413	4,625,070	10,852,483
26	30,970,722	(6,850,154)	15,970,722	6,850,154	3,971,192	10,821,346
27	23,435,553	(7,535,170)	8,435,553	7,535,170	3,251,926	10,787,095
28	15,146,866	(8,288,687)	146,866	8,288,687	2,460,733	10,749,420
29	6,029,311	(9,117,555)	(8,970,689)	9,117,555	1,590,421	10,707,976
30	0	(6,029,311)	(15,000,000)	6,029,311	633,078	6,662,388

EXHIBIT 22–4 Cash Flows to Class B and C Investors (prepayment = 0 percent PSA)

Tranche B (coupon rate = 9.25%; amount invested = $30,000,000)

Period	Amount Owed at End of Period	Principal Allocation from Pool and Z Class	Coupon Interest at 9.25%	Total Payments
0	$30,000,000			
1	30,000,000	$ 0	$2,775,000	$2,775,000
2	30,000,000	0	2,775,000	2,775,000
3	30,000,000	0	2,775,000	2,775,000
4	30,000,000	0	2,775,000	2,775,000
5	30,000,000	0	2,775,000	2,775,000
6	30,000,000	0	2,775,000	2,775,000
7	30,000,000	0	2,775,000	2,775,000
8	30,000,000	0	2,775,000	2,775,000
9	29,571,760	428,240	2,775,000	3,203,240
10	24,212,481	5,359,279	2,735,388	8,094,667
11	18,297,931	5,914,550	2,239,654	8,154,204
12	11,770,553	6,527,378	1,692,559	8,219,937
13	4,566,820	7,203,734	1,088,776	8,292,510
14	0	4,566,820	422,431	4,989,250

Tranche C (coupon rate = 9.75%; amount invested = $25,000,000)

Period	Amount Owed at End of Period	Principal Allocation from Pool and Z Class	Coupon Interest at 9.75%	Total Payments
0	$25,000,000	$ 0		
1	25,000,000	0	$2,437,500	$ 2,437,500
2	25,000,000	0	2,437,500	2,437,500
3	25,000,000	0	2,437,500	2,437,500
4	25,000,000	0	2,437,500	2,437,500
5	25,000,000	0	2,437,500	2,437,500
6	25,000,000	0	2,437,500	2,437,500
6	25,000,000	0	2,437,500	2,437,500
7	25,000,000	0	2,437,500	2,437,500
8	25,000,000	0	2,437,500	2,437,500
9	25,000,000	0	2,437,500	2,437,500
10	25,000,000	0	2,437,500	2,437,500
11	25,000,000	0	2,437,500	2,437,500
12	25,000,000	0	2,437,500	2,437,500
13	25,000,000	0	2,437,500	2,437,500
14	21,616,615	3,383,385	2,437,500	5,820,885
15	12,842,553	8,774,062	2,107,620	10,881,682
16	3,159,218	9,683,334	1,252,149	10,935,483
17	0	3,159,218	308,024	3,467,242

Exhibit 22–5 provides detail on what is referred to as the cash flow to the residual, or equity, position in the CMO offering. Recall in our example that the firm who issues the CMO securities had overcollateralized the issue by $4 million, which represents the equivalent of an equity investment in the CMO offering. Hence, the issuer is entitled to retain any excess cash flow after payments are made to all security owners and servicing fees, and so on, are paid. These cash flows represent the source of any return to the residual or equity position. Note in the exhibit that the cash flows are simply the sum of all cash flows into the pool, less all cash flows paid out to all tranches according to the

EXHIBIT 22–5   Residual Cash Flows to Issuer (prepayment = 0 percent PSA)

Residual Equity Class ($4,000,000 invested)

Period	Total Cash Flows into Pool	Total Payments to A, B, C, and Z Classes	Residual Cash Flows to Equity Class
0			($4,000,000)
1	$11,032,242	$10,119,742	912,500
2	11,032,242	10,149,689	882,553
3	11,032,242	10,182,750	849,492
4	11,032,242	10,219,246	812,995
5	11,032,242	10,259,537	772,705
6	11,032,242	10,304,016	728,225
7	11,032,242	10,353,120	679,122
8	11,032,242	10,407,328	624,914
9	11,032,242	10,467,172	565,070
10	11,032,242	10,532,167	500,075
11	11,032,242	10,591,704	440,538
12	11,032,242	10,657,437	374,805
13	11,032,242	10,730,010	302,232
14	11,032,242	10,810,135	222,107
15	11,032,242	10,881,682	150,559
16	11,032,242	10,935,483	96,759
17	11,032,242	10,994,903	37,339
18	11,032,242	11,004,072	28,170
19	11,032,242	10,988,093	44,149
20	11,032,242	10,970,517	61,725
21	11,032,242	10,951,184	81,058
22	11,032,242	10,929,917	102,325
23	11,032,242	10,906,523	125,719
24	11,032,242	10,880,790	151,452
25	11,032,242	10,852,483	179,759
26	11,032,242	10,821,346	210,896
27	11,032,242	10,787,095	245,146
28	11,032,242	10,749,420	282,822
29	11,032,242	10,707,976	324,266
30	11,032,242	6,662,388	4,369,853

Residual *IRR* = 16.83%

CMO agreement. In our example, cash flow residuals are received by the equity investor each year, even though the Z class of securities has not received any cash flows.[7] Also, the $912,500 of net cash flow to the residual interest represents a very small margin (less than 1 percent) relative to the $100 million security issue. This residual cash flow includes any servicing fees that would be earned by the issuer, who we assume also retains the servicing responsibility for the mortgage pool. This margin is important because in the event that $10 million of the mortgage pool was to unexpectedly prepay immediately after the securities were issued, that $10 million in prepayments would not provide any significant interest flow into the pool. Further, these unanticipated prepayments would have had to be reinvested at an interim rate of at least 9 percent to compensate for the loss in interest and to pay the class A tranche at the end of the year. Hence, the $912,500 cash flow to the residual would have to be used to offset the difference between interest lost because of prepayment and interest earned on interim reinvestments.

The possibility of unanticipated prepayment and the potential problem with reinvesting in a period of declining interest rates (which is also likely to cause even more prepayments) should clarify why the $4 million overcollateralization is required. Further, we have assumed that the mortgages used to form the pool for the CMO issue are FHA, VA, or conventional fixed rate mortgages. In any case, we have assumed that there is adequate insurance protection against default losses. Where there are limited or no guarantees against default losses (such as where CMOs are issued against commercial mortgages or second mortgages, etc.), the investor would have to consider the possibility of greater losses because of the impact of default on cash flows. Hence, in these latter instances we would expect to see (1) larger amounts of overcollateralization, and/or (2) pool insurance purchased by the issuer from a third party who would be willing to insure investors against part or all default loss, or (3) a provision referred to as a *calamity call,* that allows the issuer to recall all securities for a specified time after issue in the event interest rates declined sharply, prepayments accelerated, and reinvestment rates were below rates promised to investors. However, if cash flows were to occur as shown in Exhibit 22–5, the issuer would earn a BTIRR of 16.83 percent on the $4 million in equity (servicing and other fees not removed from residual cash flows). This rate obviously exceeds the rates earned by each security class which have a prior claim on all cash flows paid into the pool.

CMO Cash Flows and Prepayment Assumptions.   Because there will always be some prepayment of principal from mortgages in an underlying pool, the impact on maturity for each security class will affect profitability to the issuer. To illustrate this effect, we assume that prepayment will occur at approximately 100 percent PSA instead of zero PSA as illustrated in the preceeding exhibits.

Cash payments from the pool to each of the first three classes of security holders are shown in Exhibit 22–6. Note that in addition to normal amortization payments into the

---

[7]Some CMO provision may require that this payment be placed in reserve until termination of the issue. In this event, the internal rate of return shown at the bottom of the exhibit would be lower because residual cash flows would not be realized by the issuer until the 30th year.

EXHIBIT 22–6 Annual Cash Flows into CMO Mortgage Pool (prepayment = approximately 100 percent PSA)

Period	(1) Mortgage Pool: 30-Year Term 10% Fixed Rate	(2) Principal and Interest Payments into Pool	(3) Assumed Prepayments End of Period (approx. 100% PSA)	(4) Total Amortization Excluding Prepayments	(5) Interest	(6) Amount Owed to Security Holders	(7) Total Available for Distribution (2) + (3)
0	$104,000,000					$100,000,000	
1	101,287,758[d]	$11,032,242[a]	$2,080,000[c]	$ 632,242[b]	$10,400,000	97,287,758	$13,112,242
2	96,554,776	10,810,247	4,051,510	681,472	10,128,776	92,554,776	14,861,758
3	90,042,059	10,374,909	5,793,287	719,431	9,655,478	86,042,059	16,168,195
4	83,896,000	9,747,741	5,402,524	743,535	9,004,206	79,896,000	15,150,265
5	78,093,833	9,158,007	5,033,760	768,407	8,389,600	74,093,833	14,191,767
6	72,614,140	8,603,447	4,685,630	794,064	7,809,383	68,614,140	13,289,077
7	67,436,768	8,081,938	4,356,848	820,524	7,261,414	63,436,768	12,438,786
8	62,542,759	7,591,479	4,046,206	847,802	6,743,677	58,542,759	11,637,685
9	57,914,278	7,130,191	3,752,566	875,915	6,254,276	53,914,278	10,882,757
10	53,534,546	6,696,303	3,474,857	904,875	5,791,428	49,534,546	10,171,160
11	49,387,781	6,288,148	3,212,073	934,693	5,353,455	45,387,781	9,500,221
12	45,459,137	5,904,154	2,963,267	965,376	4,938,778	41,459,137	8,867,412
13	41,734,660	5,542,843	2,727,548	996,929	4,545,914	37,734,660	8,270,391
14	38,201,231	5,202,815	2,504,080	1,029,349	4,173,466	34,201,231	7,706,895
15	34,846,528	4,882,752	2,292,074	1,062,629	3,820,123	30,846,528	7,174,826

[a] Annual payment assuming no prepayments = $11,032,242.

[b] Principal repayment year 1 = $632,242 or ($11,032,242 − 10,400,000), assuming no prepayment, outstanding balance = $103,367,758.

[c] Prepayment assumed 2% in year 1 ($2,080,000), 4% in year 2, and 6% in year 3 and thereafter.

[d] Balance at the end of year 1 equals $103,367,758 − 2,080,000 = $101,287,758.

EXHIBIT 22–6 (Concluded)

Period	(1) Mortgage Pool: 30-Year Term 10% Fixed Rate	(2) Principal and Interest Payments into Pool	(3) Assumed Prepayments End of Period (approx. 100% PSA)	(4) Total Amortization Excluding Prepayments	(5) Interest	(6) Amount Owed to Security Holders	(7) Total Available for Distribution (2) + (3)
16	31,658,985	4,581,405	2,090,792	1,092,752	3,484,653	27,658,985	6,672,196
17	28,627,756	4,297,588	1,899,539	1,131,689	3,165,898	24,627,756	6,197,127
18	25,742,693	4,030,173	1,717,665	1,167,398	2,862,776	21,742,693	5,747,839
19	22,994,318	3,778,083	1,544,562	1,203,814	2,574,269	18,994,318	5,322,645
20	20,373,813	3,540,277	1,379,659	1,240,846	2,299,432	16,373,813	4,919,937
21	17,873,022	3,315,744	1,222,429	1,278,363	2,037,381	13,873,022	4,538,173
22	15,484,461	3,103,481	1,072,381	1,316,179	1,787,302	11,484,461	4,175,862
23	13,201,370	2,902,470	929,068	1,354,024	1,548,446	9,201,370	3,831,537
24	11,017,791	2,711,634	792,082	1,391,497	1,320,137	7,017,791	3,503,716
25	8,928,736	2,529,766	661,067	1,427,987	1,101,779	4,928,736	3,190,834
26	6,930,508	2,355,378	535,724	1,462,505	892,874	2,930,508	2,891,102
27	5,021,355	2,186,373	415,830	1,493,322	693,051	1,021,355	2,602,203
28	3,203,048	2,019,161	301,281	1,517,026	502,136	0	2,320,443
29	1,485,604	1,845,566	192,183	1,525,261	320,305	0	2,037,749
30	0	1,634,165	0	1,485,604	148,560	0	1,634,165

pool, prepayments are assumed to occur at 2 percent in year 1, 4 percent in year 2, and level off at 6 percent each year thereafter (our approximation to 100 percent PSA). Hence, prepayments in the amount of $2,080,000, or 2 percent of $104 million, are assumed to occur at the end of year 1. As shown in Exhibit 22–7, investors in tranche A receive their promised coupon payments $2,700,000 (9 percent of $30 million), plus the Z tranche portion of interest, $1,575,000 (10.5 percent of $15 million), plus all amortization and prepayments flowing into the pool during the first year ($2,080,000 + $632,242), or a total of $4,287,242. Based on this accelerated pattern of cash flows, class A investors would now be repaid after five years. This compares to nine years when no prepayment was assumed. For this reason, class A securities are sometimes referred to as the "fast pay tranche." After five years, Exhibit 22–8 shows that class B investors, who receive current interest only payments during the first five years, would begin receiving the interest accrued on the Z tranche plus all principal from mortgages paid into the pool during the fifth year. Based on this pattern of cash receipts, tranche B would now be repaid after four additional years, or a total of nine years from the date of issue. This compares to 14 years with no prepayment. The third, or C tranche, begins receiving principal payments during the ninth year and, as the pattern in the Exhibit shows, after three additional years, or a total of 12 years from the date of issue, those investors would be repaid. This compares to 17 years under the 0 percent PSA assumption.

As indicated earlier, Z tranche securities holders do not receive interest or principal payments until the A, B, and C tranches are repaid. Exhibit 22–7 shows that during the first 11 years, interest would be accrued on the Z class by compounding the $15 million invested at 10.5 percent. In year 12, cash interest payments at the coupon rate of 10.5 percent are made to the Z class security holders. Interest is calculated at the coupon rate (10.5 percent) on the accumulated investment balance, which contains $15 million plus all accrued interest. All principal payments flowing into the pool at this point are also allocated to the Z class. The Z class, based on our prepayment assumptions, will now be repaid in the 28th year.

Finally, residual cash flows remaining after all cash payments are made to each tranche of securities are retained by the issuer. As discussed before, this residual amounts to, in essence, the spread earned by the issuer for investing equity (overcollateralization) and for managing the provisions of the CMO issue. Exhibit 22–9 shows the residual cash flows, or the difference between total payments into the pool and cash payments made to all of the investor classes (based on all preceding exhibits). Recall that these residuals are based on the assumption that the repayment rate remains at 100 percent PSA. Obviously, these residuals would vary considerably at different rates of repayment. When the residual cash flows received over 30 years by the issuer are set equal to the $4 million in equity invested at the time of issue, a yield, or internal rate of return, of 13.8 percent results. As expected, this yield still represents a higher return than is earned on the A, B, C, or Z tranches. Further, this yield would obviously increase as the amount of equity used to finance the CMO issue diminishes (because of the use of financial leverage).[8]

---

[8]The reader may think of leverage in the financial structure of a CMO issue much like that of leveraging any income-producing asset with debt. Similarly, the risk assumed by the various classes of bondholders and the issuer will vary based on the amount overcollateralization.

EXHIBIT 22–7   Cash Flows to Class A and Z Investors (prepayment = approximately 100 percent PSA)

Tranche A (coupon rate = 9.00%; amount invested = $30,000,000)

Period	Amount Owed at End of Period	Principal Allocation from Pool and Z Class	Coupon Interest at 9%	Total Payments
0	$30,000,000			
1	25,712,758	$4,287,242	$2,700,000	$ 6,987,242
2	19,239,401	6,473,357	2,314,148	8,787,505
3	10,803,569	8,435,832	1,731,546	10,167,378
4	2,532,469	8,271,100	972,321	9,243,421
5	0	2,532,469	227,922	2,760,392

Tranche Z (coupon rate = 10.50%; amount invested 15,000,000)

Period	Amount Owed at End of Period	Accrued Interest	Accumulated Accrued Interest	Prepayments	Interest Payments	Total Payments
0	$15,000,000					
1	16,575,000	$ 1,575,000	$ 1,575,000			$ 0
2	18,315,375	1,740,375	3,315,375			0
3	20,238,489	1,923,114	5,238,489			0
4	22,363,531	2,125,041	7,363,531			0
5	24,711,701	2,348,171	9,711,701			0
6	27,306,430	2,594,729	12,306,430			0
7	30,173,605	2,867,175	15,173,605			0
8	33,341,834	3,168,229	18,341,834			0
9	36,842,726	3,500,893	21,842,726			0
10	40,711,213	3,868,486	25,711,213			0
11	44,985,890	4,274,677	29,985,890			0
12	41,459,137	(3,526,753)	26,459,137	$3,526,753	$4,723,518	8,250,271
13	37,734,660	(3,724,477)	22,734,660	3,724,477	4,353,209	8,077,687
14	34,201,231	(3,533,429)	19,201,231	3,533,429	3,962,139	7,495,568
15	30,846,528	(3,354,703)	15,846,528	3,354,703	3,591,129	6,945,832
16	27,658,985	(3,187,544)	12,658,985	3,187,544	3,238,885	6,426,429
17	24,627,756	(3,031,228)	9,627,756	3,031,228	2,904,193	5,935,422
18	21,742,693	(2,885,063)	6,742,693	2,885,063	2,585,914	5,470,977
19	18,994,318	(2,748,375)	3,994,318	2,748,375	2,282,983	5,031,358
20	16,373,813	(2,620,505)	1,373,813	2,620,505	1,994,403	4,614,908
21	13,873,022	(2,500,792)	(1,126,978)	2,500,792	1,719,250	4,220,042
22	11,484,461	(2,388,560)	(3,515,539)	2,388,560	1,456,667	3,845,228
23	9,201,370	(2,283,091)	(5,798,630)	2,283,091	1,205,868	3,488,960
24	7,017,791	(2,183,579)	(7,982,209)	2,183,579	966,144	3,149,723
25	4,928,736	(2,089,054)	(10,071,264)	2,089,054	736,868	2,825,923
26	2,930,508	(1,998,229)	(12,069,492)	1,998,229	517,517	2,515,746
27	1,021,355	(1,909,153)	(13,978,645)	1,909,153	307,703	2,216,856
28	0	(1,021,355)	(15,000,000)	1,021,355	107,242	1,128,597

EXHIBIT 22–8   Cash Flows to Class B and C Investors (prepayment = approximately 100 percent PSA)

Tranche B (coupon rate = 9.25%; amount invested = $30,000,000)

Period	Amount Owed at End of Period	Principal Allocation from Pool and Z Class	Coupon Interest at 9.25%	Total Payments
0	$30,000,000			
1	30,000,000	$ 0	$2,775,000	$ 2,775,000
2	30,000,000	0	2,775,000	2,775,000
3	30,000,000	0	2,775,000	2,775,000
4	30,000,000	0	2,775,000	2,775,000
5	24,382,132	5,617,868	2,775,000	8,392,868
6	16,307,710	8,074,422	2,255,347	10,329,770
7	8,263,162	8,044,547	1,508,463	9,553,010
8	200,925	8,062,237	764,343	8,826,580
9	0	200,925	18,586	219,511

Tranche C (coupon rate = 9.75%; amount invested = $25,000,000)

Period	Amount Owed at End of Period	Principal Allocation from Pool and Z Class	Coupon Interest at 9.75%	Total Payments
0	$25,000,000	$ 0		
1	25,000,000	0	$2,437,500	$ 2,437,500
2	25,000,000	0	2,437,500	2,437,500
3	25,000,000	0	2,437,500	2,437,500
4	25,000,000	0	2,437,500	2,437,500
5	25,000,000	0	2,437,500	2,437,500
6	25,000,000	0	2,437,500	2,437,500
7	25,000,000	0	2,437,500	2,437,500
8	25,000,000	0	2,437,500	2,437,500
9	17,071,552	7,928,448	2,437,500	10,365,948
10	8,823,334	8,248,218	1,664,476	9,912,695
11	401,891	8,421,443	860,275	9,281,718
12	0	401,891	39,184	441,075

Also note that in the case of faster prepayment, the *BTIRR* (Exhibit 22–9) will fall to 13.82 percent from the slower prepayment example (Exhibit 22–5), where the *IRR* was 16.83 percent. This occurs because the total interest collected from the pool will be lower if prepayment accelerates. Hence the dollar spread between interest inflow and outflow becomes smaller.

EXHIBIT 22–9 Residual Cash Flows to Issuer (prepayment = approximately 100 percent PSA)

Residual Equity Class: ($4,000,000 invested)

Period	Total Cash Flows into Pool	Total Payments to A,B,C,Z Classes	Residual Cash Flows to Equity Class
0			($4,000,000)
1	$13,112,242	$12,199,742	912,500
2	14,861,758	14,000,005	861,753
3	16,168,195	15,379,878	788,317
4	15,150,265	14,455,921	694,343
5	14,191,767	13,590,760	601,007
6	13,289,077	12,767,270	521,807
7	12,438,786	11,990,510	448,276
8	11,637,685	11,264,080	373,606
9	10,882,757	10,585,459	297,298
10	10,171,160	9,912,695	258,465
11	9,500,221	9,281,718	218,502
12	8,867,421	8,691,346	176,075
13	8,270,391	8,077,687	192,704
14	7,706,895	7,495,568	211,327
15	7,174,826	6,945,832	228,994
16	6,672,196	6,426,429	245,767
17	6,197,127	5,935,422	261,705
18	5,747,839	5,470,977	276,861
19	5,322,645	5,031,358	291,287
20	4,919,937	4,614,908	305,028
21	4,538,173	4,220,042	318,131
22	4,175,862	3,845,228	330,635
23	3,831,537	3,488,960	342,578
24	3,503,716	3,149,723	353,993
25	3,190,834	2,825,923	364,911
26	2,891,102	2,515,746	375,356
27	2,602,203	2,216,856	385,347
28	2,320,443	1,128,597	1,191,845
29	2,037,749	0	2,037,749
30	1,634,165	0	1,634,165

Residual *IRR* = 13.82%

CMOs: Pricing and Expected Maturities

To aid the reader in understanding how the patterns of cash flow payments to each tranche of securities vary with prepayment rates, Exhibit 22–10 provides additional insights. Panel A of the exhibit contains a graph showing the expected cash flows to each class of CMO investors based on 100 percent PSA. Note that four very distinct cash flow patterns emerge in the exhibit. Indeed, this is exactly the goal of the CMO issuer, that

EXHIBIT 22–10   Cash Flows to CMO Tranches at Various Prepayment Rates

Panel A: Annual cash flows to CMO tranches and residual equity at 100 percent PSA prepayment

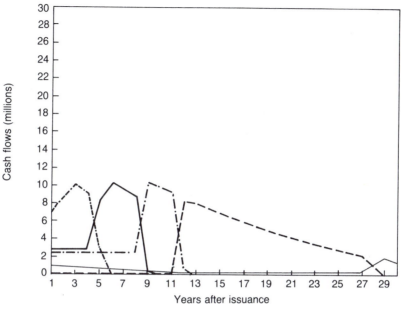

Panel B: Annual cash flows to CMO tranches and residual equity at 500 percent PSA prepayment

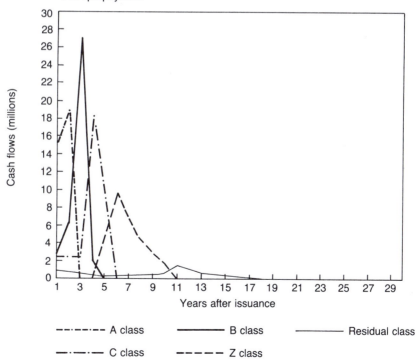

is, to reach different *market segments* of investors who have more specific maturity requirements than what would be provided by a mortgage pass-through security but who may not need an exact maturity requirement such as provided by a MBB. As indicated, however, the CMO does not completely eliminate prepayment risk. Indeed, if mortgage interest rates declined substantially, these securities may only provide investors with slightly more prepayment protection than a pass-through security. To illustrate what cash flows and the maturity of security classes may look like, assuming a significant increase in prepayment, Panel B of the exhibit shows results assuming 500 percent PSA.

By placing a priority on the distribution of cash flows to various classes of security owners, the CMO generally provides more predictability with respect to expected maturity periods and cash flows than a mortgage pass-through. Recall that with an MPT all investors could be committed for a period of up to 30 years or less, with substantial variation in cash flows received from period to period, depending on the repayment rate.

CMO securities, when issued based on a pool of FHA, VA or conventionally insured mortgages, should provide a yield in excess of U.S. Treasury securities with equivalent maturity classes[9] because of added cash flow uncertainty. In any case, if no significant decline in interest rates is expected by security holders, the pattern of cash flows shown in Panel A of Exhibit 22–10 may be appealing to some investors who would not otherwise be interested in a pass-through security. This may be particularly true for the A class or fast pay tranche, which would compete with short-term Treasury bills and notes and may be attractive to managers of money market funds. The B and C tranches may be more appealing to insurance companies and pension funds, while the Z tranche may be preferred by long-term bond mutual funds. Hence, prioritization of cash flows does create the possibility of reaching a broader class of investors with more specific maturity requirements than would be the case with MPTs.[10]

To establish some idea of the sensitivity of expected maturity to expected rates of prepayment, Exhibit 22–11 shows the outstanding amount owed for each tranche under the repayment assumption of 100 percent PSA (Panel A) and 500 percent PSA (Panel B). As expected, the balances shown for the A tranche in Panel A begins to amortize immediately, and the B and C tranches amortize in accordance with the priority allocation of cash flows. However, the amount owed to the Z class increases sharply as interest accrues (like that on a GPM mortgage). In the event that the repayment rate increases sharply, (as in Panel B), the amounts owed to each security class decrease significantly and all investors in the CMO offering would be repaid within 10 years.

To illustrate the sensitivity of the maturity of each tranche to repayment rates, we reconsider our example at increasing prepayment rates and display the results in Exhibit

---

[9]Because the investor in a CMO is dealing with an expected range in maturity, that expected maturity must be used as a basis of comparison for maturities of alternative investments.

[10]The reader may have reached the conclusion that a CMO issue with its various classes of expected maturities resembles tax-exempt serial bonds which are frequently issued by state and local municipalities. Recall that serial bond issues call for the retirement of specific amounts of bonds at specific time intervals. This pattern of different maturities appeals to many investor groups who have a specific need to match liabilities coming due on specific dates with an interest-bearing asset with the same maturity. The different pattern of CMO maturities does emulate tax-exempt offerings in this respect. However, the use of a Z class of security and residual or equity interest is the truly innovative aspect of this type of offering.

EXHIBIT 22–11   Maturity of CMO Tranches at Various Prepayment Rates

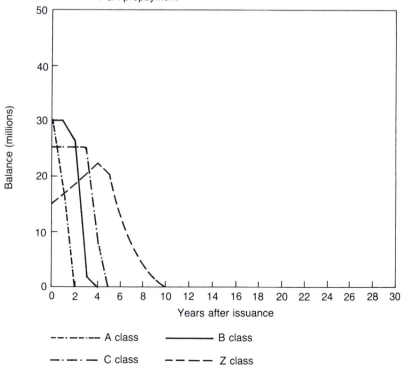

Panel A: Annual balance owed on CMO tranches at 100 percent PSA prepayment

Panel B: Annual balance owed on CMO tranches at 500 percent PSA prepayment

EXHIBIT 22–12   Estimated Maturity Periods for A,B,C, and Z Tranches at Increasing Rates of Prepayment

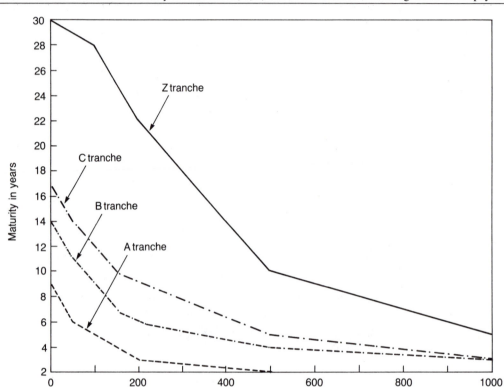

22–12. Note that, as explained, the sensitivity of the expected maturity to repayment rates is obviously greatest for the A, B, and C tranches when compared to the Z tranche. The effect of interest accrual on amounts owed to the Z class makes its expected maturity more invariant to the rate of repayment than the other classes. However, in all cases the most significant impact on expected maturity occurs as the repayment rate accelerates from 0 percent to 500 percent PSA.[11]

Expected CMO Yields and Prepayment Rates

As with mortgage pass-throughs, the price of each security class in a CMO issue will vary with movements in interest rates and the expected rate of repayment. The price of

---

[11]Based on our simplified approximation to the PSA rate at 500 percent PSA, the prepayment rate would be 10 percent (5 times 2 percent) of the pool balance in year 1, 20 percent in year 2, and 30 percent per year thereafter.

a CMO bond will equal the present value of all cash flows received by that class of investors. To illustrate the effect of both changes in interest rates and prepayment, Exhibit 22–13 contains a series of expected yields that could also be disclosed to investors at the time of issue, calculated under different rates of prepayment. The yields are calculated under two sets of assumptions. One is that the initial offering price is to contain a premium (note all cases where the securities are priced to yield a return below the coupon rate). The second is that the offering price is made at a discount (cases where the security is priced to yield a return greater than the coupon rate). These two scenarios are considered because, as previously noted, it is rarely true that the price at which security is offered will result in a yield that is equal to the coupon rate. That is, it is more common that some amount of discount or premium will be included in the offering price at the time of issue. Initial prices were calculated assuming on a 50-basis-point range above and below the coupon rate for each tranche shown in the exhibit at 100 percent PSA, which serves as a benchmark case. Those prices were then set equal to cash flows (not shown) that would occur for the range of prepayment rates considered on the internal rate of return, or yield to maturity, was calculated.

Results in Exhibit 22–13 show that when prices contain premiums (at the time of issue), expected yields will uniformly decline as prepayment rates accelerate. Further,

EXHIBIT 22–13 Expected Yields on CMOs at Offering (assuming varying rates of expected prepayment)

	Prepayment Rate % PSA			
	50	*100*	*150*	*200*
A tranche, 9% coupon				
Priced to yield 8.5%				
at 100% PSA (1.012% of par)	8.59%	8.50%	8.43%	8.36%
Priced to yield 9.5%				
at 100% PSA (0.988% of par)	9.41	9.50	9.57	9.64
B tranche, 9.25% coupon				
Priced to yield 8.75%				
at 100% PSA (1.024% of par)	8.83	8.75	8.67	8.61
Priced to yield 9.75%				
at 100% PSA (0.977% of par)	9.67	9.75	9.83	9.89
C tranche, 9.75% coupon				
Priced to yield 9.25%				
at 100% PSA (1.032% of par)	9.30	9.25	9.19	9.14
Priced to yield 10.25%				
at 100% PSA (0.970% of par)	10.20	10.25	10.31	10.36
Z tranche, 10.5% coupon				
Priced to yield 9.5%				
at 100% PSA (1.159% of par)	9.64	9.50	9.34	9.17
Priced to yield 11%				
at 100% PSA (0.930% of par)	10.93	11.00	11.08	11.16
IRR on residual class	14.87	13.39	13.30	13.00

the decline in expected yields increases as the expected maturity period for each tranche increases. This latter point can be easily seen for the Z tranche, for which the yield declines from 9.64 percent at 50 percent PSA to 9.17 percent at 200 percent PSA, while the decline for the A tranche, with its shorter maturity, ranges from 8.59 percent to 8.36 percent over the same prepayment range. With respect to the cases where securities are initially offered at a discount, the opposite result occurs; that is, expected yields increase as prepayment rates accelerate. However, those tranches with the shortest expected maturity show a greater increase in expected yield as prepayments accelerate. With respect to returns on amounts invested by the issuer as overcollateral, those yields decline as the prepayment rate accelerates (see bottom of exhibit). Hence, when the prepayment rate accelerates, expected yields on the residual class behave very much like securities issued at a premium; that is, expected yields decline. One additional observation that should be made with respect to the residual class is that expected yields are much more volatile than yields shown for other tranches of securities. This is because prepayment rates affect both the amount and timing of cash flows received by the issuer. As prepayment rates increase, the cash flow from the spread between the interest rate on mortgages in the pool and the weighted average coupon promised to CMO security classes does not persist as long as it would during periods when prepayments slow.

CMO Price Behavior and Prepayment Rates

As with MPTs, CMO prices will vary both with changes in interest rates and prepayment rates. That relationship for 100 percent PSA is shown in Panel A of Exhibit 22–14. An important characteristic of the prices is the relatively narrow range of prices (vertical axis) that result in relation to changes in demanded market rates of return (interest rates, horizontal axis) for the A, B, and C tranches. The reason is the prioritization of cash flows just discussed, which has a "smoothing effect" on prices. This effect may be compared to the pattern shown for MPTs in Exhibit 21–15, which indicates a more volatile price response as interest rates change. However, with respect to prices for the Z tranche and present value of the residual interest, they exhibit more volatility in price behavior than the A, B, and C tranches. This volatility is a by-product of the market segmentation chosen for this CMO security issue.[12]

Even when an extremely significant increase in the prepayment rate occurs, as shown in Panel B of Exhibit 22–14, the range in prices tends to narrow for all tranches in the CMO issue. This can be seen by comparing the ranges in Panels A and B. However, the reader should keep in mind that the *expected maturity period* also declines significantly as rate of prepayment increases (see Exhibit 22–12). Hence, this CMO structure is one which makes a trade-off in price stability from the Z and residual classes to the A, B, C tranches as the maturity period contracts for all classes. However, relative to mortgage

---

[12]Alternative structures may be chosen to achieve different market segmentation objectives. For example, currently there are CMO issues with multiple Z classes, some tranches with floating interest rates, and so on. These structures have been adopted to meet the needs of investors who may not otherwise invest in mortgage-related securities.

Panel A.

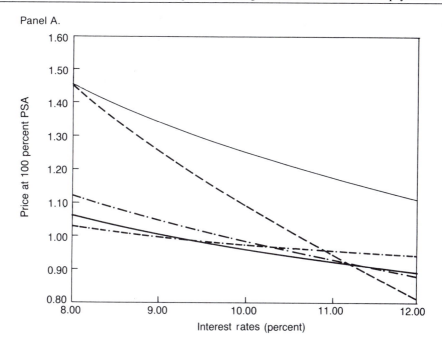

Panel B.

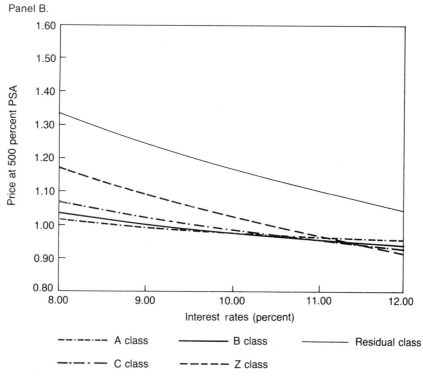

pass-through securities, the A, B, and C tranches of CMOs receive some additional prepayment and price protection that MPT security holders do not. Investors in MPTs would receive an increase in cash flows as the rate of prepayment increases, but not necessarily as dramatic a reduction in maturity (although the cash flows in the latter years may be relatively small). Consequently, structuring a CMO offering with a maturity and cash flow pattern for one Z tranche, while retaining the shorter maturities for the A and B tranche, may make it possible to appeal to investors who have a preference for shorter maturities and a strong dislike for the MPT.

RESIDENTIAL MORTGAGE-RELATED SECURITIES—A SUMMARY

We now briefly summarize some of the major characteristics of the four major types of securities covered thus far. Exhibit 22–15 is a classification of some of the more important aspects of these securities that should aid the reader in understanding cash flow and risk-bearing patterns associated with each type.

With the exception of MPTs, which represent an undivided ownership equity interest in a pool of mortgages, all other securities discussed in the chapter are actually debt. MPTs should be viewed as a stand-alone investment which is placed in trust after it is sold to investors in a securitized form. Because the mortgage pools backing the issue are usually FHA/VA or conventionally insured mortgages and a timely payment guarantee is usually provided by the issuer or GNMA, MPTs can be a stand-alone investment. That is, there is no need for overcollateralization or credit enhancements. The success of the investment is solely based on the income produced by mortgages in the pool, and the recovery of investment by investors depends on how amortization and prepayments from the mortgage pool occur. However, because of the pass-through of principal, investors bear all prepayment and reinvestment risk since they do not know exactly what cash flows will be from period to period, nor do they know when the security that they own will mature.

The debt securities listed in Exhibit 22–15 may be differentiated on the basis of (1) who bears prepayment risk and (2) the extent and type of overcollateralization and/or the use of credit enhancements. Issuers of MBBs bear all of this prepayment risk, and hence the extent of overcollateralization and/or credit enhancements for these securities must be greatest. Conversely, to the extent that the investor bears prepayment risk or, stated differently, to the extent that the pass-through of principal flows directly to investors, the need for overcollateralization and/or credit enhancements is reduced somewhat (holding all else constant). This is true because, for example, as prepayments accelerate on MPTBs and CMOs, maturities are reduced, whereas for MBBs the maturity remains constant regardless of the prepayment rate on the underlying pool. Hence, in anticipation of the possibility of prepayment in the latter case, the issuer will have to provide more collateral than with the other two debt securities. Hence, in each case, the use of overcollateralization and credit enhancements and the extent to which the investor bears prepayment risk must all be taken into account when assessing the relative attractiveness of each security type.

Finally, with respect to the issuer, the use of MBBs and MBPTs should be viewed as a method of debt financing. Although the mortgages that are securitized are placed with

EXHIBIT 22–15 Summary of Important Investment Characteristics of Mortgage-Related Securities

	MBB	*MPT**	*MPTB*	*CMO*
(a) Type of security interest acquired	Debt	Equity	Debt	Debt
(b) Number of security classes	One	One	One	Multiple
(c) Pass-through of principal	None	Direct	Direct	Prioritized
(d) Party bearing prepayment risk	Issuer	Investor	Investor	Investor
(e) Overcollateralization	Yes	No	Yes	Yes
(f) Overcollateral marked to market?	Yes	N.A.	No	No
(g) Credit enhancements used?	Yes	No	Yes	No
(h) Maturity period known?	Yes	No	No	No
(i) Call provisions?	Possibly	Cleanup	Possibly	Calamity and nuisance
(j) Off-balance-sheet financing possible?	No	Yes	No	Yes

*Assumed to be a GNMA/MPT, FNMA/MBS, or FHLMC/PC.

a trustee, they are still carried as an asset on the issuer's balance sheet, and the MBBs are categorized as debt. This would also apply to CMOs unless the issuer sells the residual interest to a third party, in which case the issuer would no longer retain an ownership interest and would not have to carry the mortgage pool as an asset or the CMO securities as liabilities. As an alternative to a CMO issue, the issuer could create a real estate mortgage investment conduit (REMIC, to be discussed) to achieve off-balance-sheet financing. With this vehicle the issuer is selling the mortgage pool to investors and the transaction is completely off-balance-sheet financing. The issuer must only recognize a gain or loss on the sale of mortgages when they are sold and securitized.

RESIDENTIAL, MORTGAGE-RELATED SECURITIES—SOME CLOSING OBSERVATIONS

Much of what has been discussed strongly suggests that there may exist some market segmentation among investors based on a strong preference for investments with specific maturities. This latter preference results from investment managers demanding interest-bearing assets with the same maturities as liabilities that come due at specified times (e.g., pension plan assets may be acquired with maturities that match liabilities coming due as a number of beneficiaries retire each year, etc.). This is also consistent with our discussion in Chapter 5, where we pointed out the market segmentation theory as one explanation of the term structure of interest rates.

Finally, because of the different cash flow patterns that are likely to be encountered when considering an MBB, MPT, MPTB, or CMO, additional questions are related to receipt of cash flows and the measurement of yields that must be addressed. For example with an MBB, a level stream of interest payments for a fixed maturity plus a lump-sum return of principal will be received, whereas an MPT may have more variable cash flows due to prepayments and the Z tranche on a CMO issue may pay cash flows to the investor toward the end of a maturity period. If we assume that each security type was offered at the same yield,[13] should an investor consider each as equivalent? Or if all three investments existed in a portfolio and payments were to be used to pay liabilities coming due at specific time periods, how can we assess the relationship between the maturity periods over which cash inflows will be received and the rate at which liabilities mature? The appendix to this chapter develops a measure that combines both cash flows constituting the yields *and* maturity into a measure called *duration*, which may be useful in assessing these questions.

MORTGAGE-RELATED SECURITIES—COMMERCIAL MORTGAGES

In this and the preceding chapters, we have dealt primarily with mortgage-related securities backed by residential mortgage pools. Essentially, the methods and structures used to issue commercial mortgage-backed securities are very similar to those used for residential-backed securities. However, the nature of the mortgage collateral, its ability to produce income, and the risk associated with commercial mortgage pools differ from a residential pool in very important ways. These differences are elaborated and contrasted in this section.

Like residential-backed securities, most commercial-backed offerings take the form of a mortgage-backed bond, pass-through security, or a collateralized mortgage obligation. The primary distinction between residential-backed and commercial-backed pools centers around the likelihood of losses due to default risk. Recall that in most residential offerings, mortgages in the pool are usually FHA insured, VA guaranteed, or conventional mortgages with private mortgage insurance. Further, in most cases, timely payment of principal and interest is usually guaranteed by a branch of the U.S. government (GNMA) or an agency (FNMA, FHLMC). While there have been many mortgage-backed and mortgage pay-through bonds issued by private entities with no government guarantees, the dollar volume of government-backed securities has been far greater in amount.

In contrast to these residential-backed issues, commercial-backed securities are secured by mortgages on income-producing properties. Tenants in these properties sign lease agreements which provide the source of income from which mortgage payments are made. Hence, the quality of properties, geographic regions in which they are located,

---

[13]Generally, the yield on the three security types would not be the same even if backed by the same pool of securities. This is because with an MBB the issuer bears repayment risk and the investor would earn a lower yield than with an MPT, where the investor bears that risk. A Z tranche security, such as the one demonstrated in the chapter, would yield more than an MPT, because not only does that investor bear prepayment risk but that interest is also accrued and paid later in the life of the security.

and the creditworthiness of the tenant must play some part in assessing the risk of a commercial-backed security offering. Clearly, if tenants default on lease payments or if the geographic market in which the property is located becomes overbuilt and rents generally decline, the income stream used to make mortgage payments will become jeopardized. Further, because such permanent mortgage loans are made on a nonrecourse basis, the lender may look only to proceeds from the sale of the property to satisfy the loan in the event of default.

The source for many of the mortgages used in forming mortgage pools comes too from insurance companies and banks who have previously originated loans on commercial (and multifamily) properties. These loans are usually "seasoned" and have a payment record spanning a number of years. These mortgages may have been made during periods of relatively high interest rates and may contain "lock-out" provisions, which prohibit refinancing or prepayment by the borrower for a specified period of time. During periods of declining interest rates, as the market value of these loans increases, many lenders want to sell them. However, because of a very thin secondary market for such individual loans, which tend to be relatively large in amount and are not standardized in terms of loan provisions, finding buyers is difficult. Hence, by placing these mortgages in a pool and issuing securities against them, the lender may issue securities in smaller denominations which are ultimately sold to many investors, thereby converting the mortgages to cash. Other motivations for lenders to securitize may be simply to obtain more funds for operating requirements by converting previously originated loans.

The security for a commercial-backed mortgage pool, therefore, can range from one mortgage on a very large mixed use, multi-tenant property to a group of smaller income producing properties on which mortgages have been made by a lender. In general, however, securities are issued based on mortgage pools owned by one lender. Further, properties serving as collateral for the mortgages are generally the same type (office buildings or retail, etc.) and are geographically diverse.

Rating Commercial-Backed Mortgage Securities

Most security offerings backed by commercial mortgages are rated by independent credit rating firms. However, because of the nature of mortgage collateral in the pool, the criteria used for rating differs dramatically from that used in rating residential pools. In cases where the securities being rated are based on the credit standing of the issuer and do not contain guarantees or insurance from third parties (to be discussed), the cash flows expected to be earned on each mortgaged property in the pool are usually subjected to a worst-case scenario regarding rents, vacancy allowances, operating expenses, and so on (in much the same way that was discussed in Chapters 10 and 12), and a judgment about the property's ability to cover debt service is made. This is particularly important when only one or a few mortgages will make up the pool. Where several mortgages are in a pool, more emphasis is placed on the past underwriting record of the lender. In other words, losses due to defaults from previous loan originations (unrelated to the mortgage pool) are given serious consideration. In order to provide the worst-case scenario, data specific to the local market area are used as input to the cash flow projections.

Because of this more complex and very different form of collateral, the risk of loss from default is more difficult to estimate. Consequently, it has been estimated that while there were approximately $800 billion in commercial mortgages in existence in 1986, only 3 percent had been securitized. This compares to $1.7 trillion in residential mortgages, of which 31 percent have been securitized.[14]

In order for a commercial-backed offering to be successful, the issuer may have to provide enough credit enhancement to the investor to reduce default risk to an acceptable level. These enhancements may include one or more of the following types of support.

1. Issuer or third party guarantees. These may include (a) a guarantee of timely payment and/or (b) a guarantee of payments to the security holder in the event of a cash flow shortfall from the mortgage pool jeopardizing promised coupon payments, and/or (c) a guarantee of repayment of principal to the security holder. Such guarantees may be limited, and they may be provided in part by the issuer with a third-party guarantee for any losses in excess of some specified limit. In any case, the ability of the issuer or third party to perform on the guarantee must be considered by the investor.

2. Surety bonds and letters of credit provided by banks and insurance companies for a fee may be used to guarantee interest and principal payments. In this case, the third-party guarantor is assuming default risk. Such guarantees may be made in addition to the guarantee provided in (1). The amount of the guarantee may also vary.

3. Advance payment agreements. These are timely payment guarantees made by the issuer and may be limited to a specified number of payments after default.

4. Loan substitutions and repurchase agreements. Some commercial-backed issues may provide that the issuer will substitute a defective mortgage with one of better quality, or that issuers stand ready to repurchase any nonperforming mortgages.

5. Lease assignments. This provision simply provides that the property owner will assign lease payments directly to the mortgage lender who, in turn, makes payments to the security holder (instead of loan payments being made first to a property manager, or owner, and then to the lender). In this way, should the property owner or manager ever become threatened with the possibility of bankruptcy, the probability that cash flow would not be received by security holders is reduced.

6. Overcollateralization. As discussed previously, this amounts to a lender providing a mortgage pool with a dollar value in excess of the value of securities being used against the pool. By doing this, more income flows into the pool from the larger amount of mortgages relative to required coupon payments to investors. Defaults would have to be approximately equal to the amount of overcollateralization before investors would suffer losses. The extent of overcollateralization necessary in commercial-backed issues is usually made based on a desired debt coverage ratio (the number of mortgages needed to provide an adequate amount of income relative to interest payment) to investors in the pool.

7. Cross-collateralization and cross-default provision. When a pool of mortgages is being used for a security issue, the lender may be able to provide a blanket mortgage or cross-collateralization agreement for all mortgages in the pool. This can occur if the

---

[14]Data provided from Salomon Brothers and FHLMC.

lender has made many loans to one developer or investor. A cross-collateralization agreement provides that all properties serving as collateral for individual loans will serve to collateralize the entire debt as represented by the blanket mortgage. Hence, in the event that one mortgage defaults, the lender may accelerate prepayments on all mortgages that are a part of the agreement. This means that any loss on one mortgage in a pool because of default may be made up by the security provided by the properties which may have appreciated in value and are now a part of the blanket mortgage security. By also accelerating on the notes secured by the appreciated properties, the owner-borrower will generally find a way (second lien, syndication) to raise additional equity and make up any payments on a defaulted loan rather than lose all of the properties.[15] Thus, a blanket mortgage or cross-collateralization agreement is usually beneficial to mortgage-backed security holders.

In the event that a third party provides a letter of credit or other guarantee of principal and interest on the mortgage pool, the ability of the third party to perform is more important than the mortgages in the underlying pool. This is because default risk is being shifted from the issuer to the third party. Hence the security holder will be more concerned with the creditworthiness of the insurer or guarantor.

Mortgage-Related Securities and REMICs

Prior to the creation of CMOs, most mortgage-related securities would have been issued as mortgage-backed bonds or mortgage pass-through securities. The federal tax treatment of these securities is relatively straightforward. For MBBs and MPTs, a grantor trust is generally utilized on which mortgages are usually placed under the administration of a trustee who oversees the provisions of the trust agreement on behalf of security owners. While such provisions may have varied, if federal income tax regulations defining a qualified trust are met, the trust avoids taxation, and interest that flows through to investors is taxed at the investor level only. The primary conditions that such a trust has to meet are (1) that it have a limited life, (2) that it be self-liquidating, and (3) that no substantive amount of management is necessary after the assets are placed in trust. In essence, to avoid classification as an association doing business as a corporation and, therefore, being subject to taxation, investment income from the trust has to be passive in nature. Hence, for MBBs and MPTs, the payment of principal and interest from a pool of mortgages under the maintenance of a trustee would generally be sufficient to avoid tax at the entity level. This means that only interest received by investors (or beneficiaries of the trust) would be taxed.

When CMOs were first offered, the IRS ruled that mortgage-backed securities with multiple tranches and an equity or residential ownership interest retained by an issuer were too similar to a corporation retaining control of the vehicle used to raise funds. In

---

[15]Cross-collateralization is used by lenders when dealing with developers who pledge previously developed properties as security to obtain financing for new developments. They do this to reduce cash equity in new developments. Lenders may also insist on this additional security because, as discussed in Chapters 17 and 18, most permanent mortgages are made on a nonrecourse basis; hence lenders must look to the real estate pledged as security for loans in the event of default.

effect, the issuing entity could use a CMO offering as financing for a business purpose, as opposed to creating a passive investment entity. Further, it required more active management than a pass-through offering. This would be particularly true with respect to selecting securities when reinvesting interim cash flows between the date of receipt from the mortgage pool and disbursement to CMO security holders. Hence, the initial position taken by the IRS was that if a mortgage-related security offering had more than one class of securities issued against a pool, it would run the risk of being classified as a corporation for tax purposes. This would result in double taxation of income, both at the entity and investor levels. If such tax treatment were applied, CMOs could obviously not complete effectively with MPTs and MBBs, the income from which was generally taxable only at the individual level.

As part of the Tax Reform Act of 1986, Congress passed legislation creating real estate mortgage investment conduits (REMICs, pronounced "remicks"). This legislation was passed to provide regulations that, if adhered to, would allow mortgage-backed offerings with multiple security classes to be issued without the risk of taxation at the entity level. Essentially, the intent of the legislation was to provide the issuer some flexibility in managing a mortgage pool and its income but to retain the basic passive character of trust and the flowthrough of income to security holders.

Regulatory Provisions.   Under the 1986 tax law, a REMIC is a tax entity (not necessarily a legal form of organization such as a corporation or partnership) that can be created by simply selecting a REMIC tax status and maintaining separate records relative to the mortgage pool and the management of funds related to the pool. A corporation, partnership, trust, or association may also elect REMIC status. In order to retain REMIC status, very stringent rules must be followed by the issuer. For example, substantially all assets must consist of "qualified mortgages," foreclosure property, cash flow investments, and a qualified reserve fund.

1. Qualified mortgages generally include any mortgages secured directly or indirectly by an interest (full or partial) in real estate (residential, commercial, and all other real estate). This definition is very broad and would encompass virtually all first mortgages, participations, seconds, other pass-through securities, and so on. Mortgages must be placed in the pool prior to its creation or within three months thereafter. New mortgages may not be acquired or sold by the REMIC after its creation; however, the REMIC is allowed to substitute new mortgages for defective mortgages for up to two years after its creation.
2. Foreclosure property may include real estate, title to which is retained only by virtue of default of a mortgage in the pool.
3. Additional investments are limited to short-term, passive, interest-bearing assets that may be used to reinvest interim cash flows received from mortgages but not yet paid out to investors (examples include T bills, guaranteed investment contracts, or GICs).
4. A qualified reserve fund may contain longer-term investments, the income from which may be used to pay expenses, if any, for managing the REMIC pool, since it may be used as added assurance to investors against losses from defaults on mortgages in the pool. These reserves may take the form of passive investments, letters of credit,

mortgage pool insurance, and other forms of credit enhancement. This fund is generally more important for commercial mortgage-backed securities or other mortgages that are not backed by the FHA, VA, or private mortgage default insurance.

Tax Status.   Generally, a REMIC must calculate net income or loss on an accrual basis at the entity level. Income must be reported for all assets in the pool, and deductions are allowed for all interest paid as regular interest (CMO security owners) and other pool expenses, in determining taxable income or loss. Any net income or loss can then be passed through to residual interests (usually the CMO issuer) as ordinary income or loss. CMO investors only pay taxes on interest income.

A REMIC retains its tax-exempt status as long as it does not engage in prohibited transactions. If it does, it is generally subject to a tax equal to 100 percent of the gross income associated with the prohibited transaction. Prohibited transactions include

1. Income received from assets that are not qualified mortgages, cash flow investments, foreclosure property or permitted investments in the reserve fund.
2. Income from fees or compensation for services performed. (This does not include servicing income on the mortgage portfolio. Such servicing income may include any excess servicing income created by a difference between income based on interest rates of mortgages in the pool less interest coupons promised on security classes.)
3. Gain from the pool of any cash flow investments, except upon liquidation of the mortgage pool. Liquidation may occur when all mortgages in the pool are fully amortized or prepaid, or, if the REMIC files a qualified plan for liquidation wherein it sells all of its assets and distributes proceeds therefrom within 90 days.
4. Sale or disposition of a qualified mortgage. Mortgages placed in a REMIC may not be sold or otherwise disposed of unless (1) a proper substitution is made in the relevant time frame, (2) a borrower defaults on a mortgage and it is disposed of, (3) bankruptcy or insolvency of the mortgage pool occurs, or (4) a complete plan for liquidation of the REMIC is filed.

Other Considerations—REMICs

Because of the pass-through nature of a REMIC, owners of residual interests in REMICs may avoid taxes at the entity level. Also, if regulations pertaining to REMICs are followed, then the owner of the residual interests (usually the issuer) may avoid including REMIC assets, liabilities and residual interests in balance-sheet reporting to the public. This may be done because REMICs are intended to be more like a passive, stand-alone entity. In theory, creation of a REMIC is akin to a sale of assets from an origination to the REMIC with a gain or loss on sale realized by the seller and subject to taxation, either immediately or over the life of the REMIC.

As such, the seller no longer carries the assets or liabilities created by the REMIC on its balance sheet. However, if it chooses not to recognize gain or loss when the sale of assets to the REMIC occurs, it will report the value of the residual interest owned in the REMIC as an asset. Generally, prior to the 1986 tax law, this off-balance-sheet accounting treatment would be allowed on issues of mortgage-related securities in which multiple classes of securities and a residual interest were created, only if the residual interest was sold or transferred by the issuer to a third party.

In sum, by providing for REMICs, a tax-exempt conduit has been created by Congress through which CMOs may be issued. This allows for the creation of mortgage-backed securities with multiple maturity classes and other investment choices that would not be available with mortgage pass-through securities. This should provide more choices to more investors and hence broaden the participation by investors in mortgage-related securities.

QUESTIONS

1. What is a mortgage pay-through bond? How does it resemble a mortgage-backed bond? How does it differ?
2. Are the overcollateralization requirements the same for mortgage pay-through bonds as for the mortgage-backed bonds?
3. Name two different ways that MPTBs can be overcollateralized.
4. What is the major difference between a CMO and the other types of mortgage-related securities?
5. Name the four major classes of mortgage-related securities. As an issuer, explain the reasons for choosing one type over another?
6. What is a CMO? Explain why a CMO has been called as much of a marketing innovation as a financial innovation?
7. Why are CMOs overcollateralized?
8. What is the purpose of the accrual tranche? Could a CMO exist without a Z class? What would be the difference between the CMO with and without the accrual class?
9. Which tranches in a CMO issue are least subject to price variances related to changes in market interest rates? Why?
10. What is the primary distinction between mortgage-related securities backed by residential mortgages and those backed by commercial mortgages?
11. Name the major types of credit enhancement used for commercial-backed mortgage securities.

PROBLEMS

The MZ Mortgage Company is issuing CMOs with three tranches. The A tranche will consist of $27 million with a coupon of 9.25 percent. The B tranche will be issued with a coupon of 10.0 percent and a principal of $15 million. The Z tranche will carry a coupon of 11.0 percent with a principal of $30 million. The mortgages backing the security issue were originated at a fixed rate of 11 percent with a maturity of 10 years (annual payments). The issue will be overcollateralized by $3 million, and the issuer will receive all net cash flows after priority payments are made to each class of securities. Priority payments will be made to the class A tranche and will include the promised coupon, all amortization from the mortgage pool, and interest that will be accrued to the Z class until the principal of $27 million is repaid. The B class securities receive interest only payments until the A class is repaid, then receive priority payments of amortization and accrued interest. The Z class will accrue interest at 11 percent until both A and B classes are repaid. It will receive current interest and principal payments at that time.

a. What will be the weighted average coupon (WAC) on the CMO when issued?

b. What will be the maturity of each tranche assuming no prepayment of mortgages in the pool?

c. What will be the WAC at the end of year 3? year 4? year 8?

d. If class A, B, and Z investors demand a 9.5 percent, 10.5 percent, and 10.75 percent yield to maturity, respectively, at the time of issue, what price should MZ ask for each security? How much will the MZ Company receive as proceeds from the CMO issue?

e. What are the residual cash flows to MZ? What rate of return will be earned on the equity overcollateralization?

f. Optional. Assume that the mortgages in the underlying pool prepay at the rate of 10 percent per year. How will your answers in (b)–(e) change?

g. Optional. Assume that immediately after the securities are issued in case (f), the price of all securities suddenly trade up by 10 percent over the issue price. What will the yield to maturity be for each security?

Appendix: Duration—An Additional Consideration in Yield Measurement

In Chapters 21 and 22, we presented four examples of mortgage-related securities. Recall that most mortgage-backed bonds (MBBs) are very much like corporate bonds, in that they promise a coupon rate of interest and repayment of principal at maturity. Mortgage pass-throughs (MPTs) also promise an interest payment; however, principal is also passed through to the investor from the mortgage pool as it is received over borrowers. Hence, repayment of principal is received over the life of the MPT security. Collateralized mortgage obligations (CMOs) differ from both of the above securities. They promise a coupon rate of interest but also promise some tranches of securities priority as to receipt of interest and principal payments as they are made into the pool. Interest on some tranches may be deferred and distributed after repayment of principal on other tranches with a higher priority.

The very different patterns of cash flows just described raise significant problems when investors are comparing yields on such securities. These problems come about because if the yield to maturity (*IRR*) is the tool used to measure return on investment, it is possible for the investments just described to have the same yield, but drastically different cash flow patterns. How should two securities with the same yield but different cash flows be compared? Should the magnitude and timing of each cash flow be taken into account as an additional consideration when comparing the investments?

As we briefly indicated in Chapter 12, many people have considered this problem. One measure that has been developed to aid in the analysis is *duration*. Recall that it is a measure that takes into account *both* size of cash flows and timing of receipt. More specifically, it is a measure of the *weighted-average time* required before all principal and interest is received on an investment.

Duration (*D*) is defined mathematically as:

$$D = \sum_{t=1}^{n} w_t(t)$$

where *t* is the time period in which a payment is received, *n* is the total number of periods during which payments will be received, and *w* is a weight representing the annual proportion of the investment's present value received each year. To illustrate, if we assume that security A has a current price of $10,000 and a coupon of 10 percent, that its maturity is five years and interest only is to be paid to investors annually, the yield to maturity, or *IRR*, would be calculated for the investment as follows:

$10,000 = $1,000 (*PVIFA*,?%, 5 years) + $10,000 (*PVIF*,?%, 5 years)

substituting an estimated interest rate of 10 percent, we have:

= $1,000 (3.790787) + $10,000 (.620921)
= $10,000

hence, we know that the yield to maturity on the bond is 10 percent.

Alternatively, if we assume that investment B is also priced at $10,000, and that five payments of principal and interest equal to $2,637.97 are to be received annually at the end of each year for five years, the yield to maturity would also be 10 percent. This can be seen as follows:

$10,000 = $2,637.97 (*PVIFA*,?%, 5 years)
= $2,637.97 (3.790787)
= $10,000

hence, by construction, both yields are 10 percent. However, when cash flows are compared, they differ dramatically. Duration provides us with a measure that can be used to determine the weighted-average time to full recovery of principal and interest payments. More specifically, for a required rate of return (*i*), the weight (*w*) for each period *t* is computed as:

$$w_t = t \left[\frac{\frac{R_t}{(1+i)^t}}{PV} \right] \quad \text{where: } PV = \sum_{t=1}^{n} \frac{R_t}{(1+i)^t}$$

Given the above defined terms, we calculate duration for any asset *j* as:

$$D_j = (1) \left[\frac{\frac{R_1}{(1+i)^1}}{PV} \right] + (2) \left[\frac{\frac{R_2}{(1+i)^2}}{PV} \right] + \ldots (n) \left[\frac{\frac{R_n}{(1+i)^n}}{PV} \right]$$

Note in this equation that the proportion that each cash flow received in each period (R_t) bears to the present value (or price) of the investment is calculated and multiplied by the year in the sequence during which each cash flow is received.

In our example, we would have for investment A:

$$D_A = (1)\left[\frac{\frac{1,000}{(1+.10)^1}}{10,000}\right] + (2)\left[\frac{\frac{1,000}{(1+.10)^2}}{10,000}\right] + (3)\left[\frac{\frac{1,000}{(1+.10)^3}}{10,000}\right] + (4)\left[\frac{\frac{1,000}{(1+.10)^4}}{10,000}\right] + (5)\left[\frac{\frac{11,000}{(1+.10)^5}}{10,000}\right]$$

$$= .0909 + .1653 + .2254 + .2732 + 3.4151$$

$$= 4.170 \text{ years}$$

for investment B we have:

$$D_B = (1)\left[\frac{\frac{2,637.97}{(1+.10)^1}}{10,000}\right] + (2)\left[\frac{\frac{2,637.97}{(1+.10)^2}}{10,000}\right] + (3)\left[\frac{\frac{2,637.97}{(1+.10)^3}}{10,000}\right] + (4)\left[\frac{\frac{2,637.97}{(1+.10)^4}}{10,000}\right] + (5)\left[\frac{\frac{2,637.97}{(1+.10)^5}}{10,000}\right]$$

$$= .2398 + .4360 + .5946 + .7207 + .8190$$

$$= 2.810$$

From the above calculations, we can see that the duration (D) for investment B is lower than the duration for investment A. This implies that although the yields and maturities on the two investments are identical, the weighted-average number of years required to realize total cash flows from investment B is far less than that for A. Hence, depending on the likelihood of better reinvestment opportunities as cash flows are received each year, the investor may choose investment B over A. For example, if the yield curve is expected to take on a more positive slope, the larger cash flows from investment B may be viewed as being more favorable, as it may be possible to reinvest them at higher rates of interest.

Duration is also a measure of the extent to which different investments expose investors to interest rate risk. For example, if interest rates were to increase suddenly, it is clear that the price of investment A, with its longer duration, is likely to decline by a greater amount than that of B. For example, if interest rates suddenly increased to 15 percent, the likely percentage change in the prices of the two securities can be approximated as follows:

$$\% \text{ decline in price of investment} = -D\left(\frac{\Delta i}{1+i_t}\right) \text{ when } \Delta i > 0 \text{ and}$$

$$D\left(\frac{\Delta i}{1+i_t}\right) \text{ when } \Delta i < 0.$$

in our example for A we have:

$$\% \text{ decline} = -4.170\left(\frac{.05}{1.10}\right)$$

$$= -.1895 \text{ or a } 18.95\% \text{ decline in price to } \$8,105;$$

for B we have:

$$\% \text{ decline} = -2.180\left(\frac{.05}{1.10}\right)$$

$$= -.0991 \text{ or a } 9.91 \text{ decline in price to } \$9,009.$$

Other applications of duration may involve a portfolio of assets and liabilities, where each component of the portfolio may have different cash flow patterns and the same, or different, maturities. Rather than relying on a simple weighted-average maturity for assets and liabilities when assessing exposure to interest rate risk, duration provides a better measure of risk exposure because it takes into account the magnitude and timing of cash flows. To illustrate, if investment A represented an asset and B represented a liability, even though the maturities for both investments are equal (five years), given a sudden interest rate change to 15%, the market value of our asset A ($8,105) would be less than that of the liability ($9,009). Depending on the circumstances, this imbalance could cause serious problems for a portfolio manager of an investment fund, or an asset-liability manager of a financial institution. Hence, in addition to making yield comparisons, duration may provide an alternative approach to matching assets and liabilities that fluctuate in value when interest rates change.

PROBLEM 22A–1

The Provincial Insurance Company has the choice of investing $100,000 either in a mortgage bond with annual payments based on a 10-year amortization schedule with a maturity of five years at 10 percent or a 5-year corporate bond with annual interest payments and a final principal payment also yielding 10 percent.

a. Find the duration of each instrument if they are issued at par.
b. If the market rate of interest on each bond fell from 10 percent to 7 percent and the durations found in part *a* remained constant, what would be the new price for each bond?

Real Estate Investment Performance

Chapter 23

Real Estate Investment Performance and Portfolio Considerations

INTRODUCTION

Thus far, our discussion of risk and required rates of return has stressed a methodology or an approach that should be used when evaluating a specific project or mortgage financing alternative. In this chapter we provide some insight into some of the contemporary issues and methods concerning the measurement of return and risk for various real estate investment vehicles and for investment portfolios.

We will apply concepts and methodologies based on financial theory and demonstrate possible applications to real estate investments. The use of many of these applications is gaining in importance by institutional investors, such as life insurance companies, investment advisors and consultants to pension funds, bank trust departments, and other entities who manage portfolios that may include real estate assets. Such managers must be able to measure the performance of real estate assets and be able to compare it to the performance of stocks, bonds, and other investments. Also, many portfolio managers are interested in knowing how well investment portfolios perform when real estate investments are *combined* with other securities.

THE NATURE OF REAL ESTATE INVESTMENT DATA

When trying to measure the investment performance of something as broadly defined as real estate, one must keep many things in mind. For example, in Chapter 10, we outlined many real estate classifications, ranging from hotels to warehouses to apartment units. Ideally, to measure the investment performance of real estate, we would like to have data on prices for all investment property transactions taking place in the economy, a detailed description of the land, improvements, and cash flows produced by such properties. We would also like to have data on repeated sales of the same properties over time. We could then calculate various measures of return on investment over time. Unfortunately, such a data series, or even an adequate sample of such transactions in the many areas of real estate, is not available.

This is because the market in which investment properties are purchased and sold is one in which the price for a relatively nonhomogeneous asset is negotiated between two parties. Generally this price does not have to be disclosed to any public or private agency. Hence unlike securities markets, there is no centralized collection of real estate transactions and operating income data.[1]

Because of these limitations, we should stress at the outset that current attempts to measure real estate investment performance are based on limited data that are made available from a few select sources. The available data may not be representative of (1) the many types of properties, (2) the many geographic areas in which commercial real estate is located, or (3) the frequency of transactions indicative of real estate investment activity in the economy as a whole. Consequently, the reader must be careful when making generalizations regarding real estate performance based on limited data because it may not be representative of general real estate performance or even the performance of all properties in a specific category of real estate (e.g., retail, hotels, office).

SOURCES OF DATA USED FOR REAL ESTATE PERFORMANCE MEASUREMENT

In this section, we provide information on four sources of real estate data that are used to a limited extent when measuring real estate investment performance. We also consider investment returns from data that are generally available on common stocks, corporate bonds, and government securities. Exhibit 23–1 summarizes the data generally available for these investments.

REIT Data

Two of the three sources of data used to produce investment returns on real estate in this chapter are based on data for REITs (see Chapter 20 for a discussion of REITs). The NAREIT (National Association of Real Estate Investment Trusts) *Equity Index* (EREIT) is a monthly index based on ending market prices for shares owned by EREIT investors. Returns are collected only on REITs that *own* real estate. Data for this series is available beginning with January of 1972 and includes all EREITs actively traded on the New York and American Stock Exchanges as well as the NASDAQ National Market System.[2]

The second REIT series shown in Exhibit 23–1 contains data compiled by Goldman Sachs & Co. for 33 *unleveraged* equity REITs only. This series, which we will refer to as ULREITs, was collected from a sample of REITs that have a policy of acquiring most properties on an

---

[1]In some states, actual transaction prices must be disclosed to property tax assessors. However, other data relating to property characteristics and operating cash flows are generally not available.

[2]Obtained from various publications of the National Association of Real Estate Investment Trusts, Washington, D.C.

EXHIBIT 23–1 Common Sources of Data Used for Measuring Investment Performance

Real Estate-Equity Returns	*Description of Data*
NAREIT—Equity REIT Share Price Index and Dividend Yield Series (EREITs)	Monthly index computed based on share prices of REITs which own and manage real estate assets. Security prices used in the index are obtained from the NYSE, AMEX, and NASDAQ system. Dividend data are collected by NAREIT. Properties owned may be levered or unlevered. Index values are available from 1972 to the present.
Goldman Sachs & Co.— Unlevered Equity REIT Total Return Index (ULREITs)	Quarterly index based on a subset of equity REITs that have used little or no financial leverage. The index is compiled from REIT security prices and dividends. Index values are available from 1974 through 1986.
Frank Russell Co.—Property Index (FRC Index)	Data is contributed by members of NCREIF, who currently own approximately 1,000 properties with an aggregate value in excess of $11 billion. The FRC Index is calculated quarterly and consists of monthly data on (1) net operating income and (2) beginning- and end-of-quarter appraised values for all properties. Actual sale prices are used, as available. All properties are owned free and clear of debt. Quarterly index values are available from 1978 to the present.
NAREIT—mortgage REIT Share Price Index and Dividend Yield Series	Monthly index computed based on share price data of REITs that make primarily commercial real estate loans (construction, development and permanent) although some make or purchase residential loans (both multifamily and single family). Prices obtained from NYSE, AMEX, and NASDAQ market system. Dividend data is collected by NAREIT. Monthly index data available from 1972 to present.
NAREIT—Hybrid REIT Index	Monthly index compiled by NAREIT based on share prices and dividends for REITs who both (1) own properties and (2) make mortgage loans. Sources of data are the same as for equity and mortgage REITs. Index values are available from 1972 to the present.
Salomon Brothers—Total Rate of Return Index—mortgage securities	Monthly index, based on over-the-counter prices obtained on mortgage pools containing $500 billion in FHA-VA residential mortgages with GNMA payment guarantees, or conventional mortgages with FNMA or FHLMC payment guarantees. Monthly index available from 1980 to present.

EXHIBIT 23–1   *(Concluded)*

Real Estate-Equity Returns	*Description of Data*
Common stocks—Standard & Poor Corp. (S&P) 500	Daily index based on common stock prices for the 500 corporations with highest market value of common stock outstanding. Data available from the financial press. Dividend data compiled by Wilshire and Associates and included in a monthly and annual total return index by Ibbotson Associates, Chicago. Daily index data available from 1926 to present.
Corporate bonds—Salomon Brothers High-Grade Corporate Bond Index	Monthly index based on high grade, long term (20 year) bond prices. Interest based on bond coupons and total returns (interest, beginning, and ending index values) compiled by Ibbotson Associates, Chicago. Daily index available from 1926 to present.
Government securities	U.S. Treasury bills and bonds. Price data obtained from *The Wall Street Journal.* A monthly total return series compiled by Ibbotson Associates, Chicago. Daily index data available from 1926 to present.

"all cash" basis and do not use a substantial amount of financial leverage in their operation.[3] ULREITs represented in this index are a *subset* of the EREIT series described in the preceding paragraph.

The data for the two equity REIT indexes just described are based on the sale of shares issued by REITs and are not based on the sale of the underlying real estate assets. In other words, these data are compiled from end-of-month transaction prices and dividends on securities owned by investors in each REIT contained in the index. Hence, the prices of REIT shares are determined by investors based on how successful they believe the trustees of an individual REIT will be in finding properties at favorable prices, managing them, and then selling them. While REIT share prices certainly reflect investor perceptions of the quality, diversity, and risk of real estate assets owned by REITs, investors are also evaluating the effectiveness of REIT trustees in their valuation of REIT securities. Further, when purchasing REIT shares, investors do not give up as much liquidity as they would if they acquired and managed real estate assets directly. This is because a continuous auction market (e.g., NYSE) exists in which REIT shares may be traded. Thus, risk may be lower when investing in a REIT when compared to investing directly in real estate.

---

[3]REITs included in this series consist of those with a debt-to-asset ratio of less than 20 percent. The authors wish to thank Mr. Randy Zisler of Goldman Sachs & Co. and Professor Steve Ross and Mr. Will Goetzmann of Yale University for providing this data.

FRC Property Index

The FRC Property Index referred to in Exhibit 23–1 measures the historic performance of income-producing properties either (1) acquired by open end commingled investment funds which sell investment units that are owned by qualified pension and profit-sharing trusts, or (2) acquired by investment advisors and managed on a separate account basis. (See Chapter 20 for a discussion of pension funds and various real estate investment vehicles.) Only *unleveraged* properties are included in the FRC Property Index. The data incorporated in the index are voluntarily contributed and based on the performance of properties managed by members of the National Council of Real Estate Investment Fiduciaries (NCREIF).[4] The index was started on December 31, 1977, with 236 properties valued at $594.4 million. As of September 30, 1987, data from approximately 1,000 properties, valued in excess of $11.0 billion, were included in the index. Quarterly rates of return are calculated for all properties included in the index based on two distinct components of return: (1) net operating income and (2) the quarterly change in property market value (appreciation or depreciation). As shown in Exhibit 23–2, the FRC Property Index contains data on four major categories of properties: office buildings, warehouses, office/showrooms/R&D facilities, and retail properties (including regional, community, and neighborhood shopping centers as well as free standing store buildings). The index is currently segmented into four geographic regions. When an FRC Index Property is sold by a participating manager, its historic performance data remains in the index. Net sales proceeds are entered as the final market value in the quarter in which the property is sold, and no further data for that property are added. The index returns represent an aggregate of individual property returns calculated quarterly before deduction of portfolio management fees. The quarterly series is calculated by summing the increase or decrease in the value of each property plus its net operating income for the quarter. To obtain changes in value, *quarterly appraisals* are made, and, in a few cases, actual transaction prices negotiated by the buyer and seller are a part of the index.

Another difference between FRC and REIT data that should be pointed out is that both indexes reflect the deduction of property management fees; however, the FRC Index does not reflect fees paid to portfolio asset managers while the REIT data does. We have provided a detailed breakdown of properties making up the FRC Index in Exhibit 23–2.

Hybrid and Mortgage REITs

There are two mortgage investment return series and a hybrid REIT index also shown in Exhibit 23–1. Like the EREIT and ULREIT indexes, the mortgage REIT index is also based on security prices of shares outstanding in REITs. However, these REITs specialize in acquiring various types of mortgage loans on many types of properties. Hence when investing in a mortgage REIT, an investor is buying equity shares in an entity whose assets are primarily mortgage loans. Also shown in the exhibit are a group of REITs referred to as hybrid REITs.

---

[4]See *The NCREIF Real Estate Performance Report,* various issues, published by National Council of Real Estate Fiduciaries (New York) and Frank Russell Co. (Tacoma, Washington).

EXHIBIT 23–2 Characteristics of Properties Making Up the FRC Property Index, as of Third Quarter 1987

Regional distribution of
property values in the FRC Index
(000,000)

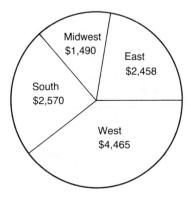

Distribution of property values
in the FRC Index by type of property
(000,000)

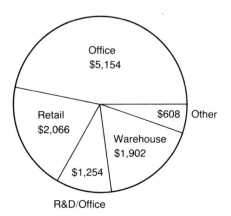

Regional distribution of
properties in the FRC Index

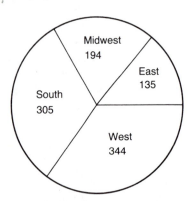

Distribution of properties in the
FRC Index by type of property

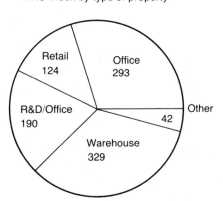

Source: Based on data provided by National Council of Real Estate Investment Fiduciaries, New York, as published by the Frank Russell Co., Tacoma, Washington.

These REITs operate by buying real estate *and* by acquiring mortgages on both commercial and residential real estate.

Residential Mortgage-Backed Security Returns

Exhibit 23–1 also contains the description of a *residential* mortgage-backed security index. The Salomon Brothers total rate of return index on mortgage securities is based on prices obtained on mortgage securities issued against residential mortgage pools with total outstanding loan balances of approximately $500 billion as of November 1987.[5] Securities selected for the index are backed by pools containing either (1) 30-year or 15-year mortgages, with timely payment guarantees made by GNMA, FNMA, or FHLMC, or (2) a limited number of mortgages made and subsequently traded on selected FHA insured projects. This monthly index was initiated in January of 1980.

Sources of Data for Other Investments.   In contrast to the scarcity of real estate return data, data on financial assets is more plentiful and easily obtainable. In this chapter, we will also develop measures of investment performance for common stocks from the Standard & Poor's 500 Index of Common Stocks, U.S. Treasury bills, longer-term U.S. Treasury bonds, and long-term corporate bonds contained in the Salomon Brothers Index of Corporate Bonds. These indexes, also referred to in Exhibit 23–1, are generally computed daily, weekly, monthly, quarterly, and annually and are published regularly in the financial press.[6]

COMPUTING OF HOLDING PERIOD RETURNS

In general, the most fundamental unit of measure used by portfolio managers to measure investment returns for individual securities, or a class of securities in a portfolio, is the holding period return (*HPR*). This is generally defined as follows:

$$HPR = \frac{P_t - P_{t-1} + D_t}{P_{t-1}}$$

where P_t is the end-of-period price for the asset, or value of an index for an investment, or index representing a class of investments, whose performance is being assessed, P_{t-1} is the beginning of period value, and D represents any dividends or other cash payouts that may have occurred during the period over which the *HPR* is being measured. We have chosen quarterly time intervals to compute *HPR*s so that comparisons can be made between the FRC Property Index, which is available only on a quarterly basis, and the

---

[5]See Research Department, Market Performance, Salomon Brothers, Inc., *Salomon Brothers Total Rate-of-Return Indexes,* November, 1987, published December 4, 1987. The authors wish to thank Professor David Hartzell for providing this data.

[6]For cumulative data since 1926 see R. G. Ibbotson Associates, Inc., *Stocks, Bonds, Bills and Inflation, 1986 Yearbook* (Chicago, 1986).

other investments.[7] Investment returns based on the FRC index are calculated as though an investor owned a unit share of all properties in the index.[8]

An example of how holding period returns are calculated is demonstrated for a small portion of the EREIT index (from the first quarter of 1984 to the fourth quarter of 1986) in Exhibit 23–3. The first quarter's return was calculated by subtracting the end-of-period index value (which already includes dividends) from the beginning-of-period value and dividing by the beginning-of-period value.[9] The arithmetic mean, variance, standard deviation, and coefficient of variation have also been calculated. These latter measures will be used in our discussion of risk later in the chapter. The *HPR* for the first quarter in the series was 4.51 percent. The mean *HPR*, or $\overline{HPR}$, of all quarterly returns in the series was 4.34 percent. Hence, an investor in a portfolio equally weighted by all shares represented in EREIT index would have earned a quarterly return of 4.34 percent, on average, from the end of 1983 through the end of 1986.

An alternative way of considering this return data is to calculate the geometric mean return. This return is calculated by finding the *n*th root of the product of each quarterly *HPR* in series multiplied together, minus 1 (see bottom of exhibit). The geometric mean return for the returns shown in Exhibit 23–3 was equal to 4.26 percent. This latter return measures the quarterly *compounded* rate of return that an investor would have earned on $1 invested in the EREIT index on the last day of 1983 and held through the end of 1986.

Although the values of the arithmetic mean and geometric mean are very close, this will not always be the case, particularly if values in the series rise and fall sharply and the series is longer than the sample shown in the exhibit. There is a distinct conceptual

---

[7]Quarterly *HPR*s for all other indexes were computed by compounding the monthly *HPR* data obtained from the sources discussed in Exhibit 23–2. The three monthly *HPR*s contained in each quarter were compounded to obtain the quarterly return series as follows: $(1 + HPR_1)(1 + HPR_2)(1 + HPR_3) - 1$.

[8]Because of the pattern of receipts, disbursements, and operating income received from leases during the quarter, quarterly changes in the FRC property index are actually computed by the Frank Russell Company as follows:

$$HPR = \frac{P_t - P_{t-1} + PS - CI + NOI}{P_{t-1} + .5(CI - PS) - .33(NOI)}$$

where P_t and P_{t-1} represent the ending and beginning quarterly values of all properties in the index, *PS* is equal to any distributions of cash from property sales, *CI* represents additional capital investments made by investors for improvements, and *NOI* represents net operating income. The term $.5(CI - PS)$ is a midpoint assumption used to take account of the timing for any net cash inflow (outflow) for *CI* and *PS* occurring during the period. By choosing the midpoint, we assume that over many quarters cash flows for *CI* and *PS* will occur, on average, midway between the beginning and end of the period. Similarly, the adjustment .33(*NOI*) is also made to reflect *monthly* receipt of income from tenant leases. These two adjustments are necessary because such cash flows may be sizable and occur during the quarter, while data on property values are available only at the *end* of each quarter. If all interim cash flows were assumed to occur at the end of the quarter, eliminating these adjustments could result in an over- or understatement of returns. For a discussion of these adjustments see W. B. Brueggeman and S. Michael Giliberto, ''Measuring Real Estate Investment Performance: A Revised Approach,'' Center for Research in Real Estate and Urban Land Economics, E. L. Cox School of Business, Southern Methodist University, Dallas, TX, May 1987.

[9]Data made available from NAREIT include both a share price index and a monthly dividend yield series which is annualized for equity, mortgage, and hybrid REITs.

EXHIBIT 23-3 Sample Computation of Holding Period Returns (*HPR*) and Related Statistics

Period Ending	Equity REITs Index	HPR_i	$(HPR_i - \overline{HPR_i})$	$(HPR_i - \overline{HPR_i})^2$
Quarter				
4: 1983	165.5736			
1: 1984	173.0439	0.0451	0.0017	0.0000
2	172.3549	−0.0040	−0.0474	0.0022
3	183.4833	0.0646	0.0212	0.0004
4	194.5444	0.0603	0.0169	0.0003
1: 1985	209.9434	0.0792	0.0358	0.0013
2	223.7473	0.0658	0.0224	0.0005
3	218.5388	−0.0233	−0.0667	0.0044
4	230.1858	0.0533	0.0099	0.0001
1: 1986	260.5604	0.1320	0.0886	0.0078
2	268.7771	0.0315	−0.0119	0.0001
3	274.0534	0.0196	−0.0238	0.0006
4	273.1348	−0.0034	−0.0467	0.0022
N = 12		Σ 0.5207		Σ 0.0200

HPR, 1Q 1984 $= (173.0439 - 165.5736)/165.5736 = 0.0451$

Mean $HPR = \overline{HPR_i} = \Sigma\, HPR_i \div n = .5207 \div 12 = .0434$

Variance $= \sigma^2 = \Sigma(HPR_i - \overline{HPR_i})^2 \div n = .02 \div 12 = 0.0017$

Standard deviation $= \sigma = \sqrt{\sigma^2} = \sqrt{.0017} = .0412$

Coefficient of variation $= .0412 \div .0434 = .9493$

Geometric mean return $= \sqrt[n]{(1 + HPR_1)(1 + HPR_2) + \ldots (1 + HPR_n)} - 1 = 0.0426$

difference between the arithmetic and geometric mean returns. The geometric mean is used by portfolio managers when considering the performance of an investment and is expressed as a compound rate of interest from the beginning to the end of a specific period of time. Arithmetic mean returns are simple averages (not compounded) and are widely used in statistical studies spanning very long periods of time.[10]

[10]The geometric mean is considered to be superior to the arithmetic mean when the past performance of an investment is being considered for a specified period of time, say from the date of purchase until the present time, or for an investment portfolio where funds are flowing in and out and the investment base is changing. For example, suppose the price of a security is 100, 110, 100 at the end of three consecutive years. The *HPR*s are 10 percent and −9.09 percent. The arithmetic mean is .45 percent however, the geometric mean is zero. The latter result occurs because the beginning and ending security prices are equal. This return better represents the performance of a security from the time of purchase until the present. Arithmetic mean returns are used in statistical studies where some inference about the future is being based on averages of past performance. In these cases, an entire series of returns may be used to justify a long-term future decision and no specific time interval is considered to be any more important than another.

Exhibit 23–4 contains summary statistics for various investments that we have chosen to include in the chapter. Note that for each of the return series, we have calculated quarterly arithmetic mean and geometric mean returns and related statistics defined at the bottom of Exhibit 23–3. The exhibit also includes data for the consumer price index (*CPI*) and gross national product (*GNP*).

Comparing Investment Returns

We can now begin to compare total returns for the various investment categories contained in Exhibit 23–4. A number of patterns should be apparent from the data shown in the exhibit. Looking to geometric mean returns (also called time weighted returns by many portfolio managers), we can see in Panel A that from 1978 to 1986, unleveraged equity REITs (ULREITs) produced quarterly returns of 6.08 percent, which exceeded all other returns shown in the exhibit. Equity (EREIT) returns were 4.32 percent, followed by returns on common stocks comprising the S&P 500, which were 3.88 percent, then by corporate bonds 3.31 percent, the FRC Index 3.25 percent, T bonds 2.59 percent, and T bills 2.32 percent. Both hybrid REITs and mortgage REITs performed very poorly, producing respective geometric mean returns of only 1.45 percent and .96 percent over the period.

HPRs, **Inflation, and Real Economic Growth.**   All returns shown in Exhibit 23–4 may also be compared with the quarterly rate of inflation, as represented by the *CPI,* which was 1.61 percent, as well as growth in nominal *GNP,* which was 2.16 percent over the same period. The comparison with the *CPI* provides some insight as to whether returns from each investment category exceeded the rate of inflation (thereby earning real returns), while the comparison with *GNP* indicates whether returns on each investment exceeded growth in the economy as a whole. Real rates of return for each security can be approximated by subtracting the rate of inflation from each return. This measure of real returns for each security can also be compared with growth in real *GNP.* Growth in real *GNP* was *approximately* 2.16 percent less the rate of inflation 1.61, or .55 percent per quarter, during the 1978–1986 period.

Comparing Risk Premiums.   In addition to returns, risk premiums may be calculated for each investment class relative to either T bills or T bonds. Risk premiums may also be calculated for each investment relative to all other investments. For example, during the 1978–1986 period, ULREITs earned an average *risk premium* of 3.76 percent per quarter in excess of T bills (6.08 % − 2.32%). T bills are generally used to represent a riskless investment; hence T bill returns provide a measure of a risk-free return. Investors in ULREITs would also have earned a premium of 2.77 percent relative to returns on corporate bonds (6.08% − 3.31%). When compared to the FRC Property Index, which provided returns of 3.25 percent compounded quarterly, both ULREIT and EREIT returns were higher than the FRC Index by 2.83 percent and 1.07 percent, respectively. We should recall, however, that the FRC Index is compiled on an *unleveraged* basis; that is,

EXHIBIT 23–4 Summary Statistics of Performance Measures For Selected Investment Groups

Panel A

Quarterly Returns (1Q)1978–(4Q)1986

	EREITS	ULREITS	FRC	Mtg. REITS	Hybrid REITS	MBS	Corp. Bonds	S&P 500	T Bills	T Bonds	CPI	GNP
Arithmetic mean	4.50%	6.37%	3.26%	1.01%	1.50%	—	3.68%	4.13%	2.32%	2.93%	1.62%	2.17%
Standard deviation	6.13%	7.87%	1.34%	3.06%	3.10%	—	8.88%	7.23%	0.62%	8.41%	1.16%	1.28%
Coefficient of variation	1.36	1.24	0.41	3.04	2.06	—	2.41	1.75	0.27	2.87	0.71	0.59
Geometric mean	4.32%	6.08%	3.25%	0.96%	1.45%	—	3.31%	3.88%	2.32%	2.59%	1.61%	2.16%
Standard deviation	6.13%	7.88%	1.34%	3.06%	3.10%	—	8.89%	7.23%	0.62%	8.42%	1.16%	1.28%
Coefficient of variation	1.42	1.30	0.41	3.18	2.13	—	2.69	1.87	0.27	3.25	0.72	0.59

Panel B

Quarterly Returns (1Q)1980–(4Q)1986

	EREITS	ULREITS	FRC	Mtg. REITS	Hybrid REITS	MBS	Corp. Bonds	S&P 500	T Bills	T Bonds	CPI	GNP
Arithmetic mean	4.26%	6.00%	2.96%	1.22%	1.66%	3.77%	4.87%	4.42%	2.37%	3.84%	1.32%	1.95%
Standard deviation	6.08%	7.25%	1.22%	3.10%	2.98%	7.39%	9.56%	7.64%	0.66%	9.21%	1.10%	1.25%
Coefficient of variation	1.43	1.21	0.41	2.54	1.80	1.96	1.96	1.73	0.28	2.40	0.83	0.64
Geometric mean	4.08%	5.74%	2.95%	1.17%	1.61%	3.51%	4.44%	4.14%	2.37%	3.44%	1.31%	1.94%
Standard deviation	6.08%	7.26%	1.22%	3.10%	2.98%	7.39%	9.57%	7.65%	0.66%	9.22%	1.10%	1.25%
Coefficient of variation	1.49	1.26	0.41	2.65	1.85	2.10	2.15	1.85	0.28	2.68	0.84	0.65

*Through 2Q. 1986.

the properties in the index were purchased on an all-cash or "free and clear" of debt. Hence, a more appropriate comparison for the FRC Index would be relative to ULREITs. This is because EREIT returns include the effects of leverage, while the FRC Index does not, hence EREITs are more risky. Therefore, holding all else constant, a premium should be earned on EREIT shares relative to returns based on the FRC Index.

When comparisons among EREITs, both ULREITs and the FRC Index are made, however, an important result emerges. Holding all else constant, we would expect that EREIT returns (leveraged) would be greater than both ULREITs and FRC returns (both of which are unleveraged). However, this was not the case for the period considered. As can be seen, ULREIT returns were 6.08 percent compared to 4.32 percent for EREITs. Further, ULREIT returns were higher than returns indicated by the FRC Index (6.08 percent versus 3.25 percent), even though properties in both of these portfolios are not leveraged. These differences may be attributable to the types of properties, their location, management, and so on, and reflected in the index for each investment. Hence, the *risk* for each investment may not be the same. More will be said about these results later in the chapter when risk-adjusted returns are discussed.

In Panel B of Exhibit 23–4, quarterly returns are shown for a slightly shorter period (1980–1986). This is because the data series for mortgage-backed securities began in 1980, and in order to make appropriate comparisons returns on all other investments had to be recalculated for the same period. A few interesting observations can be made from results in Panel B. First, as expected, the geometric mean return on MBS was greater than returns on T bonds due to prepayment risk (recall Chapters 21–22) and less favorable liquidity or marketability. However, MBS returns were less than returns on corporate bonds. The latter result may be because of U.S. agency guarantees against default losses and provide various timely payment guarantees on MBS securities. These guarantees do not exist for investors in corporate bonds.

Another important relationship that becomes apparent when Panels A and B are compared is that the time period over which returns are measured may be important when comparing returns. For example, in Panel A we see that EREIT returns exceeded returns on the S&P 500, but in Panel B, S&P returns exceed those of EREITs. This may suggest that results in Panel B are based on a period of measurement that is too short. Hence, the number of return observations (24) are too few to make a good estimate of the true mean and variability of each of the returns. Alternatively, perhaps some unanticipated economic event occurred during 1978 and 1979 which affected the S&P 500 index to a greater extent than the REIT index.

Also note the relationship between total returns earned on MBS and the FRC Index. Based on returns during the period 1980–1986, it appears that investors would have earned higher total returns on the relatively low risk MBS investments (3.51 percent) as compared to investments in riskier income properties, as represented by the FRC Index (2.95 percent). Again, this result may be caused by the relatively few quarters (24) over which the returns are calculated, or it is possible that the risk associated with both indexes bears closer examination.

Other items of importance shown in Exhibit 23–4 are that EREIT, ULREIT, and FRC real estate return indexes exceeded both growth in the economy at large (*GNP*) and the rate of inflation (*CPI*) during the period 1978–1986 (Panel A). However, both mortgage and hybrid REITs did not. From 1980 to 1986 (Panel B), arithmetic and geometric means for the EREIT, ULREIT, and the FRC indexes were lower than for the full 1978 to 1986 period, indicating a general decline in these real estate returns during the more recent period. It is also important to note that returns on T bills, T bonds, corporate bonds, and the S&P 500 were higher during the shorter period (Panel B) relative to the longer full period. This indicates a general increase in those returns during the more recent period relative to returns for the selected categories of real estate in the exhibit.

RISK, RETURN, AND PERFORMANCE MEASUREMENT

While comparing investment returns is an important starting point in evaluating investment performance, it represents only one part of the analysis. We know from material presented in earlier chapters that investments that systematically produce higher returns are generally *riskier* than investments producing lower returns. In cases involving *individual real estate* investments, such risks may be a function of the type of property, its location, design, lease structure, and so on. Those attributes, and the attendant risks associated with those attributes, can be thought of as a type of *business risk*.

Another source of risk occurs in cases where real estate investments are leveraged. In these cases, default risk is present. Finally, because of the relative difficulty and time required to sell property, liquidity risk is certainly present. As we know, when these three major sources of risk are compared among properties or among alternative investments, when more risk is taken by investors, a risk premium, or higher investment return should be earned by investors who bear that additional risk. One way of considering this risk-return relationship is to compute risk premiums, as we did above. A subjective assessment can then be made as to whether risk premiums earned on riskier assets are adequate relative to the additional risk taken. An investor may then judge whether the premium earned on EREITs when compared to corporate bonds is sufficient to compensate for the added risk taken if EREITs were purchased instead of corporate bonds.

Another way of looking at the risk-return relationship is to think about the way in which business, default, and liquidity risks affect the pattern of returns that are expected to be earned by investors. Over time, returns (dividends and price changes) on investments with more of these risks present are likely to exhibit more *variation* than for investments with fewer of these risks present. Recalling our discussion in the chapter on investment risk, we would expect a property with more risk to provide higher, but more variable investment returns than a property with less risk. The point is, greater variability in market prices and cash flows can be thought of as being commensurate with increased risk. This is because an investor owning a risky asset with a highly variable price pattern (up and down) faces having to sell this risky investment for a more unpredictable price than for a less risky asset. The assumption that variability in asset returns represents risk is the foundation for modern finance theory. It is also a premise that must be understood if the techniques for risk-adjusting returns that are described below are to be used.

Risk-Adjusted Returns—The Basic Elements

Given that the combined effects of the sources of risk described above will be reflected in the variability in investment returns, one way of taking into account investment risk when evaluating performance is to take variability of returns into account. By considering the variability of holding period returns for specific assets or classes of assets, a better comparison can be made among investments.

One approach that may be used to consider risk and returns is to compute the coefficient of variation of the returns. This is defined as the standard deviation of returns divided by the mean return (this can be done based on either the arithmetic or geometric mean returns for a given investment or investment index). Recall from Exhibit 23–3 that we demonstrated how this statistic is computed. This concept (as the reader should recall from Chapter 12) is sometimes referred to as a *risk*-to-*reward* ratio and is intended to relate total risk, as represented by the standard deviation, to the mean return. The idea is to determine how much return that an investor could expect to earn relative to the total risk taken if the investment was made. Hence, as shown in Exhibit 23–3, if an investor held a portfolio containing EREIT securities from 1984 to 1986, a quarterly mean return of 4.34 percent would have been earned. When the mean return is divided into the standard deviation of returns (4.12 percent), a coefficient of variation of .9493 results. This may be interpreted as taking .9493 units of risk for every unit of return that was earned.[11]

An interesting comparison may now be made between the investment performance of EREITs, ULREITs, and the FRC Index. Recall from Exhibit 23–4 that when compared to EREITs and ULREITs, the FRC Index produced a lower mean return. However, when mean returns for all three investment categories are risk-adjusted, the FRC Index appears to have outperformed both the EREIT and ULREIT index on a risk-adjusted basis. When the coefficient of variation for EREITs, ULREITs, and the FRC Index are compared, the FRC had the highest *risk-adjusted returns,* followed by ULREITs and EREITs. This pattern is more in keeping with the fact that both the FRC and ULREIT returns are based on unleveraged properties and hence are less risky than EREIT returns, which are riskier because of the use of leverage.[12] Of course, these are historical returns, and there is no assurance that this pattern will be repeated.

It has already been pointed out that the FRC index (1) does not include the effect of leverage in investment returns, and (2) property values used to compute the FRC index are based largely on quarterly appraisals plus a relatively small number of actual transactions. Using appraisals may have a smoothing effect on returns and hence reduce

---

[11]This calculation also assumes that the risk premium, or return, is proportional to the risk taken on all investments by all investors. This assumption clearly *does not hold* for all investors, some of whom are more risk-averse than others. Further, even for the same investor, risk aversion cannot be considered for individual assets independently of one another. Rather, risk must be assessed in terms of the additional risk assumed relative to the total portfolio of assets owned. More will be said about this later.

[12]There are many other differences in the number, quality, and geographic location of properties making up the FRC Index, EREIT, and ULREIT. Hence, leverage alone is not the only source of variation affecting the three indexes. However, if each of the three indexes were represented by a highly diversified group of properties, then leverage would be the major source of variation in returns.

variability. If property appraisals are (1) significantly different from market values and (2) affect the variation in the index, then the index may not be representative of true real estate returns, or volatility in those returns. For example, results in Exhibit 23–4 for ULREITs indicate that the mean return was 6.37 percent and the standard deviation of returns was 7.87 percent, resulting in a coefficient of variation of 1.24. This compares to a mean return of 3.26 percent for the FRC Index and a coefficient of variation which was .41. These results indicate a material difference in both return and risk for the two indexes which are both based on unleveraged property returns. This difference may be due to considerable differences in the types of properties (e.g., office, retail, apartment), in the geographic distribution of their locations (e.g., north, south, east, or west and suburban or urban sites), and in the investment strategies employed by investment managers (such as investing in raw land in predevelopment stages, or in fully leased properties only, etc.). Such differences may affect the relative risk of investments reflected in each index. Further, REIT shares are bought and sold in an *auction* market with continuous trading, whereas the individual properties that make up the FRC Index are bought and sold in a much more limited, *negotiated* market between parties. Premiums for liquidity and transaction costs when making such comparisons are really not well understood, nor have such premiums been isolated in research studies. Finally, the definition of income used in calculating the holding period returns for both indexes may not be exactly comparable because of advisory and other management fees which are deducted from REIT income, but not for properties in the FRC Index.[13] More research must be done before the nature of risk and return for investments made in REIT shares versus direct investment in real estate, as represented by the FRC Index, is well understood.

ELEMENTS OF PORTFOLIO THEORY

The preceding section dealt with one approach that may be used to compare investments by considering the investment's mean return (we used geometric) and the standard deviation of those returns. The standard deviation was used as a measure of risk when making comparisons among investments. However, an additional problem that must be considered by investors is the extent to which the acquisition of an investment affects the risk and return of a *portfolio* of assets. This question is very important because of the interaction between returns when investments are *combined* in a portfolio. Because of this interaction, the variance of the return on a portfolio may be less than the average of the individual investments. When investors add to an existing portfolio as they acquire new assets, it is important to understand how the acquisition of that new asset may *impact* the return and risk of the entire portfolio.

---

[13]The distinction being made here is that institutions reporting data for the FRC Index earn a portfolio management fee from pension plan sponsors for acquiring, managing, and disposing of assets. This fee is distinguished from a fee for property management, which involves the day-to-day management of properties. The former fee is not reflected in the FRC Index. For REITs, data are reported net of *all* management fees. Therefore, FRC returns reported in the index are probably higher than those shown for REITs.

EXHIBIT 23–5 Computation of the Mean *HPR* and Standard Deviation for a Portfolio Containing Common Stocks (S&P 500) and EREIT Shares (equally weighted), 1984–1986

Period Ending	HPR EREIT	HPR S&P 500	HPR_p (.5 EREIT + .5 S&P500)	$HPR_p - \overline{HPR_p}$	$[HPR_p - \overline{HPR_p}]^2$
Quarter					
1: 1984	.0451	−.0227	.0112	−.0335	.0011
2	−.0040	−.0258	−.0149	−.0596	.0035
3	.0646	.0968	.0807	.0360	.0013
4	.0603	.0176	.0390	−.0057	.0000
1: 1985	.0792	.0935	.0864	.0417	.0017
2	.0658	.0749	.0704	.0160	.0007
3	−.0233	−.0405	−.0319	−.0866	.0059
4	.0533	.1718	.1126	.0679	.0046
1: 1986	.1320	.1407	.1364	.0917	.0084
2	.0315	.0591	.0453	.0007	.0000
3	.0196	−.0697	−.0251	−.0600	.0036
4	−.0034	.0540	.0253	−.0194	.0004
	$\Sigma = .5207$	$\Sigma = .5497$	$\Sigma = .5354$		$\Sigma = .0325$

S&P 500 $\overline{HPR}$ = .5497 ÷ 12 = .0458
S&P 500 variance, σ^2 = .0622 ÷ 12 = .0052
S&P 500 standard deviation, σ = $\sqrt{.0052}$ = .0721
S&P 500 coefficient of variation = .0721 ÷ .0458 = 1.5742
$\overline{HPR_p}$ = .5354 ÷ 12 = .0446
Portfolio variance, $\sigma^2 = [HPR_p - \overline{HPR_p}]^2 \div n$ = .0027
Portfolio standard deviation = $\sqrt{\sigma^2}$ = $\sqrt{.0027}$ = .0520
Portfolio coefficient of variation = .0520 ÷ .0446 = 1.1659

Building a portfolio by considering the return and standard deviation of returns for *individual* investments will not always ensure that an optimum portfolio will be obtained. Indeed, any new asset being considered as an addition to a portfolio should be judged on the grounds of "efficiency," that is, whether its addition to an existing portfolio will increase expected portfolio returns while maintaining, or lowering, portfolio risk. Alternatively, the efficiency of an asset may also be judged as to whether it will lower portfolio risk while maintaining, or increasing, the expected portfolio return.[14]

To illustrate how the interaction between investment returns occurs, we consider the data in Exhibit 23–5. Returns in column 1 are the same sample of quarterly *HPR*s used

---

[14]The basis for modern portfolio theory was developed by Harry Markowitz, "Portfolio Selection," *Journal of Finance*, vol. 7, no. 1 (March 1952), pp. 77–91.

for EREITs shown in Exhibit 23–3. The returns shown in column 2 are the quarterly returns computed for the S&P 500 for common stocks over the same time period. The statistics presented at the bottom of the exhibit indicate that the quarterly mean return for the S&P 500 was 4.58 percent while the standard deviation was 7.21 percent. As previously pointed out, the mean return for EREITs was 4.34 percent, and the standard deviation of those returns was 4.09 percent. Obviously, risk and returns for these two investments are different. The S&P 500 shows both a higher mean return and a higher standard deviation (risk) when compared to the EREIT index. Assuming that at the end of 1983 an investor was holding a portfolio *comprised only of S&P 500* securities, the question that we would like to answer is, how would the addition of a real estate investment (as represented by the EREIT index) impact the quarterly mean *portfolio* return and its standard deviation?

Calculating Portfolio Returns

To demonstrate an approach that may be used to answer this question, we will use the sample of the quarterly data for 1984–1986, and we will assume that both assets would have been *weighted equally* in one portfolio over that period. We will then compute the mean return and standard deviation for the *combined portfolio* (see Exhibit 23–5). The mean return for the portfolio, $\overline{HPR}_P$, is calculated as

$$\overline{HRP}_p = W_i(\overline{HPR}_i) + W_j(\overline{HPR}_j)$$
$$= .5(.0434) + .5(.0458)$$
$$= .0217 + .0229$$
$$= .0446$$

where W represents the weights that securities i (EREIT) and j (S&P 500) will represent as a proportion of the total value of the portfolio (i.e., $W_i + W_j = 1.0$). Based on this calculation, we see that the *portfolio* return would have been 4.46 percent quarterly. This return is less than what would have been earned on the S&P 500 alone. However, we cannot really conclude much from this result before considering how portfolio *risk* may have been affected when the two investments were combined.

Portfolio Risk

To consider how total portfolio *risk* would have been affected by the addition of EREITs to an existing portfolio of S&P common stocks, the standard deviation of the *new portfolio* returns is calculated. This is also demonstrated in Exhibit 23–5. Based on the results shown in the exhibit, we can see that the portfolio standard deviation is 5.20 percent, which is far less than the standard deviation of S&P returns (7.21 percent). Further, the coefficient of variation for the portfolio (1.1659) is less than the coefficient of variation for the S&P 500 (1.5742). This implies that *adding* EREITs to our existing S&P portfolio would meet the test of "efficiency" defined earlier, in that a lower risk-to-return ratio would be achieved with EREITs in the portfolio.

Unlike the mean *HPR* for the portfolio, the standard deviation of portfolio returns for the two indexes is *not* equal to the simple weighted average of the individual standard deviations of the two indexes; that is, $[(.5)(4.12\%)] + [(.5)(7.21\%)] \neq 5.20\%$. This is because when the returns of the two assets are combined, a greater than proportionate reduction in the variation in portfolio returns is achieved. In short, there is *interaction* between the two returns in the sense that the pattern, or direction in movement, of each of the individual *HPRs* is not the same in each period.[15] Indeed, in some quarters, the *HPRs* for EREITs are positive and the *HPRs* for the S&P 500 are negative. Hence when combined in one portfolio, the returns on the portfolio are less volatile than for individual assets. The nature of this interaction is important to understand when measuring the risk of an investment portfolio.

Covariance and Correlation of Returns; Key Statistical Relationships.   When considering the variability in any portfolio return, an important aspect of individual investment returns that should be considered is how the return on an asset being considered will vary with returns on an existing portfolio. This pattern, when considered relative to mean portfolio returns, will give us an indication as to how efficient the acquisition of an asset will be when combined with another asset or with an existing portfolio. There are two statistics that provide a numerical measure of the extent to which returns tend to either move together, in opposite directions, or have no relationship to one another. These statistics are the *covariance* and *correlation* between the two return series.

The covariance between returns on two assets is an *absolute* measure of the extent to which two data series (*HPRs*) move together over time. It is calculated for our example in Exhibit 23–6. Essentially, the covariance is computed for two investments by first finding the deviation of each investment's *HPR* from its mean ($\overline{HPR}$). These deviations for each security in each period are then multiplied and summed. The summed deviations are divided by the number of observations in each series. The result is the covariance or statistic that provides an *absolute* measure of the extent to which returns between two securities move together. In our example, the covariance between EREITs and the S&P was .2 percent.

Because the result was positive, we can say that the returns on the two securities tended to move *together,* or in the same direction, during the period for which we made the calculation. Hence, we have *positive covariance* between returns on EREITs and the S&P. It is also possible to have negative covariance, indicating that returns tend to move in opposite directions. While this measure is useful, the fact that it is an *absolute* measure of the relationship between returns makes it somewhat difficult to interpret. While we would expect that very large covariance values may indicate that there is a very strong relationship (either positive or negative) between investment returns, because the covariance statistic can take on values ranging from $+\infty$ to $-\infty$, it is difficult to know when a covariance value is "large or small." Because of this problem, we need a method to gauge the importance of the statistic on a *relative* scale of importance. The coefficient

---

[15]This can be casually observed by making a simple pairwise comparison of each of the quarterly returns for the EREIT and S&P series.

EXHIBIT 23–6 Computation of Covariance of Quarterly Returns for the Equity REIT Index and the S&P 500, 1984–1986

Period Ending	HPR_i EREIT	HPR_j S&P 500	EREIT $HPR_i - \overline{HPR_i}$	S&P 500 $HPR_j - \overline{HPR_j}$	$[HPR_i - \overline{HPR_i}] \times [HPR_j - \overline{HPR_j}]$	EREIT $[HPR_i - \overline{HPR_i}]^2$	S&P 500 $[HPR_j - \overline{HPR_j}]^2$
Quarter							
1: 1984	0.0451	−0.0227	0.0017	−0.0685	−0.0001	0.0000	0.0047
2	−0.0040	−0.0258	−0.0474	−0.0716	0.0034	0.0022	0.0051
3	0.0646	0.0968	0.0212	0.0510	0.0011	0.0004	0.0026
4	0.0603	0.0176	0.0169	−0.0282	−0.0005	0.0003	0.0008
1: 1985	0.0792	0.0935	0.0358	0.0477	0.0017	0.0013	0.0023
2	0.0658	0.0749	0.0224	0.0291	0.0007	0.0005	0.0008
3	−0.0233	−0.0405	−0.0667	−0.0863	0.0058	0.0044	0.0075
4	0.0533	0.1718	0.0099	0.1260	0.0012	0.0001	0.0159
1: 1986	0.1320	0.1407	0.0886	0.0949	0.0084	0.0078	0.0090
2	0.0315	0.0591	−0.0119	0.0133	−0.0002	0.0001	0.0002
3	0.0196	−0.0697	−0.0238	−0.1155	0.0027	0.0006	0.0133
4	−0.0034	0.0540	−0.0467	0.0082	−0.0004	0.0022	0.0001
N = 12	Σ 0.5207	Σ 0.5497			Σ 0.0238	Σ 0.0200	Σ 0.0622

EREIT $\overline{HPR}$ = 0.5207 ÷ 12 = .0434

EREIT variance, σ = 0.0200 ÷ 12 = 0.0017

EREIT standard deviation, = $\sqrt{0.0017}$ = 0.0412

S&P 500 $\overline{HPR}$ = 0.5497 ÷ 12 = 0.0458

S&P 500 variance, σ^2 = 0.0622 ÷ 12 = 0.0052

S&P 500 standard deviation, σ = $\sqrt{0.0052}$ = 0.0721

$COV_{ij} = [HPR_i - \overline{HPR_i}][HPR_j - \overline{HPR_j}] \div N$
$= (0.0238) \div 12$
$= 0.0020$

Correlation between EREIT and S&P 500

$\rho_{ij} = [COV_{ij}] \div [\sigma_i \sigma_j] = .67$

of correlation (ρ) is used to obtain this *relative* measure or the extent to which one set of numbers moves in the same or opposite direction with another series. The formula for the correlation statistic is:

$$\rho_{ij} = COV_{ij} \div (\sigma_i \sigma_j)$$

In our example we have

$$\rho_{ij} = .0020 + (.0412)(.0721)$$
$$= .67$$

Because the correlation statistic only ranges between $+1$ and -1, it is a much easier way to interpret the extent to which returns are related. For example, as the coefficient of correlation approaches $+1$, two series are said to move very closely together, or be highly correlated. Hence, given a change in one of the series, there is a high likelihood of a change in the other series in the same direction.[16] Conversely, as the coefficient approaches -1, the two series are said to be negatively correlated, as they move in exactly opposite directions. Hence, given a change in one series, the other would be expected to move in the opposite direction. If the correlation coefficient is close to zero, this would imply that there is no relationship between the two series. In our example, a correlation coefficient of .67 indicates a relatively strong positive correlation between the S&P 500 and EREITs over the period considered. This is because the coefficient is equal to .67, has a positive sign, and is closer to $+1.0$ than it is to zero.[17]

What are some other relationships that are important to us at this point? It should be clear that if two investments are *highly positively correlated* then the reduction in the variance in portfolio returns (hence, risk) is likely to be smaller than if there were either no correlation or negative correlation. This is because in the latter case the distribution of two returns would be either unrelated or negatively related, and the interaction between returns would not be reinforced. In fact, if returns were negatively correlated, they would be offsetting. In this event, the sum of the deviations from the portfolio mean would be smaller after the security is added, and, hence, the standard deviation of portfolio returns would be lower (hence, lower risk). Consequently, it should be stressed that anytime the correlation between returns on two assets is less than $+1$, *some* reduction in risk (standard deviation) may be obtained by combining investments, as opposed to holding one investment (or one portfolio) with a higher standard deviation than the investment being considered. However, the potential for risk reduction is much greater as the correlation approaches -1.

Based on the foregoing analysis, it should now be clear why the standard deviation of portfolio returns in our example is not equal to a simple, weighted average of the standard

---

[16]Obviously there would have to be an underlying cause-and-effect relationship between the two series to make an assertion that any past relationship can be used to predict a future relationship.

[17]When the coefficient of correlation has a value greater than .5, the association between two series is considered to be high. There are also statistical tests of significance that enable us to say with more confidence whether two series are correlated or whether the correlation statistic calculated between the series was because of an unrepresentative sample taken from the underlying distribution of returns. For a discussion of correlation, normal distribution assumptions, and related statistics, see any standard college textbook on elementary statistics.

deviation of the two individual investment returns. Further, if variation in security returns is a reasonable representation of risk to investors, then it should become apparent to the reader that there may be some benefit in the form of risk reduction, by *diversifying* an investment portfolio to include assets with returns that are negatively correlated, or assets with returns showing little or no correlation. Of course, the other critical dimension that has to be considered is how the *mean return* of the portfolio will be affected when the individual securities are combined. For example, if two securities have the *same* positive mean returns and such returns were perfectly, negatively correlated (e.g., -1), then it may be inferred that an investor could earn a positive portfolio return with zero risk if both investments were purchased (the standard deviation of the combined returns would be zero). The likelihood of this possibility ever occurring is slight, however, because the likelihood of finding securities that are perfectly negatively correlated (-1) is small. However, there are many investments with returns that are negatively correlated, uncorrelated, or less than perfectly positively correlated that may be candidates for addition to a portfolio on the grounds of efficiency outlined above. These basic elements of portfolio analysis should make the reader aware of a framework that may be used to consider many questions regarding risk and returns.

Portfolio Weighting—Trading Off Risk and Return

To this point, we have seen that adding EREITs to a portfolio containing stocks composing the S&P 500 during the period 1984–86 would have reduced portfolio risk (standard deviation) by a greater amount than the reduction in portfolio mean return. This implies that a portfolio containing both assets (indexes) would have been more efficient than one containing only S&P 500 stocks. However, in our computations we assumed that both assets were *equally weighted*. Could a more optimal portfolio have been attained by varying the weight (proportion) of two securities in the portfolio? To answer this question, we considered the full sample of EREIT and S&P 500 returns from Exhibit 23–4, or those returns that comprised the *full period* 1978–1986. The arithmetic quarterly means *HPR* for the S&P 500 index was 4.13 percent with a standard deviation of 7.23 percent, and the *HPR* for EREITs was 4.50 percent with a standard deviation of 6.13 percent. The correlation between both return series was .69 (not shown). Because the correlation coefficient was less than 1, some reduction in risk would have been possible by combining the two assets.

To determine the optimal *weighting,* all combinations of both assets were considered in increments of 5 percent, and the mean portfolio return and standard deviation were calculated. The result is shown in Exhibit 23–7. The diagram shows all values lying between the two extreme cases, that is, the case where the portfolio would be composed entirely of S&P 500 stocks and no EREIT shares (100 percent in the exhibit) and the case where the portfolio would be composed of 100 percent EREIT securities and no S&P shares (0 percent in the exhibit). Hence, the curve in the exhibit shows the *trade-off* between return and risk for the portfolio as to the two asset classes are added in varying proportions.

EXHIBIT 23–7   Portfolio Risk and Return Equity REITs and S&P 500 1978–1986

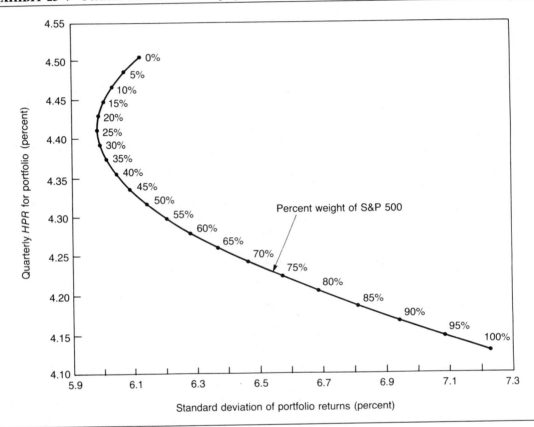

Note that even though the EREIT index had *both* a higher mean *HPR* (4.50 percent) and a lower standard deviation (6.13 percent) during this period, when compared to the S&P 500 index (see Exhibit 23–4), diversification benefits could have been realized by combining assets as opposed to holding only S&P 500 or EREIT securities. This is illustrated in Exhibit 23–7. Note that if the portfolio had consisted of 25 percent S&P and 75 percent EREIT securities, both a higher return and lower risk would be realized as opposed to holding 100 percent S&P 500 securities.

From results in Exhibit 23–7 note that as more and more EREIT shares are added to the portfolio, the mean return rises at a rate that is less than proportional to the rate at which risk increases. Further, the "backward-bending" portion of the curve (in the range of 25 percent to 0 percent) provides higher mean returns at the same level of risk than those shown on the lower portion of the curve (25 percent to 50 percent). Hence, if investors wanted to increase returns by taking more risk, they would add more EREIT shares relative to S&P 500 shares. For investors with a low aversion to risk, this small increase in return relative to risk may be acceptable. This portion of the curve is also known as the *efficient frontier,* or the combination of securities that provides investors with increasing portfolio returns as portfolio risk increases. Returns below the efficient frontier are inferior because there is always a better combination of securities that will increase returns as risk is increased. Investors will choose the combination of securities along the efficient frontier in accordance with their willingness to take risk. Investors who are risk-averse would tend to hold a mix closer to 75 percent EREIT, 25 percent S&P 500 securities in this example. Less risk-averse investors would tend to weigh EREIT shares more heavily in the portfolio.

REAL ESTATE RETURNS, OTHER INVESTMENTS, AND THE POTENTIAL FOR PORTFOLIO DIVERSIFICATION

From the above analysis, it should be clear that there are many assets that have the potential to be combined efficiently in a portfolio that will provide an optimal risk-return relationship for investors. Clearly, the example between EREITs and the S&P 500 showed this. However, many other assets can be considered by investors when selecting assets. One of the key relationships that indicates the potential for combining assets in a portfolio is the correlation between asset returns. Exhibit 23–8 is a correlation matrix or table which contains the coefficient of correlation for returns on all securities listed in Exhibit 23–4. The purpose in calculating these coefficients is to consider how various *real estate investment vehicles* might be combined with various other assets when building a portfolio.

We can gain some insights into the question of whether portfolios containing certain securities would be more efficient if a *real estate investment vehicle* was added. We will

EXHIBIT 23–8   Correlation Matrix for Selected Assets Quarterly Returns 1978–1986

	Equity REITS	ULVD. REITS*	FRC	Mtg. REITS	Hybrid REITS	MBS†	Corp. Bonds	S&P 500	T Bills	T Bonds	CPI	GNP
Equity REITS	1.000	0.764	−0.086	0.551	0.646	0.338	0.333	0.689	−0.291	0.359	−0.297	0.125
ULVD. REITS		1.000	−0.158	0.725	0.794	0.457	0.317	0.678	−0.240	0.324	0.002	−0.073
FRC			1.000	−0.401	−0.292	−0.336	−0.420	0.211	0.459	−0.385	0.503	0.352
Mortgage REITS				1.000	0.867	0.775	0.647	0.641	−0.091	0.705	−0.184	−0.312
Hybrid REITS					1.000	0.647	0.508	0.654	−0.108	0.567	−0.141	−0.168
MBS						1.000	0.846	0.500	−0.166	0.925	−0.330	−0.538
Corp. bonds							1.000	0.442	−0.159	0.849	−0.384	−0.353
S&P 500								1.000	−0.295	0.572	−0.219	0.003
T Bills									1.000	−0.117	0.506	0.045
T Bonds										1.000	−0.393	−0.489
CPI											1.000	0.312
GNP												1.000

*1Q 1978–2Q 1986
†1Q 1980–2Q 1986

focus on this more narrow question, because to consider the question of what *the* optimum portfolio *should* contain would have to include an examination of the risk and returns for all securities and assets that are available to investors. Such a portfolio might contain bonds, stock, real estate, gold, jewelry, coins, stamps, and virtually any asset that could be owned by investors. Based on mean standard deviation of returns and covariance between returns, investors would hold portfolios containing some optimum combination of available investments. An efficient frontier, such as the one shown in our two investment case in Exhibit 23–7, would also exist for this larger, diversified "market portfolio." If all investors made decisions based on whether the ratio of risk to return for the total portfolio would be improved, all investor portfolios would tend to be diversified and efficient. Returns on any additional investments would be evaluated on the basis of any incremental increases or decreases in total portfolio risk, and the risk premium paid by investors for such securities would reflect that incremental risk. In short, risk premiums for investments would be determined on the basis of the expected addition or reduction in portfolio risk and all investments would be priced in accordance with that relationship.[18]

In this section we consider the question of portfolio performance, diversification, and real estate. Real estate is an investment class that has been considered by portfolio managers for only about 10 years. This is because it has only been in recent years that (1) equity ownership in real estate has become widely available in a "securitized" form such as a REIT share or a unit of ownership in open- and closed-ended commingled investment funds, and (2) that regulatory restrictions governing pension funds have been relaxed to include real estate as an acceptable investment (see Chapter 20). However, many institutions which heretofore considered only government securities, corporate bonds, and common stock have shown increasing interest in real estate.

We now consider the question of whether real estate investments are likely to provide diversification benefits to investors with portfolios consisting of some government securities, stocks, and bonds. In other words, we begin with some assumptions about the nature of existing investment portfolios. We then consider whether such existing portfolios could have benefited from diversifying by acquiring real estate investments over the period 1978–1986. Hence, the starting point for all of the analysis that we conduct in the next sections, assume that (1) the existing portfolio must always contain 10 percent T bills for liquidity and (2) that common stocks and corporate bonds may be added to the portfolio such that any combination of weights equal 90 percent. We then consider how portfolio performance would have changed with the addition of real estate investments during that period.

Portfolio Diversification and REIT Shares.   Looking back to Exhibit 23–8, we can see what the historical (or ex post) correlation in quarterly returns for the various investments was for the entire period 1978–1986. Focusing our attention on equity investments in real estate, note, for example, that returns on EREITs tended to be positively

---

[18]For additional information regarding capital market theory and efficient markets, see W. F. Sharpe, *Investments,* 3rd ed. (Englewood Cliffs, N.J.: Prentice-Hall, 1985) and F. K. Reilly, *Investments,* 2nd ed. (New York: The Dryden Press, 1986).

correlated with both corporate bonds, common stocks (.333, .689, respectively) and negatively related to T bills (−.291). Recall from Exhibit 23–4 that EREIT returns exceeded returns on all three of these security classes. ULREIT returns show a relationship with the same three security types that is very similar to that of EREITs. The correlation coefficient between ULREITs and the three security classes carry the same signs and are of the same order of magnitude. ULREITs also had higher mean returns than both stocks and bonds. These relationships suggest that because (1) both EREITs and ULREITs have higher mean returns and lower coefficients of variation than corporate bonds and the S&P 500, (2) both ULREITs and EREITs had less than perfect correlation with both the S&P 500 and corporate bonds, and (3) the correlation coefficient between both EREITs and ULREITs and T bills is negative, there is a good chance that if either of these real estate investments were combined in a portfolio containing common stock, bonds, and T bills, diversification benefits could have been achieved.

To determine whether this is the case, we first combine the S&P 500, corporate bonds, and T bills in a portfolio. Recall that the portfolio is constrained by requiring that it will always contain 10 percent T bills. The remainder of the portfolio will be comprised of stocks and bonds. To develop the efficient frontier for this portfolio, we consider the mean return and standard deviation for different portfolios containing 10 percent T bills and all combinations (weights) of stocks and bonds (in increments of 10 percent). Mean returns and standard deviations for all portfolios are plotted in Exhibit 23–9 as *portfolio A*. Results indicate that during the period 1978–1986, a mix of 10 percent T bills, 67.5 percent S&P 500 stocks, and 22.5 percent bonds would have resulted in total portfolio returns of approximately 3.85 percent and a standard deviation of returns of 6.0 percent (calculations not shown). Also note that because the curve representing portfolio A "bends back" from this point. This means that investors would earn a higher portfolio return at higher levels of risk. Indeed, if investors were willing to take on additional risk in excess of a 6.0 percent standard deviation, they would always choose portfolios weighted in a combination corresponding to the backward bending portion (efficient frontier) of the curve. This is because they would realize higher mean returns for the same risk than the portion of the curve immediately below. For example, note that for portfolio A at a standard deviation of 6.2 percent, a mean return of either approximately 3.75 percent *or* 3.95 percent could be produced by varying the weights of investments in the portfolio. The portfolio producing the 3.95 percent return would always be chosen (dominate) over the portfolio producing the lower returns at the same level of risk.

To consider what happens when an investment in real estate *securities* is added to portfolio A, we first consider EREITs and combine them in all possible combinations with S&P stocks, bonds, and 10 percent T bills to form *portfolio B*. We then form *portfolio C* by adding ULREITs in place of EREITs. It should be clear that by adding EREITs shares, portfolio B provides a higher mean return at a lower risk (standard deviation) than does portfolio A. However, portfolio C produces a significantly higher mean return, although at higher standard deviations when compared to B. Hence, it is not clear whether investors would prefer portfolio C to B. However, portfolio C would be preferable to portfolio A because it does produce higher mean returns at *all* levels of risk (standard deviation).

The efficient frontier for portfolio C begins with a combination of 0 percent stocks, 18 percent bonds, 72 percent ULREIT shares, and 10 percent T bills. At that point the

EXHIBIT 23–9   Portfolio Simulation Results (T bills, common stock, corporate bonds, and REITs)

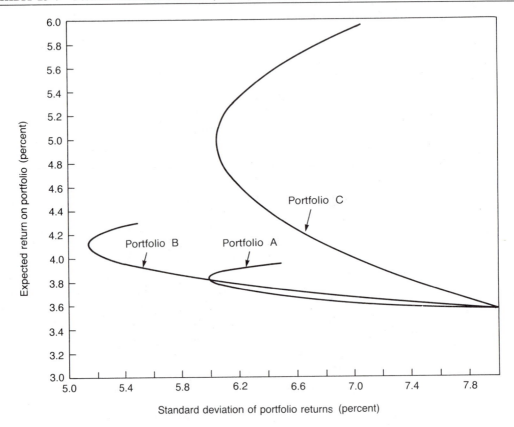

Portfolio A = 10% T bills, common stock, corporate bonds.
Portfolio B = 10% T bills, common stock, corporate bonds, EREITs.
Portfolio C = 10% T bills, common stock, corporate bonds, ULREITs.

coefficient of variation for the portfolio is lowest. The portfolio return is about 5.20 percent and the standard deviation is about 6.10 percent (calculation not shown). Should investors prefer higher portfolio returns, they would add more ULREIT shares and reduce bonds, although risk would also increase. The efficient frontier for portfolio B begins with 0 percent stock, 13.5 percent bonds and 76.5 percent EREIT shares. Should investors desire higher returns, they would do so by adding more EREIT shares in place of corporate bonds. Risk would also increase.

We should also briefly observe that portfolios B and C do not contain any S&P common stocks and are heavily weighted by REIT securities. Why is this so? Looking back to the correlation matrix, we should recall that both REIT securities are highly correlated with the S&P 500 index. This means that returns from REITs and stocks tended to *move closely together* over the past 10 years. Consequently, attempts to reduce risk in a portfolio with *both* REIT shares *and* S&P stocks would be minimal. In cases where two security returns are highly correlated, the security with the highest mean return generally remains in the portfolio with other securities. Hence, because REITs had higher mean returns than S&P stocks, REIT shares were included in portfolios while S&P 500 stocks were excluded. We should also stress that these results are based on *historical returns* over a very specific time period and may not be indicative of future performance. Indeed, should *expected* mean returns from stocks exceed those of REIT shares in the future, stocks could be the better choice to keep in the portfolio in place of REIT shares. Investors make investment decisions based on future or expected risks and returns. This example has used ex-post or past returns to illustrate concepts. There is no assurance that these results will be repeated in the future.

One other important point should be made regarding the results for REIT securities. Recall that EREITs tended to outperform ULREITs (Exhibit 23–4), and, when combined with other securities, portfolio C tended to perform very well. This is somewhat surprising because one would expect a priori that EREITs would earn higher returns than ULREITs (recall our earlier chapter on leverage and risk). We would also expect more variability in the EREIT returns because of the presence of leverage. Indeed, the opposite pattern may be seen in Exhibit 23–4; that is, ULREITs had both a higher mean return and a higher standard deviation. However, because of the nature of the data made available for use in the chapter, data for ULREIT returns are also included in EREIT returns. That is, the sample of ULREITs is a subset of the total number of EREITs in the United States. If separate data were available for *leveraged* REITs *only* then a better measure of the effect of leverage could be obtained than the one used in the chapter. Hence, the results discussed in Exhibit 23–9 may be partially due to the restrictive nature of REIT data available for this example.

Portfolio Performance and the FRC Property Index

In addition to considering REIT securities as a potential vehicle for real estate investment, we have also indicated that the FRC index may also be indicative of the performance of real estate as an asset class (however, recall the breakdown for properties in the index at the beginning of the chapter). Considering this possibility, we have also shown the correlation between the FRC index and other investments in Exhibit 23–8. Data in the exhibit show that, in general, the correlation between the FRC and all other investments (with the exception of T bills) is negative. This would imply that real estate, as represented by the FRC index, would serve as an excellent candidate for diversification when combined with any of the assets contained in the exhibit. However, it also appears that the FRC index is also slightly negatively correlated with both on EREIT and ULREIT returns. This suggests that FRC returns are either negatively correlated or unrelated to both REIT return series. Given that all three return series are based on real estate as the underlying asset, a closer, positive association between returns would be expected.

To consider the prospects of diversification with an FRC type real estate investment, quarterly returns from the FRC index were combined in portfolio A. Recall that it contained 10 percent Treasury bills, and the remainder included S&P stocks and bonds. Results for the new *portfolio D,* are compared with portfolio A in Exhibit 23–10. The implications of these results are that because of the very low standard deviation of FRC

EXHIBIT 23–10   Portfolio Simulation Results (T bills, common stock, corporate bonds, and FRC Index)

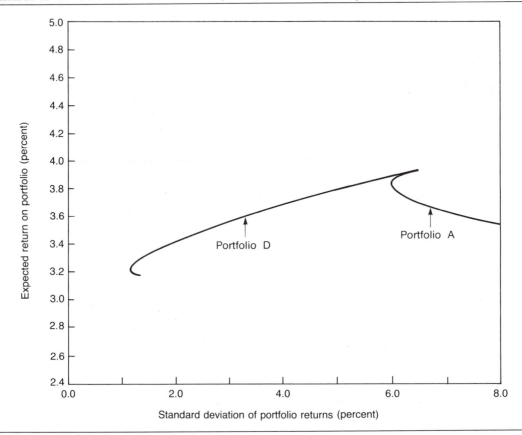

returns (see Exhibit 23–4), as more of the portfolio is weighted with those returns, the portfolio standard deviation falls at a much faster rate than does the mean return. The lowest value of the coefficient of variation for the portfolio occurs when the portfolio contained 0 percent stock, 9 percent bonds, 81 percent FRC, and 10 percent T bills. Like portfolios B and C, the real estate investment dominates the portfolio. However, in this case it is for a completely different reason. The FRC Index has a very low mean return and a very low standard deviation in returns when compared to both EREITs and ULREITs. Further, FRC returns were negatively correlated with both bonds and T bills. Both ULREITs and EREITs were positively correlated with those same securities. Does this result mean that investor portfolios could have diversified into real estate by either buying REIT shares or owning properties similar to those represented by the FRC Index? Are risk-return data for real estate best represented by security prices such as that of REIT shares or by an index representing the performance of individual properties? The answers to these questions are not clear. Some have argued the fact that because *appraised values* are used in the construction of the FRC Index, this may reduce or "smooth" the variation in returns. This does not necessarily mean that the estimates of value are erroneous. It does mean that the use of appraisals may not capture variation in period-to-period property values. In a recent study, comparing sales prices and appraised values on properties from the FRC Index, Miles, Guilkey, and Cole found that, on average, appraised values were lower than actual sale prices. The study also suggested that appraisal estimates were, on average, close to actual property values. On the other hand, Shulman has argued that parameters used in appraisals tend to be based more on *historical* economic data and not *expected* economic conditions; hence estimated values lag actual values.[19]

Relationship between Real Estate Performance and Economic Conditions. One final comparison of interest to portfolio managers is the relationship between real estate performance and general economic growth and inflation. More specifically, (1) are real estate returns related to the rate of inflation and (2) do they seem to grow at a rate which is greater or less than general economic growth? To provide some insight to these questions, we recall our earlier comparisons between the REIT and FRC indexes and the *CPI* and *GNP*. In all cases, the real estate indexes that we have used exceeded the rate of growth for both the *CPI* and *GNP*. This implies that at least for the period 1978–1986, real estate investments, as represented by the data used in Exhibit 23–4, outperformed general economic growth and exceeded the rate of inflation.

Exhibit 23–8 indicates that the correlation between these indexes and the *GNP* and *CPI* is not consistent. The FRC index had the strongest positive correlation with both *GNP* and the *CPI* (.352 and .503 respectively); however, both EREITs and ULREITs had a very weak or no relationship with *GNP* or the *CPI*. This suggests that the appraised process used in estimating property values used in the FRC Index may be more a reflection of *current economic values* instead of *expected* economy growth.

To amplify, as we know, property values are a reflection of *future* cash flows which are based on future economic expectations. Hence, it may be that the reason why EREITs and ULREITs show no relationship with *CPI* or *GNP* is that correlation may exist between *current* returns (which include price appreciation) and *future* rates of inflation and economic growth. Hence, perhaps a more appropriate model to test this possibility would be to lag investment return data and correlate it against values for the *CPI* and *GNP* for various periods coming *after* the lagged periods. This is beyond the scope of this chapter. Nonetheless, results here should *not* be used to conclude that there is no correlation between REIT prices and *expected* inflation and growth. Similarly, even though the FRC Index was correlated with the *CPI* and *GNP*, it may or may not be correlated with future values.

SUMMARY AND CONCLUSION

This chapter has introduced the measurement of investment performance and the basic elements of portfolio theory. We have also attempted to deal with the question of whether

---

[19]See M. Miles, D. Guilkey, and R. Cole, "Pension Fund Investment Managers' Unit Values Deserve Confidence," *Real Estate Review* (Spring 1987), pp. 84–89 and D. Shulman, "Appraisal-Based Returns after the RREEF Write-Offs," New York: Salomon Brothers, August 3, 1987.

real estate investments tend to provide diversification benefits to portfolios that have traditionally consisted of government securities, common stocks, and corporate bonds.

We have stressed that the nature of real estate investment return data is very limited and may not be representative of a broad measure of real estate returns. Further, some of the data are based on a group of properties owned by investment advisors. In this case, an index is calculated based on reported net operating income and appraised property values with very few actual transaction prices.

Results from the portfolio simulations conducted and reported in the latter part of the chapter indicate that based on these limited data sets, there appeared to be significant gains available from portfolio diversification into real estate *during the period 1978–1986*. In all simulations, real estate became the dominant asset in the portfolio and replaced common stock. Of course, these results are based on historical data from a limited sample of real estate investments and may *not* be indicative of future results or apply generally to all real estate investments.

QUESTIONS

1. What are some of the difficulties in obtaining data to measure real estate investment performance?
2. What are the distinguishing characteristics between REIT data and the FRC property index?
3. Differentiate between arithmetic and geometric mean returns.
4. What statistical concept do many portfolio managers use to represent risk when considering investment performance?
5. When FRC returns and REIT returns are compared, FRC returns exhibit a much lower pattern of variation. Why might this be the case?
6. Mean returns for portfolios are calculated by taking the weighted average of the mean returns for each investment in the portfolio. Why won't this approach work to calculate the standard deviation of portfolio returns?
7. What is the difference between covariance and correlation? Why are these concepts so important in portfolio analysis?
8. Results reported in the chapter showed that by including either REITs or the FRC Index in a portfolio containing S&P 500 securities, corporate bonds, and T bills, diversification benefits resulted. Why was this true? Did those benefits come about for the same reason for each category of real estate investment?
9. Results presented in the chapter are based on historical data. Of what use are these results to a portfolio manager who may be making an investment decision today? Elaborate.

PROBLEM

As an investment advisor for MREAF (Momentum Real Estate Advisory Fund) you are about to make a presentation to the portfolio manager of the ET&T pension fund. You would like to show what would have happened had ET&T made an investment in MREAF from the beginning of 1983 through the end of 1985. The ET&T manager has provided you with historical data on the performance of its portfolio, which is made up entirely of common stock. Historical data for the ET&T portfolio and the MREAF fund are as follows:

Period Ending	*ET&T* Common Stock Fund		*MREAF* Real Estate Fund	
	Unit Value	Quarterly Dividend	Unit Value	Quarterly Dividend
83 Dec	$1258.64	$14.07	$159.17	$2.93
Mar	1164.89	14.10	164.62	2.96
Jun	1132.40	14.41	168.89	3.26
Sept	1206.71	14.60	169.27	3.12
84 Dec	1211.57	15.14	168.88	3.15
Mar	1266.78	15.39	169.57	3.20
Jun	1335.46	15.39	165.49	3.21
Sept	1328.63	15.45	164.98	3.23
85 Dec	1546.67	15.51	160.41	3.22
Mar	1818.61	15.87	166.23	3.26
Jun	1892.72	16.32	172.30	3.23
Sep	1767.58	16.79	174.03	3.23
86 Dec	1895.95	16.78	176.97	3.24

a. Calculate the quarterly *HPR* for each investment.

b. Calculate the arithmetic mean *HPR*, the standard deviation of the *HPR*s, and the geometric mean for each fund. Which fund contained more risk per unit of return?

c. Was there any correlation between returns on the ET&T fund and MREAF?

d. Would a portfolio that contained equal amounts of ET&T securities and MREAF have provided any investment diversification? Why?

e. (Optional) What if each investment could have been combined in a portfolio with weights ranging from 0 percent to 100 percent. What pattern of risk and return would result if each investment was added (deleted) in increments of 10 percent (remember that the sum of the two proportions must always sum to 100 percent) What combination of securities would have comprised the ''efficient frontier'' (if any)?

f. If the manager of ET&T is considering making an investment in MREAF, of what use is this analysis?

A. Annual Compound Interest Tables

ANNUAL COMPOUND INTEREST TABLES

6.00% ANNUAL INTEREST RATE

	1 AMOUNT OF $1 AT COMPOUND INTEREST	2 ACCUMULATION OF $1 PER PERIOD	3 SINKING FUND FACTOR	4 PRESENT VALUE REVERSION OF $1	5 PRESENT VALUE ORD. ANNUITY $1 PER PERIOD	6 INSTALLMENT TO AMORTIZE $1	
YEARS							YEARS
1	1.060000	1.000000	1.000000	0.943396	0.943396	1.060000	1
2	1.123600	2.060000	0.485437	0.889996	1.833393	0.545437	2
3	1.191016	3.183600	0.314110	0.839619	2.673012	0.374110	3
4	1.262477	4.374616	0.228591	0.792094	3.465106	0.288591	4
5	1.338226	5.637093	0.177396	0.747258	4.212364	0.237396	5
6	1.418519	6.975319	0.143363	0.704961	4.917324	0.203363	6
7	1.503630	8.393838	0.119135	0.665057	5.582381	0.179135	7
8	1.593848	9.897468	0.101036	0.627412	6.209794	0.161036	8
9	1.689479	11.491316	0.087022	0.591898	6.801692	0.147022	9
10	1.790848	13.180795	0.075868	0.558395	7.360087	0.135868	10
11	1.898299	14.971643	0.066793	0.526788	7.886875	0.126793	11
12	2.012196	16.869941	0.059277	0.496969	8.383844	0.119277	12
13	2.132928	18.882138	0.052960	0.468839	8.852683	0.112960	13
14	2.260904	21.015066	0.047585	0.442301	9.294984	0.107585	14
15	2.396558	23.275970	0.042963	0.417265	9.712249	0.102963	15
16	2.540352	25.672528	0.038952	0.393646	10.105895	0.098952	16
17	2.692773	28.212880	0.035445	0.371364	10.477260	0.095445	17
18	2.854339	30.905653	0.032357	0.350344	10.827603	0.092357	18
19	3.025600	33.759992	0.029621	0.330513	11.158116	0.089621	19
20	3.207135	36.785591	0.027185	0.311805	11.469921	0.087185	20
21	3.399564	39.992727	0.025005	0.294155	11.764077	0.085005	21
22	3.603537	43.392290	0.023046	0.277505	12.041582	0.083046	22
23	3.819750	46.995828	0.021278	0.261797	12.303379	0.081278	23
24	4.048935	50.815577	0.019679	0.246979	12.550358	0.079679	24
25	4.291871	54.864512	0.018227	0.232999	12.783356	0.078227	25
26	4.549383	59.156383	0.016904	0.219810	13.003166	0.076904	26
27	4.822346	63.705766	0.015697	0.207368	13.210534	0.075697	27
28	5.111687	68.528112	0.014593	0.195630	13.406164	0.074593	28
29	5.418388	73.639798	0.013580	0.184557	13.590721	0.073580	29
30	5.743491	79.058186	0.012649	0.174110	13.764831	0.072649	30
31	6.088101	84.801677	0.011792	0.164255	13.929086	0.071792	31
32	6.453387	90.889778	0.011002	0.154957	14.084043	0.071002	32
33	6.840590	97.343165	0.010273	0.146186	14.230230	0.070273	33
34	7.251025	104.183755	0.009598	0.137912	14.368141	0.069598	34
35	7.686087	111.434780	0.008974	0.130105	14.498246	0.068974	35
36	8.147252	119.120867	0.008395	0.122741	14.620987	0.068395	36
37	8.636087	127.268119	0.007857	0.115793	14.736780	0.067857	37
38	9.154252	135.904206	0.007358	0.109239	14.846019	0.067358	38
39	9.703507	145.058458	0.006894	0.103056	14.949075	0.066894	39
40	10.285718	154.761966	0.006462	0.097222	15.046297	0.066462	40
41	10.902861	165.047684	0.006059	0.091719	15.138016	0.066059	41
42	11.557033	175.950545	0.005683	0.086527	15.224543	0.065683	42
43	12.250455	187.507577	0.005333	0.081630	15.306173	0.065333	43
44	12.985482	199.758032	0.005006	0.077009	15.383182	0.065006	44
45	13.764611	212.743514	0.004700	0.072650	15.455832	0.064700	45
46	14.590487	226.508125	0.004415	0.068538	15.524370	0.064415	46
47	15.465917	241.098612	0.004148	0.064658	15.589028	0.064148	47
48	16.393872	256.564529	0.003898	0.060998	15.650027	0.063898	48
49	17.377504	272.958401	0.003664	0.057546	15.707572	0.063664	49
50	18.420154	290.335905	0.003444	0.054288	15.761861	0.063444	50

ANNUAL COMPOUND INTEREST TABLES

7.00% ANNUAL INTEREST RATE

	1 AMOUNT OF $1 AT COMPOUND INTEREST	2 ACCUMULATION OF $1 PER PERIOD	3 SINKING FUND FACTOR	4 PRESENT VALUE REVERSION OF $1	5 PRESENT VALUE ORD. ANNUINTY $1 PER PERIOD	6 INSTALLMENT TO AMORTIZE $1	
YEARS							YEARS
1	1.070000	1.000000	1.000000	0.934579	0.934579	1.070000	1
2	1.144900	2.070000	0.483092	0.873439	1.808018	0.553092	2
3	1.225043	3.214900	0.311052	0.816298	2.624316	0.381052	3
4	1.310796	4.439943	0.225228	0.762895	3.387211	0.295228	4
5	1.402552	5.750739	0.173891	0.712986	4.100197	0.243891	5
6	1.500730	7.153291	0.139796	0.666342	4.766540	0.209796	6
7	1.605781	8.654021	0.115553	0.622750	5.389289	0.185553	7
8	1.718186	10.259803	0.097468	0.582009	5.971299	0.167468	8
9	1.838459	11.977989	0.083486	0.543934	6.515232	0.153486	9
10	1.967151	13.816448	0.072378	0.508349	7.023582	0.142378	10
11	2.104852	15.783599	0.063357	0.475093	7.498674	0.133357	11
12	2.252192	17.888451	0.055902	0.444012	7.942686	0.125902	12
13	2.409845	20.140643	0.049651	0.414964	8.357651	0.119651	13
14	2.578534	22.550488	0.044345	0.387817	8.745468	0.114345	14
15	2.759032	25.129022	0.039795	0.362446	9.107914	0.109795	15
16	2.952164	27.888054	0.035858	0.338735	9.446649	0.105858	16
17	3.158815	30.840217	0.032425	0.316574	9.763223	0.102425	17
18	3.379932	33.999033	0.029413	0.295864	10.059087	0.099413	18
19	3.616528	37.378965	0.026753	0.276508	10.335595	0.096753	19
20	3.869684	40.995492	0.024393	0.258419	10.594014	0.094393	20
21	4.140562	44.865177	0.022289	0.241513	10.835527	0.092289	21
22	4.430402	49.005739	0.020406	0.225713	11.061240	0.090406	22
23	4.740530	53.436141	0.018714	0.210947	11.272187	0.088714	23
24	5.072367	58.176671	0.017189	0.197147	11.469334	0.087189	24
25	5.427433	63.249038	0.015811	0.184249	11.653583	0.085811	25
26	5.807353	68.676470	0.014561	0.172195	11.825779	0.084561	26
27	6.213868	74.483823	0.013426	0.160930	11.986709	0.083426	27
28	6.648838	80.697691	0.012392	0.150402	12.137111	0.082392	28
29	7.114257	87.346529	0.011449	0.140563	12.277674	0.081449	29
30	7.612255	94.460786	0.010586	0.131367	12.409041	0.080586	30
31	8.145113	102.073041	0.009797	0.122773	12.531814	0.079797	31
32	8.715271	110.218154	0.009073	0.114741	12.646555	0.079073	32
33	9.325340	118.933425	0.008408	0.107235	12.753790	0.078408	33
34	9.978114	128.258765	0.007797	0.100219	12.854009	0.077797	34
35	10.676581	138.236878	0.007234	0.093663	12.947672	0.077234	35
36	11.423942	148.913460	0.006715	0.087535	13.035208	0.076715	36
37	12.223618	160.337402	0.006237	0.081809	13.117017	0.076237	37
38	13.079271	172.561020	0.005795	0.076457	13.193473	0.075795	38
39	13.994820	185.640292	0.005387	0.071455	13.264928	0.075387	39
40	14.974458	199.635112	0.005009	0.066780	13.331709	0.075009	40
41	16.022670	214.609570	0.004660	0.062412	13.394120	0.074660	41
42	17.144257	230.632240	0.004336	0.058329	13.452449	0.074336	42
43	18.344355	247.776496	0.004036	0.054513	13.506962	0.074036	43
44	19.628460	266.120851	0.003758	0.050946	13.557908	0.073758	44
45	21.002452	285.749311	0.003500	0.047613	13.605522	0.073500	45
46	22.472623	306.751763	0.003260	0.044499	13.650020	0.073260	46
47	24.045707	329.224386	0.003037	0.041587	13.691608	0.073037	47
48	25.728907	353.270093	0.002831	0.038867	13.730474	0.072831	48
49	27.529930	378.999000	0.002639	0.036324	13.766799	0.072639	49
50	29.457025	406.528929	0.002460	0.033948	13.800746	0.072460	50

ANNUAL COMPOUND INTEREST TABLES

8.00% ANNUAL INTEREST RATE

	1 AMOUNT OF $1 AT COMPOUND INTEREST	2 ACCUMULATION OF $1 PER PERIOD	3 SINKING FUND FACTOR	4 PRESENT VALUE REVERSION OF $1	5 PRESENT VALUE ORD. ANNUINTY $1 PER PERIOD	6 INSTALLMENT TO AMORTIZE $1	
YEARS							YEARS
1	1.080000	1.000000	1.000000	0.925926	0.925926	1.080000	1
2	1.166400	2.080000	0.480769	0.857339	1.783265	0.560769	2
3	1.259712	3.246400	0.308034	0.793832	2.577097	0.388034	3
4	1.360489	4.506112	0.221921	0.735030	3.312127	0.301921	4
5	1.469328	5.866601	0.170456	0.680583	3.992710	0.250456	5
6	1.586874	7.335929	0.136315	0.630170	4.622880	0.216315	6
7	1.713824	8.922803	0.112072	0.583490	5.206370	0.192072	7
8	1.850930	10.636628	0.094015	0.540269	5.746639	0.174015	8
9	1.999005	12.487558	0.080080	0.500249	6.246888	0.160080	9
10	2.158925	14.486562	0.069029	0.463193	6:710081	0.149029	10
11	2.331639	16.645487	0.060076	0.428883	7.138964	0.140076	11
12	2.518170	18.977126	0.052695	0.397114	7.536078	0.132695	12
13	2.719624	21.495297	0.046522	0.367698	7.903776	0.126522	13
14	2.937194	24.214920	0.041297	0.340461	8.244237	0.121297	14
15	3.172169	27.152114	0.036830	0.315242	8.559479	0.116830	15
16	3.425943	30.324283	0.032977	0.291890	8.851369	0.112977	16
17	3.700018	33.750226	0.029629	0.270269	9.121638	0.109629	17
18	3.996019	37.450244	0.026702	0.250249	9.371887	0.106702	18
19	4.315701	41.446263	0.024128	0.231712	9.603599	0.104128	19
20	4.660957	45.761964	0.021852	0.214548	9.818147	0.101852	20
21	5.033834	50.422921	0.019832	0.198656	10.016803	0.099832	21
22	5.436540	55.456755	0.018032	0.183941	10.200744	0.098032	22
23	5.871464	60.893296	0.016422	0.170315	10.371059	0.096422	23
24	6.341181	66.764759	0.014978	0.157699	10.528758	0.094978	24
25	6.848475	73.105940	0.013679	0.146018	10.674776	0.093679	25
26	7.396353	79.954415	0.012507	0.135202	10.809978	0.092507	26
27	7.988061	87.350768	0.011448	0.125187	10.935165	0.091448	27
28	8.627106	95.338830	0.010489	0.115914	11.051078	0.090489	28
29	9.317275	103.965936	0.009619	0.107328	11.158406	0.089619	29
30	10.062657	113.283211	0.008827	0.099377	11.257783	0.088827	30
31	10.867669	123.345868	0.008107	0.092016	11.349799	0.088107	31
32	11.737083	134.213537	0.007451	0.085200	11.434999	0.087451	32
33	12.676050	145.950620	0.006852	0.078889	11.513888	0.086852	33
34	13.690134	158.626670	0.006304	0.073045	11.586934	0.086304	34
35	14.785344	172.316804	0.005803	0.067635	11.654568	0.085803	35
36	15.968172	187.102148	0.005345	0.062625	11.717193	0.085345	36
37	17.245626	203.070320	0.004924	0.057986	11.775179	0.084924	37
38	18.625276	220.315945	0.004539	0.053690	11.828869	0.084539	38
39	20.115298	238.941221	0.004185	0.049713	11.878582	0.084185	39
40	21.724521	259.056519	0.003860	0.046031	11.924613	0.083860	40
41	23.462483	280.781040	0.003561	0.042621	11.967235	0.083561	41
42	25.339482	304.243523	0.003287	0.039464	12.006699	0.083287	42
43	27.366640	329.583005	0.003034	0.036541	12.043240	0.083034	43
44	29.555972	356.949646	0.002802	0.033834	12.077074	0.082802	44
45	31.920449	386.505617	0.002587	0.031328	12.108402	0.082587	45
46	34.474085	418.426067	0.002390	0.029007	12.137409	0.082390	46
47	37.232012	452.900152	0.002208	0.026859	12.164267	0.082208	47
48	40.210573	490.132164	0.002040	0.024869	12.189136	0.082040	48
49	43.427419	530.342737	0.001886	0.023027	12.212163	0.081886	49
50	46.901613	573.770156	0.001743	0.021321	12.233485	0.081743	50

ANNUAL COMPOUND INTEREST TABLES

9.00% ANNUAL INTEREST RATE

	1 AMOUNT OF $1 AT COMPOUND INTEREST	2 ACCUMULATION OF $1 PER PERIOD	3 SINKING FUND FACTOR	4 PRESENT VALUE REVERSION OF $1	5 PRESENT VALUE ORD. ANNUINTY $1 PER PERIOD	6 INSTALLMENT TO AMORTIZE $1	
YEARS							YEARS
1	1.090000	1.000000	1.000000	0.917431	0.917431	1.090000	1
2	1.188100	2.090000	0.478469	0.841680	1.759111	0.568469	2
3	1.295029	3.278100	0.305055	0.772183	2.531295	0.395055	3
4	1.411582	4.573129	0.218669	0.708425	3.239720	0.308669	4
5	1.538624	5.984711	0.167092	0.649931	3.889651	0.257092	5
6	1.677100	7.523335	0.132920	0.596267	4.485919	0.222920	6
7	1.828039	9.200435	0.108691	0.547034	5.032953	0.198691	7
8	1.992563	11.028474	0.090674	0.501866	5.534819	0.180674	8
9	2.171893	13.021036	0.076799	0.460428	5.995247	0.166799	9
10	2.367364	15.192930	0.065820	0.422411	6.417658	0.155820	10
11	2.580426	17.560293	0.056947	0.387533	6.805191	0.146947	11
12	2.812665	20.140720	0.049651	0.355535	7.160725	0.139651	12
13	3.065805	22.953385	0.043567	0.326179	7.486904	0.133567	13
14	3.341727	26.019189	0.038433	0.299246	7.786150	0.128433	14
15	3.642482	29.360916	0.034059	0.274538	8.060688	0.124059	15
16	3.970306	33.003399	0.030300	0.251870	8.312558	0.120300	16
17	4.327633	36.973705	0.027046	0.231073	8.543631	0.117046	17
18	4.717120	41.301338	0.024212	0.211994	8.755625	0.114212	18
19	5.141661	46.018458	0.021730	0.194490	8.950115	0.111730	19
20	5.604411	51.160120	0.019546	0.178431	9.128546	0.109546	20
21	6.108808	56.764530	0.017617	0.163698	9.292244	0.107617	21
22	6.658600	62.873338	0.015905	0.150182	9.442425	0.105905	22
23	7.257874	69.531939	0.014382	0.137781	9.580207	0.104382	23
24	7.911083	76.789813	0.013023	0.126405	9.706612	0.103023	24
25	8.623081	84.700896	0.011806	0.115968	9.822580	0.101806	25
26	9.399158	93.323977	0.010715	0.106393	9.928972	0.100715	26
27	10.245082	102.723135	0.009735	0.097608	10.026580	0.099735	27
28	11.167140	112.968217	0.008852	0.089548	10.116128	0.098852	28
29	12.172182	124.135356	0.008056	0.082155	10.198283	0.098056	29
30	13.267678	136.307539	0.007336	0.075371	10.273654	0.097336	30
31	14.461770	149.575217	0.006686	0.069148	10.342802	0.096686	31
32	15.763329	164.036987	0.006096	0.063438	10.406240	0.096096	32
33	17.182028	179.800315	0.005562	0.058200	10.464441	0.095562	33
34	18.728411	196.982344	0.005077	0.053395	10.517835	0.095077	34
35	20.413968	215.710755	0.004636	0.048986	10.566821	0.094636	35
36	22.251225	236.124723	0.004235	0.044941	10.611763	0.094235	36
37	24.253835	258.375948	0.003870	0.041231	10.652993	0.093870	37
38	26.436680	282.629783	0.003538	0.037826	10.690820	0.093538	38
39	28.815982	309.066463	0.003236	0.034703	10.725523	0.093236	39
40	31.409420	337.882445	0.002960	0.031838	10.757360	0.092960	40
41	34.236268	369.291865	0.002708	0.029209	10.786569	0.092708	41
42	37.317532	403.528133	0.002478	0.026797	10.813366	0.092478	42
43	40.676110	440.845665	0.002268	0.024584	10.837950	0.092268	43
44	44.336960	481.521775	0.002077	0.022555	10.860505	0.092077	44
45	48.327286	525.858734	0.001902	0.020692	10.881197	0.091902	45
46	52.676742	574.186021	0.001742	0.018984	10.900181	0.091742	46
47	57.417649	626.862762	0.001595	0.017416	10.917597	0.091595	47
48	62.585237	684.280411	0.001461	0.015978	10.933575	0.091461	48
49	68.217908	746.865648	0.001339	0.014659	10.948234	0.091339	49
50	74.357520	815.083556	0.001227	0.013449	10.961683	0.091227	50

ANNUAL COMPOUND INTEREST TABLES

10.00% ANNUAL INTEREST RATE

	1 AMOUNT OF $1 AT COMPOUND INTEREST	2 ACCUMULATION OF $1 PER PERIOD	3 SINKING FUND FACTOR	4 PRESENT VALUE REVERSION OF $1	5 PRESENT VALUE ORD. ANNUINTY $1 PER PERIOD	6 INSTALLMENT TO AMORTIZE $1	
YEARS							YEARS
1	1.100000	1.000000	1.000000	0.909091	0.909091	1.100000	1
2	1.210000	2.100000	0.476190	0.826446	1.735537	0.576190	2
3	1.331000	3.310000	0.302115	0.751315	2.486852	0.402115	3
4	1.464100	4.641000	0.215471	0.683013	3.169865	0.315471	4
5	1.610510	6.105100	0.163797	0.620921	3.790787	0.263797	5
6	1.771561	7.715610	0.129607	0.564474	4.355261	0.229607	6
7	1.948717	9.487171	0.105405	0.513158	4.868419	0.205405	7
8	2.143589	11.435888	0.087444	0.466507	5.334926	0.187444	8
9	2.357948	13.579477	0.073641	0.424098	5.759024	0.173641	9
10	2.593742	15.937425	0.062745	0.385543	6.144567	0.162745	10
11	2.853117	18.531167	0.053963	0.350494	6.495061	0.153963	11
12	3.138428	21.384284	0.046763	0.318631	6.813692	0.146763	12
13	3.452271	24.522712	0.040779	0.289664	7.103356	0.140779	13
14	3.797498	27.974983	0.035746	0.263331	7.366687	0.135746	14
15	4.177248	31.772482	0.031474	0.239392	7.606080	0.131474	15
16	4.594973	35.949730	0.027817	0.217629	7.823709	0.127817	16
17	5.054470	40.544703	0.024664	0.197845	8.021553	0.124664	17
18	5.559917	45.599173	0.021930	0.179859	8.201412	0.121930	18
19	6.115909	51.159090	0.019547	0.163508	8.364920	0.119547	19
20	6.727500	57.274999	0.017460	0.148644	8.513564	0.117460	20
21	7.400250	64.002499	0.015624	0.135131	8.648694	0.115624	21
22	8.140275	71.402749	0.014005	0.122846	8.771540	0.114005	22
23	8.954302	79.543024	0.012572	0.111678	8.883218	0.112572	23
24	9.849733	88.497327	0.011300	0.101526	8.984744	0.111300	24
25	10.834706	98.347059	0.010168	0.092296	9.077040	0.110168	25
26	11.918177	109.181765	0.009159	0.083905	9.160945	0.109159	26
27	13.109994	121.099942	0.008258	0.076278	9.237223	0.108258	27
28	14.420994	134.209936	0.007451	0.069343	9.306567	0.107451	28
29	15.863093	148.630930	0.006728	0.063039	9.369606	0.106728	29
30	17.449402	164.494023	0.006079	0.057309	9.426914	0.106079	30
31	19.194342	181.943425	0.005496	0.052099	9.479013	0.105496	31
32	21.113777	201.137767	0.004972	0.047362	9.526376	0.104972	32
33	23.225154	222.251544	0.004499	0.043057	9.569432	0.104499	33
34	25.547670	245.476699	0.004074	0.039143	9.608575	0.104074	34
35	28.102437	271.024368	0.003690	0.035584	9.644159	0.103690	35
36	30.912681	299.126805	0.003343	0.032349	9.676508	0.103343	36
37	34.003949	330.039486	0.003030	0.029408	9.705917	0.103030	37
38	37.404343	364.043434	0.002747	0.026735	9.732651	0.102747	38
39	41.144778	401.447778	0.002491	0.024304	9.756956	0.102491	39
40	45.259256	442.592556	0.002259	0.022095	9.779051	0.102259	40
41	49.785181	487.851811	0.002050	0.020086	9.799137	0.102050	41
42	54.763699	537.636992	0.001860	0.018260	9.817397	0.101860	42
43	60.240069	592.400692	0.001688	0.016600	9.833998	0.101688	43
44	66.264076	652.640761	0.001532	0.015091	9.849089	0.101532	44
45	72.890484	718.904837	0.001391	0.013719	9.862808	0.101391	45
46	80.179532	791.795321	0.001263	0.012472	9.875280	0.101263	46
47	88.197485	871.974853	0.001147	0.011338	9.886618	0.101147	47
48	97.017234	960.172338	0.001041	0.010307	9.896926	0.101041	48
49	106.718957	1057.189572	0.000946	0.009370	9.906296	0.100946	49
50	117.390853	1163.908529	0.000859	0.008519	9.914814	0.100859	50

ANNUAL COMPOUND INTEREST TABLES

11.00% ANNUAL INTEREST RATE

	1 AMOUNT OF $1 AT COMPOUND INTEREST	2 ACCUMULATION OF $1 PER PERIOD	3 SINKING FUND FACTOR	4 PRESENT VALUE REVERSION OF $1	5 PRESENT VALUE ORD. ANNUINTY $1 PER PERIOD	6 INSTALLMENT TO AMORTIZE $1	
YEARS							YEARS
1	1.110000	1.000000	1.000000	0.900901	0.900901	1.110000	1
2	1.232100	2.110000	0.473934	0.811622	1.712523	0.583934	2
3	1.367631	3.342100	0.299213	0.731191	2.443715	0.409213	3
4	1.518070	4.709731	0.212326	0.658731	3.102446	0.322326	4
5	1.685058	6.227801	0.160570	0.593451	3.695897	0.270570	5
6	1.870415	7.912860	0.126377	0.534641	4.230538	0.236377	6
7	2.076160	9.783274	0.102215	0.481658	4.712196	0.212215	7
8	2.304538	11.859434	0.084321	0.433926	5.146123	0.194321	8
9	2.558037	14.163972	0.070602	0.390925	5.537048	0.180602	9
10	2.839421	16.722009	0.059801	0.352184	5.889232	0.169801	10
11	3.151757	19.561430	0.051121	0.317283	6.206515	0.161121	11
12	3.498451	22.713187	0.044027	0.285841	6.492356	0.154027	12
13	3.883280	26.211638	0.038151	0.257514	6.749870	0.148151	13
14	4.310441	30.094918	0.033228	0.231995	6.981865	0.143228	14
15	4.784589	34.405359	0.029065	0.209004	7.190870	0.139065	15
16	5.310894	39.189948	0.025517	0.188292	7.379162	0.135517	16
17	5.895093	44.500843	0.022471	0.169633	7.548794	0.132471	17
18	6.543553	50.395936	0.019843	0.152822	7.701617	0.129843	18
19	7.263344	56.939488	0.017563	0.137678	7.839294	0.127563	19
20	8.062312	64.202832	0.015576	0.124034	7.963328	0.125576	20
21	8.949166	72.265144	0.013838	0.111742	8.075070	0.123838	21
22	9.933574	81.214309	0.012313	0.100669	8.175739	0.122313	22
23	11.026267	91.147884	0.010971	0.090693	8.266432	0.120971	23
24	12.239157	102.174151	0.009787	0.081705	8.348137	0.119787	24
25	13.585464	114.413307	0.008740	0.073608	8.421745	0.118740	25
26	15.079865	127.998771	0.007813	0.066314	8.488058	0.117813	26
27	16.738650	143.078636	0.006989	0.059742	8.547800	0.116989	27
28	18.579901	159.817286	0.006257	0.053822	8.601622	0.116257	28
29	20.623691	178.397187	0.005605	0.048488	8.650110	0.115605	29
30	22.892297	199.020878	0.005025	0.043683	8.693793	0.115025	30
31	25.410449	221.913174	0.004506	0.039354	8.733146	0.114506	31
32	28.205599	247.323624	0.004043	0.035454	8.768600	0.114043	32
33	31.308214	275.529222	0.003629	0.031940	8.800541	0.113629	33
34	34.752118	306.837437	0.003259	0.028775	8.829316	0.113259	34
35	38.574851	341.589555	0.002927	0.025924	8.855240	0.112927	35
36	42.818085	380.164406	0.002630	0.023355	8.878594	0.112630	36
37	47.528074	422.982490	0.002364	0.021040	8.899635	0.112364	37
38	52.756162	470.510564	0.002125	0.018955	8.918590	0.112125	38
39	58.559340	523.266726	0.001911	0.017077	8.935666	0.111911	39
40	65.000867	581.826066	0.001719	0.015384	8.951051	0.111719	40
41	72.150963	646.826934	0.001546	0.013860	8.964911	0.111546	41
42	80.087569	718.977896	0.001391	0.012486	8.977397	0.111391	42
43	88.897201	799.065465	0.001251	0.011249	8.988646	0.111251	43
44	98.675893	887.962666	0.001126	0.010134	8.998780	0.111126	44
45	109.530242	986.638559	0.001014	0.009130	9.007910	0.111014	45
46	121.578568	1096.168801	0.000912	0.008225	9.016135	0.110912	46
47	134.952211	1217.747369	0.000821	0.007410	9.023545	0.110821	47
48	149.796954	1352.699580	0.000739	0.006676	9.030221	0.110739	48
49	166.274619	1502.496533	0.000666	0.006014	9.036235	0.110666	49
50	184.564827	1668.771152	0.000599	0.005418	9.041653	0.110599	50

ANNUAL COMPOUND INTEREST TABLES

12.00% ANNUAL INTEREST RATE

YEARS	1 AMOUNT OF $1 AT COMPOUND INTEREST	2 ACCUMULATION OF $1 PER PERIOD	3 SINKING FUND FACTOR	4 PRESENT VALUE REVERSION OF $1	5 PRESENT VALUE ORD. ANNUINTY $1 PER PERIOD	6 INSTALLMENT TO AMORTIZE $1	YEARS
1	1.120000	1.000000	1.000000	0.892857	0.892857	1.120000	1
2	1.254400	2.120000	0.471698	0.797194	1.690051	0.591698	2
3	1.404928	3.374400	0.296349	0.711780	2.401831	0.416349	3
4	1.573519	4.779328	0.209234	0.635518	3.037349	0.329234	4
5	1.762342	6.352847	0.157410	0.567427	3.604776	0.277410	5
6	1.973823	8.115189	0.123226	0.506631	4.111407	0.243226	6
7	2.210681	10.089012	0.099118	0.452349	4.563757	0.219118	7
8	2.475963	12.299693	0.081303	0.403883	4.967640	0.201303	8
9	2.773079	14.775656	0.067679	0.360610	5.328250	0.187679	9
10	3.105848	17.548735	0.056984	0.321973	5.650223	0.176984	10
11	3.478550	20.654583	0.048415	0.287476	5.937699	0.168415	11
12	3.895976	24.133133	0.041437	0.256675	6.194374	0.161437	12
13	4.363493	28.029109	0.035677	0.229174	6.423548	0.155677	13
14	4.887112	32.392602	0.030871	0.204620	6.628168	0.150871	14
15	5.473566	37.279715	0.026824	0.182696	6.810864	0.146824	15
16	6.130394	42.753280	0.023390	0.163122	6.973986	0.143390	16
17	6.866041	48.883674	0.020457	0.145644	7.119630	0.140457	17
18	7.689966	55.749715	0.017937	0.130040	7.249670	0.137937	18
19	8.612762	63.439681	0.015763	0.116107	7.365777	0.135763	19
20	9.646293	72.052442	0.013879	0.103667	7.469444	0.133879	20
21	10.803848	81.698736	0.012240	0.092560	7.562003	0.132240	21
22	12.100310	92.502584	0.010811	0.082643	7.644646	0.130811	22
23	13.552347	104.602894	0.009560	0.073788	7.718434	0.129560	23
24	15.178629	118.155241	0.008463	0.065882	7.784316	0.128463	24
25	17.000064	133.333870	0.007500	0.058823	7.843139	0.127500	25
26	19.040072	150.333934	0.006652	0.052521	7.895660	0.126652	26
27	21.324881	169.374007	0.005904	0.046894	7.942554	0.125904	27
28	23.883866	190.698887	0.005244	0.041869	7.984423	0.125244	28
29	26.749930	214.582754	0.004660	0.037383	8.021806	0.124660	29
30	29.959922	241.332684	0.004144	0.033378	8.055184	0.124144	30
31	33.555113	271.292606	0.003686	0.029802	8.084986	0.123686	31
32	37.581726	304.847719	0.003280	0.026609	8.111594	0.123280	32
33	42.091533	342.429446	0.002920	0.023758	8.135352	0.122920	33
34	47.142517	384.520979	0.002601	0.021212	8.156564	0.122601	34
35	52.799620	431.663496	0.002317	0.018940	8.175504	0.122317	35
36	59.135574	484.463116	0.002064	0.016910	8.192414	0.122064	36
37	66.231843	543.598690	0.001840	0.015098	8.207513	0.121840	37
38	74.179664	609.830533	0.001640	0.013481	8.220993	0.121640	38
39	83.081224	684.010197	0.001462	0.012036	8.233030	0.121462	39
40	93.050970	767.091420	0.001304	0.010747	8.243777	0.121304	40
41	104.217087	860.142391	0.001163	0.009595	8.253372	0.121163	41
42	116.723137	964.359478	0.001037	0.008567	8.261939	0.121037	42
43	130.729914	1081.082615	0.000925	0.007649	8.269589	0.120925	43
44	146.417503	1211.812529	0.000825	0.006830	8.276418	0.120825	44
45	163.987604	1358.230032	0.000736	0.006098	8.282516	0.120736	45
46	183.666116	1522.217636	0.000657	0.005445	8.287961	0.120657	46
47	205.706050	1705.883752	0.000586	0.004861	8.292822	0.120586	47
48	230.390776	1911.589803	0.000523	0.004340	8.297163	0.120523	48
49	258.037669	2141.980579	0.000467	0.003875	8.301038	0.120467	49
50	289.002190	2400.018249	0.000417	0.003460	8.304498	0.120417	50

ANNUAL COMPOUND INTEREST TABLES

13.00% ANNUAL INTEREST RATE

	1 AMOUNT OF $1 AT COMPOUND INTEREST	2 ACCUMULATION OF $1 PER PERIOD	3 SINKING FUND FACTOR	4 PRESENT VALUE REVERSION OF $1	5 PRESENT VALUE ORD. ANNUINTY $1 PER PERIOD	6 INSTALLMENT TO AMORTIZE $1	
YEARS							YEARS
1	1.130000	1.000000	1.000000	0.884956	0.884956	1.130000	1
2	1.276900	2.130000	0.469484	0.783147	1.668102	0.599484	2
3	1.442897	3.406900	0.293522	0.693050	2.361153	0.423522	3
4	1.630474	4.849797	0.206194	0.613319	2.974471	0.336194	4
5	1.842435	6.480271	0.154315	0.542760	3.517231	0.284315	5
6	2.081952	8.322706	0.120153	0.480319	3.997550	0.250153	6
7	2.352605	10.404658	0.096111	0.425061	4.422610	0.226111	7
8	2.658444	12.757263	0.078387	0.376160	4.798770	0.208387	8
9	3.004042	15.415707	0.064869	0.332885	5.131655	0.194869	9
10	3.394567	18.419749	0.054290	0.294588	5.426243	0.184290	10
11	3.835861	21.814317	0.045841	0.260698	5.686941	0.175841	11
12	4.334523	25.650178	0.038986	0.230706	5.917647	0.168986	12
13	4.898011	29.984701	0.033350	0.204165	6.121812	0.163350	13
14	5.534753	34.882712	0.028667	0.180677	6.302488	0.158667	14
15	6.254270	40.417464	0.024742	0.159891	6.462379	0.154742	15
16	7.067326	46.671735	0.021426	0.141496	6.603875	0.151426	16
17	7.986078	53.739060	0.018608	0.125218	6.729093	0.148608	17
18	9.024268	61.725138	0.016201	0.110812	6.839905	0.146201	18
19	10.197423	70.749406	0.014134	0.098064	6.937969	0.144134	19
20	11.523088	80.946829	0.012354	0.086782	7.024752	0.142354	20
21	13.021089	92.469917	0.010814	0.076798	7.101550	0.140814	21
22	14.713831	105.491006	0.009479	0.067963	7.169513	0.139479	22
23	16.626629	120.204837	0.008319	0.060144	7.229658	0.138319	23
24	18.788091	136.831465	0.007308	0.053225	7.282883	0.137308	24
25	21.230542	155.619556	0.006426	0.047102	7.329985	0.136426	25
26	23.990513	176.850098	0.005655	0.041683	7.371668	0.135655	26
27	27.109279	200.840611	0.004979	0.036888	7.408556	0.134979	27
28	30.633486	227.949890	0.004387	0.032644	7.441200	0.134387	28
29	34.615839	258.583376	0.003867	0.028889	7.470088	0.133867	29
30	39.115898	293.199215	0.003411	0.025565	7.495653	0.133411	30
31	44.200965	332.315113	0.003009	0.022624	7.518277	0.133009	31
32	49.947090	376.516078	0.002656	0.020021	7.538299	0.132656	32
33	56.440212	426.463168	0.002345	0.017718	7.556016	0.132345	33
34	63.777439	482.903380	0.002071	0.015680	7.571696	0.132071	34
35	72.068506	546.680819	0.001829	0.013876	7.585572	0.131829	35
36	81.437412	618.749325	0.001616	0.012279	7.597851	0.131616	36
37	92.024276	700.186738	0.001428	0.010867	7.608718	0.131428	37
38	103.987432	792.211014	0.001262	0.009617	7.618334	0.131262	38
39	117.505798	896.198445	0.001116	0.008510	7.626844	0.131116	39
40	132.781552	1013.704243	0.000986	0.007531	7.634376	0.130986	40
41	150.043153	1146.485795	0.000872	0.006665	7.641040	0.130872	41
42	169.548763	1296.528948	0.000771	0.005898	7.646938	0.130771	42
43	191.590103	1466.077712	0.000682	0.005219	7.652158	0.130682	43
44	216.496816	1657.667814	0.000603	0.004619	7.656777	0.130603	44
45	244.641402	1874.164630	0.000534	0.004088	7.660864	0.130534	45
46	276.444784	2118.806032	0.000472	0.003617	7.664482	0.130472	46
47	312.382606	2395.250816	0.000417	0.003201	7.667683	0.130417	47
48	352.992345	2707.633422	0.000369	0.002833	7.670516	0.130369	48
49	398.881350	3060.625767	0.000327	0.002507	7.673023	0.130327	49
50	450.735925	3459.507117	0.000289	0.002219	7.675242	0.130289	50

ANNUAL COMPOUND INTEREST TABLES

14.00% ANNUAL INTEREST RATE

	1 AMOUNT OF $1 AT COMPOUND INTEREST	2 ACCUMULATION OF $1 PER PERIOD	3 SINKING FUND FACTOR	4 PRESENT VALUE REVERSION OF $1	5 PRESENT VALUE ORD. ANNUINTY $1 PER PERIOD	6 INSTALLMENT TO AMORTIZE $1	
YEARS							YEARS
1	1.140000	1.000000	1.000000	0.877193	0.877193	1.140000	1
2	1.299600	2.140000	0.467290	0.769468	1.646661	0.607290	2
3	1.481544	3.439600	0.290731	0.674972	2.321632	0.430731	3
4	1.688960	4.921144	0.203205	0.592080	2.913712	0.343205	4
5	1.925415	6.610104	0.151284	0.519369	3.433081	0.291284	5
6	2.194973	8.535519	0.117157	0.455587	3.888668	0.257157	6
7	2.502269	10.730491	0.093192	0.399637	4.288305	0.233192	7
8	2.852586	13.232760	0.075570	0.350559	4.638864	0.215570	8
9	3.251949	16.085347	0.062168	0.307508	4.946372	0.202168	9
10	3.707221	19.337295	0.051714	0.269744	5.216116	0.191714	10
11	4.226232	23.044516	0.043394	0.236617	5.452733	0.183394	11
12	4.817905	27.270749	0.036669	0.207559	5.660292	0.176669	12
13	5.492411	32.088654	0.031164	0.182069	5.842362	0.171164	13
14	6.261349	37.581065	0.026609	0.159710	6.002072	0.166609	14
15	7.137938	43.842414	0.022809	0.140096	6.142168	0.162809	15
16	8.137249	50.980352	0.019615	0.122892	6.265060	0.159615	16
17	9.276464	59.117601	0.016915	0.107800	6.372859	0.156915	17
18	10.575169	68.394066	0.014621	0.094561	6.467420	0.154621	18
19	12.055693	78.969235	0.012663	0.082948	6.550369	0.152663	19
20	13.743490	91.024928	0.010986	0.072762	6.623131	0.150986	20
21	15.667578	104.768418	0.009545	0.063826	6.686957	0.149545	21
22	17.861039	120.435996	0.008303	0.055988	6.742944	0.148303	22
23	20.361585	138.297035	0.007231	0.049112	6.792056	0.147231	23
24	23.212207	158.658620	0.006303	0.043081	6.835137	0.146303	24
25	26.461916	181.870827	0.005498	0.037790	6.872927	0.145498	25
26	30.166584	208.332743	0.004800	0.033149	6.906077	0.144800	26
27	34.389906	238.499327	0.004193	0.029078	6.935155	0.144193	27
28	39.204493	272.889233	0.003664	0.025507	6.960662	0.143664	28
29	44.693122	312.093725	0.003204	0.022375	6.983037	0.143204	29
30	50.950159	356.786847	0.002803	0.019627	7.002664	0.142803	30
31	58.083181	407.737006	0.002453	0.017217	7.019881	0.142453	31
32	66.214826	465.820186	0.002147	0.015102	7.034983	0.142147	32
33	75.484902	532.035012	0.001880	0.013248	7.048231	0.141880	33
34	86.052788	607.519914	0.001646	0.011621	7.059852	0.141646	34
35	98.100178	693.572702	0.001442	0.010194	7.070045	0.141442	35
36	111.834203	791.672881	0.001263	0.008942	7.078987	0.141263	36
37	127.490992	903.507084	0.001107	0.007844	7.086831	0.141107	37
38	145.339731	1030.998076	0.000970	0.006880	7.093711	0.140970	38
39	165.687293	1176.337806	0.000850	0.006035	7.099747	0.140850	39
40	188.883514	1342.025099	0.000745	0.005294	7.105041	0.140745	40
41	215.327206	1530.908613	0.000653	0.004644	7.109685	0.140653	41
42	245.473015	1746.235819	0.000573	0.004074	7.113759	0.140573	42
43	279.839237	1991.708833	0.000502	0.003573	7.117332	0.140502	43
44	319.016730	2271.548070	0.000440	0.003135	7.120467	0.140440	44
45	363.679072	2590.564800	0.000386	0.002750	7.123217	0.140386	45
46	414.594142	2954.243872	0.000338	0.002412	7.125629	0.140338	46
47	472.637322	3368.838014	0.000297	0.002116	7.127744	0.140297	47
48	538.806547	3841.475336	0.000260	0.001856	7.129600	0.140260	48
49	614.239464	4380.281883	0.000228	0.001628	7.131228	0.140228	49
50	700.232988	4994.521346	0.000200	0.001428	7.132656	0.140200	50

ANNUAL COMPOUND INTEREST TABLES

15.00% ANNUAL INTEREST RATE

	1	2	3	4	5	6	
	AMOUNT OF $1 AT COMPOUND INTEREST	ACCUMULATION OF $1 PER PERIOD	SINKING FUND FACTOR	PRESENT VALUE REVERSION OF $1	PRESENT VALUE ORD. ANNUITY $1 PER PERIOD	INSTALLMENT TO AMORTIZE $1	
YEARS							YEARS
1	1.150000	1.000000	1.000000	0.869565	0.869565	1.150000	1
2	1.322500	2.150000	0.465116	0.756144	1.625709	0.615116	2
3	1.520875	3.472500	0.287977	0.657516	2.283225	0.437977	3
4	1.749006	4.993375	0.200265	0.571753	2.854978	0.350265	4
5	2.011357	6.742381	0.148316	0.497177	3.352155	0.298316	5
6	2.313061	8.753738	0.114237	0.432328	3.784483	0.264237	6
7	2.660020	11.066799	0.090360	0.375937	4.160420	0.240360	7
8	3.059023	13.726819	0.072850	0.326902	4.487322	0.222850	8
9	3.517876	16.785842	0.059574	0.284262	4.771584	0.209574	9
10	4.045558	20.303718	0.049252	0.247185	5.018769	0.199252	10
11	4.652391	24.349276	0.041069	0.214943	5.233712	0.191069	11
12	5.350250	29.001667	0.034481	0.186907	5.420619	0.184481	12
13	6.152788	34.351917	0.029110	0.162528	5.583147	0.179110	13
14	7.075706	40.504705	0.024688	0.141329	5.724476	0.174688	14
15	8.137062	47.580411	0.021017	0.122894	5.847370	0.171017	15
16	9.357621	55.717472	0.017948	0.106865	5.954235	0.167948	16
17	10.761264	65.075093	0.015367	0.092926	6.047161	0.165367	17
18	12.375454	75.836357	0.013186	0.080805	6.127966	0.163186	18
19	14.231772	88.211811	0.011336	0.070265	6.198231	0.161336	19
20	16.366537	102.443583	0.009761	0.061100	6.259331	0.159761	20
21	18.821518	118.810120	0.008417	0.053131	6.312462	0.158417	21
22	21.644746	137.631638	0.007266	0.046201	6.358663	0.157266	22
23	24.891458	159.276384	0.006278	0.040174	6.398837	0.156278	23
24	28.625176	184.167841	0.005430	0.034934	6.433771	0.155430	24
25	32.918953	212.793017	0.004699	0.030378	6.464149	0.154699	25
26	37.856796	245.711970	0.004070	0.026415	6.490564	0.154070	26
27	43.535315	283.568766	0.003526	0.022970	6.513534	0.153526	27
28	50.065612	327.104080	0.003057	0.019974	6.533508	0.153057	28
29	57.575454	377.169693	0.002651	0.017369	6.550877	0.152651	29
30	66.211772	434.745146	0.002300	0.015103	6.565980	0.152300	30
31	76.143538	500.956918	0.001996	0.013133	6.579113	0.151996	31
32	87.565068	577.100456	0.001733	0.011420	6.590533	0.151733	32
33	100.699829	664.665524	0.001505	0.009931	6.600463	0.151505	33
34	115.804803	765.365353	0.001307	0.008635	6.609099	0.151307	34
35	133.175523	881.170156	0.001135	0.007509	6.616607	0.151135	35
36	153.151852	1014.345680	0.000986	0.006529	6.623137	0.150986	36
37	176.124630	1167.497532	0.000857	0.005678	6.628815	0.150857	37
38	202.543324	1343.622161	0.000744	0.004937	6.633752	0.150744	38
39	232.924823	1546.165485	0.000647	0.004293	6.638045	0.150647	39
40	267.863546	1779.090308	0.000562	0.003733	6.641778	0.150562	40
41	308.043078	2046.953854	0.000489	0.003246	6.645025	0.150489	41
42	354.249540	2354.996933	0.000425	0.002823	6.647848	0.150425	42
43	407.386971	2709.246473	0.000369	0.002455	6.650302	0.150369	43
44	468.495017	3116.633443	0.000321	0.002134	6.652437	0.150321	44
45	538.769269	3585.128460	0.000279	0.001856	6.654293	0.150279	45
46	619.584659	4123.897729	0.000242	0.001614	6.655907	0.150242	46
47	712.522358	4743.482388	0.000211	0.001403	6.657310	0.150211	47
48	819.400712	5456.004746	0.000183	0.001220	6.658531	0.150183	48
49	942.310819	6275.405458	0.000159	0.001061	6.659592	0.150159	49
50	1083.657442	7217.716277	0.000139	0.000923	6.660515	0.150139	50

ANNUAL COMPOUND INTEREST TABLES

16.00% ANNUAL INTEREST RATE

	1 AMOUNT OF $1 AT COMPOUND INTEREST	2 ACCUMULATION OF $1 PER PERIOD	3 SINKING FUND FACTOR	4 PRESENT VALUE REVERSION OF $1	5 PRESENT VALUE ORD. ANNUINTY $1 PER PERIOD	6 INSTALLMENT TO AMORTIZE $1	
YEARS							YEARS
1	1.160000	1.000000	1.000000	0.862069	0.862069	1.160000	1
2	1.345600	2.160000	0.462963	0.743163	1.605232	0.622963	2
3	1.560896	3.505600	0.285258	0.640658	2.245890	0.445258	3
4	1.810639	5.066496	0.197375	0.552291	2.798181	0.357375	4
5	2.100342	6.877135	0.145409	0.476113	3.274294	0.305409	5
6	2.436396	8.977477	0.111390	0.410442	3.684736	0.271390	6
7	2.826220	11.413873	0.087613	0.353830	4.038565	0.247613	7
8	3.278415	14.240093	0.070224	0.305025	4.343591	0.230224	8
9	3.802961	17.518508	0.057082	0.262953	4.606544	0.217082	9
10	4.411435	21.321469	0.046901	0.226684	4.833227	0.206901	10
11	5.117265	25.732904	0.038861	0.195417	5.028644	0.198861	11
12	5.936027	30.850169	0.032415	0.168463	5.197107	0.192415	12
13	6.885791	36.786196	0.027184	0.145227	5.342334	0.187184	13
14	7.987518	43.671987	0.022898	0.125195	5.467529	0.182898	14
15	9.265521	51.659505	0.019358	0.107927	5.575456	0.179358	15
16	10.748004	60.925026	0.016414	0.093041	5.668497	0.176414	16
17	12.467685	71.673030	0.013952	0.080207	5.748704	0.173952	17
18	14.462514	84.140715	0.011885	0.069144	5.817848	0.171885	18
19	16.776517	98.603230	0.010142	0.059607	5.877455	0.170142	19
20	19.460759	115.379747	0.008667	0.051385	5.928841	0.168667	20
21	22.574481	134.840506	0.007416	0.044298	5.973139	0.167416	21
22	26.186398	157.414987	0.006353	0.038188	6.011326	0.166353	22
23	30.376222	183.601385	0.005447	0.032920	6.044247	0.165447	23
24	35.236417	213.977607	0.004673	0.028380	6.072627	0.164673	24
25	40.874244	249.214024	0.004013	0.024465	6.097092	0.164013	25
26	47.414123	290.088267	0.003447	0.021091	6.118183	0.163447	26
27	55.000382	337.502390	0.002963	0.018182	6.136364	0.162963	27
28	63.800444	392.502773	0.002548	0.015674	6.152038	0.162548	28
29	74.008515	456.303216	0.002192	0.013512	6.165550	0.162192	29
30	85.849877	530.311731	0.001886	0.011648	6.177198	0.161886	30
31	99.585857	616.161608	0.001623	0.010042	6.187240	0.161623	31
32	115.519594	715.747465	0.001397	0.008657	6.195897	0.161397	32
33	134.002729	831.267059	0.001203	0.007463	6.203359	0.161203	33
34	155.443166	965.269789	0.001036	0.006433	6.209792	0.161036	34
35	180.314073	1120.712955	0.000892	0.005546	6.215338	0.160892	35
36	209.164324	1301.027028	0.000769	0.004781	6.220119	0.160769	36
37	242.630616	1510.191352	0.000662	0.004121	6.224241	0.160662	37
38	281.451515	1752.821968	0.000571	0.003553	6.227794	0.160571	38
39	326.483757	2034.273483	0.000492	0.003063	6.230857	0.160492	39
40	378.721158	2360.757241	0.000424	0.002640	6.233497	0.160424	40
41	439.316544	2739.478399	0.000365	0.002276	6.235773	0.160365	41
42	509.607191	3178.794943	0.000315	0.001962	6.237736	0.160315	42
43	591.144341	3688.402134	0.000271	0.001692	6.239427	0.160271	43
44	685.727436	4279.546475	0.000234	0.001458	6.240886	0.160234	44
45	795.443826	4965.273911	0.000201	0.001257	6.242143	0.160201	45
46	922.714838	5760.717737	0.000174	0.001084	6.243227	0.160174	46
47	1070.349212	6683.432575	0.000150	0.000934	6.244161	0.160150	47
48	1241.605086	7753.781787	0.000129	0.000805	6.244966	0.160129	48
49	1440.261900	8995.386873	0.000111	0.000694	6.245661	0.160111	49
50	1670.703804	10435.648773	0.000096	0.000599	6.246259	0.160096	50

ANNUAL COMPOUND INTEREST TABLES

17.00% ANNUAL INTEREST RATE

	1 AMOUNT OF $1 AT COMPOUND INTEREST	2 ACCUMULATION OF $1 PER PERIOD	3 SINKING FUND FACTOR	4 PRESENT VALUE REVERSION OF $1	5 PRESENT VALUE ORD. ANNUINTY $1 PER PERIOD	6 INSTALLMENT TO AMORTIZE $1	
YEARS							YEARS
1	1.170000	1.000000	1.000000	0.854701	0.854701	1.170000	1
2	1.368900	2.170000	0.460829	0.730514	1.585214	0.630829	2
3	1.601613	3.538900	0.282574	0.624371	2.209585	0.452574	3
4	1.873887	5.140513	0.194533	0.533650	2.743235	0.364533	4
5	2.192448	7.014400	0.142564	0.456111	3.199346	0.312564	5
6	2.565164	9.206848	0.108615	0.389839	3.589185	0.278615	6
7	3.001242	11.772012	0.084947	0.333195	3.922380	0.254947	7
8	3.511453	14.773255	0.067690	0.284782	4.207163	0.237690	8
9	4.108400	18.284708	0.054691	0.243404	4.450566	0.224691	9
10	4.806828	22.393108	0.044657	0.208037	4.658604	0.214657	10
11	5.623989	27.199937	0.036765	0.177810	4.836413	0.206765	11
12	6.580067	32.823926	0.030466	0.151974	4.988387	0.200466	12
13	7.698679	39.403993	0.025378	0.129892	5.118280	0.195378	13
14	9.007454	47.102672	0.021230	0.111019	5.229299	0.191230	14
15	10.538721	56.110126	0.017822	0.094888	5.324187	0.187822	15
16	12.330304	66.648848	0.015004	0.081101	5.405288	0.185004	16
17	14.426456	78.979152	0.012662	0.069317	5.474605	0.182662	17
18	16.878953	93.405608	0.010706	0.059245	5.533851	0.180706	18
19	19.748375	110.284561	0.009067	0.050637	5.584488	0.179067	19
20	23.105599	130.032936	0.007690	0.043280	5.627767	0.177690	20
21	27.033551	153.138535	0.006530	0.036991	5.664758	0.176530	21
22	31.629255	180.172086	0.005550	0.031616	5.696375	0.175550	22
23	37.006228	211.801341	0.004721	0.027022	5.723397	0.174721	23
24	43.297287	248.807569	0.004019	0.023096	5.746493	0.174019	24
25	50.657826	292.104856	0.003423	0.019740	5.766234	0.173423	25
26	59.269656	342.762681	0.002917	0.016872	5.783106	0.172917	26
27	69.345497	402.032337	0.002487	0.014421	5.797526	0.172487	27
28	81.134232	471.377835	0.002121	0.012325	5.809851	0.172121	28
29	94.927051	552.512066	0.001810	0.010534	5.820386	0.171810	29
30	111.064650	647.439118	0.001545	0.009004	5.829390	0.171545	30
31	129.945641	758.503768	0.001318	0.007696	5.837085	0.171318	31
32	152.036399	888.449408	0.001126	0.006577	5.843663	0.171126	32
33	177.882587	1040.485808	0.000961	0.005622	5.849284	0.170961	33
34	208.122627	1218.368395	0.000821	0.004805	5.854089	0.170821	34
35	243.503474	1426.491022	0.000701	0.004107	5.858196	0.170701	35
36	284.899064	1669.994496	0.000599	0.003510	5.861706	0.170599	36
37	333.331905	1954.893560	0.000512	0.003000	5.864706	0.170512	37
38	389.998329	2288.225465	0.000437	0.002564	5.867270	0.170437	38
39	456.298045	2678.223794	0.000373	0.002192	5.869461	0.170373	39
40	533.868713	3134.521839	0.000319	0.001873	5.871335	0.170319	40
41	624.626394	3668.390552	0.000273	0.001601	5.872936	0.170273	41
42	730.812881	4293.016946	0.000233	0.001368	5.874304	0.170233	42
43	855.051071	5023.829827	0.000199	0.001170	5.875473	0.170199	43
44	1000.409753	5878.880897	0.000170	0.001000	5.876473	0.170170	44
45	1170.479411	6879.290650	0.000145	0.000854	5.877327	0.170145	45
46	1369.460910	8049.770061	0.000124	0.000730	5.878058	0.170124	46
47	1602.269265	9419.230971	0.000106	0.000624	5.878682	0.170106	47
48	1874.655040	11021.500236	0.000091	0.000533	5.879215	0.170091	48
49	2193.346397	12896.155276	0.000078	0.000456	5.879671	0.170078	49
50	2566.215284	15089.501673	0.000066	0.000390	5.880061	0.170066	50

ANNUAL COMPOUND INTEREST TABLES

18.00% ANNUAL INTEREST RATE

	1 AMOUNT OF $1 AT COMPOUND INTEREST	2 ACCUMULATION OF $1 PER PERIOD	3 SINKING FUND FACTOR	4 PRESENT VALUE REVERSION OF $1	5 PRESENT VALUE ORD. ANNUINTY $1 PER PERIOD	6 INSTALLMENT TO AMORTIZE $1	
YEARS							YEARS
1	1.180000	1.000000	1.000000	0.847458	0.847458	1.180000	1
2	1.392400	2.180000	0.458716	0.718184	1.565642	0.638716	2
3	1.643032	3.572400	0.279924	0.608631	2.174273	0.459924	3
4	1.938778	5.215432	0.191739	0.515789	2.690062	0.371739	4
5	2.287758	7.154210	0.139778	0.437109	3.127171	0.319778	5
6	2.699554	9.441968	0.105910	0.370432	3.497603	0.285910	6
7	3.185474	12.141522	0.082362	0.313925	3.811528	0.262362	7
8	3.758859	15.326996	0.065244	0.266038	4.077566	0.245244	8
9	4.435454	19.085855	0.052395	0.225456	4.303022	0.232395	9
10	5.233836	23.521309	0.042515	0.191064	4.494086	0.222515	10
11	6.175926	28.755144	0.034776	0.161919	4.656005	0.214776	11
12	7.287593	34.931070	0.028628	0.137220	4.793225	0.208628	12
13	8.599359	42.218663	0.023686	0.116288	4.909513	0.203686	13
14	10.147244	50.818022	0.019678	0.098549	5.008062	0.199678	14
15	11.973748	60.965266	0.016403	0.083516	5.091578	0.196403	15
16	14.129023	72.939014	0.013710	0.070776	5.162354	0.193710	16
17	16.672247	87.068036	0.011485	0.059980	5.222334	0.191485	17
18	19.673251	103.740283	0.009639	0.050830	5.273164	0.189639	18
19	23.214436	123.413534	0.008103	0.043077	5.316241	0.188103	19
20	27.393035	146.627970	0.006820	0.036506	5.352746	0.186820	20
21	32.323781	174.021005	0.005746	0.030937	5.383683	0.185746	21
22	38.142061	206.344785	0.004846	0.026218	5.409901	0.184846	22
23	45.007632	244.486847	0.004090	0.022218	5.432120	0.184090	23
24	53.109006	289.494479	0.003454	0.018829	5.450949	0.183454	24
25	62.668627	342.603486	0.002919	0.015957	5.466906	0.182919	25
26	73.948980	405.272113	0.002467	0.013523	5.480429	0.182467	26
27	87.259797	479.221093	0.002087	0.011460	5.491889	0.182087	27
28	102.966560	566.480890	0.001765	0.009712	5.501601	0.181765	28
29	121.500541	669.447450	0.001494	0.008230	5.509831	0.181494	29
30	143.370638	790.947991	0.001264	0.006975	5.516806	0.181264	30
31	169.177353	934.318630	0.001070	0.005911	5.522717	0.181070	31
32	199.629277	1103.495983	0.000906	0.005009	5.527726	0.180906	32
33	235.562547	1303.125260	0.000767	0.004245	5.531971	0.180767	33
34	277.963805	1538.687807	0.000650	0.003598	5.535569	0.180650	34
35	327.997290	1816.651612	0.000550	0.003049	5.538618	0.180550	35
36	387.036802	2144.648902	0.000466	0.002584	5.541201	0.180466	36
37	456.705427	2531.685705	0.000395	0.002190	5.543391	0.180395	37
38	538.910044	2988.389132	0.000335	0.001856	5.545247	0.180335	38
39	635.913852	3527.299175	0.000284	0.001573	5.546819	0.180284	39
40	750.378345	4163.213027	0.000240	0.001333	5.548152	0.180240	40
41	885.446447	4913.591372	0.000204	0.001129	5.549281	0.180204	41
42	1044.826807	5799.037819	0.000172	0.000957	5.550238	0.180172	42
43	1232.895633	6843.864626	0.000146	0.000811	5.551049	0.180146	43
44	1454.816847	8076.760259	0.000124	0.000687	5.551737	0.180124	44
45	1716.683879	9531.577105	0.000105	0.000583	5.552319	0.180105	45
46	2025.686977	11248.260984	0.000089	0.000494	5.552813	0.180089	46
47	2390.310633	13273.947961	0.000075	0.000418	5.553231	0.180075	47
48	2820.566547	15664.258594	0.000064	0.000355	5.553586	0.180064	48
49	3328.268525	18484.825141	0.000054	0.000300	5.553886	0.180054	49
50	3927.356860	21813.093666	0.000046	0.000255	5.554141	0.180046	50

ANNUAL COMPOUND INTEREST TABLES

19.00% ANNUAL INTEREST RATE

YEARS	1 AMOUNT OF $1 AT COMPOUND INTEREST	2 ACCUMULATION OF $1 PER PERIOD	3 SINKING FUND FACTOR	4 PRESENT VALUE REVERSION OF $1	5 PRESENT VALUE ORD. ANNUINTY $1 PER PERIOD	6 INSTALLMENT TO AMORTIZE $1	YEARS
1	1.190000	1.000000	1.000000	0.840336	0.840336	1.190000	1
2	1.416100	2.190000	0.456621	0.706165	1.546501	0.646621	2
3	1.685159	3.606100	0.277308	0.593416	2.139917	0.467308	3
4	2.005339	5.291259	0.188991	0.498669	2.638586	0.378991	4
5	2.386354	7.296598	0.137050	0.419049	3.057635	0.327050	5
6	2.839761	9.682952	0.103274	0.352142	3.409777	0.293274	6
7	3.379315	12.522713	0.079855	0.295918	3.705695	0.269855	7
8	4.021385	15.902028	0.062885	0.248671	3.954366	0.252885	8
9	4.785449	19.923413	0.050192	0.208967	4.163332	0.240192	9
10	5.694684	24.708862	0.040471	0.175602	4.338935	0.230471	10
11	6.776674	30.403546	0.032891	0.147565	4.486500	0.222891	11
12	8.064242	37.180220	0.026896	0.124004	4.610504	0.216896	12
13	9.596448	45.244461	0.022102	0.104205	4.714709	0.212102	13
14	11.419773	54.840909	0.018235	0.087567	4.802277	0.208235	14
15	13.589530	66.260682	0.015092	0.073586	4.875863	0.205092	15
16	16.171540	79.850211	0.012523	0.061837	4.937700	0.202523	16
17	19.244133	96.021751	0.010414	0.051964	4.989664	0.200414	17
18	22.900518	115.265884	0.008676	0.043667	5.033331	0.198676	18
19	27.251616	138.166402	0.007238	0.036695	5.070026	0.197238	19
20	32.429423	165.418018	0.006045	0.030836	5.100862	0.196045	20
21	38.591014	197.847442	0.005054	0.025913	5.126775	0.195054	21
22	45.923307	236.438456	0.004229	0.021775	5.148550	0.194229	22
23	54.648735	282.361762	0.003542	0.018299	5.166849	0.193542	23
24	65.031994	337.010497	0.002967	0.015377	5.182226	0.192967	24
25	77.388073	402.042491	0.002487	0.012922	5.195148	0.192487	25
26	92.091807	479.430565	0.002086	0.010859	5.206007	0.192086	26
27	109.589251	571.522372	0.001750	0.009125	5.215132	0.191750	27
28	130.411208	681.111623	0.001468	0.007668	5.222800	0.191468	28
29	155.189338	811.522831	0.001232	0.006444	5.229243	0.191232	29
30	184.675312	966.712169	0.001034	0.005415	5.234658	0.191034	30
31	219.763621	1151.387481	0.000869	0.004550	5.239209	0.190869	31
32	261.518710	1371.151103	0.000729	0.003824	5.243033	0.190729	32
33	311.207264	1632.669812	0.000612	0.003213	5.246246	0.190612	33
34	370.336645	1943.877077	0.000514	0.002700	5.248946	0.190514	34
35	440.700607	2314.213721	0.000432	0.002269	5.251215	0.190432	35
36	524.433722	2754.914328	0.000363	0.001907	5.253122	0.190363	36
37	624.076130	3279.348051	0.000305	0.001602	5.254724	0.190305	37
38	742.650594	3903.424180	0.000256	0.001347	5.256071	0.190256	38
39	883.754207	4646.074775	0.000215	0.001132	5.257202	0.190215	39
40	1051.667507	5529.828982	0.000181	0.000951	5.258153	0.190181	40
41	1251.484333	6581.496488	0.000152	0.000799	5.258952	0.190152	41
42	1489.266356	7832.980821	0.000128	0.000671	5.259624	0.190128	42
43	1772.226964	9322.247177	0.000107	0.000564	5.260188	0.190107	43
44	2108.950087	11094.474141	0.000090	0.000474	5.260662	0.190090	44
45	2509.650603	13203.424228	0.000076	0.000398	5.261061	0.190076	45
46	2986.484218	15713.074831	0.000064	0.000335	5.261396	0.190064	46
47	3553.916219	18699.559049	0.000053	0.000281	5.261677	0.190053	47
48	4229.160301	22253.475268	0.000045	0.000236	5.261913	0.190045	48
49	5032.700758	26482.635569	0.000038	0.000199	5.262112	0.190038	49
50	5988.913902	31515.336327	0.000032	0.000167	5.262279	0.190032	50

ANNUAL COMPOUND INTEREST TABLES

20.00% ANNUAL INTEREST RATE

	1 AMOUNT OF $1 AT COMPOUND INTEREST	2 ACCUMULATION OF $1 PER PERIOD	3 SINKING FUND FACTOR	4 PRESENT VALUE REVERSION OF $1	5 PRESENT VALUE ORD. ANNUINTY $1 PER PERIOD	6 INSTALLMENT TO AMORTIZE $1	
YEARS							YEARS
1	1.200000	1.000000	1.000000	0.833333	0.833333	1.200000	1
2	1.440000	2.200000	0.454545	0.694444	1.527778	0.654545	2
3	1.728000	3.640000	0.274725	0.578704	2.106481	0.474725	3
4	2.073600	5.368000	0.186289	0.482253	2.588735	0.386289	4
5	2.488320	7.441600	0.134380	0.401878	2.990612	0.334380	5
6	2.985984	9.929920	0.100706	0.334898	3.325510	0.300706	6
7	3.583181	12.915904	0.077424	0.279082	3.604592	0.277424	7
8	4.299817	16.499085	0.060609	0.232568	3.837160	0.260609	8
9	5.159780	20.798902	0.048079	0.193807	4.030967	0.248079	9
10	6.191736	25.958682	0.038523	0.161506	4.192472	0.238523	10
11	7.430084	32.150419	0.031104	0.134588	4.327060	0.231104	11
12	8.916100	39.580502	0.025265	0.112157	4.439217	0.225265	12
13	10.699321	48.496603	0.020620	0.093464	4.532681	0.220620	13
14	12.839185	59.195923	0.016893	0.077887	4.610567	0.216893	14
15	15.407022	72.035108	0.013882	0.064905	4.675473	0.213882	15
16	18.488426	87.442129	0.011436	0.054088	4.729561	0.211436	16
17	22.186111	105.930555	0.009440	0.045073	4.774634	0.209440	17
18	26.623333	128.116666	0.007805	0.037561	4.812195	0.207805	18
19	31.948000	154.740000	0.006462	0.031301	4.843496	0.206462	19
20	38.337600	186.688000	0.005357	0.026084	4.869580	0.205357	20
21	46.005120	225.025600	0.004444	0.021737	4.891316	0.204444	21
22	55.206144	271.030719	0.003690	0.018114	4.909430	0.203690	22
23	66.247373	326.236863	0.003065	0.015095	4.924525	0.203065	23
24	79.496847	392.484236	0.002548	0.012579	4.937104	0.202548	24
25	95.396217	471.981083	0.002119	0.010483	4.947587	0.202119	25
26	114.475460	567.377300	0.001762	0.008735	4.956323	0.201762	26
27	137.370552	681.852760	0.001467	0.007280	4.963602	0.201467	27
28	164.844662	819.223312	0.001221	0.006066	4.969668	0.201221	28
29	197.813595	984.067974	0.001016	0.005055	4.974724	0.201016	29
30	237.376314	1181.881569	0.000846	0.004213	4.978936	0.200846	30
31	284.851577	1419.257883	0.000705	0.003511	4.982447	0.200705	31
32	341.821892	1704.109459	0.000587	0.002926	4.985372	0.200587	32
33	410.186270	2045.931351	0.000489	0.002438	4.987810	0.200489	33
34	492.223524	2456.117621	0.000407	0.002032	4.989842	0.200407	34
35	590.668229	2948.341146	0.000339	0.001693	4.991535	0.200339	35
36	708.801875	3539.009375	0.000283	0.001411	4.992946	0.200283	36
37	850.562250	4247.811250	0.000235	0.001176	4.994122	0.200235	37
38	1020.674700	5098.373500	0.000196	0.000980	4.995101	0.200196	38
39	1224.809640	6119.048200	0.000163	0.000816	4.995918	0.200163	39
40	1469.771568	7343.857840	0.000136	0.000680	4.996598	0.200136	40
41	1763.725882	8813.629408	0.000113	0.000567	4.997165	0.200113	41
42	2116.471058	10577.355289	0.000095	0.000472	4.997638	0.200095	42
43	2539.765269	12693.826347	0.000079	0.000394	4.998031	0.200079	43
44	3047.718323	15233.591617	0.000066	0.000328	4.998359	0.200066	44
45	3657.261988	18281.309940	0.000055	0.000273	4.998633	0.200055	45
46	4388.714386	21938.571928	0.000046	0.000228	4.998861	0.200046	46
47	5266.457263	26327.286314	0.000038	0.000190	4.999051	0.200038	47
48	6319.748715	31593.743576	0.000032	0.000158	4.999209	0.200032	48
49	7583.698458	37913.492292	0.000026	0.000132	4.999341	0.200026	49
50	9100.438150	45497.190750	0.000022	0.000110	4.999451	0.200022	50

B. Monthly Compound Interest Tables

MONTHLY COMPOUND INTEREST TABLES

6.00% ANNUAL INTEREST RATE   0.5000% MONTHLY EFFECTIVE INTEREST RATE

	1 AMOUNT OF $1 AT COMPOUND INTEREST	2 ACCUMULATION OF $1 PER PERIOD	3 SINKING FUND FACTOR	4 PRESENT VALUE REVERSION OF $1	5 PRESENT VALUE ORD. ANNUINTY $1 PER PERIOD	6 INSTALLMENT TO AMORTIZE $1	
MONTHS							MONTHS
1	1.005000	1.000000	1.000000	0.995025	0.995025	1.005000	1
2	1.010025	2.005000	0.498753	0.990075	1.985099	0.503753	2
3	1.015075	3.015025	0.331672	0.985149	2.970248	0.336672	3
4	1.020151	4.030100	0.248133	0.980248	3.950496	0.253133	4
5	1.025251	5.050251	0.198010	0.975371	4.925866	0.203010	5
6	1.030378	6.075502	0.164595	0.970518	5.896384	0.169595	6
7	1.035529	7.105879	0.140729	0.965690	6.862074	0.145729	7
8	1.040707	8.141409	0.122829	0.960885	7.822959	0.127829	8
9	1.045911	9.182116	0.108907	0.956105	8.779064	0.113907	9
10	1.051140	10.228026	0.097771	0.951348	9.730412	0.102771	10
11	1.056396	11.279167	0.088659	0.946615	10.677027	0.093659	11
12	1.061678	12.335562	0.081066	0.941905	11.618932	0.086066	12
YEARS							MONTHS
1	1.061678	12.335562	0.081066	0.941905	11.618932	0.086066	12
2	1.127160	25.431955	0.039321	0.887186	22.562866	0.044321	24
3	1.196681	39.336105	0.025422	0.835645	32.871016	0.030422	36
4	1.270489	54.097832	0.018485	0.787098	42.580318	0.023485	48
5	1.348850	69.770031	0.014333	0.741372	51.725561	0.019333	60
6	1.432044	86.408856	0.011573	0.698302	60.339514	0.016573	72
7	1.520370	104.073927	0.009609	0.657735	68.453042	0.014609	84
8	1.614143	122.828542	0.008141	0.619524	76.095218	0.013141	96
9	1.713699	142.739900	0.007006	0.583533	83.293424	0.012006	108
10	1.819397	163.879347	0.006102	0.549633	90.073453	0.011102	120
11	1.931613	186.322629	0.005367	0.517702	96.459599	0.010367	132
12	2.050751	210.150163	0.004759	0.487626	102.474743	0.009759	144
13	2.177237	235.447328	0.004247	0.459298	108.140440	0.009247	156
14	2.311524	262.304766	0.003812	0.432615	113.476990	0.008812	168
15	2.454094	290.818712	0.003439	0.407482	118.503515	0.008439	180
16	2.605457	321.091337	0.003114	0.383810	123.238025	0.008114	192
17	2.766156	353.231110	0.002831	0.361513	127.697486	0.007831	204
18	2.936766	387.353194	0.002582	0.340511	131.897876	0.007582	216
19	3.117899	423.579854	0.002361	0.320729	135.854246	0.007361	228
20	3.310204	462.040895	0.002164	0.302096	139.580772	0.007164	240
21	3.514371	502.874129	0.001989	0.284546	143.090806	0.006989	252
22	3.731129	546.225867	0.001831	0.268015	146.396927	0.006831	264
23	3.961257	592.251446	0.001688	0.252445	149.510979	0.006688	276
24	4.205579	641.115782	0.001560	0.237779	152.444121	0.006560	288
25	4.464970	692.993962	0.001443	0.223966	155.206864	0.006443	300
26	4.740359	748.071876	0.001337	0.210954	157.809106	0.006337	312
27	5.032734	806.546875	0.001240	0.198699	160.260172	0.006240	324
28	5.343142	868.628484	0.001151	0.187156	162.568844	0.006151	336
29	5.672696	934.539150	0.001070	0.176283	164.743394	0.006070	348
30	6.022575	1004.515042	0.000996	0.166042	166.791614	0.005996	360
31	6.394034	1078.806895	0.000927	0.156396	168.720844	0.005927	372
32	6.788405	1157.680906	0.000864	0.147310	170.537996	0.005864	384
33	7.207098	1241.419693	0.000806	0.138752	172.249581	0.005806	396
34	7.651617	1330.323306	0.000752	0.130691	173.861732	0.005752	408
35	8.123551	1424.710299	0.000702	0.123099	175.380226	0.005702	420
36	8.624594	1524.918875	0.000656	0.115947	176.810504	0.005656	432
37	9.156540	1631.308097	0.000613	0.109212	178.157690	0.005613	444
38	9.721296	1744.259173	0.000573	0.102867	179.426611	0.005573	456
39	10.320884	1864.176824	0.000536	0.096891	180.621815	0.005536	468
40	10.957454	1991.490734	0.000502	0.091262	181.747584	0.005502	480

MONTHLY COMPOUND INTEREST TABLES

6.50% ANNUAL INTEREST RATE   0.5417% MONTHLY EFFECTIVE INTEREST RATE

	1 AMOUNT OF $1 AT COMPOUND INTEREST	2 ACCUMULATION OF $1 PER PERIOD	3 SINKING FUND FACTOR	4 PRESENT VALUE REVERSION OF $1	5 PRESENT VALUE ORD. ANNUINTY $1 PER PERIOD	6 INSTALLMENT TO AMORTIZE $1	
MONTHS							MONTHS
1	1.005417	1.000000	1.000000	0.994613	0.994613	1.005417	1
2	1.010863	2.005417	0.498649	0.989254	1.983867	0.504066	2
3	1.016338	3.016279	0.331534	0.983924	2.967791	0.336951	3
4	1.021843	4.032618	0.247978	0.978624	3.946415	0.253395	4
5	1.027378	5.054461	0.197845	0.973351	4.919766	0.203262	5
6	1.032943	6.081839	0.164424	0.968107	5.887873	0.169841	6
7	1.038538	7.114782	0.140552	0.962892	6.850765	0.145969	7
8	1.044164	8.153321	0.122649	0.957704	7.808469	0.128066	8
9	1.049820	9.197485	0.108725	0.952545	8.761014	0.114142	9
10	1.055506	10.247304	0.097587	0.947413	9.708426	0.103003	10
11	1.061224	11.302811	0.088474	0.942309	10.650735	0.093890	11
12	1.066972	12.364034	0.080880	0.937232	11.587967	0.086296	12
YEARS							MONTHS
1	1.066972	12.364034	0.080880	0.937232	11.587967	0.086296	12
2	1.138429	25.556111	0.039130	0.878404	22.448578	0.044546	24
3	1.214672	39.631685	0.025232	0.823268	32.627489	0.030649	36
4	1.296020	54.649927	0.018298	0.771593	42.167488	0.023715	48
5	1.382817	70.673968	0.014149	0.723161	51.108680	0.019566	60
6	1.475427	87.771168	0.011393	0.677770	59.488649	0.016810	72
7	1.574239	106.013400	0.009433	0.635227	67.342623	0.014849	84
8	1.679669	125.477348	0.007970	0.595355	74.703617	0.013386	96
9	1.792160	146.244833	0.006838	0.557986	81.602576	0.012255	108
10	1.912184	168.403154	0.005938	0.522962	88.068500	0.011355	120
11	2.040246	192.045460	0.005207	0.490137	94.128569	0.010624	132
12	2.176885	217.271134	0.004603	0.459372	99.808260	0.010019	144
13	2.322675	244.186218	0.004095	0.430538	105.131446	0.009512	156
14	2.478229	272.903856	0.003664	0.403514	110.120506	0.009081	168
15	2.644201	303.544767	0.003294	0.378186	114.796412	0.008711	180
16	2.821288	336.237756	0.002974	0.354448	119.178820	0.008391	192
17	3.010235	371.120256	0.002695	0.332200	123.286152	0.008111	204
18	3.211836	408.338901	0.002449	0.311348	127.135675	0.007866	216
19	3.426938	448.050147	0.002232	0.291806	130.743570	0.007649	228
20	3.656447	490.420930	0.002039	0.273490	134.125004	0.007456	240
21	3.901326	535.629362	0.001867	0.256323	137.294192	0.007284	252
22	4.162605	583.865486	0.001713	0.240234	140.264456	0.007129	264
23	4.441382	635.332073	0.001574	0.225155	143.048282	0.006991	276
24	4.738830	690.245473	0.001449	0.211023	145.657372	0.006865	288
25	5.056198	748.836525	0.001335	0.197777	148.102695	0.006752	300
26	5.394821	811.351528	0.001233	0.185363	150.394529	0.006649	312
27	5.756122	878.053277	0.001139	0.173728	152.542509	0.006556	324
28	6.141620	949.222165	0.001053	0.162823	154.555664	0.006470	336
29	6.552936	1025.157366	0.000975	0.152603	156.442457	0.006392	348
30	6.991798	1106.178087	0.000904	0.143025	158.210820	0.006321	360
31	7.460052	1192.624917	0.000838	0.134047	159.868185	0.006255	372
32	7.959665	1284.861251	0.000778	0.125633	161.421521	0.006195	384
33	8.492739	1383.274822	0.000723	0.117748	162.877357	0.006140	396
34	9.061513	1488.279333	0.000672	0.110357	164.241813	0.006089	408
35	9.668379	1600.316191	0.000625	0.103430	165.520625	0.006042	420
36	10.315889	1719.856364	0.000581	0.096938	166.719167	0.005998	432
37	11.006763	1847.402364	0.000541	0.090853	167.842480	0.005958	444
38	11.743906	1983.490356	0.000504	0.085151	168.895284	0.005921	456
39	12.530417	2128.692413	0.000470	0.079806	169.882006	0.005886	468
40	13.369602	2283.618920	0.000438	0.074797	170.806793	0.005855	480

MONTHLY COMPOUND INTEREST TABLES

7.00% ANNUAL INTEREST RATE   0.5833% MONTHLY EFFECTIVE INTEREST RATE

	1 AMOUNT OF $1 AT COMPOUND INTEREST	2 ACCUMULATION OF $1 PER PERIOD	3 SINKING FUND FACTOR	4 PRESENT VALUE REVERSION OF $1	5 PRESENT VALUE ORD. ANNUINTY $1 PER PERIOD	6 INSTALLMENT TO AMORTIZE $1	
MONTHS							**MONTHS**
1	1.005833	1.000000	1.000000	0.994200	0.994200	1.005833	1
2	1.011701	2.005833	0.498546	0.988435	1.982635	0.504379	2
3	1.017602	3.017534	0.331396	0.982702	2.965337	0.337230	3
4	1.023538	4.035136	0.247823	0.977003	3.942340	0.253656	4
5	1.029509	5.058675	0.197680	0.971337	4.913677	0.203514	5
6	1.035514	6.088184	0.164253	0.965704	5.879381	0.170086	6
7	1.041555	7.123698	0.140377	0.960103	6.839484	0.146210	7
8	1.047631	8.165253	0.122470	0.954535	7.794019	0.128304	8
9	1.053742	9.212883	0.108544	0.948999	8.743018	0.114377	9
10	1.059889	10.266625	0.097403	0.943495	9.686513	0.103236	10
11	1.066071	11.326514	0.088288	0.938024	10.624537	0.094122	11
12	1.072290	12.392585	0.080693	0.932583	11.557120	0.086527	12
YEARS							**MONTHS**
1	1.072290	12.392585	0.080693	0.932583	11.557120	0.086527	12
2	1.149806	25.681032	0.038939	0.869712	22.335099	0.044773	24
3	1.232926	39.930101	0.025044	0.811079	32.386464	0.030877	36
4	1.322054	55.209236	0.018113	0.756399	41.760201	0.023946	48
5	1.417625	71.592902	0.013968	0.705405	50.501994	0.019801	60
6	1.520106	89.160944	0.011216	0.657849	58.654444	0.017049	72
7	1.629994	107.998981	0.009259	0.613499	66.257285	0.015093	84
8	1.747826	128.198821	0.007800	0.572139	73.347569	0.013634	96
9	1.874177	149.858909	0.006673	0.533568	79.959850	0.012506	108
10	2.009661	173.084807	0.005778	0.497596	86.126354	0.011611	120
11	2.154940	197.989707	0.005051	0.464050	91.877134	0.010884	132
12	2.310721	224.694985	0.004450	0.432765	97.240216	0.010284	144
13	2.477763	253.330789	0.003947	0.403590	102.241738	0.009781	156
14	2.656881	284.036677	0.003521	0.376381	106.906074	0.009354	168
15	2.848947	316.962297	0.003155	0.351007	111.255958	0.008988	180
16	3.054897	352.268112	0.002839	0.327343	115.312587	0.008672	192
17	3.275736	390.126188	0.002563	0.305275	119.095732	0.008397	204
18	3.512539	430.721027	0.002322	0.284694	122.623831	0.008155	216
19	3.766461	474.250470	0.002109	0.265501	125.914077	0.007942	228
20	4.038739	520.926660	0.001920	0.247602	128.982506	0.007753	240
21	4.330700	570.977075	0.001751	0.230910	131.844073	0.007585	252
22	4.643766	624.645640	0.001601	0.215342	134.512723	0.007434	264
23	4.979464	682.193909	0.001466	0.200825	137.001461	0.007299	276
24	5.339430	743.902347	0.001344	0.187286	139.322418	0.007178	288
25	5.725418	810.071693	0.001234	0.174660	141.486903	0.007068	300
26	6.139309	881.024427	0.001135	0.162885	143.505467	0.006968	312
27	6.583120	957.106339	0.001045	0.151904	145.387946	0.006878	324
28	7.059015	1038.688219	0.000963	0.141663	147.143515	0.006796	336
29	7.569311	1126.167659	0.000888	0.132112	148.780729	0.006721	348
30	8.116497	1219.970996	0.000820	0.123206	150.307568	0.006653	360
31	8.703240	1320.555383	0.000757	0.114900	151.731473	0.006591	372
32	9.332398	1428.411024	0.000700	0.107154	153.059383	0.006533	384
33	10.007037	1544.063557	0.000648	0.099930	154.297770	0.006481	396
34	10.730447	1668.076622	0.000599	0.093193	155.452669	0.006433	408
35	11.506152	1801.054601	0.000555	0.086910	156.529709	0.006389	420
36	12.337932	1943.645569	0.000514	0.081051	157.534139	0.006348	432
37	13.229843	2096.544450	0.000477	0.075587	158.470853	0.006310	444
38	14.186229	2260.496403	0.000442	0.070491	159.344418	0.006276	456
39	15.211753	2436.300456	0.000410	0.065739	160.159090	0.006244	468
40	16.311411	2624.813398	0.000381	0.061307	160.918839	0.006214	480

MONTHLY COMPOUND INTEREST TABLES

7.50% ANNUAL INTEREST RATE   0.6250% MONTHLY EFFECTIVE INTEREST RATE

	1 AMOUNT OF $1 AT COMPOUND INTEREST	2 ACCUMULATION OF $1 PER PERIOD	3 SINKING FUND FACTOR	4 PRESENT VALUE REVERSION OF $1	5 PRESENT VALUE ORD. ANNUINTY $1 PER PERIOD	6 INSTALLMENT TO AMORTIZE $1	
MONTHS							**MONTHS**
1	1.006250	1.000000	1.000000	0.993789	0.993789	1.006250	1
2	1.012539	2.006250	0.498442	0.987616	1.981405	0.504692	2
3	1.018867	3.018789	0.331259	0.981482	2.962887	0.337509	3
4	1.025235	4.037656	0.247668	0.975386	3.938273	0.253918	4
5	1.031643	5.062892	0.197516	0.969327	4.907600	0.203766	5
6	1.038091	6.094535	0.164081	0.963307	5.870907	0.170331	6
7	1.044579	7.132626	0.140201	0.957324	6.828231	0.146451	7
8	1.051108	8.177205	0.122291	0.951377	7.779608	0.128541	8
9	1.057677	9.228312	0.108362	0.945468	8.725076	0.114612	9
10	1.064287	10.285989	0.097220	0.939596	9.664672	0.103470	10
11	1.070939	11.350277	0.088104	0.933760	10.598432	0.094354	11
12	1.077633	12.421216	0.080507	0.927960	11.526392	0.086757	12
YEARS							**MONTHS**
1	1.077633	12.421216	0.080507	0.927960	11.526392	0.086757	12
2	1.161292	25.806723	0.038750	0.861110	22.222423	0.045000	24
3	1.251446	40.231382	0.024856	0.799076	32.147913	0.031106	36
4	1.348599	55.775864	0.017929	0.741510	41.358371	0.024179	48
5	1.453294	72.527105	0.013788	0.688092	49.905308	0.020038	60
6	1.566117	90.578789	0.011040	0.638522	57.836524	0.017290	72
7	1.687699	110.031871	0.009088	0.592523	65.196376	0.015338	84
8	1.818720	130.995147	0.007634	0.549837	72.026024	0.013884	96
9	1.959912	153.585857	0.006511	0.510227	78.363665	0.012761	108
10	2.112065	177.930342	0.005620	0.473470	84.244743	0.011870	120
11	2.276030	204.164753	0.004898	0.439362	89.702148	0.011148	132
12	2.452724	232.435809	0.004302	0.407710	94.766401	0.010552	144
13	2.643135	262.901620	0.003804	0.378339	99.465827	0.010054	156
14	2.848329	295.732572	0.003381	0.351083	103.826706	0.009631	168
15	3.069452	331.112276	0.003020	0.325791	107.873427	0.009270	180
16	3.307741	369.238599	0.002708	0.302321	111.628623	0.008958	192
17	3.564530	410.324767	0.002437	0.280542	115.113294	0.008687	204
18	3.841254	454.600560	0.002200	0.260332	118.346930	0.008450	216
19	4.139460	502.313599	0.001991	0.241577	121.347615	0.008241	228
20	4.460817	553.730725	0.001806	0.224174	124.132131	0.008056	240
21	4.807122	609.139496	0.001642	0.208025	126.716051	0.007892	252
22	5.180311	668.849794	0.001495	0.193039	129.113825	0.007745	264
23	5.582472	733.195558	0.001364	0.179132	131.338863	0.007614	276
24	6.015854	802.536650	0.001246	0.166227	133.403610	0.007496	288
25	6.482880	877.260872	0.001140	0.154252	135.319613	0.007390	300
26	6.986163	957.786129	0.001044	0.143140	137.097587	0.007294	312
27	7.528517	1044.562771	0.000957	0.132828	138.747475	0.007207	324
28	8.112976	1138.076109	0.000879	0.123259	140.278506	0.007129	336
29	8.742807	1238.849131	0.000807	0.114380	141.699242	0.007057	348
30	9.421534	1347.445425	0.000742	0.106140	143.017627	0.006992	360
31	10.152952	1464.472331	0.000683	0.098494	144.241037	0.006933	372
32	10.941152	1590.584340	0.000629	0.091398	145.376312	0.006879	384
33	11.790542	1726.486751	0.000579	0.084814	146.429801	0.006829	396
34	12.705873	1872.939621	0.000534	0.078704	147.407398	0.006784	408
35	13.692263	2030.762007	0.000492	0.073034	148.314568	0.006742	420
36	14.755228	2200.836555	0.000454	0.067773	149.156386	0.006704	432
37	15.900715	2384.114432	0.000419	0.062890	149.937560	0.006669	444
38	17.135129	2581.620647	0.000387	0.058360	150.662457	0.006637	456
39	18.465374	2794.459783	0.000358	0.054155	151.335133	0.006608	468
40	19.898889	3023.822174	0.000331	0.050254	151.959350	0.006581	480

MONTHLY COMPOUND INTEREST TABLES

8.00% ANNUAL INTEREST RATE   0.6667% MONTHLY EFFECTIVE INTEREST RATE

	1 AMOUNT OF $1 AT COMPOUND INTEREST	2 ACCUMULATION OF $1 PER PERIOD	3 SINKING FUND FACTOR	4 PRESENT VALUE REVERSION OF $1	5 PRESENT VALUE ORD. ANNUITY $1 PER PERIOD	6 INSTALLMENT TO AMORTIZE $1	
MONTHS							**MONTHS**
1	1.006667	1.000000	1.000000	0.993377	0.993377	1.006667	1
2	1.013378	2.006667	0.498339	0.986799	1.980176	0.505006	2
3	1.020134	3.020044	0.331121	0.980264	2.960440	0.337788	3
4	1.026935	4.040178	0.247514	0.973772	3.934212	0.254181	4
5	1.033781	5.067113	0.197351	0.967323	4.901535	0.204018	5
6	1.040673	6.100893	0.163910	0.960917	5.862452	0.170577	6
7	1.047610	7.141566	0.140025	0.954553	6.817005	0.146692	7
8	1.054595	8.189176	0.122112	0.948232	7.765237	0.128779	8
9	1.061625	9.243771	0.108181	0.941952	8.707189	0.114848	9
10	1.068703	10.305396	0.097037	0.935714	9.642903	0.103703	10
11	1.075827	11.374099	0.087919	0.929517	10.572420	0.094586	11
12	1.083000	12.449926	0.080322	0.923361	11.495782	0.086988	12
YEARS							**MONTHS**
1	1.083000	12.449926	0.080322	0.923361	11.495782	0.086988	12
2	1.172888	25.933190	0.038561	0.852506	22.110544	0.045227	24
3	1.270237	40.535558	0.024670	0.787255	31.911806	0.031336	36
4	1.375666	56.349915	0.017746	0.726921	40.961913	0.024413	48
5	1.489846	73.476856	0.013610	0.671210	49.318433	0.020276	60
6	1.613502	92.025325	0.010867	0.619770	57.034522	0.017533	72
7	1.747422	112.113308	0.008920	0.572272	64.159261	0.015586	84
8	1.892457	133.868583	0.007470	0.528416	70.737970	0.014137	96
9	2.049530	157.429535	0.006352	0.487917	76.812497	0.013019	108
10	2.219640	182.946035	0.005466	0.450523	82.421481	0.012133	120
11	2.403869	210.580392	0.004749	0.415996	87.600600	0.011415	132
12	2.603389	240.508387	0.004158	0.384115	92.382800	0.010825	144
13	2.819469	272.920390	0.003664	0.354677	96.798498	0.010331	156
14	3.053484	308.022574	0.003247	0.327495	100.875784	0.009913	168
15	3.306921	346.038222	0.002890	0.302396	104.640592	0.009557	180
16	3.581394	387.209149	0.002583	0.279221	108.116871	0.009249	192
17	3.878648	431.797244	0.002316	0.257822	111.326733	0.008983	204
18	4.200574	480.086128	0.002083	0.238063	114.290596	0.008750	216
19	4.549220	532.382966	0.001878	0.219818	117.027313	0.008545	228
20	4.926803	589.020416	0.001698	0.202971	119.554292	0.008364	240
21	5.335725	650.358746	0.001538	0.187416	121.887606	0.008204	252
22	5.778588	716.788127	0.001395	0.173053	124.042099	0.008062	264
23	6.258207	788.731114	0.001268	0.159790	126.031475	0.007935	276
24	6.777636	866.645333	0.001154	0.147544	127.868388	0.007821	288
25	7.340176	951.026395	0.001051	0.136237	129.564523	0.007718	300
26	7.949407	1042.411042	0.000959	0.125796	131.130668	0.007626	312
27	8.609204	1141.390571	0.000876	0.116155	132.576786	0.007543	324
28	9.323763	1248.564521	0.000801	0.107253	133.912076	0.007468	336
29	10.097631	1364.644687	0.000733	0.099033	135.145031	0.007399	348
30	10.935730	1490.359449	0.000671	0.091443	136.283494	0.007338	360
31	11.843390	1626.508474	0.000615	0.084435	137.334707	0.007281	372
32	12.826385	1773.957801	0.000564	0.077964	138.305357	0.007230	384
33	13.890969	1933.645350	0.000517	0.071989	139.201617	0.007184	396
34	15.043913	2106.586886	0.000475	0.066472	140.029190	0.007141	408
35	16.292550	2293.882485	0.000436	0.061378	140.793338	0.007103	420
36	17.644824	2496.723526	0.000401	0.056674	141.498923	0.007067	432
37	19.109335	2716.400273	0.000368	0.052330	142.150433	0.007035	444
38	20.695401	2954.310082	0.000338	0.048320	142.752013	0.007005	456
39	22.413109	3211.966288	0.000311	0.044617	143.307488	0.006978	468
40	24.273386	3491.007831	0.000286	0.041197	143.820392	0.006953	480

MONTHLY COMPOUND INTEREST TABLES

8.50% ANNUAL INTEREST RATE   0.7083% MONTHLY EFFECTIVE INTEREST RATE

	1	2	3	4	5	6	
	AMOUNT OF $1 AT COMPOUND INTEREST	ACCUMULATION OF $1 PER PERIOD	SINKING FUND FACTOR	PRESENT VALUE REVERSION OF $1	PRESENT VALUE ORD. ANNUINTY $1 PER PERIOD	INSTALLMENT TO AMORTIZE $1	
MONTHS							MONTHS
1	1.007083	1.000000	1.000000	0.992966	0.992966	1.007083	1
2	1.014217	2.007083	0.498235	0.985982	1.978949	0.505319	2
3	1.021401	3.021300	0.330983	0.979048	2.957996	0.338067	3
4	1.028636	4.042701	0.247359	0.972161	3.930158	0.254443	4
5	1.035922	5.071337	0.197187	0.965324	4.895482	0.204270	5
6	1.043260	6.107259	0.163740	0.958534	5.854016	0.170823	6
7	1.050650	7.150519	0.139850	0.951792	6.805808	0.146933	7
8	1.058092	8.201168	0.121934	0.945098	7.750906	0.129017	8
9	1.065586	9.259260	0.108000	0.938450	8.689356	0.115083	9
10	1.073134	10.324846	0.096854	0.931850	9.621206	0.103937	10
11	1.080736	11.397980	0.087735	0.925296	10.546501	0.094818	11
12	1.088391	12.478716	0.080136	0.918788	11.465289	0.087220	12
YEARS							MONTHS
1	1.088391	12.478716	0.080136	0.918788	11.465289	0.087220	12
2	1.184595	26.060437	0.038372	0.844171	21.999453	0.045456	24
3	1.289302	40.842659	0.024484	0.775613	31.678112	0.031568	36
4	1.403265	56.931495	0.017565	0.712624	40.570744	0.024648	48
5	1.527301	74.442437	0.013433	0.654750	48.741183	0.020517	60
6	1.662300	93.501188	0.010695	0.601576	56.248080	0.017778	72
7	1.809232	114.244559	0.008753	0.552721	63.145324	0.015836	84
8	1.969152	136.821455	0.007309	0.507833	69.482425	0.014392	96
9	2.143207	161.393943	0.006196	0.466590	75.304875	0.013279	108
10	2.332647	188.138416	0.005315	0.428698	80.654470	0.012399	120
11	2.538832	217.246858	0.004603	0.393882	85.569611	0.011686	132
12	2.763242	248.928220	0.004017	0.361894	90.085581	0.011101	144
13	3.007487	283.409927	0.003528	0.332504	94.234798	0.010612	156
14	3.273321	320.939504	0.003116	0.305500	98.047046	0.010199	168
15	3.562653	361.786353	0.002764	0.280690	101.549693	0.009847	180
16	3.877559	406.243693	0.002462	0.257894	104.767881	0.009545	192
17	4.220300	454.630657	0.002200	0.236950	107.724713	0.009283	204
18	4.593337	507.294589	0.001971	0.217707	110.441412	0.009055	216
19	4.999346	564.613533	0.001771	0.200026	112.937482	0.008854	228
20	5.441243	626.998951	0.001595	0.183782	115.230840	0.008678	240
21	5.922199	694.898672	0.001439	0.168856	117.337948	0.008522	252
22	6.445667	768.800112	0.001301	0.155143	119.273933	0.008384	264
23	7.015406	849.233766	0.001178	0.142543	121.052692	0.008261	276
24	7.635504	936.777024	0.001067	0.130967	122.686994	0.008151	288
25	8.310413	1032.058310	0.000969	0.120331	124.188570	0.008052	300
26	9.044978	1135.761595	0.000880	0.110559	125.568199	0.007964	312
27	9.844472	1248.631307	0.000801	0.101580	126.835785	0.007884	324
28	10.714634	1371.477676	0.000729	0.093330	128.000428	0.007812	336
29	11.661710	1505.182546	0.000664	0.085751	129.070487	0.007748	348
30	12.692499	1650.705711	0.000606	0.078787	130.053643	0.007689	360
31	13.814400	1809.091800	0.000553	0.072388	130.956956	0.007636	372
32	15.035468	1981.477780	0.000505	0.066509	131.786908	0.007588	384
33	16.364466	2169.101112	0.000461	0.061108	132.549457	0.007544	396
34	17.810936	2373.308640	0.000421	0.056145	133.250078	0.007505	408
35	19.385261	2595.566257	0.000385	0.051586	133.893800	0.007469	420
36	21.098742	2837.469426	0.000352	0.047396	134.485244	0.007436	432
37	22.963679	3100.754635	0.000323	0.043547	135.028655	0.007406	444
38	24.993459	3387.311862	0.000295	0.040010	135.527934	0.007379	456
39	27.202654	3699.198142	0.000270	0.036761	135.986665	0.007354	468
40	29.607121	4038.652333	0.000248	0.033776	136.408142	0.007331	480

MONTHLY COMPOUND INTEREST TABLES

9.00% ANNUAL INTEREST RATE   0.7500% MONTHLY EFFECTIVE INTEREST RATE

	1 AMOUNT OF $1 AT COMPOUND INTEREST	2 ACCUMULATION OF $1 PER PERIOD	3 SINKING FUND FACTOR	4 PRESENT VALUE REVERSION OF $1	5 PRESENT VALUE ORD. ANNUINTY $1 PER PERIOD	6 INSTALLMENT TO AMORTIZE $1	
MONTHS							MONTHS
1	1.007500	1.000000	1.000000	0.992556	0.992556	1.007500	1
2	1.015056	2.007500	0.498132	0.985167	1.977723	0.505632	2
3	1.022669	3.022556	0.330846	0.977833	2.955556	0.338346	3
4	1.030339	4.045225	0.247205	0.970554	3.926110	0.254705	4
5	1.038067	5.075565	0.197022	0.963329	4.889440	0.204522	5
6	1.045852	6.113631	0.163569	0.956158	5.845598	0.171069	6
7	1.053696	7.159484	0.139675	0.949040	6.794638	0.147175	7
8	1.061599	8.213180	0.121756	0.941975	7.736613	0.129256	8
9	1.069561	9.274779	0.107819	0.934963	8.671576	0.115319	9
10	1.077583	10.344339	0.096671	0.928003	9.599580	0.104171	10
11	1.085664	11.421922	0.087551	0.921095	10.520675	0.095051	11
12	1.093807	12.507586	0.079951	0.914238	11.434913	0.087451	12
YEARS							MONTHS
1	1.093807	12.507586	0.079951	0.914238	11.434913	0.087451	12
2	1.196414	26.188471	0.038185	0.835831	21.889146	0.045685	24
3	1.308645	41.152716	0.024300	0.764149	31.446805	0.031800	36
4	1.431405	57.520711	0.017385	0.698614	40.184782	0.024885	48
5	1.565681	75.424137	0.013258	0.638700	48.173374	0.020758	60
6	1.712553	95.007028	0.010526	0.583924	55.476849	0.018026	72
7	1.873202	116.426928	0.008589	0.533845	62.153965	0.016089	84
8	2.048921	139.856164	0.007150	0.488062	68.258439	0.014650	96
9	2.241124	165.483223	0.006043	0.446205	73.839382	0.013543	108
10	2.451357	193.514277	0.005168	0.407937	78.941693	0.012668	120
11	2.681311	224.174837	0.004461	0.372952	83.606420	0.011961	132
12	2.932837	257.711570	0.003880	0.340967	87.871092	0.011380	144
13	3.207957	294.394279	0.003397	0.311725	91.770018	0.010897	156
14	3.508886	334.518079	0.002989	0.284991	95.334564	0.010489	168
15	3.838043	378.405769	0.002643	0.260549	98.593409	0.010143	180
16	4.198078	426.410427	0.002345	0.238204	101.572769	0.009845	192
17	4.591887	478.918252	0.002088	0.217775	104.296613	0.009588	204
18	5.022638	536.351674	0.001864	0.199099	106.786856	0.009364	216
19	5.493796	599.172747	0.001669	0.182024	109.063531	0.009169	228
20	6.009152	667.886870	0.001497	0.166413	111.144954	0.008997	240
21	6.572851	743.046852	0.001346	0.152141	113.047870	0.008846	252
22	7.189430	825.257358	0.001212	0.139093	114.787589	0.008712	264
23	7.863848	915.179777	0.001093	0.127164	116.378106	0.008593	276
24	8.601532	1013.537539	0.000987	0.116258	117.832218	0.008487	288
25	9.408415	1121.121937	0.000892	0.106288	119.161622	0.008392	300
26	10.290989	1238.798495	0.000807	0.097172	120.377014	0.008307	312
27	11.256354	1367.513924	0.000731	0.088839	121.488172	0.008231	324
28	12.312278	1508.303750	0.000663	0.081220	122.504035	0.008163	336
29	13.467255	1662.300631	0.000602	0.074254	123.432776	0.008102	348
30	14.730576	1830.743483	0.000546	0.067886	124.281866	0.008046	360
31	16.112406	2014.987436	0.000496	0.062064	125.058136	0.007996	372
32	17.623861	2216.514743	0.000451	0.056741	125.767832	0.007951	384
33	19.277100	2436.946701	0.000410	0.051875	126.416664	0.007910	396
34	21.085425	2678.056697	0.000373	0.047426	127.009850	0.007873	408
35	23.063384	2941.784474	0.000340	0.043359	127.552164	0.007840	420
36	25.226888	3230.251735	0.000310	0.039640	128.047967	0.007810	432
37	27.593344	3545.779215	0.000282	0.036241	128.501250	0.007782	444
38	30.181790	3890.905350	0.000257	0.033133	128.915659	0.007757	456
39	33.013050	4268.406696	0.000234	0.030291	129.294526	0.007734	468
40	36.109902	4681.320273	0.000214	0.027693	129.640902	0.007714	480

MONTHLY COMPOUND INTEREST TABLES

9.50% ANNUAL INTEREST RATE   0.7917% MONTHLY EFFECTIVE INTEREST RATE

	1 AMOUNT OF $1 AT COMPOUND INTEREST	2 ACCUMULATION OF $1 PER PERIOD	3 SINKING FUND FACTOR	4 PRESENT VALUE REVERSION OF $1	5 PRESENT VALUE ORD. ANNUINTY $1 PER PERIOD	6 INSTALLMENT TO AMORTIZE $1	
MONTHS							MONTHS
1	1.007917	1.000000	1.000000	0.992146	0.992146	1.007917	1
2	1.015896	2.007917	0.498029	0.984353	1.976498	0.505945	2
3	1.023939	3.023813	0.330708	0.976621	2.953119	0.338625	3
4	1.032045	4.047751	0.247051	0.968950	3.922070	0.254967	4
5	1.040215	5.079796	0.196858	0.961340	4.883409	0.204775	5
6	1.048450	6.120011	0.163398	0.953789	5.837198	0.171315	6
7	1.056750	7.168461	0.139500	0.946297	6.783496	0.147417	7
8	1.065116	8.225211	0.121577	0.938865	7.722360	0.129494	8
9	1.073548	9.290328	0.107639	0.931490	8.653851	0.115555	9
10	1.082047	10.363876	0.096489	0.924174	9.578024	0.104406	10
11	1.090614	11.445923	0.087367	0.916915	10.494940	0.095284	11
12	1.099248	12.536537	0.079767	0.909713	11.404653	0.087684	12
YEARS							MONTHS
1	1.099248	12.536537	0.079767	0.909713	11.404653	0.087684	12
2	1.208345	26.317295	0.037998	0.827578	21.779615	0.045914	24
3	1.328271	41.465760	0.024116	0.752859	31.217856	0.032033	36
4	1.460098	58.117673	0.017206	0.684885	39.803947	0.025123	48
5	1.605009	76.422249	0.013085	0.623049	47.614827	0.021002	60
6	1.764303	96.543509	0.010358	0.566796	54.720488	0.018275	72
7	1.939406	118.661756	0.008427	0.515622	61.184601	0.016344	84
8	2.131887	142.975186	0.006994	0.469068	67.065090	0.014911	96
9	2.343472	169.701665	0.005893	0.426717	72.414648	0.013809	108
10	2.576055	199.080682	0.005023	0.388190	77.281211	0.012940	120
11	2.831723	231.375495	0.004322	0.353142	81.708388	0.012239	132
12	3.112764	266.875491	0.003747	0.321258	85.735849	0.011664	144
13	3.421699	305.898776	0.003269	0.292253	89.399684	0.011186	156
14	3.761294	348.795027	0.002867	0.265866	92.732722	0.010784	168
15	4.134593	395.948628	0.002526	0.241862	95.764831	0.010442	180
16	4.544942	447.782110	0.002233	0.220025	98.523180	0.010150	192
17	4.996016	504.759939	0.001981	0.200159	101.032487	0.009898	204
18	5.491859	567.392681	0.001762	0.182088	103.315236	0.009679	216
19	6.036912	636.241570	0.001572	0.165648	105.391883	0.009488	228
20	6.636061	711.923546	0.001405	0.150692	107.281037	0.009321	240
21	7.294674	795.116775	0.001258	0.137086	108.999624	0.009174	252
22	8.018653	886.566731	0.001128	0.124709	110.563046	0.009045	264
23	8.814485	987.092874	0.001013	0.113450	111.985311	0.008930	276
24	9.689302	1097.595994	0.000911	0.103207	113.279165	0.008828	288
25	10.650941	1219.066282	0.000820	0.093888	114.456200	0.008737	300
26	11.708022	1352.592202	0.000739	0.085412	115.526965	0.008656	312
27	12.870014	1499.370247	0.000667	0.077700	116.501054	0.008584	324
28	14.147332	1660.715659	0.000602	0.070685	117.387195	0.008519	336
29	15.551421	1838.074212	0.000544	0.064303	118.193330	0.008461	348
30	17.094862	2033.035174	0.000492	0.058497	118.926681	0.008409	360
31	18.791486	2247.345541	0.000445	0.053216	119.593820	0.008362	372
32	20.656495	2482.925693	0.000403	0.048411	120.200725	0.008319	384
33	22.706602	2741.886607	0.000365	0.044040	120.752835	0.008281	396
34	24.960178	3026.548765	0.000330	0.040064	121.255097	0.008247	408
35	27.437415	3339.462955	0.000299	0.036447	121.712011	0.008216	420
36	30.160512	3683.433122	0.000271	0.033156	122.127671	0.008188	432
37	33.153870	4061.541498	0.000246	0.030162	122.505803	0.008163	444
38	36.444312	4477.176216	0.000223	0.027439	122.849795	0.008140	456
39	40.061322	4934.061676	0.000203	0.024962	123.162729	0.008119	468
40	44.037311	5436.291914	0.000184	0.022708	123.447408	0.008101	480

MONTHLY COMPOUND INTEREST TABLES

10.00% ANNUAL INTEREST RATE   0.8333% MONTHLY EFFECTIVE INTEREST RATE

	1 AMOUNT OF $1 AT COMPOUND INTEREST	2 ACCUMULATION OF $1 PER PERIOD	3 SINKING FUND FACTOR	4 PRESENT VALUE REVERSION OF $1	5 PRESENT VALUE ORD. ANNUINTY $1 PER PERIOD	6 INSTALLMENT TO AMORTIZE $1	
MONTHS							MONTHS
1	1.008333	1.000000	1.000000	0.991736	0.991736	1.008333	1
2	1.016736	2.008333	0.497925	0.983539	1.975275	0.506259	2
3	1.025209	3.025069	0.330571	0.975411	2.950686	0.338904	3
4	1.033752	4.050278	0.246897	0.967350	3.918036	0.255230	4
5	1.042367	5.084031	0.196694	0.959355	4.877391	0.205028	5
6	1.051053	6.126398	0.163228	0.951427	5.828817	0.171561	6
7	1.059812	7.177451	0.139325	0.943563	6.772381	0.147659	7
8	1.068644	8.237263	0.121400	0.935765	7.708146	0.129733	8
9	1.077549	9.305907	0.107459	0.928032	8.636178	0.115792	9
10	1.086529	10.383456	0.096307	0.920362	9.556540	0.104640	10
11	1.095583	11.469985	0.087184	0.912756	10.469296	0.095517	11
12	1.104713	12.565568	0.079583	0.905212	11.374508	0.087916	12
YEARS							MONTHS
1	1.104713	12.565568	0.079583	0.905212	11.374508	0.087916	12
2	1.220391	26.446915	0.037812	0.819410	21.670855	0.046145	24
3	1.348182	41.781821	0.023934	0.741740	30.991236	0.032267	36
4	1.489354	58.722492	0.017029	0.671432	39.428160	0.025363	48
5	1.645309	77.437072	0.012914	0.607789	47.065369	0.021247	60
6	1.817594	98.111314	0.010193	0.550178	53.978665	0.018526	72
7	2.007920	120.950418	0.008268	0.498049	60.236667	0.016601	84
8	2.218176	146.181076	0.006841	0.450821	65.901488	0.015174	96
9	2.450448	174.053713	0.005745	0.408089	71.029355	0.014079	108
10	2.707041	204.844979	0.004882	0.369407	75.671163	0.013215	120
11	2.990504	238.860493	0.004187	0.334392	79.872986	0.012520	132
12	3.303649	276.437876	0.003617	0.302696	83.676528	0.011951	144
13	3.649584	317.950102	0.003145	0.274004	87.119542	0.011478	156
14	4.031743	363.809201	0.002749	0.248032	90.236201	0.011082	168
15	4.453920	414.470346	0.002413	0.224521	93.057439	0.010746	180
16	4.920303	470.436376	0.002126	0.203240	95.611259	0.010459	192
17	5.435523	532.262780	0.001879	0.183975	97.923008	0.010212	204
18	6.004693	600.563216	0.001665	0.166536	100.015633	0.009998	216
19	6.633463	676.015601	0.001479	0.150751	101.909902	0.009813	228
20	7.328074	759.368836	0.001317	0.136462	103.624619	0.009650	240
21	8.095419	851.450244	0.001174	0.123527	105.176801	0.009508	252
22	8.943115	953.173779	0.001049	0.111818	106.581856	0.009382	264
23	9.879576	1065.549097	0.000938	0.101219	107.853730	0.009272	276
24	10.914097	1189.691580	0.000841	0.091625	109.005045	0.009174	288
25	12.056945	1326.833403	0.000754	0.082940	110.047230	0.009087	300
26	13.319465	1478.335767	0.000676	0.075078	110.990629	0.009010	312
27	14.714187	1645.702640	0.000608	0.067962	111.844605	0.008941	324
28	16.254954	1830.594523	0.000546	0.061520	112.617635	0.008880	336
29	17.957060	2034.847258	0.000491	0.055688	113.317392	0.008825	348
30	19.837399	2260.487925	0.000442	0.050410	113.950820	0.008776	360
31	21.914634	2509.756117	0.000398	0.045632	114.524207	0.008732	372
32	24.209383	2785.125947	0.000359	0.041306	115.043244	0.008692	384
33	26.744422	3089.330596	0.000324	0.037391	115.513083	0.008657	396
34	29.544912	3425.389447	0.000292	0.033847	115.938387	0.008625	408
35	32.638650	3796.638052	0.000263	0.030639	116.323377	0.008597	420
36	36.056344	4206.761236	0.000238	0.027734	116.671876	0.008571	432
37	39.831914	4659.829677	0.000215	0.025105	116.987340	0.008548	444
38	44.002836	5160.340305	0.000194	0.022726	117.272903	0.008527	456
39	48.610508	5713.260935	0.000175	0.020572	117.531398	0.008508	468
40	53.700663	6324.079581	0.000158	0.018622	117.765391	0.008491	480

MONTHLY COMPOUND INTEREST TABLES

10.50% ANNUAL INTEREST RATE   0.8750% MONTHLY EFFECTIVE INTEREST RATE

	1 AMOUNT OF $1 AT COMPOUND INTEREST	2 ACCUMULATION OF $1 PER PERIOD	3 SINKING FUND FACTOR	4 PRESENT VALUE REVERSION OF $1	5 PRESENT VALUE ORD. ANNUINTY $1 PER PERIOD	6 INSTALLMENT TO AMORTIZE $1	
MONTHS							MONTHS
1	1.008750	1.000000	1.000000	0.991326	0.991326	1.008750	1
2	1.017577	2.008750	0.497822	0.982727	1.974053	0.506572	2
3	1.026480	3.026327	0.330434	0.974203	2.948256	0.339184	3
4	1.035462	4.052807	0.246743	0.965752	3.914008	0.255493	4
5	1.044522	5.088269	0.196530	0.957375	4.871384	0.205280	5
6	1.053662	6.132791	0.163058	0.949071	5.820455	0.171808	6
7	1.062881	7.186453	0.139151	0.940839	6.761293	0.147901	7
8	1.072182	8.249335	0.121222	0.932678	7.693971	0.129972	8
9	1.081563	9.321516	0.107279	0.924588	8.618559	0.116029	9
10	1.091027	10.403080	0.096125	0.916568	9.535126	0.104875	10
11	1.100573	11.494107	0.087001	0.908617	10.443743	0.095751	11
12	1.110203	12.594680	0.079399	0.900736	11.344479	0.088149	12
YEARS							MONTHS
1	1.110203	12.594680	0.079399	0.900736	11.344479	0.088149	12
2	1.232552	26.577337	0.037626	0.811325	21.562858	0.046376	24
3	1.368383	42.100932	0.023752	0.730789	30.766918	0.032502	36
4	1.519184	59.335280	0.016853	0.658248	39.057344	0.025603	48
5	1.686603	78.468912	0.012744	0.592908	46.524827	0.021494	60
6	1.872472	99.711137	0.010029	0.534053	53.251057	0.018779	72
7	2.078825	123.294329	0.008111	0.481041	59.309613	0.016861	84
8	2.307919	149.476469	0.006690	0.433291	64.766771	0.015440	96
9	2.562260	178.543972	0.005601	0.390280	69.682229	0.014351	108
10	2.844630	210.814814	0.004743	0.351540	74.109758	0.013493	120
11	3.158118	246.642013	0.004054	0.316644	78.097792	0.012804	132
12	3.506153	286.417494	0.003491	0.285213	81.689957	0.012241	144
13	3.892543	330.576371	0.003025	0.256901	84.925549	0.011775	156
14	4.321515	379.601707	0.002634	0.231400	87.839962	0.011384	168
15	4.797761	434.029805	0.002304	0.208431	90.465078	0.011054	180
16	5.326491	494.456068	0.002022	0.187741	92.829614	0.010772	192
17	5.913488	561.541512	0.001781	0.169105	94.959437	0.010531	204
18	6.565175	636.020005	0.001572	0.152319	96.877844	0.010322	216
19	7.288680	718.706284	0.001391	0.137199	98.605822	0.010141	228
20	8.091918	810.504876	0.001234	0.123580	100.162274	0.009984	240
21	8.983675	912.419990	0.001096	0.111313	101.564226	0.009846	252
22	9.973707	1025.566501	0.000975	0.100264	102.827014	0.009725	264
23	11.072844	1151.182148	0.000869	0.090311	103.964453	0.009619	276
24	12.293109	1290.641073	0.000775	0.081346	104.988985	0.009525	288
25	13.647852	1445.468853	0.000692	0.073272	105.911817	0.009442	300
26	15.151893	1617.359188	0.000618	0.065998	106.743045	0.009368	312
27	16.821684	1808.192431	0.000553	0.059447	107.491762	0.009303	324
28	18.675491	2020.056156	0.000495	0.053546	108.166158	0.009245	336
29	20.733595	2255.267995	0.000443	0.048231	108.773611	0.009193	348
30	23.018509	2516.400990	0.000397	0.043443	109.320766	0.009147	360
31	25.555228	2806.311742	0.000356	0.039131	109.813607	0.009106	372
32	28.371502	3128.171659	0.000320	0.035247	110.257527	0.009070	384
33	31.498139	3485.501649	0.000287	0.031748	110.657382	0.009037	396
34	34.969343	3882.210638	0.000258	0.028596	111.017546	0.009008	408
35	38.823085	4322.638325	0.000231	0.025758	111.341958	0.008981	420
36	43.101523	4811.602664	0.000208	0.023201	111.634167	0.008958	432
37	47.851460	5354.452560	0.000187	0.020898	111.897371	0.008937	444
38	53.124856	5957.126387	0.000168	0.018824	112.134448	0.008918	456
39	58.979398	6626.216950	0.000151	0.016955	112.347992	0.008901	468
40	65.479132	7369.043601	0.000136	0.015272	112.540338	0.008886	480

MONTHLY COMPOUND INTEREST TABLES

11.00% ANNUAL INTEREST RATE

0.9167% MONTHLY EFFECTIVE INTEREST RATE

	1 AMOUNT OF $1 AT COMPOUND INTEREST	2 ACCUMULATION OF $1 PER PERIOD	3 SINKING FUND FACTOR	4 PRESENT VALUE REVERSION OF $1	5 PRESENT VALUE ORD. ANNUINTY $1 PER PERIOD	6 INSTALLMENT TO AMORTIZE $1	
MONTHS							MONTHS
1	1.009167	1.000000	1.000000	0.990917	0.990917	1.009167	1
2	1.018417	2.009167	0.497719	0.981916	1.972832	0.506885	2
3	1.027753	3.027584	0.330296	0.972097	2.945829	0.339463	3
4	1.037174	4.055337	0.246589	0.964158	3.909987	0.255755	4
5	1.046681	5.092511	0.196367	0.955401	4.865388	0.205533	5
6	1.056276	6.139192	0.162888	0.946722	5.812110	0.172055	6
7	1.065958	7.195468	0.138976	0.938123	6.750233	0.148143	7
8	1.075730	8.261427	0.121044	0.929602	7.679835	0.130211	8
9	1.085591	9.337156	0.107099	0.921158	8.600992	0.116266	9
10	1.095542	10.422747	0.095944	0.912790	9.513783	0.105111	10
11	1.105584	11.518289	0.086818	0.904499	10.418282	0.095985	11
12	1.115719	12.623873	0.079215	0.896283	11.314565	0.088382	12
YEARS							MONTHS
1	1.115719	12.623873	0.079215	0.896283	11.314565	0.088382	12
2	1.244829	26.708566	0.037441	0.803323	21.455619	0.046608	24
3	1.388879	42.423123	0.023572	0.720005	30.544874	0.032739	36
4	1.549598	59.956151	0.016679	0.645329	38.691421	0.025846	48
5	1.728916	79.518080	0.012576	0.578397	45.993034	0.021742	60
6	1.928984	101.343692	0.009867	0.518408	52.537346	0.019034	72
7	2.152204	125.694940	0.007956	0.464640	58.402903	0.017122	84
8	2.401254	152.864085	0.006542	0.416449	63.660103	0.015708	96
9	2.679124	183.177212	0.005459	0.373256	68.372043	0.014626	108
10	2.989150	216.998139	0.004608	0.334543	72.595275	0.013775	120
11	3.335051	254.732784	0.003926	0.299846	76.380487	0.013092	132
12	3.720979	296.834038	0.003369	0.268747	79.773109	0.012536	144
13	4.151566	343.807200	0.002909	0.240873	82.813859	0.012075	156
14	4.631980	396.216042	0.002524	0.215890	85.539231	0.011691	168
15	5.167988	454.689575	0.002199	0.193499	87.981937	0.011366	180
16	5.766021	519.929596	0.001923	0.173430	90.171293	0.011090	192
17	6.433259	592.719117	0.001687	0.155442	92.133576	0.010854	204
18	7.177708	673.031757	0.001484	0.139320	93.892337	0.010650	216
19	8.008304	764.542228	0.001308	0.124870	95.468685	0.010475	228
20	8.935015	865.638038	0.001155	0.111919	96.881539	0.010322	240
21	9.968965	978.432537	0.001022	0.100311	98.147856	0.010189	252
22	11.122562	1104.279485	0.000906	0.089907	99.282835	0.010072	264
23	12.409652	1244.689295	0.000803	0.080582	100.300098	0.009970	276
24	13.845682	1401.347165	0.000714	0.072225	101.211853	0.009880	288
25	15.447889	1576.133301	0.000634	0.064734	102.029044	0.009801	300
26	17.235500	1771.145485	0.000565	0.058020	102.761478	0.009731	312
27	19.229972	1988.724252	0.000503	0.052002	103.417947	0.009670	324
28	21.455242	2231.480981	0.000448	0.046609	104.006328	0.009615	336
29	23.938018	2502.329236	0.000400	0.041775	104.533658	0.009566	348
30	26.708098	2804.519736	0.000357	0.037442	105.006346	0.009523	360
31	29.798728	3141.679369	0.000318	0.033558	105.429984	0.009485	372
32	33.247002	3517.854723	0.000284	0.030078	105.809684	0.009451	384
33	37.094306	3937.560650	0.000254	0.026958	106.150002	0.009421	396
34	41.386816	4405.834459	0.000227	0.024162	106.455024	0.009394	408
35	46.176050	4928.296368	0.000203	0.021656	106.728409	0.009370	420
36	51.519489	5511.216962	0.000181	0.019410	106.973440	0.009348	432
37	57.481264	6161.592447	0.000162	0.017397	107.193057	0.009329	444
38	64.132929	6887.228628	0.000145	0.015593	107.389897	0.009312	456
39	71.554317	7696.834582	0.000130	0.013975	107.566320	0.009297	468
40	79.834499	8600.127195	0.000116	0.012526	107.724446	0.009283	480

MONTHLY COMPOUND INTEREST TABLES

11.50% ANNUAL INTEREST RATE   0.9583% MONTHLY EFFECTIVE INTEREST RATE

	1 AMOUNT OF $1 AT COMPOUND INTEREST	2 ACCUMULATION OF $1 PER PERIOD	3 SINKING FUND FACTOR	4 PRESENT VALUE REVERSION OF $1	5 PRESENT VALUE ORD. ANNUINTY $1 PER PERIOD	6 INSTALLMENT TO AMORTIZE $1	
MONTHS							MONTHS
1	1.009583	1.000000	1.000000	0.990508	0.990508	1.009583	1
2	1.019259	2.009583	0.497616	0.981105	1.971613	0.507199	2
3	1.029026	3.028842	0.330159	0.971792	2.943405	0.339743	3
4	1.038888	4.057868	0.246435	0.962568	3.905973	0.256018	4
5	1.048844	5.096756	0.196203	0.953431	4.859404	0.205787	5
6	1.058895	6.145600	0.162718	0.944380	5.803784	0.172301	6
7	1.069043	7.204495	0.138802	0.935416	6.739200	0.148386	7
8	1.079288	8.273538	0.120867	0.926537	7.665737	0.130451	8
9	1.089631	9.352827	0.106920	0.917742	8.583479	0.116503	9
10	1.100074	10.442458	0.095763	0.909030	9.492509	0.105346	10
11	1.110616	11.542531	0.086636	0.900401	10.392910	0.096219	11
12	1.121259	12.653147	0.079032	0.891854	11.284764	0.088615	12
YEARS							MONTHS
1	1.121259	12.653147	0.079032	0.891854	11.284764	0.088615	12
2	1.257222	26.840607	0.037257	0.795404	21.349130	0.046840	24
3	1.409672	42.748428	0.023393	0.709385	30.325079	0.032976	36
4	1.580608	60.585221	0.016506	0.632668	38.330318	0.026089	48
5	1.772272	80.584891	0.012409	0.564248	45.469825	0.021993	60
6	1.987176	103.009708	0.009708	0.503227	51.837225	0.019291	72
7	2.228140	128.153744	0.007803	0.448805	57.516018	0.017386	84
8	2.498323	156.346728	0.006396	0.400269	62.580675	0.015979	96
9	2.801268	187.958374	0.005320	0.356982	67.097611	0.014904	108
10	3.140948	223.403228	0.004476	0.318375	71.126060	0.014060	120
11	3.521817	263.146100	0.003800	0.283944	74.718850	0.013384	132
12	3.948870	307.708167	0.003250	0.253237	77.923095	0.012833	144
13	4.427707	357.673800	0.002796	0.225851	80.780815	0.012379	156
14	4.964608	413.698232	0.002417	0.201426	83.329485	0.012001	168
15	5.566613	476.516149	0.002099	0.179642	85.602527	0.011682	180
16	6.241617	546.951324	0.001828	0.160215	87.629750	0.011412	192
17	6.998471	625.927421	0.001598	0.142888	89.437737	0.011181	204
18	7.847101	714.480107	0.001400	0.127436	91.050199	0.010983	216
19	8.798635	813.770632	0.001229	0.113654	92.488279	0.010812	228
20	9.865552	925.101060	0.001081	0.101363	93.770838	0.010664	240
21	11.061842	1049.931340	0.000952	0.090401	94.914693	0.010536	252
22	12.403194	1189.898456	0.000840	0.080624	95.934846	0.010424	264
23	13.907196	1346.837841	0.000742	0.071905	96.844673	0.010326	276
24	15.593574	1522.807696	0.000657	0.064129	97.656106	0.010240	288
25	17.484440	1720.115481	0.000581	0.057194	98.379787	0.010165	300
26	19.604591	1941.348676	0.000515	0.051008	99.025204	0.010098	312
27	21.981831	2189.408459	0.000457	0.045492	99.600823	0.010040	324
28	24.647333	2467.547806	0.000405	0.040572	100.114191	0.009989	336
29	27.636052	2779.414142	0.000360	0.036185	100.572040	0.009949	348
30	30.987181	3129.097181	0.000320	0.032271	100.980375	0.009903	360
31	34.744666	3521.182550	0.000284	0.028781	101.344550	0.009867	372
32	38.957781	3960.811927	0.000252	0.025669	101.669341	0.009836	384
33	43.681775	4453.750468	0.000225	0.022893	101.959008	0.009808	396
34	48.978598	5006.462404	0.000200	0.020417	102.217348	0.009783	408
35	54.917710	5626.195819	0.000178	0.018209	102.447750	0.009761	420
36	61.576995	6321.077691	0.000158	0.016240	102.653235	0.009742	432
37	69.043780	7100.220473	0.000141	0.014484	102.836498	0.009724	444
38	77.415982	7973.841584	0.000125	0.012917	102.999941	0.009709	456
39	86.803392	8953.397405	0.000112	0.011520	103.145709	0.009695	468
40	97.329113	10051.733506	0.000099	0.010274	103.275713	0.009683	480

MONTHLY COMPOUND INTEREST TABLES

12.00% ANNUAL INTEREST RATE   1.0000% MONTHLY EFFECTIVE INTEREST RATE

	1 AMOUNT OF $1 AT COMPOUND INTEREST	2 ACCUMULATION OF $1 PER PERIOD	3 SINKING FUND FACTOR	4 PRESENT VALUE REVERSION OF $1	5 PRESENT VALUE ORD. ANNUINTY $1 PER PERIOD	6 INSTALLMENT TO AMORTIZE $1	
MONTHS							MONTHS
1	1.010000	1.000000	1.000000	0.990099	0.990099	1.010000	1
2	1.020100	2.010000	0.497512	0.980296	1.970395	0.507512	2
3	1.030301	3.030100	0.330022	0.970590	2.940985	0.340022	3
4	1.040604	4.060401	0.246281	0.960980	3.901966	0.256281	4
5	1.051010	5.101005	0.196040	0.951466	4.853431	0.206040	5
6	1.061520	6.152015	0.162548	0.942045	5.795476	0.172548	6
7	1.072135	7.213535	0.138628	0.932718	6.728195	0.148628	7
8	1.082857	8.285671	0.120690	0.923483	7.651678	0.130690	8
9	1.093685	9.368527	0.106740	0.914340	8.566018	0.116740	9
10	1.104622	10.462213	0.095582	0.905287	9.471305	0.105582	10
11	1.115668	11.566835	0.086454	0.896324	10.367628	0.096454	11
12	1.126825	12.682503	0.078849	0.887449	11.255077	0.088849	12
YEARS							MONTHS
1	1.126825	12.682503	0.078849	0.887449	11.255077	0.088849	12
2	1.269735	26.973465	0.037073	0.787566	21.243387	0.047073	24
3	1.430769	43.076878	0.023214	0.698925	30.107505	0.033214	36
4	1.612226	61.222608	0.016334	0.620260	37.973959	0.026334	48
5	1.816697	81.669670	0.012244	0.550450	44.955038	0.022244	60
6	2.047099	104.709931	0.009550	0.488496	51.150399	0.019550	72
7	2.306723	130.672274	0.007653	0.433515	56.648453	0.017653	84
8	2.599273	159.927293	0.006253	0.384723	61.527703	0.016253	96
9	2.928926	192.892579	0.005184	0.341422	65.857790	0.015184	108
10	3.300387	230.038689	0.004347	0.302995	69.700522	0.014347	120
11	3.718959	271.895856	0.003678	0.268892	73.110752	0.013678	132
12	4.190616	319.061559	0.003134	0.238628	76.137157	0.013134	144
13	4.722091	372.209054	0.002687	0.211771	78.822939	0.012687	156
14	5.320970	432.096982	0.002314	0.187936	81.206434	0.012314	168
15	5.995802	499.580198	0.002002	0.166783	83.321664	0.012002	180
16	6.756220	575.621974	0.001737	0.148012	85.198824	0.011737	192
17	7.613078	661.307751	0.001512	0.131353	86.864707	0.011512	204
18	8.578606	757.860630	0.001320	0.116569	88.343095	0.011320	216
19	9.666588	866.658830	0.001154	0.103449	89.655089	0.011154	228
20	10.892554	989.255365	0.001011	0.091806	90.819416	0.011011	240
21	12.274002	1127.400210	0.000887	0.081473	91.852698	0.010887	252
22	13.830653	1283.065279	0.000779	0.072303	92.769683	0.010779	264
23	15.584726	1458.472574	0.000686	0.064165	93.583461	0.010686	276
24	17.561259	1656.125905	0.000604	0.056944	94.305647	0.010604	288
25	19.788466	1878.846626	0.000532	0.050534	94.946551	0.010532	300
26	22.298139	2129.813909	0.000470	0.044847	95.515321	0.010470	312
27	25.126101	2412.610125	0.000414	0.039799	96.020075	0.010414	324
28	28.312720	2731.271980	0.000366	0.035320	96.468019	0.010366	336
29	31.903481	3090.348134	0.000324	0.031345	96.865546	0.010324	348
30	35.949641	3494.964133	0.000286	0.027817	97.218331	0.010286	360
31	40.508956	3950.895567	0.000253	0.024686	97.531410	0.010253	372
32	45.646505	4464.650520	0.000224	0.021907	97.809252	0.010224	384
33	51.435625	5043.562459	0.000198	0.019442	98.055822	0.010198	396
34	57.958949	5695.894923	0.000176	0.017254	98.274641	0.010176	408
35	65.309595	6430.959471	0.000155	0.015312	98.468831	0.010155	420
36	73.592486	7259.248603	0.000138	0.013588	98.641166	0.010138	432
37	82.925855	8192.585529	0.000122	0.012059	98.794103	0.010122	444
38	93.442929	9244.292939	0.000108	0.010702	98.929828	0.010108	456
39	105.293832	10429.383172	0.000096	0.009497	99.050277	0.010096	468
40	118.647725	11764.772510	0.000085	0.008428	99.157169	0.010085	480

MONTHLY COMPOUND INTEREST TABLES

12.50% ANNUAL INTEREST RATE   1.0417% MONTHLY EFFECTIVE INTEREST RATE

	1 AMOUNT OF $1 AT COMPOUND INTEREST	2 ACCUMULATION OF $1 PER PERIOD	3 SINKING FUND FACTOR	4 PRESENT VALUE REVERSION OF $1	5 PRESENT VALUE ORD. ANNUINTY $1 PER PERIOD	6 INSTALLMENT TO AMORTIZE $1	
MONTHS							MONTHS
1	1.010417	1.000000	1.000000	0.989691	0.989691	1.010417	1
2	1.020942	2.010417	0.497409	0.979488	1.969178	0.507826	2
3	1.031577	3.031359	0.329885	0.969390	2.938568	0.340302	3
4	1.042322	4.062935	0.246127	0.959396	3.897965	0.256544	4
5	1.053180	5.105257	0.195877	0.949506	4.847470	0.206293	5
6	1.064150	6.158437	0.162379	0.939717	5.787187	0.172796	6
7	1.075235	7.222588	0.138455	0.930029	6.717216	0.148871	7
8	1.086436	8.297823	0.120514	0.920441	7.637657	0.130930	8
9	1.097753	9.384258	0.106561	0.910952	8.548609	0.116978	9
10	1.109188	10.482011	0.095402	0.901561	9.450170	0.105818	10
11	1.120742	11.591199	0.086272	0.892266	10.342436	0.096689	11
12	1.132416	12.711940	0.078666	0.883068	11.225504	0.089083	12
YEARS							MONTHS
1	1.132416	12.711940	0.078666	0.883068	11.225504	0.089083	12
2	1.282366	27.107146	0.036891	0.779809	21.138383	0.047307	24
3	1.452172	43.408507	0.023037	0.688624	29.892126	0.033454	36
4	1.644463	61.868431	0.016163	0.608101	37.622274	0.026580	48
5	1.862216	82.772744	0.012081	0.536995	44.448517	0.022498	60
6	2.108803	106.445124	0.009395	0.474203	50.476552	0.019811	72
7	2.388043	133.252107	0.007505	0.418753	55.799715	0.017921	84
8	2.704258	163.608765	0.006112	0.369787	60.500428	0.016529	96
9	3.062345	197.985131	0.005051	0.326547	64.651476	0.015468	108
10	3.467849	236.913480	0.004221	0.288363	68.317132	0.014638	120
11	3.927048	280.996567	0.003559	0.254644	71.554154	0.013975	132
12	4.447052	330.916961	0.003022	0.224868	74.412664	0.013439	144
13	5.035913	387.447618	0.002581	0.198574	76.936921	0.012998	156
14	5.702748	451.463840	0.002215	0.175354	79.166011	0.012632	168
15	6.457884	523.956837	0.001909	0.154849	81.134449	0.012325	180
16	7.313011	606.049070	0.001650	0.136743	82.872712	0.012067	192
17	8.281371	699.011633	0.001431	0.120753	84.407717	0.011847	204
18	9.377958	804.283930	0.001243	0.106633	85.763229	0.011660	216
19	10.619750	923.495968	0.001083	0.094164	86.960239	0.011500	228
20	12.025975	1058.493594	0.000945	0.083153	88.017279	0.011361	240
21	13.618407	1211.367071	0.000826	0.073430	88.950717	0.011242	252
22	15.421703	1384.483450	0.000722	0.064844	89.775006	0.011139	264
23	17.463783	1580.523215	0.000633	0.057261	90.502909	0.011049	276
24	19.776269	1802.521791	0.000555	0.050566	91.145697	0.010971	288
25	22.394964	2053.916541	0.000487	0.044653	91.713322	0.010904	300
26	25.360417	2338.599989	0.000428	0.039432	92.214573	0.010844	312
27	28.718543	2660.980094	0.000376	0.034821	92.657212	0.010792	324
28	32.521339	3026.048499	0.000330	0.030749	93.048092	0.010747	336
29	36.827686	3439.457817	0.000291	0.027153	93.393265	0.010707	348
30	41.704262	3907.609164	0.000256	0.023978	93.698077	0.010673	360
31	47.226576	4437.751261	0.000225	0.021175	93.967246	0.010642	372
32	53.480132	5038.092678	0.000198	0.018699	94.204941	0.010615	384
33	60.561760	5717.928933	0.000175	0.016512	94.414841	0.010592	396
34	68.581108	6487.786416	0.000154	0.014581	94.600198	0.010571	408
35	77.662348	7359.585384	0.000136	0.012876	94.763880	0.010553	420
36	87.946089	8346.824524	0.000120	0.011371	94.908422	0.010536	432
37	99.591562	9464.789968	0.000106	0.010041	95.036063	0.010522	444
38	112.779083	10730.791976	0.000093	0.008867	95.148778	0.010510	456
39	127.712843	12164.432965	0.000082	0.007830	95.248314	0.010499	468
40	144.624073	13787.911025	0.000073	0.006914	95.336210	0.010489	480

MONTHLY COMPOUND INTEREST TABLES

13.00% ANNUAL INTEREST RATE   1.0833% MONTHLY EFFECTIVE INTEREST RATE

	1 AMOUNT OF $1 AT COMPOUND INTEREST	2 ACCUMULATION OF $1 PER PERIOD	3 SINKING FUND FACTOR	4 PRESENT VALUE REVERSION OF $1	5 PRESENT VALUE ORD. ANNUINTY $1 PER PERIOD	6 INSTALLMENT TO AMORTIZE $1	
MONTHS							MONTHS
1	1.010833	1.000000	1.000000	0.989283	0.989283	1.010833	1
2	1.021784	2.010833	0.497306	0.978680	1.967963	0.508140	2
3	1.032853	3.032617	0.329748	0.968192	2.936155	0.340581	3
4	1.044043	4.065471	0.245974	0.957815	3.893970	0.256807	4
5	1.055353	5.109513	0.195713	0.947550	4.841520	0.206547	5
6	1.066786	6.164866	0.162210	0.937395	5.778915	0.173043	6
7	1.078343	7.231652	0.138281	0.927349	6.706264	0.149114	7
8	1.090025	8.309995	0.120337	0.917410	7.623674	0.131170	8
9	1.101834	9.400020	0.106383	0.907578	8.531253	0.117216	9
10	1.113770	10.501854	0.095221	0.897851	9.429104	0.106055	10
11	1.125836	11.615624	0.086091	0.888229	10.317333	0.096924	11
12	1.138032	12.741460	0.078484	0.878710	11.196042	0.089317	12
YEARS							MONTHS
1	1.138032	12.741460	0.078484	0.878710	11.196042	0.089317	12
2	1.295118	27.241655	0.036708	0.772130	21.034112	0.047542	24
3	1.473886	43.743348	0.022861	0.678478	29.678917	0.033694	36
4	1.677330	62.522811	0.015994	0.596185	37.275190	0.026827	48
5	1.908857	83.894449	0.011920	0.523874	43.950107	0.022753	60
6	2.172341	108.216068	0.009241	0.460333	49.815421	0.020074	72
7	2.472194	135.894861	0.007359	0.404499	54.969328	0.018192	84
8	2.813437	167.394225	0.005974	0.355437	59.498115	0.016807	96
9	3.201783	203.241525	0.004920	0.312326	63.477604	0.015754	108
10	3.643733	244.036917	0.004098	0.274444	66.974419	0.014931	120
11	4.146687	290.463399	0.003443	0.241156	70.047103	0.014276	132
12	4.719064	343.298242	0.002913	0.211906	72.747100	0.013746	144
13	5.370448	403.426010	0.002479	0.186204	75.119613	0.013312	156
14	6.111745	471.853363	0.002119	0.163619	77.204363	0.012953	168
15	6.955364	549.725914	0.001819	0.143774	79.036253	0.012652	180
16	7.915430	638.347406	0.001567	0.126336	80.645952	0.012400	192
17	9.008017	739.201542	0.001353	0.111012	82.060410	0.012186	204
18	10.251416	853.976825	0.001171	0.097548	83.303307	0.012004	216
19	11.666444	984.594826	0.001016	0.085716	84.395453	0.011849	228
20	13.276792	1133.242353	0.000882	0.075319	85.355132	0.011716	240
21	15.109421	1302.408067	0.000768	0.066184	86.198412	0.011601	252
22	17.195012	1494.924144	0.000669	0.058156	86.939409	0.011502	264
23	19.568482	1714.013694	0.000583	0.051103	87.590531	0.011417	276
24	22.269568	1963.344717	0.000509	0.044904	88.162677	0.011343	288
25	25.343491	2247.091520	0.000445	0.039458	88.665428	0.011278	300
26	28.841716	2570.004599	0.000389	0.034672	89.107200	0.011222	312
27	32.822810	2937.490172	0.000340	0.030467	89.495389	0.011174	324
28	37.353424	3355.700690	0.000298	0.026771	89.836495	0.011131	336
29	42.509410	3831.637843	0.000261	0.023524	90.136227	0.011094	348
30	48.377089	4373.269783	0.000229	0.020671	90.399605	0.011062	360
31	55.054699	4989.664524	0.000200	0.018164	90.631038	0.011034	372
32	62.654036	5691.141761	0.000176	0.015961	90.834400	0.011009	384
33	71.302328	6489.445641	0.000154	0.014025	91.013097	0.010987	396
34	81.144365	7397.941387	0.000135	0.012324	91.170119	0.010969	408
35	92.344923	8431.839055	0.000119	0.010829	91.308095	0.010952	420
36	105.091522	9608.448184	0.000104	0.009516	91.429337	0.010937	432
37	119.597566	10947.467591	0.000091	0.008361	91.535873	0.010925	444
38	136.105914	12471.315170	0.000080	0.007347	91.629487	0.010914	456
39	154.892951	14205.503212	0.000070	0.006456	91.711747	0.010904	468
40	176.273210	16179.065533	0.000062	0.005673	91.784030	0.010895	480

MONTHLY COMPOUND INTEREST TABLES

13.50% ANNUAL INTEREST RATE   1.1250% MONTHLY EFFECTIVE INTEREST RATE

	1 AMOUNT OF $1 AT COMPOUND INTEREST	2 ACCUMULATION OF $1 PER PERIOD	3 SINKING FUND FACTOR	4 PRESENT VALUE REVERSION OF $1	5 PRESENT VALUE ORD. ANNUITY $1 PER PERIOD	6 INSTALLMENT TO AMORTIZE $1	
MONTHS							MONTHS
1	1.011250	1.000000	1.000000	0.988875	0.988875	1.011250	1
2	1.022627	2.011250	0.497203	0.977874	1.966749	0.508453	2
3	1.034131	3.033877	0.329611	0.966995	2.933745	0.340861	3
4	1.045765	4.068008	0.245821	0.956238	3.889982	0.257071	4
5	1.057530	5.113773	0.195550	0.945600	4.835582	0.206800	5
6	1.069427	6.171303	0.162040	0.935080	5.770662	0.173290	6
7	1.081458	7.240730	0.138108	0.924677	6.695339	0.149358	7
8	1.093625	8.322188	0.120161	0.914391	7.609730	0.131411	8
9	1.105928	9.415813	0.106204	0.904218	8.513948	0.117454	9
10	1.118370	10.521741	0.095041	0.894159	9.408107	0.106291	10
11	1.130951	11.640110	0.085910	0.884211	10.292318	0.097160	11
12	1.143674	12.771061	0.078302	0.874375	11.166693	0.089552	12
YEARS							MONTHS
1	1.143674	12.771061	0.078302	0.874375	11.166693	0.089552	12
2	1.307991	27.376998	0.036527	0.764531	20.930567	0.047777	24
3	1.495916	44.081434	0.022685	0.668487	29.467851	0.033935	36
4	1.710841	63.185871	0.015826	0.584508	36.932637	0.027076	48
5	1.956645	85.035127	0.011760	0.511079	43.459656	0.023010	60
6	2.237765	110.023563	0.009089	0.446874	49.166717	0.020339	72
7	2.559275	138.602198	0.007215	0.390736	54.156827	0.018465	84
8	2.926977	171.286853	0.005838	0.341649	58.520052	0.017088	96
9	3.347509	208.667457	0.004792	0.298730	62.335146	0.016042	108
10	3.828460	251.418698	0.003977	0.261202	65.670968	0.015227	120
11	4.378512	300.312201	0.003330	0.228388	68.587726	0.014580	132
12	5.007593	356.230450	0.002807	0.199697	71.138066	0.014057	144
13	5.727056	420.182722	0.002380	0.174610	73.368018	0.013630	156
14	6.549887	493.323301	0.002027	0.152674	75.317832	0.013277	168
15	7.490939	576.972311	0.001733	0.133495	77.022700	0.012983	180
16	8.567195	672.639547	0.001487	0.116724	78.513394	0.012737	192
17	9.798082	782.051719	0.001279	0.102061	79.816818	0.012529	204
18	11.205816	907.183624	0.001102	0.089239	80.956500	0.012352	216
19	12.815805	1050.293785	0.000952	0.078029	81.953009	0.012202	228
20	14.657109	1213.965218	0.000824	0.068226	82.824331	0.012074	240
21	16.762961	1401.152054	0.000714	0.059655	83.586193	0.011964	252
22	19.171370	1615.232853	0.000619	0.052161	84.252345	0.011869	264
23	21.925805	1860.071591	0.000538	0.045608	84.834813	0.011788	276
24	25.075983	2140.087398	0.000467	0.039879	85.344107	0.011717	288
25	28.678761	2460.334319	0.000406	0.034869	85.789421	0.011656	300
26	32.799166	2826.592538	0.000354	0.030489	86.178793	0.011604	312
27	37.511568	3245.472702	0.000308	0.026658	86.519249	0.011558	324
28	42.901021	3724.535238	0.000268	0.023309	86.816936	0.011518	336
29	49.064802	4272.426817	0.000234	0.020381	87.077226	0.011484	348
30	56.114160	4899.036412	0.000204	0.017821	87.304817	0.011454	360
31	64.176330	5615.673790	0.000178	0.015582	87.503816	0.011428	372
32	73.396828	6435.273643	0.000155	0.013625	87.677816	0.011405	384
33	83.942077	7372.629046	0.000136	0.011913	87.829958	0.011386	396
34	96.002408	8444.658462	0.000118	0.010416	87.962986	0.011368	408
35	109.795500	9670.711105	0.000103	0.009108	88.079303	0.011353	420
36	125.570307	11072.916176	0.000090	0.007964	88.181007	0.011340	432
37	143.611551	12676.582277	0.000079	0.006963	88.269935	0.011329	444
38	164.244860	14510.654207	0.000069	0.006088	88.347692	0.011319	456
39	187.842648	16608.235397	0.000060	0.005324	88.415680	0.011310	468
40	214.830836	19007.185391	0.000053	0.004655	88.475127	0.011303	480

MONTHLY COMPOUND INTEREST TABLES

14.00% ANNUAL INTEREST RATE   1.1667% MONTHLY EFFECTIVE INTEREST RATE

	1 AMOUNT OF $1 AT COMPOUND INTEREST	2 ACCUMULATION OF $1 PER PERIOD	3 SINKING FUND FACTOR	4 PRESENT VALUE REVERSION OF $1	5 PRESENT VALUE ORD. ANNUITY $1 PER PERIOD	6 INSTALLMENT TO AMORTIZE $1	
MONTHS							MONTHS
1	1.011667	1.000000	1.000000	0.988468	0.988468	1.011667	1
2	1.023469	2.011667	0.497100	0.977069	1.965537	0.508767	2
3	1.035410	3.035136	0.329475	0.965801	2.931338	0.341141	3
4	1.047490	4.070546	0.245667	0.954663	3.886001	0.257334	4
5	1.059710	5.118036	0.195387	0.943654	4.829655	0.207054	5
6	1.072074	6.177746	0.161871	0.932772	5.762427	0.173538	6
7	1.084581	7.249820	0.137934	0.922015	6.684442	0.149601	7
8	1.097235	8.334401	0.119985	0.911382	7.595824	0.131651	8
9	1.110036	9.431636	0.106026	0.900872	8.496696	0.117693	9
10	1.122986	10.541672	0.094862	0.890483	9.387178	0.106528	10
11	1.136088	11.664658	0.085729	0.880214	10.267392	0.097396	11
12	1.149342	12.800745	0.078120	0.870063	11.137455	0.089787	12
YEARS							MONTHS
1	1.149342	12.800745	0.078120	0.870063	11.137455	0.089787	12
2	1.320987	27.513180	0.036346	0.757010	20.827743	0.048013	24
3	1.518266	44.422800	0.022511	0.658646	29.258904	0.034178	36
4	1.745007	63.857736	0.015660	0.573064	36.594546	0.027326	48
5	2.005610	86.195125	0.011602	0.498601	42.977016	0.023268	60
6	2.305132	111.868425	0.008939	0.433815	48.530168	0.020606	72
7	2.649385	141.375828	0.007073	0.377446	53.361760	0.018740	84
8	3.045049	175.289927	0.005705	0.328442	57.565549	0.017372	96
9	3.499803	214.268826	0.004667	0.285730	61.223111	0.016334	108
10	4.022471	259.068912	0.003860	0.248603	64.405420	0.015527	120
11	4.623195	310.559534	0.003220	0.216301	67.174230	0.014887	132
12	5.313632	369.739871	0.002705	0.188195	69.583269	0.014371	144
13	6.107180	437.758319	0.002284	0.163742	71.679284	0.013951	156
14	7.019239	515.934780	0.001938	0.142466	73.502950	0.013605	168
15	8.067507	605.786272	0.001651	0.123954	75.089654	0.013317	180
16	9.272324	709.056369	0.001410	0.107848	76.470187	0.013077	192
17	10.657072	827.749031	0.001208	0.093834	77.671337	0.012875	204
18	12.248621	964.167496	0.001037	0.081642	78.716413	0.012704	216
19	14.077855	1120.958972	0.000892	0.071034	79.625696	0.012559	228
20	16.180270	1301.166005	0.000769	0.061804	80.416829	0.012435	240
21	18.596664	1508.285522	0.000663	0.053773	81.105164	0.012330	252
22	21.373928	1746.336688	0.000573	0.046786	81.704060	0.012239	264
23	24.565954	2019.938898	0.000495	0.040707	82.225136	0.012162	276
24	28.234683	2334.401417	0.000428	0.035417	82.678506	0.012095	288
25	32.451308	2695.826407	0.000371	0.030815	83.072966	0.012038	300
26	37.297652	3111.227338	0.000321	0.026811	83.416171	0.011988	312
27	42.867759	3588.665088	0.000279	0.023328	83.714781	0.011945	324
28	49.269718	4137.404359	0.000242	0.020296	83.974591	0.011908	336
29	56.627757	4768.093467	0.000210	0.017659	84.200641	0.011876	348
30	65.084661	5492.970967	0.000182	0.015365	84.397320	0.011849	360
31	74.804537	6326.103143	0.000158	0.013368	84.568442	0.011825	372
32	85.975998	7283.656968	0.000137	0.011631	84.717330	0.011804	384
33	98.815828	8384.213825	0.000119	0.010120	84.846871	0.011786	396
34	113.573184	9649.130077	0.000104	0.008805	84.959580	0.011770	408
35	130.534434	11102.951488	0.000090	0.007661	85.057645	0.011757	420
36	150.028711	12773.889538	0.000078	0.006665	85.142966	0.011745	432
37	172.434303	14694.368868	0.000068	0.005799	85.217202	0.011735	444
38	198.185992	16901.656478	0.000059	0.005046	85.281792	0.011726	456
39	227.783490	19438.584899	0.000051	0.004390	85.337989	0.011718	468
40	261.801139	22354.383358	0.000045	0.003820	85.386883	0.011711	480

MONTHLY COMPOUND INTEREST TABLES

14.50% ANNUAL INTEREST RATE   1.2083% MONTHLY EFFECTIVE INTEREST RATE

	1 AMOUNT OF $1 AT COMPOUND INTEREST	2 ACCUMULATION OF $1 PER PERIOD	3 SINKING FUND FACTOR	4 PRESENT VALUE REVERSION OF $1	5 PRESENT VALUE ORD. ANNUITY $1 PER PERIOD	6 INSTALLMENT TO AMORTIZE $1	
MONTHS							MONTHS
1	1.012083	1.000000	1.000000	0.988061	0.988061	1.012083	1
2	1.024313	2.012083	0.496997	0.976264	1.964325	0.509081	2
3	1.036690	3.036396	0.329338	0.964609	2.928934	0.341421	3
4	1.049216	4.073086	0.245514	0.953092	3.882026	0.257597	4
5	1.061894	5.122302	0.195225	0.941713	4.823739	0.207308	5
6	1.074726	6.184197	0.161702	0.930470	5.754209	0.173786	6
7	1.087712	7.258922	0.137761	0.919361	6.673570	0.149845	7
8	1.100855	8.346634	0.119809	0.908385	7.581955	0.131892	8
9	1.114157	9.447490	0.105848	0.897539	8.479495	0.117932	9
10	1.127620	10.561647	0.094682	0.886824	9.366318	0.106766	10
11	1.141245	11.689267	0.085549	0.876236	10.242554	0.097632	11
12	1.155035	12.830512	0.077939	0.865774	11.108328	0.090023	12
YEARS							MONTHS
1	1.155035	12.830512	0.077939	0.865774	11.108328	0.090023	12
2	1.334107	27.650207	0.036166	0.749565	20.725634	0.048249	24
3	1.540940	44.767478	0.022338	0.648954	29.052051	0.034421	36
4	1.779841	64.538532	0.015495	0.561848	36.260850	0.027578	48
5	2.055779	87.374798	0.011445	0.486434	42.502042	0.023528	60
6	2.374497	113.751493	0.008791	0.421142	47.905507	0.020874	72
7	2.742628	144.217508	0.006934	0.364614	52.583688	0.019017	84
8	3.167833	179.406832	0.005574	0.315673	56.633938	0.017657	96
9	3.658959	220.051745	0.004544	0.273302	60.140540	0.016628	108
10	4.226227	266.998057	0.003745	0.236618	63.176466	0.015829	120
11	4.881441	321.222707	0.003113	0.204858	65.804893	0.015196	132
12	5.638237	383.854095	0.002605	0.177360	68.080518	0.014688	144
13	6.512363	456.195562	0.002192	0.153554	70.050696	0.014275	156
14	7.522010	539.752513	0.001853	0.132943	71.756425	0.013936	168
15	8.688187	636.263747	0.001572	0.115099	73.233202	0.013655	180
16	10.035163	747.737633	0.001337	0.099650	74.511757	0.013421	192
17	11.590968	876.493913	0.001141	0.086274	75.618698	0.013224	204
18	13.387978	1025.211968	0.000975	0.074694	76.577058	0.013059	216
19	15.463588	1196.986579	0.000835	0.064668	77.406782	0.012919	228
20	17.860991	1395.392327	0.000717	0.055988	78.125136	0.012800	240
21	20.630076	1624.557981	0.000616	0.048473	78.747069	0.012699	252
22	23.828467	1889.252413	0.000529	0.041967	79.285522	0.012613	264
23	27.522721	2194.983839	0.000456	0.036334	79.751701	0.012539	276
24	31.789716	2548.114445	0.000392	0.031457	80.155306	0.012476	288
25	36.718246	2955.992779	0.000338	0.027234	80.504738	0.012422	300
26	42.410872	3427.106674	0.000292	0.023579	80.807267	0.012375	312
27	48.986057	3971.259878	0.000252	0.020414	81.069189	0.012335	324
28	56.580627	4599.776067	0.000217	0.017674	81.295954	0.012301	336
29	65.352625	5325.734484	0.000188	0.015302	81.492281	0.012271	348
30	75.484592	6164.242121	0.000162	0.013248	81.662256	0.012246	360
31	87.187373	7132.748085	0.000140	0.011470	81.809416	0.012224	372
32	100.704498	8251.406712	0.000121	0.009930	81.936824	0.012205	384
33	116.317255	9543.496975	0.000105	0.008597	82.047130	0.012188	396
34	134.350542	11035.906907	0.000091	0.007443	82.142630	0.012174	408
35	155.179625	12759.693140	0.000078	0.006444	82.225312	0.012162	420
36	179.237953	14750.727180	0.000068	0.005579	82.296896	0.012151	432
37	207.026173	17050.441884	0.000059	0.004830	82.358871	0.012142	444
38	239.122549	19706.693669	0.000051	0.004182	82.412528	0.012134	456
39	276.194997	22774.758387	0.000044	0.003621	82.458982	0.012127	468
40	319.014986	26318.481600	0.000038	0.003135	82.499201	0.012121	480

MONTHLY COMPOUND INTEREST TABLES

15.00% ANNUAL INTEREST RATE   1.2500% MONTHLY EFFECTIVE INTEREST RATE

	1 AMOUNT OF $1 AT COMPOUND INTEREST	2 ACCUMULATION OF $1 PER PERIOD	3 SINKING FUND FACTOR	4 PRESENT VALUE REVERSION OF $1	5 PRESENT VALUE ORD. ANNUINTY $1 PER PERIOD	6 INSTALLMENT TO AMORTIZE $1	
MONTHS							MONTHS
1	1.012500	1.000000	1.000000	0.987654	0.987654	1.012500	1
2	1.025156	2.012500	0.496894	0.975461	1.963115	0.509394	2
3	1.037971	3.037656	0.329201	0.963418	2.926534	0.341701	3
4	1.050945	4.075627	0.245361	0.951524	3.878058	0.257861	4
5	1.064082	5.126572	0.195062	0.939777	4.817835	0.207562	5
6	1.077383	6.190654	0.161534	0.928175	5.746010	0.174034	6
7	1.090850	7.268038	0.137589	0.916716	6.662726	0.150089	7
8	1.104486	8.358888	0.119633	0.905398	7.568124	0.132133	8
9	1.118292	9.463374	0.105671	0.894221	8.462345	0.118171	9
10	1.132271	10.581666	0.094503	0.883181	9.345526	0.107003	10
11	1.146424	11.713937	0.085368	0.872277	10.217803	0.097868	11
12	1.160755	12.860361	0.077758	0.861509	11.079312	0.090258	12
YEARS							MONTHS
1	1.160755	12.860361	0.077758	0.861509	11.079312	0.090258	12
2	1.347351	27.788084	0.035987	0.742197	20.624235	0.048487	24
3	1.563944	45.115505	0.022165	0.639409	28.847267	0.034665	36
4	1.815355	65.228388	0.015331	0.550856	35.931481	0.027831	48
5	2.107181	88.574508	0.011290	0.474568	42.034592	0.023790	60
6	2.445920	115.673621	0.008645	0.408844	47.292474	0.021145	72
7	2.839113	147.129040	0.006797	0.352223	51.822185	0.019297	84
8	3.295513	183.641059	0.005445	0.303443	55.724570	0.017945	96
9	3.825282	226.022551	0.004424	0.261419	59.086509	0.016924	108
10	4.440213	275.217058	0.003633	0.225214	61.982847	0.016133	120
11	5.153998	332.319805	0.003009	0.194024	64.478068	0.015509	132
12	5.982526	398.602077	0.002509	0.167153	66.627722	0.015009	144
13	6.944244	475.539523	0.002103	0.144004	68.479668	0.014603	156
14	8.060563	564.845011	0.001770	0.124061	70.075134	0.014270	168
15	9.356334	668.506759	0.001496	0.106879	71.449643	0.013996	180
16	10.860408	788.832603	0.001268	0.092078	72.633794	0.013768	192
17	12.606267	928.501369	0.001077	0.079326	73.653950	0.013577	204
18	14.632781	1090.622520	0.000917	0.068340	74.532823	0.013417	216
19	16.985067	1278.805378	0.000782	0.058875	75.289980	0.013282	228
20	19.715494	1497.239481	0.000668	0.050722	75.942278	0.013168	240
21	22.884848	1750.787854	0.000571	0.043697	76.504237	0.013071	252
22	26.563691	2045.095272	0.000489	0.037645	76.988370	0.012989	264
23	30.833924	2386.713938	0.000419	0.032432	77.405455	0.012919	276
24	35.790617	2783.249347	0.000359	0.027940	77.764777	0.012859	288
25	41.544120	3243.529615	0.000308	0.024071	78.074336	0.012808	300
26	48.222525	3777.802015	0.000265	0.020737	78.341024	0.012765	312
27	55.974514	4397.961118	0.000227	0.017865	78.570728	0.012727	324
28	64.972670	5117.813598	0.000195	0.015391	78.768713	0.012695	336
29	75.417320	5953.385616	0.000168	0.013260	78.939236	0.012668	348
30	87.540995	6923.279611	0.000144	0.011423	79.086142	0.012644	360
31	101.613606	8049.088447	0.000124	0.009841	79.212704	0.012624	372
32	117.948452	9355.876140	0.000107	0.008478	79.321738	0.012607	384
33	136.909198	10872.735858	0.000092	0.007304	79.415671	0.012592	396
34	158.917970	12633.437629	0.000079	0.006293	79.496596	0.012579	408
35	184.464752	14677.180163	0.000068	0.005421	79.566313	0.012568	420
36	214.118294	17049.463544	0.000059	0.004670	79.626375	0.012559	432
37	248.538777	19803.102194	0.000050	0.004024	79.678119	0.012550	444
38	288.492509	22999.400699	0.000043	0.003466	79.722696	0.012543	456
39	334.868983	26709.518627	0.000037	0.002986	79.761101	0.012537	468
40	388.700685	31016.054774	0.000032	0.002573	79.794186	0.012532	480

MONTHLY COMPOUND INTEREST TABLES

16.00% ANNUAL INTEREST RATE   1.3333% MONTHLY EFFECTIVE INTEREST RATE

	1 AMOUNT OF $1 AT COMPOUND INTEREST	2 ACCUMULATION OF $1 PER PERIOD	3 SINKING FUND FACTOR	4 PRESENT VALUE REVERSION OF $1	5 PRESENT VALUE ORD. ANNUINTY $1 PER PERIOD	6 INSTALLMENT TO AMORTIZE $1	
MONTHS							MONTHS
1	1.013333	1.000000	1.000000	0.986842	0.986842	1.013333	1
2	1.026844	2.013333	0.496689	0.973857	1.960699	0.510022	2
3	1.040536	3.040178	0.328928	0.961043	2.921743	0.342261	3
4	1.054410	4.080713	0.245055	0.948398	3.870141	0.258389	4
5	1.068468	5.135123	0.194737	0.935919	4.806060	0.208071	5
6	1.082715	6.203591	0.161197	0.923604	5.729665	0.174530	6
7	1.097151	7.286306	0.137244	0.911452	6.641116	0.150577	7
8	1.111779	8.383457	0.119283	0.899459	7.540575	0.132616	8
9	1.126603	9.495236	0.105316	0.887624	8.428199	0.118649	9
10	1.141625	10.621839	0.094146	0.875945	9.304144	0.107479	10
11	1.156846	11.763464	0.085009	0.864419	10.168563	0.098342	11
12	1.172271	12.920310	0.077398	0.853045	11.021609	0.090731	12
YEARS							MONTHS
1	1.172271	12.920310	0.077398	0.853045	11.021609	0.090731	12
2	1.374219	28.066412	0.035630	0.727686	20.423539	0.048963	24
3	1.610957	45.821745	0.021824	0.620749	28.443811	0.035157	36
4	1.888477	66.635803	0.015007	0.529527	35.285465	0.028340	48
5	2.213807	91.035516	0.010985	0.451711	41.121706	0.024318	60
6	2.595181	119.638587	0.008359	0.385330	46.100283	0.021692	72
7	3.042255	153.169132	0.006529	0.328704	50.347235	0.019862	84
8	3.566347	192.476010	0.005195	0.280399	53.970077	0.018529	96
9	4.180724	238.554316	0.004192	0.239193	57.060524	0.017525	108
10	4.900941	292.570569	0.003418	0.204042	59.696816	0.016751	120
11	5.745230	355.892244	0.002810	0.174057	61.945692	0.016143	132
12	6.734965	430.122395	0.002325	0.148479	63.864085	0.015658	144
13	7.895203	517.140233	0.001934	0.126659	65.500561	0.015267	156
14	9.255316	619.148703	0.001615	0.108046	66.896549	0.014948	168
15	10.849737	738.730255	0.001354	0.092168	68.087390	0.014687	180
16	12.718830	878.912215	0.001138	0.078624	69.103231	0.014471	192
17	14.909912	1043.243434	0.000959	0.067069	69.969789	0.014292	204
18	17.478455	1235.884123	0.000809	0.057213	70.709003	0.014142	216
19	20.489482	1461.711177	0.000684	0.048806	71.339585	0.014017	228
20	24.019222	1726.441638	0.000579	0.041633	71.877501	0.013913	240
21	28.157032	2036.777427	0.000491	0.035515	72.336367	0.013824	252
22	33.007667	2400.575011	0.000417	0.030296	72.727801	0.013750	264
23	38.693924	2827.044294	0.000354	0.025844	73.061711	0.013687	276
24	45.359757	3326.981781	0.000301	0.022046	73.346552	0.013634	288
25	53.173919	3913.043898	0.000256	0.018806	73.589534	0.013589	300
26	62.334232	4600.067404	0.000217	0.016043	73.796809	0.013551	312
27	73.072600	5405.444997	0.000185	0.013685	73.973623	0.013518	324
28	85.660875	6349.565632	0.000157	0.011674	74.124454	0.013491	336
29	100.417742	7456.330682	0.000134	0.009958	74.253120	0.013467	348
30	117.716787	8753.759030	0.000114	0.008495	74.362878	0.013448	360
31	137.995952	10274.696396	0.000097	0.007247	74.456506	0.013431	372
32	161.768625	12057.646856	0.000083	0.006182	74.536375	0.013416	384
33	189.636635	14147.747615	0.000071	0.005273	74.604507	0.013404	396
34	222.305489	16597.911700	0.000060	0.004498	74.662626	0.013394	408
35	260.602233	19470.167508	0.000051	0.003837	74.712205	0.013385	420
36	305.496388	22837.229116	0.000044	0.003273	74.754498	0.013377	432
37	358.124495	26784.337116	0.000037	0.002792	74.790576	0.013371	444
38	419.818887	31411.416562	0.000032	0.002382	74.821352	0.013365	456
39	492.141422	36835.606677	0.000027	0.002032	74.847605	0.013360	468
40	576.923018	43194.226353	0.000023	0.001733	74.870000	0.013356	480

MONTHLY COMPOUND INTEREST TABLES

17.00% ANNUAL INTEREST RATE   1.4167% MONTHLY EFFECTIVE INTEREST RATE

	1 AMOUNT OF $1 AT COMPOUND INTEREST	2 ACCUMULATION OF $1 PER PERIOD	3 SINKING FUND FACTOR	4 PRESENT VALUE REVERSION OF $1	5 PRESENT VALUE ORD. ANNUINTY $1 PER PERIOD	6 INSTALLMENT TO AMORTIZE $1	
MONTHS							MONTHS
1	1.014167	1.000000	1.000000	0.986031	0.986031	1.014167	1
2	1.028534	2.014167	0.496483	0.972258	1.958289	0.510650	2
3	1.043105	3.042701	0.328655	0.958676	2.916965	0.342822	3
4	1.057882	4.085806	0.244750	0.945285	3.862250	0.258916	4
5	1.072869	5.143688	0.194413	0.932080	4.794330	0.208580	5
6	1.088068	6.216557	0.160861	0.919060	5.713391	0.175027	6
7	1.103482	7.304625	0.136900	0.906222	6.619613	0.151066	7
8	1.119115	8.408107	0.118933	0.893563	7.513176	0.133100	8
9	1.134969	9.527222	0.104962	0.881081	8.394257	0.119129	9
10	1.151048	10.662191	0.093789	0.868774	9.263031	0.107956	10
11	1.167354	11.813238	0.084651	0.856638	10.119669	0.098817	11
12	1.183892	12.980593	0.077038	0.844672	10.964341	0.091205	12
YEARS							MONTHS
1	1.183892	12.980593	0.077038	0.844672	10.964341	0.091205	12
2	1.401600	28.348209	0.035276	0.713471	20.225611	0.049442	24
3	1.659342	46.541802	0.021486	0.602648	28.048345	0.035653	36
4	1.964482	68.081048	0.014688	0.509040	34.655988	0.028855	48
5	2.325733	93.581182	0.010686	0.429972	40.237278	0.024853	60
6	2.753417	123.770579	0.008079	0.363185	44.951636	0.022246	72
7	3.259747	159.511558	0.006269	0.306704	48.933722	0.020436	84
8	3.859188	201.825006	0.004955	0.259122	52.297278	0.019121	96
9	4.568860	251.919548	0.003970	0.218873	55.138379	0.018136	108
10	5.409036	311.226062	0.003213	0.184876	57.538177	0.017380	120
11	6.403713	381.438553	0.002622	0.156159	59.565218	0.016788	132
12	7.581303	464.562540	0.002153	0.131903	61.277403	0.016319	144
13	8.975441	562.972341	0.001776	0.111415	62.723638	0.015943	156
14	10.625951	679.478890	0.001472	0.094109	63.945231	0.015638	168
15	12.579975	817.410030	0.001223	0.079491	64.977077	0.015390	180
16	14.893329	980.705566	0.001020	0.067144	65.848648	0.015186	192
17	17.632089	1174.029800	0.000852	0.056715	66.584839	0.015018	204
18	20.874484	1402.904761	0.000713	0.047905	67.206679	0.014879	216
19	24.713129	1673.867935	0.000597	0.040464	67.731930	0.014764	228
20	29.257669	1994.658995	0.000501	0.034179	68.175595	0.014668	240
21	34.637912	2374.440878	0.000421	0.028870	68.550346	0.014588	252
22	41.007538	2824.061507	0.000354	0.024386	68.866887	0.014521	264
23	48.548485	3356.363651	0.000298	0.020598	69.134261	0.014465	276
24	57.476150	3986.551756	0.000251	0.017399	69.360104	0.014418	288
25	68.045538	4732.626240	0.000211	0.014696	69.550868	0.014378	300
26	80.558550	5615.897651	0.000178	0.012413	69.712000	0.014345	312
27	95.372601	6661.595368	0.000150	0.010485	69.848104	0.014317	324
28	112.910833	7899.588246	0.000127	0.008857	69.963067	0.014293	336
29	133.674202	9365.237774	0.000107	0.007481	70.060174	0.014273	348
30	158.255782	11100.408126	0.000090	0.006319	70.142196	0.014257	360
31	187.357711	13154.661953	0.000076	0.005337	70.211479	0.014243	372
32	221.811244	15586.676066	0.000064	0.004508	70.270000	0.014231	384
33	262.600497	18465.917458	0.000054	0.003808	70.319431	0.014221	396
34	310.890557	21874.627526	0.000046	0.003217	70.361184	0.014212	408
35	368.060758	25910.171179	0.000039	0.002717	70.396451	0.014205	420
36	435.744087	30687.817929	0.000033	0.002295	70.426241	0.014199	432
37	515.873821	36344.034396	0.000028	0.001938	70.451403	0.014194	444
38	610.738749	43040.382285	0.000023	0.001637	70.472657	0.014190	456
39	723.048553	50968.133160	0.000020	0.001383	70.490609	0.014186	468
40	856.011201	60353.731845	0.000017	0.001168	70.505773	0.014183	480

MONTHLY COMPOUND INTEREST TABLES

18.00% ANNUAL INTEREST RATE   1.5000% MONTHLY EFFECTIVE INTEREST RATE

	1 AMOUNT OF $1 AT COMPOUND INTEREST	2 ACCUMULATION OF $1 PER PERIOD	3 SINKING FUND FACTOR	4 PRESENT VALUE REVERSION OF $1	5 PRESENT VALUE ORD. ANNUNITY $1 PER PERIOD	6 INSTALLMENT TO AMORTIZE $1	
MONTHS							**MONTHS**
1	1.015000	1.000000	1.000000	0.985222	0.985222	1.015000	1
2	1.030225	2.015000	0.496278	0.970662	1.955883	0.511278	2
3	1.045678	3.045225	0.328383	0.956317	2.912200	0.343383	3
4	1.061364	4.090903	0.244445	0.942184	3.854385	0.259445	4
5	1.077284	5.152267	0.194089	0.928260	4.782645	0.209089	5
6	1.093443	6.229551	0.160525	0.914542	5.697187	0.175525	6
7	1.109845	7.322994	0.136556	0.901027	6.598214	0.151556	7
8	1.126493	8.432839	0.118584	0.887711	7.485925	0.133584	8
9	1.143390	9.559332	0.104610	0.874592	8.360517	0.119610	9
10	1.160541	10.702722	0.093434	0.861667	9.222185	0.108434	10
11	1.177949	11.863262	0.084294	0.848933	10.071118	0.099294	11
12	1.195618	13.041211	0.076680	0.836387	10.907505	0.091680	12
YEARS							**MONTHS**
1	1.195618	13.041211	0.076680	0.836387	10.907505	0.091680	12
2	1.429503	28.633521	0.034924	0.699544	20.030405	0.049924	24
3	1.709140	47.275969	0.021152	0.585090	27.660684	0.036152	36
4	2.043478	69.565219	0.014375	0.489362	34.042554	0.029375	48
5	2.443220	96.214652	0.010393	0.409296	39.380269	0.025393	60
6	2.921158	128.077197	0.007808	0.342330	43.844667	0.022808	72
7	3.492590	166.172636	0.006018	0.286321	47.578633	0.021018	84
8	4.175804	211.720235	0.004723	0.239475	50.701675	0.019723	96
9	4.992667	266.177771	0.003757	0.200294	53.313749	0.018757	108
10	5.969323	331.288191	0.003019	0.167523	55.498454	0.018019	120
11	7.137031	409.135393	0.002444	0.140114	57.325714	0.017444	132
12	8.533164	502.210922	0.001991	0.117190	58.854011	0.016991	144
13	10.202406	613.493716	0.001630	0.098016	60.132260	0.016630	156
14	12.198182	746.545446	0.001340	0.081979	61.201371	0.016340	168
15	14.584368	905.624513	0.001104	0.068567	62.095562	0.016104	180
16	17.437335	1095.822335	0.000913	0.057348	62.843452	0.015913	192
17	20.848395	1323.226308	0.000756	0.047965	63.468978	0.015756	204
18	24.926719	1595.114630	0.000627	0.040118	63.992160	0.015627	216
19	29.802839	1920.189249	0.000521	0.033554	64.429743	0.015521	228
20	35.632816	2308.854370	0.000433	0.028064	64.795732	0.015433	240
21	42.603242	2773.549452	0.000361	0.023472	65.101841	0.015361	252
22	50.937210	3329.147335	0.000300	0.019632	65.357866	0.015300	264
23	60.901454	3993.430261	0.000250	0.016420	65.572002	0.015250	276
24	72.814885	4787.658998	0.000209	0.013733	65.751103	0.015209	288
25	87.058800	5737.253308	0.000174	0.011486	65.900901	0.015174	300
26	104.089083	6872.605521	0.000146	0.009607	66.026190	0.015146	312
27	124.450799	8230.053258	0.000122	0.008035	66.130980	0.015122	324
28	148.795637	9853.042439	0.000101	0.006721	66.218625	0.015101	336
29	177.902767	11793.517795	0.000085	0.005621	66.291930	0.015085	348
30	212.703781	14113.585393	0.000071	0.004701	66.353242	0.015071	360
31	254.312506	16887.500372	0.000059	0.003932	66.404522	0.015059	372
32	304.060653	20204.043526	0.000049	0.003289	66.447412	0.015049	384
33	363.540442	24169.362788	0.000041	0.002751	66.483285	0.015041	396
34	434.655558	28910.370554	0.000035	0.002301	66.513289	0.015035	408
35	519.682084	34578.805589	0.000029	0.001924	66.538383	0.015029	420
36	621.341343	41356.089521	0.000024	0.001609	66.559372	0.015024	432
37	742.887000	49459.133344	0.000020	0.001346	66.576927	0.015020	444
38	888.209197	59147.279782	0.000017	0.001126	66.591609	0.015017	456
39	1061.959056	70730.603711	0.000014	0.000942	66.603890	0.015014	468
40	1269.697544	84579.836287	0.000012	0.000788	66.614161	0.015012	480

MONTHLY COMPOUND INTEREST TABLES

19.00% ANNUAL INTEREST RATE   1.5833% MONTHLY EFFECTIVE INTEREST RATE

	1 AMOUNT OF $1 AT COMPOUND INTEREST	2 ACCUMULATION OF $1 PER PERIOD	3 SINKING FUND FACTOR	4 PRESENT VALUE REVERSION OF $1	5 PRESENT VALUE ORD. ANNUINTY $1 PER PERIOD	6 INSTALLMENT TO AMORTIZE $1	
MONTHS							MONTHS
1	1.015833	1.000000	1.000000	0.984413	0.984413	1.015833	1
2	1.031917	2.015833	0.496073	0.969070	1.953483	0.511906	2
3	1.048256	3.047751	0.328111	0.953965	2.907449	0.343944	3
4	1.064853	4.096007	0.244140	0.939096	3.846545	0.259974	4
5	1.081714	5.160860	0.193766	0.924459	4.771004	0.209599	5
6	1.098841	6.242574	0.160190	0.910050	5.681054	0.176024	6
7	1.116239	7.341415	0.136214	0.895865	6.576920	0.152047	7
8	1.133913	8.457654	0.118236	0.881902	7.458822	0.134069	8
9	1.151866	9.591566	0.104258	0.868156	8.326978	0.120092	9
10	1.170104	10.743433	0.093080	0.854625	9.181602	0.108913	10
11	1.188631	11.913537	0.083938	0.841304	10.022906	0.099771	11
12	1.207451	13.102168	0.076323	0.828191	10.851097	0.092157	12
YEARS							MONTHS
1	1.207451	13.102168	0.076323	0.828191	10.851097	0.092157	12
2	1.457938	28.922394	0.034575	0.685900	19.837878	0.050409	24
3	1.760389	48.024542	0.020823	0.568056	27.280649	0.036656	36
4	2.125583	71.089450	0.014067	0.470459	33.444684	0.029900	48
5	2.566537	98.939196	0.010107	0.389630	38.549682	0.025941	60
6	3.098968	132.566399	0.007543	0.322688	42.777596	0.023377	72
7	3.741852	173.169599	0.005775	0.267247	46.279115	0.021608	84
8	4.518103	222.195973	0.004501	0.221332	49.179042	0.020334	96
9	5.455388	281.392918	0.003554	0.183305	51.580735	0.019387	108
10	6.587114	352.870328	0.002834	0.151812	53.569796	0.018667	120
11	7.953617	439.175798	0.002277	0.125729	55.217118	0.018110	132
12	9.603603	543.385424	0.001840	0.104128	56.581415	0.017674	144
13	11.595879	669.213441	0.001494	0.086238	57.711314	0.017328	156
14	14.001456	821.144606	0.001218	0.071421	58.647086	0.017051	168
15	16.906072	1004.594042	0.000995	0.059150	59.422084	0.016829	180
16	20.413254	1226.100247	0.000816	0.048988	60.063930	0.016649	192
17	24.648004	1493.558135	0.000670	0.040571	60.595501	0.016503	204
18	29.761257	1816.500430	0.000551	0.033601	61.035743	0.016384	216
19	35.935259	2206.437425	0.000453	0.027828	61.400348	0.016287	228
20	43.390065	2677.267240	0.000374	0.023047	61.702310	0.016207	240
21	52.391377	3245.771169	0.000308	0.019087	61.952393	0.016141	252
22	63.260020	3932.211806	0.000254	0.015808	62.159509	0.016088	264
23	76.383375	4761.055238	0.000210	0.013092	62.331041	0.016043	276
24	92.229102	5761.843068	0.000174	0.010843	62.473102	0.016007	288
25	111.362218	6970.245332	0.000143	0.008980	62.590755	0.015977	300
26	134.464421	8429.331851	0.000119	0.007437	62.688195	0.015952	312
27	162.359199	10191.107326	0.000098	0.006159	62.768894	0.015931	324
28	196.040777	12318.364881	0.000081	0.005101	62.835728	0.015915	336
29	236.709632	14886.924139	0.000067	0.004225	62.891079	0.015901	348
30	285.815282	17988.333579	0.000056	0.003499	62.936920	0.015889	360
31	345.107947	21733.133503	0.000046	0.002898	62.974886	0.015879	372
32	416.700935	26254.795909	0.000038	0.002400	63.006328	0.015871	384
33	503.145960	31714.481694	0.000032	0.001987	63.032369	0.015865	396
34	607.524092	38306.784745	0.000026	0.001646	63.053935	0.015859	408
35	733.555571	46266.667644	0.000022	0.001363	63.071796	0.015855	420
36	885.732406	55877.836195	0.000018	0.001129	63.086589	0.015851	432
37	1069.478478	67482.851256	0.000015	0.000935	63.098840	0.015848	444
38	1291.342856	81495.338274	0.000012	0.000774	63.108986	0.015846	456
39	1559.233220	98414.729710	0.000010	0.000641	63.117389	0.015843	468
40	1882.697708	118844.065787	0.000008	0.000531	63.124348	0.015842	480

MONTHLY COMPOUND INTEREST TABLES

20.00% ANNUAL INTEREST RATE   1.6667% MONTHLY EFFECTIVE INTEREST RATE

	1 AMOUNT OF $1 AT COMPOUND INTEREST	2 ACCUMULATION OF $1 PER PERIOD	3 SINKING FUND FACTOR	4 PRESENT VALUE REVERSION OF $1	5 PRESENT VALUE ORD. ANNUITY $1 PER PERIOD	6 INSTALLMENT TO AMORTIZE $1	
MONTHS							MONTHS
1	1.016667	1.000000	1.000000	0.983607	0.983607	1.016667	1
2	1.033611	2.016667	0.495868	0.967482	1.951088	0.512534	2
3	1.050838	3.050278	0.327839	0.951622	2.902710	0.344506	3
4	1.068352	4.101116	0.243836	0.936021	3.838731	0.260503	4
5	1.086158	5.169468	0.193444	0.920677	4.759408	0.210110	5
6	1.104260	6.255625	0.159856	0.905583	5.664991	0.176523	6
7	1.122665	7.359886	0.135872	0.890738	6.555729	0.152538	7
8	1.141376	8.482551	0.117889	0.876136	7.431865	0.134556	8
9	1.160399	9.623926	0.103908	0.861773	8.293637	0.120574	9
10	1.179739	10.784325	0.092727	0.847645	9.141283	0.109394	10
11	1.199401	11.964064	0.083584	0.833749	9.975032	0.100250	11
12	1.219391	13.163465	0.075968	0.820081	10.795113	0.092635	12
YEARS							MONTHS
1	1.219391	13.163465	0.075968	0.820081	10.795113	0.092635	12
2	1.486915	29.214877	0.034229	0.672534	19.647986	0.050896	24
3	1.813130	48.787826	0.020497	0.551532	26.908062	0.037164	36
4	2.210915	72.654905	0.013764	0.452301	32.861916	0.030430	48
5	2.695970	101.758208	0.009827	0.370924	37.744561	0.026494	60
6	3.287442	137.246517	0.007286	0.304188	41.748727	0.023953	72
7	4.008677	180.520645	0.005540	0.249459	45.032470	0.022206	84
8	4.888145	233.288730	0.004287	0.204577	47.725406	0.020953	96
9	5.960561	297.633662	0.003360	0.167769	49.933833	0.020027	108
10	7.268255	376.095300	0.002659	0.137585	51.744924	0.019326	120
11	8.862845	471.770720	0.002120	0.112831	53.230165	0.018786	132
12	10.807275	588.436476	0.001699	0.092530	54.448184	0.018366	144
13	13.178294	730.697658	0.001369	0.075882	55.447059	0.018035	156
14	16.069495	904.169675	0.001106	0.062230	56.266217	0.017773	168
15	19.594998	1115.699905	0.000896	0.051033	56.937994	0.017563	180
16	23.893966	1373.637983	0.000728	0.041852	57.488906	0.017395	192
17	29.136090	1688.165376	0.000592	0.034322	57.940698	0.017259	204
18	35.528288	2071.697274	0.000483	0.028147	58.311205	0.017149	216
19	43.322878	2539.372652	0.000394	0.023082	58.615050	0.017060	228
20	52.827531	3109.651838	0.000322	0.018930	58.864229	0.016988	240
21	64.417420	3805.045193	0.000263	0.015524	59.068575	0.016929	252
22	78.550028	4653.001652	0.000215	0.012731	59.236156	0.016882	264
23	95.783203	5686.992197	0.000176	0.010440	59.373585	0.016843	276
24	116.797184	6947.831050	0.000144	0.008562	59.486289	0.016811	288
25	142.421445	8485.286707	0.000118	0.007021	59.578715	0.016785	300
26	173.667440	10360.046428	0.000097	0.005758	59.654512	0.016763	312
27	211.768529	12646.111719	0.000079	0.004722	59.716672	0.016746	324
28	258.228656	15433.719354	0.000065	0.003873	59.767648	0.016731	336
29	314.881721	18832.903252	0.000053	0.003176	59.809452	0.016720	348
30	383.963963	22977.837794	0.000044	0.002604	59.843735	0.016710	360
31	468.202234	28032.134021	0.000036	0.002136	59.871850	0.016702	372
32	570.921630	34195.297782	0.000029	0.001752	59.894907	0.016696	384
33	696.176745	41710.604726	0.000024	0.001436	59.913815	0.016691	396
34	848.911717	50874.703014	0.000020	0.001178	59.929321	0.016686	408
35	1035.155379	62049.322767	0.000016	0.000966	59.942038	0.016683	420
36	1262.259241	75675.554472	0.000013	0.000792	59.952466	0.016680	432
37	1539.187666	92291.259933	0.000011	0.000650	59.961018	0.016678	444
38	1876.871717	112552.303043	0.000009	0.000533	59.968032	0.016676	456
39	2288.640640	137258.438381	0.000007	0.000437	59.973784	0.016674	468
40	2790.747993	167384.879555	0.000006	0.000358	59.978500	0.016673	480

C.   *Mortgage Balance Factors*

MORTGAGE BALANCE FACTORS
Monthly Payments

7.00% INTEREST RATE

	BALANCE 10 YR LOAN	BALANCE 15 YR LOAN	BALANCE 20 YR LOAN	BALANCE 25 YR LOAN	BALANCE 30 YR LOAN	
MONTHS						MONTHS
1	0.994222	0.996845	0.998080	0.998766	0.999180	1
2	0.988411	0.993672	0.996149	0.997524	0.998356	2
3	0.982566	0.990480	0.994207	0.996275	0.997527	3
4	0.976687	0.987269	0.992254	0.995019	0.996692	4
5	0.970773	0.984040	0.990289	0.993755	0.995853	5
6	0.964825	0.980792	0.988313	0.992484	0.995010	6
7	0.958843	0.977525	0.986325	0.991206	0.994161	7
8	0.952825	0.974239	0.984326	0.989920	0.993307	8
9	0.946772	0.970934	0.982314	0.988627	0.992448	9
10	0.940684	0.967609	0.980292	0.987326	0.991585	10
11	0.934561	0.964265	0.978257	0.986018	0.990716	11
12	0.928402	0.960902	0.976210	0.984702	0.989842	12
YEARS						MONTHS
1	0.928402	0.960902	0.976210	0.984702	0.989842	12
2	0.851627	0.918978	0.950701	0.968298	0.978949	24
3	0.769303	0.874023	0.923348	0.950708	0.967270	36
4	0.681028	0.825818	0.894017	0.931846	0.954745	48
5	0.586371	0.774128	0.862566	0.911622	0.941316	60
6	0.484871	0.718702	0.828842	0.889935	0.926916	72
7	0.376034	0.659269	0.792679	0.866680	0.911474	84
8	0.259329	0.595539	0.753902	0.841744	0.894917	96
9	0.134188	0.527203	0.712322	0.815005	0.877162	108
10	0.000000	0.453926	0.667737	0.786334	0.858124	120
11		0.375352	0.619928	0.755590	0.837709	132
12		0.291099	0.568663	0.722623	0.815819	144
13		0.200754	0.513692	0.687274	0.792347	156
14		0.103879	0.454747	0.649368	0.767178	168
15		0.000000	0.391541	0.608723	0.740189	180
16			0.323766	0.565140	0.711249	192
17			0.251092	0.518405	0.680217	204
18			0.173164	0.468293	0.646942	216
19			0.089602	0.414557	0.611261	228
20			0.000000	0.356938	0.573001	240
21				0.295152	0.531975	252
22				0.228901	0.487983	264
23				0.157860	0.440811	276
24				0.081683	0.390229	288
25				0.000000	0.335991	300
26					0.277832	312
27					0.215468	324
28					0.148596	336
29					0.076890	348
30					0.000000	360

MORTGAGE BALANCE FACTORS
Monthly Payments

7.50% INTEREST RATE

	BALANCE 10 YR LOAN	BALANCE 15 YR LOAN	BALANCE 20 YR LOAN	BALANCE 25 YR LOAN	BALANCE 30 YR LOAN	
MONTHS						MONTHS
1	0.994380	0.996980	0.998194	0.998860	0.999258	1
2	0.988725	0.993941	0.996377	0.997713	0.998511	2
3	0.983034	0.990883	0.994548	0.996559	0.997760	3
4	0.977308	0.987806	0.992708	0.995397	0.997003	4
5	0.971546	0.984709	0.990857	0.994229	0.996243	5
6	0.965748	0.981594	0.988994	0.993053	0.995477	6
7	0.959913	0.978459	0.987119	0.991869	0.994707	7
8	0.954043	0.975304	0.985233	0.990679	0.993931	8
9	0.948135	0.972129	0.983334	0.989481	0.993151	9
10	0.942191	0.968935	0.981424	0.988275	0.992366	10
11	0.936209	0.965721	0.979502	0.987062	0.991576	11
12	0.930191	0.962486	0.977568	0.985841	0.990782	12
YEARS						MONTHS
1	0.930191	0.962486	0.977568	0.985841	0.990782	12
2	0.854962	0.922061	0.953395	0.970583	0.980848	24
3	0.773893	0.878496	0.927345	0.954140	0.970142	36
4	0.686530	0.831550	0.899273	0.936420	0.958606	48
5	0.592385	0.780959	0.869021	0.917325	0.946174	60
6	0.490931	0.726441	0.836421	0.896748	0.932777	72
7	0.381601	0.667690	0.801290	0.874573	0.918340	84
8	0.263784	0.604378	0.763432	0.850677	0.902783	96
9	0.136820	0.536152	0.722634	0.824926	0.886017	108
10	0.000000	0.462628	0.678670	0.797175	0.867950	120
11		0.383397	0.631292	0.767270	0.848480	132
12		0.298015	0.580237	0.735044	0.827499	144
13		0.206005	0.525218	0.700315	0.804889	156
14		0.106851	0.465927	0.662891	0.780524	168
15		0.000000	0.402034	0.622561	0.754267	180
16			0.333180	0.579101	0.725971	192
17			0.258981	0.532266	0.695479	204
18			0.179022	0.481795	0.662620	216
19			0.092856	0.427407	0.627210	228
20			0.000000	0.368796	0.589051	240
21				0.305635	0.547930	252
22				0.237570	0.503616	264
23				0.164222	0.455863	276
24				0.085179	0.404401	288
25				0.000000	0.348945	300
26					0.289184	312
27					0.224783	324
28					0.155382	336
29					0.080594	348
30					0.000000	360

MORTGAGE BALANCE FACTORS
Monthly Payments

8.00% INTEREST RATE

	BALANCE 10 YR LOAN	BALANCE 15 YR LOAN	BALANCE 20 YR LOAN	BALANCE 25 YR LOAN	BALANCE 30 YR LOAN	
MONTHS						**MONTHS**
1	0.994534	0.997110	0.998302	0.998949	0.999329	1
2	0.989031	0.994201	0.996593	0.997890	0.998654	2
3	0.983492	0.991273	0.994873	0.996824	0.997974	3
4	0.977916	0.988324	0.993141	0.995752	0.997289	4
5	0.972303	0.985357	0.991397	0.994672	0.996600	5
6	0.966652	0.982369	0.989642	0.993585	0.995906	6
7	0.960964	0.979362	0.987876	0.992491	0.995208	7
8	0.955237	0.976334	0.986097	0.991389	0.994505	8
9	0.949473	0.973287	0.984307	0.990280	0.993798	9
10	0.943670	0.970219	0.982504	0.989164	0.993085	10
11	0.937828	0.967131	0.980690	0.988040	0.992368	11
12	0.931948	0.964022	0.978863	0.986909	0.991646	12
YEARS						**MONTHS**
1	0.931948	0.964022	0.978863	0.986909	0.991646	12
2	0.858247	0.925057	0.955972	0.972731	0.982599	24
3	0.778429	0.882858	0.931181	0.957377	0.972801	36
4	0.691986	0.837157	0.904333	0.940748	0.962190	48
5	0.598369	0.787663	0.875256	0.922739	0.950699	60
6	0.496981	0.734060	0.843765	0.903236	0.938253	72
7	0.387178	0.676009	0.809661	0.882113	0.924774	84
8	0.268262	0.613139	0.772727	0.859238	0.910177	96
9	0.139476	0.545052	0.732727	0.834464	0.894368	108
10	0.000000	0.471313	0.689406	0.807633	0.877247	120
11		0.391453	0.642491	0.778576	0.858705	132
12		0.304966	0.591681	0.747107	0.838624	144
13		0.211300	0.536654	0.713025	0.816876	156
14		0.109860	0.477060	0.676116	0.793323	168
15		0.000000	0.412519	0.636142	0.767816	180
16			0.342622	0.592851	0.740191	192
17			0.266923	0.545967	0.710273	204
18			0.184941	0.495192	0.677872	216
19			0.096155	0.440202	0.642782	228
20			0.000000	0.380648	0.604780	240
21				0.316151	0.563623	252
22				0.246300	0.519050	264
23				0.170653	0.470778	276
24				0.088726	0.418499	288
25				0.000000	0.361881	300
26					0.300564	312
27					0.234158	324
28					0.162239	336
29					0.084352	348
30					0.000000	360

MORTGAGE BALANCE FACTORS
Monthly Payments

8.50% INTEREST RATE

	BALANCE 10 YR LOAN	BALANCE 15 YR LOAN	BALANCE 20 YR LOAN	BALANCE 25 YR LOAN	BALANCE 30 YR LOAN	
MONTHS						MONTHS
1	0.994685	0.997236	0.998405	0.999031	0.999394	1
2	0.989332	0.994452	0.996799	0.998055	0.998784	2
3	0.983941	0.991649	0.995181	0.997073	0.998170	3
4	0.978512	0.988826	0.993552	0.996083	0.997551	4
5	0.973045	0.985983	0.991912	0.995086	0.996928	5
6	0.967538	0.983119	0.990260	0.994082	0.996300	6
7	0.961993	0.980236	0.988596	0.993072	0.995668	7
8	0.956409	0.977331	0.986920	0.992054	0.995032	8
9	0.950785	0.974407	0.985232	0.991028	0.994391	9
10	0.945121	0.971461	0.983533	0.989996	0.993745	10
11	0.939417	0.968495	0.981821	0.988956	0.993095	11
12	0.933673	0.965508	0.980098	0.987909	0.992440	12
YEARS						MONTHS
1	0.933673	0.965508	0.980098	0.987909	0.992440	12
2	0.861483	0.927967	0.958436	0.974749	0.984213	24
3	0.782912	0.887108	0.934860	0.960426	0.975257	36
4	0.697396	0.842638	0.909200	0.944837	0.965511	48
5	0.604321	0.794236	0.881272	0.927870	0.954903	60
6	0.503019	0.741557	0.850875	0.909403	0.943357	72
7	0.392763	0.684221	0.817791	0.889304	0.930790	84
8	0.272762	0.621817	0.781784	0.867429	0.917113	96
9	0.142153	0.553897	0.742593	0.843619	0.902227	108
10	0.000000	0.479974	0.699938	0.817706	0.886025	120
11		0.399516	0.653513	0.789501	0.868392	132
12		0.311947	0.602985	0.758804	0.849199	144
13		0.216637	0.547990	0.725393	0.828310	156
14		0.112903	0.488134	0.689030	0.805574	168
15		0.000000	0.422987	0.649452	0.780829	180
16			0.352082	0.606375	0.753897	192
17			0.274910	0.559491	0.724584	204
18			0.190916	0.508463	0.692680	216
19			0.099498	0.452925	0.657956	228
20			0.000000	0.392477	0.620163	240
21				0.326687	0.579029	252
22				0.255081	0.534260	264
23				0.177146	0.485533	276
24				0.092322	0.432499	288
25				0.000000	0.374778	300
26					0.311954	312
27					0.243577	324
28					0.169157	336
29					0.088158	348
30					0.000000	360

MORTGAGE BALANCE FACTORS
Monthly Payments

9.00% INTEREST RATE

	BALANCE 10 YR LOAN	BALANCE 15 YR LOAN	BALANCE 20 YR LOAN	BALANCE 25 YR LOAN	BALANCE 30 YR LOAN	
MONTHS						MONTHS
1	0.994832	0.997357	0.998503	0.999108	0.999454	1
2	0.989626	0.994695	0.996994	0.998209	0.998903	2
3	0.984381	0.992012	0.995474	0.997304	0.998349	3
4	0.979096	0.989310	0.993943	0.996392	0.997790	4
5	0.973772	0.986587	0.992401	0.995473	0.997228	5
6	0.968407	0.983844	0.990846	0.994547	0.996661	6
7	0.963003	0.981080	0.989280	0.993614	0.996089	7
8	0.957558	0.978295	0.987703	0.992674	0.995514	8
9	0.952072	0.975490	0.986113	0.991727	0.994934	9
10	0.946545	0.972663	0.984512	0.990773	0.994350	10
11	0.940976	0.969816	0.982898	0.989812	0.993761	11
12	0.935366	0.966947	0.981273	0.988844	0.993168	12
YEARS						MONTHS
1	0.935366	0.966947	0.981273	0.988844	0.993168	12
2	0.864669	0.930793	0.960789	0.976641	0.985695	24
3	0.787340	0.891247	0.938384	0.963293	0.977521	36
4	0.702757	0.847992	0.913877	0.948694	0.968581	48
5	0.610240	0.800679	0.887070	0.932724	0.958801	60
6	0.509044	0.748928	0.857750	0.915257	0.948105	72
7	0.398355	0.692323	0.825679	0.896151	0.936405	84
8	0.277282	0.630407	0.790599	0.875253	0.923607	96
9	0.144853	0.562683	0.752229	0.852395	0.909609	108
10	0.000000	0.488606	0.710259	0.827392	0.894297	120
11		0.407581	0.664352	0.800044	0.877550	132
12		0.318954	0.614139	0.770131	0.859231	144
13		0.222014	0.559215	0.737411	0.839194	156
14		0.115980	0.499140	0.701622	0.817277	168
15		0.000000	0.433428	0.662476	0.793305	180
16			0.361553	0.619657	0.767083	192
17			0.282935	0.572822	0.738402	204
18			0.196942	0.521594	0.707031	216
19			0.102883	0.465560	0.672716	228
20			0.000000	0.404269	0.635183	240
21				0.337229	0.594128	252
22				0.263900	0.549223	264
23				0.183693	0.500105	276
24				0.095961	0.446379	288
25				0.000000	0.387614	300
26					0.323336	312
27					0.253028	324
28					0.176125	336
29					0.092008	348
30					0.000000	360

MORTGAGE BALANCE FACTORS
Monthly Payments

9.50% INTEREST RATE

	BALANCE 10 YR LOAN	BALANCE 15 YR LOAN	BALANCE 20 YR LOAN	BALANCE 25 YR LOAN	BALANCE 30 YR LOAN	
MONTHS						**MONTHS**
1	0.994977	0.997474	0.998595	0.999180	0.999508	1
2	0.989914	0.994929	0.997180	0.998353	0.999012	2
3	0.984811	0.992363	0.995753	0.997520	0.998513	3
4	0.979668	0.989777	0.994314	0.996680	0.998009	4
5	0.974484	0.987171	0.992865	0.995833	0.997501	5
6	0.969259	0.984543	0.991404	0.994980	0.996990	6
7	0.963992	0.981895	0.989931	0.994120	0.996474	7
8	0.958684	0.979227	0.988446	0.993253	0.995954	8
9	0.953334	0.976537	0.986950	0.992379	0.995430	9
10	0.947941	0.973825	0.985442	0.991499	0.994902	10
11	0.942506	0.971092	0.983923	0.990611	0.994370	11
12	0.937028	0.968338	0.982391	0.989716	0.993834	12
YEARS						**MONTHS**
1	0.937028	0.968338	0.982391	0.989716	0.993834	12
2	0.867806	0.933534	0.963034	0.978412	0.987055	24
3	0.791714	0.895275	0.941755	0.965986	0.979604	36
4	0.708070	0.853219	0.918365	0.952326	0.971413	48
5	0.616124	0.806989	0.892654	0.937311	0.962410	60
6	0.515053	0.756172	0.864391	0.920805	0.952513	72
7	0.403951	0.700310	0.833322	0.902662	0.941633	84
8	0.281823	0.638905	0.799171	0.882717	0.929674	96
9	0.147573	0.571405	0.761629	0.860794	0.916528	108
10	0.000000	0.497206	0.720362	0.836694	0.902077	120
11		0.415643	0.675000	0.810203	0.886192	132
12		0.325985	0.625135	0.781082	0.868731	144
13		0.227428	0.570321	0.749071	0.849536	156
14		0.119090	0.510067	0.713883	0.828436	168
15		0.000000	0.443833	0.675203	0.805243	180
16			0.371025	0.632684	0.779747	192
17			0.290991	0.585945	0.751721	204
18			0.203015	0.534568	0.720913	216
19			0.106306	0.478091	0.687048	228
20			0.000000	0.416009	0.649822	240
21				0.347766	0.608902	252
22				0.272749	0.563920	264
23				0.190288	0.514473	276
24				0.099642	0.460120	288
25				0.000000	0.400371	300
26					0.334693	312
27					0.262497	324
28					0.183135	336
29					0.095897	348
30					0.000000	360

MORTGAGE BALANCE FACTORS
Monthly Payments

10.00% INTEREST RATE

	BALANCE 10 YR LOAN	BALANCE 15 YR LOAN	BALANCE 20 YR LOAN	BALANCE 25 YR LOAN	BALANCE 30 YR LOAN	
MONTHS						MONTHS
1	0.995118	0.997587	0.998683	0.999246	0.999558	1
2	0.990196	0.995154	0.997355	0.998486	0.999112	2
3	0.985232	0.992701	0.996016	0.997720	0.998662	3
4	0.980228	0.990228	0.994666	0.996947	0.998208	4
5	0.975181	0.987734	0.993305	0.996168	0.997751	5
6	0.970093	0.985219	0.991932	0.995383	0.997290	6
7	0.964962	0.982683	0.990548	0.994591	0.996825	7
8	0.959788	0.980126	0.989152	0.993792	0.996356	8
9	0.954571	0.977547	0.987745	0.992986	0.995883	9
10	0.949311	0.974948	0.986326	0.992174	0.995407	10
11	0.944007	0.972326	0.984895	0.991355	0.994926	11
12	0.938658	0.969683	0.983453	0.990530	0.994441	12
YEARS						MONTHS
1	0.938658	0.969683	0.983453	0.990530	0.994441	12
2	0.870893	0.936191	0.965173	0.980068	0.988300	24
3	0.796032	0.899192	0.944978	0.968510	0.981516	36
4	0.713332	0.858319	0.922669	0.955742	0.974022	48
5	0.621972	0.813166	0.898024	0.941638	0.965743	60
6	0.521046	0.763285	0.870799	0.926056	0.956597	72
7	0.409551	0.708181	0.840722	0.908843	0.946494	84
8	0.286382	0.647306	0.807497	0.889827	0.935332	96
9	0.150315	0.580058	0.770792	0.868820	0.923002	108
10	0.000000	0.505767	0.730243	0.845614	0.909380	120
11		0.423697	0.685449	0.819977	0.894332	132
12		0.333033	0.635964	0.791656	0.877709	144
13		0.232876	0.581297	0.760369	0.859344	156
14		0.122231	0.520906	0.725806	0.839057	168
15		0.000000	0.454191	0.687624	0.816646	180
16			0.380490	0.645444	0.791887	192
17			0.299072	0.598847	0.764536	204
18			0.209128	0.547371	0.734321	216
19			0.109766	0.490505	0.700943	228
20			0.000000	0.427683	0.664069	240
21				0.358284	0.623333	252
22				0.281618	0.578333	264
23				0.196923	0.528620	276
24				0.103360	0.473701	288
25				0.000000	0.413032	300
26					0.346010	312
27					0.271970	324
28					0.190177	336
29					0.099819	348
30					0.000000	360

MORTGAGE BALANCE FACTORS
Monthly Payments

10.50% INTEREST RATE

	BALANCE 10 YR LOAN	BALANCE 15 YR LOAN	BALANCE 20 YR LOAN	BALANCE 25 YR LOAN	BALANCE 30 YR LOAN	
MONTHS						MONTHS
1	0.995257	0.997696	0.998766	0.999308	0.999603	1
2	0.990471	0.995372	0.997522	0.998610	0.999202	2
3	0.985645	0.993027	0.996266	0.997906	0.998797	3
4	0.980776	0.990662	0.995000	0.997196	0.998389	4
5	0.975864	0.988277	0.993722	0.996480	0.997978	5
6	0.970909	0.985870	0.992433	0.995757	0.997563	6
7	0.965911	0.983442	0.991133	0.995028	0.997144	7
8	0.960869	0.980994	0.989822	0.994293	0.996722	8
9	0.955783	0.978523	0.988499	0.993551	0.996296	9
10	0.950653	0.976031	0.987165	0.992803	0.995866	10
11	0.945478	0.973518	0.985819	0.992048	0.995432	11
12	0.940257	0.970982	0.984461	0.991287	0.994995	12
YEARS						MONTHS
1	0.940257	0.970982	0.984461	0.991287	0.994995	12
2	0.873930	0.938766	0.967209	0.981613	0.989438	24
3	0.800294	0.903000	0.948056	0.970874	0.983269	36
4	0.718543	0.863292	0.926792	0.958951	0.976421	48
5	0.627783	0.819208	0.903185	0.945714	0.968817	60
6	0.527020	0.770267	0.876977	0.931018	0.960375	72
7	0.415153	0.715931	0.847880	0.914703	0.951004	84
8	0.290958	0.655608	0.815576	0.896590	0.940599	96
9	0.153077	0.588637	0.779713	0.876480	0.929048	108
10	0.000000	0.514285	0.739897	0.854155	0.916224	120
11		0.431739	0.695693	0.829369	0.901986	132
12		0.340097	0.646618	0.801851	0.886180	144
13		0.238356	0.592135	0.771302	0.868631	156
14		0.125402	0.531648	0.737385	0.849149	168
15		0.000000	0.464495	0.699731	0.827520	180
16			0.389941	0.657927	0.803507	192
17			0.307171	0.611516	0.776847	204
18			0.215279	0.559991	0.747250	216
19			0.113261	0.502787	0.714391	228
20			0.000000	0.439279	0.677911	240
21				0.368772	0.637411	252
22				0.290496	0.592447	264
23				0.203593	0.542528	276
24				0.107112	0.487108	288
25				0.000000	0.425581	300
26					0.357273	312
27					0.281437	324
28					0.197244	336
29					0.103772	348
30					0.000000	360

MORTGAGE BALANCE FACTORS
Monthly Payments

11.00% INTEREST RATE

	BALANCE 10 YR LOAN	BALANCE 15 YR LOAN	BALANCE 20 YR LOAN	BALANCE 25 YR LOAN	BALANCE 30 YR LOAN	
MONTHS						MONTHS
1	0.995392	0.997801	0.998845	0.999366	0.999643	1
2	0.990741	0.995581	0.997679	0.998725	0.999284	2
3	0.986048	0.993341	0.996502	0.998079	0.998920	3
4	0.981312	0.991081	0.995315	0.997427	0.998554	4
5	0.976532	0.988800	0.994117	0.996769	0.998184	5
6	0.971709	0.986498	0.992908	0.996105	0.997811	6
7	0.966841	0.984175	0.991688	0.995435	0.997434	7
8	0.961929	0.981831	0.990456	0.994758	0.997054	8
9	0.956971	0.979465	0.989214	0.994076	0.996671	9
10	0.951968	0.977077	0.987959	0.993387	0.996284	10
11	0.946920	0.974668	0.986694	0.992692	0.995893	11
12	0.941825	0.972236	0.985417	0.991991	0.995499	12
YEARS						MONTHS
1	0.941825	0.972236	0.985417	0.991991	0.995499	12
2	0.876918	0.941260	0.969146	0.983054	0.990477	24
3	0.804500	0.906699	0.950992	0.973084	0.984873	36
4	0.723702	0.868138	0.930738	0.961960	0.978622	48
5	0.633554	0.825116	0.908139	0.949549	0.971646	60
6	0.532974	0.777115	0.882926	0.935701	0.963864	72
7	0.420756	0.723559	0.854795	0.920251	0.955181	84
8	0.295551	0.663806	0.823409	0.903013	0.945494	96
9	0.155858	0.597138	0.788391	0.883781	0.934685	108
10	0.000000	0.522755	0.749320	0.862322	0.922626	120
11		0.439766	0.705728	0.838381	0.909171	132
12		0.347172	0.657092	0.811669	0.894159	144
13		0.243864	0.602828	0.781867	0.877410	156
14		0.128601	0.542284	0.748615	0.858722	168
15		0.000000	0.474735	0.711516	0.837873	180
16			0.399368	0.670123	0.814610	192
17			0.315281	0.623941	0.788656	204
18			0.221462	0.572414	0.759698	216
19			0.116788	0.514925	0.727389	228
20			0.000000	0.450784	0.691342	240
21				0.379220	0.651123	252
22				0.299374	0.606250	264
23				0.210289	0.556185	276
24				0.110896	0.500325	288
25				0.000000	0.438002	300
26					0.368467	312
27					0.290886	324
28					0.204327	336
29					0.107751	348
30					0.000000	360

MORTGAGE BALANCE FACTORS
Monthly Payments

11.50% INTEREST RATE

MONTHS	BALANCE 10 YR LOAN	BALANCE 15 YR LOAN	BALANCE 20 YR LOAN	BALANCE 25 YR LOAN	BALANCE 30 YR LOAN	MONTHS
1	0.995524	0.997901	0.998919	0.999419	0.999680	1
2	0.991005	0.995783	0.997828	0.998832	0.999358	2
3	0.986442	0.993644	0.996726	0.998239	0.999032	3
4	0.981836	0.991484	0.995614	0.997641	0.998703	4
5	0.977186	0.989304	0.994491	0.997037	0.998371	5
6	0.972491	0.987103	0.993357	0.996427	0.998036	6
7	0.967751	0.984881	0.992212	0.995812	0.997698	7
8	0.962966	0.982637	0.991057	0.995190	0.997356	8
9	0.958135	0.980372	0.989890	0.994563	0.997011	9
10	0.953257	0.978086	0.988712	0.993929	0.996663	10
11	0.948333	0.975777	0.987523	0.993290	0.996311	11
12	0.943362	0.973447	0.986322	0.992644	0.995956	12

YEARS						MONTHS
1	0.943362	0.973447	0.986322	0.992644	0.995956	12
2	0.879856	0.943673	0.970986	0.984396	0.991422	24
3	0.808649	0.910290	0.953791	0.975148	0.986338	36
4	0.728808	0.872858	0.934510	0.964778	0.980638	48
5	0.639285	0.830887	0.912891	0.953151	0.974247	60
6	0.538907	0.783827	0.888650	0.940115	0.967080	72
7	0.426357	0.731061	0.861471	0.925497	0.959044	84
8	0.300159	0.671896	0.830995	0.909107	0.950035	96
9	0.158659	0.605557	0.796824	0.890729	0.939932	108
10	0.000000	0.531174	0.758509	0.870123	0.928605	120
11		0.447771	0.715549	0.847018	0.915904	132
12		0.354254	0.667379	0.821112	0.901662	144
13		0.249398	0.613368	0.792064	0.885694	156
14		0.131827	0.552808	0.759494	0.867790	168
15		0.000000	0.484904	0.722974	0.847714	180
16			0.408766	0.682026	0.825205	192
17			0.323396	0.636113	0.799965	204
18			0.227673	0.584632	0.771666	216
19			0.120344	0.526909	0.739934	228
20			0.000000	0.462187	0.704355	240
21				0.389616	0.664462	252
22				0.308245	0.619731	264
23				0.217007	0.569576	276
24				0.114706	0.513340	288
25				0.000000	0.450284	300
26					0.379582	312
27					0.300307	324
28					0.211419	336
29					0.111752	348
30					0.000000	360

MORTGAGE BALANCE FACTORS
Monthly Payments

12.00% INTEREST RATE

MONTHS	BALANCE 10 YR LOAN	BALANCE 15 YR LOAN	BALANCE 20 YR LOAN	BALANCE 25 YR LOAN	BALANCE 30 YR LOAN	MONTHS
1	0.995653	0.997998	0.998989	0.999468	0.999714	1
2	0.991262	0.995977	0.997968	0.998930	0.999425	2
3	0.986828	0.993935	0.996937	0.998387	0.999133	3
4	0.982349	0.991872	0.995895	0.997839	0.998838	4
5	0.977825	0.989789	0.994844	0.997285	0.998540	5
6	0.973257	0.987686	0.993781	0.996726	0.998240	6
7	0.968642	0.985561	0.992708	0.996161	0.997936	7
8	0.963981	0.983415	0.991624	0.995590	0.997629	8
9	0.959274	0.981247	0.990530	0.995014	0.997319	9
10	0.954520	0.979058	0.989424	0.994432	0.997006	10
11	0.949718	0.976847	0.988308	0.993844	0.996690	11
12	0.944868	0.974614	0.987180	0.993250	0.996371	12

YEARS						MONTHS
1	0.944868	0.974614	0.987180	0.993250	0.996371	12
2	0.882744	0.946008	0.972734	0.985644	0.992282	24
3	0.812741	0.913774	0.956455	0.977073	0.987675	36
4	0.733860	0.877452	0.938112	0.967415	0.982483	48
5	0.644974	0.836523	0.917443	0.956532	0.976632	60
6	0.544816	0.790404	0.894153	0.944269	0.970040	72
7	0.431955	0.738436	0.867908	0.930451	0.962611	84
8	0.304781	0.679877	0.838336	0.914880	0.954241	96
9	0.161478	0.613891	0.805012	0.897335	0.944808	108
10	0.000000	0.539536	0.767463	0.877564	0.934180	120
11		0.455751	0.725151	0.855286	0.922204	132
12		0.361341	0.677473	0.830182	0.908708	144
13		0.254956	0.623748	0.801895	0.893501	156
14		0.135080	0.563210	0.770020	0.876366	168
15		0.000000	0.494994	0.734103	0.857057	180
16			0.418126	0.693630	0.835300	192
17			0.331510	0.648025	0.810783	204
18			0.233908	0.596635	0.783156	216
19			0.123928	0.538728	0.752026	228
20			0.000000	0.473477	0.716948	240
21				0.399951	0.677422	252
22				0.317100	0.632882	264
23				0.223740	0.582693	276
24				0.118541	0.526139	288
25				0.000000	0.462413	300
26					0.390605	312
27					0.309690	324
28					0.218512	336
29					0.115771	348
30					0.000000	360

MORTGAGE BALANCE FACTORS
Monthly Payments

12.50% INTEREST RATE

MONTHS	BALANCE 10 YR LOAN	BALANCE 15 YR LOAN	BALANCE 20 YR LOAN	BALANCE 25 YR LOAN	BALANCE 30 YR LOAN	MONTHS
1	0.995779	0.998091	0.999055	0.999513	0.999744	1
2	0.991514	0.996163	0.998101	0.999021	0.999486	2
3	0.987205	0.994214	0.997136	0.998524	0.999224	3
4	0.982851	0.992246	0.996162	0.998022	0.998960	4
5	0.978451	0.990256	0.995177	0.997514	0.998694	5
6	0.974006	0.988246	0.994182	0.997002	0.998424	6
7	0.969514	0.986215	0.993177	0.996484	0.998152	7
8	0.964975	0.984163	0.992161	0.995960	0.997876	8
9	0.960390	0.982090	0.991134	0.995431	0.997598	9
10	0.955756	0.979995	0.990097	0.994897	0.997318	10
11	0.951074	0.977878	0.989049	0.994357	0.997034	11
12	0.946344	0.975739	0.987991	0.993811	0.996747	12

YEARS						MONTHS
1	0.946344	0.975739	0.987991	0.993811	0.996747	12
2	0.885582	0.948265	0.974391	0.986802	0.993063	24
3	0.816775	0.917153	0.958990	0.978865	0.988891	36
4	0.738856	0.881921	0.941550	0.969878	0.984167	48
5	0.650620	0.842024	0.921801	0.959700	0.978818	60
6	0.550700	0.796844	0.899437	0.948175	0.972760	72
7	0.437549	0.745681	0.874112	0.935123	0.965899	84
8	0.309416	0.687744	0.845432	0.920343	0.958131	96
9	0.164315	0.622135	0.812956	0.903606	0.949333	108
10	0.000000	0.547838	0.776179	0.884653	0.939371	120
11		0.463703	0.734532	0.863190	0.928090	132
12		0.368427	0.687370	0.838885	0.915315	144
13		0.260535	0.633963	0.811362	0.900848	156
14		0.138357	0.573485	0.780194	0.884465	168
15		0.000000	0.504998	0.744899	0.865914	180
16			0.427442	0.704930	0.844905	192
17			0.339617	0.659669	0.821115	204
18			0.240162	0.608415	0.794175	216
19			0.127537	0.550373	0.763667	228
20			0.000000	0.484646	0.729120	240
21				0.410216	0.689998	252
22				0.325930	0.645696	264
23				0.230483	0.595527	276
24				0.122398	0.538715	288
25				0.000000	0.474380	300
26					0.401527	312
27					0.319026	324
28					0.225601	336
29					0.119805	348
30					0.000000	360

MORTGAGE BALANCE FACTORS
Monthly Payments

13.00% INTEREST RATE

MONTHS	BALANCE 10 YR LOAN	BALANCE 15 YR LOAN	BALANCE 20 YR LOAN	BALANCE 25 YR LOAN	BALANCE 30 YR LOAN	MONTHS
1	0.995902	0.998181	0.999118	0.999555	0.999771	1
2	0.991760	0.996342	0.998226	0.999105	0.999540	2
3	0.987573	0.994483	0.997324	0.998650	0.999307	3
4	0.983341	0.992605	0.996413	0.998191	0.999070	4
5	0.979063	0.990705	0.995491	0.997726	0.998832	5
6	0.974738	0.988786	0.994560	0.997257	0.998590	6
7	0.970367	0.986845	0.993619	0.996782	0.998346	7
8	0.965948	0.984883	0.992667	0.996302	0.998100	8
9	0.961481	0.982901	0.991705	0.995817	0.997851	9
10	0.956966	0.980896	0.990733	0.995326	0.997599	10
11	0.952402	0.978870	0.989750	0.994831	0.997344	11
12	0.947789	0.976822	0.988757	0.994330	0.997087	12

YEARS						MONTHS
1	0.947789	0.976822	0.988757	0.994330	0.997087	12
2	0.888371	0.950445	0.975961	0.987877	0.993771	24
3	0.820751	0.920427	0.961400	0.980533	0.989998	36
4	0.743798	0.886265	0.944828	0.972176	0.985703	48
5	0.656222	0.847389	0.925970	0.962665	0.980817	60
6	0.556559	0.803145	0.904508	0.951842	0.975255	72
7	0.443138	0.752795	0.880083	0.939524	0.968926	84
8	0.314062	0.695495	0.852287	0.925506	0.961723	96
9	0.167169	0.630286	0.820655	0.909554	0.953526	108
10	0.000000	0.556075	0.784656	0.891399	0.944198	120
11		0.471621	0.743688	0.870738	0.933582	132
12		0.375510	0.697065	0.847226	0.921501	144
13		0.266132	0.644007	0.820467	0.907752	156
14		0.141657	0.583625	0.790016	0.892105	168
15		0.000000	0.514909	0.755361	0.874299	180
16			0.436707	0.715923	0.854034	192
17			0.347711	0.671041	0.830973	204
18			0.246431	0.619963	0.804728	216
19			0.131170	0.561836	0.774861	228
20			0.000000	0.495685	0.740871	240
21				0.420403	0.702189	252
22				0.334729	0.658168	264
23				0.237230	0.608070	276
24				0.126273	0.551058	288
25				0.000000	0.486176	300
26					0.412338	312
27					0.328308	324
28					0.232679	336
29					0.123851	348
30					0.000000	360

MORTGAGE BALANCE FACTORS
Monthly Payments

13.50% INTEREST RATE

MONTHS	BALANCE 10 YR LOAN	BALANCE 15 YR LOAN	BALANCE 20 YR LOAN	BALANCE 25 YR LOAN	BALANCE 30 YR LOAN	MONTHS
1	0.996023	0.998267	0.999176	0.999594	0.999796	1
2	0.992000	0.996514	0.998343	0.999183	0.999589	2
3	0.987933	0.994742	0.997501	0.998767	0.999381	3
4	0.983820	0.992949	0.996649	0.998347	0.999170	4
5	0.979660	0.991137	0.995788	0.997922	0.998956	5
6	0.975454	0.989304	0.994916	0.997492	0.998740	6
7	0.971201	0.987450	0.994035	0.997057	0.998522	7
8	0.966899	0.985576	0.993145	0.996617	0.998301	8
9	0.962549	0.983681	0.992244	0.996173	0.998078	9
10	0.958151	0.981764	0.991333	0.995723	0.997852	10
11	0.953702	0.979826	0.990411	0.995269	0.997624	11
12	0.949204	0.977865	0.989480	0.994809	0.997393	12

YEARS						MONTHS
1	0.949204	0.977865	0.989480	0.994809	0.997393	12
2	0.891110	0.952551	0.977448	0.988873	0.994412	24
3	0.824669	0.923599	0.963688	0.982083	0.991002	36
4	0.748683	0.890487	0.947951	0.974318	0.987102	48
5	0.661779	0.852618	0.929953	0.965438	0.982642	60
6	0.562389	0.809309	0.909368	0.955281	0.977542	72
7	0.448720	0.759777	0.885827	0.943665	0.971708	84
8	0.318719	0.703128	0.858903	0.930381	0.965037	96
9	0.170040	0.638341	0.828111	0.915187	0.957406	108
10	0.000000	0.564245	0.792895	0.897811	0.948680	120
11		0.479503	0.752619	0.877938	0.938700	132
12		0.382587	0.706556	0.855211	0.927286	144
13		0.271745	0.653876	0.829217	0.914232	156
14		0.144979	0.593626	0.799489	0.899302	168
15		0.000000	0.524721	0.765490	0.882227	180
16			0.445915	0.726606	0.862700	192
17			0.355787	0.682136	0.840366	204
18			0.252710	0.631276	0.814824	216
19			0.134824	0.573109	0.785612	228
20			0.000000	0.506585	0.752203	240
21				0.430503	0.713994	252
22				0.343491	0.670296	264
23				0.243976	0.620319	276
24				0.130164	0.563162	288
25				0.000000	0.497792	300
26					0.423031	312
27					0.337528	324
28					0.239741	336
29					0.127905	348
30					0.000000	360

MORTGAGE BALANCE FACTORS
Monthly Payments

14.00% INTEREST RATE

	BALANCE 10 YR LOAN	BALANCE 15 YR LOAN	BALANCE 20 YR LOAN	BALANCE 25 YR LOAN	BALANCE 30 YR LOAN	
MONTHS						**MONTHS**
1	0.996140	0.998349	0.999231	0.999629	0.999818	1
2	0.992235	0.996679	0.998454	0.999254	0.999634	2
3	0.988284	0.994990	0.997667	0.998874	0.999447	3
4	0.984288	0.993281	0.996872	0.998490	0.999259	4
5	0.980245	0.991551	0.996067	0.998101	0.999068	5
6	0.976154	0.989802	0.995252	0.997708	0.998875	6
7	0.972016	0.988032	0.994428	0.997311	0.998680	7
8	0.967829	0.986242	0.993595	0.996908	0.998483	8
9	0.963594	0.984431	0.992751	0.996501	0.998283	9
10	0.959309	0.982598	0.991898	0.996090	0.998081	10
11	0.954975	0.980745	0.991035	0.995673	0.997876	11
12	0.950589	0.978869	0.990162	0.995252	0.997670	12
YEARS						**MONTHS**
1	0.950589	0.978869	0.990162	0.995252	0.997670	12
2	0.893800	0.954583	0.978855	0.989794	0.994991	24
3	0.828529	0.926669	0.965859	0.983522	0.991913	36
4	0.753511	0.894587	0.950923	0.976312	0.988375	48
5	0.667289	0.857714	0.933755	0.968026	0.984308	60
6	0.568190	0.815334	0.914024	0.958503	0.979634	72
7	0.454293	0.766624	0.891347	0.947558	0.974262	84
8	0.323385	0.710641	0.865282	0.934977	0.968088	96
9	0.172927	0.646296	0.835326	0.920518	0.960992	108
10	0.000000	0.572343	0.800895	0.903900	0.952836	120
11		0.487345	0.761322	0.884800	0.943462	132
12		0.389653	0.715840	0.862847	0.932689	144
13		0.277372	0.663565	0.837616	0.920306	156
14		0.148322	0.603483	0.808617	0.906074	168
15		0.000000	0.534428	0.775287	0.889716	180
16			0.455061	0.736980	0.870916	192
17			0.363841	0.692952	0.849308	204
18			0.258997	0.642348	0.824472	216
19			0.138497	0.584187	0.795928	228
20			0.000000	0.517341	0.763122	240
21				0.440511	0.725415	252
22				0.352207	0.682078	264
23				0.250716	0.632268	276
24				0.134068	0.575020	288
25				0.000000	0.509223	300
26					0.433598	312
27					0.346680	324
28					0.246782	336
29					0.131965	348
30					0.000000	360

MORTGAGE BALANCE FACTORS
Monthly Payments

14.50% INTEREST RATE

	BALANCE 10 YR LOAN	BALANCE 15 YR LOAN	BALANCE 20 YR LOAN	BALANCE 25 YR LOAN	BALANCE 30 YR LOAN	
MONTHS						MONTHS
1	0.996255	0.998428	0.999283	0.999662	0.999838	1
2	0.992464	0.996838	0.998558	0.999319	0.999674	2
3	0.988628	0.995228	0.997824	0.998973	0.999507	3
4	0.984745	0.993598	0.997081	0.998622	0.999339	4
5	0.980815	0.991949	0.996329	0.998267	0.999169	5
6	0.976838	0.990280	0.995568	0.997908	0.998997	6
7	0.972813	0.988591	0.994798	0.997544	0.998822	7
8	0.968739	0.986882	0.994018	0.997176	0.998646	8
9	0.964616	0.985152	0.993230	0.996804	0.998467	9
10	0.960443	0.983401	0.992431	0.996427	0.998287	10
11	0.956220	0.981628	0.991623	0.996046	0.998104	11
12	0.951945	0.979835	0.990805	0.995659	0.997919	12
YEARS						MONTHS
1	0.951945	0.979835	0.990805	0.995659	0.997919	12
2	0.896440	0.956543	0.980185	0.990646	0.995514	24
3	0.832330	0.929640	0.967918	0.984855	0.992738	36
4	0.758281	0.898566	0.953749	0.978167	0.989530	48
5	0.672751	0.862675	0.937383	0.970441	0.985826	60
6	0.573961	0.821220	0.918481	0.961518	0.981547	72
7	0.459856	0.773337	0.896647	0.951212	0.976604	84
8	0.328059	0.718031	0.871429	0.939307	0.970896	96
9	0.175830	0.654150	0.842301	0.925557	0.964302	108
10	0.000000	0.580366	0.808657	0.909676	0.956686	120
11		0.495142	0.769798	0.891332	0.947889	132
12		0.396706	0.724913	0.870144	0.937729	144
13		0.283009	0.673070	0.845671	0.925993	156
14		0.151684	0.613189	0.817404	0.912438	168
15		0.000000	0.544025	0.784755	0.896782	180
16			0.464138	0.747043	0.878698	192
17			0.371866	0.703486	0.857810	204
18			0.265288	0.653175	0.833684	216
19			0.142186	0.595064	0.805818	228
20			0.000000	0.527945	0.773631	240
21				0.450419	0.736455	252
22				0.360874	0.693514	264
23				0.257446	0.643917	276
24				0.137984	0.586630	288
25				0.000000	0.520461	300
26					0.444034	312
27					0.355759	324
28					0.253797	336
29					0.136028	348
30					0.000000	360

MORTGAGE BALANCE FACTORS
Monthly Payments

15.00% INTEREST RATE

	BALANCE 10 YR LOAN	BALANCE 15 YR LOAN	BALANCE 20 YR LOAN	BALANCE 25 YR LOAN	BALANCE 30 YR LOAN	
MONTHS						MONTHS
1	0.996367	0.998504	0.999332	0.999692	0.999856	1
2	0.992688	0.996990	0.998656	0.999380	0.999709	2
3	0.988963	0.995456	0.997971	0.999063	0.999561	3
4	0.985191	0.993903	0.997278	0.998743	0.999411	4
5	0.981373	0.992331	0.996576	0.998419	0.999260	5
6	0.977506	0.990740	0.995865	0.998091	0.999106	6
7	0.973592	0.989128	0.995146	0.997759	0.998950	7
8	0.969628	0.987496	0.994417	0.997423	0.998793	8
9	0.965615	0.985844	0.993679	0.997082	0.998633	9
10	0.961552	0.984171	0.992933	0.996738	0.998472	10
11	0.957437	0.982477	0.992176	0.996389	0.998308	11
12	0.953272	0.980763	0.991411	0.996035	0.998142	12
YEARS						MONTHS
1	0.953272	0.980763	0.991411	0.996035	0.998142	12
2	0.899032	0.958433	0.981440	0.991433	0.995986	24
3	0.836073	0.932513	0.969868	0.986091	0.993484	36
4	0.762993	0.902427	0.956434	0.979890	0.990578	48
5	0.678165	0.867504	0.940841	0.972692	0.987206	60
6	0.579700	0.826967	0.922742	0.964337	0.983292	72
7	0.465407	0.779914	0.901733	0.954639	0.978749	84
8	0.332741	0.725297	0.877347	0.943382	0.973475	96
9	0.178748	0.661899	0.849040	0.930316	0.967353	108
10	0.000000	0.588311	0.816184	0.915149	0.960248	120
11		0.502892	0.778045	0.897544	0.952000	132
12		0.403743	0.733775	0.877109	0.942426	144
13		0.288654	0.682389	0.853388	0.931313	156
14		0.155065	0.622742	0.825855	0.918414	168
15		0.000000	0.553507	0.793895	0.903441	180
16			0.473142	0.756798	0.886061	192
17			0.379858	0.713737	0.865887	204
18			0.271578	0.663754	0.842470	216
19			0.145891	0.605736	0.815289	228
20			0.000000	0.538392	0.783738	240
21				0.460221	0.747116	252
22				0.369485	0.704606	264
23				0.264162	0.655263	276
24				0.141907	0.597987	288
25				0.000000	0.531504	300
26					0.454333	312
27					0.364758	324
28					0.260782	336
29					0.140092	348
30					0.000000	360

MORTGAGE BALANCE FACTORS
Monthly Payments

15.50% INTEREST RATE

	BALANCE 10 YR LOAN	BALANCE 15 YR LOAN	BALANCE 20 YR LOAN	BALANCE 25 YR LOAN	BALANCE 30 YR LOAN	
MONTHS						MONTHS
1	0.996476	0.998577	0.999378	0.999719	0.999871	1
2	0.992906	0.997135	0.998748	0.999435	0.999741	2
3	0.989290	0.995675	0.998109	0.999147	0.999609	3
4	0.985627	0.994196	0.997463	0.998855	0.999476	4
5	0.981917	0.992698	0.996808	0.998559	0.999341	5
6	0.978159	0.991180	0.996145	0.998260	0.999204	6
7	0.974352	0.989643	0.995473	0.997957	0.999065	7
8	0.970497	0.988086	0.994792	0.997649	0.998924	8
9	0.966591	0.986509	0.994103	0.997338	0.998782	9
10	0.962635	0.984911	0.993404	0.997023	0.998638	10
11	0.958628	0.983293	0.992697	0.996704	0.998492	11
12	0.954570	0.981654	0.991980	0.996381	0.998344	12
YEARS						MONTHS
1	0.954570	0.981654	0.991980	0.996381	0.998344	12
2	0.901575	0.960254	0.982626	0.992159	0.996411	24
3	0.839757	0.935290	0.971713	0.987234	0.994157	36
4	0.767646	0.906170	0.958984	0.981489	0.991528	48
5	0.683529	0.872201	0.944135	0.974787	0.988461	60
6	0.585406	0.832577	0.926814	0.966970	0.984884	72
7	0.470946	0.786355	0.906609	0.957851	0.980710	84
8	0.337429	0.732437	0.883040	0.947213	0.975842	96
9	0.181680	0.669542	0.855547	0.934805	0.970163	108
10	0.000000	0.596175	0.823476	0.920331	0.963539	120
11		0.510592	0.786065	0.903446	0.955812	132
12		0.410760	0.742425	0.883751	0.946798	144
13		0.294306	0.691519	0.860776	0.936284	156
14		0.158462	0.632138	0.833976	0.924018	168
15		0.000000	0.562869	0.802713	0.909711	180
16			0.482068	0.766246	0.893022	192
17			0.387813	0.723706	0.873553	204
18			0.277864	0.674084	0.850844	216
19			0.149609	0.616200	0.824353	228
20			0.000000	0.548678	0.793451	240
21				0.469913	0.757404	252
22				0.378035	0.715356	264
23				0.270858	0.666306	276
24				0.145837	0.609090	288
25				0.000000	0.542347	300
26					0.464491	312
27					0.373673	324
28					0.267733	336
29					0.144154	348
30					0.000000	360

MORTGAGE BALANCE FACTORS
Monthly Payments

16.00% INTEREST RATE

MONTHS	BALANCE 10 YR LOAN	BALANCE 15 YR LOAN	BALANCE 20 YR LOAN	BALANCE 25 YR LOAN	BALANCE 30 YR LOAN	MONTHS
1	0.996582	0.998646	0.999421	0.999744	0.999886	1
2	0.993118	0.997275	0.998834	0.999485	0.999770	2
3	0.989609	0.995885	0.998239	0.999223	0.999653	3
4	0.986052	0.994476	0.997636	0.998957	0.999534	4
5	0.982448	0.993049	0.997026	0.998688	0.999413	5
6	0.978796	0.991602	0.996407	0.998415	0.999291	6
7	0.975096	0.990137	0.995780	0.998138	0.999168	7
8	0.971346	0.988652	0.995144	0.997858	0.999042	8
9	0.967545	0.987147	0.994500	0.997573	0.998915	9
10	0.963695	0.985621	0.993848	0.997286	0.998787	10
11	0.959793	0.984076	0.993186	0.996994	0.998656	11
12	0.955839	0.982510	0.992516	0.996698	0.998524	12

YEARS						MONTHS
1	0.955839	0.982510	0.992516	0.996698	0.998524	12
2	0.904070	0.962007	0.983743	0.992827	0.996794	24
3	0.843382	0.937972	0.973459	0.988290	0.994765	36
4	0.772240	0.909797	0.961403	0.982971	0.992388	48
5	0.688843	0.876768	0.947270	0.976735	0.989600	60
6	0.591078	0.838048	0.930702	0.969426	0.986333	72
7	0.476471	0.792659	0.911280	0.960857	0.982502	84
8	0.342121	0.739450	0.888513	0.950812	0.978012	96
9	0.184626	0.677075	0.861823	0.939036	0.972748	108
10	0.000000	0.603955	0.830536	0.925232	0.966578	120
11		0.518238	0.793858	0.909050	0.959344	132
12		0.417754	0.750862	0.890080	0.950864	144
13		0.299961	0.700459	0.867842	0.940924	156
14		0.161874	0.641373	0.841773	0.929271	168
15		0.000000	0.572108	0.811213	0.915610	180
16			0.490911	0.775389	0.899596	192
17			0.395726	0.733393	0.880823	204
18			0.284144	0.684163	0.858817	216
19			0.153339	0.626452	0.833019	228
20			0.000000	0.558798	0.802777	240
21				0.479490	0.767325	252
22				0.386520	0.725766	264
23				0.277533	0.677048	276
24				0.149771	0.619937	288
25				0.000000	0.552987	300
26					0.474504	312
27					0.382500	324
28					0.274647	336
29					0.148214	348
30					0.000000	360

MORTGAGE BALANCE FACTORS
Monthly Payments

16.50% INTEREST RATE

	BALANCE 10 YR LOAN	BALANCE 15 YR LOAN	BALANCE 20 YR LOAN	BALANCE 25 YR LOAN	BALANCE 30 YR LOAN	
MONTHS						MONTHS
1	0.996686	0.998713	0.999461	0.999768	0.999899	1
2	0.993326	0.997408	0.998915	0.999532	0.999796	2
3	0.989920	0.996085	0.998361	0.999293	0.999691	3
4	0.986467	0.994744	0.997799	0.999051	0.999586	4
5	0.982967	0.993385	0.997230	0.998805	0.999478	5
6	0.979418	0.992007	0.996653	0.998556	0.999370	6
7	0.975821	0.990610	0.996068	0.998304	0.999260	7
8	0.972174	0.989194	0.995475	0.998048	0.999148	8
9	0.968478	0.987758	0.994873	0.997789	0.999035	9
10	0.964730	0.986303	0.994264	0.997526	0.998920	10
11	0.960931	0.984827	0.993646	0.997260	0.998804	11
12	0.957079	0.983332	0.993020	0.996990	0.998686	12
YEARS						MONTHS
1	0.957079	0.983332	0.993020	0.996990	0.998686	12
2	0.906516	0.963695	0.984796	0.993443	0.997138	24
3	0.846949	0.940562	0.975109	0.989266	0.995314	36
4	0.776775	0.913310	0.963696	0.984344	0.993165	48
5	0.694105	0.881205	0.950251	0.978546	0.990634	60
6	0.596714	0.843383	0.934412	0.971715	0.987651	72
7	0.481981	0.798826	0.915752	0.963668	0.984138	84
8	0.346817	0.746336	0.893770	0.954188	0.980000	96
9	0.187586	0.684498	0.867874	0.943021	0.975124	108
10	0.000000	0.611649	0.837366	0.929864	0.969380	120
11		0.525827	0.801426	0.914365	0.962614	132
12		0.424724	0.759086	0.896106	0.954642	144
13		0.305617	0.709206	0.874595	0.945251	156
14		0.165301	0.650445	0.849254	0.934188	168
15		0.000000	0.581220	0.819401	0.921155	180
16			0.499668	0.784232	0.905801	192
17			0.403594	0.742800	0.887712	204
18			0.290413	0.693991	0.866403	216
19			0.157078	0.636490	0.841300	228
20			0.000000	0.568750	0.811726	240
21				0.488948	0.776886	252
22				0.394935	0.735843	264
23				0.284182	0.687490	276
24				0.153708	0.630528	288
25				0.000000	0.563423	300
26					0.484368	312
27					0.391236	324
28					0.281521	336
29					0.152268	348
30					0.000000	360

MORTGAGE BALANCE FACTORS
Monthly Payments

17.00% INTEREST RATE

	BALANCE 10 YR LOAN	BALANCE 15 YR LOAN	BALANCE 20 YR LOAN	BALANCE 25 YR LOAN	BALANCE 30 YR LOAN	
MONTHS						MONTHS
1	0.996787	0.998777	0.999499	0.999789	0.999910	1
2	0.993528	0.997536	0.998990	0.999574	0.999819	2
3	0.990224	0.996278	0.998475	0.999357	0.999726	3
4	0.986872	0.995002	0.997952	0.999137	0.999632	4
5	0.983473	0.993707	0.997421	0.998913	0.999537	5
6	0.980026	0.992395	0.996883	0.998686	0.999440	6
7	0.976530	0.991064	0.996338	0.998457	0.999342	7
8	0.972984	0.989714	0.995785	0.998223	0.999243	8
9	0.969388	0.988345	0.995224	0.997987	0.999142	9
10	0.965741	0.986956	0.994655	0.997747	0.999039	10
11	0.962043	0.985548	0.994078	0.997504	0.998936	11
12	0.958292	0.984120	0.993492	0.997257	0.998831	12
YEARS						MONTHS
1	0.958292	0.984120	0.993492	0.997257	0.998831	12
2	0.908914	0.965319	0.985788	0.994010	0.997446	24
3	0.850457	0.943062	0.976667	0.990166	0.995807	36
4	0.781249	0.916711	0.965868	0.985615	0.993867	48
5	0.699314	0.885515	0.953084	0.980226	0.991570	60
6	0.602313	0.848582	0.937949	0.973847	0.988850	72
7	0.487474	0.804857	0.920031	0.966295	0.985630	84
8	0.351516	0.753092	0.898817	0.957355	0.981818	96
9	0.190558	0.691808	0.873703	0.946770	0.977305	108
10	0.000000	0.619253	0.843970	0.934238	0.971963	120
11		0.533357	0.808770	0.919402	0.965637	132
12		0.431665	0.767097	0.901838	0.958149	144
13		0.311273	0.717760	0.881044	0.949284	156
14		0.168742	0.659351	0.856427	0.938788	168
15		0.000000	0.590201	0.827282	0.926362	180
16			0.508334	0.792778	0.911651	192
17			0.411413	0.751928	0.894235	204
18			0.296669	0.703567	0.873617	216
19			0.160825	0.646313	0.849207	228
20			0.000000	0.578530	0.820308	240
21				0.498283	0.786094	252
22				0.403278	0.745589	264
23				0.290803	0.697636	276
24				0.157645	0.640864	288
25				0.000000	0.573653	300
26					0.494082	312
27					0.399878	324
28					0.288352	336
29					0.156316	348
30					0.000000	360

Index

G–H